The Good Hotel Guide 2005

The Good Hotel Guide 2005

Continental Europe

Editors:

Adam and Caroline Raphael

Editor for Benelux, Iberia and Scandinavia:
Desmond Balmer

Editor for Italy:
Bing Taylor

Contributing editors:
Bill Bennett, Lottie Moggach, Tracey Taylor

Founding editor:
Hilary Rubinstein

EBURY PRESS
LONDON

The Good Hotel Guide
50 Addison Avenue, London W11 4QP
or (posted in UK only)
Freepost PAM 2931, London W11 4BR
Tel/fax: (020) 7602 4182
Email: Goodhotel@aol.com
Website: www.goodhotelguide.com

This edition first published in 2005 by Ebury Press,
Random House, 20 Vauxhall Bridge Road,
London SW1V 2SA

The Random House Group Limited Reg. No. 954009

www.randomhouse.co.uk

3 5 7 9 10 8 6 4

Cover design by Main Artery

Managing editor for Ebury Press: Alison Wormleighton
Text editor: Daphne Trotter
Editorial assistant: Nicola Davies

A CIP catalogue record for this book may be found in the British Library.

ISBN 0 09 189191 4

Typeset from author's disks by
MATS, Southend-on-Sea, Essex
Printed and bound in Great Britain by
Cox and Wyman Ltd, Reading, Berkshire

Contents

A note for new readers

This is a truly independent guide. Contributors are not paid for writing to us; hotels do not pay for their entry; the editors and their staff accept no free hospitality, and no payments from hotels. This book covers continental Europe; Volume I, covering Great Britain and Ireland, was published in September 2004.

The *Guide* is best described as word-of-mouth in print, since every place has been recommended by correspondents or inspectors who have spent at least one night there. It includes hotels, inns, guest houses and B&Bs of unusual character and quality. Most are quite small, but none has fewer than three rooms. Almost all the hotels, especially in rural areas, are managed by resident owners. We update the commentaries each year, using reports from readers, on whose generous support we depend. We verify and collate the reports, making an anonymous overnight inspection where necessary, and select those hotels that we consider make the grade. Hotels are dropped if critical reports outweigh those in favour, or if we have had no recent reports. They are also dropped following a change of ownership, unless we are certain that standards have been maintained.

We do not attempt to be comprehensive, because that would involve lowering standards. There are many blank areas on our maps. We almost never include chain hotels, because our readers prefer the personal style of individually owned places. We try to convey the flavour of each, so that you will find one that suits your tastes, needs and purse. Our definition of a good hotel is: 'Where the guest comes first.'

How to contact the *Guide*:
By mail: From anywhere in the UK write to: *Good Hotel Guide*, Freepost, PAM 2931, London W11 4BR (no stamp needed)
From outside the UK: *Good Hotel Guide*, 50 Addison Avenue, London W11 4QP, England
By telephone or fax: (020) 7602 4182
By email: Goodhotel@aol.com
Via our website: www.goodhotelguide.com

Introduction

Finding the perfect hotel gets no easier. Newspapers and magazines devote acres of space to reports on hotels. But how reliable is such information, linked, as it invariably is, to advertising and paid-for trips? The Internet is also a much-used source of information. But again, it pays to be cautious about the facts and pictures provided. One of our readers wrote to us recently: 'More and more people now wish to travel independently rather than take a package tour; many book via the Internet, and need good independent reports about hotels. For less than the cost of a breakfast for two people on holiday, your guide helps us pick hotels that we can rely on.'

It won't surprise you that we say we think this is wise advice. We often hear from travellers who have taken the gamble of booking a hotel via its website, not always with happy results. It must be remembered that a website is like a brochure, produced by the hotel's owners or publicity agent. It may well present an over-rosy view of the place, and it will certainly gloss over facts like noisy nearby roads, thin walls and small single bedrooms. Some hotel websites are both informative and entertaining. The *Château de Saint Paterne*, at St-Paterne, for example, gives a picture of each room as you click on the windows of the château (www.chateau-saintpaterne.com). With *Le Vieux Castillon*, at Castillon-du-Gard, you get birdsong as well as an excellent preview (www.vieuxcastillon.com). In other websites, butterflies flap across the screen accompanied by music by Mozart. But most hotel websites are woefully inadequate when it comes to hard facts like postal and email addresses and tariffs. Infuriatingly, even Google often leads the visitor not to the hotel itself, but to a parasitical accommodation agency which withholds these vital details, making it impossible for you to contact the hotel direct.

Thank you

Once again we thank the many readers who have reported to us this year on their visits to continental hotels already in the *Good Hotel Guide*, and on their new discoveries. As a result, we have 199 new entries in this edition and 225 hotels have been omitted (due to change of owner, lack of recent reports or critical comments).

France, with its many small hotels, often run by one family for generations, remained our readers' favourite country. As one of them put it: 'Traditions of good hotel management are still alive and well in provincial France, and at very reasonable prices.' Individual hoteliers were praised: take Christophe Beeuwsaert of *Hostellerie Les Aiguillons* at St-Martial-Viveyrols, of whom one couple wrote: 'He is always on hand, never obtrusive. He takes great pride in the food, changes the menus often. All the dishes are made on the premises. He is dedicated, professional, with no outward signs of commercialism.

Surely the very best in *Good Hotel Guide* criteria. We would give it all the awards. This man dedicates his life to perfection.'

Deinflationary euro

Prices on the whole seem not to have risen much this year. As the economic slowdown in France and Germany continued, many hotels have again held their tariffs. One Italian hotelier told an inspector: 'At this time of year [June] we would normally see many French and German visitors. This year, there are far fewer.' Americans seem still to be travelling abroad less, too, due to economic as well as international factors.

We find nowadays that some hotels are deliberately vague about their tariffs; some are increasing their range of special offers, and some are adjusting prices for last-minute reservations and bookings via the Internet.

Muzak

This is still a major irritant for many *Guide* readers. As one visitor wrote, after suffering 'non-stop and very intrusive' Norah Jones: 'I loathe wallpaper music, but it seems to be everywhere. I wish it was a fashion that had passed its sell-by date. It's the sort of brain-softening thing which makes me suspicious; an attempt at calming, so I won't notice how clean the linen is, etc.'

Farewell to John

Regular readers will notice that for the first time in many years, John Ardagh's name does not appear on the title page. John, now aged 77 and not in the best of health, has decided to put away his pen. He wrote the Irish and Welsh entries in the volume of the *Guide* that covers Great Britain and Ireland, but did not feel up to the huge task of writing the entries for France and Germany in this volume. We greatly miss his enthusiasm and his encyclopaedic knowledge of continental Europe.

Adieu

Sadly also, unless a fairy godparent intervenes, this will be the final edition of the continental Europe volume of the *Good Hotel Guide*. The *Guide* has always been run as a labour of love, but though the edition for Great Britain and Ireland is flourishing, a point has been reached where the revenues of the continental volume lag seriously behind the considerable costs of compiling it. We are proud of our independence which prevents us, unlike many of our competitors, from accepting advertising, hospitality or payment from hotels. But this means that we live or die according to the numbers of copies sold. Despite the loyalty of a small group of readers to whom we are hugely grateful, sales have not been good enough to sustain the continental volume. The only good news is that its demise will enable us to devote more time, resources and effort to the Great Britain and Ireland edition.

ADAM AND CAROLINE RAPHAEL NOVEMBER 2004

Special hotels to match low-cost flights

The low-cost airlines have transformed the way we travel to Europe. It is possible to pick up a cheap flight from airports across Britain to a bewildering range of European destinations. With its unrivalled selection of hotels of character, the continental volume of the *Guide* has never been more useful. This listing will help you find a hotel within a reasonable distance of most of the airports used by the low-cost carriers. At the smaller airports, you may wish to hire a car to reach some of the more interesting places.

AUSTRIA

GRAZ (Ryanair)
Hotel Burg Bernstein, Bernstein
Family welcome at massive fortress in wooded hills page 3
Schlossberg Hotel, Graz
Architect's stylish B&B in renovated historic building page 8

KLAGENFURT (Ryanair)
Hotel Die Forelle, Millstatt am See
Family-run hotel on promontory in lakeside resort page 13
Schloss Leonstain, Pörtschach am Wörthersee
Sophisticated hotel, excellent food, in fashionable resort page 14

SALZBURG (FlyBE, Thomsonfly)
Gasthof-Hotel Doktorwirt, Salzburg
A helpful family runs this ancient inn page 16
Hotel Goldener Hirsch, Salzburg
Traditional flavour in famous city centre street page 17

BELGIUM

BRUSSELS (Ryanair)
Le Dixseptième, Brussels
Characterful B&B in former home of Spanish ambassador page 30
Hotel Rembrandt, Brussels
Amazing value at modest but professional B&B page 31

CZECH REPUBLIC

PRAGUE (bmibaby, easyJet, FlyBE, Jet2)
Hotel Hoffmeister, Prague
Stylish hotel in smart district below the castle page 51
Hotel U Páva, Prague
Baroque house with easy access to both sides of city page 52

Romantik Hotel U raka, Prague
Welcoming guest house in artist's colony near castle page 53
Hotel 16, Prague
Admired B&B hotel with terraced garden, helpful staff page 53

DENMARK

COPENHAGEN (easyJet)
Skovshoved Hotel, Charlottenlund
Romantic seaside feel in village close to city page 55
71 Nyhavn, Copenhagen
Converted warehouses at junction of canal and harbour page 56

ESBJERG (Ryanair)
Sønderho Kro, Sønderho
Delicious food at elegant hotel in pretty village page 58

FRANCE

BERGERAC (FlyBE, Ryanair)
Hostellerie des Ducs, Duras
Restaurant-with-rooms in wine-growing town page 131
Hôtel du Centenaire, Les Eyzies-de-Tayac
Fine dining at first-rate hotel by River Vézère page 133
La Métairie, Mauzac
Genial hospitality, superb food, in pretty countryside page 168

BIARRITZ (Ryanair)
Lehen Tokia, Ciboure
Marvellous Art Deco villa, full of character page 116
Hôtel Arcé, St-Étienne-de-Baïgorry
Beautiful country hotel by a trout river in Basque country page 219
Hôtel Parc Victoria, St-Jean-de-Luz
Luxurious hotel near beach of upmarket fishing port page 223

BORDEAUX (bmibaby, FlyBE)
Hauterive Saint-James, Bordeaux
Luxury hotel built around 17th-century *maison vigeronne* page 88
Château Cordeillan-Bages, Pauillac
Sophisticated hotel set among Médoc vineyards page 193
Au Logis des Remparts, St-Émilion
Popular B&B hotel in medieval wine town page 218

CARCASSONNE (Ryanair – see also Toulouse)
La Bastide Cabezac, Bize-Minervois
Regional touches at *relais de poste* among vineyards page 86
La Ferme de la Sauzette, Cazilhac
Children welcomed in tranquil rural hideaway page 102
Auberge de l'Arbousier, Homps
Good value at restaurant-with-rooms by a towpath page 148

RODEZ (Ryanair)
Hôtel Restaurant du Vieux Pont, Belcastel
Excellent regional cooking in beautiful hamlet page 83
Hôtel Sainte-Foy, Conques
17th-century timbered inn opposite famous abbey page 123
Auberge du Fel, Le Fel
Chic rural inn in attractive Aveyron hill village page 134

ST-ÉTIENNE (Ryanair)
Domaine de Clairefontaine, Chonas L'Amballan
Fine food in former country home of bishops of Lyon page 116
Hôtellerie Beau Rivage, Condrieu
Smart, newly modernised family hotel on banks of Rhône page 122
Hôtel Restaurant Le Bellevue, Les Roches-de-Condrieu
Good food – and value – at welcoming riverside hotel page 212

TOULOUSE (bmibaby, easyJet, FlyBE, Ryanair)
La Réserve, Albi
Blissful retreat with lawns sloping down to the Tarn page 65
Château Cap de Castel, Puylaurens
Family-run 13th-century château in Cathar stronghold page 207
Hôtel des Couteliers, Toulouse
Distinctive modern hotel in quiet street in old city page 246

TOURS (Ryanair)
Château de Pray, Amboise
Cosy small 13th-century château in park above Loire page 67
Hôtel Agnès Sorel, Chinon
Warm welcome, excellent value, in château country page 113
Les Hautes Roches, Rochecorbon
Imposing mansion with rooms carved out of rock page 211

GERMANY

ALTENBURG/LEIPZIG (Ryanair)
Hotel Bülow Residenz, Dresden
Baroque mansion within walking distance of main sights page 282
Hotel Kreller, Freiberg
Friendly family-run hotel in Saxon university city page 287
Romantic Hotel am Brühl, Quedlinburg
Warmth, elegance and value in historic old town page 301

BERLIN (easyJet, Ryanair)
art'otel Berlin Mitte, Berlin
Minimalist, elegant hotel in the lively city centre page 276
Bleibtreu Hotel, Berlin
Funky designer hotel with eco-friendly emphasis page 277
Hotel Jurine, Berlin
Welcoming B&B hotel with trilingual staff page 277

Palazzo Sasso, Ravello
Pink 12th-century palace on cliff above the Amalfi coast page 403

PALERMO (Ryanair)
Hotel Elimo, Erice
Family-run hotel in ancient mountain village page 363
Villa Esperia, Mondello
Authentic Sicilian two-star hotel in seaside suburb page 386
Palazzo Conte Federico, Palermo
The count welcomes B&B guests to his ancestral home page 394

PESCARA (Ryanair)
Villa Vignola, Marina di Vasto
Fish restaurant-with-rooms in white seaside villa page 383

PISA (Jet2, Ryanair, Thomsonfly)
Loggiato dei Serviti, Florence
Much-loved 16th-century monastery in attractive square page 368
Locanda L'Elisa, Lucca
Striking 19th-century villa near famous walled city page 379
Hotel Armonia, Pontedera
Renovated 19th-century *palazzo* in attractive small town page 400

ROME (easyJet, Ryanair, Thomsonfly)
Hotel Due Torri, Rome
Good value at friendly B&B, well situated but quiet page 405
Hotel Portoghesi, Rome
Family-run *palazzo* close to main attractions page 407
Villa del Parco, Rome
Pleasant B&B in 19th-century villa in embassy district page 408

VENICE (easyJet, Jet2, Ryanair to Treviso, Thomsonfly)
Pensione Accademia – Villa Maravege, Venice
Authentic *pensione* well placed near Accademia bridge page 424
Hotel Colombina, Venice
Restored 17th-century *palazzo* near Piazza San Marco page 426
Hotel Flora, Venice
Old-fashioned hospitality at much-liked traditional hotel page 426

VERONA (Ryanair to Brescia)
Villa del Quar, Pedemonte
Patrician dwelling, a national monument, among vineyards page 396
Hotel Gabbia d'Oro, Verona
Luxurious B&B hotel in *centro storico* page 427

THE NETHERLANDS

AMSTERDAM (bmibaby, easyJet, Jet2, Thomsonfly)
Ambassade Hotel, Amsterdam
Well-managed B&B hotel formed from ten gabled houses page 434

Canal House Hotel, Amsterdam
Amiable Irish-owned B&B in Jordaan district page 435
Hotel d l'Europe, Amsterdam
Imposing Victorian building at junction of two canals page 436

PORTUGAL

FARO (bmibaby, easyJet, FlyBE, Jet2, MyTravelLite, Ryanair)
Monte do Casal, Estoi
Tranquil hotel on edge of medieval market town page 450
Casa Três Palmeiras, Praia do Vau
Stress-free B&B in a dream setting on cliff edge page 456
Quinta da Lua, Santo Estêvão
Rustic style in the rural eastern Algarve page 458

SPAIN

ALMEIRA (easyJet, FlyBE, MyTravelLite)
Alquería de Morayma, Cádiar
Informal welcome on large organic farm page 479
Hotel Taray, Órgiva
Much-praised hotel in gardens beside Guadalfeo river page 500

BARCELONA (easyJet, Jet2, MyTravelLite, Ryanair to Girona and Reus)
Hotel Claris, Barcelona
Posh designer hotel, off main shopping strip page 471
Hotel Neri, Barcelona
Contemporary restoration of 18th-century palace page 472
Hotel Sant Agustí, Barcelona
Simple comfort in former convent just off La Rambla page 472

BILBAO (easyJet)
Iturrienea Ostatua, Bilbao
Simple, eccentric family-run *pension* in old town page 475
López de Haro, Bilbao
Well-run city hotel near Guggenheim museum page 476
Petit Palace Arana, Bilbao
Ultra-modern conversion of 19th-century building page 476

GIRONA (Ryanair)
Hotel Aigua Blava, Begur
Much-loved hotel on lovely stretch of Costa Brava page 473
Castell d'Empordà, La Bisbal d'Empordà
Restored Gothic castle with wonderful views page 477
Hotel Mas de Torrent, Torrent
Luxury hideaway surrounded by fields of wheat page 512

JEREZ DE LA FRONTERA (Ryanair)
Hotel El Convento, Arcos de la Frontera
Good value at converted convent with stunning views page 469

Berns Hotel, Stockholm
Exclusive hotel with Conran-designed restaurant page 519
Victory Hotel, Stockholm
Quirky hotel, dedicated to Nelson, in old town page 521

Useful websites
www.bmibaby.com
www.easyjet.com
www.flybe.com
www.jet2.com
www.mytravellite.com
www.ryanair.com
www.thomsonfly.com

How we choose our hotels

A hotel is considered for an entry in the *Guide* only if the nominator or an inspector has spent a night there and had the opportunity to discover details that a tour with a clipboard does not reveal: whether breakfast is as good as dinner; how good the beds, soundproofing, plumbing and lighting are, and so on. Of course, such a system is open to error, but we are pleased that positive reports from readers far outweigh the negative ones.

The hotels, inns and B&Bs included differ widely. The final selection is not easy, as they have been nominated by a collection of individuals, not all of whose tastes and standards of judgment are familiar to us, and the only thing that they have in common is that the editors would be happy to stay in them. But the process of selection is not arbitrary. Among the factors which influence us are the following:

– The consensus of recent reports on a hotel that has an entry in the *Guide*, and the tone of the letter recommending a hotel for the first time. If someone whose judgment we know and trust tells us of a new find, or that a particular hotel does not deserve its entry, he or she carries more influence than someone writing to us for the first time.

– The hotel's brochure/website, and its reply to our questionnaire: we ask them to tell us what sort of guests they hope to attract. Many do not take the trouble to write back; the replies of those who do are helpful.

– Menus. Instructive in many ways.

– Whether, and how, a hotel features in other guides.

– Inspections. In cases of doubt (due to conflicting or ambivalent reports), we carry out an anonymous inspection. We have a limited inspection budget, but a number of readers have generously volunteered to do unreimbursed inspections for us.

We drop a hotel when there has clearly been a fall in standards or – a tricky issue – if we feel that it no longer offers value for money. Hotels are omitted after a change of ownership or management, unless we have evidence that the new regime is maintaining previous standards. And hotels are dropped – often unfairly – when we have had inadequate feedback. We often get letters asking: 'Why have you left out — ?' If the case is convincing, we reinstate it in the next edition.

Some hotels ask their guests to send us an 'unsolicited' recommendation. Sometimes we receive a flurry of fulsome reports, from people who have never written to us before, about a particular hotel. Some hotels photocopy our report form, and ask their guests to fill it in. One hotelier designed a special postcard for the purpose. These collusive practices are counter-productive.

How to read the entries

Length Entries vary greatly. A long one does not necessarily imply an especially good hotel, nor a short one a marginal case. Sometimes it takes many words to convey a place's special flavour, and sometimes we quote at length from an amusing report. Country hotels usually get more space than city ones, because we like to comment on the location when a hotel is in a remote or little-known area.

Names At the end of each entry are the names of people who have nominated the hotel or endorsed its entry in an earlier edition of the *Guide*. We don't give the names of inspectors, correspondents who wish to be anonymous, or those who have written an adverse report, though their contributions are just as important as the enthusiastic ones.

Maps These are in the colour section of the book. Hotels are listed country by country under the name of the town or village. If you remember the hotel's name but not its location, please consult the alphabetical list of hotels at the back.

Facilities The factual material varies in length. If a hotel does not return our questionnaire, we don't always know exactly what it offers. About a quarter of the hotels in this volume ignored the questionnaire or returned it after the *Guide* went to press. So the information may be briefer and less accurate than we would like. We don't give details about bedroom facilities: most hotel bedrooms nowadays have a telephone, a TV and an *en suite* bathroom. If any of these is vital to you, please discuss it with the hotel. A 'double room' may be double- or twin-bedded; mention your preference when booking. We try to give accurate information about opening times, but hotels, particularly small ones, sometimes close on the spur of the moment. Hotels on the Continent often close one day a week, but don't always tell us which day. And they don't always give us reliable information about which credit cards they take. Please check with the hotel if this is vital to you.

Italic entries These describe hotels which we feel are worth considering but which, for various reasons – inadequate information, lack of feedback, ambivalent reports – do not at the moment deserve a full entry.

Traveller's tales These tales of disaster are for the amusement of readers, and none of them relates to hotels currently in the *Guide*. They have *no connection* with the adjacent entries.

Symbols We avoid giving information in hieroglyphic form. Days and months are abbreviated; 'B&B' means bed and breakfast, 'D,B&B' means dinner, bed and breakfast, and 'alc' is *à la carte*. 'Full alc' is the hotel's estimate per person for a three-course meal including a half bottle of modest wine, service and taxes; 'alc' is the price excluding wine. A 'set meal' could be no-choice or *table d'hôte*. We say 'Unsuitable for ♿' when a hotel tells us that, and we give information, when we can, about lifts, ramps, etc. But wheelchair-users *must* check details with the hotel. The 'New' label indicates hotels making their debut in the *Guide* or being readmitted after an absence. 'Budget' indicates hotels that offer half board at around the foreign equivalent of £50 per person, or B&B for about £30 and dinner for about £20.

Vouchers The Voucher scheme offers an opportunity to get a discount at any hotel with ***V*** at the end of its entry. Each of the six vouchers on the tear-out card in the centre of the book entitles you to a discount of 25 per cent from the normal price for bed and breakfast (or the price of a room if the hotel charges for breakfast separately). You can't use it if you are already on a special deal, and you will be expected to pay the full price for all other services. The discount will apply whether you use the voucher for one night or for a longer visit, and is for one room. You must produce two vouchers if you are booking two rooms. The vouchers remain valid until 12 January 2006. **You MUST request a voucher booking at the time of reservation, and participating hotels may refuse a voucher reservation, or accept the voucher for one night only, if they expect to be fully booked at the normal room price at that time.**

Tariffs These can be complicated. Some hotels have a standard rate for all rooms regardless of season and length of stay. But many, particularly resort hotels, operate a complicated system which varies from off-season to high, and according to length of stay and facilities. The figures given without mention of a single or a double room indicate the range of tariffs per person; otherwise we give a room rate. Lowest rates are for the simplest room, for a person sharing a double, or out of season, or both; highest rates are for the 'best' rooms, and for high season if the hotel has one. Meal prices are per person. We cannot guarantee the tariffs given in the *Guide.* We ask hotels, in the summer of one year, to make an informed guess at their tariffs for the following year. This is not easy, and many prefer to quote their current rates. Please *don't* rely on the figures printed. You should *always* check tariffs at the time of booking, and not blame the hotel or the *Guide* if prices are different from those printed.

Join the *Good Hotel Guide* Readers' Club

Send us a brief review of your favourite British or Irish hotel.

As a member of the club, you will be entitled to:

1. Special pre-publication discount offers
2. Personal advice on hotels
3. Advice if you are in dispute with a hotel

The best review will win a bottle of vintage champagne.

Send your review via:

Our website: www.goodhotelguide.com
or email: goodhotel@aol.com
or fax: 020-7602 4182
or write to: *Good Hotel Guide*
Freepost PAM 2931
London W11 4BR
or
from outside the UK:
Good Hotel Guide
50 Addison Avenue
London W11 4QP
England

Austria

Raffelsberger Hof, Weissenkirchen

Though the big chains such as Holiday Inn and Mercure are represented, most hotels in Austria are smaller and individually run, of the kind the *Guide* prefers. Many are in lovely settings. Some are chalet-style ski-hotels, or picturesque old inns with folksy decor and a jovial ambience. Many simple country inns have the official label of the *Gasthof* or the smaller *Gasthaus*. In the cities, some of the best smaller hotels are *Pensionen*, personal in character but not offering full hotel facilities (eg, the reception desk may not always be staffed).

A small group called Schlosshotels and Herrenhäuser includes a number of hotels in historic buildings, some of which are in these pages. These places vary greatly in size and degree of luxury, from the atmospheric but quite simple *Hotel Burg Bernstein*, near the Hungarian border at Bernstein, to *Schloss Leonstain*, with its sophisticated restaurant, at Pörtschach am Wörthersee.

As in Germany, duvets, rather than sheets and blankets, are the norm; beds can be a little hard, since this is thought healthy. Except in the smallest places, breakfast is a buffet, generally included in the room price. Service, too, is included, but it is usual to leave a small tip if it has pleased you. Some city restaurants now leave a line open for *Trinkgeld* on the credit card slip. Food is generally copious, with a regional touch; in cities it can be sophisticated, often with an emphasis on natural ingredients.

ALPBACH 6236 Tirol **Map 10:F2**

Romantikhotel Böglerhof
Tel (05336) 52270
Fax (05336) 5227402
Email boeglerhof@telecom.at
Website www.boeglerhof.com

'Well organised for skiers', this 'small, pretty village' is in a lovely valley between Kitzbühel and Innsbruck. In summer, its houses and hotels have flower-bedecked balconies, and there are 'delightful walks on the Wiedersbergerhorn, reached by the gondola-bahn'. Owned for three generations by the Duftner family, this hotel gives a 'warm, personal welcome', say admirers. It has 'perfect family accommodation', and children are well looked after. Returning visitors 'were welcomed as friends. Our son received a certificate from the mayor because he has visited more than five times.' Earlier guests wrote: 'Our immaculate large bedroom had a sitting area with bench seating and a table. Furnishings were attractive in traditional style.' The half-board meals, in a series of rustic-style small rooms, are 'varied and interesting'. 'The food was even better this year.' Sometimes there is entertainment by a local folk group. In summer there is a weekly grill evening in the garden. Breakfast is a buffet. In the large lounge, drinks and snacks can be ordered. There is a 'very attractive' indoor swimming pool. Staff wear traditional costume. 'Good value.' (*Alex and Beryl Williams, and others*)

Open 20 Dec–Oct. **Rooms** 11 suites, 10 family, 33 double, 6 single. **Facilities** Lift. Lounge, reading room, TV room, bar, restaurant; indoor swimming pool, sauna, massage, table tennis; children's playroom; conference rooms. Garden: terrace (dancing sometimes), tennis, children's play area; mountain bikes. **Location** Central, opposite church and ski bus-stop. Garage. Parking. **Credit cards** MasterCard, Visa. **Terms** [2004] D,B&B €65–€124.

ALTAUSSEE 8992 Steiermark **Map 10:E3**

Herrenhaus Hubertushof
Puchen 86
Tel (03622) 71280
Fax (03622) 7128080
Email hubertushof@a1.net
Website www.herrenhaus-hubertushof.at

Owned by Gräfin Rose-Marie Strasoldo, this 'upmarket B&B', in a peaceful area of Styria, is an old hunting lodge filled with 'furniture of a leisured and aristocratic age', antlers, family portraits, etc. At breakfast, in a panelled room, 'the marmalade is a winner', according to visitors returning in 2004. Earlier they wrote: 'Our room was spacious; exquisitely decorated. Its balcony was excellent; chocolates and other goodies were provided. The walks down to the village are as tasteful as the lodge; the lake is peaceful and Chekovian. The countess, who wears traditional dress, is assisted by Anna Ebner, stylish and helpful: she provides extra touches like lighting a candle in the porch for late returnees. The views of mountain and village are perfection. High-class meals in the village are difficult to find, but the *Gasthof Loser* specialises in fish, or you can visit the *Konditorei*.' (*Michael and Jennifer Hodge*)

Open All year, except Nov. **Rooms** 3 suites, 4 double, 3 single. **Facilities** Lounge, breakfast room. Terrace. Garden. Walking, fishing nearby. **Location** Above village. 80 km SE of Salzburg. Parking. **Credit cards** Probably some accepted. **Terms** [2004] B&B: single €40–€50, double €85–€110, suite €120–€140.

BERNSTEIN 7434 Burgenland — Map 10:E5

Hotel Burg Bernstein
Schlossweg 1

Tel (03354) 6382
Fax (03354) 6520
Email burgbernstein@netway.at
Website www.burgbernstein.at

Amid rolling wooded hills above a village near the Hungarian border, this massive fortress was the birthplace in 1895 of Count Lázlo Almásy, of *The English Patient* fame. It dates back over 800 years; the current building is mostly 17th-century. Despite stuccoed ceilings, flagstone floors, huge fireplaces and stone staircase, paintings and antiques, it is not grand. Alexander and Andrea Berger-Almásy, whose family have owned it since 1892, say that guests 'should not expect the standard of a four- or five-star hotel; they are received as members of the family'. He welcomes visitors, carries cases, serves at table; she produces a simple no-choice dinner, in a 'splendid banqueting hall', lit only by candles, and with Renaissance hunting friezes. 'Someone is always around when needed', and the host 'has the knack of chatting to visitors without being intrusive'. The large bedrooms have no telephone, TV, minibar or door key; heating is mostly by antique wood-burning stoves. Some rooms have wide views; one has a terrace on the battlements. Bathrooms are bright, with Carrara marble. Suits of armour, ancient weaponry, old china, etc, are dotted about; there is an open-air swimming pool. In winter, the castle offers B&B only (breakfast is served in a room with an open fire). (*A and CR*)

Open All year. Dining room closed Oct–May, and midday. **Rooms** 6 suites, 4 double. Some on ground floor. **Facilities** Ramps. Salon, lounge, bar, dining room; chapel; sauna. No background music. 16-hectare park: garden, unheated swimming pool; pond, fishing. Tennis, golf, riding, hunting nearby. **Location** 300 m above Bernstein (signposted from village square). 13 km N of Oberwart. Bus from Vienna. **Credit cards** All major cards accepted. **Terms** [2004] B&B double €160–€262. Set dinner €33.

BERWANG 6622 Tirol — Map 10:E1

Sporthotel Singer

Tel (05674) 8181
Fax (05674) 818183
Email office@hotelsinger.at
Website www.hotelsinger.at

On a pine-studded slope on the edge of this busy summer and ski resort, west of the towering Zugspitze, stands this 'luxurious and wonderful' hotel (Relais & Châteaux), 76 years old this year. Composed of two big adjacent chalets, it is run by 'hands-on' owners, Günter and Gerti Singer. 'Standards of decor, service, cuisine and friendliness have endured,' wrote a couple who have been visiting for over four decades. 'Nowhere have we had such a good welcome,' was another recent comment. 'We liked the spacious feel.' From the large entry hall, a curved, wrought iron, red-carpeted staircase leads to a galleried first-floor lounge. There are beams and much wood in the bedrooms; many have a balcony. 'Our suite had windows with superb views on three sides, two settees and a fireplace.' Thomas Kunath, formerly *sous-chef*, serves a 'well-balanced menu' in the candlelit restaurant, with its beautiful painted ceiling. There is a large terrace for summer meals, a big Tyrolean-style *Stüberl* with open fire, a lively après-ski bar, dancing and all-night music in season. Children are welcomed (reduced rates, parties, etc). In summer, the hotel offers 'very good value', and there are 'lots of easy walks'. (*A, B and JW, and others*)

Open 18 Dec–2 Apr, 13 May–4 Oct. **Rooms** 23 suites, 22 double, 11 single. Some no-smoking. **Facilities** Lift. Lounge, 2 bars, 2 restaurants; children's play room; fitness centre, whirlpool, sauna; boutique; ski room. Small garden: terrace. **Location** 75 km NW of Innsbruck, off B179. Garages, parking. **Credit cards** All major cards accepted. **Terms** D,B&B €70–€145. Set lunch €16.50, dinner €24.

BEZAU 6870 Vorarlberg — Map 10:F1

Hotel Gasthof Gams
Platz 44

Tel (05514) 2220
Fax (05514) 222024
Email info@hotel-gams.at
Website www.romantik.cc

Facing green fields and wooded hills (good walking), the ever-popular *Gams* is run 'with enthusiasm and efficiency' by its owner, Ellen Nenning. A hotel since 1648, it belongs to the group Austria Kuschelhotels, offering special arrangements for 'romantic guests'. It stands by the fountain in the middle of a village that 'is far more than a tourist venue'. Recent praise: 'A pleasant welcome, most helpful staff'; 'Comfortable accommodation at value-for-money prices'; 'Excellent food'. The attractive public rooms have wooden floors, ceilings and furniture. The bedrooms vary in size: most have a contemporary decor. Some can be noisy when one of the hotel's lively events is going on. The suites are suitable for a family – children are welcomed. The five-course half-board dinners include 'innovative vegetarian dishes'. They are served in small, candlelit rooms or, on warm nights, on a terrace looking over the gardens and swimming pool. Breakfast, a buffet with 'delicious local cheeses', is accompanied by the *Morgenpost*, the hotel's newspaper with advice about local attractions.

Open Mid-Dec–mid-Nov. **Rooms** 10 suites, 18 double, 5 single. **Facilities** Lift. 5 *Stuben*, library, bar, dining room; conference/function room; sauna, Turkish bath, solarium, whirlpool. No background music. Large garden: terraces, swimming pool (heated May–Oct), tennis, children's play area. Unsuitable for ♿. **Location** Central, by church. 35 km SE of Bregenz. Bus from Bregenz. Parking. **Credit cards** MasterCard, Visa. **Terms** [2004] D,B&B: single €83–€166, double €152–€177, suite €198. B&B €10 deducted per person. Set lunch €25, dinner €45.

Hotel Post
Brugg 35

Tel (05514) 22070
Fax (05514) 220722
Email office@hotelpostbezau.com
Website www.hotelpostbezau.com

'We just had to go back,' say returning visitors in 2004 to Susanne Kaufmann's sophisticated hotel (her family has owned it for five generations). Composed of two gabled wooden houses, it has flowery balconies, and much wood panelling in the public areas. Other comments: 'Light-hearted, friendly.' 'Facilities are superb.' 'Service professional and friendly; good value; generous breakfasts.' Some bedrooms are 'traditional cosy'; others, in cool, contemporary style, are in a modern extension: 'Glass walls enclose the bathroom in one corner, glass doors at the other end open on to a balcony with views of countryside and distant mountains.' A 'magnificent high-tech structure' has tennis courts, a 'beautiful, warm' swimming pool, sauna, etc. Exhibitions are held. 'They have a daily programme, like a cruise ship.' In the large restaurant, the chef, Wolfgang Mäzler, serves 'excellent food with strong organic emphasis'. (*Florence and Russell Birch, and others*)

Open Mid-Dec–mid-Nov. Restaurant closed Sun evening/Mon. **Rooms** 23 suites, 21 double, 9 single. Some on ground floor. Some no-smoking. **Facilities** Lift, ramps. Salons, bar, restaurant; background music; children's playroom; function facilities; fitness and beauty facilities; indoor swimming pool, indoor and outdoor tennis. Garden. **Location** Central, by church. 35 km SE of Bregenz. Bus from Bregenz. Parking. **Credit cards** All major cards accepted. **Terms** [2004] B&B €70–€113; D,B&B €27 added.

BILDSTEIN 6858 Vorarlberg — Map 10:E1

Hotel Traube NEW
Dorf 85

Tel (05572) 58369
Fax (05572) 583693
Email office@hotel-traube.at
Website www.hotel-traube.at

A good base for the Schubertiade at Schwarzenberg, the Zanghellini family's small hotel is in a village (with an imposing pilgrimage church) above Bregenz. From its dining terrace there are magnificent views, and the food is 'excellent, quite refined', says this year's nominator, 'marvellous fish from the lake; interesting starters, very good puds. The spacious bedrooms, all with balcony, are very comfortable. Decor a bit OTT, but it makes a change from the usual sober style. Herr Zanghellini cannot do too much for you: if we have an evening concert, he stays up to cook for us on our return; his wife is glamorous.' (*Anne Weizmann*)

Open Mar–15 Jan. **Rooms** 1 suite, 7 double. **Facilities** Lounge, restaurant, dining terrace. **Location** 7 km from Bregenz. **Credit cards** All major cards accepted. **Terms** [2004] B&B: single €72–€90, double €122–€140, suite €220–€250; D,B&B €25 added per person.

BRAND 6708 Vorarlberg — Map 10:F1

Hotel Valschena BUDGET

Tel (05559) 331
Fax (05559) 331113
Email hotel.valschena@cable.vol.at
Website www.tiscover.com/hotel-valschena

In a village at the head of a quiet, green valley near Bregenz, the Schedler family run their 'small, cosy' chalet-style hotel, much admired: 'Good value; standards are high; hospitality is exceptional,' was one comment. The owners join guests for afternoon tea or coffee with cake (included in the price) on the balcony every afternoon. At their restaurant, the *Brandner Hof*, across the street, 'very good food' is served with silver, flowers and candles. 'The daily menu was written in English just for us. Excellent house wine.' Breakfast is a buffet. The indoor swimming pool looks on to the garden. For children there are toys and a playground. Marked walks lead from the village in summer; free tennis is available nearby; special rates are available at a local golf club, and ski packages are offered in winter.

Open 20 Dec–10 Apr, 22 May–10 Oct. **Rooms** 15 double, 2 single. **Facilities** Lounge/library, breakfast room, restaurant (across road); background music, live music sometimes; indoor swimming pool, sauna, spa bath. 2 terraces. Garden: children's playground. Golf, free tennis, skiing nearby. Unsuitable for ♿. **Location** Village centre. 12 km SW of Bludenz. Parking. **Credit cards** MasterCard, Visa. **Terms** B&B €37–€60; D,B&B €65–€90. Full alc €40.

ELLMAU 6352 Tirol — Map 10:E2

Hotel der Bär
Kirchbichl 9

Tel (05358) 2395
Fax (05358) 239556
Email info@hotelbaer.com
Website www.hotelbaer.com

'A fantastic hotel for a family stay,' says a visitor in 2004 to the Windisch family's 'extremely comfortable, though down-to-earth' hotel (Relais & Châteaux). 'We could not fault the service, food, cleanliness or facilities. They organised our taxi transfers, ski school for the children and ski passes.' Built like a village, with chalets in its large grounds, the hotel has a smallish indoor swimming pool and one outdoors, a fitness centre, and indoor tennis courts. It is down a short but steep slope from the centre of this resort, which has access to 'one of the largest conjoined ski areas in Austria'. An earlier visitor wrote: 'Some of the best food we've had in a ski hotel, though vegetarians are not particularly catered for. The Austrian wines were good. Hosts much in evidence.' Once a week, there is a five-course gala dinner. There is a 'mini-club' for children in school holidays. 'Ellmau is attractive; walking is superb.' (*Anna Ralph, and others*)

Open 21 Dec–3 Apr, 18 May–23 Oct. **Rooms** 26 suites, 26 double, 5 single. 14 in annexe. **Facilities** Lounge, bar, restaurant; live/background music; meeting room; swimming pool, sauna, beauty centre; children's club (school holidays). Garden: swimming pool. Golf nearby. Unsuitable for ♿. **Location** SW of Salzburg. From Innsbruck: A12, Wörgl-Ost exit, B178 to Ellmau. **Credit cards** Amex, MasterCard, Visa. **Terms** B&B €85–€125; D,B&B €95–€135. Set dinner €35–€50; full alc €45. 1-night bookings sometimes refused.

GARGELLEN 6787 Vorarlberg — Map 10:F1

Alpenhotel Heimspitze
Gargellen 53

Tel (05557) 6319
Fax (05557) 631920
Email hotel@heimspitze.com
Website www.heimspitze.com

In the highest resort (good for both a summer and a winter holiday) in the Montafon valley, this chalet hotel stands 'idyllically', well back from the road, in large grounds. It has uninterrupted views across meadows to the surrounding mountains. The 'welcoming' Thoeny family owners have 'created a special atmosphere', say recent guests. 'Attractive collectibles everywhere contribute to the homely feel. The food was exceptional; families come from far for Sunday lunch. Frau Thoeny, much in evidence, supervises the meals; her husband takes guests on a guided walk several times a week. Our rooms were most comfortable; bedroom balconies have superb views.' The breakfast buffet has a wide choice. In summer there are loungers in the garden. The gondola lift, well hidden by trees, is five minutes' walk away. (*A,B and JW*)

Open Early Dec–mid-Apr, June–early Oct. **Rooms** 7 suites, 36 double, 13 single. **Facilities** Lift. 2 lounges (1 with balcony), restaurant; sauna, massage. Garden. **Location** Central. Gargellen is 28 km S of Bludenz. Parking. **Credit cards** All major cards accepted. **Terms** [2004] D,B&B €62–€122; B&B €14.50 reduction per person.

GERSBERG 5020 Salzburger Land — Map 10:E3

Die Gersberg Alm NEW
Salzburg-Gnigl

Tel (0662) 641257
Fax (0662) 644278
Email office@gersbergalm.at
Website www.gersbergalm.at

Ten mins' drive SE of Salzburg, 'delightful' Romantik hotel. 'Warm and comfortable. Our modern yet traditional room had large glass doors on to terrace. Well-cooked Austrian food,' say nominators.

Lounge, restaurant, breakfast room; terrace (outside dining). Most major credit cards accepted. 46 bedrooms. B&B: single €91–€117, double €134–€275; D,B&B €35 added per person [2004].

GRAZ 8010 Steiermark **Map 10:F4**

Schlossberg Hotel
Kaiser-Franz-Josef-Kai 30

Tel (0316) 80700
Fax (0316) 807070
Email office@schlossberg-hotel.at
Website www.schlossberg-hotel.at

The architect owner, Dr Helmut Marko, has turned this old building, on the edge of the *Altstadt*, into a stylish B&B hotel. Painted blue, it stands at the foot of Schlossberg, above the River Mur. 'Beautifully renovated and furnished', it has beamed and vaulted ceilings, rambling corridors, country-style antiques and traditional fabrics, modern and old paintings, inner courtyards and terraced gardens. 'Reception was by two charming girls,' say recent guests. 'A smiling porter took charge of the car and gave us delicious apples. We had tea in the bright sitting area. Our small bedroom, with lovely pine wardrobe and marble bathroom, was like a small suite.' Some rooms are large; some have a sofa. Breakfast (which can include a boiled egg) is served in the 'lovely' winter garden. 'The strawberries and other delicacies were a delight, as was this city of culture.' There is a rooftop terrace with a small swimming pool and city views. Many restaurants nearby. (*M and JH*)

Open All year, except Christmas/New Year. **Rooms** 4 suites, 50 double. Some on ground floor. 1 floor no-smoking. Air conditioning. **Facilities** Lift. Reception/lounge, clubroom, bar (background CDs), breakfast room/conservatory; wellness room, solarium; conference/function facilities. Courtyards, gardens; rooftop terrace: unheated swimming pool, sauna. Unsuitable for ♿. **Location** 5 mins' walk from centre. Garage. **Credit cards** All major cards accepted. **Terms** [2004] B&B: single €102–€309, double €146–€379.

GRIES IM SELLRAIN 6182 Tirol **Map 10:F2**

Sporthotel Antonie BUDGET
Haus Nr 16

Tel (05236) 203
Email info@hotel-antonie.at
Website www.hotel-antonie.at

A 'classically good hotel', says its nominator. In this summer and winter resort, it is run by the Denifle and Oberegelsbacher families, 'who seem to work all hours'. Mainly built of wood, and much extended over the years, it has a spacious bar much patronised by locals, and three interlinked eating areas. 'The set menu is somewhat better than "good honest fare". It starts with a salad buffet from a very fine spread. I remember particularly a spinach dumpling dish. A highlight is the reasonably priced wine list. Half board is excellent value.' Most bedrooms are spacious; some have a balcony 'from which you can watch the sun set over the peaks'; all have ample storage space. On Thursday there is a *fondueabend* with candlelight and zither music. Cross-country ski tracks start from the door. (*SW*)

Open 18 Dec–3 Apr, 26 May–2 Oct. **Rooms** 8 family, 27 double, 7 single. 3 on ground floor. **Facilities** Lift, ramps. Lounges, bar, café, restaurant; background music; children's games room, fitness facilities: sauna, etc. Sun terrace (summer grills). Garden: heated swimming pool, children's playground. Free ski bus. **Location** In Sellraintal, 22 km SW of Innsbruck. **Credit cards** MasterCard, Visa. **Terms** [2004] D,B&B €42–€76. Set lunch €9, dinner €11.50; full alc €30. *V*

INNSBRUCK 6020 Tirol **Map 10:F2**

Gasthof-Hotel Weisses Kreuz
Herzog-Friedrichstrasse 31

Tel (0512) 594790
Fax (0512) 5947990
Email hotel@weisseskreuz.at
Website www.weisseskreuz.at

The wrought iron sign still hangs outside this 15th-century inn: inside are Gothic ceilings and old furniture, and 'creaking wooden floors and pleasantly rustic rooms in the older part', says a visitor this year. 'My single room (without *en suite* facilities) was small but rather comfortable; the shared bathroom was spotless.' Other visitors stayed in the newer part. 'Our bedroom was light, modern and stylish, in a simple, almost Scandinavian way. The bathroom had high-quality fittings.' 'Perfectly placed on a pedestrian street in the old town', this friendly hotel is run by its owner and manager, Josef Ortner and Sabine Schennach, with an 'efficient staff'. Some rooms have a view of the Golden Roof. Rear ones are quietest; front ones hear passers-by during the day, and traffic is allowed between 6 and 10.30 am. Breakfast, in a pleasant panelled room, is a 'very good buffet'. The garage is three minutes' walk away; a trolley is provided for luggage. In 1769, Mozart (aged 13) and his father stayed here. Leopold wrote to his wife: 'Wir sind, Gott Lob, wohl auf. Wir logieren beym weisen Kreutz.' (*Charles Belair, and others*)

Open All year. **Rooms** 28 double, 8 single. Some no-smoking. Most with facilities *en suite*. **Facilities** Lift. TV room/lobby, 2 breakfast rooms (classical background music); meeting room. Unsuitable for ♿. **Location** Central; pedestrian zone. Garage 3 mins' walk (€9 a day). **Credit cards** Amex, MasterCard, Visa. **Terms** B&B: single €57–€85, double €85–€110.

KALS AM GROSSGLOCKNER 9981 Tirol **Map 10:F3**

Hotel Taurerwirt
Burg 12

Tel (04786) 8226
Fax (04786) 822611
Email info@taurerwirt.at
Website www.taurerwirt.at

In Hohe Tauern national park (lovely scenery, much wildlife, good walking): Rogl family's 'excellent hotel', dedicated to fitness. 'Very friendly, well appointed; good and varied food.' Reading room, winter garden (both no-smoking), bar, 2 dining rooms; background music; children's games room; swimming pool, sauna, etc; terrace. Garden: children's playground. Open 29 May–9 Oct, 18 Dec–Easter. 34 bedrooms (most are spacious). D,B&B €66–€108 [2004].

KITZBÜHEL 6370 Tirol Map 10:E3

Romantikhotel Tennerhof
Griesenauweg 26

Tel (05356) 63181
Fax (05356) 6318170
Email tennerhof@kitz.net
Website www.tennerhof.com

At the foot of the Kitzbühel Horn stands the Pasquali family's extended Renaissance manor house, 'smart yet cosy'; a cable-car station is nearby. 'Very good value in summer', and popular with golfers and bridge players, it has a 'welcoming feel'. Frau Pasquali 'keeps a keen eye on things'. The decor is typically Tyrolean: family antiques, hand-painted armoires, wooden floors. In the bedrooms are pastel-coloured duvet covers, chairs in flowered fabrics. 'Our "superior" double had a large sitting area with *chaise longue*, and patio doors to a balcony with a lovely view.' There is a 'very comfortable' lounge. 'Flowers everywhere.' 'Service is unobtrusive, by young men and women in local dress.' The dining rooms are 'relaxed', with subtle lighting: one has an *à la carte* menu, the other serves the 'high-quality' *en pension* dinner. In summer guests eat on a panoramic terrace. 'Healthy ingredients' are grown in the garden ('protected by ducks'); milk comes from the cows that graze in the pasture behind the hotel. The buffet breakfast includes home-made breads, stewed fruit. There is a coolish outdoor swimming pool and a very warm one indoors.

Open Mid-Dec–early Apr, mid-May–mid-Oct. **Rooms** 18 suites (some in annexe), 18 double, 5 single. **Facilities** Lobby bar (pianist), residents' dining room, restaurant; conference facilities; indoor swimming pool, steam room, sauna, solarium, massage. No background music. Garden: terrace, swimming pool. Unsuitable for ♿. **Location** 1 km from centre; 500 m from Hornbahn cable-car station. Parking. **Credit cards** All major cards accepted. **Terms** [2004] B&B double €253–€404; D,B&B €26 added per person. Set meals €42.

LECH AM ARLBERG 6764 Vorarlberg Map 10:F1

Gasthof Post
Dorf 11

Tel (05583) 22060
Fax (05583) 220623
Email info@postlech.com
Website www.postlech.com

In the middle of this upmarket little resort, the former imperial post house is now a smart hotel (Relais & Châteaux). Florian and Sandra Moosbrugger (their family has owned it since 1937) run it, 'faultlessly', entertaining European royalty among others. Frescoes, embroidered cushions, painted wooden furniture, hunting trophies, log fires, flowers and cuckoo clocks combine with 'state-of-the-art facilities', including wireless Internet access and a ski-repair station. Bedrooms (some have a big sitting area) are 'beautifully furnished in Alpine style'. *Guide* readers enjoy the 'understated luxury' and 'homely feel'. 'Our delightful rooms had wonderful views. Dinner [men are asked to wear jacket and tie] was of high quality [try the ox-tail ravioli or the deer medallions]; so was breakfast.' 'Excellent Austrian wines.' Staff are 'fantastic'. Neighbouring buildings overlook some rooms, but the chalet suite offers extra privacy. The large indoor swimming pool has mountain views. The garden has a tea house, and lawns for sunbathing. Not cheap, but in summer all transport (buses and lifts) is free to guests; 'in the morning you can pick up the ingredients for a picnic, and you get a complimentary newspaper'. Ski packages are offered; also summer activities, eg, 'a spectacular walk and a charming lunch at a mountain hut'. Dogs are welcomed, and the village has children's programmes and an outdoor swimming pool.

Open 2 Dec–25 Apr, 24 June–26 Sept. **Rooms** 6 suites (1 across street), 28 double, 5 single. **Facilities** Lift. Salon/library, bar, restaurant; background music; weekly zither/piano evening; children's games room; conference facilities; indoor swimming pool, sauna. Garden: tea house. Unsuitable for ♿. **Location** Central. Parking, garage (free in summer). **Credit cards** MasterCard, Visa. **Terms** B&B: single €200–€310, double €370–€630, suite €520–€840. Set dinner €60–€85; alc €35–€70. 1-night bookings often refused in winter (normal booking Sun–Sun).

LIENZ 9900 Tirol **Map 10:F3**

Parkhotel am Tristachersee

Tel (04852) 67666
Fax (04852) 67699
Email tristachersee@osttirol.com
Website www.parkhotel-tristachersee.at

Under the 'charismatic leadership' of owner/chef Josef Kreuzer, this chalet-style hotel has a 'gorgeous setting' on a small lake, beside wooded hills with the Dolomites in the background. Herr Kreuzer and his wife, Christl, 'are true professionals', say regular visitors. The 'excellent' food is served in 'cosy' Tyrolean-style dining rooms or on the large dining terrace (with movable glass panels) over the lake. Asparagus mousse; trout with potato cake; vanilla and chocolate bananas were enjoyed; also the 'wonderful cheeseboard' and 'excellent Austrian wines'. A champagne gala dinner is held on Sunday. Mineral water comes from the hotel's spring. The public rooms have pale wood panelling. Bedrooms (some have just been renovated) are simple. Most have lake views and a flowery balcony. 'Ours was a long way from the lift (no porter service).' A small single is above the car park. Breakfast is 'sumptuous' (scrambled eggs, strudel, etc). 'The garden, with its fisheries, is beautiful' (loungers stand under mature trees). There is a 'lovely' indoor swimming pool and a spa; yoga classes and birdwatching expeditions are arranged. 'Lienz is very attractive', and an 18-hole golf course is near. (*M and JH, and others*)

Open May–Oct, Dec/Jan. **Rooms** 3 suites, 45 double, 2 single. **Facilities** Lift, ramps. Reception lounge, bar, restaurant (no smoking at breakfast); classical background music, live music sometimes; sauna, swimming pool; fitness facilities. Garden: dining terrace, lake, fishing. Golf nearby. **Location** 5 km E of Lienz. Parking. **Credit cards** All major cards accepted. **Terms** [2004] D,B&B €60–€135; B&B €10 reduction. Set lunch €27, dinner €31; full alc €35.

LOIBICHL AM MONDSEE 5311 Oberösterreich — Map 10:E3

Hotel Seehof

Tel (06232) 5031
Fax (06232) 503151
Email seehof@nextra.at
Website www.seehof-mondsee.com

The original nominator of this sophisticated hotel returned this year and found it 'even more enjoyable'. Owned, and 'immaculately supervised', by Hans and Jutta Nick, it stands by the lake in the gentle mountain scenery of the Salzkammergut, not far from charming Mondsee town. Lawns lead down to a private beach with jetty. The bedrooms, 'some rather grand', and of varying sizes, are in separate buildings. Suites have two baths and a lounge. 'All is beautifully done, comfortable, old-fashioned yet modern looking, bright and clean, in white, yellow, green. Flowers everywhere.' The food is 'hotel Austrian, enjoyable, not expensive'. Summer meals can be taken on a terrace. Service is 'efficient but unobtrusive'. Prices rise at festival time (Salzburg is 30 kilometres away), but are reasonable in early and late season. Minibar drinks are free. (*Felix Singer*)

Open May–Oct. **Rooms** 30 suites, 35 double. In 5 houses. **Facilities** Lounge, bar, breakfast room, restaurant; function facilities; terrace. Garden: beach, waterskiing school, boats, bar, sauna; tennis. Golf nearby. **Location** Shore of Mondsee, 6 km SE of Mondsee town. Off A1 to Salzburg. Garage. **Credit cards** All major cards accepted. **Terms** [2004] Room: double €155–€469, suite €212–€905; D,B&B (min. 3 nights) €30–€38 added per person.

MAUERBACH BEI WIEN 3001 Vienna — Map 10:D5

Berghotel Tulbingerkogel NEW
Tulbingerkogel 1

Tel (02273) 7391
Fax (02273)739173
Email hotel@tulbingerkogel.at
Website www.tulbingerkogel.at

In the middle of the Vienna Woods, this hilltop hotel (Relais du Silence) was built in 1930: the Bläuel family have presided since 1951. 'The location is superb, some 20–30 minutes from the centre of Vienna,' says this year's nominator. 'The lovely terrace, where alfresco meals are served, has uninterrupted views of the Alps and the Danube valley. You can step out of the grounds on to a number of trails through the woods. The architecture of the annexe is less attractive than that of the main house, and rooms are quite simple.' Traditional dishes are served in the restaurant. 'The food is excellent and varied, and there are some very good local wines. An ideal refuge from Vienna's summer heat.' The swimming pool on the terrace, covered in winter, can be used all year round. (*Andrey Kidel*)

Open All year. **Rooms** 2 suites, 24 double, 18 single. Some no-smoking. **Facilities** Lift, ramps. Lobby, TV room, bar, restaurant (classical background music), wintergarden. Garden: terraces, heated swimming pool, sauna, steam bath, solarium. **Location** 8 km NW of Vienna (25 km from city centre) towards Tulln. Leave A1 at Wien Auhof. **Credit cards** Amex, MasterCard, Visa. **Terms** B&B: single €63–€88, double €90–€260, suite €210–€432; D,B&B €25 added per person. Set meals €28–€45; full alc €42. *V*

MILLSTATT AM SEE 9872 Kärnten — Map 10:F3

Hotel Die Forelle
Fischergasse 65

Tel (04766) 2050
Fax (04766) 205011
Email office@hotel-forelle.at
Website www.hotel-forelle.at

In a 'delightful' setting, on a promontory on the lake in this 'unspoilt, friendly' resort, this long-established family hotel is owned by Mathias and Christa Aniwanter. They and their staff 'keep a watchful eye on proceedings', says a regular visitor. 'There is a splendid dining terrace, a small outdoor pool, a sun terrace, a reasonably priced and delightful bar, and an excellent restaurant: don't miss the fillet of rabbit. Service is first rate. A senior member of staff always tours the dining room to check that all is well.' The bedrooms are spacious, and most have a 'wonderful' balcony looking over the lake. Upper Millstatt, five minutes' drive away, has spectacular views; within a half-hour drive is 'magnificent Alpine scenery'. (*SP*)

Open May–Oct. **Rooms** 60. **Facilities** Lounges, bar, restaurant; dining terrace; beauty treatments. Garden: sun terrace, swimming pool, beach: fishing, water sports. **Location** On lake. NW of Klagenfurt, 4 km E of Seeboden. **Credit cards** MasterCard, Visa. **Terms** [2004] D,B&B €57.50–€136. No single surcharge in low season.

OBERALM BEI HALLEIN 5411 Salzburger Land — Map 10:E3

Schloss Haunsperg
Hammerstrasse 51

Tel (06245) 80662
Fax (06245) 85680
Email info@schlosshaunsperg.com
Website www.schlosshaunsperg.com

Fifteen minutes by car from Salzburg, in a village not far from the motorway, this 'very special place' is run by its owners, Eike and Georg von Gernerth-Mautner Markhof, in house-party style. They write: 'Children and pets are always welcomed in this multilingual family home.' Inside the ivy-clad 14th-century *Schloss* are elegant public rooms, family antiques and pictures, Persian rugs, chandeliers, vaulted ceilings. There is a baroque chapel and a music room with a grand piano – a von Gernerth ancestor wrote the words to *The Blue Danube*. The 'cheerful hosts' are full of local information. Some bedrooms are up three flights of stairs (no lift). Spacious suites have a large lounge, 'beautiful old furniture, interesting objects'. Bathrooms, if on the small side, 'contain much luxury'. Copious breakfasts are served with good china, crystal and silver. Snacks and drinks are available, and help is given with dinner and ticket reservations. 'Good restaurants are a short walk away.' There is a big playground and a clay tennis court in the park. Nearby is 'spectacular Alpine walking'.

Open All year. **Rooms** 4 suites, 4 double. **Facilities** 2 lounges, breakfast room. Garden: tennis, children's playground. Unsuitable for ♿. **Location** 15 km S of Salzburg, 1 km N of Hallein. *Autobahn* A10, exit 16 (Hallein). **Credit cards** All major cards accepted. **Terms** B&B: single €96, double €160, suite €200. 10% reduction in low season.

OETZ 6433 Tirol — Map 10:F2

Villa Agnes NEW/BUDGET
Dorfstrasse 34

Tel/Fax (05252) 6205
Email villaagnes@utanet.at
Website www.villa-agnes.com

In 'excellent skiing and hiking country', Oetz is at the north end of an attractive valley leading from the River Inn to the high mountains along the Italian frontier. Astrid Wolf's three-storey *pension*, in the centre, has good-sized bedrooms in rustic style, says the nominator. 'My bathroom was adequate; the street goes nowhere important, so there was little outside noise. But the owners played loud music in the evening, limiting the relaxation value of the residents' lounges. Breakfast was a satisfactory buffet, served in an attractive room. Very inexpensive, but you must bring your own soap, shampoo, etc.' There are red-and-white tablecloths in the wood-panelled public rooms, and antlers on walls. Balconies and windows are flower-bedecked in summer. (*Charles Belair*)

Open 19 Dec–10 Apr, 15 May–20 Oct. **Rooms** 1 suite, 10 double, 2 single. No telephone. **Facilities** 2 lounges, bar, breakfast room. Garden: table tennis, children's playground. **Location** Central. 50 km W of Innsbruck. Parking. **Credit cards** None accepted. **Terms** B&B (min. 7 nights in season) €22–€28.

PÖRTSCHACH AM WÖRTHERSEE 9210 Kärnten — Map 10:F4

Schloss Leonstain
Leonstainerstrasse 1

Tel (04272) 2816
Fax (04272) 2823
Email info@leonstain.at
Website www.leonstain.at

Dinner was found 'outstanding' by a visitor in 2004 to Christoph Neuscheller's sophisticated hotel/restaurant on the main street of this fashionable Wörthersee resort. 'Characterful and sprawling', the former monastery has wooden beams, white walls, pictures and antiques. The bedrooms vary from 'Biedermeier' to 'rural elegance'. 'Ours had a balcony with chairs and tables, good bathroom (under-floor heating).' 'Thick walls kept my room cool in summer.' Some rooms hear the railway at the back. The minimalist decor of the restaurant (14 *Gault Millau* points) matches the modern cuisine. 'The buffet breakfast was excellent; the friendly restaurant staff were efficient.' Summer meals are served in the arcaded courtyard where there are vines, a fountain and a bust of Brahms (he once stayed). In the 'well-being area', Florian Neuscheller offers yoga, breathing therapy, etc. On the other side of the road is a private beach, with surfboards, deckchairs, parasols, bathing in the lake's cool, clear water, and views of snow-capped mountains. Eight golf courses are nearby. (*John Collier, and others*)

Open May–Oct. **Rooms** 5 suites, 24 double, 2 single. Some in garden villa. **Facilities** Lobby (computer access), bar, restaurant; 'chill out' background music; games room; sauna, solarium, well-being centre; conference room. Courtyard, garden: children's play area; private beach across road (summer restaurant). Unsuitable for ♿. **Location** Main street of resort (windows double glazed). 20 km W of Klagenfurt. Parking. **Credit cards** Diners, MasterCard, Visa. **Terms** B&B: single €84–€110, double €94–€114, suite €99–€134; D,B&B (min. 3 days) €19–€25 added per person. Full alc €37.

REIFNITZ 9081 Kärnten — Map 10:F4

Strandhotel Sille NEW
am Corso 108

Tel (04273) 2237
Fax (04273) 244853
Email reservierung@hotel-sille.com
Website www.hotel-sille.com

'Beautifully situated' on S side of Wörthersee: Botzenhart family's white-walled, red-roofed hotel. 'A welcome find. Our pleasant suite faced the lake. Good food,' say nominators. Sophisticated, uncluttered decor. Lounge, restaurant, lovely lakeside terrace (meal service), lawn with loungers; 2 seminar rooms. All major credit cards accepted. 2 suites, 24 bedrooms. B&B €44–€95; D,B&B €57–€109 [2004].

ST GILGEN 5340 Salzburger Land — Map 10:E3

Gasthof Fürberg BUDGET
Winkl 19

Tel (06227) 23850
Fax (06227) 238535
Email gasthof@fuerberg.at
Website www.fuerberg.at

East of Salzburg, 2 km from delightful village (30 mins' walk or 8 mins by ferry), on shore of Wolfgangsee, amid spectacular scenery: Karin and Bernhard Ebner's white-walled hotel with flowery balconies, lawn with parasols, lakeside walk, free boating and fishing. Warmly endorsed this year. 'Beautiful, peaceful setting; excellent food, notably fresh fish; good service. Half board excellent value' (it includes soup-and-salad lunch, 4-course dinner). Wood panelling, carved wooden pillars in public rooms. Stüberl *(beautiful carved ceiling), restaurant (no smoking at breakfast). Open week before Easter–mid-Oct. All major credit cards accepted. 30 bedrooms, some no-smoking; some fairly luxurious, others quite simple, some suitable for ♿; most have balcony and lake views. B&B double €76–€172; D,B&B €25 added per person [2004].*

SALZBURG Map 10:E3

Hotel Astoria Salzburg BUDGET
Maxglaner Hauptstrasse 7
5020 Salzburg

Tel (0662) 834277
Fax (0662) 83427740
Email hotel.astoria@aon.at
Website www.astoriasalzburg.com

Illinger family's reasonably priced hotel, 15 mins' walk from historic centre. Tasteful, modern decor, friendly staff. Café; lovely terrace for breakfast ('excellent buffet') and light meals (available all day). Some traffic noise. Private parking. All major credit cards accepted. 30 bedrooms (some with small glassed-in balcony). B&B €44–€75 [2004].

Gasthof-Hotel Doktorwirt
Glaserstrasse 9
5026 Salzburg-Aigen

Tel (0662) 6229730
Fax (0662) 62297325
Email schnoell@doktorwirt.co.at
Website www.doktorwirt.co.at

A 'lovely traditional hotel', much enjoyed in 2004: 'We can't give it enough accolades,' one reader wrote. Another adds: 'What a delightful place. Some of the nicest, most professional hoteliers I have come across.' An ancient creeper-covered inn, with panelling, beamed ceilings and carved wooden furniture, it is in a residential suburb a short ride by trolley bus from the centre. The 'extremely helpful' Karl and Anneliese Schnöll (his family have owned it for over a century) run it with their identical twin daughters and younger son. 'The people, the service and the menus reflect the finest that Salzburg offers. Beautiful walking area, sounds of cowbells,' says this year's reporter. Others wrote: 'You can combine visits to the city with a relaxing setting against wooded hills.' 'Delightful dogs.' Breakfast is in a conservatory. For dinner you can eat *à la carte* or choose a simple set menu. 'Food of a high standard.' There is a swimming pool in the garden, and also one indoors. Some bedrooms have a balcony. Ten minutes' walk away is the Von Trapp family home. (*Bruce McFadden, Jennifer Harte*)

Open All year, except 2nd/3rd week Feb, mid-Oct–end Nov. Restaurant closed Mon, and Sun night in low season. **Rooms** 5 junior suites, 32 double, 4 single. Some no-smoking. **Facilities** Bar, 3 *Stüberl* (1 no-smoking), restaurant, conservatory; conference room; indoor swimming pool, sauna, solarium, fitness room. No background music. Garden: terrace, heated swimming pool, children's play area, table tennis. Unsuitable for ♿. **Location** 4 km S of centre (10 mins by bus). **Credit cards** All major cards accepted. **Terms** B&B: single €68–€90, double €105–€160; D,B&B €15 added per person; full board €30 added per person. Set lunch €12.50, dinner €28; full alc €35. 1-night bookings sometimes refused during festival.

> Important: Please regard the terms printed as only a rough guide to the sort of bill you can expect at the end of your stay. You *must* check the tariffs when booking.

Hotel Goldener Hirsch NEW

Getreidegasse 37
5020 Salzburg

Tel (0662) 80840
Fax (0662) 843349
Email welcome@goldenerhirsch.com
Website www.goldenerhirsch.com

In this famous street in the pedestrianised centre, this old hotel, opposite the festival hall, has long been managed by Herbert Pöcklhofer. Composed of several tall, narrow houses, it has a lift, also 'rather a lot of stairs and creaky floorboards'. Antlers, wood-carved statues and old furniture adorn its public areas. 'Excellently run', 'very friendly; great attention to detail,' say this year's visitors restoring it to the *Guide* after a time without feedback. The bedrooms on various levels are 'comfortable and decorated with taste': most are furnished with antiques. The main restaurant, 'very Austrian in feel', serves 'good meat courses', veal, venison, etc; the Austrian wines (but not the others) are 'reasonably priced'. In the 'atmospheric' tavern, *Herzl*, 'jolly female staff serve hearty local fare'. The Green Bar, with its covered courtyard and 'folksy atmosphere', is frequented by locals. Breakfast has 'plenty of choice'. 'Some traffic noise.' (*IGC Farman, FH Potts*)

Open All year. **Rooms** 4 suites, 63 double, 2 single. 6 in nearby annexe. Some no-smoking. Air conditioning. **Facilities** Lift. Bar (classical background music), 2 restaurants; conference/banqueting rooms. Unsuitable for ♿. **Location** Inner city, 400 m W of Residenz. Valet parking. **Credit cards** All major cards accepted. **Terms** Room: single €119–€660, double €150–€660, suite €335–€1,110. Breakfast €25. Set meals €51; full alc €65.

Altstadthotel Weisse Taube

Kaigasse 9
5020 Salzburg

Tel (0662) 842404
Fax (0662) 841783
Email hotel@weissetaube.at
Website www.weissetaube.at

Run by its friendly owners, Doris and Helmut Wollner and their family, this B&B hotel is a converted 14th-century *Burgerhaus* in an 'outstanding' location, near the Mozartplatz. 'Staff are efficient; bedrooms are simple but pleasant,' say recent visitors. The rooms have minibar and TV. 'Good breakfast (not a buffet): extras at reasonable cost. Highly recommended.' Guests with a car should get advance instructions about parking. (*Y and KF*)

Open All year, except 6–21 Jan. **Rooms** 25 double, 6 single. **Facilities** Lift. Breakfast room. No background music. Unsuitable for ♿. **Location** Central, near Mozartplatz. Street parking nearby; public garage 8 mins' walk. **Restrictions** No smoking in breakfast room. No pets. **Credit cards** All major cards accepted. **Terms** B&B: single €61–€82, double €96–€165. Min. 2 nights at New Year. *V*

The *V* sign at the end of an entry indicates that the hotel has agreed to take part in our Voucher scheme and to give *Guide* readers a 25% discount on its room or B&B rates, subject to the conditions explained in *How to read the entries*, and on the back of the vouchers.

Altstadthotel Wolf-Dietrich
Wolf-Dietrich-Strasse 7
5020 Salzburg

Tel (0662) 871275
Fax (0662) 8712759
Email office@salzburg-hotel.at
Website www.salzburg-hotel.at

On the edge of the *Altstadt*, the Schmelzle family's 'pleasant hotel' is near Schloss Mirabell and the Kapuzinerberg. Some bedrooms (several have a balcony) look over the adjacent St Sebastian's church and Italianate cloister (where Mozart's father and widow lie buried). 'Staff were friendly; the receptionists spoke excellent English. All is quiet at night, but bell-ringing starts early,' wrote recent guests. 'Our mini-suite had a canopied bed, crystal chandeliers, a nice sitting area. The ceiling was studded with little lights like stars. Adequate breakfasts.' In the basement is a small swimming pool with murals, chlorine-free water and jet stream. The organic restaurant, *Ährlich*, serves salads, vegetarian dishes, goulash, braised steak, etc. In summer, there is a pavement café.

Open All year. Restaurant closed 30 Jan–14 Mar, Sun/Mon, midday except July/Aug. **Rooms** 4 suites, 18 double, 5 single. 14 in annexe opposite. **Facilities** Small lounge, breakfast room, restaurant (classical background music); swimming pool, sauna; courtyard, pavement café. Unsuitable for ♿. **Location** *Altstadt*, pedestrian zone near Kapuzinerberg. Garage 200 m (€12 daily). **Credit cards** All major cards accepted. **Terms** B&B: single €69–€109, double €109–€184, suite €154–€209; D,B&B €20 added per person. Set lunch €8, dinner €20.

SCHRUNS 6780 Vorarlberg — Map 10:F1

Hotel Krone BUDGET
Ausserlitzstrasse 2

Tel (05556) 722550
Fax (05556) 7225522
Email hotelkrone@austria-urlaub.com
Website www.hotelkrone-schruns.com

'Superb and reasonably priced.' Near railway station of lively capital of lovely Montafon valley: 180-year-old hotel owned by Armin Gmeiner and family, who have extensively renovated. 'Still a pleasure to visit,' say returning visitors. 'Friendly service; delicious half-board dinner.' Lift, bar; beamed breakfast room; panelled restaurant (closed in summer); small conference room; Internet facilities. Sauna, ski room. Garden with chestnut trees. Parking. MasterCard, Visa accepted. 12 bedrooms with rustic antiques (1 suitable for ♿). B&B €36.50–€61; D,B&B €52–€76.50 [2004].

SEEFELD 6100 Tirol — Map 10:F2

Hotel Seelos NEW
Wettersteinstrasse 226

Tel (05212) 2308
Fax (05212) 204541
Email info@hotel-seelos.at
Website www.hotel-seelos.at

'We were very impressed,' says the 2004 nominator of the Seelos family's chalet-hotel, quietly set above this well-heeled mountain resort: David Seelos is owner/manager. 'Lovely room with balcony providing superb view of Seefeld and surrounding mountains. Spotlessly clean. Superb service. Cuisine above average. Our package in June included buffet breakfast, packed lunch, afternoon tea with cake, four- or five-course dinner (with choice of main course) and Austrian wine. Our only criticism: we thought the beef and lamb less good than the veal.' There is entertainment once a week, trips in the hotel minibus, etc. Guests have free access to Seefeld's Olympic swimming pool. (*David Ayres-Regan*)

Open 15 Dec–5 Apr, 15 May–4 Oct. **Rooms** 4 suites, 26 double, 5 single. 10 no-smoking. **Facilities** Lift. Lobby, lounge, American bar (pianist), restaurant; music and dancing; fitness room: sauna, massage, etc. Garden: sun terrace. **Location** 10 mins' walk from centre. 21 km NW of Innsbruck. Garage, car park. **Credit cards** MasterCard, Visa. **Terms** B&B: single €47–€112, double €94–€224, suite €138–€246; D,B&B €57–€122 per person. Set lunch €15, dinner €20; full alc €29. *V*

Aktivhotel Veronika
Riehlweg 161

Tel (05212) 2105
Fax (05212) 3787
Email veronika@seefeld.at
Website www.hotel-veronika.at

'We found both hotel and resort charming,' say visitors in 2004 to the Kirchmair family's chalet-hotel, liked for its 'genuine Tyrolean character' (staff wear local costume). Flowery window boxes adorn its balconies in summer. It provides many sporting activities; the cable car to the Rosshütte/Seefelderspitze is near; there is good winter skiing and summer walking. Families are welcomed: there is a 'Kiddy-Club', a playroom, and entertainments ('Family Olympics', etc) are organised. The half-board menu has limited choice (you select your main course at breakfast). 'The standard was high.' 'Tasty dishes, colourfully presented. But wines, apart from the acceptable house wines, were expensive.' The generous breakfast buffet, served until noon, includes cold meats, fruit, boiled eggs. Most bedrooms have a balcony. 'Our room was excellent. Bathroom with separate loo.' 'Ours was spacious, but the small bathroom had only a half-bath.' At night a chocolate is left on your pillow. 'Some noise from trains.' 'Great value in summer.' (*Florence and Russell Birch, Carolyn and Robin Orme*)

Open 21 Nov–31 Mar, 15 May–31 Oct. **Rooms** 6 suites, 40 double, 3 single. **Facilities** Lift. Lobby, billiard room, bar (pianist), restaurant; background music; swimming pool, sauna, whirlpool, massage; children's club (Sun–Fri, 3–10 pm); 4 meeting rooms. Garden. **Location** 300 m from station. 18 km NW of Innsbruck. Garage, car park. **Credit cards** All major cards accepted. **Terms** D,B&B €62–€167. Set lunch €25, dinner €30; full alc €25–€30.

Don't trust out-of-date editions of the *Guide*. Hotels change hands, deteriorate or go out of business. Each year many hotels are dropped and many new ones are added.

SEEHAM 5164 Salzburger Land — Map 10:E3

Hotel Walkner BUDGET
Eisenharting 4

Tel (06217) 5550
Fax (06217) 555022
Email hotel.walkner@eunet.at
Website www.hotel-walkner.at

Salzburg is only 15 minutes' drive away, but this family-friendly hotel is in a 'sleepy little village'. It stands on a small hill amid beautiful scenery in large and lovely grounds on the Trumer Lake. Two other bathing lakes are near, and the open countryside around is good for cycling. The 'most agreeable' owners, Hilda and Bernhard Haberl, have many devotees, attracted by the 'consistent high standards'. 'Still great value; lovely breakfast buffet,' one wrote. Others said: 'We have been visiting for a mere 18 years. We are outstripped by guests from France, Germany and Austria whom we first met here as children and who are now coming with *their* children.' There are games, table football, etc, for the young. The restaurant and terrace café look over the large garden (with swimming pool) to the lake, as do the bedrooms (best ones have a living area and balcony). The small attic rooms can be 'airless' in summer. 'Traffic by day, but quiet at night.' On the menus much local produce is used. Two new chefs arrived this year: 'They are very creative,' the Haberls tell us. The hotel's dairy provides the basis of a cheese menu. The summer Sunday barbecue is popular with locals.

Open All year, except Christmas, 14 days Nov. **Rooms** 17 double, 5 single. **Facilities** TV room, bar, games room, restaurant (background music/live music), breakfast room (no-smoking); conference room; sauna, solarium, fitness room; children's playroom. Garden: terraces (summer café), swimming pool (heated May–Oct), children's playground. Lake (sailing, fishing, bathing) 400 m. Unsuitable for ♿. **Location** 18 km N of Salzburg, by Mattighofen road. Parking. **Credit cards** Amex, MasterCard, Visa. **Terms** B&B €33–€54; D,B&B €47–€68. Set lunch €10, dinner €14; full alc €23.30. *V* (1 night)

VIENNA — Map 10:E5

Hotel Austria BUDGET
Am Fleischmarkt 20
1010 Vienna

Tel (01) 51523
Fax (01) 51523506
Email office@hotelaustria-wien.at
Website www.hotelaustria-wien.at

'Good value, good location, extremely helpful staff,' says a returning visitor to this B&B hotel managed by Christian Zeidler. 'Recent refurbishment has turned it into a gem.' It is in a pedestrianised cul-de-sac between St Stephan's cathedral and the Danube. 'Amazingly quiet', 'very friendly', it has a modern decor: much maroon, dark wood furnishings and oriental rugs. 'Our room was extremely comfortable,' wrote a couple who appreciated the large bathroom 'with *bath*'. The 'good, basic continental' breakfast, in a 'lovely room' with chandeliers and a fountain, is accompanied by newspapers in several languages. 'The lift is small', sometimes necessitating a short wait. There is a roof garden, and an Internet corner. Children are welcomed (babysitters available). (*Simon Routh, and others*)

Open All year. **Rooms** 4 suites, 38 double, 4 single. 38 with facilities *en suite*. Some no-smoking. **Facilities** Lift. 2 lounges, TV room, breakfast room (no-smoking). Roof garden. Unsuitable for ♿. **Location** Central, near cathedral. Garage 50 m. (Metro: Stephansplatz) **Credit cards** All major cards accepted. **Terms** [2004] B&B: single €49–€95, double €78–€136, suite €119–€185. *V*

Hotel Kaiserin Elisabeth NEW
Weihburggasse 3
1010 Vienna

Tel (01) 515260
Fax (01) 515267
Email info@kaiserinelisabeth.at
Website www.kaiserinelisabeth.at

'The location could not be better,' says a visitor this year to this 'lovely, smart hotel', 'central but quiet', liked for both 'elegance and value'. Privately owned, and managed by Norbert Klindert, it is in a small pedestrianised street close to St Stephan's cathedral. 'One of the most immaculately maintained hotels I have stayed in,' was one comment in 2004. Other visitors found Reception 'particularly helpful'. Public areas are traditional: oriental rugs on marble floors, big armchairs in the 'delightful lounge', with its glass dome and portrait of the empress. Most bedrooms overlook a quiet courtyard. 'Our large, well-furnished room had two armchairs and excellent lighting.' 'A glorious bathroom.' But one single was 'small and overheated', another had a 'depressing outlook'. And 'the heavy wooden doors echo loudly when guests open and close them'. Breakfast (7 to 11 am), in a 'very Viennese' room, is a buffet. Snacks are available during the day, and many restaurants are close by: *Zum Weissen Rauchfangkehrer* (the White Chimney Sweep) is particularly recommended. 'Take all you need from your car: access to the garage is not easy.' (*Mark Gross, and others*)

Open All year. **Rooms** 3 suites, 42 double, 18 single. 50% air conditioned. **Facilities** Lift. Lobby/bar, lounge, computer corner; small conference room. No background music. **Location** In pedestrian zone near cathedral. Parking in nearby contract garage, pick-up and delivery service (€28 per day, cash). Airport shuttle. (Metro: Stephansplatz) **Credit cards** All major cards accepted. **Terms** B&B: single €119, double €205, suite €225. 3 nights for price of 2: weekends 4 Nov–28 Mar (except New Year, 23 Feb).

Hotel König von Ungarn
Schulerstrasse 10
1010 Vienna

Tel (01) 515840
Fax (01) 515848
Email hotel@kvu.at
Website www.kvu.at

Much loved by *Guide* readers, this is said to be the oldest hotel in Vienna (opened 1815). 'Full of character', it is close to St Stephan's cathedral and 'very good shopping'. It has a yellow exterior and a vaulted reception area that opens on to a glassed-over courtyard, now the lounge/bar, with trees, plants and easy chairs. Here, guests can enjoy *Wiener Kaffeespezialitäten*. Service 'is very good'. All the bedrooms are different; most are 'nice and roomy'. Some look on to the atrium; street-facing ones are lighter. Bathrooms are modern. There are some two-bedroom duplex apartments. Breakfast, served until noon, includes 'healthy options'. The vaulted restaurant is separately owned. The house next door, where *The Marriage of Figaro* was composed, contains a charming Mozart museum. The air terminal is a short walk away. (*M and JH, and others*)

Open All year. Restaurant closed midday. **Rooms** 8 apartments, 21 double, 4 single. Air conditioning. **Facilities** Lift, ramps. Lobby, bar, restaurant (separately owned); Viennese background music; conference room. **Location** Central; near St Stephan's cathedral, in maze of 1-way streets. Special rates at nearby garage. (Metro: Stephansplatz) **Credit cards** All major cards accepted. **Terms** [2004] B&B: single €135–€155, double €192, apartment (3–4 people) €270–€320.

Mailberger Hof NEW
Annagasse 7
1010 Vienna

Tel (01) 5120641
Fax (01) 512064110
Email reception@mailbergerhof.at
Website www.mailbergerhof.at

A stone's throw from the Opera, in a pedestrianised street, this 'very friendly', family-run hotel is composed of two Gothic gabled listed buildings formerly owned by the Knights of Malta. 'Very much a *Guide* hotel,' says its nominator this year. 'It has style and is quiet. Reserve a room on the nice, leafy inner courtyard, a pleasant place for meals in fine weather.' There is a 17th-century fresco in the lounge. The small restaurant serves 'Vienna specialities and Naturküche'. (*Andrey Kidel*)

Open All year. **Rooms** 6 apartments, 40 double. Some no-smoking. **Facilities** Lounge, restaurant; meeting room. Courtyard. **Location** Central, just off Kaertnerstrasse. (Metro: Stephansplatz) **Credit cards** All major cards accepted. **Terms** [2004] B&B: single €125–€140, double €195–€230.

Pension Nossek
Graben 17
1010 Vienna

Tel (01) 53370410
Fax (01) 5353646
Email reservation@pension-nossek.at
Website www.pension-nossek.at

'Amazing value. Genuinely friendly.' 'Our spacious, nicely decorated room had a newly refurbished, attractive bathroom.' Always liked for its old-fashioned ambience, this *pension* (for over 100 years) is on the upper floors of a 19th-century office/apartment block in the main pedestrian and shopping area. It is run by two sisters, Theresia Bernad and Susanne Gundolf, whose family has owned it since 1914. The high-ceilinged bedrooms have homely furnishings; some have a balcony; some see St Stephan's spire, and buildings on and around the Graben. Double glazing cuts out street noise; flowers come from the owners' garden. Rooms at the back are small. Breakfast is 'a rich buffet'. 'Cars and taxis cannot get right to the building: arrive with the minimum of luggage.' (*MM*)

Open All year. **Rooms** 3 suites, 22 double, 5 single. Not all singles have a WC. **Facilities** Lift. Lounge with TV, breakfast room (background music). Unsuitable for ♿. **Location** Central; corner of Graben/Habsburgergasse. Underground car park (MQ) nearby. (Metro: Stephansplatz) **Credit cards** None accepted. **Terms** B&B: single €54–€70, double €105, suite €130.

Hotel Zur Wiener Staatsoper NEW *Tel* (01) 5131274
Krugerstrasse 11 *Fax* (01) 513127415
1010 Vienna *Email* office@zurwienerstaatsoper.at
Website www.zurwienerstaatsoper.at

'A charming and stately old *pension*,' say visitors in 2004. In a pedestrianised street near the Karntner Strasse, this 19th-century building, with its baroque facade, flowery window boxes and wrought iron doors, is close to St Stephan's cathedral. 'Graceful entrance, friendly welcome. The large Reception has a beautiful chandelier. Our room, attractive and bright, if a bit small, faced the front but was quiet. Wonderfully comfy large bed, lovely linens, antique furniture; good shower room. Very generous breakfasts (fresh fruit, good rolls, sausages, eggs if wanted). Great value.' The bedroom decor is quite simple. The manager is Claudia Neumann-Ungersböck, and the hotel is child- and pet-friendly. (*Sue Ann and Martin Marcus*)

Open All year, except 3 weeks Nov. **Rooms** 16 double, 6 single, all with shower. **Facilities** Lift. Reception hall, Lounge/breakfast room (no smoking during breakfast). Unsuitable for ♿. **Location** Pedestrian zone near St Stephan's. Parking in nearby garage: hotel provides tickets. (Metro: Stephansplatz) **Credit cards** All major cards accepted. **Terms** [2004] B&B: single €78–€95, double €111–€140, triple €133–€160.

WEISSENKIRCHEN 3610 Niederösterreich Map 10:D4

Raffelsberger Hof *Tel* (02715) 2201
Weissenkirchen 54 *Fax* (02715) 220127
Email raffelsberger@nextra.at
Website www.raffelsbergerhof.at

This wine-producing village near the Danube in the unspoilt Wachau is 'a historic and gastronomic paradise', say visitors this year, and the Anton family's B&B hotel (a lovely arcaded Renaissance shipmaster's house, filled with antiques) is 'magical'. Claudia Anton is the 'excellent' manager. 'Our rooms on the ground floor were ideal. We were treated to candles, fresh flowers, swallows flying into the courtyard.' On a previous occasion they had a 'spacious, spotless bedroom looking over the lovely garden and its fruit trees'. The help-yourself breakfast includes eggs, ham, local jams and the odd cake. 'Good value.' No restaurant, but the wine bar, in the vaults, is 'good for a snack (delicious local salami) and a glass of local wine', and the *Hotel Jamek*, 20 minutes' walk away, has 'welcoming atmosphere and quality food'. (*Michael and Jennifer Hodge*)

Open Easter–end Nov. **Rooms** 2 suites, 11 double, 2 single. **Facilities** Salon, breakfast room, wine bar. Garden. **Location** Centre of village, W of Krems. Parking. **Credit cards** Diners, MasterCard, Visa. **Terms** B&B: single €62–€80, double €98–€112, suite €128–€152.

The 'New' label is used both for new entries and for hotels that have been readmitted to the *Guide* this year.

Belgium

Romantik Hotel Le Val d'Amblève

ANTWERP 2000 **Map 3:C4**

Villa Mozart
Handschoenmarkt 3

Tel 03 231 30 31
Fax 03 231 56 85
Email info@villamozart.be
Website www.bestwestern.com

Opposite cathedral ('great if you don't mind the bells'): 'friendly, efficient' hotel (Best Western). 'Good value.' Bar/brasserie Metropool*; terrace for summer meals; sauna; banqueting/meeting facilities; lift. All major credit cards accepted. Secure parking nearby. 25 bedrooms: €109–€119. Breakfast €12. D,B&B €15 added per person [2004].* *V*

De Witte Lelie
Keizerstraat 16–18

Tel 03 226 19 66
Fax 03 234 00 19
Email hotel@dewittelelie.be
Website www.dewittelelie.be

Near the magnificent 14th-century cathedral, this attractive conversion of a group of gabled 17th-century town houses is a 'luxurious but not stuffy' B&B hotel, managed by the 'splendid' Monica Bock. It is liked for the 'understated style', 'high levels of service, and genuinely warm welcome', and is full of 'light, calm and quiet'. The entrance hall, with black and white floor tiles and a baby grand piano, leads to a striking floodlit patio. Bedrooms, done in white, have a mix of antique and contemporary furniture, and free port and sherry; some have a CD-player. 'One of the best continental breakfasts we have had': served in the room, on a terrace, or in the white kitchen, it has hams, cheeses, sausages, freshly baked croissants, scrambled eggs. 'Pricey but worth it.' (*G and VB, and others*)

Open 9 Jan–21 Dec. **Rooms** 3 suites, 6 double, 1 single. Some no-smoking. 1 with terrace. 5 air conditioned. **Facilities** Lift. Lobby, 2 lounges; breakfast room (no-smoking); background music. Patio garden. **Location** Central, just E of cathedral. Private underground garage. **Credit cards** Amex, MasterCard, Visa. **Terms** [2004] B&B: single €180, double €240, suite €250–€420.

BOUILLON 6830 Luxembourg Belge — Map 3:E4

La Ferronnière
Voie Jocquée 44

Tel 061 23 07 50
Fax 061 46 43 18
Email info@laferronniere.be
Website www.laferronniere.be

The 'fabulous food and gentle atmosphere' were enjoyed again in 2004 at this 'gorgeous' restaurant-with-rooms (*Michelin Bib Gourmand*). Set above a steep valley on a loop of the River Semois, it is owned and managed by Angélique Maqua (of the family who run the popular *Hotel des Ardennes*, Corbion, *qv*), and her Dutch husband, Wim Philips (the chef). She has 'all the splendid attributes of her family', say fans, and he is a 'splendid cook'. 'Angélique was nursing her newborn son, but Wim and the staff kept everything together charmingly. He worked with unruffled grace front-of-house and in the kitchen, speaking many languages.' The old villa has been renovated this year, losing some of its creeper cover. The restaurant is Art Deco in style: 'its windows were filled with greenness from the valley opposite'. There is a comfortable conservatory/lounge, and a 'delightful' outside eating area. The bedrooms are thought 'charming'. 'We loved the home-made rhubarb jam at breakfast. Wim gave us a pot to take home.' Bouillon, on the edge of a forest, 'was down at heel, but has been galvanised into new life'. (*Mari Roberts and Christian Gotsch, BG*)

Open All year, except 9–27 Jan, 13–24 Mar, 19 June–7 July, Mon/Tues midday. **Rooms** 7 double. **Facilities** Lounge/conservatory, restaurant (no-smoking; classical background music). Garden. **Location** 500 m from centre. 8 km E of Corbion. Parking. **Credit cards** MasterCard, Visa. **Terms** [2004] B&B €75–€110; D,B&B €69–€128. Set lunch €25–€30, dinner €30–€55. *V*

BRUGES 8000 West-Vlaanderen — Map 3:C3

Hotel Adornes

Sint-Annarei 26

Tel 050 34 13 36
Fax 050 34 20 85
Email info@adornes.be
Website www.adornes.be

'Unpretentious, spotless, good value', Nathalie Standaert's B&B hotel consists of four gabled houses on a corner by a canal bridge. They have been updated in a style 'perfectly suited' to their age; a lift has been 'craftily fitted' into a medieval space. Within walking distance are all the main sights, but one visitor preferred using one of the bicycles which the hotel provides free of charge: 'We found the streets less crowded than the pavements.' An earlier comment: 'Our spacious, quiet room faced the inner courtyard and had everything we could want. Reception staff were young, courteous and knowledgeable.' The best bedrooms are oak-beamed. 'Our third-floor double was airy, very comfortable.' Some rooms are 'small and functional'; some hear comings and goings at a nearby school. The good breakfast, in a room with a high ceiling, candles, flowers, open fire, includes 'cereals, six types of home-made bread, yogurt, fruit purées'. In the 17th-century cellar are a bar, a small library, videos and children's games. 'Good-mannered' dogs are accepted (not in the breakfast room). For meals, *Cafedraal*, 'in a beautiful shady garden', is recommended. (*Trevor Sanderson, and others*)

Open 9 Feb–1 Jan. **Rooms** 20 double. Some on ground floor. **Facilities** Lift, ramp. Lounge, TV room, breakfast room (no-smoking); background music. Courtyard. Free bicycles. **Location** From ring road enter via Dampoort; follow canal towards centre; hotel signposted. Free parking 200 m. **Credit cards** All major cards accepted. **Terms** B&B: single €90–€115, double €95–€120. No weekend 1-night block bookings.

Hotel Anselmus

Riddersstraat 15

Tel 050 34 13 74
Fax 050 34 19 16
Email info@anselmus.be
Website www.anselmus.be

A 'quiet, tasteful' B&B just four minutes' walk from the Markt. It was liked again this year for its reasonable prices and 'the kindness of the owners', Magda Maenhoudt and her husband, and their staff. Help is given with parking and luggage. The handsome old gabled house has a fine staircase, chandeliers and a 'cosy yet elegant' breakfast room which faces a rose garden with a cupid statue. Some bedrooms share this view. The best rooms are large. 'Ours, at the back, reached up steep winding steps (no lift), was pin-drop quiet.' Seven new rooms opened in 2004. The substantial breakfast has squeezed orange juice, fresh rolls, ham, salami, cheese and 'a surprise' for children. (*John and Alice Severs, Carol Godfrey, Luisa Nobili*)

Open 4 Feb–31 Dec. **Rooms** 1 suite, 15 double, 1 single. 2 on ground floor. **Facilities** Lounge, Internet room, breakfast room (classical background music). Garden. **Location** On foot: leave Burg Square via Hoogstraat; 3rd street on left. By car: enter at Kruispoort. Riddersstraat (one-way) is just after old bridge (*c.* 800 m); to enter it, take Boomgaardstraat (2nd right); turn left twice, 1st street on left. Parking. **Restrictions** No smoking: breakfast room, bedrooms. No dogs. **Credit cards** Amex, MasterCard, Visa. **Terms** B&B: single €77–€81, double €92–€102, suite €102. 4 nights for 3 for Sun/Mon arrivals, except July/Aug.

Hotel Bryghia *Tel* 050 33 80 59
Oosterlingenplein 4 *Fax* 050 34 14 30
Email info@bryghiahotel.be
Website www.bryghiahotel.be

Liked for its good value and its quiet location, on one of the city's prettiest canals, Guido Lebacq's red brick 15th-century merchant's house is just five minutes' walk from the town square. The best bedrooms face the canal. The buffet breakfast is served in a pink-walled room with a beamed ceiling. The lounge, with its bright checked armchairs, is 'pleasant', and there is free parking a short walk away. (*SH*)

Open 18 Feb–16 Dec. **Rooms** 18 double. **Facilities** Salon, bar; breakfast room (no-smoking). Unsuitable for ♿. **Location** Central. Free parking in front. **Credit cards** All major cards accepted. **Restriction** No dogs. **Terms** B&B: single €67–€98, double €95–€135. 1-night bookings refused Sat. *V*

Hotel Ter Duinen *Tel* 050 33 04 37
Langerei 52 *Fax* 050 34 42 16
Email info@terduinenhotel.be
Website www.terduinenhotel.be

This B&B hotel is a trim white house by a canal, north of the centre. It is well run by its friendly owners, Marc and Lieve Bossu-Van Den Heuvel, say visitors this year. And, 'a bonus in a city where taxis are scarce', it is on two bus routes. The bedrooms (most are decent-sized) have striped bedspreads and matching curtains. 'From our balcony we enjoyed the moonlight over the canal.' But cheaper rooms are small, and some have an 'uninspiring outlook'. Reception is found 'charming'; the conservatory-style lounge and breakfast room look over the flowery patio garden. For dinner, *L'Hermitage*, nearby, was thought 'great'. (*AW, and others*)

Open All year. **Rooms** 20 double. Some on ground floor. Air conditioning. **Facilities** Lift. Lounge/bar with TV, breakfast room. Patio garden. Unsuitable for ♿. **Location** 10 mins' walk from centre (windows double glazed). By car enter from Dampoort. Street parking, garage (€10 per night). **Restrictions** No smoking: breakfast room, some bedrooms. No dogs. **Credit cards** All major cards accepted. **Terms** B&B: single €89–€149, double €89–€199. *V*

Hotel Egmond *Tel* 050 34 14 45
Minnewater 15 *Fax* 050 34 29 40
Email info@egmond.be
Website www.egmond.be

'Our favourite Bruges hotel,' says a regular visitor after 'another comfortable stay' at the Van Laere family's B&B. Overlooking the 'lake of love' in Minnewater Park, it is a gabled 18th-century manor house decorated in traditional Flemish style. 'We first went because of the excellent parking facilities. Little did we know that we would return so often over the years.' Earlier guests wrote of the 'excellent value', 'helpful owners', and peaceful, well-tended garden. There are beamed ceilings and a large fireplace in most public rooms. Bedrooms are 'spotless'; those in the main building overlook the lake. 'Good buffet breakfast in a lovely room.' Free coffee and tea are available in the lobby each afternoon, and there is an honesty bar. The Beguinage is close by, and the station is an easy walk away. (*Mary Fradgley*)

Open Mid-Feb–early Jan. **Rooms** 7 double, 1 single. 1 on ground floor. Apartments/studios (air-conditioned) 100 and 300 m. **Facilities** Lounge, games room, breakfast room; classical background music. Terrace, garden. Unsuitable for ♿. **Location** 700 m S of centre. Leave ring road at Katelijnepoort; cross bridge; 4th left off Katelijnestr into Arsenaalstr; Minnewater 2nd left. Parking. **Restrictions** Smoking in lounge only. No dogs. **Credit cards** None accepted. **Terms** [2004] B&B: single €92, double €98–€120, triple €150. Min. 2 nights at weekends.

De Snippe
Nieuwe Gentweg 53

Tel 050 33 70 70
Fax 050 33 76 62
Email info@desnippe.be
Website www.desnippe.be

On a quiet street near the centre, Luc and Francine Huysentruyt's 'superbly run' hotel and restaurant was again enjoyed by readers in 2003/4. 'The staff do not change; by now we know quite a few of them.' 'A delightful, friendly welcome.' The 18th-century town house has antiques, unusual pieces of furniture, original murals, candelabra, gold leather wallpaper. 'We had a lovely room at the back, with a large bathroom; good toiletries and bathrobes. We were slightly less impressed this time by the five-course dinner [*Michelin* calls the dishes '*classiques innovants*'], but it was still very good.' Pre-dinner drinks come with an 'amazing' array of *amuse-gueule*. There is a pretty garden under big trees, and a conservatory lounge. Most bedrooms are spacious and well appointed (two now have a spa bath and hammam), but some may be dark. 'Exceptional' breakfast (fresh fruit salad, eggs, croissants; 'delicious Belgium waffles with home-made jams'). Difficult to find by car ('we used satellite navigation'), but the brochure has a map. (*Wolfgang Stroebe, Anthony Rosen, Maybel King*)

Open All year, except 16 Jan–11 Feb, Sun Nov–Easter. Restaurant closed Sun/Mon midday. **Rooms** 1 suite, 4 junior suites, 3 double. Air conditioning. **Facilities** Lift, ramps. Lounge, conservatory, bar, restaurant. No background music. Small garden: terrace. **Location** Central. Parking. **Credit cards** All major cards accepted. **Terms** B&B: double €145–€275, suite €310. Set lunch €38–€69, dinner €69; full alc €100.

Hotels are dropped if we lack positive feedback.

Hotel De Tuilerieën
Dijver 7

Tel 050 34 36 91
Fax 050 34 04 00
Email info@hoteltuilerieen.com
Website www.hoteltuilerieen.com

By the Groeninge museum, Luc Rammant's luxurious little B&B hotel is a 15th-century mansion on one of Bruges's main canals. It is 'visually delightful', says a recent visitor: traditional Flemish colours, dark grey/blue walls, polished wood, and black-and-white marble chequerboard floors, and crystal chandeliers. The staff are 'young, smart and professional'. Most bedrooms are spacious; some overlook the canal: 'Our superior double, in the adjacent building, had wooden beams, brick walls, lovely furnishings, sumptuous bathroom, great views towards the town square.' An attic room was 'smallish but well equipped'. A canal-facing room was found noisy at the weekend. Breakfast, in a pleasant room, with big sash windows facing the street and canal, has meats, cheeses, fruit, omelettes, yogurt, 'even champagne'. There is a small indoor swimming pool and sauna. The free bicycles and ample parking are appreciated. 'Good for a swanky, child-free break.' (*FC-H, and others*)

Open All year. **Rooms** 4 suites, 41 double. 6 in annexe. 1 on ground floor. Air conditioning. **Facilities** Lift. Bar, breakfast room (no-smoking, classical background music); 2 conference rooms; covered terrace; swimming pool, sauna; free bicycles. **Location** Central. Parking (€5). **Credit cards** All major cards accepted. **Terms** [2004] Room: single €182–€233, double €208–€312, suite €390. Breakfast €24.

BRUSSELS — Map 3:D4

Le Dixseptième
Rue de la Madeleine 25
1000 Brussels

Tel 02 517 17 17
Fax 02 502 64 24
Email info@ledixseptieme.be
Website www.ledixseptieme.be

'Brilliantly located', on a side street between the Grand'Place and the central station, this B&B hotel was once the home of the Spanish ambassador. It was mostly liked this year: 'Enjoyable as ever, an oasis of good taste and efficiency.' 'A place of character, much nicer than the business hotels nearby.' The bedrooms, each named after a Belgian artist, are all different, some period (one has a *trompe l'œil* mural), some modern. The suites have a spacious lounge with 32-inch plasma TV screen; some have a kitchenette, some a sun terrace; but some of their bedrooms are small. Some rooms face the pretty courtyard, where visitors sit on summer nights; front rooms get street noise. Some criticisms: 'There was little service.' 'Housekeeping was lax.' The hot and cold buffet breakfast, served in a 'lovely' room, has been called 'overpriced' by some visitors, 'lavish' by others. Difficult to find by car. (*Andrew Warren, and others*)

Open All year. **Rooms** 12 suites, 12 double. In 2 houses. Air conditioning. **Facilities** Lift. Lobby, bar, breakfast room; classical background music; conference room. Courtyard. Unsuitable for ♿. **Location** Central, near Grand'Place. Public car park nearby. **Restrictions** No smoking: restaurant, bedrooms. No dogs. **Credit cards** All major cards accepted. **Terms** B&B: single/double €180–€230, suite €280–€330.

Hotel Rembrandt BUDGET
42 rue de la Concorde
1050 Brussels

Tel 02 512 71 39
Fax 02 511 71 36
Email rembrandt@brutele.be
Website www.hotel-rembrandt.be

In a 'superb' location, just off Avenue Louise, the Grasset-Gallais family's B&B, modest but 'professionally run', offers 'amazing value', say its fans. The manager, Jacqueline Grasset ('formal and polite'), is 'prepared to emerge in her dressing gown to let you in as midnight approaches'. 'Every room is spotless; those with shower and loo are spacious. A marvellous collection of old photographs and/or jigsaws of Old Masters adorns the walls.' A large dresser separates the sitting room/reception from the breakfast area: 'Breakfast may be fairly basic, but bread is always fresh; service is punctilious.' The street is quiet at night; on weekdays there can be traffic noise quite early. (*AW*)

Open 10 Jan–31 July, 1 Sept–20 Dec. **Rooms** 12 double, 1 single. **Facilities** Small lift. Sitting room, breakfast room (no-smoking); classical background music. Unsuitable for ♿. **Location** Off Ave Louise, near Pl. Stéphanie. (Metro: Place Louise, Porte de Namur) **Restriction** No dogs. **Credit cards** MasterCard, Visa. **Terms** B&B: single €40, double €95.

Stanhope Hotel
Rue du Commerce 9
1000 Brussels

Tel 02 506 91 11
Fax 02 512 17 08
Email summithotels@stanhope.be
Website www.stanhope.be

'Agreeable' large luxury hotel, near Royal Palace and European Parliament, but quiet. 'Elegant hall, sitting areas, windows to lovely inner court with fountain.' 'My sensibly sized room had comfortable bed, good lighting, great bathroom. Nice touches like free shoe cleaning.' 2 lounges, bar, restaurant; 2 conference rooms; fitness centre; classical background music. Garden. Valet parking. No smoking: restaurant, some bedrooms. No dogs. All major credit cards accepted. 43 suites (1 in garden pavilion), 43 double, 9 single. B&B: single from €140, double from €150, suite from €255. Set meals from €37; full alc €50 [2004].

CORBION SUR SEMOIS 6838 Luxembourg Belge Map 3:E4

Hotel des Ardennes BUDGET
Rue de la Hate 1

Tel 061 25 01 00
Fax 061 46 77 30
Email contact@hoteldesardennes.be
Website www.hoteldesardennes.be

'The best place we know,' says the greatest fan of the Maqua family's Logis de Belgique, in a 'beautiful part of the southern Ardennes' near the French border. 'The best hotel of our holiday'; 'Perfect;

professional without pomposity', were other comments. Most of the bedrooms are admired ('well appointed; plenty of storage space'). The best, 'large, quiet' rooms at the rear, have 'magical views' over the gardens (with pools and fountains) to hills. But a front room was 'very noisy' due to traffic both morning and evening. The bar, which serves as a local, and the lounge, have 'welcoming seating'. Drinks and 'tasty snacks' are served in the large conservatory, 'good for reading in wet weather'. The food (*Michelin Bib Gourmand*) is also acclaimed: 'What is extraordinary is how they produce different menus for each meal, of high quality and remarkable value. If something on the *pension* menu doesn't suit, they cheerfully change it.' Abundant breakfasts have fresh and preserved fruits, cheese, meats, 'excellent coffee'. Around is 'great walking country; glorious in autumn'. Paul Verlaine lived in Corbion from 1881 to 1883. (*Rebecca Goldsmith, Malcolm Roots, and others*)

Open All year, except 2–15 Mar. **Rooms** 1 suite, 25 double, 3 single. 4 in villa. **Facilities** Lift. Salon, conservatory, bar, 2 dining rooms (no-smoking); background music; conference facilities; snooker room, games room; terrace. 1-hectare garden: tennis, children's play area. **Location** 7 km W of Bouillon. **Credit cards** All major cards accepted. **Terms** B&B: single €70–€90, double €105, suite €140; D,B&B €67–€82 per person. Set meals €25–€55; full alc €60.

CORROY-LE-GRAND 1325 Brabant — Map 3:D4

Le Grand Corroy
Rue de l'Église 13

Tel 010 68 98 98
Fax 010 68 94 78
Email legrandcorroy@wannado.be
Website www.legrandcorroy.be

Old farmhouse 'nicely renovated' as restaurant with 4 rooms: 35 km SE of Brussels, off motorway to Luxembourg. 'Excellent food. Large, luxurious bedrooms with pleasing mixture of modern and antique furniture, table by window where great breakfast is served; sizeable bathroom.' Garden (meal service). Parking. Closed 12–20 Apr, 13–21 Sept, 20 Dec–4 Jan, Sat midday, Sun night/Mon. All major credit cards accepted. B&B double €100. Set lunch €24, dinner €36–€87 [2004].

FALAËN 5522 Namur — Map 3:D4

Casa Bo NEW
12 rue du Château-Ferme

Tel/Fax 082 69 98 69
Email info@casabo.be
Website www.casabo.be

Owned by an Anglo-Belgian couple, film-makers Jessica Woodworth and her husband, Peter Brosens, this small four-star B&B, formerly a girls' boarding school, is in a classified village in the Ardennes. Facing the château-ferme, it stands in a 'beautifully kept' garden with pond, ducks and 'two lovely geese'. Each of the three bedrooms is dedicated to a famous film-maker: Pasolini (with four-poster), Kitano (with futon) and Almodóvar (red walls, large wooden bed). Guests who occupied the last-named reported: 'It was spacious, with fresh flowers, fruit, CDs, flip-flops and chocolates. Breakfast was healthy, tasty and abundant (lots of local produce). One night we enjoyed the platter of local meats and cheeses. Recommended to anyone who enjoys good food and beer, peace and quiet.' Guests have access to a large collection of films, music and books. For full meals, the adjacent restaurant, *La Fermette*, is recommended. Wine tastings are sometimes held here. The surrounding area has pretty villages, lovely countryside with footpaths, horse riding, etc. (*Chiara and Nic Harker*)

Open All year, except infrequent breaks for filming, etc. **Rooms** 3 double. **Facilities** Living room/library/TV room, dining room; background music; film archive. Terrace. Garden: pond. Walking, cycling, fishing, climbing, etc, nearby. **Location** 12 km NW of Dinant (guests can be met at train station). 99 km from Brussels. **Restrictions** Smoking discouraged in bedrooms. No pets. **Credit cards** None accepted (cash only). **Terms** [2004] (min. 2 nights) B&B: single €78–€110, double €90–€125. Special rates for film-makers/students.

GENT 9000 Oost-Vlaanderen — Map 3:D3

Hotel Monasterium PoortAckere
Oude Houtlei 56

Tel 092 69 22 10
Fax 092 69 22 30
Email info@monasterium.be
Website www.monasterium.be

'The staff were especially helpful,' say visitors this year to this unusual hotel in the medieval centre of the city. 'Clean, friendly, with atmosphere and charm', it is a recent conversion of a 13th-century convent: the last six nuns left in 1998. It offers two types of accommodation: fully fledged hotel rooms (with *en suite* facilities, TV, telephone, Internet connection) in the main house ('ours was spacious, with dressing room, large bathroom; plain but comfortable furnishings'), and simpler guest house-style accommodation in the original convent cells which are named after the nuns who lived here. Most of these rooms have only a washbasin; bathroom facilities are shared. Dinner (weekends only) and a 'very good' buffet breakfast ('wide choice of cereals, fruit, meats, cheeses, breads') are served in the chapter house or the walled garden. Well placed for elegant shops ('some splendid confiseries'), 'wonderful' Gravensteen castle, and St Bavo's cathedral (with Van Eyck's *Adoration of the Mystic Lamb*). (*J and AS*)

Open All year. Restaurant open Fri and Sat evenings; for groups, by reservation, at other times. **Rooms** 34 double, 20 single. 36 with facilities *en suite*. 1 on ground floor. **Facilities** Ramp. Bar with TV, restaurant; classical background music; chapel (conference room). Garden. **Location** Follow signs to Gent Centrum (yellow parking route); at Hoogstraat, take last street on right. Hotel halfway up on right. Courtyard parking. **Restriction** No dogs. **Credit cards** All major cards accepted. **Terms** B&B: single €46–€98, double €90–€125. Set meals €24; full alc €32.

> When a hotel has failed to return its questionnaire, we quote the 2004 prices.

KORTRIJK 8500 West-Vlaanderen Map 3:D3

Village Gastronomique
Eddy Vandekerckhove
Sint-Anna 5

Tel 056 22 47 56
Fax 056 22 71 70
Email info@evdk.be
Website www.evdk.be

'The best dinner and breakfast ever' were enjoyed this year at owner/chef Eddy Vandekerckhove's restaurant-with-rooms in a hamlet south of an affluent Flemish town (Courtrai in French), just across the border from Lille. M. Vandekerckhove serves modern cooking 'with a traditional touch'. 'Dinner was a set-piece gourmet affair with wine; no one else was having it, so we had all the wine. We came down late to breakfast to find a feast of food and flowers. We were the only overnight guests, and felt the most privileged couple alive.' A motorway is near, 'but the only noise is from the fountain in the lovely conservatory' (with fishpond, tropical plants, tables and chairs for coffee/drinks). In summer, dinner is served in the garden. The bedrooms, around a patio, are spacious and modern: 'Ours was well appointed, imaginatively decorated.' 'Ours was a little on the luxurious side.' Sound insulation is not always perfect. Difficult to find: M. Vandekerckhove has been known to drive out to rescue lost visitors. An earlier verdict: 'Quite expensive, but worth every penny.' (*Jon Hughes, Bob and Kate Flaherty*)

Open All year, except 1 week before Easter, last 2 weeks Aug. **Rooms** 7 double. All on ground floor. **Facilities** Lounge, bar, conservatory (no-smoking), restaurant; background music; meeting room. Small garden. **Location** In hamlet 3 km S of Kortrijk. From E17 exit 2, go towards Tournai (Doornik). Right at next roundabout, bear left through Marionettenburg. At crossroads, right towards Sint-Anna (signposted Don Bosco/Kinderland), left at T-junction; hotel on left at village entrance. Parking. **Credit cards** All major cards accepted. **Terms** B&B: single €112, double €118. Set meals €50–€100.

MARCHE-EN-FAMENNE 6900 Luxembourg Belge Map 3:E5

Château d'Hassonville
Route d'Hassonville 105
Marloie

Tel 084 31 10 25
Fax 084 31 60 27
Email info@hassonville.be
Website www.hassonville.be

Built as a hunting lodge for Louis XIV, this 17th-century pepperpotted château is run by two generations of the Rodrigues family. Visitors like the 'comfort and quality, appropriate to the price'. It stands in a huge park with formal gardens, peacocks, a lake and a large fountain: footpaths wind through woods, and there is a barn with animals. Game is on Christophe Poard's menus in the 'beautiful *Grand Pavillon* restaurant in an orangery', where the 'delicious meals' are enjoyed. A buffet breakfast is served (from 9 am) in a conservatory. Open fires burn in the public rooms. Spacious bedrooms (the best ones are said to be in the annexe) have elegant period decor and original paintings. Hot-air ballooning and guided tours of the surrounding region can be arranged. (*AG, and others*)

Open All year, except 1–10 Jan, Tues. Restaurant closed Wed midday. **Rooms** 1 suite, 20 double. 7 in annexe. **Facilities** Lift. 3 lounges, breakfast conservatory, wine cellar, restaurant; classical background music; function facilities; snooker room. 55-hectare park: putting, bicycles, lake. Unsuitable for ♿. **Location** 3 km SW of Marche by N836. **Restrictions** Smoking in bar only. No dogs in restaurant. **Credit cards** All major cards accepted. **Terms** [2004] B&B: single €115, double €130–€180, suite €280. Set meals €55–€85; full alc €135. 1-night bookings sometimes refused weekends. *V*

DE PANNE 8660 West-Vlaanderen — Map 3:D2

Hostellerie Le Fox
Walckierstraat 2

Tel 058 41 28 55
Fax 058 41 58 79
Email hotelfox@pandora.be
Website www.hotelfox.be

Owner/chef Stéphane Buyens has long had a *Michelin* star for his 'light, inventive, unpretentious' cooking at his restaurant-with-rooms just off the long promenade of this seaside resort (popular in summer with Belgian families). This year's reports: 'One of the most memorable meals we've had. We chose the fish menu, served with champagne, with lobster as the main course. It was beautifully presented, totally delicious. Staff were relaxed, friendly, efficient. Our room was basic but adequate.' 'Lunch was perfection; service and surroundings were superb.' In summer, meals are served under green-and-white parasols on the pavement. Mme Buyens and her family speak fluent English and 'are very nice'. 'The promenade was lively after dinner, with no hint of the yob culture found in similar English resorts.' *Guide* readers get a complimentary drink on arrival. Calais is 40 minutes' drive away. (*J and AS, R and KF, and others*)

Open All year. Restaurant closed Mon/Tues midday. **Rooms** 11 double, 2 single. **Facilities** Salon, bar, restaurant (no-smoking); classical background music. Beach 20 m. **Location** Central (rear rooms quietest), off promenade. 31 km SW of Ostend. Garages. **Credit cards** All major cards accepted. **Terms** Room: single €50–€95, double €90–€110. Breakfast €11. D,B&B €100–€135 per person. Set meals €50–€75. 1-night bookings sometimes refused.

LA ROCHE-EN-ARDENNE 6980 Luxembourg Belge — Map 3:E5

Les Genêts BUDGET
Corniche de Deister 2

Tel 084 41 18 77
Fax 084 41 18 93
Email info@lesgenetshotel.com
Website www.lesgenetshotel.com

Patrick and Myriam Defays-Joie's 'small, friendly', quiet hotel, high on hill above pretty Ardennes town. 'Excellent food (residents only); helpful service.' Terrace, garden. Closed 1–15 July, 1 week Sept, 3 weeks Jan, Thurs low season. MasterCard, Visa accepted. 7 bedrooms, all with views of ruined castle and river. B&B €36–€37; D,B&B €64–€66 [2004].

STAVELOT 4970 Liège Map 3:D5

Romantik Hotel Le Val d'Amblève
Route de Malmedy 7

Tel 080 28 14 40
Fax 080 28 14 59
Email info@levaldambleve.com
Website www.levaldambleve.com

In some of the most beautiful Ardennes countryside, this old half-timbered house stands in well-kept grounds amid ancient trees. The owners, Ruud and Marion Roxs-Spoelder, run it as a restaurant-with-rooms. Recent praise: 'Superb food: innovative use of fresh ingredients; personal service from *le patron* and his staff.' Bedrooms in the extension at the back are larger than those in the main house, whose front rooms face the road (it was renovated in 2004, and given new windows). Six rooms are in *Le Jardin des Princes*, a villa in the grounds which has a small salon where guests can make coffee or tea. The restaurant has large windows opening on to a wide terrace with parasols, where drinks and meals are served in fine weather. Beyond are sloping lawns. A 'very good' buffet breakfast is taken in 'a pleasant room with soft music'. (*VC*)

Open All year, except Jan. Restaurant closed to non-residents on Mon. **Rooms** 18 double. 4 in annexe, 6 in villa. **Facilities** 3 lounges (1 in villa), breakfast room, restaurant/winter garden (no-smoking); background music. Terrace. 1-hectare garden. Golf, spa, walking nearby. Unsuitable for ♿. **Location** Outskirts of Stavelot. 9 km SW of Malmedy (bus/free taxi service). Garages, car park. **Credit cards** All major cards accepted. **Terms** [2004] B&B: single €76–€90, double €102–€115. Set meals €35–€75. 1-night bookings sometimes refused long weekends/Francorchamps motor races. *V*

TROIS-PONTS 4980 Liège Map 3:D5

Le Beau Site BUDGET
Rue des Villas 45

Tel 080 68 49 44
Fax 080 68 49 60
Email info@beausite.be
Website www.beausite.be

On an outcrop in the Ardennes, with 'stunning' views of the sleepy little town and the valleys of the rivers Amblève and Salm, Dennis and Christine Fluijter's Logis de Belgique provides 'exceptional value', say its admirers. Reached via a hairpin bend, it is 'charming if eccentric'; the welcome is 'friendly in the extreme'. Drinks are served on a panoramic terrace. The 'excellent' dinner (with menus of four to seven courses) is 'solicitously served, with good French wines'. Bedrooms vary in size, and decoration ('I counted 11 different wallpaper patterns'). 'The sunrise, and the buffet breakfast in such relaxed surroundings, made a perfect start to the day,' was one recent comment.

Open 21 Jan–18 Dec. Restaurant closed Wed. **Rooms** 15 double, 2 single. **Facilities** Bar/salon, restaurant; classical background music; meeting room. Dining terrace. Unsuitable for ♿. **Location** Village centre. 6 km SW of Stavelot. E40, exit 11. Car park. Guests met at station (1 km). **Credit cards** All major cards accepted. **Terms** [2004] B&B €39.50–€57; D,B&B (min. 2 nights) €67.50–€85. Set lunch €15, dinner €31–€62. 1-night bookings sometimes refused.

WIERDE 5100 Namur Map 3:D4

Le Petit Marais
Rue Lambaitienne 7

Tel 081 40 25 65
Fax 081 40 20 72
Email lepetitmarais@tiscali.be

'A superb stop; a lovely setting,' say visitors this year to owner/chef Jean-Philippe Vanderschueren's restaurant-with-rooms in quiet countryside near Namur. The house is new, but built in old style. It stands in a neat garden with herbs above the green valley of the Tronquoy. 'The welcome is pleasant. Monsieur remembered my mobility problem from a previous visit and came to help with luggage. The bedrooms are excellently furnished. We best like one with windows on three sides. Large, superb bathrooms. The meal was superb, *haute cuisine*, with wide choice of rolls, lovely chocolate delicacies to end. Monsieur and his waiter were very patient, keen to be sure we understood the menus, which are all in French.' Earlier visitors chose a menu in which all courses featured lobster: 'Very good apart from one course: unusual flavours and textures.' Breakfast has freshly squeezed juices, 14 different teas, freshly baked breads, home-made jams, ham, etc. A swimming pool is new this year.

Open All year, except 1–15 Sept. Closed Tues/Wed, except holidays. **Rooms** 4 double. **Facilities** Lounge, restaurant; terrace. Garden: swimming pool. Cycling, golf, tennis nearby. **Location** 9 km SE of Namur. Exit 16 off E411. At Wierde, 1st right at church; follow signs. Parking. **Credit cards** MasterCard, Visa. **Terms** [2004] Room €80. Breakfast €10. Set lunch from €24, dinner €45–€55; alc €56–€68.

Croatia

Hotel Park, Split

The long and lovely Dalmatian coast of Croatia, with its thousand islands, was a major Mediterranean holiday venue before 1990, and is now one again: with a mix of government and private investment, tourism is accelerating. There are still many hotels that are relics of Yugotours from the 1970s, but many of the larger state-owned hotels on the coast have been privatised and refurbished by their new owners. A new generation of small private hotels of quality is now emerging, and there are plenty of good, if simple, restaurants.

Jill Benderly, an American living in Croatia, writes: 'Many hotels have been renovated, and some new ones are opening. In Dubrovnik, where the hotel capacity is still too small for the number of guests, the *Hotel Argentina* [155 bedrooms, set in a large park] has been completely remodelled with Italianate elegant marble bathrooms, and warm wood furnishings and fabrics. Prices have been raised to match. Breakfast buffet is outstanding. Private small *Agriturizam* have been developing in Istria.'

Some resorts are now attracting the glitterati, and may be losing sight of their customers by raising prices and reducing standards, but this chapter includes attractive hotels at all prices, ranging from the *Villa Dubrovnik*, which entered the *Guide* years ago when we had a chapter for Yugoslavia, to the charismatic *Palmižana Meneghello Reservation* on an island in the south Adriatic. As we went to press, we received an attractive nomination, the *Villa Vilina*, on the island of Lopud, offshore of Dubrovnik.

DUBROVNIK 20000 Dalmatia-Dubrovnik **Map 14:E6**

Villa Dubrovnik
Vlaha Bukovca 6

Tel (020) 42 29 33
Fax (020) 42 34 65
Email villa.dubrovnik@laus.hr
Website www.villa-dubrovnik.hr

Terraced on to a cliff on the southern side of Dubrovnik, this striking modern building faces the old walled town and the island of Lokrum. Pine trees, flowers and blue awnings give a Riviera flavour. 'The views are outstanding,' say visitors this year. 'Management was friendly, if impersonal.' Others wrote: 'Truly magic, with excellent service.' 'An excellent hotel.' 'Our room was sparkling clean.' Summer meals are served on the vine-covered terrace facing the old town. Breakfast is continental, but other items can be ordered for an extra charge. 'A pianist played nightly as we dined on the covered patio.' Most visitors have found the cooking 'cheap and decent' with 'good local seafood'. The bedrooms, all sea-facing, have a balcony and 'fabulous views'. Some are quite small. Swimming is in crystal-clear water off rocks in front of the hotel (sunbeds and umbrellas provided). But the 'beach' is concrete, and 66 steep steps lead from the hotel to the road above. You can walk to the city in 20 minutes, or take the hotel's motorboat. (*Colin Parker, and others*)

Open 1 Apr–30 Oct. **Rooms** 1 suite, 39 double. Air conditioning. **Facilities** Lift. Lounge, bar/café, restaurant, dining terrace; background music all day; fitness room. Garden, private beach. **Location** S side of town. Garages, parking. Airport transfer. **Credit cards** MasterCard, Visa. **Terms** B&B: single €140–€244, double €190–€280, suite €290–€470; D,B&B €35 added per person.

LOPUD 20222 Dalmatia-Dubrovnik **Map 14:E6**

Villa Vilina NEW
Obala Iva Kuljevana 5
Hrvatska

Tel (020) 75 93 33
Fax (020) 75 90 60
Email villa-vilina@inet.hr
Website www.villa-vilina.hr

On the small island of Lopud, 45 minutes by ferry from Dubrovnik, this 'charming hotel', run by its owners, the Vilina family, is warmly recommended in 2004. It stands on a bay, by a medieval Franciscan monastery. 'The building has recently been refurbished to a high standard. Bedrooms in the front have wonderful views over the small port. Meals are taken on a terrace with this view. The owners' daughter, Ivona Simunovic, is an artist: her paintings hang in all the rooms, and there are many artistic touches. The delightful staff go out of their way to help, and they speak English to a high level. The breakfasts are first class: freshly cooked eggs and bacon plus the usual offerings. Speciality for the *en pension* dinners is fish, freshly caught.' Modern touches include Internet connection, satellite TV, safes and minibars in the bedrooms, and the family promise figs, grapes, tangerines and olives from the garden, and 'a cup of home-made rose brandy'. Lopud is traffic-free and has 'fabulous sandy beaches', 20 minutes' walk from the hotel. 'For those who find Dubrovnik too crowded with tourists, this is an ideal retreat.' (*AD Canning-Jones*)

Open Probably May–Nov. **Rooms** 3 suites, 14 double. **Facilities** Bar, restaurant; meeting room. Terraces. Garden: swimming pool. **Location** N side of island. NW of Dubrovnik. **Credit cards** Probably some accepted. **Terms** [2004] B&B: single €101–€125, double €119–€216, suite €170–€330.

MALI STON 20230 Dalmatia-Dubrovnik **Map 14:E6**

Hotel Ostrea

Tel (020) 75 45 55
Fax (020) 75 45 75
Email ostrea.info@ostrea.hr
Website www.ostrea.hr

In south Dalmatia, this ancient stone-built fishing village is off the main coast road north-west of Dubrovnik. It is 'quiet, and gorgeous, with lots of narrow streets suitable only for pedestrians'. On the waterfront, the Kralj family's old stone home is now an elegant little hotel, 'ably managed by Ante Kralj'. 'A delightful setting, very friendly welcome, good-quality fittings,' say visitors this year. Some bedrooms are small; the best ones have a sea view. 'All are beautifully furnished, and have shutters against the summer sun.' Other praise: 'The English-speaking staff looked after us well.' 'Excellent buffet breakfasts, on the terrace: delicious mountain ham.' The family own two restaurants: the *Mlinica* on the hotel ground floor, and the *Kapetanova Kuća* on the waterfront: it specialises in local fish and seafood, such as the region's famed oysters. 'The harbour, close by, is a nursery for shellfish and quite clean: you can swim from the hotel's jetty.' Nearby also are many islets and coves. The hotel's minibus will take guests on outings. (*Chris and Nancy Head, and others*)

Open All year. **Rooms** 1 suite, 9 double. **Facilities** Lounge, conference room. Terrace. Adjacent restaurant (live music nightly). **Location** 60 km NW of Dubrovnik. W of main coast road, 1 km from Ston, at E end of Pelješac peninsula. Parking. **Credit cards** Most major cards accepted. **Terms** [2004] B&B: single €67–€116, double €94–€135.

> We asked hotels to estimate their 2005 tariffs, but many preferred not to think so far ahead, and gave their 2004 tariffs. Prices should *always* be checked when booking.

MARCANA 52206 Istria — Map 14:D4

Stancija Negricani BUDGET
Divsici

Tel (052) 39 10 84
Fax (052) 58 08 40
Email konoba-jumbo@pu.tel.hr
Website www.stancijanegricani.com

On a rural estate, this 'beautiful old house' in north-west Croatia stands amid woods where aromatic and medicinal herbs grow, and fields with olives, vines and tobacco. Mario ('Jumbo') and Mirjana Modrusan run it in relaxed style as an *Agriturizam*. 'He has basic Italian, she speaks English.' 'A delightful setting,' say recent visitors. 'Little sound except birdsong, the odd dog, and cars arriving during the day for the excellent cooking.' Pretty bedrooms have old furniture, oleographs of saints, etc. Some have a terrace with sea view. Bathrooms are modern. Summer meals are served alfresco. 'Food, locally sourced, comes in generous proportions, eg, very fresh sea bass (one per person). Much is cooked on the giant barbecue at the back of the house. House wine in jugs is good, and there is a selection of posher wines by the bottle. Grappa is on the house. Coffee is Turkish or instant, but there is a wide range of teas, including infusions of local plants.' 'In autumn, the fire in the restaurant hearth was an essential element in the meal: prsut (prosciutto) and sheep's cheese; home-baked bread, and incredible brandy made from herbs.' Local attractions include the Roman amphitheatre in Pula (20 minutes' drive). (*MH and SN, JB*)

Open All year. **Rooms** 9. **Facilities** Lounge, restaurant. Terrace. Large estate: garden: swimming pool, tennis court, bicycle hire. **Location** 15 km NE of Pula. **Credit cards** Probably none accepted. **Terms** [2004] Room €54–€95. Breakfast €5. Alc from €20.

OPATIJA 51410 Kvarner & Highlands — Map 14:C4

Hotel Villa Ariston
Marsala Tita 179

Tel (051) 27 13 79
Fax (051) 27 14 94
Email villa-ariston@ri.hinet.hr

This classic seaside resort was popular with the aristocracy of the Austro-Hungarian Empire. Just outside, this handsome 19th-century villa stands in 'delightful' terraced gardens facing the sea. 'It is almost unspoilt,' says a 2004 visitor, 'the quality of the workmanship is a delight.' Others wrote of a 'fabulous atmosphere', 'an excellent stay'. One couple had a room on the attic floor: 'Plain and a bit brown, but good; it had a lovely view across the bay. The bathroom was well equipped, but the basin had no plug.' Another couple had a first-floor junior suite: 'Enormous bedroom with wonderful view, reading room, spacious bathroom with small balcony (and plugs).' You can bathe in the clear, unpolluted water from a ladder reached down 110 steps. The restaurant has now been leased to separate owners, and the food is thought 'average and expensive'. You can walk to town by the Lungomare, a footpath stretching 12 kilometres along the Kvarner

Riviera. Not much to do in Opatija, but trips can be made to various islands. (*Margaret Batstone, AD Canning-Jones, MH and SN*)

Open All year. **Rooms** 2 suites, 8 double. Air conditioning. **Facilities** Lounge, bar, dining rooms; terraces. **Location** On seafront, just outside the town. **Credit cards** All major cards accepted. **Terms** [2004] B&B: single €53–€73, double €82–€164, suite €178–€247.

PALMIŽANA 21450 Dalmatia-Split — Map 14:E5

Palmižana Meneghello Reservation BUDGET
Palmižana-Hvar

Tel (021) 71 72 70
Fax (021) 71 72 68
Email palmizana@palmizana.hr
Website www.palmizana.hr

On a small private island in the south Adriatic, off the coast of the island of Hvar, this 'splendid' complex ('my favourite place for a weekend break', says a fan) is owned and run by Dagmar Meneghello, journalist and arts patron, with her three adult children, Djenko, Romina and Tarin. Accommodation is in stone villas, each one different, each with a terrace, in a subtropical botanical garden. Most have a lounge with an extra bed. 'I love the white villa on the waterfront,' one fan wrote. No cars: numerous taxi boats run from Hvar, or you can anchor your boat in their harbour. 'The terrace restaurant serves some of the best food in the country (delicious lobster and shellfish risotto) with local wine.' The other restaurant, *Toto's*, is on the beach. 'In this sophisticated place you can attend small Sunday classical concerts, meet artists and see their works and many ancient amphorae in Dagmar's art gallery.' A child-friendly and pet-friendly place. There is a small beach below the hotel, but much of the swimming is from flat rocks around the bay. Activities include fishing, diving, water sports, etc. Guests are expected to take their meals in the resort's restaurants. (*Jill Benderly*)

Open 1 Apr–15 Nov. **Rooms** 13 double rooms in bungalows and villas, 6 apartments. **Facilities** Bar, 2 restaurants; terraces (meal service). 320-hectare estate. Garden, beach; bicycle hire; boat hire; water sports. **Location** Paklina archipelago, S of Hvar island. **Credit cards** All major cards accepted. **Terms** [2004] (Min. 1 week, Sat–Sat, in high season) B&B €28–€48; D,B&B €50–€75.

PLITVIČE 53231 Kvarner & Highlands — Map 14:D5

Hotel Plitvičе BUDGET
Plitvička jezera

Tel (053) 75 11 00
Fax (053) 75 11 65
Email plitvice@np-plitvicka-jezera.hr
Website www.np-plitvice.com

The Plitviče national park, in wooded hills way south of Zagreb, is famed for its 'seventeen lakes of a beautiful turquoise colour, linked by waterfalls and cascades: one of the great natural wonders of Europe'. It contains a big holiday complex, with a nightclub for dancing, an indoor swimming pool, sporting amenities and three hotels: this is the smallest. 'Very much at the upper end of a typical communist bloc state-run hotel: simple, but friendly, clean and convenient,' says a recent guest. The architecture and decor may be unappealing, but another visitor wrote: 'Our double room was palatial, with immaculate bathroom, top-quality linen. Food was good and inexpensive, and service was attentive, notably in the restaurant.' From a nearby bus-stop, you can reach Zagreb in about two hours. (*EA, and others*)

Open All year. **Rooms** 1 suite, 51 double. **Facilities** Lounge, piano bar, restaurant; terrace. In hotel complex: bar for dancing, cinema, conference hall, heated indoor swimming pool, sauna, sports centre, bowling. Near lake: safe bathing. **Location** In national park. 140 km SW of Zagreb. **Credit cards** All major cards accepted. **Terms** [2004] B&B €33–€65; D,B&B €41–€76.

PULA 52100 Istria — Map 14:D4

Hotel Restaurant Valsabbion BUDGET *Tel/Fax* (052) 21 80 33
Pješèana uvala IX/26
Email valsabbion@valsabbion.net
Website www.valsabion.com

Near S tip of Pula: pink boutique hotel with famous Slow Food restaurant, thought to be the best in town (eg, mushroom carpaccio with truffles; risotto with scampi baked in cheese). On inlet by marina: outdoor seating, 'sublime sunsets'. Bar. Top-floor indoor swimming pool; beauty/health treatments. Air conditioning. Garden. Closed Jan. All major credit cards accepted. 10 bedrooms (5 with terrace and sea view): €59–€149. Breakfast €9.50. D,B&B double €80–€122 [2004].

ROVINJ 52210 Istria — Map 14:D4

Hotel Angelo d'Oro *Tel* (052) 84 05 02
Via Švalba 38–42 *Fax* (052) 84 01 11
Email hotel.angelo@vip.hr
Website www.rovinj.at

Rovinj, a beautiful Venetian port capped by a huge baroque church, was the setting for some chapters of Jules Verne's *Mathias Sandorf*. This 18th-century bishop's palace, now an upmarket hotel managed by Dario Božac, is named after the 17th-century statue in its stone-walled dining room. The hotel stands in a narrow street in a pedestrianised area of the old town: staff meet guests nearby, by arrangement, and cars are left in reserved parking spaces. There are stone-flagged floors, antiques in the public rooms and bedrooms, 'lots of paintings and *objets d'art*'. The small loggia on the top floor has a sea view. Recent visitors wrote: 'Our room, moderately sized and well equipped, with parquet floor, looked on to the pretty garden. We heard enthusiastic bell-ringing at 7 am from St Eufemia's church. In our modern bathroom were robes and lots of towels. Dinner by candlelight was excellent, especially the fish. You can choose your wine direct from the cellar, which is fun. Grappa comes on the house.' In summer, meals and all-day snacks are served in the garden. Breakfast has 'excellent coffee, fresh fruit, good breads and pastries'. The hotel has a boat for trips to the islands. (*MH and SN*)

Open Mar–Jan. **Rooms** 1 suite, 19 double, 3 single. Some on ground floor. Air conditioning. **Facilities** Lounge, bar, restaurant; 24-hour background music; sauna, spa bath, solarium. Garden: bar. Beach 200 m. **Location** Old town. **Restriction** No smoking: restaurant, some bedrooms. **Credit cards** All major cards accepted. **Terms** B&B: single €71–€113, double €116–€200, suite €205–€270; D,B&B €25 added per person. Full alc €40.

SPLIT 21000 Dalmatia-Split — Map 14:D5

Hotel Park
Hatzeov perivoj 3

Tel (021) 40 64 00
Fax (021) 40 64 01
Email info@hotelpark-split.hr
Website www.hotelpark-split.hr

This historic city/port is the cultural and economic centre of Dalmatia, and this 'lovely old stone building', managed by Joze Tomaš, is used by business people, but other travellers love it too. It has a terrace with palm trees and a 'true Mediterranean atmosphere'. The 'delightful' open-air café and restaurant face the wide panorama of the Adriatic. Many bedrooms face the sea too: they are 'elegant' and air conditioned. It's a one-minute walk to the Bačvice beach, a bit longer to the ferry harbour and to the old town built into Diocletian's palace (AD 300). 'A pleasant place to stay en route to the islands.' (*JB*)

Open All year. **Rooms** 3 suites, 33 double, 21 single. Some no-smoking. Air conditioning. **Facilities** Lift, ramps. Lounges, bar, restaurant; background music all day; conference facilities; health club, beauty centre. Terrace (café). Beach nearby. **Location** Central, near harbour. Parking. **Credit cards** All major cards accepted. **Terms** [2003] B&B: single €104–€128, double €132–€156, suite €227–€332. Set meals €17; full alc €25. *V*

****

Traveller's tale Hotel in France. In this hotel you should avoid the ground-floor rooms on hot evenings, the first-floor rooms if you want to avoid the noise of the kitchen at night and the children at the nearby school if you want a lie-in after a gastronomic excess.

****

Traveller's tale Hotel in Germany The much-vaunted restaurant was disappointing. The waiters were dismissive of anyone not wanting the intricate *à la carte* menu. The wine we selected from a pretentious list was very expensive and served with condescension. The food was fussily presented, blobs of paste everywhere. We thought the flavours lacked precision. At breakfast, service was slow, the coffee was cold and stewed, and people were complaining.

****

Czech Republic

Hotel Růže, Český Krumlov

The Czech Republic became a full member of the European Union in confident mood in 2004. Prague remains one of the most popular of European capitals for short-break visitors, in part because of the number of low-cost flights from British regional airports. The *Guide* has a varied selection of hotels here, including a newcomer, *Casa Marcello*, a town house 'out of earshot of the louder British visitor'. But an old favourite, *U Tří Pštrosů*, by the Charles Bridge, has been dropped this year for lack of feedback.

Standards outside Prague are more variable, but we include some interesting country hotels. We have an appealing new entry this year, *Dům Bedřicha Smetany*, an Art Nouveau hotel in Luhačovice, a car-free spa town near the Moravian border.

While hotel prices tend to be on the high side, restaurants (which cater for locals as well as visitors) offer rather better value. Expect generous amounts of food at meals, particularly outside Prague; 'I'm sure there is no Czech word for snack,' comments a *Guide* hotelier. Half-board deals can offer astonishing value.

BRNO 602 00 Moravia — Map 13:A6

Hotel Royal Ricc
Starobrněnská 10

Tel (5) 42 21 92 62
Fax (5) 42 21 92 65
Email hotelroyalricc@brn.inecnet.cz
Website www.romantichotels.cz

Near the 11th-century Romanesque cathedral, in the old part of the Czech Republic's second city, this pink 16th-century baroque building belongs to the small KK group (see also *u Páva*, Prague). With a 'medieval feel' (decorative ironwork and quirky frescoes), it is 'a stylish haven in a quiet pedestrianised area', say recent visitors. 'Our room had a huge ceramic tiled stove, beamed ceiling painted with traditional Moravian patterns, and stained-glass casement windows facing a tiny square. The dining room was elegant, the dinner delicious: cooking not Czech, but varied, fish especially good. Service was charming.' Good Moravian wines on the list. Brno has an interesting castle but is not overpowered by tourism; it is busiest during a huge annual trade fair.

Open All year. **Rooms** 1 suite, 30 double. Some no-smoking. **Facilities** Lift. Lobby/bar, restaurant, wine cellar; terrace; background music 8 am–10 pm. **Location** Central, near cathedral. Garage. **Credit cards** Amex, MasterCard, Visa. **Terms** [2004] B&B: single €101–€155, double €111–€165, suite €190–€206; D,B&B €10 added per person. *V*

ČESKÝ KRUMLOV 381 01 Bohemia — Map 13:B5

Hotel Růže NEW
Horní 154

Tel (380) 77 21 00
Fax (380) 71 31 46
Email info@hotelruze.cz
Website www.hotelruze.cz

Set dramatically above a loop of the River Vltava, in this 'prettiest of cities', a 16th-century Jesuit seminary has been turned into this 'special hotel' ('the Rose'). 'The rooms are not over-decorated or comfy; tapestries and coats of arms predominate,' say visitors in 2004 (long-standing *Guide* hoteliers). 'But the welcome was charming, and staff were happy to help in any way.' Other guests felt 'in a time warp', in both the unspoilt medieval town centre and the hotel. 'Dinner was above-average for the Czech Republic: good-quality meat and subtle flavours; substantial portions; excellent wines.' The buffet breakfast 'should suit all tastes, apart from the nasty orange juice'. The restaurants and banqueting hall are in Renaissance style. On the panoramic terrace above the river, live music is sometimes played. (*John and Sue Jenkinson, Eva and Alexander Aldbrook*)

Open All year, except 28 Dec–2 Jan. **Rooms** 8 suites, 53 double, 10 single. **Facilities** Lounge, bar, restaurant; banqueting hall; fitness centre: indoor swimming pool, sauna, etc. Terrace **Location** Central. Car park (€9.50 a day). **Credit cards** All major cards accepted. **Terms** [2004] B&B: single €76–€146, double €108–€203, suite €152–€273; D,B&B €13 added per person.

JINDŘICHŮV HRADEC 377 01 Bohemia — Map 13:B5

Hotel Bílá Paní NEW/BUDGET
Dobrovského 5/1

Tel/Fax (384) 36 26 60
Email recepce@hotelbilapani.cz
Website www.hotelbilapani.cz

In interesting south Bohemian town: small hotel ('White Lady') in 16th-century stucco building facing huge 13th/18th-century castle, across quiet small square. 'Charmingly low-key; good service.' Honesty minibar in corridor. Formal restaurant, tavern ('good food from large menu'); buffet breakfast. Unsuitable for ♿. 9 bedrooms on first floor. B&B €17.50–€35 [2004].

KARLOVY VARY 360 01 Bohemia — Map 13:A4

Hotel Embassy
Nová Louka 21

Tel (353) 32 21 161
Fax (353) 22 31 46
Email info@embassy.cz
Website www.embassy.cz

Once known as Carlsbad, this lovely Bohemian spa town has been much restored. 'Tasting the waters and walking about is fun in summer or winter,' says a recent visitor. This 'very central' family-run hotel, 'comfortable and pleasant', has an 'atmospheric' restaurant (small rooms, a big tiled stove, traditional decor), 'probably the best in town'. One couple ate outside on a tiny bridge over the river, and enjoyed pheasant with honey sauce, braised red cabbage and bacon dumplings. Bedrooms vary: 'Ours was a little over-decorated, but we have never had a bad one,' says a regular visitor. 'The OK breakfast is abundant.' (*JP, A and RM*)

Open All year. **Rooms** 40. **Facilities** Lounge, bar, restaurant; fitness room: sauna, massage. Terrace. Tennis, golf nearby. **Location** Central. Parking (free). **Credit cards** MasterCard, Visa. **Terms** [2004] B&B: single €58–€70, double €82–€108.

KAŠPERSKÉ HORY 341 92 Bohemia — Map 13:B4

Parkhotel Tosch BUDGET
Okres Klatovy

Tel (376) 58 25 92
Fax (376) 58 25 00
Email info@tosch-parkhotel.cz
Website www.tosch-parkhotel.cz

Converted 15th-century brewery, off main square of small town in pretty Bohemian countryside, popular with holidaying Czechs. Lobby bar, lounge facing garden with pretty views. 'Friendly, efficient staff; good value in area short of suitable places.' Vaulted restaurant. Buffet breakfast ('everything out of a packet'); conference facilities; fitness centre: indoor swimming pool, sauna. Diners, MasterCard, Visa accepted. 4 suites, 39 double rooms. B&B: single €57, double €78, suite €124; D,B&B €9 added per person [2004].

LEDNICE 691 44 Moravia — Map 13:B6

My Hotel BUDGET
21 Dubna 657

Tel (519) 34 01 30
Fax (519) 34 01 66
Email info@myhotel.cz
Website www.myhotel.cz

Modern hotel, white and 'a bit "international"', by castle in southern Moravian town (with neighbouring Valtice a UNESCO World Cultural Heritage Site). Amid fascinating artificially created landscape with baroque and neo-Gothic buildings. 'Comfortable beds, friendly staff, quite a good restaurant.' 2 lounges, bar; night bar/ disco; conference hall. Terrace. Amex, MasterCard, Visa accepted. 2 apartments, 15 triple rooms, 28 double. B&B: single €57, double €63, apartment €95; D,B&B €8 added per person [2004].

LUHAČOVICE 763 26 Moravia — Map 13:A6

Dům Bedřicha Smetany NEW
Lázeňské náměstí 436

Tel (577) 68 21 11
Fax (577) 13 25 26
Email info@lazneluhacovice.cz
Website www.lazneluhacovice.cz

'Full of fresh air and friendly people', this small spa town, on the Moravian border with Slovakia, has 'no cars, just bridges, a bandstand, cafés, and numerous springs'. Overlooking the promenade is this imposing Art Nouveau hotel, named after the composer Smetana, considered to be the father of Czech national music. Restored in the 1990s, it has 'huge well-appointed rooms, each with a well-equipped bathroom': they face the promenade or the woods behind. The design 'is restrained, yet bold', says the 2004 nominator. A grand staircase has stained-glass windows; there are friezes, reliefs, patterns on floors, walls and ceiling. 'Staff are quiet and careful in a spa-like way.' In the small dining room, with terrace, the 'excellent Czech breakfast' has cold meats, eggs, cheese, local jam, sweet buns. 'Freshly cooked meals' are served here ('good fish, tasty stews, delicious pancakes'), and the town has 'some reasonably priced restaurants'. 'Don't expect night life, just peace and quiet.' (*David Sulkin*)

Open 1 Jan–20 Dec. **Rooms** 1 suite, 14 double, 22 single. 2 suitable for ♿. **Facilities** Lift. Lobby bar, restaurant, dining room. Garden. **Location** Central. 20 km S of Zlín. **Credit cards** Amex, MasterCard, Visa. **Terms** [2004] B&B €29–€53. Dinner €5. Spa packages.

> The 'Budget' label by a hotel's name indicates an establishment where dinner, bed and breakfast are offered at around the foreign currency equivalent of £50 per person, or B&B for about £30 and an evening meal for about £20. These are only a rough guide and do not always apply to single accommodation, nor do they necessarily apply in high season.

PRAGUE **Map 13:A5**

Hotel Casa Marcello NEW
Řasnovka 783
110 00 Prague 1

Tel (2) 22 31 02 60
Fax (2) 22 31 33 23
Email booking@casa-marcello.cz
Website www.casa-marcello.cz

Quietly set by St Agnes Monastery, this hotel (part of the French Concorde group), composed of two listed buildings, is 'a good place for peaceful collapse after exploring the city', say its nominators this year. The bedrooms are 'stylish and spacious'; there is a pleasant courtyard for summer meals and drinks. 'Slow service at breakfast, but the buffet choice was excellent.' Well placed for the Old Town Square, but 'out of earshot of the louder British visitors', it offers 'particularly good deals in July, August and winter'. (*Paul and Nicky Tyler*)

Open All year. **Rooms** 12 suites, 20 double. **Facilities** Bar, restaurant; sauna. Courtyard garden: café. **Location** Central, by St Agnes monastery. **Credit cards** All major cards accepted. **Terms** [2004] Room: double €178–€202, suite €251–€291.

Hotel Hoffmeister
Pod Bruskou 7
118 00 Prague 1

Tel (2) 51 01 71 11
Fax (2) 51 01 71 20
Email hotel@hoffmeister.cz
Website www.hoffmeister.cz

'Service is impeccable yet friendly,' say visitors in 2004 to this stylish white-fronted hotel (Relais & Châteaux), 'one of the best we have stayed in.' Owner/manager Martin Hoffmeister has dedicated it to his father Adolf, painter, writer and diplomat, whose avant-garde paintings and drawings, including caricatures (Salvador Dalí, Samuel Beckett and others), adorn the walls. The location is 'just right'; near the left bank of the Vltava, on a busy boulevard below the castle, in the Malá Strana district of offices, embassies and smart restaurants. New this year: eight bedrooms and a wellness centre. Street-facing rooms have double glazing; there is a flowery inner courtyard where meals are served, and in summer, the *Café Ria* (offering light meals) opens on to a terrace with parasols and potted plants. The *Ada* restaurant provides Czech and international fare: 'Really good food, expensive for Prague, but good value for us. Our spacious suite was well furnished, immaculate; public areas were comfortable, though short of seating, except for the large bar/breakfast room.' (*Christopher Smith, and others*)

Open All year. **Rooms** 17 suites, 24 double, 3 single. 1 equipped for ♿. Air-conditioning. **Facilities** Lift. Lobby, bar, wine cellar, café (summer terrace), restaurant; background music; wellness centre. **Location** Near Charles Bridge (windows double glazed). Garage. **Credit cards** All major cards accepted. **Terms** [2004] B&B: single €185–€285, double €215–€325, suite €315–€595. Full alc €45.

The maps can be found in the colour section of the *Guide*.

Hotel Paříž
U Obecního Domu 1
110 00 Prague 1

Tel (2) 22 19 51 95
Fax (2) 24 22 54 75
Email booking@hotel-pariz.cz
Website www.hotel-pariz.cz

The Art Nouveau interior of this neo-Gothic mansion, built in 1904, is 'delightful and beautifully maintained', say visitors this year. Near the Old Town Square, it was the meeting place for the city's café society between the wars. The Brandejs family owners have renovated and filled it with paintings, and it is now a five-star member of the French group, Concorde. One couple in 2004 praised the 'friendly staff and caring service', but another wrote: 'It caters to tour operators; individual visitors do not feel especially welcome.' A fourth-floor room was 'not large but comfortable, beautifully decorated, with high standard of housekeeping; excellent modern bathroom apart from a quirky fixed shower screen'. Light meals, coffee, cakes and desserts can be taken in the *Café de Paris*. In the graceful *Sarah Bernhardt* restaurant, 'meals, with good live piano music, were superb, and service was efficient and unfussy'. (*A and EA, Jean and Alan Stokes, and others*)

Open All year. **Rooms** 17 suites, 69 deluxe/executive. 1 no-smoking floor. Air conditioning. **Facilities** Bar, 2 restaurants; background music; Relax Club: sauna, massage; 2 meeting rooms. Unsuitable for ♿. **Location** Central, 400 m E of Staroměstské náměstí. Parking. **Credit cards** All major cards accepted. **Terms** Room €150–€320, suite €300–€3,700. Breakfast €20. Set lunch €30, dinner €60; full alc €60.

Hotel U Páva
U Lužického semináře 32
118 00 Prague 1

Tel (2) 57 53 33 60
Fax (2) 57 53 09 19
Email hotelupava@iol.cz
Website www.romantichotels.cz/upava

'Pleasant, quiet and convenient', this historic building ('At the Peacock') belonged to the Benedictine order and was rebuilt in 1639 as a baroque house. On Kampa island, near Charles Bridge, it has 'easy access to both sides of the city'. Antique furniture, crystal chandeliers, works of art and an impressive staircase with stone pillars, combine with modern comforts (sauna, spa bath, etc). Staff are 'helpful, friendly', but one visitor, a hotelier himself, was 'amazed that they ran everything without any sign of management over four days. Our rooms were attractively decorated; we had a lovely castle view. Our son's room had no window – but no traffic disturbance either. Breakfast was a good buffet, dinner was slow, huge, but freshly prepared and good quality.' A sister Prague hotel, *U Krále Karla* ('At the King Charles'), is similar in style. The *Royal Ricc*, Brno (*qv*), is also in the KK group. (*Michael Jay, John and Sue Jenkinson*)

Open All year. **Rooms** 8 suites, 19 double. Some on ground floor. **Facilities** Lift. Breakfast room, wine cellar, restaurant, café; spa bath, sauna, solarium. No background music. **Location** Central, on Kampa island. **Credit cards** Amex, MasterCard, Visa. **Terms** [2004] Room: single €138–€202, double €142–€218, suite €228–€250.

Hotel Pohoda BUDGET
Královická 27
100 00 Prague 10

Tel (2) 74 82 21 98
Fax (2) 74 81 44 19
Email pohoda@telecom.cz
Website www.hotelpohoda.cz

Šimon family's simple, well-modernised, little, white B&B hotel, in Strašnice suburb (residential district), 4 km E of centre, near Metro Skalka (15 minutes from centre). 'Clean, well run; excellent buffet breakfast.' Fitness room, sauna; garden. Parking. Small dogs only. Unsuitable for ♿. Amex, MasterCard, Visa accepted. 12 well-designed, quiet bedrooms. B&B: single €39–€80, double €49–€99. *V*

Romantik Hotel U raka
Černínská 10/93
118 00 Prague 1

Tel (2) 20 51 11 00
Fax (2) 33 35 80 41
Email uraka@login.cz
Website www.romantikhotel-uraka.cz

In an artists' colony up a hill near the castle (a 'charming spot'), this stylish little guest house ('At the Sign of the Crayfish') is a tasteful recreation of two wooden 18th-century farm buildings, in cobbled courtyards, on this site. The 'extremely helpful' Paul family have preserved many original features – tiled floors, open hearths – alongside modern metal and wooden furnishings. Visitors like the 'quiet, welcoming atmosphere', the 'unique style'. 'The perfect place to unwind,' one wrote. In the kitchen/bar, with its wooden ceiling and open fire, an ample breakfast (fruit, cereals, yogurts, ham, eggs, etc) is served with damask napkins, on 'exquisite' blue and white Czech porcelain. Also praised: the 'impeccable cleanliness', and the quality of the fittings, eg, a modern shower room. 'Our bedroom, quite small, had luxurious bedding.' 'My spacious room had excellent lighting, a ceiling with great beams.' One room has a well and a winter garden. The small two-tiered garden 'has an element of the Japanese': snacks can be served here. (*SM, and others*)

Open All year. **Rooms** 6 double. In 2 buildings. **Facilities** Lounge, snack bar/breakfast room; background music. Garden terrace. Unsuitable for ♿. **Location** Off Loreta Sq, 500 m W of castle. Parking. Airport transit arranged. **Restrictions** No smoking during breakfast and in some bedrooms. No children under 10. Dogs in public rooms only. **Credit cards** Amex, MasterCard, Visa. **Terms** [2004] B&B: single €190–€210, double €210–€230, suite €240–€265.

Hotel 16
Katerinská 16
128 00 Prague 2

Tel (2) 24 92 06 36
Fax (2) 24 92 06 26
Email hotel16@hotel16.cz
Website www.hotel16.cz

A returning visitor to this well-run small B&B hotel thought it 'the best I've experienced in the Czech Republic'. Earlier praise: 'It is so welcoming you wouldn't want to stay anywhere else.' Recently renovated, it is near the botanical gardens. It has a small skylit atrium and a pleasant terraced rear garden; the multilingual staff are 'very friendly'. A junior suite was 'nicely furnished, with small sitting room; good bathroom lighting; double-glazed windows kept out most of the noise of cars on the cobbled street'. A ground-floor single at the back has a small walled garden, 'but some noise from Reception'. A 'fine buffet breakfast' is served in a room with four clocks 'which did not agree on when to chime'. Wenceslas Square and the 'wonderful' *Café Slavia* on the riverbank are about ten minutes' walk away. 'Not all taxi drivers know the hotel (they sometimes mistake it for the nearby *Novotel*): ask the staff how to say the address in Czech.' (*Charles K Belair, CG*)

Open All year. **Rooms** 7 junior suites, 5 double, 2 single. Air conditioning. **Facilities** Bar, lounge, breakfast room (no-smoking); background music all day. Garden. Antique shop. Unsuitable for ♿. **Location** 1 km SW of Wenceslas Square. Parking. Airport transfer (book in advance). **Credit cards** Amex, MasterCard, Visa. **Terms** [2004] B&B: single €83–€91, double €111–€122, junior suite €101–€140.

STARÉ SPLAVY 471 63 Bohemia — Map 13:A5

Pension Rut BUDGET — *Tel* (487) 87 32 13
Lázeňský vrch 97 — *out of season* (327) 31 35 65

Máchovo jezero (Lake Mácha), in a holiday area about an hour's drive north of Prague, was created in 1366 by King Charles IV to improve the view from Castle Bezděz. This 'simple but charming' *pension* stands on the shore in this lakeside village, which has a small port with boats for hire. 'The Forman family are welcoming owners,' says a regular visitor. 'There is a shady wide terrace, a garden where children can play. Nice home-made breakfast. Drinks and ice creams are served on the terrace. Dinner is sometimes provided; when it is not, try *Hostinec Na Rychtě*, Jestřebí: (487) 87 70 20. Charming paintings by an uncle who now lives in Australia hang throughout.' Visitors in 2004 add: 'The welcome and location exceeded all expectations. The view from our balcony was romantic. Supper on the terrace was a delight. We much enjoyed our conversations with the owners.' The *Pension Rut* should not be confused with the *Pension Ruch*, lower down in the village. (*JP, and others*)

Open Apr–Oct (depends on weather). **Rooms** 10. **Facilities** TV room, conservatory, breakfast room; terrace. Garden on lake. **Location** 80 km N of Prague. **Credit cards** MasterCard, Visa. **Terms** [2004] B&B €90–€115.

****

Traveller's tale Hotel in France. In this newly renovated, posh hotel, we checked into a two-bedroom suite. There was only one closet, which contained only six clothes hangers. We asked for more hangers and were told the rule was 'six hangers per closet'. At dinner we chose the salad with gambas for €18. It turned out to be three whole tomatoes still tied to each other on the vine, a piece of cheese, a small, tiny heart of some green, and a tiny fried shrimp. The oddest and most expensive salad we have ever eaten.

****

Denmark

Steensgaard Herregårdspension, Millinge

CHARLOTTENLUND 2920 North Zealand **Map 1:C3**

Skovshoved Hotel
Strandvejen 267

Tel 39 64 00 28
Fax 39 64 06 72
Email reception@skovshovedhotel.com
Website www.skovshoved-hotel.dk

In an exclusive seaside commuter village north of Copenhagen, this is one of Denmark's oldest hotels (1660). It was taken over in 2003 by Tofa and Ivan Nadelmann (he owns AVIS in Denmark and Poland). Both are new to hotel-keeping, but full of enthusiasm; she 'likes to greet her guests'. They have redecorated with a modern touch, aiming to maintain a 'romantic seaside feel'; all is light and airy; furniture has been specially designed. Some bedrooms are large; some have a balcony facing the sea. The restaurant serves good brasserie-style food, a mix of Spanish, Italian and French; in summer, guests can eat on a terrace facing thatched-roofed cottages. The building also includes an inn where snacks and beer are served, and in the lobby bar 'the hottest DJs in Denmark' perform at the weekend. Two of Copenhagen's best beaches are near, and so is *Dyrehavsbakken*, one of the world's oldest amusement parks. (*Trina Hahnemann*)

Open All year. **Rooms** 2 suites, 20 double. **Facilities** Lounge, inn, restaurant; terrace. **Location** Coast road, 7 km N of Copenhagen. **Credit cards** All major cards accepted. **Terms** [2004] B&B: single 1,100–1,300 Dkr, double 1,300–2,800 Dkr. Set meal with wines 440 Dkr.

COPENHAGEN — Map 1:C3

Hotel Christian IV
Dronningens Tværgade 45
1302 Copenhagen K

Tel 33 32 10 44
Fax 33 32 07 06
Email hotelchristianiv@arp-hansen.dk
Website www.hotelchristianiv.com

White 1950s building near Rosenborg Castle and King's Garden; under same ownership as 71 Nyhavn *(*qv*). 'Spotlessly clean, well maintained, with friendly staff; reasonably disabled-friendly. Excellent breakfasts.' Lift. TV room. 'Pleasant, if expensive' restaurant next door. 42 bedrooms with modern Danish design, all with shower, some no-smoking. B&B: single 795–1,190 Dkr, double 995–1,490 Dkr [2004].*

Ibsens Hotel NEW
Vendersgade 23
1363 Copenhagen K

Tel 33 13 19 13
Fax 33 13 19 16
Email hotel@ibsenshotel.dk
Website www.ibsenshotel.dk

In quiet setting in Nansensgade, by lakes (near Nørreport rail/metro station): Brøchner-Mortensen family's 'good-value' hotel, 'popular with Danes'. 'Comfortable room of adequate size; friendly staff. High-quality Italian restaurant.' Buffet breakfast. Lift, reception/bar, atrium garden. All major credit cards accepted. 118 rooms (some no-smoking), ranging from 'simple' to 'exuberant'. B&B: single 925–1,025 Dkr, double 1,100–1,300 Dkr, suite 2,100 Dkr [2004].

---

71 Nyhavn Hotel
Nyhavn 71
1051 Copenhagen K

Tel 33 43 62 00
Fax 33 43 62 01
Email 71nyhavnhotel@arp-hansen.dk
Website www.71nyhavnhotel.com

Standing among coloured gabled houses at the junction of the Nyhavn canal and the harbour, this conversion of two old spice warehouses is within walking distance of most of the main sights. 'Great hotel; best reception desk in Europe,' wrote one recent visitor. Others admired the 'delightful young staff' and the decor: 'Huge, bright abstract paintings, thick fir beams and posts in public areas and bedrooms. Our medium-sized room had an efficient small shower room, excellent soundproofing (thick walls).' The long, narrow *Pakhuskælderen* restaurant serves 'sophisticated dinners, with formal presentation (dome-lifting, etc) by charming young waiters'. Breakfast is a large buffet. Some rooms get noise from street and wharf. Package tours and business visitors are accommodated: good weekend rates. (*DJS, and others*)

Open All year. Restaurant closed Sun, public holidays. **Rooms** 17 suites, 124 double, 9 single. **Facilities** Lobby/lounge, bar, restaurant; background music. Unsuitable for ♿. **Location** Central. Free parking. **Restriction** No smoking at breakfast, and in 70 bedrooms. Small dogs only (not in restaurant) **Credit cards** All major cards accepted. **Terms** [2004] Room: single 1,025–2,385 Dkr, double 1,325–2,385 Dkr, suite 3,835–5,035 Dkr. Breakfast 125 Dkr.

MILLINGE 5642 Funen — Map 1:C2

Falsled Kro
Assensvej 513

Tel 62 68 11 11
Fax 62 68 11 62
Email info@falsledkro.dk
Website www.falsledkro.dk

In lovely grounds on the garden island of Funen (Fyn), this cluster of thatched buildings, once a smugglers' inn, has been run as a luxury hotel (Relais & Châteaux) for over 30 years by chef Jean-Louis Lieffroy from the Vosges (co-owner with the Grønlykke family). His French cooking in the glass-walled restaurant, which faces the pretty harbour, is highly regarded in Denmark. Seasonal ingredients include cod, lumpfish roe and langoustine in March; wild duck, Jerusalem artichokes and cèpes in September. Recent visitors praised the 'civilised style', the 'enormously nice' Danish/French staff, and the 'high level of accommodation and food'. The suites, around three sides of a courtyard, are across the road. 'Ours was splendid: big half-timbered living room with sofas by the fireplace, fine old prints; charming Spanish-tiled bathroom, breakfast room and private patio. A grand and delicious breakfast was wheeled over each morning.' Some rooms are small, with a steep stairway leading to a loft sleeping area. 'Not cheap, but full value – and more.'

Open All year, except Christmas. Restaurant closed Mon, except dinner May–Oct. **Rooms** 8 suites (across road), 9 double, 2 single. Some on ground floor. **Facilities** Lounge, bar, restaurant; conference facilities; terrace, courtyard. No background music. Large grounds. Sea 50 m. Unsuitable for ♿. **Location** 8 km NW of Fåborg, on Road 329. Garage, car park. **Credit cards** All major cards accepted. **Terms** [2004] Room: single 850 Dkr, double 1,250–2,350 Dkr, suite 2,600–2,900 Dkr. Breakfast 150–200 Dkr. Set lunch 360 Dkr, dinner 540–875 Dkr, full alc 1,050 Dkr.

****

Traveller's tale Hotel in Germany. Halfway through the excellent breakfast, the owner presented us with our bill, asking if we could pay before she left at 9.45 am. She would not accept our MasterCard. Cash we did not have, so we had to abandon our breakfast and go into the village, in driving rain, to find a cash machine. We found one. When we returned, our breakfast had been cleared away.

****

Steensgaard Herregårdspension
Steensgaard 4

Tel 62 61 94 90
Fax 63 61 78 61
Email steensgaard@herregaardspension.dk
Website www.herregaardspension.dk

'An escapist's retreat', this 'marvellous' old brick and half-timbered 14th-century moated manor house on the island of Funen (Fyn) wins yet more praise in 2004: 'A most charming, relaxing place.' Approached up an avenue of trees and through an imposing courtyard, it stands in a large park with a lake and a reserve for deer. Public rooms have antiques, portraits, chandeliers, much panelling; hunting trophies are in the hall, and leather-bound volumes in the library. The owners, Niels Raahauge and Anne Bille-Brahe (the chef), are supported by a 'well-informed, humorously helpful' staff. The large candlelit dining room is popular with locals: 'The food is the best possible combination of contemporary Danish/French cuisine. Much of the produce, especially dairy, comes from the beautiful contiguous farm. The good wine list, strong on New World wines, is sensibly priced for Denmark.' The best bedrooms have 'a faded Danish charm' and windows on several sides; a smaller, cheaper room under the eaves, with its bathroom down the hall, was found 'airy and attractive'. Breakfast is 'the usual Scandinavian buffet, elegantly done'. (*Peter Dell, DJS*)

Open All year, except New Year. **Rooms** 20 double. 6 in annexe. **Facilities** Hall, 4 lounges, bar, billiard room, restaurant (classical background music); small conference facilities. 6-acre grounds: tennis, lake, fishing; game reserve. Beaches 2 km; golf, riding nearby. Unsuitable for ♿. **Location** NW of Millinge, a village NW of Fåborg. Garage, car park. **Restriction** No smoking: restaurant, some bedrooms. **Credit cards** All major cards accepted. **Terms** [2004] B&B: single 835–1,325 Dkr, double 1,100–1,625 Dkr. Full alc 550 Dkr. *V*

SØNDERHO 6720 Fanø — Map 1:C2

Sønderho Kro
Kropladsen 11

Tel 75 16 40 09
Fax 75 16 43 85
Email mail@sonderhokro.dk
Website www.sonderhokro.dk

'Simply lovely; one of the most delightful places we have been to.' High praise in 2004 from a trusted *Guide* correspondent for Birgit and Niels Steen Sørensen's elegant hotel (Relais & Châteaux). Built in traditional style, it is in the grounds of one of the oldest inns in Denmark (1722) in a pretty village near the southern tip of the island of Fanø. In the restaurant ('a beautifully restored room in the original inn'), the young chef, Mette Hyldegaard, serves 'delicious' Danish/international dishes on a no-choice half-board menu and a short *carte*. 'The Sørensens are in the restaurant from morning to evening, and service is good.' 'Excellent' light lunches include local smoked herring. Meals are served under tall trees in the garden in summer. Each bedroom is named after a boat built on Fanø; each is different. Most are in new buildings ('in old style'). 'Our fisherman's cottage had a bedroom, two small sitting areas, one with an open fire.' The island, with its ten-mile beach of fine, firm sand, is reached by frequent ferries. 'You can rent bicycles in the village to ride on the beach and explore the nature reserve.' (*Wolfgang Stroebe*)

Open All year, except 20–27 December, 15 Jan–1 Feb, occasional other periods in winter. **Rooms** 14 double. 8 on ground floor. **Facilities** Hall, salons, restaurant (background music); small conference facilities. Garden. By estuary. Sandy beach, bathing 2 km. **Location** In SE Sønderho, by church. Ferry from Esbjerg. 12 km to Sønderho. Towards centre 400 m; right 100 m, left 25 m. **Credit cards** All major cards accepted. **Terms** [2004] Room: single (not available July/Aug) 810–1,100 Dkr, double 1,030–1,410 Dkr. Breakfast from 125 Dkr. Set lunch 198–248 Dkr, dinner 298–378 Dkr; full alc 550 Dkr.

France

Le Manoir les Minimes, Amboise

Last year saw the centenary of the *Entente cordiale* and, if tourism is an indicator, it is alive and well. France remains our readers' most popular holiday destination on the Continent, and this chapter includes over 360 hotels, varying from glossily converted châteaux and mill houses to the simpler rural *auberges* and small town inns that have long been the glory of our French selection. We also include some *chambres d'hôtes*. Many are farmhouses offering simple bedrooms, maybe an evening meal, and a glimpse of French rural life; others may be châteaux, grander but just as personal: they may be run by the ancestral owners, who sometimes dine with their guests. We are stringent with our choices; this year we have dropped 90 entries and added 71 new or readmitted ones. Apart from Paris, which has 24 recommendations, few of our hotel entries are in big cities: Bordeaux and Marseille have one each, Lyon has two, and Nice has three.

We do not include chain hotels: though generally efficient and offering acceptable accommodation, they tend to be impersonal. The

Accor group, with brands such as Sofitel, Novotel, Mercure, Ibis and Formule 1, dominates this market.

The smaller hotels of character that *Guide* readers prefer are nearly all individually owned and run, but many group together (at a price) for marketing and promotion. The superior Relais & Châteaux association has over 450 members in 50 countries, 137 in France: most are good, if expensive, and many are featured here. Châteaux et Hôtels de France members, generally middle-priced, are often very attractive. Logis de France is a fraternity of some 4,000 family-owned small town hotels and rural *auberges*, identifiable by their green-and-yellow signboard. They tend to be fairly simple, but on the whole they are well run, and good value. Relais du Silence members are mostly in an isolated setting; many are marked by a red rocking chair in *Michelin*, which also bestows red print on a hotel whose looks or ambience it likes.

We say if a place has an award for its cuisine from *Michelin* or from the *Gault Millau* guide. Even one *Michelin* star indicates a high standard; the top rating, three stars, was in 2004 given to only 18 places in France. *Gault Millau*, which in 1969 pioneered the interest in modern cooking (*nouvelle cuisine*), with its avoidance of rich sauces, and an emphasis on fresh ingredients and attractive presentation, gives a mark out of 20: 18 points are for what it sees as the best restaurants. Anything above 12 denotes very good food by its standards. For 'good-value, moderately priced menus' look out for restaurants awarded *Michelin*'s *Bib Gourmand* (there are over 450). *Michelin* also has a blue *Bib Hotel* sign for good-value accommodation, and it now includes a thumbnail description of each hotel.

Almost always, you get better value by taking a *prix-fixe* menu than by going *à la carte*. But the former may have limited choice, while the *carte* can offer more interesting dishes. Some hotels now make their *prix-fixe* menus more flexible, for clients who want just two courses. *Demi-pension* rates, which include breakfast and an evening meal, generally offer good value; some hotels now allow guests on these terms to choose dishes from the *à la carte*.

In many French hotels, notably smaller ones, the owner does the cooking or has a chef who stays for many years. But the French catering industry continues to lament the dearth of talented recruits, and young chefs are becoming more mobile. So French culinary standards are now more erratic; some hotels are recommended here more for ambience and comfort than for food. Generally, though, food is still taken seriously and is one of the main reasons that so many of us return again and again. Where else but in France would you get such wonderfully specialised culinary 'brotherhoods' as the Confrérie des Prunes in Aquitaine or the Confrérie des Chevaliers de la Coquille St-Jacques in Brittany?

Most hotels with a restaurant do not insist that residents dine there. But some do, notably smaller hotels in high season; you should check this when booking. Breakfast, except for *demi-pension* bookings, is generally an optional extra. Traditionally, it will be fresh bread, croissants (not necessarily warm), jams (often home made) and coffee, but more French hotels nowadays offer a copious buffet.

The price of hotel bedrooms is generally far lower than in Britain, and many of the hotels in this chapter carry our 'Budget' sign. Moreover, the year-on-year increase in rates, away from the more popular seaside resorts, has been slight. In Paris, there are many special offers available, particularly if you book online. France is a family-friendly country. It's rare for a hotel to impose age restrictions on children; one of the few we have seen this year is British-owned. French children are taught from an early age that mealtimes are a social occasion, to be enjoyed with patience.

The often tricky subject of gratuities is simple in France: by law these are included in hotel and restaurant bills. You need leave nothing more than a few coins if service has been really good.

AÏNHOA 64250 Pyrénées-Atlantiques — Map 4:D2

Hôtel Ithurria
Rue Principale

Tel 05.59.29.92.11
Fax 05.59.29.81.28
Email hotel@ithurria.com
Website www.ithurria.com

On pilgrim route to Santiago de Compostela, near pretty Basque village in Pyrenean foothills behind St-Jean-de-Luz, 28 km S of Bayonne: 'welcoming hotel', owned by Isabal family for 3 generations, recently renovated. 'A precision-run operation; charming staff and management; modern stylish rooms, good food,' say visitors in 2004. Lift. 2 salons, bar, breakfast room, restaurant (Basque specialities); conference facilities; sauna, fitness room. No background music. 1-hectare garden: terrace, palm trees, large unheated swimming pool. Unsuitable for ♿. Open 8 April–1 Nov. All major credit cards accepted. Air conditioning. 27 bedrooms (some with balcony facing hills; roadside ones hear traffic): single €89–€95, double €115–€130, suite €220–€250. Breakfast €10. D,B&B €95–€125 per person. Set meals €28–€48 [2004].

AIX-EN-PROVENCE Bouches-du-Rhône — Map 6:E3

Le Pigonnet
5 avenue du Pigonnet
13090 Aix-en-Provence

Tel 04.42.59.02.90
Fax 04.42.59.47.77
Email reservation@hotelpigonnet.com
Website www.hotelpigonnet.com

'One of the nicest hotels we've stayed in,' say visitors in 2004. 'Staff were particularly helpful. Food was excellent.' This 19th-century mansion has been owned and run since 1924 by the Swellen family, who 'take a personal interest in their guests'. It is decorated in sophisticated Provençal style, and has a much-praised garden: Cézanne sometimes painted Mont Ste-Victoire from here. There are rose bowers, fountains, ornamental ponds, and a terrace with a swimming pool surrounded by loungers. The chandeliered dining room, *Le Riviera*, is attractive, with much yellow, and on warm evenings guests dine under chestnut trees on its terrace. Most bedrooms have antiques and cheerful fabrics, many have been renovated this year, and a steam room, fitness room and business centre are new. Some traffic noise, and the area, south of the historic centre ('a brisk walk away'), is 'slightly dull, with 1960s university buildings opposite'.

Open All year. Restaurant closed Sat/Sun midday. **Rooms** 1 ground-floor suite (in villa), 49 double. Air conditioning. **Facilities** 2 lifts. 3 lounges, bar, TV room, restaurant (no-smoking) with terrace; business centre; hammam, fitness room. 1-hectare garden: heated swimming pool (May–Sept). **Location** 1 km SW of centre. From motorway: Pont de l'Arc exit towards centre; turn left after 3rd traffic light. Parking. **Credit cards** All major cards accepted. **Terms** Room: single €140–€300, double €180–€380, suite €450–€500. Breakfast €15. D,B&B €50 added per person. Set meals €38–€48; full alc €94. *V*

Hôtel St-Christophe
2 avenue Victor-Hugo
13100 Aix-en-Provence

Tel 04.42.26.01.24
Fax 04.42.38.53.17
Email saintchristophe@francemarket.com
Website www.hotel-saintchristophe.com

'Wonderful', 'excellent value', are comments this year on the Bonnet family's hotel in the centre, near the Cours Mirabeau. Léopold Bonnet turned a garage into a restaurant in 1936, and later added guest rooms. The Art Deco-style *Brasserie Léopold* still has some paintings by '*les amis des arts*', local painters of the 1930s. It serves dishes from Alsace (eg, varieties of choucroute) and Provence (eg, fish soup). 'The food was not brilliant, but the New Year celebrations were such fun.' The bar provides teas, ice creams and 'colourful cocktails'. 'The breakfast buffet has lots of choice. Bedrooms can be smallish, but furnishings are excellent, and *insonorisation* means there is almost no traffic noise.' Some rooms have a terrace; some suites have a view of Mont Ste-Victoire. (*BR*)

Open All year. **Rooms** 7 suites, 51 double. 1 suitable for ♿. Air conditioning. **Facilities** Lift. Bar, breakfast room, restaurant; conference rooms. **Location** Central, near W end of Cours Mirabeau. Private parking (reserve). Garage €9.50. **Credit cards** All major cards accepted. **Terms** [2004] Room: single €64–€100, double €70–€109. Breakfast €8.50.

> The *V* sign at the end of an entry indicates that the hotel has agreed to take part in our Voucher scheme and to give *Guide* readers a 25% discount on its room or B&B rates, subject to the conditions explained in *How to read the entries*, and on the back of the vouchers.

ALBI 81000 Tarn — Map 4:D5

La Réserve — *Tel* 05.63.60.80.80
Route de Cordes — *Fax* 05.63.47.63.60
Email lareservealbi@wanadoo.fr
Website www.relaischateaux.com/reservealbi

'Delightfully set' in a large park on the banks of the Tarn, just outside the city, the Rieux family's smart hotel (Relais & Châteaux) has a terrace and large swimming pool above lawns that slope down to the river. Quietest bedrooms have a balcony overlooking the river (good birdwatching). Some rooms might hear traffic, but others are found 'amazingly quiet, even in season'. In the 'lavish' colonial-style restaurant 'food was lovely, staff were genuinely friendly'. 'A superb lunch.' The family also own the *Hostellerie Saint-Antoine* (see next entry). (*NP and EB, and others*)

Open 1 May–31 Oct. Restaurant closed Mon midday, Tues/Wed midday. **Rooms** 1 suite, 23 double. All no-smoking. Air conditioning. **Facilities** Lift. 2 lounges, bar, restaurant; conference room. Garden: terrace, swimming pool, tennis; river, fishing. **Location** 3 km N of town, on Cordes road (rooms soundproofed; garden-facing ones quietest). **Credit cards** All major cards accepted. **Terms** [2004] Room €130–€280, suite €380. Breakfast €16. Set meals €35–€75.

Hostellerie Saint-Antoine — *Tel* 05.63.54.04.04
17 rue St-Antoine — *Fax* 05.63.47.10.47
Email hotel@saint-antoine-albi.com
Website www.saint-antoine-albi.com

Run by the Rieux family for five generations, this hotel (opened in 1734 on the site of an 11th-century monastery) is one of the oldest in France. 'Quiet, despite its central location' (in a small street fairly near the superb cathedral and the Toulouse Lautrec collection), it has 'beautiful, spacious' bedrooms (some were renovated this year) and 'nice public areas'. Service is 'personal and helpful', say fans. The 'excellent restaurant' serves dishes like carpaccio de canard aux épices; délice de pigeonneau Toulouse Lautrec. One correspondent was disappointed that 'no food of any kind was available on Sunday evening'. Breakfasts are thought 'exceptional'. Drinks are served on a terrace. Guests have free use of the swimming pool and tennis court at the smart sister hotel, *La Réserve* (see previous entry). (*David Lodge, and others*)

Open All year. Restaurant closed Sun, Sat midday, Mon midday. **Rooms** 5 suites, 39 double. Some no-smoking. Air conditioning. **Facilities** Lift. Bar, restaurant (no-smoking); 4 conference rooms; terrace. Garden. **Location** Central, behind theatre. Double glazing. Parking. **Credit cards** All major cards accepted. **Terms** Room €80–€165, suite €185–€220. Breakfast €13. Set meals €25–€55. *V*

> All our inspections are anonymous.

ALGAJOLA 20220 Haute-Corse **Map 11:D1**

Hotel Stella Mare BUDGET
Chemin Santa Lucia

Tel 04.95.60.71.18
Fax 04.95.60.69.39
Email stellamare2@wanadoo.fr
Website www.hotel-stellamare.com

'Modest, but extremely good value for money', this coastal hotel was liked again in 2004: 'Excellent bedroom and shower room. The young owner/manager, Sandrine Levy, and her father give a wonderfully warm welcome.' Fifteen minutes' drive from Calvi, it stands, backed by mountains, above a 'charming village'. Other regular *Guide* correspondents write: 'All is peaceful. Smiling, helpful staff. Front rooms tastefully equipped.' Larger, cheaper rooms face mountains at the rear ('they might get road noise, but are great value'). Air conditioning is new this year. A four-course set menu (main courses like brochette d'agneau grillé avec ratatouille) is served on a terrace overlooking the sea. 'A great base to relax and explore': there are good beach facilities at nearby Casarena, and opposite the hotel is a small station, from which electric single-track trains run along the coast between 8 am and 8 pm. (*Michael Green, D and GB*)

Open 12 Apr–12 Oct. **Rooms** 16 double. Air conditioning. **Facilities** Salon, TV room, bar, restaurant (background music); dining terrace. Garden. Unsuitable for ♿. **Location** Edge of village, opposite station. 16 km NE of Calvi. Parking, garage. **Restrictions** No children under 4. No dogs. **Credit cards** MasterCard, Visa. **Terms** Room €46–€90. Breakfast €7.50. D,B&B (obligatory July/Aug) €30 added per person. Set lunch €16, dinner €27. 1-night bookings refused Aug.

ALOXE-CORTON 21420 Côte d'Or **Map 5:D3**

Villa Louise NEW
9 rue Franche

Tel 03.80.26.46.70
Fax 03.80.26.47.16
Email hotel-villa-louise@wanadoo.fr
Website www.hotel-villa-louise.fr

Near Corton vineyards, in classic Burgundy wine village, 4 km N of Beaune: B&B in 17th-century maison de maître *built above old wine cellars. Helpful owner, viticulturist Véronique Perrin. 'Breakfast in lovely garden, looking towards vineyards.' 3 salons (1 with fireplace, 1 with piano); tiny indoor swimming pool, Turkish bath, sauna. No background music. Amex, MasterCard, Visa accepted. Parking. 12 bedrooms (some no-smoking, 1 on ground floor, 1 air conditioned): €92–€190. Breakfast €13.*

> The *Good Hotel Guide* has its own small Internet site: www.goodhotelguide.com. Anyone may visit it, but the *Guide*'s full Internet site can be accessed only by members of AOL. If you have access to AOL, put in the keyword GHG, or go to AOL's travel pages where the *Guide* is featured.

AMBOISE 37400 Indre-et-Loire — Map 2:F4

Château de Pray
Route de Chargé

Tel 02.47.57.23.67
Fax 02.47.57.32.50
Email chateau.depray@wanadoo.fr
Website http://praycastel.online.fr

In a wooded park outside Amboise, facing the Loire, this small château was built in 1244 by Geoffrey de Pray; later, the wife of Alphonse Daudet lived here. Now a highly regarded hotel, it is managed by Graziella and Ludovic Laurenty (he is the chef). 'Staff very friendly, but not OTT; the food was outstanding; our fellow guests were cosmopolitan,' says a 2004 visitor. Earlier comments: 'A beautiful old building, interesting and full of heraldry.' 'A comfortable bedroom, good bathroom, good housekeeping, cosy atmosphere.' 'Good value.' Public rooms have suits of armour, stained glass, timbered ceilings, panelling. The Menu des Gourmets, in the Renaissance-style dining room, might include langoustines bretonnes, tomates confites; agneau au poêlon, financier d'olives, tomates et courgettes; crémet maison. There is a panelled tea room. Concerts of classical music are held; balloon and helicopter trips can be arranged. (*Rodney Baker-Bates, and others*)

Open All year, except Christmas, 3–20 Jan, 15–30 Nov. **Rooms** 2 suites, 17 double. Some in pavilion. **Facilities** Salons, tea room, restaurant; *orangerie*; *caveau*; conference room. 4-hectare grounds: terrace, garden, heated swimming pool. **Location** 3 km E of Amboise, by route de Chargé, D751. Closed parking. **Restrictions** No smoking: restaurant, some bedrooms. No dogs. **Credit cards** All major cards accepted. **Terms** Room: double €98–€165, suite €190–€230. Breakfast €11. D,B&B double €100–€146.50. Set meals €30–€50; full alc €65. *V*

Le Manoir les Minimes NEW
34 quai Charles Guinot

Tel 02.47.30.40.40
Fax 02.47.30.40.77
Email manoir-les-minimes@wanadoo.fr
Website www.manoirlesminimes.com

'Excellently situated, next to the château', this 18th-century residence stands on the banks of the Loire. 'Our suite was truly exceptional,' say visitors in 2004, 'walls covered in a delightful Jouy fabric; luxurious bathroom.' Another couple had a double room with 'beautiful decor, firm beds and good lighting'. The cheaper rooms at the top are thought good value. 'We liked the safe parking, the free Internet access and the greeting from Olga, the sheepdog.' There is a spacious salon, and the breakfast room is 'lovely', but the breakfast 'is not lavish'. 'Despite this, and the relatively high price, we would revisit for a touch of luxury.' No restaurant: plenty in Amboise (the hotel keeps menus). (*Geoff and Val Barrow, Claire Lavery*)

Open 1 Mar–4 Jan. **Rooms** 2 suites, 13 double. Air conditioning. **Facilities** Salon, breakfast room, bar; terrace. Garden. **Location** River bank, S of bridge. Private (enclosed) parking. **Restrictions** Smoking in bar only. No pets. **Credit cards** MasterCard, Visa. **Terms** [2004] Room €90–€170. Breakfast €11.50–€16.

Le Manoir Saint-Thomas NEW *Tel* 02.47.23.21.82
1 Mail Saint-Thomas *Fax* 02.47.23.24.96
Email info@ manoir-saint-thomas.com
Website www.manoir-saint-thomas.com

Opened in 2004 by Antonella and Bertrand Pautout: 12th-century turreted building, sympathetically restored, now B&B hotel 'de grand standing', *2 mins' walk from centre. Salon with large fireplace, 'British' decor, background music. Garden: heated swimming pool; safe parking. Closed Mar; possibly closed Tues/Wed. Amex, MasterCard, Visa accepted. 10 bedrooms (1 on ground floor, 1 family, some no-smoking): €70–€160, suite €135–€230. Breakfast €10–€15.*

AMBONNAY 51150 Marne Map 5:A3

Auberge St-Vincent *Tel* 03.26.57.01.98
1 rue St-Vincent *Fax* 03.26.57.81.48
Email info@auberge-st-vincent.com
Website www.auberge-st-vincent.com

In small medieval town amid Champenois vineyards 29 km SE of Reims: Logis de France run by owner/chef, Jean-Claude Pelletier, and 'charming wife', Anne-Marie, both 'warmly welcoming'. 2 lounges, restaurant (old cooking utensils; background music), popular with locals: 'high-quality regional cooking'. Vegetarians catered for. On busy road: rear rooms quietest. Parking nearby. Closed Christmas, 30 Jan–1 Mar, 16–31 Aug, Sun night/Mon, Easter/Whitsun. Amex, MasterCard, Visa accepted. 10 bedrooms (small, simple, 'adequate'): €50–€64. Breakfast €9. Set meals €29–€70 [2004].

L'AMÉLIE-SUR-MER 33780 Gironde Map 4:B3

Hôtel des Pins BUDGET *Tel* 05.56.73.27.27
Fax 05.56.73.60.39
Website www.hotel-des-pins.com

On the edge of a pine forest, near the southern tip of the Médoc peninsula, 'Soulac is a proper little seaside town', and l'Amélie is a 'sort of suburb'. Here, this Logis de France, white-fronted, red-roofed, is 'very well run' by its owners, M. and Mme Moulin, say visitors this year. 'They have a fine sense of humour and an excellent staff. At breakfast each day we received the *demi-pension* dinner menu with a request to tell Monsieur by 10 am if any dish did not meet our wishes. Twice we asked for an alternative and this was readily agreed. The menu was never repeated. The restaurant [with a huge fish tank] was always full, but residents were not given short shrift. Large wine list (lots of Bordeaux, of course). We were the only British.' The garden has a wide lawn, pine trees, deckchairs and parasols. Close by is a vast sandy beach ('cleaned daily by the municipality; no deckchairs; bring your own'). (*W and AR, and others*)

Open 19 Mar–7 Nov. Closed Sat midday, Sun/Mon Oct–May. **Rooms** 31. 10 in annexe. **Facilities** Salon, restaurant; seminar room. Garden (outdoor dining). Beach 100 m. **Location** 5 km SW of Soulac-sur-Mer. 99 km NW of Bordeaux. Frequent ferries from Royan. Secure parking. **Credit cards** All major cards accepted. **Terms** [2004] Room €40–€82. Breakfast €6.50–€7.50. D,B&B (obligatory 31 July–24 Aug) €59–€68 per person. Set meals €22–€45.

LES ANDELYS 27700 Eure — Map 2:D5

La Chaîne d'Or
27 rue Grande
Le Petit Andely

Tel 02.32.54.00.31
Fax 02.32.54.05.68
Email chaineor@wanadoo.fr
Website www.lachainedor.com

'Still the best and still our favourite,' says one of the many fans of this restaurant-with-rooms, now owned by Sylvia and Gérard Millet. Originally an 18th-century coaching inn, it stands on a loop of the wide Seine, by the village square; above are the ruins of Château Gaillard, built by Richard Cœur de Lion in 1196. Other comments: 'Superb in all respects.' 'The large rooms overlooking the river cannot be bettered. Beds and sofas blissfully comfortable. Nothing beats sitting by the French windows watching the river traffic.' 'Staff are caring, highly professional.' In the 'charming' beamed restaurant, most tables have a river view. 'Food is excellent but unfussy, and they leave the wine on the table for you to pour.' 'Breakfast, in a delightful room, was good, with fresh fruit.' 'The suave *maître d'* brought our breakfast to the bedroom.' The 'cosy salon' has lots of books. The few rooms that face the courtyard with its flowery window boxes can hear cars. (*Rosemary Winder, Bob and Kate Flaherty, and many others*)

Open Apr–Oct. Restaurant closed Tues midday, and Sun night–Wed off-season. **Rooms** 2 suites, 8 double. **Facilities** Salon, breakfast/TV room, restaurant (background music). Courtyard, terrace. Unsuitable for ♿. **Location** Le Petit Andely, on river. 39 km SE of Rouen. Parking. **Credit cards** Amex, MasterCard, Visa. **Terms** [2004] Room €72–€110, suite €122. Breakfast €12. Set meals €27–€86.50; alc €62–€79.

ANGERS 49100 Maine et Loire — Map 2:F3

Hotel du Mail NEW/BUDGET
8–10 rue des Ursules

Tel 02.41.25.05.25
Fax 02.41.86.91.20
Email hoteldumailangers@yahoo.fr

'Bang in the middle of decent-sized, pleasant town', behind Hôtel de Ville: 'peaceful, efficiently run, reasonably priced' B&B hotel, 17th-century former convent. Salon, breakfast room (background music), inner courtyard where cars can park. All major credit cards accepted. For meals try La Ferme *('packed with serious local eaters'),* Les Templiers *('quality and value'). 26 bedrooms, 'decorated with taste' (3 on ground floor): single €42, double €51–€66. Breakfast €7.50.*

ANNOT 04240 Alpes-de-Haute-Provence — Map 6:D5

Hôtel de l'Avenue BUDGET
Avenue de la Gare

Tel 04.92.83.22.07
Fax 04.92.83.33.13
Email hot.avenue@wanadoo.fr

An unassuming hotel/restaurant, on a quiet, shady avenue in this charming little town, south of the mighty Gorges du Verdon. It offers 'marvellous value', say admirers. 'Our bedroom was modern, with great views.' The rooms are a bit small, but some have a spacious balcony. Owner/chef Jean-Louis Genovesi and his family are 'hospitable and kind' and the food is 'excellent' (*Michelin Bib Gourmand,* 13 *Gault Millau* points for '*cuisine à l'accent régional'*, eg, escalope de foie gras poêlé; cuisse de lapin rôtie aux gnocchis). Meals are taken on the terrace in fine weather. 'Everything is clean and freshly painted; the place has a homely air.' 'Some of the decor is a bit twee, some a bit dazzling.' The lavish breakfast buffet includes muesli, cakes, home-made marmalade. The town has ancient archways, tall Renaissance houses, neatly paved alleyways with streams: 'perfect for strolling'. (*BW Ribbons, and others*)

Open 1 Apr–1 Nov. Restaurant closed Wed midday, Fri midday. **Rooms** 11 double. 1 in annexe. **Facilities** Lounge with TV, restaurant. No background music. Unsuitable for ♿. **Location** Central. Annot is 32 km NE of Castellane. Street parking. **Restrictions** No smoking: restaurant, some bedrooms. No dogs. **Credit cards** MasterCard, Visa. **Terms** Room €45–€53. Breakfast €7.50. D,B&B (obligatory July/Aug) double €94. Set lunch €16, dinner €25.

ANTIBES 06600 Alpes-Maritimes — Map 6:E5

Mas Djoliba
29 avenue de Provence

Tel 04.93.34.02.48
Fax 04.93.34.05.81
Email hotel.djoliba@wanadoo.fr
Website www.hotel-djoliba.com

Ten minutes' walk from the busy old town and its beaches, this converted 1920s *mas* has something of the air of a private home: 'handsome, quiet and comfortable'. Stéphanie Boulesteix runs the office and serves breakfast; her husband, Sylvain, cooks and tends the 'exquisite flowering shrubs' in the garden. Each bedroom is different, with Provençal fabrics, 'pleasant pictures', TV, safe and minibar. One couple first had a 'very small' room but then moved to one that was 'excellent'. Some rooms have a balcony; some are suitable for a family. Upper ones are the sunniest. The 'relaxed atmosphere' is liked, and 'food and service are good'. Meals are served on a covered terrace by the kidney-shaped pool with its loungers, parasols and views over the pine-forested peninsula of Cap d'Antibes. In season, guests are expected to take dinner, which is 'at 7.30 sharp'. The simple seasonal menus are Provençal: eg, soupe de poissons; canard à la confiture d'oignons; fromages; tiramisu.

Open 4 Feb–4 Nov. **Rooms** 2 suites, 10 double, 1 single. 2 in adjacent villa. 3 air conditioned. **Facilities** Salon, bar, dining terrace; background music. Garden: unheated swimming pool. Sandy beach 500 m. Unsuitable for ♿.

Restriction No dogs. **Location** 1.5 km S of centre, off Blvd Wilson (signposted). Free closed parking. **Credit cards** MasterCard, Visa. **Terms** [2004] Room: single €80, double €80–€120, suite €160–€210. Breakfast €10. D,B&B (obligatory 1 May–30 Sept) €74–€114 per person.

ARBOIS 39600 Jura — Map 5:D4

Jean-Paul Jeunet — *Tel* 03.84.66.05.67
9 rue de l'Hôtel-de-Ville — *Fax* 03.84.66.24.20
Email jpjeunet@wanadoo.fr
Website www.jeanpauljeunet.com

In a small town in the Jura hills stands Jean-Paul Jeunet's famous restaurant-with-rooms. He has two *Michelin* stars, 17 points from *Gault Millau* (it compares his creations to *haute couture*). The surrounding vineyards produce an unusual *vin jaune* which can accompany M. Jeunet's dishes, based on local produce. 'A culinary experience well worth the detour,' says a reader this year. 'A lovely meal in a superb restaurant,' writes another. The welcome is 'very friendly', and the decor is 'a confident blend of old stone with modern fabrics'. The dining room has a baronial stone fireplace, vivid abstract collage pictures, bleached beams and Japanese-style blinds. 'Unostentatious' bedrooms range from 'light and airy' to 'dark, somewhat old-fashioned, but quiet and comfortable'. Two rooms open on to a private garden, and there is a lovely flowery courtyard. Mme Jeunet supervises the dining room and serves the 'delicious breakfast' (yogurt, cheese, etc; boiled eggs on request). Children are welcomed. Visit Arbois's small museum devoted to Pasteur (he spent his youth here). (*Christopher McCall, and others*)

Open 1 Feb–30 Nov. Closed Tues/Wed, except July/Aug when open Wed night. **Rooms** 19 doubles. 7 in annexe. **Facilities** Lift. 2 salons, restaurant; classical background music. **Location** Opposite *Hôtel de Ville* (windows double glazed). Public parking across bridge. **Credit cards** All major cards accepted. **Terms** Room €85–€110, suite €125–€135. Breakfast €15. Set meals €45–€125.

LES ARCS SUR ARGENS 83460 Var — Map 6:E4

Le Logis du Guetteur NEW — *Tel* 04.94.99.51.10
Place du Château — *Fax* 04.94.99.51.29
Email le.logis.du.guetteur@wanadoo.fr
Website www.logisduguetteur.com

An 11th-century fortified castle at the top of a medieval village in the hills south of Draguinon has been turned into this small hotel where, say the nominators in 2004, 'everything was correct'. The best bedrooms, in the main building, have a four-poster bed and view. 'Ours, outside the gate, was fairly basic. All dining facilities are below courtyard level. You eat on the terrace (spectacular view) or behind a glazed cover. In really cold weather you go into an interesting labyrinth [where a wood fire burns]. The meal was excellent, with impeccable service.' Benjamin Collombat, the chef, serves seasonal dishes. (*Martin and Karen Oldridge*)

Open 8 Mar–15 Jan. **Rooms** 12. **Facilities** Salon, dining room, terrace (meal service). Garden: swimming pool. Tennis, riding nearby. **Location** 11 km S of Draguinon, 29 km W of St Raphaël. **Credit cards** All major cards accepted. **Terms** [2004] Room €128. Breakfast €15. D,B&B €123 per person.

ARLES 13200 Bouches-du-Rhône — Map 6:D2

Hôtel Calendal BUDGET
5 rue Porte de Laure

Tel 04.90.96.11.89
Fax 04.90.96.05.84
Email contact@lecalendal.com
Website www.lecalendal.com

'A lovely little hotel,' says a visitor in 2004 to Cécile Lespinasse-Jacquemin's quiet, friendly B&B in three buildings in the old town. Other comments: 'Excellent. Good value. Nice ambience.' 'Helpful staff.' 'There is a beautiful patio and eating area where you can have breakfast, lunch or tea. The colours are Provençal yellows and blues. Our room looked directly at the Roman arena.' Other rooms face the theatre or the hotel's garden. Most are large; some have a modern decor, some a beamed ceiling. The tea room serves a buffet lunch from noon to 4 pm, and crêpes sucrées, ice cream and drinks between noon and 8 pm). An evening meal is available in winter. (*Frank Deis, Peter and Ann Moran*)

Open All year, except 6–26 Jan. Restaurant closed at night in summer. **Rooms** 38. In 3 buildings. Air conditioning. **Facilities** Tea room. Garden. **Location** Central, between theatre and arena. Parking adjacent – reserve in advance. **Credit cards** All major cards accepted. **Terms** [2004] Room €45–€99. Breakfast €7.

Hôtel Le Cloître BUDGET
16 rue du Cloître

Tel 04.90.96.29.50
Fax 04.90.96.02.88
Email hotel_cloitre@hotmail.com
Website www.hotelcloitre.com

Near Roman theatre and cloister of Église Ste-Trophime: 'excellent' B&B hotel, 'not luxurious but full of character, with helpful staff'. Rambling building, 12th-century in origin (exposed thick stone wall, ancient beams), recently restored by owners, Agnès and Jean-François Hugly. Provençal decor. Reception lounge, TV room, breakfast room. Terrace. Parking (€5). Open 1 Nov–15 Mar. 30 bedrooms: €45–€70. Breakfast €5.75 [2004].

ASTAFFORT 47220 Lot-et-Garonne — Map 4:D4

Hôtel Le Square
Restaurant Michel Latrille
5 place de la Craste

Tel 05.53.47.20.40
Fax 05.53.47.10.38
Email latrille.michel@wanadoo.fr
Website www.latrille.com

The village, south-west of Agen, 'is not very interesting in itself', write recent visitors, but this small, chic hotel, owned by the singer

Francis Cabrel, is 'charming'. Composed of two adjacent town houses, it is decorated in warm colours: a series of small public rooms lends it a 'small-scale feeling'. *Michelin* gives a star to manager/chef, Michel Latrille (for, eg, raviolis de langoustines aux truffes; côte de veau aux champignons), and *Gault Millau* awards 15 points, also commending the large selection of local wines on the list. 'You can dine on the first-floor terrace (no views). Wonderful regional dishes and marvellous desserts, and the service was relaxed and friendly. Breakfast is good, especially the confiture de pêches. Our bedroom, with a view of the village square, had a marvellous bathroom, good sitting room, country-style decor.' Latrille's wife Sylvie, front-of-house, is 'very friendly', and happy to suggest walking routes in the surrounding hills. (*KB and NJ*)

Open All year, except 1 week May, 3 weeks Nov, 25 Dec, Sun night. Restaurant also closed Mon/Tues midday. **Rooms** 14 double. No smoking. Air conditioning. **Facilities** Lift. Breakfast room, 2 dining rooms (1 no-smoking); background music; function room. Large dining terrace. Parking. **Location** 18 km SW of Agen by N21. **Credit cards** MasterCard, Visa. **Terms** Room: single €50–€100, double €60–€120. Breakfast €10. Set meals €22–€55.

AUDRIEU 14250 Calvados — Map 2:D3

Château d'Audrieu

Tel 02.31.80.21.52
Fax 02.31.80.24.73
Email audrieu@relaischateaux.com
Website www.chateaudaudrieu.com

'A truly delightful place. The garden and park provide pleasure from every point,' says a report in 2004: in 1976, this 18th-century château, a historic monument in a large park near Bayeux, was turned into an elegant hotel (Relais & Châteaux) by its owners, the Livry-Level family. 'The decor, with some antiques, is brilliant,' another visitor wrote: there are original fireplaces, chandeliers and wood panelling in large and formal lounges (one is rococo-panelled). The manager, Willy Grevin, provides 'understated service' and a 'relaxing atmosphere'; his staff are 'courteous and friendly'. Bedrooms range from 'cosy' attic rooms to 'monumental' spaces with original beams and panelling. 'Our apartment was modern and good.' Most bathrooms are luxurious, done in marble. But one couple had a 'cramped' bedroom with an 'old-fashioned' bathroom. Specialities of Cyril Haberland, promoted this year to head chef, include John Dory with liquorice juice and baby leeks; duck liver with mushrooms, apricots and white truffles. In the 'delightful' garden there are a sheltered swimming pool ('it just passes our minimum length test') and a children's play area with tree house. (*Peter and Moira Smith*)

Open 4 Feb–18 Dec. Restaurant closed Mon to non-residents, and midday, except Sat, Sun, public holidays. **Rooms** 4 suites, 25 double. Some on ground floor. 2 in adjacent house. **Facilities** 3 lounges, bar, 3 dining rooms. 60-hectare park: garden, heated swimming pool. **Location** 13 km SE of Bayeux, E of D6 to Tilly. Parking. **Credit cards** All major cards accepted. **Terms** Room €120–€400, suite €305–€425. Breakfast €17–€23. D,B&B €191–€466 per person. Set meals €35–€90; full alc €60–€90.

AUXERRE 89000 Yonne — Map 5:C2

Le Parc des Maréchaux

6 avenue Foch

Tel 03.86.51.43.77
Fax 03.86.51.31.72
Email contact@hotel-parcmarechaux.com
Website www.hotel-parcmarechaux.com

In a pretty riverside town in northern Burgundy, Pascal and Marie-Jeanne Leclerc run a stylish B&B hotel in a white 1850s mansion. The bedrooms, each named after a French marshal, now have air conditioning; those facing the road have double glazing. 'Our lovely, well-furnished room had a luxuriously large bathroom,' say guests this year, 'but some chipped paint indicated that maintenance could be better.' Others had 'an elegant second-floor room with a balcony above the tranquil grounds and pool'. 'Breakfast on the terrace was delightful,' said one visitor. Another thought the buffet 'not particularly impressive'. In the public rooms, furnishings and decor are opulent (lots of crimson); the bar has an open fire. No restaurant, but light dishes (eg, soupe de poisson, tarte aux poireaux, pavé de saumon) are served in the breakfast room, on the terrace or in the bedrooms. Recommended restaurants: *Le Barnabet* (*Michelin* star), by the Yonne and near the cathedral; *Salamandre* (cheaper; 13 *Gault Millau* points). (*SS, B and AF, J Oldham, and others*)

Open All year. **Rooms** 25. 4 on ground floor. Air conditioning. **Facilities** Lift. Lounge, bar (background CDs), breakfast room; conference room. Large garden: heated swimming pool, children's play area. Unsuitable for ♿. **Location** 500 m W of centre. Private parking. **Credit cards** All major cards accepted. **Terms** B&B: single €70–€90, double €80–€110.

AVALLON 89200 Yonne — Map 5:C2

Château de Vault de Lugny NEW

Vault de Lugny

Tel 03.86.34.07.86
Fax 03.86.34.16.36
Email hotel@lugny.com
Website www.ila-chateau.com/lugny

Built in the 12th century, demolished in the 15th, and restored by the present owners, the Audan-Bourzeix family, in the 20th, this impressive building is now a small luxury hotel. 'One of our favourites in all France,' says an American traveller this year. The rooms and suites, individually designed, are 'ravishing and superbly furnished', says *Michelin*. All have a safe and satellite TV. Housekeeping is twice daily. The huge garden, where peacocks roam, is extensively landscaped, and activities on offer include hot-air ballooning and private wine tastings. The restaurant (residents only) serves regional specialities and uses vegetables, fruit, eggs and jam from the premises, 'but we do not eat our chickens or ducks since we regard them as our pets'. Dinner is served in the refectory, with all guests at one long table, or in the courtyard at separate tables in fine weather. Children have their own menu, and babysitters can be arranged. (*Marshall S Harris*)

Open 19 Mar–14 Nov. Restaurant closed midday and Wed. **Rooms** 7 junior suites, 5 double. **Facilities** Salon, bar, restaurant (no-smoking). Garden:

tennis, river, trout fishing, hot-air balloon. **Location** 10 km W of Avallon, towards Vézelay. In Pontaubert take D142 (1st road on right after church). Parking. **Credit cards** All major cards accepted. **Terms** [2004] Rooms: double €160–€290, suite €350–€460. Breakfast €5–€10. D,B&B €45 added per person. Set meals €50–€90.

Hostellerie du Moulin des Ruats *Tel* 03.86.34.97.00
Vallée du Cousin *Fax* 03.86.31.65.47
Email contact@moulin-des-ruats.com
Website www.moulin-des-ruats.com

Visitors returning in 2004 were greeted warmly at this attractive conversion of an old flour mill (the wheel is still in place) in the leafy valley of the River Cousin. Chef Jean-Pierre Rossi, a Citroën devotee from Corsica, runs it with his wife, Jocelyne. 'Many model cars are on display; also photographs of their fawn cat draped over the bonnet of an old Citroën.' The bedrooms are in traditional style; some have a terrace: 'We sat outside, watching wagtails and finches on the riverbank.' *Demi-pension* allows guests choice from both *table d'hôte* menus. Enjoyed this year: 'Snails with garlic; trout with almonds; casserole of monkfish.' 'Good value.' Service is usually found 'excellent, unflustered', but one couple suffered excessive delays at dinner, and disliked their room in the modern part of the building. 'Housekeeping and flower arrangements were admirable, and the lounge is comfortable and spacious.' Breakfasts, stylishly served, are 'old-style French, with home-made croissants and brioches'. There is a riverside terrace for summer meals. 'The woods were full, in late March, of anemones, bluebells and violets.' You can buy wines (including some powerful Corsican ones) from the hotel at half the restaurant price. Avallon is not particularly attractive, but Vézelay, to the west, has a stunning Romanesque abbey. Also nearby is the Château de Bazoches, home of Vauban, the military engineer whose work is seen all over France. (*Sir William and Lady Reid, Ann Mathews, and others*)

Open 15 Feb–11 Nov. Restaurant closed Mon, midday except Sun. **Rooms** 1 suite, 24 double. **Facilities** Lounge/bar, restaurant (no-smoking); background music. Garden on river, fishing. Unsuitable for ♿. **Location** 4 km SW of Avallon, towards Pontaubert/Vézelay by D427. Parking. **Credit cards** All major cards accepted. **Terms** Room €73–€126, suite €147. Breakfast €11. D,B&B €82–€119 per person. Set meals €28–€41; full alc €60.

AVIGNON 84000 Vaucluse **Map 6:D3**

Hôtel d'Europe *Tel* 04.90.14.76.76
12 place Crillon *Fax* 04.90.14.76.71
Email reservations@hotel-d-europe.fr
Website www.hotel-d-europe.fr

A hotel since 1799, this elegant 16th-century building has long been a favourite of *Guide* readers. Earlier visitors include Napoleon, Victor Hugo, Tennessee Williams, Picasso and the Brownings. In summer, it is a 'cool, expensive haven' in the noisy, hot city. It is 'beautifully furnished': tapestries hang in the stairwell; public rooms have flowers and antiques. The 'impeccable welcome' (bags carried, valet parking, smiling reception) is praised, and so are most bedrooms: 'Ours was exquisite.' 'A lovely bathroom.' The rooms vary in size; quiet ones face an inner court; some at the back get slight traffic noise. Some first-floor suites have a large private terrace looking towards the palace. *Michelin* gives a star to chef Bruno d'Angelis for, eg, St-Pierre cuit à l'étouffé de figues et girolles, au parfum des Garrigues. On warm days guests eat under a huge old plane tree by a fountain in the small courtyard, candlelit at night. But 'the set menus don't change; so if you eat in several times you have to go expensively to the *carte*'. The buffet breakfast is 'lavish'. (*Rosemary Woodhill, MF*)

Open All year. Restaurant closed 9–24 Jan, 14–29 Aug, 20–28 Nov, Sun/Mon midday. **Rooms** 3 suites, 41 double. Some on ground floor. Air conditioning. **Facilities** Lift. TV room, bar, restaurant; conference facilities; free Internet access. No background music. Small garden; terrace, courtyard. **Location** By Porte de l'Oulle (W side of city). Garage (€14). **Credit cards** All major cards accepted. **Terms** Room €135–€429, suite €646–€732. Breakfast €23. Set meals €33–€95; full alc €69. *V*

BAGNOLES-DE-L'ORNE 61140 Orne — Map 2:E4

Le Manoir du Lys
La Croix Gautier
Route de Juvigny

Tel 02.33.37.80.69
Fax 02.33.30.05.80
Email manoirdulys@voila.fr
Website www.manoir-du-lys.fr

'Excellent accommodation, a beautiful setting.' Admired again this year, Paul and Marie-France Quinton's gabled, half-timbered manor house (Relais du Silence) is in a forest just outside a Normandy spa resort. Though modernised, with picture windows and electrically operated shutters, it retains a rustic air and has rambling corridors and little flights of stairs. This year, the restaurant has been renovated in contemporary style. Guests enjoyed the 'polite pampering' by 'charming staff', and the 'delicious food' (*Michelin* star, 14 *Gault Millau* points for the Quinton's son, Franck). For summer meals there is a 'delightful terrace'. 'First-class buffet breakfast.' Some bedrooms are small, but there are spacious suites, each with terrace, in an annexe; some rooms have a balcony facing the 'lovely' gardens. One couple had a 'fabulous room on stilts', at a 'very reasonable price'. There are swimming pools indoors and out, and much else for the active (see below). In autumn, there are mushroom weekends: guests are taken into the forest and taught the difference between the edible and the poisonous; then Franck Quinton gives lessons in cooking the former (you might find confiture de cèpes on the breakfast table). (*G and K Tarr, CPD, DJH*)

Open 13 Feb–2 Jan. Closed Sun night/Mon 1 Nov–1 Apr. **Rooms** 7 air-conditioned suites (in annexe), 30 double. 1 suitable for ♿. **Facilities** Lift, ramp. Lounge, bar (pianist Fri night), restaurant; background music; private dining rooms; billiard room, indoor swimming pool; conference facilities. 1-hectare garden: terrace, children's play area, heated swimming pool, tennis, golf practice, mountain bike rentals. **Location** 2 km NW of Bagnoles, towards Juvigny (near golf course). Garage, parking. **Restriction** No smoking: restaurant, some public rooms, bedrooms. **Credit cards** All major cards accepted. **Terms** Room: single €60–€84, double €78–€185, suite €190–€240. Breakfast €13. D,B&B (min. 3 nights) €87–€140 per person. Set meals €27–€76; full alc €60–€70.

BARCELONNETTE 04400 Alpes-de-Haute-Provence Map 6:C5

Hôtel Azteca BUDGET

3 rue François-Arnaud

Tel 04.92.81.46.36
Fax 04.92.81.43.92
Email hotel-azteca@wanadoo.fr
Website www.hotel-azteca.fr.st

'An unexpected chunk of Mexico' in upper Provence, Anne Marie Chabre's B&B (managed by Hervé Graff) is filled with furniture and craftworks which globetrotting residents of this medieval town collected in the 19th century. It was liked again recently: 'Staff very friendly. Delicious breakfast on the wide terrace. Our annexe room was quite dark, but spotless, very comfortable.' Many rooms are in Mexican style, and beds are large. 'The decorations everywhere are attractive.' 'Service was efficient.' Afternoon tea has a wide choice of teas, and hot pastries. In the evening there is a happy hour at the bar with *tapas*, 'which may make it unnecessary to go to a restaurant'. Nearby are golf, lakes, fishing and *sports d'air,* and the hotel's *navette* will take guests free to nearby ski resorts such as Le Sauze and Pra Loup. (*AC, and others*)

Open 1 Dec–11 Nov. **Rooms** 5 duplex, 22 double. 2 suitable for ♿. **Facilities** Lift. Salon (no-smoking), bar/library, breakfast room (no-smoking); background radio; conference room. Terrace. **Location** Behind Pl. de la Poste. Town is 146 km NW of Nice (pass closed in winter), 69 km SE of Gap. Safe parking. **Credit cards** All major cards accepted. **Terms** Room: single/double €49–€95, quadruple €90–€120. Breakfast €8.

BARCUS 64130 Pyrénées-Atlantiques Map 4:E3

Hôtel Chilo BUDGET

Tel 05.59.28.90.79
Fax 05.59.28.93.10
Email martine.chilo@wanadoo.fr
Website www.hotel-chilo.com

South-west of Pau, in a tiny village on the edge of the Pays Basque, this old inn has been turned into a smart restaurant-with-rooms by owner/chef Pierre Chilo. Praised by readers for its 'excellent food, remarkable value and attractive furnishings', it has 13 *Gault Millau* points for the regional cuisine served in a *néo-rustique* dining room: eg, brochette de chipirons et gambas; crépinette d'agneau aux pieds de porc et champignons sauvages. Meals are served in winter by a fire, in summer on a terrace by the flowery garden, facing mountains. The pool and loungers are 'very good'. Bedrooms and bathrooms vary in size: the cheaper annexe rooms are said to be 'basic', and rooms facing the street can suffer early-morning traffic noise.

Open All year. Restaurant closed Sun evening/Mon, Tues midday. **Rooms** 1 suite, 10 double. 1 on ground floor. 2 in annexe. Air conditioning. **Facilities** Salon, bar, restaurant (smoking discouraged; background music); function facilities. Garden: unheated swimming pool. **Location** Village centre (rear rooms quietest). 18 km W of Oloron-Ste-Marie. Closed parking. **Credit cards** All major cards accepted. **Terms** Room €46–€85, suite €120–€140. Breakfast €8–€10. D,B&B €59–€108 per person. Set meals €18–€62; full alc €55.

BARJAC 30430 Gard — Map 6:C2

Le Mas du Terme
Route de Bagnols-sur-Cèze

Tel 04.66.24.56.31
Fax 04.66.24.58.54
Email welcome@mas-du-terme.com
Website www.mas-du-terme.com

A short way from the gorges of the Ardèche, this converted 18th-century stone *mas*, surrounded by vineyards and fields of lavender, is now a Logis de France, run by its owners, Fabienne and Thierry Marron. They promise: 'Only cicadas disturb the peace.' The decor is Provençal, as is the cooking. Meals (no choice) are served in the arched restaurant or on the patio in fine weather. 'The food was good, with pleasant service,' say recent guests. 'Buffet breakfast also good.' There is an 'excellent swimming pool'. Some of the simple bedrooms are in the main house, some in the garden. Some are small. Visits can be arranged to grottos, vineyards, picturesque villages, etc. (*Ann Mathews, and others*)

Open Apr–Oct. Restaurant closed midday. **Rooms** 22 double. 1 suitable for ♿. 10 in annexe. **Facilities** 2 salons, bar, TV room, restaurant; conference room; fitness room; dining patio. Garden: swimming pool. **Location** 34 km NE of Alès, 4 km SE of Barjac by D901. **Credit cards** MasterCard, Visa. **Terms** [2004] Room €62–€100, suite €130–€160. Breakfast €9. D,B&B €78–€116 per person. Set meals €27–€35.

BARNEVILLE-CARTERET 50270 Manche — Map 2:D3

La Marine
11 rue de Paris

Tel 02.33.53.83.31
Fax 02.33.53.39.60

'Seven days of great comfort in a superb location' were enjoyed in 2004 at the Cesne family's holiday hotel in a *pieds dans l'eau* position on the Cotentin peninsula, south of Cherbourg. On a tidal estuary in a small fishing port/summer resort, it is near superb beaches and a marina. The food is thought 'exceptional' (*Michelin* star, 15 *Gault Millau* points for Laurent Cesne's 'inventive cuisine', eg, huîtres en nage glacée de cornichons; volaille à la créançoise, sauce foie gras). 'Delicious desserts.' 'Mme Cesne and her staff are charming'; 'she works hard to ensure everything is perfect.' 'The waiters were professional but amusing.' The lounge, 'like an ocean liner', the terrace, and the restaurant all face the water. Breakfast is 'standard French'. Bedrooms facing the estuary are 'spacious, warm, well equipped'; best ones have a balcony. Annexe ones have good facilities but not the views. Some rooms are small and basic. Many guests are British. (*Antony TR Fletcher, and others; also Nigel and Olga Wikeley*)

Open 1 Apr–11 Nov. Restaurant closed Mon midday, Thurs midday Apr–Sept except July/Aug; Sun night/Mon and Thurs midday Oct–mid-Apr. **Rooms** 28 double, 2 single. 3 in annexe. **Facilities** Salon (background music), restaurant. Terrace. Beach 200 m. Unsuitable for ♿. **Location** Carteret village. 37 km SW of Cherbourg. Small car park (unguarded). **Credit cards** Amex, MasterCard, Visa. **Terms** [2004] Room: €78–€138. Breakfast €10. D,B&B €79–€109 per person. Set meals €28–€81; alc €55.

LE BARROUX 84330 Vaucluse — Map 6:D3

Hôtel Les Géraniums BUDGET
Place de la Croix

Tel 04.90.62.41.08
Fax 04.90.62.56.48
Email les-geraniums@wanadoo.fr
Website www.avignon-et-provence.com/hotels/les-geraniums

Owned by Huw Awada (former London hotelier) and his Irish wife, and with chef Jacques Roux: handsome old stone building in village perché *(with 12th-century castle, fine views, llamas) near Mont Ventoux (10 km NE of Carpentras, by D938). 'Excellent value; great room in annexe, with wonderful views; excellent restaurant; attentive staff.' Open 5 Mar–15 Nov. Salon with TV, bar, restaurant; function room. No background music. Garden: 2 terraces, solarium. Only restaurant suitable for ♿. Parking. All major credit cards accepted. 22 bedrooms (4 with terrace, 9 in nearby annexe): €45–€50. Breakfast €8. D,B&B €43–€46 per person.*

LA BAULE 44504 Loire-Atlantique — Map 2:F2

Castel Marie-Louise
1 avenue Andrieu

Tel 02.40.11.48.38
Fax 02.40.11.48.35
Email marielouise@relaischateaux.com
Website www.castel-marie-louise.com

Built a century ago as a private house, this *belle époque* mansion (Relais & Châteaux) was turned into a hotel by François André in 1926: he named it after his wife. It stands in a large garden (with pine trees, white parasols and loungers) across the road from La Baule's magnificent beach. It was found 'marvellous, relaxing' by a recent visitor. 'The staff were superb. Our attractive room faced the garden.' In the beamed restaurant, 'the food and service were so good that we ate in every night' (*Michelin* star for Éric Mignard). There are antiques in public areas and in the bedrooms (some are large and sumptuous, with heavily patterned matching wallpaper and bedspread). Breakfast has 'a good buffet' and cooked dishes. The hotel offers an hour's free tennis each day for children, and bicycles are provided. La Baule has water sports, riding, golf, a casino and a *Centre de Thalassothérapie*. The valet parking is 'a boon' in season. (*JB*)

Open All year, except 14 Nov–24 Dec. Restaurant closed midday, except Sun, in off-season. **Rooms** 2 suites, 29 double. 1 suitable for ♿. **Facilities** Lift. Lobby, lounge, bar, restaurant; classical background music; meeting/banqueting rooms. Terrace (lunches May–mid-Sept). Large garden. Bicycles. Access to swimming pools of sister hotels *Royal* and *Hermitage*, 200 m. Sandy beach 30 m; tennis nearby. **Location** 1.5 km W of centre (shuttle available). Car park. **Restriction** No smoking: restaurant, some bedrooms. **Credit cards** All major cards accepted. **Terms** [2004] Room €253–€465, suite €485–€525. Breakfast €18. Set meals €40–€86; alc €89.

LES BAUX-DE-PROVENCE 13520 Bouches-du-Rhône Map 6:D2

La Cabro d'Or

Tel 04.90.54.33.21
Fax 04.90.54.45.98
Email contact@lacabrodor.com
Website www.lacabrodor.com

Well away from the tourist crowds which flock to this spectacular hilltop village, the Charial family's 'Golden Goat' is a sophisticated modern hotel (Relais & Châteaux). Built in the style of a Provençal *mas*, it has rooms in houses in the luxuriant Mediterranean gardens, and a locally inspired decor. There is a large swimming pool, but no bar and no real lounges. The ambience is 'relaxed', 'very peaceful', and the accent is on sport (tennis, riding, etc). Chef Jean-André Charial is manager with his wife, Geneviève. The food, served in the country-style dining room or outside under lime trees, is thought 'excellent' (*Michelin*, 14 *Gault Millau* points for, eg, ravioles de queues de langoustines aux courgettes; pigeonneau contisé au chèvre frais). Other comments: 'The set half-board menu was uniformly good. Service was cheerful.' 'Our bedroom was well equipped.' A horse-drawn taxi takes guests up to the village, where the family own the even more luxurious *Oustau de Baumanière* (two *Michelin* stars, 15 *Gault Millau* points). (*ND*)

Open 20 Dec–11 Nov. Closed Mon Dec–Mar. Restaurant also closed Tues midday. **Rooms** 8 suites, 22 double, 1 single. Air conditioning. **Facilities** Ramps. Restaurant; function rooms. No background music. Large grounds: terrace, swimming pool, tennis, riding. Unsuitable for ♿. **Location** 1 km W of village. Parking. **Credit cards** All major cards accepted. **Terms** [2004] Room €134–€205, suite €278–€350. Breakfast €16. D,B&B €137–€276 per person. Set meals €38–€80; alc €80–€95.

BAYEUX 14400 Calvados Map 2:D3

Le Lion d'Or
71 rue St-Jean

Tel 02.31.92.06.90
Fax 02.31.22.15.64
Email lion.d-or.bayeux@wanadoo.fr
Website www.liondor-bayeux.fr

Run since 1928 by the Jouvin-Bessière family, this Logis de France (also Relais du Silence) is a short walk from the famous tapestry (really an embroidery). A much-modernised old coaching inn, it was enjoyed again in 2004. 'Staff were friendly, efficient. The food was excellent and good value.' But another visitor found the ambience 'not very French' and staff 'overworked'. Bedrooms lead off rambling corridors ('well lit, done in pleasant green fabric'). With their colourful window boxes, they look on to a paved courtyard (with flowers and palm trees) where cars are parked ('the transition is amazing, from the busy street to this quiet oasis'). Some rooms are up many stairs (no lift, but help is given); most are spacious. 'Ours was cheerful. From the bed we could see the floodlit cathedral.' Smaller rooms are 'adequate'. Sound insulation may not always be perfect. Chef Patrick Mouilleau wins 14 *Gault Millau* points (one more this year) for seasonal dishes, eg, courgette flowers with Dublin Bay prawns; red mullet with citronella, roast fennel and aniseed. 'The buffet breakfast had wide choice.' (*Roy and Jenny May, BW, and others*)

Open 21 Jan–18 Dec. **Rooms** 1 suite, 18 double, 6 single. **Facilities** Salon, bar, restaurant; classical background music; meeting room. Courtyard. Unsuitable for ♿. **Location** Central (quiet), NE of cathedral. Courtyard parking (€4). **Credit cards** All major cards accepted. **Terms** [2004] Room €62–€118, suite €136–€165. Breakfast €11–€12. D,B&B €76–€167 per person. Set meals €25–€45; full alc €60.

BEAULIEU-SUR-MER 06310 Alpes-Maritimes — Map 6:D5

Le Métropole

15 boulevard du Maréchal Leclerc

Tel 04.93.01.00.08
Fax 04.93.01.18.51
Email metropole@relaischateaux.com
Website www.le-metropole.com

An opulent gold and white villa built in the style of an Italian *palazzo*, in this small, chic resort. Now a luxury hotel (Relais & Châteaux), but less expensive than its neighbour, *La Réserve* (see below), it stands in magnificent gardens which lead to a private beach and pier. The restaurant looks on to large sea-facing terraces where meals are served. The sea-water swimming pool is heated all year to 30°. 'Staff are friendly,' say visitors who spent a week. 'In our good seaview room we could find nothing to criticise. A strong point is the spacious and pleasant public rooms.' The regional cuisine of Christian Métral (15 *Gault Millau* points) is thought 'excellent', and 'some nice restaurants are nearby'. Bedrooms are in Louis XVI style. Some cheaper ones face inland: they are small and can be noisy. (*M and AF*)

Open 20 Dec–20 Oct. **Rooms** 5 suites, 35 double. Air conditioning. **Facilities** Lift. Lounges, bar, restaurant; dining terrace. Garden: heated swimming pool, beach. **Location** Seafront. 10 km E of Nice. Parking. **Credit cards** All major cards accepted. **Terms** [2004] Rooms: single €160–€230, double €170–€280, suite €460–€1,020. Breakfast €23–€33. D,B&B €60–€70 added per person. Set meals €56–€86.

La Réserve de Beaulieu

5 boulevard Maréchal Leclerc

Tel 04.93.01.00.01
Fax 04.93.01.28.99
Email reserve@wanadoo.fr
Website www.reservebeaulieu.com

By the rocky shore, the Delion family's pink, Florentine-style villa (Relais & Châteaux) was a favourite of prewar Riviera society: Garbo and Scott Fitzgerald were among its habitués. 'It is my idea of the perfect hotel,' says an aficionado. 'One is pampered with professionalism yet one feels at home.' Devotees admire the 'magnificent position', the flower-filled courtyard, the 'excellent concierges'. 'Our room, large and nicely furnished, looked over the busy little harbour, the mountains, the coast as far as Èze. Public areas are gorgeous. Superb flowers.' The heated sea-water swimming pool, overlooking the sea and Cap Ferrat, 'is a jewel at sunrise and sunset'. Chef Christophe Cussac has a *Michelin* star (one fewer than last year) for, eg, melba de foie gras poivré; loup de Méditerranée au bellet rouge et poire épicée. Front-facing rooms may hear traffic.

Open 18 Dec–7 Nov. **Rooms** 11 suites, 28 double. Air conditioning. **Facilities** Lift. Lounge, piano bar, billiard room, restaurant; meeting rooms. Garden: courtyard, outdoor dining, heated swimming pool, health spa; diving, sailing, waterskiing. **Location** Seafront. 10 km E of Nice. Parking. **Credit cards** All major cards accepted. **Terms** [2004] Room €170–€1,000, suite €1,125–€2,400. Breakfast €28–€38. Set meals €65–€130; alc €105–€150.

BEAUNE 21206 Côte-d'Or — Map 5:D3

Hôtel Le Cep
27 rue Maufoux

Tel 03.80.22.35.48
Fax 03.80.22.76.80
Email resa@hotel-cep-beaune.com
Website www.hotel-cep-beaune.com

The most famous hotel in Burgundy's wine capital continues to win praise from *Guide* readers: 'Nice, characterful, comfy', 'we always find it excellent', say visitors this year. Owned by the Bernard family, the stately building, mainly 17th-century, part 14th, has outside stone staircases, a superb spiral stairway, a medieval courtyard, Louis XV decor, a tower with views of the old town. 'Our room was well furnished, the air conditioning worked (a bit noisily); staff were excellent.' Some bedrooms, though small, have 'delightful furniture'; some, more modern, are less interesting. A few rooms face the one-way street; most face the garden or a courtyard. Five apartments are new this year. Public rooms are 'sumptuously furnished'. A 'super' breakfast (fresh orange juice, pastries, cheese, hams) is served in the vaulted former wine cellar. 'The highlight was a German egg-boiler, great fun!' No restaurant: *Bernard Morillon*, next door, is found 'excellent, if expensive'. (*Charlie Nairn, Maybel King; also Michael Burns*)

Open All year. Restaurant closed Jan. **Rooms** 21 suites, 34 double, 7 single. 2 suitable for ♿. 18 in pavilions. Air conditioning. **Facilities** Lift, ramps. 2 lounges, library, bar; background jazz; breakfast room; conference/function facilities. Courtyards. Garden. **Location** Central, near Notre Dame church. Parking, garage. **Credit cards** All major cards accepted. **Terms** [2004] Room: single €125, double €160–€190, suite €240–€320, apartment €500. Breakfast €18.

> We quote either price per room, or else the range of prices per person – the lowest is likely to be for one person sharing a double room out of season, the highest for a single room in high season.

BEAURECUEIL 13100 Bouches-du-Rhône — Map 6:E3

Relais Sainte-Victoire

Tel 04.42.66.94.98
Fax 04.42.66.85.96
Email relais-ste-victoire@wanadoo.fr
Website www.relais-sainte-victoire.com

In 'lovely countryside, like a Cézanne painting', the Jugy-Bergès family's converted *mas*, now a stylish restaurant, stands amid corn-fields east of Aix-en-Provence. Its terrace has charming rural views. The bedrooms, all different, have names (Rodolphe, Bossy, Magali, etc); some have a spa bath, some a terrace. They are 'good value, spacious and peaceful, if rather plain', says a visitor this year. Other comments: 'Everyone was very welcoming.' 'Wonderful; Madame couldn't be more helpful. Lovely dining rooms; marvellous food; exquisite table decorations.' The decor is Provençal: so is René Bergès's cuisine (13 *Gault Millau* points, *Michelin* star), eg, nougat de pigeon confit; filet de rouget poêlé de nos côtes françaises. Service is 'very correct', but the limited menu changes infrequently. The list of local wines is huge. There is a 'little, tucked-away' pool in the garden. (*Beverley Adams, Rose Woodhill, and others*)

Open All year, except 1st week Jan, 10 days Nov, Feb school holidays, Sun night/Mon, Fri, except evenings Mar–Oct. **Rooms** 15 double. In adjacent building. Some on ground floor. 14 air conditioned. **Facilities** Reception, restaurant. No background music. Park: garden, terrace, unheated swimming pool. **Location** Outside village. 10 km E of Aix-en-Provence. **Credit cards** Amex, MasterCard, Visa. **Terms** Room €61–€122. Breakfast €14. D,B&B €130–€150 per person. Set meals €25–€65; full alc €70.

BELCASTEL 12390 Aveyron — Map 4:C5

Hôtel Restaurant du Vieux Pont

Tel 05.65.64.52.29
Fax 05.65.64.44.32
Email hotel-du-vieux-pont@wanadoo.fr
Website www.hotelbelcastel.com

'Wonderful.' 'My favourite of our trip.' Much praise again for this tiny 'French dream hotel'. Converted from the childhood home of the owners, Michèle and Nicole Fagegaltier, it stands amid 'rich countryside' in an old Massif Central hamlet ('lovely after the crowds have left'), which rises on the sides of a steep cliff topped by a feudal castle. Below, a 15th-century cobbled bridge crosses the swift-flowing Aveyron. On one side is the *Vieux Pont*, formerly the village café where the Fagegaltiers fried tiny fish from the river. Today, Michèle is the elegant front-of-house, while Nicole and her husband, Bruno Rouquier, win a *Michelin* star, 14 *Gault Millau* points for their 'staggering', 'fantastically presented' regional cooking, eg, l'agneau de l'Aveyron avec une petite purée de citron; poitrine de pigeon rissolée. The *menu d'enfant* offers smaller portions of the same dishes. Dinner is in a room with 'relaxed upmarket chic' and picture windows facing the river. The five spacious, modern bedrooms, in a building across the river, are 'imaginatively designed' with white walls, curtains and bedspreads and wooden floors. Breakfast is taken in the 'delightful' little garden. 'Delicate white umbrellas' are on hand should the weather prove inclement. (*Hugh Willbourn, Karin Bronsaer and Nico Janssen, DD*)

Open 15 Mar–1 Jan. Restaurant closed Sun night/Mon/Tues midday. **Rooms** 7 double. 1 on ground floor. Air conditioning. **Facilities** Restaurant (no-smoking); terrace. No background music. Garden: river. **Location** Centre of village. 23 km W of Rodez, off D994 to Villefranche. Parking nearby. **Credit cards** MasterCard, Visa. **Terms** Room €73–€87. Breakfast €11. Set meals €26–€75; alc €50–€72.

BELLEGARDE-SUR-VALSERINE 01200 Ain — Map 5:E4

Hôtel Le Fartoret — *Tel* 04.50.48.07.18
Place de la Mairie, Éloise — *Fax* 04.50.48.23.85

'A lovely hotel, with a nice pool.' This Relais du Silence/Logis de France was liked again in 2004. A collection of buildings, it is in a small hillside hamlet (no shops or café) amid fine scenery. The Bachmann-Gassilloud family owners, 'lovely warm people', create 'a happy atmosphere'. The 'large and airy' dining room, 'most attractive', has views of the Jura. Here, one couple had 'a superb meal, with impeccable service'. Rooms in the main building are judged better than those in the annexe, where one visitor had a 'rather drab bedroom, with poor upkeep'. The large terrace faces the hills, and there is a swimming pool surrounded by hedges. Quiet, apart from church bells and the occasional aircraft. (*Frank Deis, Jane Couchman, and others*)

Open 4 Jan–22 Dec. Closed Sun night off-season. **Rooms** 38 double, 2 single. 20 in garden. **Facilities** Lift. Salon, bar, restaurant; conference room; dining terrace. 5-hectare grounds: swimming pool, tennis, children's playground. Unsuitable for ♿. **Location** In Éloise. 5 km SE of Bellegarde, 35 km SW of Geneva. From A40, exit Éloise. Garage. **Credit cards** All major cards accepted. **Terms** Room €63–€83.50. Breakfast €9.50. D,B&B €52–€75 per person. Set meals €20–€45.

BERZÉ LA VILLE 71960 Saône-et-Loire — Map 5:E3

Relais du Mâconnais NEW/BUDGET — *Tel* 03.85.36.60.72
La Croix Blanche — *Fax* 03.85.36.65.47
Email resa@lannuel.com
Website www.lannuel.com

In tiny village on D17 between Cluny and Mâcon: restaurant-with-rooms owned by Christian Lannuel; his son, Arnaud, is the 'exceptional' chef (14 Gault Millau *points). 'Roasted lobster with garlic purée was memorable,' says nominator. Attractive, beamed restaurant; meeting room. Big, shady garden, terrace, parking. Good walking nearby. Closed Jan, Sun night/Mon. 10 bedrooms ('pleasant, reasonably priced', but road-facing ones hear traffic): €59–€90; D,B&B €63–€93 per person. Set meals €24–€58.*

BEUZEVILLE 27210 Eure — Map 2:D4

Le Petit Castel et L'Auberge du Cochon d'Or BUDGET
Place du Général de Gaulle

Tel 02.32.57.76.08
Fax 02.32.42.25.70
Email auberge-du-cochon-dor@wanadoo.fr
Website www.le-cochon-dor.fr

*On main square of charming small town 15 km SE of Honfleur: 'small and simple' Logis de France (*Petit Castel*) opposite 'excellent' Norman restaurant (closed Mon, and Sun evening Oct–end Mar) in old auberge (*Cochon d'Or*), both owned by Catherine and Olivier Martin. 'Warm welcome, good French breakfast, good service.' 2 lounges, breakfast room, restaurant, terrace (meal service). Open 15 Jan–15 Dec. Free, secure parking. MasterCard, Visa accepted. 20 bedrooms (quietest ones face pretty rear garden): €38–€54. Breakfast €7. Set meals €14–€40 [2004].*

BEZANCOURT 76220 Seine-Maritime — Map 2:D5

Château du Landel NEW

Tel 02.35.90.16.01
Fax 02.35.90.62.47
Email contact@chateau-du-landel.fr
Website www.chateau-du-landel.fr

In wooded grounds near the Forêt de Lyons in Haute Normandie, this 18th-century house (Relais du Silence) was once a staging post on the pilgrimage route to Santiago de Compostela. 'We stayed a second night because it was so good,' says the reader who discovered it in 2004. 'It is lovely, unpretentious, decorated in soft colours, with elegant furniture and wonderful floors of marble, flagstones and brick. Our comfortable, pretty room, all blue, was on the second floor.' The owners, Yves and Annick Cardon, are 'friendly, charming, not obsequious': he is the chef, she runs front-of-house. 'The food was excellent, fairly simple by French château standards, with limited choice (eg, poached artichoke hearts with smoked salmon; turbot with sorrel). 'Excellent breakfasts: the best croissants of our holiday.' Children are welcomed. (*Hilary J Chapman*)

Open Mid-Mar–mid-Nov. Restaurant closed midday on Mon and Thurs, Sun night off-season. **Rooms** 17 double. **Facilities** Salon, 2 dining rooms (1 no-smoking; classical background music); snooker room; meeting rooms. 2-hectare grounds: garden (outdoor meals): heated swimming pool, tennis. **Location** 12 km SW of Gournay-en-Bray, by D62, off D316. **Credit cards** All major cards accepted. **Terms** B&B: single €89.50–€189, double €99–€189. Breakfast €9.50. D,B&B €79.50–€209.50 per person. Set meals €26–€42.

> Italicised entries indicate hotels that are worth considering but which, for various reasons – inadequate information, lack of feedback, ambivalent reports – do not at the moment warrant a full entry.

BILLIERS 56190 Morbihan — Map 2:F2

Domaine de Rochevilaine
Pointe de Pen Lan-Sud
Tel 02.97.41.61.61
Fax 02.97.41.44.85
Email domaine@domainerochevilaine.com
Website www.domainerochevilaine.com

On a rocky spur of the south Brittany coast, this luxurious hotel (Relais & Châteaux) is owned by Bertrand Jaquet. A romantic collection of buildings, including a 13th-century stone gateway, old manor houses and cottages, it stands in pretty gardens by the sea. Bedrooms with a sitting room (good for a family) are in palatial modern pavilions; some have a private terrace. There are old stone carvings, beams, modern paintings and sculptures, a huge fireplace. The furniture is antique Breton (large carved wardrobes, etc). The spa, which offers all manner of health treatments, has a large indoor swimming pool overlooked by the spacious breakfast room and a circular balcony. A small, shallow, outdoor pool is set above rocks. The dining room has huge picture windows facing the sea. You can also dine outdoors, in a courtyard. Patrice Caillault has 15 *Gault Millau* points, for, eg, côte d'agneau en croûte de chorizo, jus d'un navarin. Or you could take the Menu Homard. Service is formal, with much dome-lifting. 'The staff were particularly efficient and charming,' says a visitor this year. (*A and SC, and others*)

Open All year. **Rooms** 3 suites, 33 double. In several houses. 2 on ground floor. **Facilities** Lift. Salon/bar, restaurant, breakfast room; background music; health centre: swimming pool, sauna, massage, beauty treatments; conference facilities. Garden: heated swimming pool. Beaches, safe bathing nearby. **Location** Pointe de Pen Lan, 5 km S of Muzillac, 33 km SE of Vannes. Parking. **Credit cards** All major cards accepted. **Terms** Room €120–€340, suite €195–€490. Breakfast €17. D,B&B (min. 3 nights) €58 added per person.

BIZE-MINERVOIS 11120 Aude — Map 4:D6

La Bastide Cabezac
18–20 Hameau de Cabezac
Tel 04.68.46.66.10
Fax 04.68.46.66.29
Email contact@labastidecabezac.com
Website www.labastidecabezac.com

'A gem': opened in 2001, this renovated 18th-century post house stands amid Minervois vineyards. 'Reasonably priced, stylish, very French', it has 'charming hosts', says a visitor this year. Sabine dos Santos was responsible for the 'regionally inspired' decor (pale distressed wood, ochre, yellow and blue, coir matting, white linen; 'all clean and fragrant'); her husband, Hervé, is the chef. 'He cooks seasonal food with a light touch.' The restaurant, *L'Olivier*, earns 13 *Gault Millau* points for, eg, cannellonis de poivrons rouges et fromage de brousse; queue de lotte rôtie aux olives noires. Meals are also served outdoors. 'Staff are attentive but not overbearing. A busy road is near, but we were not bothered by traffic noise. In the heat of August we were grateful for the clean, adequate-sized swimming pool and the air conditioning in our bedroom.' (*SH*)

Open All year, except 24/25 Dec. Restaurant closed Sat midday, Sun night/Mon. **Rooms** 2 suites, 10 double. 1 on ground floor. Some no-smoking. Air conditioning. **Facilities** Restaurant; conference room in basement. Patio. Garden: terrace, heated swimming pool. **Location** 18 km NW of Narbonne, 3 km S of Bize-Minervois on D5. Parking. **Credit cards** MasterCard, Visa. **Terms** [2004] Room: €69–€84, suite €107–€199. Breakfast €10. Set lunch €16, dinner €23–€43; full alc €45.

LE BLANC 36300 Indre — Map 4:A4

Domaine de l'Étape BUDGET
Route de Bélâbre

Tel 02.54.37.18.02
Fax 02.54.37.75.59
Email domainetape@wanadoo.fr
Website www.domaineetape.com

A '*belle demeure bourgeoise*', says *Michelin*: Jean-Pierre Seiller's 19th-century château hotel stands in a huge park, with horses and a lake for fishing and boating, down a country lane east of Poitiers. The manager is Philippe Dujardin. The 'quiet location', 'old-fashioned' aura and welcome to children are all commended. The bedrooms vary: some, 'up a lot of stairs', are on the maids' floor, 'still with service bells in the corridors'. One reader had 'a lovely big attic room'. Some rooms in the modern *pavillon* have been renovated in 2004. The cheapest ('not fancy, but comfortable') are in a farmhouse. The food is thought 'delicious'. Potage maison is 'served by the gallon in tureens'. 'Wonderful desserts, sumptuous cheeseboard.' The continental breakfast is 'more than pleasant'. There is a terrace for summer meals. Lots of wildlife nearby, in the Parc de la Brenne. (*MH*)

Open All year. **Rooms** 35 double (11 in *pavillon*, 9 in farm). 7 on ground floor. **Facilities** Lounge with TV, 2 dining rooms (background music); conference facilities. 220-hectare park: terraces, lake, fishing, canoeing. **Location** 5 km SE of Le Blanc, off D10 to Bélâbre, 60 km E of Poitiers. **Credit cards** All major cards accepted. **Terms** [2004] Room €40–€110. Breakfast €10. Set meals €20–€54; full alc €30–€50.

LE BOIS-PLAGE-EN-RÉ 17580 Charente-Maritime — Map 4:A3

Hôtel Restaurant L'Océan
172 rue de St-Martin
Île de Ré

Tel 05.46.09.23.07
Fax 05.46.09.05.40
Email info@re-hotel-ocean.com
Website www.re-hotel-ocean.com

The magnificent white beaches of Île de Ré, offshore from La Rochelle, attract hordes of French holidaymakers in season: advance booking is essential for Noël and Martine Bourdet's two-star Logis de France. Five hundred metres from a prime stretch of sand, in 'a pretty, sleepy village', it has 'seaside ambience and rural charm'. 'I loved it,' writes one 2004 visitor. The public rooms are 'attractive in a hip-seaside way': muted colours, wood panelling, Lloyd Loom chairs, earthenware pots and paintings by local artists. The bar, with its 'ocean-liner feel', is particularly liked. Bedrooms, with curved doors, gingham curtains, beach hut-style wardrobes, have similarly 'wonderful decor', but some might be small and 'basic'. Some overlook the garden. Chef Yoann Leraut's menus centre on fresh fish, simply prepared, and meals are served in the beamed restaurant or on a patio. Breakfast is a buffet. Service is efficient, but one couple complained of a 'brusque welcome' and another would have liked help with suitcases up two flights of stone steps. A heated swimming pool is new this year. The island has miles of salt-marsh, cycle and hiking trails, good birdwatching. (*Liz Reason, Sally Holloway, and others*)

Open All year, except 24/25 Dec, 3 Jan–9 Feb, Wed except school holidays. **Rooms** 28 double, 1 single. 1 on ground floor. **Facilities** Salon, bar, restaurant; background jazz; meeting room. Garden: heated swimming pool. **Location** Village halfway along island. 23 km W of La Rochelle. Private parking (unsupervised) for 10 cars 50 m. **Restrictions** No smoking in some bedrooms. No dogs. **Credit cards** Amex, MasterCard, Visa. **Terms** Room €70–€150. Breakfast €10. D,B&B €66–€150 per person. Set meals €22–€32.

BOLLEZEELE 59470 Nord — Map 3:D2

Hostellerie Saint-Louis BUDGET
47 rue de l'Église

Tel 03.28.68.81.83
Fax 03.28.68.01.17
Email contact@hostelleriesaintlouis.com
Website www.hostelleriesaintlouis.com

The 'very good food' and 'warm welcome' continue to impress visitors to this 'Flemish country inn' (Logis de France), where Philippe and Bea Dubreucq have presided for 25 years. 'We had a super time,' was one comment. The handsome building, in a village near Dunkerque, has modern interiors and stained-glass windows. The fixed-price menus are thought 'excellent value for money' (they include scallops in an aromatic broth; chicken waterzooi). Wines are 'reasonably priced', staff are 'cheerful, even at breakfast' ('an adequate buffet'). 'Our "superior" room was spacious, quiet, well decorated.' There is a big garden with a fountain. Many visitors are British, and conferences and functions are held. The fine, large village church has 'impressive altars'. (*M Roots, RG, WR*)

Open All year, except 23 Dec–15 Jan, 19– 25 July. **Rooms** 2 suites, 7 superior, 19 standard; 19 with bath, 9 with shower. 4 on ground floor. **Facilities** Lift. Lounge, restaurant (no-smoking, background music); 6 private dining rooms; conference/exhibition facilities; games room, billiard room. 3-hectare garden. **Location** 24 km SW of Dunkerque. Free parking. **Credit cards** Amex, MasterCard, Visa. **Terms** Room: single €40–€48, double €51–€60, suite €76. Breakfast €9. D,B&B €28 added per person. Set dinner €23–€40; full alc €47.

BORDEAUX 33270 Gironde — Map 4:C3

Hauterive Saint-James
3 place Camille Hostein
Bouliac

Tel 05.57.97.06.00
Fax 05.56.20.92.58
Email reception@saintjames-bouliac.com
Website www.saintjames-bouliac.com

An unusual and stylish modern hotel (Relais & Châteaux) on a hillside in the south-eastern suburb of Bouliac. Inspired by tobacco dryers, it has been created around a 17th-century *maison vigneronne.* It stands in large grounds with vines and a warm, black swimming pool. 'Food is delicious, service as friendly as ever,' says a returning visitor (*Michelin* star, 16 *Gault Millau* points – one more this year – for Michel Portos, eg, mullet, artichokes and carrots with basil and spiced Feta cheese). A glass of appropriate wine accompanies each of the first two courses. There is a new, big, multi-level dining room. The 'Zen-like' bedrooms, theatrically lit, vary in size and shape. Each has a vast bed on a plinth; all face the river. Summer meals are served on a large terrace, and there are two cheaper eateries, the *Bistroy* (fish restaurant/wine bar), by the gates, and the *Café de l'Espérance*, in the style of an old-fashioned village café. Breakfast comes with little delicacies like pistachio crème brulée. (*Brian, Lesley and Fenella Knox*)

Open All year. Main restaurant closed Jan, Sun, Mon off-season. **Rooms** 3 suites, 15 double. In 4 buildings. 2 equipped for ♿. Air conditioning. **Facilities** Lift. 2 salons, bar, 3 restaurants; conference room. 16-hectare grounds: dining terrace, heated swimming pool, sauna. **Location** Bouliac, 7 km SE of centre, off Ave G. Cabannes. Parking. **Credit cards** All major cards accepted. **Terms** [2004] Room: single €137–€168, double €153–€183, suite €236–€267. Breakfast €15–€18. Café alc €25. *Bistroy* alc €35. Restaurant: set meals (with wine) €28–€80.

BOULOGNE-SUR-MER 62200 Pas-de-Calais — Map 3:D2

La Matelote
7080 boulevard Ste-Beuve

Tel 03.21.30.33.33
Fax 03.21.30.87.40
Email tolestienne@nordnet.fr
Website www.la-matelote.com

By the harbour entrance and near Boulogne's 'odd little beach', the Lestienne family's restaurant-with-rooms is in two converted 1930s houses. Tony Lestienne, who specialises in seafood (14 *Gault Millau* points), continues to win accolades from *Guide* correspondents. 'By far the best meal of our holiday,' say visitors in 2004. 'Well organised and stylish.' The grand, 'rather masculine' decor – red and gold colour scheme, Louis XVI furniture, and 'two adjacent staircases which climb up the centre' – is offset by eccentric touches. 'In the bar, an automatic piano plays; in the restaurant are angels, cherubs and teddy bears.' 'Bedrooms are comfortably modern, with good bathroom.' Front rooms have views of the 'amazing' Nausicaa marine life centre next door, and sea and sunsets, but hear traffic. Breakfast is a generous buffet: 'A hard-working waitress coped pretty well when everyone descended to eat at once.' (*D and E Gardner, R and EU, and others*)

Open All year. Restaurant closed 23 Dec–15 Jan, Sun night, Thurs midday. **Rooms** 29. Some air conditioned. Some suitable for ♿. **Facilities** Lift. Lounge, bar, TV room, breakfast room, restaurant (background music). **Location** By harbour entrance, 800 m NW of centre. Garage (€12). **Credit cards** Amex, MasterCard, Visa. **Terms** Room: single €80–€115, double €95–€140, suite €180–€205. Breakfast €11–€12. Set meals €33–€71.

BOURDEILLES 24310 Dordogne — Map 4:B4

Château de la Côte
Biras-Bourdeilles

Tel 05.53.03.70.11
Fax 05.53.03.42.84
Email chateau@chateaudelacote.com
Website www.chateaudelacote.com

In a park with century-old trees bordered by box tree walkways, this Renaissance château near Brantôme looks across a valley. Graceful and romantic, it is creeper-covered, pepperpot-towered. The owners, Michel and Olivier Guillaume, are 'very friendly, lovely people', one guest wrote. The bedrooms are in period style; some are large; some have a fireplace; some have exposed beams: 'Ours, in the turret, had a large round bathroom, amazing views.' One suite has private access to the dungeon terrace. The new chef, Stéphane Cholière, serves, eg, slices of Granny Smith apple and duck liver fried in Banyuls, encased in flaky pastry; salmon steak stuffed with cèpes in a spiced chicken stock.

Open 26 Dec–4 Jan, 15 May–15 Nov. Restaurant closed midday, except Sun, public holidays. **Rooms** 8 suites, 8 double. 3 in annexe. **Facilities** Lounge, bar, breakfast room, dining rooms; classical background music; billiard room; terrace. 6-hectare garden: unheated swimming pool. Unsuitable for ♿. **Location** 10 km SW of Brantôme, between Bourdeilles and Biras. Parking. **Credit cards** Amex, MasterCard, Visa. **Terms** [2004] Room €60–€106, suite €108–€195. Breakfast €11–€14. D,B&B €76–€129 per person. Set meals €29–€52; full alc €68.

Hostellerie Les Griffons NEW

Tel 05.53.45.45.35
Fax 05.53.45.45.20
Email griffons@griffons.fr
Website www.griffons.fr

Beneath the 13th/16th-century château of this village near Brantôme, this 17th-century *maison bourgeoise* stands by the River Dronne. Owned by Lucile and Bernard Lebrun, it has old beams and stones, wooden ceilings and antique furniture. 'The hotel is elegant, the management and service could not be bettered, and the food is excellent,' says a visitor in 2004. 'Our room was in the attic but was spacious, comfortable and well equipped.' Traditional Périgord cuisine is served on a flowery riverside terrace or in a dining room that 'has *cachet*', according to *Michelin*. (*Warren Bagust*)

Open 9 Apr–15 Oct. Closed midday on Mon and Fri July/Aug; closed midday except weekends and holidays Sept–June. **Rooms** 10. Some no-smoking. **Facilities** Lounge, bar, restaurant. Terrace. Garden. **Location** 10 km SW of Brantôme. Car park. **Credit cards** Amex, MasterCard, Visa. **Terms** [2004] Room €84–€94. Set meals €21.50–€38.

The 2006 edition of the *Guide*, covering Great Britain and Ireland, will appear in the autumn of 2005. Reports are particularly useful in the spring, and they need to reach us by 15 May 2005 at the very latest if they are to help the 2006 edition.

BRANCION 71700 Saône-et-Loire — Map 5:E3

La Montagne de Brancion — *Tel* 03.85.51.12.40
Col de Brancion — *Fax* 03.85.51.18.64
Email lamontagnedebrancion@wanadoo.fr
Website www.brancion.com

'A lovely creeper-covered building overlooking vineyards and farmland as far as the eye can see': Jacques and Nathalie Million's hotel is on a slope of the Mâconnais hills, near a hamlet with a Romanesque church and ruined castle. 'On a clear night we could see the Swiss mountains and Mont Blanc.' The restaurant has panoramic views, and 15 *Gault Millau* points for the cooking of Gilles Bérard. His 'classic regional' cuisine was found 'outstanding' by visitors in 2004. 'Dishes like a work of art on the plate. But when we asked for steak, chips, green salad and profiteroles we were told "*pas de problème*".' Wine prices, however, 'have to be seen to be believed'. There's a terrace for lunch, and drinks are served by the large swimming pool in well-tended gardens. Staff are 'delightful', service is 'impeccable'. The 'very comfortable' bedrooms (many have been upgraded this year) have splendid views; most have a small terrace. The Millions recently founded an association, Brancion Air Tourisme: Jacques Million takes sightseers (one at a time) over Burgundy in a ULM ('ultra-light motorglider'). They have also created some marked walks from the hotel. 'The area is great for dogs.' (*Janice Carrera, and others*)

Open 15 Mar–10 Nov. Restaurant closed midday Mon–Fri. **Rooms** 1 suite, 18 double. 7 on ground floor. **Facilities** Ramps. Salon, bar, restaurant (no-smoking); background music; function room. Garden: terrace, heated swimming pool, children's play area. **Location** 1.5 km from village. 13 km W of Tournus by D14. Parking. **Credit cards** Diners, MasterCard, Visa. **Terms** Room €98–€150, suite €200. Breakfast €15. D,B&B (obligatory holiday weekends/in season) €173–€205 per person. Set meals €45–€68; full alc €65.

BRANTÔME 24310 Dordogne — Map 4:B4

Le Moulin de l'Abbaye — *Tel* 05.53.05.80.22
1 route de Bourdeilles — *Fax* 05.53.05.75.27
Email moulinabbaye@moulin-abbaye.com
Website www.moulin-abbaye.com

Staying here is 'a very good experience', says a visitor this year to this creeper-clad 16th-century mill, now a luxurious hotel owned by Régis Bulot, president of the Relais & Châteaux association. Its managers are Bernard and Yvette Dessum. It stands at the foot of a cliff in this beautiful, if touristy, little Périgord town. On one side is the 11th-century abbey, on the other the River Dronne, surging over a weir. Other comments: 'Delightful.' 'Not cheap, but you get what you pay for.' 'Excellent food and service.' In the gourmet restaurant, Bernard Villain, who formerly worked at the *Manoir d'Hautegente*, Coly (*qv*), retains his predecessor's *Michelin* star, 16 *Gault Millau* points for, eg, langoustines en carpaccio, pistou thaï; escalope de foie gras poché.

There are two simpler eating places, *Au Fil de l'Eau*, a fish bistro by the river, and *Fil du Temps* (grill/Périgord specialities). All have a dining terrace. Many of the rustic-style bedrooms face the river. Rooms in the annexes, *La Maison du Meunier* and *La Maison de l'Abbé*, may be quieter than those in the mill but 'have less atmosphere', according to our inspector. 'The salons are welcoming in a clubby way.' (*JB, and others*)

Open May–Oct. Restaurant closed midday Mon–Fri except bank holidays. **Rooms** 3 suites, 16 double. In 3 buildings. 1 on ground floor. Some air conditioned. **Facilities** Salon, smoking room, 3 restaurants; dining terraces. Garden. Unsuitable for ♿. **Location** Edge of town. 27 km N of Périgueux. Free garage. **Credit cards** All major cards accepted. **Terms** [2004] Room €220, suite €295. Breakfast €19. D,B&B €195–€232 per person. Set meals €50–€70.

LE BREUIL-EN-BESSIN 14330 Calvados — Map 2:D3

Château de Goville

Tel 02.31.22.19.28
Fax 02.31.22.68.74
Email chateaugoville@wanadoo.fr
Website www.chateaugoville.com

A collection of antique doll's houses lines a corridor of this 18th-century château: at night, each house has rooms lit up. Quirky touches such as this distinguish Jan-Jacques Vallée's hotel near Bayeux. 'Not a run-of-the-mill hotel experience, more like a large home with paying guests,' says one regular visitor. 'Peaceful, and geared to adults', it has striking colour schemes and is 'stuffed with ornaments, photos, *objets d'art*: no surface is left uncluttered'. The period furniture is elaborate; there are some creaky wooden floors. Guest bedrooms are named after members of the family. 'Angélique, not large but comfortable, was done in green, even the door was papered to match the walls. Best feature was the large bathroom with proper bath and big windows.' Another room, mostly blue, has a large canopied bed, but a small bath. Drinks are served in the attractive garden. 'Breakfast, in the bedroom, has a good choice of breads and preserves.' Main meals are no longer served. The château stands back from a busy main road, so traffic noise is muffled. (*ST*)

Open All year. **Rooms** 2 suites, 8 double. **Facilities** Salon, bar, games room. 3-hectare grounds. Unsuitable for ♿. **Location** 10 km SW of Bayeux, off D5. Parking. **Restriction** No smoking in some bedrooms. **Credit cards** MasterCard, Visa. **Terms** Room €115–€155, suite €140–€180. Breakfast €12. €12 supplement for dogs.

How to contact us:
From anywhere in the UK write to: *Good Hotel Guide*, Freepost, PAM 2931, London W11 4BR (no stamp is needed). From abroad, write to: *Good Hotel Guide*, 50 Addison Avenue, London W11 4QP, England. *Tel/Fax* (020) 7602 4182. *Email* goodhotel@aol.com.

BRINON-SUR-SAULDRE 18410 Cher — Map 2:F5

La Solognote
34 Grande Rue

Tel 02.48.58.50.29
Fax 02.48.58.56.00
Email la.solognote@wanadoo.fr
Website www.lasolognote.com

Owned since March 2004 by Sandrine de Passos, with Aurélie Artault as chef; old auberge *(Relais du Silence): low brick building, with rear bedroom extension. By river, in village on edge of marshlands and forests of the Sologne, 57 km SE of Orléans. Bar/*salon d'hiver, *'handsome restaurant'. Long list of local wines. No background music. Patio garden for drinks and breakfasts. Private open parking. Good cycling (bicycles for hire across road). Closed 21 Feb–9 Mar. Amex, MasterCard, Visa accepted. 13 bedrooms (5 on ground floor): €58–€78. Breakfast €10. D,B&B €75–€90 per person. Set meals €19.50–€45; full alc €70. 'Excellent food, friendly service, our room was fairly basic but adequate,' says endorser in 2004.*

BRIOUDE 43100 Haute-Loire — Map 4:B6

Hôtel de la Poste et Champanne BUDGET
1 boulevard Docteur Devins

Tel 04.71.50.14.62
Fax 04.71.50.10.55

A long-time *Guide* favourite, the Chazal family's 'seriously good' small hotel/restaurant is on the main street of a pleasant market town in the Auvergne. One daughter, Hélène, is chef; her sister, Agnès, runs the front desk; Agnès's husband is in the bar. Guests in 2004 were impressed by the welcome and value: 'The receptionist even walked up the hill with us to show us the private parking. Our entire bill was €154.' Other praise: 'Charming, friendly.' 'Unpretentious, warm-hearted.' 'What a delight to be in the company of the Chazal family.' 'The jewel is the restaurant' ('packed each night with locals'): *Michelin Bib Gourmand* for '*cuisine cent pour cent auvergnate*'. 'We had the top menu, which included pan-fried foie gras with a pear compôte; lotte with a magnificent Puy lentil sauce; boned quail with cèpes. A basket of walnuts and another of fruit were left on the table – such rare generosity!' On half board, guests choose from any menu. Breakfast is 'an excellent buffet'. Some bedrooms are small, but most are a good size, and two have been redecorated this year. Quietest rooms (with balcony) are up the hill in an annexe, 'warm and comfortable', which has a garden. Guests may use the outdoor swimming pool of the family's other, pricier hotel, *La Sapinière*, 'central but quiet'. (*Graham Avery, Janet and Dennis Allom, Alan Brownlow*)

Open 1 Mar–20 Jan. Restaurant closed Sun night/Mon midday. **Rooms** 4 quadruple, 19 double. 14 in annexe, 5 in park. **Facilities** Reading room, bar, 4 dining rooms (classical background music); conference facilities. Terrace. Garden in annexe. Swimming pool at *Sapinière*. Unsuitable for ♿. **Location** Central. Brioude is 71 km SE of Clermont-Ferrand. Parking. **Restriction** No smoking: 1 dining room, 8 bedrooms. **Credit cards** MasterCard, Visa. **Terms** Room €30–€44, suite €55. Breakfast €6.50. D,B&B €44 per person. Set meals €14–€37; full alc € 37.

CABRIÈRES D'AVIGNON 84220 Vaucluse — Map 6:D3

La Bastide de Voulonne

Tel 04.90.76.77.55
Fax 04.90.76.77.56
Email sophie@bastide-voulonne.com
Website www.bastide-voulonne.com

A honey-coloured 18th-century *bastide*, transformed by its owners, Sophie and Alain Rebourg Poiri, into a charming small hotel. Light and airy, full of Provençal colour, it is in the valley between Gordes and the Luberon hills. For this expensive area, popular with artists and holiday sun-seekers, rates are relatively modest. Rooms are all different; some have a patio. At the good-sized pool, you help yourself to drinks from a fridge on an honesty basis and look towards the Luberon over the garden full of lavender bushes. There's an ample buffet breakfast. Dinner is cooked five nights a week (the menu is displayed after breakfast). After free aperitifs in the courtyard, guests dine together around a large farmhouse table. 'English, French, Belgians and Germans got on famously.' If you feel shy about such multilingual conversation, a table for two can be arranged. There are tiled floors and potted plants, and ancient plane trees in the spacious grounds.

Open All year, except 24 Nov–26 Dec. Restaurant closed Sun, Wed. **Rooms** 2 suites, 9 double. Some on ground floor. **Facilities** Salon, dining room. 5-hectare grounds: garden: outdoor dining; heated swimming pool. **Location** 1.5 km S of Cabrières-d'Avignon, 32 km E of Avignon. At Coustellet, turn off D2 towards Gordes. **Restriction** No smoking: restaurant, bedrooms. **Credit cards** MasterCard, Visa. **Terms** [2004] Room €122–€145, suite from €152. Breakfast €11. Set dinner €29.

CAHORS 46000 Lot — Map 4:C5

Hôtel Terminus
5 avenue Charles de Freycinet

Tel 05.65.53.32.00
Fax 05.65.53.32.26
Email info@balandre.com
Website www.balandre.com

Cahors, in a famous wine region, has some characterless modern buildings but also some interesting old ones, eg, the fortified 14th-century Pont Valentré over the Lot. Opposite the station, this classic town hotel, run by the Marre family for nearly a century, was found 'totally enjoyable' by recent guests. A converted 19th-century mansion, it has 'wild' stucco carvings outside, and an Art Deco interior of rich woods, stained glass, furniture covered in primary colours. The emphasis is on the chandeliered, candlelit restaurant, *Le Balandre* (16 *Gault Millau* points). Gilles Marre's specialities include sandre grillé avec une poêlée de cuisses de grenouille. The vast cellar includes 70 Cahors wines. Front bedrooms are light, but hear traffic noise. 'Our slightly more expensive, large one at the top, with attic windows leading on to a private terrace, was quiet. Breakfast, in an attractive Art Nouveau room, included freshly pressed fruit juice, sweet plum jam.' (*SH*)

Open All year, except 15–30 Nov. Restaurant closed Sun/Mon except evenings July/Aug. **Rooms** 1 suite, 19 double, 2 single. Air conditioning. **Facilities** Lift. Salon/bar, restaurant, brasserie; outside dining; function room. No background music. Unsuitable for ♿. **Location** By station (windows double glazed). Parking. **Credit cards** All major cards accepted. **Terms** [2004] Room: €45–€130, suite €130–€160. Breakfast €7.62–€10. Set meals €40–€90.

CAJARC 46160 Lot — Map 4:C5

La Ségalière NEW/BUDGET
Route de Cadrieu

Tel 05.65.40.65.35
Fax 05.65.40.74.92
Email hotel.segaliere@wanadoo.fr
Website pro.wanadoo.fr/hotelsegaliere

In a 'delightfully quiet' setting, on the edge of a pleasant old *bourg* on the River Lot, east of Cahors, this modern two-storey hotel/restaurant looks quite glamorous, but it is modestly priced. Its 'astonishing design' is said to have been influenced by Georges Pompidou, who lived in Cajarc. Not everyone is keen on the modern design, but a visitor in 2004 wrote: 'Extraordinarily good value. Top-class service.' Food may not be a strong point. The 'hands-on' owners, Alain and Virginia Massabie, have a new chef this year, Stéphane Delporte. The 'practical' bedrooms all have a balcony looking over the quiet road or the large, unusually shaped pool. All were redecorated this year, and there are six new rooms. The vast open-plan ground floor has a large lounge on one side, a big dining room, with picture windows, on the other. Outside is a large terrace for fine-weather dining, facing the pool and the tree-lined hills beyond. (*Richard Parish, and others*)

Open 20 Mar–10 Nov. Restaurant closed for lunch on weekdays, except 15 July–15 Aug. **Rooms** 1 suite, 23 double. Some no-smoking. Some on ground floor. **Facilities** Salon/bar, restaurant; pianist sometimes; classical background music throughout. 1-hectare garden: dining terrace; unheated 20 by 12-metre swimming pool, children's play area. Unsuitable for ♿. **Location** Outskirts of Cajarc. 25 km SW of Figeac. Parking. **Credit cards** All major cards accepted. **Terms** Room: single €45–€65, double €56–€80. Breakfast €8. D,B&B €51–€88 per person. Set meals €14–€50; full alc €40. *V*

CALLAS 83830 Var — Map 6:D4

Hostellerie Les Gorges de Pennafort NEW

Tel 04.94.76.66.51
Fax 04.94.76.67.23
Email info@hostellerie-pennafort.com
Website www.hostellerie-pennafort.com

Opposite the dramatic gorges of Pennafort, in wooded country near Draguignan, this former *relais de poste* is now a luxurious hotel/restaurant managed by chef Philippe Da Silva and his wife, Martine. Its dining terrace is above the road which, say visitors in 2004, 'can be busy during the day, but traffic drops to a trickle in the evening. Our suite, well away from the road, was completely quiet. It opened on to a shared balcony with recliners and tables.' Across the road is a garden with a 'large, attractive' swimming pool surrounded by trees, and hard tennis courts. M. Da Silva has a *Michelin* star, 16 *Gault Millau* points for, eg, raviolis de foie gras; perdreau aux champignons. 'We ordered the *menu dégustation* (€110); somehow ten courses came, every one exquisite in taste and presentation. We asked Madame why we had been honoured with the extra dishes: she smiled and said her husband was sometimes *coquin*.' Many wine estates in the area. (*Martin and Karen Oldridge*)

Open 15 Mar–15 Jan. Restaurant closed Sun night, Mon, except evenings July/Aug, Wed midday. **Rooms** 5 junior suites, 11 double. Air conditioning. **Facilities** Salon, restaurant. Garden, dining terrace; swimming pool, tennis. Unsuitable for ♿. **Location** 7 km SE of Callas, 7 km NE of Draguignan. Exit A8 at Le Muy, D25 to Callas. Parking. **Credit cards** Amex, MasterCard, Visa. **Terms** [2004] Room: double €150–€175, junior suite €180–€210. Breakfast €16. D,B&B €140–€170 per person. Set meals €49–€110.

CALVI 20260 Haute-Corse — Map 11:D1

La Villa
Chemin de Notre-Dame-de-la-Serra

Tel 04.95.65.10.10
Fax 04.95.65.10.50
Email reservation@hotel-lavilla.com
Website www.hotel-lavilla.com

'Extremely luxurious', Jean-Pierre Pinelli's hilltop hotel (Relais & Châteaux) stands in lovely grounds above this fortified harbour town (its 15th-century citadel, built by the Genoese, was bombarded by the British in 1794, when Nelson lost his right eye). The design is part Roman villa, part Corsican monastery: cloisters, mosaics, tiled floors, and a 'superb terrace' for outdoor meals ('romantic sunsets'). A family in 2004 'had an elegant two-bedroom suite with lovely balcony'. Some rooms face the citadel, floodlit at night, some are in villas, each with its own swimming pool, in the garden. There is a large main pool, too. 'Friendly reception, restaurant staff excellent: young, affable, not too matey.' 'Food so light we enjoyed every meal and every course' (*Michelin* star, 15 *Gault Millau* points for the Mediterranean cuisine of Christophe Bacquié). At the beach, about 20 minutes' walk down and also open to the paying public, the hotel has a restaurant that serves 'good, reasonably priced' snacks. Calvi is also 20 minutes' walk downhill. 'The road is unlit at night, but taxis are cheap.' (*VM, T and MH*)

Open 1 Apr–31 Oct. **Rooms** 20 suites, 32 double. Some in villas. Air conditioning. **Facilities** Lift. 4 salons, bar, restaurant; background jazz; conference room. Large garden: terrace, 4 swimming pools (1 heated), tennis. Beach 1 km. **Location** 1 km SW of centre, by sea. Parking. **Restriction** No dogs. **Credit cards** Diners, MasterCard, Visa. **Terms** [2004] Room €300–€420, suite €460–€750. Breakfast €23–€30. Set meals €70.

> We asked hotels to quote 2005 prices. Not all were able to predict them. Some of our terms will be inaccurate. Do check latest tariffs at the time of booking.

CAMBRAI 59400 Nord Map 3:E3

Hôtel Beatus
718 avenue de Paris

Tel 03.27.81.45.70
Fax 03.27.78.00.83
Email hotel.beatus@wanadoo.fr
Website www.hotel.beatus.fr

A guest returning in 2004 to this ever-popular hotel found standards 'as high as ever'. The 'hands-on owner', Philippe Gorczynski (an expert on the battles and campaigns of the First World War), is regularly praised. 'Courtesy and service are the rule,' was another comment. Bicycles are provided free, and Internet access is now available. The white-fronted building is shielded from a 'rather grim' road by its large garden, 'peaceful apart from birdsong'. Many bedrooms (styles range from Louis XV to contemporary) overlook garden or drive. 'Ours opened on to a small private patio.' The 'lovely' breakfast, with 'first-class preserves', is in an airy room facing the garden. In the restaurant, chef Sébastien Dessolle provides 'good, simple, food (we particularly liked his onion soup) with reasonably priced wines'. On his days off, try *Chez Dan* nearby. In this interesting old town the church of St-Géry has a fine *La Mise au tombeau* by Rubens. (*Wendy Christian, Marilyn Frampton, Ann Mathews, Jean and Alan Stokes; also Roger and Jean Cook*)

Open All year. Restaurant closed midday, Sat/Sun, Aug. **Rooms** 1 suite, 32 double. 12 on ground floor. **Facilities** Ramp. Salon, bar, restaurant (background music); conference room. Garden. **Location** 1 km SW of centre on N44 to St-Quentin. Parking, garages. **Restriction** No smoking except in designated zone in public areas. **Credit cards** Amex, MasterCard, Visa. **Terms** [2004] Room €58–€74, suite €99. Breakfast €9. Set dinner €22; full alc €39.

CAMON 09500 Ariège Map 4:E5

L'Abbaye-Château de Camon

Tel/Fax 05.61.60.31.23
Email peter.katielawton@wanadoo.fr

'Just as lovely as we remembered,' says a returning visitor to this converted 10th-century abbey, part of a castle in this lovely old fortified village, way south-west of Carcassonne. New owners, Peter and Katie Lawton, had taken over since her last visit. At the time of writing they are operating as a *chambres d'hôtes*. 'They are warm, friendly and helpful. The meals, all taken on a lovely terrace, were excellent: traditional dishes nicely cooked; plentiful breakfasts.' Earlier praise still holds good: 'The situation is idyllic; the views of wooded hills, Pyrenees in the distance, are splendid. The building exudes ancient character, and the bedrooms are superb, light, spacious, tastefully decorated, with lovely views.' The more expensive rooms are former monks' cells. The dining room has tapestry-like murals; there is a pleasant inner terrace, a large terraced garden with a pool. Weddings are sometimes held. The château of Montségur and the caves of Niaux are not far away. (*Mrs A Mathews*)

Open Mar–Nov. House parties only Christmas/New Year. **Rooms** 1 suite, 10 double, 2 single. All on 1st floor. **Facilities** Lounge, dining room (background music), dining terrace. Garden: unheated swimming pool. **Location** 12 km SE of Mirepoix, 5 km NW of Chalabre, on D7. Follow signs to cemetery; go up slope. Parking. **Restriction** No smoking in some bedrooms. **Credit cards** MasterCard, Visa. **Terms** [2004] B&B: single €95–€125, double €140–€180; D,B&B €97–€152 per person. *V*

CANCALE 35260 Ille-et-Vilaine — Map 2:E3

Maisons de Bricourt
1 rue Duguesclin

Tel 02.99.89.64.76
Fax 02.99.89.88.47
Email bricourt@relaischateaux.com
Website www.maisons-de-bricourt.com

Owner/chef Olivier Roellinger and his wife, Jane, preside over their collection of *maisons* (Relais & Châteaux) in and around this picturesque fishing port renowned for its oysters. They provide 'extreme comfort, superb food and exciting views across the bay', says a fan. They have two *Michelin* stars, 19 *Gault Millau* points for the restaurant, converted from Roellinger's childhood home. Recent visitors wrote of their dinner: 'A grand affair, but without pomposity: the ten-course *dégustation* menu was a stunning sequence of flavours, subtly spiced. Super service, notably by the porter who acted as our waiter and driver.' 'The attractive young staff seemed to care about perfection.' There are five 'rustic' bedrooms in the cottage-style *Les Rimains* in Cancale: 'Its small garden with chairs extends to the cliff-top.' *Château Richeux*, 'a lovely little 1920s villa', is in a lush park, at St-Méloir-des-Ondes, six kilometres away. It has its own *bistrot marin*, *Le Coquillage.* 'Our room, Anise Etoilée, was superb, mosaics around the walls, a lovely bathroom tiled to match. Art Deco furniture, super bed, CD-player (Breton folk music), stunning sunrise view across to Mont-St-Michel.' 'Children of all ages are welcome.'

Open Feb–Dec. Restaurant closed Mon/Tues midday. **Rooms** 2 suites, 11 double. 1 on ground floor. **Facilities** Lift. Salon, 2 restaurants (no-smoking). No background music. 3-hectare garden. **Credit cards** All major cards accepted. **Terms** [2004] Room €160, suite €310. Breakfast €16. Set meals €25; alc €44.

CANGEY 37530 Indre-et-Loire — Map 2:F5

Le Fleuray NEW

Tel 02.47.56.09.25
Fax 02.47.56.93.97
Email lefleurayhotel@wanadoo.fr
Website www.lefleurayhotel.com

Near the Loire valley and Amboise, a pink 19th-century farmhouse, 'very isolated and blessedly quiet', has been converted into a small country hotel by its English owners, Hazel and Peter Newington. They run it with son and daughter, Jordan and Cassie. It doesn't suit everyone: one correspondent thought the annexe unappealing and the local countryside 'nondescript', and staying here may be 'not a very French experience', but visitors in 2004 enjoyed their stay. 'The owners are very friendly, efficient and bilingual. Our room was well equipped and nicely decorated. There is a good, sensibly fenced swimming pool which seems to be used by people with children and/or dogs.' Earlier praise: 'Our large room had its own terrace facing miles of rolling farmland, where they served us drinks. We enjoyed a good dinner served romantically by candlelight, under the trees in the garden. Breakfast, in the cosy dining room, came with fresh orange juice, good coffee, warm rolls and croissants.' 'It was great to find an excellent *English* library in the comfortable lounge. Our large room was pretty.' The 'classic French' cooking is admired: 'Starters up to *Michelin* star standard.' 'Cheerful young waiters.' Children get special menus. Bedrooms are named after local flowers, five are in a converted barn; some beds have a canopy. You can explore the Loire châteaux, or ride on an old steam train at Richelieu. (*Warren Bagust, and others*)

Open All year, except early Nov, Christmas/New Year, 1 week Feb. **Rooms** 15 double/family. 6 in annexe. 1 adapted for ♿. **Facilities** Lounge, conservatory, restaurant. No background music. Garden: terrace (meal service), swimming pool, orchards, pond. **Location** 7 km NE of Cangey (on D74 Dame-Marie road), which is 12 km NE of Amboise. Exit 18 from A10 motorway (7 km). **Credit cards** MasterCard, Visa. **Terms** [2004] Room €84–€102. Breakfast €9. D,B&B €78–€98 per person.

CANNES 06400 Alpes-Maritimes — Map 6:E5

California's Hotel
8 traverse Alexandre III

Tel 04.93.94.12.21
Fax 04.93.43.55.17
Email nadia@californias-hotel.com
Website www.hotel-californias.com

Just off the eastern end of La Croisette, this four-star B&B hotel is 'a splendid place with helpful staff', says its fans. Owned by Claude Fauré, it is managed by Nadia Moussalem, 'a great character, always around, dashingly dressed, on friendly terms with her guests, proud of the hotel'. This consists of two buildings, white with blue awnings. Between them, a paved area (renovated in 2004) with flowerpots, lemon and olive trees holds a medium-sized swimming pool; a wall is covered by a mural of a Riviera scene. 'Our smallish room had blue-and-white decor, smart bathroom, excellent lighting.' The bar serves salads and snacks. 'Nadia will arrange free transport within Cannes, and is very security conscious (codes to the doors, etc).' Also on offer: free boat trips (a new boat this year), free Internet access with wireless connection. The hotel is at the junction of two streets, amid blocks of flats, and the breakfast terrace is near a main railway line.

Open All year. **Rooms** 7 mini-suites (with terrace), 26 double. 11 in annexe. Some on ground floor. **Facilities** Lift, ramp. 2 lounges, bar, breakfast room; background music; seminar room; Internet room. Terrace. Garden: unheated swimming pool. **Location** 1.5 km E of harbour. Take Croisette towards Palm Beach; left at 1st light after the Martinez, then immediately right. Free street parking. **Restrictions** No smoking: breakfast room, some bedrooms. Generally no dogs. **Credit cards** All major cards accepted. **Terms** [2004] Room: single €101–€147, double €116–€214, suite €136–€300. Breakfast €14–€18. Snacks €16. *V*

Hôtel de Provence NEW/BUDGET
9 rue Molière

Tel 04.93.38.44.35
Fax 04.93.39.63.14
Email contact@hotel-de-provence.com
Website www.hotel-de-provence.com

'Slap bang between the seafront and rue d'Antibes (great for shopping)', Xavier Portier's 'little gem' of a Logis de France, newly decorated in Provençal style, is warmly recommended this year. 'You enter through a delightful garden with pots and ancient palm trees. Rooms are small but stylish. Ours had a small balcony facing the garden. The shower room was white and very clean.' The suite has a roof garden. 'Breakfast, in the garden, was of a high standard. The friendly owners, who speak good English, are happy to provide the odd bottle of chilled wine as you relax after a hard day at the beach, and will bring coffee and brandy before you go to bed.' The hotel has an arrangement with the Long Beach plage (with restaurant). For dinner, *Astoux & Brun*, 21 rue Félix Faure, is recommended. (*Deb Gardner*)

Open 26 Dec–22 Nov. **Rooms** 1 suite, 23 double, 6 single. Air conditioning. **Facilities** Reception (background music), salon, bar, restaurant. Unsuitable for ♿. Terrace. Garden. Arrangement with private beach. **Location** Central. 100 m from La Croisette. Parking (on reservation). **Credit cards** All major cards accepted. **Terms** [2004] Room: single €53–€69, double €69–€99, suite €109–€129. Breakfast €7.50. 1-night bookings sometimes refused. *V*

CAP D'ANTIBES 06160 Alpes-Maritimes — Map 6:E5

Hotel du Levant NEW
Plage de la Garoupe

Tel 04.92.93.72.99
Fax 04.92.93.72.60
Email levant@lecapdantibes.com
Website www.lecapdantibes.com/levant

Overlooking Plage de la Garoupe (where it has a bar and restaurant): 'attractive, comfortable' hotel (1970s building, recently renovated) on quiet road. 'Helpful staff. Good value in an expensive area.' Open Mar–Oct. Small garden. Parking. No dogs. No restaurant, nominator recommends nearby Keller. *25 air-conditioned bedrooms of varying sizes ('ours, not large, was tasteful'), with balcony or terrace, sea views: €110–€170. Breakfast €10 [2004].*

CASTILLON-DU-GARD 30210 Gard — Map 6:D2

Le Vieux Castillon
Rue Turion Sabatier

Tel 04.66.37.61.61
Fax 04.66.37.28.17
Email vieux.castillon@wanadoo.fr
Website www.vieuxcastillon.com

In a medieval village between Avignon and Nîmes, this group of ancient stone houses has been turned, 'with charm and imagination', by the Walser family into a luxurious hotel (Relais & Châteaux). 'Comfortable, with such helpful staff' (say recent visitors), it is near the Pont du Gard. The flowery garden, where the 'high-quality' breakfasts can be taken, is sheltered from the *mistral*; the terrace and the beautiful, large swimming pool enjoy wide views over a plain with vineyards. Across a bridge is the beamed restaurant where chef Patrick Walser took up the reins in 2004. Will he keep the *Michelin* star won by his predecessor? Children and dogs are welcomed. Bedrooms vary in size and quality: most are elegant, with period furniture and flowery fabrics; some look over a narrow village street. 'Though two clocks can be heard, this is a peaceful place.' In the lounge are wooden floors, oriental rugs and striped armchairs.

Open Early Mar–early Jan. Restaurant closed midday on Mon and Tues. **Rooms** 3 junior suites, 30 double. Some in annexe across alley. Air conditioning. **Facilities** 2 salons, TV room, bar, restaurant; conference facilities; billiards, sauna, hammam. No background music. Small patio, terrace: unheated swimming pool. Unsuitable for ♿. **Location** 4 km N of Pont-du-Gard, 26 km W of Avignon. Parking 300 m (€16 a night). **Credit cards** All major cards accepted. **Terms** Room €180–€300, suite €325. Breakfast €17. Set lunch €48 (Wed–Fri), dinner €72–€105.

CAVALAIRE-SUR-MER 83240 Var — Map 6:E4

Hôtel de la Calanque
Rue de la Calanque

Tel 04.94.01.95.00
Fax 04.94.64.66.20
Email mario.lacalanque@wanadoo.fr
Website www.hotel-la-calanque.com

On a 'beautiful piece of coast', secluded in a cove in a resort near St-Tropez, this 'spick-and-span' modern hotel is run by its owner, Louis Pantaleo, with a 'very friendly staff'. It has lovely views over the bay of the Corniche des Maures, and is close to superb beaches. The bedrooms, newly renovated, are 'comfortable, large, with terrace and first-class bathroom'. Swimming is from rocks easily accessible by steps, and the 'immaculate' pool above the sea is well equipped with loungers and parasols: its restaurant provides a 'modest lunch'. In the main restaurant, Jacques Guerrier specialises in seafood: the *carte* is expensive, and one couple complained: 'On half board we were consigned to the rather dreary breakfast room. Service was abrupt.' But 'there are some good fish restaurants at the port'. Breakfast, which can be served on the bedroom terrace, is 'excellent – best croissants'. (*David and Georgina Bennett, MDF, and others*)

Open 15 Mar–4 Jan. Restaurant closed Mon Oct–Jan. **Rooms** 1 suite, 3 apartments, 24 doubles. **Facilities** Lift. 2 salons, bar, restaurant. Garden: terraces: outdoor restaurant; heated swimming pool, spa bath, steam room, solarium; tennis; rocky beach, bar, grill. Unsuitable for ♿. **Location** 10 mins' walk from centre. 15 km SW of St-Tropez. Parking. **Credit cards** All major cards accepted. **Terms** Room €155–€240, suite €320–€345, apartment €360–€415. Breakfast €14–€18. Set meals €25–€50; full alc €75.

> In the case of EMU members, we quote the rates in euros. Sterling equivalents of other foreign currencies at the date of going to press will be found at the back of the *Guide*.

CAZILHAC 11570 Aude — Map 4:E5

La Ferme de la Sauzette BUDGET
Route de Villefloure
Palaja

Tel 04.68.79.81.32
Fax 04.68.79.65.99
Email info@lasauzette.com
Website www.lasauzette.com

'A perfect rural hideaway.' 'Excellent. Such welcoming owners.' Chris and Diana Gibson's *chambres d'hôtes* stands amid vineyards near Carcassonne, within easy driving distance of the wild Cathar country further south. Two granaries of the old stone farmhouse, with original exposed beams, have been turned into five bedrooms and a large living/dining room with open fire. 'The decor is earthily artistic, the bedrooms are pretty and rustic, and their lighting is good.' 'Our two-year-old daughter loved the woodland, the resident cats and most of all the huge, amiable Newfoundland, Monty,' says a 2004 visitor. At the 'convivial' dinner, the all-inclusive no-choice menu, 'a bargain', is served (alfresco in fine weather) round one large table, after an aperitif at 8 pm. 'Chris doesn't skimp on the wines.' 'Breakfast [fresh breads, home-made jams, local honey, yogurt] was delicious.' (*Claire Hadjipetrou, S and RW, Russell England*)

Open Feb–Oct, Dec, except Christmas. Dinner available by arrangement, 4 nights a week. **Rooms** 5 double. 1 suitable for ♿. Also *gîte*, let weekly. **Facilities** Living/dining room. No background music. Veranda, terrace. 2-hectare garden. **Location** S of Cazilhac on Villefloure road; 5 km S of Carcassonne. Parking. **Restrictions** No smoking: bedrooms, at table during meals. Guide dogs only. **Credit cards** None accepted. **Terms** (Min. 2 nights May–Sept) B&B: single €55–€66, double €62–€73. Set dinner (with wine and coffee) €28. *Gîte* €310–€405 per week.

CÉRET 66400 Pyrénées-Orientales — Map 4:E5

Hotel des Arcades NEW/BUDGET
1 place Picasso

Tel 04.68.87.12.30
Fax 04.68.87.49.44
Email hotelarcades.ceret@wanadoo.fr
Website www.hotel-arcades-ceret.com

'We were very happy in this genuine, simple, family-run hotel,' say its 2004 nominators. Owned by the Astrou brothers, it is in the centre, close to the Museum of Modern Art to which Picasso donated 50 works of art. It contains a collection of posters and lithographs by local artists. Some of the air-conditioned bedrooms face the square. 'Ours was light and spacious. Breakfast, served in the ground-floor breakfast room by one of the cheery female family members, included freshly toasted baguette, juicy Spanish oranges.' Parasols stand under old plane trees outside the hotel and the associated *Bar Le Pablo*, next door. No restaurant, plenty in town and across the Spanish border in Figueras. (*Jan and Diana Stern*)

Open All year. **Rooms** 30. Some with kitchenette. 10 air conditioned. **Facilities** Lift. Breakfast room. No background music. Unsuitable for ♿. **Location** Central (double glazing). 31 km SW of Perpignan. Parking. Garage. **Credit cards** MasterCard, Visa. **Terms** Room €42–€56. Breakfast €6.50.

La Terrasse au Soleil
Route de Fontfrède

Tel 04.68.87.01.94
Fax 04.68.87.39.24
Email terrasse-au-soleil.hotel@wanadoo.fr
Website www.la-terrasse-au-soleil.fr

'A lovely hotel, run by friendly, efficient staff,' says one of this year's visitors to this old *mas* which Charles Trénet once owned. But another visitor found service sometimes 'under-motivated'. Nicely converted by the Leveillé-Nizerolle family, it stands on a hill amid cherry orchards, outside this little town in the Pyrenean foothills. In the background is Mont Canigou. 'The setting and view are glorious, and there is a delightful small garden.' The swimming pool is liked. Inside, 'the bright, bold colours in the bedrooms are appealing, and much attention has been paid to the decor'. 'Our large, comfortable room had a balcony with an amazing view.' The restaurant, *La Cerisaie*, has beamed ceiling and colourful faience. In summer, guests are expected to dine in. Comments on the food vary from 'wonderful' to 'a bit pretentious'. Breakfasts are ample. One reader thought incidentals (coffee, beer, etc) expensive, and maintenance may not be perfect. Best arrive in daylight: 'The approach road is tortuous and narrow.' (*Suzanne Dalton, and others*)

Open All year. Restaurant closed midday, except Sat and Sun. **Rooms** 5 suites, 33 double. Some in 4 annexes. Some on ground floor. 1 suitable for ♿. Air conditioning. **Facilities** 1 lounge, bar, 3 dining rooms, breakfast room; classical background music; relaxation centre (hammam, massage, etc); conference room. 4-hectare grounds: terrace (meal service); heated swimming pool, tennis, golf practice. **Location** 1 km W of Céret, 31 km SW of Perpignan. Parking. **Restriction** No smoking: 1 dining room, some bedrooms. **Credit cards** All major cards accepted. **Terms** [2004] B&B: single €110–€217, double €159–€265, suite €190–€296; D,B&B €140–€178.50 per person. Set meals €43–€52; full alc €55. *V*

CHABLIS 89800 Yonne — Map 5:C2

Hostellerie des Clos
Rue Jules-Rathier

Tel 03.86.42.10.63
Fax 03.86.42.17.11
Email contact@hostellerie-des-clos.fr
Website www.hostellerie-des-clos.fr

'If wine touring takes you to Chablis, this should be your hotel of choice,' says a travel expert of chef/*patron* Michel Vignaud's converted almshouse (Logis de France) in this 'adorable little town'. The restaurant is locally famous (*Michelin* star, 15 *Gault Millau* points for, eg, bisque glacée de homard; cuisson confite de la poitrine de canette fermière). 'The cuisine was excellent, elegant.' Other comments: 'Service like a ballet, with synchronised dome-lifting.' 'Huge wine list', but 'mark-ups are steep'. The bedrooms ('some are on the small side') face the village, or the pretty courtyard garden where drinks and tea are served. 'Our big, quiet room had two nice beds, plenty of hanging space but little storage.' 'Room 10 is the best disabled room I have come across.' 'Buffet breakfast in the garden was gorgeous.' 'A very good hotel with amiable service.' Wine tastings are held. (*Marshall S Harris, MH, and others*)

Open 17 Jan–21 Dec. **Rooms** 32. 1 suitable for ♿. **Facilities** Lift, salon, bar, restaurant; conference room; terrace. Garden. **Location** Central, near *mairie*. 19 km E of Auxerre. Limited private parking. **Credit cards** Amex, MasterCard, Visa. **Terms** [2004] Room €50–€122. Breakfast €10. D,B&B €82–€150 per person. Set meals €35–€70.

CHAGNY 71150 Saône-et-Loire Map 5:D3

Hostellerie du Château de Bellecroix
RN6

Tel 03.85.87.13.86
Fax 03.85.91.28.62
Email info@chateau-bellecroix.com
Website www.chateau-bellecroix.com

Near Beaune, this former residence of the Knights of Malta, turreted and creeper-covered, dates in part from the 12th century, but the château itself is 19th-century. Owned and run by Delphine Gautier, and much renovated in the last few years, it stands in its own lovely park, with a 'romantic' ornamental pond and a sizeable swimming pool. Visitors in 2004 'happily endorsed' last year's praise by a returning visitor: 'We had a lovely stay, we were made so welcome. Our meal was superb' (local Burgundian dishes). Guests are asked to eat in once a day: there is a beautiful dining room, with white tablecloths, pink flowers, panelling, wooden floor, a large fireplace. Aperitifs and breakfasts can be served in the garden. The cheapest bedrooms are small; the best rooms, in the annexe, the 12th-century *commanderie*, are large and luxurious; some have a four-poster. Front rooms hear a busy road. (*Michael and Wendy Dods, LB*)

Open 14 Feb–19 Dec. Closed Wed 1 Oct–30 May. Restaurant closed Wed/Thurs midday. **Rooms** 1 suite, 19 double. 8 (air conditioned) in annexe. **Facilities** Lounge, bar, restaurant (background music). Garden: outside dining; swimming pool. Unsuitable for ♿. **Location** N6, 2 km S of Chagny, 17 km SW of Beaune. **Credit cards** All major cards accepted. **Terms** [2004] Room €88–€168, suite €229. Breakfast €12.50. D,B&B €94–€137 per person. Set meals €42–€56.

LA CHAISE-DIEU 43160 Haute-Loire Map 6:A1

Hôtel Écho et Abbaye BUDGET
Place de l'Écho

Tel 04.71.00.00.45
Fax 04.71.00.00.22
Website www.auvergne-alc.com

In a picturesque village amid the 'great countryside' of the Massif Central, this 'delightful small hotel' stands on a quiet square behind a lovely abbey (fine Flemish tapestries). It is efficiently run by its owners, Lionel and Estelle Degreze, say recent enthusiastic visitors. He is the 'accomplished chef'; she looks after front-of-house. Other praise: 'We loved it. Decor old-fashioned, and none the worse for that. Dinner in the small, pretty dining room was serious, and amazing value: good use of local Auvergne ingredients; delicious *amuse-gueule*; lavish dessert trolley, like the window of a patisserie: exquisite cakes. Waiters wear a bow tie but are not stuffy.' Some bedrooms face the abbey cloister. 'Our room, rather small, was very comfortable: good linen and towels, etc.' Breakfast is a substantial buffet. The village has a classical music festival in late summer. (*BWR, MH*)

Open All year, except 11 Nov–5 Dec, 10 Jan–10 Feb. Closed Wed. **Rooms** 10. **Facilities** Restaurant. Garden. **Location** Village square. 30 km S of Ambert. Ample free parking. **Credit cards** All major cards accepted. **Terms** [2004] Room €49–€60. Breakfast €8. Set meals €16.50–€60.

CHALLES-LES-EAUX 73190 Savoie — Map 6:A4

Château des Comtes de Challes — *Tel* 04.79.72.72.72
247 montée du Château — *Fax* 04.79.72.83.83
Email info@chateau-alpes.com
Website www.chateau-alpes.com

'Delightfully located', outside Challes thermal station (casino, etc), 6 km SE of Chambéry: superb 15th-century castle, renovated by the Trèves family owners. Lift, ramp. Salon, bar, beamed restaurant (no smoking), breakfast room; conference room; background music. 'Standard room excellent; very pleasing atmosphere; food a bit rich.' 6-hectare wooded grounds: alfresco meals, unheated swimming pool, tennis, children's playground, herons; wide views. Amex, MasterCard, Visa accepted. 46 bedrooms (2 air conditioned, some no-smoking) in 3 buildings of character: €58–€185, suite €165–€235. Breakfast €12. D,B&B from €70 per person. Set meals €25; full alc €40 [2004]. *V*

CHÂLONS-EN-CHAMPAGNE 51000 Marne — Map 5:A3

Hôtel d'Angleterre — *Tel* 03.26.68.21.51
19 place Monseigneur Tissier — *Fax* 03.26.70.51.67
Email hot.angl@wanadoo.fr
Website www.hotel-dangleterre.fr

'A super place. Dining here is to be savoured: food, setting, service all extremely satisfying.' 'Even better this time.' Praise this year from returning visitors for owner/chef Jacky Michel's hotel in this market town on the edge of the Champagne district. He has a *Michelin* star for his 'original, delicious' cooking. *Gault Millau* awards 15 points, commending his commitment to fresh local produce and sensitivity to evolving tastes. The set menu 'has varied only slightly over the last few years', so regulars might need to go to the *carte*. Specialities, served in an elegant white-and-yellow room, include langoustines à la nage au Chardonnay; carré d'agneau rôti au parfum d'orange. 'Very friendly staff.' 'Sophisticated public rooms.' 'Buffet breakfast, with huge choice, the best we have had in France.' Bedrooms vary: some are quite small, but one couple had a 'huge room and bathroom'. Triple glazing keeps out noise from the busy road. Only drawback: 'The lack of outside space.' The town has 'boring postwar streets', but a fine Gothic cathedral. (*Janet Wilmslow, Brenda and Owen Gape, and others*)

Open All year, except 17 July–8 Aug, Christmas/New Year, Sun. Restaurant closed Sat midday, Mon midday. **Rooms** 25 double. 2 suitable for ♿. Air conditioning. **Facilities** Lift, ramp. Salon, bar, restaurant; conference room. No background music. Terrace (outdoor dining). **Location** By *église* Notre-Dame-en-Vaux, across river from town hall. Parking, garage (€10). **Credit cards** All major cards accepted. **Terms** Room: single €85–€130, double €100–€150. Breakfast €15. Set meals €32–€90; full alc €75.

CHAMALIÈRES 63400 Puy-de-Dôme — Map 6:A1

Hôtel Radio
43 avenue Pierre et Marie Curie

Tel 04.73.30.87.83
Fax 04.73.36.42.44
Email resa@hotel-radio.fr
Website www.hotel-radio.fr

Built in 1930 as a radio station, this homage to Art Deco sits on a hillside in this residential suburb of Clermont-Ferrand. Owned for many years by Michel Mioche, it is now run by his daughter, Caroline: she and her staff are found 'genuinely helpful'. *Guide* reporters received 'a warm welcome' and an 'excellent dinner'. The striking white building is full of period features including 'a super old lift' and, in the hall, a mosaic depicting radio waves. The restaurant (*Michelin* star, 16 *Gault Millau* points for Frédéric Coursol for, eg, lobster with truffle jus; roast pigeon casserole) is the most prestigious in the area. 'Fantastic home-made bread' and a wine list specialising in Languedoc-Roussillon. 'Our good-sized room, bright and attractive, had excellent fabrics, large bed, bathroom with 1930s touches. Excellent housekeeping.' Good breakfast, too: fresh orange juice. The garden is 'lovingly tended'. The baths and casinos of Royat are nearby; also the Golf des Volcans, and Vulcania, the European centre of vulcanology.

Open 23 Jan–30 Apr, 9 May–31 Oct, 8 Nov–31 Dec. Restaurant closed Sat midday, Sun/Mon midday. **Rooms** 1 suite, 24 double. Some no-smoking. 10 air conditioned. **Facilities** Lift. Salon, restaurant (no-smoking); background jazz; conference room. Garden. **Location** 3 km W of central Clermont-Ferrand, towards Royat. Parking. Garage. **Credit cards** All major cards accepted. **Terms** Room: single €74–€117, double €86–€127, suite €166–€178. Breakfast €12. Set meals €33–€85. *V*

CHAMONIX-MONT-BLANC Haute-Savoie — Map 6:A5

Hôtel L'Aiguille du Midi
479 chemin Napoléon
Les Bossons
74400 Chamonix

Tel 04.50.53.00.65
Fax 04.50.55.93.69
Email hotel-aiguille-du-midi@wanadoo.fr
Website www.hotel-aiguilledumidi.com

In a village midway between the town and the Mont Blanc Tunnel entrance, this cheerful chalet-style hotel (Logis de France) is owned and run by Bernard and Martine Farini, the fourth generation of a hotel-keeping family. In a large park (with big swimming pool and tennis), it faces Mont Blanc and the Bossons glacier, the largest icefall in Europe. 'Excellent value, beautifully kept, with good service, friendly staff,' say recent guests. 'Madame is delightful.' An earlier comment: 'Very good food: the five-course *table d'hôte* menu for the *pensionnaires* included a generous dessert table. Copious buffet breakfast.' But there is a new chef this year, Giles Dunand, formerly *sous-chef.* The public rooms are 'very well furnished'; bedrooms are 'plain, but comfortable'. A free shuttle takes guests to the ski slopes, 'minutes away'. There is a new terrace with wooden decking, and a giant parasol which shades 60 people. 'Noise from the road could be a problem but great views compensate. Rear rooms might be quieter, but lack the dramatic outlook.' (*RDM, Carie Roots*)

Open 20 Dec–4 Apr, 12 May–20 Sept. **Rooms** 2 family, 35 double, 3 single. 8 in adjacent chalet. **Facilities** Lift, ramps. Salon/bar, restaurant, lobby/card room; background radio; seminar room; table-tennis room, pool room; sauna, spa bath. Terraces. 2-hectare grounds: tennis, heated swimming pool. Winter sports. Golf nearby. Parking. Unsuitable for ♿. **Restriction** No smoking in some bedrooms. **Location** 3 km from centre. **Credit cards** MasterCard, Visa. **Terms** Room: single €60–€80, double €68.50–€80, family room €100–€116. Breakfast €12. D,B&B €62.50–€123 per person. Min. 3 nights peak season. Set meals €19.90–€43; full alc €42. *V* (off-season)

Le Hameau Albert 1er
119 impasse du Montenvers
74402 Chamonix

Tel 04.50.53.05.09
Fax 04.50.55.95.48
Email infos@hameaualbert.fr
Website www.hameaualbert.fr

Owned since 1903 by the Carrier family, this luxury hotel (Relais & Châteaux) is named after the Belgian king who loved this ski resort. It has 'wonderful views' and, says a visitor this year, 'it is extremely well and unobtrusively run'. In a big flowery garden on the edge of town (some noise from the new bypass), it consists of a large brown building and three chalets. The best bedrooms are in *La Ferme* (Italian designer furniture; shiny modern bathrooms). 'Our room had eight windows facing Mont Blanc.' 'Ours, with sitting area and balcony, was in Alpine style.' The inventive cooking of chef/*patron* Pierre Carrier wins two *Michelin* stars, 17 *Gault Millau* points. His wife, Martine, manages. The set menus are 'good value', both in the main restaurant and the rustic *Maison Carrier*, where regional dishes are served informally around a huge fireplace. Also enjoyed: 'generous breakfasts', lunch on the terrace, the *après-ski* ambience, the half-covered heated swimming pool, the fitness centre. 'The staff are terrific.' In summer, 'there are comfortable chairs in garden, and lots of shade'. Children are welcomed. Ski passes and lessons are arranged, and there is a free shuttle around the valley. (*JH, and others*)

Open Early Dec–mid-Nov. Restaurant *Albert 1er* closed early Oct–early Dec, Wed/Thurs midday except holidays. **Rooms** 1 chalet, 1 suite, 40 double. 12 in annexe. 1 equipped for ♿. **Facilities** Lift. 3 lounges, 2 bars, 2 restaurants (*Albert 1er* no-smoking); background music; beauty centre. Large garden: terrace, swimming pool, golf practice. **Location** 500 m from centre. Underground parking. **Credit cards** All major cards accepted. **Terms** [2004] Room €150–€565, suite €503–€625, chalet €808–€1,250. Breakfast €17. D,B&B €63 added per person. *Albert 1er*: set meals €54–€136; alc €80–€150; *Maison Carrier*: set meals €13–€50.

CHAMPAGNAC-DE-BELAIR 24530 Dordogne Map 4:B4

Le Moulin du Roc

Tel 05.53.02.86.00
Fax 05.53.54.21.31
Email moulinroc@aol.com
Website www.moulinduroc.com

Michelin awards a star to owner/chef Alain Gardillou, admiring also the 'magic' setting of his 17th-century oil mill on the Dronne. *Guide* readers, too, call it a 'wonderful, bucolic spot'. In a village near Brantôme, it is 'a sophisticated place with a cosmopolitan clientele'. The mill machinery is still there, in the 'charming' sitting rooms. All bedrooms face the river (fringed by banana trees); they have antiques and fresh flowers. 'Our large ground-floor room had a four-poster bed, and a spa bath in its bathroom.' A 'lovely spacious suite' is up a spiral staircase. Gardillou's specialities include fois gras rôti en cocotte, salade truffée. 'Reception was courteous, the surroundings were calm and elegant, the cooking was refined.' Only criticism: 'The menus seldom change.' The list has 900 wines. On fine days, the 'excellent' breakfast is taken on a lawn by the water: a bridge leads to a swimming pool and tennis courts.

Open 6 Mar–31 Dec. Restaurant closed Tues, and Wed except evenings June–Sept. **Rooms** 1 suite, 12 double. Air conditioning. **Facilities** Reception. Lounge, 2 dining rooms (classical background music). 1-hectare garden: heated swimming pool; tennis, stream. Unsuitable for ♿. **Location** 6 km NE of Brantôme by D78, D83. Parking. **Credit cards** Diners, MasterCard, Visa. **Terms** Room €135, suite €170; D,B&B: single €200, double €268, suite €369. Breakfast €16. Set meals €33–€85; full alc €80.

CHASSEY-LE-CAMP 71150 Saône-et-Loire Map 5:D3

Auberge du Camp Romain BUDGET

Tel 03.85.87.09.91
Fax 03.85.87.11.51
Email auberge.du.camp.romain@wanadoo.fr

Between woodlands and vineyards on a Burgundy hillside, M. and Mme Dressinval's holiday hotel (Logis de France) stands on a minor road, below an old Neolithic settlement. Its leisure facilities (see below) include a 'first-class outdoor swimming pool, well away from the main buildings'. Not all rooms have views: annexe ones are larger and more modern than those in the main building; some have a balcony. One dissenting report came this year, but all others are positive: 'A very pleasant place at a good price.' 'The food was excellent' (*Michelin Bib Gourmand* for *cuisine traditionelle généreuse*). 'First-class buffet breakfast.' 'Our third stay. We are still very happy with all that it offers.' At weekends, and during school holidays, the hotel is 'crowded with families'; at other times it is 'very quiet'. 'The atmosphere is relaxed, and our dog was welcomed everywhere, except by the pools.' 'Madame creates a personal touch.' (*Bob and Kate Flaherty, and others*)

Open 10 Feb–1 Jan. **Rooms** 5 suites, 36 double. 17 in annexe. **Facilities** Lift. Bar, breakfast room, restaurant (classical background music); conference rooms; children's games room; billiards; indoor swimming pool, fitness facilities. Garden: dining terrace, swimming pool, tennis, table tennis, mini-golf, badminton, *pétanque*. **Location** 6 km SW of Chagny: take D974, then D109 to Remigny, turn sharp left (signposted). **Credit cards** MasterCard, Visa. **Terms** [2004] Room €61–€79. Breakfast €8.50. D,B&B (min. 3 nights) €60–€72 per person. Set meals €24–€43.

CHÂTEAUBERNARD 16100 Charente — Map 4:B3

Château de l'Yeuse
65 rue de Bellevue
Quartier de l'Échassier

Tel 05.45.36.82.60
Fax 05.45.35.06.32
Email reservations.yeuse@wanadoo.fr
Website www.yeuse.fr

With unspoilt views over the Charente from its dining terrace, this 19th-century *gentilhommière* stands among oak trees (*yeuses*). It has a 'romantic atmosphere', say fans, despite a 'slightly incongruous modern extension'. Managed by Céline Desmazières, it attracts visitors to the brandy towns of Cognac and Jarnac (free tours of distilleries, with tastings, can be arranged). Public rooms, traditionally furnished, have large mirrors and chandeliers. In the '*cognathèque*', there is a 'remarkable selection' of local brandies, and a vast range of Havana cigars. *Gault Millau* awards 14 points (one more this year) for Pascal Nebout's imaginative cooking, eg, râble de lapin au thym, brochette de rognons, pommes de terre et girolles. 'All the staff were helpful.' The *sommelier* is 'superb'. The half-board menu has no choice, but substitutes are offered. 'A good buffet breakfast.' Bedrooms, though not large, are comfortable. 'The immediate area is a bit boring', but Saintes, with the remains of a Roman amphitheatre, is near.

Open All year. Restaurant closed Sat midday, and Sun night off-season. **Rooms** 3 suites, 21 double. Air conditioning. **Facilities** Lift. 2 lounges, breakfast room, restaurant (background music); meeting rooms. Terrace. Garden: 2 unheated swimming pools; by river, bathing. **Location** 3 km S of Cognac, off D15. Parking. **Credit cards** All major cards accepted. **Terms** Room €92–€157, suite €205–€314. Breakfast €14. D,B&B €105.50–€188.50 per person. Set meals €25–€65.

CHÂTEAUNEUF 21320 Côte-d'Or — Map 5:D3

Hostellerie du Château BUDGET

Tel 03.80.49.22.00
Fax 03.80.49.21.27
Email infos@hostellerie-chateauneuf.com
Website www.hostellerie-chateauneuf.com

Enjoyed again this year, André and Florence Hartmann's old hostelry is in this ramparted medieval hamlet on a hilltop west of Dijon: 'a most attractive location; fine views over countryside'. Though modernised, it is picturesque, with its beamed ceilings, rough stonework, and small, pretty garden which faces the château. 'The food and service were excellent, and we loved eating outside on the flowery patio,' say recent guests. The candlelit dinners and the trays of drinks in the reception/hall/bar (with flagstone floors, tapestry rugs, a fine old fireplace) are liked. But several visitors agreed that breakfast 'in a rather gloomy cellar, and with coffee in a thermos flask' was disappointing. Bedrooms (some are small) are on several floors (no lift). Some have beams, old stones and period furnishings; some overlook countryside. The most spacious rooms are in the annexe. The motorway is near, but out of earshot. (*BH, and others*)

Open 15 Feb–1 Dec. Closed Wed Oct–Mar, Mon/Tues except July/Aug. Restaurant closed Tues midday. **Rooms** 1 suite, 15 double, 1 single. 6 in annexe. **Facilities** 2 salons, restaurant; function room; terrace. Garden: children's play area. **Location** 10 km SE of Pouilly-en-Auxois. Pouilly exit from A6 motorway. **Credit cards** All major cards accepted. **Terms** [2004] Room €45–€70. Breakfast €8. D,B&B (min. 2 nights) €52–€90 per person. Set meals €23–€36.

CHAUNY 02300 Aisne — Map 3:E3

La Toque Blanche
24 avenue Victor Hugo

Tel 03.23.39.98.98
Fax 03.23.52.32.79
Email info@toque-blanche.fr
Website www.toque-blanche.fr

A 'charming couple', Vincent and Véronique Lequeux, own and run this restaurant-with-rooms in a small town near Noyon. It is popular with locals for functions. An 'impressive classic house' (1920s) in a garden with mature trees, it has a balustraded terrace for drinks and summer meals, and a 'cosy' bar. The 'very smart' restaurant has a *Michelin* star, 15 *Gault Millau* points for cuisine which 'combines tradition with invention', eg, escalopes de foie gras de canard; étuvée de homard aux sauternes. *Guide* correspondents have written of 'a fine selection of cheeses, excellent wine list, generous breakfast', 'a spacious room with blue-and-gold colour scheme and large bathroom', 'immaculate housekeeping'. 'Eight out of ten,' say visitors in 2004. Excellent walking and cycling nearby, particularly in the Forêt de Compiègne. Noyon has a 'fabulous Saturday market'. (*Bob and Kate Flaherty, and others*)

Open All year, except 15 days Feb, 3 weeks Aug, Sun/Mon. Restaurant closed Sat midday. **Rooms** 5 double, 1 single. Some no-smoking. **Facilities** Ramp. Lounge/bar, 4 dining rooms; function facilities; terrace. Large garden: tennis. Unsuitable for ♿. **Location** Central. 30 km S of St-Quentin, 18 km from Noyon. Parking. **Restriction** No dogs. **Credit cards** MasterCard, Visa. **Terms** Room €60–€87. Breakfast €12. Set meals €31–€70.

****

Traveller's tale Hotel in Venice. When presented with a bill for nearly £20 for two coffees and a piece of cake, by a Brian Ferry lookalike waiter in a white DJ, I asked whether the bill included service. His deadpan and well-practised reply, in perfect English, was: 'Yes, sir, it does include service but it does not include the tip.' I left him the rest of the change for his chutzpah!

****

CHÊNEHUTTE-LES-TUFFEAUX 49350 Maine-et-Loire — Map 2:F4

Le Prieuré

Tel 02.41.67.90.14
Fax 02.41.67.92.24
Email contact@prieure.com
Website www.prieure.com

On a bluff above the Loire, west of Saumur, this luxurious hotel was built as a lodge in the 12th century. Later a Benedictine priory, it was abandoned during the revolution. A hotel since 1957, it is managed by Stéphane Cateux. The gardens, in a large wooded park, are lovely, and the terrace, where drinks and meals are served, looks over the river, as does the elegant dining room with its tall windows. Bedrooms vary: one is the former 10th-century chapel, 'large, bright, with ceiling-high drapes, king-size bed, river view'. Some rooms have a private patio; two have a fireplace. 'Wonderful position. Charming, well-trained staff. Very good food,' says this year's reporter. 'But the menu choice seems limited if you stay more than four nights. In our good, south-facing bungalow there was only one bedside light, and the burglar-proof coat-hangers fell from their worn-out plastic mounts.' Concerts are held on some Saturdays in winter; there are tastings in the wine cellar. Some coach tours come. In the tufa cliffs nearby you can visit the caves, some used for mushroom-growing, some with ancient sculptures, some still inhabited. (*Malcolm Levitt, and others*)

Open Mar–early Jan. **Rooms** 2 suites, 31 double, 3 single. 15 in 6 cottages, 400 m. **Facilities** Lounge/bar, breakfast room, restaurant; background music; 2 function rooms. 35-hectare park: garden, mini-golf, tennis, *pétanque*, heated swimming pool, bicycles; river, fishing. Unsuitable for ♿. **Location** 7 km W of Saumur, off D751. **Credit cards** All major cards accepted. **Terms** [2004] Room €125–€270, suite €295–€320. Breakfast €21. D,B&B €78 added per person. Set meals €41–€70.

CHENONCEAUX 37150 Indre-et-Loire — Map 2:F5

Le Bon Laboureur
6 rue du Dr Bretonneau

Tel 02.47.23.90.02
Fax 02.47.23.82.01
Email laboureur@wanadoo.fr
Website www.bonlaboureur.com

'Lovely-looking and efficiently run,' say visitors this year. At the château gates, this 18th-century post house (Relais du Silence) has been owned by the Jeudi family since 1902. It consists of five small houses, each with garden. There is a shady terrace for summer meals, and a charming beamed dining room. Antoine Jeudi is chef (*Michelin* star, 16 *Gault Millau* points for, eg, terrine de foie gras, asperges vertes grillées; cochon de lait, sauce aux épices douces). 'Everything was beautifully presented, and tasted wonderful.' But menus are short and change infrequently, so guests staying more than a few days may need to choose from the fairly expensive *carte*. Some correspondents thought service was 'cool', and detected 'a touch of complacency'. Most bedrooms have antiques and air conditioning; some face a rose garden; the ones on the main road have double glazing. The large lounges have a modern décor, 'a bit out of kilter with the old-world charm'. The swimming pool is in a secluded garden across the road. (*B and EU, and others*)

Open Early-Feb–mid-Nov, mid-Dec–early Jan. Closed 25 Dec, 1 Jan. Restaurant closed Wed and Thurs off-season, Tues midday high season. **Rooms** 3 suites, 21 double. 2 suitable for ♿. Air conditioning. **Facilities** 2 salons, bar, 3 dining rooms. No background music. Terrace. 1.5-hectare garden: heated swimming pool. **Location** By château gates (roadside windows double glazed). Parking. **Credit cards** Amex, MasterCard, Visa. **Terms** [2004] Room €75–€135, suite €145–€175. Breakfast €10. D,B&B €50 added per person. Set meals €21–€69; full alc €75.

Hostellerie de la Renaudière BUDGET *Tel* 02.47.23.90.04
24 rue du Dr Bretonneau *Fax* 02.47.23.90.51
Email gerhotel@club-internet.fr
Website www.chenonceaux-renaudiere.com

'Beguilingly idiosyncratic', this 19th-century mansion (Logis de France) stands in a large garden with sequoias and cedars of Lebanon, near the château. The former residence of the doctor who gave his name to the street, it is owned, and managed with enthusiasm, by Joël Camus; his wife, Isabelle, cooks, basing many of her 'exquisite' dishes on 17th-century recipes. From the dining room there are views through tall windows of the lawn where, on fine days, meals are served under white-and-red parasols. Small hens and cats might be in attendance, and there is a heated swimming pool. 'The welcome was good and the food was excellent,' says a visitor in 2004. Others wrote: 'All is relaxed, but service, food and wines were all excellent.' Stuffed animals share landing space with antiques. 'Don't expect luxurious bedrooms' – and one visitor wrote: 'Management is not a strong point' – but some bedrooms have an outdoor seating area with deckchairs. (*Terry Herbert, and others*)

Open All year, except 2 Jan–14 Feb. **Rooms** 4 suites, 14 double, 2 single. Some in 2 annexes. Some on ground floor. **Facilities** Salon, breakfast room, restaurant. 2-hectare garden: heated swimming pool, children's play area. **Location** Edge of village. Closed parking. **Credit cards** All major cards accepted. **Terms** [2004] Room €40–€95, suite €120–€185. Breakfast €6. D,B&B €20 added per person. Set meals €20–€40. *V*

CHÉPY 80210 Somme Map 3:E2

L'Auberge Picarde BUDGET *Tel* 03.22.26.20.78
95 place la Gare *Fax* 03.22.26.33.34
Email auberge-picarde@wanadoo.fr
Website www.auberge-picarde.com

Logis de France, owned and managed by Anne and Alain Henocque, SW of Abbeville, near motorway to Rouen. 'Welcoming, cheap and cheerful, amazingly good value, with pleasant, brisk meal service.' Smart new annexe ('splendidly spacious bathrooms'). Michelin Bib Gourmand *for popular rustic-style restaurant with extension.*

Adequate breakfast in room with coal-mining memorabilia. Billiard room; meeting room. Unsuitable for ♿. Garage. Closed 23 Aug–8 Sept, 26 Dec–12 Jan. Restaurant closed Sat midday, Sun night. 25 bedrooms (9 no-smoking): €40–€44. Breakfast €6. D,B&B €51.50–€75 per person. Set meals €14–€34.50; full alc €40 [2004].

CHINON 37500 Indre-et-Loire — Map 2:F4

Hôtel Agnès Sorel BUDGET
4 quai Pasteur

Tel 02.47.93.04.37
Fax 02.47.93.06.37
Email info@agnes-sorel.com
Website www.agnes-sorel.com

Named after a mistress of Charles VII who was also an enthusiastic cook, this 'sweet, unpretentious little place, astonishingly cheap', has long been loved by *Guide* readers. Owned and run by the 'smart, polite and welcoming' Catherine Raoust and her husband, it stands by the Vienne, below the great castle. Rooms are in two buildings. 'Ours, separate from the main one, had a little terrace with tables, chairs and creepers, delightful in summer.' 'Our good-sized room had two narrow balconies facing the river. Inevitably it heard traffic; earplugs helped.' 'Our beamed room across a side alley lacked a view, but had character to compensate.' 'Room service was charming. Accommodation is homely. A fine modern bathroom.' Breakfast (fresh orange juice, nothing packaged, lots of croissants, etc) in a 'tastefully decorated, high-ceilinged room' on the terrace or in the bedroom is 'graciously served'. For dinner *L'Océanic*, a seafood restaurant in the pedestrianised area, and *Au Plaisir Gourmand* (*Michelin* star) are both warmly recommended. (*Josie Mayers, B and RK, and others*)

Open All year. **Rooms** 1 suite, 10 double. In 2 different houses. 1 on ground floor. **Facilities** Reception, breakfast room; background music. Terrace. Small garden. Bicycle hire. **Location** Central, between castle and river (rear rooms quietest). Free public parking adjacent. **Credit cards** MasterCard, Visa. **Terms** [2004] Room €46–€72, suite €95–€140. Breakfast €8.

Château de Marçay
Route du Château
Marçay

Tel 02.47.93.03.47
Fax 02.47.93.45.33
Email marcay@relaischateaux.com
Website www.chateaudemarcay.com

Built as a fortress in about 1150, the town of Marçay was originally inside the walls of this splendid château, now a smart hotel (Relais & Châteaux). The present structure, with pepperpot towers and a formal garden, dates from the 15th century. Owned by Philippe Mollard, managed by Bernard Beteille, it stands in a large park. Its impressive public rooms have beamed ceilings, panelling, log fires, flowers and paintings. Some bedrooms are in the towers ('our delightful, if smallish, room had a massive bathroom,' one couple wrote). Some rooms are large, and have antique prints and period furniture. The ones in the pavilion annexe are cheaper, and visitors during a heatwave found theirs 'hot, and lacking privacy'. Chef Marc de Passorio earns 16 *Gault Millau* points for cooking, which this year's visitors found 'mostly excellent, with amazing presentation'. 'Wonderful smell of lime blossom, as we sat outside for the exceptional breakfast: cherries, tiny pots of porridge and crème fraîche.' You can buy the château's wine from Reception. (*JW*)

Open Early Mar–mid-Jan. Restaurant closed Sun night/Mon except high season, Thurs midday in season, Mon midday, Tues midday. **Rooms** 6 suites, 28 double. 7 in pavilion. **Facilities** Lift. 2 salons, bar, TV room, restaurant; conference facilities. No background music. 15-hectare grounds: terrace, heated swimming pool, tennis. **Location** 6 km S of Chinon, by D116. **Credit cards** All major cards accepted. **Terms** [2004] Room €114–€255, suite €290. Breakfast €18. D,B&B €177–€379 per person. Set meals €48–€77.

Hôtel Diderot BUDGET
4 rue de Buffon/7 rue Diderot

Tel 02.47.93.18.87
Fax 02.47.93.37.10
Email hoteldiderot@hoteldiderot.com
Website www.hoteldiderot.com

Near the famous, near-derelict (but open for visits) château of this well-known wine town on the Vienne, Laurent and Françoise Dutheil's B&B 'continues to be a delightful place to stay', says a fan. The fine old building (15th-century, remodelled in the 18th) is full of character: a spiral stairway on the facade leads to a wrought iron balcony. At the communal breakfast (served in summer in the garden, under an olive tree), over 50 kinds of home-made conserves, from fig and banana jam to lavender jelly, are served. The bedrooms (four were renovated this year) vary in style and size. Some are beamed; some face a road; some may be a little dark; some, 'light and modern', are in the courtyard. Bathrooms are 'spotless'. For meals, the *Michelin*-starred *Au Plaisir Gourmand* is recommended; also *L'Océanic* ('specialises in seafood'), and *La Bonne France* ('good value'). (*TH*)

Open All year. **Rooms** 27 double. 5 in courtyard, 4 in annexe (10 metres). Some on ground floor. 1 equipped for ♿. **Facilities** Bar (7.30 am–10 pm), breakfast room. No background music. Courtyard. Garden. **Location** 800 m E of château, near St Mexme church. Limited parking. **Restrictions** Smoking in bar only. No dogs. **Credit cards** All major cards accepted. **Terms** Room: single €40–€51, double €50–€71. Breakfast €6.50. *V*

CHISSAY-EN-TOURAINE 41400 Loir-et-Cher — Map 2:F5

Château de Chissay NEW

Tel 02.54.32.32.01
Fax 02.54.32.43.80
Email chissay@leshotelsparticuliers.com
Website www.leshotelsparticuliers.com

In the Cher valley, near Chenonceaux and Blois, this 'idyllic' medieval château stands on a hillside. Owned by Alain Guinoiseau, and part of the small Savray group, it is 'a perfect example of traditional local architecture', according to its 2004 nominators. Earlier visitors have been Charles VII, Louis XI and Charles de Gaulle.

With a round tower on each of three corners, it is set round a courtyard with a Renaissance loggia looking over the valley. Rooms are spacious and quietly furnished in traditional style; many have an *en suite* bathroom in a tower. 'The atmosphere is extremely civilised: high-quality restoration has kept the feel of a large private house. No TVs in bedrooms but a small, pleasant TV room on the ground floor. Lots of places to sit: courtyard, terrace, by the 25-metre pool which is designed in keeping with its surroundings.' Some bedrooms near the pool, with parking nearby, are suitable for those unable to walk up the spiral staircases in the main building. 'The food is superb, beautifully presented, served in the vaulted dining room or on the terrace. The menus, for all sizes of appetite, use local, seasonal products. Good range of local wines. Breakfast is light and tasty.' A main-line railway runs through the valley: occasional trains can be heard. The road beneath the château is audible from pool and rooms, but has little traffic at night. 'There is some parkland round the building, enough for a short stroll.' (*George and Kay Brock*)

Open 15 Mar–15 Nov. **Rooms** 11 suites, 21 double. **Facilities** Lift. Salon with TV, tea room, restaurant; conference facilities. Courtyard, terrace. Garden: swimming pool. **Location** 4 km W of Montrichard. **Credit cards** All major cards accepted. **Terms** [2004] Room: €91–€229. Breakfast €13. Set meals €18–€52.

CHITENAY 41120 Loir-et-Cher — Map 2:F5

Auberge du Centre BUDGET
Place de l'Église

Tel 02.54.70.42.11
Fax 02.54.70.35.03
Email aub-centr@wanadoo.fr
Website www.auberge-du-centre.com

Convenient for visiting the Loire châteaux, this 'cool and pleasant' inn (Logis de France) is in a peaceful village south of Blois. It is the family home of the owner, Gilles Martinet. 'He is much in command, visiting the tables at breakfast and dinner,' one couple wrote. The cooking of Cédric Botte, served in the beautiful dining room or on the terrace by the garden, is thought 'really good'. His dishes include terrine de homard et légumes de saison; magret de canard poêlé. There is 'a terrific selection of local wines'. On Monday, only the menu du jour (€19) is served, by arrangement. Breakfasts, in a rustic room, 'are excellent, with figs, greengages and strawberries in season, and home-made jams'. There are big fireplaces, beamed ceilings, a spacious salon. One couple had a 'compact bedroom, very pretty, with an equally attractive bathroom'. (*W and AR*)

Open Mar–end Jan. Restaurant closed midday on Mon and Tues (Mon dinner by arrangement) May–Sept, Sun evening/Mon Oct–Apr. **Rooms** 2 suites, 24 double. 7 (some no-smoking) in annexes. **Facilities** Lounge, restaurant. Garden, dining terrace. **Location** In village. 12 km S of Blois. Parking. **Credit cards** Amex, MasterCard, Visa. **Terms** [2004] Room: single €47.40–€65, double €51.50–€72. Breakfast €7.50. D,B&B €47–€92 per person. Set meals €19–€38.

CHONAS L'AMBALLAN 38121 Isère Map 6:A3

Domaine de Clairefontaine *Tel* 04.74.58.81.52
Chemin des Fontanettes *Fax* 04.74.58.80.93
Email domaine.de.clairefontaine@gofornet.com
Website domaine-de-clairefontaine.fr

Owned by the Girardon family, this lovely 18th-century mansion, once the country home of the bishops of Lyon, is on the edge of a Rhône valley village. It has a 'beautiful terrace', a big garden with a pond, a steeple dating from 1736, and a walnut-drying house. It was found 'wonderfully rewarding, relaxing and peaceful' by one couple, but another guest thought the welcome 'offhand'. 'The food was fantastic, my room was large, comfortable and inexpensive,' says a report this year. Chef Philippe Girardon's *Michelin*-starred dishes include nénuphar de homard en salade; truite aux parfums de citronelle. 'The chocolate desserts have to be seen to be believed.' The best bedrooms are in the annexe, *Les Jardins de Clairefontaine*, which has a sleek lift, automatic sliding glass doors, electronically operated shutters, smart bathrooms. The family also own the ten-bedroom *Marais St-Jean*, nearby. (*M and KO, Terry Herbert, and others*)

Open All year, except 15 Dec–15 Jan, 1 May, Tues except evenings July/Aug. **Rooms** 2 suites, 25 double. 18 in annexe. 2 suitable for ♿. Some air conditioned. **Facilities** Lift. Salon/bar, 2 dining rooms (no-smoking); background music; terrace. 3-hectare grounds: tennis. **Location** 9 km SW of Vienne: from N, leave *autoroute* at Vienne; follow N7 to roundabout at Chonas d'Amballon (hotel is signposted); from S, leave *autoroute* at exit 12; follow N7. **Credit cards** All major cards accepted. **Terms** [2004] Room €43–€110. Breakfast €11–€20. Set meals €42–€85; alc €65.

CIBOURE 64500 Pyrénées-Atlantiques Map 4:D2

Lehen Tokia NEW *Tel* 05.59.47.18.16
Chemin Achotarreta *Fax* 05.59.47.38.04
Email info@lehen-tokia.com
Website www.lehen-tokia.com

A 'marvellous house', recommended by visitors in 2004. This Art Deco villa (its Basque name translates into French as 'premier endroit', ie, 'first place') stands on a hill above the bay of St-Jean-de-Luz, close to the Spanish border. It has been turned by its owner, Yan Personnaz, into a 'guest house': he promises 'un confort merveilleux à l'Anglaise'. With flowery balconies, a sloping roof, and stained-glass windows by Jacques Grüber, it is full of character. Each bedroom is named after a precious stone: the suite is Diamant. The best rooms have sea views; others face the garden; one opens on to the swimming pool by which 'the good breakfast is served on the terrace at any time'. The 'very nice staff' are 'easy-going', and good local restaurants are a ten-minute drive away. (*Brian and Sandra Richards*)

Open All year, except 12 Nov–21 Dec, 6–20 Jan. **Rooms** 1 suite, 6 double. **Facilities** Salons. Garden: terrace, swimming pool. **Location** 5 km SW of St-Jean-de Luz. **Credit cards** All major cards accepted. **Terms** [2004] Room €80–€145, suite €185–€215. Breakfast €10.

CLÉCY 14570 Calvados — Map 2:E4

Le Moulin du Vey
Le Vey

Tel 02.31.69.71.08
Fax 02.31.69.14.14
Email reservations@moulinduvey.com
Website www.moulinduvey.com

'Especially lovely in autumn, ivy glowing red, wheel slowly turning', this creeper-covered mill stands by the River Orne, in the hilly Suisse Normande. 'A gorgeous setting', 'delightful', are other comments. Owned by Denise Leduc, and run with 'care and attention' by her 'charming daughter', Chantal, the hotel has cosy rustic decor and a distinct Norman ambience. 'Dogs are warmly welcomed' and 'service is excellent'. The half-board meals are thought 'very good' ('excellent fish'; 'we gasped at the sweet trolley'), but choice is limited. In summer, coach tours come for lunch. The beamed dining room opens on to a riverside terrace where guests can eat alfresco. Some bedrooms enjoy this view. Rooms in the mill, reached by a narrow staircase, can be small but have character and hear 'the soothing sound of the mill wheel'. Other, 'functional', rooms are in an annexe. Quality and soundproofing may vary. Breakfast includes cereal, eggs and yogurt. There is good climbing and walking nearby, but on summer weekends the river and its banks can be 'chock-a-block' with pedalos, kayaks, canoes, picnickers and crêpe stalls, 'and the singing of rock climbers can be heard until late'. (*JC, J and SC*)

Open 1 Feb–30 Nov. Closed Sun night (restaurant also closed Mon midday) Nov, Feb/Mar. **Rooms** 12 double. 1 family, 5 in annexe (400 m). **Facilities** Salons, tea room, restaurant; breakfast room in annexe; function facilities. No background music. Garden: terrace (meals served), table tennis. By river: fishing, canoeing. Unsuitable for ♿. **Location** D133a, 1 km E of Clécy, 37 km S of Caen. Parking. **Credit cards** All major cards accepted. **Terms** Room €75–€105. Breakfast €10.50. D,B&B (min. 3 days) €88.50–€118.50 per person. Set meals €23.70–€64; full alc €58.

CLIOUSCLAT 26270 Drôme — Map 6:C3

La Treille Muscate

Tel 04.75.63.13.10
Fax 04.75.63.10.79
Email latreillemuscate@wanadoo.fr
Website www.latreillemuscate.com

Easily accessible from the A7 *Autoroute du Soleil*, and just 24 kilometres from Montélimar (which has a TGV station), the Delaitre family's 'exquisite' ivy-covered, ochre-walled *auberge* is in a Rhône valley *village perché* known for its glazed pottery. Inside are tiled floors, wrought iron, and dried flowers. Each room is different: 'Ours, small but charming, had Provençal fabrics, nice linens, geraniums in the window.' Another reader says, 'It was the favourite hotel of our trip, also the least expensive.' Katy Delaitre offers 'a warm welcome', and chef Jean-Luc Dunan provides 'delicious' regional food, eg, soupe glacée de tomates, brousse aux herbes; onglet de bœuf au pistou, pignons de pin grillés. There is an attractive lounge ('lots of books and games'), and a 'lovely shaded terrace', with superb views over vineyards and hills, where drinks and breakfast can be served.

Open 1 Mar–15 Dec. Restaurant closed Wed. **Rooms** 12. 1 on ground floor. **Facilities** Lounge, dining room. Terrace. Garden. **Location** In village, 24 km NE of Montélimar. Parking. **Credit cards** MasterCard, Visa. **Terms** [2004] Room €60–€115. Breakfast €8. D,B&B €32 added per person. Set meals €13–€26.

COCURÈS 48400 Lozère — Map 4:C6

La Lozerette BUDGET

Tel 04.66.45.06.04
Fax 04.66.45.12.93
Email lalozerette@wanadoo.fr

Found 'outstanding' this year by a regular correspondent, this *auberge*, in a medieval village high in the Cévennes, is run with brio by Pierrette Agulhon, the 'hands-on' granddaughter of the founder. 'She and her staff looked after us splendidly,' say visitors in 2004. Earlier praise: 'Excellent housekeeping.' 'Madame's welcome was warm, our bedrooms were delightful: each had a balcony looking down over the village.' 'The bar/lounge, warm and comfortable, had plenty of newspapers, guides, etc' (also deep leather armchairs, a fire on chilly days). There is a tiny shady garden 'where it is bliss to sit after a day's walking'. Some bedrooms are fair-sized, some very small, 'with minute bathroom'; five were redecorated this year. Mme Agulhon tells us that she has upgraded the breakfasts after last year's comments. She 'is a trained *sommelier*'; her wine list 'is well chosen, at fair prices'. The restaurant has 13 *Gault Millau* points: there is a new chef this year. Around are orchards and vineyards; the Tarn is 200 metres away. (*FH Potts, Michael and Betty Hill, and others*)

Open Easter–1 Nov. Restaurant closed to non-residents Tues/Wed midday. **Rooms** 20 double, 1 single. 2 on ground floor. **Facilities** Salon, TV lounge, bar, restaurant; background music. Garden. **Location** 4 km NE of Florac, by D998. Parking, garage. **Credit cards** All major cards accepted. **Terms** Room: single €46–€68, double €51–€72. Breakfast €7.50. D,B&B €64–€87 per person. Set meals €15–€22; full alc €43–€60.

COLLIOURE 66190 Pyrénées-Orientales — Map 4:E6

Casa Païral

Impasse des Palmiers

Tel 04.68.82.05.81
Fax 04.68.82.52.10
Email contact@hotel-casa-pairal.com
Website www.hotel-casa-pairal.com

'A good, sound hotel in a fine position.' Owned by Alix Guiot, this 19th-century *demeure* (Relais du Silence) is part of a small group of Roussillon hotels. It is in a traffic-free area of the charming old town centre, 'down a quiet, hidden lane'. Near port and beach, it has an attractive walled garden, with flowers, palm trees, fountain and swimming pool. Of the bedrooms (all are air conditioned), the best are said to be those in the main house; some rooms are in an annexe in the garden; some ground-floor courtyard rooms, though comfortable, may be 'rather small and dark'. 'Caring staff, good breakfast; nice relaxing atmosphere,' say visitors this year. But a dissenter wrote of a 'gloomy' bedroom that faced the street, and a poor welcome. B&B only: many restaurants are close by. (*Michael Hill, D and GB, and others*)

Open 26 Mar–1 Nov. **Rooms** 2 junior suites, 26 double. 18 in garden annexe, some on ground floor. Air conditioning. **Facilities** 2 lounges, breakfast room. No background music. Garden: swimming pool. **Location** 150 metres from port. Pay-parking 50 m. **Credit cards** All major cards accepted. **Terms** [2004] Room €73–€138, suite €154–€170. Breakfast €10.

Hôtel Madeloc
24 rue Romain-Rolland

Tel 04.68.82.07.56
Fax 04.68.82.55.09
Email hotel@madeloc.com
Website www.madeloc.com

Away from the crowded waterfront of this old fishing port near the Spanish border, the Pouchairet-Ramona family's modestly priced B&B hotel, 'not luxurious, but good value', is up a steep side street. 'The owners were exceedingly helpful,' say visitors in 2004, endorsing earlier praise: 'Christine, her husband and mother-in-law all seem genuinely interested in your well-being; son Jean-Laurent, a cat and two dogs complete the picture.' Rooms vary, but all have air conditioning. Street-facing ones hear traffic, and one visitor thought the lighting 'poor'. But most rooms are praised: 'My front room was decorated in fresh yellow.' My third-floor room, up steep stairs, had French windows opening on to its own little terrace surrounded by lavender bushes.' Public areas have Catalan paintings. There is a large high-ceilinged reception area, and a 'pleasant, smallish' swimming pool with bar. 'The views over mountains are beautiful, especially as the sun sets.' For meals, *Le Trémail*, *El Capillo* and *Le Puits* are recommended. (*Mary and Brian Morris, Vivienne Menkes-Ivry, DT, and others*)

Open 19 Mar–13 Nov. **Rooms** 22 double. 1 in annexe. Some with terrace. Air conditioning. **Facilities** Bar/breakfast room. No background music. Garden: heated swimming pool, bar. Unsuitable for ♿. **Location** 500 m from centre. Parking. **Credit cards** All major cards accepted. **Terms** Room €60–€93. Breakfast €10. *V*

COLMAR 68000 Haut-Rhin — Map 5:C5

Le Colombier
7 rue de Turenne

Tel 03.89.23.96.00
Fax 03.89.23.97.27
Email info@hotel-le-colombier.fr
Website www.hotel-le-colombier.fr

Run by Anne-Sophie Heitzler with a 'helpful staff', this modern hotel is a conversion of three half-timbered Renaissance buildings in Colmar's beautiful Petite Venise area. It has a four-storey spiral staircase, contemporary furniture, a fax/modem connection in each bedroom, and modern art works including a sculpture by England's

David Jacobson. New this year are three more bedrooms and a breakfast room: the 'excellent' buffet breakfast includes fresh orange juice and charcuterie. The 'very good central location', on a cobbled street, means that nearby parking is difficult (the two garages in a stable must be reserved in advance), and the bedrooms, apart from the four that face the courtyard, hear street noise. There is double glazing, but one visitor found the air-conditioning unit 'very noisy', and another room was found 'cramped and smelling of cigarettes'. Others wrote: 'Our room was large, well furnished, with a good bathroom.' No restaurant: plenty nearby. *Aux Trois Poissons*, medium priced, is liked for its seafood, and *JY's* (*Michelin* star), round the corner, is also recommended. (*AW, and others*)

Open All year. **Rooms** 1 suite, 23 double, 3 single. 2 suitable for ♿. Air conditioning. **Facilities** Lift. Salon/bar, breakfast room; meeting room; background radio. Courtyard. **Location** Centre of Old Colmar. 2 garages; street parking. **Credit cards** All major cards accepted. **Terms** [2004] Room €75–€180, suite €180. Breakfast €10.

La Maison des Têtes
19 rue des Têtes

Tel 03.89.24.43.43
Fax 03.89.24.58.34
Email les-tetes@calixo.net
Website www.la-maison-des-tetes.com

In the old town, between the Dominican church and the Unterlinden museum, this ornate mansion (1609), owned by Carmen and Marc Rohfritsch, is decorated with 100 sculpted *têtes* (heads). A restaurant since 1898, it now has guest accommodation. 'Our rooms were spacious, comfortable, with very nice bathroom,' said one reader; others appreciated the welcome: 'The proprietor (he is also the chef), his wife and their staff were dedicated to making our stay pleasant. They work hard to keep standards high.' 'An excellent meal': in the pale-panelled dining room lit by chandeliers, the *carte* offers regional specialities, eg, escalope de foie d'oie poêlée aux pommes caramelisées; le baeckaoffa de caille. Breakfast, in the lovely courtyard with Virginia creeper, is 'superb', and includes cheeses and hams. Works by a local contemporary sculptor are displayed in corridors. Some bedrooms have beams and sloping ceiling. The largest rooms are in an extension. Colmar has dull suburbs, but in its centre are many medieval and Renaissance buildings. (*MH, G and MG*)

Open All year, except Feb. Restaurant closed Sun evening, Mon/Tues midday. **Rooms** 1 duplex, 20 double. 1 on ground floor. Air conditioning. **Facilities** Lift, ramps. Hall, restaurant (background music); banqueting room; terrace. **Location** Centre of Old Colmar. Parking. **Restriction** No smoking: some bedrooms, part of restaurant. **Credit cards** All major cards accepted. **Terms** [2004] Room: single €98–€110, double €100–€169, duplex €209–€231. Breakfast €13.50. Set meals €29–€65. *V*

COLY 24120 Dordogne — Map 4:C4

Manoir d'Hautegente

Tel 05.53.51.68.03
Fax 05.53.50.38.52
Email hotel@manoir-hautegente.com
Website www.manoir-hautegente.com

'Delightful', 'peaceful and idyllic', say visitors this year to this long-time *Guide* favourite. Owned by one family for over 300 years, now run by the 'charming' Patrick Hamelin and his Canadian wife, Marie Josee, it stands peacefully by a trout stream in pretty countryside north of Sarlat. The creeper-clad former forge is fronted by a stream with pools and weirs. Bedrooms are in the main house and a nearby annexe. 'Ours, luxurious, had first-rate lighting. The bathroom had a spa bath and high-tech shower.' Another room was 'beautiful, comfortable and spacious'. The lounge has a large open fireplace, where logs are burned and ducks are smoked. Dining is in two interconnected rooms. The chef, Ludovic Lavaud, serves 'cooking of the highest order'. 'Canard foie gras was superb. Service is formal (lids lifted, ingredients recited, menus without prices for the women). Staff were impeccable: efficient and congenial.' Summer meals are served on a flowery terrace by the water, ducks in attendance ('as dusk fell, candles were lit, music played softly'). Breakfast is a copious buffet. The swimming pool 'is in a kind of secret garden, behind hedges'. The Lascaux caves are near. (*Jim Clarke, HR, and others*)

Open 1 Apr–1 Nov. Restaurant closed midday Mon–Thurs. **Rooms** 7 suites (in separate building 50 m), 10 double. 2 on ground floor. 13 with air conditioning. **Facilities** Lounge, restaurant; conference facilities. Large garden: terrace, unheated swimming pool, pond; river, fishing (trout). **Location** 25 km N of Sarlat. From N89: D704, D62. Parking. **Restriction** No smoking: restaurant, bedrooms. **Credit cards** All major cards accepted. **Terms** [2004] Room €83–€160, suite €152–€160. Breakfast €13. D,B&B €90–€160 per person. Set meals from €45.

COMPIÈGNE 60200 Oise — Map 5:A1

Hostellerie du Royal-lieu

9 rue de Senlis
Tel 03.44.20.10.24
Fax 03.44.86.82.27
Email hostellerieduroyallieu@bigfoot.com
Website www.hostellerie-du-royal-lieu.com

On the edge of this historic town stands owner/chef Angelo Bonechi's substantial half-timbered inn. It is on a dull main road, but bedrooms (in Louis XVI to Louis-Philippe style) face a quiet rear garden which has a dining terrace. Visitors this year had an enjoyable stay: 'The host was welcoming. Our first-floor room was nicely furnished. The *demi-pension* dinners were good, alternatives offered for any dish we didn't fancy.' The wine list has a good selection of half bottles. 'Traditional French breakfast with the bonus of fresh orange juice.' Visit the 17th/18th-century Palais National with Marie-Antoinette's lavish rooms. Nearby are the forests of Compiègne. (*EH and SW*)

Open All year, except 15 days Feb, 15 days Aug. Restaurant closed Sun evening/Mon midday. **Rooms** 15 double. 1 suitable for ♿. **Facilities** Bar, 2 dining rooms; conference room. No background music. Terrace. Garden. **Location** 3 km SW of town, on Senlis road. Private parking. **Credit cards** All major cards accepted. **Terms** [2004] Room €83–€105. Breakfast €9. D,B&B €107–€145 per room. Set meals €23–€33.50.

CONDRIEU 69420 Rhône — Map 6:A3

Hôtellerie Beau Rivage NEW
2 rue du Beau Rivage

Tel 04.74.56.82.82
Fax 04.74.59.59.36
Email infos@hotel-beaurivage.com
Website www.hotel-beaurivage.com

'Very smart' and 'beautifully situated' (on the Rhône, in a famous vineyard), the Humann-Donet family's hotel was omitted from the *Guide* last year because of major building works. Devotees returned in 2004 and report: 'Still highly recommended. Modernisation has lost little of the old fisherman's cottage atmosphere, but prices are higher.' Staff are 'very efficient and most welcoming', says another guest. Some annexe rooms may be 'a bit basic', but their bathrooms are new. 'Our very comfortable suite had a spacious bedroom and a conservatory with magnificent views of river and surrounding hills.' Everyone admires the food (*Michelin* star for Reynald Donet). It is served on a river-facing terrace or in the 'very attractive' dining room, 'run with calm efficiency'. 'One of the best meals we have eaten. French food at its finest.' 'Super turbot and lamb, many small courses, incredible puds. Good wine list (including Condrieu).' The 'excellent breakfast' has home-made jams. There's a lovely garden with statuary. Some rooms hear cargo trains night and day, but double glazing is efficient. Condrieu is 'not an attractive town'. (*IGC Farman, Dr and Mrs A Naylor, and others*)

Open All year. **Rooms** 12 suites, 16 double. 15 in annexe. Some no-smoking. 1 on ground floor. 11 with air conditioning. **Facilities** Lift. Salon, bar, restaurant, conservatory; 2 meeting rooms. No background music. Garden: terrace on river. **Location** On N86, 40 km SW of Lyon. A7 exit Condrieu (from N) or Chanas (from S). Garages, free closed parking. **Restriction** No smoking: restaurant, some bedrooms. **Credit cards** Diners, MasterCard, Visa. **Terms** Room €90–€135, suite €195–€240. Breakfast €15. Set lunch €36, dinner €52; full alc €70.

CONNELLES 27430 Eure — Map 2:D5

Le Moulin de Connelles
RD 19

Tel 02.32.59.53.33
Fax 02.32.59.21.83
Email moulindeconnelles@moulindeconnelles.com
Website www.moulindeconnelles.com

'A peaceful spot, stunningly beautiful,' say visitors this year to the Petiteau family's 20th-century 'Anglo-Norman' half-timbered mill house. With towers and turrets, it straddles an arm of the Seine near Les Andelys. A series of islands splits the river into channels, and the hotel forms a bridge: you can watch boats pass below as you dine. 'The river, with willows, is at its most beautiful here.' The bedrooms vary in size – some are a bit poky: one couple this year had a room where 'you needed to be a gymnast to get into the bed'; another thought the 'shabby chic had gone a little too far', though they liked the 'charming touches' such as complimentary liqueur, and the 'amazing circular sunken bath' in their tower suite. Others had a 'lovely, spacious room with balcony above the water'. 'Reception is welcoming, but often overstretched.' The half-board menu is 'good value and tasty'. In the lovely park are fine old trees and birds; there is a heated swimming pool on an island, and 'you can use the rowing boats free for an hour'. Some traffic noise, morning and early evening, from the nearby road. (*R and EU, AB, and others*)

Open All year. Closed Sun night/Mon Oct–Mar. **Rooms** 6 suites, 7 double. **Facilities** Reception, bar, restaurant; classical background music; function facilities; veranda (no-smoking). 3-hectare grounds: dining terrace, 2 heated swimming pools (1 covered), tennis; river, fishing, rowing. Unsuitable for ♿. **Location** Outside village. 13 km W of Les Andelys. Parking. **Credit cards** All major cards accepted. **Terms** Room €110–€150, suite €150–€230. Breakfast €13. D,B&B €101–€196 per person. Set meals €33; full alc €75. *V*

CONQUES 12320 Aveyron **Map 4:C5**

Hôtel Sainte-Foy
Rue Principale

Tel 05.65.69.84.03
Fax 05.65.72.81.04
Email hotelsaintefoy@hotelsaintefoy.fr
Website www.hotelsaintefoy.fr

On a pilgrim route, this 'magical village', spectacularly situated on a wooded hillside above a gorge, is one of the most romantic in south-west France. Opposite its famous Romanesque abbey, which houses jewelled relics dating back to the fifth century, is the Garcenot family's 17th-century timbered inn. 'A lovely place,' was one recent comment. Old stones, beams and rustic furniture 'add to the cosy feel'. One couple had a 'big, handsome' front room facing the abbey, but a 'superior room' was found 'very small'. The food is enjoyed. 'A delicious dinner, beautifully presented', but one visitor complained of 'lengthy waits at table'. Chef Laurent Dufour offers a series of menus, one based on truffles. There is a pretty garden dining area, and a more formal beamed dining room. 'Most of the staff are female.' (*SH, and others*)

Open Easter–1 Nov. **Rooms** 5 suites, 12 double. 4 air conditioned. **Facilities** Lift, ramp. Lounges, TV lounge, bar, restaurant (classical background music), breakfast room; conference facilities; patio; rooftop terrace. **Location** Central, opposite abbey church. 5 garages. **Restriction** No smoking: 1 lounge, some bedrooms. **Credit cards** All major cards accepted. **Terms** Room €110–€199, suite €185–€217. Breakfast €14. D,B&B €48–€50 added per person. Set meals €17–€51; full alc €49.

CORDES-SUR-CIEL 81170 Tarn — Map 4:D5

Le Grand Écuyer
Rue Voltaire

Tel 05.63.53.79.50
Fax 05.63.53.79.51
Email grand.ecuyer@thuries.fr
Website www.thuries.fr

Best approached from the south ('it could be a mirage,' says an inspector), this hilltop village was built in the 13th century as a defence against Simon de Montfort and his crusaders. Now, it is packed with boutiques and craft shops, and tourists in season. Through high stone walls, and up a narrow street, this Gothic former *résidence de chasse* of the counts of Toulouse opened as a chic hotel/restaurant in 1980. It has antiques, tapestries, chandeliers, baronial furnishings and mullioned windows. Owner Yves Thuriès (who has two other hotels in the village) is famous throughout France as a '*grand spécialiste de la pâtisserie-chocolaterie*'. With his son Damien, he wins a *Michelin* star, 14 *Gault Millau* points for, eg, croustillant de rouget, chutney de fruits au vinaigre de framboise; pigeonneau de Mont Royal, cuisse fondante au Banyuls. Desserts are 'spectacular'. 'The medieval town is amazing. The hotel is historic. Our room was fantastic. Food to die for,' says a recent visitor. The best bedrooms have a four-poster bed, antiques, large fireplace. 'Staff love to dramatically draw the curtains on to the stunning view, as they show guests to their room.' The bar is 'charming'. (*JH, and others*)

Open 18 Mar–mid-Oct. Restaurant closed Mon, midday except Sun. **Rooms** 1 suite, 12 double. Air conditioning. **Facilities** 2 salons, bar (background music), 3 dining rooms (1 no-smoking). Terrace. Unsuitable for ♿. **Location** Central. 25 km NW of Albi. Public car park at bottom of hill. **Credit cards** All major cards accepted. **Terms** [2004] Room €90, suite €230. Breakfast €13. Set meals €59–€73; alc €75–€80.

COUFFOULEUX 81800 Tarn — Map 4:D5

Le Manoir de la Maysou BUDGET

Tel 05.63.33.85.92
Fax 05.63.40.64.24
Email marianne.silver@wanadoo.fr
Website www.manoir-maysou.com

Endorsed in 2004: 18th-century former hunting lodge of wealthy Toulouse family, now small guest house run by owners Tony and Marianne Silver. NE of Toulouse off A68 (exit 6/7), on D13 from St-Sulpice. Attractive decor: original fireplaces, stained glass, pottery, pictures, etc. No-choice communal meals, with hosts, on terrace in good weather. 'Breakfast and dinner excellent. Lovely, shady grounds, super swimming pool.' 3 lounges, TV room, dining room. 3-hectare garden: table tennis, boules, *badminton, bicycle hire. Unsuitable for ♿. No pets. No credit cards. 1 suite, 5 bedrooms (some no-smoking). B&B double €80–€105. Set dinner (with house wine) €31 [2004].*

COURCELLES-SUR-VESLE 02220 Aisne — Map 5:A2

Château de Courcelles
8 rue du Château

Tel 03.23.74.13.53
Fax 03.23.74.06.41
Email reservation@chateau-de-courcelles.fr
Website www.chateau-de-courcelles.fr

In a 'lovely, tranquil' setting, this stately, white-fronted 17th-century *demeure* (Relais & Châteaux) stands in a *jardin à la française* in its own park, between Reims and Soissons. Managed by Franck Dulong, it was 'much enjoyed' by *Guide* correspondents again this year. An earlier guest, Jean Cocteau, designed the staircase banister. The public rooms have 'quaint old-fashioned charm'. Most bedrooms and bathrooms are spacious. All but two rooms look over the park: best ones have luxurious furnishings and a fine ceiling. The restaurant, candlelit and much beamed, has a *Michelin* star for, eg, pigeonneau rôti, jus aux arômes de cacao. The list of champagnes is long. 'A superb meal,' said one couple; but another wrote of disorganised service at dinner. Breakfast is now a buffet. There's a pleasant conservatory for summer meals and a heated swimming pool beside the terrace. (*Pat and Jeremy Temple, and others*)

Open All year. **Rooms** 3 suites, 15 double. **Facilities** Salon/bar, 2 dining rooms (1 no-smoking). No background music. 23-hectare park: garden: swimming pool (heated May–mid-Sept), tennis, jogging course, mountain bikes. **Location** 20 km E of Soissons, on N31 to Reims. Parking. **Credit cards** All major cards accepted. **Terms** [2004] Room €155–€305, suite €345–€395. Breakfast €18. D,B&B €165–€240 per person. Set meals €45–€80; alc €75–€95.

COUR-CHEVERNY 41700 Loir-et-Cher — Map 2:F5

Hôtel des Trois Marchands BUDGET
Place de l'Église

Tel 02.54.79.96.44
Fax 02.54.79.25.60
Email hotel-des-trois-marchands@tiscali.fr
Website www.hoteldes3marchands.com

On square of village SE of Blois, 800 m from château: old inn owned by Bricault family since 1865. 'Friendly, helpful staff; decent bedrooms; very good traditional food' (fish, game, foie gras). Public rooms 'richly decorated' in Louis XIII style: beams, panelling, antlers. Foyer/lounge; grill room, restaurant; 2 function rooms, banqueting room; shady terraces, garden. Car park. Closed Mon and 16 Feb–17 Mar. All major credit cards accepted. 24 bedrooms: €42–€55; D,B&B €46–€52 per person [2004].

The *Good Hotel Guide* has its own small Internet site: www.goodhotelguide.com. Anyone may visit it, but the *Guide*'s full Internet site can be accessed only by members of AOL. If you have access to AOL, put in the keyword GHG, or go to AOL's travel pages where the *Guide* is featured.

COURSEGOULES 06140 Alpes-Maritimes — Map 6:D5

Auberge de l'Escaou BUDGET
Place de l'Escaou

Tel 04.93.59.11.28
Fax 04.93.59.13.70
Email escaou@wanadoo.fr
Website www.hotel-escaou.com

Pleasant, modern Logis de France, run by owner Serge Granoux with friendly staff. In remote medieval perched village, 17 km NW of Vence. 'Wonderfully easy' for wheelchair guests (one room adapted). 'Magical, with excellent food (copious regional cooking, eg, rabbit stuffed with chicken liver); good view from dining terrace. Lift. TV room. Background music. Open 5 Jan–30 Nov. Amex, MasterCard, Visa accepted. 10 modern bedrooms: €40–€84. Breakfast €6. D,B&B €48–€58 per person [2004].

CRÉPON 14480 Calvados — Map 2:D3

Ferme de la Rançonnière BUDGET
Route d'Arromanches

Tel 02.31.22.21.73
Fax 02.31.22.98.39
Email ranconniere@wanadoo.fr
Website www.ranconniere.com

'We thought it excellent value, and a very French experience, so close to the UK,' says a report in 2004. Near Bayeux and Arromanches, this Logis de France is a 'large and sprawling' fortified medieval farm, still working, run by its owners, the Sileghem-Vereecke family, as a hotel/restaurant. Old farm implements are dotted around. Converted barns have large public rooms below and bedrooms above, some reached by twisting stairways. The rooms are said to vary from 'tiny' to 'palatial': best ones are in the *Ferme de Mathan*. 'Our compact room had a wonderful old carved wardrobe, colourful matching fabrics, a tiled bathroom.' Beside the huge flagged courtyard is the main dining room, rustic and timber-ceilinged. In the large restaurant, service is prompt, and chef Bruno Champion serves 'tasty and well-cooked' dishes, 'of the *terroir*', eg, soupe de poisson; suprême de volaille au parfums de Normandie. The breakfast room, with terrace, gets the morning sun: breakfast is 'a great buffet'. Groups are catered for (they have a separate dining room). (*Sally Holloway*)

Open All year. Restaurant closed 3–27 Jan. **Rooms** 35 double. 14 in annexe, 600 m. 1 on ground floor. **Facilities** Lift. Salon, breakfast room, restaurant (classical background music); conference room. Large grounds. Sandy beach 5 km. **Location** 7 km SE of Arromanches. Caen Péripherique Nord; exit 7. **Credit cards** Amex, MasterCard, Visa. **Terms** Room: single/double €45–€50, junior suite €140–€180. Breakfast €10. D,B&B €58–€112 per person. Set meals €15–€40; full alc €35. *V* (off-season)

> Don't trust out-of-date editions of the *Guide*. Hotels change hands, deteriorate or go out of business. Each year many hotels are dropped and many new ones are added.

CRILLON-LE-BRAVE 84410 Vaucluse — Map 6:D3

Hostellerie de Crillon le Brave
Place de l'Église

Tel 04.90.65.61.61
Fax 04.90.65.62.86
Email crillonbrave@relaischateaux.com
Website www.crillonlebrave.com

Below Mont Ventoux, in a tiny Provençal *village perché*, this smart hotel (Relais & Châteaux), owned by Peter Chittick and Craig Miller, is managed by David Candillon, formerly at *Claridge's*, London. Composed of seven 16th/17th-century houses up a 'twisty drive', it has sweeping views across orchards, vineyards and olive groves, and is 'most attractive', says a visitor this year. Another called it 'delightful in all respects, setting, service, facilities and food. Staff helpful but not pushy.' The 'inspired', if expensive, Provençal cooking of Philippe Monti (15 *Gault Millau* points) is served on a panoramic terrace with cypresses, or in a vaulted stone dining room. There is also a bistro, an Italianate garden, and a 'rather small' swimming pool. 'Charming' bedrooms have oak beams, local antiques. Some have a balcony facing the mountain. 'Our bathroom had two freestanding tubs and a champagne cooler in between. The bed's mattress was excellent.' Church bells ring between 7 am and 10 pm. (*Andrew Hillier, WC, and others*)

Open Mid-Mar–early Jan. Restaurant closed midday, Tues evening Nov–Apr. **Rooms** 8 suites, 24 double. In 7 buildings. 1 on ground floor. 15 air conditioned. **Facilities** Lounges, breakfast room, bar, restaurant, bistro. No background music. Garden: terraces, heated swimming pool; bicycles. **Location** 14 km NE of Carpentras, off D974 to Bédoin. Parking. **Credit cards** All major cards accepted. **Terms** Room €155–€430, suite €475–€560. Breakfast €17. Set dinner €74; full alc €40–€75. *V*

LE CROTOY 80550 Somme — Map 3:E2

Hotel-Restaurant Les Tourelles BUDGET
2–4 rue Pierre Guerlain

Tel 03.22.27.16.33
Fax 03.22.27.11.45
Email lestourelles@nhgroupe.com
Website www.lestourelles.com

Ten years old as a hotel this year, this *fin-de-siècle* villa is a former home of the *parfumier* Pierre Guerlain. 'Winningly eccentric', it has a '*pieds-dans-l'eau* position' on the north side of the Somme estuary (excellent birdwatching and 'very special, pearly light'). Its Belgian owners have created a 'chic Nordic feel'. French families crowd it in holiday time, creating 'cheerful mayhem'. 'Pure *Monsieur Hulot*; we loved it,' said one couple. 'Room 4 was superb: lovely views.' The dark red exterior is crowned by two blue pointed turrets; interiors are 'balneo-rustic': wooden floors, sculptures made from driftwood, wooden boats, the odd rococo antique and chandelier. 'Loads of books and scrapbooks.' Front bedrooms are the priciest. In the '*dortoir matelots*', adventurous children can sleep away from their parents. Chef Philippe Carré serves 'good-value, well-cooked' meals with the accent on seafood, but service can be pressed at times. The managers,

Dominique and Gilles Ferreira da Silva, organise entertainments (a Christmas party, a golf tournament, art exhibitions, etc). (*R and KF, and others*)

Open All year, except 4–25 Jan. **Rooms** 25 double, 2 single. 2 on ground floor. Dormitory for children (14 beds). 6-bedroom annexe planned for 2005. **Facilities** Ramp. Lounge, library/bar, TV room, games room, children's playroom; restaurant; background music; meeting room. Terrace. **Location** Central, opposite beach. **Credit cards** MasterCard, Visa. **Terms** Room: single €39–€44, double €57– €74.50. Breakfast €7.50. D,B&B €24 added per person. Set lunch €19.80, dinner €29; full alc €40. Min. 2-night bookings at weekends.

CUISERY 71290 Saône-et-Loire — Map 5:E3

Hostellerie Bressane NEW
56 route de Tournus

Tel 03.85.32.30.66
Fax 03.85.40.14.96
Email hostellerie.bressane@worldonline.fr
Website hostellerie-bressane.fr

'Well located, a few miles away from the busy A6', this restaurant-with-rooms (Logis de France) is recommended by a visitor in 2004 for 'peaceful nights and fabulous meals, all at reasonable prices'. The quietest bedrooms are in a 'bungalow' around 'a pleasant flowery garden with a pond'; others are on two storeys (no lift) in the old main building. Owner/chef Jean-Francis Beaufays, *Maître Cuisinier de France*, offers regional specialities in his 'light, modern, semi-conservatory dining room' or in the garden under a 200-year-old plane tree. 'We were served by a young and enthusiastic team led by his charming wife.' The village, near Tournus, is the 'French equivalent of Hay-on-Wye, full of bookshops'. The local website describes it as a '*village du livre*', and it holds a book fair on the first Sunday of August and September. It also has its own 'Eden Project', *le Centre Eden*, dedicated to the nature and environment of Burgundy. (*Mrs J Oldham*)

Open All year, except 22 Dec–3 Feb, midday on Wed and Thurs. **Rooms** 2 suites (air conditioned), 13 double. 6 (on ground floor) in annexe. **Facilities** Lounge, restaurant. Garden (meal service). **Location** 7 km E of Tournus. Parking. Garage. **Credit cards** MasterCard, Visa. **Terms** [2004] Room: double €60–€75, family €84–€105. Breakfast €9. D,B&B (min. 3 nights) €74–€78 per person. Set lunch €18, dinner €22–€60; alc €37–€60.

CURZAY-SUR-VONNE 86600 Vienne — Map 4:A4

Château de Curzay
Route Jazeneuil

Tel 05.49.36.17.00
Fax 05.49.53.57.69
Email info@chateau-curzay.com
Website www.chateau-curzay.com

*On banks of River Vonne: Cachart family's 18th-century château (Relais & Châteaux) in 120-hectare park (with swimming pool), 29 km SW of Poitiers. 'Good welcome, excellent food' (*Michelin *star, 14* Gault Millau *points for Eric Jan in* La Cédraie *restaurant). Huge, beautiful salon/bar; chapel; function facilities; terrace with old* *cedars. 'Magnificent, high-ceilinged bedroom' liked by recent honeymooners. Open 13 May–2 Nov, closed Mon/Tues off-season. All major credit cards accepted. 22 bedrooms: €150–€260. Breakfast €20. Set meals €40–€92 [2004].*

CUZANCE 46600 Lot — Map 4:C5

Manoir de Malagorse NEW

Tel/Fax 05.65.27.15.61
Email acongratel@manoir-de-malagorse.fr
Website www.manoir-de-malagorse.fr

In the rolling hills of the Lot, this 19th-century manor house, approached by a long and narrow country road, has been turned by Abel and Anna Congratel into a *chambres d'hôtes*. They are very welcoming, say the nominators; the house is 'comfortable and well appointed' and 'service is second to none'. He, the chef, is French (in winter they run a restaurant, *Le Ya-Ca*, in Courchevel); she is English and a qualified physiotherapist (aromatherapy and massages are available to guests). The emphasis is on food and wine: gastronomic weekends and 'laid-back' cookery courses are held. Dinner, booked in advance, might include foie gras poêlé aux figues; parmentier de confit de canard; petite tarte Tatin. An aperitif and wine are included. Meals are taken around a large table in the kitchen/dining room, or on a panoramic terrace. Breakfast has fresh orange juice, home-made jams and yogurts. The bedrooms, all different (you can study them on the website), have rustic furniture and wooden beams. Children are warmly welcomed (the Congratels are parents of young twins). (*Tricia and Dudley Robshaw, Sam Lewis*)

Open 1 May–30 Oct. Possibly Christmas/New Year. Dinner by arrangement. **Rooms** 6 double. 2 in annexe. All no-smoking. **Facilities** Lounge/library, dining room/kitchen; background music. 5-hectare garden: dining terrace, unheated swimming pool; free mountain bikes. Unsuitable for ♿. **Location** 12 km NE of Souillac. **Credit cards** MasterCard, Visa. **Terms** [2004] B&B €100–€125. Set dinner (with aperitif/wine) €36.

DIJON 21000 Côte-d'Or — Map 5:D3

Hôtel Wilson

Place Wilson
1 rue de Longvic

Tel 03.80.66.82.50
Fax 03.80.36.41.54
Email hotelwilson@wanadoo.fr
Website www.wilson-hotel.com

Owned by Mme Descaillot and Mme Etievant, this 17th-century post house has been nicely converted into a B&B. It stands on a pretty square a short walk from the historic centre. 'A very good place,' one couple wrote. 'We were greeted warmly. The decor was unappealing, but our room was clean and comfortable.' Most bedrooms are large, some have exposed beams. The best face a quiet courtyard with hanging flower baskets. Rooms that face the road are triple glazed, but recent visitors found this 'useless when you have to keep the windows open because of warm weather'. 'Breakfast, in a charming beamed room (with fresh flowers and a roaring fire), was fairly good: boiled egg if wished. The enclosed parking was a relief.' Next door is a *Michelin*-starred restaurant, *Stéphane Derbord*. (*C and GR, and others*)

Open All year. **Rooms** 27 double. Some on ground floor. **Facilities** Lift. Salon (drinks served). No background music. **Location** 800 m S of centre. Secure parking (€9). **Restriction** No smoking in some bedrooms. **Credit cards** Amex, MasterCard, Visa. **Terms** Room €70–€88. Breakfast €11.

DOMME 24250 Dordogne — Map 4:C4

Hôtel de l'Esplanade
Le Bourg

Tel 05.53.28.31.41
Fax 05.53.28.49.92
Email esplanade.domme@wanadoo.fr
Website www.chateauxhotels.com/esplanade

High above the Dordogne, in this picturesque medieval village (full of trippers by day, quieter at night), the Gillard family's 'upmarket' hotel has spectacular views. 'Comfortable, pleasant, with fine wood panelling,' says one report. In the dining room, 'resplendent in blue and yellow', or on the flowery terrace overlooking the valley below, chef Pascal Bouland serves 'superb dinners' (14 *Gault Millau* points), eg, duo de langoustines et de foie gras poêlé; pintade farcie; pyramide de chocolat, compote d'orange tiède. 'Service was attentive, with painstaking explanation of dishes where needed.' The breakfast/bar area overlooks the village's small terrace-like park. The salon is elegant, with parquet flooring and antiques. 'Our room was comfortable, but furnishings were a bit frayed. Its French doors opened on to a small balcony.' Some bedrooms are in old houses in the village. (*Dr Alec Frank, Peter Crichton, and others*)

Open 1 Mar–12 Nov. Restaurant closed Mon and Wed midday, also Mon night Mar–May, Oct. **Rooms** 20 double. 5 in 3 village houses, 50 m. 15 air conditioned. **Facilities** Salon, bar, restaurant (classical background music). Terraces, garden. Unsuitable for ♿. **Location** Centre of village. 12 km S of Sarlat. Public parking nearby. **Credit cards** All major cards accepted. **Terms** Room: single €72–€77, double €77–€128. Breakfast €11. D,B&B €91–€116 per person. Set meals €30–€80; alc €55.

DUCEY 50220 Manche — Map 2:E3

Auberge de la Sélune
2 rue St-Germain

Tel 02.33.48.53.62
Fax 02.33.48.90.30
Email info@selune.com
Website www.selune.com

In a beautiful setting on the Sélune (one of the last salmon rivers in France), where the N176 crosses an old bridge, this unsophisticated Logis de France is run by its owners, Jean-Pierre and Josette Girres. 'Madame is warmly welcoming and much in evidence,' says a visitor this year. 'Monsieur smiled with genuine delight when we praised his superb cuisine.' The blue-and-white restaurant, which faces the small garden and river, is locally popular (seasonal dishes include fish soup;

stuffed saddle of young rabbit with a cider-vinegar sauce). There is a terrace for drinks and summer meals. Some bedrooms are spacious; some have garden views; three are in a pavilion. 'Our room was tiny, but the bathroom was a good size, and we heard no noise from the road.' 'Our bath was four feet long; we washed using the shower attachment.' 'Good value for money.' Breakfast is 'fairly basic'. Opposite is the small, flowery municipal garden. (*Peter Stattersfield, Bob and Kate Flaherty, R and JM*)

Open All year, except early Nov–mid-Dec, end Jan–mid-Feb, Mon Oct–Mar. **Rooms** 20 double. 3, on ground floor, in pavilion. **Facilities** Salon, bar, restaurant; 2 meeting rooms. No background music. Garden: dining terrace. Unsuitable for ♿. **Location** On N176, 11 km SE of Avranches. Small car park. **Credit cards** All major cards accepted. **Terms** [2004] Room: double €52–€55. Breakfast €7.50. D,B&B (min. 2 nights) €55–€56.50 per person. Set meals €15–€36.

DURAS 47120 Lot-et-Garonne — Map 4:C4

Hostellerie des Ducs BUDGET
Boulevard Jean Brisseau

Tel 05.53.83.74.58
Fax 05.53.83.75.03
Email hostellerie.des.ducs@wanadoo.fr
Website www.hostellerieducs-duras.com

In a 'delightful' small wine-growing town between the rivers Garonne and Dordogne, the Blanchet family's restaurant-with-rooms has a terrace facing Duras's 14th-century fortress which looks across a vast plain. It stands in a quiet garden with a good pool. In the dining room (with 18th-century decor), *Gault Millau* awards 14 points for M. Blanchet's cooking, eg, terrine d'homard; escalope de foie gras aux pêches. Service is 'pleasant, smiling', if sometimes 'slow'. Mixed views of the rooms: 'Ours, on the ground floor in the annexe, had plenty of space, easy wheelchair access, well-adapted shower and bathroom.' But another couple thought their small room 'nothing special (bathroom with plastic sliding door)'. Marguerite Duras, *née* Donnadieu, chose her *nom-de-plume* because her parents once lived near here. Also near is the Lac de Castelgaillard with water sports, horse riding, etc. (*Alec Frank, and others*)

Open All year. Restaurant closed Sat midday; also Sun night/Mon Oct–June, Mon midday July–Sept. **Rooms** 13 double, 2 single. 5 air conditioned. 1 suitable for ♿. **Facilities** Lounge, TV room, restaurant (classical background music); billiard room; terrace (meal service). Garden: unheated swimming pool. Lake: swimming, fishing, water sports 7 km. **Location** By château. 23 km N of Marmande. Locked car park. **Credit cards** All major cards accepted. **Terms** Room: single €43.50, double €54.50–€84. Breakfast €8.50. D,B&B €59–€73 per person. Set meals €15–€56; full alc €75.

DURFORT-LACAPELETTE 82390 Tarn-et-Garonne Map 4:D4

Aube Nouvelle NEW/BUDGET

Tel 05.63.04.50.33
Fax 05.63.04.57.55
Email aubenouvelle@chez.com
Website www.chez.com/aubenouvelle

On road to Compostela, with friendly Belgian owners, Marc and Claudine de Smet-Bruneel: former maison de maître, *now two-star hotel/restaurant. Outside nondescript village amid orchards and vines in Quercy countryside, 10 km N of Moissac. 'Very quiet; good dinner' (some Belgian dishes; Belgian beers; local wines). Alfresco meals in summer. Hall, 2 dining rooms, terrace, garden. Closed 3 weeks Dec/ Jan, Sat midday. MasterCard, Visa accepted. 7 simple bedrooms (some family), some with beamed ceiling. B&B €39–€55 [2004].*

ÉPERNAY-SOUS-GEVREY 21220 Côte d'Or Map 5:D3

La Vieille Auberge NEW/BUDGET
2 place des Tilleuls

Tel 03.80.36.61.76
Fax 03.80.36.64.68
Email bacchus.neil@wanadoo.fr
Website http://hote.bourgogne.free.fr

Old farmhouse, later an inn, renovated in 2000 as B&B by Scottish owner/managers, Neil and Pam Aitken, 'welcoming, helpful'. In quiet village NE of Nuits-St-Georges by D109. 'As good as some of the posh hotels I've stayed at,' says nominator in 2004 after 4th visit. Reservations made at local restaurants. Breakfast room, patio, garden: children's swings, slides. No credit cards. 5 bedrooms (some family, some face village green). B&B: single from €45, double from €60, triple from €75 [2004]. Gîte *also available.*

ÉTOGES 51270 Marne Map 5:A2

Château d'Étoges
4 rue Richebourg

Tel 03.26.59.30.08
Fax 03.26.59.35.57
Email contact@etoges.com
Website www.etoges.com

A 'ravishing building', a 17th-century château, with pepperpot tower, moat with swans, 'hens and cockerels strutting in the grounds'. This 'imposing place with imposing prices' (a comment in 2004) is a historic monument: the French kings sometimes stayed here on their way east. It has been turned into a 'really wonderful hotel' by Filliette Neuville, whose family has a champagne estate in the village. 'We lugged our suitcase up a magnificent marble staircase past diverse statues; our large room had marble fireplace, wall paintings, wood panelling, a half-tester bed. Like staying in a National Trust house, but it felt lived in. On a second visit we had a tower room with gorgeous decor and views in two directions.' Some 'attic-style' rooms are small (some bathrooms too), and some rooms can hear noise from the ones above. Staff 'are helpful'. There is a new chef this year: 'The food was delicious, light, not too rich, but service can be slow.' However, one couple found the breakfast disappointing. A new restaurant is planned for 2005. (*Margaret Cooper, Matthew Hamlyn, Felicity M Peto, JD Toff, and others*)

Open 12 Feb–22 Jan. Restaurant closed midday, except Sat, Sun. **Rooms** 1 suite, 19 double. **Facilities** Lounge, bar, 2 dining rooms (1 no-smoking; background music); conference room. 18-hectare grounds: children's playground. Unsuitable for ♿. **Location** Outside village, SE of Montmort. 25 km S of Épernay. Parking. **Credit cards** All major cards accepted. **Terms** [2004] Room €80–€260, suite €160–€260. Breakfast €12. D,B&B €82–€172 per person. Set meals €30–€65; alc €50. *V*

EUGÉNIE-LES-BAINS 40320 Landes — Map 4:D3

Les Prés d'Eugénie

Tel 05.58.05.06.07
Fax 05.58.51.10.10
Email guerard@relaischateaux.com
Website www.michelguerard.com

In this spa town north of Pau, Michel and Christine Guérard's 'exquisite, tiny village' stands in a park full of flowers and statues. It includes a spa treating obesity and rheumatism, a gym, shops, an inn, an *auberge*, and M. Guérard's famous hotel/restaurant (Relais & Châteaux). *Curistes* eat his *cuisine minceur*, but other visitors feast on the much-admired *cuisine gourmande* (three *Michelin* stars, 18 *Gault Millau* points). The restaurant, in four rooms, has cane chairs, chandeliers, pale colours, oil paintings. Bedrooms have lots of white wood, 'admirable bathroom; three perfect red roses in vases – more came on the breakfast trays, loaded with delicious things'. The suites are in an 18th-century nunnery, the *Couvent des Herbes*. Drinks are taken on a patio with illuminated fountains and statues. In the *auberge, La Ferme aux Grives,* the restaurant (15 *Gault Millau* points) is like a medieval banqueting hall, roasts turning on spits. The 'cordial' Guérards are often around; their manager is Olivier Pollard.

Open All year, except 4 Jan–26 Mar, 29 Nov–17 Dec. Gourmet restaurant closed Mon night, midday except Sat, Sun, holidays. **Rooms** 10 suites, 30 double. 8 in *Couvent*. Air conditioning. **Facilities** Lift. 2 salons, gallery, billiard room, bar, 2 restaurants; 3 function rooms; beauty salon, thermal baths, sauna. Garden: terrace, heated swimming pool, tennis. **Location** Off D944, near St-Sever-Aubagnan, 53 km N of Pau. **Credit cards** All major cards accepted. **Terms** [2004] Room €265–€375, suite €400–€500. Breakfast €28. Set meals €40–€175; alc €115–€160.

LES EYZIES-DE-TAYAC 24620 Dordogne — Map 4:C4

Hôtel du Centenaire

Rocher de la Penne

Tel 05.53.06.68.68
Fax 05.53.06.92.41
Email hotel.centenaire@wanadoo.fr
Website www.hotelducentenaire.com

On the edge of this village, famous for the discovery of the cave of Cro-Magnon man nearby, and very touristy in summer, this 'first-rate' hotel (Relais & Châteaux) stands by the winding River Vézère.

Though on the main road, it is quiet, protected by a high stone wall and backed by limestone cliffs. It is owned by Alain and Geneviève Scholly with chef Roland Mazère whose *cuisine périgourdine* (two *Michelin* stars, 18 *Gault Millau* points) includes langoustines rôties à la broche, fleurs de courgettes du jardin. Decor is modern and sleek. In the small, shady garden is an 'excellent' swimming pool. 'Rooms good value, service excellent,' is a recent comment. Many bedrooms are large, with modern bathroom. Some have a balcony facing hills. Breakfast ('a fine buffet') is in a glass-ceilinged atrium. Loungers and parasols stand on the lawn. (*Marshall S Harris*)

Open Early Apr–early Nov. Restaurant closed midday, except Thurs, Sat, Sun and holidays. **Rooms** 5 suites, 14 double. Air conditioning. **Facilities** Salon, bar, restaurant; dining terrace; fitness room. Garden: heated swimming pool. Unsuitable for ♿. **Location** Edge of village. 20 km NW of Sarlat. Parking. **Restriction** No dogs. **Credit cards** All major cards accepted. **Terms** [2004] Room €138–€230, suite €260–€381. Breakfast €20. D,B&B €145–€230 per person. Set meals €62–€120; full alc €100. *V*

LE FEL 12140 Aveyron — Map 4:C5

Auberge du Fel NEW/BUDGET

Tel 05.65.44.52.30
Fax 05.65.48.64.96
Email info@auberge-du-fel.com
Website www.auberge-du-fel.com

This 'immaculate, tiny village, like a film set' stands high on an escarpment above the valleys of the Lot and the Truyère, north of Rodez. It has a 360-degree panorama, and its pretty cottages, most now holiday homes, have retained their roofs tiled with authentic grey *lauzes*. Here, this rural inn (Logis de France), fronted by a pergola, is run 'with efficiency' by its owner, Elizabeth Albespy, say the readers who discovered it in 2004. 'It has largely been refurbished in chic, modern style. Four rooms are in the original part of the building, up creaky stairs, the rest are newer, and most have a balcony, high above the chestnut trees. There are amazing views from the dining room, and several areas for outside eating. Madame is always to be seen in her chef's apron, often at work in her gleaming kitchen.' She promises 'good family cooking based on traditional recipes'. 'Her menus are interesting, there is one for vegetarians; another, *du terroir*, features the pig in most courses (oreille du cochon avec pounti; mignon de porc; truite farcie aux lardoons, etc)'. Breakfast is 'traditional and copious'. 'The area is unspoilt, there is plenty of good walking from the door, and chairs and loungers for the less active can be found in the large, wild grounds.' A picnic lunch can be provided for hikers, a '*stage de yoga*' is offered in summer, and in autumn there is a *weekend gastronomique autour des vendanges*. (*Janet and Dennis Allom*)

Open 3 Apr–3 Nov. Restaurant closed midday except Sat, Sun and holidays. **Rooms** 10. 1 suitable for ♿. **Facilities** Breakfast room, restaurant, veranda. Terrace. Large garden. Fishing, walking, etc, nearby. **Location** 10 km W of Entraygues-sur-Truyère, 46 km N of Rodez. **Credit cards** MasterCard, Visa. **Terms** [2004] Double room €52–€58. Breakfast €6.50. D,B&B (min. 3 nights) €48–€53 per person.

FIGEAC 46100 Lot — Map 4:C5

Château du Viguier du Roy
52 rue Droite
Tel 05.65.50.05.05
Fax 05.65.50.06.06
Email hotel@chateau-viguier-figeac.com
Website www.chateau-viguier-figeac.com

'Like a film set', this fascinating ensemble of buildings, from the 12th, 14th and 18th centuries, stands amid a maze of alleys in a beautifully preserved town on the River Célé. It has a colonnaded exterior, medieval keep, vaulted chapel, and a tiny swimming pool behind the lovely cloister. It has been 'intelligently restored' by the 'charming' owner/manager, Anne Secordel-Martin. The 'splendid dinner', provided by chef Daniel Authié, is served 'flamboyantly, but without pretension', in a smallish beamed room with a huge carved stone fireplace, or in the tiny courtyard. Bedrooms vary in size; some are huge, with period furniture. 'Our interconnecting rooms, facing the main street, were a delight.' 'Ours, high up, was light, with a long balcony, views to the cathedral, and hills across the river. Luxurious four-poster bed.' Bathrooms are modern. No noise, save church bells. Breakfast, in a vaulted room, has plenty of choice. The Tudor-style garden has roses, herbs and box hedging.

Open 8 Apr–30 Oct. **Rooms** 2 suites, 18 double, 1 single. 13 no-smoking. Some on ground floor. Air conditioning. **Facilities** Lift. Lounges, library, bar, 3 dining rooms (1 no-smoking); chapel; spa bath. Background music. Garden: heated swimming pool. Parking, garage. Unsuitable for ♿. **Location** Central. Figeac is 69 km E of Cahors. Garage. **Restriction** No pets. **Credit cards** All major cards accepted. **Terms** Room €155–€235, suite €275–€450. Breakfast €17–€20. Set meals €28–€68; full alc €39.50–€68.

FLAGY 77940 Seine-et-Marne — Map 5:B1

Hostellerie du Moulin
2 rue du Moulin
Tel 01.60.96.67.89
Fax 01.60.96.69.51

Idyllically located, in pretty village 23 km SE of Fontainebleu: Claude Scheidecker's 13th-century mill house, charmingly converted into rustic restaurant-with-rooms. 'Very nice staff. Good food.' Pleasant lounge with old mill machinery, bar, dining room; summer meals by stream in garden. Open 21 Jan–17 Sept, 29 Sept–17 Dec. 10 bedrooms ('old-fashioned but comfortable', some large, some up spiral staircase): €54–€110. Simple breakfast: €11. Set meals €15–€18.50 [2004].

LA FLOTTE 17630 Charente-Maritime — Map 4:A3

Le Richelieu
44 avenue de la Plage
Île de Ré
Tel 05.46.09.60.70
Fax 05.46.09.50.59
Email info@hotel-le-richelieu.com
Website www.hotel-le-richelieu.com

Connected to the mainland at La Rochelle, by a three-kilometre toll bridge, the Île de Ré has sandy beaches, oyster beds and, out of season, 'an air of tranquillity'. On its north side, the Gendre family's 'very fine', modern, white hotel (Relais & Châteaux) was thought 'expensive, but worth every penny' by recent visitors. 'Our bedroom, beautifully decorated, with ships, etc, painted direct on whitewashed walls, had a big balcony with sea views, and a splendid bathroom.' Some rooms are in 'rather motel-like' bungalows, fronted by table, chairs and loungers. 'Luxurious yet relaxing' public areas include a small library. There is some 'splendid' stained glass, notably a depiction of Richelieu above the lovely staircase. 'Half-board guests are herded into one part of the panoramic dining room, but service was attentive and the atmosphere unstuffy.' 'A wonderful dinner': *Michelin* star, 14 *Gault Millau* points, for Dominique Bourgeois (eg, homard grillé au beurre de corail; trilogie de St-Jacques). Local wines are on the list. 'Breakfast the best of our trip.' The gardens are lovely; the swimming pool is large, with loungers. There is a thalassotherapy centre with various treatments. The beach is across the road: tides go far out, and bathing can be shallow. (*R and EU, and others*)

Open 10 Feb–5 Jan. **Rooms** 6 suites, 34 double. All air conditioned. Some on ground floor. 30 in 3 annexes. **Facilities** Lounge, bar, restaurant (pianist sometimes), breakfast room; meeting room; thalassotherapy centre. Garden: heated swimming pool, tennis. Beach 20 m. **Location** NE coast of island. 16 km NW of La Rochelle. Parking. **Credit cards** Amex, MasterCard, Visa. **Terms** [2004] Room €125, suite €370. Breakfast €20. D,B&B €125–€325 per person. Set meals €50–€65; full alc €100–€120.

FONTANGES 15140 Cantal — Map 4:C5

Auberge de l'Aspre NEW/BUDGET
Le Bourg

Tel 04.71.40.75.76
Fax 04.71.40.75.27
Email auberge.aspre@worldonline.fr
Website www.auberge-aspre.com

In a 'delightful position' on the edge of a tiny, historical village in the valley of the Aspre near Salers in the Cantal, this simple *auberge* is efficiently run by its owners, Brigitte and Christophe Landau, say the nominators in 2004. 'He is the talented chef [*Michelin Bib Gourmand*], she is the friendly, always smiling *patronne*.' 'The converted farmhouse has only eight bedrooms: each has a smart bathroom in the roof space above it; each has a pastoral view.' There is a small salon with guidebooks and maps, and the peaceful garden has a good-sized swimming pool. The seasonal menus use local pork and veal; foie gras is home made. 'The menus had not much variety: lots of meat dishes, few salads, and the food was hearty. Barbary duck en civet was delicious but rich. Staff are friendly. Service is very good. Excellent value.' (*Janet and Dennis Allom*)

Open 1 Feb–15 Nov. Closed Sun night/Mon and Wed night off-season. **Rooms** 1 family, 7 double. **Facilities** Salon, dining room. Garden: swimming pool. Tennis, riding nearby. **Location** 5 km S of Salers by D35, 43 km W of Murat. **Credit cards** MasterCard, Visa. **Terms** [2004] Room €48–€79. Breakfast €8. D,B&B (min. 3 nights) €52 per person. Set meals €16–€32.

FONTJONCOUSE 11360 Aude — Map 4:E5

Auberge du Vieux Puits

Tel 04.68.44.07.37
Fax 04.68.44.08.31
Email aubergeduvieuxpuits@wanadoo.fr

Michelin awards two stars, *Gault Millau* 18 points (one more this year) to the brilliant cooking of the 'warmly welcoming' owner/chef Gilles Goujon in the stylish restaurant-with-rooms which he runs with his wife, Marie-Christine. Set in this remote hamlet ('a cluster of stone houses') south-west of Narbonne, it is reached by a 'long but charming drive on small roads in parts winding and potholed' through the Corbières vineyards. The six-course set meal might include risotto aux asperges, brochette de langoustine; dos de sanglier en croûte de pomme de terre croustillante. 'Breakfast superb, too.' The bedrooms (six are new this year) are also liked: 'They are bo-bo (bohemian bourgeois), and very enjoyable: pink-washed walls, pictures of flowers, super bed, modern bathroom, high-tech lighting. One switch opens the blinds, another brings an outsize TV up from a chest.' Some rooms have a terrace looking over the swimming pool. Cathar castles and the Canal du Midi are nearby. M. Goujon also runs cookery courses. (*FS*)

Open Mar–Jan. Closed 25 Dec evening, Mon midday all year; Sun night/Mon/Tues 15 Sept–15 June. **Rooms** 2 suites, 12 double. 6 in separate building. Some suitable for ♿. Air conditioning. **Facilities** Ramps. Salon, restaurant; classical background music. Garden: terraces; heated swimming pool. **Location** 30 km SW of Narbonne (directions on website). Parking. **Credit cards** All major cards accepted. **Terms** [2004] Room €80–€170, suite €170–€230. Breakfast €15. D,B&B €150–€260 per person. Set meals €50–€100.

FONT-ROMEU 66120 Pyrénées-Orientales — Map 4:E5

Le Grand Tétras

14 avenue Emmanuel Brousse

Tel 04.68.30.01.20
Fax 04.68.30.35.67
Email hotelgrandtetras@wanadoo.fr
Website www.hotelgrandtetras.free.fr

*Near cable car, in centre of large Pyrenean ski resort in the Cerdagne, W of Perpignan, on D618: M. and Mme Sarda's three-star hotel: 'Real French atmosphere; remarkable value; warmth and comfort. Attractive lounge with log fire. Good food in smart restaurant [*La Potinière*, separately managed]. Everything worked.' Some south-facing rooms have panoramic views. Lift. Lounge with open fire, bar, conference room. Indoor swimming pool, sauna; billiards. Terrace. 36 bedrooms (including 4 suites), some with balcony or loggia: €53–€116. Breakfast €7 [2004].*

> Always let a hotel know if you have to cancel a booking, whether you have paid a deposit or not. Hotels sustain huge losses because of 'no-shows'.

FONTVIEILLE 13990 Bouches-du-Rhône Map 6:D2

Auberge La Régalido
Rue Frédéric Mistral

Tel 04.90.54.60.22
Fax 04.90.54.64.29
Email la-regalido@wanadoo.fr
Website www.laregalido.com

Down a quiet side street, this former oil mill is in a small town east of Arles, made famous by the writer Alphonse Daudet. Outwardly unassuming, it is luxurious inside. Public rooms are 'chic rustic'; bedroom decor varies from period to 'starkly modern'; some rooms have a beamed ceiling. 'Our large room had a rather shut-in terrace.' The Provençal cooking of owner/chef Jean-Pierre Michel and Philippe Huot earns a *Michelin* star, 13 *Gault Millau* points ('*très beaux légumes*'). M. Michel is much in evidence. 'Dinner and breakfast were most enjoyable,' say recent visitors. 'Reception is friendly.' Breakfast is 'varied and good'. Meals are served in an elegant vaulted dining room or on the 'charming' terrace facing the 'exuberant' garden. Lots of steps, and the hotel can be difficult to find. There are views of the Alpilles, and Daudet's windmill (or rather, one of his windmills) is on a hill nearby.

Open 28 Feb–4 Jan. Restaurant closed Sat midday and Mon. **Rooms** 15 double. 1 on ground floor. Air conditioning. **Facilities** 2 small salons, bar, restaurant. No background music. Garden: terrace (meals served). Unsuitable for ♿. **Location** 10 km NE of Arles. Down one-way street; entrance not easily visible. Parking. **Credit cards** All major cards accepted. **Terms** [2004] Room €97–€280. Breakfast €8–€16. D,B&B €60 added per person.

Hostellerie Saint-Victor NEW
Chemin des Fourques

Tel 04.90.54.66.00
Fax 04.90.54.67.88
Email aps@hotel-saint-victor.com
Website www.hotel-saint-victor.com

'Perfectly located for touring Provence': on a hill on the edge of this picturesque town near Arles, this spacious *mas* was discovered this year by a regular *Guide* correspondent. It has wide views (Alpilles, Camargue, Les Baux), and a large swimming pool in its 'well-landscaped' garden. The owners, Philippe and Agnes Sourisseau, who 'run it almost single-handed', have two small children, a dog, two cats and two donkeys. 'They do an exceptional job. Philippe carried our luggage up to the room (no lift). It was immaculate, lighting was adequate, and the bathroom had the best tub I have ever used. Breakfast [in the salon, or by the pool in summer] had an ample buffet, including pastries, yogurt, fresh orange juice, and eggs of our choice. They gave us restaurant recommendations. At the *Cuisine au Planet* we had the best meal of our trip.' (*Claire Lavery*)

Open All year. **Rooms** 13 double. Some with private terrace. Air conditioning. **Facilities** Salon with TV; billiards. Terraces: swimming pool, garden. **Location** 1 km SW of centre. 10 km NE of Arles. Parking. **Credit cards** All major cards accepted. **Terms** [2004] Room €80–€170. Breakfast €11.

FORCALQUIER 04300 Alpes-de-Haute-Provence Map 6:D4

Auberge Charembeau
Route de Niozelles (N100)

Tel 04.92.70.91.70
Fax 04.92.70.91.83
Email contact@charembeau.com
Website www.charembeau.com

Tastefully converted by its owners Sandra and André Berger, this group of 18th-century stone farm buildings is now an inexpensive B&B hotel. It stands in a large park of woods and rolling fields, amid wonderful Provençal scenery. Some bedrooms have a large private terrace, others a balcony; the rooms in the *Résidence* (let weekly) have a kitchenette. 'Our large, uncluttered room was attractive, high-ceilinged; lots of storage space, good plumbing.' 'Excellent breakfasts.' No restaurant, but advice is given about local eating places. In fine weather, you can picnic under walnut trees on the wide lawn, near the big swimming pool. Forcalquier, on a hillside nearby, was the medieval capital of Upper Provence. Its 13th-century Franciscan monastery has a museum of early religious art.

Open 15 Feb–15 Nov. **Rooms** 2 suites, 19 double, 3 single. 10, with kitchenette, in annexe. 1 suitable for ♿. **Facilities** Breakfast room. 2-hectare grounds: terrace, heated swimming pool, tennis, table tennis, badminton. **Location** 4 km E of town (towards Niozelles) by N100 and private road. 80 km NE of Aix-en-Provence. **Credit cards** Amex, MasterCard, Visa. **Terms** Room €50–€88, suite €86–€115. Breakfast €8.

FORGES-LES-EAUX 76440 Seine-Maritime Map 2:D5

Auberge du Beau Lieu
2 route du Montadet
Le Fossé (D915)

Tel 02.35.90.50.36
Fax 02.35.90.35.98
Email aubeaulieu@aol.com
Website www.auberge-du-beau-lieu.com

Returning to this restaurant with only three rooms (in 'simple country style'), visitors this year praised 'the superb food' and 'charming wee garden' (where breakfast, with fresh orange juice, is served on fine days). Owner/chef Patrick Ramelet and his wife, Marie-France, have run this former cider press for over 20 years in this small spa town north-east of Rouen (its casino is popular with Parisians). *Gault Millau* awards 14 points for Norman dishes (eg, turbot au cidre), served in the restaurant with its big stone fireplace, log fire and candlelight. The wine cellar is admired, too. In 2005 a bypass will divert much of the traffic from the road in front. The bedrooms are in a cottage facing the garden. The rooms are attractive, with coloured floor tiles, modern bathroom. The forest is across the road. (*B and KF*)

Open 11 Feb–13 Jan, except 1 May. **Rooms** 3. On ground floor. **Facilities** Salon, restaurant (background music). Garden: patio. Unsuitable for ♿. **Location** 2 km SE of town, on D915. 46 km NE of Rouen. **Credit cards** All major cards accepted. **Terms** Room €45–€55. Breakfast €6–€10. Set meals €17.75–€53.50; full alc €66.

FOX-AMPHOUX 83670 Var — Map 6:E4

Auberge du Vieux Fox — *Tel* 04.94.80.71.69
Place de l'Église — *Fax* 04.94.80.78.38

On a wooded bluff in a tiny (deserted, but for weekenders) hill village of the upper Var, Nicole and Rudolf Staudinger's small Logis de France, once the priory of a 12th-century church, has beamed ceilings and Provençal decor. From its tree-shaded terrace (where summer meals are served), you can look across open countryside to Mont Ste-Victoire, 'magical in the evening light'. 'There was an atmosphere of bonhomie. Our host most convivial, his wife very pleasant,' say recent visitors. 'Our room at the top had a huge bed, nice modern bathroom and the same splendid views. The food was good, with copious helpings.' The dining room has red tablecloths, blue-and-white china ornaments and an open fire. There is a new chef, Thierry Allard, this year. His 'market menu' includes anchoïade with fresh vegetables; red mullet with black olives in pastry. (*DJH*)

Open All year. Restaurant closed Thurs Oct–Mar. **Rooms** 8 double. **Facilities** Salon, restaurant (no-smoking); classical background music. 2 terraces; outdoor dining. Unsuitable for ♿. **Location** By church in village. 35 km W of Draguignan, 35 km N of Brignoles. Parking in square. **Credit cards** Amex, MasterCard, Visa. **Terms** Room €65–€100. Breakfast €8. Set meals €32.

FUTEAU 55120 Meuse — Map 5:A4

À L'Orée du Bois — *Tel* 03.29.88.28.41
Courupt — *Fax* 03.29.88.24.52
Email oreedubois@free.fr

On a hillside in the Argonne forest (deer are sometimes seen), owner/chef Paul Aguesse and his wife, Roselyne, 'an excellent hostess', run this smart restaurant-with-rooms (Logis de France; Relais du Silence). 'We sat with drinks under apple trees, very peaceful,' say visitors this year. Other comments: 'A fabulously quiet, rural setting.' 'Fantastic food.' 'Excellent breakfast.' In the dining room, 'sophisticated yet rustic', with a huge fireplace, you can watch the sun setting over hills while you sample the modern cooking (14 *Gault Millau* points for, eg, médaillons de lotte au coulis de crustacés). Service is 'cheerful and efficient'. 'I fondly remember the cheese trolley.' But one guest thought his lobster main course 'tough and tasteless'. *Gault Millau* writes of '*chambres adorables*', but there are mixed views from correspondents: 'Awkward design, odd choice of furnishings.' 'Rather dark.' 'A cool room in a Swiss-chalet-type building.' 'We were very satisfied with our "*charme*" room with spa bath.' 'Nice breakfast: very good orange juice, croissants, etc, and *le patron* will do eggs if asked.' (*Brenda and Owen Gape, Matthew Hamlyn, Mr and Mrs RH Down, JH, and others*)

Open Jan–Nov. Closed Mon midday and Tues midday in season. **Rooms** 1 suite, 13 double. 8 in annexe. Some no-smoking. Some on ground floor. **Facilities** Ramp. 2 lounges, 2 dining rooms (classical background music); 2 meeting rooms. Garden: sauna. **Location** 1 km S of Futeau. Turn S off N3 at

Les Islettes. 80 km SE of Reims. Car park. **Credit cards** MasterCard, Visa. **Terms** Room €70–€130. Breakfast €11–€12. Set meals €20–€65; full alc €70–€75.

LA GARDE-ADHÉMAR 26700 Drôme — Map 6:C3

Le Logis de l'Escalin NEW

Tel 04.75.04.41.32
Fax 04.75.04.40.05
Email info@lescalin.com
Website www.lescalin.com

'A lovely discovery', by a regular *Guide* correspondent in 2004. Just outside this medieval *village perché* north of Orange, above the Rhône, it is only a kilometre from the A7, 'but it could be a world away'. The owners, Serge and Nadège Fricaud, have recently refurbished the old *bastide* in 'hand-painted Provençal' style. 'Dinner was a relaxed three-hour affair, many courses, professionally served, owner/chef much in evidence; Provençal dishes like tomato and olive pissaladière, lavender honey ice cream on the €30 menu; huge selection of cheeses. Breakfast perfect, not a packet to be seen, bowls of butter, jam and honey, hot croissants and a pile of fruit. The shower was stunning but we could not make it work in spite of written instructions. Plenty of safe parking.' There is a large terrace, shaded by plane trees, where summer meals are served. (*Rosemary Winder*)

Open All year, except 3–10 Jan, 13–22 Apr, 18–28 Oct. Closed Sun night/ Mon/Tues midday. **Rooms** 15. **Facilities** 4 dining rooms; conference room. Garden: terrace, swimming pool. **Location** 1 km N of village, E of A7, off D458. 24 km S of Montélimar. **Credit cards** Amex, MasterCard, Visa. **Terms** [2004] Room €58–€100. Breakfast €10. D,B&B (min. 3 days) €35 added per person. Set meals €21–€63.

GÉMENOS 13420 Bouches-du-Rhône — Map 6:E3

Relais de la Magdeleine
Rond-point de la Fontaine

Tel 04.42.32.20.16
Fax 04.42.32.02.26
Email contact@relais-magdeleine.com
Website www.relais-magdeleine.com

'A lovely hotel in a beautiful setting'; 'calm and quiet'. It is one of the *Guide*'s best-loved hotels, owned by the Marignane brothers: Christophe and Vincent manage; Philippe is the 'accomplished chef'. Their 'beautiful, old *bastide*', outside a delightful small town below the Massif de la Sainte Baume, stands in a large walled garden with swimming pool and fountain. It is liked for its 'special atmosphere, created by grounds, building and above all by the charming owners and helpful staff', and 'air of faded gentility'. Magnificent plane trees shade the terrace: at one end are sofas where drinks are served to classical music. You dine at the other end, or in the 'superb' restaurant. 'The half-board menu was no-choice, but alternatives were readily offered. Food is tasty, not rich.' 'Professional service from discreet staff.' 'They are totally flexible about children's meals.' The spacious bedrooms are 'beautifully furnished'. 'I liked our green-flecked marble bathroom.' 'Dogs and a donkey wander in the garden: the latter joined us for tea on the terrace.' A 'shopping salon' is planned for 2005. (*Maybel King, Andrew and Christine McManus, Carolyn and Robin Orme*)

Open 15 Mar–1 Dec. Restaurant sometimes closed Wed midday off-season. **Rooms** 1 suite, 2 apartments, 21 double. 15 air conditioned. **Facilities** Lift, ramps. 2 salons, 2 dining rooms (1 no-smoking); background music; function room. Garden: unheated swimming pool. Unsuitable for ♿. **Location** Outskirts of Gémenos. 23 km E of Marseille, 10 km NE of Cassis. A52 exit Pont de l'Étoile. Parking. **Credit cards** All major cards accepted. **Terms** [2004] Room: €80–€185, suite €190–€220. Breakfast €13–€14. D,B&B €98–€146 per person. Set meals €30–€55; full alc €75.

GÉRARDMER 88400 Vosges — Map 5:C5

Hostellerie des Bas Rupts et Chalet Fleuri NEW
181 route de la Bresse

Tel 03.29.63.09.25
Fax 03.29.63.00.40
Email basrupts@relaischateaux.com
Website www.bas-rupts.com

Owner/chef Michel Philippe has long had a *Michelin* star for his cooking which 'combines *terroir* and inventiveness'; *Gault Millau* awards 14 points. His Relais du Silence stands amid pine woods and hilly meadows, just outside this lake resort. His daughter, Sylvie Philippe-Witdouck, is manager. The best bedrooms are in the flower-bedecked chalet facing the small swimming pool; ones in the main house are good also; a third building connects the two. 'The food was superb,' says a visitor this year. 'Terrine de canette aux foie gras et pistaches; pavé de cabillaud à la fleur de sel; scrummy pud of Mirabelle ice cream and eglantine sorbet. Brilliant service in the long, narrow dining room. Glassed along one side it has the feel of a balcony which has somehow merged with a splendid old railway carriage. The *maître d'* wanders about, calmly greeting and chatting, in a way which is kind and polite. The phone booking and arrival were excellent. You feel you are in the hands of people who know what they are doing. Our bill for one night was a hefty €365.' Earlier visitors wrote: 'The flowery decor, thick textiles and solid, comfortable furnishings created a warm nest. Our bathroom was opulent.' Breakfast includes pastries, ham, cheese, 'luscious home-made jams'. Some visitors have disliked the background music. There are parasols in the garden, terraces with wide views. 'A long way from any main roads. Great for cross-country skiing in winter.' A wine bar and fitness facilities, including an indoor swimming pool, are planned for 2005. (*Carie Roots, and others*)

Open All year. **Rooms** 3 suites, 23 double. 13 in *Chalet*, 17 in *Hostellerie*. Some on ground floor. **Facilities** Salon (piano bar), wine bar, conservatory, 4 dining rooms; conference room; fitness facilities; background music throughout. Garden: swimming pool, tennis. Lake 3 km. Unsuitable for ♿. **Location** On D486, 3 km S of Gérardmer towards La Bresse. Parking. **Credit cards** Amex, MasterCard, Visa. **Terms** Room €110–€168, suite €190–€250. Breakfast €14–€18; D,B&B €130–€198 per person. Set meals €32–€85; alc €100.

GIGONDAS 84190 Vaucluse Map 6:C3

Les Florets
Route des Dentelles

Tel 04.90.65.85.01
Fax 04.90.65.83.80
Website www.hotel-lesflorets.com

Against a background of the craggy Dentelles de Montmirail, this old-fashioned hotel has a superb setting high in a wooded valley, near some of the best Côtes du Rhône vineyards. 'Thierry and Martine Bernard [the third-generation owners] are perfect hosts,' say returning fans. 'Welcome as warm as ever.' Residents are expected to dine in. Summer meals are served on the flowery terrace (13 *Gault Millau* points for Daniel Chiocca). 'A real gastronomic treat; tuna carpaccio; fantastic fish soup; duck in rich orange sauce.' The 'excellent selection of local wines' includes some from M. Bernard's prize-winning vineyards. 'Lavender fields, a scent of flowers. Silence reigns.' There's 'not much of a lounge', and the bedrooms (some are in a chalet) may be 'dowdy' but the recently renovated bathrooms are liked. 'Breakfast was moderate, with heart-stopping coffee.' The owners and their English-speaking staff have 'a dry humour'. (*S and DC, RG*)

Open 20 Mar–1 Jan. Closed Mon evening–Wed Nov–Mar. Restaurant closed Wed. **Rooms** 1 suite, 14 double. 5, on ground floor with terrace, in annexe. **Facilities** Salon/bar, restaurant (smoking discouraged). No background music. Garden: dining terrace, loungers. **Location** 2 km NE of village (signposted). Parking. **Credit cards** All major cards accepted. **Terms** Room €90, suite €125. Breakfast €12. D,B&B: single €127, double €178–€213. Set meals €24–€60; full alc €60.

GILLY-LES-CÎTEAUX 21640 Côte-d'Or Map 5:D3

Château de Gilly NEW

Tel 03.80.62.89.98
Fax 03.80.62.82.34
Email gilly@grandesetapes.fr
Website www.chateau-gilly.com

In a hamlet midway between Dijon and Beaune, this magnificent 14th/16th-century Cistercian abbey is now a luxury hotel. 'Truly excellent; we had a very comfortable room,' says a regular correspondent, restoring it to the *Guide*. The terrace, where drinks and meals can be taken, faces a large garden laid out in formal French fashion with flowerbeds, gravel paths and a central fountain. Beyond this, sheltered by low hedges, is an attractive swimming pool. There are two dining rooms: the bistro-style *Côté Terroirs*, for lunch, and for dinner the *Clos Prieur* in a splendidly vaulted cellar approached by an underground passageway ('the ambience was a pleasure'). This year, there is a new chef, Olivier Dupart, Burgundian by birth, who has worked with Alain Chapel and Joël Robuchon. The 30,000 bottles in the wine cellar include 28,000 from Burgundy. There is plenty to do and see in the region, and reception staff, who 'offer excellent advice', can arrange for a 'prodigious' picnic hamper to be made up. (*David Crowe*)

Open All year. **Rooms** 9 suites, 39 double. **Facilities** Lift. Salon, breakfast room, 2 restaurants (no-smoking); conference room. Garden: terrace (meal service); swimming pool. **Location** 2 km E of Vougeot, on D251. **Credit cards** All major cards accepted. **Terms** [2004] Room €135–€290, suite €390–€610. Breakfast €22. D,B&B €78 added per person. Set lunch €16–€19, dinner €39–€75.

GORDES 84220 Vaucluse — Map 6:D3

Auberge de Carcarille NEW/BUDGET — *Tel* 04.90.72.02.63
Route d'Apt — *Fax* 04.90.72.05.74
Email carcaril@club-internet.fr
Website www.auberge-carcarille.com

Informally run by friendly Rambaud family owners: 'pleasing stone building' (Logis de France), set back from road, E of village 26 km SE of Carpentras, 38 km E of Avignon, in 'fairly spacious' grounds. Bar, large restaurant (white walls, colourful chairs, flowery curtains), outside dining area; 'reasonable-sized' swimming pool. 'Enjoyable half-board meals (no choice), good buffet breakfast, very good value.' Closed 30 Nov–1 Feb; restaurant closed Fri except evenings Apr–Sept. MasterCard, Visa accepted. 11 bedrooms, most with terrace or balcony: €60–€70. Breakfast €10. D,B&B €68–€73 per person. Set meals €17–€40 [2004].

GRAY 70100 Haute-Saône — Map 5:D4

Château de Rigny NEW — *Tel* 03.84.65.25.01
Route de la vallée de la Saône — *Fax* 03.84.65.44.45
Rigny — *Email* chateau-de-rigny@wanadoo.fr
Website www.hotels-tradition.com/rigny

Run by its owners, Brigitte and Jacques Maupin, this 17th-century château (Relais du Silence) stands by the upper Saône, in a village outside Gray. 'The approach is unpromising,' says a visitor this year. 'When you enter a shady courtyard through tall wrought iron gates, the balanced facade of the pale stone building comes as a surprise. The welcome is polite, the scented flowers in the hall are voluptuous. The feel is of slightly faded grandeur, more home than hotel. No lift: our second-floor room, up wide wooden stairs, was cool and quiet, with a huge bathroom.' Another guest loved the park, with its statues, stream, bridges, ducks, 'peaceful atmosphere, super swimming pool'. There is a terrace for drinks and meals; also two ornate dining rooms. 'Food was copious (delicious pintade), not expensive for such splendid surroundings. Service was slow. Madame, young and attentive, constantly made sure all was well. On a hot night, some of the staff looked uncomfortable, others were friendly. Upkeep must be demanding; some repairs were a bit makeshift.' Breakfast is in a 'curious glass room, like a Paris café' which has 'an efficient machine for boiling eggs'. (*Carie Roots, Barbara Hill*)

Open All year. **Rooms** 4 suites, 25 double. Some in 2 *pavillons*. 4 on ground floor. **Facilities** Hall, 2 salons, conservatory, bar, restaurant; function/ conference room. 5-hectare park: garden, dining terrace, heated swimming pool, tennis, river. **Location** Outside Rigny. 4 km NE of Gray, 46 km NW of Besançon. **Credit cards** All major cards accepted. **Terms** [2004] Room €73–€190. Breakfast €10.50. D,B&B €75–€130 per person. Set meals dinner €30–€56.

GRESSE-EN-VERCORS 38650 Isère — Map 6:B3

Le Chalet BUDGET

Tel 04.76.34.32.08
Fax 04.76.34.31.06
Email lechalet@free.fr
Website lechalet.free.fr

Amid the 'breathtaking scenery' of the eastern Vercors, where, say recent visitors, 'sheer mountain cliffs rise majestically above trees and meadows', is this 'gem' of a hotel (Logis de France). Owned by the Prayer family for four generations, it is an unassuming white building with a modern annexe across the road. Mother and daughter-in-law are front-of-house; father and son prepare the 'very good, varied' food (*Michelin Bib Gourmand*, 12 *Gault Millau* points). Meals are served on the terrace, in the *jardin intérieur* (with glazed roof) or in one of several smaller rooms. 'Staff are welcoming; help offered with luggage.' One couple liked the 'luscious blue and raspberry fabrics' in their bedroom. Others wrote: 'Ours was really a suite, comfortable, if starkly decorated, and with amazing views.' The *demi-pension* menu, with little choice, changes nightly. 'Breakfast DIY, but plenty of it. Good pool with sliding roof.' In winter the village attracts skiers; in summer, 'for wild flowers, birdwatching, painting, it is *sans pareil*'. (*BW Ribbons, C and RO*)

Open 8 May–10 Oct, 18 Dec–6 Mar. Restaurant closed Wed, except school holidays. **Rooms** 25. Some in annexe opposite, 50 m. **Facilities** Lift. Bar, lounge, restaurant; background music; conference room. Garden: terrace, heated swimming pool, solarium, tennis. **Location** 14 km SW of Monestier-de-Clermont, W of N75. Garage, parking. **Restriction** No dogs. **Credit cards** MasterCard, Visa. **Terms** [2004] Room €54–€78. Breakfast €8.50. D,B&B €57–€65 per person. Set meals €17–€48.

GRÉSY-SUR-ISÈRE 73460 Savoie — Map 6:A4

La Tour de Pacoret
Montailleur

Tel 04.79.37.91.59
Fax 04.79.37.93.84
Email info@hotel-pacoret-savoie.com
Website www.hotel-pacoret-savoie.com

Above the Isère valley outside this 'tiny, quaint' Alpine village near Albertville, a 14th-century stone watchtower, with views of the Alps, has been turned into this restaurant-with-rooms (Relais du Silence). Owned and run by Gilles and Laurence Chardonnet, it was recently enjoyed: 'Great value.' 'Fairly modest, unusual and romantic.' 'Excellent food and service; delicious breakfast pastries.' 'Our lovely room had restored antiques and rich tapestries.' Less than agile visitors may find the steep circular staircase a challenge. A *potager* supplies the kitchen, and some dishes are *Savoyard*, eg, filet de féra des lacs juste poêlé, amandes hachées. A selection of wines of the day can be had by the glass. The dining room has wide views, and a terrace, shaded by a 100-year-old wisteria, where drinks and food are served. The lounge has tapestries and upholstered chairs. In the garden is a swimming pool with loungers. In winter the Chardonnets run the *Hôtel Alba* in Méribel.

Open 1st Sun in May–3rd Sun Oct. Restaurant closed Tues, and Wed midday except July/Aug. **Rooms** 8 double, 2 single. **Facilities** Salon (background music), restaurant (no-smoking); function facilities. 4-hectare garden: dining terrace, swimming pool, *boules*. Unsuitable for ♿. **Location** 1.5 km NE of Grésy, 12 km SW of Albertville. Helipad. Parking. Garage (€6). **Credit cards** MasterCard, Visa. **Terms** [2004] Room: single €55–€58, double €64–€94. Breakfast €9. D,B&B €60–€80 per person. Set meals €19–€45; full alc €50.

GRIGNAN 26230 Drôme — Map 6:C3

Manoir de la Roseraie NEW
Route de Valréas

Tel 04.75.46.58.15
Fax 04.75.46.91.55
Email roseraie.hotel@wanadoo.fr
Website www.manoirdelaroseraie.com

'You can tick all the "Good Hotel" boxes for this one,' say the nominators of this 'beautiful house, away from traffic on the edge of a spectacular village'. The elegant 19th-century building, below the Renaissance château where the Marquise de Sévigny often stayed, is owned by the 'omnipresent' Hartmut and Michèle Alberts ('he is gentle and thoughtful, she adds a touch of glamour'). 'His background is the theatre, hers dancing,' explains the brochure. They are helped by their son, an enthusiastic chef. They provide 'comfortable, modern rooms, not OTT, a first-rate restaurant, a quality breakfast'. The rotunda dining room looks through big windows to the garden where summer meals are served, roses grow and there is a 'nice pool'. The menu might include loup rôti en jus de coquillage; agneau de lait, millefeuille de pommes de terre aux olives. And all this is 'not too expensive'. (*Martin and Karen Oldridge*)

Open 13 Feb–31 Dec, closed Tues/Wed off-season. **Rooms** 21. Some no-smoking. 1 on ground floor. **Facilities** Bar/lounge, restaurant/conservatory; conference room. Garden: outside dining; heated swimming pool, tennis. **Location** 52 km NE of Orange. **Credit cards** All major cards accepted. **Terms** Room €162–€213. Breakfast €19. D,B&B €125–€280 per person. Set meals €34–€63. *V*

> The *V* sign at the end of an entry indicates that the hotel has agreed to take part in our Voucher scheme and to give *Guide* readers a 25% discount on its room or B&B rates, subject to the conditions explained in *How to read the entries*, and on the back of the vouchers.

HALLINES 62570 Pas-de-Calais — Map 3:D2

Hostellerie St-Hubert NEW
1 rue du Moulin

Tel 03.21.39.77.77
Fax 03.21.93.00.86

19th-century manor house, now restaurant-with-rooms, on edge of small village 6 km SW of St-Omer, 30 mins' drive from Calais. 'Pleasant garden with river, lawns, flowering trees. No traffic noise.' Parking. Good-value food in dining room up 'majestic' marble staircase. Closed Sun night/Mon/Tues midday. 8 bedrooms ('ours, large, well-lit, faced the garden): €61–€122. Breakfast ('excellent bread, croissants, brioches, orange juice') €10. Set meals €25–€54; alc €45–€62 [2004].

HAMBYE 50450 Manche — Map 2:E3

Auberge de l'Abbaye BUDGET
5 route de l'Abbaye

Tel 02.33.61.42.19
Fax 02.33.61.00.85
Email aubergedelabbaye@wanadoo.fr

Near the superb ruins of a Gothic abbey, in a lovely valley south-east of Coutances, Jean and Micheline Allain's grey stone restaurant-with-rooms (Logis de France) is always admired: 'Welcoming, efficient, very comfortable'; 'Amazing value'; 'Madame was charming, and most helpful'. Though modestly priced, it is quite smart, and prettily decorated. The flower arrangements 'are lovely', and 'attention to detail is apparent'. 'A warm dining room and traditional cuisine,' says *Michelin*, and *Guide* readers agree: 'Soft colours, pretty curtains; food was superb.' 'Continental breakfast the nicest we had in France: delicious jams.' 'We felt like house guests rather than hotel guests.' Most bedrooms have shower rather than bath. The parterre, with lawn and flowers, is admired, and 'we loved walking in the country lanes'. (*Lesley Goodden, G and K Tarr*)

Open All year, except 9–25 Feb, 1–15 Oct. **Rooms** 7 double. **Facilities** Salon, restaurant. No background music. Terrace, fishing. Unsuitable for ♿. **Location** 3.5 km S of Hambye by D21. 21 km SE of Coutances. Parking. **Credit cards** MasterCard, Visa. **Terms** Room €44–€51. Breakfast €8. D,B&B €52 per person. Set meals €21–€54; full alc €30.

HAUT-DE-CAGNES 06800 Alpes-Maritimes — Map 6:D5

Le Cagnard
Rue Sous Barri

Tel 04.93.20.73.21
Fax 04.93.22.06.39
Email resa@le-cagnard.com
Website www.le-cagnard.com

The Barel-Laroche family's unusual hotel (Relais & Châteaux) is a clever conversion of medieval houses on the side of a cliff, by the ramparts of this fashionable hill village, inland from Nice. Admirers who returned in 2004 report: 'Lovely family, professional staff, a comfortable place to stay. M. and Mme Barel are still in evidence; Minou and Jean-Marc Laroche now run it, hands-on every day. The atmosphere is easy-going. Many guests don't arrive for breakfast before 11 am, and a very good breakfast can be served in the bedroom at any time.' The 'beautiful hand-painted ceiling' of the restaurant slides away to reveal the sky. Meals are also served in a graceful, candlelit former guardroom, or on the terrace. Jean-Yves Johany is the chef (*Michelin* star, 14 *Gault Millau* points). 'Meals are excellent. The daily menu is good value; the *carte* can be expensive, but for the quality of the cooking and ingredients not too frightening for this part of the Côte, and as residents you can switch between the two menus without penalty.' Rooms are regularly refurbished in contemporary Provençal style. Most are spacious, 'save for some in the older building'. They are reached along 'higgledy-piggledy corridors' or by an alley. Some have a balcony with views to the sea and mountains. A suite has a sunny terrace. 'Haut-de-Cagnes has narrow, bendy streets, mostly one-way': it may be best to use the car park below the village, or let the hotel park your car. The feudal castle-cum-museum has Chagalls, Dufys, etc. Down the hill is Auguste Renoir's old house, uniquely evocative. (*Pat and Jeremy Temple*)

Open All year. Restaurant closed mid-Nov–mid-Dec. **Rooms** 8 suites, 16 double. 10 in 2 annexes. Some no-smoking. Air conditioning. **Facilities** Lift. Lounge/bar, 2 dining rooms (background music). Terrace (outdoor dining). 10 mins' drive from stony/sandy beach (shuttle). Unsuitable for ♿. **Location** Near château. Follow signs: *Bourg Mediéval* from Cagnes centre. Valet parking, garage. **Credit cards** All major cards accepted. **Terms** Room €135–€200, suite €190–€280. Breakfast €16. D,B&B €150–€246 per person. Set meals €56–€90.

HOMPS 11200 Aude — Map 4:E5

Auberge de l'Arbousier BUDGET — *Tel* 04.68.91.11.24
50 avenue de Carcassonne — *Fax* 04.68.91.12.61
Email auberge.arbousier@wanadoo.fr

The curious name of this Minervois wine village, between Narbonne and Carcassonne, comes from a Gallo-Roman villa called Ulmos (elms). Just outside it, reached by a towpath under plane trees, is Virginie Rosado's restaurant-with-rooms (Logis de France), where you can sample the local vintages while eating on a terrace beside the Canal du Midi. A former *chai* (for storing wine that is not yet bottled), it was once a *commanderie* of the Order of Malta. 'Amazing value and a delightful situation,' say visitors in 2004. 'The outside was somewhat scruffy and the tables and chairs are simple and rustic. We enjoyed dining under trees watching the boats glide by. Every table was filled with locals. At dusk the tree lights were switched on and all was transformed. Excellent meals were much enjoyed: they included foie gras and smoked salmon anèthe. Breakfast was a typically basic French affair with stewed coffee from an urn, milk and water kept warm in flasks. Our room was large and simply furnished, but everything was well thought-out, it was carpeted throughout and the bathroom was well equipped.' Winter meals are served in a large dining room. You can walk to the village and the port of Minervoise, some 200 yards along the towpath. (*Dennis and Janet Allom*)

Open All year except 15 Feb–15 Mar, 25 Oct–30 Nov, 23 Dec–5 Jan. Restaurant closed Tues midday, Mon July/Aug, Sun evening and Wed Sept–June. **Rooms** 11 double. **Facilities** Small salon, large restaurant. Garden (outdoor dining). **Location** 1 km from village on Canal du Midi, off Carcassonne–Béziers road. 11 km N of Lézignan-Corbières. Parking. **Credit cards** MasterCard, Visa. **Terms** [2004] Room €43–€70. Breakfast €6. D,B&B €40–€50 per person. Set meals €20–€34.

HONFLEUR 14600 Calvados — Map 2:D4

L'Absinthe Hôtel
1 rue de la Ville

Tel 02.31.89.23.23
Fax 02.31.89.53.60
Email reservation@absinthe.fr
Website www.absinthe.fr

To visitors in 2004, this sympathetically converted 16th-century presbytery 'felt more like a home than a hotel'. Central, but 'with no extraneous noise at night', it combines traditional style with contemporary touches. 'Our attractive bedroom had a beamed ceiling and an excellent modern bathroom with spa bath.' Other visitors liked the little box of chocolates on arrival. 'Our fabulous suite had the most palatial bathroom ever.' The small lounge has magazines, sofas and a big fireplace. 'In the breakfast room, good warm croissants and excellent juice were served by quietly friendly staff.' Under the same ownership, 'two hops away', are the brasserie, *La Grenouille*, 'where the meals are tasty and reasonably priced', and *L'Absinthe* restaurant. The secure parking, though 'slightly inconveniently' situated half a mile away, is appreciated, 'given the popularity of the resort'. (*Roy and Jenny May, Rosemary Winder, R and EU*)

Open 13 Dec–13 Nov. **Rooms** 1 suite, 6 double. **Facilities** Lounge, breakfast room. **Location** S of Vieux Bassin. Parking (€10). **Credit cards** All major cards accepted. **Terms** [2004] Room €95–€125, suite €215. Breakfast €10.

Hôtel L'Écrin
19 rue Eugène-Boudin

Tel 02.31.14.43.45
Fax 02.31.89.24.41
Email hotel.ecrin@honfleur.com
Website www.honfleur.com

'Honfleur is a delight in its shabby but beautiful way, and *L'Écrin* fits in well,' says a visitor in 2004 to this 18th-century manor house. It stands up a hill, in a garden dotted with statuary. Run by the 'charming, urbane' Jean-Luc Blais, with a 'Siamese aide with exquisite manners', it is an 'upmarket B&B' with 'a slightly faded grandeur, reminiscent of a previous elegant age'. 'A wonderful place,' says another correspondent. 'The public rooms are crammed with good paintings, orientalia, wood carvings, ship models, etc.' Bedrooms, all different, are in five buildings. Those in the main house are opulent, with Louis XV furniture and canopied beds; simpler but pleasant rooms are in the converted stables. But one room had 'a bed that was almost as ancient as some of the furniture, and with an off-putting rubber mattress cover'. Another had crimson walls 'and we could hear nearly every noise made by our neighbours'. Reports on breakfast (served in the conservatory) vary: 'fresh orange juice, nice jams, good yoghurt', but 'coffee the worst we had in France'. The staff are 'kind to children'. 'No need for a restaurant: Honfleur is full of them.' (*Felix Singer, Michael Hodge, and others*)

Open All year. **Rooms** 1 apartment, 1 suite, 26 double. In 5 buildings. 5 on ground floor. Some air conditioned. **Facilities** 2 lounges, breakfast room, conservatory; meeting room; sauna, spa. No background music. Garden. **Location** 300 m W of centre. Parking. **Restrictions** No smoking. No dogs. **Credit cards** All major cards accepted. **Terms** Room €90–€160, suite €180. Breakfast €10–€15.

LES HOUCHES 74310 Haute-Savoie — Map 6:A5

Hôtel du Bois BUDGET
475 avenue des Alpages
La Griaz

Tel 04.50.54.50.35
Fax 04.50.55.50.87
Email reception@hotel-du-bois.com
Website www.hotel-du-bois.com

In village 5 km SW of Chamonix-Mont-Blanc: modern chalet-style hotel (Logis de France) just off motorway from Mont Blanc tunnel (some traffic noise). Liked for 'service and charm'. Barry's Bar; *2 restaurants:* Le Caprice *with fireplace;* Terrasse du Bois *(with pizzas) in summer; buffet breakfast. 'Friendly multilingual staff, excellent breakfast.' 'Very good steaks' at dinner. Small indoor swimming pool, sauna; meeting room. Open 1 Dec–10 May, 1 June–31 Oct. MasterCard, Visa accepted. 43 bedrooms (small but adequate, all with balcony; best ones at rear, below Mont Blanc). B&B: single €59–€91, double €68–€100; D,B&B €20 added per person [2004].*

HUSSEREN-LES-CHÂTEAUX 68420 Haut-Rhin — Map 5:C5

Hôtel Husseren-les-Châteaux
Rue du Schlossberg

Tel 03.89.49.22.93
Fax 03.89.49.24.84
Email mail@hotel-husseren-les-chateaux.com
Website www.hotel-husseren-les-chateaux.com

In the foothills of the Vosges mountains, overlooking the highest village on the Alsatian wine trail, is this large, modern, Scandinavian-style hotel. Public rooms are light, and the 'very friendly' Dutch owners, Karin and Lucas de Jong, have brightened up the 'slightly institutional' long corridors and expanses of bare concrete with Oriental prints, and pictures by members of their family. 'It is good for visitors with children,' says a report in 2004 (large indoor pool, games room, good walking and biking nearby). Other reporters 'had a comfortable and enjoyable stay'. In the restaurant, *Au Sapin Doré*, which has a heated terrace (with views over the Rhine plain) for alfresco meals, 'the good, basic food' is accompanied by local wines. The split-level bedrooms, each with lounge and south-facing terrace, are spacious. The buffet breakfasts are admired. There are extensive conference/function facilities, and coach parties are accommodated. Charming villages are close by. (*Simon Routh, CEA*)

Open All year. Restaurant closed Sun evening/Mon in Aug. **Rooms** 1 suite, 37 double. Some on ground floor. Some no-smoking. **Facilities** Lift. Lounge, bar, breakfast room, restaurant; classical background music; 10 seminar/function rooms; indoor swimming pool, sauna, fitness room, billiard room. Garden: terraces, tennis, children's playground. Secure parking. **Location** Edge of village, 6 km SW of Colmar. Turn off N83 at Eguisheim; follow road 2.5 km. Parking. **Credit cards** All major cards accepted. **Terms** Room: single €83–€98, double €103–€165, suite €220. Breakfast €12. D,B&B €104.50 per person. Set meals €21–€52.

IGÉ 71960 Saône-et-Loire — Map 5:E3

Château d'Igé

Tel 03.85.33.33.99
Fax 03.85.33.41.41
Email ige@chateauxhotels.com
Website www.chateaudige.com

'A delightful family-run hotel in an exquisite building,' says a visitor in 2004. 'With its thick, honey-coloured stone walls, it looks every inch a medieval manor house,' says our inspector. Now a luxury hotel owned by Françoise Germond-Lieury, 'a very sympathetic hostess', this 13th-century château stands in wooded grounds in a small village amid the vineyards and forests of the Mâconais wine region (Mâcon d'Igé is an *appellation* in its own right). It has ivy-covered walls, stone-flagged floors and spiral stairways; corridors are dark and winding. It stands in 'lovely gardens, full of corners', with chairs, 'posh loungers', huge goldfish pond with ducks. The suites in the turrets are particularly attractive, with their circular rooms. 'At dinner and breakfast, Madame came to each table, chatting with guests – so nice.' Food is thought 'good, if a little fussy'. One main course is roasted pigeon with gingerbread and baby carrots. Lunch is informal; summer drinks and meals are served on a terrace by a stream. Breakfast, with fruit salad and yogurt, is in a conservatory. (*Andrew Hillier, and others*)

Open 25 Feb–1 Dec. Restaurant closed midday Mon–Fri except holidays. **Rooms** 6 suites, 8 double. **Facilities** Salon, 3 restaurant rooms (background music); conservatory; conference facilities; function room. Large grounds: garden: terrace (outdoor dining). Unsuitable for ♿. **Location** 6.5 km N of N79, exit 4 via La Roche Vineuse; 14 km NW of Mâcon. **Credit cards** All major cards accepted. **Terms** [2004] Room €95–€144, suite €175–€210. Breakfast €14. D,B&B €50 added per person. Set menus €35–€72; alc €100. ***V***

ILLHAEUSERN 68970 Haut-Rhin — Map 5:C6

Hôtel des Berges
4 rue de Collonges

Tel 03.89.71.87.87
Fax 03.89.71.87.88
Email hotel-des-berges@wanadoo.fr
Website www.hotel-des-berges.fr

'Guests enjoy really personal service' at this small hotel run by Marco Baumann and his wife, Danielle Haeberlin. Designed to accommodate guests of the Haeberlin family's renowned restaurant *L'Auberge de l'Ill*, it has a pastoral setting on the river bank (*berge*) in a village north of Colmar. *L'Auberge* has long been the most distinguished restaurant in Alsace (three *Michelin* stars, 17 *Gault Millau* points), and the hotel 'runs elegantly and effortlessly'. The building was once a barn for drying tobacco leaves (rooms are named after cigars); and the decor is 'tasteful throughout', says a visitor this year. 'Our large room had a sitting area, wide balcony, views to the distant Vosges mountains, state-of-the-art bathroom.' Two new suites have a sauna. In the grounds are vegetables, herbs and flowers; inside is a spacious country atmosphere, antiques, modern cane chairs, rough stone tile floors, modern lighting. Paul Haeberlin is *chef de cuisine*, aided by son Marc, serving, eg, mousseline de grenouilles; volaille de Bresse rôtie à la broche. Paul's brother, Jean-Pierre, directs. The dining rooms open on to a terrace. 'At night, the illuminated riverside complex looks fantastic.' Breakfast, 'one of the best in France', can be taken on a punt or by the water, 'watching kingfishers darting between the willows'. (*Adrian Turner, CM*)

Open All year, except Christmas, Feb, Mon/Tues. **Rooms** 6 suites, 7 double. Some in *Fisherman's Cottage*. Air conditioning. **Facilities** Lift. Lobby, bar (background music); meeting room. Garden: 'Swedish bath'; river: swimming, fishing. **Location** 15 km NE of Colmar. Parking, garage. **Credit cards** All major cards accepted. **Terms** Room €252–€287, suite €342–€497. Breakfast €27. Set meals €138–€210.

INXENT 62170 Pas-de-Calais — Map 3:D2

Auberge d'Inxent BUDGET — *Tel* 03.21.90.71.19
318 rue de la Vallée (D127) — *Fax* 03.21.86.31.67
Email auberge.inxent@wanadoo.fr

Jean-Marc Six was a *sommelier* in Lille when he won a million francs in a bottle-top collecting competition sponsored by Perrier. He bought this *auberge* in a village (famous for its ancient churches) in the pretty Course valley, south-east of Boulogne. He runs it with his wife, Laurence, and their teenage son. 'A very pleasant family,' say visitors in 2004. Monsieur Six and his waitress serve 'with calm efficiency'; he 'takes time to chat'; Madame's housekeeping is 'excellent'. The small, whitewashed building, with blue-and-white shutters, offers 'excellent value'. Rooms are 'simple but well cared for'; towels are 'the big fluffy sort'. A garden (with roses, fruit and walnut trees and pond) leads to the river, where M. Six farms trout. The chef, Carole Gérard, serves 'good, relatively simple' meals: 'excellent guineafowl with puréed celeriac'. 'Superb wine list.' 'Breakfast also simple and good' (fresh orange juice, fruit, yogurts, home-made jams). Meals are served outdoors in fine weather. One visitor in poor weather found 'nowhere to sit indoors'. Near a main road, but '*relativement calme*', say the Sixes. (*Bob and Kate Flaherty, William and Ann Reid, MC*)

Open Feb–June, 12 July–mid-Dec. Closed Tues/Wed. **Rooms** 5 double. **Facilities** Breakfast room, restaurant (background music). Terrace (outdoor dining). Garden. Unsuitable for ♿. **Location** Village centre. 12 km N of Montreuil-sur-Mer, towards Desvres. Unguarded parking. **Credit cards**

MasterCard, Visa. **Terms** [2004] Room €54–€70. Breakfast €8. D,B&B €54–€80 per person. Set meals €14.50–€37; full alc €36.

ISBERGUES 62330 Pas-de-Calais — Map 3:D2

Le Buffet NEW/BUDGET
Rue de la Gare, Molinghem

Tel 03.21.25.82.40
Fax 03.21.27.86.42
Website www.le-buffet.com

Owned by chef Thierry Wident and his wife (with a Labrador in attendance), this restaurant-with-rooms is the former buffet of a railway station in a 'dull town' (says its nominator) west of Lille. 'The food was superb [*Michelin Bib Gourmand*], French cooking at its best, professionally if somewhat formally served, in a delightful conservatory. Our medium-priced menu (€38) included delicious "surprises" between courses. The delicious continental breakfast had freshly squeezed orange juice, home-made jams and *hot* croissants. An excellent last-night stop in France.' Meals are served in a pretty panelled room or on a terrace. (*Kay Birchley*)

Open All year, except Feb holidays, 2–26 Aug, Mon except midday bank holiday, Sun night. **Rooms** 5. **Facilities** Restaurant, conservatory. Garden (meal service). **Location** 6 km SE of Aire-sur-la-Lys, 62 km W of Lille. **Credit cards** MasterCard, Visa. **Terms** [2004] Room €45–€52. Breakfast €9. D,B&B €65 per person. Set meals €19–€50.

LES ISSAMBRES 83380 Var — Map 6:E5

Villa Saint-Elme NEW
Corniche des Issambres

Tel 04.94.49.52.52
Fax 04.94.49.63.18
Email info@saintelme.com
Website www.saintelme.com

In a 'magnificent setting facing the Mediterranean', this luxury hotel is a 1930s villa between the sea and the main coast road on the edge of a pleasant village east of Ste-Maxime. Everyone agrees that 'the welcome is good'. One couple thought their suite 'overpriced' and the decor 'tired in a luxurious way', but a regular *Guide* correspondent found much to admire: 'A modern period piece with discreet service, beautiful wood panelling, comfortable seating. The bar has a nice small terrace; the pool on the sea's edge has super views to St-Tropez.' There is an open-air café for lunch. 'Dinner had an interesting menu, good fish; wonderful chocolate tart; sensible wine list. Waiting staff very helpful.' The suites ('ours, Frou Frou, was OTT, frills everywhere, but fun') share a terrace where the 'good and plentiful' breakfast can be served. The rooms in the annexe across the road are less liked, and hear traffic. (*IGC Farman, and others*)

Open All year. **Rooms** 3 suites, 9 junior suites, 17 double. **Facilities** Lift. Salons, café, restaurant; health centre; conference facilities. Garden: outside dining, swimming pool. **Location** 19 km N of St-Tropez. From A8 turn off to N98 at Fréjus. **Credit cards** All major cards accepted. **Terms** [2004] Room with breakfast: double €150–€332, junior suite €279–€478, €340–€599. D,B&B €21 added per person.

ITTERSWILLER 67140 Bas-Rhin Map 5:B6

Hôtel Arnold BUDGET
98 route des Vins

Tel 03.88.85.50.58
Fax 03.88.85.55.54
Email arnold-hotel@wanadoo.fr
Website www.hotel-arnold.com

'Still one of our favourites.' Set among vineyards near this old village, the Arnold family's hotel (Logis de France) is typically Alsacien, with its yellow-painted half-timbered walls and flower-covered balconies. Its setting, with views as far as the Black Forest, 'is superb'. Owned by the family for three generations, it is now run by an Arnold daughter and her husband, M. and Mme Simon. Rooms are traditionally furnished and many have a balcony facing vineyards or woodland. 'Ours was impeccable for space, comfort and shower.' Breakfast has home-baked *kugelhopf*. The restaurant, across the street, is a big operation. Half board includes three courses from the *à la carte* menu: huge portions of Alsatian food, 'all of high quality'. There are four open wines to choose from, at fair prices, and a large wine list; tastings are often held. (*Malcolm Roots*)

Open All year, except Christmas. Restaurant closed Sun night Nov–June, and Mon. **Rooms** 2 suites (for 4), 27 double. 6 plus 1 apartment in annexe. 1 suitable for ♿. **Facilities** Salon, breakfast room (no-smoking), restaurant; boutique. No background music. Small garden: terrace. **Location** Opposite church. 47 km SW of Strasbourg. Parking. **Credit cards** Amex, MasterCard, Visa. **Terms** Room €77–€111, suite €99–€160 (€220 for 4). Breakfast €10. D,B&B (min. 3 nights) €54.50–€129 per person. Set meals €24–€48; full alc €54.

JOIGNY 89300 Yonne Map 5:C2

La Côte Saint-Jacques
14 Faubourg de Paris

Tel 03.86.62.09.70
Fax 03.86.91.49.70
Email lorain@relaischateaux.com
Website www.cotesaintjacques.com

'It keeps on improving' according to a visitor returning in 2004 to the Larain family's glamorous hotel (Relais & Châteaux), on the banks of the Yonne. 'Difficult to criticise,' was another comment, though a third reporter found the atmosphere 'a little impersonal'. Manager/chef Jean-Michel Lorain has 19 *Gault Millau* points and three *Michelin* stars (one more this year) for inventive dishes like genèse d'un plat sur le thème de l'huître; homard 'pattes bleues' rôti et carottes fanes à la bourguignonne. Ten 'traditional' bedrooms are in the main building; the best ones are reached by a tunnel (decorated with Roman remains) under the noisy N6. 'Ours, overlooking the river, had a balcony with table and two chairs, a bed large enough for a family of four.' There is a summer lounge with terrace, a winter lounge with fireplace and library. The large indoor swimming pool opens on to the garden. Children have their own menu, *Initiation à la Gourmandise*, and babysitters can be arranged. Breakfast is 'wonderfully imaginative'. There is a boat for river trips. The family's other hotel, *La Rive Gauche*, is across the river. (*Val Morgan, M and AF, and others*)

Open 5 Feb–5 Jan. **Rooms** 9 suites, 23 double. 22 (air conditioned) in *La Résidence*. **Facilities** 2 lounges, bar, 2 dining rooms (no-smoking areas); children's games room; shop; indoor swimming pool, sauna; function facilities. Garden, by river: boat trips. **Location** 27 km NW of Auxerre, on N6 (Sens exit). Parking. **Credit cards** All major cards accepted. **Terms** Room €135–€278, suite €330–€490. Breakfast €18–€27. Set meals €72–€140.

JULIÉNAS 69840 Rhône — Map 5:E3

Chez La Rose NEW
Le Bourg

Tel 04.74.04.41.20
Fax 04.74.04.49.29
Email info@chez-la-rose.fr
Website www.chez-la-rose.fr

'The food is excellent,' say visitors this year. In a wine village in the Beaujolais, this restaurant-with-rooms is run by its owners, Sylvette Alizer ('she has a lively presence') and her husband, Bertrand. He has a *Michelin Bib Gourmand* for his '*cuisine du terroir soignée*', served in a rustic dining room or on a flowery terrace. Accommodation consists of spacious modern suites in a pavilion, or double rooms in a simpler *auberge* down the road. Here, the nominators had a room that was 'small and short on drawer space, but otherwise well equipped, with a good shower room'. At dinner they enjoyed dos de saumon sauce ciboulette; coq au vin de Juliénas; cassis sorbet; figues rôties et glace basilique. 'The restaurant is always bursting at the seams with a French/European clientele. Good use is made of herbs. We ate in the no-smoking dining room where breakfast is served: in the evening it is quite elegant: white tablecloths, subtle lighting. Breakfast is a buffet with a wide choice: croissants, pastries and jams are home made.' Meals are also served on a veranda which becomes a terrace in summer, and parasols stand in the garden. (*Brian and Rosalind Keen*)

Open All year, except 10–25 Dec, 3 weeks Feb. Restaurant closed Mon night Oct–Apr, midday except Wed, Sat, Sun. **Rooms** 2 suites, 8 double. In 2 buildings. **Facilities** Bar, 2 dining rooms; background music; function facilities; terrace. Garden. **Location** Centre of town. 14 km SW of Mâcon. Limited courtyard parking; public parking opposite. **Restriction** No smoking. **Credit cards** All major cards accepted. **Terms** Room €60–€70, suite €68–€150. Breakfast €10. D,B&B €55–€100 per person. Set meals €25–€55.

LACAVE 46200 Lot — Map 4:C5

Château de la Treyne

Tel 05.65.27.60.60
Fax 05.65.27.60.70
Email treyne@relaischateaux.com
Website www.chateaudelatreyne.com

Superbly set above the River Dordogne, this 17th-century château is now a luxury hotel (Relais & Châteaux), 'sympathetically restored' by its owner, Michèle Gombert-Devals. 'Everything was as smooth as always,' wrote a visitor returning in 2004. 'The best meal we have ever had: simple ingredients combined and cooked superbly.' *Michelin* awards a star, *Gault Millau* 16 points, for the inventive cooking of Stéphane Andrieux (eg, pot-au-feu de canard; nage de lotte au curry et saffron; savarin au chocolat Manjari), served at impeccably set tables with engraved glasses, silver candelabra, Limoges porcelain. In fine weather, dinner is served on the terrace above the water as the sun sets, and breakfast may be taken under a giant cedar of Lebanon. An earlier report: 'Our bedroom, overlooking the river and the fabulous garden, had beamed ceilings, faded oriental rugs, antique armoire, superb carved doors, and on the walls old silk damask.' Cheaper rooms are in the *Château du Bastit*, in the grounds. Concerts and exhibitions are held in a Romanesque chapel. (*Rodney Baker-Bates, P and JW*)

Open Easter–Nov, New Year. Restaurant closed midday Tues–Fri. **Rooms** 3 suites, 18 double. 5 in *Château du Bastit*. Air conditioning. **Facilities** Lift. 2 lounges (classical background music), bar, breakfast room, restaurant. 120-hectare park: garden, 2 terraces, tennis, spa, heated swimming pool. **Location** 3 km W of Lacave, 6 km SE of Souillac. **Restriction** No smoking: restaurant, some public rooms. **Credit cards** All major cards accepted. **Terms** [2004] Room €180–€360, suite €480. Breakfast €18. D,B&B €180–€270 per person. Set meals €42–€118; full alc €115.

Le Pont de l'Ouysse

Tel 05.65.37.87.04
Fax 05.65.32.77.41
Email pont.ouysse@wanadoo.fr
Website www.lepontdelouysse.fr

On the site of a former farm, the Chambon family's famous restaurant-with-rooms started life as a hotel/café in 1886 when a stone bridge was built over the River Ouysse. The bridge is no longer usable (damaged by floods), but the setting, below Château Belcastel (on a cliff), is delightful. The riverside terrace, where meals are taken under walnut and lime trees in fine weather, 'is particularly attractive', says our inspector, 'ideal for an aperitif, before sampling Daniel Chambon's cuisine' (*Michelin* star, 17 *Gault Millau* points). His inventive dishes, regionally inspired, include queues de langoustines aux truffes. Earlier praise: 'A lovely spot, delicious meal, friendly owners.' The wine list is 'remarkable'. But visitors in 2004 had a 'disastrous' stay: 'A local wedding was celebrated, with amplified sound, in a large tent in the grounds. It went on until 7.15 am.' Bedrooms face the terrace; some are up a spiral staircase. 'Ours, bright and fresh, had strong colours, French windows, a narrow spa bath.' 'Superb breakfasts.' 'A delightful swimming pool', with views, loungers and parasols. (*K and JC, and others*)

Open Early Mar–mid-Nov. Restaurant closed midday Mon and Tues, Mon night off-season. **Rooms** 2 suites, 12 double. 2 in annexe. 2 on ground floor. Air conditioning. **Facilities** TV room, salon/bar, restaurant; classical background music. Garden: dining terrace, heated swimming pool. Unsuitable for ♿. **Location** 10 km SE of Souillac. Private parking. **Restriction** No smoking in some bedrooms. **Credit cards** All major cards accepted. **Terms** [2004] Room €138–€160. Breakfast €15. D,B&B €153–€165 per person. Set meals €35–€120; full alc €60.

LANDÉDA 29870 Finistère — Map 2:E1

Hôtel La Baie des Anges
350 route des Anges
Port de l'Aber Wrac'h

Tel 02.98.04.90.04
Fax 02.98.04.92.27
Email contact@baie-des-anges.com
Website www.baie-des-anges.com

A stylish yellow 1900s building in a 'great' location on the Pays des Abers coast in north-west Finistère, this Relais du Silence is run by its owners, France Barre and Jacques Briant. 'A very good team: he is an absolute charmer,' says a recent visitor. Interiors are light and airy, with an Art Deco flavour and 'cool, chic seaside decor' (wicker, striped and checked fabrics, 'carefully chosen *objets*'). Most of the 'delightful' bedrooms have a sea view. 'Fabulous breakfast.' There is a small spa area with sauna and whirlpool (€10). No restaurant: plenty at the port, a few minutes' walk away: *Le Brennig* is recommended. (*AF*)

Open All year, except Jan. **Rooms** 2 suites, 16 double, 2 single. 1 suitable for ♿. **Facilities** Reception with TV, salon/bar (classical background music), breakfast room; sauna, hydromassage, spa bath; conference facilities. Terrace. Beach opposite. **Location** 24 km N of Brest. Parking. **Restriction** Smoking in bar only. **Credit cards** Amex, MasterCard, Visa. **Terms** [2004] Room €68–€136, suite €154–€176. Breakfast €12.

LANGRES 52200 Haute-Marne — Map 5:C3

Le Cheval Blanc
4 rue de l'Estres

Tel 03.25.87.07.00
Fax 03.25.87.23.13
Email info@hotel-langres.com
Website www.hotel-langres.com

Spectacularly situated above the Marne, this hilltop town north of Dijon has ancient ramparts, gateways, a 13th-century cathedral, and a statue of Diderot (he was born here) surrounded by volumes of his encyclopaedia. Down a quiet side street, this Logis de France, an old converted church, is run by its owners, Yves and Brigitte Chevalier. It has vaulted ceilings, well-proportioned public rooms, interesting antiques and country-style furnishings. 'A lovely stay,' one couple wrote. Rooms vary: 'Ours was spacious and comfortable.' 'Ours, very good value though small, had character.' But one room was thought 'shabby'. Three have been redecorated this year. Everyone praises the food: 'Outstanding, even the cheapest menu.' 'Dinner on the terrace was delicious.' Menus change every four months, and might include trilogie de foie gras de canard; carré d'agneau rôti aux épices. The large terrace is pleasant for drinks and breakfast. (*Mary and Brian Morris, Bob and Kate Flaherty, and others*)

Open All year, except 7–30 Nov, Christmas/New Year. Restaurant closed Wed midday. **Rooms** 3 family, 19 double. 11 in annexe, 10 m. Some on ground floor. **Facilities** Salon/bar, restaurant; background music. Terrace. Unsuitable for ♿. **Location** Central. 25 km SE of Chaumont. Garage (€7; valet parking only). **Credit cards** Amex, MasterCard, Visa. **Terms** Room: single €50, double €65–€85, family €90–€98. Breakfast €8. Set meals €24–€70.

Grand Hôtel de l'Europe BUDGET
23–25 rue Diderot

Tel 03.25.87.10.88
Fax 03.25.87.60.65
Email hotel-europe.langres@wanadoo.fr
Website www.relais-sud-champagne.com

On the main street of this 'attractive little cathedral town', Roger Chiarla's stone-fronted Logis de France, a former *relais de poste*, is always much liked. 'As good as ever,' wrote one visitor over two decades. The 'welcoming owners' and 'good value' are often mentioned. 'Delicious and varied' food is served in the 'lovely panelled dining room': it is often busy with locals, but 'the service copes admirably'. Staff are 'chatty and humorous'. There is a good wine list, and the local Pinot Noir in carafes is 'very acceptable'. The bedrooms, decorated in blue and white, are attractive (some are large). Bathrooms are 'efficient, modern'. Ask for one of the quiet rooms, in the rear annexe, on a courtyard. Breakfast is a generous buffet. Tables, chairs and parasols are on the pavement in summer. The private parking is appreciated. The town's museum holds Roman antiquities and Egyptian mummy cases. (*J Ekins-Daukes, and others*)

Open All year. Closed Sun night in winter. **Rooms** 26 double. 8 in rear annexe. **Facilities** Lounge, bar, restaurant; courtyard. No background music. Unsuitable for ♿. **Location** Central (windows double glazed, rear rooms quietest). Parking. **Credit cards** MasterCard, Visa. **Terms** [2004] Room €45–€65. Breakfast €7.50. D,B&B €68 per person. Set meals €15–€46.

LES LAVAULTS 89630 Yonne — Map 5:D2

L'Auberge de l'Âtre

Tel 03.86.32.20.79
Fax 03.86.32.28.25
Email laubergedelatr@free.fr
Website www.auberge-de-latre.com

In a village amid the 'wonderful scenery' of the Morvan national park, this is a restaurant-with-rooms for mushroom enthusiasts (*Michelin* star, 14 *Gault Millau* points). The owners, chef/*patron* Francis Salamolard and his wife, Odile, are charming, say fans: 'They work hard to make their guests welcome.' He is '*fou de champignons*': fricassée of mushrooms is a speciality, and each bedroom is named after a species of mushroom. Inside the 18th-century farmhouse, a 'lovely fire burns, even in August' (*âtre* means 'hearth'). There is a wide stone staircase, wooden panelling, period furniture. Bedrooms are 'modern rustic', 'large, well decorated, well kept'. 'At Sunday lunch, the beamed dining rooms heaved with French families. Excellent five-course menu; choice of 20 fabulous desserts. Attentive young staff. Enormous wine list.' 'Good breakfast, served with Staffordshire china.' You can eat in the garden (with gnomes). Dogs are welcomed. Some traffic on the country road by day, quiet at night. The Salamolards recently bought another hotel in the village centre. (*FW, and others*)

Open All year, except Feb, Tues night/Wed off-season. **Rooms** 7. 1 suitable for ♿. **Facilities** Ramps. 2 salons, tea room, bar, 3 dining rooms; background music; dining terrace. Big garden: children's play area; garden room for adults.

Location 5 km SE of Quarré-les-Tombes by D10, 22 km SE of Avallon. Parking. **Credit cards** All major cards accepted. **Terms** [2004] Room: single €38–€58, double €69–€91. Breakfast €8.50. D,B&B €84 per person. Set meals €23.50–€40.

LIGNY-EN-CAMBRÉSIS 59191 Nord — Map 3:E3

Château de Ligny — *Tel* 03.27.85.25.84
2 rue Pierre Curie — *Fax* 03.27.85.79.79
Email contact@chateau-de-ligny.fr
Website www.chateau-de-ligny.fr

Liked again this year, Paulette and Jean Lenglet's small, lovely old château stands in a walled garden near the ancient walled town of Cambrai. It has a 12th-century pepperpot tower; the rest is pure Flemish Renaissance. Inside are carved wood, marble, panelling, a red and gold colour scheme, crystal chandeliers. All is done in 'excellent taste', say admirers. The 'refined' restaurant, headed by Gérard Fillaire and Raymond Brochard, has a *Michelin* star, 16 *Gault Millau* points for, eg, tourte de volaille de Licques au foie gras. The food is enjoyed, but the set menu changes only weekly, and 'choosing from the *carte* is rather expensive'. 'At breakfast, tea and coffee were in communal pots.' 'Staff are attentive.' Parties and conferences are held. Some rooms are in a modern annexe, but decorated in traditional style. Nearby is the Musée Matisse in Cateau-Cambrésis, where the painter was born. (*Michael Burns, Pat and Jeremy Temple, A and IN*)

Open All year, except Feb, also Mon. **Rooms** 3 suites, 23 double. 13 in building in park. Some on ground floor. **Facilities** 3 salons, bar, restaurant (classical background music); function facilities. 2-hectare park. **Location** 4 km SW of Caudry, 17 km SE of Cambrai. **Restrictions** No smoking: restaurant, some bedrooms. No dogs. **Credit cards** All major cards accepted. **Terms** Room €120–€440, suite €220–€440. Breakfast €15. Set meals €48–€82; full alc €113.

LIGNY-LE-CHÂTEL 89144 Yonne — Map 5:C2

Relais Saint Vincent BUDGET — *Tel* 03.86.47.53.38
14 Grande Rue — *Fax* 03.86.47.54.16
Email relais.saint.vincent@libertysurf.fr
Website www.logis-de-bourgogne.com

Found 'very good value' by a visitor this year, this 17th-century half-timbered former bailiff's house of 'old-world charm' (Logis de France) stands on a quiet street in a village near Chablis. Jacky Vuillemin is a helpful proprietor ('he lent us a pamphlet on local walks'), and the *auberge* is 'lovely and quiet' (no music). In the Renaissance-style dining room, traditional Burgundian dishes are served, eg, rognons de veau flambés au marc. 'First-class food, good choice in each menu, all reasonably priced.' 'We had a lovely spacious beamed bedroom.' Some rooms at the back, more modern, face a courtyard where you can take drinks. Breakfast is 'standard French: home-made jams, honey, good coffee'. (*Terry Herbert, J and AS, and others*)

Open 3 Jan–19 Dec. **Rooms** 15. Some suitable for ♿. **Facilities** Lounge, restaurant, private dining room; conference room. No background music. Courtyard. **Location** In village. 22 km NE of Auxerre. Parking. **Credit cards** All major cards accepted. **Terms** [2004] Room €42–€68. Breakfast €7.50. D,B&B (min. 3 days) €41–€53 per person. Set meals €13–€26.

LILLE 59800 Nord **Map 3:D3**

Hôtel de la Paix BUDGET
46 bis rue de Paris

Tel 03.20.54.63.93
Fax 03.20.63.98.97
Email hotelpaixlille@aol.com
Website www.hotel-la-paix.com

200-year-old building, now 'friendly, efficient no-frills' B&B hotel, central but quiet. 'Eclectic' decor: red and pink, dark wood, iron balustrades, reproductions of famous paintings. Sizeable bedrooms (named after artists and writers) and bathrooms. Helpful staff. Lift. Breakfast room with fresco. Restaurants close by. All major credit cards accepted. 35 rooms: €70–€102. Breakfast €8.50 [2004].

LOCQUIREC 29241 Finistère **Map 2:E2**

Grand Hôtel des Bains
15 bis rue de l'Église

Tel 02.98.67.41.02
Fax 02.98.67.44.60
Email hotel.des.bains@wanadoo.fr
Website www.grand-hotel-des-bains.com

'A terrific place,' said a recent visitor. Gloriously positioned on a peninsula in a fishing port on the north Brittany coast, this handsome white 1900s hotel is decorated in 'contemporary *balnéaire*' style: polished floorboards, grey and honey panelled walls, wooden furniture, original wicker chairs, and colourful modern fabrics: 'the apogee of casual chic'. The garden, with an alley of lime trees, leads down to the sea. There is a large indoor saltwater swimming pool and a health and beauty spa. Most bedrooms face south-east across the bay; others overlook a church; some have a terrace. 'Ours was not large, but airy, light and comfortable.' But one couple complained of a smell of cooking in their room above the kitchen. The gourmet restaurant, with sea view, is mostly enjoyed, though the *table d'hôte* menu may have 'too many dishes' for some; you can also eat at the hotel's bistro at the port, a short walk away. (*AF, NP and EB, and others*)

Open All year, except 5–30 Jan. Restaurant closed midday. **Rooms** 36 double. Some on ground floor. **Facilities** Lift, ramps. Salon with bar, breakfast room, restaurant; classical background music; health/beauty treatments; function facilities; indoor swimming pool. Terrace; direct access to sandy/rocky beach. **Location** In village. 26 km NE of Morlaix. Parking. **Credit cards** All major cards accepted. **Terms** [2004] B&B: single €157–€173, double €179–€197; D,B&B: single €186–€205, double €237–€261.

Every entry in the *Guide* is based on a stay of at least one night.

LOISON-SUR-CRÉQUOISE 62990 Pas-de-Calais — Map 3:D2

La Commanderie BUDGET — *Tel* 03.21.86.49.87
3 Allée des Templiers — *Website* www.gites-de-france.fr

In a rural setting, just outside a small village between Montreuil-sur-Mer and Hesdin, Marie-Hélène Flament runs this 'superb' *chambres d'hôtes*. 'She is a joy,' say readers on a return visit in 2004. The building, which has its origins in a 12th-century fort of the Knights Templar (she showed our inspector a stone cannon ball found on site), is in a garden bordering on the pretty little River Créquoise. Earlier comments: 'Magical.' 'Charming. The vivacious owner is a mine of local information.' The rooms, furnished in French country style, face the garden and river. One has a conservatory and kitchen. The suite, with two bedrooms, bathroom and games room, is ideal for a family. 'Delicious breakfasts' with home-made jams are served in a room with a log fire. At weekends Mme Flament often bakes a cake for her guests: 'She insisted that we take some home.' She will make reservations for dinner: there are plenty of restaurants in nearby towns. Within easy reach are the medieval centre at Azincourt (a 'must' for lovers of history), and the Abbey of Valloires (superb rose gardens). (*Bob and Kate Flaherty, BB*)

Open All year except Feb. **Rooms** 1 suite, 2 double. **Facilities** Lounge/breakfast room, games room. Garden. **Location** 12 km E of Montreuil-sur-Mer, 2 km NE of Beaurainville, off D349. **Restriction** No animals. **Credit cards** None accepted. **Terms** [2004] B&B: double €54–€61, suite (for 4) €84.

LOURMARIN 84160 Vaucluse — Map 6:D3

Le Mas de Guilles — *Tel* 04.90.68.30.55
Route de Vaugines — *Fax* 04.90.68.37.41
Email hotel@guilles.com
Website www.guilles.com

'We cannot adequately praise this hotel,' say visitors in 2004 to this 17th-century *mas* (Relais du Silence). It stands up a private road on a large estate, outside this beautiful village on the southern slopes of the Luberon. 'The cross-vaulted arches in the lounge and restaurant, combined with the traditional Provençal colours, are a feast for the senses. This was matched with the artistry of Patrick Lherm in a series of faultless meals. His wife, Michèle, runs front-of-house with style.' An earlier report: 'The extraordinary old building has had bits added on all sides. Five steep, narrow stone staircases creep up the outside to some rooms (an internal staircase is more secure).' Rooms are graded from 'comfort' to 'luxe'; they are traditionally furnished, some have a terrace, most have 'wonderful views'. A large Lurçat tapestry hangs at reception. The restaurant is a light, modern extension with a panoramic terrace. 'Menus are original; prices are moderate. It is a privilege to stay in such an interesting place.' The swimming pool is surrounded by lawns and potted plants. (*Patrick and Berenice D'Arcy, FS*)

Open 1 Mar–15 Nov. Restaurant closed midday. **Rooms** 1 suite, 28 double. **Facilities** Salon, bar, restaurant; conference facilities. No background music. 25-hectare grounds: terraces; unheated swimming pool, tennis. **Location** 2 km from village. 38 km NW of Aix-en-Provence. **Credit cards** All major cards accepted. **Terms** [2004] Room €80–€110. Breakfast €12. D,B&B €90–€105 per person.

LOUVIERS 27400 Eure **Map 2:D5**

Le Pré Saint-Germain NEW *Tel* 02.32.40.48.48
7 rue St-Germain *Fax* 02.32.50.75.60
Email le.pre.saint.germain@wanadoo.fr
Website www.le-pre-saint-germain.com

'Useful, civilised hotel', an easy drive from Normandy Channel ports, in town 33 km S of Rouen. 'Quiet, yet central; used for business symposiums, etc, but none the worse for that. Superb food.' Bar, restaurant (closed Sat midday, Sun), bistro; traiteur*; 2 conference rooms. Garden: terrace (meal service). Amex, MasterCard, Visa accepted. 30 bedrooms with contemporary decor: single €69–€83, double €80–€100; D,B&B: single €104–€118, double €150–€170 [2004].*

LUCHÉ-PRINGÉ 72800 Sarthe **Map 2:F4**

Auberge du Port des Roches NEW/BUDGET *Tel* 02.43.45.44.48
Port des Roches *Fax* 02.43.45.39.61

On the banks of Le Loir (*not* La Loire, further south), this small country restaurant-with-rooms (Logis de France) was discovered by readers in 2004. 'The setting is most attractive, the young owners [Thierry and Valérie Lesiourd] were quietly welcoming' (he cooks, she is front-of-house). There is a small salon and a 'very pleasant terrace and garden' leading down to the river. 'Our room was attractively wallpapered and furnished in a rather English style. We dined well from a modestly priced set menu, and enjoyed an excellent bottle of St Nicholas de Bourgueil.' Nearby is the handsome town of La Flèche. (*Jane and Christopher Couchman*)

Open 11 Mar–23 Jan. Closed Sun night/Mon, midday on 25 Dec and 1 Jan. Restaurant closed Tues midday. **Rooms** 12 double. **Facilities** Salon, 2 dining rooms (no-smoking); background music. Garden: terrace, fishing. Unsuitable for ♿. **Location** 13 km E of La Flèche by D13 and D214. 2 km from village: take Mansigne road, then 1st road to right. Parking. **Credit cards** MasterCard, Visa. **Terms** Room €44–€54. Breakfast €6. Set meals €21–€42.

The 'Budget' label by a hotel's name indicates an establishment where dinner, bed and breakfast are offered at around the foreign currency equivalent of £50 per person, or B&B for about £30 and an evening meal for about £20. These are only a rough guide and do not always apply to single accommodation, nor do they necessarily apply in high season.

LUNÉVILLE 54300 Meurthe-et-Moselle — Map 5:B5

Château d'Adoménil
Rehainviller

Tel 03.83.74.04.81
Fax 03.83.74.21.78
Email adomenil@relaischateaux.com
Website www.adomenil.com

This Lorraine town has a 'mini-Versailles' of a château, worth visiting (damaged by a fire in 2003, but due to reopen in 2005). And in a wooded park to the south, this handsome, turreted 19th-century mansion is now a luxurious hotel (Relais & Châteaux). Owner/manager Michel Million welcomes guests. Geese and ducks swim in the moat and there is a resident Great Dane. 'It has a nice family atmosphere,' says a report this year, 'and great style. Our room was in a wing; its bathroom was ultra modern, the bedroom a lovely blend of modern and antique. To welcome us was a little tray containing three delectable mini-meringues and two shiny apples. Dinner was a marvellously balanced menu of the day: wonderful value at €41.' M. Million's son-in-law, Cyril Leclerc, is the chef (*Michelin* star, 16 *Gault Millau* points, for Alsatian cooking with a modern touch, eg, homard bleu en vinaigrette d'orange et olives noires; blanc de turbot poché). The glass-walled restaurant faces the river. There is a terrace for alfresco meals and drinks. Some bedrooms face the park; some are in Provençal style; there are some duplex suites. Many bedrooms have a terrace where the copious breakfast can be served, on the beautiful china for which Lunéville is famous. The 'state-of-the-art' swimming pool is in an impeccable walled garden.

Open All year, except 2 Jan–8 Feb. Closed Mon/Tues midday, and Sun night 1 Nov–14 Apr. **Rooms** 5 suites, 9 double. 4 in *Maison du Vigneron*. Air-conditioning. **Facilities** Lounge, bar, restaurant; conference room; veranda, dining terrace. No background music. 7-hectare grounds: heated swimming pool, chapel, golf practice. Unsuitable for ♿. **Location** 3 km S of Lunéville, off D914 to Épinal. Follow signs for Adoménil. **Credit cards** All major cards accepted. **Terms** [2004] Room €150–€185, suite €210–€250. Breakfast €17. D,B&B €86 added per person. Set meals €41–€85.

LUSSAC-LES-CHÂTEAUX 86320 Vienne — Map 4:A4

Les Orangeries BUDGET
12 avenue du Docteur Dupont

Tel 05.49.84.07.07
Fax 05.49.84.98.82
Email orangeries@wanadoo.fr
Website www.hotel-lesorangeries.com

'A place to unwind and experience a little of the magic France still offers,' says a visitor in 2004. Jean-Philippe Gautier, an architect, and his wife, Olivia, have restored their manor house, in a town south of Poitiers, while preserving its old character. 'Madame loves her beautiful 18th-century home. It is not for those who want a standard hotel experience (bars, room service, etc). The feel is almost Tuscan: mellow stone, eau de nil paintwork, large terracotta pots, all in a lovely walled garden cocooned from the outside world, though it is on a busy Route Nationale.' You should avoid the rooms that face the road. There are exposed stone walls, parquet floors and paving; an iron balustrade, lit by wall sconces, curves up from the entrance hall; oak stairs are highly polished. Stone walls surround the garden, with its 'amazing, long' (35-metre) swimming pool, tubs of clipped box trees, and orchard. On fine evenings, the no-choice dinner is served outdoors by candlelight: 'We found the food well thought out and tasty.' Vegetarians should give prior notice. Breakfast, also alfresco, has 'delicious jams made with fruits from the garden'. In the games room, a 'beautifully converted' beamed attic the length of the house, are old board games, and antique snooker and billiard tables. (*Sally Holloway*)

Open 15 Jan–15 Dec. **Rooms** 3 suites, 7 double. **Facilities** Salon, games room, dining room; function facilities. Garden: outdoor dining, swimming pool. **Location** 35 km SE of Poitiers on N147 to Limoges (rear rooms quietest), 12 km SW of Montmorillon. **Credit cards** MasterCard, Visa. **Terms** [2004] Room €85–€100, suite €90–€120. Breakfast €12. Set meals €25.

LYON Rhône — Map 6:A3

Hôtel des Artistes
8 rue Gaspard-André
69002 Lyon

Tel 04.78.42.04.88
Fax 04.78.42.93.76
Email hartiste@club-internet.fr

By Théâtre des Célestins, B&B much used by visiting actors. 'Friendly, unpretentious, very central' (near Place Bellecour). Lift. Lounge, bar, breakfast room with Cocteau-style mural. All major credit cards accepted. 45 double-glazed bedrooms, 'small but nicely decorated' (but showers can be awkward): €72–€111. Breakfast €9.

Cour des Loges
6 rue du Bœuf
69005 Lyon

Tel 04.72.77.44.44
Fax 04.72.40.93.61
Email contact@courdesloges.com
Website www.courdesloges.com

'What a remarkable place,' says one of this year's visitors to this designer hotel in the lively narrow streets of the trendy St-Jean quarter of Vieux Lyon. Four adjacent Renaissance mansions have been converted by Jocelyne and Jean-Louis Sibuet to give a 'breathtakingly contemporary interior'. There is a 'magnificent atrium, with dark red cloisters and stunning modern paintings' and 'lovely gardens are scattered behind at all levels: many can be entered directly from the rooms'. It can take time to learn to operate the high-tech fittings in bedrooms and bathrooms (one visitor called the hotel 'a triumph of design over function'). But 'everything was immaculate'; the staff are 'helpful', 'warm and bright'. The restaurant has lost its *Michelin* star and *Gault Millau* points (there is a new chef), but there are plenty of other restaurants nearby. There is a roof garden, a wine cellar (tastings are held), a small mosaic-tiled swimming pool. (*SH, and others*)

Open All year. **Rooms** 10 suites, 37 double, 15 single. All air conditioned. Some no-smoking. **Facilities** Lifts. Lobby (background music), atrium, bar, restaurant; conference facilities; swimming pool, sauna. Terraces/hanging garden. **Location** Vieux Lyon, 1 km NW of main station. Garage (€30 a day),

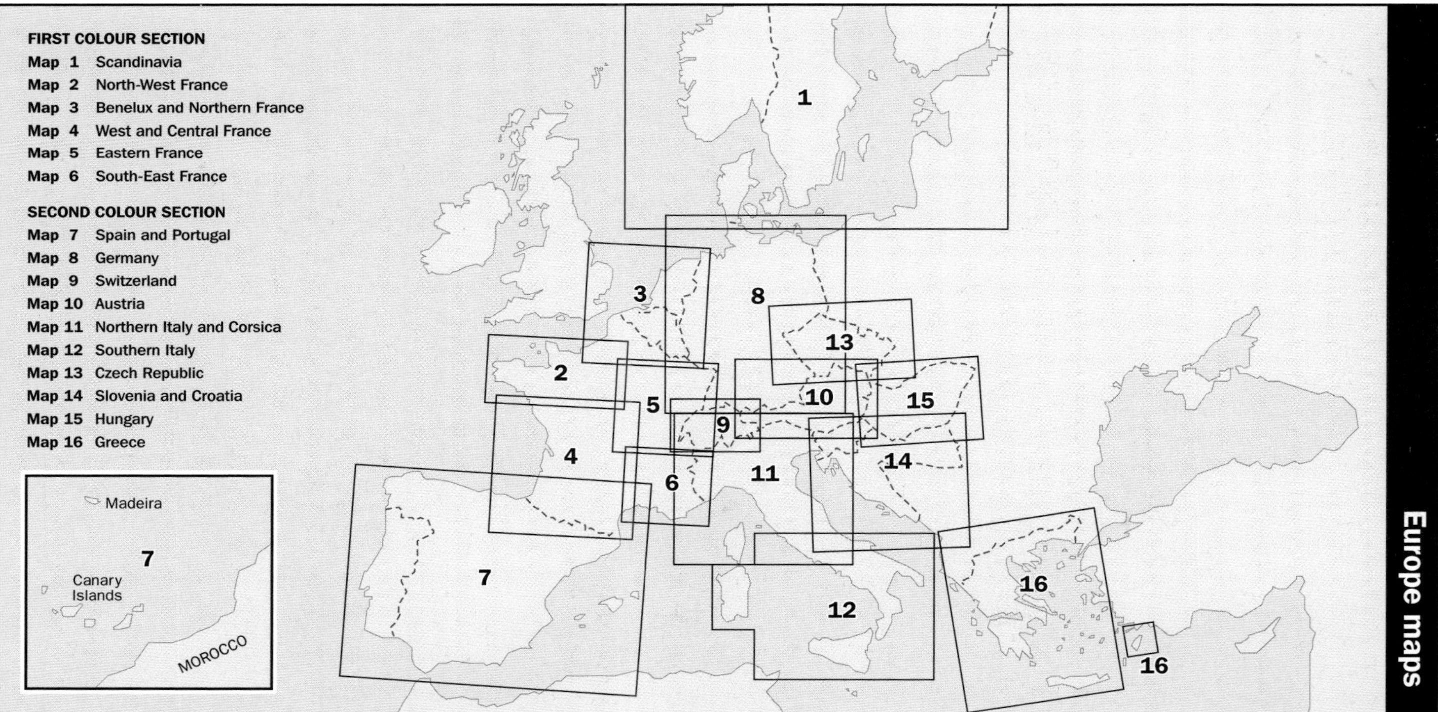
Europe maps
FIRST COLOUR SECTION
Map 1 Scandinavia
Map 2 North-West France
Map 3 Benelux and Northern France
Map 4 West and Central France
Map 5 Eastern France
Map 6 South-East France
SECOND COLOUR SECTION
Map 7 Spain and Portugal
Map 8 Germany
Map 9 Switzerland
Map 10 Austria
Map 11 Northern Italy and Corsica
Map 12 Southern Italy
Map 13 Czech Republic
Map 14 Slovenia and Croatia
Map 15 Hungary
Map 16 Greece
Madeira
7
Canary Islands
MOROCCO
1
2
3
4
5
6
7
8
9
10
11
12
13
14
15
16
16

1 Scandinavia

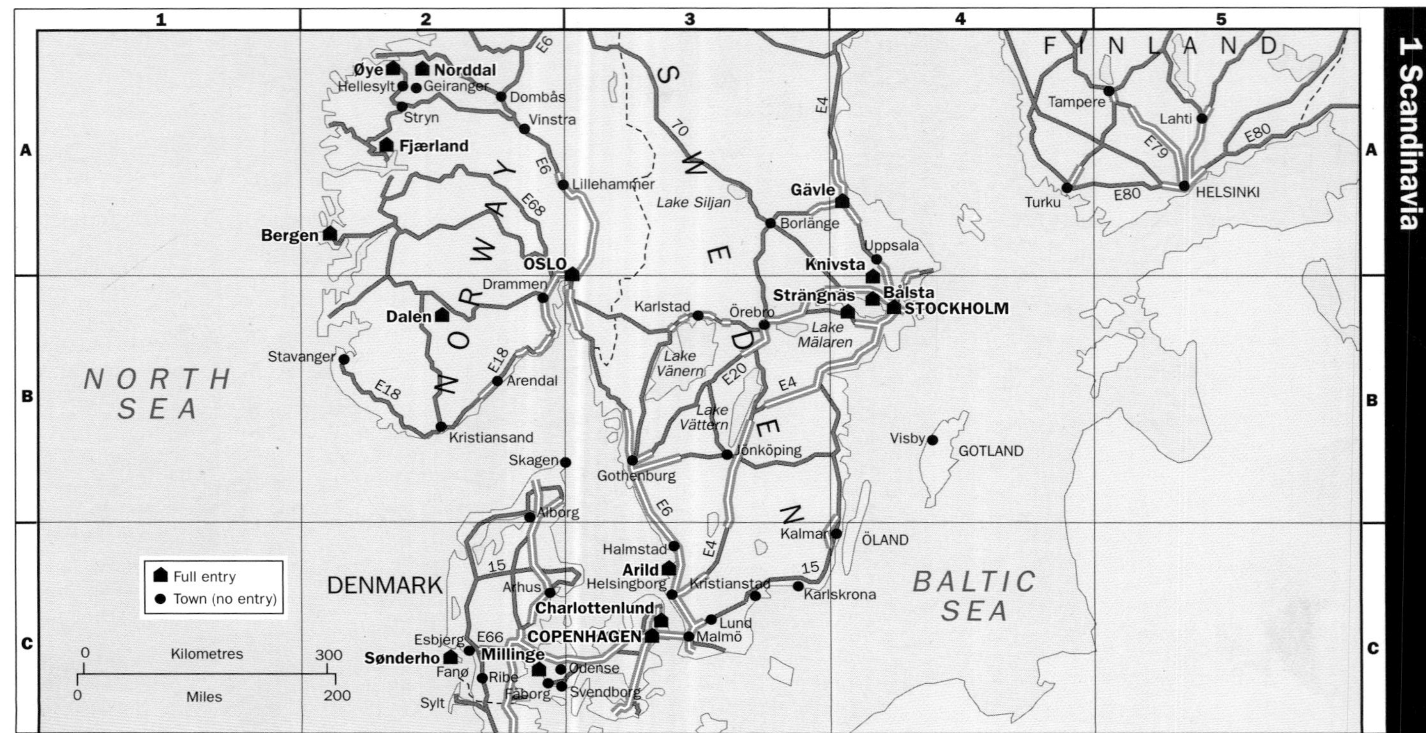

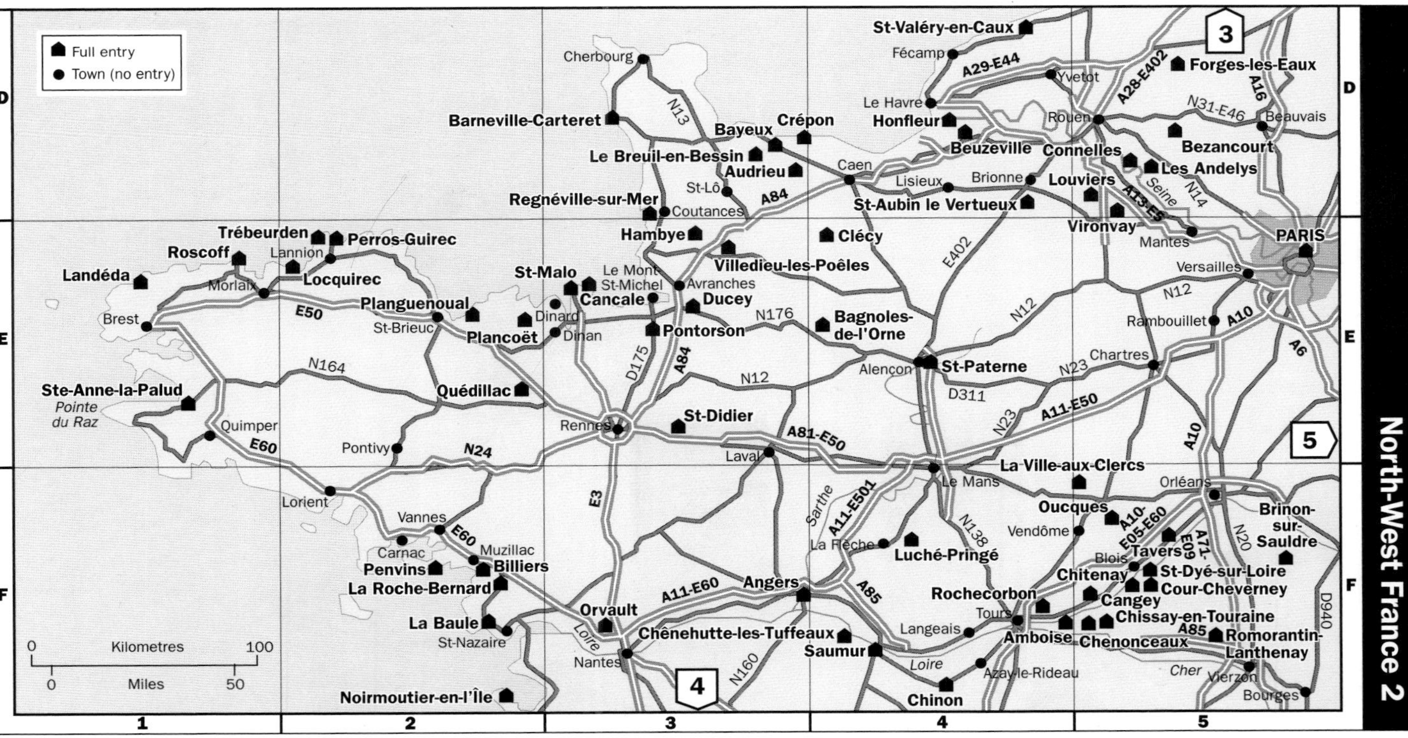

Full entry
Town (no entry)
D
E
F
1
2
3
4
5
3
4
5
Kilometres
Miles
0
50
100
St-Valéry-en-Caux
Fécamp
A29-E44
Yvetot
A28-E402
Forges-les-Eaux
A16
Beauvais
N31-E46
Bezancourt
Les Andelys
N14
Seine
Rouen
Connelles
Louviers
A13-E5
Vironvay
Mantes
PARIS
Versailles
A10
A6
Rambouillet
N12
Chartres
N23
A11-E50
Le Havre
Honfleur
Beuzeville
Brionne
Lisieux
St-Aubin le Vertueux
E402
Caen
Clécy
Villedieu-les-Poêles
Bagnoles-de-l'Orne
Alençon
St-Paterne
D311
N23
Le Mans
La Ville-aux-Clercs
Oucques
Vendôme
Orléans
A10-E05-E60
A71-E09
Tavers
Blois
St-Dyé-sur-Loire
Cour-Cheverney
Chitenay
Cangey
Chissay-en-Touraine
Chenonceaux
A85
Romorantin-Lanthenay
Brinon-sur-Sauldre
N20
D940
Bourges
Vierzon
Cher
Amboise
Azay-le-Rideau
Tours
Rochecorbon
N138
Luché-Pringé
Langeais
Loire
Chinon
Saumur
A85
A11-E501
La Flèche
Sarthe
Cherbourg
N13
Crépon
Bayeux
Audrieu
Le Breuil-en-Bessin
A84
St-Lô
Coutances
Barneville-Carteret
Regnéville-sur-Mer
Hambye
Avranches
Ducey
Pontorson
N176
N12
A81-E50
Laval
St-Didier
A84
Le Mont St-Michel
Cancale
St-Malo
Dinard
Dinan
D175
Rennes
E3
Angers
Chênehutte-les-Tuffeaux
N160
A11-E60
Orvault
Nantes
Loire
Plancoët
Quédillac
N24
Muzillac
Billiers
E60
Vannes
Carnac
Penvins
La Roche-Bernard
La Baule
St-Nazaire
Noirmoutier-en-l'Île
Perros-Guirec
Locquirec
Planguenoual
St-Brieuc
Pontivy
Lorient
Trébeurden
Lannion
E50
N164
Roscoff
Morlaix
Quimper
E60
Landéda
Brest
Ste-Anne-la-Palud
Pointe du Raz

3 Benelux and Northern France

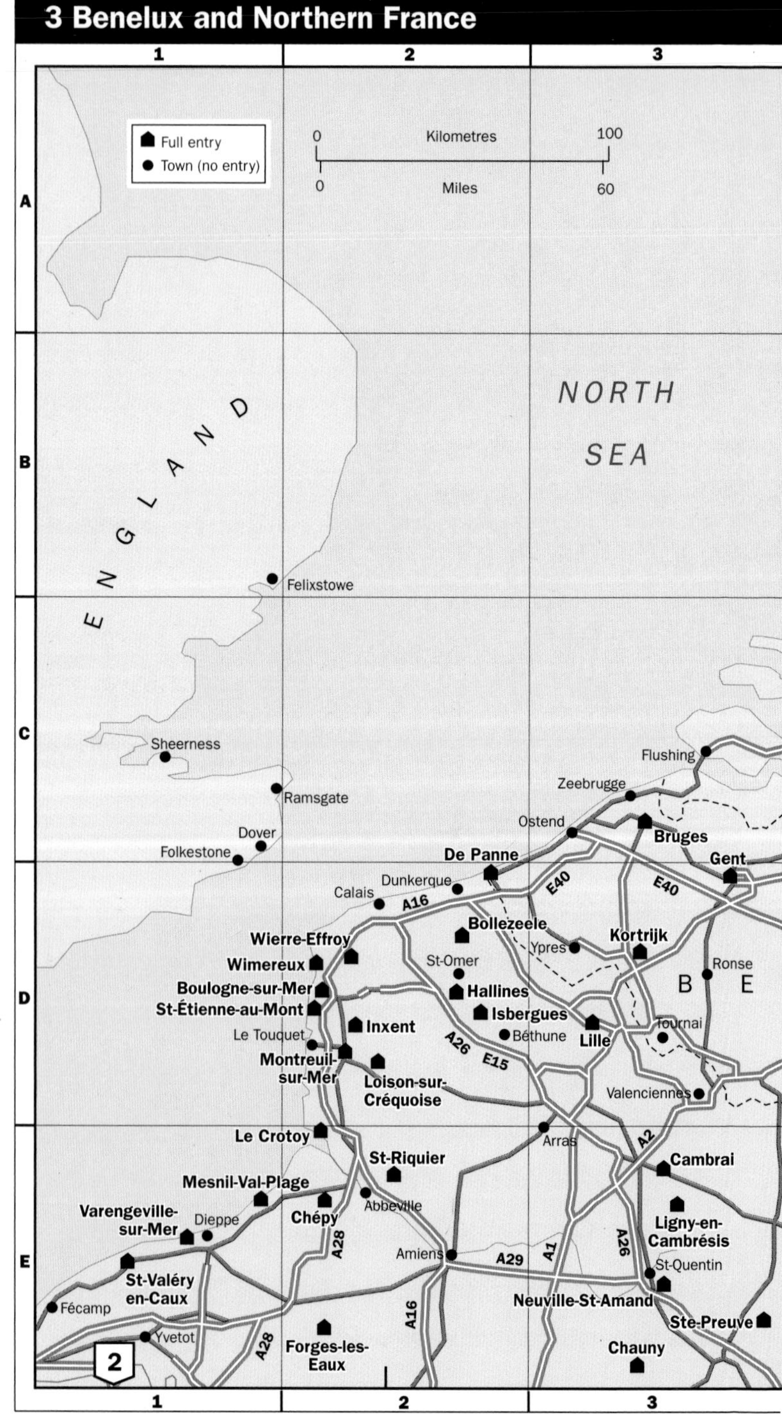

1
2
3
A
B
C
D
E
Full entry
Town (no entry)
0
Kilometres
100
0
Miles
60
NORTH SEA
ENGLAND
Felixstowe
Sheerness
Ramsgate
Dover
Folkestone
Flushing
Zeebrugge
Ostend
Bruges
De Panne
Gent
Dunkerque
Calais
A16
E40
E40
Bollezeele
Wierre-Effroy
Ypres
Kortrijk
Wimereux
St-Omer
Ronse
Boulogne-sur-Mer
Hallines
B E
St-Étienne-au-Mont
Isbergues
Inxent
Tournai
Le Touquet
Béthune
Lille
A26
E15
Montreuil-sur-Mer
Loison-sur-Créquoise
Valenciennes
Le Crotoy
Arras
A2
Cambrai
St-Riquier
Mesnil-Val-Plage
Abbeville
Varengeville-sur-Mer
Dieppe
Chépy
Ligny-en-Cambrésis
A28
A26
Amiens
A29
A1
St-Valéry en-Caux
St-Quentin
Neuville-St-Amand
Fécamp
A16
Ste-Preuve
Yvetot
A28
Forges-les-Eaux
Chauny
2

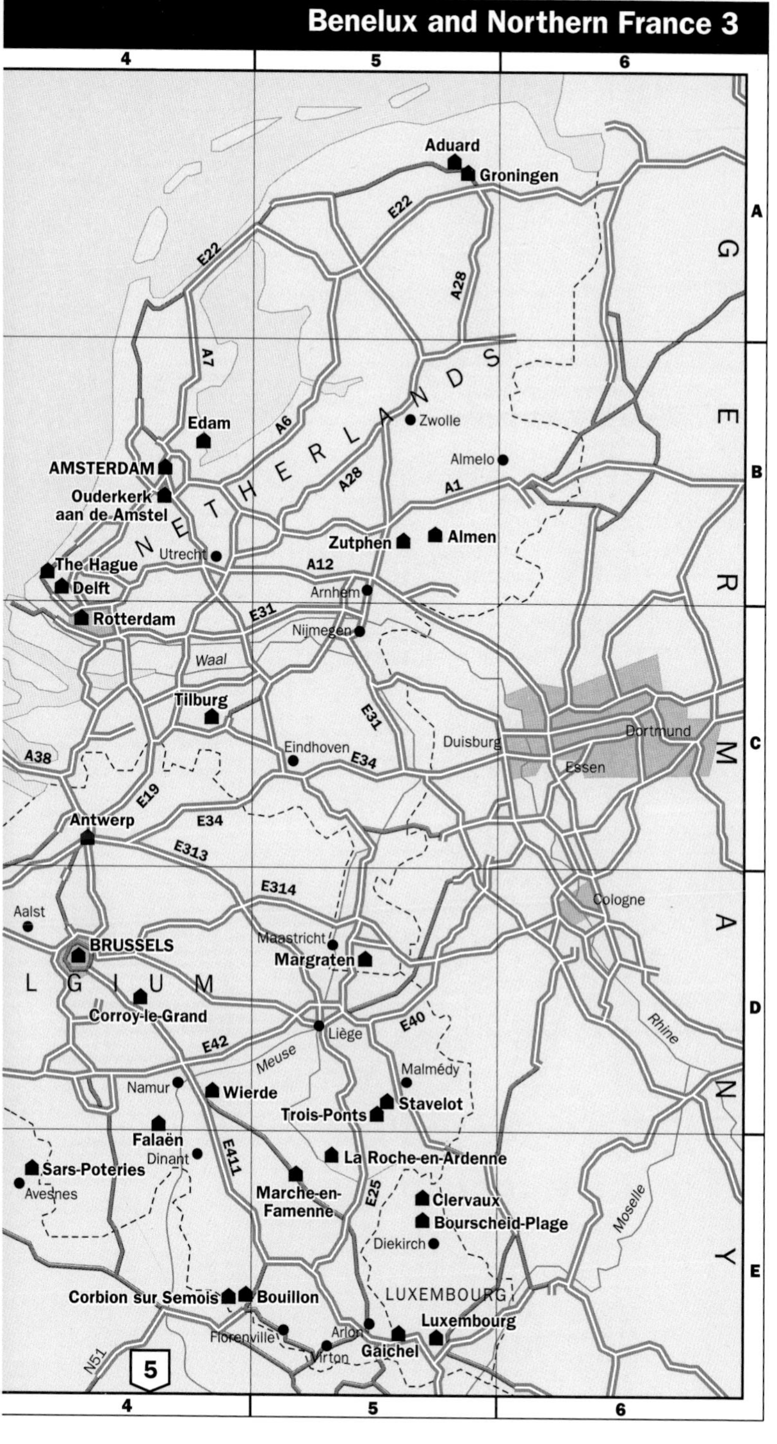
4
5
6
A
B
C
D
E
NETHERLANDS
BELGIUM
GERMANY
Aduard
Groningen
E22
A28
A7
A6
Edam
Zwolle
AMSTERDAM
Ouderkerk aan de Amstel
Almelo
A1
Zutphen
Almen
Utrecht
The Hague
Delft
A12
Arnhem
Rotterdam
E31
Nijmegen
Waal
Tilburg
Eindhoven
E34
Duisburg
Dortmund
Essen
A38
E19
Antwerp
E313
E314
Aalst
Cologne
BRUSSELS
Maastricht
Margraten
Corroy-le-Grand
E40
Liège
E42
Meuse
Rhine
Malmédy
Namur
Wierde
Stavelot
Trois-Ponts
Falaën
Dinant
E411
La Roche-en-Ardenne
Sars-Poteries
Avesnes
Marche-en-Famenne
E25
Clervaux
Bourscheid-Plage
Moselle
Diekirch
LUXEMBOURG
Corbion sur Semois
Bouillon
Luxembourg
Arlon
Florenville
Virton
Gaichel
N51
5

4 West and Central France

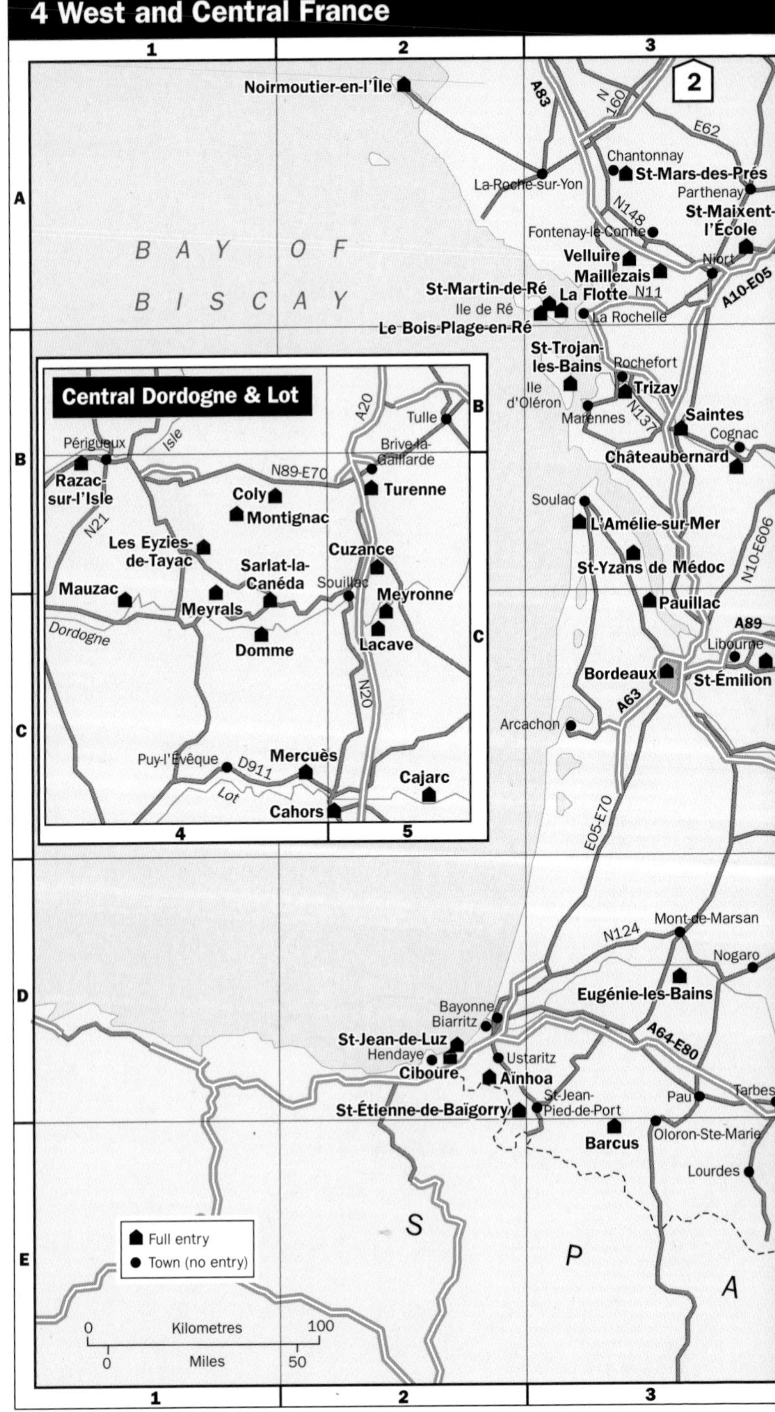

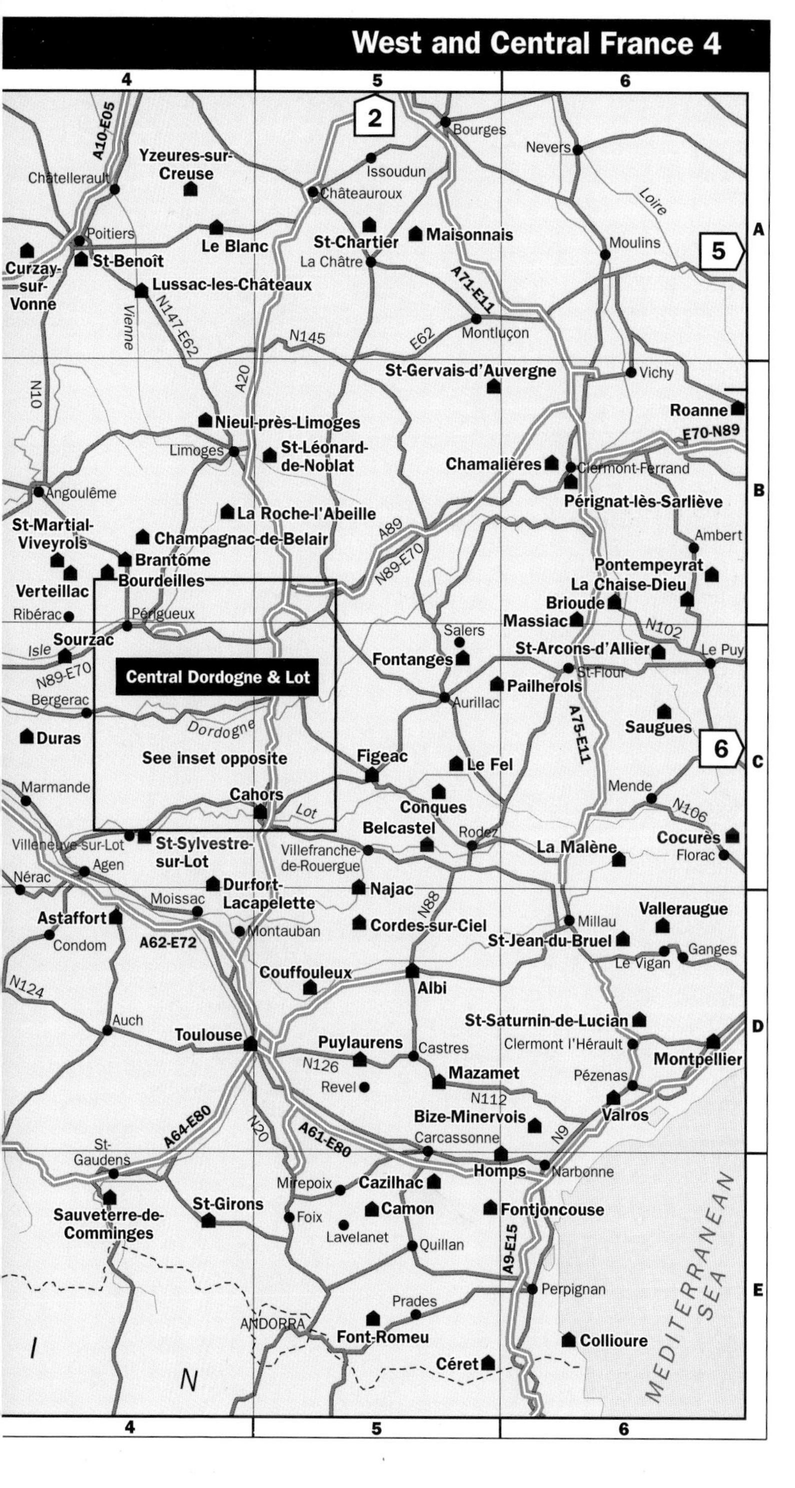

4
5
6
A
B
C
D
E
2
5
6
Bourges
Nevers
Yzeures-sur-Creuse
Châtellerault
Issoudun
Châteauroux
Loire
Poitiers
Le Blanc
St-Chartier
Maisonnais
Moulins
Curzay-sur-Vonne
St-Benoît
La Châtre
Lussac-les-Châteaux
A71-E11
Vienne
N147-E62
N145
E62
Montluçon
A10-E05
St-Gervais-d'Auvergne
Vichy
N10
A20
Roanne
E70-N89
Nieul-près-Limoges
Limoges
St-Léonard-de-Noblat
Chamalières
Clermont-Ferrand
Angoulême
Pérignat-lès-Sarliève
La Roche-l'Abeille
St-Martial-Viveyrols
A89
Ambert
Champagnac-de-Belair
Brantôme
N89-E70
Pontempeyrat
Verteillac
Bourdeilles
La Chaise-Dieu
Brioude
Ribérac
Périgueux
Massiac
Salers
N102
Sourzac
St-Arcons-d'Allier
Isle
Fontanges
Le Puy
N89-E70
Central Dordogne & Lot
St-Flour
Pailherols
Bergerac
Aurillac
A75-E11
Saugues
Duras
Dordogne
See inset opposite
Figeac
Le Fel
Marmande
Mende
Cahors
Conques
N106
Lot
Belcastel
Cocurès
Villeneuve-sur-Lot
St-Sylvestre-sur-Lot
Rodez
Villefranche-de-Rouergue
La Malène
Florac
Agen
Nérac
Durfort-Lacapelette
Najac
Moissac
N88
Valleraugue
Astaffort
Millau
Montauban
Cordes-sur-Ciel
St-Jean-du-Bruel
Condom
A62-E72
Ganges
Le Vigan
Couffouleux
Albi
N124
St-Saturnin-de-Lucian
Auch
Clermont l'Hérault
Toulouse
Puylaurens
Castres
Montpellier
N126
Mazamet
Pézenas
Revel
N112
Valros
Bize-Minervois
A64-E80
N20
A61-E80
N9
Carcassonne
St-Gaudens
Homps
Narbonne
Mirepoix
Cazilhac
St-Girons
Camon
Fontjoncouse
Sauveterre-de-Comminges
Foix
Lavelanet
Quillan
A9-E15
MEDITERRANEAN SEA
Perpignan
Prades
ANDORRA
Font-Romeu
Collioure
Céret
I
N

5 Eastern France

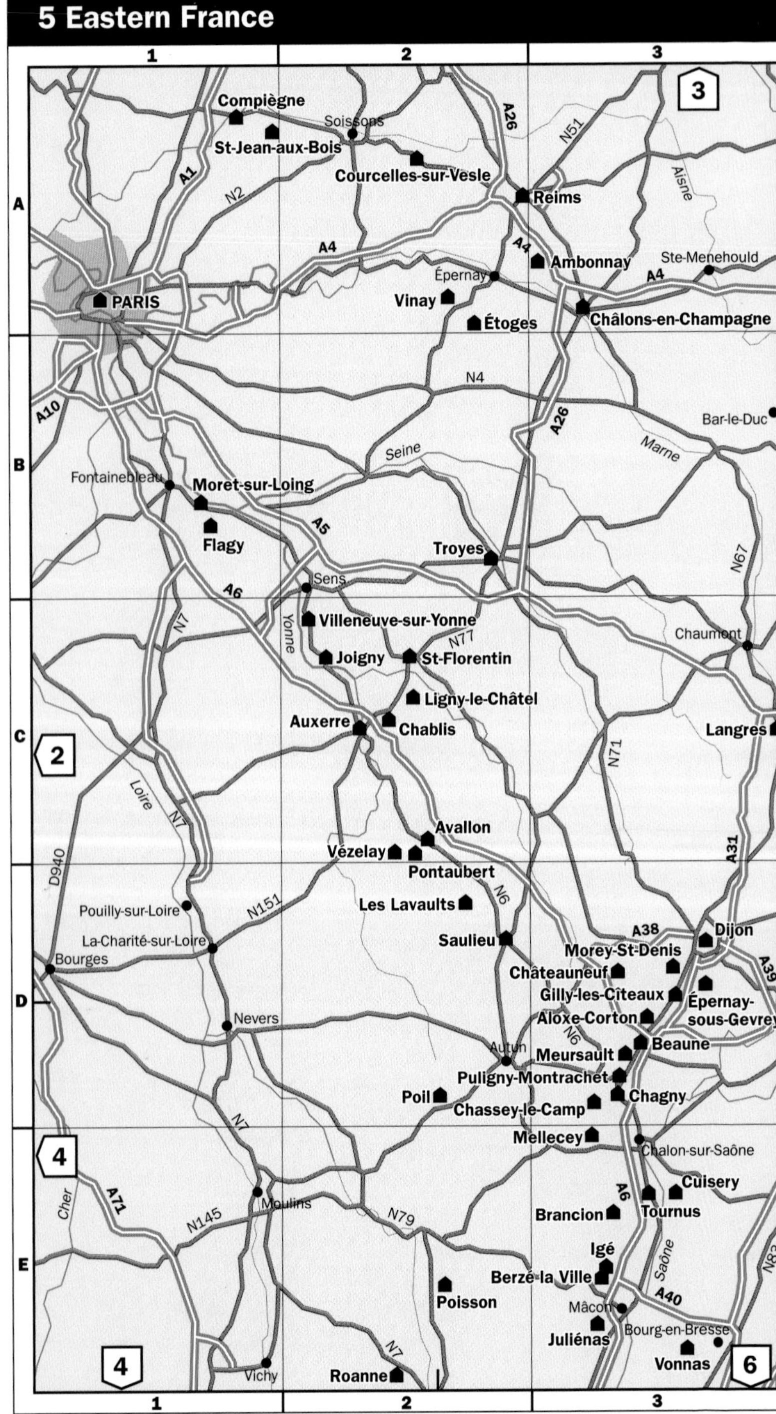

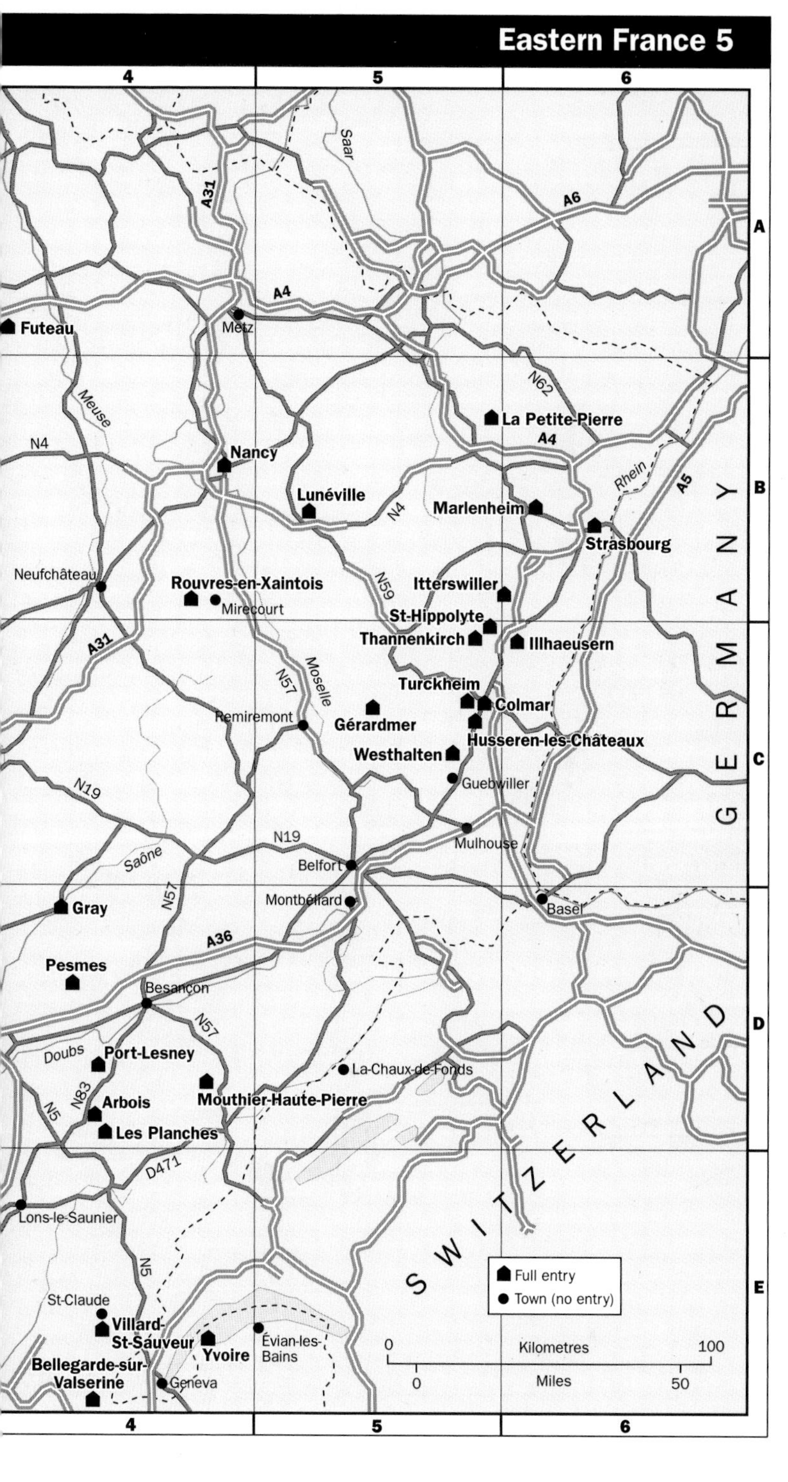
4
5
6
A
B
C
D
E
Saar
A31
A6
A4
Metz
Futeau
N62
Meuse
La Petite-Pierre
A4
N4
Nancy
Rhein
A5
Lunéville
N4
Marlenheim
Strasbourg
GERMANY
Neufchâteau
Rouvres-en-Xaintois
Mirecourt
N59
Itterswiller
St-Hippolyte
Thannenkirch
Illhaeusern
A31
N57
Moselle
Turckheim
Colmar
Remiremont
Gérardmer
Husseren-les-Châteaux
Westhalten
Guebwiller
N19
Mulhouse
N19
Saône
Belfort
Montbéliard
N57
Gray
Basel
A36
Pesmes
Besançon
N57
Doubs
Port-Lesney
La-Chaux-de-Fonds
N83
Arbois
Mouthier-Haute-Pierre
N5
Les Planches
SWITZERLAND
D471
Lons-le-Saunier
N5
Full entry
Town (no entry)
St-Claude
Villard-St-Sauveur
Yvoire
Évian-les-Bains
Bellegarde-sur-Valserine
Geneva
0
Kilometres
100
0
Miles
50
4
5
6

6 South-East France

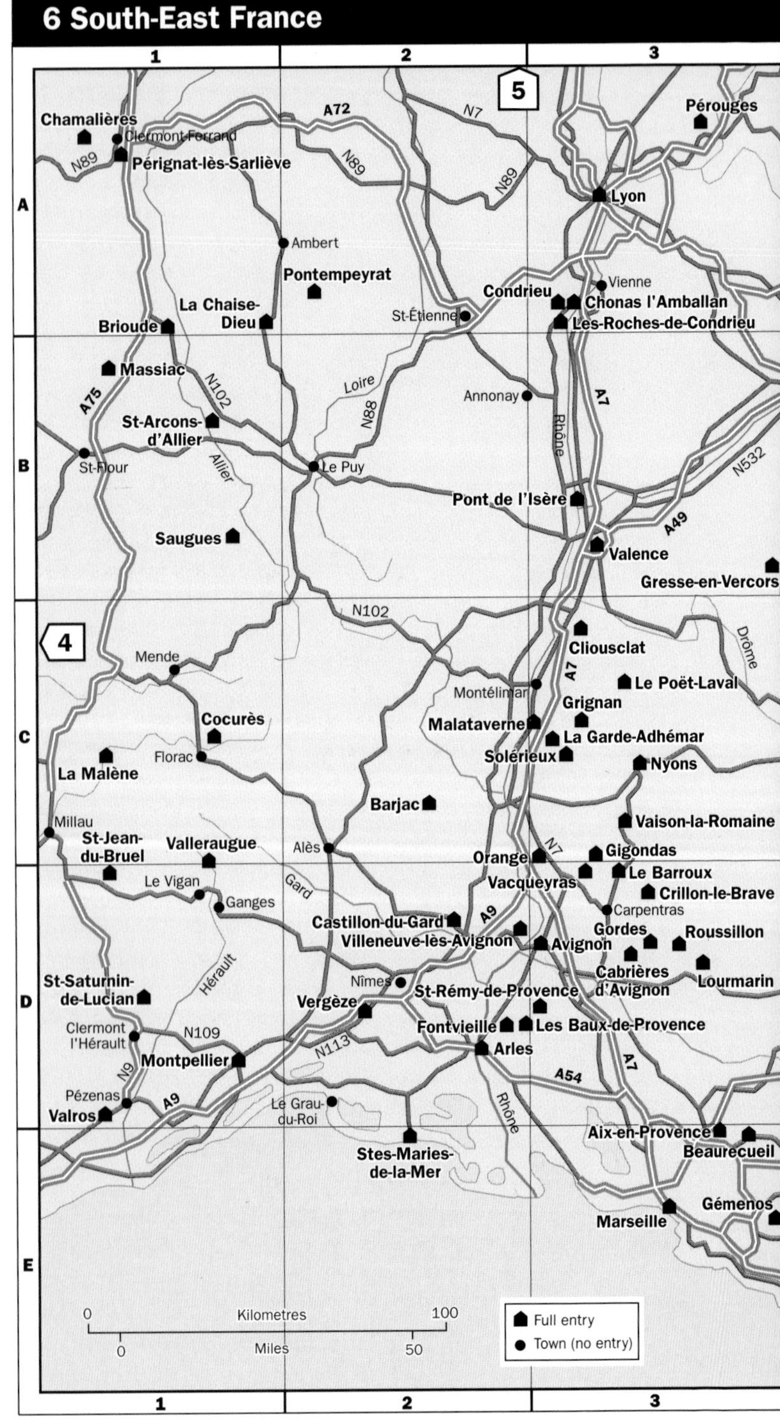

1
2
3
A
B
C
D
E
5
4
Chamalières
Clermont-Ferrand
Pérignat-lès-Sarliève
A72
N7
N89
Pérouges
Lyon
Ambert
Pontempeyrat
La Chaise-Dieu
Brioude
St-Étienne
Condrieu
Vienne
Chonas l'Amballan
Les-Roches-de-Condrieu
Massiac
A75
N102
Loire
N88
Annonay
Rhône
A7
St-Arcons-d'Allier
Allier
St-Flour
Le Puy
N532
Pont de l'Isère
Saugues
A49
Valence
Gresse-en-Vercors
N102
Cliousclat
Drôme
Mende
Montélimar
Le Poët-Laval
Grignan
Cocurès
Malataverne
La Garde-Adhémar
Florac
Solérieux
Nyons
La Malène
Barjac
Vaison-la-Romaine
Millau
St-Jean-du-Bruel
Valleraugue
Alès
Orange
Gigondas
Le Barroux
Vacqueyras
Crillon-le-Brave
Le Vigan
Ganges
Gard
Carpentras
Castillon-du-Gard
A9
Gordes
Roussillon
Villeneuve-lès-Avignon
Avignon
Hérault
Cabrières d'Avignon
Lourmarin
St-Saturnin-de-Lucian
Nîmes
St-Rémy-de-Provence
Vergèze
Clermont l'Hérault
N109
Fontvieille
Les Baux-de-Provence
N113
Arles
Montpellier
N9
A54
Pézenas
A9
Valros
Le Grau-du-Roi
Aix-en-Provence
Beaurecueil
Stes-Maries-de-la-Mer
Marseille
Gémenos
0
Kilometres
100
0
Miles
50
Full entry
Town (no entry)

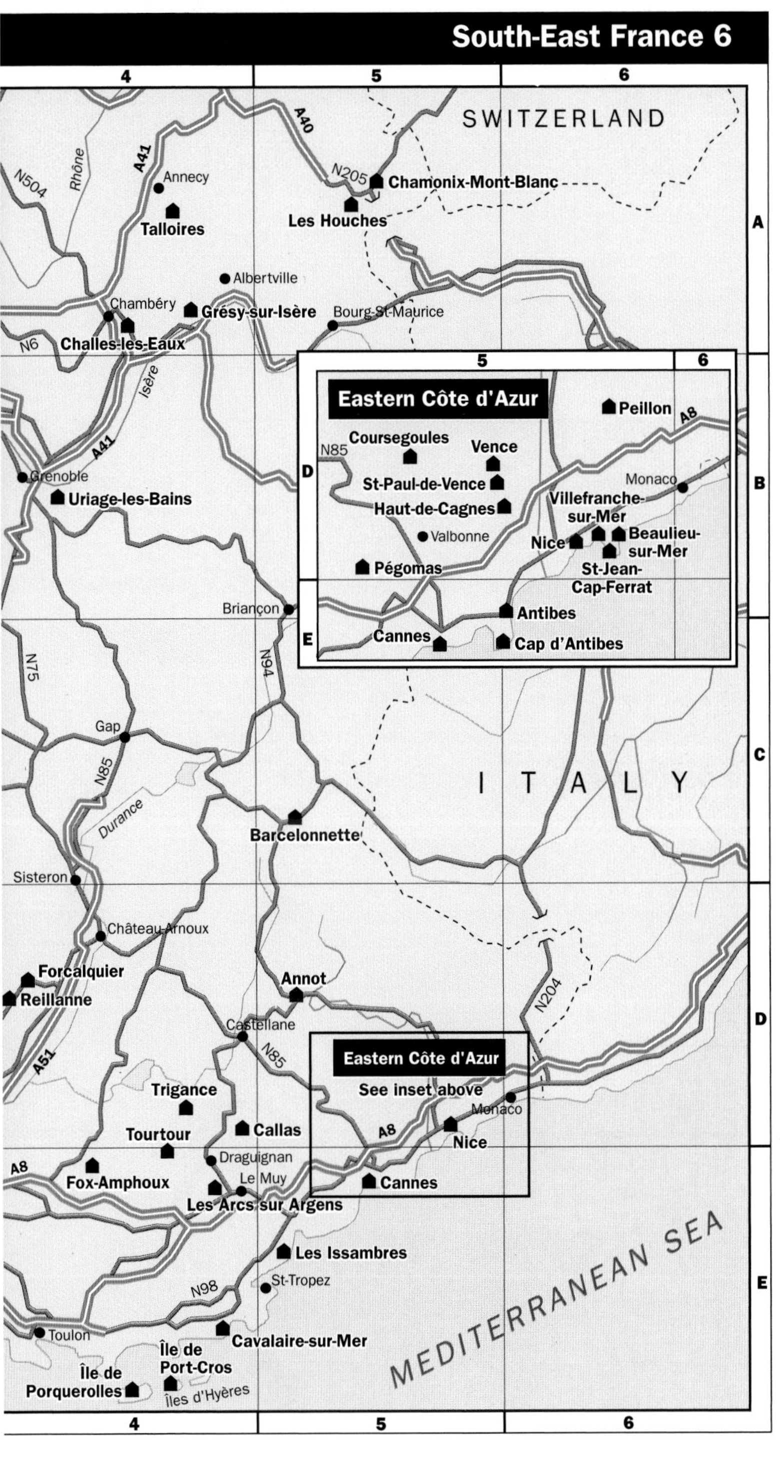
SWITZERLAND
ITALY
MEDITERRANEAN SEA
Annecy
Talloires
Chamonix-Mont-Blanc
Les Houches
Albertville
Chambéry
Grésy-sur-Isère
Bourg-St-Maurice
Challes-les-Eaux
Grenoble
Uriage-les-Bains
Briançon
Gap
Barcelonnette
Sisteron
Château-Arnoux
Forcalquier
Reillanne
Annot
Castellane
Trigance
Callas
Tourtour
Draguignan
Fox-Amphoux
Le Muy
Les Arcs sur Argens
Les Issambres
St-Tropez
Toulon
Cavalaire-sur-Mer
Île de Port-Cros
Île de Porquerolles
Îles d'Hyères
Eastern Côte d'Azur
See inset above
Monaco
Nice
Cannes
Eastern Côte d'Azur
Peillon
Coursegoules
Vence
St-Paul-de-Vence
Haut-de-Cagnes
Valbonne
Villefranche-sur-Mer
Beaulieu-sur-Mer
St-Jean-Cap-Ferrat
Pégomas
Antibes
Cap d'Antibes
Rhône
Isère
Durance
N504
A41
A40
N205
N6
N75
N94
N85
N204
A51
A8
N98
4
5
6
A
B
C
D
E

valet parking (car access with map, ask for access code). **Credit cards** All major cards accepted. **Terms** [2004] Room: single €230, double €250–€370, suite €440–€590. Breakfast €22. Set meals €60–€110; full alc €90.

MAILLEZAIS 85420 Vendée — Map 4:A3

Liliane Bonnet BUDGET
69 rue de l'Abbaye

Tel 02.51.87.23.00
Fax 02.51.00.72.44
Email liliane.bonnet@wanadoo.fr
Website www.acceuilvendee.com

Crisscrossed by canals and slow-moving rivers, the Marais Poitevin (*la Venise verte*) is a strange landscape of marshland and meadows. Punts are a common form of transport, even for weddings or moving cows. In a village in its north is this 'delightful' 19th-century house. 'Large and gracious', 'full of antiques', it is run as a *chambres d'hôtes* by its 'splendid' owner, Liliane Bonnet, whom recent visitors called 'one of the most charming and sympathetic hostesses we have met in France'. 'Our pleasant room overlooked the large garden', which is 'wonderful', with ancient trees. Other guests wrote of 'lovely breakfasts' with 'exquisite home-made jams'. 'We walked through a tunnel to the kitchen garden/orchard and tennis court, and to the river where we took a punt to explore the local waterways.' There is a large salon/library; a conservatory holds a small museum, with ancient local tools. 'In the village's restaurants we had good, honest, country cooking' (*Gault Millau* awards 11 points to *Le Collibert*). Nearby is a Benedictine abbey where Rabelais once lived.

Open All year. **Rooms** 4 double, 1 single. 1 on ground floor. **Facilities** Salon/library/TV room, orangerie (tool museum). No background music. 1-hectare garden: orchard, tennis, swings; cycling, boating, fishing, riding nearby. Unsuitable for ♿. **Location** In village 26 km NW of Niort, 14 km SE of Fontenay. Parking. **Restriction** No smoking: bedrooms, some public rooms. **Credit cards** None accepted. **Terms** (Min. 2 nights in season) B&B: single €57, double €64.

MAISONNAIS 18170 Cher — Map 4:A5

La Maison d'Orsan
Jardins du Prieuré Notre-Dame d'Orsan

Tel 02.48.56.27.50
Fax 02.48.56.39.64
Email prieuredorsan@wanadoo.fr
Website www.prieuredorsan.com

In 1995, two architects, Sonia Lesot and Patrice Taravella, re-created a remarkable medieval garden in an old priory, south of Bourges. It has orchards, medicinal herbs, rose garden, kitchen garden, espaliered fruit trees and much more. Some of the outbuildings (dining halls, dormitories, etc) have been turned into guest rooms 'of a high standard', 'all white, simple, extremely comfortable; lovely bathrooms'. There are wide beds and beamed ceilings. Two rooms have a little private garden. 'The decor, architectural renovation and cuisine are perfect; the kindness of the owners is marvellous,' say guests this year. The host's cooking (12 *Gault Millau* points) uses much home-grown produce and reflects his Italian origins (dishes like tortiglioni à la tomate). In fine weather, guests eat alfresco, under vine-clad pergolas. The public areas are an *enfilade* of spaces, inspired by a French château. There is an exhibition centre and a shop selling home-made jams, books, etc. 'A lovely scullery, too, with boot- and shoe-cleaning materials.' Nearby are the Sancerre vineyards. (*JMT*)

Open 26 Mar–31 Oct. Restaurant closed Mon–Fri midday April/May, Sept/Oct, except holidays. **Rooms** 7 double. 2 on ground floor. **Facilities** Salons (classical background music if wanted), Internet room, 3 dining rooms. 4-hectare garden (outside dining). Unsuitable for ♿. **Location** 45 km S of Bourges on D65; from A71: St-Amand-Montrond exit towards Lignières, then follow signs. **Restrictions** No smoking: restaurant, some bedrooms. No dogs. **Credit cards** MasterCard, Visa. **Terms** [2004] Room €160–€210. Breakfast €18. D,B&B €85 (with wine, water, coffee) added per person. Set meals €45–€54; full alc €60. (€10 reduction after 3 nights.)

MALATAVERNE 26780 Drôme — Map 6:C3

Domaine du Colombier
Route de Donzère

Tel 04.75.90.86.86
Fax 04.75.90.79.40
Email domainecolombier@voila.fr
Website www.domainecolombier.com

In open country south of Montélimar, this creeper-covered 14th-century *bastide* was once an overnight stop for pilgrims. It is now a stylish little hotel, owned and run by Anne and Thierry Chochois. The 'cheerful decor' is liked. 'Our huge room, mainly white, with pink and blue splashes of soft furnishing, had a huge balustraded balcony with tables, chairs and loungers,' writes one correspondent, who, on a previous visit, stayed in 'a green-and-pink bedroom, with wallpaper with roses, small, attractive bathroom and a loo in a cupboard'. The dining room is 'large and pretty, with a fireplace, pale blue chairs and orange-flowered tablecloths'. Guests can take drinks on the lawn by the 'delightful' swimming pool, and dine on a lamp-lit patio. Food is 'superb' (eg, ris de veau aux girolles et truffes blanches d'été; filets de rouget en duo de langoustines) and service is friendly. There is a lovely walled garden at the back. 'Close to the *autoroute*, yet quiet.' (*LB*)

Open All year, except Mon Oct–Feb, 16 Feb–2 Mar, 25 Oct–8 Nov. **Rooms** 3 suites, 22 doubles. Air conditioning. **Facilities** 2 salons, restaurant; dining terrace. No background music. 4-hectare garden: patio, unheated swimming pool. Unsuitable for ♿. **Location** 10 km S of Montélimar, S of Malataverne village, just W of N7 (signposted). Parking. **Credit cards** All major cards accepted. **Terms** Room: double €58–€204, suite €135–€204. Breakfast €12. D,B&B €43 added per person. Set lunch €24, dinner €32–€58; full alc €48.

> 'Set meals' refers to fixed-price meals, which may have ample, limited or no choice on the menu. 'Full alc' is the hotel's estimated price per person of a three-course *à la carte* meal with a half bottle of house wine. 'Alc' is the price without wine.

LA MALÈNE 48210 Lozère — Map 4:C6

Château de la Caze
Route des Gorges du Tarn

Tel 04.66.48.51.01
Fax 04.66.48.55.75
Email ilacaze@ila-chateau.com
Website www.ila-chateau.com/caze

'An excellent centre for touring one of the most spectacular areas of France.' In a large park, beneath the cliffs of the mighty gorge of the Tarn (a 'fantastic landscape'), this 15th-century château stands right by the river. 'A most attractive place', it is managed by Sandrine and Jean-Paul Lecroq (he is the chef). Their staff are 'very friendly', says a recent visitor. 'Our comfortable mini-suite had modern furnishings: its balcony faced the river.' Some bedrooms are in antique style, with tapestries and painted ceiling. In the annexe, some rooms face the swimming pool and river, and bathrooms have a large sunken corner bath. 'Enjoyable meals' are served in the little former chapel, with Gothic fireplace, or on a lovely terrace above the moat. 'Breakfast was a wonderful spread, including fried eggs.' Concerts and gourmet dinners are held.

Open Mid-Mar–mid-Nov. Restaurant closed Wed night/Thurs midday except 14 May–17 Sept and holidays. **Rooms** 6 suites, 13 double. **Facilities** Salons, dining room; outdoor dining terrace. Large grounds with garden; swimming pool. **Location** 5 km NE of La Malène, which is 45 km NE of Millau. **Credit cards** All major cards accepted. **Terms** [2004] Room €95–€150. Breakfast €14. D,B&B €104–€155 per person. Set meals €30–€76.

MARLENHEIM 67520 Bas-Rhin — Map 5:B6

Hôtel Restaurant Le Cerf
30 rue du Général de Gaulle

Tel 03.88.87.73.73
Fax 03.88.87.68.08
Email info@lecerf.com
Website www.lecerf.com

'We very much enjoyed our stay,' say visitors in 2004 to this half-timbered post house in a small town at the end of the Route des Vins west of Strasbourg. Owner/chef Michel Husser and his wife run it with a 'very helpful' staff. The regional cooking is among the finest in Alsace (two *Michelin* stars, 17 *Gault Millau* points, for, eg, salade gourmande aux écrevisses; pigeonneau d'Alsace; soupe au chocolat). 'Super food.' 'The young *sommelier* helped us choose from the vast wine list.' Meals are taken in a panelled dining room 'of immense character' or the 'charming courtyard, cascading with flowers'. Comments on the bedrooms vary: 'Our room was delightfully furnished.' 'My small double had little space to manoeuvre around the bed, and there was no hot water before dinner.' And some rooms hear 'constant traffic' (the inn stands back from the busy main road, windows are double glazed). Other comments: 'A beautiful hotel.' 'A plate of fresh berries and delicious petits fours was in our room.' 'Excellent breakfast.' There is a pleasant walk above the hotel to a small chapel among vineyards. (*JBB, and others*)

Open All year. Closed Tues/Wed, New Year. Air conditioning. **Rooms** 2 suites, 11 double. Some on ground floor. **Facilities** Salon, restaurant (no-smoking section), 2 banqueting rooms. Garden (outdoor dining): terrace. **Location** Central. 20 km W of Strasbourg. Parking in adjoining yard. **Credit cards** All major cards accepted. **Terms** [2004] Room €90–€140, suite €200. Breakfast €15. Set lunch €39, dinner €85–€125; alc €115. *V*

MARSEILLE 13002 Bouches-du-Rhône — Map 6:E3

Résidence du Vieux Port
18 quai du Port

Tel 04.91.91.91.22
Fax 04.91.56.60.88
Email hotel.residence@wanadoo.fr
Website www.hotelmarseille.com

'Splendidly located' on quayside by mairie, *facing S over* Vieux Port: *modern 7-storey B&B hotel, no beauty, but comfortable, surprisingly quiet. Helpful staff. 40 air-conditioned, soundproofed bedrooms (1 suitable for ♿), with huge window, balcony: panoramic views of port and hilltop Notre Dame de la Garde. Lift, bar; conference room. No background music. Sandy beach 15 mins' walk. Arrangement with public garage (200 m). All major credit cards accepted. Room: single €100.50, double €118.50, suite €199. Buffet breakfast €11 [2004].*

MASSIAC 15500 Cantal — Map 4:B6

Grand Hôtel de la Poste BUDGET
26 avenue Charles de Gaulle

Tel 04.71.23.02.01
Fax 04.71.23.09.23
Email hotel.massiac@wanadoo.fr

In small, pretty Auvergne town, on N9, W of the A75: Lucette and Jean-Pierre Delmas's old hotel, in imposing building, well maintained. Large dining room with 'family atmosphere'. 'Wonderful traditional menu (wild boar, fantastic cheeseboard). Amazingly reasonable prices, good breakfast, safe parking.' Bar, brasserie; small leisure centre: indoor and outdoor swimming pools; hammam, squash, gym; shady garden. Safe parking. Closed 15 Nov–15 Dec. All major credit cards accepted. 33 bedrooms in contemporary style: €40–€52. Breakfast €6.50. D,B&B €43–€49. Set meals €12.50–€34 [2004].

MAUZAC 24150 Dordogne — Map 4:C4

La Métairie

Tel 05.53.22.50.47
Fax 05.53.22.52.93
Email metairie.la@wanadoo.fr
Website www.la-metairie.com

In the Périgord Noir, this 'true gem' is run by its 'genial' Swiss owner, Heinz Johner. An ivy-covered 18th-century house, it stands amid pretty countryside, in a park above the Cingle de Trémolat, a spectacular loop in the Dordogne. 'Our room opened on to the garden. Super food; advice given on local (inexpensive) wine. One day we walked to Trémolat, sat on the bank, and watched buzzards gliding on the thermals – magic.' All bedrooms are different. One first-floor suite has its own stone staircase and a sunny balcony, with chairs, looking over the garden. Housekeeping and breakfast are 'excellent'. Regional dishes are served in a wood-beamed dining room with a beautiful fireplace, or on a terrace. Half-board guests have a daily-changing set five-course menu, or they can choose from the *carte* (dishes like ballotin d'asperges, petit rôti de lotte). The 'lovely pool' (renovated this year) is surrounded by a lawn and loungers. Popular in summer with families. (*J and HW, and others*)

Open 1 April–31 Oct. **Rooms** 1 suite, 9 double. 4 on ground floor. Some no-smoking. **Facilities** Salon, bar, restaurant; meeting room. No background music. 7-hectare park: garden, terrace, unheated swimming pool. Unsuitable for ♿. **Location** 3 km N of Mauzac, by C301, 7 km W of Trémolat, by C303. Parking. **Credit cards** All major cards accepted. **Terms** Room €90–€150, suite €170–€230. Breakfast €15. D,B&B €75–€165 per person. Set lunch €20, dinner €40; full alc €60.

MAZAMET 81660 Tarn — Map 4:D5

Marican NEW/BUDGET — *Tel/Fax* 05.63.98.16.60
Pont de l'Arn — *Email* marican@wanadoo.fr
Website www.marican.com

A renovated *maison de maître*, run as a guest house by an English couple, John and Kate Orr (he is front-of-house, she cooks). On a hill in the Haut-Languedoc between Albi and Carcassonne, it has superb views of the Mazamet valley and the Montagne Noire. 'Everything was outstanding,' say visitors in 2004. 'Our large room, beautifully appointed, had sweeping drapes, big, solid wardrobes, large bed; also coffee-making facilities, fridge, bookcase with about 200 books.' There is a residents' lounge, a large swimming pool and a smaller, safe pool for children. The no-choice dinner menu (discussed at breakfast) might include seared scallops in pastis; fillet of beef wrapped in ham. Aperitifs, wine and coffee are included in the price. 'All dishes were beautifully cooked and presented. The puddings made me drool. There appeared to be a waiting list of local French wanting to eat here (non-resident diners are catered for at quiet times).' In this unspoilt region of the Tarn there is much to see, excellent walking. (*John and Pamela Clarke*)

Open All year. **Rooms** 1 family, 5 double. 3 in annexe. **Facilities** Salon with TV, dining room. No background music. 2.2-hectare grounds: terrace, unheated 20 by 8-metre swimming pool, children's pool. Unsuitable for ♿. **Location** 5 mins' drive S of Mazamet, 24 km SE of Castres. **Credit cards** MasterCard, Visa. **Terms** B&B: double €47–€68, family €88; D,B&B €28 added per person. Set dinner (with drinks and coffee) €28. *V*

> Inevitably, some hotels change hands or close after we have gone to press. Please check the ownership when booking, particularly in the case of small places.

MELLECEY 71640 Saône-et-Loire Map 5:E3

Le Clos Saint-Martin
Route de la Vallée
Le Bourg

Tel/Fax 03.85.45.25.93
Email stephan.murraysykes@freesbee.fr

'Our third visit. We enjoy it more each time we stay,' say devotees of this part 13th-century house by the green of a village near Chalon-sur-Saône. Rambling and creeper-covered, it has a peaceful setting. The 'charming' owners, Stephan and Kate Murray-Sykes, run it as a *chambres d'hôtes*. Visitors are welcomed with a glass of wine. 'All is spotless, beds are comfy.' The 'excellent' breakfast includes cereals, cheeses and fruit. 'Our suite in the stable block had sofas, luxurious shower, well-equipped kitchenette.' Some rooms can interconnect to make family accommodation. 'The garden is lovely', and the swimming pool is 'a joy'. Around are vineyards: the host runs a wine business and holds tastings. 'His cellar is magnificent.' There is a large selection of videos in English. Good restaurants nearby: *Le Vendangerot*, Rully, *Hostellerie du Val d'Or* (*Michelin* star), Mercurey. (*Anni Corbett, JFH, and others*)

Open 3 Jan–22 Dec. Closed 2 weeks Feb, 1 week end Oct, Christmas/New Year. **Rooms** 3 suites, 4 double. 4 in stables. Some with kitchenette. **Facilities** Lounge/TV room/kitchen (for guests in main house), breakfast room. No background music. Garden: heated swimming pool. Unsuitable for ♿. **Restrictions** No smoking. No dogs. **Location** Centre of village, 150 m, near pond and *boules* pitch. On D48 10 km W of Chalon-sur-Saône. Parking. **Credit cards** MasterCard, Visa. **Terms** B&B: single €70–€100, double €90–€120, suite €120–€170. *V* (not peak season/holiday weekends)

MERCUÈS 46090 Lot Map 4:C4

Château de Mercuès
Route de Villeneuve-sur-Lot

Tel 05.65.20.00.01
Fax 05.65.20.05.72
Email mercues@relaischateaux.com
Website relaischateaux.com/mercues

Dating in part from the 12th century, this 'truly beautiful', many-turreted castle stands high on a cliff above the River Lot, in 'beautiful formal gardens' on a wine-growing estate: the views from the terrace are 'magic'. Once the residence of the *comtes-éveques* of Cahors, it is now a luxury hotel (Relais & Châteaux), owned by Georges Vigouroux ('his wines are splendid'). It has been tastefully modernised. Recent comments: 'Expensive, but worth every euro: a very honeymoony sort of place.' 'Wonderful, with every comfort, splendid, very rich food.' *Michelin*-starred dishes, eg, turbot with black truffles, are served in the large, high-ceilinged Louis XV restaurant, or in a courtyard. There are tiled floors in public areas, and flowery fabrics in bedrooms (the best ones are said to be those in a tower). An Olympic-size swimming pool is 'discreetly hidden at the bottom of the park'. Some noise from the railway in the valley. (*JBH*)

Open Easter–Nov. Restaurant closed Mon, and midday Tues, Wed and Thurs. **Rooms** 6 suites, 22 double. Some on ground floor. **Facilities** Lift. 3 salons, bar, restaurant; wine cellar; conference facilities. 22-hectare park: garden, swimming pool, tennis. **Location** 6 km NW of Cahors, off D911. Helipad. **Credit cards** All major cards accepted. **Terms** [2004] Room €160–€260, suite €270–€400. Breakfast €18. D,B&B (min. 2 nights) €150–€200 per person. Set meals €52–€90; alc €65–€95.

MESNIL-VAL-PLAGE 76910 Seine-Maritime — Map 3:E1

Hostellerie de la Vieille Ferme NEW/BUDGET

Tel 02.35.86.72.18
Fax 02.35.86.12.67

In a small seaside resort in a gap in high chalk cliffs on the Normandy coast between Le Tréport and Dieppe, this Logis de France is on the main street, which has 'splendid examples of French seaside architecture of around 1900'. The large rustic-style restaurant is on the ground floor of an 18th-century half-timbered house. Here, says the nominator, 'the serious action takes place. We had a terrific plateau des fruits de mer, served on a kind of three-tier castle, most impressive and one of the tastiest we have had in France. Breakfast was more modest, but had a boil-it-yourself contraption for eggs.' The bedrooms, in three separate buildings, vary in size. 'Ours was simple and small.' There is a pleasant shady terrace. (*Graham Avery*)

Open All year, except early Dec–mid-Jan, Sun/Mon Oct–mid-Mar. **Rooms** 33. In 3 buildings. **Facilities** Small lounge, bar, restaurant; conference facilities. Terrace. Garden. **Location** NE of Criel sur Mer, 25 km NE of Dieppe. Free car park. **Credit cards** All major cards accepted. **Terms** [2004] B&B: single €52, double €74. Breakfast €8. D,B&B €50–€70 per person. Set meals €17–€37.

MEURSAULT 21190 Côte-d'Or — Map 5:D3

Les Magnolias
8 rue Pierre-Joigneaux

Tel 03.80.21.23.23
Fax 03.80.21.29.10
Email hotel@les-magnolias.com
Website www.les-magnolias.fr

'It was a pleasure to return to this small hotel,' says a correspondent in 2004. An 18th-century residence with a flowery courtyard, it is run by its 'charming' half-English owner, Antonio Delarue. 'When we arrived he was making apricot jam.' This is served at the 'delicious' breakfast along with leaf tea, freshly squeezed orange juice, and 'croissants, brioches and bread delivered at 7.45 am'. The 'family atmosphere' is liked, and the bedrooms are 'very attractive with some antiques'. Some rooms are large; some face 'gorgeous countryside', but front ones hear early agricultural traffic, and lighting can be dim. For meals, the *Hôtel du Centre* ('good simple cooking') and the *Hôtel des Arts* ('pleasant garden'), both in the square, are recommended (*Marilyn Frampton; also Roger and Jean Cook, Jennifer and Michael Hodge*)

Open 15 Mar–30 Nov. **Rooms** 1 suite, 11 double. 3 on ground floor. In 2 buildings. Some no-smoking. **Facilities** Salon/bar/library. No background music. Terrace, courtyard. **Location** Central (signposted). 8 km SW of Beaune. Courtyard parking. **Restriction** No pets. **Credit cards** Amex, MasterCard, Visa. **Terms** [2004] Room €86–€128. Breakfast €9.

MEYRALS 24220 Dordogne — Map 4:C4

Hôtel de la Ferme Lamy NEW

Tel 05.53.29.62.46
Fax 05.53.59.61.41
Email ferme-lamy@wanadoo.fr
Website www.ferme-lamy.com

Michelin finds Michel and Nelly Bougon's extended 17th-century farmhouse in the Périgord Nord near Sarlat, 'ravishing' and tells of its '*ambiance cosy*'. And this year's nominator found it, in good weather, 'a perfect place to do nothing'. Surrounded by fields and woods, it is 'very pleasant, totally quiet'. Many of the bedrooms have a terrace, some have old beams, most have antiques; the best one, Prestige, has a fireplace. 'Our room had a shower, and an extra bed in a gallery. Breakfast [with home-baked breads and home-made jams] was on a shaded area by the large swimming pool which has good views.' There is a 'nice lounge'. The 'family atmosphere' is liked. 'An excellent restaurant is just down the lane, there are two in the village, two kilometres away, and Les Eyzies-de-Tayac is an easy ten-minute drive.' (*Stephen Hugh-Jones, and others*)

Open All year. **Rooms** 12. Most on ground floor. Air conditioning. **Facilities** Lounge, breakfast room. Garden: terraces, swimming pool. **Location** 8 km SE of Les Eyzies, towards Sarlat by D47. **Credit cards** All major cards accepted. **Terms** [2004] Room €90–€200. Breakfast €10–€15.

MEYRONNE 46200 Lot — Map 4:C5

La Terrasse

Tel 05.65.32.21.60
Fax 05.65.32.26.93
Email terrasse.liebus@wanadoo.fr
Website www.hotel-la-terrasse.com

Formerly the summer residence of the bishops of Tulle, this 11th-century château stands above the Dordogne, near Rocamadour: it has 'glorious views'. 'We loved the personal care and the informality; Françoise Liebus is a charming hostess,' say recent visitors. Her husband, Gilles, is the chef, serving regional cooking in a vaulted room above the river, eg, escalope de foie gras de canard frais; tournedos de bœuf aux morilles. Summer meals are served on a shady riverside veranda; a sunny terrace contains the swimming pool. Breakfast is an 'excellent buffet'. The building is 'eccentric, with ancient beams, creaky floorboards and spiral staircases', and bedrooms vary greatly. Some are large; some are in an adjacent 9th-century castle. 'Ours was in the keep, approached by a winding stone staircase.' Dissenters found their rooms 'awkwardly designed', and the lounge 'small and unwelcoming'. (*Stephen Holman, and others*)

Open Mar–10 Nov. Restaurant closed Tues midday. **Rooms** 5 suites, 12 double. 1 on ground floor. 4 air conditioned. **Facilities** Ramps. 2 salons, TV room, bar, 3 dining rooms; function facilities. No background music. Small garden: dining terrace, unheated swimming pool. Unsuitable for ♿. **Location** On Dordogne, 13 km SE of Souillac, 12 km NW of Rocamadour. **Credit cards** All major cards accepted. **Terms** [2004] Room €60–€125, suite €155–€230. Breakfast €10. D,B&B €75–€122 per person. Set meals €25–€49; full alc €50.

MONTIGNAC 24290 Dordogne — Map 4:C4

Hostellerie La Roseraie
Place d'Armes

Tel 05.53.50.53.92
Fax 05.53.51.02.23
Email laroseraie@fr.st
Website www.laroseraie.fr.st

By the River Vézère in this medieval village, this handsome 19th-century building has 'delightful, hands-on' owners, Vincent and Isabelle Nourrisson, who run it with a 'light touch'. She has a 'lovely, bubbly personality' and speaks good English, and the ambience is friendly, say recent visitors. 'Our room faced the river; the bathroom had lots of toiletries.' Traditional meals are served in the *coquette salle à manger bourgeoise* (*Michelin*'s description), or under parasols on a lawn. 'The grounds are large and peaceful: ivy-covered walls, mature trees, a goldfish pond, lots of roses.' Palms stand beside the attractive curving swimming pool; there is a paddling pool for tinies. 'Lots of garden furniture; a waitress came round offering drinks. On a scorching hot day, all was cool, quiet. Breakfast, a self-service buffet, was great.'

Open 2 Apr–7 Nov. Restaurant closed midday weekdays 15 Sept–15 June. **Rooms** 14. **Facilities** Bar, restaurant. Large grounds: garden, swimming pool, mountain bikes. Tennis nearby. **Location** 25 km N of Sarlat. Garage. **Credit cards** MasterCard, Visa. **Terms** [2004] Room €80–€130. Breakfast €10. D,B&B €75–€100 per person.

MONTPELLIER 34000 Hérault — Map 6:D1

Hôtel Le Guilhem
18 rue Jean-Jacques Rousseau

Tel 04.67.52.90.90
Fax 04.67.60.67.67
Email hotel-le-guilhem@mnet.fr
Website www.leguilhem.com

Montpellier has some grandiose modern architecture but is full of historical interest too, and has a charming *Vieille Ville*, well restored. Here, down a narrow street, this group of fine 16th/17th-century buildings is an appealing B&B hotel owned by Eric Charpentier, liked again in 2004: 'Most welcoming staff. A very comfortable stay.' 'The same bedroom as last year, looking on to gardens and cathedral. As nice and quiet as ever.' 'Good continental breakfast.' Some rooms are small. Access by car is tricky, particularly on a Sunday, and one reader advises: 'Phone for advice about parking.' Some nearby garages offer special rates. No restaurant: try *Le Petit Jardin*, next door ('excellent'); *Isadora*, in a vaulted 13th-century cellar; *Pomme d'Or*. (*Michael and Betty Hill, Andrew Semple; also FH Potts*)

Open All year. **Rooms** 33 double, 3 single. 9 in adjacent annexe. Air conditioning. **Facilities** Lifts. Breakfast room; terrace. Unsuitable for ♿. **Location** *Centre historique*. Approach from W, via Promenade du Peyrou. Public car parks nearby (Peyrou-Pitot, Foch). **Credit cards** All major cards accepted. **Terms** [2004] Room €71–€135. Breakfast €11.

MONTREUIL-SUR-MER 62170 Pas-de-Calais Map 3:D2

Château de Montreuil
4 chaussée des Capucins

Tel 03.21.81.53.04
Fax 03.21.81.36.43
Email reservations@chateaudemontreuil.com
Website www.chateaudemontreuil.com

'Unqualified excellence all round. It is always a delight to stay here.' 'The most comfortable of hotels.' Again there is enthusiasm for this 1930s house (Relais & Chateaux), turquoise-shuttered, in a walled garden near the ruined citadel of this medieval hilltop town near Le Touquet. Christian and Lindsay Germain have presided for over 20 years. He earns a *Michelin* star, 15 *Gault Millau* points for, eg, mi-cuit de thon rouge en croûte de pain d'épices; grouse d'Écosse rôtie aux haricots cocos. She is responsible for the decor. The bedrooms are liked: 'Not too frilly.' 'Our delightful room had a balcony facing garden and ramparts, fantastic bathroom with copper ceiling.' But an inspector found a hand-held shower 'temperamental'. The 'excellent' breakfast includes 'hot loaves and rich jams'. Service, though formal, is friendly. Many residents are British, but French locals patronise the restaurant. 'The staff are very good with children' (there is a babysitting service). Azincourt (Agincourt) village (with fine *Centre Médiéval*) is half an hour's drive away. (*David Crowe, Rodney Baker-Bates, and others*)

Open Feb–mid-Dec. Closed Mon. Restaurant also closed Thurs midday, and Tues midday except July/Aug. **Rooms** 4 suites (3 in air-conditioned cottages), 10 double, 4 single. **Facilities** Lounge, bar, restaurant (no-smoking). No background music. Garden: terrace, small swimming pool (heated all year). Unsuitable for ♿. **Location** 1 km from centre, opposite Roman citadel. 38 km S of Boulogne, off N1 and A16. Parking. Garage (€8). **Credit cards** All major cards accepted. **Terms** [2004] Room €170–€255, suite €255. Breakfast €15. D,B&B double €350–€410. Set meals €38–€75; full alc €75. *V* (Sat night and Tues night Nov/Dec, Feb/Mar)

Auberge de la Grenouillère
La Madelaine-sous-Montreuil

Tel 03.21.06.07.22
Fax 03.21.86.36.36
Email auberge.de.la.grenouillere@wanadoo.fr
Website www.lagrenouillere.fr

'Idyllically' set on the little River Canche, below the citadel, this restaurant-with-rooms is very personally run by its owner, Roland Gauthier. 'He is concerned for guests' comfort,' one visitor wrote. He and his son, Alexandre, serve 'classic French cooking' (15 *Gault Millau* points for, eg, St-Jacques en coquilles; carré d'agneau aux fruits de saison; 'inspired regional desserts'). Their speciality, of course, is cuisses de grenouilles à l'ail. Meals are served in three dining rooms (one with 1920s frog murals) and a flowery courtyard. 'M. Gauthier took our telephone booking (in good English), greeted us on arrival, took us to our lovely room: it had all we could need.' Of the bedrooms (in an annexe): the main one is beamed; another has striped wallpaper; two smaller cottage rooms open on to a courtyard. 'Above-average pine-clad bathroom; good lighting.' 'Wonderful breakfast: perfect coffee, fruit salad, freshly squeezed juice, home-made preserves.' (*J and JM, D and JB*)

Open All year, except Jan. Closed Tues/Wed except July/Aug. **Rooms** 1 suite, 3 double. All on ground floor, in annexe. **Facilities** Salon, bar, 3 dining rooms (no-smoking); background music. Garden on river (outdoor dining). **Location** 2.5 km W of Montreuil, by D917, D139. Parking. **Credit cards** All major cards accepted. **Terms** [2004] Room €75–€100, suite €100. Breakfast €10–€13 or alc. Set meals €30–€70; full alc €100.

MORET-SUR-LOING 77250 Seine-et-Marne — Map 5:B1

Hostellerie du Cheval Noir NEW
47 avenue Jean Jaurès

Tel 01.60 70 80 20
Fax 01.60.70.80 21
Email chevalnoir@chateauxhotels.com
Website www.chevalnoir77.com

Just W of western gate of 'amazingly picturesque', tiny home town of Impressionist painter Alfred Sisley, 11 km SE of Fontainebleau: former 18th-century relais de poste, *now Gilles de Crick's restaurant-with-rooms. 'His imaginative dishes are worth the visit: "Yeux fermés" [surprise] menu, the best I had in France. Very nice room with balcony,' says nominator. Bar, restaurant,* Les Impressionistes, *hung with paintings and with huge picture window facing garden (closed Mon midday, Tues midday); alfresco meals. Closed 3–14 Jan, 26 July–12 Aug. Amex, MasterCard, Visa accepted. 10 bedrooms: €80–€110. Breakfast €10. D,B&B €80–€190 per person. Set meals €20–€68 [2004].*

MOREY-ST-DENIS 21220 Côte d'Or — Map 5:D3

Castel de Très Girard
7 rue de Très Girard

Tel 03.80.34.33.09
Fax 03.80.51.81.92
Email info@castel-tres-girard.com
Website www.castel-tres-girard.com

Quietly set amid noble Burgundy vineyards, 4 km S of Gevrey-Chambertin: handsome 18th-century manor house in large garden with unheated swimming pool. Now restaurant-with-rooms, owned by Didier and Lionnel Petitcolas and Sébastien Pilat. Renovated in 2000, keeping old beams, original stonework; 'comfortable, well run and quiet, with friendly service, good food' (regional dishes); long wine list. Bar, lounge bar, restaurant (closed Sat midday, Mon/Tues midday); background music; dining terrace. Parking. Closed 1–26 Feb. All major credit cards accepted. 2 suites €160, 8 'adequate' double rooms €85–€120. Buffet breakfast €11. Set meals €21–€100 [2004]. Endorsed this year.

MOUTHIER-HAUTE-PIERRE 25920 Doubs Map 5:D4

Hôtel Restaurant la Cascade NEW/BUDGET *Tel* 03.81.60.95.30
4 route des Gorges de Noailles *Fax* 03.81.60.94.55
Email hotellacascade@wanadoo.fr

Traditional country inn, modernised by owner/managers René and Madeleine Savonet, in beautiful part of the Jura. Renominated this year: 'Very comfortable, delicious food. Balconies of nearly every room overlook River Loue flowing through fantastic limestone gorge.' Marvellous views from no-smoking restaurant. Parking. No dogs. Unsuitable for ♿. Open 11 Mar–2 Nov. Amex, MasterCard, Visa accepted. 19 comfortable, rustic bedrooms: €48–€62. Breakfast €8. D,B&B €60–€69 per person. Set meals €19–€42.

NAJAC 12270 Aveyron Map 4:D5

L'Oustal del Barry BUDGET *Tel* 05.65.29.74.32
Place du Bourg *Fax* 05.65.29.75.32
Email oustal@caramail.com
Website www.oustaldelbarry.com

In a remote spot above the Aveyron gorges, this well-preserved *bastide* village (population 250) was founded in the 13th century below a hilltop fortress, now a ruin. In the square is this 'extremely well-run' Logis de France, owned by chef Rémy Simon. He wins a *Michelin Bib Gourmand*, 13 *Gault Millau* points for, eg, pavé de veau du Bas Rouergue; l'astet najacois et aligot de Laguiole. His cooking is 'nothing short of excellent', wrote one correspondent, who also praised the wines, service and 'exceptional value for money'. 'The no-choice *pension* menu is interestingly varied from day to day, and the food is presented with great artistry,' says another. The restaurant, with rustic decor, is 'filled with locals', and you can dine out on the terrace. The breakfast (not a buffet) is also enjoyed. It includes home-made jams, yogurt, 'very good bread'. Bedrooms (many were refurbished this year) are 'simple but comfortable'. 'Ours had a good view over the garden.' (*Colin and Stephanie McFie, SH, CS*)

Open 1 Apr–15 Nov. Restaurant closed midday Mon and Tues, to non-residents Mon night. **Rooms** 18 doubles. **Facilities** Lift. 2 lounges, seminar room, 2 dining rooms; background music throughout. Garden: terraces, children's playground. Free access to public swimming pool and tennis courts. **Location** Centre of village. 19 km SW of Villefranche-de-Rouergue, off D122. Train from Paris; station 0.5 km (hotel will meet). Parking. **Restriction** No smoking. **Credit cards** All major cards accepted. **Terms** Room €43–€60. Breakfast €8.70. D,B&B €24.50–€34 added per person. Set meals €22.80–€48.

We give details about the credit cards which the hotels tell us that they accept. But please check with them, when booking, that this is still the case.

NANCY 54000 Meurthe-et-Moselle **Map 5:B4**

Grand Hôtel de la Reine
2 place Stanislas

Tel 03.83.35.03.01
Fax 03.83.32.86.04
Email nancy@concorde-hotels.com
Website www.hoteldelareine.com

This 18th-century palace is where Marie-Antoinette stayed on her way to meet her husband-to-be, Louis XVI. Now a hotel, 'in the best discreet French tradition', it belongs to the Concorde group. The decor is in Louis XV style: high ceilings, chandeliers, panelling. 'The faded grandeur is appealing,' says a visitor this year. The best, 'Royal' rooms overlook the 'stunningly beautiful' Place Stanislas; quietest ones face the inner courtyard. 'Ours,' wrote a recent guest, 'was well furnished, with a smart bathroom, and was always in excellent order. In the restaurant, elegantly laid out, cooking and presentation were very good. The local Toul wine is pleasant. A good and varied buffet breakfast. Service was impeccable.' Another visitor recommends dining at the *Brasserie Excelsior Flo*, 'a gloriously buzzy Art Deco joint with great food at reasonable prices'. (*AT*)

Open All year. Restaurant closed Sun 1 Nov–1 Apr, Sat midday. **Rooms** 7 suites, 35 double. **Facilities** Lift. Salon, bar, restaurant; conference room. **Location** Central (windows double glazed). Public parking nearby. **Credit cards** All major cards accepted. **Terms** [2004] Room €140–€270, suite €370. Breakfast €14. Set meals €30–€43.

NEUVILLE-ST-AMAND 02100 Aisne **Map 3:E3**

Le Château de Neuville-St-Amand BUDGET
St-Quentin

Tel 03.23.68.41.82
Fax 03.23.68.46.02
Email chateaudeneuville.st.amand@wanadoo.fr
Website www.chateauneuvillestamand.com

In Picardy village off A26, 2 km SE of St-Quentin: Claude and Sébastien Meiresonne's 1900s handsome white manor house (Logis de France), endorsed this year. 'Friendly staff. High-quality food.' Lounge, bar, restaurant; dining terrace. No background music. 3-hectare well-kept grounds. Closed 2 weeks Christmas/New Year, 3 weeks Aug, Sat midday, Sun night/Mon. Amex, MasterCard, Visa accepted. 15 bedrooms (large, quiet; best on ground floor by garden, 9 in annexe): single €60, double €70. Breakfast €8.50. Set meals €25–€55; full alc €65 [2004].

NICE Alpes-Maritimes **Map 6:D5**

Le Grimaldi
15 rue Grimaldi
06000 Nice

Tel 04.93.16.00.24
Fax 04.93.87.00.24
Email zedde@le-grimaldi.com
Website www.le-grimaldi.com

On a street near the old town and the seafront, Yann and Joanna Zedde (she is English) run this much-admired B&B in two *belle époque* houses. 'One of the most stylish hotels in town' and 'We loved it' are recent comments. Visitors find it 'comfortable, quiet', 'high quality, with interesting decor'. Reception staff are 'unfailingly helpful'. 'They served us a complimentary bottle of champagne when we booked three rooms for two nights.' The 'excellent' (if 'pricey') buffet breakfast, served on Limoges porcelain, includes freshly squeezed orange juice, fresh pastries, and you can boil your own eggs. All is neat and elegant: white-tiled bathrooms, bright colours, Provençal fabrics, flower and fruit prints on walls. Windows are double glazed and bathrooms have recently been renovated.

Open All year. **Rooms** 2 junior suites, 46 double. Air conditioning. **Facilities** 2 lounge/bar/breakfast rooms (background music); business centre. Beach 10 mins' walk. Unsuitable for ♿. **Location** 4 blocks back from seafront, behind casino. Public car park opposite. **Credit cards** All major cards accepted. **Terms** Room: single €80–€155, double €90–€185, suite €190–€230. Breakfast €15–€20. *V*

La Pérouse
11 quai Rauba-Capeu
06300 Nice

Tel 04.93.62.34.63
Fax 04.93.62.59.41
Email lp@hroy.com
Website www.hroy.com/la-perouse

'Perfect location, perfect staff, perfect pool and loads of delightful Provençal fabrics and artefacts.' A returning visitor again enjoyed what last year she called 'the best all-round hotel experience I can remember'. On a hill at the east end of the Promenade des Anglais, it has stunning views over the Baie des Anges. It stands back from the busy road, so most bedrooms are quiet. 'Ours looked over proper French houses.' 'Our lovely room had tall windows on to a small balcony: like a Matisse painting.' 'A good marble bathroom.' Some small rear rooms have no view. Yellow-painted corridors are hung with marine and Impressionist prints. The big heated swimming pool is set below high rocks. 'On the charming terrace, with lemon trees, breakfast had good choice (quiche, fruit salad, etc); a salad lunch was adequate.' On the roof is a solarium, with deckchairs and wide views, spa bath and small gym. Staff are 'charming, particularly the receptionists'; 'the brilliant *bagagiste* parked our car'. The beach is 15 metres away. 'Dinner was tasty and well presented', and countless restaurants are near. (*Anne Douglas, and others*)

Open All year. Restaurant closed 20 Sept–10 May. **Rooms** 4 suites, 56 double, 2 single. Air conditioning. **Facilities** Lifts. Lounge, bar, restaurant; background music; conference room. Terrace: meal service, heated swimming pool; rooftop terrace: sauna, solarium. Beach across road. Unsuitable for ♿. **Location** E end of Promenade des Anglais, by *Hôtel Suisse*. For loading/unloading, brief kerbside parking tolerated (make a U-turn at the port). Public car park nearby (€18 a night). **Restriction** No dogs. **Credit cards** All major cards accepted. **Terms** Room €155–€420, suite €630–€840. Breakfast €19. Set meals from €35. 1-night bookings occasionally refused. *V*

For details of the Voucher scheme, see page xxvi.

Hôtel Windsor
11 rue Dalpozzo
06000 Nice

Tel 04.93.88.59.35
Fax 04.93.88.94.57
Email reservation@hotelwindsornice.com
Website www.hotelwindsornice.com

Visitors this year 'had a great stay' at the Redolfi-Strizzot family's unusual hotel, not far from the seafront, behind the mighty *Hôtel Negresco*. Others called it 'a delight'. Fairly quiet, yet lively, it has a quirky style. 'A mother-of-pearl-inlaid bed is in the corner of the foyer, where one evening a zither player performed.' 'The lift says "seven, six, five, start main engines, four, three, two, one, lift off". Then the doors open.' Artists have decorated many of the bedrooms: 'Our large room, done in great style and overlooking the garden, had a Buddha mural and an open-plan bathroom.' The 'splendid Moroccan garden', 'overgrown, charming', has taped ('rather scratchy') bird-song and a very small swimming pool ('often in the shade'). 'In the exercise room in the attic, my daughter had an enjoyable massage.' 'In late October, dinner outdoors, with lights in the trees, was delightful. Good food, charming service.' On cool days, guests dine by a fire in the panelled dining room. There is a 'congenial' small bar. 'Breakfast was good.' (*Anna Ralph, J and VP, and others*)

Open All year. Restaurant closed midday and Sun. **Rooms** 56 double, 1 single. Air conditioning. **Facilities** Lounge/bar (jazz/classical background music), restaurant; fitness centre, hammam, sauna. Garden: dining terrace; unheated swimming pool. Beach nearby. Unsuitable for ♿. **Location** Central, 400 m from Promenade des Anglais. **Restriction** No smoking: restaurant, some bedrooms. **Credit cards** Amex, MasterCard, Visa. **Terms** Room €75–€155. Breakfast €10. D,B&B: single €108–€138, double €141–€221. Full alc €43.

NIEUL-PRÈS-LIMOGES 87510 Haute-Vienne Map 4:B4

La Chapelle Saint-Martin
33 Saint-Martin du Fault

Tel 05.55.75.80.17
Fax 05.55.75.89.50
Email chapelle@relaischateaux.com
Website www.chapellesaintmartin.com

North-west of Limoges, this *gentilhommière* (Relais & Châteaux) stands in a large park on the edge of a wood. The old grey house is 'not impressive from the road', but its 'calm comfort' beguiled recent visitors. 'It is something special, small, with beautifully furnished, very comfortable bedrooms; one feels one is staying in a private house. Service and food very enjoyable.' In the elegant restaurant, with wall hangings and large fireplaces, chef/*patron* Gilles Dudognon has a *Michelin* star for, eg, déclinaison de foies gras; ris de veau farc de truffes. There is a wide selection of Bordeaux wines. At the rear, a modern conservatory faces the extensive lawns and forests of the estate, and there is a swimming pool. (*FS*)

Open 1 Feb–end Dec. Restaurant closed Mon/Tues midday, Wed midday, Sun night 1 Nov–31 Mar. **Rooms** 3 suites, 7 double. 2 in annexe, 50 m. 5 on ground floor. **Facilities** Bar, restaurant; seminar room; terrace (meal service). No background music. 35-hectare park: swimming pool, tennis, lakes, horse riding. **Location** S of Nieul, by D20, at St-Martin-du-Fault. 10 km NW of

Limoges by D35. **Credit cards** All major cards accepted. **Terms** [2004] Room €80–€160, suite €190. Breakfast €14. D,B&B €133–€198 per person.

NOIRMOUTIER-EN-L'ÎLE 85330 Vendée — Map 4:A2

Fleur de Sel
Rue des Saulniers
Île de Noirmoutier

Tel 02.51.39.09.07
Fax 02.51.39.09.76
Email contact@fleurdesel.fr
Website www.fleurdesel.fr

The island of Noirmoutier, north-west of La Rochelle, was a monastic settlement in the seventh century; now tourism is its main industry. Linked to the mainland by a bridge and, at low tide, by a 'spectacular causeway', it is a peaceful place which has been spared the high-rise developments of other holiday coastal resorts. In the north-east, on the edge of its main town, this white-fronted hotel, an 'oasis of calm' (say fans), is run by its owners, Pierre and Annick Wattecamps, with son Pierrick. Built in 1982 in marine/Vendéen style, it has attractive gardens and a good-sized swimming pool. Much renovation and redecoration took place in early 2004. 'All is fresh, full of character (the odd antique, good textiles, judicious use of natural materials). Our first-floor room had distant views of castle and church; traditional pine furniture, quilted bedspreads, nice pictures gave a feel of summery comfort.' 'Superior' rooms have a small terrace and direct access to garden and swimming pool. The restaurant has two sections: one has white-painted wood panelling, and paintings of local scenes by the owners' daughter, Céline; the other has a large window ('spectacular sunsets'). 'Simple, light' dishes by Eric Pichou (13 *Gault Millau* points) include steak de thon, fondue de tomates aux anchois et olives. Wines are fairly priced. Breakfast has an 'adequate buffet'. (*F and IW*)

Open Mid-Mar–1 Nov. Restaurant closed Mon midday and Thurs midday off-season. **Rooms** 2 suites, 31 double, 2 single. 2 suitable for ♿. **Facilities** Lobby (free Internet connection), lounge, restaurant (background jazz). 1.5-hectare garden: tennis, heated swimming pool, whirlpool, golf practice. Bicycle hire. Beaches 1 km. **Location** 500 m behind church. 87 km SW of Nantes. Parking. **Restrictions** No smoking in restaurant. No babies/young children in restaurant. No dogs over 17 kg. **Credit cards** Amex, MasterCard, Visa. **Terms** Room: single €77–€130, double €77–€150, suite €150–€230. Breakfast €11. D,B&B €71–€170 per person. Set lunch €25–€45, dinner €34–€45; full alc €40. 1-night bookings sometimes refused July/Aug.

NYONS 26110 Drôme — Map 6:C3

Hôtel La Picholine BUDGET
Promenade de la Perrière

Tel 04.75.26.06.21
Fax 04.75.26.40.72
Email picholine@wanadoo.fr

On hillside 1 km N of Nyons (self-styled 'olive capital of the world') M. and Mme Romanet's Logis de France, 'utterly peaceful; silent at night'. Lounge, bar, restaurant (closed Mon Oct–Apr, Tues), meeting room. 'Delightful meals on terrace.' Swimming pool amid olive trees. Closed 24 Oct–17 Nov, 7 Feb–1 Mar. MasterCard, Visa accepted.

11 bedrooms (6 with terrace): €55–€69. Breakfast €7.50. D,B&B €58–€65 per person. Set meals €22.50–€39 [2004].

ORANGE 84100 Vaucluse **Map 6:C3**

Mas des Aigras BUDGET
Chemin des Aigras
Russamp Est (RN7 Nord)

Tel 04.90.34.81.01
Fax 04.90.34.05.66
Email masdesaigras@free.fr
Website www.avignon-et-provence.com

Creeper-clad stone mas, *now welcoming three-star* demeure d'hôtes, *quietly set amid fields, vineyards and orchards, 4 km N of Orange, off RN7. Sylvie and Alain Davi and family provide 'friendly service, excellent dinners, very good buffet breakfast' (organic produce). Provençal decor. Smoking lounge, restaurant. No background music. Garden: swings, slides, unheated swimming pool. Closed Nov school holidays, 3 weeks Christmas, Tues/Wed off-season. Restaurant closed Wed midday and Sat midday in season, Tues/Wed off-season. MasterCard, Visa accepted. 13 bedrooms (all no-smoking, 9 air conditioned): €70–€106. Breakfast €11. D,B&B €72–€143f per person. Set lunch €18, dinner €26; full alc €70.* *V*

Hôtel Saint-Jean BUDGET
1 cours Pourtoules

Tel 04.90.51.15.16
Fax 04.90.11.05.45
Email saint-jean@avignon-et-provence.com
Website www.avignon-et-provence.com

Near Roman theatre, at foot of St-Eutrope hill: 17th-century coaching inn, now pink, green-shuttered two-star B&B with 'welcoming' owner/managers, Agnès and Jean-Louis Sornin de Leysat; salon cut into the rock; 'interesting antiques'. Breakfast in summer on tree-shaded terrace. Safe courtyard parking (€3). Closed Jan. MasterCard, Visa accepted. 23 bedrooms: €38–€80. Breakfast €6 [2004].

ORVAULT 22700 Loire-Atlantique **Map 2:F3**

Le Domaine d'Orvault NEW
Chemin des Marais du Cens

Tel 02.40.76.84.02
Fax 02.40.76.04.21
Email contact@domaine-orvault.com
Website www.domaine-orvault.com

Built in the 1970s, this large white villa, with its sloping red-tiled roof, looks more Basque than Breton. Managed by Sylvain Lejeune, it is in a north-west suburb of Nantes: 'So much nicer than going to the city centre,' says a visitor in 2004. 'A charming hotel. Excellent cuisine served on a lovely terrace under lime trees. Room clean and quiet. Friendly staff.' In the restaurant facing the wooded grounds, the chef, Thierry Bouhier, serves 'classic cuisine'. Each bedroom is different: decor ranges from 'rustic' through 'romantic' to contemporary; most are spacious. The atmosphere is 'relaxed', says a recent report. Children under 16 stay free. (*Mary Tilden-Smith, and others*)

Open All year. Restaurant closed Sun night Sept–June, Sat midday. **Rooms** 29. **Facilities** Lift. Lounge, bar, restaurant; winter garden; conference/function rooms. Garden: terrace (meal service); swimming pool, tennis, children's playground. **Location** 7 km NW of centre of Nantes, off N137 to Rennes. **Credit cards** All major cards accepted. **Terms** [2004] Room €80–€134. Breakfast €14. Set meals €22–€38.

OUCQUES 41290 Loir-et-Cher — Map 2:F5

Hôtel du Commerce NEW/BUDGET
9 route de Beaugency

Tel 02.54.23.20.41
Fax 02.54.23.02.88
Email hotelrestaurantcommerce@wanadoo.fr

In quiet street of simple village off D924 27 km N of Blois: small hotel/restaurant (Logis de France, Michelin Bib Gourmand*) owned by chef M. Lanchais: 'He and his wife are warm and friendly. Our large second-floor room was huge, with good bathroom. Dinner well balanced, beautifully presented; sensible wine list. Traditional breakfast, very adequate,' say nominators. 1970s-style dining room decor; bedrooms more modern. Parking. Closed 20 Dec–15 Jan, Sun night/ Mon except holidays. Amex, MasterCard, Visa accepted. 11 bedrooms: €58–€62. Breakfast €7.50. D,B&B €55 per person. Set meals €18–€54.*

PAILHEROLS 15800 Cantal — Map 4:C5

Auberge des Montagnes BUDGET

Tel 04.71.47.57.01
Fax 04.71.49.63.83
Email info@auberge-des-montagnes.com
Website www.auberge-des-montagnes.com

Returning visitors to the Combourieu family's converted farmhouse (Logis de France) again found it 'outstanding'. 'Surprisingly sophisticated' yet inexpensive, it is on the edge of a village in the remote Cantal uplands. 'The fourth-generation owners are so proud of their *auberge*. Madame and her team are always smiling. Service in the restaurant, always filled with locals, is first class, even under pressure.' The food and wines are 'excellent value'. André Combourieu's cuisine (*Michelin Bib Gourmand*) comes in generous portions. Special dishes can be ordered the day before (one reader recommends this rather than half board). Bedrooms in the old building are 'rustic'. 'We sat on our sunny balcony, enjoying birdsong and views of green scenery.' More modern rooms are in the 'mini-château annexe', *Le Clos des Gentianes*, which faces a lake. 'In the attractive bar/lounge, a log fire was lit on cool evenings.' The outdoor pool has a 'bucolic setting'; the indoor one is 'rather shallow'. Breakfast is 'a bit of a DIY bun-fight; generous, but with "make your own toast", and "serve your own coffee" from an urn, huge croissants which you can smell baking after 7 am'. There are mountain bikes for hire, marked walks and cross-country skiing. (*J and DA, BWR, and others*)

Open 20 Dec–10 Oct. Restaurant closed Tues off-season. **Rooms** 22. 7 in annexe. 2 suitable for ♿. **Facilities** 3 salons, bar, 2 dining rooms (1 no-smoking); gym, indoor swimming pool. Garden: dining terrace, swimming pool, children's playground; fitness centre: gym, sauna, hammam. **Location** 14 km SE of Vic-sur-Cère, 34 km E of Aurillac. **Credit cards** MasterCard, Visa. **Terms** [2004] Room €35–€48. Breakfast €6.50. D,B&B €42–€49 per person. Set meals €17–€29.

PARIS **Map 2:E5**

Hôtel de l'Abbaye
10 rue Cassette
75006 Paris

Tel 01.45.44.38.11
Fax 01.45.48.07.86
Email abbaye@wanadoo.fr
Website www.hotel-abbaye.com

Returning in 2004 to Pierre and Gisèle Lafortune's hotel, a former 17th-century convent near St-Sulpice, a visitor wrote: 'Expensive, but worth every euro. The people are charming.' Set back from a small street behind large wooden gates, across a small courtyard lit by carriage lamps at night, it has long been admired by *Guide* readers. 'Our room had its own private garden, and a delightful seating area.' Breakfast, in a conservatory-style room, comes with a free English newspaper and is thought 'excellent'. Some suites have recently been given a 'very contemporary' decor. The duplexes have a terrace with view over rooftops. There is a small mirrored lift. One visitor enjoyed tea with biscuits by the fire in a salon full of flowers: 'How civilised, like being in someone's country home. Wonderful squishy armchairs.' (*Carol Heaton, JH, and others*)

Open All year. **Rooms** 4 suites, 42 double. Some no-smoking. Air conditioning. **Facilities** Salon, TV room, bar, breakfast room. No background music. Small patio garden. Unsuitable for ♿. **Location** Central, near St-Sulpice church. (Métro: St-Sulpice) **Restriction** No dogs. **Credit cards** Amex, MasterCard, Visa. **Terms** [2004] B&B: single/double €211–€313, suite €393–€449.

Hôtel d'Aubusson NEW
33 rue Dauphine
75006 Paris

Tel 01.43.29.43.43
Fax 01.43.29.12.62
Email reservationmichael@hoteldaubusson.com
Website www.aubusson-paris-hotel.com

'Not cheap, but the style, decor, service and fabulous location make it a winner': this 17th-century mansion is within easy walking distance (via Pont Neuf) of the Louvre and Notre Dame. 'It combines warmth and tradition with modern comforts,' says a visitor in 2004. Housekeeping is 'immaculate'; staff are 'very friendly'. Bedrooms are 'comfortable, not OTT, with traditional French flowered fabrics and soothing shades of beige; mine, at the top, overlooked rooftops'. At weekends, when there is jazz in the cocktail bar ('enjoyable, but not conducive to sleep'), you should ask for a room at the back. The *grand salon* has a magnificent beamed ceiling; the breakfast room is hung with tapestries; there is a patio with fountain where drinks are served in fine weather. (*Victoria T Allen*)

Open All year. **Rooms** 3 suites, 50 double. Some no-smoking. Some suitable for ♿. Air conditioning. **Facilities** Lift. Salon, breakfast room. Patio. **Location** Left Bank, near Pont Neuf. Garage. (Metro: Odéon) **Credit cards** All major cards accepted. **Terms** [2004] Room €260–€410. Breakfast €23.

Hôtel de Buci
22 rue de Buci
75006 Paris

Tel 01.55.42.74.74
Fax 01.55.42.74.44
Email hotelbuci@wanadoo.fr
Website www.hotelbuci.fr

Near St-Germain-des-Prés, this small, luxurious B&B hotel is in a 16th-century building facing the well-known outdoor market (which some rooms overlook) of the narrow rue de Buci. 'Comfortable, discreet', it has 'sleek' public rooms with leather chairs and contemporary paintings. There are coordinated fabrics and repro furniture in the bedrooms: each has a different theme, some have a canopy bed. 'Our double-glazed window had a flowery window box.' Room-service snacks are available. Breakfast can be continental (with yogurt), 'fitness' or 'American'.

Open All year. **Rooms** 4 suites, 11 double, 9 single. Air conditioning. **Facilities** Salon, bar, breakfast room (no-smoking). Unsuitable for ♿. **Location** Off boulevard St-Germain. (Métro: Mabillon, St-Germain-des-Prés) **Restriction** No dogs. **Credit cards** All major cards accepted. **Terms** [2004] Room: single €190–€250, double €230–€315, suite €360–€650. Breakfast €17–€22.

Hôtel Cambon NEW
3 rue Cambon
75001 Paris

Tel 01.44.58.93.93
Fax 01.42.60.30.59
Email contact@cambon-hotel.com
Website www.cambon-hotel.com

Near Tuileries, Madeleine, Champs-Élysées, Louvre, etc: four-star B&B hotel, recommended by visitors of over 20 years. 'Highly efficient, courteous patronne. *Agreeable rooms. Excellent restaurant across road.' Modern furnishings, old paintings and engravings. (Métro: Concorde) No dogs. 43 bedrooms (with air conditioning, Internet connection): €190–€317. Breakfast €15 [2004].*

Hôtel Caron de Beaumarchais
12 rue Vieille-du-Temple
75004 Paris

Tel 01.42.72.34.12
Fax 01.42.72.34.63
Email hotel@carondebeaumarchais.com
Website www.carondebeaumarchais.com

'Well managed, charming; the location is superb,' says a visitor this year to father and son Étienne and Alain Bigeard's elegant small hotel in the trendy Marais district. 'Very romantic', 'lovely' were earlier comments. Pierre-Augustin Caron de Beaumarchais, who wrote *Le Mariage de Figaro* in 1778, lived next door, and the hotel's decor is in 18th-century style with a Mozart theme: recordings of his operas are played in public areas. It was extensively renovated in 2004, with top-quality fabrics, wall-hangings, carpets and bedlinen. The foyer has tapestries, old opera programmes, an Erard piano (1793), an antique card table with hand-made cards, and a fireplace. Some bedrooms are beamed; all have a chandelier, flat-screen satellite TV and high-speed Internet connection. 'The owners are friendly. Reception was helpful. Our sixth-floor room, tiny but cosy, had flowers and a balcony.' Breakfast, 'smilingly served in an intimate basement room', includes fresh orange juice, pastries, home-made jams, and newspapers, including, of course, *Le Figaro*. (*Mary Hanson, and others*)

Open All year. **Rooms** 19 double. Air conditioning. **Facilities** Lift. Lobby, breakfast room; classical background music. Tiny garden. Unsuitable for ♿. **Location** Central (Marais). Public car park (Baudoyer, rue de Rivoli) nearby. (Métro: Hôtel de Ville, St-Paul-le-Marais) **Restriction** No dogs. **Credit cards** Amex, MasterCard, Visa. **Terms** Room €122–€152. Breakfast €10. *V*

Châtillon Hôtel BUDGET

11 square de Châtillon
75014 Paris

Tel 01.45.42.31.17
Fax 01.45.42.72.09
Email chatillon.hotel@wanadoo.fr

'Outstanding value, nearly perfect in its class.' Ever popular, Luce and Bernard Lecoq's quirky little hotel is off the beaten track, in an 'amazingly quiet' square near the Porte d'Orléans. It offers 'perhaps the best value in Paris', say fans. Transport links to the centre are good. The Lecoqs are 'lovely people', 'uniformly courteous and helpful'. 'Madame was wonderful, providing a bouquet of roses for my wife's birthday breakfast.' Corridors are 'brightly decorated in ochres, greens and dark yellows'. The simple bedrooms are 'clean, large, bright', with furniture 'in Habitat 1970s style'. Bathrooms, too, are spacious, 'with hot, hot water, but hip-size bath' (a hand-held shower was found awkward to use this year). Breakfast, which includes a newspaper, is usually liked: 'Fresh orange juice and pains chocolat.' Recommended local restaurants (both *Michelin Bib Gourmand*): *La Régalade*, avenue Jean Moulin; *La Bonne Table*, rue Friant. (*Simon Willbourn, Frank Deis, MW Roots, and others*)

Open All year. **Rooms** 31 double. 1 on ground floor. 2 no-smoking. **Facilities** Lift. Lounge, bar/TV room, breakfast room. No background music. Unsuitable for ♿. **Location** Entrance to square by 33 ave Jean Moulin. Garage parking nearby. (Métro: Alésia) **Restriction** No dogs. **Credit cards** MasterCard, Visa. **Terms** Room €62–€78. Breakfast €6.

Hôtel Chopin

10 boulevard Montmartre
(46 passage Jouffroy)
75009 Paris

Tel 01.47.70.58.10
Fax 01.42.47.00.70

Liked again in 2004 ('a lovely visit, value for money'), Philippe Bidal's modest hotel (a listed historic monument) stands at the end of a glass-roofed 19th-century arcade with shops, near the junction of boulevards Haussmann, Montmartre and des Italiens. It has been open for business every day since 1846. Many bedrooms and bathrooms are small, but it is liked for its 'cheerful staff' and 'faded elegance'. 'The quietest hotel we have found in Paris.' Idiosyncrasies include creaky lifts and antiquated plumbing, and one top-floor bedroom has 'a window facing a shaft: the low balustrade looked a bit dangerous'. The buffet breakfast has an electric juice maker and 'plentiful, good hot coffee'. *Chartier*, 7 rue du Faubourg Montmartre, one of Paris's best traditional budget restaurants, is nearby: 'It buzzes with life, and you might have to share a table.' (*Rosalind Draper, HW, and others*)

Open All year. **Rooms** 31 double, 5 single. **Facilities** Lift. Breakfast room (no-smoking). Unsuitable for ♿. **Location** Central. Public parking rue Chauchat. (Métro: Richelieu-Drouot) **Credit cards** MasterCard, Visa. **Terms** Room €58–€86. Breakfast €7.

Hotel Le Clément NEW
6 rue Clément
75006 Paris

Tel 01.43.26.53.60
Fax 01.44.07.06.83
Email info@hotel-clement.fr
Website www.hotel-clement.com

M. and Mme Charrade's 'typical Parisian small hotel, narrow, on 6 floors', just off Boulevard St-Germain. 'Quiet, comfortable, scrupulously clean; reasonable rates; high-standard decor, unfailingly helpful service.' Lift, salon, courtyard. No dogs. (Métro: Mabillon, Odéon) 31 air-conditioned bedrooms: €117–€145. 'Adequate' breakfast €10 [2004].

Hôtel Duc de Saint-Simon
14 rue de St-Simon
75007 Paris

Tel 01.44.39.20.20
Fax 01.45.48.68.25
Email duc.de.saint.simon@wanadoo.fr
Website www.hotelducdesaintsimon.com

'Full of character, delightfully decorated and a haven of peace': this 17th-century mansion is in a side street off Boulevard St-Germain. Managed by its owner, Göran Lindqvist, it has old beams, rough stone walls, tiles, antique furniture, bright colours. The basement bar/breakfast room has 'a series of arched stone vaults, delightfully lit and furnished', and in summer, the good breakfast ('lots of coffee, freshly squeezed orange juice for a small supplement') and drinks are served in the small, pretty garden. Half the bedrooms overlook the garden. Rooms vary in size: 'Ours was relatively small, but well appointed,' say visitors in 2004. The tiny cobbled forecourt has shrubs and trelliswork. (*Sheila and John Cotton*)

Open All year. **Rooms** 5 suites, 29 double. Some on ground floor. 5 in annexe. 50% air conditioned. **Facilities** Lift. Lounge, bar/breakfast room; background music. Unsuitable for ♿. **Location** Left Bank. 2 private parking places (€30). (Métro: Rue du Bac) **Restrictions** No smoking in lounge. No dogs. **Credit cards** All major cards accepted. **Terms** Room €220–€280, suite €335–€375. Breakfast €15.

Most hotels nowadays provide telephone, TV, etc, in the bedrooms. To save space, we do not give such details. If any of these is vital to you, check about availability in advance.

Hotel de Fleurie NEW
32–34 rue Grégoire-de-Tours
75006 Paris

Tel 01.53.73.70.00
Fax 01.53.73.70.20
Email bonjour@hotel-de-fleurie.fr
Website www.hotel-de-fleurie.fr

Run by the Marolleau family, this well-restored 18th-century building is in a narrow street, full of cheap restaurants, near St-Germain-des-Prés. It was liked again in 2004 by visitors on their fourth stay. 'Standards as high as ever. Our "luxury" room, quite spacious, and quiet, had tea- and coffee-making facilities. On an earlier visit we had a small attic room kept cool by wonderfully efficient air conditioning.' Some rooms may hear street noise; all have Internet connection. The 'friendly staff', 'excellent location', and 'small, comfortable lounge' are appreciated. The 'good-value' buffet breakfast is served in a vaulted room. A museum pass is offered to guests staying more than a week. (*Alex and Beryl Williams, CJ Pearson*)

Open All year. **Rooms** 29 double (some family). Air conditioning. **Facilities** Lift. Lounge, bar, breakfast room. **Location** 500 m E of St-Germain-des-Prés. (Métro: Odéon) **Restriction** No dogs. **Credit cards** All major cards accepted. **Terms** [2004] Room: single €130–€145, double €165–€265, family €290–€325. Breakfast €10.

Hôtel des Grands Hommes
17 place du Panthéon
75005 Paris

Tel 01.46.34.19.60
Fax 01.43.26.67.32
Email reservation@hoteldesgrandshommes.com
Website www.hoteldesgrandshommes.com

Liked again in 2004 ('good, quiet, exceptional value'; 'an excellent hotel in a very good location'), this converted town house is named after the 'great men' entombed in the Panthéon opposite. It claims also to be the birthplace of Surrealism: many Surrealist writers and painters stayed here. Furnished in 'high empire neo-classical style', it is thought 'great fun'. 'It is small, and the landings are difficult to negotiate when the chambermaids have their trolleys in place. But the reception staff could not have been more helpful.' Bedrooms vary in size. 'Ours had textile wall-covering depicting scenes of ancient Egypt; pleasant, if somewhat bizarre.' 'Our lovely, small fifth-floor room had a view of the Panthéon, floodlit at night, two pairs of French windows: we slept with them open and all was quiet at night. But the shower was not up to 2004 standards.' From the top-floor rooms you can see to Sacré-Cœur. Breakfast in a small vaulted cellar is a buffet, or it can be brought to the room. The Moncelli family also owns the *Hôtel Panthéon*, next door, similar in price, with 'pretty, feminine' bedrooms, and the *Résidence Henri IV*, nearby (many of its rooms have a tiny kitchenette). (*Allan Kelly, John and Jane Holland, and others*)

Open All year. **Rooms** 2 suites, 28 double, 1 single. 1 on ground floor. Air conditioning. **Facilities** Lift. Reception (background music), bar, breakfast room; meeting room. Small courtyard. **Location** Opposite Panthéon. Free parking in square Sat night/Sun; underground car park 100 m. (Métro: Maubert-Mutualité) **Credit cards** All major cards accepted. **Terms** [2004] Room €168–€213, suite €275–€382. Breakfast €10.

Grand Hôtel Malher
5 rue Malher
75004 Paris

Tel 01.42.72.60.92
Fax 01.42.72.25.37
Email ghmalher@yahoo.fr
Website www.grandhotelmalher.com

'Excellently located', in the Marais, this 'very friendly' hotel has for three generations been owned and run by Didier Fossiez's family ('he and his wife, Pamela, are delightful'). It has a 'stylish' entrance hall. The bedrooms are 'fine, given the relatively low prices', says a visitor this year. 'Our room was small, but adequate; the shower room was good and spacious,' say others. The lift to the upper floors is 'tiny and slow'. Bedrooms at the back get virtually no noise from outside: but soundproofing between rooms can be poor. The 'excellent' breakfast, in a 17th-century vaulted wine cellar, has 'lots of good croissants, good coffee, bottled orange juice; slow service, but a winning smile'. Many small restaurants nearby. (*Caroline Pudney, Carolyn and Robin Orme, Bob and Kate Flaherty, and others*)

Open All year. **Rooms** 1 suite, 30 double. 2 on ground floor. **Facilities** Lift. Breakfast room (no-smoking). Unsuitable for ♿. **Location** Off E end of rue de Rivoli. 3 public garages nearby. (Métro: St-Paul) **Restriction** No dogs. **Credit cards** All major cards accepted. **Terms** Room: single €90–€123, double €107–€148, suite €160–€175. Breakfast €8.

Hôtel Montalembert
3 rue de Montalembert
75007 Paris

Tel 01.45.49.68.68
Fax 01.45.49.69.49
Email welcome@montalembert.com
Website www.montalembert.com

'Still smart and very comfortable,' say visitors in 2004 to this ultra-modern hotel near Boulevard St-Germain. 'Only the cost is likely to make us stay elsewhere in Paris.' The latest make-over, in 2002 by Grace Leo-Andrieu, has made it 'super-trendy, a fascinating mix of modern and traditional styles'. It has gleaming marble floors, dramatic flower displays, a colour scheme of taupe, olive and cinnamon, and Art Deco design in its public areas. Staff wear 'Prada-style sand-and-gunpowder-grey uniform'. 'Service is friendly.' Every bedroom has a flat-screen TV, DVD-player and Internet access. But one party found the rooms too small: 'We had a problem opening our suitcases.' The top-floor suites have spectacular views. The bar/grill serves breakfast, and light meals all day. In the oak-panelled restaurant, the chef, Alain Lecompte, allows guests to 'compose their own menu and decide size of portion'. The outdoor dining terrace has 'Alice in Wonderland-style banquettes', camellias and box trees. (*Brian and Lesley Knox, and others*)

Open All year. **Rooms** 8 suites, 48 double. Air conditioning. **Facilities** Salon, bar/café, restaurant, terrace; 'classical/trendy' background music; meeting room. Unsuitable for ♿. **Location** Near junction of blvds St-Germain/Raspail/rue du Bac. Valet parking at public car park nearby. (Métro: Rue du Bac) **Credit cards** All major cards accepted. **Terms** [2004] Room €340–€430, suite €560–€750, 2-bedroom suite €1,180. Breakfast €20.

Hôtel du Palais Bourbon
49 rue de Bourgogne
75007 Paris

Tel 01.44.11.30 70
Fax 01.45.55.20.21
Email htlbourbon@aol.com
Website www.hotel-palais-bourbon.com

Near Assemblée Nationale, Invalides and Musée Rodin: Thierry Claudon's B&B hotel, fairly inexpensive despite grand name: elegant old building in quiet, pleasant street, much renovated this year. 'Classically frugal French breakfast. Helpful staff. Good lighting.' No muzak. Salons (some in newly converted cellars). Unsuitable for ♿. No dogs. Amex, MasterCard, Visa accepted. 30 air-conditioned bedrooms (4 in annexe; some are large). B&B: single €70–€105, double €120–€130, family €155–€175.

Le Pavillon de la Reine
28 place des Vosges
75003 Paris

Tel 01.40.29.19.19
Fax 01.40.29.19.20
Email contact@pavillon-de-la-reine.com
Website www.pavillon-de-la-reine.com

'Romantically set' in the Marais on one of Paris's loveliest squares, this handsome 17th-century building, with creeper-draped facade and pretty front courtyard, is an elegant hotel, now managed by Yves Monnin. The large, attractive lobby has heavy drapes, antiques, open fireplace, and lounge area. All bedrooms are different: some are spacious, with a modern four-poster bed, beams, striped fabrics; some are small. Quietest rooms overlook a courtyard; a few face the street. 'Our duplex suite on the top floor had beautiful decor, elegant bathroom.' Breakfast, in a basement room, includes eggs and bacon, fruits, cereals, etc. There is 24-hour room service. Plenty of good restaurants are near.

Open All year. **Rooms** 15 suites, 41 double. Some on ground floor. Air conditioning. **Facilities** Lobby, lounge, honesty bar, breakfast room; conference room. Flowery courtyard. Unsuitable for ♿. **Location** Central (Marais). Free garage. (Métro: St-Paul, Bastille) **Credit cards** All major cards accepted. **Terms** Room €335–€410, suite €480–€780. Breakfast €20–€25.

Hôtel de la Place des Vosges NEW
12 rue de Birague
75004 Paris

Tel 01.42.72.60.46
Fax 01.42.72.02.64
Email hotel.place.des.vosges@gofornet.com
Website www.hotelplacedesvosges.com

In the Marais, on one-way street two mins' walk from Place des Vosges: former stable for mules of Henry IV, now an 'attractive, honest, reasonable' small hotel. 'My fifth-floor room, small, comfortable, clean, had smart decor, state-of-the-art bathroom.' Lift (1st–4th floor), salon, breakfast room. Amex, MasterCard, Visa accepted. (Métro: St-Paul, Bastille) 15 bedrooms (rear ones 'very quiet'): €105–€250. 'Decent' breakfast €7 [2004].

> Hotels are dropped if we lack positive feedback.

Hôtel Pratic NEW/BUDGET
9 rue d'Ormesson
75004 Paris
Tel 01.48.87.80.47
Fax 01.48.87.40.04
Email practic.hotel@wanadoo.fr
Website www.hotelpratic.com

'Wonderfully located' in the Marais: inexpensive, newly renovated hotel. 19th-century building with wood-beamed lobby, modern bedrooms (best ones face lively Place du Marché-Ste-Catherine). 'Very nice staff.' No restaurant; plenty in the square. MasterCard, Visa accepted. (Métro: St-Paul) 23 bedrooms: €52–€109. Breakfast €6. *V*

Relais Christine
3 rue Christine
75006 Paris
Tel 01.40.51.60.80
Fax 01.40.51.60.81
Email contact@relais-christine.com
Website www.relais-christine.com

Built on the site of a 13th-century abbey, this converted 16th-century mansion is now a luxurious hotel in a side street in St-Germain-des-Prés. Recent praise: 'Service is impeccable.' 'A wonderful atmosphere.' 'Like a small country house. Our room looked over the garden, where the only noise was the birds' dawn chorus.' Some bedrooms have a terrace by the garden; some others face the courtyard, with its topiary shrubs and magnolia. But front rooms hear street noise. Some rooms are small, but all are well furnished, with 'sumptuous' fabrics and wireless Internet access; many have beams. A buffet breakfast is served in the former refectory; even the continental breakfast is 'generous and delicious'. The panelled lounge has an honesty bar, board games, English newspapers and a log fire, and there is a spa in the vaults. 'Nice dogs' are welcomed. (*DMT, and others*)

Open All year. **Rooms** 19 suites, 32 double. Air conditioning. **Facilities** Lounge with honesty bar, breakfast room; meeting room; spa: sauna, massage, etc. Small garden. Courtyard. Unsuitable for ♿. **Location** Left Bank. Private garage (free). (Métro: Odéon, St-Michel) **Credit cards** All major cards accepted. **Terms** Room €345–€595. Breakfast €20–€25. *V*

Relais du Louvre
19 rue des Prêtres-St-Germain-l'Auxerrois
75001 Paris
Tel 01.40.41.96.42
Fax 01.40.41.96.44
Email contact@relaisdulouvre.com
Website www.relaisdulouvre.com

'Well placed for visits to central Paris', this 18th-century building is where Puccini set *La Bohème*. 'Quietly elegant', it is in a small street opposite the Louvre, by the lovely old church of St-Germain-l'Auxerrois (its bells are silent at night). It is now a small hotel, owned by Roger Thiery, where 'modern comfort accompanies ancient grace'. Recent comments: 'Courteous reception'; 'We were made very welcome'. 'Everything on a small scale; our small bedroom, with small bathroom, was reached by a tiny lift. It had flowery fabrics, flower prints, a comfortable bed with cotton sheets.' No public rooms apart from Reception ('very pretty: red walls, old beams, nice old chairs, mirrors'); the 'good breakfast' is brought on a tray with dainty china to the bedroom. The manager, Sophie Aulnette, is 'particularly helpful'. If you need a parking place you should mention this when booking. (*Christopher Born, Michael and Betty Hill, and others*)

Open All year. **Rooms** 3 suites, 9 double, 9 single. Some no-smoking. 2 on ground floor. Air conditioning. **Facilities** Lift. Lobby (with Internet access). No background music. Small patio. Unsuitable for ♿. **Location** Near Seine and Pont Neuf. **NB** address: do *not* go to Rue St-Germain-l'Auxerrois. 2 safe parking places (€17). (Métro: Pont Neuf, Louvre Rivoli; RER: Châtelet-les-Halles) **Restriction** No smoking: lobby, most bedrooms. **Credit cards** All major cards accepted. **Terms** Room: single €99–€128, double €145–€180, suite €205–€244. Breakfast €10. *V*

Hôtel Le Sainte-Beuve
9 rue Sainte-Beuve
75006 Paris

Tel 01.45.48.20.07
Fax 01.45.48.67.52
Email saintebeuve@wanadoo.fr
Website www.hotel-sainte-beuve.fr

'Agreeable' small hotel in quiet street at NW end of Jardin du Luxembourg (2 mins' walk), near St-Sulpice and Montparnasse. Owned and managed by Jean-Pierre Egurreguy, decor by David Hicks, a 'tasteful blend of antique and contemporary comfort'. 'Intimate atmosphere.' Air conditioning. Ground-floor sitting/breakfast room with deep sofas, open fire; bar. Lift. No dogs. All major credit cards accepted. (Métro: Vavin, Notre-Dame-des-Champs) 22 bedrooms: €130–€272. Breakfast €14 [2004].

Hôtel Tilsitt Étoile NEW
23 rue Brey
75017 Paris

Tel 01.43.80.39.71
Fax 01.47.66.37.63
Email info@ tilsitt.com
Website www.tilsitt.com

Liked for 'peace, comfort, reasonable rates and accessibility': hotel in side street near Étoile. (Métro: Charles de Gaulle) 'Decor artistic yet practical. Very good buffet breakfast (fresh orange juice, large selection of rolls and croissants). Helpful receptionist.' Reception lounge, breakfast room, seminar room. All major credit cards accepted. 38 'cosy' bedrooms: single €110–€128, double €125–€192. Breakfast €12 [2004].

Hôtel de l'Université
22 rue de l'Université
75007 Paris

Tel 01.42.61.09.39
Fax 01.42.60.40.84
Email hoteluniversite@wanadoo.fr
Website www.hoteluniversite.com

'Civilised' little Left Bank hotel (former Benedictine convent). Hemingway wrote Moveable Feast *here. Fine staircases and fire-places; antiques and tapestries in public rooms (in crypt); beamed ceilings. 'Helpful staff.' Breakfast (€10) by tiny patio, or in bedrooms. Lift. Salon. Unsuitable for ♿. All major credit cards accepted. No dogs. 27 air-conditioned bedrooms (best ones open on to terrace; street-facing ones spacious, but can be noisy): €85–€190.*

Hôtel de Varenne NEW
44 rue de Bourgogne
75007 Paris

Tel 01.45.51.45.55
Fax 01.45.51.86.63
Email info@hoteldevarenne.com
Website www.hoteldevarenne.com

Close to the Invalides and the Rodin museum with its fascinating garden, this former *hôtel particulier* changed hands in 2002. The new owner, Jean-Marc Pommier, much in evidence, has extensively renovated in Louis XVI and Empire style. Furniture has been specially made for the hotel. 'The rooms are comfortable and clean,' says a Canadian visitor on his second visit in 2004. 'Bathrooms are spacious.' Most bedrooms face the 'quiet, lovely' courtyard with its creepers, bushes and flowers; all have an Internet connection. The continental breakfast, served until midday, and taken in the bedroom or in summer in the courtyard, has fresh-baked pastries, etc; eggs, yogurt and fresh juices cost extra. Front rooms may hear traffic. The Assemblée Nationale is close by, so many guests are politicians, embassy staff, etc. (*Alfred Seekamp*)

Open All year. **Rooms** 20 double, 4 single. Air conditioning. **Facilities** Lift. Lounge, breakfast room. Courtyard. Unsuitable for ♿. **Location** Just E of Invalides. (Métro: Varenne) **Credit cards** Amex, MasterCard, Visa. **Terms** [2004] Room €117–€147. Breakfast €9. Winter discounts.

Hôtel Verneuil NEW
8 rue de Verneuil
75007 Paris

Tel 01.42.60.82.14
Fax 01.42.61.40.38
Email hotelverneuil@wanadoo.fr
Website www.hotelverneuil.com

'Small and personal, with attentive staff', this B&B hotel is in a quiet street in St-Germain-des-Prés: 'A lovely location, close to shops and the local market,' says a visitor in 2004. Bedrooms, all are different, vary in size; all have toile de Jouy wall coverings. 'Mine, small but well equipped, had a comfortable bed and a large marble bathroom (superb tub). My aunt's deluxe double was much larger, with nice canopied bed and beautiful bedspread.' One bathroom has a shower only. There is a 'beautiful' sitting room, filled with books. 'Good, if expensive, continental breakfast. On Valentine's Day, a heart-shaped box of chocolates was left on each bed, with a card from the owner, Mme de Lattre.' Only drawback: 'The lift is up one flight of stairs from Reception.' (*Cheryl Lum*)

Open All year. **Rooms** 26 double. 15 air conditioned. **Facilities** Lift. Reception (background radio), salon/library/TV room, breakfast room. Unsuitable for ♿. **Location** Between Blvd St-Germain and river. (Métro: Rue du Bac, St-Germain-des-Prés) Public parking nearby (€25). **Restriction** No dogs. **Credit cards** All major cards accepted. **Terms** Room: single €125, double €140–€190. Breakfast €12.

> The 'New' label is used both for new entries and for hotels that have been readmitted to the *Guide* this year.

PAUILLAC 33250 Gironde Map 4:C3

Château Cordeillan-Bages *Tel* 05.56.59.24.24
Route des Châteaux *Fax* 05.56.59.01.89
Email cordeillan@relaischateaux.com
Website www.cordeillanbages.com

A 17th-century Carthusian monastery is now this 'serious hotel with a formal atmosphere' (Relais & Châteaux). It stands amid famous vineyards in the Médoc, a boring stretch of gravel-based land north-west of Bordeaux which produces some of the world's finest red wines: Pauillac is a top *appellation*. Manager/chef Thierry Marx wins two *Michelin* stars, 18 *Gault Millau* points (one more this year) for, eg, pressé d'anguille fumée; agneau de lait en trois façons. Service is 'a good mix of friendly and sophisticated', say recent visitors. There are 'lovely, rather clubby' public rooms, and a charming grassy courtyard where meals are served. Breakfasts and bedrooms are admired. 'Our "superior" room had fine furniture, and a patio with parasols.' Some beds are king-size. 'Superb bath.' Wine-tasting courses are offered.

Open 14 Feb–15 Dec. Restaurant closed Mon, Sat midday, Tues midday. **Rooms** 4 suites, 25 double. Some on ground floor. 4 in annexe. Some air conditioned. 1 designed for ♿. **Facilities** Lift, ramp. 3 lounges, breakfast room, restaurant; background music; seminar room; fitness room, sauna; wine shop. Courtyard, terrace. Garden: heated swimming pool. **Location** 1 km S of Pauillac, 53 km N of Bordeaux. **Restriction** No smoking: restaurant, some bedrooms. **Credit cards** All major cards accepted. **Terms** [2004] Room €142–€275, suite €300–€425. Breakfast €18–€22. Set lunch €60, dinner €95; full alc €110.

PÉGOMAS 06580 Alpes-Maritimes Map 6:D5

Le Bosquet BUDGET *Tel* 04.92.60.21.20
74 chemin des Périssols *Fax* 04.92.60.21.49
Email hotel.lebosquet@wanadoo.fr
Website www.pegomas.com

Between Cannes and Grasse, on the edge of a village in mimosa country, this informal and 'convivial' holiday hotel, long popular with readers, is owned and run by Chantal Cattet. It is a *Michelin Bib* hotel ('good accommodation at moderate prices'). *Guide* readers have called it 'a haven of quiet from the busy coast'. The bedrooms have recently been redecorated, bathrooms renewed. The one-bedroom studios have a kitchen. In summer, you can breakfast (with home-made jams) in the large garden full of apricot and plum trees and lavender bushes. There is a good hard tennis court. The smallish swimming pool and its area are immaculate: plenty of loungers. But in high season, bedrooms near the pool could hear noise from children. No restaurant: try *L'Écluse* outside the village, 'with an attractive riverside dining terrace', or the 'more expensive, but fascinating' *Auberge de la Vignette Haute* in nearby Auribeau.

Open All year. **Rooms** 7 studios, 16 double. **Facilities** Salon, TV room, breakfast room. No background music. Garden: terrace, swimming pool, tennis. Golf nearby. Unsuitable for ♿. **Location** Edge of village. 10 km NW of Cannes on road to Mouans-Sartoux. Covered parking. **Credit cards** Amex, MasterCard, Visa. **Restriction** No dogs. **Terms** Room €45–€60, studio €75–€80. Breakfast €6.50.

PEILLON 06440 Alpes-Maritimes **Map 6:D5**

Auberge de la Madone
2 place Auguste Arnulf

Tel 04.93.79.91.17
Fax 04.93.79.99.36
Email madone@chateauxhotels.com
Website www.chateauxhotels.com/madone

'Between sea and sky' in the hills behind Nice, this well-known *village perché* is up a winding road, on a rocky spur. At its gates, the Millo family's 'rather special' hotel has a 'wonderful setting'. Service is 'friendly but professional, with a hint of humour', said one guest. Others wrote of 'stunning food, elegantly presented'. *Père et fils*, Christian and Thomas Millo, win a *Michelin* star, 14 *Gault Millau* points for, eg, gratin de macaroni au foie gras et truffes; carré d'agneau rôti au fleur de thym. Guests dine in the pink-beamed restaurant or on the broad, flowery terrace with a view of the valley. House wines are fairly priced. Bedrooms have tiled floors, pastel colours, Provençal fabrics, rustic furniture; many are spacious, and have a balcony facing the panorama. Antiques are on landings and in odd corners. Breakfast, with cakes and strong coffee, is in a room with chandeliers and velvet drapes. Six simpler bedrooms are in the annexe, *Lou Pourtail*.

Open All year, except 7–31 Jan, 20 Oct–20 Dec, Wed. **Rooms** 3 suites, 14 double. 6 more in annexe, *Lou Pourtail*, 50 m. **Facilities** Salon, TV room, bar, restaurant; background music. 5-hectare grounds: tennis, *boules*. Unsuitable for ♿. **Location** 19 km N of Nice. From A55: D2204 towards Sospel, then D121, D21. **Restrictions** No smoking in some bedrooms. No dogs. **Credit cards** MasterCard, Visa. **Terms** [2004] Room €95–€240, suite €215–€390. Breakfast €16. Set meals €45–€75; alc €65.

PENVINS 56370 Morbihan **Map 2:F2**

Hôtel Le Mur du Roy BUDGET

Tel 02.97.67.34.08
Fax 02.97.67.36.23
Email le-mur-du-roy@wanadoo.fr
Website www.lemurduroy.com

The setting of M. and Mme Boyère's modern hotel is 'splendid', say visitors to the lovely Rhuys peninsula. Others wrote of 'a spacious feel, a friendly *patron*'. 'A rough lawn leads to the sandy, rocky, seaweedy beach, almost empty at the end of June. Bathing was safe: lots of little boats to swim to.' Many of the 'small, plain' rooms face the sea, as do the sunny dining areas. Monsieur's cooking, specialising in *fruits de mer*, is 'accomplished', menus are 'perfectly balanced', and 'service, from a young girl, was faultless'. One guest, who wanted a change from the no-choice menu, was offered a steak 'immediately, with no question of extra charge'. 'Delicious breakfast pastries.' 'Excellent value, highly recommended.' (*L and CR, and others*)

Open All year, except Jan. **Rooms** 10. 1 on ground floor. **Facilities** 2 dining rooms (1 no-smoking), dining terrace. Garden; beach. **Location** 7 km SE of Sarzeau, by D198, 24 km S of Vannes. Parking. **Credit cards** Amex, MasterCard, Visa. **Terms** Room €57. Breakfast €10. D,B&B €35 added per person. Set meals €31–€42, full alc €56.

PÉRIGNAT-LÈS-SARLIÈVE 63170 Puy-du-Dôme Map 6:A1

Hostellerie Saint-Martin
Allée de Bonneval

Tel 04.73.79.81.00
Fax 04.73.79.81.01
Email reception@hostellerie-st-martin.com
Website www.hostellerie-st-martin.com

Jacques Brugère's imposing white-fronted hotel (16th-century Cistercian abbey, later an 18th-century château): 8 km SE of Clermont-Ferrand, just W of A75. 'Warm and welcoming; huge panelled rooms; true Auvergnat food (large helpings), fine cheese-board.' Lift. Conference/function rooms. 7-hectare park: lawn, shady terrace (outdoor dining), heated swimming pool, tennis; distant views of Auvergne volcanoes. Amex, MasterCard, Visa accepted. Restaurant closed Sun night Oct–Mar. 34 bedrooms (annexe ones refurbished, but small). B&B €95–€119. Set meals €25–€59 [2004].

PÉROUGES 01800 Ain Map 6:A3

Ostellerie du Vieux Pérouges
Place du Tilleul

Tel 04.74.61.00.88
Fax 04.74.34.77.90
Email thibaut@ostellerie.com
Website www.ostellerie.com

This lovely medieval village, with its ramparts, half-timbered houses, and cobbled streets, is often the setting for historical films. Here, the Thibaut family have presided since 1912 at their hotel, converted from 14th-century and Renaissance buildings on the square. 'Magical and peaceful: recommended for the *bastide* experience,' was one comment. Other visitors told of 'excellent food'. Regional dishes, eg, foie gras de canard; médaillons de veau aux asperges, are served by waitresses in medieval costume; menus are on parchment scrolls. The bedrooms are in four houses, those in the *Manoir* are said to be the best. 'Ours, tastefully restored, very quiet, had a marvellous view over the garden by the church (its bells are turned off at night).' Some rooms have their own garden where you can breakfast.

Open All year. **Rooms** 2 suites, 26 double. In 4 different houses. 2 on ground floor. **Facilities** 2 salons, bar, 4 dining rooms; 4 meeting rooms. No background music. 2 terraces. Unsuitable for ♿. **Location** Village square. 40 km NE of Lyon. Parking. 2 garages. **Restriction** No smoking in some public rooms. **Credit cards** MasterCard, Visa. **Terms** [2004] Room: single €75–€115, double €110–€250, suite €220. Breakfast €13. Set meals €35–€70; full alc €50.

PERROS-GUIREC 22700 Côtes-d'Armor Map 2:E2

Manoir du Sphinx NEW
67 chemin de la Messe

Tel 02.96.23.25.42
Fax 02.96.91.26.13
Email lemanoirdusphinx@wanadoo.fr
Website www.lemanoirdusphinx.com

Built as a private villa in the early 20th century and 'tastefully extended' in the 1960s, Anne-Catherine Lavallière's hotel on the north Brittany coast 'stands dramatically above pink granite rocks that lead to the sea's edge, which one can scramble down to'. *Michelin* likes the 'charming garden'. *Gault Millau* describes the bedrooms as '*claires et élégantes*'. 'Ours, good sized, had a tiny balcony with views of the bay and one of the larger offshore islands.' In the panoramic restaurant, *L'Étape des Gourmets*, food (with an emphasis on seafood) 'was excellent, supported by a good wine list. Service of a high standard. An appealing balance between French formal correctness and family friendliness.' (*Christopher and Felicity Macy*)

Open 24 Feb–16 Jan. Restaurant closed Sun night Oct–Mar, Mon midday and Fri midday except holidays. **Rooms** 20. **Facilities** Salon/bar, restaurant. Garden. Sandy beach. Tennis, golf, horse riding nearby. **Location** Plage de Trestrignel. 12 km N of Lannion. **Restriction** No dogs. **Credit cards** Amex, MasterCard, Visa. **Terms** Room €104–€122. Breakfast €9.50. D,B&B (min. 3 days) €97–€116 per person. Set meals €21–€50.

PESMES 70140 Haute-Saône Map 5:D4

Hôtel de France BUDGET
Rue Vannoise

Tel 03.84.31.20.05
Fax 03.84.31.29.85

Between Dijon and Besançon, this 'very beautiful' village has a 'wonderful setting' on the River Ognon. By the water, this 'real, simple country hotel' (Logis de France), owned since 1940 by the Vieille family, is 'not for lovers of luxury', says a fan. 'The emphasis is on good food at reasonable prices.' '*Demi-pension* was an amazing bargain. Mme Vieille controls the operation, assisted by two daughters, two grandfathers and various grandchildren. By the end of our stay, we knew them all as friends.' Other comments: 'The family, all fine advertisements for good eating, bustled around, serving a five-course dinner with plenty of choice.' 'Towards the end, Madame comes to chat, shake hands, and where such familiarity is appropriate, to kiss.' The bar is 'full of locals'. The restaurant stands on a busy road, but the bedrooms (some visitors find them too basic) are in a nearby house in a large, quiet garden. 'Plumbing a bit erratic, housekeeping a little random, but everything one needs.' Breakfast (baguette, large block of butter, home-made jam, unlimited coffee) is served under fruit trees on fine days. Close by is an island with *buvette* and bathing area. (*CB, BWR*)

Open All year, except 15 days Nov, 24 Dec evening, Sun night Nov–Easter. Restaurant closed Sun night. **Rooms** 10 double. All in annexe. **Facilities** Lounge, bar, breakfast room, restaurant; meeting room; terrace. No background music. Large garden. Unsuitable for ♿. **Location** In village. 19 km S of Gray, 26 km N of Dole. Parking. **Credit card** Visa. **Terms** [2004] Room €36–€45. Breakfast €6. D,B&B €40 per person. Set meals €20; full alc €28.

LA PETITE-PIERRE 67290 Bas-Rhin — Map 5:B5

Auberge d'Imsthal BUDGET
3 route forestière d'Imsthal

Tel 03.88.01.49.00
Fax 03.88.70.40.26
Email auberge.imsthal@wanadoo.fr
Website www.petite-pierre.com

The Michaely family's trim and 'delightful' little Relais du Silence is in a valley just below this hilltop village amid the rolling forests of the North Vosges national park. 'A total switch-off from humdrum life,' wrote one satisfied guest. Gabled and half-timbered, it faces a small lake ('good swimming, and fun for children who love to spot the fish,' says our inspector). Others add: 'Good value in a charming setting. We had a lovely walk in the woods. An interesting German-style breakfast. Staff friendly, rooms well equipped, food excellent.' Local dishes, such as coq au riesling, are on the menu. The bedrooms are quite simple; some are small; most have a spacious modern bathroom.

Open All year, except 30 Aug–9 Sept, 15 Nov–16 Dec. Restaurant closed Tues. **Rooms** 23 double. **Facilities** Lift. Lounge, bar, 2 dining rooms; function facilities; background music; sauna, spa bath; games room. Garden. By lake: bathing, fishing. **Location** 3 km SE of village, by D178. Parking. **Restrictions** No smoking in 1 dining room. No dogs in restaurant. **Credit cards** All major cards accepted. **Terms** Room €45–€92. Breakfast €9. D,B&B €56–€78 per person.

LES PLANCHES 39600 Jura — Map 5:D4

Moulin de la Mère Michelle
Domaine de la Venne

Tel 03.84.66.08.17
Fax 03.84.37.49.69
Email moulin@mere-michelle.com
Website www.mere-michelle.com

A 'wonderfully sited, quiet hotel' (says a visitor in 2004). A converted 15th-century mill (Relais du Silence), it is at the foot of a waterfall in the Cirque du Fer à Cheval (high cliff horseshoe), near the source of the River Cuisance. An unpretentious place, it has red-tiled roofs and a highly praised restaurant, with wood panelling, a tapestry, and upholstered chairs. Some bedrooms are in the mill. 'Ours, in another block, was smallish, clean, with lovely view.' One visitor thought that apart from the 'well-cared-for dining room', the hotel looked 'rather unfinished'. Ingredients for the kitchen come from the farm of co-owner Jean-Claude Delavenne. Rachelle and Pascal Mathieu produce 'first-class food with great variety' (they are members of the 900-strong *Confrérie de la poularde au vin jaune et aux morilles*). 'Our excellent dinner included foie gras maison; locally caught fish cooked to perfection.' 'Plenty of Jura wines, on an extensive list.' There is a 'nice covered swimming pool with a basic bar', a shop selling farm produce. Local activities include mushroom gathering. (*Kay Birchley, PH, and others*)

Open All year, except 5–31 Jan. Restaurant closed midday Mon–Fri unless reservation made. **Rooms** 2 family, 22 double. In 3 buildings. **Facilities** Lift. Salon, restaurant. Shop. Garden: covered swimming pool, tennis, archery, ping-pong. **Location** 4 km SE of Arbois, 52 km S of Besançon. Parking **Credit cards** Amex, MasterCard, Visa. **Terms** [2004] Room €96–€175. Breakfast €10. D,B&B €95–€115 per person. Set meals €37–€65.

PLANCOËT 22130 Côtes-d'Armor — Map 2:E2

Hôtel L'Écrin
et Restaurant Jean-Pierre Crouzil
20 les quais

Tel 02.96.84.10.24
Fax 02.96.84.01.93
Email jean-pierre.crouzil@wanadoo.fr
Website www.crouzil.com

'Again we had a wonderful time,' say trusted correspondents after their third visit to Jean-Pierre Crouzil's restaurant-with-rooms in a village west of Dinan. Earlier they wrote: 'It has vitality, panache, and a warmth we have met nowhere else.' 'After showing us to our cosy first-floor room, the receptionist produced tea and Breton pancakes. Madame as affable as ever. Personable staff.' Public rooms have bronzes, good fabrics and carpets. M. Crouzil wins two *Michelin* stars, 16 *Gault Millau* points for, eg, St-Jacques poêlées au verjus de tokay; homard rôti, brûlé au lambic. 'On half board you can take any menu; the wine list is fine if a bit costly; breads, all home made, are also fine.' In the 'striking' dining room, 'dazzlingly lit glassed alcoves display attractive china', and there are 'exquisite flower arrangements, elegant glasses and cutlery'. Breakfast has fresh pastries, home-made jams. 'Though between the busy main road and a branch line, the hotel is quiet. No views of note.' (*Francine and Ian Walsh, and others*)

Open All year, except evenings of 25 Dec, 1 Jan. **Rooms** 1 suite, 6 double. **Facilities** Salon, restaurant (background music); sauna, solarium. Sea 7 km. Unsuitable for ♿. **Location** Main road, by station (double glazing). 15 km SW of Dinard. Parking. **Credit cards** Amex, MasterCard, Visa. **Terms** Room: single €78, double €110, suite €168. Breakfast €15–€25. D,B&B (min. 3 days) €137–€153 per person. Set meals €70–€100; full alc €96.

PLANGUENOUAL 22400 Côtes-d'Armor — Map 2:E2

Manoir de la Hazaie

Tel 02.96.32.73.71
Fax 02.96.32.79.72
Email manoir.hazaie@wanadoo.fr
Website www.manoir-hazaie.com

'Superbly restored' by owners Jean-Yves and Christine Marivin, and with 'furnishings tastefully selected to create an authentic contemporary ambience', this stone-built manor house was found 'delightful' by regular *Guide* correspondents: 'Our welcome could not have been warmer.' The bedrooms are romantically named: Typhaine, Brocéliande, etc: some have a fireplace and beamed ceiling; two are in a watermill by a lake. Also in the grounds are fountains, a medieval garden, a large swimming pool with '*aqua-musique*'. 'Personal service' is provided by the owners. 'Breakfast, one of the best we have had in France, was in the large main hall.' The setting is rural, well away from the nearest main road, and the house is 'very quiet at night'. Ten minutes' drive away is the 'rather smart' resort of Pléneuf-Val-André with many good seafood restaurants, eg, *Au Biniou* (*Michelin Bib Gourmand*). (*I and GE*)

Open All year. **Rooms** 1 junior suite, 5 double, 1 apartment (for 4). 2 in watermill. 1 on ground floor, accessible to ♿. **Facilities** Salon (classical background music). 3-hectare grounds: medieval garden, heated swimming pool, lake. Beach 5 km. **Location** SW of Pléneuf-Val-André, which is 43 km NW of Dinan. **Restrictions** No smoking: salon, some bedrooms. No dogs. **Credit cards** Amex, MasterCard, Visa. **Terms** [2004] Room €130–€197, suite €214–€240. Breakfast €13.

LE POËT-LAVAL 26160 Drôme — Map 6:C3

Les Hospitaliers
Le Vieux Village

Tel 04.75.46.22.32
Fax 04.75.46.49.99
Email contact@hotel-les-hospitaliers.com
Website www.hotel-les-hospitaliers.com

Visitors returning this year to the Morin family's hilltop hotel found it 'delightful as ever'. In a medieval village east of Montélimar, it is built on the ruins of a much older building (once owned by the Knights of St John). It has a beamed and vaulted lounge in front of a ruined 12th-century chapel. 'The views from the terrace are magnificent. Our large annexe room had old furniture and a view down the valley. But we would have liked help with luggage.' Most bedrooms and bathrooms have been renovated this year. The dining terrace is 'superb', and the food (14 *Gault Millau* points) is always enjoyed. 'M. Morin a constant presence at dinner. Service, and the local Côtes du Rhône, both very good.' At night, there is 'only the sound of birds'. (*Matthew Hamlyn, John Holland, Dr and Mrs A Naylor, and others*)

Open 18 Mar–13 Nov. Restaurant closed to non-residents Mon/Tues 1 July–15 Sept. **Rooms** 2 suites, 20 double. In 4 buildings. 11 on ground floor. **Facilities** Ramps. Salon, bar, restaurant; conference facilities. No background music. Garden: terraces, unheated swimming pool. Unsuitable for ♿. **Location** Top of old village on D540. 5 km W of Dieulefit, 25 km E of Montélimar. Car park opposite. **Credit cards** All major cards accepted. **Terms** Room €65–€140, suite €150–€160. Breakfast €10–€15. D,B&B €35 added per person. Set meals €40–€53; full alc €85.

POIL 58170 Nièvre — Map 5:D2

Château de Villette NEW

Tel 03.86.30.09.13
Fax 03.86.30.26.03
Email catherinestork@wanadoo.fr
Website www.stork-chateau.com

In the Morvan nature reserve in southern Burgundy, this 16th/18th-century château has been run for three years as a *chambres d'hôtes* by its English-speaking owners Catherine and Coen Stork (she is Belgian, he is Dutch). 'They made us feel like their personal guests,' one couple wrote. The bedrooms are 'of the highest standard; old-fashioned, but with modern comforts'. The setting, with panoramic views, is 'stunning' and tranquil: it is in a huge park (designed by Le Nôtre), with woods, streams, ponds and fields. 'The owners' chocolate Labrador, Timber, went with us on walks, and we saw roe deer, partridges and hares.' The five-course set dinner (chosen the day before) is served in the candlelit dining room ('decorated in warm colours') or on a terrace. 'Dining with the owners was a treat.' Breakfasts are 'lavish'. House parties are catered for. (*Arent and Marthe Foch, May Rademaker, DJ Andriesse*)

Open All year. **Rooms** 3 double. **Facilities** 2 salons, dining room; table-tennis room. 200-hectare park: 2 terraces, heated swimming pool, tennis. Golf nearby. **Location** 20 km SW of Autun. On D192, off N81. Parking. **Credit cards** MasterCard, Visa. **Terms** [2004] B&B double €145–€195. Set dinner €38 with wine.

POISSON 71600 Saône-et-Loire — Map 5:E2

Hôtel La Reconce et Restaurant de la Poste
Le Bourg

Tel 03.85.81.10.72
Fax 03.85.81.64.34

In a relatively unexplored area of south-west Burgundy, this Charolais house is now a restaurant-with-rooms (Relais du Silence). Run by owner/chef Jean Noël Dauvergne and his wife, Denise, in a 'uniquely delightful' way, say admirers, it 'exemplifies all that is good about France', at modest prices. 'We were enchanted,' was one comment. The restaurant, liked by *Michelin* for its use of *les produits du terroir*, earns 13 *Gault Millau* points for, eg, carpaccio de bœuf, julienne de céleri et gingembre; daurade à la plancha. 'The meal was great. Lots of locals.' Service, by 'cheerful young waitresses', may not be swift, 'but we preferred to linger over such a good meal'. The local burgundies are at fair prices. 'Eccentric decor; a giant aquarium in the dining room.' There is a 'nice big garden' at the back, and a shady terrace and veranda for summer meals. The small bedrooms, in a separate building, are modern and well designed, but some facing the village can be 'rather noisy in the morning', and one is by a kitchen vent. 'High-class breakfast: fruit and clafoutis.' Many Romanesque churches are nearby. (*C and GR*)

Open All year, except 1–20 Oct, and Mon/Tues. **Rooms** 1 suite, 4 double, 2 single. 1 on ground floor. **Facilities** Salon, bar/breakfast room, restaurant (no-smoking; background music). Veranda; terrace; garden: swing, table tennis. **Location** 68 km W of Mâcon, 8 km S of Paray-le-Monial. Parking. **Credit cards** Amex, MasterCard, Visa. **Terms** Room: single €54, double €76, suite €120. Breakfast €11. Set meals €25–€75; full alc €55.

> In the case of EMU members, we quote the rates in euros. Sterling equivalents of other foreign currencies at the date of going to press will be found at the back of the *Guide*.

PONT DE l'ISÈRE 26600 Drôme — Map 6:B3

Michel Chabran NEW
25 avenue du 45ème parallèle N7

Tel 04.75.84.60.09
Fax 04.75.84.59.65
Email chabran@michelchabran.fr
Website www.michelchabran.fr

'In a nondescript little town', near picturesque Valence, 'Michel Chabran's hotel/restaurant is impossible to miss,' says a visitor in 2004. At the foot of the famous vineyards of Hermitage, where 'amazing' wines are produced, the 100-year-old house stands on a major road. It was bought by M. Chabran's grandparents as a café in 1935. Now, he has a *Michelin* star, 16 *Gault Millau* points for 'brilliant and subtle' dishes like St-Jacques sautées aux poireaux à l'huile de truffe; pigeonneau en cocotte et cuisse en pastilla. 'Monsieur is much in evidence; Madame is charming. You feel part of the family while staying here.' The dining room is 'warmly attractive'; summer meals are served in the small garden. Breakfast comes with home-made jams. The bedrooms (with double glazing) are all different; quietest ones face the garden. (*Frank Deis*)

Open All year, except Sun night and Wed Nov–Mar, Wed midday and Thurs midday July–Sept. **Rooms** 12 double. Air conditioning. **Facilities** 2 salons, bar, restaurant. Garden (meal service). Unsuitable for ♿. **Location** 9 km N of Valence on N7. **Credit cards** All major cards accepted. **Terms** [2004] Room €77–€120. Breakfast €16. Set meals €45–€120.

PONTAUBERT 89200 Yonne — Map 5:C2

Les Fleurs BUDGET
69 route de Vézelay

Tel 03.86.34.13.81
Fax 03.86.34.23.32
Email info@hotel-lesfleurs.com
Website www.hotel-lesfleurs.com

In a village in rolling Burgundy country between Avallon and Vézelay, Claire and Régis Tatraux's small white-fronted restaurant-with-rooms (Logis de France) 'offers good value in a pleasant environment', says a visitor this year. 'Charming, simple: everything that mattered was perfect,' was another comment. It is on a busy road, but quiet at night, and most of the 'well-maintained' bedrooms are at the rear, facing the pretty garden, full of trees, shrubs and flowers. 'Toiletries (though minimal) are replenished daily.' The *patron*'s menu was found 'most appealing': 'We could have chosen anything from it' (eg, confit de canard fermier et ses pommes Sarladaises). There is a terrace for summer meals ('not a midge or mosquito in sight'). 'Good, simple breakfast – excellent toasted brioche and country baguette, real jams, freshly made coffee.' The national park of the Morvan is nearby. (*Mrs JM Turner, Eva Jacobs, and others*)

Open 26 Jan–14 Dec. Restaurant closed Thurs, and Wed except 15 June–15 Sept. **Rooms** 7 double. **Facilities** Salon, restaurant; background music. Garden: terrace. Unsuitable for ♿. **Location** D957, 3 km W of Avallon. Parking. **Credit cards** Amex, MasterCard, Visa. **Terms** Room €47. Breakfast €7. D,B&B (min. 3 nights) €47–€58 per person. Set meals €15–€37; full alc €50.

PONTEMPEYRAT 43500 Haute-Loire — Map 6:A2

Moulin de Mistou
Craponne-sur-Arzon

Tel 04.77.50.62.46
Fax 04.77.50.66.70
Email moulin.de.mistou@wanadoo.fr
Website www.mistou.fr

A vine-covered former watermill (1720), this cheerful small hotel, run by chef/*patron* Bernard Roux and his wife, Jacqueline, 'sits in gardens by a tree-lined river', in the eastern Auvergne. The first of the Logis de France, it is mostly liked: 'A lovely spot, very quiet, on a country road.' 'It has all the virtues of a hands-on family operation,' say regular correspondents. In the 'delightful' garden is a 'fine open-air pool' (no shallow end). 'Our nice room had blue-and-yellow decor, good bed, decent lighting, even tea/coffee-making facilities.' The pretty dining room has a river view, and there is a veranda for summer meals. Many dishes (gazpacho, mignons de porc, etc) were enjoyed, but several visitors complained of a lack of salads and vegetables. 'No choice on the half-board menu, but you can negotiate for dishes from other menus.' Service can be 'slightly fussy', but staff are 'helpful about local walks'. Breakfast, served after 8.30 am, includes fresh orange juice, good pastries. Terraces open on to lawns with garden furniture. (*Matthew Hamlyn, and others*)

Open May–Oct. Restaurant closed midday, except Sun, public holidays. **Rooms** 14 double. Some no-smoking. 1 on ground floor. **Facilities** Salon, 2 restaurants (no-smoking, background music); conference room; fitness room. 2-hectare garden: heated swimming pool, spa bath. Unsuitable for ♿. **Location** On D498 7 km NE of Craponne, 36 km N of Le Puy. **Credit cards** Amex, MasterCard, Visa. **Terms** B&B double €95–€130. Breakfast €12. D,B&B €95–€110 per person. Set meals €32–€58.

PONTORSON 50170 Manche — Map 2:E3

Hotel Montgomery BUDGET
13 rue Couesnon

Tel 02.33.60.00.09
Fax 02.33.60.37.66
Email info@hotel-montgomery.com
Website www.hotel-montgomery.com

Built in 1526, this creeper-covered building was the home of the Earl of Montgomery, who accidentally killed the French king, Henry II, in a tournament. Now a hotel 'full of character' (Best Western), owned by Joël and Marie-Christine Petit, it has many original features: carved wooden staircase, painted ceilings, 16th-century paintings; one room has an amazing four-poster bed. 'Our entire stay was a pleasure,' say recent visitors. 'Stairs are narrow and twisty, floors squeak; the decor is old-fashioned, but the renovated bathrooms work beautifully.' Some rooms face the town, some the garden; some have a spa bath, a new junior suite has a double bath. The orange-walled restaurant serves local cuisine. Five minutes' drive from Mont-Saint-Michel; an hour from D-Day beaches. (*S and EH*)

Open All year, except 13–25 Feb, 14–26 Nov. Restaurant closed midday and 25 Dec. **Rooms** 2 junior suites, 28 double, 2 single. **Facilities** Lift. Bar,

2 dining rooms (background music), conservatory. Garden. **Location** 0.2 km from centre. 59 km N of Rennes. Garage. **Restriction** No smoking: restaurant, 6 bedrooms. **Credit cards** All major cards accepted. **Terms** Room: single €48–€55, double €60–€100, suite €120–€225. Breakfast €10. D,B&B (min. 3 nights) €29 added per person. Set dinner €15–€25; full alc €28. *V*

ÎLE DE PORQUEROLLES 83400 Var — Map 6:E4

Le Mas du Langoustier

Tel 04.94.58.30.09
Fax 04.94.58.36.02
Website www.langoustier.com

The middle, and most easily accessible, of the three Îles d'Hyères, the island of Porquerolles (the name means 'lavender port') is a car-free national park, with wooded cliffs and sandy beaches. At its western end, amid pines and eucalyptus trees in its own large park, is this luxury hotel, 'close to paradise' according to a reader. Best bedrooms, with a balcony and views, are in an annexe. The older rooms, in a courtyard, are judged 'adequate', and are furnished in Provençal style. Meals are served to *en pension* residents in the *Pinède* terrace restaurant, with a view 'too good to miss', and to others in the more expensive *Olivier*, glass-panelled, with an olive tree in its centre: residents can pay extra to eat here. Chef Joël Guillet has a *Michelin* star, 16 *Gault Millau* points for dishes like soupe de poissons de roche; filet de loup grillé, coulis d'artichauts. Food in both restaurants is thought 'excellent'. The generous breakfast is served in the terrace restaurant. The hotel manages a 100-metre strip of sandy beach nearby, for which a charge is made, and a swimming pool is planned for 2005.

Open Mid-April–mid-Oct. **Rooms** 5 suites, 44 double. 1 on ground floor. Air conditioning. **Facilities** Lift, ramps. 3 salons, bar, 2 restaurants (1, no-smoking, for residents). Terrace, garden, park, tennis; mountain bike hire. Beach (paying) 200 m: boat hire, jet skis. **Location** 3.5 km W of port of Porquerolles (15 mins by boat from La Tour Fondue: frequent services). No cars on island. Free bus service from port. Helipad. **Credit cards** All major cards accepted. **Terms** [2004] D,B&B (obligatory) €180–€337 per person.

ÎLE DE PORT-CROS 83400 Var — Map 6:E4

Le Manoir

Tel 04.94.05.90.52
Fax 04.94.05.90.89
Email le manoir-portcros@wanadoo.fr

'Does one endorse Paradise?' asks a visitor in 2004 to this handsome, white 18th-century manor house. Its 'charming owner', Pierre Buffet, say other guests, 'has with great *élan* combined the old, "bashed-up" look with the new (modern bathrooms, exquisite swimming pool)'. It stands by the sea in large grounds among palms, oleanders and eucalyptus trees, on the loveliest of the three Îles d'Hyères, a hilly, densely wooded nature reserve, with subtropical vegetation, and a population of only about 30. No traffic (not even bicycles) is allowed, nor is fishing. 'Noisy crickets overlay the deep silence of the island.' Some rooms have a private terrace, all face south. 'You can feel really private, yet they have thought of everything you could want.' Meals (no-choice) are served on the terrace or by the pool. 'The food, formerly heavy, is now delicious, imaginative and light.' 'Games, newspapers and books are provided in the comfortable lounge. Excellent breakfast.' It is a 25-minute trek to sandy beaches: but the *Manoir*'s motor dinghy will take guests, with a picnic, to rocky bays nearby. (*Jean Chotia, MK, and others*)

Open 10 Apr–3 Oct. **Rooms** 4 suites (air conditioned), 15 double, 4 single. 2 in pavilion. **Facilities** Lounge, salon, TV room, restaurant. No background music. 2-hectare grounds: terrace, garden, bar, swimming pool. Unsuitable for ♿. **Location** 300 m from island's small port. Port-Cros is *c.* 1 hr by ferry from Le Lavandou/Hyères. **Restrictions** No smoking in some bedrooms. No dogs. **Credit cards** MasterCard, Visa. **Terms** [2004] D,B&B (obligatory) €150–€195. Set meals €43–€53. 1-night bookings sometimes refused.

PORTICCIO 20166 Corse-du-Sud — Map 11:E1

Hôtel Le Maquis
BP 94

Tel 04.95.25.05.55
Fax 04.95.25.11.70
Email info@lemaquis.com
Website www.lemaquis.com

Named after the scrub-like bushes which cover Corsica and gave their name to the French Resistance, this 'very well-run hotel' (say inspectors this year) is a collection of buildings by the sea. It was founded by a local woman, Catherine (Ketty) Salini, after the Second World War: 'She is still much in evidence.' It backs on to a busy road, but most bedrooms are quiet. 'Our delightful room had a small terrace with sea view, splendid lighting: one standard lamp was a Nubian bearing a chandelier dripping crystals.' 'Service and food of the highest order: delicious local fish and game.' Meals are served on the poolside terrace, or in the beamed restaurant, *L'Arbousier* ('elegant dress' is required for dinner). 'The charming staff speak English but were willing to indulge our attempts at French.' Only downside: 'Ever-present piped music.' There is a sea-water swimming pool in a conservatory. Porticcio, a 'thin, boring strip of hotels', is well placed for forays into the spectacular mountainous interior. 'Ajaccio holds the sunshine record for France, 2,900 hours per year,' says the hotel. The airport is 20 minutes' drive away. (*G and AM, and others*)

Open Feb–end Dec. **Rooms** 5 suites, 19 double. Air conditioning. **Facilities** Lounges, bar, restaurant; background music; function facilities; indoor swimming pool (hydromassage); shop, hairdresser. Terrace: meal service; unheated swimming pool; garden: tennis, private beach. Unsuitable for ♿. **Location** 5 mins' drive from Porticcio. Car park. **Credit cards** All major cards accepted. **Terms** [2004] Room €150–€490, suite €290–€970. Breakfast €21. Set dinner €58; full alc €95. 1-night bookings sometimes refused.

PORT-LESNEY 39600 Jura — Map 5:D4

Château de Germigney
Rue Edgar Faure

Tel 03.84.73.85.85
Fax 03.84.73.88.88
Email chateau.de.germigney@wanadoo.fr
Website www.chateaudegermigney.com

In a large park with statues, benches, and lily pond with fountain, this 18th-century manor house, former home of the Marquis de Germigney, is now a luxury hotel (Relais & Châteaux). Renovated from a semi-ruin by Roland Schön, a Swiss architect, and his wife, Verena, it is in a holiday village by the River Loue. Furnishings are antique and contemporary; modern fabrics combine with original features, pictures and sculptures. Recent comments: 'Dinner was excellent, with superb service. Interesting furnishings throughout.' 'Everything was light and bright.' 'Fantastic flowers. Our room was huge and peaceful.' But one couple found their bathroom 'poky, with a difficult-to-use hand shower', and added: 'The food and staff are good, but the garden needs a lot of TLC.' For meals, there is a formal dining room, with chandeliers, an orangery, and a 'huge and elegant' covered dining terrace. The chef, Pierre Basso Moro, wins a *Michelin* star, 15 *Gault Millau* points, for his contemporary cuisine. 'A plus point: half-portions of some dishes could be ordered.' The owners also have a bistro in the village. (*J Hanford, Pat and Jeremy Temple, and others*)

Open All year, except Jan. Restaurant closed Tues. **Rooms** 3 suites, 17 double. 1 suitable for ♿. **Facilities** Lift. Reception, bar, restaurant; background music; conference facilities. 3-hectare park: terrace, garden; croquet, river, swimming, fishing. **Location** In village. 37 km SW of Besançon. Parking. **Credit cards** All major cards accepted. **Terms** [2004] Room €125–€275. Breakfast €20. D,B&B (min. 3 days) €75 added per person. Set meals €35–€80.

PORTO-VECCHIO 20137 Corse-du-Sud — Map 11:E2

Belvédère NEW
Route de la Plage de Palombaggia

Tel 04.95.70.54.13
Fax 04.95.70.42.63
Email info@hbcorsica.com
Website www.hbcorsica.com

Five km E of Porto-Vecchio: 'enjoyable' modern hotel amid pine and eucalyptus trees on lagoon (private beach). Open 7 Mar–1 Jan. Michelin-*starred gastronomic restaurant by rocks: 'good food, good view'. Informal grill restaurant,* Mari e Tarra, *June–Oct. Lovely garden: panoramic terrace, 'magnificent' swimming pool, 2 spa baths. Insects can be a problem in summer. Excellent public beaches nearby. 19 bedrooms (most in pavilions) 'well furnished', air conditioned. B&B: double €100–€395, suite €180–€985. Set meals €49–€79; alc €45–€70 [2004].*

The maps can be found in the colour section of the *Guide*.

PROPRIANO 20110 Corse-du-Sud — Map 11:E1

Grand Hôtel Miramar
Route de la Corniche

Tel 04.95.76.06.13
Fax 04.95.76.13.14
Email miramar@wanadoo.fr
Website www.miramarcorse.com

In an area popular with tourists attracted by the fine beaches, this small luxury hotel stands high above the sea, in sumptuous gardens with superb views across the Gulf of Valinco. All bedrooms (some are rather small) are soundproofed and have a sea-facing balcony or terrace. Suites and an apartment (with private sauna) are in the park. 'Breakfast in the garden, looking across the bay, was delightful,' said one recent visitor. Lunch and dinner ('gourmet food, good Corsican wines') are served by the good-sized swimming pool (surrounded by loungers and parasols), which is floodlit at night. 'The climb to it is steep (no lift).' Public rooms are spacious and elegant. An 'excellent' beach is below the hotel. So is the coast road, where traffic is noisy, 'but if you close the windows, the air-conditioning is efficient'.

Open 25 Apr–3 Oct. **Rooms** 3 suites, 25 double. **Facilities** Lounge/bar, restaurant; conference room. Garden: terrace, swimming pool. **Location** Outside Propriano. 72 km SE of Ajaccio. Parking. **Credit cards** All major cards accepted. **Terms** [2004] Room €260–€370, suite €495–€830. Breakfast €18. D,B&B €73 added per person.

PULIGNY-MONTRACHET 21190 Côte-d'Or — Map 5:D3

Le Montrachet NEW
10 place des Marronniers

Tel 03.80.21.30.06
Fax 03.80.21.39.06
Email info@le-montrachet.com
Website www.le-montrachet.com

In the 'charming, quiet setting' of the tree-filled main square of this famous Burgundy wine village, this well-modernised old hostelry is owned by Thierry and Suzanne Gazagnes. The emphasis is on the food; there is no residents' lounge and the bedrooms vary: some are 'huge and luxurious'; smaller ones at the top are 'functional'. A new chef, Thierry Berger, took over in May 2004, and visitors soon after wrote: 'There was a generous welcome into the restaurant, and dinner was a delight. We were left in peace to enjoy the experience, but friendly waiters arrived when needed. Our small room was adequate for an overnight. The small bathroom was modern but the bath was short.' Breakfast, in the restaurant, or at tables under the canopy on the terrace facing the square, 'was of the same high standard as dinner: ample choice, smiling, attentive service'. The list of white Montrachets is 'of telephone-directory size', and many are 'hugely expensive'. Yet the place is 'unpretentious, charming'. The bar/lounge has a wood fire. (*Gareth Gunning, and others*)

Open 17 Jan–1 Dec. **Rooms** 3 suites, 28 double. 10 in annexe opposite. Some on ground floor. 1 adapted for ♿. **Facilities** Lounge/bar, restaurant (classical background music). Terrace. **Location** 10 km SW of Beaune. Enclosed parking. **Credit cards** All major cards accepted. **Terms** Room €100, suite €165–€170. Breakfast €14. D,B&B (min. 3 nights) €118–€154 per person. Set meals €38–€75. *V*

PUYLAURENS 81700 Tarn — Map 4:D5

Château Cap de Castel
Le Bourg

Tel 05.63.70.21.76
Fax 05.63.75.77.18
Email hotel@chateau-capdecastel.com
Website www.chateau-capdecastel.com

In the old centre of this former Cathar stronghold, this converted 13th-century château has 'fabulous views' over surrounding countryside and bedrooms in two 17th-century buildings. It is 'delightful, family-run, tasteful and clean', said a recent visitor. 'We were shown to enormous high-ceilinged rooms, with antiques. Bathrooms are spacious. Simple furnishings, but no tat.' Meals are served on the 'lovely terrace' by the small swimming pool, or in a room with a large fireplace. Ingredients include 'products of the *terroir* produced by our neighbours'. One menu is '*tout canard*'. Breakfast, on the terrace, was 'basic, but bread was fresh and croissants were hot'. A good base for viewing other castles in the area, such as Quéribus, and the Cathars' final stronghold at Montségur. (*SP*)

Open All year, except Nov. **Rooms** 10 bedrooms. 3 in annexe. 1 suitable for ♿. **Facilities** Salon, restaurant. Garden: dining terrace, swimming pool. **Location** Centre of town. W of Castres on N126. Public garage nearby. **Credit cards** Diners, MasterCard, Visa. **Terms** [2004] Room €39–€82. Breakfast €6. Set meals €17–€26.

QUÉDILLAC 35290 Ille-et-Vilaine — Map 2:E2

Relais de la Rance BUDGET
6 rue de Rennes

Tel 02.99.06.20.20
Fax 02.99.06.24.01
Email relaisdelarance@21s.fr

A smart restaurant-with-rooms (Logis de France) in a village north-west of Rennes, just off the main road to Brest. This old granite *maison bourgeoise* is run by its 'charming and sophisticated' owners, André Guitton and Joël Chevrier. It has a *Michelin Bib Gourmand* for regional dishes, much enjoyed by *Guide* correspondents: 'We had the Menu de Terroir Bretagne: crêpe de pomme avec saumon frais et beurre citron; civet de porc; fraise gourmandise. The interesting set menus vary widely in price, and there is an extensive *carte*. The wine list is good.' The bedrooms were recently refurbished: 'Ours was immaculate and thoughtfully equipped. Chantal, the granddaughter of the first hotelier, makes a most friendly hostess.' (*D and JA*)

Open All year, except 20 Dec–20 Jan, Fri evening, Sun evening. **Rooms** 13. **Facilities** TV room, bar, restaurant. **Location** 39 km NW of Rennes, off N12. Parking. **Credit cards** All major cards accepted. **Terms** [2004] Room €44–€59. Breakfast €8. D,B&B €46–€70 per person. Set meals €19–€65.

RAZAC-SUR-l'ISLE 24430 Dordogne — Map 4:C4

Château de Lalande NEW
Annesse et Beaulieu

Tel 05.53.54.52.30
Fax 05.53.07.46.67
Email lalande.chateau@wanadoo.fr
Website www.chateau-lalande-perigord.com

Between Bordeaux and the Dordogne, this small château, 'with slightly faded elegance', is a modestly priced hotel-restaurant (Logis de France), run by its owners, Louis and Michèle Sicard. A 'happy find', by a regular *Guide* correspondent, it is an impressive building, in 'rather neglected' parkland, but with a good swimming pool. 'Our room was palatial, bathroom also. The plumbing worked and water was hot.' One suite has a terrace and private entrance. In the restaurant, *Le Tilleul Cendré*, the chef, Louis Sicard, offers traditional dishes of the Périgord and of his native Provence. 'A really excellent, good-value meal; a wide-ranging, inexpensive wine list. The dining room was almost full, in midweek, and families with babies were well treated. Very few British visitors.' Summer meals are served on a lawn, under trees. Furnishing and colour schemes in the public rooms are 'rather unusual'. (*Alec Frank*)

Open 16 Mar–10 Nov. Restaurant closed Wed midday off-season. **Rooms** 3 suites, 15 double. **Facilities** Salon, bar, restaurant. 3-hectare grounds: swimming pool. **Location** 12 km W of Périgueux (N89 towards Bordeaux). Cross bridge at Razac-sur-l'Isle towards Gravelle, then left on D3. **Credit cards** Amex, MasterCard, Visa. **Terms** [2004] Room €53–€83, suite €90–€150. Breakfast €7. D,B&B €60–€75 per person. Set meals €25–€49; alc €40.

REGNÉVILLE-SUR-MER 50590 Manche — Map 2:D3

L'Hostellerie de la Baie NEW/BUDGET
Le Port

Tel 02.33.07.43.94
Fax 02.33.07.64.09
Website www.hostellerie-de-la-baie.com

Visitors this year raved about this 'heavenly place'. 'Splendidly located' in a pretty sailing village south of Cherbourg, this modest little seaside hotel has a cheerful owner, Didier Lecureur, who gives a warm welcome. But things can be disorganised, according to several readers, so it lost its place in the *Guide* last year. This year's reports have been mainly enthusiastic: 'Wonderful, inexpensive food. The best breakfast we had this year in France: proper bowls of coffee. Views of the tide coming and going, birds, boats and marshes. Ask for the room with the red striped bath, basin, bidet and loo. It's a hoot.' The elegant sea-facing dining room, often full of French families, serves a 'huge range of fish dishes'. A large birthday party enjoyed 'excellent festive food, appropriate to the region'. Specialities include seafood stew, and duck fillet with blackcurrants. Meals are also served in the garden facing the water. There is a big bar, and some 'very comfortable' bedrooms, looking out to sea, with a good bathroom and Louis XV or Louis XVI repro furniture. 'We could sunbathe while in bed, and with binoculars could see thousands of seabirds.' Some cheaper bedrooms may be less good. Tables and chairs stand on the grass by the bay, where there are lots of sailing boats. Nearby is Coutances, with its superb Gothic cathedral. (*Caroline Dalrymple, and others*)

Open All year, except Jan. **Rooms** 7 double. **Facilities** Bar, tea room, restaurant. Garden. **Location** In village. 11 km SW of Coutances. **Credit cards** MasterCard, Visa. **Terms** [2004] Room €49–€59. Breakfast €6. Set meals €14–€32.

REILLANNE 04110 Alpes-de-Haute-Provence — Map 6:D4

Auberge de Reillanne BUDGET *Tel/Fax* 04.92.76.45.95
Départementale 214 *Website* www.reillanne-en-luberon.com/auberge

Monique Balmand's small hotel: 'beautifully refurbished' old bastide *in ancient fortified village, set back from D214 off N100 between Apt (26 km) and Forcalquier. 'Calm, quiet, relaxing; simply furnished, spacious rooms.' Large salon; big garden. No-choice dinner (residents only), 'simple and good'. Good breakfast (orange juice, yogurt, etc). Open 1 Apr–20 Oct. Restaurant closed Wed. Unsuitable for ♿. MasterCard, Visa accepted. 6 bedrooms: single €48, double €68–€72. Breakfast €8. D,B&B €65 per person.*

REIMS 51430 Marne — Map 5:A2

L'Assiette Champenoise *Tel* 03.26.84.64.64
40 avenue Paul Vaillant-Couturier *Fax* 03.26.04.15.69
Tinqueux *Email* assiette.champenoise@wanadoo.fr
Website www.assiettechampenoise.com

Though not particularly attractive, apart from its splendid Gothic cathedral, Reims has some excellent restaurants and hotels, including this one, owned by the Lallement family. Set in large grounds, it has a typically north French exterior: white rendering with timbers, red brickwork, grey roof tiles. Fairly grand and sizeable, it has 'splendid' public rooms and 'many delightful sitting areas, indoors and out'. 'Our bedroom, and the dining room, were warm and welcoming on a winter's night,' say recent guests. The cooking of Arnaud Lallement (*Michelin* star, 16 *Gault Millau* points) is thought 'excellent', eg, asperges vertes de Robert Blanc; filet d'agneau cuit à la rôtissoire. The wine list is enormous. There is an opulent dining room and, in fine weather, you can eat on the 'idyllic' terrace. 'Breakfast was a generous buffet' (but served in the bedroom, it might come on an 'overweight tray'). Some suites have a patio (good wheelchair access) or terrace. The 'excellent' indoor swimming pool looks through large windows on to the garden. 'Expensive but worth it.' (*A and EA, and others*)

Open All year, except 24 Dec. Restaurant closed Tues/Wed midday. **Rooms** 55. Some air conditioned. Some suitable for ♿. **Facilities** Lift. 3 lounges, 2 bars, 2 dining rooms; conference facilities; swimming pool. Garden, dining terrace. **Location** 5 km W of Reims, signposted. Parking. **Credit cards** All major cards accepted. **Terms** [2004] Room €125–€237, suite €155–€245. Breakfast €14. D,B&B €69 added per person. Set meals €55–€85; full alc €120.

ROANNE 42300 Loire Map 4:B6

Hôtel Restaurant Troisgros
Place Jean-Troisgros

Tel 04.77.71.66.97
Fax 04.77.70.39.77
Email troisgros@avo.fr
Website www.troisgros.com

For three generations, since 1968, the Troisgros family, pioneers of *nouvelle cuisine*, have won three *Michelin* stars at their famous restaurant (Relais & Châteaux), which stands opposite *la gare* of a provincial town. It is said that the station is painted rose and green in honour of the escalope de saumon à l'oseille created by Michel Troisgros, *patron*/chef, grandson of the founder, Jean-Baptiste. He has 19 points from *Gault Millau*, too. He and his wife, Marie-Pierre, have created a 'beautiful' contemporary decor. On the roundabout outside is a sculpture of huge forks; there is a glass exterior lift; inside is a collection of modern art, and an 'amazing' library for food lovers. Bedrooms have soft colours, natural materials; 'superb lighting, fresh flowers, fruit brought daily, huge, very comfortable bed, vast marble bathroom with every extra', say recent visitors. 'The staff and family are lovely: our welcome was warm, and when we left, both Troisgros senior and junior shook our hands, and staff carried our bags to the station.' The restaurant, 'a relaxing room', has views of the garden and the kitchen. 'Fantastic puddings; some local wines were not too pricey.' The 'beautiful' breakfast buffet includes tomato with snails, scrambled eggs with caviar. 'A super, light bar lunch.' Next door is the Troisgros's café/grocery, *Le Central*.

Open All year, except Feb school holidays, 1st 2 weeks Aug, Tues/Wed. **Rooms** 5 suites, 13 double. Air conditioning. **Facilities** Salon, bar (background music), breakfast room, restaurant (no-smoking). Garden. Café adjacent. Unsuitable for ♿. **Location** Central (windows double glazed). Car park. **Credit cards** All major cards accepted. **Terms** [2004] Room €220–€300, suite €360–€440. Breakfast €24. Set meals €135–€170.

LA ROCHE-L'ABEILLE 87800 Haute-Vienne Map 4:B4

Au Moulin de la Gorce
St-Yrieix-la-Perche

Tel 05.55.00.70.66
Fax 05.55.00.76.57
Email moulindelagorce@wanadoo.fr
Website www.moulindelagorce.com

'Our visit could not have been more enjoyable,' says a regular *Guide* correspondent, returning in 2004 to Pierre and Isabelle Bertranet's 16th-century mill house, now an elegant small hotel (Relais & Châteaux). Deep in wooded Limousin countryside, 'an oasis of calm', it stands by a big pond with ducks and a stream, surrounded by old trees. M. Bertranet's cuisine, served in the galleried dining room or outdoors, has a *Michelin* star, 16 *Gault Millau* points for, eg, œufs brouillés aux truffes; bar de ligne grillé, piqué a l'ail. Another visitor wrote: 'It is like a mini-château, set before water so smooth that you see two buildings, one upside down, surrounded by trees. Beautiful, comfortable rooms, really excellent food. Madame is so kind.' The bedrooms, named after flowers, are in the main house and the mill ('the sound of the millrace lulls one to sleep'); some have old beams, some, reached up twisty stairs, are small but 'elegantly furnished'. The decor (expensive fabrics, bright colours, antiques and bibelots) 'is more château than mill'. Nearby are the two porcelain centres of Limoges (sprawling and ugly) and St-Yrieix (small and lovely). (*Humphrey Potts, James L Clarke, and others*)

Open 11 Mar–14 Nov. Restaurant closed Mon/Tues/Wed midday. **Rooms** 1 suite (in garden), 9 double. 3 in main building, 6 in mill. **Facilities** Salon, 2 dining rooms. No background music. Garden: pond, stream, fishing. Unsuitable for ♿. **Location** 2 km S of La Roche, off D17, 12 km NE of St-Yrieix, off D704. **Credit cards** All major cards accepted. **Terms** [2004] Room: double €70–€135, suite €210–€244 (3/4 people). Breakfast €14. D,B&B (min. 3 nights) €117–€147 per person. Set meals €40–€59, €105–€250 (inc fine wines).

LA ROCHE-BERNARD 56130 Morbihan — Map 2:F2

L'Auberge Bretonne
2 place Duguesclin

Tel 02.99.90.60.28
Fax 02.99.90.85.00
Email jacques.thorel@wanadoo.fr
Website www.auberge-bretonne.com

'Pretty close to perfection' was one couple's verdict on this luxurious hotel (Relais & Châteaux) in a busy market village near the south Brittany coast. Owner/chef Jacques Thorel has two *Michelin* stars, 19 *Gault Millau* points for his 'really extraordinary' creations. His wife, Solange, is 'very welcoming'. The restaurant, in an enclosed cloister, is 'smart, not cosy', filled with sculptures and paintings. It has a walled, glassed-in garden where spectacular vegetables and herbs are grown. 'Our table faced an illuminated fountain.' Dishes are 'artful, yet still in touch with their Breton roots', eg, homard de nos côtes en cocotte. 'The *sommelier* really cares.' Bedrooms, 'elegant spartan', have a chic bathroom and Breton fabrics. Public rooms have 'twinkling lights in window boxes and local antiques'. There is an 'atmospheric bar' with inglenook fireplace.

Open All year, except 15 Nov–26 Dec and 5–20 Jan. Restaurant closed Thurs, midday on Mon, Tues and Fri. **Rooms** 11 double. 1 suitable for ♿. **Facilities** Lift. Lounge, bar, restaurant, terrace; conference room. Background music. **Location** Central. 41 km SE of Vannes, 70 km NW of Nantes. Parking (€8). **Credit cards** All major cards accepted. **Terms** Room €100–€275. Breakfast €17. D,B&B €185–€260 per person. Set lunch €55, dinner €105–€137; alc €110.

ROCHECORBON 37210 Indre-et-Loire — Map 2:F4

Les Hautes Roches NEW
86 quai de la Loire

Tel 02.47.52.88.88
Fax 02.47.52.81.30
Email hautes.roches@wanadoo.fr
Website www.leshautesroches.com

On the site of a monastery, this imposing 18th-century mansion (Relais & Châteaux), facing the Loire near Tours, stands back from the fairly busy N152, up a curving drive. A unique feature is its twelve *chambres troglodytiques* carved out of the chalky rock (*tuffeau*), adjacent to the main building. Inspectors in 2004 were entranced: 'Our huge *de luxe* double was reached by steps leading to a terrace with river views. With its two large wardrobes, each with full-length mirror, and chest of drawers, it was one of the few hotel rooms in which we've been able properly to unpack. It had also a large settee, two armchairs, a table and a desk.' Public rooms include a 'rather plain' small salon, and a 'cosy' candlelit bar, originally the monastery's summer kitchen, hollowed out of the rock. The restaurant, in pale yellow and coral, is in three sections. The largest has river views, and there is a fish tank: manager/chef Didier Edon, from Brittany (*Michelin* star, 15 *Gault Millau* points) specialises in lobster. 'Our superb meal started with foie gras de canard à la façon d'un nougat, and ended with tarte fine aux figues caramelisées. With a glass of Vouvray *moelleux* to accompany the former, and Sancerre with the lobster, we were in heaven. Without exception, the staff were friendly and efficient. Outside the restaurant is a terrace with tables and chairs. To one side there is a lawn and, a little further down the slope, a heated swimming pool sheltered by trees and a hedge. A perfect base for visiting the central Loire châteaux and the Vouvray vineyards.' The owners, brothers Philippe and François Mollard, also own two other hotels in the region, *Château de Noizay*, Noizay, and *Château de Marçay*, Chinon (*qv*).

Open 27 Mar–18 Jan. **Rooms** 15 double. 12 in 'troglodyte' annexe, adjacent. **Facilities** Lift. Salon, bar, restaurant. Garden: terrace, lawn, heated swimming pool. Unsuitable for ♿. **Location** 7 km E of Tours, on N152 towards Vouvray. A10, exit 20. **Restriction** No dogs in restaurant. **Credit cards** All major cards accepted. **Terms** [2004] Double room €125–€255. Breakfast €17. D,B&B €76 per person added. Set meals €46–€65. Alc €56–€81.

LES ROCHES-DE-CONDRIEU 38370 Isère — Map 6:A3

Hôtel Restaurant Le Bellevue BUDGET
Quai du Rhône

Tel 04.74.56.41.42
Fax 04.74.56.47.56
Website www.le-bellevue.net

In a 'wonderful position on the Rhône', Josiane and Jean Paret's 'excellent', 'welcoming' small hotel, modern and creeper-covered, stands right on the majestically curving river in a village south of Vienne. On the opposite bank are the famous vineyards of Condrieu and the Côte Rôtie. 'Staff were friendly, and the food was the best of our holiday,' writes a visitor this year. In the pleasant restaurant, with huge fireplace and large windows facing a yachting harbour, there is a choice of menus, Tradition, Découverte, Saveur, and a *carte*. Dishes range from râble de lapin rôti à l'ail rosé to queue de homard en fricassée. The chef, Antoine Amalou, has worked with, among others, Gordon Ramsay at *Claridge's* in London. Breakfast is a 'substantial buffet'. Another reader liked her large room: 'From its balcony, with seating, we looked at the river and the vineyards beyond. But the towels were thin and rough.' Some road-facing rooms may be noisy. (*JA Harvey, Shirley Tennent, and others*)

Open 2 Mar–14 Feb. Restaurant closed Sun night/Mon Nov–Mar. **Rooms** 2 suites, 14 double. Some no-smoking. Some on ground floor. 3 in annexe. **Facilities** Salon, bar, restaurant. Terrace. Sports centre nearby. Unsuitable for ♿. **Location** 13 km SW of Vienne. On river, by marina. Safe parking. **Credit cards** Amex, MasterCard, Visa. **Terms** [2004] Room €46–€70. Breakfast €8. Set meals €17–€75.

ROMORANTIN-LANTHENAY 41200 Loir-et-Cher Map 2:F5

Grand Hôtel du Lion d'Or NEW
69 rue Georges-Clemenceau

Tel 02.54.94.15.15
Fax 02.54.88.24.87
Email info@hotel-liondor.fr
Website www.hotel-liondor.fr

In the main street of an old market town south of Orléans, this ravishing Renaissance manor house, a hotel since 1774, is now a very stylish one (Relais & Châteaux), run by the Barrat-Clément family owners. Didier Clément, the talented chef for 20 years, has two *Michelin* stars, 17 *Gault Millau* points for his 'subtle classical' cooking. Behind a rather plain exterior is a flowery courtyard with fountain, where breakfast and drinks are served in summer. Visitors on a return visit in 2004 found cuisine and service 'still of a high standard'. There are 'stunning reception rooms' with floor-to-ceiling mirrors, lighted candelabra on a grand piano, 'glorious flowers'. The dining room has 18th-century panelling and a giant, low-slung chandelier. 'The quality of the china, cutlery and glassware is a pleasure in itself.' Most bedrooms ('ours was hard to fault,' said another guest) face the courtyard; some have 'a lovely view of country and old tiled roofs'; those facing the street can be noisy, but have double glazing. 'Ours was well endowed with mirrors. Amazing bathroom: the shower had six faucets.' Parking (for which you pay) comes with windscreen cleaning. Romorantin has some ancient houses and a fascinating folk museum. Close by is the Sologne forest (Alain-Fournier country – you may find a copy of *Le Grand Meaulnes* by your bed). (*Peter and Moira Smith, and others*)

Open All year, except 14 Feb–24 Mar, 14–25 Nov. Restaurant closed Tues midday. **Rooms** 3 suites, 13 double. Air conditioning. **Facilities** Lift. 2 salons (background jazz), restaurant. Courtyard, terrace. **Location** Central (street-facing windows double glazed). 67 km SW of Orléans. Car park (€11 daily). **Credit cards** All major cards accepted. **Terms** [2004] Room €125–€350, suite €250–€450. Breakfast €20. Set meals €85–€130.

ROSCOFF 29681 Finistère Map 2:E1

Le Brittany
Boulevard Sainte-Barbe
BP 47

Tel 02.98.69.70.78
Fax 02.98.61.13.29
Email hotel.brittany@wanadoo.fr
Website www.hotel-brittany.com

Right by the sea, this 17th-century manor house, just east of the port, is now an attractive hotel whose owner, Mme Chapalain, 'is very kind', says a returning visitor this year. The best bedrooms, with views of sea or town, are in the main house. 'Ours, white and spacious, had four windows with long yellow curtains: one opened on to a private terrace with loungers. Stylish bathroom.' The rooms in the extension by the covered swimming pool, which have in the past been disliked, have been renovated this year. The sea-facing restaurant, *Le Yachtman*, with its huge fireplace, serves Loïc Le Bail's '*cuisine du terroir*', eg, cochon de lait saucisse et boudin noir; bar de ligne, galette de blé noir. 'Delicious food, especially the puddings.' There is a terrace by the sea for summer meals. Breakfast, with fresh pastries, orange juice, yogurt, is mostly enjoyed. The car-free Île de Batz, opposite (with bicycles for hire), is worth visiting. (*EH, and others*)

Open Mid-Mar–early Nov. Restaurant closed midday. **Rooms** 2 suites, 23 double. 6 in extension. Some no-smoking. 1 suitable for ♿. **Facilities** Lift. Lounge/bar, breakfast room, restaurant (background music); meeting room. Garden: covered heated swimming pool, sauna, solarium; café. Sandy beach opposite. **Location** Near ferry terminal, 2 km E of centre. Parking. **Restriction** No smoking: restaurant, some bedrooms. **Credit cards** Amex, MasterCard, Visa. **Terms** [2004] Room €90–€155, suite €155. Breakfast €12. D,B&B €99–€167 per person. Set dinner €29–€59.

ROUSSILLON 84220 Vaucluse **Map 6:D3**

Le Mas de Garrigon
Route de St-Saturnin d'Apt

Tel 04.90.05.63.22
Fax 04.90.05.70.01
Email mas.de.garrigon@wanadoo.fr
Website www.masdegarrigon-provence.com

This old hill village, popular with artists, is full of arty boutiques. Its name means 'russet': it is famous for its ochre quarries, and its buildings are in shades of red, pink and orange. Just outside, Christiane Druart's converted farmhouse (Relais du Silence) has fine views. It is 'enjoyable and relaxing', says a recent visitor. 'We were welcomed with a revitalising tray of melon and Parma ham. Our small room, named after the author St-John Perse, was deep red and a little dark.' The owners' daughter, Sandrine Kanza, cooks the no-choice dinner which might include terrine de poisons; pot au feu de canard. 'A good choice of local wines.' The pool is 'small, but inviting'. Each bedroom has a terrace. There is a library and, in winter, a log fire in the lounge.

Open All year. Dining rooms closed Mon/Tues, and 4 Nov–15 Mar. **Rooms** 1 suite, 8 double. Some air conditioned. **Facilities** Salon, library, bar, 3 dining rooms; classical background music. 3-hectare garden: unheated swimming pool, solarium. Unsuitable for ♿. **Location** 3 km N of village, 14 km NW of Apt. **Restrictions** No smoking: restaurant, some bedrooms. No children under 10. Dogs by arrangement only. **Credit cards** All major cards accepted. **Terms** Room: single €100–€125, double €110–€135, suite €135–€175. Breakfast €16. D,B&B (obligatory Easter–end Sept) €60 added per person. Set dinner €45. *V*

ROUVRES-EN-XAINTOIS 88500 Vosges — Map 5:B4

Hôtel Burnel & La Clé des Champs BUDGET
22 rue Jeanne-d'Arc

Tel 03.29.65.64.10
Fax 03.29.65.68.88
Email hotelburnel@burnel.fr
Website www.burnel.fr

Mme Burnel's friendly Logis de France in Joan of Arc country, in small peaceful village, 9 km W of Mirecourt (where violins and lace are made). 'Country pub atmosphere.' Best bedrooms in modern Hôtel Burnel*; bar, restaurant, gym, across road.* Michelin Bib Gourmand *for 'classic cuisine': seafood and game specialities, served in pretty dining room or on flowery terrace. 'Very good buffet breakfast with prompt service.' Closed Nov holidays, 14–31 Dec, Sun night and Sat midday off-season. MasterCard, Visa accepted. 22 spacious bedrooms (some with balcony or terrace): €34–€68. Breakfast €10. D,B&B €35–€47 per person. Set meals €14–€25 [2004].*

ST-ARCONS-D'ALLIER 43300 Haute-Loire — Map 4:C6

Les Deux Abbesses
Le Château

Tel 04.71.74.03.08
Fax 04.71.74.05.30
Email direction@les-deux-abbesses.fr
Website www.les-deux-abbesses.fr

'Unusual and charming', this is a '*hôtel éclaté*' (spread): the rooms and suites are in houses (Atelier du Peintre, Maison Blanche, Bonne Maman, etc) in an old *village perché*. Reception, salons and restaurant are in the 9th/11th-century château, by the church. Dinner, using home-grown ingredients, is taken in the candlelit *Salle Seigneuriale*, after aperitifs in the garden. The setting is 'stunning', above the River Allier. 'Perhaps the most peaceful hotel I've experienced in France,' was one comment. Co-owner Laurence Perceval-Hermet ('much in evidence, very helpful') runs it 'with a minimum of staff'. The spacious bedrooms are well equipped, and decorated in minimalist style. Some windows are small and high. Breakfast (with yogurt, fresh fruit, *confitures artisanales*) is served in the château, the rooms or the gardens. There is a small, traditional café, *Au Rendez-vouz des Pêcheurs*, at the village entrance, and a swimming pool above the river. A path leads down to the beach. Arriving guests park in the village car park, and walk up through the narrow cobbled streets; cars are later brought to an allotted place. Idyllic in fine weather; on rainy days 'the place can seem rather gloomy'. (*JBH*)

Open May–Nov. Closed Mon/Tues in May/June, Sept/Oct. Restaurant closed midday, Mon and Tues, except July/Aug, and to non-residents. In winter B&B only, weekends only. **Rooms** 2 suites, 12 double. 7 in small houses. No telephone/TV, etc. **Facilities** Reception, library, music room, café, restaurant (background music); auditorium. Gardens; unheated swimming pool (15 June–15 Sept); by river: beach, fishing. Unsuitable for ♿. **Location** From Langeac go towards St-Flour. At roundabout take D585 towards Sauges/Prades. 1 km after Chanteuges turn left to village. Right after bridge. Follow river 500 m. Village entrance on left. Leave car in village car park for valet parking.

Restrictions No smoking: restaurant, some bedrooms. No children under 10. No dogs. **Credit cards** Amex, MasterCard, Visa. **Terms** Room: single €100, double €140–€250, suite €200–€350. Breakfast €20–€25. Set dinner €45. Min. 2-night stay at weekends.

ST-AUBIN LE VERTUEUX 27300 Eure — Map 2:D4

Hostellerie du Moulin Fouret BUDGET
Route St-Quentin-des-Isles
Tel 02.32.43.19.95
Fax 02.32.45.55.50
Email lemoulinfouret@wanadoo.fr

Old mill, straddling large stream, in quiet, picturesque valley between Rouen and Caen, 3 km S of Bernay. Handsome dining room (background music), terrace (summer dining). 'Lovely garden; friendly Labradors.' Closed parking. Excellent Norman cooking by owner/chef François Déduit (14 Gault Millau *points); his wife, Edwige ('welcoming, helpful'), fronts. Closed Christmas, Sun night/Mon except holidays, and Tues midday Oct–Mar. Unsuitable for ♿. Amex, MasterCard, Visa accepted. 8 bedrooms ('cosy if dated'; some small with tiny shower room; some hear 'soothing gurgle of millstream'): €47. Breakfast €8.50. Set meals €30–€60; alc €75 [2004].*

ST-BENOÎT 86280 Vienne — Map 4:A4

Le Chalet de Venise BUDGET
6 rue du Square
Tel 05.49.88.45.07
Fax 05.49.52.95.44

Near Romanesque church of old village 4 km S of Poitiers by D88: Serge and Margaret Mautret's restaurant-with-rooms. Elegant salon/breakfast room/bar and restaurant face flowery terrace (summer meals) and 'delightful' garden, with ancient chestnut trees, by River Clain. 'Food excellent, good management.' Traditional French breakfast. Background music. Closed Feb holidays, last week Aug. Restaurant closed Sun night/Mon/Tues midday. Amex, MasterCard, Visa. 12 small bedrooms (some with balcony, 1 suitable for ♿): €46–€54. Breakfast €7. D,B&B €114 per person. Set meals €19–€45; full alc €50. *V*

ST-CHARTIER 36400 Indre — Map 4:A5

Château de la Vallée Bleue
Route de Verneuil
Tel 02.54.31.01.91
Fax 02.54.31.04.48
Email valleebleu@aol.com
Website www.chateauvalleebleue.com

In the Vallée Noire, on the George Sand tourist circuit, this village is where she set several scenes in her novels. The family château of Nohant (open to visitors) is nearby. Her doctor's home, an imposing 19th-century mansion in large grounds, is now this hotel owned by the 'very pleasant' Gérard Gasquet. Each bedroom has the name of a Sand novel: some face the village, others the park. Three 'rustic-style' rooms are in a building in the grounds; there is a duplex in a pigeonnier. One visitor wrote of 'helpful staff', adding: 'Our bathroom was eccentric (loo in a cupboard), and the bath was recessed in a niche so that one stepped over the taps to get in.' Before an 'excellent dinner' (eg, feuilleté de cuisses de grenouilles aux pleurotes; suprême de pintade, sauce berrichonne), you can have a 'Cocktail George Sand' (champagne and *crème de pêche*). 'The *patron*'s real passion is his wine cellar.' Background Chopin, of course. There are two swimming pools (one for children), a terrace for outdoor dining. Some traffic noise. (*JBH*)

Open End Mar–early Nov. Closed Sun evening/Mon, except May–Aug. **Rooms** 2 suites, 13 double. 3 in annexe. **Facilities** Salon, 2 dining rooms; background Chopin; conference facilities; terraces. 4-hectare grounds: 2 unheated swimming pools, practice golf, *boules*; bicycles. Unsuitable for ♿. **Location** 1 km E of St-Chartier, on Verneuil road; 9 km N of La Châtre. Parking. **Restriction** No dogs. **Credit cards** Amex, MasterCard, Visa. **Terms** Room: double €95–€130, suite €185–€200. Breakfast €12. Set lunch €29, dinner €39; full alc €50.

ST-DIDIER 35221 Ille-et-Vilaine — Map 2:E3

Hôtel Pen'Roc NEW
La Peinière, Châteaubourg

Tel 02.99.00.33.02
Fax 02.99.62.30.89
Email hotellerie@penroc.fr
Website www.penroc.fr

In a hamlet east of Rennes, this Relais du Silence is a converted farmhouse with old beams and thick walls. 'A stunning meal and fabulous rooms' were enjoyed this year. 'The building may be functional,' say other correspondents, but it has a delightful, quiet location. 'Without exception, staff are efficient and friendly.' The owners, Joseph and Mireille Froc, are 'very kind'. In the last two years, all bedrooms have been renovated and given air conditioning; some have a hydro-shower, some a *bain bouillant*, some a terrace. 'Ours was comfortable, well furnished, if a bit small.' 'Ours was tidy and spacious.' Summer meals are served under large parasols on a terrace. Herbs and vegetables come from the garden. Wines are reasonably priced. Breakfast is buffet-style. The bells of the pilgrimage church nearby chime regularly, but only until 10 pm. The swimming pool is 'rather cramped', according to one correspondent. The splendid medieval town of Vitré, with its great fortress, is near. (*Alison Hodge, Geoff and Val Barrow, and others*)

Open 10 Jan–18 Dec. Restaurant closed Fri evening, Sun evening off-season. **Rooms** 2 suites, 26 double, 1 single. 2 on ground floor. Air conditioning. **Facilities** Lift, ramps. Lounge, bar, 3 dining rooms (1 air conditioned); classical background music; conference facilities; fitness room. Large grounds: garden; heated swimming pool, sauna, children's play area. **Location** 4 km E of Châteaubourg. Turn off D857 at St-Jean-sur-Vilaine, then left to La Peinière. **Credit cards** All major cards accepted. **Terms** Room: single €67–€105, double €78–€121, suite €118–€183. Breakfast €11. D,B&B €77.50–€130.50 per person. Set meals €20.50–€64. *V*

ST-DYÉ-SUR-LOIRE 41500 Loir-et-Cher — Map 2:F5

Manoir Bel Air

Tel 02.54.81.60.10
Fax 02.54.81.65.34
Email manoirbelair@free.fr
Website www.manoirdebelair.com

Guests in 2004 had 'an altogether enjoyable stay' at this low, creeper-covered, 17th-century manor house on the banks of the Loire between Blois and Orléans, well placed for touring the châteaux. Another visitor wrote: 'Superb as ever. Peaceful. A memorable sunset.' Once owned by a governor of Guadeloupe, it is now an unpretentious hotel where readers on their third visit liked their 'large and excellently decorated room with a superb bathroom'. Another couple were offered a small room on arrival: 'We demurred and were offered, without fuss, one much superior at no extra cost.' Most rooms have far-reaching views of the river. 'The large, bustling restaurant was full, mostly with local families. The food was ample and beautifully presented. Prices are gentle. Worth every euro.' But: 'They appear to do a flourishing line in catering for business groups.' (*Nigel and Olga Wikeley, Rosemary Winder*)

Open 20 Feb–20 Jan. **Rooms** 43. **Facilities** Salon, TV room, restaurant; conference facilities. Garden. **Location** 200 m from village, which is 4 km W of Chambord. **Credit cards** MasterCard, Visa. **Terms** [2004] Room €69–€75. Breakfast €7. D,B&B €75 per person. Set meals €22–€43.

ST-ÉMILION 33330 Gironde — Map 4:C3

Au Logis des Remparts
18 rue Guadet

Tel 05.57.24.70.43
Fax 05.57.74.47.44
Email logis-des-remparts@wanadoo.fr
Website www.saint-emilion.org

In this famous medieval wine town, surrounded by vineyards, this popular B&B hotel was recently enlarged: four new suites have been created. 'Staff were helpful, breakfast was good,' is one recent comment. Earlier guests wrote of the 'happy atmosphere', created by the 'charming owners', M. and Mme Yonnet. The bedrooms have modern furniture and a few antiques; some are hung with tapestries. The lounge is 'both comfortable and stylish'. There is a handsome terrace, with an olive tree, where the 'delightful' breakfast is served. 'Everything, including the large swimming pool and shady garden (with discreet bar service), was immaculate.' On the lawns are tables and chairs under parasols. For meals, *Le Tertre* is liked: 'Excellent, and reasonably priced.' (*John Holland, and others*)

Open Mid-Jan–mid-Dec. **Rooms** 4 suites, 17 double. 2 on ground floor. **Facilities** Salon, bar, breakfast conservatory (no-smoking); conference room. No background music. Garden: terrace, swimming pool. Unsuitable for ♿. **Location** Main street (rooms soundproofed). Parking (reservation necessary, inaccessible 11 pm–7 am; €10 a night). **Restriction** No dogs. **Credit cards** Amex, MasterCard, Visa. **Terms** Room €70–€180. Breakfast €12.

ST-ÉTIENNE-AU-MONT 62360 Pas-de-Calais Map 3:D2

Hostellerie de la Rivière BUDGET
17 rue de la Gare
Pont-de-Briques la gare

Tel 03.21.32.22.81
Fax 03.21.87.45.48
Email hostelleriedelariviere@wanadoo.fr
Website www.hostelleriedelariviere.com

In an unexceptional southern suburb of Boulogne-sur-Mer, this smart and 'hospitable' restaurant-with-rooms stands by the little River Liane. Owner/chef Dominique Martin presides: *Gault Millau* awards 14 points for his traditional seasonal cooking, eg, cuisse de canard rôti, choux au lard paysans; gigot d'agneau en croûte de pomme de terre. His wife, Sybille, is front-of-house. Smart dress is expected of diners. The decor is rustic, and visitors wrote of 'a comfortable room, charming owners and staff, excellent food at eminently reasonable prices'. The bedrooms, with river or garden view, are quiet. The bar and dining room are 'inviting'; the garden at the back, sheltered by neat hedges, has tables, chairs and parasols. The Channel Tunnel is 20 minutes' drive away.

Open All year, except 24 Jan–10 Feb, 22 Aug–8 Sept, Sun night/Mon, nights of 25 Dec and 1 Jan. **Rooms** 8 double. **Facilities** Bar, restaurant. No background music. Small garden by river. Beach 4 km; golf nearby. Unsuitable for ♿. **Location** Near Pont-de-Briques station, just N of St-Étienne-au-Mont. 5 km S of Boulogne. Parking. **Restrictions** No smoking in restaurant. No dogs. **Credit cards** All major cards accepted. **Terms** Room €59–€60. Breakfast €10. Set meals €27–€50.

ST-ÉTIENNE-DE-BAÏGORRY 64430 Pyrénées-Atlantiques Map 4:E2

Hôtel Arcé
Route du Col d'Ispéguy

Tel 05.59.37.40.14
Fax 05.59.37.40.27
Email reservations@hotel-arce.com
Website www.hotel-arce.com

Near the Spanish border, in the remote Aldudes valley, this village is a key Basque folklore centre. Here, Pascal and Christine Arcé's 'beautiful country hotel', by a trout river, is much admired. 'Sublime location, very good value, one of our favourite hotels in France,' say guests returning in 2004. Others wrote: 'Deeply wonderful: a centre of gourmet cooking which retains the character of an old-fashioned family-run *auberge*.' A three-generation group was treated with 'great friendliness'. 'Every detail lovingly attended to – pleasing room decor, copious breakfasts (fruit, eggs, etc).' Pascal Arcé, whose family have been here since 1870, wins 13 *Gault Millau* points for, eg, foie gras mi-cuit au Jurançon; croustillants de langoustines jus crémé au gingembre. 'Service is friendly, informal. Interesting wines.' 'In a week on demi-pension, we never had a repeated dish. Madame Arcé was superb: hands-on leadership of her all-woman team. Her staff are so well trained, so pleasant. The food was good, wholesome, not very innovative – just what we like.' 'Only problem: lack of green veg.' There is a large dining room, and a vine-covered terrace for outdoor meals. 'Our spacious annexe room had interesting old furniture, a large balcony.' A 'gorgeous' swimming pool, across a footbridge, stands in its own sunny garden. 'Eccentric church bells' ring at night. Good walking in the hills. (*Matthew Hamlyn and Sallie Nicholas, Jessica Mann, William and Ann Reid, HN, and others*)

Open Mid-Mar–mid-Nov. Restaurant closed Mon midday and Wed midday 15 Sep–15 July, except holidays. **Rooms** 2 suites, 21 double, 1 single. 6 in villa. 1 on ground floor. **Facilities** Ramp. Salon, restaurant, billiard room (no-smoking); veranda. No background music. Garden: terrace, heated swimming pool, tennis, river, fishing. Unsuitable for ♿. **Location** Near church. 11 km W of St-Jean-Pied-de-Port. Private parking nearby. **Credit cards** Diners, MasterCard, Visa. **Terms** Room: single €65–€71, double €115–€135, suite €200–€215. Breakfast €10. D,B&B (min. 3 nights) €75–€125 per person. Set meals €24–€36; full alc €48.

ST-FLORENTIN 89600 Yonne — Map 5:C2

La Grande Chaumière — *Tel* 03.86.35.15.12
3 rue des Capucins — *Fax* 03.86.35.33.14
Email lagrandechaumiere@wanadoo.fr
Website www.chateauxhotels.com/lachaumiere

'As always, our stay here was excellent,' report regular visitors to Jean-Pierre Bonvalot's smart restaurant-with-rooms in this small town between Troyes and Auxerre. Rooms are 'comfortable and well maintained', although the plumbing is 'not the world's best'. The main attraction is the 'super cuisine' of M. Bonvalot, considered 'extremely good value' (*Michelin* star, 15 *Gault Millau* points for, eg, soufflé de brochet au Chablis; filet de charolais à l'Irancy). 'The sauces are delicate and delicious, the wine list is impressive', the dining room is 'a gracious space', and Mme Bonvalot supervises 'quietly and efficiently, ably assisted by her amiable young staff'. 'The big mirrors in the corridors can be disorienting', but bedrooms are 'well furnished', in contemporary style, if 'lacking frills'. Quietest ones face the large and lovely formal garden where aperitifs may be taken; some others get street noise. No lounge, but 'the reception area is large and immaculate'. The town has an impressive cathedral; nearby are Chablis vineyards. (*Dr and Mrs A Naylor*)

Open 19 Jan–1 Sept, 8 Sept–19 Dec. Restaurant closed Wed/Thurs midday. **Rooms** 11 double. 2 in annexe. **Facilities** Lounge, restaurant (classical background music). Garden: terrace. Unsuitable for ♿. **Location** Central. 31 km NE of Auxerre. Parking. **Restriction** No dogs. **Credit cards** All major cards accepted. **Terms** Room €56–€131. Breakfast €12. Set meals €28–€49; full alc €95.

****

Traveller's tale Hotel in Austria. You shouldn't come to this ancient inn for the food. Dinner was adequate in size but not in content. And getting information out of the owners was like drawing teeth. Should non-residents wish to dine, the time is decided by the host not the guest.

****

ST-GERVAIS-D'AUVERGNE 63390 Puy-de-Dôme Map 4:B5

Castel Hotel 1904 NEW/BUDGET
Rue du Castel
Tel 04.73.85.70.42
Fax 04.73.85.84.39
Email info@castel-hotel-1904.com
Website www.castel-hotel-1904.com

This 17th-century *demeure* was turned into a hotel (now Logis de France) by the Mouty family in 1904. 'In many ways it seems not to have changed since then,' writes the nominator in 2004. 'It hasn't been "refurbished", a great relief. But it is not shabby; all is spotless. Old-fashioned and comfortable, it has large, generous rooms with good old French furniture, high bedsteads, thick mattresses, bedside lights that are really bedside, not somewhere up in the air. The well-appointed bathrooms have been squeezed out of the bedrooms but this hasn't cramped them.' Others wrote of a 'grand hotel feeling of another era'. In the restaurant (*Michelin Bib Gourmand*), with heavy damask tablecloths and napkins, 'Madame, bent with arthritis, keeps the sharpest of eyes on proceedings; she is friendly too. The best menu, with widest choices, costs €35.' 'The cooking is excellent. From the dessert trolley you can sample as many of the delights as you can manage.' The bistro, *Comptoir à Moustaches*, serves regional dishes. The 'remarkably comprehensive' wine list 'includes all the best producers at reasonable prices'. Breakfast is 'excellent', with 'perfect croissants', home-made jams. 'A wonderful family atmosphere.' (*Alexander Schouvaloff, Janet and Dennis Allom*)

Open All year. Restaurant closed Mon/Tues/Wed. **Rooms** 17. **Facilities** Bar, bistro, restaurant. **Location** 47 km SE of Montluçon, 55 km NW of Clermont-Ferrand. **Restriction** No dogs. **Credit cards** MasterCard, Visa. **Terms** [2004] Room €57–€70. Breakfast €7.50. D,B&B €50 per person. Set meals €13–€35.

ST-GIRONS 09200 Ariège Map 4:E4

Hôtel Eychenne
8 avenue Paul-Laffont
Tel 05.61.04.04.50
Fax 05.61.96.07.20
Email eychen@club-internet.fr
Website www.ariege.com/hotel-eychenne

For one family, this hotel/restaurant, owned by the Bordeau family for six generations, was 'the highlight of our holiday: the accommodation was excellent, the wine list better, the food better still'. 'Efficiently run' was another plaudit. A former *relais de poste*, it stands down a side street in a pleasant old market town in the Pyrenean foothills. 'Sublime' regional food is served in the traditional beamed, red-walled dining room. Bedrooms are 'decorated and furnished in slightly shabby but cosy French late 19th-century style: lots of dark, highly polished antique furniture that had seen better days, a huge, squidgy old sleigh bed'. The best bedrooms have a balcony facing the flowery garden; all rooms around the courtyard are quiet. The large, 'lovely' swimming pool is surrounded by loungers. (*J, I and FK, and others*)

Open 1 Feb–30 Nov. Closed Sun night/Mon Nov–Mar. **Rooms** 2 suites, 30 double, 4 single. 7 air conditioned. **Facilities** Lounge, restaurant. No background music. Garden: children's play area; heated swimming pool. **Location** 99 km S of Toulouse. Parking. **Credit cards** Amex, MasterCard, Visa. **Terms** Room: single €46–€97, double €65–€112, suite €130–€180. Breakfast €9. D,B&B €61–€103 per person. Set meals €24–€53; full alc €40–€60.

ST-HIPPOLYTE 68590 Haut-Rhin — Map 5:C5

Hostellerie Munsch aux Ducs de Lorraine
16 route du Vin

Tel 03.89.73.00.09
Fax 03.89.73.05.46
Email hotel.munsch@wanadoo.fr
Website www.hotel-munsch.com

In a quiet, attractive village on the Route du Vin north of Colmar, this vine-clad Relais du Silence, run by the Munsch-Meyer family, was liked by readers again this year. Typically Alsatian, the building has balconies covered in geraniums, wide views of the Vosges and of the château of Haut-Koenigsbourg, and smart decor. Bedrooms are furnished in various period styles. 'Our lovely room faced the vineyards.' 'Ours had a flower-bedecked terrace.' But 'the coded door locks are not illuminated; take a torch'. There is a pleasant dining terrace, a beamed and panelled dining room with carved wooden figures, and (for residents) a no-smoking one with an elaborate wooden ceiling. 'Good honest cooking, based on excellent produce' (eg, coq au Riesling, avec spaetzle). 'A bit overwhelming, but typical of the area.' 'An excellent choice of local wines.' 'Some traffic noise, and no outside sitting areas.' (*Mr and Mrs RH Down, and others*)

Open All year, except 5 Jan–12 Feb, 26 July–5 Aug, 8–25 Nov. Restaurant closed Tues midday Nov–mid-May, Fri midday, Sat night/Mon. **Rooms** 4 suites, 34 double, 4 single. 14 air conditioned. Some in annexe. **Facilities** Salon, bar, breakfast room, 2 dining rooms (1 no-smoking); background music. **Location** Centre of village. 20 km N of Colmar (A35 exit 12). Parking. **Credit cards** MasterCard, Visa. **Terms** [2004] Room: single €50–€67, double €76–€118, suite €150–€175. Breakfast €11.50. D,B&B €78.50–€129 per person. Set menus €21–€54.

ST-JEAN-AUX-BOIS 60350 Oise — Map 5:A1

Auberge à la Bonne Idée
3 rue des Meuniers

Tel 03.44.42.84.09
Fax 03.44.42.80.45
Email a-la-bonne-idee.auberge@wanadoo.fr
Website www.a-la-bonne-idee.fr

In a picturesque village in the forest of Compiègne, Yves Giustiniani's restaurant-with-rooms was liked again in 2003/4: 'A lovely suite with large bedroom, very nice bath and shower, large sitting room. Lovely food too.' 'A warm welcome; help with luggage. Our room, up steep stairs, had low eaves.' Some rooms are in the main building; others in an annexe in the grounds. 'The gardens are well tended'; in summer, meals are served on the terrace. 'In the elegant beamed dining room, dinner was a gastronomic experience.' Chef Baptiste Bisiaux has 13 *Gault Millau* points for, eg, tarte fine aux sardines fraîches; onglet de veau, risotto crémeux aux champignons. Breakfast is thought 'exceptional'. Staff are friendly. At nearby Pierrefonds, the feudal castle was much restored by Viollet-le-duc. (*Bob and Kate Flaherty, EB*)

Open All year. **Rooms** 3 suites, 20 double. 9 in annexe. 1 on ground floor. **Facilities** Salon/bar, restaurant; dining terrace. No background music. Park with animals. **Location** 8 km W of Pierrefonds, 10 km SE of Compiègne, by D85. Parking. **Credit cards** Amex, MasterCard, Visa. **Terms** Room €61–€79, suite €90–€142. Breakfast €8.50. D,B&B €74.50–€115 per person. Set meals €29–€65; full alc €60.

ST-JEAN-CAP-FERRAT 06230 Alpes-Maritimes Map 6:D5

Hôtel Clair Logis *Tel* 04.93.76.51.81
12 avenue Centrale *Fax* 04.93.76.51.82
Email hotelclairlogis@orange.fr
Website www.hotel-clair-logis.fr

On this magnificent peninsula, full of expensive villas, Pierre Melon's B&B is a 'lovely old house' in a large garden with huge old trees and safe parking. 'An easy and tranquil place to stay' (says a recent guest), it is on a hill in a residential area. Rooms are in several buildings of different styles: most have a terrace or balcony. Some are 'basic', but spacious. 'Our two large windows looked on to the garden. Breakfast, alfresco, came with good bread and croissants; for extra we got delicious yogurt, and freshly squeezed juice from the orange trees in the garden. At night all was quiet, once the tree frogs and cicadas had gone to sleep.' It is a steep climb down to the beaches (small and crowded) and the many restaurants around the port. Local sights include the Ephrussi de Rothschild villa (beautiful rose garden, museum and tea room).

Open 1 Feb–1 Nov, 15 Nov–5 Jan. **Rooms** 3 suites, 11 double, 2 single. 7 in 2 annexes. 4 air conditioned. 1 suitable for ♿. **Facilities** TV lounge, breakfast room. No background music. Garden. **Location** 1 km from centre, near zoo and stadium, off Blvd de Gaulle. 10 km E of Nice. Parking. **Credit cards** Amex, MasterCard, Visa. **Terms** Room: single €90–€160, double €110–€180, suite €180. Breakfast €12.

ST-JEAN-DE-LUZ 64500 Pyrénées-Atlantiques Map 4:D2

Hôtel Parc Victoria *Tel* 05.59.26.78.78
5 rue Cépé *Fax* 05.59.26.78.08
Email parcvictoria@relaischateaux.com
Website www.parcvictoria.com

In this upmarket little town near the Spanish border, Roger Larralde's white, late 19th-century mansion (Relais & Châteaux) stands quietly near the broad sandy beach and pedestrianised shopping streets. Furnishing is a mix of Art Nouveau and Art Deco. Some of the 'sumptuous' rooms have a private garden or terrace. 'If there is heaven on earth this is it,' said visitors in 2004. 'Our brand-new room was luxurious. The gardens are truly beautiful, and well kept under the watchful eyes of management, assorted birds, red squirrels,

Victor, the cat and Vanille, the golden retriever. Food was excellent and ample. Service was professional.' But a dissenting couple thought the service 'impersonal', and the food 'too rich'. The 'beautiful' pool area 'is the lively hub of the hotel': here drinks and meals (Basque and Landaise cooking by Eric Jorge) are served. On cool days, guests eat in the formal restaurant with conservatory (which 'shelters a unique collection of owls'). Breakfast, 'a delicious spread', if 'a bit pricey', can be taken on the terrace, with roses. There is a summer house with children's games, under venerable yew trees. (*Robert Marks, and others*)

Open 15 Mar–15 Nov. Restaurant closed 15 Nov–31 Mar, Tues off-season. **Rooms** 9 suites, 9 double. 8 in 2 cottages (1 adapted for ♿). Air conditioning. **Facilities** Lounge, bar, 3 dining rooms (1 no-smoking), conservatory; 2 conference rooms. No background music. 1-hectare garden: terrace, unheated swimming pool, pool house; summer house. Beach 350 m. **Location** From A63 *autoroute*, exit St-Jean-de-Luz Nord, follow direction 'Centre Ville'. At 4th traffic light turn right, signposted Quartier du Lac. Hotel on right. Parking. **Credit cards** All major cards accepted. **Terms** Room €130–€305, suite €245–€410. Breakfast €16. D,B&B double €251–€506. Set meals €37–€75; full alc €80–€110.

ST-JEAN-DU-BRUEL 12230 Aveyron — Map 6:D1

Hôtel du Midi-Papillon BUDGET — *Tel* 05.65.62.26.04 *Fax* 05.65.62.12.97

For over 150 years, four generations of Papillons have owned and run this former *relais de poste* (now Logis de France). It stands by a humpbacked medieval bridge in an old village on the River Dourbie, in the western Cévennes. For the last quarter-century, Jean-Michel and Maryse Papillon have presided. Devotees (many of them British) return again and again. 'It just gets better and better,' says one, on his fourth visit. 'We re-meet old friends: it is like a wonderful club.' Other comments: 'Amazing value.' 'Total charm and efficiency.' 'What an ambience!' The best bedrooms have 'delightful views of the river' and, writes Madame, 'we still have no TV in the rooms: our guests come for the peace'. M. Papillon's *cuisine du terroir*, on the short *en pension* menu, 'gets better and better'. He raises his own chickens, makes charcuterie from local pork, and jams from the fruit in his garden. One visitor thought the wines 'relatively expensive'. By the swimming pool in the small garden, guests hear 'birdsong and the lullaby of the river'. (*Peter Stattersfield, Trevor Sanderson, and others*)

Open Mid-Apr–11 Nov. **Rooms** 2 suites, 15 double, 1 single. 2 pairs of communicating rooms in annexe. **Facilities** Ramps. Salon, TV room, bar, 3 dining rooms (2 no-smoking; classical background music). Garden: terrace, heated swimming pool, whirlpool; river, fishing, bathing. Unsuitable for ♿. **Location** Entrance to village, on D999. 20 km E of N9, 40 km SE of Millau. Public parking. **Credit cards** MasterCard, Visa. **Terms** Room: single €16.10–€34.50, double €31.90–€35.50, suite €57.50. Breakfast €4.80. D,B&B €20.60–€22.10 added per person. Set meals €13–€36.20; full alc €25.50.

ST-LÉONARD-DE-NOBLAT 87400 Haute-Vienne Map 4:B5

Hostellerie Le Grand St-Léonard *Tel* 05.55.56.18.18
23 avenue du Champs de Mars *Fax* 05.55.56.98.32
Email grandsaintleonard@wanadoo.fr

East of Limoges, this charming little medieval market town has narrow winding streets and a 'fantastic' granite church (part 11th-century). On the outskirts is this inexpensive, large, white, former coaching inn run by owner/chef Jean-Marc Vallet, 'very helpful and jolly'. In the beamed rustic restaurant with its shining copperware and Limoges porcelain, he produces classic dishes like gateau de lapin au foie gras, parfum basilic; cassolette de langoustines sur fondue de poireaux. 'Excellent food, good value. A budget room,' said one reader. Another wrote: 'Our bedroom (No. 1) was excellent, with a good bathroom. Not a great view, but fun for one night: we could overhear the cooks and waitresses chatting.' (*MM, and others*)

Open 21 Jan–19 Dec. Closed Mon except evenings 15 June–15 Sept. Restaurant closed Mon/Tues midday 15 June–15 Sept. **Rooms** 14 double. **Facilities** Lounge, restaurant (classical background music); conference room. Unsuitable for ♿. **Location** Edge of town. 20 km E of Limoges. Garage. **Credit cards** All major cards accepted. **Terms** [2004] Room €54–€59. Breakfast €10. D,B&B €78–€90 per person. Set meals €25–€59; full alc €59–€75.

ST-MAIXENT-L'ÉCOLE 79400 Deux-Sèvres Map 4:A3

Le Logis St-Martin *Tel* 05.49.05.58.68
Chemin de Pissot *Fax* 05.49.76.19.93
Email contact@logis-saint-martin.com
Website www.logis-saint-martin.com

The town may be 'ordinary', but Bertrand and Ingrid Heintz's hotel on the outskirts is 'very attractive', says a visitor this year. It stands quietly across a road from parkland along the banks of the small River Sèvre. The large, white 17th-century manor house has been renovated in 'blissfully simple' style: tiled floors, beamed ceilings, good paintings, furniture and glass from Bohemia and Murano. A stone staircase leads to 'beautiful' bedrooms off a narrow whitewashed corridor. 'Ours had exquisite wall coverings of blue-patterned fabric.' The suite is a duplex in a tower with exposed stone walls. The 'elegant and charming' owners are 'helpful with advice about what to do'. Madame's small dog, Sushi, lives in a filing cabinet in Reception. 'A superb meal': chef Guy Robin uses only organically produced ingredients in his ambitious dishes: eg, transparence à la mousseline de choux-fleur et piment d'Espelette. Service is formal, with much dome-lifting. 'Excellent breakfast' (not a buffet), but with 'irritating muzak'. In summer, drinks are served on a terrace under large white parasols. (*J and HW, JH, A and CR*)

Open All year, except Jan, Mon night. Check-in after 3 pm. Restaurant closed midday on Mon, Tues and Sat. **Rooms** 1 suite, 10 double. Some air conditioned. **Facilities** Salon, restaurant (no-smoking; background music);

small conference room. 2-hectare grounds: terrace, stream, heated swimming pool. Unsuitable for ♿. **Location** Edge of town. W of A10, between Poitiers and Niort. **Restriction** No dogs. **Credit cards** All major cards accepted. **Terms** Room €105–€145, suite €145. Breakfast €15. D,B&B €117.50–€200 per person. Set lunch €35, dinner €48–€75; full alc €75.

ST-MALO 35400 Ille-et-Vilaine — Map 2:E3

Le Valmarin — *Tel* 02.99.81.94.76
7 rue Jean XXIII, St-Servan — *Fax* 02.99.81.30.03
Email levalmarin@wanadoo.fr
Website www.levalmarin.com

'Such a wonderful building; good value,' says a visitor this year to Françoise and Gérard Nicolas's 18th-century house, elegantly renovated in period style. South of the old town, in wooded grounds, it has 'stacks of character and a friendly welcome'. 'Our lovely high-ceilinged room overlooked the enchanting garden. The charming staff got up early to give us breakfast when we had to leave at 7 am.' The bedrooms have antique furniture; some are up stairs (no lift); the spacious ones on the first floor are particularly liked. Breakfast, served alfresco on fine days, includes cake, fruit, 'superb croissants'. No restaurant: *L'Atre*, near the port, serves 'excellent fish'; *La Corderie,* inexpensive, is enjoyed for its food, art show and sea view. The hotel can be awkward to find: they will send directions. There is secure parking, but if you arrive after 10.30 pm, you have to leave the car in the street. (*Alison Hodge, J and HW, AF*)

Open All year. **Rooms** 12 double. **Facilities** Reception, bar/tea room, breakfast room. Garden. Beach, casino, golf, tennis, horse riding nearby. Unsuitable for ♿. **Location** In St-Servan, near church of Ste-Croix. 2 km S of old St-Malo. Car park. **Credit cards** Amex, MasterCard, Visa. **Terms** Room €95–€135. Breakfast €10.

ST-MARS-DES-PRÉS 85110 Vendée — Map 4:A3

Manoir de Ponsay — *Tel* 02.51.46.96.71
Chantonnay — *Fax* 02.51.46.80.07
Email ponsay@chateaux-france.com
Website www.chateaux-france.com

'A haven of rural peace and quiet', this 15th-century red brick château has been owned by the de Ponsay family since 1644. Now they offer paying guests '*la vie du château*', and the 'family feel' was enjoyed by inspectors in 2004. Other comments: 'The place has great charm. The two fox terriers are well behaved; one of them took us for a walk.' 'A friendly welcome; a good meal. Our room was lovely, comfortable.' 'Ours had a delightful canopied bed, superb modern bathroom, view of Charollais cattle in a field.' Meals are often served communally, in a candlelit room with pale blue walls hung with blue plates, a big chandelier with blue candles. 'We were the only guests: we dined at a small table in the salon.' 'Breakfast had a good choice of breads, croissants, jams; excellent coffee.' The remarkable *son-et-lumière* of

Vendée history is at Le Puy-du-Fou (25 km). (*Michael Wace, Mick Brammer, and others*)

Open 1 Apr–1 Dec. **Rooms** 1 suite, 7 double. **Facilities** Salon, restaurant, breakfast room. Garden: outdoor dining, swimming pool. Unsuitable for ♿. **Location** 2 km NW of St-Mars (signposted), 6 km E of Chantonnay, 80 km SE of Nantes. Parking. **Credit cards** None accepted. **Terms** Room €58–€105, suite €110. Breakfast €9. Set dinner (by arrangement) €32, inc wine, coffee.

ST-MARTIAL-VIVEYROLS 24320 Dordogne — Map 4:B4

Hostellerie Les Aiguillons — *Tel* 05.53.91.07.55
Le Beuil — *Fax* 05.53.91.00.43
Email lesaiguillons@aol.com
Website www.hostellerielesaiguillons.com

In the Périgord Blanc, south-east of Angoulême, this 'extremely well-kept' little Logis de France is built on the ruins of an old farm. White-walled and red tile-roofed, 'it has a wonderful situation on a hill'. The owner, Christophe Beeuwsaert, is 'the perfect host', say visitors this year. 'We would give his hotel every award. The cooking is excellent. Monsieur takes great pride in it. He changes the menu often, makes all the preserves, canapés and petits fours himself.' Regional dishes include terrine de foie gras de canard au Pineau des Charentes; cassolette de sole au Monbazillac. 'Desserts are wicked: triumphs of spun sugar. The wine list is fairly priced.' Good breakfast, too. 'Our room, attractive and comfortably furnished, looked over rolling countryside. Complete silence, apart from cooing pigeons and the occasional tractor. The large garden is immaculate, the swimming pool beyond the rose beds is bliss.' No salon, but there is a terrace for drinks, and the beamed dining room is pleasant. (*J and DA*)

Open 2 Apr–31 Oct. Closed Sun night off-season. Restaurant closed midday and Sun night off-season. **Rooms** 1 suite, 7 double. Some no-smoking. 1 equipped for ♿. **Facilities** Bar, restaurant (classical background music). Garden: terrace, ponds, unheated swimming pool. Horse riding, tennis nearby. **Location** 5 km NW of Verteillac, 47 km SE of Angoulême. Car park. **Credit cards** All major cards accepted. **Terms** [2004] B&B: €62–€101. D,B&B €78–€92 per person. Set meals €25–€42.

ST-MARTIN-DE-RÉ 17410 Charente-Maritime — Map 4:A3

Le Corps de Garde — *Tel* 05.46.09.10.50
1 quai Georges Clemenceau — *Fax* 05.46.09.76.99
Île de Ré — *Email* info@lecorpsdegarde.com
Website www.lecorpsdegarde.com

The Île de Ré, offshore from La Rochelle, is a popular bolthole for wealthy Parisians. It has miles of glorious sandy beaches, an interior of pine forests and vineyards, and plenty of charm (planning regulations forbid unsightly hoardings and oversized buildings). In this little fortified town, still a busy port, the former harbourmaster's house is now a 'supremely stylish' *maison d'hôtes*. By the quay, it looks on to sea and fortifications on one side, the harbour on the other. 'The setting could not be more picturesque,' say inspectors. The decor, described by the owners, M. and Mme Bressy (who live on the first floor), as '*faite dans un esprit de maison de famille*', has featured in interior design magazines. Each room is different, decorated with light colours, natural fabrics, seagrass matting and plain wood. All have a view; most have a sitting area and sofa. The salon, in the former boathouse, has an open fire, potted plants. Breakfast is served here, or in the bedroom, '*sans limite d'heure*'. Only 'very small' dogs are accepted. Plenty of restaurants at the port: the *Bistro Marin* was enjoyed this year. (*DC, and others*)

Open All year. **Rooms** 2 suites, 3 double. **Facilities** 2 salons. No background music. Unsuitable for ♿. Parking. **Location** By harbour. **Credit cards** MasterCard, Visa. **Terms** Room €90–€180. Breakfast €10. 1-night bookings refused holiday weekends.

ST-PATERNE 72610 Orne — Map 2:E4

Château de Saint Paterne

Tel 02.33.27.54.71
Fax 02.33.29.16.71
Email paterne@club-internet.fr
Website www.chateau-saintpaterne.com

'A wonderful antidote to faceless mid-Atlantic hotels', this beautiful Renaissance château stands in its own lovely park on the eastern edge of Alençon. 'What it lacks in the glossier hotel facilities,' says a visitor this year, 'it more than makes up for with a wonderfully nostalgic atmosphere.' 'Romantic, quirky, charming', it has been in the family of the 'delightful English-speaking owners', Charles-Henry and Ségolène de Valbray, for generations. Salons are filled with antiques, paintings and family artefacts; open fires burn in winter. Bedrooms, up a curved wooden staircase, are all different. One has a set of engravings given by Napoleon; in another are beams decorated in the 16th century with the crest of Henri IV and his paramour Diane de Courtemanche (this was his hideaway). In the 'lovely' dining room, the candlelit dinner is served by arrangement: guests take an aperitif together, but eat at separate tables. 'Charles-Henry is passionate about cooking, and his four-course menus are excellent; second helpings of main course usually offered.' Vegetables are home grown. Breakfast, a buffet, is in a former kitchen, 'with the feel of an upmarket *brocante*'. In the magnificent grounds are woodland walks, huge lawns, a large *potager*, a swimming pool. (*Peter Jowitt; also Michael and Wendy Dods, Peter Stattersfield*)

Open Probably 1 May–1 Oct. Closed Christmas. Rooms 2 suites, 6 double. 1 on ground floor. **Facilities** 2 lounges, breakfast room, dining room (no-smoking; background music). Terrace. 10-hectare grounds: woodland walks, heated swimming pool, table tennis, bicycles. Unsuitable for ♿. **Location** Village centre. 1.5 km E of Alençon by D311. Parking. **Credit cards** MasterCard, Visa. **Terms** Room €105–€210. Breakfast €10. Set dinner (by arrangement) €40, incl. aperitif and coffee. 1-night bookings refused during Le Mans 24-hour races.

ST-PAUL-DE-VENCE 06570 Alpes-Maritimes Map 6:D5

La Colombe d'Or

Tel 04.93.32.80 02
Fax 04.93.32.77.78
Email contact@la-colombe-dor.com
Website www.la-colombe-dor.com

At the entrance of this old walled town, this 'beautiful and special' hotel is run by François Roux with his wife, Daniele. His artist grandfather, Paul Roux, founded it in 1931, and famous artist guests left works of art in lieu of payment, hence the Braque mosaic and Calder mobile by the secluded swimming pool, the Léger mural dominating the terrace, the paintings by Picasso, Miró, etc, in the dining room. Film and pop stars visit nowadays, but, says a regular *Guide* correspondent, 'the avant-garde atmosphere and simple Provençal style remain'. It is 'relaxed, charming, and fun', writes a visitor in 2004. Residents must book for the 'blessedly unmodernised' dinners, taken on the terrace under ancient fig trees. The 'old-fashioned, appetising *petit déjeuner*' consists of freshly squeezed orange juice, bread, croissants, etc; an omelette can be had as extra. 'Service is efficient.' The bedrooms 'face in all directions; glorious countryside in the distance'. The best rooms, in the main building, are 'simply furnished, rather than luxurious'; some have a private terrace. Others are in an annexe by the car park. (*AB, Charlie Nairn*)

Open All year, except 1–10 Jan, 28 Oct–20 Dec. **Rooms** 10 suites, 16 double. 6 in annexe. Air conditioning. **Facilities** Bar, restaurant, dining terrace. Garden: heated swimming pool, sauna. Unsuitable for ♿. **Location** Entrance to village. 21 km NE of Nice. Parking. **Credit cards** All major cards accepted. **Terms** [2004] Room €265–€320. Breakfast €10. D,B&B €40 added per person. Full alc €60.

****

Traveller's tale Hotel in Italy. On arrival we found no heating whatsoever in our bedroom. I went down and told the receptionist that the room was cold. She said she would have the heating turned on. Twenty minutes later the room was still cold, so I asked to be moved to another room. The receptionist flatly refused, and said the room would warm up soon. Eventually it did, but they had turned the heating full on, and there was no way of controlling it in our room. We discovered when we went to bed that the heating was controlled from downstairs. The room became stifling. We could get no sleep. At 4.45 am I opened the door to the passage and sat on a chair by the door, but that had no effect. Next morning, when paying the bill, I told the receptionist (a thoroughly unpleasant person) that it was the worst room I had ever slept in, to which she replied: 'You said you wanted heat in your room last night, so we put it on Full.'

****

Hôtel Le Saint-Paul
86 rue Grande

Tel 04.93.32.65.25
Fax 04.93.32.52.94
Email stpaul@relaischateaux.com
Website www.lesaintpaul.com

'For warmth of reception combined with lovely rooms, it cannot be beat,' writes a travel expert about Olivier Borloo's luxurious and stylish little hotel (Relais & Châteaux). Within the ramparts of this famous car-free old village, this conversion of three 16th-century houses has a flowery terrace for meals in fine weather. 'It is a jewel, very welcoming,' one couple wrote. 'Our room had a magnificent view over the valley. Staff are friendly. Super cuisine.' One dining room has frescoes of fruit and flowers, the other a fountain. *Michelin* awards a star for, eg, suprême de pigeon rôti au baton de réglisse. The decor (Souleïado fabrics) is as Provençal as the cuisine. Some bedrooms are small; many have a mural; a suite has a large fireplace. 'Small, well-educated dogs' are accepted. (*Marshall S Harris, Michael Burns*)

Open All year. **Rooms** 4 suites, 15 double. 1 suitable for ♿. Air conditioning. **Facilities** Lift. Lounge/bar (piano), library, restaurant; dining terrace; background music. **Location** In village, above ramparts. 21 km NE of Nice. Public parking 50 m. **Credit cards** All major cards accepted. **Terms** Room €170–€300, suite €270–€560. Breakfast €20. D,B&B (min. 3 nights) €85 added per person. Set lunch €45, dinner €65–€82; full alc €80–€99.

Villa St-Maxime
390 route de la Colle

Tel 04.93.32.76.00
Fax 04.93.32.93.00
Email riviera@villa-st-maxime.com
Website www.villa-st-maxime.com

A 'very friendly' American couple, John and Ann Goldenberg, run this *villa d'hôtes* just outside the village. It makes 'an ideal base for touring the Côte d'Azur', said one recent visitor. Large open public areas have 'a wonderful combination of antiques and modern furnishings'. In the evening, complimentary aperitifs are served, including the house speciality, an Orange Max. The bedrooms, all with terrace or balcony overlooking the sea, are brightly furnished in primary colours. 'Very comfortable bed, good linens; large marble bathroom: great shower head.' A guest in 2004 adds: 'It was fun – sort of. The owners told me the house was built about ten years ago by a Middle-Eastern arms dealer. Breakfast includes champagne opened with a sabre': served in fine weather on a panoramic terrace, it also has eggs, yogurt and cheese. There are palm trees, and a swimming pool surrounded by blue loungers. (*CN, SR, and others*)

Open All year. **Rooms** 2 suites, 4 double. Air conditioning. **Facilities** 2 lounges, bar. No background music. Large garden: terrace, unheated swimming pool. **Location** 7 mins' walk from village (or bus). Large blue sign off main road to La Colle sur Loup. Parking. **Restrictions** Smoking out of doors only. No dogs. No children under 10. **Credit cards** Amex, MasterCard, Visa. **Terms** B&B: single €130–€190, double €140–€195, suite €180–€340. 1-night advance bookings refused May–Sept.

ST-RÉMY-DE-PROVENCE 13210 Map 6:D3

Sous les Figuiers NEW
3 avenue Taillandier

Tel 04.32.60.15.40
Fax 04.32.60.15.39
Email hotel.souslesfiguiers@wanadoo.fr
Website www.hotel-charme-provence.com

'A little French gem, full of charm and character': Gisèle and Denise Lafuente's *chambres d'hôtes* stands quietly in 'beautifully kept gardens', near the centre. The spacious bedrooms, all different, are 'decorated in tasteful modern style, with great attention to detail' (original furniture, quilted bedcovers, etc). Ten rooms have a private terrace and garden with fig tree. Bathrooms are 'well designed', showers 'a delight to use'. Breakfast, served outside in good weather, was 'the best we came across in our travels', say the nominators. 'Top-quality ingredients, beautifully presented and prepared.' The 'enthusiastic and friendly' owners are painters: their work is in evidence on furniture and walls, and they run workshops on decorative paint techniques. (*Josephine and Alan Dougall*)

Open 18 Mar–4 Jan. **Rooms** 3 family, 9 double. 4 in annexe, 8 in separate building. **Facilities** Salon, bar, breakfast room; background music. Garden: unheated swimming pool. **Location** 5 mins' walk from centre. Secure parking. **Credit cards** MasterCard, Visa. **Terms** Room: single €52–€100, double €67–€115, family €110–€125. Breakfast €10.50. *V*

ST-RIQUIER 80135 Somme Map 3:E2

Hôtel Jean de Bruges
18 place de l'Église

Tel 03.22.28.30.30
Fax 03.22.28.00.69
Email jeandebruges@wanadoo.fr
Website www.hotel-jean-de-bruges.com

'Stylish and characterful', Bernadette Stubbe's white-stoned, former abbot's house (17th-century) is named after a medieval Flemish prince who lived in nearby Abbeville. Madame Stubbe 'gives a warm welcome', say visitors; 'the decor is tasteful, bathtowels are fluffy'. Bedrooms (three are in the beamed loft) are comfortable; 'excellent bathrooms'. Some face a busy road, but triple glazing is effective. The substantial breakfast can be taken on the elegant patio, where snacks are also served. For meals, there is a reasonable choice of restaurants in Abbeville. St-Riquier, a pleasant little town, has a flamboyant Gothic church, part of a former 7th-century Benedictine abbey which the hotel faces. For a meal, *L'Auberge la Corne* in Abbeville is recommended. (*Brian and Pat Lloyd*)

Open 1 Feb–31 Dec, except Christmas. No snacks Sun night. **Rooms** 2 suites, 9 double. 2 air conditioned. **Facilities** Lift. Lounge, bar, tea room, patio; background radio. Courtyard. **Location** Central. 8 km NE of Abbeville, A16 exit 22 (5 km). Parking on main square. **Restrictions** No smoking: tea room, some bedrooms. No dogs. **Credit cards** Amex, MasterCard, Visa. **Terms** Room: single €90, double €99, suite €195. Breakfast €13.

ST-SATURNIN-DE-LUCIAN 34725 Hérault Map 6:D1

Ostalaria Cardabela
et Restaurant Le Mimosa
10 place de la Fontaine

Tel 04.67.88.62.62
Fax 04.67.88.62.82
Email ostalaria.cardabela@free.fr

In a village near Clermont-l'Hérault, Bridget Pugh, from New Zealand, and her Welsh husband, David, run their 'delightfully informal' small hotel. Their restaurant, *Le Mimosa* (16 *Gault Millau* points), is in another village, St-Guiraud, nearby. 'The rooms are simple and comfortable,' says a reader this year. 'The two overlooking the square are much the best' (the others are said to be very dark, and one guest thought them overpriced!). But church bells strike the hour all night 'and ring a noisy angelus at seven in the morning'. 'Breakfast was very good!' 'Bridget is delightful, and a fine cook', but portions might be small for hearty appetites, and mark-ups on the wine are said to be high. You can walk to the restaurant from the hotel, but in hot weather, it may not be advisable 'in clothes that you would wish to wear in that smart establishment'. Next door to the hotel is Virgile Joly's tiny *cave*, immortalised in Patrick Moon's *Virgile's Vineyard*; opposite is an *auberge* recommended for grills, casseroles and 'superb local wines at reasonable prices'. (*NP and EB, and others*)

Open 11 Mar–30 Oct. *Le Mimosa* open Sun midday, evenings Tues–Sat, Sun night July/Aug. **Rooms** 7 double. **Facilities** Breakfast room; garden. Restaurant *Le Mimosa* 2.5 km. Unsuitable for ♿. **Location** 10 km N of Clermont-l'Hérault. **Restriction** No dogs. **Credit cards** Diners, MasterCard, Visa. **Terms** [2004] Room €65–€90. Breakfast €9.50. Set meals €52–€78.

ST-SYLVESTRE-SUR-LOT 47140 Lot-et-Garonne Map 4:C4

Château Lalande

Tel 05.53.36.15.15
Fax 05.53.36.15.16
Email chateau.lalande@wanadoo.fr
Website www.chateau-lalande.com

Opened as a luxury hotel in 1992 by owner Yves Prenat, this 13th/18th-century house stands in a superb park just north of the village and the River Lot. Mansarded and red-roofed, it has elegant salons with chandeliers and period furniture. Two lovely outdoor swimming pools, surrounded by striped loungers and parasols, are to be found on a broad patio (meals are served here in fine weather), and there are huge water lilies in the pond by the gate. The staff were found 'charming' by recent visitors: 'There is an appealing individuality and humour here. Food was good French.' There are two restaurants (one *gastronomique,* one for *cuisine légère*). (*P and JW, and others*)

Open All year. Restaurant closed midday 1 Nov–31 Mar. **Rooms** 22. **Facilities** Lift. Salons, 2 bars, 2 restaurants; conference/function facilities. 9-hectare grounds: 2 swimming pools, tennis, children's playground; fitness centre: gym, hammam, *balnéothérapie*, massage, etc. **Location** 8 km E of Villeneuve-sur-Lot. Helipad. **Credit cards** All major cards accepted. **Terms** [2004] Room €145–€250, suite €270–€350. Breakfast €15. D,B&B double (min. 3 nights) €225–€450. Set meals €37–€99.

ST-TROJAN-LES-BAINS 17370 Charente-Maritime Map 4:B3

Le Homard Bleu
10 boulevard de la Plage
Île d'Oléron

Tel 05.46.76.00.22
Fax 05.46.76.14.95
Email homard.bleu@wanadoo.fr
Website www.homardbleu.fr

Facing the sea, near the spectacular bridge which links Oléron to the mainland, this white-fronted Logis de France is in a village in the south-east of the island. Owned by Mme Nelly Ratier, it is an unsophisticated hotel, popular with French holidaymakers. 'The restaurant [13 *Gault Millau* points], crammed with tables, each with a dark blue tablecloth, is renowned for its seafood fresher than fresh, and sumptuous puddings,' says a recent visitor (to sit by the large bay windows you must book in advance). 'Breakfast, in a conservatory with bright yellow paper tablecloths, is copious. Madame is lively, obviously liked by her friendly, hard-working staff: they were attentive to the elderly and disabled.' There is a terrace for alfresco meals. The 19th-century building has been renovated, in 'somewhat stark' style: 'minimalist' bedrooms have modern textiles; bathrooms are well appointed. Half of the rooms face the sea, the others look on to a '*petite forêt*' of pine and mimosa. 'The busy road between hotel and sea quietens at night, and double glazing is effective against the noise of wind and rain in stormy weather.' (*F and IW*)

Open All year, except 1 Nov–22 Dec, 2 Jan–15 Feb, Tues/Wed 25 Sept–Easter. **Rooms** 20. **Facilities** Foyer, TV room, bar, restaurant; gym. Dining terrace. Garden. **Location** On coast road in SE corner of island. **Credit cards** All major cards accepted. **Terms** [2004] B&B double €64–€78. D,B&B (obligatory in high season) €52–€65 per person. Set meals €18–€59; light meal €12.

ST-VALÉRY-EN-CAUX 76460 Seine-Maritime Map 2:D4

Les Hêtres
24 rue des Fleurs Le Bourg
Ingouville-sur-Mer

Tel 02.35.57.09.30
Fax 02.35.57.09.31
Email leshetres@wanadoo.fr
Website www.leshetres.com

Named after the beech trees in its 'glorious, secluded' garden, this smart restaurant-with-rooms has a rural setting near this small fishing port. 'Such a serene place,' say fans in 2004, after their fourth visit. 'One of the few where both hospitality and cuisine are first class.' The 17th-century half-timbered Norman farmstead is owned by Eric Liberge ('genuinely affable') and Bertrand Warin ('the charming and gifted chef'). Much admired are the 'tasteful dining room' with log fire, attractive table settings, 'delicate food, excellent, fairly priced wines, attentive service'. 'The lowest-price menu offers enough alternatives to eat differently for several nights, avoiding the need to go to the more expensive *carte*.' Most bedrooms are liked, but one couple wrote: 'Our large first-floor room in the annexe had a sloping wall/ceiling, so sitting up entailed a great deal of caution. The spa bath was also under a slope. Head-banging was the order of the day.'

Breakfasts in the garden are 'wonderful'. 'The house dogs took us for a walk.' (*Francine and Ian Walsh, and others*)

Open All year, except 10 Jan–10 Feb, 27 Sept–7 Oct, Mon/Tues/Wed off-season. **Rooms** 1 suite, 4 double. 1 on ground floor. **Facilities** Lounge, breakfast room, restaurant. Garden. **Location** Ingouville, 3 km SW of St-Valéry, towards Fécamp by D925. Parking. **Credit cards** MasterCard, Visa. **Terms** [2004] Room €105–€145. Breakfast €15. Set meals €36–€76; alc €60–€79.

ST-YZANS DE MÉDOC 33340 Gironde — Map 4:B3

Château Loudenne NEW — *Tel* 05 57 00 02 17
Domaines Lafragette — *Email* loudenne@receptif.org
Website www.lafragette.com

NW of Bordeaux, SW of Cognac, amid famous Médoc vineyards, in 46-hectare wine-growing estate on the wide Gironde (private port): 'magical' maison d'hôtes *where reporters on 'gastronomic/romantic escapade' felt 'like guests not hotel clients'. Salons, library in former chapel; flowers everywhere, panelling, family antiques; courtyards. Breakfast on lovely terrace (stunning river views); large lawn bordered by flowerbeds.* Dégustation *in Victorian* chai. *15 bedrooms (best ones in main château, others in west wing): €120–€190. Breakfast €13 [2004].*

STE-ANNE-LA-PALUD 29550 Finistère — Map 2:E1

Hôtel de la Plage — *Tel* 02.98.92.50.12
À la plage — *Fax* 02.98.92.56.54
Email laplage@relaischateaux.com
Website www.plage.com

Run 'with panache' by its owners, Anne and Jean Milliau Le Coz, this upmarket beach hotel (Relais & Châteaux) was found 'delightful' again this year. It stands beside a huge, secluded sandy beach. 'The food was sublime,' was another comment (Hervé Pachoud, 'who enjoys strong flavours', has a *Michelin* star). 'Our four-year-old daughter was made as welcome as we were, even at the evening meal. We watched glorious sunsets as we ate.' The extensive wine list is reasonably priced. The spectacular tiered conservatory dining room is for residents; the older dining room, with Venetian crystal chandeliers, is for locals. 'Guests were dressed informally', and 'the young staff, in black and white uniforms, are friendly'. Public rooms are 'quite smart'; the spacious bar has sea views from 'comfy sofas'. 'Our nice-size bedroom had a great view of the beach.' Breakfast is a buffet ('good but not great'). The gardens are 'immaculate', and the swimming pool is useful at low tide when the sea goes far out (the rapid incoming tide makes caution necessary). (*Michael Burns, Julie Grant, WS*)

Open 25 Mar–5 Nov. Restaurant closed midday on Tues, Wed and Fri. **Rooms** 4 suites, 26 double. 6 in annexe, 50 m. 2 on ground floor. **Facilities** Lift. 2 salons, games room, bar (background music), restaurant; conference facilities;

sauna. Garden: tennis, heated swimming pool; safe, sandy beach. Unsuitable for ♿. **Location** On coast, W of Plonevez-Porzay by D61. Car park. **Credit cards** All major cards accepted. **Terms** Room €87–€290, suite €220–€300. Breakfast €16. D,B&B €147.50–€215 per person. Set meals €50–€85.

STE-PREUVE 02350 Aisne — Map 3:E3

Château de Barive

Tel 03.23.22.15.15
Fax 03.23.22.08.39
Email contact@lesepicuriens.com
Website www.chateau-de-barive.com

Behind imposing wrought iron gates, and fronted by a courtyard with a central fountain and lawns, this big, honey-coloured, former 18th-century hunting lodge was liked again by visitors returning in 2004. 'Very peaceful. There is a nice new dining terrace. Gardens have been improved.' 'Smooth, redecorated; the cuisine is even better.' Others wrote: 'An exceptional hotel. Everything faultless. A memorable dinner.' Owned by Senator Helmut Aurenz, and managed by Nicolas Froment and Pascal Leromain, it has 'charming staff', and 'comfortable, well-equipped' bedrooms. But there is no air conditioning and the rooms under the eaves, though attractive (exposed beams, etc), 'can be very hot in summer'. 'Food is delicious and very well served.' Meals are taken in the chandeliered dining room or a spacious garden room, looking on to a big lawn that stretches to a stream and pond. Breakfasts, in a 'new, well-designed room', include cold meats, cheeses, 'outstanding croissants'. The 'fabulous swimming pool' is in a converted barn, and bicycles can be borrowed. (*IGC Farman, Dr and Mrs RF Barrett, R Selbie, Dr and Mrs A Naylor, Peter Scott-Edeson, Carie Roots*)

Open All year. **Rooms** 2 apartments (in annexe), 12 double. **Facilities** Salon, 2 restaurants (no-smoking), bar, library; conservatory; conference facilities; heated swimming pool, sauna, gym. No background music. Terrace. 500-hectare park: tennis. Unsuitable for ♿. **Location** 23 km NE of Laon, 4 km W of Ste-Preuve, off Sissonne road. From A26 take exit 13, then D977. **Credit cards** All major cards accepted. **Terms** [2004] Room €115–€200. Breakfast €16. D,B&B €45–€70 added per person. Set meals €30–€85; full alc €60.

****

Traveller's tale B&B in Switzerland. This place, which I found on a B&B website, is on the floor above the bakery in a small, remote village which is reached via a complicated route over steep and snow-covered roads. I arrived, having made a telephone booking six weeks earlier. It was 5.30 pm on a Saturday afternoon. The bakery was closed, so I rang the bell. A teenage girl came to the door. When I said why I was there, she said they did not take guests. She closed and locked the door and went away. I recovered from my surprise and (there being no alternative accommodation in the village) retraced my steps to the Zürich airport area.

****

SAINTES 17100 Charente-Maritime — Map 4:B3

Relais du Bois Saint-Georges
Parc Atlantique
Cours Genêt

Tel 05.46.93.50.99
Fax 05.46.93.34.93
Email info@relaisdubois.com
Website www.relaisdubois.com

Created from an old farm, this unusual hotel is run with brio by its owner, Jérôme Emery. Spacious grounds with mature trees and hedges protect it from the 'industrial surroundings'. Most reviews remain positive: 'All our visits have been first class: the bedrooms, the staff, the grounds, the food.' 'We loved it.' 'We felt pleasurably pampered.' The open-plan foyer/salon/restaurant has a decor of beams, old candlesticks, tapestries, a big fireplace and, at one end, a small swimming pool with Roman statuary: you can dine beside it, looking through picture windows to a floodlit lake with swans and ducks. Summer meals are taken on a terrace. In the *restaurant gastronomique*, chef Michaël Gallas earns 15 *Gault Millau* points for, eg, St-Pierre avec sa crème aux arômes de coquillages. One couple, while finding the food reasonably priced, was 'astounded' by the prices of water, aperitifs and coffee. The bistro, *La Table du Bois*, produces 'delicious, lighter food'. Bedrooms in the older wing are well equipped (music system, etc): some face the lake. In the newer block are themed rooms: Carnet de voyage, Country life, etc. Saintes has narrow streets, medieval houses and the ruins of a Roman amphitheatre. (*Harold Metcalfe, Stephen Holman, and others*)

Open All year. **Rooms** 3 suites, 27 double. 6 on ground floor. Some no-smoking. Some air conditioned. **Facilities** 4 lounges, bar, tea room, restaurant, bistro; indoor swimming pool; massage, beauty treatment; classical background music; conference facilities. 7-hectare grounds: gardens, terrace (meals), croquet, *boules*, table tennis, lake, jogging track. **Location** W outskirts of Saintes. 2 km from A10 exit 35. Garage. **Credit cards** All major cards accepted. **Terms** [2004] Room: single €58–€130, double €160–€195, suite €235–€305. Breakfast €10–€20. Set meal: bistro from €20; restaurant (with wine) €41–€120. *V*

STES-MARIES-DE-LA-MER 13460 Bouches-du-Rhône — Map 6:E2

Le Mas de la Fouque
Route du Petit Rhône

Tel 04.90.97.81.02
Fax 04.90.97.96.84
Email info@masdelafouque.com
Website www.masdelafouque.com

'An idyllic luxury hotel in the Camargue', M. and Mme Regis's neat whitewashed *mas* is isolated by a lagoon just north of the Camargue's little seaside capital. All around are sea, beaches and much wildlife. This sophisticated place attracts many French celebrities (Daniel Auteuil, Émmanuelle Béart, Bernadette Chirac have stayed). Our reporter wrote: 'Our room was like a cool cave. A curtain separated the bedroom from a spectacular bathroom with a large, low-walled ceramic bath/shower in vaguely Roman style. There was a small sitting area, and a private terrace overlooking the salt marshes. We saw swallows and swifts skimming the water, flamingos flying overhead and a couple of creamy Camargue horses cropping the grass nearby. Dinner was excellent, a simple menu with limited choice, but all delicious.' On Saturdays there is a Flamenco dinner, with gypsy singers and guitar players. The hotel's boat takes visitors on trips round the coast to see wild bulls, herons, etc; other activities include horse riding on the beach and cycling (free bicycles). (*DL*)

Open 19 Dec–5 Jan, 20 Mar–11 Nov. **Rooms** 5 suites, 12 double. Some on ground floor. **Facilities** 2 salons, bar, restaurant; terrace with café. 3-hectare park: garden: heated swimming pool, putting; lake: fishing; free bicycles. Large sandy beach 2 km. **Location** 4 km NE of Stes-Maries-de-la-Mer by D38. **Restriction** No smoking: some bedrooms. **Credit cards** All major cards accepted. **Terms** Room €180–€270, suite €310–€440. Breakfast €18. Set meals €48–€62.

SARLAT-LA-CANÉDA 24200 Dordogne — Map 4:C4

Hôtel La Hoirie BUDGET — *Tel* 05.53.59.05.62
Rue Marcel Cerdan — *Fax* 05.53.31.13.90
Email lahoirie@club-internet.fr
Website www.lahoirie.com

Now owned by M. and Mme Pruvot, this 'most attractive building' is in a quiet residential area just outside Sarlat: 'a peaceful and beautiful setting'. It is a part 13th-century hunting lodge, 'truly romantic'. 'Dinner and breakfast both excellent. The welcome was warm on a chilly night,' says a visitor this year. The bedrooms are in three old stone buildings around a pretty courtyard; they vary in size and lightness; many have old beams. 'Our spacious room looked over neighbouring gardens to distant hills.' 'Ours, beautifully decorated, had good furniture, plenty of wardrobe space, a large bathroom.' Meals are served in a 13th-century room with a 'monumental fire-place' or in the garden, by candlelight. (*Alison Hodge, and others*)

Open 1 Mar–20 Dec. Restaurant closed midday and Tues. **Rooms** 3 suites, 16 double. All air conditioned. In 3 buildings. **Facilities** Salon, restaurant (classical background music). Garden (outdoor dining); unheated swimming pool. Unsuitable for ♿. **Location** 3 km S of Sarlat, off D704 towards Cahors. **Credit cards** Amex, MasterCard, Visa. **Terms** Room €48–€52, suite €84–€105. Breakfast €9.15. D,B&B (obligatory in summer) €60–€135 per person. Set dinner €22–€40. *V*

SARS-POTERIES 59216 Nord — Map 3:E4

Auberge Fleurie — *Tel* 03.27.61.62.48
67 rue du Général de Gaulle — *Fax* 03.27.61.56.66
Email fauberge@wanadoo.fr
Website www.auberge-fleurie.net

'The highlights of our stay were the welcome and the food,' say visitors in 2004. In the Avesnois *bocage* country in north-east France, relatively untouched by tourism, owner/chef Alain Leguy and his wife run this restaurant-with-rooms in a former glassworks ('poterie'). It stands in a garden full of roses, and flowers are everywhere, outside and in (fabrics and fresh flower arrangements). An earlier comment: 'Madame Leguy, full of charm, is immensely proud of her spacious bedrooms, in outbuildings, which she has decorated with antiques and expensive, co-ordinated English-style textiles. Our bathroom was large, superbly tiled.' 'Our rear room was quiet (a long, straight road runs through the village).' In the colourful beamed restaurant, 'sophisticated rustic, with pink tablecloths', M. Leguy has a *Michelin* star, 15 *Gault Millau* points for, eg, carpaccio de thon à l'huile d'olives et basilic frais; tournedos Rossini, sauce aux truffes. 'A masterly cheeseboard; delicious home-made bread.' 'Our Santenay and St-Amour were good, service was effective. Breakfast included petits pains au chocolat, home-made jams, cherries.' (*Brian and Rosalind Keen, and others*)

Open All year, except 8–25 Jan, 20–30 Aug, Sun night. Restaurant closed Mon. **Rooms** 8. 1 suitable for ♿. **Facilities** Restaurant. Garden (outside dining). **Location** Village on D962. 10 km NE of Avesnes-sur-Helpe. Parking. **Credit cards** All major cards accepted. **Terms** [2004] Room €60–€90. Breakfast €8. D,B&B €62.50–€95 per person. Set lunch €23, dinner €54; alc €43–€63.

SAUGUES 43170 Haute-Loire — Map 6:B1

La Terrasse BUDGET
Cours Docteur Gervais

Tel 04.71.77.83.10
Fax 04.71.77.63.79
Email laterrasse.saugues@wanadoo.fr
Website www.chemindecompostelle.com

A former *maison de notaire*, this inexpensive Logis de France is in a small town, surrounded by mountain pastures, on the pilgrims' route to Santiago de Compostela. The two Fargier brothers (their family has owned it since 1795) 'try hard to please', writes a visitor in 2004 (one brother is chef, the other front-of-house). The hotel is found 'comfortable', though one guest thought the interior was 'gloomy, with mushroom-coloured wallpaper and dark wood panelling in the bedrooms'. But earlier visitors wrote: 'The bedrooms are good (they even provide towelling bathrobes).' The food was this year thought 'simple, but generally pleasing, with wine both good and cheap'. But Saugues itself has 'a down-at-heel look, with many boarded-up shops and cafés', and the road outside the Logis can be busy with traffic (front rooms have effective double glazing). 'Breakfast was lavish: muesli, mountain ham, melon, etc.' (*Marilyn Frampton, GA, and others*)

Open Feb–15 Nov. Closed Sun night/Mon off-season. **Rooms** 1 suite, 6 double, 2 single. Some no-smoking. **Facilities** Bar, restaurant (air conditioning; background music). Unsuitable for ♿. **Location** In town, 43 km SW of Le Puy. Parking. **Credit cards** MasterCard, Visa. **Terms** [2004] Room €50–€55, suite €69. Breakfast €8. D,B&B €36–€50 per person. Set meals €20–€50.

All our inspections are anonymous.

SAULIEU 21210 Côte-d'Or Map 5:D2

Le Relais Bernard Loiseau *Tel* 03.80.90.53.53
2 rue Argentine *Fax* 03.80.64.08.92
Email loiseau@relaischateaux.com
Website www.bernardloiseau.com

'A splendid place, tasteful, comfortable, with exquisite food,' wrote regular correspondents about this famous Burgundian restaurant-with-rooms (Relais & Châteaux). The elegantly converted old post hotel is now run by Dominique Loiseau, widow of its founder, with a 'well-trained, considerate' staff. Behind its traditional facade are 'superb' interiors which make much use of local materials (stone, tiles, and wooden beams). Fireplaces are 'imposing', there are 'breathtaking' mirrors, and distinctive pictures and antiques. In the two dining rooms, chef Patrick Bertron keeps the three *Michelin* stars, 17 *Gault Millau* points awarded to the late Bernard Loiseau (specialities include jambonnettes de grenouille à la purée d'ail; blanc de volaille fermière, foie gras poêlé, purée de pommes de terre truffée). 'Our spacious room made judicious use of warm woods and traditional textiles.' The building is on the N6, but most rooms face the immaculate *jardin à l'anglaise* (with a 'small but good' swimming pool), so are quiet. 'Hard to imagine a hotel with higher standards or higher prices' is another recent comment. (*F and IW, JH*)

Open All year except 3–25 Jan. **Rooms** 12 suites, 20 double. Air conditioning. **Facilities** Lift. 2 lounges, restaurant. Garden: heated swimming pool, sauna, hammam. **Location** Central. 39 km SE of Avallon. **Credit cards** All major cards accepted. **Terms** [2004] Room €210–€330, suite €330–€470. Breakfast €28. Set lunch €92 (with wine), dinner €120–€172; alc €118–€196.

SAUMUR 49400 Maine-et-Loire Map 2:F4

Hôtel Anne d'Anjou *Tel* 02.41.67.30.30
32 quai Mayaud *Fax* 02.41.67.51.00
Email anneanjou@saumur.net
Website www.hotel-anneanjou.com

Beneath the white and turreted château built by Louis X, home of the French Cavalry Academy since 1763, is Jean-René and Mary Lyn Camus's stylish hotel, an 18th-century listed building overlooking the Loire. 'The reception is warm, the lounges are beautifully comfortable. Our elegant, sumptuous room faced the château,' says a visitor in 2004. An earlier guest had a delightful room facing the river, and added: 'Staff were attentive and unobtrusive.' Others had a 'lovely second-floor room, with king-size bed and large bathroom'. Some rooms have a landscape mural by the bed; a suite is in *style Empire*. The restaurant in the garden, *Les Ménestrels,* is separately owned by its chef, Christophe Hosselet, whose 'excellent' cuisine (13 *Gault Millau* points) might include carpaccio de thon et piment; filet de féra (a local freshwater fish) à la crème d'écrevisses. Local wines, such as Saumur, Chinon and Vouvray, are available by the glass. Not far away is the 12th-century Abbaye de Fontevraud, burial place of

Eleanor of Aquitaine and Richard the Lionheart. (*Jim Clarke, Anne Folkes, and others*)

Open All year. Restaurant closed Sun, Christmas. **Rooms** 2 suites, 37 double, 6 single. 5 in courtyard. 1 designed for ♿. **Facilities** Lift. Reception (classical background music), bar, restaurant; conference room. Garden. **Location** Central. Car park (€8). **Credit cards** All major cards accepted. **Terms** Room: single €76, double €85, suite €130. Breakfast €10. Set meals €31; full alc €70. *V*

SAUVETERRE-DE-COMMINGES 31510 Haute-Garonne — Map 4:E4

Hostellerie des 7 Molles
Gesset

Tel 05.61.88.30.87
Fax 05.61.88.36.42
Email contact@hotel7molles.com
Website www.hotel7molles.com

Amid the 'fabulous scenery' of the Pyrenean foothills, the Ferran family's hotel is named after the seven watermills (*molles = moulins*) which once stood nearby. Their millstones are now tables in its rose-scented garden, which has a stream, a well-kept swimming pool, and a 'perfectly playable' clay tennis court. The 1960 building 'has the ambience of a large family home'. 'Standards are high,' say fans. 'Staff are friendly', and the bucolic setting is liked. In the large dining room are chandeliers, 'charming' local china, and service by 'solemn young waiters in black'. Gilles Ferran is the chef, serving dishes like truite à la belle meunière aux amandes, accompanied by local wines. There is a separate restaurant, *La Table du Meunier*, for lunch. 'Our room was large, light and airy. Birds provided a dawn chorus.' Some rooms have a balcony facing the landscape; others overlook a road. Visit the beautiful cathedral of St-Bertrand-de-Comminges, in a medieval hilltop village, and the elegant spa town of Bagnères-de-Luchon near the Spanish border. (*Harold Metcalfe*)

Open 15 Mar–15 Feb, except Tues/Wed off-season. Restaurant closed midday Thurs, midday Fri off-season. **Rooms** 2 suites, 15 double, 2 single. **Facilities** Lift, ramps. Lounge/bar, billiard room, breakfast room, 2 restaurants. Garden: unheated swimming pool, tennis, table tennis. Unsuitable for ♿. **Location** At Gesset, 2 km SE of Sauveterre, 13 km SW of St-Gaudens. **Credit cards** All major cards accepted. **Terms** Room €64–€128, suite €187–€200. Breakfast €12. D,B&B €89–€178 per person. Set meals €29–€39. Full alc €50. *V*

SOLÉRIEUX 26130 Drôme — Map 6:C3

La Ferme St-Michel
Route de la Baume (D341)

Tel 04.75.98.10.66
Fax 04.75.98.19.09
Website www.fermesaintmichel.com

'Charming as ever,' says a visitor this year, returning to this 16th-century stone *mas* in vineyards and lavender fields in rolling country east of the Rhône valley. 'No airs and graces, casual and welcoming. The grounds are a joy, just what a true Provençal estate should be.' There is statuary, a massive plane tree, tables and chairs dotted about, and a large swimming pool. The beamed and vaulted dining room is 'small and welcoming'; meals are served in the courtyard in fine weather. Regional dishes include les ravioles d'olives sur une piperade de poivrons; noisette de selle d'agneau au romarin. In season you can take the truffle menu: 'It ended with crème brûlée with slices of truffle – a triumph.' There is a tiny bar; furniture is 'rustic'. 'Our room, with white walls and pretty painted furniture, was blissfully warm (but there was some traffic noise). Breakfast with fluffy croissants served gracefully in the bedroom. Superb value.' Nearby is Mme de Sévigné's château at Grignan. (*Rosemary Winder, LB*)

Open All year. Restaurant closed 20 Dec–20 Jan, midday, Sun night. **Rooms** 12 double. 5 air conditioned. **Facilities** 2 lounges, bar, restaurant. No background music. Garden: outdoor dining, unheated swimming pool. Unsuitable for ♿. **Location** On D341, between Solérieux and La Baume de Transit, 38 km N of Orange. Parking. **Restrictions** No smoking in restaurant. No dogs. **Credit cards** Amex, MasterCard, Visa. **Terms** [2004] Room €65–€75. Breakfast €7. D,B&B €75–€103 per person. Set meals €21–€42.

SOURZAC 24400 Dordogne — Map 4:C4

Le Chaufourg en Périgord — NEW

Tel 05.53.81.01.56
Fax 05.53.82.94.87
Email info@lechaufourg.com
Website www.lechaufourg.com

Between Bergerac and Périgueux, this 17th-century manor house was the childhood home of Georges Dambier, one of France's great fashion photographers. Now he runs it very personally as a luxury hotel: 'A delightful place,' says a travel expert. It stands amid gardens and meadows in a large park, facing the River Isle. 'Georges knows the area well and will arrange local tours, bicycles and canoes. He has a marvellous eye. All the bedrooms are distinctive. Most are done in white or pale pastel. Even the smallest one is correct in every detail. Our wonderful suite, on the second floor, had windows overlooking the pool in one direction and the river in the other.' No separate dining room: tables are placed in a large salon and adjacent billiard room for the residents-only evening meals provided by chef Alain Civire. The house is just off the N89, but most traffic now uses the A89 *autoroute*. (*Marshall S Harris*)

Open 15 Feb–15 Nov. **Rooms** 4 suites, 5 double. In 3 buildings. 5 air conditioned. 2 no-smoking. **Facilities** Salon, billiard room. Terrace. 4-hectare garden: swimming pool. **Location** 4 km NE of Mussidan, 30 km N of Bergerac. Exit 13 from A89/N89. **Credit cards** All major cards accepted. **Terms** [2004] Room: double €150–€205, suite €310. Breakfast €16. Dinner (alc, residents only) €40–€65.

> We quote either price per room, or else the range of prices per person – the lowest is likely to be for one person sharing a double room out of season, the highest for a single room in high season.

STRASBOURG 67000 Bas-Rhin — Map 5:B6

Hôtel de la Cathédrale
12–13 place de la Cathédrale

Tel 03.88.22.12.12
Fax 03.88.23.28.00
Email reserv@hotel-cathedrale.fr
Website www.hotel-cathedrale.fr

In the historic centre, on the traffic-free square in front of the cathedral, this 'tastefully decorated' hotel, managed by its owners, Alain Céziard and Simone Ligier, offers 'good value', say *Guide* readers. Many of the 'characterful' bedrooms have been renovated this year. They are priced according to position and size; most are quiet ('the cathedral bells are not overpowering, thanks to double glazing'). Room 48 is the former chapel. Colours are bright; bathrooms are modern. The good buffet breakfast is served in a 'delightful' room. A porter/driver helps with luggage, and bicycles are provided free.

Open All year. **Rooms** 47. Some no-smoking. Air conditioning. **Facilities** Lift (1st–6th floor). Lounges, bar, breakfast room; background music; conference facilities; Internet room. Unsuitable for ♿. **Location** Central, opposite cathedral. 5 private parking spaces, 3 public car parks nearby. **Credit cards** All major cards accepted. **Terms** B&B: single €75–€100, double €85–€150.

Hôtel du Dragon
2 rue de l'Écarlate

Tel 03.88.35.79.80
Fax 03.88.25.78.95
Email hotel@dragon.fr
Website www.dragon.fr

'Pleasant, very convenient.' 'A gem! Peaceful, comfortable, relaxing.' The latest reports on this B&B hotel in a quiet cul-de-sac in the old centre of this busy city. A 17th-century house, but dating back to 1345, it has a modern minimalist decor. 'My stylish room on the fourth floor was soothing in pale grey and cream. Small attic windows looked over the cathedral on one side, top floors of houses on the other, giving a pleasant feel of being part of the community.' The small courtyard garden, with plants in terracotta pots, 'is a delight, particularly in hot weather'. The 'cordial' owner, Jean Zimmer, runs the house with a 'charming team', and the atmosphere is 'very friendly'. On the courtyard, breakfast (with fresh fruit and yogurt, boiled eggs), drinks and light lunches are served. Recommended restaurants include *Maison des Tanneurs* and *Zum Strissel*. (*Florence and Russell Birch, VM-I*)

Open All year. **Rooms** 2 suites, 30 double. **Facilities** Lift. Salon, bar, breakfast room; background music; seminar room. Courtyard. **Location** Central: off Quai St-Nicolas, near Pl. d'Austerlitz. Public car park; 4 private spaces. **Restrictions** No smoking: some bedrooms, breakfast room. No dogs. **Credit cards** All major cards accepted. **Terms** Room €69–€112, suite (3 or 4 people) €129–€145. Breakfast €10.

> Before making a long detour to a small hotel, do check that it is open. Some are known to close on impulse.

TALLOIRES 74290 Haute-Savoie **Map 6:A4**

Hôtel Beau Site
Rue André Theuriet

Tel 04.50.60.71.04
Fax 04.50.60.79.22
Email hotelbeausite@free.fr
Website www.hotel-beausite-fr.com

The lawns of this hotel (with loungers and plenty of space for sunbathing) run down to a private beach on the shore of Lake Annecy. Long owned (like Les Prés du Lac, *qv*, also in Talloires) by the Conan family, and run by Anne Conan, it has many devotees. The building is 'handsome, both inside and out,' says one. The decor is modern; public rooms are 'cosy', with good pictures; some bedrooms are large; some have a balcony. In the large dining room, 'Italianate in feel', and 'with lovely views', the staff are 'very welcoming' and Patrick Durand's cooking is 'of a high standard'. The set meal is good value, but the cooking is better, with more sophisticated ingredients, if you go *à la carte*. 'Local wines of a high standard.' For 'the small gastronomist', there is a separate short menu. 'Breakfast, in the garden, was lovely.' Guests on B&B terms tend to stay in the annexe, *La Tournette*. (*PH*)

Open 20 May–2 Oct. **Rooms** 1 suite (air conditioned), 27 double, 1 single. In 3 buildings. **Facilities** Lounge, lounge/bar, breakfast room, restaurant; function room. No background music. 1-hectare garden: terrace, tennis, table tennis; private beach. Unsuitable for ♿. **Location** Village centre, on E side of lake. 12 km S of Annecy. Parking. **Restriction** No smoking in breakfast room, bedrooms. **Credit cards** Amex, MasterCard, Visa. **Terms** Room: single €64–€66, double €94–€144, suite €138–€180. Breakfast €12–€12.50. D,B&B €98–€126 per person. Set meals €27.50–€28.50; full alc €43.50.

Hôtel Restaurant Le Cottage

Tel 04.50.60.71.10
Fax 04.50.60.77.51
Email cottagebise@wanadoo.fr
Website www.cottagebise.com

'Family-run and it shows,' say visitors this year to this chalet-style building ('like a 1930s English cottage with a touch of Gallic flair'). Everyone agrees that the owners, Christine and Jean-Claude Bise, and their staff are 'charming'. Madame is 'much in evidence'. The large dining room faces the water, and in fine weather guests eat under trees on the 'wonderful' lake-facing terrace. Bedrooms, 'done with charm and individuality', are in the main building (many here have a balcony) and (newer ones) in two tall villas in the gardens. 'The excellent tiled bathrooms are spacious.' Public rooms are light, cheerful and smart. Diners were 'very impressed by the care and attention we received'. In the attractive restaurant, with 'comfortable seating, crisp napery, good china and glass', the food is 'probably the best in Talloires: the fish dishes are superb'. The flowery gardens are pretty; by the pool are lots of loungers and parasols. Pedalos, rowing boats and kayaks are available, plus guided walks in the mountains. Children are welcomed. (*Roger and Jean Cook, PH*)

Open 25 Apr–2 Oct. **Rooms** 35. In 3 buildings. **Facilities** Lift (main building). Lounge, restaurant; conference room; no background music. Garden: 2 terraces (outdoor dining); heated swimming pool. Tennis, mini-golf, swimming, boating, water sports, horse riding, cycling all nearby. **Location** E bank of lake, 300 m from village centre. Garages, private parking. **Restriction** No dogs. **Credit cards** All major cards accepted. **Terms** [2004] Room €130–€220. Breakfast €15. D,B&B €110–€165 per person. Set menus €33–€50.

Les Prés du Lac
Rue André Theuriet

Tel 04.50.60.76.11
Fax 04.50.60.73.42
Email les.pres.du.lac@wanadoo.fr
Website www.lespresdulac.com

'We just love it,' write visitors on their sixth visit to this hotel composed of three handsome 19th-century villas. It shares grounds with the *Beau Site* (above), also owned by the Conan family. 'The closest I'm going to get to heaven on earth,' was another comment. The manager, Marie-Paule Conan, and her mother, are 'very welcoming', service is 'gentle, cheerful', 'any request is greeted with a smile', and 'the charm and utter peace never fail to restore flagging spirits'. Bedrooms, all with views of lake and mountains, some with balcony or terrace, have 'soft colours, stunning rugs, dramatic pictures, huge vases of flowers'. 'A tray never arrives without a tiny posy. Breakfast, at any time, is superb: strong coffee, delicate tea, fresh fruit, home-made jams, lavender honey.' It is taken in the room or on the terrace, 'perfect also for a drink'. 'The birdlife in the garden is a delight. We enjoyed swimming in the lake, beside the friendly swans.' No restaurant: a snack lunch (eg, omelette and salad) can be served, and you can dine at the *Beau Site* (*qv*) or in the village. (*Padi and John Howard*)

Open 30 Apr–9 Oct. **Rooms** 16 double. Some in 2 villas. 6 air conditioned. **Facilities** 2 salons, library. No background music. 1-hectare lakeside garden: private beach, swimming, tennis. Unsuitable for ♿. **Location** 3 mins' walk from centre. E side of lake. 12 km S of Annecy. Garages, parking. **Credit cards** All major cards accepted. **Terms** Room €154–€267. Breakfast €18 or alc.

TAVERS 45190 Loiret — Map 2:F5

La Tonnellerie
12 rue des Eaux Bleues

Tel 02.38.44.68.15
Fax 02.38.44.10.01
Email tonelri@club-internet.fr.com
Website www.tonelri.com

Once the home of a 19th-century wine merchant, this vine-covered building is now a 'charming small hotel', says a visitor in 2004. 'The friendly staff were very helpful.' The owner, Marie-Christine Pouey, has decorated it in 19th-century style. An earlier visitor wrote of 'a very comfortable room and good food'. In the 'delightful garden', drinks are served under white parasols in summer, and a 'lovely' swimming pool, with loungers, is set amid chestnut trees. All is quiet, apart from church bells and birdsong. There's a courtyard for summer meals, and a pretty dining room. The young chef, Daniel Ferreira, puts a new spin on old classics, eg, lobster couscous. 'The head waiter was extremely knowledgeable about his wine list.' A good base for visiting the Loire châteaux, and events such as the '*soupe des chiens*' at Cheverny; the old wine town of Beaugency is nearby. (*Sir Timothy Harford, MB*)

Open 1 Mar–23 Dec. Restaurant closed midday except Sun. **Rooms** 2 suites, 18 double. Some (family) in annexe. 4 on ground floor. **Facilities** Lift. Lounge, restaurant; 2 meeting rooms. No background music. Garden: heated swimming pool. Golf, tennis, riding nearby. Unsuitable for ♿. **Location** In village, by Loire. 3 km SW of Beaugency. Parking. **Credit cards** Amex, MasterCard, Visa. **Terms** Room: single €70–€140, double €102–€178, suite €162–€208. Breakfast €12. D,B&B €127–€197 per person. Set meals €27–€49; full alc €87. *V*

THANNENKIRCH 68590 Haut-Rhin — Map 5:C5

Auberge la Meunière BUDGET
30 rue Ste-Anne

Tel 03.89.73.10.47
Fax 03.89.73.12.31
Email info@aubergelameuniere.com
Website www.aubergelameuniere.com

With the impressive castle of Haut-Koenigsbourg on the horizon and visible from some bedrooms, this modernised, but traditionally styled Alsatian *auberge* (Logis de France) is run by owner/chef Jean-Luc Dumoulin and his wife, Francesca. It caters for families and 'fulfils its function well', say correspondents in 2004. Its wooden facade is bedecked in summer with geraniums. 'The food is delicious, hearty and plentiful,' say recent visitors (eg, suprême de pintade sur écorce de sapin; onglet de veau au citron et gingembre. One couple found the no-choice half-board menu 'quite plain', but 'the meat was always exceptionally tender'. Others wrote: 'Our room had a lovely view. We awoke each morning to church bells. The wood panelling is rich and attractive. Service was exceptional.' 'A huge and comfy bedroom.' Rear rooms can be 'cramped and dark', but all rooms are quiet. The 'good breakfast' is served in a bright room ('you can make your own pancakes'); there is a glass lift, and a large panoramic terrace for summer meals. Showpiece wine villages, eg, Riquewihr, Kaysersberg, are near. (*Brian and Rosalind Keen, and others*)

Open 25 Mar–22 Dec. Restaurant closed Mon/Tues/Wed midday. **Rooms** 13 family, 12 double. **Facilities** Lift. 3 salons, TV room, billiard room, breakfast room, restaurant (background music); conference room; spa bath, sauna. Garden: terrace; children's playground. Mountain bike hire. Unsuitable for ♿. **Location** 24 km NW of Colmar. Parking. **Restriction** No smoking in some bedrooms, part of restaurant. **Credit cards** Amex, MasterCard, Visa. **Terms** B&B double €61–€102; D,B&B €45–€70 per person. Set meals €17–€33; full alc €30.

> Important: Please regard the terms printed as only a rough guide to the sort of bill you can expect at the end of your stay. You *must* check the tariffs when booking.

TOULOUSE 31000 Haute-Garonne — Map 4:D4

Hôtel des Couteliers
22 Descente de la Halle aux Poissons

Tel 05.34.31.94.80
Fax 05.34.31.94.81
Email contact@hoteldescouteliers.com
Website www.hotelsdecharmetoulouse.com

A reader whose flight was cancelled due to a strike was consoled by the discovery of Pierre Courtois de Viçose's small, newish hotel (formerly the Hôtel des Capitouls) in a quiet, narrow street in the old city. 'What a haven: cool (air conditioned), chic and classic,' she writes. Other recent praise: 'Distinctive and impressive'; 'very special'. In the public areas are lots of red, designer furniture and contemporary artwork. Drinks are served in the lounge by 'outstandingly helpful' staff. Two bedrooms have views of the Garonne. A continental breakfast can be brought to the room; a buffet breakfast is taken in the 'fine restaurant' opposite, *Le 19*, under the same ownership (like the cheaper *Hôtel des Beaux Arts*, nearby). In a vaulted cellar, *Le 19* has two dining rooms, a 'remarkably comprehensive wine cellar' and a smokers' lounge. Each dish on the *Menu Dégustation* comes with the suggestion of an appropriate wine. 'The fish was excellent.' Also nearby is the Hôtel d'Assézat, a glorious Renaissance mansion, now a cultural centre.. (*Patricia Brown, KMY*)

Open All year. Restaurant closed Sun, Sat and Mon midday, 3 weeks Aug, Christmas/New Year. **Rooms** 3 suites, 11 doubles. Some no-smoking. 1 suitable for ♿. Air conditioning. **Facilities** Lobby ('smooth' background music), lounge, restaurant (30 m). **Location** Central, near river (windows double glazed). Public underground car park (Esquirol) 200 m. **Restriction** No pets. **Credit cards** All major cards accepted. **Terms** Room €155–€175, suite €209–€259. Breakfast €18. Set lunch €31, dinner €55.

TOURNUS 71700 Saône-et-Loire — Map 5:E3

Hôtel de Greuze
5 place de l'Abbaye

Tel 03.85.51 77.77
Fax 03.85.51.77.23

In painter Jean-Baptiste Greuze's birthplace, overlooked by bell tower of Romanesque abbey of St-Philibert: Renaissance 'Bressane' building restored as elegant, luxurious hotel. 'Excellent breakfast, courteous service.' Lift. Air conditioning, double glazing. Salon, breakfast room; conference room. Adjacent is Jean Ducloux's Restaurant Greuze *(Relais & Châteaux,* Michelin *star, 15* Gault Millau *points). Open 8 Dec–13 Nov. All major credit cards accepted. 21 comfortable bedrooms in different styles (Louis XVI, Directoire, etc); some face abbey, others main road and railway. €130–€285. Breakfast €20 [2004].*

Aux Terrasses
18 avenue du 23 janvier (N6)

Tel 03.85.51.01.74
Fax 03.85.51.09.99

'One of our best hotel experiences in 15 years,' write visitors in 2004 to this creeper-covered Logis de France just south of this lovely medieval town. Others wrote: 'A wonderful discovery.' 'The ideal stop-over, if you want to eat well and stay cheaply.' It is close to the busy road, but the soundproofed, air-conditioned rooms are 'very quiet'. 'A superb room; we've never had a better shower.' 'The food was exquisite. Even the children's menu was excellent. Service was calmly efficient.' Michel Carrette, chef/*patron* for over 20 years, presides with his wife, Henriette. He wins a *Michelin* star, 13 *Gault Millau* points for his Burgundian food, eg, poulet de Bresse à la crème aux morilles et vin jaune. Meals are served by 'pleasant staff' in three 'discreetly elegant' dining rooms. (*Bob and Kate Flaherty, Susan and David Lawler, and others*)

Open All year, except 4 Jan–2 Feb, 6–14 June, 14–21 Nov. **Rooms** 18 double. 1 on ground floor. Air conditioning. **Facilities** 3 dining rooms (1 no-smoking); classical background music. Unsuitable for ♿. **Location** On N6, 800 m S of centre. Parking. Garage. **Credit cards** Amex, MasterCard, Visa. **Terms** Room €58–€68. Breakfast €8. Set meals €22–€60.

TOURTOUR 83690 Var — Map 6:E4

Auberge St-Pierre
Route d'Ampus

Tel 04.94.50.00.50
Fax 04.94.70.59.04
Email aubergestpierre@wanadoo.fr
Website www.guideprovence.com/hotel/saint-pierre

High in the mountains in Upper Provence, outside a lovely but touristy village, is this 'special place'. René Marcellin's converted 16th-century *bastide* stands in a large estate: lush fields dotted with grazing sheep, cattle and horses, forests, and a small lake. 'Utter tranquillity. We enjoyed listening to silence,' says a visitor in 2004. 'Marvellous as ever,' says a regular guest; other visitors mention the 'friendly atmosphere' and the 'helpful, personable' staff. 'Madame Marcellin was charming.' The bedrooms, mostly in a new wing, are spacious, some with a sofa and balcony. Food is simple: goat's cheese salad; grilled lamb, dessert from the trolley. 'All very good; quantities not vast.' Many ingredients are home produced. 'Excellent breakfast: home-made jams and yogurt.' 'Our room, decorated in pretty sky blue, faced the *piscine*, which has a large hood allowing off-season swimming.' A whirlpool bath has been added this year. Tables and chairs, for drinks, etc, are in the garden and on the poolside patio. 'Lovely walks nearby.' (*Brian Beach, HN, and others*)

Open April–Nov. Restaurant closed Wed, and midday Mon, Tues and Thurs. **Rooms** 16 double. **Facilities** Salon, TV room, bar, restaurant; meeting room. No background music. 90-hectare grounds: swimming pool (covered spring/autumn), tennis, gym, table tennis, sauna; lake, fishing, archery, mountain bikes. Unsuitable for ♿. **Location** 3 km NE of Tourtour on Ampus road, 20 km NW of Draguignan. Parking. **Credit cards** All major cards accepted. **Terms** Room €70–€92.50. Breakfast €8.50. D,B&B €74–€116 per person. Set meals €23.50–€31.50; full alc €45. *V* (except July/Aug)

For details of the Voucher scheme, see page xxvi.

TRÉBEURDEN 22560 Côtes-d'Armor **Map 2:E2**

Manoir de Lan-Kerellec
Allée centrale

Tel 02.96.15.00.00
Fax 02.96.23.66.88
Email manoir.lankerellec@wanadoo.com
Website www.lankerellec.com

'A beautiful hotel,' one reader wrote. Built of local pink granite, this 19th-century Breton manor house (Relais & Châteaux) stands on a wooded headland on the edge of this popular resort. 'Luxurious without being stuffy', it is within walking distance of fine, sandy beaches. All bedrooms look south over sea and islands. 'The view from our room was breathtaking. Our elegantly appointed bathroom had spa bath, separate shower, loads of fluffy towels, renewed twice daily.' The 'charming' garden, with blue-and-white loungers and parasols, faces the sea, as does the *Michelin*-starred restaurant where the 'warmly welcoming' owners, Gilles and Luce Daubé, are 'always present' and chef Marc Briand specialises in fish, eg, filet de turbot doré au beurre demi-sel. Staff are 'discreet yet friendly'; 'at dinner they are formally dressed: splendid long jackets'. Half-board guests eat off the *carte*. 'Breakfast in the bedroom, served until noon, was delicious: fresh orange juice, croissants, lovely crêpes and eggs.' It is served until 10 am in the restaurant. (*RB, WS, and others*)

Open Mid-Mar–mid-Nov. Restaurant closed midday on Mon, Tues and Thurs. **Rooms** 3 suites, 16 double. **Facilities** 3 salons, bar, restaurant; conference facilities; beauty salon. Garden: terrace; beach. Water sports, golf nearby. **Location** Edge of village. 10 km NW of Lannion. Parking. **Credit cards** All major cards accepted. **Terms** [2004] Room €95–€320, suite €300–€400. Breakfast €16. D,B&B (obligatory 25 June–15 Sept) €150–€273 per person. Set meals €40–€60; alc €58–€92.

Ti al Lannec
14 allée de Mézo-Guen

Tel 02.96.15.01.01
Fax 02.96.23.62.14
Email resa@tiallannec.com
Website www.tiallannec.com

A visitor this year 'greatly enjoyed' Gérard and Danielle Jouanny's handsome, white 19th-century mansion (Relais de Silence). 'Still very nice: a relaxing visit,' was another plaudit. It stands in a large flowery garden (where meals are served under parasols and cypress trees) high above the beach, on the 'granite rose coast', arguably the loveliest stretch of north Brittany, where large pink rocks lie offshore. 'Well organised for small children', it has 'a family feel'. Service is 'impeccable', 'very friendly'. The restaurant has a panoramic terrace. The food (plenty of local fish and seafood) is much liked. 'A remarkable wine cellar.' Breakfast, a generous buffet, comes with a bulletin giving times of tides, local markets and events. Some bedrooms have a balcony with views of the coast. Some, under the gables, can be hot in summer. The spa offers beauty treatments. Steps lead down to the big public beach, which is sometimes crowded, and one guest mentioned noise from a disco on the seafront on a summer weekend. Residents are expected to dine in. (*Michael Burns, AF*)

Open 1 Mar–15 Nov. **Rooms** 8 suites, 22 double, 3 single. 2 suitable for ♿. **Facilities** Lift, ramps. 3 salons, billiard room, bar, restaurant (no-smoking); background music; conference facilities; fitness centre. Park: garden, terrace, outdoor chess, children's play area, table tennis, *boules*. Path to sandy beach: safe bathing, fishing. **Location** Hilltop above resort. 10 km N of Lannion. Parking. **Credit cards** Diners, MasterCard, Visa. **Terms** [2004] Room: single €78–€97, double €144–€231, suite €166–€317. Breakfast €14. D,B&B €123–€205 per person. Set meals €21–€66; alc €50.

TRIGANCE 83840 Var — Map 6:D4

Château de Trigance

Tel 04.94.76.91.18
Fax 04.94.85.68.99
Email chateautrigance@wanadoo.fr
Website www.chateau-de-trigance.fr

'Magical.' 'Delightful.' This former 10th-century fortress, near the awesome Gorges du Verdon, is owned by the family of Claude Thomas; his 'charming' son manages. 'The welcome is warm and genuine,' say visitors this year. High above the village, it has 'sensational' views from the battlements where breakfast (a 'theatrical event' with fruit, pastries, yogurt, home-made jams) and aperitifs are served by 'attentive' staff. In the 'gorgeous' medieval dining room, formerly an armoury, 'we had the best meal of our week' (12 *Gault Millau* points for Philippe Joffroy). Staying here, 'you need the agility of a mountain goat': the bedrooms, 'superbly decorated in fitting style', are reached from the battlements, by a path along a wooden gangplank above a steep drop, down solid rock steps (no lift or fitted carpets). 'Our room had superb views, stone semi-vaulting, brocade-canopied bed, TV.' 'Ours, in a tower, was spacious and comfortable.' 'The silence is breathtaking.' Guests are expected to dine in. (*David and Georgina Bennett, Anni Corbett, and others*)

Open 25 Mar–31 Oct. Restaurant closed Wed midday Mar and Oct. **Rooms** 2 suites, 8 double. **Facilities** Salon, restaurant (no-smoking); classical background music; terrace. Unsuitable for ♿. **Location** 20 km SW of Castellane, 12 km NW of Comps-sur-Artuby. Parking. **Credit cards** All major cards accepted. **Terms** Room €105–€165, suite €185. Breakfast €13. D,B&B: double €201–€261, suite €281. Set meals €25–€65.

The 2006 edition of the *Guide*, covering Great Britain and Ireland, will appear in the autumn of 2005. Reports are particularly useful in the spring, and they need to reach us by 15 May 2005 at the very latest if they are to help the 2006 edition.

TRIZAY 17250 Charente — Map 4:B3

Les Jardins du Lac NEW
au lac du Bois Fleuri

Tel 05.46.82.03.56
Fax 05.46.82.03.55
Email hotel@jardins-du-lac.com
Website www.jardins-du-lac.com

Outside a village in the Saintonge, Sabine and Michel Suire (he is the chef) run their purpose-built restaurant-with-rooms (Relais du Silence) by a lake. Composed of two red-roofed single-storey buildings, it is in a large garden with trees, flowers, a stream and a swimming pool. 'The light, airy bedrooms have *en suite* facilities of a high standard.' Designed to catch the morning sun, they are simply furnished and pleasant: 'Ours had a lake view and terrace. Dinners were excellent, with good choice of local and national dishes.' The dining room has a ceiling shaped like a boat's hull, large picture windows, and tables facing the water. Meals are served in the garden in summer. Home-grown vegetables and herbs are used in dishes like craquant de langoustines en salade de mesclun; noisettes d'agneau rôties au crumble d'herbes du jardin. Traditional breakfasts: 'Warm croissants, rolls etc.' (*Alison Hodge, and others*)

Open All year, except Feb, Sun night/Mon Nov–Mar. **Rooms** 8 double. **Facilities** Salons, bar, restaurant (air conditioned); conference room. Garden: meal service, swimming pool. **Location** 15 km SE of Rochefort, 2.5 km W of Trizay on D238. Parking. **Credit cards** All major cards accepted. **Terms** [2004] Room €143.50–€167.50. Breakfast €12. D,B&B €88.50–€97.50 per person. Set meals €24–€64.

TROYES 10000 Aube — Map 5:B2

Le Champ des Oiseaux
20 rue Linard-Gonthier

Tel 03.25.80.58.50
Fax 03.25.80.98.34
Email message@champdesoiseaux.com
Website www.champdesoiseaux.com

Owned by the much-admired Monique Boisseau, this B&B hotel, named after storks that once nested nearby, is in two 15th/16th-century oak-framed buildings in a cobbled street near the cathedral of this lovely medieval town. 'Heaven on earth, one of the pleasantest hotels we've stayed in, run by immensely nice people,' writes a visitor in 2004. Large bedrooms surround a beautiful pillared courtyard: 'We had two nights in a cool ground-floor room, one night in the slightly eccentric Chambre Bleue, with loo between bedroom and sitting room, but all charmingly decorated.' But dissenters had a 'basic' room with poor sound insulation ('thanks to the tiled floor, we heard everything from the rooms above and adjacent'). The 'old-fashioned French hotel breakfast' (with fresh strawberries and good croissants) in the courtyard is liked: 'A treat not to have the endless walk-about of the modern buffet.' 'The helpful receptionist parked our car and offered to carry our bags.' Madame will advise on local restaurants. The bedrooms in the new sister hotel, *Maison de Rhodes*, were less liked: 'The suite had a large, almost empty, bedroom, and expensive-looking lights pointed everywhere but in a useful direction.' A restaurant, with a fixed-price menu (€40), and a medieval garden in the *Maison de Rhodes* are planned. (*Charlie Nairn, and others*)

Open All year. **Rooms** 6 suites, 17 double. Some on ground floor. In two buildings. **Facilities** Ramps. 3 salons, bar, breakfast room; classical background music; courtyard garden. **Location** Central, near cathedral (map on brochure). Parking nearby (€12). **Credit cards** All major cards accepted. **Terms** Room €95–€168, suite €170–€200. Breakfast €15.

TURCKHEIM 68230 Haut-Rhin — Map 5:C5

Berceau du Vigneron BUDGET
10 place Turenne

Tel 03.89.27.23.55
Fax 03.89.30.01.33
Email infos@berceau-du-vigneron.com
Website www.berceau-du-vigneron.com

In a 'lovely little' medieval town on the Route du Vin, west of Colmar, this old half-timbered building is now a 'charming' small hotel. Recently redecorated, it is built into the 14th-century ramparts by the city gates. 'It can be recommended,' says a visitor who stayed three nights, 'to tourists who are keen not on luxury but on a friendly atmosphere and good service.' Another guest found it 'simple, very clean, extraordinarily good value for plain accommodation'. The bedrooms are 'quite spacious, well lit'; quietest ones are at the back. The good buffet breakfast is served in a galleried inner courtyard or a stone-walled, beamed room. No restaurant, but a good choice in the village: 'We liked the *Caveau du Vigneron*: a typical Alsatian atmosphere, like the hotel.' (*Helmut Poensgen, Iain Elliott*)

Open All year, except Jan. **Rooms** 16. **Facilities** Breakfast room. **Location** 5 km W of Colmar. Public parking. **Credit cards** MasterCard, Visa. **Terms** [2004] Room €42–€70. Breakfast €7.50.

TURENNE 19500 Corrèze — Map 4:C5

La Maison des Chanoines BUDGET
Route de l'Église

Tel/Fax 05.55.85.93.43
Email maisondeschanoines@wanadoo.fr
Website www.maison-des-chanoines.com

This 'jewel of a medieval village' sits below a spectacular ruined Knights Templar castle on a huge rock, north of the Dordogne. The oldest building in its square is Chantal and Claude Cheyroux's 16th-century hotel, found 'delightful' and 'excellent value' again, in 2004. Earlier praise: 'Our room had yellow walls, antique chests (the TV seemed out of place), an amazing medieval window in the loo.' 'Ours, in the attractive building across the road, was large, very comfortable, with distant rural views', but these rooms are reached up a stone spiral staircase with no hand rail, so are suitable only for the 'really sure-footed'. Madame is 'so friendly'; Monsieur's cooking is 'delicious', served under vines in the courtyard garden or in a former wine cellar which contains 'an eclectic collection of paintings, prints, pottery and lamps'. *Gault Millau* awards 14 points, recommending moules au jus de noix vertes; côte de veau aux girolles. Breakfast has 'brioches, excellent pain de campagne, crisp toast, superb coffee' but 'commercial orange juice and no fruit'. Views are 'magnificent'. (*Humphrey Potts, PMS, and others*)

Open Easter–end-Sept. Closed Wed evening in June. Restaurant closed midday except Sun, public holidays, Wed evening in June. **Rooms** 1 suite, 5 doubles. 3 in garden house. **Facilities** Bar, restaurant (background music). Garden, terrace. Unsuitable for ♿. **Location** By church in village. 16 km S of Brive. Public parking. **Restriction** No dogs. **Credit cards** MasterCard, Visa. **Terms** Room €60–€85, suite €85. Breakfast €9. D,B&B (min. 3 nights) €64–€74 per person. Set meals €30–€36.

URIAGE-LES-BAINS 38410 Isère — Map 6:B4

Hôtel Les Mésanges — *Tel* 04.76.89.70.69
Route St-Martin-d'Uriage — *Fax* 04.76.89.56.97
Email prince@hotel-les-mesanges.com
Website www.hotel-les-mesanges.com

Visitors in 2004 found this white-walled, red-roofed Logis de France, run by the 'warm and helpful' Prince family owners, 'ideal' for a walking holiday in the French Alps. A *mésange* is a tit, and 'lots of them' have been seen 'singing and dancing about' on its wide lawn. High above a small spa town near Grenoble, in a wooded sub-Alpine setting, it has superb views from some rooms (most have a balcony). 'Ours did not have much furniture, but there was a well-fitted bathroom, separate loo, plenty of hot water and a view of the Vercors.' On the spacious garden terrace, tables are grouped round a pond under plane trees. 'The bright, attractive restaurant deserves its excellent local reputation. There was a happy hum of well-behaved conversation. The cooking was thoughtful, confident and accurate. For *demi-pension* guests, a four-course menu is recited. If the prospect of something displeases, there may be a choice. Nothing displeased us.' Specialities include marbré de foie gras et d'artichauts, senteur noisette; filet de sandre, sauce à l'échalotte. 'Service was observant. A family member is always in front-of-house.' The swimming pool is surrounded by parasols and loungers. 'In this very French area, we heard only one other English voice in nine days.' (*Gareth and Ros Gunning, and others*)

Open 1 Feb–20 Oct. Restaurant closed Sun night/Mon midday/Tues, and Mon night Feb–Apr. **Rooms** 33 double. **Facilities** Restaurant; 2 conference rooms. No background music. Garden: terrace, heated swimming pool, table tennis, *boules*. Tennis, riding, mountain walks, winter sports nearby. Unsuitable for ♿. **Location** 11 km SE of Grenoble, 1 km NE of Uriage. Parking. **Restrictions** No smoking in restaurant. No dogs. **Credit cards** Amex, MasterCard, Visa. **Terms** Room €54–€66. Breakfast €7.50. D,B&B €53–€59 per person. Set meals €22–€50; full alc €40.

> Please never tell a hotel you intend to send a report to the *Guide*. Anonymity is essential for objectivity.

VACQUEYRAS 84190 Vaucluse Map 6:D3

Hôtel Montmirail BUDGET
Montmirail

Tel 04.90.65.84.01
Fax 04.90.65.81.50
Email hotel-montmirail@wanadoo.fr
Website www.hotelmontmirail.com

In a 'delightful location' near Vacqueyras, at the head of a wooded ravine below the rocky Dentelles de Montmirail, this 19th-century building was once a spa centre. 'We once again enjoyed its friendly atmosphere,' says a visitor returning in 2004. 'The food and wine remain good.' The 'charming' owner, Marc Nicolet, 'never stops working, whether clearing the table before breakfast or waiting at table in the evening'. Jean Padilla's no-choice *menu du jour* is served under an ancient plane tree on a lovely dining terrace by the swimming pool, or in a rustic dining room with Provençal fabrics. (*Terry Herbert, and others*)

Open Mid-Mar–end Oct. Restaurant closed Thurs midday, Sat midday. **Rooms** 32 double, 7 single. Some on ground floor. **Facilities** Salon, restaurant; conference room. No background music. 3-hectare garden: heated swimming pool. **Location** E of Vacqueyras, 6 km S of Gigondas. Guarded parking. **Credit cards** MasterCard, Visa. **Terms** [2004] Room: single €52–€57, double €72–€99. Breakfast €8.50. D,B&B €58–€93.50 per person. Set meals €20–€33; full alc €48.

VAISON-LA-ROMAINE 84110 Vaucluse Map 6:C3

Hostellerie le Beffroi BUDGET
Rue de l'Évêché

Tel 04.90.36.04.71
Fax 04.90.36.24.78
Email contact@le-beffroi.com
Website www.le-beffroi.com

This old town has fascinating Roman remains, not public buildings but patrician villas, shops, a bridge and an amphitheatre; nearby is the modern section, with shops and restaurants. To the south, across the River Ouvèze, the *Haute Ville* is the medieval quarter with narrow, winding streets, entered by a 14th-century gateway. Here, Yann and Christine Christiansen are the owner/managers (the family has presided for over 50 years) of a conversion of 16th/17th-century houses. 'Quiet and comfortable', according to recent visitors, it has 'lovely rooms, lovely views, reasonable prices'. The restaurant serves dishes like scampi salad and foie gras ravioli; rabbit roasted with sea-salt crystals, caramelised with white wine. 'Our breakfast tray was brought to our room up a stone spiral staircase. Furniture and decoration are good.' There is a pretty garden, a swimming pool, a salad bar on the terrace in summer, and a tea room. Parking is at the foot of the old city. Local attractions include the medieval villages of Séguret and Crestet.

Open End Mar–end Jan. Restaurant open Apr–Oct; closed midday, except Sat, Sun, Tues in summer. **Rooms** 1 suite, 18 double, 3 single. In 2 buildings. **Facilities** Salon, bar, tea room, restaurant; classical background music; conference facilities. Garden: terrace, swimming pool. Unsuitable for ♿. **Location** *Haute Ville*, near Beffroi arch. 27 km NE of Orange. 11 parking spaces in front of hotel; garage at foot of old city. **Credit cards** All major cards accepted. **Terms** [2004] Room €68–€125. Breakfast €10. D,B&B €72–€112 per person. Set meals €26–€41.

VALENCE 26000 Drôme — Map 6:B3

Pic
285 avenue Victor Hugo

Tel 04.75.44.15.32
Fax 04.75.40.96.03
Email pic@relaischateaux.com
Website www.pic-valence.com

In a shady garden on the edge of this Rhône valley town, this famous restaurant-with-rooms (Relais & Châteaux) was founded by Sophie Pic almost a century ago. Now, her great-granddaughter, Anne-Sophie, is chef, continuing the tradition of this 'gourmand dynasty' (Anne-Sophie's father, Jacques, was one of the great masters of modern French cuisine). She wins two *Michelin* stars, 17 *Gault Millau* points for, eg, filet de bœuf et foie gras. Her husband, David Sinapian, is director. 'Dinner was brilliant, inventive, beautifully served in an attractive room,' one couple wrote. 'Anne and David, much in evidence, both delightful, speak good English.' Others admired the 'warm and generous ambience', the 'excellent service' and the 'superb wines'. The bedrooms, finely decorated, are 'comfortable, practical and quiet, very good for a short stay'. Each has a marble bathroom; many have a balcony overlooking a courtyard where meals are served. Breakfast, which comes with a bottle of *marc*, is also praised. Across the garden, the family has a second, simpler restaurant, *L'Auberge du Pin*, with rustic cuisine.

Open All year, except 3–22 Jan. Restaurant closed Sun night/Mon/Tues Nov–Mar. **Rooms** 3 suites, 10 double, 2 single. Some on ground floor. 1 equipped for ♿. Air conditioning. **Facilities** Lift, ramps. 2 lounges (1 no-smoking, 1 with billiards), bar, restaurant (no-smoking); background music; 2 conference rooms. Garden: terrace, unheated swimming pool. **Location** 1 km S of centre. *Autoroute* A7 exit Valence Sud; follow signs for *Centre Ville*. Free underground garage. **Credit cards** All major cards accepted. **Terms** Room €145–€280, suite €280–€350. Breakfast €23. Set meals €52–€145; alc €130.

VALLERAUGUE 30570 Gard — Map 6:C1

Hôtel Les Bruyères BUDGET — *Tel/Fax* 04.67.82.20.06
Rue André Chamson

At confluence of Hérault and Clarou rivers: former coaching inn, now informal Logis de France, run by friendly Bastide family, in untouristy village in narrow, steep-sided valley, 22 km N of Le Vigan. 'Good atmosphere; pleasant staff.' 'Our large bedroom was peaceful and typically French. Dinner was simple, breakfast was good,' say visitors in 2004. Café/bar, restaurant, 'charming' covered dining terrace. Garden: swimming pool. Garage. MasterCard, Visa accepted. Open 1 May–30 Sept. 24 bedrooms (some no-smoking): €52–€60. Breakfast €7. D,B&B €46–€67 per person. Set meals €15–€30.

VALROS 34990 Hérault Map 6:D1

Auberge de la Tour BUDGET *Tel* 04.67.98.52.01
N113 *Fax* 04.67.98.65.31

In 2 buildings, separated by garden with swimming pool, on busy N9, 18 km NE of Béziers, 62 km SW of Montpellier: M. and Mme Grasset's 'relatively modern' Logis de France, popular with golfers. 'Cheap and cheerful, with better food than one would expect; fantastically convenient location, agreeably shaded terrace.' Bar, TV room, restaurant. 'Wines from local vigneron, *attractively priced.' Closed holidays and Wed. MasterCard, Visa accepted. 18 bedrooms (with balcony or terrace; 'basic, but adequate, cool in summer'; some on ground floor; all face garden): €48–€55. Breakfast €6. D,B&B €47–€50 per person. Set meals €16–€38 [2004].*

VARENGEVILLE-SUR-MER 76119 Seine-Maritime Map 3:E1

Hotel-Restaurant de la Terrasse BUDGET *Tel* 02.35.85.12.54
Route de Vasterival *Fax* 02.35.85.11.70
Email francois.delafontaine@wanadoo.fr
Website www.hotel-restaurant-la-terrasse.com

A short drive west of Dieppe, this village has 'solid, would-be bourgeois *châteaux* and one of France's best gardens' (the Parc Floral des Moutiers, partly designed by Lutyens). Here, Anne and François Delafontaine's Logis de France is reached 'along a steep, narrow road leading to a dramatic position on top of chalk cliffs'. The gabled white building (1902), in a large shady garden, 'has a relaxed summer holiday atmosphere: shrimping nets by the entrance, donkey and ponies in the field below'. The 'delightfully traditional' panoramic restaurant ('looped curtains, solid wooden chairs') serves 'very reasonably priced' food, says a trusted *Guide* correspondent (emphasis on seafood, eg, fish stew with saffron; sole Dieppoise). There are 'several wines at under £10' and 'no canned music, a great relief'. The bedrooms are 'cheerfully, simply done with nice fabrics'; sea-facing ones cost the most. 'Not super-luxury, but a good bed, adequate furniture including a vast wardrobe, a spacious bathroom. All was spotless.' There is a terrace for alfresco meals. A shingle beach is ten minutes' walk away, down a steep path. (*Michael Bourdeaux, and others*)

Open 15 Mar–15 Oct. **Rooms** 4 family, 18 double. **Facilities** TV lounge, restaurant, dining terrace; conference facilities. No background music. Garden: tennis. **Location** 3 km NW of Varengeville, at Vasterival, 12 km W of Dieppe. **Credit cards** MasterCard, Visa. **Terms** [2004] D,B&B €45–€50. Set meals €16–€30.

The international dialling codes for the countries represented in this volume are at the end of the book.

VELLUIRE 85770 Vendée Map 4:A3

Auberge de la Rivière

Tel 02.51.52.32.15
Fax 02.51.52.37.42

'A blissfully quiet retreat', 'an idyllic spot', Robert and Luce Pajot's rustic restaurant-with-rooms (Logis de France) is on the north-west edge of the Marais Poitevin (*Venise Verte*). It stands on the banks of a small river in a 'sleepy, nondescript' village. Local fishermen supply produce for the kitchen. There are two limited-choice menus and a short *carte*, with dishes like huîtres spéciales d'Oléron; pigeonneau aux morilles. 'The dining room facing the river was pleasant,' say visitors in 2004. Other guests found Monsieur 'welcoming, charming, always bustling to carry cases, serve at table, etc'. Some visitors found service slow at mealtimes, but 'everything was fresh and cooked to order. Breakfast was most civilised'. Most bedrooms also look over the water. 'Ours was simply, but adequately, furnished; its bathroom was splendidly lit.' (*Hilary Rubinstein, Dennis and Janet Allom, and others*)

Open 2 Mar–20 Dec. Closed Sun night/Mon except Mon night July/Aug. **Rooms** 11 double. 9 in annexe. **Facilities** Bar, restaurant. No background music. By river, fishing. Bicycle hire. Unsuitable for ♿. **Location** 11 km SW of Fontenay-le-Comte, by D938 and D68. **Credit cards** MasterCard, Visa. **Terms** Room €75–€94. Breakfast €11. D,B&B €86–€106 per person. Set meals €36–€48; full alc €64.

VENCE 06140 Alpes-Maritimes Map 6:D5

Hôtel Cantemerle
258 chemin Cantemerle

Tel 04.93.58.08.18
Fax 04.93.58.32.89
Email info@hotelcantemerle.com
Website www.hotelcantemerle.com

Owned by Christine Dayan, this 'very peaceful' hotel has Art Deco-inspired decor. It stands on a hill amid pine trees, in a well-kept garden with swimming pool (where snacks are served in summer). 'It is architecturally pleasing, in Provençal style,' say recent visitors, 'and comfortably equipped for good-weather living.' The solarium, with indoor pool and hammam, overlooks the Mediterranean. The lounge, bar and restaurant open on to a large terrace. A limited dinner menu is served (eg, asperges tièdes à l'œuf poché; dorade grillée, émincée d'artichauds violets), and many restaurants are nearby. Most bedrooms are duplex, with terrace. 'Staff are pleasant.' (*GC*)

Open Easter–mid-Oct. Restaurant closed Mon except July/Aug. **Rooms** 17 suites, 10 double. 9 in annexe. Air conditioning. **Facilities** Reception lounge, lounge, bar, restaurant; background music; function facilities; indoor swimming pool, hammam; terrace. 1-hectare grounds: unheated swimming pool. Sea 15 mins' drive. Unsuitable for ♿. **Location** Central. Cagnes-sur-Mer exit off A8. Parking. **Credit cards** Amex, MasterCard, Visa. **Terms** Room: double €170–€190, suite €195–€265. Breakfast €15. D,B&B €48 added per person. Set meals €40; full alc €58. *V*

VERGÈZE 30310 Gard — Map 6:D2

La Passiflore BUDGET
1 rue Neuve
Tel 04.66.35.00.00
Fax 04.66.35.09.21

In a pretty village between Nîmes and Montpellier, Anthony and Linda Booth run this Logis de France, a renovated, creeper-covered, old farmhouse. All the air-conditioned bedrooms face the central courtyard or a garden: some are small; two have been refurbished this year. The 'sheer cosiness' and good value are praised. The 'above-average' dinner, cooked by Mrs Booth, is served by candlelight, in the 'delightful small dining room' with its large fireplace, or in the courtyard in summer. The set menu has five choices for each stage (main courses include noisettes d'agneau et son jus parfumé au romarin, or magret de canard, sauce Calvados. There is also a *carte*. Regional wines, many costing less than €20, dominate the short list. The host is 'entertaining, helpful, very professional'.

Open All year. Restaurant closed midday, 2 Oct–30 Mar, Sun/Mon. **Rooms** 11 double. 1 on ground floor. Air conditioning. **Facilities** Lounge, breakfast room, restaurant (classical background music). Courtyard (meal service), garden. **Location** Centre of village. 20 km SW of Nîmes. Parking. **Restriction** No smoking in breakfast room. **Credit cards** Amex, MasterCard, Visa. **Terms** Room €43–€62. Breakfast €7. D,B&B (min. 3 days): single €68–€86, double €100–€118. Set dinner €26; full alc €40.

VERTEILLAC 24320 Dordogne — Map 4:B4

La Guide
Cherval
Tel/Fax 05.53.91.53.54

Guests this year at Pat and Geoffrey Burnstone's guest house, deep in the Périgord Blanc, in a hamlet west of Brantôme, found it 'wonderfully relaxing, with friendly owners'. A former stone farmhouse, complete with *pigeonnier*, it is run with 'a charming mix of hospitality and privacy which allowed us to enjoy the quiet of the countryside'. The best accommodation is in the Barn House, with galleried bedroom, large sitting room, books, magazines. 'Outside, a hammock hung between a wild plum and a walnut tree.' 'As we sat by the pool we were brought grapes from the vine, and invited to help ourselves to figs from two huge trees in the garden.' Dinner (by arrangement) is served 'under the starry sky' or in the 'splendid dining room': home-grown organic produce is much used. There are several restaurants in the area, some rooms have a kitchenette, and there is a barbecue. At night, bats and owls can be heard. (*H Haddon, MH*)

Open 7 May–15 Oct. **Rooms** 7 double. In 3 buildings. 2 on ground floor. All no-smoking. **Facilities** 2 sitting rooms, TV room, dining room. No background music. 0.8-hectare garden (outdoor dining): 12 by 6-metre heated swimming pool. Free bicycles. Tennis, riding, lake nearby. Parking. Unsuitable for ♿. **Location** 4 km N of Verteillac, 15 km N of Ribérac. **Restrictions** No smoking. No dogs in bedrooms. **Credit cards** None accepted. **Terms** (Min. 3 nights; weekly July/Aug) B&B double €68–€96. Dinner (with aperitif and wine) €29.

VÉZELAY 89450 Yonne Map 5:C2

L'Espérance
St-Père-sous-Vézelay

Tel 03.86.33.39.10
Fax 03.86.33.26.15
Email marc.meneau@wanadoo.fr
Website www.marc-meneau-esperance.com

'Very good, expensive but commensurate with the degree of perfection offered.' Regular correspondents' praise for Marc Meneau's famous restaurant/hotel (Relais & Châteaux, 3 *Michelin* stars – one more this year, 18 *Gault Millau* points). Outside this hilltop hamlet (superb Romanesque abbey church), it is in three buildings separated by a road. The original *Espérance*, surrounded by trees and gardens, is an imposing house with '*chambres bourgeoises*'; *Le Moulin*, rustic and creeper-covered, is a former mill house; *Le Pré des Marguerites* is modern, with larger rooms than the others. 'Ours, sober in style, painted pale pink, had a well-equipped bathroom.' Other visitors said: 'Our room was well fitted, but things were well hidden. We hunted for towels, pillows and the minibar.' 'Monsieur, mellow and hefty, and Madame, pencil-slim and brisk', are much in evidence, and the food 'defies description', says a guest who enjoyed baby red snapper with a concassé of orange and tomato; 'historic' Bresse pigeon; 'cheeses in prime condition; the ultimate tray of petits fours'. Meneau's wine from his own vineyard 'was the cheapest on a staggering list'. (*Francine and Ian Walsh, and others*)

Open Early Mar–end Jan. Restaurant closed Tues (except evening high season), Wed midday. **Rooms** 6 suites, 20 double. In 3 buildings. Some air conditioned. **Facilities** Salon, bar, restaurant (air conditioning); conference room. Garden: terrace, swimming pool. Unsuitable for ♿. **Location** 3 km SE of Vézelay. Parking. **Credit cards** All major cards accepted. **Terms** [2004] Room €70–€250, suite €180–€385. Breakfast €25–€30. D,B&B €150–€200 per person. Set lunch (with wine) €87, dinner €127–€170.

Résidence Hôtel Le Pontot
Place du Pontot

Tel 03.86.33.24.40
Fax 03.86.33.30.05

Surrounded by a bucolic patchwork of vineyards and sunflower fields, this walled medieval town is one of France's architectural gems. A block away from the Romanesque Basilique Ste-Madeleine is this 'very special' B&B. A 15th-century fortified house, with tower and walled flower garden, it is owned and run by Christian Abadie, who, say admirers, 'takes enormous trouble with his guests'. Bedrooms vary in size: some are up a stone-flagged spiral stairway; some have antiques; one has an old oven. 'Our big room, down the road in a *dépendance*, had an ancient fireplace, old kitchen pans, modern bathroom; views over the hills.' A 'simple but delicious breakfast' is served on blue-and-gold Limoges china, in a blue-panelled Louis XVI salon or alfresco. Guests can arrive by helicopter, and hot-air ballooning and canal-boat cruises can be arranged. Recommended for meals: *St-Étienne* and *L'Auberge de la Coquille* nearby, and Marc Meneau's luxurious *L'Espérance* (*Michelin* three stars, see previous entry) at the foot of the hill.

Open 15 Apr–15 Oct. **Rooms** 3 suites, 8 double, 2 single. **Facilities** Salon, bar, breakfast room. No background music. Garden: bar. Unsuitable for ♿. **Location** Central. Public car park adjacent; private parking by reservation. **Restriction** No children under 8. **Credit cards** Diners, MasterCard, Visa. **Terms** Room €105–€180, suite €160–€180. Breakfast €12.

VILLARD-ST-SAUVEUR 39200 Jura — Map 5:E4

Au Retour de la Chasse NEW/BUDGET
St-Claude

Tel 03.84.45.44.44
Fax 03.84.45.13.95
Email retour-de-la-chasse@wanadoo.fr
Website www.golf-saint-claude.com

'A reminder that France can do good food without pretension or fuss, at a good price': this Logis de France is part of a cluster of steep-roofed houses on the eastern side of the valley of the Tacon, across which the quiet main road to St-Claude is hidden in trees. Adjacent is St-Claude's golf club; nearby are skiing, walking, canyoning and much else for the active guest. 'The building is gaunt and rather tall,' says the nominator. 'Arriving on a hot afternoon, we were struck by the silence. Our annexe room was a splendid mix of brown carpeted walls, wallpapered ceiling, pink plastic-topped furniture, comfortable bed and clean shower room.' Gérard Vuillermoz is the chef/*patron*; his wife, Anny ('charming and hospitable'), is front-of-house. 'Dinner was excellent. Everything done with quiet pride. Huge amounts of food for our €32 menu, starting with Tatin of shellfish and vegetables, unusual and fresh. The restaurant decor is uncoordinated mayhem, rather dark, with stone floors and walls, pink tablecloths, but when filled with diners, it has a homely feel. Breakfast was adequate. Some people might think this too simple, but it was great for a night stop (less than £120).' (*Carie Roots*)

Open Mid-Feb–mid-Jan. Closed Sun night/Mon/Tues midday. **Rooms** 14. Some in annexe. **Facilities** Restaurant; meeting room. **Location** 4 km S of St-Claude by D290, 60 km NW of Geneva. Parking. **Credit cards** Amex, MasterCard, Visa. **Terms** [2004] Room €50–€65. Breakfast €5.50. D,B&B €52 per person.

LA VILLE-AUX-CLERCS 41160 Loir-et-Cher — Map 2:F5

Le Manoir de la Forêt
Fort-Girard

Tel 02.54.80.62.83
Fax 02.54.80.66.03
Email manoirdelaforet@wanadoo.fr

Between Orléans and Le Mans, outside village 18 km N of Vendôme: handsome, ivy-covered 19th-century former hunting lodge of Duc de La Rochefoucauld, now owned by Maryse and Guy Redon. Reached down side road past a lake, in beautiful valley. 'Suitable for stop-over, good value, good atmosphere, lovely setting.' Bedrooms pleasant, though decor 'a bit passé*'. Elegant dining room, wide dining terrace;* 'cuisine classique'*; meeting room. 2-hectare wooded grounds.*

Unsuitable for ♿. Amex, MasterCard, Visa accepted. Closed Sun night/Mon Oct–Easter. 18 bedrooms: €51–€73. Breakfast €9. D,B&B €76 per person. Set meals €26–€46 [2004].

VILLEDIEU-LES-POÊLES 50800 Manche **Map 2:E3**

Manoir de l'Acherie NEW/BUDGET *Tel* 02.33.51.13.87
Rue Michel de l'Épinay, L'Acherie *Fax* 02.33.51.33.69
Ste-Cécile *Email* manoir@manoir-acherie.fr

Amid quiet Normandy farmland NE of Avranches: M. and Mme Bernard Cahu's restaurant-with-rooms (Logis de France, Michelin Bib Gourmand*), 2 km E of village by N175/D554. 17th-century manor house and small chapel grouped around flowery garden. Rustic interior;* cuisine du terroir. *'Excellent meat (owner is a retired butcher), nice family atmosphere, warm, comfortable rooms, reasonable prices,' say regular visitors. Closed 14 Feb–2 Mar, 1–17 Nov, Sun night Oct–Easter, Mon except evenings 11 July–31 Aug. Amex, Visa accepted. No dogs. 15 bedrooms: €36–€58. Breakfast €6.50. D,B&B €57–€65 per person. Set meals €16–€34 [2004].*

VILLEFRANCHE-SUR-MER 06231 Alpes-Maritimes **Map 6:D5**

Hôtel Welcome *Tel* 04.93.76.27.62
3 quai Amiral Courbet *Fax* 04.93.76.27.66
Email guide@welcomehotel.com
Website www.welcomehotel.com

Between Nice and Monte Carlo, this 'impeccable hotel', owned by Gérard Galbois, has been totally refurbished over the last few years. It stands opposite the fishermen's chapel decorated by Cocteau. 'He wrote *Orphée* in the *Welcome*,' says a reader, 'and his shadow lies long across it, with pictures, sketches, even a mosaic signature on the lobby floor.' All bedrooms face the bay and Cap Ferrat; some are small, but all have a balcony. 'Our large room had three easy chairs, and a view across the bay to the fabulous Rothschild villa.' Another room was pale blue with 'jolly striped curtains, newly done bathroom'. There is a wine bar. Breakfast is a buffet. No restaurant, but there are 12 nearby, ranging from 'casual' to 'refined'. *Mère Germaine*, and *L'Échalote* (12 *Gault Millau* points), both medium-priced, are liked. There is a popular diving club in front of the hotel. Villefranche is a 'gem' of a town, and there's an 'excellent coastal walk on paved footpaths westward'. (*C and SW, LB*)

Open 23 Dec–11 Nov. **Rooms** 2 suites, 32 double, 2 single. 2 no-smoking. 2 suitable for ♿. Air conditioning. **Facilities** Lift. Salon, wine bar (background music); veranda. **Location** From A8, exits 50/58 go towards main square; follow signs: Plages, Chapelle St-Pierre. Garage, on reservation, €12–€16. **Credit cards** All major cards accepted. **Terms** [2004] Room: single €62–€82, double €85–€184, suite €220–€330. Breakfast €12.

THE 2005 GOOD HOTEL GUIDE

Use this voucher to claim a 25% discount off the normal price for bed and breakfast at hotels with a *V* sign at the end of their entry. **You must request a voucher discount at the time of booking and present this voucher on arrival. Further details and conditions overleaf.** Valid to 12th January 2006.

THE 2005 GOOD HOTEL GUIDE

Use this voucher to claim a 25% discount off the normal price for bed and breakfast at hotels with a *V* sign at the end of their entry. **You must request a voucher discount at the time of booking and present this voucher on arrival. Further details and conditions overleaf.** Valid to 12th January 2006.

THE 2005 GOOD HOTEL GUIDE

Use this voucher to claim a 25% discount off the normal price for bed and breakfast at hotels with a *V* sign at the end of their entry. **You must request a voucher discount at the time of booking and present this voucher on arrival. Further details and conditions overleaf.** Valid to 12th January 2006.

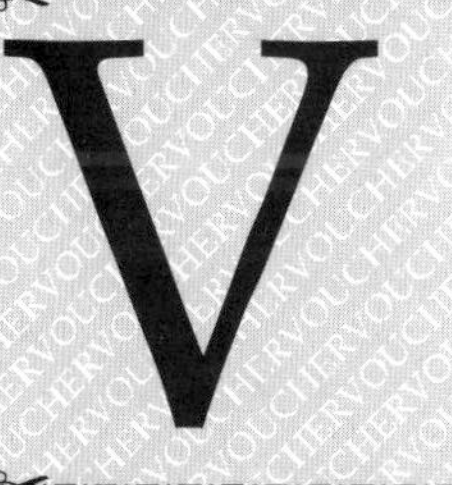

THE 2005 GOOD HOTEL GUIDE

Use this voucher to claim a 25% discount off the normal price for bed and breakfast at hotels with a *V* sign at the end of their entry. **You must request a voucher discount at the time of booking and present this voucher on arrival. Further details and conditions overleaf.** Valid to 12th January 2006.

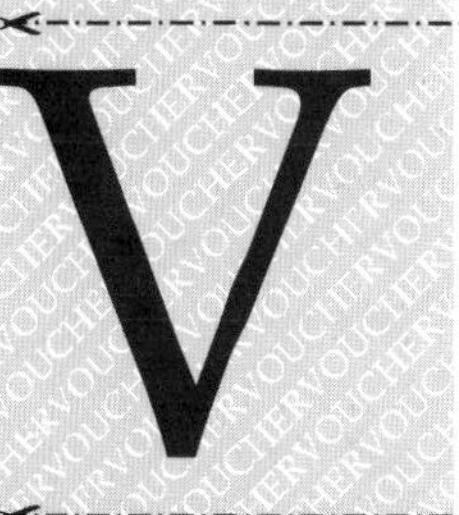

THE 2005 GOOD HOTEL GUIDE

Use this voucher to claim a 25% discount off the normal price for bed and breakfast at hotels with a *V* sign at the end of their entry. **You must request a voucher discount at the time of booking and present this voucher on arrival. Further details and conditions overleaf.** Valid to 12th January 2006.

THE 2005 GOOD HOTEL GUIDE

Use this voucher to claim a 25% discount off the normal price for bed and breakfast at hotels with a *V* sign at the end of their entry. **You must request a voucher discount at the time of booking and present this voucher on arrival. Further details and conditions overleaf.** Valid to 12th January 2006.

CONDITIONS

1. Hotels with a ***V*** have undertaken to give readers a discount of 25% off their normal bed-and-breakfast rate (or their room rate if breakfast is charged separately). You will be expected to pay full prices for other meals and all other services.
2. You may use one voucher for a single-night stay or for a longer visit, and for yourself alone or for a partner sharing your room. But you will need two vouchers if you are booking more than one room.
3. Participating hotels may refuse a voucher reservation if they expect to be fully booked at the full room price nearer the time, or accept a voucher for one night only.

CONDITIONS

1. Hotels with a ***V*** have undertaken to give readers a discount of 25% off their normal bed-and-breakfast rate (or their room rate if breakfast is charged separately). You will be expected to pay full prices for other meals and all other services.
2. You may use one voucher for a single-night stay or for a longer visit, and for yourself alone or for a partner sharing your room. But you will need two vouchers if you are booking more than one room.
3. Participating hotels may refuse a voucher reservation if they expect to be fully booked at the full room price nearer the time, or accept a voucher for one night only.

CONDITIONS

1. Hotels with a ***V*** have undertaken to give readers a discount of 25% off their normal bed-and-breakfast rate (or their room rate if breakfast is charged separately). You will be expected to pay full prices for other meals and all other services.
2. You may use one voucher for a single-night stay or for a longer visit, and for yourself alone or for a partner sharing your room. But you will need two vouchers if you are booking more than one room.
3. Participating hotels may refuse a voucher reservation if they expect to be fully booked at the full room price nearer the time, or accept a voucher for one night only.

CONDITIONS

1. Hotels with a ***V*** have undertaken to give readers a discount of 25% off their normal bed-and-breakfast rate (or their room rate if breakfast is charged separately). You will be expected to pay full prices for other meals and all other services.
2. You may use one voucher for a single-night stay or for a longer visit, and for yourself alone or for a partner sharing your room. But you will need two vouchers if you are booking more than one room.
3. Participating hotels may refuse a voucher reservation if they expect to be fully booked at the full room price nearer the time, or accept a voucher for one night only.

CONDITIONS

1. Hotels with a ***V*** have undertaken to give readers a discount of 25% off their normal bed-and-breakfast rate (or their room rate if breakfast is charged separately). You will be expected to pay full prices for other meals and all other services.
2. You may use one voucher for a single-night stay or for a longer visit, and for yourself alone or for a partner sharing your room. But you will need two vouchers if you are booking more than one room.
3. Participating hotels may refuse a voucher reservation if they expect to be fully booked at the full room price nearer the time, or accept a voucher for one night only.

CONDITIONS

1. Hotels with a ***V*** have undertaken to give readers a discount of 25% off their normal bed-and-breakfast rate (or their room rate if breakfast is charged separately). You will be expected to pay full prices for other meals and all other services.
2. You may use one voucher for a single-night stay or for a longer visit, and for yourself alone or for a partner sharing your room. But you will need two vouchers if you are booking more than one room.
3. Participating hotels may refuse a voucher reservation if they expect to be fully booked at the full room price nearer the time, or accept a voucher for one night only.

VILLENEUVE-LÈS-AVIGNON 30400 Gard — Map 6:D2

Le Prieuré
7 place du Chapître

Tel 04.90.15.90.15
Fax 04.90.25.45.39
Email leprieure@relaischateaux.com
Website www.leprieure.fr

On the west bank of the Rhône, this historic little town above Avignon has a splendid charterhouse and other noble buildings, including this 14th-century priory, now a luxurious hotel (Relais & Châteaux). Owned by Marie-France Mille, and managed by her 'charming son', François, it stands in a big flower-scented garden with a spacious swimming pool and shady dining patio. 'We had a great stay,' says a visitor this year. 'Excellent food, which we ate in the courtyard. But we had to include the *sommelier* in our toast to absent friends: he was preoccupied by a small conference.' Others wrote: 'Dinner is serious: an army of waiters and waitresses.' Serge Chenet, the chef for 17 years, wins a *Michelin* star, 16 *Gault Millau* points for, eg, méli-mélo de légumes au jus de rôti; carré d'agneau en croûte. There is a 'fine dessert trolley', and a 'splendid' array of breads. Breakfast is a buffet. Two old buildings, approached on foot down a long rose arbour, contain the public rooms, 'all charming', with some antiques; but their bedrooms are quite small. The '70s annexe, the *Atrium*, has large rooms of quality, many with balcony. Some train noise at night. (*Michael Hague, and others*)

Open 19 Mar–31 Oct. Restaurant closed Tues/Wed except July/Aug. **Rooms** 10 suites, 26 double. In 3 buildings. 2 no-smoking. Air conditioning. **Facilities** Lift. 4 lounges, library, TV room, restaurant; dining patio; conference facilities. Garden: unheated swimming pool, tennis. **Location** Central, behind church. 3 km N of Avignon. Secure parking. **Credit cards** All major cards accepted. **Terms** [2004] Room: single €95, double €120–€220, suite €248–€295. Breakfast €16. Set lunch €36, dinner €60–€88.

VILLENEUVE-SUR-YONNE 89500 Yonne — Map 5:C2

La Lucarne aux Chouettes
Quai Bretoche

Tel 03.86.87.18.26
Fax 03.86.87.22.63
Email lesliecaron-auberge@wanadoo.fr
Website www.lesliecaron-auberge.com

A 'delightful' small *auberge*, stylish, but not posh, created by the actress Leslie Caron from four 17th-century boat houses on the Yonne. 'The Owl's Nest' is in an attractive little town with honey-coloured stone buildings in northern Burgundy, where Mme Caron lives part of the year. She 'sometimes invites herself to stay': when she does, she chats to guests and keeps an eye on the garden. The conversion has kept the old character: stones, beams, flagged floors and old tiles. One suite has a river view and a portrait of Sarah Bernhardt above the bed. In the 'superb' dining room, created from a 17th-century warehouse, you can eat by a fire under a vaulted ceiling. Summer meals are on a riverside terrace with parasols. Dominique Inagaki is manager; her husband, the chef, Daïsuke Inagaki, is

Japanese: his dishes are mainly French, sometimes with oriental overtones (eg, brochettes de lotte façon 'Yakitori'). 'The food is excellent; service is good and friendly.' 'A bargain.' (*Marshall S Harris, and others*)

Open Mid-Dec–mid-Nov. Closed Sun, Mon. Restaurant open for lunch Christmas, New Year. **Rooms** 3 suites, 1 double. **Facilities** Bar/salon (background music), restaurant. Riverside dining terrace; bathing, fishing, boating; bicycles available. Unsuitable for ♿. **Location** Central, by bridge. 13 km S of Sens. **Credit cards** MasterCard, Visa. **Terms** Room €95–€135, suite €155. Breakfast €10. Set meals €19–€36.

VINAY 51530 Marne — Map 5:A2

Hostellerie La Briqueterie
4 route de Sézanne

Tel 03.26.59.99.99
Fax 03.26.59.92.10
Email info@labriqueterie.com
Website www.labriqueterie.com

In champagne country, near Épernay, this luxurious hotel, surrounded by a lovely landscaped garden and vineyards, is 'highly recommended' by recent guests. Owned by the Trouillard family, it is built on the site of an old brickworks in neo-rustic style ('with old wooden fairground horses, the odd antique'). It stands at the apex of two roads, one a busy *route nationale*. In the beamed restaurant, with large fireplace and elegant table settings, the chef, Christophe Bernard, has a *Michelin* star for, eg, gaspacho de légumes glacés et petite tartare de homard et concombre; suprême de poulet fermier, pané aux herbes. The most expensive menu, the *Trentenaire* (€85), includes champagne. Glass-plated corridors give a sense of light and space. 'Our spacious, quiet room had a smart seating area, a large bathroom with generous toiletries. Breakfast was a copious buffet.' 'The welcome is charming and sophisticated.' You can play volleyball in the garden, and there is a large indoor swimming pool.

Open All year, except 21–26 Dec. **Rooms** 2 suites, 40 double. 2 on ground floor. Air-conditioning. **Facilities** Salon, bar, breakfast room, restaurant; classical background music; conference facilities; indoor swimming pool, sauna, gym. 6-hectare grounds: garden, table tennis, volleyball, *pétanque*; helipad. **Location** 5 km SW of Épernay towards Sézanne. Parking. **Credit cards** Amex, MasterCard, Visa. **Terms** [2004] Room: double €190–€220, suite €250. Breakfast €14. Set meals €40–€85.

VIRONVAY 27400 Eure — Map 2:D5

Les Saisons NEW

Tel 02.32.40.02.56
Fax 02.32.25.05.26
Website www.deauville-france.com/lessaisons

Two regular correspondents this year nominate this restaurant-with-rooms in a village south of Rouen. 'Wish we'd stayed longer,' one wrote. Another adds: 'We often come early or late in the year and enjoy the wood fire.' Owned by the 'jaw-droppingly handsome' Henry-Louis Portier, son of the founders, the former coaching inn stands in large, flowery grounds. The bedrooms are in cottages; each is different; the recent renovation is 'brilliant'. Dinner is served in a 'glamorous new building', or in the garden in warm weather. M. Portier's sophisticated Norman cuisine wins a *Michelin* star for, eg, soupière de crustacés et coquillages en croûte; pomme de ris de veau braisée aux légumes de saison; his 'elegant wife' is in charge of the dining room. 'One cannot resist the temptation to finish every meal with his tarte fine aux pommes et amandine – delicious!' Others found the food 'excellent, though pretty rich'. There is a 'large, attractive' swimming pool. Monet's garden at Giverny is within easy reach. (*Gillian and Richard Treen, Felix Singer*)

Open All year, except 16–26 Aug, 20–27 Dec; Sun night/Mon, Wed night 23 Feb–11 Mar. **Rooms** 4 suites, 10 double. In cottages. **Facilities** Salon, bar, restaurant; conference room. Garden: dining terrace, heated swimming pool, tennis. **Location** 5 km SE of Louviers, by N155. Parking. **Restriction** No dogs. **Credit cards** All major cards accepted. **Terms** [2004] Room €130–€185. Breakfast €12. Set meals €39–€54, alc €62–€80.

VONNAS 01540 Ain — Map 5:E3

Georges Blanc

Tel 04.74.50.90.90
Fax 04.74.50.08.80
Email blanc@relaischateaux.com
Website www.georgesblanc.com

'Worth going to France for,' was one comment on Georges Blanc's distinguished hotel/restaurant (Relais & Chateaux) in a village near Mâcon. The half-timbered *auberge*, in a garden by the River Veyle, was opened by his family in 1872: it is now a sizeable building with annexes and shops. The restaurant (with beams, tapestried chairs) has had three *Michelin* stars since 1981. *Gault Millau* awards 18 points. M. Blanc, with sons, Frédéric and Alexandre, cooks in local Bresse style (eg, embrouillade de grenouilles aux épices; poulet aux gousses d'ail). He 'is usually around, in ebullient form'. Mme Blanc's welcome is 'elegant'. 'Our table faced the river lit by the slanting rays of the evening sun. Atmosphere of calm efficiency. Our young waitress was informative and amusing. The wine list is daunting, but the house wine was excellent and reasonably priced.' The breakfast buffet is 'amazing'. Bedrooms and suites, many facing the river, are in the 'winter garden' area: the lounge has a log fire in winter and becomes a riverside terrace in summer. 'Standard of accommodation was high; the bathroom was neat and shiny.' Cheaper rooms, in *La Résidence des Saules*, are 'spacious, yet cosy'; each has a terrace facing the market square. M. Blanc's simpler eating place, *L'Ancienne Auberge* (*Michelin Bib Gourmand*), serves 'food as it used to be in rural France'. (*J and JH*)

Open All year, except Jan. Main restaurant closed Mon/Tues/Wed midday. **Rooms** 9 suites, 29 double. Also 10 in *Résidence des Saules*. Air conditioning. **Facilities** Lift. 2 lounges, bar, breakfast room, dining room; conference room; shops; winter garden/river terrace. No background music. Garden: heated swimming pool, tennis, mountain bikes; helipad. **Location** 20 km SE of Mâcon, *autoroute* A6 from N: exit Mâcon Nord; from S: exit Villefranche.

Parking. **Credit cards** All major cards accepted. **Terms** [2004] Room €150–€330 (*Saules* €110–€135), suite €360–€520. Breakfast €23. Set meals €98–€190.

WESTHALTEN 68250 Haut-Rhin — Map 5:C5

Auberge du Cheval Blanc
20 rue de Rouffach

Tel 03.89.47.01.16
Fax 03.89.47.64.40
Email chevalblanc.west@wanadoo.fr
Website www.auberge-chevalblc.com

'What a good stop-over,' say visitors in 2004. 'Super dinner, comfy room, lovely village.' Owned since 1785 by the wine-producing Koehler family ('much in evidence'), this cheerful restaurant-with-rooms stands in a 'pretty, peaceful' village amid the orchards and vineyards of the Vosges foothills. The panelled dining room, with low-beamed ceiling, is much patronised by locals. Gilbert Koehler wins a *Michelin* star, 14 *Gault Millau* points. 'Ten courses, all of them excellent.' 'Veal cutlets au jus truffé were spot on.' Madame Koehler is front-of-house: she and her staff are found 'charming', 'not over-formal'. Aperitifs are taken on a terrace with parasols. Breakfast, a generous buffet, includes local honey and cold meats. Bedroom decor is 'modern French floral'; the largest rooms, each with a big sliding window, are in an annexe. Lower ones have a little patio, upper ones a balcony and a view of farm animals. But a basement room was 'a bit dark', and another room had a 'poor outlook'. There are 'fantastic walks' around, and 'a *dégustation* in the family's *cave* is recommended'. (*Pat and Jeremy Temple*, *E and P Thompson, and others*)

Open All year, except Feb, 10 days end June, Sun night/Mon/Tues midday. **Rooms** 2 suites, 10 double. All in courtyard annexe. Some on ground floor. Air conditioning. **Facilities** Lift, ramp. 2 lounges, restaurant; conference room. No background music. Terrace, courtyard; outdoor dining. Tennis, swimming, horse riding nearby. **Location** Off N83, 21 km SW of Colmar, 10 km N of Guebwiller. Secure parking. **Credit cards** MasterCard, Visa. **Terms** [2004] Room €76–€87. Breakfast €11. Set meals €35–€72.

****

Traveller's tale Hotel in Germany. I booked a three-night stay at this hotel three months in advance. Our ground-floor room, whose broom-cupboard-like door opened straight on to Reception, was gloomy and depressing. Its two net-curtained windows faced a small street edged by a busy road, compromising privacy, peace and security in one hit. The air conditioning was ineffective: water trickled down the walls. We asked to be moved and were told: 'Not possible. You should have asked for a different room when booking.' I pointed out that I hadn't known the hotel before, and if they were intending to allocate such a poor room they should have had the courtesy to warn us. Breakfast was poor: staff were like museum pieces, and the manageress was more concerned with a dining room photo shoot (posing as a guest) than the guests themselves. We checked out.

****

WIERRE-EFFROY 62720 Pas-de-Calais Map 3:D2

La Ferme du Vert
Route du Paon

Tel 03.21.87.67.00
Fax 03.21.83.22.62
Email ferme.du.vert@wanadoo.fr
Website www.fermeduvert.com

Much loved by *Guide* readers, the Bernard family's farm guest house (Logis de France) has a pleasant rural setting near Boulogne and Calais. 'The accommodation and cooking continue to delight,' says one visitor this year. 'A first-class stop-over,' was another comment. It is good for a family holiday, too, having a piano for guests' use, a half-wild garden, a Labrador, a courtyard with pond, ducks and geese, doves, kittens and much else (see below). Dinner, in two rustic dining rooms (one has a large open fire), might include soupe de poisson et sa rouille; cuisse de canard à la bière. Cheeses are made by two of the four sons of the owners, using milk from a nearby farm. Dogs have now been banned from the restaurant. Some bedrooms are in converted barns; the best are large, smart rather than rustic; others are 'quaint and cosy'. Five new rooms, 'grand, traditional and comfortable', are in a 'very beautiful' château, five minutes' walk away, in a park. Breakfast, in a 'charming room', is a generous buffet. The facade was renovated this year and there is a new terrace. (*Peter Stattersfield, Anthony Rosen, and many others*)

Open 20 Jan–15 Dec. Closed Sun Nov–Mar. Restaurant closed Sun/Mon midday. **Rooms** 1 suite, 15 double. In 4 buildings. 3 on ground floor (1 suitable for ♿). **Facilities** Salon, bar, breakfast room, 2 dining rooms (background music); 2 conference rooms. Garden: terrace, table tennis, putting, mini-tennis; bicycle hire. **Location** A16 exit Marquise–Rinxent. From Marquise D238 to Wierre-Effroy; follow signs. **Restrictions** No smoking: breakfast room, 1 dining room, some bedrooms. No dogs in restaurant. **Credit cards** All major cards accepted. **Terms** [2004] Room: single €53–€84, double €58–€91, suite from €117. Breakfast €9. D,B&B (min. 2 nights) €57–€111 per person. Set meals €22–€39; full alc €35.

WIMEREUX 62930 Pas-de-Calais Map 3:D2

Atlantic Hôtel
& Restaurant La Liégeoise
Digue de Mer

Tel 03.21.32.41.01
Fax 03.21.87.46.17
Email reception.hotelatlantic@tiscali.fr
Website www.atlantic-delpierre.com

In this small seaside resort, close to busy Boulogne, Alain Delpierre's 'excellent' Art Deco-fronted hotel stands on the pedestrianised promenade on to which some of the sea-facing bedrooms lead. They have 'panoramic views', and 'enjoy radiant sunsets'. Visitors this year had a 'simple, but well-designed room with lots of space, lovely bathroom, sheltered balcony with seats and a table'. Another guest who arrived in the dark wrote: 'A sea view was unnecessary; my small, but comfortable room at the back was exceptional value.' One couple enjoyed 'breakfast on our balcony, with pretty Limoges china' and the 'fun marine decor': fish sculptures, shell-patterned bedspreads, etc. The elegant first-floor restaurant has huge picture windows facing the Channel. Most visitors think the seafood cuisine 'wonderful' (14 *Gault Millau* points for, eg, oysters on a bed of crushed garlic, tomatoes and courgette purée; sea bass with an almond and lemon zest crust), but one thought it 'competent, rather than spectacular'. Another found the service 'very slow'. Fish dishes and fruits de mer are also served in the downstairs brasserie, decorated in white and turquoise, which offers 'excellent value'. The wide, sandy beach is popular with French families. (*R and EU, Nigel Fletcher, David Ayres-Regan, and others*)

Open All year, except Feb. Restaurant closed Sun night/Mon midday. **Rooms** 18 double. **Facilities** Lift. Lounge, bar, 2 restaurants; conference room. **Location** On seafront. 6 km N of Boulogne. Secure parking. **Credit cards** All major cards accepted. **Terms** [2004] Room €70–€117. Breakfast €10. D,B&B €74–€118 per person. Set meals €32–€61.

YVOIRE 74140 Haute-Savoie — Map 5:E4

Hôtel Restaurant du Port

Tel 04.50.72.80.17
Fax 04.50.72.90.71
Email hotelduport.yvoire@wanadoo.fr
Website http://hotelrestaurant.port.online.fr

On the shore of Lake Geneva, in a 'delightful' medieval village, Jeannine and Jean-François Kung's chalet-style restaurant-with-rooms, with its flowery facade, was thought 'charming', and 'welcoming' by recent visitors. 'We loved our room. Cream and white, it had a little sitting area and a balcony overlooking the lake. Robes and slippers were provided in the wonderful bathroom. It was blissfully quiet, and we slept soundly. Food was superb.' The restaurant, which specialises in fish, and the terrace, surrounded by trees, also face the water. The large foyer, which doubles as bar and breakfast area, is 'well designed'. 'Not cheap, but worth it,' is one verdict. (*JR, and others*)

Open 2 Mar–1 Nov. Closed Wed off-season. **Rooms** 1 suite, 7 double (2 interconnecting). Air conditioning. **Facilities** Lift. Salon, bar, 3 dining rooms; conference room. 2 terraces on lake. **Location** In village. 30 km NE of Geneva. Cars allowed for access only (hotel arranges parking). **Restriction** No pets. **Credit cards** Amex, MasterCard, Visa. **Terms** [2004] Room €100–€190, suite €220–€280. Breakfast €10. Set meals €29–€45; alc €41.

YZEURES-SUR-CREUSE 37290 Indre-et-Loire — Map 4:A4

La Promenade BUDGET

1 place du 11 novembre

Tel 02.47.91.49.00
Fax 02.47.94.46.12
Website www.touraine-gourmande.com

'Usefully close to the A10', south of Tours, this is 'a delightful old inn, full of character', say visitors this year. A former *relais de poste* (1780), it stands on the quiet square of a small village at the border of Touraine,

Poitou and Berry. There are old beams, exposed stone, 'cosy sitting areas, charming soft furnishings'. Some bedrooms look over the village square: 'Ours was good; its window boxes were filled with flowering pansies.' Another guest loved her 'beamed loft room, spacious, very clean'. But one reader had a bathroom that was poorly maintained. 'In the pretty pink dining room, with candles and a huge fireplace, the wines are excellent, the food is delicious' (lobster and asparagus in spring and summer, wild game and mushrooms in autumn and winter, free-range poultry all year). Geneviève Bussereau, 'very friendly', is owner/chef; her 'chic, delightful' daughter, Sévérine, serves, and will advise on local sights. Breakfast, a buffet, has muesli, fresh juices, 'fabulous breads'. Many English guests (the hotel is used by an English tour operator). (*Janet and Dennis Allom, and others*)

Open 14 Feb–12 Jan. Closed to non-residents Mon/Tues. **Rooms** 15 double. **Facilities** Lounge, restaurant; background music. Unsuitable for ♿. **Location** By church. 25 km E of Châtellerault, 85 km S of Tours. Parking. **Credit cards** MasterCard, Visa. **Terms** [2004] Room €45–€52. Breakfast €9.50. Set meals €20–€47.

Germany

Der Eichenhof, Worpswede

Chain hotels are far less numerous in Germany than in Great Britain or the United States. The leading upmarket German chains are Maritim, with hotels in all the major cities, and Steigenberger. Their members are generally efficient but impersonal. Nearly all German hotels are individually owned and run, and many have charm and personality. Some group together, as in France, for joint marketing. The best of these associations is, perhaps, Romantik Hotels: many of its members are in old buildings of character. The Gast im Schloss association consists of converted castles, some still run by their family owners: several are in this book. Standards of hotels in former East Germany are rapidly improving.

Most German hotels have a friendly ambience, especially in rural areas. Standards of service are usually high. As in most of central Europe, duvets (*Federbetten*) are the norm. German beds tend to be rather hard, with small, thin pillows (this is considered healthy). Most double rooms have twin beds, often placed close together. Often, a chocolate or a sweet will be left on the pillow at night. Breakfast is generally a copious buffet, included in the room price. You need leave nothing extra for room service, though in a restaurant it is usual to give a tip of about three to five per cent to the waiter or waitress when paying the bill. Some hotels are now leaving credit card slips open for service to be added by the guest.

We indicate *Michelin*'s awards for cuisine. As John Ardagh, formerly editor of this chapter, wrote: 'At the top gourmet level, food in Germany may lag far behind France, but at the middle level, authentic German dishes are well cooked and presented, with interesting regional variations, and they come in robust portions.'

Wine is sold by the bottle or by the *Viertel* (a large glassful, equalling a quarter bottle) – useful for light drinkers, visitors on their own, or motorists.

AMORBACH 63916 Bavaria — Map 8:E2

Der Schafhof Amorbach
Schafhof 1

Tel (09373) 9 73 30
Fax (09373) 41 20
Email info@schafhof.de
Website www.schafhof.de

Amorbach is a small town with some baroque architecture, on the eastern slopes of the hilly Odenwald forest. Just outside it stands this former Benedictine monastery. 'A superior hotel with superior prices, comfort and food to match,' say visitors in 2004. Part of the Gast im Schloss group, it is owned by Vera Ullrich; her husband, Herbert, is manager. The setting, surrounded by woods and sheep, is peaceful. 'The *Schafhof* (sheep farm) motif is much in evidence (even the soap tablets are little sheep).' Two restaurants: the gourmet *Abt- & Schäferstube*, with chef Achim Krutsch, has a *Michelin* star. 'Excellent, delicate food'; 'impeccable service'. The *Benediktinerstube* serves local and Mediterranean dishes. There is a dining terrace with views. Bedrooms (most are spacious) have 'a high level of designer comfort'. 'Ours had character and a well-appointed bathroom.' 'Our attic had the usual heads/beams problem.' Breakfast is 'lavish even by German standards'. There are extensive conference/function facilities. Plenty to do on the estate (see below).

Open All year. *Abtstube* closed end Jan–mid-Feb, Mon/Tues, *Benediktinerstube* closed 3 weeks Jan, Wed/Thurs. **Rooms** 8 suites, 16 double. 9 in *Kelterhaus* (♿ access), 2 in *Waldhaus*. **Facilities** Lift. Salons, bar, 2 restaurants (classical background music); 3 function rooms; solarium, sauna, health/beauty treatments. Large estate: garden, lake (bathing), tennis, *boules*, small menagerie, horse riding, bicycle hire. **Location** 4 km SW of Amorbach, 20 km E of Erbach. **Credit cards** All major cards accepted. **Terms** [2004] B&B: single €105–€250, double €130–€170, suite €210–€275. Set meals €43–€74; alc from €30.

Hotels are dropped if we lack positive feedback.

ANDERNACH 56626 Rheinland-Pfalz — Map 8:D1

Hotel Meder: die Residenz am Rhein
Konrad-Adenauer-Allee 36

Tel (02632) 4 26 32
Fax (02632) 3 01 11
Email info@hotel-meder.de
Website www.hotel-meder.de

'Pleasant, friendly and well appointed', and 'excellent value for money', this neat town house (*c.* 1900) is an upmarket B&B hotel, yellow-painted and fronted by flowery window boxes. 'A good base for Rhine and Mosel trips,' say visitors this year. Owned by Brigitte Schauss, and managed by her husband ('charming, most helpful, he speaks excellent English'), it is on the promenade near the boat jetty, facing the broad Rhine, and with the *Altstadt* just behind. 'Each room is different; some furniture is rustic.' 'Our very nice, river-facing room was large, pleasantly furnished but noisy (road and railway).' Windows are double glazed, and rear rooms are quieter. The next-door restaurant is 'very good'. Andernach has many medieval buildings: the castle ruins are 14th-century; the Rheintor, a fortified gateway, dates from the 12th century. (*Florence and Russell Birch, J Hanford*)

Open All year. **Rooms** 9 double, 1 single. **Facilities** Breakfast room (background music). Terrace. Unsuitable for ♿. **Location** Edge of old town, by Rhine. 19 km NW of Koblenz. Garage. **Restriction** No dogs. **Credit cards** All major cards accepted. **Terms** B&B: single €67, double €87.

ARZBERG BEI TORGAU 04886 Sachsen — Map 8:C4

Hotel Rittergut Adelwitz NEW/BUDGET

Tel (03422) 24 39 00
Fax (03422) 24 39 20
Email info@rittergut-adelwitz.de
Website www.rittergut-adelwitz.de

On a large 'knight's estate' in Saxony, this collection of buildings stands amid farmland. It comprises a former palace and its outbuildings. Much activity takes place, including weddings, and there is a school for dogs and their owners. This former hunting lodge is now a small hotel, liked for its quiet setting and welcoming atmosphere. 'The bedrooms vary greatly,' says this year's nominator (some face the car park). 'My good-sized double overlooked the landscaped grounds at the back where an apple tree was in blossom. It was pleasantly furnished, though the bed squeaked a lot. Breakfast was a very interesting buffet; they seemed to share my penchant for unusual variations on regular food items: jams like pear-apple-cinnamon and peach-orange-almond, plus yoghurt with pieces of orange and chocolate.' There is a restaurant, with a good range of menus, and a pleasant garden terrace café. 'The owner speaks some English, but she is happier talking French or German.' Torgau, nearby, is an attractive town with a huge castle and 'excellent beer from a famous old brewery'. (*Charles Belair*)

Open All year. Restaurant open weekends only (meals for residents available all week). **Rooms** 12. **Facilities** Restaurant, café; function facilities. Terrace. Garden: children's playground. **Location** 10 km E of Torgau. **Credit cards** All major cards accepted. **Terms** [2004] B&B: single €45, double €65, suite €85.

ASCHAU IM CHIEMGAU 83229 Bavaria — Map 8:F4

Residenz Heinz Winkler
Kirchplatz 1

Tel (08052) 1 79 90
Fax (08052) 17 99 66
Email info@residenz-heinz-winkler.de
Website www.residenz-heinz-winkler.de

At the foot of the Chiemgau Alps, in a 'charming, unspoilt' little town, this is 'a place to feel self-indulgent', says an enthusiastic visitor in 2004. A 14th-century building has been turned into this large and imposing hotel/restaurant (Relais & Châteaux), famed for owner/chef Heinz Winkler's cuisine (*Michelin* three stars). The decor is '1980s luxury-style'; murals decorate the public rooms. No lounge, but a 'big, rather ostentatious lobby'. In the restaurant, smart evening wear is expected, and 'ladies are given a small stool on which to place their handbag'. 'The food did not disappoint. Herr Winkler came to say hello, reinforcing the impression that this is very much his personal creation.' Some guests find the 'army of staff' a bit 'over-attentive', but others wrote: 'Service is fantastic. We were greeted by name, though we had not visited before. A superb weekend treat.' The wine list 'contains some true greats at great prices'. 'Stunning buffet breakfast: 16 different savoury foods.' 'Large, stylish' bedrooms face the mountains, or the attractive gardens (with loungers and pond). There's a patio for drinks in summer, a winter garden, and a spa with a Roman-style bathing area. Peaceful, apart from early church bells. (*Simon Routh*, *OS, and others*)

Open All year. **Rooms** 13 suites, 19 double. Some on ground floor. **Facilities** Lift. Lobby, bar, TV room, winter garden, restaurant, *Stube*; conference facilities; spa: swimming pool, saunas, aromatherapy, shiatsu, etc, beauty salon. Garden: terrace. Golf, horse riding, tennis, ballooning, rafting. Not really suitable for ♿. **Location** By church. 82 km SE of Munich. Garage, private parking. **Credit cards** All major cards accepted. **Terms** Room: single €140–€230, double €160–€235, suite €250–€340. Breakfast €17. Set meals €110–€138.

AUGSBURG 86152 Bavaria — Map 8:F3

Dom-Hotel
Frauentorstrasse 8

Tel (0821) 34 39 30
Fax (0821) 34 39 32 00
Email info@domhotel-augsburg.de
Website www.domhotel-augsburg.de

Down quiet side street on N side of cathedral: modern B&B hotel, owned and run by Illig family. Best rooms have balcony facing patio. Buffet breakfast, served outdoors in summer. 'Modest but adequate' reading room; indoor swimming pool, sauna, solarium; free Internet access. Several restaurants within walking distance. Unsuitable for ♿. Parking, underground garage. Closed 22 Dec–12 Jan. All major credit cards accepted. 34 bedrooms, 8 suites (some no-smoking). B&B: single €65–€105, double €75–€125, suite €100–€145.

BAD ELSTER 08645 Sachsen — Map 8:D4

AmbienteHotel Quellenpark BUDGET
Ascher Strasse 20

Tel (037437) 56 00
Fax (037437) 5 60 56
Email info@quellenpark.de
Website www.quellenpark.de

One of the oldest and most attractive spa towns in Germany, Bad Elster, near the Czech border, south of Plauen, hit a rocky period after unification, but has now been restored to its former glory. It is a 'special place', according to a regular *Guide* correspondent. For accommodation, he recommends this small VCH (Lutheran church)-affiliated hotel, which opened in 2001. It stands in large grounds by a main road but in 'a quiet area of a quiet town'. Dating from the 1880s, it was formerly the town's electricity generating station and outbuildings. Now decorated in 'modern but pleasing' style, it stands in a rose-filled garden. 'My oddly shaped single bedroom, long and narrow, had windows along two sides; its door opened on to the terrace. Its bathroom was fine and well lit. Double rooms are just as pleasant.' Breakfast, in a winter garden, was thought 'only standard', but dinner is 'well prepared, beautifully presented; portions small by German standards, normal for the rest of the world'. Unusually for a VCH hotel, there is a full range of drinks. The hotel's restaurant, *La Bodega*, serves Spanish cuisine (on a terrace in summer). (*CKB*)

Open All year. **Rooms** 21. Most on ground floor. Some no-smoking. **Facilities** Winter garden/breakfast room, restaurant; terrace. Large grounds: garden: sauna, solarium, bowls, grill. **Location** S edge of spa. 50 km E of Hof. Garage (€4) **Credit cards** MasterCard, Visa. **Terms** [2004] B&B: single €45–€85, double €75–€128. Alc €15–€30.

BAD TÖLZ 83646 Bavaria — Map 8:F3

Altes Fährhaus NEW
An der Isarlust 1

Tel (08041) 60 30
Fax (08041) 7 22 70
Email info@altes-faehrhaus-toelz.de
Website www.altes-faehrhaus-toelz.de

On the bank of the River Isar which flows through this spa town (its iodine-rich waters provide the basis for treatments), this former ferry house is now a restaurant-with-rooms run by its owners, Peter Kluge and Elly Reisser-Kluge. 'It offers good value,' says the nominator in 2004. 'Though only a ten-minute walk from the attractive main street, the pedestrianised Marktstrasse, it is quiet, almost rural, and quite difficult to find. Our room, done in 1970s *café au lait* tones, was huge, with large balcony facing the river. Good buffet breakfasts include lots of fruit, freshly squeezed juice, cheese, ham, etc. You dine on the riverside terrace or in one of two dining rooms' ('elegant rustic' or 'classic'). 'The set menu was quite elaborate; dishes from the *carte* included good salad of wild mushrooms, and red fruit salad with lemon sorbet.' A footbridge across the river leads to a footpath along the bank, through a park to the centre of town. There are walking and cycling trails in all directions. (*Matthew Hamlyn*)

Open All year, except 2 weeks Feb, 2 weeks Nov. Restaurant closed Mon/Tues. **Rooms** 5. **Facilities** 2 dining rooms. Terrace (outside dining). **Location** 53 km S of Munich, 54 km NE of Garmisch-Partenkirchen. **Credit cards** Probably some accepted. **Terms** [2004] B&B: single €69–€87, double €100–€118. Alc €28–€49.

BAMBERG Bavaria — Map 8:D3

Hotel Brudermühle
Schranne 1
96049 Bamberg

Tel (0951) 95 52 20
Fax (0951) 9 55 22 55
Email info@brudermuehle.de
Website www.brudermuehle.de

With its baroque palaces and splendid four-towered Gothic cathedral on a hilltop, Bamberg is one of the loveliest of all German cities. In its centre, on an arm of the River Regnitz, with 'evocative views of the town', is Georg and Erna Vogler's handsome beamed mill house, dating from the 14th century. Now a 'very good' little hotel, it has a large dining terrace above the river, and a beamed multi-level restaurant ('popular with upmarket locals'), with scrubbed rustic tables. Local Franconian dishes are served: carp, trout, game, etc. 'Our room was immaculate and well modernised,' says a visitor in 2004. Earlier praise: 'The food was excellent.' 'Delicious desserts.' 'Lots of character, superb situation, and fairly quiet. Reception was helpful. Our room was comfortable, if a bit dark.' Bedrooms vary in size. Some have a window above the river – 'the noise of rushing water is balm to the ear'. 'Very good breakfast with friendly service.' The price includes a welcome drink. There are small bicycles, games and special menus for children. (*J Hanford, and others*)

Open All year. Restaurant closed 24/25 Dec. **Rooms** 3 apartments, 17 double, 4 single. Some no-smoking. **Facilities** Restaurant (background music); conference room. Large dining terrace. Unsuitable for ♿. **Location** Central, by cathedral and river. Public parking 50 m. **Credit cards** Diners, MasterCard, Visa. **Terms** [2004] B&B: single €75–€80, double €105–€120; D,B&B €16 added per person. Set lunch €15, dinner €20–€25; full alc €25–€30.

Romantikhotel Weinhaus Messerschmitt
Langestrasse 41
96047 Bamberg

Tel (0951) 29 78 00
Fax (0951) 2 97 80 29
Email hotel-messerschmitt@t-online.de
Website www.hotel-messerschmitt.de

Behind its gold-and-white 'wedding cake' facade, this 15th-century wine house is now a comfortable hotel, owned and run by Otto and Lydia Pschorn, descendants of Professor Willy Messerschmitt, the engineer who built the model of his first aircraft here. It stands at the east end of a westbound one-way street. 'Excellent in all respects,' was a recent comment, endorsed by visitors in 2004. The decor of dark wood beams, carved stair-rails and oriental rugs is 'pleasantly old-fashioned'. Old portraits adorn hallways. 'Staff were helpful, notably with luggage; we appreciated the pre-booked parking. In our light, good-sized room, a free drink was waiting.' 'Our room faced the busy road, but double glazing helped cut out noise.' The 'elegant-rustic' restaurant serves local fish dishes, and game and asparagus in season. 'Service was professional, food and Franconian wines were very good. Excellent dessert trolley.' Summer meals are served on the terrace, with fountain. Some bedrooms have antique or rustic furniture; some are large; front ones can be noisy. Breakfast is a generous buffet. The centre of this superb old city is a short walk away. The home of the writer ETA Hoffmann is now a remarkable museum. (*EH Whitaker, and others*)

Open All year, except 12–18 Jan. **Rooms** 14 double, 3 single. 8 no-smoking. **Facilities** Restaurant, *Stube*, wine cellar; background music; conference/function rooms. Patio: summer restaurant. Unsuitable for ♿. **Location** Central. 3 private parking spaces (must be pre-booked); underground car park nearby. **Restriction** No dogs. **Credit cards** All major cards accepted. **Terms** [2004] B&B: single €55–€80, double €120–€160. Alc €24–€40.

BERCHTESGADEN 83471 Bavaria — Map 8:F4

Hotel Krone BUDGET
Am Rad 5

Tel (08652) 9 46 00
Fax (08652) 94 60 10
Email grafe@hotel-krone-berchtesgaden.de
Website www.hotel-krone-berchtesgaden.de

Built in traditional chalet-style, this modest hotel, 'typically Bavarian and slightly old-fashioned', has 'stunning views across the valley' and 'very helpful' owner/managers, Grit and Jörg Grafe: 'She is charming. A lovely welcome,' say visitors in 2004. It stands on a hill in the northern outskirts of this famous resort. White-walled and green-shuttered, it has flower-bedecked balconies, and hand-painted furniture in the snug, wood-panelled public rooms and the 'charming' bedrooms. Most rooms are large, and have a balcony facing valley and mountain. 'But not all bathrooms have been modernised: our shower hardly worked.' 'Enjoyable' meals are served on a terrace with the same extensive views, or in a room with paintings and flowers. Frau Grafe and her daughter-in-law wear local costume. Dinner (5.30–7 pm) includes local specialities, eg, asparagus and trout. 'The *en pension* menus, if not exciting, were good value. Breakfast is an adequate buffet.' There is a fitness centre: the indoor swimming pool has panoramic views. 'Ask for directions: the hotel is in a narrow one-way street, and it is difficult to find your way back if you overshoot.' Berchtesgaden, surrounded by lakes, has a big *Schloss* and fascinating salt mines. (*Alex, Beryl and Jonathan Williams, PG*)

Open 20 Dec–30 Oct. Closed Mon after midday. Restaurant closed Mondays for lunch. **Rooms** 2 suites, 12 double, 6 single. Some no-smoking. **Facilities** Lift. Lounge, 2 dining rooms (1 no-smoking); background music; sauna, whirlpool, steam bath. Garden: terrace, children's play area. **Location** 1 km N of centre, off Salzburg road, via Locksteinstrasse. Parking. Bus-stop 300 m. **Restriction** No dogs. **Credit cards** MasterCard, Visa. **Terms** B&B €29–€45; D,B&B €40–€56.

BERGEN 86633 Bavaria — Map 8:E3

Zum Klosterbräu BUDGET
Kirchplatz 1, Neuburg

Tel (08431) 6 77 50
Fax (08431) 4 11 20
Email boehm@zum-klosterbraeu.de
Website www.zum-klosterbraeu.de

In a former convent, later a brewery (hence its name), Otto and Martina Böhm's pink-fronted hotel/restaurant was found 'very peaceful' by a visitor this year. Some buildings are 300 years old: they enclose a garden where meals can be taken; or you can eat in one of several atmospheric, low-ceilinged rooms. Dinner, 'very good, with a light touch', might include spring lamb with caramelised peach and rhubarb; roast pork with potato noodles. Meat and fish come from the family's estate. Breakfast is 'above average'. Staff ('women in traditional dress') are helpful. 'Large, attractive' bedrooms, in a newish building, have parquet floors and white stucco walls. Marble bathrooms have under-floor heating. The village has a lovely baroque church ('church bells add atmosphere') and 'extremely tidy farms'. Nearby Neuburg, with its 16th-century castle, is a fine town on the upper Danube. (*Kay Brock*)

Open 6 Jan–22 Dec. **Rooms** 16 double, 8 single. 6 in annexe. Some on ground floor. Some no-smoking. **Facilities** Lift. 4 dining rooms (1 no-smoking). Garden: children's play area, library, fishpond, sauna, tennis. **Location** 8 km NW of Neuburg, 60 km N of Augsburg. **Credit cards** MasterCard, Visa. **Terms** B&B: single €52–€61, double €72–€89. Set meals €17–€37; full alc €22.

BERLIN — Map 8:B4

art'otel Berlin Mitte
Wallstrasse 70–73
10179 Berlin

Tel (030) 24 06 20
Fax (030) 24 06 22 22
Email aobminfo@artotels.de
Website www.artotel.de

'Comfortable, minimalist and elegant,' say its fans. This hotel was built seven years ago by Austrian architect Johanne Nalbach in the lively Berlin-Mitte area. It is filled with original pictures by Georg Baselitz. 'We are still enamoured,' writes a regular reader. 'We go for the top-floor back rooms where large windows look silently to sky and much of Berlin.' Some find the designer style hard to take: 'Tiny, uncomfortable armchairs, sinks with hard-to-use taps and no plug; little space around the bed.' 'No luggage carriers: trolley by door.' 'The air conditioning was so noisy we could not sleep; service was poor.' But those in favour feel that 'the most important things' are right. 'Great beds, soft towels, lots of hot water, friendly staff.' 'Excellent breakfast: copious fruit salad, 12 types of tea.' The bar/restaurant, *The Factory*, serves 'innovative dishes'; the short room-service menu 'is great'. Nearby is an arm of the Spree, where the hotel has a boat with a summer restaurant. The sister hotel, *art'otel city centre west*, is filled with works by Andy Warhol. (*G Smith, Felix Singer, Susan Hanley, and others*)

Open All year. Restaurant closed midday, July/Aug, Sun/Mon. **Rooms** 10 'art suites' (2 with kitchen), 4 suites, 82 double, 13 single. Some no-smoking. Some equipped for ♿. Air conditioning. **Facilities** Lift. Reception (contemporary music), bar/restaurant, dining terrace; conference/banqueting/function facilities; art gallery; discounts at nearby health centre. **Location** SE side of Berlin-Mitte. Garage, free parking permit. (U-Bahn: Märkisches Ufer) **Credit cards** All major cards accepted. **Terms** [2004] B&B: single €130–€180, double €160–€210. Alc €23–€31.

Bleibtreu Hotel
Bleibtreustrasse 31
10707 Berlin

Tel (030) 88 47 40
Fax (030) 88 47 44 44
Email info@bleibtreu.com
Website www.bleibtreu.com

In the Charlottenburg district, this 'funky' designer hotel is run with an emphasis on healthy living. Eco-friendly materials have been used throughout (organic paint, etc), and there is a fitness centre. An old town house has been given a contemporary decor and a 'youthful feel'. 'It is in a street of attractive shops, just off the Ku'Damm yet quiet: we could sleep with the windows open,' write recent guests. A glass lift takes you up to the bedrooms: 'Ours had oatmeal-coloured fabrics, bathroom dashingly tiled in shades of blue and with a deep tiled bath.' The remote-control switches in the bedrooms may be confusing, housekeeping is not always perfect, but the 'supremely comfortable' beds are admired, and 'reception staff are helpful'. The espresso bar and the New York-style *Deli 31* serve snacks. *Restaurant 31* offers a 'no-sugar, low-carbohydrate' menu. 'Very good fish and vegetarian dishes. Breakfast good, too, nothing packaged.' (*CR and ANR*)

Open All year. **Rooms** 45 double, 15 single. Some no-smoking. Some air-conditioned. 1 suitable for ♿. **Facilities** Lift. Lobby, sitting area, deli, coffee shop, bar/restaurant (background music); wellness centre: steam bath, plunge pool, massage. **Location** Central, off Ku'Damm, near Savignyplatz. Public parking across street. (U-Bahn: Savignyplatz) **Credit cards** All major cards accepted. **Terms** B&B: single €157–€237, double €182–€262; D,B&B €30 added per person.

Hotel Jurine NEW
Schwedter Strasse 15
10119 Berlin

Tel (030) 4 43 29 90
Fax (030) 44 32 99 99
Email mail@hotel-jurine.de
Website www.hotel-jurine.de

In the past five years, this three-star B&B hotel has doubled in size, but it is still 'welcoming and quiet', says its nominator. The buffet breakfast is 'unusually good: eggs and bacon, a great variety of cold cuts, cheese, fruit, jams, 12 different teas and decent coffee'. It is served in a pleasant room with conservatory or, in fine weather, in the 'flourishing' rear garden. Six bedrooms have balcony and bath; the others have a shower. The owner/managers are 'a charming couple';

he is French, she is German, 'and the helpful reception staff are trilingual'. 'All sorts of restaurants nearby.' (*Maria Goldberg*)

Open All year. **Rooms** 56. Some no-smoking. **Facilities** Lift. Reception, breakfast room; sauna; business centre. Garden. **Location** Berlin-Mitte. Garage (€12). (U-Bahn: Senefelder Platz) **Credit cards** All major cards accepted. **Terms** [2004] B&B: single €77– €127, double €97–€137. Breakfast €13.

Hotel Seehof
Lietzensee-Ufer 11
14057 Berlin

Tel (030) 32 00 20
Fax (030) 32 00 22 51
Email info@hotel-seehof-berlin.de
Website www.hotel-seehof-berlin.de

In Charlottenburg, near conference centre: 'excellent' hotel: large white building, 'civilised, peaceful', quite smart and formal, with pleasant staff. Most bedrooms (some with balcony) overlook Lietzensee and its small park. Good modern cooking, and excellent buffet breakfast, served till late, in gourmet restaurant, Au Lac *(closed 4–14 Jan); lovely terrace facing lake. Lift; cosy bar, indoor swimming pool ('slightly spartan'), sauna; function facilities. Garage (€13.50). (U-bahn: Sophie-Charlotten-Platz) All major credit cards accepted. 75 rooms. B&B: single €135–€245, double €165–€275, suite €195–€320. Alc €21–€34 [2004].*

BRAUBACH 56338 Rheinland-Pfalz — Map 8:D2

Landgasthof Zum Weissen Schwanen
Brunnenstrasse 4

Tel (02627) 98 20
Fax (02627) 88 02
Email zum-weissen-schwanen@rz-online.de
Website www.zum-weissen-schwanen.de

'Like a museum, 14th-century documents displayed, and the waterwheel still turning', the Kunz family's inn, composed of a 17th-century half-timbered wine house and watermill, is in a Rhineside village crowned by a superb castle. Inside are wooden beams and tiled floors. Some bedrooms have country antiques; some are in the former stables; bathrooms are modern. Recent visitors were enthusiastic: 'The formidable landlady gave us an excellent room,' said one. 'We slept in a four-poster bed in the miller's original bedroom,' wrote another. 'There was more noise from the stream than from traffic.' The 'excellent meals' are served in the busy restaurant and the pretty garden. A new brasserie, *Brentano*, has just been opened. 'Service was good. Everyone was friendly.' 'Breakfast good, too.' (*KB, and others*)

Open All year. Main restaurant closed Jan, Karneval (Feb), Wed. **Rooms** 1 suite, 16 double, 3 single. Some in mill house, 20 m. 10 no-smoking. 1 on ground floor. **Facilities** 4 lounges, TV room, bar, brasserie, restaurant; classical background music throughout; conference room. Small garden: museum; children's play area. **Location** In village, on E bank of Rhine. 13 km SE of Koblenz. Parking. **Credit cards** All major cards accepted. **Terms** B&B: single €55–€65, double €80–€95, suite €90–€105. Set lunch €20, dinner €25–€50; full alc €45. *V*

BREMEN 28203 Map 8:B2

Hotel Lichtsinn
Rembertistrasse 11

Tel (0421) 36 80 70
Fax (0421) 32 72 87
Email reservierung@hotel-lichtsinn.com
Website www.hotel-lichtsinn.de

In quiet side street, c. *800 m SW of main station, 800 m NE of historic centre (on foot across gardens and canal): pleasant modern, inexpensive B&B hotel, owned and run by friendly owner, Ralf Lichtsinn, and wife. Striking glass-enclosed lift in front. Bedrooms, some with four-poster, vary in size; all are comfortable with glossy bathroom. Excellent buffet breakfast; swift service. Bar; fitness room, solarium. Garage (€10). All major credit cards accepted. 36 rooms. B&B: single €80, double €105 [2004].*

CELLE 29221 Niedersachsen Map 8:B3

Hotel Utspann
Im Kreise 13–14

Tel (05141) 9 27 20
Fax (05141) 92 72 52
Email info@utspann.de
Website www.utspann.de

On the south side of the splendid *Altstadt* of this lovely old city is this 'fine collection of old buildings with gardens'. Now a hotel and wine tavern owned by Ulla Mehls, it is 'full of character', 'nicely warren-like'. The main building (1644) was first an inn, then a tannery. The bedrooms are all different: three have a balcony, two a patio. Four suites are new this year. 'Reception was helpful, very friendly,' said admirers. 'Our large room was delightfully and somewhat eccentrically furnished: strong colours, bold patterns; homely touches, eg, kettle and herbal teas; period fittings like an Art Deco phone stand, *and* a computer modem facility. Good bed with double mattress, unlike the side-by-side single mattresses usual in Germany.' 'A good buffet breakfast with fresh orange juice.' Light evening meals are served. And you can eat well at Celle's *Ratskeller* or the *Michelin*-starred *Endtenfang* (at the glamorous *Fürstenhof Celle*). In the grounds are a sun deck, a gazebo and a stream.

Open 5 Jan–23 Dec. Restaurant closed midday and Sun/Mon. **Rooms** 4 suites, 15 double, 3 single. Some no-smoking. Some air conditioned. Some on ground floor. **Facilities** Lounge, wine bar; background music; breakfast room (no-smoking); conference room; terrace. Garden: solarium, sauna. Unsuitable for ♿. **Location** 600 m SE of *Altstadt*. Outdoor parking nearby. **Credit cards** All major cards accepted. **Terms** Room: single €67.50–€130, double €94–€155, suite €145–€235. Breakfast €7.50–€10. Set dinner €20; full alc €30. *V*

You should always check latest tariffs with a hotel when you make your booking.

CLAUSTHAL-ZELLERFELD 38678 Niedersachsen Map 8:C3

Parkhotel Calvör BUDGET
Treuerstrasse 6

Tel (05323) 95 00
Fax (05323) 95 02 22
Email parkhotel.calvoer@t-online.de
Website www.parkhotel.calvoer.harz.de

In a holiday area, Zellerfeld (attached to Clausthal) is a former silver- and copper-mining town. It has an interesting museum of mining and a spa centre, and it is full of wooden buildings in Norwegian style (immigrant Norwegian miners rebuilt it in their country's image after a major fire in the 18th century). This hotel has sizeable rooms with 'lots of light', pale pine furniture, parquet flooring and oriental rugs, and extra-long beds (which pleased one tall visitor). It is in a quiet residential area, with big trees. 'Staff are friendly.' Breakfast, in a pleasant room, is a 'normal German buffet'. The cellar bar, *Dream No. 1*, serves evening drinks and snacks. Dinner is offered only from Thursday to Saturday, by prior arrangement, but several restaurants are nearby.

Open All year. Restaurant open evenings Thurs–Sat. **Rooms** 35. 15 no-smoking. Some on ground floor. **Facilities** Wine cellar/bar, breakfast room, restaurant; sauna; conference/function facilities. **Location** Central. 19 km SW of Goslar. Parking. **Credit cards** MasterCard, Visa (not accepted for packages). **Terms** [2004] B&B: single €40–€70, double €50–€80, suite €89; D,B&B €12 added per person. Alc €15–€30.

COLOGNE Nordrhein-Westfalen Map 8:D1

Antik Hotel Bristol NEW
Kaiser-Wilhelm-Ring 48
50672 Cologne

Tel (0221) 12 01 95
Fax (0221) 13 14 95
Email hotel@antik-hotel-bristol.de
Website www.antik-hotel-bristol.de

Privately owned and operated, this B&B hotel is on a ring road, 'but it is set back quietly, behind a narrow green belt', says the 2004 nominator. 'A collection of antique works determines the atmosphere. Most of the bedrooms have at least one or two items stemming from different parts of Germany.' Some have a four-poster. Baths, mini-bars, safes, etc, are modern. 'Service is friendly and the clientele is international. Reception staff speak good English and provide useful local information. The buffet breakfast is varied and generous.' Next door, in the pedestrian zone, is a large café, and a 'brisk local restaurant', *Jan von Werth*, is round the corner. (*George Blythe*)

Open 2 Jan–21 Dec. **Rooms** 44. Some no-smoking. **Facilities** Lift. Breakfast room; conference room. **Location** By MediaPark and pedestrian zone. 5 mins by taxi from station. Public underground car park opposite. **Credit cards** All major cards accepted. **Terms** [2004] B&B: single from €69, double from €92. 'Pay for ten nights, get one free.'

Every entry in the *Guide* is based on a stay of at least one night.

Buchholz Downtown Hotel
Kunibertsgasse 5
50668 Cologne

Tel (0221) 16 08 30
Fax (0221) 1 60 83 41
Email info@hotel-buchholz.de
Website www.hotel-buchholz.de

In the city centre, this listed building (with peach facade and white awnings) just north of the cathedral has newly renovated bedrooms and wireless Internet access. Run as a small B&B hotel by Sascha Buchholz and his Welsh-born mother, Carole Ann, it is 'friendly, comfortable, quiet, good value', say fans. Bedrooms (some are large) have Lloyd Loom furniture, a big sofa, free 24-hour room service. Back rooms are quietest. The 'copious breakfast' is served in a pleasant, rustic-style room, next to the small bar. No restaurant; plenty nearby.

Open 4 Jan–23 Dec. **Rooms** 3 suites, 9 double, 7 single. 3 on ground floor. Some no-smoking. **Facilities** Lift. Internet surfstation; bar, breakfast room (no-smoking). Small garden. **Location** Central, near station and cathedral. Public parking. Airport transfer (€29). **Credit cards** All major cards accepted. **Terms** B&B: single €55–€105, double €66–€195, suite €88–€195. *V*

Hotel im Wasserturm
Kaygasse 2
50676 Cologne

Tel (0221) 2 00 80
Fax (0221) 2 00 88 88
Email info@hotel-im-wasserturm.de
Website www.hotel-im-wasserturm.de

This 19th-century water tower, a listed monument, was turned in 1990 into a luxury hotel with ultra-modern decor, by the French interior designer Andrée Putman. It stands in large grounds (with chairs, tables and parasols in summer) in a residential area, barely a kilometre from the *Dom*. It is 'full of excellent modern art', as befits this modern art capital. Some *Guide* readers dislike the 'austere design'. One wrote: 'The bath was in a black hole (no light to read by). No stand for our suitcase.' Others think it 'magnificent'. 'Our wedge-shaped junior suite was a fine creation: a single orchid adorned each black wood table.' Regular visitors wrote in 2004: 'Our room was exemplary. Housekeeping is good. Service is impeccable, and the free car park is a boon.' The split-level suites have a spiral staircase. Double beds only. In *La Vision*, the rooftop restaurant on the 11th floor (*Michelin* star), Hendrik Otto serves 'French food with a Mediterranean twist': it was thought 'excellent, if a little fussy'. There is a 'superb wine list'. A second restaurant named *dʌblju W* has now opened. It serves 'light seasonal cooking'. 'Very attractively designed, it has nice views over the garden, a summer terrace, and an interesting and reasonably priced menu.' The 'fabulous buffet breakfast' is served here. *Harry's Bar* provides informal food. (*Pat and Jeremy Temple, D and AS, and others*)

Open All year. *La Vision* closed 2–27 Jan, end July–mid-Aug, Sun/Mon. **Rooms** 34 suites, 44 double, 10 single. Some no-smoking. Air conditioning. **Facilities** Lift. Lounge, piano bar, 2 restaurants; roof terrace; conference centre; sauna, solarium. Garden: terrace (outdoor dining). Unsuitable for ♿. **Location** Central, 1.5 km SW of cathedral. Underground garage. **Credit cards** All major cards accepted. **Terms** [2004] Room: single €180–€265, double €210–€335, suite €240–€840. Breakfast €18. Set dinner €48; alc €52–€60.

DETMOLD 32756 Nordrhein-Westfalen — Map 8:C2

Ringhotel Detmolder Hof
Lange Strasse 19

Tel (05231) 9 91 20
Fax (05231) 99 12 99
Email info@detmolder-hof.de
Website www.detmolder-hof.de

This well-preserved 16th-century small town, former capital of the principality of Lippe, has a fine *Residenz*, and a superb market on Thursday and Saturday. In a quiet pedestrian zone, the Schuster family's 'friendly, well-run hotel' is a conversion of a building in Weser Renaissance style. A returning visitor writes of 'a general atmosphere of well-being'. Service is 'unfailingly courteous'. Of the two restaurants, the Italian-orientated *Le Fonti* has 'ingenious pasta dishes' and 'good service'. The *Bistro*, favoured by local young people, can be crowded at night: it serves traditional German fare, eg, liver Berlin style. There is also a lively pavement café. 'The rooms in the old building are not luxurious, but all needs are catered for.' The buffet breakfast includes 'delicious local bread and sausages'. There is good walking in the unspoilt countryside nearby, and 'if you have a car, several appealing inns are within easy reach'. (*AB*)

Open All year, except 24 Dec. **Rooms** 1 suite, 26 double, 12 single. 18 in annexe (*Weinhaus*). 3 no-smoking. **Facilities** Lift. Bar, bistro, restaurant; conference room; café, dining terrace; background music. **Location** Central (pedestrian zone). Public parking. **Credit cards** All major cards accepted. **Terms** B&B: single €77–€93, double €99–€121, suite €155; D,B&B €16.50 added per person. Full alc €25.

DRESDEN 01097 Sachsen — Map 8:D5

Hotel Bülow Residenz
Rähnitzgasse 19

Tel (0351) 8 00 30
Fax (0351) 8 00 31 00
Email info@buelow-residenz.de
Website www.buelow-residenz.de

'Elegant', and 'very well situated' in a quiet street of old town houses and smart shops, Horst and Monika Bülow's 18th-century baroque mansion, yellow-fronted, is across the Elbe from the historic centre (all the sights are within walking distance). A small luxury hotel (Relais & Châteaux), it is 'pricey but good value', says a visitor in 2004. 'Charming staff, lovely public spaces. Our dinner was wonderful.' In the smart *Caroussel* restaurant (*Michelin* star), the chef, Stefan Hermann, produces French and Swabian cuisine. Earlier guests liked their large room, 'with pale curtains, masses of storage space, bowl of fresh fruit, lovely bathroom, softest duvets ever; excellent lights above the beds. Dinner, in the modern manner, had so many *amuse-bouche* and petits fours we needed to order only two courses, and when we thought we had finished, a huge tray of chocolate truffles was brought. Breakfast was a wonderful buffet. Only caveat: the piped music was out of character.' There is a vaulted cellar bar. Alfresco meals are served in a leafy courtyard. 'Everything can be reached by wheelchair,' the hotel tells us. (*John Stege, CR, and others*)

Open All year, except 4–19 Jan. Restaurant closed Sun/Mon. **Rooms** 5 suites, 24 double, 1 single. **Facilities** Lift. Salon, cellar bar, restaurant (no-smoking; background music); conference/function facilities. Courtyard (meal service). **Location** Central. Parking 50 m. **Credit cards** All major cards accepted. **Terms** Room: single €120–€180, double €180–€220, suite €270–€410; dogs €20 extra. Breakfast €17. D,B&B €60 added per person. Set lunch €39, dinner €64; full alc €90.

Hotel Martha Hospiz *Tel* (0351) 8 17 60
Nieritzstrasse 11 *Fax* (0351) 8 17 62 22
Email marthahospiz.dresden@vch.de
Website www.vch.de/marthahospiz.dresden

Century-old house, across Elbe from historic centre, near Bülow Residenz *(above): discreet, green-fronted hotel owned by Lutheran churches (VCH), managed by Winfrid Tilp; equipped throughout for* ♿. *'Excellent value; very friendly.' 'Rooms slightly spartan (uncarpeted), but warm, nicely furnished. Excellent buffet breakfast on covered terrace.' The Kartoffelkeller ('must be visited at least once'), open evenings, popular locally (no-smoking), serves potato-based dishes ('even potato ice cream') at low prices. Closed 22–27 Dec. Amex, MasterCard, Visa accepted. No dogs. Private parking nearby (€5). 50 well-appointed bedrooms. B&B: single €54–€84, double €102–€118. Set meal €12–€22 [2004].*

EISENACH 99817 Thüringen Map 8:D3

Schlosshotel Eisenach *Tel* (03691) 21 42 60
Markt 10 *Fax* (03691) 21 42 59
Email schlosshotel@eisenachonline.de
Website www.schlosshotel-eisenach.de

Built on the ruins of a 13th-century Franciscan monastery, this tall, white, gabled building, thoroughly modernised in 1994, is now a small city-centre hotel run by its owners, the Reinel family. 'Very quiet', because of the traffic-free zones nearby, it has an 'attractive interior design', says a recent guest. 'My nice corner room, facing an outdoor café, was well decorated, with a fine bathroom. Breakfast, good even by German standards, was served in a cosy modern dining room.' There is a vaulted cellar restaurant. This historic city is best known for its hilltop Wartburg fortress, where Luther translated the Bible. It has museums devoted to Bach (he was born here) and Wagner, and a 'fine small exhibition of wooden religious statuary'.

Open All year. **Rooms** 2 suites, 30 double, 11 single. Some no-smoking. Some on ground floor. **Facilities** Lift. 2 wine cellars, 3 dining rooms; background music; fitness facilities: whirlpool, sauna, solarium, etc. **Location** Central, by Lutherhaus. Garages, street parking. **Credit cards** Amex, MasterCard, Visa. **Terms** B&B: single €70–€75, double €92–€110, suite €110–€180; D,B&B €15 added per person.

ESSEN-KETTWIG 45219 Nordrhein-Westfalen Map 8:C1

Schloss Hugenpoet
August-Thyssen-Strasse 51

Tel (02054) 1 20 40
Fax (02054) 12 04 50
Email info@hugenpoet.de
Website www.hugenpoet.de

An imposing, moated 17th-century castle, this luxurious hotel (Relais & Châteaux, four red gables in *Michelin*) lies between Düsseldorf and Essen in beautiful wooded parkland. It is also near the River Ruhr whose curving valley is no industrial eyesore but quite rural (the big mines and steelworks are to its north). The owner is Michael Lübbert: 'Affable and impressive, much in evidence, he speaks perfect English,' says an inspector. He has appointed a new chef, Erika Bergheim, for the *Nesselrode* gourmet restaurant (one visitor found her cooking 'sophisticated, well presented, quite *nouvelle*, served by suave young men'). There is an informal bistro/*Weinkeller*, *Hugenpöttchen*, in a stable block in the courtyard. Meals, including the good buffet breakfast, can be taken on the terrace in fine weather. The bedrooms are 'sumptuous', though some are 'smallish'; those on the second floor have Asian antiques. Some furnishings are baronial. A main road is nearby, and aircraft fly above to Düsseldorf airport, 'but the noises cease at night'. The nearby Krupp family mansion, Villa Hügel, now a museum, is worth a visit. (*JA, and others*)

Open All year. *Nesselrode* closed Tues. **Rooms** 5 suites, 14 double, 6 single. 6 in annexe. Some air conditioned. **Facilities** Lift, ramps. Lobby, salon, library/billiard room, restaurant, bistro (background music); conference facilities; terrace. Park: garden, tennis, river; golf nearby. **Location** 18 km SW of Essen. Ratingen-Breitscheid exit at A3/A52 interchange, B227 towards Velbert, then Essen-Kettwig. Parking, garage. **Credit cards** All major cards accepted. **Terms** B&B: single €189–€205, double €225–€270, suite €350. Set meals: bistro €29–€42; *Nesselrode* (dinner only) €75–€106.

FELDBERG-BÄRENTAL 79868 Baden-Württemberg Map 8:F2

Schwarzwaldgasthof Adler BUDGET
Feldbergstrasse 4

Tel (07655) 93 39 33
Fax (07655) 93 05 21
Email info@adler-feldberg.de
Website www.adler-feldberg.de

A traditional mountain hotel run by Walter Wimmer and his wife, Sabine, who is also the chef. More than 200 years old, this large brown chalet with flowery balconies is in the Black Forest near the high Feldberg peak. The 'warm personal style, good meals, lovely setting' and comfortable rooms have been enjoyed. Furnishings are rustic, in local style. No lounge, but most bedrooms have a sitting area; some have a four-poster; some are split-level, with the bed in the eaves and a mini-kitchen below, hidden in a painted wardrobe. All rooms are different, with unusual lighting effects, such as tiny star-like lights in the ceiling. Bathrooms tend to be small. In the 'large, attractive' restaurant, lively with locals, the waitresses wear folk costume. There is a separate *Pfifferlinge* (chanterelles) menu. Breakfast is 'beautifully presented', with a wide-ranging buffet. Families are welcomed. Two roads, one fairly busy, run alongside. (*MM, B and LA*)

Open All year. **Rooms** 7 suites, 8 double, 1 single. Some no-smoking. **Facilities** Bar, restaurant (background music), breakfast room (no-smoking); games room. Garden. Unsuitable for ♿. **Location** 40 km SE of Freiburg, SW of Titisee. Parking. **Credit cards** MasterCard, Visa. **Terms** B&B: double €90–€130, suite €100–€150; D,B&B €23 added per person. Set meals €25–€30; full alc €31.

FLECKL 95485 Bavaria — Map 8:D4

Sporthotel Fleckl NEW/BUDGET
Fleckl 5
Warmensteinach

Tel (09277) 99 90
Fax (09277) 9 99 99
Email voit@sporthotel-fleckl.de
Website www.sporthotel-fleckl.de

Simple holiday hotel, partly in chalet-style, with an extension, run since 1876 by Voit family. In quiet resort village 29 km NE of Bayreuth, 5 km NE of Warmensteinach, amid scenic upland country of Fichtelgebirge. Large, handsome garden with trees, 'lots of lawn for children', terrace, games; indoor swimming pool, sauna. Simple furnishings, pleasant bedrooms; no lunches, good home-cooked dinners (residents only): €25. No background music. Parking, 8 garages. Unsuitable for ♿. Closed 2 weeks spring, 1 week early Sept, Nov–mid-Dec. 4 suites, 15 rooms. B&B: single €40–€50, double €70–€98, suite €90.

FLINTSBACH AM INN 83126 Bavaria — Map 8:F4

Hotel Gasthof Dannerwirt NEW
Kirchplatz 4

Tel (08034) 9 06 00
Fax (08034) 90 60 50
Email info@dannerwirt.de
Website www.dannerwirt.de

'Good value, well run', the Schweinsteiger family's hotel is in a small farming village with a pretty baroque church whose bells are silent at night, 'but light sleepers may be awakened in time for the 6.30 am church service', says a seasoned traveller in 2004. Otherwise the village ('a few houses and farms, a couple of small shops, the town hall') is peaceful. 'Highly recommended', this three-storey chalet-style building 'has a pleasing, semi-rustic decor' with some antique furniture. 'My single room was larger than normal, quite comfortable with unpainted pine furniture and an armchair.' In the restaurant, traditional German dishes ('local special events can fill the place'). Breakfast, part buffet, is in an attractive, panelled room. 'My requests were handled with quiet efficiency.' (*Charles Belair*)

Open All year. Restaurant closed Thurs. **Rooms** 1 suite, 17 double, 6 single. **Facilities** Restaurant; conference room. Unsuitable for ♿. **Location** 16 km S of Rosenheim, 70 km SE of Munich. *Autobahn* Munich–Salzburg, exit 8. Car park. **Credit cards** MasterCard, Visa. **Terms** [2004] B&B: single €38.50–€41, double €57–€63, suite €77–€82; D,B&B €12.50 added per person. Full alc €25.

FRANKFURT AM MAIN 60325 Hessen — Map 8:D2

Hotel Westend
Westendstrasse 15

Tel (069) 78 98 81 80
Fax (069) 74 53 96
Email hotel_westend@t-online.de
Website www.hotelwestend.com

Small and personal, the Mayer family's B&B hotel makes a welcome change from Frankfurt's mostly big, brash modern ones. It is in a quiet, mainly residential area, ten minutes' walk from the centre: 'An excellent situation,' says a visitor in 2004. Others had 'an agreeable welcome'. There is a pleasant garden where drinks can be served, and 'the staff are mostly very helpful'. The 'tasteful decor' includes antiques, old paintings, brass chandeliers and oriental rugs. 'We liked the old-style decor of our room (No. 12): the bathroom had been ingeniously fitted in without much harm to the proportions.' But there's no lift in this 'lovely old listed building', and you may have to carry your bags up four flights of 'pretty steep' stairs if your room is on the top floor. Some of the rooms are 'poky', and two share a bathroom. Breakfast, 'unusually eclectic', with 'terrific coffee', is served in the lounges or on the terrace. (*EH Whitaker, AW, and others*)

Open All year, except 23 Dec–3 Jan. **Rooms** 1 suite, 9 double, 10 single. 2 with shared bathroom. **Facilities** TV lounge, bar; business room. No background music. Garden: terrace. Unsuitable for ♿. **Location** Central, off Mainzer Landstrasse, between trade fair venue and station. Parking. **Credit cards** All major cards accepted. **Terms** B&B: single €50–€190, double €100–€240, suite €170–€420. *V*

FRASDORF 83112 Bavaria — Map 8:F4

Landgasthof Karner NEW
Nussbaumstrasse 6

Tel (08052) 40 71
Fax (08052) 47 11
Email info@landgasthof-karner.de
Website www.landgasthof-karner.de

West of the Chiemsee, five minutes' drive from the A8, this 'handsome old building with the feel of a coaching inn' is in a small, fairly quiet village between Munich and Salzburg, at the foot of the Alps. It was discovered by regular correspondents this year. 'A fine carved wooden door leads into a long hall-cum-corridor off which open dining rooms. Our room was on the second floor (no lift and no help with baggage). It was large and airy, high ceilinged and rather pink. It lacked effective curtains but was a nice room in a nice hotel, and good value. Dinner was in a wood-panelled dining room, highly decorated in Bavarian Alpine style. Food was not quite so Bavarian, but very good, and technically accomplished, starters of kebab of rabbit with rabbit cannelloni, or lasagne of roast vegetables. Long and serious wine list. The restaurant is obviously popular with locals.' Meals are served outdoors in summer, and there is also a 'cosy pub'. 'A very good overnight stop, or a base for a few days' rambling.' (*Matthew Hamlyn*)

Open All year. **Rooms** 26. **Facilities** Restaurant; indoor swimming pool, sauna. Garden (meal service). **Location** 78 km SE of Munich, 64 km W of Salzburg. **Credit cards** All major cards accepted. **Terms** [2004] B&B: single €55–€80, double €90–€150; D,B&B €28 added per person. Alc €35–€49.

FREIBERG 09599 Sachsen — Map 8:D4

Hotel Kreller BUDGET
Fischerstrasse 5

Tel (03731) 3 59 00
Fax (03731) 2 32 19
Email kontakt@hotel-kreller.de
Website www.hotel-kreller.de

Freiberg, a Saxon university city south-west of Dresden, is famous for its 16th-century baroque Marienkirche and its museums, and it makes a good base for exploring the former mining centres and present-day makers of wooden Christmas ornaments in the towns of the nearby Erzgebirge mountains. In its centre, yet quiet, this old hotel is run by its owners, the Kreller family. 'It is friendly and good value,' says a returning visitor. 'Staff are helpful.' The restaurant, popular with locals, serves local cuisine: 'My fish ragout was tasty, and service was good. The buffet breakfast is excellent, even by German standards. The plastic plants are kept well dusted.' (*CB*)

Open All year. **Rooms** 37. Some in adjacent building. No smoking. **Facilities** Lift. Lounge, bar, restaurant; conference room. Beer garden. **Location** 49 km SW of Dresden. In historic centre, at main post office, turn left at 1st street; hotel 50 m on left. Car park. **Credit cards** All major cards accepted. **Terms** [2004] B&B: single €45–€65, double €68–€88. Alc €16–€38.

FREIBURG IM BREISGAU 79098 Baden-Württemberg — Map 8:F2

Hotel Oberkirch
Münsterplatz 22
Schusterstrasse 11

Tel (0761) 2 02 68 68
Fax (0761) 2 02 68 69
Email info@hotel-oberkirch.de
Website www.hotel-oberkirch.de

In the pedestrianised *Altstadt*, opposite the great cathedral of this fine old university city, Doris Hunn's hotel/restaurant/*Weinstube* was recently much admired: 'Absolutely wonderful. Staff exceptionally helpful. The waiter shown in the brochure became our mentor. Our room looked through double-glazed windows on to the *Dom* and the Saturday Easter market, the loveliest we have seen anywhere. The food was remarkable. No non-smoking areas in the restaurant, so they put us in a first-floor dining room.' Seasonal dishes, such as asparagus in May, game in October, feature on the menus of chef Armando Noiosi; dishes with chanterelles are a speciality. In summer, you can eat under oleander trees on the pavement. In winter, the panelled restaurant is warmed by a tiled stove. Hard to find (they send a map). (*S and EH*)

Open All year. Gourmet restaurant closed 3 weeks in Jan. **Rooms** 3 suites, 13 double, 10 single. Some no-smoking. 17 in adjacent building. **Facilities** Lift. 2 restaurants; function facilities; terrace. Unsuitable for ♿. **Location** Pedestrian zone: market place. Go through Schwabentor gate. Garage. **Credit cards** Amex, MasterCard, Visa. **Terms** B&B: single €89–€125, double €138–€148, suite €163. Set meals €16–€19; full alc €40.

HAMBURG — Map 8:B3

Garden Hotels
Magdalenenstrasse 60
20148 Hamburg

Tel (040) 41 40 40
Fax (040) 4 14 04 20
Email garden@garden-hotels.de
Website www.garden-hotels.de

In the trendy Pöseldorf district on the west bank of the Alster Lake, which some bedrooms overlook, stands this chic, modern, B&B hotel. Composed of three houses surrounded by trees, it is in a quiet street. It is 'attractively decorated' and hung with modern pictures. Some bedrooms have a balcony facing a garden. Electronic blinds can be controlled from the bed. Bathrooms, some in natural stone, have under-floor heating. 'Our comfortable room had two sofas,' one couple wrote. The 'good breakfast', available all day, is served in a conservatory in the main house or, in summer, on the balconies or in the pleasant gardens. Within easy reach are restaurants and shops.

Open All year. **Rooms** 6 apartments with kitchenette, 2 suites, 37 double, 20 single. In 3 buildings. **Facilities** Lifts. Breakfast conservatory; conference room. Small gardens. **Location** W side of Aussenalster lake, 1 km N of centre. Parking. (U-Bahn: Hallerstrasse) **Credit cards** All major cards accepted. **Terms** [2004] Room: single €125–€145, double €145–€185, suite €230–€280. Breakfast €9.

HÄUSERN 79837 Baden-Württemberg — Map 8:F2

Schwarzwald-Hotel Adler
St-Fridolinstrasse 15

Tel (07672) 41 70
Fax (07672) 41 71 50
Email hotel-adler-schwarzwald@t-online.de
Website www.adler-schwarzwald.de

In a village in the southern Black Forest, this stylish hotel (Relais & Châteaux) has been owned and run for five generations by the Zumkeller family. On its facade are ornate wooden balconies and a heavily gilded inn sign. It has gables, wooden ceilings, local folklore touches, but some furnishings are modern. 'There is a genuine desire to please and look after the guest,' one visiting couple wrote. 'A smooth and superbly run operation.' The Baden-based cooking, 'delicate and delicious', wins a *Michelin* star. Staff wear folk dress. Bedrooms are in rustic style. In the garden are tables with parasols, and ornamental ponds. There is a good indoor swimming pool. Lots of activities locally for sports and fitness fans (see below).

Open 18 Dec–21 Nov. Restaurant closed Mon/Tues, 10 Nov–18 Dec. **Rooms** 4 suites, 45 double. **Facilities** Lift. Lounge, bar, restaurant; seminar facilities; swimming pool, whirlpool, sauna, hammam, beauty salon; bowling alley.

Garden: outdoor dining, tennis. Hiking, mountain biking, sailing, skiing, etc nearby. **Location** 22 km N of Waldshut, 58 km SE of Freiburg. **Credit cards** MasterCard, Visa. **Terms** [2004] B&B: single €76–€92, double €113–€162, suite €176–€236. Set meals €30–€82; alc €33–€53.

HORBRUCH IM HUNSRÜCK 55483 Rheinland-Pfalz Map 8:D1

Liller's Historische Schlossmühle
An der Landstrasse 190
Tel (06543) 40 41
Fax (06543) 31 78
Email info@historische-schlossmuehle.de

There is an air of whimsy to this 17th-century mill house (its waterwheel still turns in the stream by the dining room). In its gardens are painted statuettes of children, sitting on steps, and a fountain with a frog prince and a princess. Inside are 'pictures and knick-knacks everywhere' (many are for sale). Added to this are a 'genuine welcome' from the 'delightful hosts', Anne and Rüdiger Liller, and a 'high class of comfort'. Rooms in the main house (some open on to a little patio) may be small and crowded with furniture and ornaments: one couple found 'six religious tomes' in their room, but wrote: 'We enjoyed our stay immensely'. Some rooms are in a cottage annexe. The food is 'excellent, in modern German style (nothing to do with small portions)', eg, glazed duck with noodles and almond broccoli; artichoke and ricotta ravioli with lemon butter. Dinner is served in the big garden (with pond) on warm evenings. 'First-class breakfast.' At weekends, the Lillers organise visits in the area (Bernkastel and other lovely old towns on the winding Mosel). (*NF, P and JW*)

Open 16 Jan–31 Dec. Restaurant closed to non-residents Mon. **Rooms** 2 suites, 16 double. 8 in annexe. **Facilities** Lounge, library, breakfast room, restaurant (classical background music); conference room. Large garden: pond, children's playground. **Location** 12 km SE of Bernkastel-Kues. Hotel (signposted) just outside village. Car park. **Restrictions** No smoking: breakfast room, restaurant, bedrooms. No dogs. **Credit cards** MasterCard, Visa. **Terms** B&B: double €120–€160, suite €180. Set lunch €30, dinner €41; full alc €65.

LIMBURG AN DER LAHN 65549 Hessen Map 8:D2

Romantik Hotel Zimmermann
Blumenröder Strasse 1
Tel (06431) 46 11
Fax (06431) 4 13 14
Email zimmermann@romantikhotels.com
Website www.romantik-hotel-zimmermann.de

Few German cities are as well preserved as Limburg: its *Altstadt*, with Gothic hilltop cathedral, has survived largely intact since medieval times. Recommended 'for those who appreciate adventurous eating and an ultra-personal approach', this 50-year-old hotel stands near the station. It looks a bit dull outside, but inside, say recent visitors, the Zimmermann family 'have taken endless care to furnish the bedrooms and small public spaces to a high standard' (much brass, marble, mirrors, pictures, drapes, Art Deco fittings). 'Dinner, for residents only, was prepared with loving care by Herr Zimmermann junior, and discussed with equal passion by his father. No written menu or wine list, and no price was mentioned. The four-course meal was excellent and beautifully balanced, if a little slow in coming. We chose wine from a number of half bottles brought to the table for us to inspect. Considerable trouble was taken to provide a one-course meal for two American children in a larger party at another table.' Breakfast, not a buffet, is 'elegantly served'. (*R and AS*)

Open 10 Jan–20 Dec. Dining room closed Sat/Sun. **Rooms** 20. Some no-smoking. **Facilities** Small sitting areas, dining room; background music. Tiny courtyard. **Location** Central, near station (windows triple glazed). Exit Limburg-Süd from A3. Parking. **Credit cards** Amex, MasterCard, Visa. **Terms** B&B: single €80–€115, double €85–€165. Set meal €35–€44; full alc €45.

MALCHOW 17213 Mecklenburg-Vorpommern — Map 8:B4

Inselhotel Malchow BUDGET
An der Drehbrücke

Tel (039932) 86 00
Fax (039932) 8 60 30
Email inselhotel-malchow@t-online.de
Website www.insel-hotel-malchow.m-vp.de

By a small harbour of this attractive small town, this 'delightful' hotel, white-walled and red-roofed, has been nicely converted from a white 19th-century warehouse. Its friendly owners, Anke and Olaf Bernhard, formerly worked for the GDR state airline Interflug. 'Rooms on the street were a bit noisy with the windows open during a heatwave,' says a visitor in 2004. 'But everything else was excellent and not expensive.' The large bedrooms, in white and pale green, have light-coloured furniture. Many have a lake view. Bathrooms are large, too. Meals are served outdoors in fine weather, and a returning visitor enjoyed 'copious fish stew, and good rote Grütze' (stew of berries, topped with crumbled dried flower petals). 'Breakfast, above average, in a cheerful room with a nautical air.' Malchow, perched on an island between two lakes, is in the flat Mecklenburg district with woods and scenic lakes much used for boating and swimming. (*Simon Boyd, and others*)

Open All year. **Rooms** 16 double. **Facilities** Breakfast room, restaurant; dining terrace. Access to local *Relax-Therme* and golf course. **Location** Central, by lake. 79 km SE of Rostock. Parking. **Credit cards** MasterCard. **Terms** [2004] B&B: single €46–€59, double €62–€76. Alc €12–€24.

Every entry in the *Guide* is updated every year. If we get no feedback on a hotel, we drop it.

MARIA GERN 83471 Bavaria **Map 8:F4**

Hotel Maria Gern BUDGET
Kirchplatz 3

Tel (08652) 34 40
Fax (08652) 6 62 76
Email info@mariagern.de
Website www.mariagern.de

In quiet village, 4 km N of Berchtesgaden: Uschi and Bartl Walch-Plenk's chalet-style hotel by beautiful little village church. Wonderful mountain views. 'Charming room, friendly owners.' Good Bavarian food in beamed dining room; adequate breakfasts; background music; musical evenings in summer. Terrace. Fitness room, sauna, solarium, massage. Unsuitable for ♿. No dogs. Closed 1 week Mar, 20 Oct–12 Dec, Sat; restaurant sometimes closed at quiet times. Amex, MasterCard, Visa accepted. 13 attractive bedrooms in Alpine style, some large, most with flowery balcony. B&B €33–€40; D,B&B €15 added per person. Alc from €19.

MEERSBURG 88709 Baden-Württemberg **Map 8:F2**

Gasthof zum Bären BUDGET
Marktplatz 11

Tel (07532) 4 32 20
Fax (07532) 43 22 44
Email gasthofzumbaeren@t-online.de
Website www.meersburg.de/baeren

On the small market square of this 'beautiful town, a fun place to visit', on Lake Constance, this 17th-century inn is regularly praised. Owned for five generations by the Gilowsky family, it is now a 'charming hotel', run by Michael Gilowsky. 'He parked our car as well as providing a good simple meal' (his cooking of zander fresh from the lake is praised). Visitors this year enjoyed eating on the pavement, 'watching the world go by'. 'Rustic, warm and comfortable', the inn has antiques, steep, creaking stairways (no lift); and there are carvings and flowerpots on its picturesque corner tower, whose best bedrooms have an alcove where you can sit and watch the lively scene below. Each room is different: 'Ours was a romantic ensemble of celadon-green antiques. The smart modern bathroom was small; others are larger. Breakfast was a nice buffet; staff were friendly.' One dining room has carved beams and chandeliers. The Obertor, next door, chimes the hour until 11 pm and starts again at 7 am: 'It added to the ambience.' Annette von Droste-Hülshoff, probably Germany's finest poetess, died of consumption and a broken heart in 1848, in the local fortress (now open to visitors). (*Kay Brock, S and EH*)

Open 15 Mar–15 Nov. Restaurant closed Mon. **Rooms** 17 double, 3 single. **Facilities** Restaurant (no-smoking at breakfast). No background music. Unsuitable for ♿. **Location** Central, in pedestrian zone (free car access for hotel guests). 20 garages. **Credit cards** None accepted. **Terms** B&B: single €46–€65, double €76–€104; D,B&B €17 added per person. Set meals €18–€27.

Hotel Weinstube Löwen BUDGET

Marktplatz 2

Tel (07532) 4 30 40
Fax (07532) 43 04 10
Email info@hotel-loewen-meersburg.de
Website www.hotel-loewen-meersburg.de

The 'location, friendly staff, and excellent restaurant' are all enjoyed by visitors to Sigfrid Fischer's red-fronted, flower-bedecked 15th-century inn, in the pedestrianised section of this old walled town. The breakfast buffet is also liked. Locals patronise the *Weinstube*, with its carved woodwork and tiled stove, and the panelled restaurant which serves traditional dishes. In summer, meals are also served under canopies on the cobbled square. Public rooms have antiques and heirlooms. Bedrooms vary: some are 'ultra-modern, with a sparkling marble bathroom', others 'characterful, with a creaking floor'; all have a sofa and easy chairs. 'Ours, spacious and clean, was perhaps slightly tired, especially the bathroom.' (*SE and others*)

Open All year. Restaurant closed Wed Nov–Apr. **Rooms** 18 double, 3 single. **Facilities** Restaurant, *Weinstube*; classical CDs; function room; terrace restaurant in summer. Unsuitable for ♿. **Location** Pedestrian zone of upper town. Public parking. **Credit cards** All major cards accepted. **Terms** [2004] B&B: single €44–€67, double €80–€105; D,B&B €20 added per person. Alc €24–€40.

MORAAS 19230 Mecklenburg-Vorpommern — Map 8:B3

Hotel Heidehof NEW/BUDGET

Hauptstrasse 15

Tel (03883) 72 21 40
Fax (03883) 72 91 18
Email hotel-heidehof@m-vp.de
Website www.hotel-heidehof.m-vp.de

Created from two old half-timbered thatched houses in a quiet farming village near Hagenow, Hans-Joachim Schulte's small hotel offers 'excellent value', says its nominator in 2004. He liked his room. 'Its balcony, shared with an adjacent room, overlooked the small ornamental fishpond, and would be good for relaxing on a warm day.' Only reservations: 'Somewhat dim lighting, and the newish pine furniture, though of good quality, looked as though it had been recently assembled from a kit.' In the ground-floor restaurant, main courses cost €10 to €12; many are regional specialities. 'My meal centred on fine roast pork stuffed with apples and prunes.' (*Charles Belair*)

Open Thurs–Mon 11 am–11 pm, Tues/Wed 3 pm–11 pm. **Rooms** 9 double, 2 single. 8 in annexe 4 m. **Facilities** Restaurant, grill; function/conference facilities. Beer garden: fishpond. **Location** By fire station. 11 km E of Hagenow by B321 towards Schwerin. Parking. **Credit cards** All major cards accepted. **Terms** B&B: single €39–€49, double €59–€69, suite €69–€79. Set meals €17. *V* (1 night)

The Voucher scheme is valid for a year from the publication of this volume of the *Guide* in January 2005.

MUNICH Bavaria **Map 8:F4**

Hotel Daniel's BUDGET
Hauptstrasse 11
Hallbergmoos-Goldach
85399 Munich
Tel (0811) 5 51 20
Fax (0811) 55 12 13
Email info@hotel-daniels.de
Website www.hotel-daniels.de

Fifteen mins' drive from airport, 20 km from city centre, in quiet suburb: Helga Held and Rainer Feldkamp's gabled white B&B hotel: 'good-value, welcoming, comfortable.' Excellent breakfast in attractive room. Meeting facilities. No background music. Terrace. Free car park. Open 7 Jan–23 Dec. All major credit cards accepted. 28 bedrooms with Italian period furniture, some no-smoking ('ours, good-sized, had a good bathroom'). Room: single from €43, double from €66. Breakfast €9 [2004].

Hotel Marienbad
Barerstrasse 11
80333 Munich
Tel (089) 59 55 85
Fax (089) 59 82 38
Email info@hotelmarienbad.de
Website www.hotelmarienbad.de

In a business area but fairly quiet, the Grüner family's down-to-earth B&B hotel, a red-roofed mansion, is near the Alte Pinakothek and other major museums. Visitors in 2004 endorsed earlier praise: 'Pleasant and unpretentious.' 'Service is friendly, breakfast is good, prices are moderate.' The helpful owners and their staff 'always have interesting titbits of gossip about Munich'. Most rooms are good sized, 'if a bit old-fashioned': they have sturdy pine furniture, plenty of cupboard space. Some may need renovation ('a shower handle came away in my hand'), but all now have Internet access. On the top floor is a flat with kitchen and splendid views. (*Simon Routh, and others*)

Open All year, except Christmas/New Year. **Rooms** 2 suites, 17 double, 11 single. Internet access in rooms. Some on ground floor. **Facilities** Lift. Breakfast room/lounge (no-smoking); terrace. **Location** 1 km NW of centre, near Alte Pinakothek. Free private parking. (U-Bahn: Karlsplatz) **Credit cards** MasterCard, Visa. **Terms** B&B: single €50–€95, double €105–€125, suite €135–€155.

Hotel Torbräu
Tal 41
80331 Munich
Tel (089) 24 23 40
Fax (089) 24 23 42 35
Email info@torbraeu.de
Website www.torbraeu.de

Said to be Munich's oldest hotel (500 years), owned by Werner and Walter Kirchlechner, directed by Manfred Fritsch: large yellow building, 'very central, very quiet; extremely helpful, ungrand management'. Small lift. Air conditioning. Bar, La Cantinetta*; restaurant,* La Famiglia *(closed 25 Dec);* Café am Isartor *(open all day: 'delicious' buffet breakfast, salads,* Kaffee und Kuchen, *etc; pavement service under parasols). Conference facilities. Unsuitable for ♿. Garage/parking adjacent. (S-Bahn: Isartor) Hotel closed 23–26 Dec.*

Amex, MasterCard, Visa accepted. 92 bedrooms (38 are singles), some no-smoking. B&B: single €135–€215, double €170–€280, suite €230–€305. Alc €32.50–€40.

MÜNSINGEN 72525 Baden-Württemberg — Map 8:F2

Gasthof Herrmann NEW/BUDGET
Am Marktplatz

Tel (07381) 1 82 60
Fax (07381) 62 82
Email info@hotelherrmann.de
Website www.hotelherrmann.de

*Run by Autenrieth family for 4 generations: hotel/restaurant (*Michelin Bib Gourmand*) in small town in pretty countryside south-east of Stuttgart. 'A very good pit stop. Excellent dinner in dining room bursting with locals. Very comfortable bedroom, quiet at night. Vigilant owner/head chef. Free drink on arrival.' Lift. Restaurant; function room; sauna. Garden (meal service). Parking. Amex, MasterCard, Visa accepted. 33 bedrooms: single €40–€46, double €46–€76. Set meals €20–€32 [2004].*

NECKARGEMÜND 69151 Baden-Württemberg — Map 8:E2

Hotel zum Schwanen
Uferstrasse 16
Kleingemünd

Tel (06223) 9 24 00
Fax (06223) 24 13
Email info@hotel-schwanen.com
Website www.hotel-schwanen.com

Backed by a wooded hill, this 200-year-old inn looks across the River Neckar to the village with its pretty churches. 'Not a place for a lie-in,' says a visitor this year. 'We were awoken at 6.30 am every day by a long peal of bells from said churches.' She liked her spacious room with big sofa, satellite TV, 'very nice bathroom' and minibar. Another visitor found his room 'somewhat anonymous' but enjoyed the 'good, simple fare, especially the Pfifferlingen omelette and a couple of blue trout, served under chestnut trees in the garden'. The 'superb local beer and wine' have also been praised. There is a smart panoramic restaurant, and a conservatory, full of potted plants, where the buffet breakfast is taken. Owner/chef, Günter Ehrenhold, and his wife, Miwako (Japanese but brought up in Paris), are thought 'charming and considerate'. Barges, ducks and swans on the river add to the atmosphere. No lift in this old building: some rooms are up lots of stairs. Good walks nearby. (*NW*, *John Stege*, *SL*)

Open All year. **Rooms** 1 suite, 12 double, 6 single. **Facilities** Foyer, winter garden, restaurant; classical background music; conference facilities. Garden (outdoor dining): beer garden, children's playground. Unsuitable for ♿. **Location** On river, across from Neckargemünd. 9 km SE of Heidelberg. Open parking. **Credit cards** All major cards accepted. **Terms** B&B: single €75–€79, double €99–€125, suite €145; D,B&B €18 added per person. Set meals €20–€25; full alc €30–€40. *V* (1 Oct–31 Mar)

NEUSTADT BEI COBURG 96465 Bavaria — Map 8:D3

Hotel Am Markt
Markt 3

Tel (09568) 92 02 20
Fax (09568) 92 02 29
Email info@hotelgarni-am-markt.de
Website www.hotelgarni-am-markt.de

Liked by returning visitor in 2004, notably for 'excellence and international character' of buffet breakfast: stylish small, green-fronted, gabled hotel in town in toy-making area, 17 km NE of Coburg: on market square but quiet at night. Quality furnishings, marble bathrooms; 20 bedrooms in modern minimalist style; big beds. All major credit cards accepted. Conference room, parking. Restaurant across square, Beim Thomas, *under same ownership, has 'excellent food and service' (dinner only; closed Sun and Sept). B&B: single €40–€50, double €82–€87. Alc €21–€31 [2004].*

NEUWEIER 76534 Baden-Württemberg — Map 8:E2

Hotel Heiligenstein
Heiligensteinstrasse 19a

Tel (07223) 9 61 40
Fax (07223) 96 14 50
Email gast@hotel-heiligenstein.de
Website www.hotel-heiligenstein.de

In a big wine village on the *Badische Weinstrasse*, this chalet-style hotel, near vineyards, is 'very pleasant with attractive rooms and a delicious buffet breakfast', say recent admirers. Others wrote: 'Our welcome was warm; the comfortable bedroom was well furnished.' Owned by Barbara Beck and managed by Bettina Fundinger, it has a fire in the lounge bar, and a sunny terrace for drinks and coffee. The evening meal can be a *Vesper* (snack), or you can take the menu of the day. 'Delicious local wines.' Some bedrooms are large, with massive wood furnishings and a balcony ('splendid views') and 'quiet, except for birdsong'. (*SL, and others*)

Open Apr–Dec, except Christmas. Restaurant closed Tues. **Rooms** 3 suites, 18 double, 9 single. Some on ground floor. **Facilities** Lift. Lobby, TV room, bar, restaurant; background music; 2 conference rooms; billiard room; sauna, whirlpool, solarium. Terrace. Garden. **Location** Edge of village. 10 km SW of Baden-Baden, 7 km NE of Bühl. Parking. **Restriction** No smoking: breakfast room, whirlpool, some bedrooms. **Credit cards** MasterCard, Visa. **Terms** B&B: single €48–€62, double €87–€104, suite €140–€160; D,B&B €24 added per person.

OBERAMMERGAU 82487 Bavaria — Map 8:F3

Hotel Alte Post
Dorfstrasse 19

Tel (08822) 91 00
Fax (08822) 91 01 00
Email info@altepost.com
Website www.altepost.com

In the Ammer valley, this pretty, if touristy, town is famed for its passion play and its tradition of woodcarving. In the centre is Anton

Preisinger's 400-year-old hotel. Behind its intricately painted facade is a rustic decor (beams, wood panelling, antlers, etc). 'The staff were uniformly helpful: most were fluent in English,' says a recent visitor. 'My adequately sized room, with large brass chandelier, looked over the main street: one of the better views I have had from a hotel window. Some street noise, not overpowering.' Other rooms look on to car parks or 'mundane buildings'. 'Dinner was standard German fare. Breakfast had delicious pastries with apple filling.' Tables on the front terrace allow guests to watch the world go by in the town square. 'Good value off-season.' (*CKB*)

Open All year. **Rooms** 6 suites, 22 double, 4 single. Some no-smoking. 6 in annexe. **Facilities** Lift, ramps. Internet café. Lounge, bar, restaurant. No background music. **Location** Central. 10 mins' walk from station. Parking. **Credit cards** All major cards accepted. **Terms** B&B: single €40–€45, double €60–€80, suite €80–€90; D,B&B €52–€57 per person. Set meals €10–€15; full alc €17–€22.

OBERWESEL 55430 Rheinland-Pfalz — Map 8:D2

Burghotel Auf Schönburg

Tel (06744) 939 30
Fax (06744) 16 13
Email huettl@hotel-schoenburg.com
Website www.hotel-schoenburg.com

Romantically set above the Rhine (stunning views), this medieval castle is reached by 'quite a walk up, on cobblestones' (luggage follows by tractor). Outwardly severe, it is cosy inside, 'a warren of nooks and crannies': small courtyards and dining rooms, a lounge in a tower, a handsome library. 'Everything is tasteful: superb etchings/paintings.' The owner/managers, Wolfgang and Barbara Hüttl, are 'excellent hosts', say their guests. Their English-speaking staff are friendly, and the bedrooms are 'lovely'. The best ones are in the tower. 'Our huge room had windows on all four sides, a small balcony. Furnishings were homely.' One 'very nice' bathroom was 'built over the roof and hidden by a bookcase'. Some rooms are small; back ones are quietest; river-facing ones get noise from the trains below. The 'superb' food is elaborate, eg, lamb in a thyme and Parmesan crust with ratatouille tart. Guests dine in the courtyard in fine weather. 'A lovely lunch on the terrace facing the Rhine. The local white wine is wonderful.' There is smoked salmon with Sekt for breakfast, and free sherry in bedrooms. Toys, etc, are provided for children. Some tour groups. (*SBH*)

Open 17 Mar–31 Dec. **Rooms** 2 suites, 18 double, 2 single. 3 on courtyard level. **Facilities** Sitting room, library, restaurant (classical background music); conference/function room; chapel. Courtyard (alfresco meals), riverside terraces. Unsuitable for ♿. **Location** 2 km S of town. E of A61, 49 km S of Koblenz; take Laudert/Oberwesel exit. Car park below castle. **Credit cards** MasterCard, Visa. **Terms** B&B: single €65–€98, double €150–€210, suite €210. Set lunch €25, dinner €78 (7 courses); full alc €36.

OEVERSEE 24988 Schleswig-Holstein — Map 8:A3

Romantik Hotel Historischer Krug
Grazer Plaz 1 (B76)

Tel (04630) 94 00
Fax (04630) 7 80
Email krug@romantikhotels.com
Website www.historischer-krug.de

In a pretty village near Flensburg, by the River Treene, Frau Lenka Hansen-Mörck has turned her ancestral home (since 1519), a low, white, thatched building, into this attractive hotel complex, with guest accommodation in houses in the garden, and thermal baths and a beauty farm. It was recently much admired: 'A beautiful and well-restored house. We were impressed by our room, the friendliness and service of the staff, and the restaurant. The breakfast buffet was typical German with lots of choice. Prices were reasonable.' There are lounges in rustic style, and two restaurants, the gourmet *Privileg* and the simpler *Krugwirtschaft*. Some bedrooms are pine-panelled; some have flowery fabrics. (*DJS*)

Open All year. *Privileg* restaurant open Thurs–Mon, evenings only, closed 15 Jan–15 Feb. **Rooms** 35 double, 5 single. Some no-smoking. In 6 buildings. **Facilities** 3 salons, bar/lounge, 2 restaurants (classical background music). 3-hectare grounds on river: thermal baths, wellness/beauty facilities. Tennis, riding, golf nearby. **Location** 9 km S of Flensburg on B76. On A7, Tarp exit. **Restriction** No smoking at breakfast. **Credit cards** All major cards accepted. **Terms** [2004] B&B: single €59–€111, double €102–€155. Set meals €26–€74; alc €27–€39.

OLZHEIM 54597 Rheinland-Pfalz — Map 8:D1

Haus Feldmaus BUDGET
Knaufspescher Strasse 14

Tel (06552) 9 92 20
Fax (06552) 99 22 22
Email info@feldmaus.de
Website www.feldmaus.de

Visitors this year enthused about 'the delights of the kitchen and cellar' at this old converted farmhouse (it calls itself a *Hotelschen*). It stands amid trees and fields outside a village near the Belgian border, on the edge of the Schneifel mountains ('great walking and wildlife watching'). 'Delightful and distinctive', it is liked for its 'excellent welcome', reasonable prices, big beds and collection of modern art. The 'helpful owner', Stephan Trierweiler, puts the accent on healthy living and ecology. The bedrooms, all different, simple but stylish, have names like Nostalgie (with old oak furniture), Budoar (like a French boudoir), Kafavis (for the Greek poet; it has two baths). Meals are served outdoors in summer in a charming forecourt with white parasols, or in a conservatory. 'Good home cooking: vegetarian dishes a speciality'; 'some of the wines are real finds'. 'Splendid breakfast buffet: excellent home-made muesli.' (*CG*)

Open All year. Restaurant closed midday, to non-residents Sun. **Rooms** 6 double, 4 single. **Facilities** Lounge, TV room, 2 dining rooms; conservatory; seminar room, sauna. No background music. Gardens: terrace. Unsuitable for ♿. **Location** W edge of Olzheim, which is 65 km N of Trier, 8 km N of Prüm.

Parking. **Restriction** No smoking: lounge, sun room, 1 dining room, 6 bedrooms. **Credit cards** MasterCard, Visa. **Terms** B&B: single €44, double €78–€98; D,B&B €14 added per person. Set dinner €15; full alc €20. 1-night bookings refused some weekends.

PALLING 83349 Bavaria — Map 8:F4

Gasthof Michlwirt NEW/BUDGET
Steiner Strasse 1–3

Tel (08629) 9 88 10
Fax (08629) 98 81 81
Email michlwirt@t-online.de
Website www.michlwirt.de

In market town NW of Salzburg: large building, half old, half new, at fairly busy traffic intersection. Owned and 'personally run' by Rudolf and Marianne Trinkberger and family. 'Nice room of character in country style; good pine furniture. Excellent buffet breakfast, even by German standards.' Closed 11–25 Jan, 12 Sept–3 Oct. Restaurant closed Sun. Lift. Restaurant (locally popular; booking advised); children's play area; sauna, whirlpool; function rooms. Location 92 km N of Munich. Car park. MasterCard, Visa accepted. 42 bedrooms (newer, best ones in annexe). B&B: single €33–€41, double €55–€67. Alc €12–€23 [2004].

PASSAU 94032 Bavaria — Map 8:E4

Hotel König BUDGET
Untere Donaulände 1

Tel (0851) 38 50
Fax (0851) 38 54 60
Email info@hotel-koenig.de
Website www.hotel-koenig.de

With its smart pink facade and cheerful window boxes, Franz Kralj's modern hotel is in the centre of this lovely old town, on the banks of the Danube. It is liked for its 'efficient service' and 'club-like feel'. 'My room,' says a returning visitor, 'was good as ever; lots of quality furnishing, large, well-designed bathroom. Breakfast was varied.' Double glazing makes even the riverside rooms fairly quiet (all rooms have new windows this year). No restaurant: you can eat at the yellow-fronted sister hotel, *Zum König*, close by: it has a terrace for summer meals. And there are good eating places in the *Altstadt*. Passau was the setting of *The Nasty Girl*, the film and book about its Nazi past. Its cathedral is said to contain the world's largest organ. (*CKB*)

Open All year. **Rooms** 41 double, 8 single. 20 in annexe. 3 suitable for ♿. **Facilities** Lift. Lobby, bar, breakfast room; sauna, solarium. **Location** Central, by Danube. Garage; parking close by. **Credit cards** All major cards accepted. **Terms** [2004] B&B: single €57–€85, double €85–€130.

> We asked hotels to quote 2005 prices. Not all were able to predict them. Some of our terms will be inaccurate. Do check latest tariffs at the time of booking.

PEGNITZ 91257 Bavaria — Map 8:E4

Pflaums Posthotel Pegnitz
Nürnbergerstrasse 8–16

Tel (09241) 72 50
Fax (09241) 8 04 04
Email info@ppp.com
Website www.ppp.com

'Eccentric, excellent, exceptional (and expensive); quite unlike any other hotel,' says a regular *Guide* correspondent on his third visit. 'Nothing changes. It is unique, the Pflaums in particular.' Dedicated to Wagner, this handsome post house (where Napoleon once stayed) is on the edge of a small town south of Bayreuth. Owned and run since 1707 by the Pflaum family, it is now a famous and ambitious hotel: its cosmopolitan clientele includes opera singers and their audience. Wagner's works are played on a giant screen in the lobby. Traditional outside (flowery window boxes), '*PPP*' has 'enthusiastic postmodern' decor inside. 'In your room, it is a conundrum how to control the lights,' one visitor wrote. The eccentricity doesn't suit everyone, but 'the young staff are charming', and Hermann Pflaum's cooking is 'exceptional'. He runs a smart gourmet restaurant, and a rustic *Stube* for Franconian food. His brother, Andreas, with wife Wilhelmina ('very warm'), is manager. Meals can be served in the 'lovely garden'. All bedrooms have a CD- and a DVD-player (Wagner operas can be borrowed). Some rooms are in rustic style; others, named after Wagnerian characters, are 'futuristic'. Plácido Domingo and Michael Jackson have stayed in the Parsifal room, lit by a thousand blue stars. Some rooms have a private garden. A few hear traffic. There are games, etc, for children. (*J Hanford*)

Open All year. **Rooms** 25 suites (2 suitable for ♿), 25 double. Air conditioning. **Facilities** Lift. Lounges, TV room, Internet café, bar, restaurant, *Stube*; classical background music; conference facilities; spa: swimming pool, sauna, indoor golf; *Kindergarten*. Garden: dining terrace. Golf nearby. **Location** 1 km SW of Pegnitz. 15 mins' drive from Bayreuth. **Restriction** No smoking: restaurants, some bedrooms. **Credit cards** All major cards accepted. **Terms** B&B: single €118–€268, double €185–€336, suite €350–€750. Set meals €39–€115. *V*

PERLEBERG 19348 Brandenburg — Map 8:B4

Hotel Deutscher Kaiser NEW
Bäckerstrasse 18

Tel (03876) 7 91 40
Fax (03876) 79 14 79
Email info@deutscherkaiser.de
Website www.deutscherkaiser.de

In town with attractive pedestrianised centre, on S edge of Mecklenburg lake district ('a good base for touring; try the local mustard Perleberger Senf'), 75 km SE of Schwerin: traditional hotel, built 1913, recently restored to former elegance. Buffet breakfast in period room. Restaurant, tavern (locally popular), 'wonderful' ballroom; small meeting room; terrace café (by river) in summer. Parking. Garage. MasterCard, Visa accepted. 10 bedrooms (the most interesting) in old part, 15 in modern extension. B&B: single €52–€77, double €61–€98. Alc €21–€33 [2004].

PFINZTAL-SÖLLINGEN 76327 Baden-Württemberg Map 8:E2

Villa Hammerschmiede NEW
Hauptstrasse 162

Tel (07240) 60 01
Fax (07240) 6 01 60
Email info@villa-hammerschmiede.de
Website www.villa-hammerschmiede.de

A large red villa once owned by the Krupp family is now this smart hotel (Relais & Châteaux), owned by the Schwalbe family. Chef Markus Nagy has a *Michelin* star for the food, elegantly served in a conservatory or a vaulted cellar restaurant (where breakfast also takes place). Visitors in 2004 had a 'delicious dinner: asparagus served three ways; zander fillet with garden vegetables; mullet with olives and grilled peppers. The wine list is huge; we chose a *Weissburgunder* from a local vineyard. Service by girls in rustic dresses was efficient. All the staff were friendly.' Some bedrooms are in a modern steel and glass annexe, 'very stylish', with contemporary art along the corridors. 'Our room was huge and comfortable. Huge windows faced a wooded hillside. Furnishings were mainly cherry wood (so popular in Germany). The large, supremely comfortable bed had lovely linen and fluffy duvets. Huge, amazing bathroom. Breakfast was a vast buffet: fruit, eggs, cooked dishes and much more.' There is an indoor swimming pool carved out of rock. 'Everything is immaculate. Professional staff. Superb food. Lovely building.' (*Pat and Jeremy Temple*)

Open All year. **Rooms** 30. **Facilities** Lift. Salon, restaurant, conservatory; conference facilities; indoor swimming pool. Garden: meal service. **Location** 15 km E of Karlsruhe, 50 km N of Baden-Baden. **Credit cards** All major cards accepted. **Terms** [2004] Room €160–€230, suite €260–€440. Breakfast €16. Set meals €38–€84; alc €41–€56.

PFRONTEN 87459 Bavaria Map 8:F3

Berghotel Schlossanger Alp
Am Schlossanger 1
Obermeilingen

Tel (08363) 91 45 50
Fax (08363) 91 45 55 55
Email ebert@schlossanger.de
Website www.schlossanger.de

'Particularly enjoyed' this year, the Schlachter-Ebert family's modern chalet-style hotel has a 'spectacular setting' amid fields, facing 'a panorama of peaks', on the edge of a ski and summer resort in the Allgäu Alps. Behind is the high Falkenstein mountain with its gaunt ruined castle. 'Not slick but very comfortable' and 'professionally run', it has a rustic decor: wood carvings, and 'some whimsy'. A panoramic winter garden is new this year. Barbara Schlachter-Ebert's cooking (*Michelin Bib Gourmand*) is 'good with hearty portions'. Her husband, Bernard, is in charge of the wine. Meals are taken alfresco in fine weather. Service, by waitresses in local dress, 'can be slow, but is friendly'. Breakfast is a 'wonderful' buffet. Geraniums on balconies; deer in the meadows; 'cowbells by day, croaking frogs in the evening, otherwise peace'. There is good accommodation for families, and a 'very small' indoor swimming pool. (*Michael Burns, Dawn Mitchell, G and VB*)

Open All year. **Rooms** 6 suites, 24 double. Some no-smoking. **Facilities** Lounge, winter garden, breakfast rooms, restaurant (pianist sometimes); small conference room; children's playroom; swimming pool, sauna, solarium, whirlpool, fitness room. Garden: terrace/café; children's playground. Unsuitable for ♿. **Location** 4 km E of Pfronten, towards Füssen. **Credit cards** MasterCard, Visa. **Terms** B&B €78–€210; D,B&B €20 added per person. Set lunch €14–€20, dinner €20–€58; full alc €35. *V*

PIESPORT 54498 Rheinland-Pfalz Map 8:D1

Hotel Piesporter Goldtröpfchen BUDGET *Tel* (06507) 24 42
Am Domhof 5 *Fax* (06507) 68 79
Email weingut-hain@t-online.de
Website www.weingut-hain.de

For more than four centuries, the Hain family has produced award-winning Riesling wines in this attractive village on the Mosel. Their 'delightful hotel' has a pleasant terrace facing the river: drinks and meals are served here in fine weather. 'Excellent cleanliness, facilities, etc,' says a visitor in 2004. 'Our newly refurbished room across the courtyard was of a high standard, albeit a little bare. Food was adequate; small printed menu. The friendly owners showed us the cellars: we bought some wine.' Some bedrooms face the river. Some rooms get 'substantial traffic noise'. Other comments: 'Excellent value, more a home than a hotel.' 'We dined among local families – very happy-making,' one couple wrote. 'Good breakfasts.' Children are welcomed: there is a playroom. Good riverside walking. (*J Hanford, and others*)

Open All year. **Rooms** 1 suite, 13 double. **Facilities** *Weinstube*, restaurant; terrace; sauna. **Location** In village, across river from main road, by westerly bridge. 18 km W of Bernkastel-Kues. Public parking opposite. **Restriction** No smoking: breakfast room, 5 bedrooms. **Credit cards** MasterCard, Visa. **Terms** B&B: single €38, double €51–€65. Full alc €20.

QUEDLINBURG 06484 Sachsen-Anhalt Map 8:C3

Romantik Hotel am Brühl *Tel* (03946) 9 61 80
Billungstrasse 11 *Fax* (03946) 9 61 82 46
Email hotelambruehl@t-online.de
Website www.hotelambruehl.de

One of a group of listed houses in a quiet street in this 'remarkably preserved' old town (a UNESCO historic site), this half-timbered building has been lovingly restored. In the lounge are alcoves, subtle lighting, terracotta-coloured armchairs and sofas, an open wood fire. All contribute to a 'feeling of warmth' created by the 'hands-on' owner, Ursula Schmidt. Visitors write of 'elegant decor and value for money'. 'Our double room was compact, but decorated with taste, as was the gleaming bathroom. The family dined each evening and chatted with guests in the high-quality restaurant, a former "cow parlour" across the flower-filled courtyard. Food and wine (accent on seasonal and local produce) and service were excellent.' Breakfast is a copious buffet. Quedlinburg, north of the Harz mountains, has a summer music festival and a lively pre-Christmas market. (*R and AS*)

Open All year. Restaurant closed midday. **Rooms** 5 suites, 33 double, 7 single. Some no-smoking. **Facilities** Lifts. Lounge, Breakfast room (no-smoking), restaurant; classical background music; 2 conference rooms; sauna, solarium. Courtyard garden. **Location** Near historic centre, S of castle. 71 km SW of Magdeburg. Parking. **Credit cards** All major cards accepted. **Terms** [2004] B&B: single €85–€90, double €100–€145, suite €145–€165. Set meal €25–€38; full alc €45.

QUERFURT 06268 Sachsen-Anhalt — Map 8:C4

Querfurter Hof BUDGET
Merseburger Strasse 5

Tel (034771) 52 40
Fax (034771) 52 41 99
Email info@querfurterhof.de
Website www.querfurterhof.de

In centre of small, historic town 25 km SW of Halle (huge fortress, Renaissance and baroque buildings): Volker Hartmann's stylish 3-star hotel (built 1998), 'quiet, competently run'. Good public rooms, pleasant, if 'slightly austere', bedrooms with light wood furnishings. Much-praised restaurant; 'buffet breakfast exceptional, even by German standards'. Fitness room, sauna, lift. Locked car park (free) close by. Closed 24 Dec. All major credit cards accepted. 25 bedrooms. B&B: single from €55, double from €75. Alc €23–€29 [2004].

ROTHENBURG OB DER TAUBER 91541 Bavaria — Map 8:E3

Gasthof Glocke
Am Plönlein 1

Tel (09861) 95 89 90
Fax (09861) 9 58 99 22
Email glocke.rothenburg@t-online.de
Website www.glocke-rothenburg.de

Pleasant old inn, owned and run by Thürauf family since 1898. 'Cosy and gemütlich', *with several levels and staircases. Friendly staff, 'excellent' Bavarian food, good breakfasts. 3 dining rooms,* Weinstube *(family owns vineyards). Parking. Some traffic noise. All major credit cards accepted. Closed 22 Dec–7 Jan. Restaurant closed Sun night. 24 comfortable bedrooms, some with balcony above garden, some no-smoking. B&B: single €61–€77, double €72–€103. Alc €14–€35 [2004].*

Hotel garni Hornburg NEW/BUDGET
Hornburgweg 28

Tel (09861) 84 80
Fax (09861) 55 70
Email info@hotel-hornburg.de
Website www.hotel-hornburg.de

'An excellent, good-value B&B,' says a visitor in 2004, restoring it to the *Guide* after a time with no reports. Set peacefully in a large garden just outside the city walls, but an easy walk from the centre, this big Jugendstil villa (1903), much gabled and timbered, is run by its 'very friendly' owners, Martin and Gabriele Wetzel. The original glass doors, panelling and stucco ceilings have been restored. Earlier comments: 'A superb mansion.' 'Fabulous.' The bedrooms are individually decorated and well kept. Some are suitable for a family. 'Ours, very spacious, with a small conservatory, was done in yellow with prints of butterflies and flowers.' A 'bountiful buffet breakfast' is served in a cheery room. No restaurant, but the large garden can be used for barbecues. The owners' golden retrievers 'play their part in the hospitality', and visiting 'friendly dogs' are welcomed (no charge). Cots and high chairs are provided for babies. (*J Hanford*)

Open All year, except Christmas. **Rooms** 1 suite, 9 double. 3 on ground floor. 5 no-smoking. **Facilities** 2 lounges, 2 breakfast rooms (no-smoking; background radio). Garden. Unsuitable for ♿. **Location** E of city walls, near Galgentor. Follow signs for Stadtmitte; turn left in front of Würzburger Gate. Large car park in front (€3 per day). **Credit cards** Amex, MasterCard, Visa. **Terms** B&B: single €52–€67, double €69–€98, suite €98. 3-night rates. 1-night bookings refused public holidays, festivals.

Kloster-Stüble BUDGET
Heringsbronnengasse 5

Tel (09861) 67 74
Fax (09861) 64 74
Email hotel@klosterstueble.de
Website www.klosterstueble.de

Central but quiet, in side street near city walls (views over wooded Tauber valley): Hammel family's cheerful, unpretentious Gasthof, *recently refurbished. Tall gabled mansion, once a farmhouse. Friendly staff (valet parking); 'hearty, fresh, generous breakfasts'. Franconian food in cosy restaurant with outdoor terrace. Wine cellar. Bavarian pine furnishings. Comfortable bedrooms. Children warmly welcomed. Unsuitable for ♿. MasterCard, Visa accepted. 13 rooms, including suite with four-poster. B&B: single €50–€55, double €75–€85, suite €110–€155. Set lunch €13, dinner €22; alc €30 [2004].*

RÜDESHEIM-ASSMANNSHAUSEN 65385 Hessen Map 8:D2

Hotel Alte Bauernschänke
Niederwaldstrasse 18–23

Tel (06722) 4 99 90
Fax (06722) 4 79 12
Email altebauernschaenke@t-online.de
Website www.altebauernschaenke.de

A simpler, jollier and less expensive alternative to the august *Krone* (now omitted from the *Guide* for lack of reports), in this famous Rhineside village near Rüdesheim. This *Old Peasant Pub* is now a characterful hotel, made up of two old mansions, one 15th-century. It has flower-bedecked windows, half-timbering, beamed ceilings. 'A really enjoyable place to stay,' recent visitors wrote. 'We ate well.' The Berg family (Konrad is owner, Jürgen is chef) are proud of their dance halls and bars which attract a lively young crowd. The large bedrooms are decorated in rustic style; the big bathrooms are well equipped; staff are helpful. There are three restaurants and a dining terrace. Children have their own menu.

Open Mid-Mar–mid-Dec. **Rooms** 3 suites, 45 double, 5 single. In 2 buildings. **Facilities** Lift. Bar, 3 restaurants; terrace restaurant; background/live music; skittle alley; 2 dance halls; conference rooms. Unsuitable for ♿. **Location** Central. Free parking. **Credit cards** Amex, MasterCard, Visa. **Terms** [2004] B&B: single €59–€91, double €80–€108, suite €110–€140; D,B&B €19 added per person. Alc €16–€31.

SCHNEEBERG 08289 Sachsen — Map 8:D4

Hotel-Restaurant Büttner BUDGET
Markt 3

Tel (03772) 35 30
Fax (03772) 35 32 00
Email hotel-restaurant_buettner@t-online.de
Website www.hotel-buettner.de

Just behind Schneeberg's city hall, this little hotel, formerly the Büttner family's *Konditorei*, is known for the cuisine of chef Uwe Tögel; his 'charming' wife, Birgit, is front-of-house. Its gourmet restaurant is in a vaulted wine cellar decorated with old culinary utensils. 'Breakfast, in a charming room, was a bit above German average in content, and much above average in presentation,' says a recent visitor. 'Spacious, well-equipped' bedrooms have flower paintings, but curtains may be thin. Some rooms look over the lively market square where a splendid Christmas fair is held: these get street noise 'most of the time'. The baroque centre of this small hilltop city near Chemnitz – which grew wealthy through its silver mines – is a listed historic monument. The cathedral, dedicated to St Wolfgang, has a Cranach altarpiece and bells that are active on Sunday. (*CB*)

Open All year. Restaurant closed 2 weeks Jan, 2 weeks Aug. **Rooms** 1 apartment in annexe, 11 double, 1 single. **Facilities** Breakfast room, wine cellar, restaurant (classical background music); terrace café. Courtyard. Unsuitable for ♿. **Location** Behind city hall. Courtyard parking. **Credit cards** MasterCard, Visa. **Terms** B&B: single €46–€50, double €66–€80; D,B&B €22 added per person. Full alc €41.50. 1-night bookings sometimes refused.

SCHÖNAICH 71101 Baden-Württemberg — Map 8:E2

Waldhotel Sulzbachtal BUDGET
Im Sulzbachtal 2

Tel (07031) 7 57 80
Fax (07031) 75 78 10
Email hotel-sulzbachtal@schoenbuch.de
Website www.schoenbuch.de/hotel-sulzbachtal/hotel

In 'idyllic rural location' of Sulzbachtal, 15 km SW of Stuttgart, just NE of Böblingen, towards Steinenbronn: Knittel family's hotel with warm welcome, good value. 'About 15 minutes' drive from Stuttgart airport; a fine alternative to the airport hotels.' Double glazing reduces aircraft noise; no planes midnight–6 am. Honesty bar. Good buffet breakfast. In adjacent restaurant, good hot food (limited menu) served till 10 pm, then 'generous' cold dishes. Terrace: meal service; children's play area; meeting facilities. Schönbuch nature reserve adjacent. Unsuitable for ♿. Closed 27 Dec–mid-Jan; restaurant closed 13–19 Sept, Mon/Tues midday. All major credit cards accepted. 20 bedrooms (no-smoking; some with balcony and view). B&B: single €54–€62, double €76–€93. Set meals €18 [2004].

SCHÖNWALD 78141 Baden-Württemberg Map 8:F2

Hotel Dorer BUDGET
Schubertstrasse 20

Tel (07722) 9 50 50
Fax (07722) 95 05 30
Email hotel-dorer-schoenwald@t-online.de
Website www.hotel-dorer.de

The Scherer family's chalet-style hotel sits on a quiet street next to a park in this picturesque Black Forest village. Rolf Scherer is chef, his daughter is front-of-house. All is in traditional style: public rooms have wood panelling, stylish furnishings, ornate ceilings; even the 'pristine' small indoor swimming pool is beamed. Bedrooms, some with a balcony, are all different. 'Marvellous buffet breakfast. Wonderful dinner,' was one comment. The food, a mix of local specialities and dishes with a Mediterranean flavour, is 'delicately cooked and presented'. Outside is an ornate bandstand where local musicians perform in summer. Around is 'gorgeous scenery'. *Wild- und Wander-Wochen* packages are offered in spring and summer. 'Still lovely' and 'very welcoming', say returning visitors. (*V and MR*)

Open All year. **Rooms** 4 suites, 10 double, 5 single. **Facilities** Lounge/bar, restaurant (no-smoking); background music; beauty salon, massage, etc; indoor swimming pool. Garden: solarium. Unsuitable for ♿. **Location** 56 km NE of Freiburg. Parking. **Credit cards** All major cards accepted. **Terms** B&B: single €45–€50, double €82–€90, suite €95; D,B&B €20 added per person. Set meals €20; full alc €33.50.

Hotel zum Ochsen NEW
Ludwig-Uhland-Strasse 18

Tel (07722) 86 64 80
Fax (07722) 8 66 48 88
Email ringhotel@ochsen.com
Website www.ochsen.com

On a residential road on the edge of this stylish resort village in the Black Forest, the Martin family have owned and run this hotel for five generations. It is a series of chalet-like buildings, decorated in folksy local style (lots of light wood). It backs on to its own nine-hole golf course and has a 'smallish but good' indoor pool surrounded by picture windows facing greenery. Bedrooms are modern. Visitors in 2004 had a 'large room, simply and well decorated', with sitting area and French windows opening on to a balcony, adequate shower room. The restaurant consists of three adjoining rooms, one almost a conservatory, opening on to the garden, and the Baden cooking includes local wild boar, fish from Lake Constance. 'The food was very good (poussin with mushroom risotto; excellent puddings). Herr and Frau Martin are much in evidence (she prepared an amazing zabaglione for a large party). Service throughout the hotel was friendly. Fabulous breakfast: buffet stretching as far as the eye could see.' There are good facilities for children. (*Matthew Hamlyn*)

Open All year, except 10–28 Jan. **Rooms** 7 suites, 30 double. **Facilities** Lounge, restaurant (background music; live music once a week); conference room; indoor swimming pool, sauna, solarium. Large grounds: terrace, tennis, 9-hole golf course, bicycles, lake, fishing. Unsuitable for ♿. **Location** Edge of village. 56 km NE of Freiburg. Parking. Garage (€7). **Credit cards** All major cards accepted. **Terms** [2004] B&B €38; D,B&B €21 added per person.

SCHWANGAU 87645 Bavaria — Map 8:F3

Hotel Rübezahl BUDGET
Am Ehberg 31

Tel (08362) 88 88
Fax (08362) 8 17 01
Email hotel-ruebezahl@t-online.de
Website www.neuschwanstein-hotel.com

'We were very satisfied.' 'It never lets us down. The owners continually refresh and improve.' Praise in 2004 for Erhard and Giselle Thurm's chalet-style hotel. Set back from a main road, it represents 'a wonderful mixture of Bavarian *Gemütlichkeit* and Latin flair' (she is a former Brazilian ice-skating champion). 'Delightful staff. Superb buffet breakfast': in summer it can be taken outside, with views of King Ludwig II's castle, and 'the gentle sounds of grazing cows and their bells'. The 'excellent dinners' are served in 'cosy' dining rooms; 'helpings are generous'. Theme evenings (Bavarian, Italian, etc), with appropriate buffet, are held. The *Residenz* has junior suites with 'superb design'. In the *Landhaus* are 'high-quality' bedrooms and suites. The original building has good rooms, too, but most have only a shower. The Thurms say they 'love children' (games, videos, etc, provided). They belong to the group 'Ludwig Musical Hotels', and have live music, dancing and fashion shows in the winter garden. 'The new Therme Romana' (spa with saunas, whirlpools, etc) 'really enhances the hotel,' say visitors this year. (*Maureen and Jack Sharkey, Oliver Schick*)

Open All year. *À la carte* restaurant closed Wed. **Rooms** 11 suites, 24 double, 5 single. In 3 buildings. Some on ground floor. Some no-smoking. **Facilities** Lift. *Wintergarten*/bar (dancing twice monthly), *Stube*, restaurant; classical background music throughout; children's games room; spa: beauty treatments; sauna, etc. Terrace; lawn. Unsuitable for ♿. **Location** 3 km E of Füssen. Car park. **Restriction** No smoking in 1 dining room. **Credit cards** MasterCard, Visa. **Terms** B&B: single €55–€75, double €100–€125, suite €140–€210. Set lunch €18, dinner €25; full alc €35.

SEIFFEN 09548 Sachsen — Map 8:D4

Hotel Berghof NEW/BUDGET
Kurhausstrasse 36

Tel (037362) 77 20
Fax (037362) 77 22 20
Email berghof@nussknackerbaude.de
Website www.berghof-seiffen.de

In a small valley in eastern Germany, amid the rolling hills of the Erzgebirge along the frontier with the Czech Republic, this town has long been the centre of a cottage industry producing traditional wooden decorations for Christmas and Easter. Many visitors come from Germany and elsewhere between mid-November and Christmas, but for the rest of the year, the town is quiet. 'Many of its hotels seem to cater to bus tour groups,' says a visitor this year, 'but this converted farm building and its sister hotel, the *Knussknackerbaude*, seem to be more interested in the individual traveller. The *Berghof* sits amid farmland high above Seiffen and has good views. A sympathetic1960s addition fits well with the rural surroundings. My room had rustic but unfussy decor in green and natural wood.' The restaurant is in three sections, each different, one rustic, one semi-sophisticated, one in modern café style. In summer there is a patio café. 'Breakfast was a fine buffet, served with Rosenthal china.' Picnics, horse riding, etc, can be arranged. (*Charles Belair*)

Open All year. **Rooms** 3 suites, 24 double, 3 single. **Facilities** Lift. Lounge, bar, 3 dining rooms (background music); sauna. Garden: patio, summer café. **Location** 2 km from centre. 65 km S of Dresden, 56 km SE of Chemnitz. **Credit cards** MasterCard, Visa. **Terms** B&B €35–€55; D,B&B €10 added per person. *V* (cash only)

SONDERSHAUSEN 99706 Thüringen — Map 8:C3

Hotel-Restaurant Zum Erbprinzen — *Tel* (03632) 75 03 36
Im Loh 1 — *Fax* (03632) 75 03 38

In small eastern city between Harz mountains and Weimar: Henze family's restaurant-with-rooms in one end of long, low building in quiet spot below huge baroque palace (now an interesting museum). 'Breakfast above average, dinner good and nicely served: ambitious menu: venison, wild pig, duck, beef, turkey and several fish dishes.' Closed 2 weeks in summer. Amex, MasterCard, Visa accepted. 8 bedrooms, quite small, but adequately furnished. B&B: single €40–€46, double €50–€56. Set dinner from €15 [2004].

THIERHAUPTEN 86672 Bavaria — Map 8:E3

Klostergasthof BUDGET — *Tel* (08271) 8 18 10
Augsburger Strasse 3 — *Fax* (08271) 81 81 50
Email info@hotel-klostergasthof.de
Website www.hotel.klostergasthof.de

In a small town north of Augsburg (easily reached by regular trains from nearby Meitingen), this gabled, white 17th-century building, part of a former monastery, has been imaginatively converted into a hotel. It is owned and managed by Josef and Inge Riss. A returning visitor advises: 'Ask for one of the rooms in the old part; they have every comfort, some are split-level. The modern annexe is fine, but could be anywhere, its rooms are smaller, and those by the road get traffic noise.' There is a 'fabulous' sauna/steam room. The breakfast buffet is 'wholesome, served in vaulted crypt-like surroundings'. The dinner is 'noteworthy: food cooked to order, but no excessive delays or defeatingly large portions. Pork and beef were perfectly cooked and suitably accompanied. The wine list is good and good value.' Meals are served outdoors in summer. (*SW*)

Open All year. Restaurant closed Sun evening. **Rooms** 19 double, 28 single. Some no-smoking. **Facilities** Lift. Breakfast room, restaurant with terrace; classical background music; conference room; sauna. **Location** 29 km N of Augsburg, E of road to Donauwörth. Parking, underground garage. **Credit cards** Amex, MasterCard, Visa. **Terms** [2004] B&B: single €58–€73, double €80–€92. Set lunch €18, dinner €20, alc €22–€33.

TRIER Rheinland-Pfalz — Map 8:D1

Hotel Petrisberg
Sickingenstrasse 11/13
54296 Trier

Tel (0651) 46 40
Fax (0651) 4 64 50
Email info@hotel-petrisberg.de
Website www.hotel-petrisberg.de

'Full of character', this modern hotel stands on a hillside amid woods, vineyards and meadows. The owners, Wolfgang and Helmut Pantenburg, run it in personal style. One visitor wrote of a 'very friendly welcome', another 'loved the magnificent view of the city': you can look down to the Mosel (30 minutes' walk away) and Trier's superb Roman monuments. The finely landscaped grounds contain much religious iconry, eg, a re-creation of Jesus's empty tomb (Trier draws many pilgrims). 'This iconry is in the public rooms too, and we found it also in our bedroom, which had a small balcony at the front.' The breakfast buffet (a gnome presides) 'offers great choice', including smoked salmon and trout, 'exceptional omelettes'. No restaurant, but a 'delicious' light supper is available. The bedrooms are mostly admired: many are spacious. 'Our bathroom was exceptionally nice.' Annexe rooms can be 'ordinary'. (*Nikki Wild, SL, and others*)

Open All year. **Rooms** 4 suites, 29 double, 2 single. 2 on ground floor. 14 in annexe, 100 m. **Facilities** Lift. Bar/TV room, music room, breakfast room (background music), wine bar. Garden: terrace. Unsuitable for ♿. **Location** 20–30 mins' walk from centre (uphill from Roman amphitheatre). Parking, garages. **Restrictions** No smoking: breakfast room, bedrooms. No dogs. **Credit cards** MasterCard, Visa. **Terms** [2004] B&B: single €65, double €90, suite €135–€160.

Hotel Villa Hügel
Bernhardstrasse 14
54295 Trier

Tel (0651) 3 30 66
Fax (0651) 3 79 58
Email info@hotel-villa-huegel.de
Website www.hotel-villa-huegel.de

Owned and run as a B&B hotel by the Schütt family, this large, white, Jugendstil villa (1914) stands high amid trees in the southern suburbs, with wide views over city, countryside and the River Mosel. The historic centre is a ten-minute walk away. 'We had a most pleasant stay,' says a visitor this year. 'Our top-floor room, comfortable and clean, had a beautiful view. My husband has a passion for trains and was delighted to hear and see them from our room.' Others wrote: 'The proprietor was kindness itself.' The staff are thought 'charming'. The 'lavish breakfast buffet' is admired. A short supper menu is available for residents until 9 pm on weekdays. The bar is open until 1 am. For meals the *Schlemmereule*, downtown, is warmly recommended. There's an indoor swimming pool with a conservatory, and an 'excellent' patio, and the park has 'romantic spots'. Some rooms have a balcony. An annexe with two-room apartments is new this year. (*Joan Faulk and Jonathon Greggs*)

Open All year, except Christmas/New Year. No evening meal at weekends. **Rooms** 6 suites, 26 double, 1 single. Some on ground floor. **Facilities** Ramps. Lounges, bar, breakfast/dining rooms (background music); winter garden; indoor swimming pool, spa bath, sauna; roof terrace. Garden: terrace. Unsuitable for ♿. **Location** In S suburbs, 10 mins' walk from centre. Follow ERA signs. Garage, parking. **Restriction** No smoking in 2 dining rooms, 16 bedrooms. **Credit cards** Amex, MasterCard, Visa. **Terms** B&B: single €72–€88, double €99–€139, suite €145–€149. Full alc €42.

UNTERREICHENBACH 75399 Baden-Württemberg Map 8:E2

Mönchs Waldhotel
Kapfenhardt Mühle

Tel (07235) 79 00
Fax (07235) 79 01 90
Email moenchs.waldhotel@t-online.de
Website moenchs-waldhotel.de

Liked for its 'friendly welcome' and 'hunting-lodge atmosphere', the Mönch family's modern hotel is a timbered, chalet-type building in traditional style, with panelled wooden ceilings. It has a leafy setting on the north-east edge of the Black Forest, near the pretty town of Calw. Though quite large, 'it does not feel like a big hotel', according to one fan. Another told of 'a huge, comfortable family room; superb, attractive indoor pool and spa' (with two large saunas, plunge pool, soft music). 'Our balcony with loungers looked over the forest. The restaurant was fine'; 'enormous portions of well-prepared food' on an extensive menu; many local dishes. 'Wonderful buffet breakfast.' 'Fruit crumble at tea was exceptional.' You can eat on the terrace in summer.

Open All year, except Christmas. **Rooms** 4 suites, 42 double, 19 single. Some suitable for ♿. **Facilities** Lift. Lounge, TV room, bar, restaurant; conservatory; indoor swimming pool, sauna, jacuzzi, gym; terrace. Garden: bowls, children's play area. **Location** 14 km N of Calw, at Kapfenhardt. Parking. **Credit cards** All major cards accepted. **Terms** B&B €49.50–€90; D,B&B €20 added per person. Set lunch €17, dinner €23; full alc €25.

VIECHTACH 94234 Bavaria Map 8:E4

Hotel Schmaus BUDGET
Stadtplatz 5

Tel (09942) 9 41 60
Fax (09942) 94 16 30
Email info@hotel-schmaus.de
Website www.hotel-schmaus.de

31 km N of Deggendorf, near Czech border, Schmaus family's busy hotel, in quiet setting outside pleasant little town in beautiful Bayerischer Wald. Smart cream facade. 'Excellent' large bedrooms; good indoor swimming pool. Conference rooms. Lift, ramps; sauna; 4 dining rooms (background music); garden (outdoor dining). 'Very good dinner, bountiful breakfast.' Parking. Closed 7 Jan–1 Feb,

21–24 Dec. All major credit cards accepted. 41 bedrooms. B&B: single €58, double €85; D,B&B €18 added per person. Alc €32.

WALLERFANGEN 66798 Saarland **Map 8:E1**

Villa Fayence NEW
Hauptstrasse 12

Tel (06831) 9 64 10
Fax (06831) 6.20.68
Email info@villafayence.de
Website www.villafayence.de

Within two minutes of the motorway towards south Germany and Switzerland, this 'gem' of a restaurant-with-rooms was discovered in 2004 by regular *Guide* correspondents. The pink-washed 1835 villa stands in a large, shady garden off the main road. 'The decor throughout is elegant', with good pictures, beautiful antiques, chandeliers, plants and *objets d'art*. There is a cellar bistro, a fine high-ceilinged lounge, and a 'fantastic' white conservatory restaurant, furnished in modern style, on the ground floor. Upstairs are just four bedrooms, with traditional decor. 'The suite is worth the extra: it is palatial, with elegant antiques, comfortable modern settee, and a Persian rug on a shining parquet floor. Its marvellous white bathroom has a wonderful deep bathtub as well as a shower cubicle.' Owner/chef Bernhard Michael Bettler has 16 *Gault Millau* points. 'The best meal of our nine-day trip: it included fish soup; leg and breast of poussin stuffed with foie gras; home-made choc chip ice cream decorated with the chef's initials in bitter chocolate. Breakfast in the elegantly classic breakfast room had several types of bread, cooked meats, cheese, etc, and we were offered eggs cooked any way: Frau Bettler, who is American, presided. Her lovely little Scottie, Gismo, likes to play on the lawn with her husband's little cat.' (*Francine and Ian Walsh*)

Open All year. Restaurant closed Sun/Mon. **Rooms** 1 suite, 3 double. **Facilities** Lounge, bar, restaurant, bistro, breakfast room. Garden. Unsuitable for ♿. **Location** 4 km W of Saarlouis, which is 27 km NW of Saarbrücken, 70 km S of Trier. Parking. **Restriction** No dogs. **Credit cards** Amex, MasterCard, Visa. **Terms** [2004] B&B: single €79.50–€112.50, double €123–€154. Set meals €32–€45; alc €32–€50.

WEHRSDORF 02689 Sachsen **Map 8:D5**

Residenz Hotel Trügelmann NEW
Oppacher Strasse 1

Tel (035936) 45 00
Fax (035936) 4 50 29
Email info@residenzhotel-trueggelmann.de
Website www.residenzhotel-trueggelmann.de

Wehrsdorf is almost on the Czech frontier, an hour's drive east of Dresden. The area is known for its textiles of former days and its *umgebinde* houses: their architectural style developed from the textile production as a cottage industry, with production on the ground floor, and living quarters above, supported by an arched timber construction. Behind its 250-year-old facade, this hotel (formerly the *Landgasthof Erbgericht*) has 'large, very comfortable' bedrooms, varying in decor from traditional to modern. 'It stands by the highway but is very quiet at night, thanks to double glazing and good construction techniques,' says the reader who visited it in 2004. 'My room was in "Queen Anne" style, a bit ornate. The bathroom was excellent. The staff speak several languages and try very hard to be helpful. Breakfast was average, but enjoyable, served in an attractive room.' The reception areas have chequered floors and gilt-framed mirrors; suites have a large draped double bed. There is a large and attractive wellness suite. (*Charles Belair*)

Open All year. **Rooms** 1 apartment, 1 junior suite, 11 double. 1 suitable for ♿. **Facilities** Lift. Lounge areas, restaurant; wellness facilities: sauna, whirlpool, massage, etc; meeting room. **Location** 3 km NW of Sohland an der Spree. Near Czech frontier, 58 km E of Dresden. **Credit cards** Amex, MasterCard, Visa. **Terms** [2004] **Room**: single €45–€100, double €82–€121, junior suite €136, apartment €151. Breakfast €6. Alc €15–€27.

WEIMAR 99423 Thüringen — Map 8:D3

Hotel zur Sonne BUDGET

Rollplatz 2

Tel (03643) 80 04 10
Fax (03643) 86 29 32
Email hotelzursonne@web.de
Website www.thuringia-online.de/hotel-zur-sonne

Well located, in quiet square near Stadtkirche*: neat, unpretentious hotel in 19th-century red-brick building. 'Nice staff, fine breakfast, good value,' says recent visitor. 'Simple but excellent' small restaurant, with cheerful service, local cooking; background radio. Parking nearby. Unsuitable for ♿. No smoking in breakfast room. All major credit cards accepted. 21 modern bedrooms. B&B: €33–€51; D,B&B €10 added. Alc €11.50–€17.50 [2004].*

WEINGARTEN 88250 Baden-Württemberg — Map 8:F3

Hotel Altdorfer Hof

Burachstrasse 12

Tel (0751) 5 00 90
Fax (0751) 50 09 70
Email hotel@altdorfer-hof.de
Website www.altdorfer-hof.de

In baroque 'overgrown village' (with great abbey basilica) 85 km SW of Ulm: Unglert family's quite smart hotel, much enjoyed in 2004: 'Very pleasant reception. Excellent, spacious room with very good bathroom. Dinner and breakfast of a high standard. Warm, comfortable atmosphere.' Closed 20 Dec–10 Jan. Lift, ramps, bar, restaurant (closed Sun night/Mon); terrace; business facilities (free Internet access, etc). Garages. All major credit cards accepted. 50 bedrooms (some traditional, some contemporary; some in Gasthaus *opposite). B&B: single from €76, double from €98, suite €199. Alc €18.50–€30 [2004].*

The maps can be found in the colour section of the *Guide*.

WILDESHAUSEN 27793 Niedersachsen — Map 8:B2

Landhaus Thurm-Meyer BUDGET
Dr-Klingenberg-Strasse 15

Tel (04431) 9 90 20
Fax (04431) 99 02 99
Email info@thurm-meyer.de
Website www.thurm-meyer.de

'Spruce, stylish', and not expensive, this country hotel, in a town south-west of Bremen, is in a quiet residential area, full of large houses and big trees. 'A pleasant stay. A bit like visiting friends,' one visitor wrote. 'There are various nooks and crannies. My ground-floor room was comfortable; most others are one floor up.' The very pretty 'wedding bedroom' has a white-canopied bed. The buffet breakfast is served in a pleasant room facing the garden. The white-fronted building has a lawn and plants in front, a garden and terrace at the back, below a bar and dining area. There is a 'charming' little garden annexe. Meals are for residents only.

Open All year. Dining room (residents only) closed midday, Sun. **Rooms** 25 double. 3 on ground floor. Some in annexe. **Facilities** Lounge, winter garden/bar, breakfast room, dining room; conference room. Small garden: terrace. **Location** Edge of town. 37 km SW of Bremen, off A1 (signposted). Car park. **Credit cards** All major cards accepted. **Terms** [2004] B&B: single €40–€45, double €55–€65. Alc €7–€17.

WORPSWEDE 27726 Niedersachsen — Map 8:B2

Hotel Buchenhof BUDGET
Ostendorfer Strasse 16

Tel (04792) 9 33 90
Fax (04792) 93 39 29
Email info@hotel-buchenhof.de
Website www.hotel-buchenhof.de

'Picturesque, if artsy-touristy', Worpswede, in beautiful countryside near Bremen, was established as an artists' colony shortly after the First World War. This B&B hotel, a Jugendstil villa 'with the feel of a country house', was the home of Hans am Ende, one of the colony's founders. Tastefully restored, owned and run by Petra Neuber and Jochen Semken, it stands in a leafy garden up an oak-tree lane, on the edge of a forest. 'Our beautiful, fairly large room was extremely nice, furnished with antiques,' said the nominator. 'The small staff is very friendly.' No restaurant, but 'the buffet breakfast was excellent: nice breads, cold meat, cereals, etc', and there is an honesty bar. Some bedrooms are traditional, some 'designer'. Good walks through woods from the door. (*WS*)

Open All year. **Rooms** 2 suites, 24 double, 2 single. 16 in guest house (10 m). Some no-smoking. Some on ground floor. **Facilities** Lobby, TV room, bar; meeting room. No background music. Garden. Unsuitable for ♿. **Location** 26 km NE of Bremen. Map on brochure. Parking. Bus-stop 30 m. **Credit cards** Amex, MasterCard. **Terms** B&B: single €35–€80, double €70–€115, suite €100–€115.

Der Eichenhof
Ostendorfer Strasse 13

Tel (04792) 26 76
Fax (04792) 44 27
Email eichenhof-hotel@t-online.de
Website www.worpswede.de/eichenhof

This 'oasis of peace' is reached by a long, paved lane off the main road. A traditional, one-storey house and some smaller buildings are set in lovely grounds with mature trees and a lawn with sun loungers. Inside, the contemporary decor – bold colours, streamlined furniture – is, says the manager, Dörte Köhnke, intended to be 'modern not modish'. The nominator thought it 'well done' and found the hotel 'very comfortable'. The *ARTisst* restaurant has a 'small but very interesting' menu, eg, saffron pasta with mushrooms and pesto; rabbit with asparagus and thyme potatoes; there are good vegetarian dishes and organic wines. In summer, guests eat on the terrace. The breakfast buffet, 'not huge, but excellent', includes fresh fruit salad and home-made muesli. 'Our lovely little apartment, on two levels, had cooking facilities.' The most expensive bedrooms are modern, others are traditional *norddeutsch*. 'Wellness treatments' are now available. (*WS*)

Open All year. Restaurant closed midday. **Rooms** 20. In 3 buildings. Some no-smoking. Most on ground floor. **Facilities** Lounges, restaurant; conference room. Indoor pool. Terrace. Extensive grounds. Bicycle hire. Wellness Institut. **Location** 25 km NE of Bremen. Parking. Bus-stop 30 m. **Credit cards** Diners, MasterCard, Visa. **Terms** [2004] B&B: single €76, double €143–€161. Set dinner €35; alc €55. *V* (3 or more nights)

WÜRGAU 96110 Bavaria — Map 8:D3

Brauerei-Gasthof Hartmann BUDGET
Fränkische-Schweizstrasse 26

Tel (09542) 92 03 00
Fax (09542) 92 03 09
Email info@brauerei-hartmann.de
Website www.brauerei-hartmann.de

'Full of local character' and 'amazingly cheap', this 'attractive stucco building' is part of the Hartmann family's 450-year-old brewery, in a village on the edge of the 'hilly, gently attractive' area known as Franconian Switzerland. Though on the road through the town (four kilometres from the A70), it is quiet at night. The restaurant is popular locally for its 'down-to-earth Franconian cooking'. 'The food is excellent, plentiful, and great value,' says a recent guest. 'The bedrooms, one floor up, are well maintained and nicely decorated, but dimly lit.' Breakfast is a country-style affair with meats, cheese, butter and home-made jam. (*CKB*)

Open All year. Closed Tues. Restaurant closed 23–29 Dec. **Rooms** 9. **Facilities** Café, dining room; conference room. Beer garden. **Location** Main street. 4 km from the A70; 5 km E of Schesslitz, which is 14 km E of Bamberg. Parking. **Credit cards** MasterCard, Visa. **Terms** [2004] Room: single €28–€30, double €48.50–€51, triple €64. Alc €14–€35.

WÜRZBURG 97070 Bavaria — Map 8:D3

Hotel Walfisch
Am Pleidenturm 5

Tel (0931) 3 52 00
Fax (0931) 3 52 05 00
Email walfisch@hotel-walfisch.com
Website www.hotel-walfisch.com

On the Main, within easy walking distance of all the sights 'both cultural and vinous', this 'very personally run' hotel was liked again this year. 'Our compact, well-furnished bedroom had a beautiful view across the river to the fortress opposite. The shower room was miniscule, but well designed and perfectly adequate. There was plentiful choice for the breakfast buffet.' The 'cheerful' bearded owner, Elmar Schwarzmeier, whose family has owned it since 1919, runs it with his wife, Ulrike. Rebuilt after the war, it has 'attractive modern decor and good modern paintings'. 'The best bedrooms, and the elegant dining room, face the river, the fortress, and the vineyards on the slope beneath.' There is a pleasant bar/lounge. One visitor thought the restaurant 'lacked atmosphere', but others wrote: 'The cuisine is *nouvelle*, prettily arranged on the plate; excellent local wines.' 'Very good value', all agree, and 'the garaging is much appreciated'. (*DG and AMS, and others*)

Open All year. Restaurant closed Sun evening. **Rooms** 20 double, 20 single. **Facilities** Lift. Bar/lounge, restaurant; conference facilities. **Location** Central (windows double glazed), on river. Garage (€8 per day). **Restriction** No dogs. **Credit cards** All major cards accepted. **Terms** [2004] B&B: single €85–€126, double €116–€155. Alc €19–€32.

Greece

Hotel Ganimede, Galaxídhi

The customary way of finding accommodation in Greece, especially on the islands, is to ask around, and inspect the rooms before choosing. The reports in the *Guide* offer a less taxing alternative. But perhaps because a higher proportion of visitors to Greece go on a package tour, we receive fewer reports on Greek hotels than we would like. Nonetheless, we are pleased with this selection of hotels, guest houses and B&Bs, spread across the mainland and the islands.

Greek accommodation can be simple, but at its best is spotlessly clean. Some of the most interesting places to stay are in old buildings in rural settings: towers in the Máni, wooden houses on Mount Pelion and entire small villages on Santorini have been converted under the auspices of the Tourism Office, taking care to maintain their authentic feeling. The *Londas Tower Guest House* at Areópoli is an example of these.

Many of our hotels are run with charm by (often extended) families. In the best of them, the welcome is warm and the cooking is authentically Greek.

AGHIOS NIKÓLAOS Crete — Map 16:E3

St Nicolas Bay Hotel
PO Box 47
Aghios Nikólaos
721 00 Lassíthi

Tel 28410 25041
Fax 28410 24556
Email stnicolas@otenet.gr
Website www.stnicolasbay.gr

Consisting of bungalows and buildings in gardens around a small bay (with a Blue Flag beach) on Crete's north coast this large resort hotel stands in 'beautifully designed' gardens with 'wonderful views'. It has been managed for many years by Costas Zarbalas. Visitors who returned for the third time in 2004 report: 'It undoubtedly deserves its place in the *GHG*. There have been considerable improvements: the outdoor pools have been redesigned; much of the outdoor furniture has been replaced with more attractive items. Housekeeping is fairly efficient. There was muzak at the Bay Café during lunch; at dinner we had live music. Breakfast was excellent: a great variety of fruits, a variety of pancakes, as well as the usual cooked assortment.' Another 2004 visitor wrote that the family suites (two bedrooms and a living room) are 'ideal'. Most rooms face the sea, away from the busy road behind the hotel; some suites have a small private pool. Staff are friendly. Spacious lounges have colourful rugs, paintings and flowers. The bar/café serves light lunches ('slightly pricey'). Guests on half-board eat in a large dining room. There are two *à la carte* restaurants: the open-air *Kafenion* (Cretan dishes) by the beach, and the more formal *Minotaure* (with tables by the sea-water swimming pool). There are many health and sports facilities (see below), and exhibitions are sometimes held. Aghios Nikólaos nearby, on a salt lake by a large bay, has cafés and tavernas. One tip: 'If you go on a package tour from London you can fly directly to Heraklion; if you travel independently, you have to fly via Athens.' (*Conrad and Marilyn Dehn, Sara Martin, and others*)

Open Apr–Oct. **Rooms** 48 suites (24 with private pool), 50 double, 10 single. Some no-smoking. Air conditioning. **Facilities** 2 lounges, 3 bars, 5 restaurants; background music; piano bar nightly, folklore dancers weekly; games room; health club: indoor swimming pool, spa bath, gym, sauna, massage; conference facilities. Large grounds: terraces, tennis, 3 swimming pools, 2 children's pools, children's playground; private beach: restaurant; water sports, sea excursions. Unsuitable for ♿. **Location** 1.5 km N of Aghios Nikólaos. Bus-stop 500 m. **Credit cards** All major cards accepted. **Terms** [2004] B&B: single €90–€280, double €130–€300, suite €180–€415; D,B&B €95–€310 per person. Set lunch €30, dinner €45; full alc €55.

****

Traveller's tale Hotel in Italy. In this modern hotel, we felt that design had taken precedence over practicality. The curtains and blinds were too thin, the towel rail was so high that water ran down one's arm as one reached for a towel. And the room for two had only one chair. The staff were invisible – too few and too laid-back. The place is inflexibly run, and we felt that all would be well were it not for the guests.

****

AGIA PELAGIA Kythera, Lakonian Islands Map 16:E2

Hotel Pelagia Aphrodite BUDGET
Agia Pelagia
802 00 Kythera

Tel 27360 33926
Fax 27360 34242
Email pelagia@otenet.gr
Website www.kythera.com

On a sand and rock beach ('fine swimming'), in an old fishing village on the north-east coast of lovely Kythera island, stands this small white B&B hotel, built in traditional style. The owners, Theodore and Eleni Chlampeas, are 'charming and helpful', says a recent enthusiastic report. 'Their two daughters speak excellent English.' The bedrooms are 'spotless'; each has a balcony. 'Fresh and delicious' breakfasts are served on the terrace. The village has several good restaurants ('some very fine fish to be had'). The island is 'full of wonders: magnificent scenery, exquisite Byzantine churches, even the beach where Aphrodite rose from the sea'. (*CB*)

Open All year. **Rooms** 4 triple, 10 double, 1 single. Some on ground floor. Air conditioning. **Facilities** Lift. Bar, reception/lounge, breakfast room, terrace. On beach. **Location** NE coast of island. **Restrictions** 'We prefer that no one smokes on the premises.' No dogs. **Credit cards** MasterCard, Visa (but cash preferred). **Terms** [2004] Room: single €41–€65, double €50–€80, triple €60–€95. Breakfast €6.

APOLLONÍA Sifnos, Cycladic Islands Map 16:D2

Hotel Petali BUDGET
Ano Petali, Apollonía
840 03 Sifnos

Tel 22840 33024
Fax 22840 33391
Email petali@par.forthnet.gr
Website www.hotelpetali.gr

On a hill above the capital of this 'traditional Greek island', this 'very attractive hotel' (said the nominator) is managed by Georgios Troullos. Built in local style, 'like a village within a village', it is composed of four whitewashed buildings covered with bougainvillaea. It stands in large grounds with roses and white canvas chairs and sunshades, and has wide views across to the Aegean, the islands, and Mount Profitis Ilias. The 'unusually good' food and the 'magnificent terrace' are praised. Breakfast is 'rich continental' (cold meats, fruit, cereals, etc). The coffee shop, open all day, provides snacks. The restaurant serves fresh-caught fish, and *Mastelo*, a local dish of young lamb or goat, cooked for several hours in an earthenware pot. The 'good-sized' bedrooms all have a balcony or terrace. 'Superior' ones have a sitting area with sofa bed. Not suitable for the infirm: lots of steps. There is a bus service to the beaches (15–20 minutes' drive).

Open All year. Restaurant closed Oct–Apr. **Rooms** 7 suites, 11 double, 1 single. **Facilities** Lounge, TV room, coffee shop, restaurant (background music). Dining terrace. Large grounds: unheated swimming pool, bar, hydromassage. **Location** Centre of island. **Credit cards** MasterCard, Visa. **Terms** B&B €63–€85. Full alc €25. *V*

AREÓPOLI Peloponnese — Map 16:E2

Londas Tower Guest House BUDGET
Areópoli
230 62 Lakonía

Tel 27330 51360
Fax 27330 51012
Email londas@otenet.gr
Website http://users.otenet.gr/~londas/

In the capital of the Inner Máni, on a plateau 250 metres above the Gulf of Messinia, this traditional tower house has been turned into a sophisticated small guest house by Iakovos Xenakis, a painter (the chef), and Hans Jakob Kleiner. They say they cater for guests who 'prefer a friendly, discreet atmosphere to the usual anonymous tourist accommodation'. *Guide* readers agree, praising the conversion for its 'respect for tradition', and for the decor ('an outstanding eye for comfort, colour and fabric'). There are pale blue wooden ceilings, ochre and dark yellow in alcoves, modern lighting, simple wooden furniture. Stone artefacts and earthenware pots stand on marble floors; bright paintings hang on white walls. Thick walls and narrow windows keep the small bedrooms cool; views are limited, but the terraces look across rooftops to sea and mountains. 'Our beds were comfortable (rare in the Peloponnese).' Breakfast (with home-made marmalade and local honey) and an informal dinner, by arrangement, are served in a room with a barrel-vaulted ceiling. A rocky beach is three minutes away by car, a sand/pebble beach slightly further.

Open All year, except owners' holidays. **Rooms** 1 triple, 3 double (2 share bath/shower). No telephone/TV. **Facilities** Lounge, living/dining room; classical background music sometimes, 'if wanted'. 2 terraces. Unsuitable for ♿. **Location** Central, signed from main church. **Restrictions** Not very suitable for small children. No dogs. **Credit cards** MasterCard, Visa. **Terms** [2004] B&B: double €80, triple €100. Evening meal €20–€35. 10% surcharge for stay of less than 3 nights. 1-night bookings sometimes refused.

ATHENS Central Greece — Map 16:D2

The Athenian Inn NEW
22 Xaritos Street
Kolonaki 106 75 Athens

Tel 210 7238097
Fax 210 7242268
Website http://athens.hotelguide.net

In the chic, leafy area near Kolonaki Square (with some of the best shopping in Athens), this 'small and welcoming' family-run B&B hotel is liked for its simple, traditional Greek style. It was a favourite of the writer Lawrence Durrell (he described it as 'good and modest in scale, but perfect in service and goodwill'). Many of the main sights are near, also good restaurants, and the Acropolis is a 20-minute (steep) walk away. All bedrooms have air conditioning and an *en suite* shower room; the best, on the top floor, have a balcony and view of the summit of Mount Lykavetus. Some others may be 'a bit gloomy'. The buffet breakfast, served in a small lounge with fireplace, is 'basic, but you can order fresh orange juice or bacon and eggs, for a bit extra'. The funicular lift to the top of the smallest of the city's seven hills is close.

Open All year. **Rooms** 3 suites, 25 double. Air conditioning. **Facilities** Lounge/bar/breakfast room. No background music. **Location** Central, but quiet, near Kolonaki Square. **Credit cards** All major cards accepted. **Terms** [2004] B&B: single €100, double €125.

Herodion Hotel
Rovertou Galli 4
117 42 Athens

Tel 210 9236832
Fax 210 9211650
Email herodion@herodion.gr
Website www.herodion.com

'So central, yet quiet', this modern, quite large, much-balconied hotel is in a pleasant residential/working neighbourhood to the south of the Acropolis. 'To relax in a deckchair on the rooftop terrace, looking at the Acropolis, is a bonus after a day's tramping round the sights.' Some back bedrooms (these are the quietest) share this view. Air conditioning and room lighting have been upgraded this year. 'Our room was small, but efficiently designed.' The 'very good public areas' have a 'cool Mediterranean decor'. A 'semi-indoor' coffee shop, in an atrium with pistachio trees, leads off the bar and lounge, and there is a taverna-style dining room. The 'excellent breakfast buffet' includes eggs, bacon, cheese, etc – 'as much as you want'. 'Staff are courteous,' say *Guide* correspondents. (*S and RW, and others*)

Open All year. **Rooms** 4 mini-suites, 77 double, 9 single. Air conditioning. **Facilities** Lift. Lounge, bar, coffee shop, taverna (no-smoking area); background music; conference hall; gift shop. Rooftop terrace. Unsuitable for ♿. **Location** 10 mins' walk from centre; near Acropolis. **Restriction** No dogs. **Credit cards** All major cards accepted. **Terms** [2004] B&B: single €154–€210, double €200–€270, triple €220–€310. Set meals €25; full alc €35. *V*

CHÓRA Kythera, Lakonian Islands — Map 16:E2

Margarita Hotel BUDGET
Chóra
801 00 Kythera

Tel 27360 31711
Fax 27360 31325
Email margarita@hotel-margarita.com
Website www.hotel-margarita.com

In Kythera's 'very pretty' old administrative capital, this white-walled, blue-shuttered, two-storey 19th-century mansion stands on a hill. There are 'breathtaking sea views', from the terrace where breakfast is served under white parasols, and from many of the spacious bedrooms. With stone arches and tiled floors, they are simply furnished in local style. The owner/managers, Frédéric Ferrière-Urvanowitz and François Crépeaux, and their staff are friendly. The breakfast buffet has ham, boiled eggs, fresh fruit, and French touches (home-baked fruitcake or chocolate cake, sometimes croissants); there is a large choice of teas. Steps lead up from a road: 'No cars at night,' we are assured, 'only cicadas and doves disturb the peace.' Kapsáli beach, safe and sandy, is a short walk away. 'The island, birthplace of Aphrodite, is quiet and unspoilt.' No public transport: rent a car, take a taxi or walk ('wonderful paths').

Open Apr–Nov. **Rooms** 1 triple, 1 suite, 9 double, 1 single. Air conditioning. **Facilities** Bar/café, 2 terraces. No background music. Kapsáli beach 1.5 km. Unsuitable for ♿. **Location** In town on S side of island. **Credit cards** MasterCard, Visa. **Terms** B&B: single €40–€70, double €50–€90, suite €74–€132. *V* (max. 2 days; not July/Aug, Greek national holidays)

CORFU Ionian Islands — Map 16:C1

Corfu Palace
Leoforos Democratias 2
491 00 Corfu

Tel 26610 39485
Fax 26610 31749
Email info@corfupalace.com
Website www.corfupalace.com

By the old city wall of Corfu's Venetian capital, this large five-star hotel provides an escape from the heat and crush of the town. Devotees returning in 2004 found 'all well at one of the most comfortable hotels we stay at'. In beautiful subtropical gardens, it looks over Garitsa Bay. Konstantinos Dendrinos is the manager: 'He was away, but his long-serving staff recognised us and gave a good welcome.' The grill room serves international and local specialities; summer meals are taken on a terrace. 'The excellent four-course half-board dinner is still a bargain at €25. Brunch by the pool had large portions, good napkins.' The 'very good' breakfast can be served on a trolley in the bedroom: all rooms have a balcony or terrace, and double glazing (there can be aircraft noise). There is an indoor swimming pool, and a 'first-class' outdoor one; across the road is sea bathing from rocks. (*David and Georgina Bennett*)

Open All year. **Rooms** 11 suites (for 2–4), 90 double, 11 single. Some on ground floor. Air conditioning. **Facilities** Lift, ramps. TV room, 2 bars, 2 restaurants; 24-hour background music; live music/folklore dances weekly; function rooms; indoor swimming pool. Dining terrace. Garden: unheated swimming pool, 2 bars. Beach 2 km. **Location** 1.5 km from harbour/airport. Parking. **Credit cards** All major cards accepted. **Terms** [2004] B&B: single €95–€195, double €115–€265, suite €190–€710; D,B&B €25 added per person. Set lunch €32, dinner €38; full alc €65. *V*

GALAXÍDHI Central Greece — Map 16:D2

Hotel Ganimede BUDGET
Gurguris 16
Galaxídhi 330 52 Fokis

Tel 22650 41328
Fax 22650 42160
Email bruno@gsp.gr
Website www.gsp.gr/ganimede.gr

In an ancient port on the Gulf of Corinth near Delphi, Costas and Chrisoula Papalexi have bought this admired *pensione* from Brunello Perocco, who has retired to Italy. 'He visits us often,' they tell us. And a rave report came in 2004. 'The enchanting young Chrisoula studied under the revered Bruno for a year "to learn the secrets of making guests special".' She has renovated, 'with refined taste'. Each bedroom now has TV, hairdryer, fridge and central heating, and there is a new suite. The rooms are in three buildings, one a 19th-century captain's house. Some are small, 'but the plumbing works: marvellous hot showers'. 'The epicentre is a flower-filled courtyard, with traditional blue Greek furniture. Here, reviving cocktails are served; also the famous breakfasts, which have five exotic home-made preserves, including a devastating lemon curd.' No restaurant, but *Mesedopolein o Bebelis*, five minutes' walk away, is 'one of the best "slow food" restaurants in Greece' (though it closes in high season when 'people are not serious about food'). 'The tiny town, with cobbled streets, old-fashioned shops, and two harbours, is being sensitively restored.' The sea, with pebble beaches, is a short walk away. (*Dawn Mitchell*)

Open All year. **Rooms** 1 suite, 4 triple, 3 double, 1 single. 4 across garden. 2 on ground floor. Some no-smoking. Air conditioning. No telephone. **Facilities** TV room, bar/breakfast room; 'chill-out' background music. Garden: bar. **Location** Central. 33 km SW of Delphi via Itéa and coast road. Safe street parking. Daily buses from Athens. **Restriction** Dogs by arrangement. **Credit cards** MasterCard, Visa. **Terms** [2004] Room: single €35, double €54, triple €65, suite €170. Breakfast €8.50.

HANIÁ Crete — Map 16:E2

Porto Veneziano Hotel
Akti Enosseos
731 32 Haniá

Tel 28210 27100
Fax 28210 27105
Email hotel@portoveneziano.gr
Website www.portoveneziano.gr

'A wonderfully relaxed place,' say visitors returning in 2004 to this large, much-balconied hotel (Best Western), by the water on the old Venetian harbour, is run by its 'charming' owner, Yannis Platsidakis. Earlier praise: 'Incredibly quiet, in a marvellous position.' 'Very welcoming', it has 'happy and smiling staff'. 'We slept with the windows open; the only sounds came from the odd fishing boat setting off.' Breakfast ('very good'), served outdoors or in the bedroom, has fresh juices, boiled eggs, cheese, avocados and yogurt. Drinks and snacks are available in the café/bar, with tables on a waterfront terrace. There is a walled garden. Dozens of tavernas around. (*Anne and Philip Eastwood*)

Open All year. **Rooms** 6 suites, 45 double, 6 single. Some no-smoking. Air conditioning. **Facilities** Lounge, Internet café/bar; background music; terrace. Garden. Beach 1.5 km. Unsuitable for ♿. **Location** 300 m from centre. Free public parking 300 m. **Restriction** No dogs (house cat). **Credit cards** All major cards accepted. **Terms** [2004] B&B: single €70–€90, double €95–€125, suite €140–€200.

HYDRA Saronic Islands **Map 16:D2**

Bratsera Hotel
180 40 Hydra

Tel 22980 53971
Fax 22980 53626
Email bratsera@yahoo.com
Website www.greekhotel.com/saronic/hydra/bratsera

With 'bags of character', this converted 19th-century sponge trading post is 'in many ways the perfect small Greek island hotel', according to a visitor in 2004. It stands, overlooking hills, in the tiny streets behind the harbour of the capital of this beautiful car-free island. Reception is in a huge atrium with open fire and grand piano. Staff are thought 'first rate'. 'Bedrooms have whitewashed walls, high ceiling, white muslin curtains. 'Our pleasant, simple room off the courtyard was available only for three days. On our last night, we were moved to a two-level room with a futon-like bed on a platform, and a shower room down precipitous steps. They told us: "These rooms are really for our younger guests."' Only reservation: 'Not enough hot water for the shower.' Tables and chairs for summer meals stand by the large, deep swimming pool ('the only full-sized hotel pool on the island') in a 'charming' walled garden with bougainvillaea, oleanders, jacaranda, cypress trees and amphorae. 'Too few sunbeds – you have to be nippy to get one in the morning.' The restaurant is said to be 'one of the best on Hydra', and the buffet breakfast is 'superb'. (*Edward Alcock, SC*)

Open 20 Feb–end Oct. **Rooms** 4 suites, 19 double. 10 in annexe opposite. Some on ground floor. Air conditioning. **Facilities** Ramps. Lounge, bar/restaurant; background music all day; function facilities; courtyard (dining); unheated swimming pool. Pebble/rock/sand beach 10 mins' walk. **Location** 2 mins' walk from harbour. Regular ferry/hydrofoil from Piraeus. No cars on Hydra. **Credit cards** All major cards accepted. **Terms** [2004] B&B: double €108–€195, suite €188–€215. Full alc €32. 1-night bookings sometimes refused.

Hotel Miranda
180 40 Hydra

Tel 22980 52230
Fax 22980 53510
Email mirhydra@hol.gr
Website www.miranda-hotel.com

Valued for its 'relaxed atmosphere', the Sofianou family's 'civilised' B&B hotel is a listed 19th-century sea captain's mansion, 'a fine example of Hydriot architecture'. It has some hand-painted ceilings, and a collection of 18th/19th-century furniture, prints and artefacts. Front rooms have a large balcony facing the sea. 'Excellent breakfasts' are served in a flowery courtyard. Close by is 'the best taverna in town, *Christina & Manolis*'. There is a gallery where art exhibitions are sometimes held. (*NP and EB, and others*)

Open 1 Apr–31 Oct. **Rooms** 1 suite, 10 double, 3 single. Some on ground floor. Air conditioning. **Facilities** Lounge area with TV; courtyard garden; background music at breakfast; art gallery. Pebble/rock/sand beach 10 mins' walk. **Location** Central; turn left by church clock tower. Regular ferry/hydrofoil from Piraeus. No cars on Hydra. **Restriction** No pets. **Credit cards** MasterCard, Visa. **Terms** B&B: single €83, double €101–€156, suite €156.

IGOUMENÍTSA Epirus Map 16:C1

Angelika Pallas NEW/BUDGET
Agion Apostolon
461 00 Igoumenítsa

Tel 26650 26100
Fax 26650 22105
Email hotel@angelikapallas.gr
Website www.angelikapallas.gr

Igoumenítsa is 'an enormous new port' in northern Greece, linking traffic from high-speed ferries from Italy with the new motorway (under construction) across the mountains to Thessaloniki, and beyond. This 'pristine' new hotel (built 2000), opposite the port, is warmly recommended. 'The friendly family owners are constantly on hand to make sure everything runs smoothly. A spacious glass lobby extends into an attractive café, where an excellent breakfast and snacks are served. Our large, modern room had a comfortable bed, sitting area, small balcony, smart marble bathroom.' No restaurant, but a nearby fish taverna, *O Timoz*, 'was packed with locals; excellent seafood, the best ever calamari'. (*John and Barbara Gittings*)

Open All year. **Rooms** 1 suite, 37 double. Air conditioning. **Facilities** Lift. 2 lobbies, bar, breakfast room, restaurant; conference facilities. Roof garden. **Location** Opposite harbour. Parking. **Credit cards** MasterCard, Visa. **Terms** [2004] Room: single €60–€75, double €85–€105, suite €120–€170.

KARDAMÍLI Peloponnese Map 16:E2

Kalamitsi Hotel BUDGET
Kardamíli, 240 22 Messíni

Tel 27210 73131
Fax 27210 73135
Email info@kalamitsi-hotel.gr
Website www.kalamitsi-hotel.gr

In the lush Messinian part of the Máni, this friendly hotel, backed by an olive grove and built in local pink stone, was recently extended. Visitors returning in 2004 liked it as much as ever. The Ponireas family owners 'are charming', say fans, and the new rooms 'combine the best features of the original ones, such as deep stone balconies, with improved facilities – lots of storage space, good tiled bathroom'. A no-choice dinner ('well-cooked local dishes' – 'Mama Ponireas excels herself with regard to vegetables and salads') is served in the attractive dining area. The menu is posted at breakfast: 'If you don't like the day's selection, it's a short walk into Kardamíli [a town popular with wealthy Athenians], which has many restaurants and tavernas (our favourite is *Kiki's*).' Breakfast includes 'fresh fruit (including home-grown figs), jam, cheese, cake, yogurt, bacon and eggs'. A path of 70 steps leads down to a sheltered small cove with a pebble beach, and the sand and pebble beach of Kalamitsi Bay is ten minutes' walk away. Good accommodation for families, in bungalows. 'If you take a studio apartment, it is serviced only every three days.' Credit cards are not accepted for meals. (*SP, Christine Hughes*)

Open Apr–Oct. **Rooms** 34. 15 in bungalows. **Facilities** Lounge, restaurant. Garden; beach. **Location** W coast of Máni peninsula. 1.5 km from Kardamíli, SE of Kalamáta. **Credit cards** MasterCard, Visa (*for accommodation only*). **Terms** [2004] Room: double €80–€100, suite €120–€140, family bungalow €180–€200. Breakfast €8. Set dinner €15.

LÉFKES Paros, Cycladic Islands — Map 16:D3

Léfkes Village Hotel NEW
PO Box 71
844 00 Léfkes

Tel 2840 41827
Fax 2840 42398
Email lefkesvl@otenet.gr
Website www.lefkesvillage.gr

Outside a charming inland village, this 'most attractively situated' small hotel is designed to look like a village itself. It stands in gardens with flowers, vines and fruit trees, and has fine views of countryside and sea, and a good-sized swimming pool. 'Our room had air conditioning, fridge, and balcony with views,' say visitors in 2004. 'The food was very good, though the mark-up for drinks is relatively high. Some refurbishment may be necessary (the building is ten years old), but overall it is excellent.' Some rooms are suitable for a family. The restaurant serves traditional Greek dishes, and the bar serves drinks and snacks all day. The hotel has its own small museum of Aegean civilisation. (*Neil and Claire Butter*)

Open Check with hotel. **Rooms** 20. **Facilities** Lounges, bar, restaurant; museum; terraces. Garden: whirlpool, swimming pool. **Location** 5 mins' walk from centre of Léfkes. 10 km SE of Parikía. **Credit cards** Probably MasterCard, Visa. **Terms** [2004] B&B double €100–€140.

METHÓNI Peloponnese — Map 16:E1

Achilles Hotel BUDGET
Platia Eleftherias
Methóni
240 06 Messíni

Tel 27230 31819
Fax 27230 28734
Email achilefs@conxion.gr
Website www.methoni.gr

Built in neo-classical style, this small, modern hotel has 'very friendly' owners, Helen and Panagiotis Georgopolou, and a 'nice local atmosphere, villagers sitting in the reception rooms chatting and drinking'. It is in a large, pretty village with a 'marvellously evocative' Venetian/Turkish fortress, in the south-west Peloponnese. 'It is our favourite place to stay in Greece,' one devotee writes. 'The proprietress takes a keen interest in all aspects of housekeeping. The good-sized bedrooms are decorated to a high standard. Ours had a balcony with a lovely view of bay and castle; the roomy bathroom was attractively tiled.' Breakfast, under a wooden pergola on the veranda that flanks the building on two sides, has fresh orange juice and a wide choice of bread, hams, cheese, cakes. The staff are 'extremely helpful'. No restaurant: *Klimataria*, five minutes' walk away, is recommended. The 'almost deserted' beaches north of Pylos and Koroni can be easily reached from here. (*SP*)

Open All year. **Rooms** 1 triple, 11 double, 1 single. **Facilities** Lounge/TV room, bar/café; large veranda; background music. Garden. Beach 100 m. **Location** Central square, opposite town hall. **Credit cards** None accepted. **Terms** [2004] Room: single €35–€45, double €40–€60. Breakfast €5.

MONEMVASSÍA Peloponnese — Map 16:E2

Malvasia Hotel BUDGET

Kastro, Monemvassía
230 70 Lakonía

Tel 27320 61160
Fax 27320 61722
Email malvasia@otenet.com

B&B hotel, named after local wine, on SE coast of Peloponnese. On 300-metre-high rock in sea, linked to mainland by narrow causeway: 3 'exquisitely converted' Venetian houses on narrow cobbled car-free lanes inside half-ruined Byzantine fortress. 'Lovely', 'atmospheric', reasonably priced. Small lounge with TV, bar (Apr–Oct). No background music. Air conditioning. Breakfast in flower-filled courtyard. Small garden. Rocky beach 105 m. No dogs. MasterCard, Visa accepted. 6 apartments (for 3 or 4), 20 double rooms, nicely furnished (hand-woven rugs, antiques): some have balcony; most have sea view, one has large private terrace. B&B double €60–€131 [2004].

NÁFPLIO Peloponnese — Map 16:D2

Byron Hotel BUDGET

Platonos 2, Platia Agiou Spiridona
Náfplio
211 00 Argolis

Tel 27520 22351
Fax 27520 26338
Email byronhotel@otenet.gr
Website www.byronhotel.gr

Two neo-classical buildings, one pink, the other green, form Aristidis Papaioannou's small B&B hotel in this 'enchanting old town', in the traffic-free area of the port at the foot of Citadel Hill. The 'small but pretty' rooms in the older section have 'marvellous views of town and harbour'. Smarter rooms, with vaulted, beamed ceiling, oriental rugs, polished wooden floor, antique furniture and minibar, lack the view but are 'comfortable and elegant'. All rooms have an efficient bathroom; some have a small patio. The continental breakfast, on a terrace with geraniums and bougainvillaea, has fresh orange juice, home-made jam, 'lovely croissants', newly baked bread. Plenty of restaurants nearby.

Open All year. **Rooms** 17 double. In 2 buildings. All with shower. Some air conditioned. **Facilities** Breakfast room/bar (classical background music); hammam. Terrace. Rock beach nearby. Unsuitable for ♿. **Location** Near Catholic church. Public parking 30 m. **Credit cards** Amex, MasterCard, Visa. **Terms** [2004] Room: single €61, double €67–€87. Breakfast €6.

> Always let a hotel know if you have to cancel a booking, whether you have paid a deposit or not. Hotels sustain huge losses because of 'no-shows'.

NÁXOS Cycladic Islands **Map 16:D3**

Hotel Grotta NEW/BUDGET
7 lak, Kampaneli Street
843 00 Chora (Náxos Town)
Tel 22850 22101
Fax 22850 22000
Email info@hotelgrotta.gr
Website www.hotelgrotta.gr

On a hillside, about seven minutes' walk from the harbour and within a short distance of the Venetian castle, the museum and many *tavernas* and shops, 'this is one of the nicest hotels we have stayed in,' say visitors this year. A modest B&B hotel, run by the 'exceptionally charming' Lianos family, 'who go out of their way to make everyone welcome', it has spectacular views over the Temple of Apollo towards Paros. 'All is spotless. A good breakfast is available from 8 until 10 am.' Each bedroom has a fridge and a balcony or terrace (most face the sea), and there is a large indoor spa bath. Transport is provided free of charge to the ferry, and excursions around Naxos and to neighbouring islands are arranged. (*Neil and Claire Butter*)

Open Mar–Oct. **Rooms** 22. Air conditioning. **Facilities** Bar, breakfast room; spa bath; Internet access. Courtyard. Bicycle hire. **Location** Side street above harbour. Airport 2 km. **Credit cards** MasterCard, Visa. **Terms** [2004] B&B: single €30–€70, double €40–€85.

OLYMPIA Peloponnese **Map 16:D1**

Hotel Europa
Drouva 1
Olympia 270 65 Ilia
Tel 26240 22650
Fax 26240 23166
Email hoteleuropa@hellasnet.gr
Website www.hoteleuropa.gr

'It is always a treat to go back,' says a regular visitor to this modern hotel (Best Western), 'delightfully set' on a hill above ancient Olympia. Owned by the Spiliopoulos family, and with Ernestos Spiliopoulos as manager, it is composed of several large, white buildings. It has 'marble everywhere', and 'civilised bedrooms with effective air conditioning': some have a split-level sitting area; many have a balcony with views over the pool, the hills, and the plain of Olympia. The hotel's greatest fan calls it 'a haven of comfort, charm and friendliness; tremendous value for a quality of accommodation that we have not seen bettered in our visits to mainland Greece'. It does a large coach party trade, but 'somehow manages to absorb them so they don't dominate' (they eat in the restaurant). Independent travellers get 'friendly, personal service', and eat in the taverna by the pool. 'A good choice of well-cooked dishes; excellent buffet breakfast.' (*SP*)

Open All year. **Rooms** 2 suites, 66 double, 12 single. All air conditioned. Some on ground floor. 3 suitable for ♿. **Facilities** Lift, ramps. 2 lounges (24-hour background music), 2 bars, restaurant; Internet room; jewellery shop. Garden: taverna, bar; unheated swimming pool, tennis. Sea 20 km. **Location** 0.8 km from centre. Parking. **Restriction** No smoking: much of restaurant, 50% of bedrooms. **Credit cards** All major cards accepted. **Terms** B&B: single €75–€110, double €95–€140, suite €250. Set meals €16. *V*

SÁMI Cephallonia, Ionian Islands — Map 16:D1

Sámi Beach Hotel BUDGET
Sámi
280 80 Cephallonia

Tel 26740 22824
Fax 26740 22846
Email samibeah@otenet.gr
Website www.samibeachhotel.gr

On a beautiful bay, with a river on either side, on the beautiful island of Cephallonia, this 'blissful' B&B hotel, owned by the 'genuinely welcoming' Dorizas family, was liked again this year. Ioannis (Janni) Dorizas runs it with his wife, Maryann; brother Periklis is the chef; a nephew, Forti, does the bar. 'On arrival, there is an ouzo on the house. A bottle of wine and a hand-written note of welcome wait in the bedroom.' 'Our spotless room and bathroom were simply furnished.' The small bedroom balconies look over the Ionian Sea. There is a 'Rolls-Royce of a lift'. In the 'immaculately maintained' grounds are palm trees, bamboos and eucalyptus, and a sizeable L-shaped pool with a 'very nice' bar which serves lunchtime snacks. Breakfast is 'a plentiful buffet'. Children are welcomed. Sámi, a 'pleasant 15-minute stroll away' and surrounded by hills, has several restaurants facing its harbour. It is on the less touristy side of the island (most of the filming of *Captain Corelli's Mandolin* took place around here, in sets that were subsequently dismantled). A regular car ferry operates to the nearby island of Ithaca ('totally unspoilt with spectacular scenery: a car is essential'). (*Emma Hart, PJ, JC*)

Open Mid-Apr–mid-Oct. **Rooms** 44 double, 5 single. All air conditioned. **Facilities** Lift. 2 lounges, library, TV room; radio background music. Garden: unheated swimming pool, bar, tennis, table tennis, children's playground. Sea 20 m: pebble/sandy beach, fishing. Unsuitable for ♿. **Location** 2.5 km from Sámi, towards Karavomilos. **Restriction** No dogs. **Credit cards** MasterCard, Visa. **Terms** [2004] B&B: single €55–€78, double €70–€95.

SÍMI Symi Dodecanese Islands — Map 16:E1

Hotel Aliki
Akti Gennimata
856 00 Sími

Tel 22460 71665
Fax 22460 71655
Email info@simi-hotelaliki.gr
Website www.simi-hotelaliki.gr

Restored neo-classical mansion (built by wealthy 19th-century sea captain), now a sympathetic and 'exquisite' B&B hotel. On picturesque waterfront of Yialos (lower town) of lovely little port/capital of small island between Rhodes and Turkish coast. Tasteful decor; airy lounge, bar, roof terrace (fine views); tables with parasols by waterfront; ladder to water for bathing. 'Friendly staff.' Open Apr–Oct. 15 bedrooms, air conditioned, with antiques: best have sea view (top ones have balcony). B&B: single €65–€105, double €80–€130, suite €120–€160 [2004].

Every entry in the *Guide* is updated every year.

SPARTA Peloponnese — Map 16:D2

Menelaion Hotel NEW/BUDGET
91 K Paleologou
231 00 Sparta

Tel 27310 22161
Fax 27310 26332
Email info@menelaion.com
Website www.menelaion.com

On the main, 'most interesting', palm tree-lined street of this pleasant small town stands this neo-classical hotel, built in 1935 and recently refurbished. 'The best feature is the reception rooms,' says this year's nominator. 'A wide lobby opens to a smart lounge and bar to one side and an imaginative open-air swimming pool at the back. The most expensive bedrooms are on the front, with balcony, but I think that those at the back, overlooking the pool, are better. Ours was good-sized, comfortable, with efficient double glazing. The bathroom, attractively tiled, had (unusual for Greece) a decent bath.' Meals can be taken by the pool or in the adjacent dining room: 'Excellent food, with a good range of Greek and international dishes; breakfast was fine, apart from the orange juice.' The 'atmospheric, if not extensive' remains of the ancient city state are a short walk away. The Byzantine city of Mistrás is near. (*Steve Potts*)

Open All year. Restaurant closed Sun. **Rooms** 40 double or triple, 8 single. 3 suitable for ♿. Air conditioning. **Facilities** Ramp. Lounge, bar, café, restaurant; background music; assembly room; bank. Terrace: unheated swimming pool with bar. **Location** Central. **Credit cards** Diners, MasterCard, Visa. **Terms** [2004] Room: single €61, double €74. Breakfast €9. *V*

THERMÍ Lesbos, North-east Aegean Islands — Map 16:C3

Hotel Votsala BUDGET
Pyrgi Thermí, Mitilíni
811 00 Lesbos

Tel 22510 71231
Fax 22510 71179
Email votsalah@otenet.gr
Website www.greekhotel.com

By the beach, in a garden of flowers and fruit trees, this 'very relaxed' hotel on the coast north of Mitilíni (capital of Lesbos). The owners, Iannis and Daphni Troumbounis, promise 'no Greek nights, no TV in rooms, no disco'. They and their staff are 'endlessly helpful', says a recent visitor. The simply furnished bedrooms are in four low buildings: all have a balcony or terrace; most have a fridge. No air conditioning: 'The Aegean breeze does the trick.' Pedal boats and canoes are provided free. An alfresco breakfast has 'everything you want'; salads are available at lunchtime, and though the hotel has 'no Greek taverna', dinner may be served twice a week. A restaurant is a short walk away; slightly further is the old fishing village of Thermí, which has shops, eating places and regular buses to Mitilíni. (*JC*)

Open Apr–Oct. **Rooms** 45 double. No TV. Some on ground floor. **Facilities** Bar, terraces; background music. 9-acre grounds: garden, children's playground, pebble/sand beach. Unsuitable for ♿. **Location** 11 km N of Mitilíni (regular buses). Airport 20 km. **Credit cards** MasterCard, Visa. **Terms** [2004] B&B: single €54–€80, double €38–€80.

TOLÓ Peloponnese Map 16:D2

Hotel Minoa BUDGET
56 Aktis, Toló
210 56 Argolis

Tel 27520 59207
Fax 27520 59707
Email kingmino@otenet.gr

'Perfect for families with children', this holiday hotel is on the beach at the 'better' end, near the harbour, of this 'rather commercial' resort near Náfplio. Owner/manager Yannis Georgidakis 'takes an interest in all that goes on', says an admirer this year. He is supported by other members of the family and a 'helpful staff'. An earlier visitor wrote: 'Teamwork is the key factor: everyone seems personally involved.' The best bedrooms have a balcony ('the moon on the sea is beautiful'); back ones overlook a sprawl of houses. All rooms are 'well furnished, immaculate', with 'good bathroom, constant hot water'. Some are in the annexe, *Hotel Knossos* (the family also owns *King Minos* and *Apollon*). The restaurant faces the beach through picture windows. 'The food has improved since Kostas, Yannis's son, joined the staff.' Guests on half board choose from an extensive hot and cold buffet. On the *carte* are 'fresh fish, tender pork and lamb, all cooked to order'. Drinks and snacks, from the 'perpetually open bar', are taken on a sheltered patio. Breakfast has fruit, yogurt, cheese, cold meats, etc. In summer, blue wooden tables and chairs stand on the sand by the shallow, clean sea. Water sports are available, and boat trips start from the nearby jetty. An 8% discount is offered to any *Guide* reader who arrives with a copy of the book in hand. (*REB Sears, and others*)

Open Mar–Nov. **Rooms** 1 suite, 56 double, 6 single. 18 in *Knossos* (80 m). Some on ground floor. Air conditioning. **Facilities** Lift. Lounge/TV room, bar (background music 10 am–11 pm), indoor restaurant (no-smoking), outdoor restaurant; Greek evening weekly in season. Terrace (with bar), beach; unheated swimming pool at *King Minos Hotel*, nearby. Unsuitable for ♿. **Location** 5 mins' walk from centre, near old port. 12 km SE of Náfplio. Free parking nearby. Hourly bus from Náfplio; hydrofoil from Piraeus in summer. **Restrictions** No smoking: restaurant, bedrooms. Small dogs only. **Credit cards** Amex, MasterCard, Visa. **Terms** B&B: single €51–€57, double €64–€75, suite €80–€100; D,B&B €39–€65 per person. Set meals €12; full alc €20. 1-night bookings refused high season.

****

Traveller's tale Hotel in the Czech Republic. It was a quiet Sunday night, and I was the only customer in the hotel's restaurant. The only other people there were the woman working in the bar and her female friend (not a customer), with whom she was engrossed in conversation. The radio was on, tuned to a station that favoured bouncy talk and fast rock music. This foreground music was even worse than the background music would be during dinner. I managed to get the bartender's attention and asked that the radio be turned off. She emphatically said, 'No', and went back to her conversation. At breakfast next morning there was no radio playing: a similar talk and music TV show had replaced it.

****

Hungary

Hotel Senátor Ház, Eger

BUDAPEST **Map 15:A2**

art'otel
Bem Rakpart 16–19
1011 Budapest

Tel (1) 487 9487
Fax (1) 487 9488
Email budapest@artotel.hu
Website www.artotel.hu

Six hundred works of art by a minimalist American artist, Donald Sultan, fill this designer hotel, a conversion of four 18th-century baroque houses on the Danube embankment, opposite the Parliament building. A recent visitor called it 'really nice, with very helpful English-speaking staff'. This year's reporter adds: 'A memorable stay in a stylish hotel, from champagne on the house at midnight on New Year's Eve, watching from the front door the superb display of fireworks arching over the Danube and the Parliament building, to the friendly reception staff who booked us on a comprehensive tour of Budapest and recommended a splendid restaurant, *Kisbuda Gyöngye*, a short taxi ride away.' Most bedrooms face the river; large suites are at the back. All are quiet, thanks to effective double glazing. The decor is 'modern and cheerful' (much red and grey): 'rich red bathrobes with a mauve tie' echo the colours of carpets and curtains. The 'very good' restaurant serves Hungarian and international food. Breakfast is a huge hot and cold buffet. There are extensive function facilities. Other art'otels are in Berlin (*qv*) and Dresden. The Castle district is an easy walk away. (*DT*)

Open All year. **Rooms** 9 suites, 147 double, 8 single. Some suitable for ♿. 2 floors no-smoking. Air conditioning. **Facilities** Lift, ramps. Lobby, lounge/breakfast room, café, restaurant (pianist 3 or 4 nights a week); background music all day; fitness room, sauna; business centre. Terrace (grills in summer). **Location** On Danube, in Buda, near Chain Bridge. Garage. (Metro: Batthyány Sq) **Credit cards** All major cards accepted. **Terms** [2004] B&B: single €120–€168, double €140–€188, suite €240–€340; D,B&B €18 added per person.

Hotel Astra Vendégház
Vám utca 6
1011 Budapest

Tel (1) 214 1906
Fax (1) 214 1907
Email hotelastra@euroweb.hu
Website www.hotelastra.hu

A stylish conversion of a white 18th-century house, with rooms arranged round a geranium-covered courtyard, below the Castle district of Buda. It is a 'charming' small B&B hotel, 'a bargain at the price', say admirers. The public rooms are tall, airy; 'house plants much in evidence'. 'I loved it. Wonderfully quiet. My spacious room, with lovely warm bathroom, led on to the courtyard. It was like having my own little house.' Suites have 'lavish furniture and equipment, good modern bathroom'. Some rooms face the street, 'a cul de sac with little traffic'. The buffet breakfast, in a 'pleasant room', is 'adequate, if not startling'. Good Hungarian eating nearby. (*A and MK, and others*)

Open All year. **Rooms** 3 suites, 8 double. Some no-smoking. **Facilities** Lounge, cellar bar with snooker; breakfast room; background radio; meeting room. Courtyard. Unsuitable for ♿. **Location** In Buda, just N of castle. **Credit cards** None accepted. **Terms** B&B: single €80–€90, double €95–€105, suite €125–€135.

Beatrix Panzió Hotel BUDGET
Széher u. 3
1021 Budapest

Tel (1) 275 0550
Fax (1) 394 3730
Email beatrix@pronet.hu
Website www.beatrixhotel.hu

A pleasant three-star *pension* in a trim white villa in a residential area in the western suburbs, easily reached by tram. It has long been liked by *Guide* readers, particularly for the 'warm welcome' from the Martinecz family owners, who 'speak fairly good English'. This year there is a new double room, and a new breakfast room, but rates have been held. Terracotta sculptures and pictures are on the staircase; bedrooms are simple but clean; all have TV and minibar; suites have a balcony. A good selection of local drinks and a snack menu is available in the small bar. The small front garden, with a fishpond and gazebo, is sometimes used for barbecues or goulash parties; there's a terrace for drinks in summer. Breakfast is a buffet. Traffic on the road, but quiet at night.

Open All year. **Rooms** 7 suites (with kitchenette and ♿ access), 11 double. 5 on ground floor. 2 in adjacent building. **Facilities** Lounge, snack bar, breakfast room (no-smoking); background radio; sauna. Garden: coffee terrace. **Location** 2 km W of centre; tram/bus service. Secure parking. **Credit cards** None accepted. **Terms** B&B: single €45–€55, double €50–€60, suite €60–€105.

City Hotel Pilvax
Pilvax köz 1–3
1052 Budapest

Tel (1) 266 7660
Fax (1) 317 6396
Email pilvax@taverna.hu
Website www.taverna.hu

Occupying the lower floors of a 1930s-style block in the business district of Pest, this medium-priced hotel (part of the small Taverna chain) is on a traffic-free street near the main shopping street (Váci utca). The air-conditioned rooms vary in size: 'Ours was an unusual trapezoid shape, but very comfortable,' say recent visitors. 'Rooms at the back may be even quieter, but perhaps a bit gloomy. Housekeeping was excellent, and staff were very friendly and efficient: most spoke English.' Breakfast, in the panelled restaurant, is 'the usual Hungarian cold buffet, plus one hot dish on offer'. The *Pilvax* restaurant 'offers good food and reasonable value'. The Danube is five minutes' walk away.

Open All year. Restaurant closed 24 Dec. **Rooms** 30 double, 2 single. 8 no-smoking. Air conditioning. **Facilities** Lounge, bar, restaurant (no-smoking; live/background music after 6 pm). Unsuitable for ♿. **Location** Central, in Pest. Airport shuttle. (Metro: Ferenciek ter) **Credit cards** All major cards accepted. **Terms** [Up to 31 Mar 2005] B&B: single €55–€75, double €75–€99. Set lunch €10, dinner €12; full alc €14.

Hotel Gellért
Szent Gellért tér 1
1111 Budapest

Tel (1) 889 5500
Fax (1) 889 5505
Email gellert.reservation@danubiusgroup.com
Website www.danubiusgroup.com/gellert

A visitor in 2004 loved this imposing Art Nouveau white palace (1918) of 'faded charm'. 'Perfectly positioned' on the right bank of the Danube, it has 'slightly echoey' public rooms, marbled halls, stained-glass windows, wrought ironwork, a splendid stairway. 'With its wonderful baths, it felt like an old-fashioned seaside hotel. Staff were (mostly) charming.' The best, spacious front bedrooms, with old-fashioned furniture and big windows, have 'wonderful' views of the river, but their double glazing does not quite blot out the clanging of trams. Some other rooms can be 'poky'. At the buffet breakfast, in two hill/river-facing rooms, the young staff are 'eager if sometimes a bit disorganised; some items run out at busy times'. The coffee shop is a local meeting place. Rich local dishes are served in the restaurant. Hotel guests have access by a lift to the famous thermal baths: these are separately managed, often crowded. In summer, the world's first wave machine still operates in the big outdoor swimming pool surrounded by arbours and statues. 'Sun terraces built into the hill are well protected from the winds that often blow up and down the Danube.' 'The anonymous chain or fashionable boutique hotels nearby may offer more modern comforts, but only at the *Gellért* will one feel truly at home in Budapest,' says a regular visitor. (*Mari Roberts and Christian Gotsch, and others*)

Open All year. **Rooms** 13 suites, 129 double, 92 single. Some no-smoking. **Facilities** Lounges, bar, brasserie, café, restaurant (background music; live folk music); 6 banqueting halls; business centre; beauty parlour; recreation centre: thermal baths. Garden: terraces, swimming pool. Unsuitable for ♿. **Location** 3 km from centre (foot of Gellért hill). Guarded parking opposite. **Credit cards** All major cards accepted. **Terms** [2004] B&B: single €75–€130, double €190–€240, suite €300.

Hotel Victoria NEW
Bem rakpart 11
1011 Budapest

Tel (1) 457 8080
Fax (1) 457 8088
Email victoria@victoria.hu
Website www.victoria.hu

On Buda bank of Danube, close to Chain Bridge: 'straightforward', modern B&B hotel. 'Excellent, convenient location. Friendly no-frills service. All necessary amenities.' Lounge, bar, free sauna. Air conditioning. Parking (€9). 'More than adequate' buffet breakfast. All major credit cards accepted. 27 'generous-sized' rooms; all with superb view through big windows across river to Parliament building. B&B: single €74–€97, double €79–€102 [2004].

EGER 3300 — Map 15:A2

Hotel Senátor Ház BUDGET
Dobó tér 11

Tel/Fax (36) 32 04 66
Email senator@egerhotels.com
Website www.holidayhungary.com

'Warmly endorsed' in 2004, this 18th-century town house was once owned by a local senator. An earlier visitor called it 'an absolute gem'. In the well-preserved baroque quarter of this attractive old town (famed for its Bull's Blood wine), it is on the stately main square near the historic castle, where the Magyars halted the Ottoman march on Europe in 1552. 'The owners are very friendly. Levels of comfort and service are high.' The hotel is quaint inside, with a cosy lobby of arched, whitewashed walls and some period furniture. Bedrooms, up an old staircase, are 'above average by Hungarian standards', with minibar, satellite TV, Internet connection, etc. Breakfast, in an 'airy yet intimate' room, is a varied and generous spread. 'The hotel's restaurant lacks real character, but on either side of it are authentic Magyar eateries with dazzling wall hangings, occasional gypsy music.' (*James Sutton, and others*)

Open All year. **Rooms** 9 double, 2 single. Some no-smoking. Some suitable for ♿. **Facilities** Lounges, bar, café, restaurant; function rooms. Patio. **Location** On main square, below castle. Parking, garage. **Credit cards** MasterCard, Visa. **Terms** [2004] B&B: single €35–€50, double €48–€70.

GYÖR 9021 — Map 15:A1

Hotel Schweizerhof BUDGET
Sarkantyú köz 11–13

Tel (96) 329 171
Fax (96) 326 544
Email info@schweizerhof.hu
Website www.schweizerhof.hu

This town, near the Danube and the borders with Austria and Slovakia, makes a good base for sightseeing. Though now industrialised, it has a beautiful baroque centre. Below the ancient castle wall, this Swiss/ Hungarian hotel, which opened in 1995 and is managed by its owner, Erwin Gross, is 'a real find in provincial Hungary', said a well-travelled correspondent. It consists of three 'charmingly renovated' listed buildings in a network of pedestrianised streets. Some bedrooms lead on to a pair of charming little flowery roof terraces. 'My room, in cheerful yellow tones, had a small but immaculate bathroom.' Modern, light versions of traditional Hungarian dishes are served by cheerful young staff in the *Bacchus* restaurant. Breakfast has a 'very generous' buffet. There is a health centre with a small pool, etc. (*VM-I*)

Open All year. **Rooms** 9 suites, 10 double, 13 single. Some no-smoking. In 3 buildings. Air conditioning. **Facilities** Lift. Lounge, bar, restaurant, wine cellar; background music; meeting rooms; health centre: solarium, indoor swimming pool; roof terraces. **Location** Old town, below castle. Parking. Garage. **Credit cards** All major cards accepted. **Terms** [2004] B&B: single €67–€71, double €76, suite €81; D,B&B €44–€83 per person. Set meals €14; full alc €22.

KECSKEMÉT 6000 — Map 15:B2

Fábián Panzió BUDGET
Kápolna Utca 14

Tel (76) 477 677
Fax (76) 477 175
Email panziofabian@freemail.hu
Website www.hotels.hu/fabian

'Quite exceptional', this guest house is run by the Fábián family at their home, a short walk from the centre of this attractive city south-east of Budapest. Zsuzsa Fábián, the manager, writes: 'We do our best to help guests feel at home.' 'She is an amazing linguist, very helpful,' say recent visitors. 'The place gleams, it is so clean. Bedrooms are small but well equipped, nicely designed.' Single rooms, and the breakfast room, are in the main house by the road; the double rooms are in a one-storey building round a pretty courtyard garden. Many walls are pale pink; most furniture is white, simple, modern. Fresh flowers on the table at breakfast, 'nicely served' (not a buffet); 'the usual Hungarian (ham, cheese, salami), but each day we were asked what we wanted, and there was usually a "surprise", perhaps delicious watermelon, or fresh biscuits made by one of the cleaners.' Zoltán

Kodály, the composer, was born in the city, which is 'worth a visit if you like Art Nouveau architecture'.

Open All year. **Rooms** 6 double, 4 single. **Facilities** Reception, breakfast room. No background music. Terrace. Garden. Bicycle hire. Unsuitable for ♿. **Location** 80 km SE of Budapest. Centre of town. Car park. **Restrictions** No smoking: breakfast room, bedrooms. No dogs. **Credit cards** None accepted. **Terms** B&B: single €28–€32, double €36–€38.

Italy

Hotel Cannero, Cannero Riviera

Italy has some of the finest hotels in Europe. They are furnished and decorated with true Italian flair, whether modern or traditional, and can be strikingly lovely. This chapter has a good selection. In Tuscany and Umbria especially, villas and manor houses, tastefully converted, are run as personal hotels, sometimes by their ancestral owners. Or old farmhouses, rural dwellings and even complete hamlets have been restored, keeping the rustic style but adding modern comforts. *Agriturismo* is a movement that encourages this trend.

First-time visitors will notice differences between Italian hotels and those, for example, in France. It is usual in rural areas for rooms to have a tiled floor – they are more practical and cooler than carpet. Showers are more common than baths in simple inns, and often don't have a shower curtain, so water floods the shower room floor. Don't panic, it will have been designed that way; the water will drain away.

Hotels are officially classified, and range from five-star deluxe to small one-star inns and guest houses. The big international chains are represented in this classification, but the vast majority of Italian hotels, and most of those featured in the *Guide*, are individually owned. Some, as in other countries, group together in associations – Relais & Châteaux, Romantik Hotels, etc. Logis d'Italia, a branch of the excellent Logis de France association, has over 100 members. The *locanda* is a country inn, similar to a French *auberge*. We include a number of these, run with a typically Italian combination of informal warmth, style and panache. The number of good individual hotels in big cities is gradually increasing.

Prices include a service charge; you need leave only a token tip, if service has been especially good. A double room usually costs 30 to 50 per cent more than a single one. If you stay in an inexpensive hotel, breakfast might be sparse, and it can be better value, and more fun, to go to a nearby café. A growing number of smarter hotels are now offering a more substantial buffet breakfast to keep their American and German visitors happy.

Food is taken seriously, and the Slow Food Movement is gathering strength. Every Italian is an expert on pasta. We quote the *Michelin* ratings of star and *Bib Gourmand*: these are more frequent in northern Italy than in the south. Wine is similarly held in high esteem and it is usually most rewarding to drink the wines of the region, since they properly complement the local cuisine.

A new law banning smoking in public places in Italy is due to come into effect at the beginning of 2005. From that date, smokers will be allowed to smoke only in designated places. Individual hotels' interpretation of this law may vary. Some are now banning smoking in all their bedrooms as well as in all public rooms. The information about smoking in the entries that follow may not always be accurate. If it is important to you, please check directly with the hotel in question.

ACQUAFREDDA DI MARATEA 85041 Potenza — Map 12:B4

Romantik Hotel Villa Cheta Elite
Via Timpone 46

Tel (0973) 878134
Fax (0973) 878135
Email villacheta@tin.it
Website www.villacheta.it

In this 'old-fashioned summer resort' on the dramatic north Tyrrhenian coast, this 18th-century 'Liberty-style' building stands in lush grounds. Family antiques, portraits and paintings, and the original Art Nouveau glass panels give it 'the feel of a private house', say fans. Best bedrooms have sea views, others face the garden where alfresco meals are served on terraces under bougainvillaea, parasols and trees. Visitors in poor weather complained of 'abysmal lighting' in their bedroom, but additional lamps were provided on request: 'Management and staff are extremely willing.' 'Quite a few steps and no lift, but the porter is helpful.' The owner, Stefania Aquadro, is 'much in evidence', and the food is 'simple but excellent' (lots of local fish). Half board is 'a bargain'. Breakfast is 'very good, if rather formal (waiters in dinner jackets)'. There is a roof terrace, with sunbeds, and a small rocky beach below the hotel: its boat will take guests on trips on 'the water once crossed by Ulysses'. Yoga lessons are available. A 'well-used railway line' is nearby, 'but, oddly, you don't really hear the trains'. (*CH and CE*)

Open Apr–Nov. **Rooms** 24 double. Air-conditioning. **Facilities** Lounge, indoor and outdoor bars and dining areas; background music. Garden: solarium; rock/pebble beach below. **Location** 10 mins' walk from centre. 8 km NW of Maratea. Parking. **Restriction** No smoking: public areas, some bedrooms. **Credit cards** All major cards accepted. **Terms** B&B (off-season only): single €80–€130, double €120–€240; D,B&B €100–€150 per person. Set meals €30; full alc €45.

ALASSIO 17021 Savona — Map 11:C2

Villa della Pergola NEW
Via Privata Montagù 9/1

Tel (0182) 640414
Fax (0182) 554969
Email info@villadellapergola.it
Website www.villadellapergola.it

A former haunt of English noblemen, this B&B is a conversion of two pink colonial-style villas once owned by Sir Daniel Hanbury. It stands above the town in a park with magnolias, eucalyptus, cypresses, olive trees and jacaranda, and panoramic views of the Baia del Sole on the Ligurian coast. 'Not a ritzy glitzy place but an absolute joy,' says its nominator. 'Bountiful breakfast on the terrace: good coffee, wonderful home-baked cakes, fruits, yogurts, freshly squeezed orange juice. Good value.' Some bedrooms have a fireplace, some open on to a loggia or patio, some have a private sitting-out area. One large room has its own small children's room and a huge spa bath. 'The owner, Marcella Demartini, is very hospitable, and we enjoyed aperitifs on the terrace with the other guests on Saturday evening. The architecture is stunning [beams, arches, old windows and a handsome Carrara marble staircase], and the buildings are full of historical interest.' The beach is a ten-minute walk down ('you have to feel energetic for the walk back'). (*Wendy Ashworth*)

Open All year. **Rooms** 6 double. 3 in main villa, 3 in annexe. Some air conditioned. **Facilities** 2 lounges (1 with TV, 1 in annexe), breakfast room. Large grounds: breakfast terrace. 10 mins' walk from sea. Unsuitable for ♿. **Location** Above Alassio town; between Ventimiglia and Genoa. Parking. **Restrictions** No smoking: public areas, some bedrooms. No dogs. **Credit cards** All major cards accepted. **Terms** [2004] B&B (min. 2 days): double €150–€180, suite €200.

ALGHERO 07041 Sassari, Sardinia — Map 12:A1

Villa Las Tronas NEW
Lungomare Valencia 1

Tel (079) 981818
Fax (079) 981044
Email info@hvlt.com
Website www.hvlt.com

Until the 1940s a holiday home of the Italian royal family, this rectangular pink 19th-century villa, renovated in 2000, retains a 'charming air of gently fading elegance', says its nominator this year. 'It stands proudly apart from the bustling town on a promontory that juts into the Mediterranean.' In its large park are a big swimming pool with 'breathtaking' views of rocky coastline, and it has a mooring area for small boats. 'The public rooms are rather grand and furnished with antiques, but the atmosphere was warm and welcoming, rather than intimidating.' Some bedrooms have a terrace. 'Our corner room, tastefully restored, had wide views of town and Mediterranean. Dinner in the softly lit dining room was unforgettable: the immaculately dressed waiters were friendly, and the cuisine was exceptional. A grand finale to our stay in Sardinia.' Alghero's international airport (flights from Stansted) is 30 minutes' drive away. (*John Collier*)

Open All year. **Rooms** 5 suites, 18 double, 2 single. Air conditioning. **Facilities** Salon, bar, restaurant (live music during dinner); gym; meeting room. Park: terraces; unheated swimming pool; piers to sea. Unsuitable for ♿. **Location** 5 mins' walk from centre. NW part of island, 35 km SW of Sassari. **Restriction** No smoking in public areas. **Credit cards** All major cards accepted. **Terms** B&B: single €180–€215, double €210–€350, suite €410–€520; D,B&B €140–€295 per person. Set meals €55–€130; full alc €60.

AMALFI 84011 Salerno — Map 12:B3

Luna Convento
Via Pantaleone Comite 33

Tel (089) 871002
Fax (089) 871333
Email info@lunahotel.it
Website www.lunahotel.it

Run for many years as a hotel by the Barbaro family, this former medieval convent, founded by St Francis of Assisi in 1222, has long been popular with *Guide* readers. 'A great place: lots of style'; 'very romantic', are recent comments. It stands above the busy coast road, but its cloisters, with lemon and kumquat trees, bougainvillaea and an ivy-clad well with goldfish and terrapins, are tranquil. The bedrooms 'may not be the height of modern comfort – heavy old beds and cold floor – but they have real architectural interest'. 'Our big room had a lovely painted ceiling (flowers and local scenes), huge balcony with tables, chairs and deckchairs, but we weren't keen on the plastic towel rails and miserable little soaps.' Public areas 'have character'. 'Staff are good humoured.' The buffet breakfast includes fresh fruit. The panoramic restaurant serves 'local dishes, freshly cooked, with good local wines'. In summer you can dine *à la carte* across the road, on the terrace of the *Torre Saracena*, an old Moorish tower. Below it is the swimming pool, carved into rocks, with sunbathing spots and ladders down to the sea. When settling the bill, you must use cash for taxis and laundry. (*S and SS, and others*)

Open All year. *Torre Saracena* open Apr–Oct. **Rooms** 5 suites, 38 double. Air conditioning. **Facilities** Lift. Lounge, TV room, bar, 2 restaurants (1 no-smoking); function facilities; cloister. Swimming pool. Unsuitable for ♿. **Location** On coast road, 500 m E of centre. Garage or unguarded road parking. **Restrictions** No smoking in public areas. No dogs. **Credit cards** Amex, MasterCard, Visa. **Terms** [2004] Room with breakfast €220–€240; D,B&B €160 per person. Alc €43–€71.

AOSTA 11100 Aosta — Map 11:B1

Hotel Milleluci
Località Porossan Roppoz

Tel (0165) 235278
Fax (0165) 235284
Email info@hotelmilleluci.com
Website www.hotelmilleluci.com

The nominator had a 'wonderful stay' at this 'very welcoming' B&B hotel which the Galassi family have converted from their stone and wood farmhouse complex. The name, 'a thousand lights', refers to the night-time views of Aosta below. 'We felt at home. We were delighted with our spacious, comfortable accommodation.' The house is filled with locally made period furnishings, and antiquities, and 'the prosecco in the minibar alleviated the exhaustion of the long day's travel'. The suites are 'plush', and there is a 'stylish yet cosy' lounge with flower-upholstered chairs and sofas, and a terrace for breakfast: this includes local cheeses, ham, sausage, fruit, and a 'dizzying array of breads and pastries'. There is a garden with swimming pool, and a health club is new this year. This attractive winter and summer resort has narrow cobbled streets and easy access to the Gran Paradiso national park. The Mont Blanc tunnel is 40 minutes' drive away. (*HA*)

Open All year. **Rooms** 31. **Facilities** Lift. Lounge, breakfast room; health club: sauna, etc; terrace. Garden: swimming pool. **Location** 1 km from historic centre. Parking. **Restriction** No smoking in public areas. **Credit cards** All major cards accepted. **Terms** [2004] Room with breakfast €95–€150.

ARGEGNO 22010 Como — Map 11:A3

Villa Belvedere
Via Milano 8

Tel (031) 821116
Fax (031) 821571
Email capp.belvedere@libero.it
Website http://go.to/belvedere

'It has returned to its old form,' says one of the many fans of the Cappelletti family's hotel by Lake Como. Dinners are offered again, 'and the menus are as extensive as before'. Other comments: 'The meals are first class' (mushroom risotto, osso buco, etc). 'Dining on the terrace, inches away from the lake, can't be beaten.' 'We feel at home in a hotel with one of the best views in the world.' The bedrooms are simple but immaculate. Breakfast on the terrace is enjoyed (fresh fruit, fresh rolls, eggs if wanted). Ask for a lake-facing room ('we woke with sun streaming through the windows and glittering on the water; the occasional storms are spectacular'). Traffic noise can be heard, especially in the roadside rooms (these have no outlook but are now air conditioned). As we went to press, we were sad to hear that Giorgio Cappelletti, whose family has owned this 18th-century villa since 1951, and who was regularly praised for his warmth and humour, has suddenly died. His Scottish wife, Jane, is supported by two daughters and a son-in-law, all admired for their professionalism. (*Wolfgang Stroebe, Bing and Jess Taylor, Esler Crawford*)

Open 1 Apr–5 Nov. **Rooms** 16 double. Some no-smoking. Some air conditioned. **Facilities** Lift, ramp. Lounge, bar/TV room, restaurant (no-smoking;

background music). Terrace. Garden on lake; swimming. **Location** 20 km N of Como. Parking. **Restriction** No smoking in public areas. **Credit cards** MasterCard, Visa. **Terms** B&B: single €80–€110, double €100–€130. Set lunch €30, dinner €35. 1-night bookings sometimes refused Sept.

ASOLO 31011 Treviso — Map 11:B4

Albergo Al Sole
Via Collegio 33

Tel (0423) 951332
Fax (0423) 951007
Email info@albergoalsole.com
Website www.albergoalsole.com

Once a bolt hole for wealthy Venetians escaping the summer heat (plus Robert Browning, Freya Stark, Igor Stravinsky *et al.*), this charming little medieval hill town in the Veneto is known as 'the town of a hundred horizons'. Standing quietly in an elevated position is Silvia and Elena De Checchi's pink-and-cream 16th-century villa. Some of the junior suites have views, but all the bedrooms are liked: 'Ours was large, with fresh fruit, lovely bedlinen, a wonderful shower. The owners' enthusiasm for high tech includes electronically controlled "Do not disturb" signs, and fabulous automatic loos for the public areas.' Other praise: 'The ambience is relaxed, but attention to detail is paramount. Standards of housekeeping are high.' Chef Marco Valletta uses local ingredients (asparagus, mushrooms, radicchio di Treviso, etc) in *La Terrazza*, the panoramic restaurant. Breakfast is served on a balcony with views, or in a 'nicely thought-out' room on cool days. The three-night packages are 'good value'. There is a grotto with 16th-century frescoes; art exhibitions are held. (*WA*)

Open All year. Restaurant may close in Jan. **Rooms** 1 suite, 14 double, 8 single. 2 suitable for ♿. Some no-smoking. Air conditioning. **Facilities** Lift. Hall, restaurant (no-smoking), breakfast room; classical background music; fitness centre; conference room. Terrace. Access to local golf club with swimming pool. **Location** Central. 66 km NW of Venice. Private parking nearby. **Restriction** No smoking in public areas. **Credit cards** Amex, MasterCard, Visa. **Terms** B&B: single €110–€150, double €170–€255, suite €205–€255. Full alc €30.

BAGNO VIGNONI 53027 Siena — Map 11:D4

Hotel Posta Marcucci
Via Ara Urcea 43

Tel (0577) 887112
Fax (0577) 887119
Email info@hotelpostamarcucci.it
Website www.hotelpostamarcucci.it

An ancient open-air hot sulphur spring dominates the central square of this 'magical' village: from an arcade built along one side by the Romans, steam rises, even in winter. The Marcucci family's 'very well-run' spa hotel, facing the Val d'Orcia, caters for 'a mix of holidaymakers and the elderly taking the waters'. It has a 'wonderful' open-air swimming pool (open to the public and sometimes crowded), and two indoor thermal pools for residents only. 'Still a hotel of high quality in our favourite area of Italy,' says a returning visitor in 2004.

'Best pool I ever swam in,' adds his 11-year-old son. But there were also caveats: 'Our room, next to a lift, was noisy, and some economies had been made at the expense of service.' 'High-quality Italian cooking with regional specialities' is served in the large, scenic dining room. There is a wide range of mainly Tuscan wines. 'Delightful breakfast on the terrace: home-made bread and cakes, and a conveyor belt-style super-toaster.' The village is 'quite lively', with bars and restaurants, but closed to traffic. Around is unspoilt countryside, with good walking (lots of footpaths). (*Donald Reid, Graham and Nicholas Avery, and others*)

Open All year. **Rooms** 10 suites, 25 double. Air conditioning. **Facilities** Lift. 2 lounges, card room, bar, restaurant; classical background music; 2 indoor thermal pools, sauna, Turkish bath; conference facilities; terrace. Garden: thermal pool, sauna, gym, tennis, bowling. **Location** Edge of village. 5 km S of San Quirico d'Orcia, 44 km SE of Siena. **Restrictions** No smoking: public areas, some bedrooms. No dogs in restaurant or pool areas. **Credit cards** All major cards accepted. **Terms** B&B double €138–€200; D,B&B €87–€95 per person. Set lunch €14–€25, dinner €25–€30; full alc €30–€33.

BARBIANO 39040 Bolzano **Map 11:A4**

Albergo Bad Dreikirchen BUDGET
S Giacomo 6

Tel (0471) 650055
Fax (0471) 650044
Email info@baddreikirchen.it
Website www.baddreikirchen.it

High above the Isarco valley between Bressanone and Bolzano, this hamlet consists of *le tre chiese*, three curious little attached medieval churches and this unspoilt 14th-century chalet, now a modest hotel. Run by Matthias Wodenegg ('all goodness', says a fan), with his wife, Annette, it has been owned by his family for 200 years. 'Everything revolves around nature,' they write. 'No television, telephones or automobiles.' Arriving guests are met at the car park in Barbiano, a small tourist village. 'Herr Wodenegg took us on a hair-raising journey in his minibus up the mountain.' Or you can arrive on foot, 'an exhilarating half-hour uphill trek'. There are 'spectacular views' of the valley on one side, Castle Trostburg on the other side. Around are meadows, mountains, streams and woods. 'All is constructed of wood,' say recent guests. 'Our room at the back looked on to the three ancient churches. We loved the scrubbed pine floors, the vases of wild flowers. The swimming pool is tastefully placed, and the public areas are excellent.' Earlier visitors admired the 'beautiful hand-painted furniture' in their bedroom and its large terrace 'where we could sit and admire the scenery'. There is a library, a lounge with a grand piano, and a spacious panoramic veranda. The food 'is as good as you can expect up a mountain', and there is excellent walking all around. (*J and MH*)

Open 1 May–24 Oct. **Rooms** 2 suites, 16 double, 8 single. **Facilities** Lounge with piano, library, restaurant; table tennis room. No background music. Garden: heated swimming pool. Unsuitable for ♿. **Location** From E45 Ponte Gardena exit: 4 km W to Barbiano. At Barbiano telephone the inn. **Restriction** No smoking. **Credit cards** Amex, MasterCard, Visa. **Terms** B&B: single €33–€51, double €66–€103; D,B&B €47–€65.50 per person.

BASSANO DEL GRAPPA 36061 VICENZA — Map 11:B4

Villa Ca' Sette NEW
Via Cunizza da Romano 4

Tel (0424) 383350
Fax (0424) 393287
Email info@ca-sette.it
Website www.ca-sette.it

Despite its famous Palladian covered bridge and medieval castle and its *grappa*, Bassano is a relatively unexplored but lovely old town near Vicenza. The Zonta family's hotel, about 20 minutes' walk from the centre, is a recent conversion of the Sette family's 18th-century summer home. Decor is a blend of modern (furnishings, modem links, etc) and antique (frescoed ceilings, wooden beams). The nominator, on his second visit, wrote of 'large rooms, most with real character (some in the villa, some in the adventurously designed annexe), huge beds, large cupboards, well-appointed bathrooms'. In the big conservatory restaurant, *Ca' 7*, the 'very good' food (vegetarian, local and seafood dishes) includes zucchini flowers filled with scampi and pesto; guineahen with wild mushrooms; filo pastry with aubergine, mozzarella and candied tomatoes. 'Relatively expensive but good value; staff are friendly.' Both Venice and Verona are an hour away. (*David Medcalf*)

Open All year. Restaurant closed 10 days Aug. **Rooms** 1 triple, 2 suites, 11 double, 5 single. 1 designed for ♿. Air conditioning. **Facilities** Lift. Salon, bar, restaurant (no-smoking; background music); meeting rooms; Internet link. Large garden. Free bicycles. **Location** 1 km N of Bassano (driver service provided). 35 NE of Vicenza; SS 47 exit Pove del Grappa. Garage. **Restriction** No smoking in public areas. **Credit cards** All major cards accepted. **Terms** B&B: single €110–€130, double €170–€206, suite €250–€400. Set meals €25; full alc €40.

BAVENO 28831 Verbania — Map 11:B2

Hotel Rigoli BUDGET
Via Piave 48

Tel (0323) 924756
Fax (0323) 925156
Email hotel@hotelrigoli.com
Website www.hotelrigoli.com

In a 'rare, quiet position', and with a private beach on Lake Maggiore, this modest hotel, fronted by a flowery terrace shaded by palm trees, faces the Borromeo islands and the distant Alps. 'The approach does not do it justice (it is by an unobtrusive campsite),' says a regular visitor. Recently renovated, it has bedrooms that 'are basic but not primitive': they vary in size, and some bathrooms are 'poky'. Lakeside bedrooms have a balcony. 'The public rooms are pleasant, especially the large, sunny dining room which runs the length of the building by the water. The food is unpretentious, often exceptional, with a cheeseboard to die for, and a display of calorific cakes.' Half board is 'especially good value': set menus offer good choice, including 'super hors d'œuvre' and a salad buffet. The owners, the 'delightful' sisters Claudia and Patrizia Bezzoli, and their staff are 'attentive and helpful, yet unobtrusive'. The town centre (busy in season) and landing stage are close by. (*DB, SP*)

Open Apr–Oct. **Rooms** 28 double, 3 single. **Facilities** TV room, bar, restaurant; background music. Air conditioning. Garden, private beach. Tennis, sailing, windsurfing, waterskiing, fishing, golf nearby. Unsuitable for ♿. **Location** 200 m from centre. Parking. **Restriction** No smoking. **Credit cards** Amex, MasterCard, Visa. **Terms** B&B: single €65–€80, double €100–€115; D,B&B €50–€80 per person. Set meals €25; full alc €35–€40.

BELLAGIO 22021 Como **Map 11:B3**

Albergo Belvedere *Tel* (031) 950410
Via Valassina 31 *Fax* (031) 950102
Email belveder@tin.it
Website www.belvederebellagio.com

An 'excellent, well-run hotel': this large, white building stands in terraced gardens, 'full of birdsong', above a picturesque little harbour and small stony beach on Lake Como. Owned by Tiziana Martinelli Manoni, whose ancestors founded a simple *albergo* here in 1880, it is liked for the 'courteous staff' and 'lovely setting'. Bellagio, with its tree-shaded promenade and narrow streets, is a short walk away. There are views across the water from many bedrooms, the restaurant, the terrace where alfresco meals are served, and the swimming pool (surrounded by loungers and lawns). The suite, on the top floor, has a terrace and balcony. Some rooms look on to a quiet side street. Visitors in 2004 had 'a fabulous fourth-floor bedroom with stunning lake views'. Another couple's room, with large bathroom and dressing room, opened on to lawn and garden. Most visitors find the half-board meals 'good value, with plenty of choice', but one was critical of the restaurant service. Another wrote: 'In high season there were lots of package tours.' (*Trish and Mike Winder, MS, and others*)

Open 1 Apr–31 Oct. **Rooms** 4 suites, 56 double, 3 single. Some in annexes. Some suitable for ♿. Some no-smoking. Most air conditioned. **Facilities** Lift. Lounge, reading room, TV room, breakfast room, bar, restaurant (no-smoking); conference room. No background music. Garden: terrace restaurant; unheated swimming pool, children's playground. 30 m above lake: small stony beach. **Location** 300 m from centre. Parking. **Restriction** No smoking in public areas. **Credit cards** All major cards accepted. **Terms** [2004] B&B: single €100–€115, double €140–€249, suite €290–€357; D,B&B €96.50–€142 per person. Set meals €33; full alc €50.

Grand Hotel Villa Serbelloni *Tel* (031) 950216
Via Roma 1 *Fax* (031) 951529
Email inforequest@villaserbelloni.com
Website www.villaserbelloni.com

'Airy and opulent', this famous old hotel 'sprawls along the shoreline' on a promontory, looking across Lake Como to the distant Alps. It has large, flowery grounds; behind is a park with magnolias and pomegranate trees; on the private beach are palm trees and cabins. Frescoed ceilings, marble columns, gilt furnishings, putti and crystal chandeliers 'lend a baroque theatricality to the public rooms', says a visitor this year, bowled over by the 'sense of regal space and excess'. The *à la carte* restaurant, *Mistral*, faces the lake; so do many bedrooms. 'Our suite had lovely fabrics, sitting room with antiques, huge bath with marble tiles.' In 'one of the world's most grandiose dining rooms', or on the terrace, the four-course daily menu (lots of choice) is accompanied by a 'lively' trio. 'Meals are like state occasions', and 'if the food does not quite rise to this', service 'by squads of speed-walking waiters' is attentive. 'Five generations of ownership by the Bucher family ensure that behind the grand facade, a personal regime holds sway.' 'Skimpy beach towels, canned orange juice, tired furnishings in our suite', were negative points this year, and some bedrooms were thought 'small and spartan', but the consensus is: 'Quite expensive, but value for money.' Children are welcomed. (*John Hillman, Michael Burns, BB, and others*)

Open 24 Mar–20 Nov. Closed Christmas/New Year. **Rooms** 20 suites, 59 double, 2 single. Some on ground floor. 13 apartments in *Residence* in park. Air conditioning. **Facilities** Lift. Lounge, 2 bars, reading room, TV room, restaurant (no-smoking), terrace restaurant; live/background music; spa: swimming pool, massage, etc; conference/function facilities. Large grounds: dining terrace, children's playground, heated swimming pool, tennis; on lake: beach, pier. **Location** Central. Parking, garage. **Restriction** No smoking in public areas. **Credit cards** All major cards accepted. **Terms** B&B: single €150–€230, double €250–€485, suite €495–€850; D,B&B: single €207–€287, double €364–€599, suite €609–€964. Set meals €65–€75; full alc €85.

BOLOGNA — Map 11:C4

Hotel dei Commerciante
Via de' Pignattari 11
40124 Bologna

Tel (051) 7457511
Fax (051) 7457522
Email commercianti@inbo.it
Website www.bolognarthotels.it

'Remarkably silent for its position', this 'high-class hotel, just off the main square' is under the same ownership as the *Corona d'Oro* (now omitted for lack of feedback), the *Novecento* and the *Orologio* (see next entry). It has 'friendly, helpful staff', and guests like the 'nice touches such as bicycles – great for cycle-friendly Bologna', and the Internet access. From some bedrooms, with 'lovely beams under the eaves', you can practically see into the cathedral; other rooms have a little balcony. The hotel is in a traffic-free side street, near most of the main tourist attractions, the Via dell'Indipendenza (great shopping), and many of the best restaurants in the 'food capital of Italy', such as *Battibecco* (*Michelin* star), *Rodrigo* and *Cesari*. (*NM, and others*)

Open All year. **Rooms** 2 studio apartments (2 mins' walk), 27 double, 7 single. Air conditioning. **Facilities** Lift. Hall, lounge; Internet point; breakfast room; classical background music. Unsuitable for ♿. **Location** Centre of old town, near Piazza Maggiore. Garage (€26 a night). **Restriction** No smoking: public areas, some bedrooms. **Credit cards** All major cards accepted. **Terms** B&B: single €136–€300, double €189–€320, suite €281–€468.

Hotel Orologio
Via IV Novembre 10
40123 Bologna

Tel (051) 7457411
Fax (051) 7457422
Email orologio@inbo.it
Website www.bolognarthotels.it

'Perfectly situated for getting around the old town, and for buses and trains', this 'well-managed' B&B hotel stands by the main square, facing the clock (*orologio*) on the civic tower. 'The staff are helpful,' say fans who spent 'a lovely couple of days'. 'Much thought has been given to making guests comfortable' (eg, free Internet use). 'Lovely bedrooms', some with a balcony, are distributed over five floors (but 'the small lift does not serve the ground floor; it begins after a flight and a half of stairs'). Newspapers are available in the first-floor lounge, and in the adjacent breakfast room there is 'an extensive buffet with freshly squeezed juices', sometimes marred by 'loud conversations carried on, almost on top of one, by the staff'. The area is pedestrianised, but cars are allowed in for unloading. (*Sara Price, A and EA*)

Open All year. **Rooms** 1 mini-flat, 31 double, 2 single. Air conditioning. **Facilities** Hall, sitting room (free Internet access), breakfast room; classical background music. Unsuitable for ♿. **Location** Near main square in pedestrianised zone. Garage, parking (expensive) nearby. **Restriction** No smoking: public areas, some bedrooms. **Credit cards** All major cards accepted. **Terms** B&B: single €130–€300, double €179–€320, suite €271–€468.

BOLVEDRO DI TREMEZZO 22019 Como — Map 11:A3

Hotel Villa Edy BUDGET
Via Febo Sala 18

Tel (0344) 40161
Fax (0344) 40015
Email villaedy@libero.it
Website www.lakecomo.org/www/hotelvillaedy

On a hill, back from the busy waterfront outside Tremezzo, a fairly sedate resort, the Fasoli family's modern villa-style hotel offers 'very good value for money', says a visitor this year. The bedrooms are 'comfortable and well maintained'. Bathrooms have an 'excellent shower'. Each room has a balcony: some have 'breathtaking views' of the mountains, lake and hilltop towns; some face the large swimming pool. But the villa is not for the less nimble. A visitor without a car reports that it is quite a steep climb up from Tremezzo, 'and no lift: our room was on the second floor'. One report told of 'attentive staff and family atmosphere', but another guest found the welcome 'cool'. And 'the adjacent campsite could be noisy in summer'. No meals apart from breakfast ('a generous buffet') in the garden or on a terrace (one visitor was put out to discover that this had to be paid for separately, in cash), but the bar serves 'very good' drinks and snacks (pasta, salads, etc) until midnight, and there are plenty of restaurants in Tremezzo and in Bellagio across the lake. *Al Vellu*, on the road to Rogaro, is also recommended: 'We sat outside with stunning views of the lake. The food was very good: it was worth the climb to get there.' (*MT, HA*)

Open Apr–Oct. **Rooms** 10. **Facilities** Breakfast room (no-smoking), bar; terrace. Garden: swimming pool, tennis. Unsuitable for ♿. **Location** 1 km W of Tremezzo. Parking. **Restrictions** No smoking in public areas. No dogs. **Credit cards** All major cards accepted. **Terms** [2004] Double room with breakfast €62–€75.

BOLZANO 39100 Map 11:A4

Hotel Greif NEW
Piazza Walther

Tel (0471) 318000
Fax (0471) 318148
Email info@greif.it
Website www.greif.it

Behind the restored facade of the medieval *Black Griffin Inn*, a protected building in the pedestrianised old part of town, is a 'stunning modern high-tech interior, including free Internet access in all bedrooms', say visitors who discovered it in 2004. 'Great room facing the square, wonderful people-watching. Great bath. Breakfast was hearty.' The Staffler family owners recently carried out a major renovation: each room contains a specially commissioned contemporary work of art. Only B&B is offered: guests have access to the larger sister *Park Hotel Laurin*, nearby, with its bar, restaurant and large grounds with swimming pool. The station and the main shopping street are also near. (*Sue Ann and Martin Marcus*)

Open All year. **Rooms** 33. Air conditioning. **Facilities** Lift. Lounge area, breakfast room; rooftop garden. Access to *Park Hotel Laurin*: bar, restaurant; large grounds: outdoor meals; swimming pool. **Location** Central. A22 exit Bolzano S or Bolzano N. Parking (€15). **Restriction** No smoking in public areas. **Credit cards** All major cards accepted. **Terms** [2004] B&B: single €105–€160, double €158–€235, suite €280–€330.

BORGO SAN LORENZO 50032 Firenze Map 11:C4

Locanda degli Artisti NEW
Piazza Romagnoli 2

Tel (055) 8455359
Fax (055) 8450116
Email info@locandartisti.it
Website www.locandartisti.it

In the small main town of the Mugello, north-east of Florence (45 minutes away by train), this small, 'quite simple' B&B is an 1846 building, recently redecorated by its owner, Anna Benvenuti, in Liberty style. The themed bedrooms (Wisteria, Sunflowers, Mimosa, etc) are 'nice, spacious, clean and quiet', says the nominator in 2004, 'and the central position is perfect'. Each room is decorated with an oil painting and ceramics appropriate to its name. Breakfast is 'really good, with fruit from the owners' garden, and home-made cakes': in summer it is served under a pergola. The restaurant downstairs (www.ristorantedegliartisti.it) is separately owned, and well reputed in the area. Children under six get a free soft toy. (*Litta Sohi*)

Open All year. **Rooms** 5 double, 2 single. Air conditioning. **Facilities** Reception, bar; background music. **Location** Central, in traffic-free zone. 27 km NE of Florence. **Restrictions** No smoking. No pets. **Credit cards** MasterCard, Visa. **Terms** B&B: single €70–€80; double €110–€130.

BRESSANONE 39042 Bolzano — Map 11:A4

Hotel Elephant
Via Rio Bianco 4

Tel (0472) 832750
Fax (0472) 836579
Email info@hotelelephant.com
Website www.hotelelephant.com

In 1551, the King of Portugal sent an elephant from Goa via Genoa to Archduke Ferdinand of Austria in Vienna. Tired by its long walk, it lodged overnight at this tavern, then called *Am hohen Feld*. The landlord renamed the building and commissioned an elephant fresco for the outside wall. Now it is a 'very traditional hotel with modern touches', much liked by recent visitors: 'Two helpful porters in green baize aprons are always around. Our suite in a villa in the large garden across the road had an enormous bed, plenty of seating, wonderful bathroom with spa bath. The owner, Elisabeth Heiss, was around most of the day, helping in the restaurant, and arranging flowers.' Tyrolean dishes, cooked to order, are served in three dining rooms and on a terrace. 'The famous *Piatto Elephant* consists of an enormous platter of meats and vegetables on a bed of rice, plus a starter and dessert: wonderful value at €30 per person. Breakfasts, the best we have experienced, includes many hot and cold dishes, and an exquisite home-made yogurt in a crystal glass swirled with fresh raspberries and juice.' The 'lovely' swimming pool is surrounded by lawns. Gentle hill walks and adventurous mountain climbs are nearby. (*JC*)

Open 6 Mar–7 Nov, 1 Dec–6 Jan. **Rooms** 25 double, 19 single. 14 in annexe in park, 50 m across main road. 1 suitable for ♿. **Facilities** Lift (in annexe). Lounge, reading room, bar, 3 dining rooms (no-smoking). No background music. Large garden; heated swimming pool, tennis. **Location** Near historic centre. Parking. **Restriction** No smoking in public areas. **Credit cards** All major cards accepted. **Terms** B&B: single €96–€105, double €192–€215; D,B&B single €127–€130, double €254–€274. Set lunch €33, dinner €40; full alc €45.

Hotel Goldener Adler
Adlerbrückengasse 9

Tel (0472) 200621
Fax (0472) 208973
Email info@goldener-adler.com
Website www.goldener-adler.com

'It was outstanding: wonderful value and quality.' 'Thoroughly professional.' Endorsements this year for the Mayr family's crenellated, cream-painted hotel. Originally a 16th-century palace, it is in the pedestrianised centre of this charming little medieval town (Brixen in German) just off the *autostrada* from the Brenner Pass: a good base for walking or winter sports, or touring in the mountains. Earlier visitors, equally enthusiastic, wrote: 'It has a friendly, multilingual staff, and very elegant furnishings including many antique pieces.' 'Our spacious bedroom was well equipped.' Some rooms have cooking facilities. The rooms with a balcony overlooking the River Isalco are particularly liked. 'Bathrooms are luxurious.' Breakfast, in an 'elegant first-floor salon', is a 'superb buffet', including hot dishes and Tyrolean pastries. For meals there are the *Künstlerstübele*, the

Kapitelschenke, with garden (open all day), or the *Finsterwirt*. Dogs are welcomed. A 'fabulous' sun terrace, approached by a spiral staircase, is new this year. Splendid mountain views all around. But 'shops in the South Tyrol are closed on Saturday afternoon and Monday morning'. (*FH Potts, Janice Carrera*)

Open All year. **Rooms** 5 suites, 20 double, 3 single. Some no-smoking. **Facilities** Lift. Bar/lounge; background music; breakfast room (no-smoking), 3 restaurants; sauna. **Location** Central, in pedestrianised zone. Courtyard parking (€5.50). **Restriction** No smoking in public areas. **Credit cards** All major cards accepted. **Terms** [2004] B&B €47–€75. Meals alc.

BRISIGHELLA 48013 Ravenna — Map 11:C4

Relais Torre Pratesi
Via Cavina 11

Tel (0546) 84545
Fax (0546) 84558
Email info@torrepratesi.it
Website www.torrepratesi.it

Loved by fans for its rustic feel, this 'wonderful, relaxing get-away with fabulous food included in the not-tiny price' was enjoyed by most visitors this year, though its style and food won't suit everyone. A collection of old buildings on a ridge in the Romagna hills, it is personally run by the 'genial' owner/chef, Nerio Raccagni, and his wife, Letizia ('who leaves you in no doubt that you play by her rules'): neither speaks English. Earlier visitors 'loved the view and the walk through the orchard to the swimming pool': here 'on-tap Fanta was a hit with the kids (and the beer with me)'. The best bedrooms are in the 16th-century fortified tower' (it has a small lift to the third floor, and a spiral staircase). One enormous room occupies each of its four floors: each has a comfortable bed, efficient shower, and the original slits for windows. Other rooms, not particularly attractive, but comfortable, are in a farmhouse. In the grounds are a bar in one shed, a mini-gym in another, a playground ('two rustic swings and a slide'), and a 'zoo' ('a few interesting farm animals'). Dinner (no choice) by candlelight is between five and eight courses. 'Home cooking, rather than gourmet', it ends with 'exquisite desserts'. Breakfasts include small omelettes, home-made bread and yogurt, cheese and sausages. All drinks are included in the price. Brisighella is a 'charming town' with a picturesque piazza. (*Keith Conlon, D and AD*)

Open All year. **Rooms** 6 suites (3 in annexe, 150 m), 3 double. 3 on ground floor. Some no-smoking. **Facilities** 2 lounges, bar, restaurant; gym. 18-hectare grounds: unheated swimming pool, spa bath, children's play area; mountain bikes. **Location** 8 km W of Brisighella. From A14 Faenza exit: trunk road S302 to Florence/Brisighella, 4 km beyond Brisighella, on far side of Fognano, turn right to Zattaglia; house *c*. 4 km further, on left. **Restriction** No smoking in public areas. **Credit cards** All major cards accepted. **Terms** [2004] B&B: double €150–€180, suite €180–€210; D,B&B €115–€145 per person. Set meals (with drinks) €40–€45.

CALASETTA 09011 Cagliari, Sardinia — Map 12:B1

Hotel Luci del Faro NEW
Località Mangiabarche Sud

Tel (0781) 810089
Fax (0781) 810091
Email hotel.lucidelfaro@tiscali.it
Website www.lucidelfaro.com

Tastefully designed modern complex of bungalows built in semi-circle round large swimming pool, on island of Sant'Antioco off SW Sardinia. 'Immaculate bedroom with balcony; informally dressed, welcoming staff; calm atmosphere. Delightful dinner (interesting local dishes) on terrace lit by candles and restaurant oil lamps. Excellent breakfast.' Air conditioning. Cocktail bar, restaurant; meeting facilities; tennis. Navette to nearby beach. Families welcomed. No smoking in public areas; no dogs. Ristorante da Nicolò *on harbour at Calasetta also liked. Open Mar–Oct. All major credit cards accepted. 38 rooms. B&B €40–€90; D,B&B €70–€130. Set meals (residents only) €25–€30 [2004].*

CAMAIORE 55041 Lucca — Map 11:C3

Peralta NEW
Pieve di Camaiore

Tel/Fax (0584) 951230
Email peraltusc@aol.com
Website www.peraltatuscany.com

High above the valley of Camaiore in the Alpi Apuane hills of Tuscany, this hamlet was acquired 30 years ago by the late, renowned sculptress, Fiore de Henriquez. It now offers B&B accommodation and also some self-catering houses and flats. The old stone buildings, connected by steep steps and sunny terraces, are surrounded by bougainvillaea, lemon trees and jasmine. A simple three-course dinner is served by arrangement twice weekly in summer, on a panoramic terrace, from which 'you can see Corsica on a clear day'. Many guests are British. Dinah Voisin manages, supported by Kate Simova and the 'ebullient Italian-American Ron', who will collect luggage from the car park. 'They run the place like an extension of their family. Fiore's spirit, her studio and sculptures are much in evidence.' A small swimming pool stands amid olive groves. The road up the hill is steep, especially the last 200 metres. 'Not for the faint hearted, but you get used to it', and if you can't face it, you can leave your car at the bottom of the track, and they will fetch you. Courses are held (art, writing, cookery). (*Bing Taylor*)

Open B&B 1 Mar–30 Nov; self-catering all year. **Rooms** 1 family, 5 double. Also 6 self-catering apartments/houses (for 2–8 people). **Facilities** Sitting room, bar, dining room; studio. Garden: terraces (outside dining), swimming pool. Unsuitable for ♿. **Location** 22 km NW of Lucca; 10 km from exit A11/A12 at Viareggio, follow signs: Camaiore, Pieve di Camaiore, Peralta. **Restriction** No smoking in public areas. **Credit cards** None accepted. **Terms** Room €60–€110. Weekly rates.

CAMOGLI 16032 Genova — Map 11:C3

Hotel Cenobio dei Dogi
Via N Cuneo 34

Tel (0185) 7241
Fax (0185) 772796
Email reception@cenobio.it
Website www.cenobio.it

'We cannot think of a nicer, better-run seaside hotel,' says a devotee of this large hotel, built on the site of a villa once owned by the aristocratic Dogi family. 'Well run, though easy-going' and 'mildly luxurious', it stands above the sea in spacious grounds with pine trees and exotic plants, at the southern end of this fishing village on the Ligurian coast south of Genoa. The views are 'enchanting'. It has an 'excellent' sea-water pool, spacious lounges and terrace, and service is 'both efficient and very friendly'. 'We had a magical week,' says a report this year. 'Our wonderfully large, well-appointed bedroom had beautiful marble bathroom, two large windows and balcony facing excellent pool and bar area.' Other rooms face the garden. 'The beach is pebbly, but bathing in the clean sea is marvellous.' 'Lots of choice for breakfast' and the half-board dinners are 'good if unexciting', with limited choice. 'We preferred *La Playa*, open to non-residents.' There could be noise from nearby trains, but they make travelling up and down Liguria easy. Conferences are held off-season. Good walks in the surrounding hills. (*Anne Weizmann, Marsha Benson, Wolfgang Stroebe*)

Open All year. **Rooms** 4 suites, 88 double, 15 single. 2 suitable for ♿. Air conditioning. **Facilities** Lift. Lounges, dining room, restaurant; terrace; chapel; function/conference facilities. No background music. Garden: swimming pool; private beach with seasonal restaurant. Tennis, golf, water sports nearby. **Location** Central. 15 km NW of Portofino. Parking. **Restriction** No smoking in public areas. **Credit cards** All major cards accepted. **Terms** [2004] B&B: single €108–€151, double €150–€348, suite €361–€425; D,B&B €35 added per person.

CANALICCHIO 06050 Perugia — Map 11:D5

Relais Il Canalicchio
Via della Piazza 4

Tel (075) 8707325
Fax (075) 8707296
Email relais@relaisilcanalicchio.it
Website www.relaisilcanalicchio.it

'Very comfortable', 'delightful', with 'magnificent views in all directions', this medieval *castello*, managed by Dorine Kunst, is nicely placed for exploring Umbrian hill towns (Spello, Assisi, Trevi, etc): a car is essential. It stands on a large estate amid woods, olive trees and vineyards. The bedrooms with terrace are especially recommended, but all the rooms are 'comfortable, beautifully appointed'. Decorated in what the hotel calls 'English country' style, they have names like Countess of Oxford, Duchess of Norfolk, and there is a Sir Winston Churchill smoking room. 'The hotel seems to cater unashamedly for the English tourist,' one guest wrote. But the atmosphere is 'congenial', staff are 'friendly', and 'room service is prompt'. 'Excellent cuisine, good wine cellar.' A new building with 14 apartments, each with its own entrance, and a second swimming pool, is connected to the hotel by a little wooden bridge.

Open 25 Mar–30 Nov, 27 Dec–6 Jan. **Rooms** 14 apartments (in separate building), 3 suites, 31 double, 1 single. Air conditioning. **Facilities** Lift, ramp. Reception, lounge, library, TV room, billiard room, piano bar, restaurant with terrace; background jazz; conference room; gym, sauna. 25-hectare grounds: 2 unheated swimming pools, hydromassage; tennis, mountain bikes, horse riding. **Location** 35 km SE of Perugia. E45, exit Ripabianca–Foligno; follow signs for 6 km. Parking. Garage. **Restriction** No smoking: public areas, except cigar smokers' room, some bedrooms. **Credit cards** All major cards accepted. **Terms** (Min. 3 nights) B&B: single €150, double €188, suite €209–€253; D,B&B €39 added per person. *V* (1st night only)

CANNERO RIVIERA 28821 Verbania — Map 11:A2

Hotel Cannero
Lungo Lago 2

Tel (0323) 788046
Fax (0323) 788048
Email info@hotelcannero.com
Website www.hotelcannero.com

An unexpected haven of peace', this 'delightful hotel' stands across a 'small, cobbled, almost pedestrianised road' facing Lake Maggiore. A converted 19th-century monastery, owned by the Gallinotto family since 1902, it is run by Maria Carla Gallinotto with her three sons and daughter. 'They and their staff are very friendly,' says a visitor in 2004. The hotel 'retains features of a former age, eg, the original staircase with wrought iron balustrade, and a delightful inner courtyard'. The lake 'dominates every aspect of life', and upper front rooms have a balcony over the water. 'Our rooms faced the landing stage but were never noisy.' Rear rooms get the last of the sun. There is a five-course *demi-pension* menu and a good *carte*, and 'several restaurants are nearby'. Lunch can be taken on the lakeside terrace; snacks are served in the bar. Breakfast is thought 'excellent'. The 'lovely swimming pool', in a garden with orange and lemon trees, can be crowded in summer. (*Pamela Haley, Michael Burns, LG, Daniel Wentz*)

Open 10 Mar–3 Nov. **Rooms** 10 junior suites, 42 double, 1 single. In 2 buildings. Some air conditioned. Also 10 self-catering apartments. **Facilities** Lift, ramps. Lounge, library, bar, restaurant; background music/pianist; small meeting room. Garden: lakeside terrace, heated swimming pool, solarium, tennis, water sports. **Location** In village. 30 km N of Stresa. Turn off main road to mini roundabout by lake; then left. Hotel opposite landing stage. Garage, parking. **Restrictions** No smoking in public areas. No dogs in public areas. **Credit cards** All major cards accepted. **Terms** B&B €53–€108; D,B&B €73–€128. Set lunch €20, dinner €25; alc €25. *V*

> 'Set meals' refers to fixed-price meals, which may have ample, limited or no choice on the menu. 'Full alc' is the hotel's estimated price per person of a three-course *à la carte* meal with a half bottle of house wine. 'Alc' is the price without wine.

CAPRI 80073 Napoli — Map 12:B3

Villa Sarah
Via Tiberio 3/a

Tel (081) 8377817
Fax (081) 8377215
Email info@villasarah.it
Website www.villasarah.it

Once the summertime day-trippers have left, Capri becomes a different place: it has 'charm, beauty, many fabulous sights'. A short walk from its *centro storico*, Domenico de Martino's white-painted hotel stands quietly amid orchards and vineyards. It was found 'absolutely delightful' by a visitor in 2004: 'Every member of staff was helpful.' Like most of Capri, it must be approached on foot: the island's transport service will (for a fee) bring your luggage from the harbour. Though 'plainly decorated', the villa's bedrooms 'have everything necessary for comfort', said other guests. Many have a sea view; some have a terrace. 'Ours overlooked a garden in which grew a remarkable range of fruits and vegetables. We were invited by the friendly management to wander round it and help ourselves to grapes': guests may also sample the house wine. All the rooms have a view; some have a balcony. A good breakfast is served on the terrace. No restaurant; lots nearby. (*Caroline Pudney, and others*)

Open 15 Mar–30 Oct. **Rooms** 15 double, 4 single. Air conditioning. **Facilities** Bar, breakfast room. Garden: terrace. Unsuitable for ♿. **Location** 800 m E of centre of Capri town, 1.5 km from harbour. **Restrictions** No smoking. No dogs. **Credit cards** All major cards accepted. **Terms** B&B: single €80–€125, double €165–€190.

Hotel La Tosca BUDGET
Via Dalmazio Birago 5

Tel/Fax (081) 8370989
Email h.tosca@capri.it
Website www.latoscahotel.com

Overlooking the ancient monastery of San Giacomo, a few minutes' walk from the café-lined *piazzetta*, this simple *pensione* is owned by Ettore Castelli. 'The bedrooms are a cool (in every sense), immaculate white,' says a recent visitor. 'Very good bathrooms and beds.' Most rooms have a balcony with the 'stunning views' that are seen also from the tiny terrace where drinks and breakfast are served. The 'friendly, amusing' staff speak English. The transfer of luggage from the harbour can be arranged. Sgr Castelli writes that the *Guide* voucher discount of 25% is a bit too high for him, but 'we always try to offer a good rate to guests'. (*NR*)

Open 15 Mar–6 Nov. **Rooms** 10 double, 1 single. All air conditioned. **Facilities** Bar with terrace, breakfast room. No background music. Unsuitable for ♿. **Location** Near Giardini di Augusto. No parking (pedestrianised area). **Restrictions** No smoking: public areas, some bedrooms. No dogs. **Credit cards** MasterCard, Visa. **Terms** Room: single €40–€80, double €63–€125.

All our inspections are anonymous.

Villa Brunella
Via Tragara 24a

Tel (081) 8370122
Fax (081) 8370430
Email villabrunella@capri.it
Website www.villabrunella.it

A bit of a walk from Capri's small main square, Piazza Umberto, in a pleasant residential area, this small modern villa is 'stylish, efficient and vertiginous', says a visitor this year. Earlier guests wrote of its 'personal atmosphere and pleasant staff'. Owned by Vincenzo Brunella and his wife, it stands in a flowery garden. 'A series of beautiful rooms and suites, each with terrace, most with spectacular views, cascades down a steep hill towards the sea.' 'There were 80 steps down from the entrance to the deluxe room where we spent three nights. It was excellent, spacious, with two trees and comprehensive bathroom.' The restaurant, with panoramic dining terrace, serves traditional Caprese dishes. Breakfast is taken by the swimming pool. Porters will collect guests' luggage from the boat. 'Beyond the *Brunella* is only one hotel and then just the spectacular south coast.' (*Stephen Wright, CH and CE*)

Open 19 Mar–5 Nov. **Rooms** 20. Air conditioning. **Facilities** Lift. Lounge, bar, restaurant. Garden: dining terrace, heated swimming pool. Unsuitable for ♿. **Location** 15 mins' walk from centre. **Restrictions** No smoking in public areas. No dogs. **Credit cards** All major cards accepted. **Terms** [2004] B&B double €240–€320. Alc €38–€56.

CARPESICA DI VITTORIO VENETO 31029 Treviso Map 11:A4

Alice Relais nelle Vigne NEW
Via Giardino 94

Tel (0438) 561173
Fax (0438) 920754
Email info@alice-relais.com
Website www.alice-relais.com

In the hills between Conegliano and Vittorio Veneto where Prosecco is produced, this old farmhouse stands quietly amid vines. It is filled with tapestries, antique wooden furniture and ornaments. 'The personal service and myriads of little touches made our stay memorable,' says the 2004 nominator. 'Arriving late, we were welcomed with a glass of Prosecco by Umberto Cosmo, *Alice*'s amazing host. Our immaculate room, in converted stables, had a picture-perfect view of the pretty surrounding countryside. All the facilities are brand new and high-tech, but entirely in sympathy with the rural Italian style. Breakfast was stylish. Umberto drove us round his vineyards. He holds wine tastings accompanied by local delicacies.' All rooms have a 'green tea aromatherapy set'; some have a spa bath. Children are welcomed (playground, babysitters provided). In the grounds are a 'fitness path' and a 'sensorial path'. Arrival is by appointment only. *Alice* has special arrangements with local restaurants of all kinds. (*Natalie Malevsky-Price*)

Open All year. **Rooms** 5 junior suites, 5 double. Air conditioning. **Facilities** Lift. Lounge; background music; courtyard. 20-hectare grounds: fitness paths, children's playground. **Location** S of Vittorio Veneto towards Conegliano.

1.3 km from A27, exit Vittorio Veneto Sud, direction Carpesica. Hotel on right. **Restrictions** No smoking. No pets. **Credit cards** All major cards accepted. **Terms** [2004] B&B: single €80–€102.50, double €100–€145.

CASTELLINA IN CHIANTI 53011 Siena — Map 11:D4

Palazzo Squarcialupi
Via Ferruccio 26

Tel (0577) 741186
Fax (0577) 740386
Email info@chiantiandrelax.com
Website www.chiantiandrelax.com

In the pedestrianised historic centre of this fortified hill village, the most important civil building has been 'sensitively converted while retaining its traditional character' by the Targioni family. Monica Targioni is the manager. A visitor this year had 'a very pleasant stay' and endorsed earlier praise: 'Staff could not have been more helpful.' Wine cellars, and a shop selling the family's wine, La Castellina, are on the ground floor. Above are the bedrooms, 'traditionally furnished and quiet', the breakfast room with its panoramic terrace, and the 'beautifully furnished' lounges (one has frescoed walls, another a large fireplace; oriental rugs lie on wooden floors). Rear rooms have 'stunning views' over the surrounding hills. A swimming pool in the garden is new this year. No restaurant: three good ones are within walking distance, and there is a pizzeria opposite. (*Gillian Seel*)

Open 21 Mar–1 Nov. **Rooms** 17 double. Air conditioning. **Facilities** Lift. 2 lounges, bar, breakfast room; background music; games room; terrace; wine cellar; shop. Garden: swimming pool. Unsuitable for ♿. **Location** Centre of village. 24 km N of Siena. Free parking. **Restrictions** No smoking in public areas. Small dogs only. **Credit cards** All major cards accepted. **Terms** B&B double €88–€160.

CATANIA 95131 Sicily — Map 12:C3

Hotel Pensione Rubens NEW/BUDGET
Via Etnea 196

Tel (095) 317073
Fax (095) 7151713
Email rubens@simail.it
Website www.hotelrubenscatania.com

In the main shopping street of this 'splendidly baroque' city, this small B&B has an 'exuberant', multilingual owner/manager, Signor Caviezel, Swiss in origin. 'The city fathers should name a street after him,' says the nominator. 'His bonhomie and fund of stories make a visit to Catania worthwhile. He offers advice, information, even bus tickets. His small but comfortable hotel is not luxurious, but most rooms are quiet (a premium in Sicily): looking inwards, they have air conditioning and mini-fridge.' Some have a balcony facing Mount Etna. (*Nigel Rodgers*)

Open All year. **Rooms** 7. Air conditioning. **Facilities** Breakfast room. **Location** Central. **Restriction** No smoking in public areas. **Credit cards** Amex, MasterCard, Visa. **Terms** [2004] B&B: single €45, double €52–€68.

CENERENTE 06070 Perugia Map 11:D4

Castello dell'Oscano
Strada della Forcella 37

Tel (075) 584371
Fax (075) 690666
Email info@oscano.com
Website www.oscano.com

'Imaginatively converted', this neo-Gothic castle stands amid pine trees in hilly countryside near Perugia. From the west side there are views over the Umbrian countryside. 'The decor is lovely,' says a recent warm commendation, 'handmade carpets everywhere, antiques, comfortable chairs. Our room in the turret, not large, and with narrow windows, was pleasingly decorated. Its attractive bathroom was in a shed built on to the turret: the shower fluctuated, but the water temperature remained constant.' Some cheaper rooms are in the adjoining *Villa Ada*, and there are self-contained flats in *La Macina* (mill) in the huge park. In the hotel's *Ristorante Turandot*, the five-course fixed-price dinner, at 8.30 pm, was thought 'terrific, in the best Italian style, sophisticated, imaginative, but of the region' (eg, pheasant tortelli; young boar fillet). The cellar contains over 200 Umbrian wines. Breakfast is an 'ample if unexceptional' buffet. There is a 'charming library', and a 'beautiful secluded terrace' for summer meals. Lake Trasimeno is ten minutes' drive away.

Open All year. Meals for residents only. **Rooms** 13 suites, 31 double, 3 single. 11 in castle, 23 in *Villa Ada*. 1 on ground floor. Air conditioning. Also 13 flats in *La Macina*. **Facilities** Hall, lounges, library, piano bar, restaurant; background music; games room; meeting room. 252-hectare park: 2 unheated swimming pools. Horse riding, tennis, lake (fishing), mountain bikes; golf nearby. **Location** 7 km NW of Perugia towards Gubbio (E45 exit Madonna Alta). **Restriction** No smoking: public areas, some bedrooms. **Credit cards** All major cards accepted. **Terms** B&B: single €115–€130, double €150–€160, suite €290–€320; D,B&B €30 added per person. Set lunch €30, dinner €38; full alc €40. *V*

CERTALDO ALTO 50052 Firenze Map 11:D4

Il Castello BUDGET
Via G della Rena 6

Tel/Fax (0571) 668250
Email info@albergoilcastello.it
Website www.albergoilcastello.it

Midway between Empoli and Siena, 'one of Italy's best-preserved hill towns' rises above the bustling and undistinguished modern village below. This *albergo familiare*, creeper-covered and crenellated, is in a 13th-century *palazzo* which is part of the city walls (Boccaccio's birthplace is outside the door). 'The furniture is blissfully unreformed 19th-century,' one couple wrote. Half of the bedrooms, which are of moderate size, have a panoramic view over lower town and countryside. Others, quieter, have more restricted views, of the old town. The restaurant is on a lovely terrace with fountain, palm trees, flowers and views of the Val d'Elsa towards San Gimignano. The 'kind and knowledgeable' owner/chef, Romana Marcori, is proud of her *cucina tradizionale*, using mushrooms, local fresh fish, etc. 'Food and service are good.' 'At breakfast, a kettle is on the buffet table, and you make your own tea. No charge for morning coffee and afternoon tea.'

Open All year, except Nov. Restaurant closed Tues. **Rooms** 12. **Facilities** Bar, 3 dining rooms; 2 cellar function rooms. No background music. Large garden. Unsuitable for ♿. **Location** Certaldo old town. 42 km NW of Siena. Public parking 300 m. **Restriction** No smoking in public areas. **Credit cards** All major cards accepted. **Terms** [2004] B&B: single €60, double €100; D,B&B €70 per person.

Osteria del Vicario
Via Rivellino 3

Tel/Fax (0571) 668228
Email info@osteriadelvicario.it
Website www.osteriadelvicario.it

*Attractive 'restaurant-with-lodgings', 51 years old, in former monastery (1212). 'Creative' Tuscan cooking (*Michelin *star) served in beamed restaurant or alfresco in lovely cloister. 'Quiet. Good welcome and dinner. Excellent service. Satisfying breakfast.' Closed Wed, and Mon/Tues in Jan/Feb. Unsuitable for ♿. No smoking in public areas; no dogs. All major credit cards accepted. 8 bedrooms (4 in monks' cells, 4 in guest house): with breakfast €60–€90; D,B&B €75 per person. Alc €46–€63 [2004].*

CHIAVERANO DI IVREA 10010 Torino — Map 11:B2

Castello San Giuseppe NEW
Località Castello San Giuseppe

Tel (0125) 424370
Fax (0125) 641278
Email info@castellosangiuseppe.it
Website www.castellosangiuseppe.it

Historic building (former 17th-century convent), now hotel of character. Spectacular, peaceful setting on hill surrounded by 11-hectare parkland, small lakes, hills and mountains, 6 km NE of Ivrea. 'Very welcoming staff. The New Year's Eve dinner was an amazing banquet.' Salons, frescoed, candlelit restaurant, Il Cenobio, *outdoor dining; meeting facilities. Closed 7–20 Jan; restaurant closed midday and Sun. No smoking in public areas. All major credit cards accepted. 21 bedrooms, all different, some have frescoed arched ceiling, chandelier, four-poster. B&B: single €88–€129, double €140–€180; D,B&B €36 added per person [2004].*

CIOCCARO DI PENANGO 14030 Asti — Map 11:B2

Locanda del Sant'Uffizio
Strada Sant'Uffizio 1

Tel (0141) 916292
Fax (0141) 916068
Email santuffizio@thi.it

Found 'absolutely marvellous' by a returning visitor in 2004, this converted 17th-century monastery has a 'dream location' amid the vine-clad Monferrato hills north-east of Asti. It stands in large grounds (with roses, geraniums, orange and lemon trees in large pots, and a big swimming pool surrounded by parasols and loungers). 'Truly "*vaut-le-voyage*". A wonderful room in the old part, basking lizard on the balcony. Superb food [Fabrizio Donna is chef]. *Maître d'* the best we have encountered. Charming welcome.' Another visitor recommends: 'Make sure you earn enough money to enjoy the experience', and adds: 'The seven-course meals will long be remembered.' An earlier report told of 'lovely quiet walks with outstanding views'. The bedrooms are decorated in pale colours; bathrooms are spacious. Breakfast is a 'superb buffet with reasonable (for Italy) juice'. Children are welcomed; bicycles and mountain bikes can be hired. Truffle exhibitions are held in winter. (*Christopher McCall, Alan Brownlow, MG*)

Open All year. **Rooms** 5 suites, 5 junior suites, 21 double, 2 single. Some on ground floor. Air conditioning. **Facilities** Lift. Salons, bar, orangery (breakfast/lunch), restaurant; games room; billiard room; small gym; conference/banqueting facilities. No background music. 1-hectare grounds: swimming pool, tennis. **Location** Off SS457 Asti–Casale, 5 km S of Moncalvo, 20 km NE of Asti. Parking. **Restriction** No smoking: public areas, some bedrooms. **Credit cards** All major cards accepted. **Terms** [2004] B&B: single €118–€165, double €161–€230; D,B&B €50–€57 added per person. Set meals €50–€60; full alc €55.

COGNE 11012 Aosta — Map 11:B1

Hotel Bellevue NEW
Rue Grand Paradis 22

Tel (0165) 74825
Fax (0165) 749192
Email bellevue@relaischateaux.com
Website www.hotelbellevue.it

Spectacularly located in the Gran Paradiso national park, the Jeantet-Roullet family's luxurious hotel (Relais & Chateaux, *Michelin* star) is in a French-speaking mountain valley, south of Aosta. It returns to the *Guide* after a time with no reports: visitors in 2004 had 'a perfect week' of cross-country skiing, while staying here. 'Our room was delightful and spacious, with balconies overlooking Cogne (a charming town) and Gran Paradiso mountain. The restaurant was a nightly treat after a day's fresh air and exercise: wonderful five-course dinners, beautifully presented. Free afternoon tea, and buffet breakfasts as good as could be wished for. Staff the most agreeable and helpful that we have encountered. Excellent value.' Brightly coloured fabrics and typical Valdostana furniture create an atmosphere 'both smart and cosy'. Some rooms have a spa bath; some a fireplace. There are two restaurants, a brasserie and a cheese cellar, and a spa offering aromatic, hay and steam baths, massages, etc. (*Sheila and Christopher Richards*)

Open All year. Reduced service 3 Oct–17 Dec. **Rooms** 3 chalets, 7 suites, 31 double. **Facilities** Lounge, piano bar, 4 restaurants; background/live music; children's play room; spa: heated swimming pool, sauna, massage; cinema. Garden: terrace (bar). **Location** 27 km S of Aosta (A5 exit Aosta West). **Restrictions** No smoking in public areas. **Credit cards** All major cards accepted. **Terms** B&B: single €110–€200, double €140–€300, chalet €285–€360; D,B&B €25 added per person. Set meals €30–€59.

COLLE DI VAL D'ELSA 53034 Siena — Map 11:D4

Ristorante Arnolfo NEW
Via XX Settembre 52

Tel/Fax (0577) 920549
Email arnolfo@arnolfo.com

Colle di Val d'Elsa has modern suburbs, but its medieval *città alta*, on a ridge, is 'an impressive string of medieval buildings'. One of them is this 16th-century *palazzo*, now a 'superb' restaurant with only four rooms. It was discovered by regular *Guide* correspondents in 2004. Owned by Giovanni Trovato (front-of-house, 'amazingly warm and competent') and his brother, Gaetano (the *Michelin* two-starred chef), it has an 'elegant, simple' decor, contemporary paintings throughout, and 'delightfully furnished' bedrooms. 'Ours was cool, light, spotless, with a bowl of fresh fruit, ample storage space. A large window looked over rolling hills and down to neighbouring gardens far below. The spacious shower cubicle was colourfully tiled.' The restaurant has white walls, stone floor, two crystal chandeliers, smart table settings. In fine weather meals are served on a 'lovely terrace with views across a valley'. The menus change regularly. 'Creative versions of Tuscan dishes, eg, ravioli stuffed with aubergine purée. Choices for meat lovers and vegetarians.' 'Don't expect full hotel facilities,' another visitor warns. 'At times it may be difficult to gain admission.' There is an unrelated *Hotel Arnolfo* on the main square. (*Pat and Jeremy Temple, Kate and David Wooff*)

Open All year, except 13 Jan–11 Feb, 27 July–11 Aug. Restaurant closed Tues/Wed, 25 Dec night, 31 Dec midday. **Rooms** 4. **Facilities** Sitting area, restaurant; terrace (meal service). **Location** Village. 24 km NW of Siena. **Restrictions** No smoking in public areas. No dogs. **Credit cards** All major cards accepted. **Terms** [2004] Room with breakfast €130–€160. Alc €74–€100.

CORTEMILIA 12074 Cuneo — Map 11:C2

Villa San Carlo NEW
Lungomare Roma 82

Tel (0173) 81546
Fax (0173) 81235
Email info@hotelsancarlo.it
Website www.hotelsancarlo.it

'In an area famous for wine, truffles and hazelnuts', this simple, pink-walled hotel/restaurant has 'a kitchen and cellar of outstanding quality', says a report this year. Owner/chef Carlo Zarri, whose family have been hoteliers for four generations, produces 'wonderful, tasty, elegant food from simple ingredients, many of them local', including 'incredibly light' spinach gnocchi with tomato sauce. He has over 700 wines in his cellar and 'it is absolutely safe to trust his recommendations'. Wine and cookery courses are held, and also gourmet evenings with live classical music. There is a swimming pool in the peaceful garden. Mountain bikes can be borrowed for exploring the hills and valleys of the Langhe region of Piedmont. Dogs are allowed in the restaurant, but not in the bedrooms. (*Mrs G Oldham*)

Open 3 Mar–4 Jan, except 19–28 Dec. **Rooms** 2 suites, 17 double, 2 single. Some air conditioned. **Facilities** Lounge, bar, restaurant. Garden: unheated swimming pool. Unsuitable for ♿. **Location** 36 km E of A6 Carcare exit.

100 km NW of Genoa. **Restrictions** No smoking in public areas. Dogs in bedrooms only. **Credit cards** All major cards accepted. **Terms** B&B: single €55–€75, double €84–€102; suite €115–€160. Set dinner €38; full alc €40–€45. *V*

CORTINA D'AMPEZZO 32043 Belluno — Map 11:A4

Hotel Restaurant da Beppe Sello NEW
Via Ronco 68

Tel (0436) 3236
Fax (0436) 3237
Email beppesello@dolomiti.org
Website cortina.dolomiti.org/beppesello

Five mins' drive from centre of 'chi-chi' ski resort: good-value family-run restaurant ('one of the best in town: sublime steak tartare'). Unassuming decor (lots of wood). Bar snacks available. Open Dec–Mar, 20 May–20 Sept. Restaurant closed Mon off-season. No smoking in public areas. All major credit cards accepted. 13 good, simple bedrooms (power shower, crisp sheets, comfortable bed, balcony) in adjacent chalet. Room with breakfast €93–€180. Set meals €32–€45 [2004].

CORTONA 52044 Arezzo — Map 11:D4

Relais Il Falconiere
Località S. Martino 370

Tel (0575) 612679
Fax (0575) 612927
Email info@ilfalconiere.com
Website www.ilfalconiere.com

Surrounded by olive trees and vineyards, the Baracchi family's elegant hotel (Relais & Chateaux) was enjoyed again in 2004. 'From the garden of our little suite, the views were magical: Tuscan hillsides, fields, church spires and beautiful Cortona. Reception staff were marvellous, elegantly dressed, welcoming and knowledgeable.' Earlier visitors wrote of 'charming owners'. The 14th-century building, sympathetically restored, stands in large grounds with cypress trees, an avenue of horse chestnut trees, and two swimming pools. 'The main road and railway are in sight but not intrusive.' The 'lovely' bedrooms are in the main villa (a tiny tower room is 'most romantic') and (more luxurious) in an old restored house in the garden, 'quite a distance away'. Dinner is served in the 'beautifully vaulted lemon-house' or on its terrace, lit by oil lamps. The cooking (modern Tuscan cooking, *Michelin* star) was thought 'good but not excellent'. In summer, light lunches and drinks are taken in a poolside bar. Wine and olive oil are home produced. Ascent to the main building from the car park by gravelled ramps may be 'somewhat slippery'. Cookery courses and wine tours are available. (*MG, and others*)

Open All year. Restaurant closed Mon/Tues midday Jan/Feb. **Rooms** 6 suites, 13 double. Some in dependence, 300 m. Air conditioning. **Facilities** Lift. Lounge, restaurant; terrace. Large grounds: 2 unheated swimming pools, bar (snack lunches). **Location** 2 km N of Cortona. From A1, Valdichiana exit, towards Perugia, exit 2 to Cortona. From Camucia take SS71 towards Arezzo; after 2 km, right at 1st crossroads. Parking. **Restriction** No smoking in public areas. **Credit cards** All major cards accepted. **Terms** [2004] B&B: double €260–€320, suite €420–€560. Set meals €60–€65; alc €57–€95.

COURMAYEUR 11013 Aosta — Map 11:B1

Romantik Hotel Villa Novecento NEW
Viale Monte Bianco 64

Tel (0165) 843000
Fax (0165) 844030
Email info@villanovecento.it
Website www.villanovecento.it

Cavaliere family's newly opened (2002) 'fairy-tale' hotel: renovated tall 'villa Liberty' in peaceful setting in mountain resort, 35 km W of Aosta, 24 km SE of Chamonix. 'Every detail perfect, from food to service, ambience to fitness centre,' says nominator. Salon/bar, restaurant serving 'revisited valdostana' cuisine; cinema; meeting facilities; spa bath, gym. Garden: outdoor dining. Parking. Closed May and Nov. No smoking in public areas. All major credit cards accepted. 26 bedrooms, some no-smoking. B&B €90–€280; D,B&B €110–€305. Set lunch €32, dinner €39; full alc €42. *V*

ERBUSCO 25030 Brescia — Map 11:B3

L'Albereta NEW
Via Vittorio Emanuele 11

Tel (030) 7760550
Fax (030) 7760573
Email info@albereta.it
Website www.albereta.it

'We would not hesitate to recommend *L'Albereta*,' say visitors this year. Surrounded by mature trees, the Moretti family's luxurious hotel (Relais & Châteaux) stands on a hill, facing Lake Iseo, in a large Franciacorta wine-growing estate (tours and tastings can be arranged). A former lodge and its surrounding buildings, its decor combines Gothic and modern, pillars, murals and frescoes. Furniture is a mix of antique and contemporary. Public rooms are large. So are most bedrooms: some have a patio or a balcony; some have an open fire; all have 'much technical gimmickry'. The suites face vineyards or lake; some have a spa bath. Staff are 'attentive', 'welcoming'. In the restaurant, separately owned, Gualtiero Marchesi ('father of *l'alta cucina*') has two *Michelin* stars for food that is 'light on the palate'. 'Dinners and breakfasts were superlative.' But one couple was disappointed by the 'somewhat chilly, modern dining room'. The gardens are 'beautifully planted' and the indoor swimming pools open on to sun terraces.

Open All year. Restaurant closed mid-Jan–mid-Feb, Sun night/Mon. **Rooms** 9 suites, 45 double, 3 single. Air conditioning. **Facilities** Lift. Chess room, library/bar (pianist), restaurant; background music; billiard room; 2 function rooms; spa: 2 indoor swimming pools, sauna, etc; terrace. Park: garden, health trail, horse riding, mountain bikes, tennis. Helipad. Unsuitable for ♿. **Location** 2 km from Erbusco via Viale Vittoria. A4 exit Rovato. 20 km NW of Brescia. Garages. **Restrictions** No smoking: public areas, some bedrooms. Small dogs only. **Credit cards** All major cards accepted. **Terms** [2004] Room: single €160–€200, double €230–€505, suite €500–€820. Breakfast €25. Full alc €90–€100.

ERICE 91016 Sicily — Map 12:B2

Hotel Elimo
Via Vittorio Emanuele 75

Tel (0923) 869377
Fax (0923) 869252
Email hotelelimo@siciliaindettaglio.it
Website www.charmerelax.com

The Tilotta family's hotel (fully renovated in 2003) is in the *centro storico* of this ancient mountain village (with 'magnificent' views of Trápani below) in north-west Sicily. 'Not cheap, but probably the best value of our tour,' said a reader who found 'a warm welcome and excellent family-based service'. 'Our excellent double room, newly furnished, had a sitting area and a comfortable, large bed. The superb dinner was enlivened by an invitation to the kitchen where chef/ proprietor Carmelo Tilotta, an Albert Einstein lookalike, showed us how to cook tuna on a volcanic stove. Breakfast was above average.' There is a panoramic terrace for summer meals. The hotel, a 'clever blend of new (bedrooms) and old (public areas, with pictures and books)', is in a narrow street: best park in the public car park and walk up (100 metres); luggage will be fetched. (*MG*)

Open All year. Restaurant closed Jan. **Rooms** 3 suites, 17 double, 1 single. Air conditioning. **Facilities** Lift. Hall (background music), lounge, bar, restaurant. Terrace; small garden. **Location** Central. 96 km W of Palermo. **Restrictions** No smoking in public areas. No dogs. **Credit cards** All major cards accepted. **Terms** B&B: single €90–€129, double €100–€170, suite €220; D,B&B €30 added per person. Full alc €30–€40. *V*

FALCADE 32020 Belluno — Map 11:A4

Belvedere Hotel NEW
Via Garibaldi 28

Tel (0437) 599021
Fax (0437) 599081
Email belvedere@dolomiti.com

'Delightful, family-run hotel with splendid service. Nice old Alpine-style building in beautiful, peaceful setting. Good, limited-choice daily-changing menu.' 52 km NW of Belluno, 62 km SE of Bolzano. Panelled lounges with old stue *(stoves), dining room. Dolomite ski slopes nearby. No smoking in public areas. Amex, MasterCard, Visa accepted. 37 bedrooms: with breakfast €130. Set meals €21–€31 [2004].*

****

Traveller's tale Hotel in France. In the grounds, directly under the hotel, was a tent for a wedding. The evening was a disaster. The wedding guests had to pass the diners and later stagger back to the hotel toilets. Service was so pressed that the residents' meals took even longer than usual (65 minutes for a simple dessert). They could not cope. The noise was amplified to such an extent that guests could not sleep. It lasted until 7.13 am when the remnants of the party staggered past the early breakfast guests with their champagne bottles. When we complained, Madame had lost command of her normally very good English.

****

FERRARA 44100 Map 11:B4

Locanda Borgonuovo
Via Cairoli 29

Tel (0532) 211100
Fax (0532) 246328
Email info@borgonuovo.com
Website www.borgonuovo.com

A 'charming B&B in this wonderful city': run by a 'welcoming couple', the Orlandinis, it is in a small street near the *duomo*. 'A model of an elegant town house lodging,' was one visitor's comment. 'Intimate and friendly,' was another. Breakfasts, in a shady courtyard, include home-made bread and jams, a special cake baked daily. 'Our room was small but well equipped'; others are larger; some have antiques. Internet access is available, and bicycles can be borrowed free of charge. There is a 17th-century room for conferences, concerts, etc. Recommended restaurants: *Zafferano* (local specialities), *Quel Fantastico Giovedì* (for fish and 'the experience'). 'For a lunchtime snack try *Pasticceria Leon d'Oro* in the main square for its sweet pastry pies of béchamel sauce, macaroni and mushrooms – said to be a recipe from Renaissance days. Ferrara, in a fruit-growing region north of Bologna, makes a good base for exploring Emilia-Romagna and the Veneto. (*DWR Clarke, Christopher Maycock*)

Open All year. **Rooms** 2 apartments in annexe, 2 double, 2 single. Air conditioning. **Facilities** Sitting room/library, breakfast room (background music); meeting/concert room. Courtyard garden. Unsuitable for ♿. **Location** Pedestrianised zone near *duomo*. Parking (€5 per day, permit from *Locanda*). **Restriction** No smoking: public areas, some bedrooms. 'Small, quiet dogs only.' **Credit cards** Amex, MasterCard, Visa. **Terms** B&B: single €55–€65, double €85–€105.

Hotel Principessa Leonora
Via Mascheraio 39

Tel (0532) 206020
Fax (0532) 242707
Email principessaleonora@tin.it
Website www.principessaleonora.it

Liked again this year, this conversion of a 16th-century listed building is a short walk from Ferrara's historic centre. It has antiques, beamed ceilings, French tapestries, monumental staircase and 'exceedingly helpful staff'. The suites are named after famous former visitors to the house, eg, Montgolfier of hot-air balloon fame; bedrooms are called after their earlier use (stable, olive store, etc). 'Ours, spacious, spotless, had efficient plumbing.' Breakfast, on a 'pleasant lawn' or in an 'intimate' room, was thought 'rather disappointing, mostly cakes and over-sugared brioches'. No restaurant: plenty nearby, including that of the sumptuous sister hotel, *Duchessa Isabella* (Relais & Châteaux). There is a fitness centre, and a horse and carriage for excursions. The surrounding area 'is on the flat, ideal for wheelchairs', according to a disabled visitor who was 'well looked after' by the hotel. (*FH Potts, E and AA, and others*)

Open All year. **Rooms** 3 suites, 13 double, 6 single. Air conditioning. **Facilities** Lift. Lounge, bar, breakfast room; congress hall; fitness centre. Garden. **Location** Central, near Piazza Ariostea. Garage (€13 a day).

Restriction No smoking in public areas. **Credit cards** All major cards accepted. **Terms** [2004] Room: single €47–€94, double €77–€154, suite €180–€207. Breakfast €13.

San Girolamo dei Gesuati BUDGET
Via Madama 40/a

Tel (0532) 207448
Fax (0532) 207264
Email reception@sangirolamodeigesuati.it
Website www.sangirolamodeigesuati.it

A 'super-budget hotel of great character'. It is a converted monastery in a narrow, quiet street ten minutes' walk from the centre. 'A great find. The bedrooms, of adequate size, have an ample well-equipped bathroom,' says a recent visitor. 'Staff are helpful. The buffet breakfast has excellent coffee from a self-service dial-your-choice machine; also cereals, yogurt, fruit and croissants, but uninteresting bread.' A light but adequate evening meal is available (pasta, meat dish, dessert; wine for 'amazingly little money'). No lounge/sitting area, but there is a pleasant garden, and ample parking. (*NBF, ARF*)

Open Probably all year. **Rooms** 38. Air conditioning. **Facilities** Lift. Bar, restaurant. **Location** 10 mins' walk from centre. **Restriction** No smoking in public areas. **Credit cards** All major cards accepted. **Terms** [2004] B&B: single €38.50, double €71; D,B&B €48.50–€51.50 per person.

FIDENZA 43036 Parma — Map 11:B3

Hotel Astoria
Via Gandolfi 5

Tel (0524) 524314
Fax (0524) 527263
Email info@hotelastoriafidenza.it
Website www.hotelastoriafidenza.it

In charming, untouristy, small town (magnificent Romanesque cathedral) 21 km NW of Parma: newly modernised hotel between railway station and centre, managed by Nicola Nardiello. 'Large, comfortable bedroom, first-rate bathroom; no traffic noise, but distant rumbling of trains.' Lift, ramp, TV room, breakfast room, restaurant, pizzeria (background music). Air conditioning. Secure parking nearby (€8). No smoking in public areas. No dogs. MasterCard, Visa accepted. 34 bedrooms: single €54, double €80, suite €105. Breakfast €8. Full alc €18 [2004].

FIESOLE 50014 Firenze — Map 11:C4

Pensione Bencistà
Via Benedetto da Maiano 4

Tel/Fax (055) 59163
Email pensionebencista@iol.it
Website www.bencista.com

Ever-popular, Simone Simoni's 'blissfully quiet' *pensione* in a residential area on a hilltop just north-west of Florence represents 'amazing value', say its devotees. 'Breathtaking' views over the city are seen from the dining room and many bedrooms, notably Room 21 ('usually reserved a year in advance'). 'A pre-dinner bottle of Chianti, with canapés, can be taken on the charming terrace [with a huge, gnarled wisteria and pots of flowers] as you watch the sun set over Florence.' Dinner, at 7.30 pm, is 'unsophisticated Tuscan family fare; the staff are anxious that guests have plenty to eat'. 'The cheeseboard is magnificent.' 'Inexpensive house wines.' 'Dining with fellow guests creates a friendly atmosphere' – so does the lack of television. 'Great choice for breakfast.' There are 'beautiful small sitting rooms' on several floors. Bus 7 to the city goes from the top of the road, and 'there is good walking in the hills nearby, a nice change from pounding the pavements'. (*B and LA, and many others*)

Open 1 Feb–30 Nov. Dining room open only to residents and their guests. **Rooms** 3 suites, 26 double, 11 single. 2 in annexe, 10 m. Some on ground floor. **Facilities** Lift, 3 lounges, restaurant. No background music. Garden. **Location** Hillside 8 km NE of Florence. Bus 7 from railway station. Parking. **Restrictions** No smoking. No dogs in restaurant. **Credit cards** MasterCard, Visa. **Terms** D,B&B: single €90, double €176. Set lunch €28, dinner €30.

FILICUDI 98050 Messina, Sicily — Map 12:B3

La Sirena BUDGET
Via Pecorini Mare
Filicudi, Isole Eolie

Tel (090) 9889997
Fax (090) 9889207
Email lasirena@netnet.it
Website www.pensionelasirena.it

'Lovely, spacious, comfortable rooms. Spectacular views. Staff are friendly.' A comment this year on this little restaurant-with-rooms near the pebble beach and tiny harbour of Pecorino, on one of the more distant Aeolian Islands. Run by owner/chef Antonio Pellegrino and his 'very pleasant' wife, Alina Maslowski, from England, it serves 'the best food in the islands, making brilliant use of the region's riches'; 'swordfish, and pasta with almond sauce and shrimp particularly good'. Another visitor called *La Sirena* 'casual in the extreme', and the welcome may not always be warm. 'Simple but well-planned' bedrooms (shower, no bath) have 'stylish touches' like Sicilian antiques. Rooms in the hotel have a tiny balcony and air conditioning. Some rooms are in houses (with kitchen and terrace) nearby, facing the sea. Filicudi, 'beautiful and virtually unspoilt', has 'wild flowers, sheep, steep walks on donkey trails, exhilarating views'. No public transport: there are scooters for hire; tourists may bring a car only with a permit (15 days minimum). (*Maeve and Philip Vickery, and others*)

Open 1 Feb–30 Nov. **Rooms** 10 suites, 6 double, 3 single. Some in houses 5 and 10 mins' walk away. Air conditioning. **Facilities** Restaurant, bar. Terrace (meal service). No background music. Unsuitable for ♿. **Location** On beach on island NE of Milazzo (hydrofoil; ferry). **Restriction** No smoking in public areas. **Credit cards** All major cards accepted. **Terms** B&B: single €30–€55, double €60–€110; D,B&B (obligatory 1 July–30 Aug) €55–€85 per person. Full alc €35. *V*

FLORENCE **Map 11:C4**

Villa Belvedere
Via Benedetto Castelli 3
50124 Florence

Tel (055) 222501
Fax (055) 223163
Email reception@villa-belvedere.com
Website www.villa-belvedere.com

With 'stunning views' over Florence and the surrounding hills, this family friendly hotel 'couldn't be faulted' by a visitor in 2004. Run by two generations of the Ceschi-Perotto family ('always around'), it stands in well-kept gardens and provides 'good service by caring people' and 'excellent value'. The 1930s villa may lack 'antique charm', but all is 'spotless', and 'facilities are excellent'. Open-plan public rooms have picture windows. Bedrooms have a smart colour scheme, wood fittings, spacious bathroom. 'Metal window shutters keep out city noise and early sunlight.' Some rooms, good for a family, are in a little house by the small swimming pool. The 'excellent breakfast' ('any kind of egg, cooked to order') is served on a veranda facing the *duomo*. 'More than adequate' snacks (soup, pasta, etc) are available until 8.30 pm. 'Tea and biscuits or toast brought whenever we wanted.' 'You can sip a drink in the garden at night, roses scenting the air, the city lights twinkling below.' Guests' laundry is returned 'beautifully washed and ironed, often the same day'. The city is a short bus ride away: 'popping to and fro makes you feel part of the local scene'. (*Jane Smith, and others*)

Open 1 Mar–30 Nov. **Rooms** 3 suites, 21 double, 2 single. Some no-smoking. Air conditioning. **Facilities** Lift. 2 lounges, TV room, bar, breakfast room, snack room; veranda. 3-hectare grounds: unheated swimming pool, tennis. Unsuitable for ♿. **Location** E of Siena road, 1.5 km S of Ponte Vecchio. Bus 11/36 from centre. Parking. **Restrictions** No smoking in public areas. No dogs. **Credit cards** All major cards accepted. **Terms** B&B: single €100–€130, double €155–€207, suite €235–€260. Light alc meal €15.

Hotel Hermitage
Vicolo Marzio 1
50122 Florence

Tel (055) 287216
Fax (055) 212208
Email florence@hermitagehotel.com
Website www.hermitagehotel.com

Overlooking the Arno, between the Ponte Vecchio and the Uffizi, this 'very peaceful' B&B hotel has 'marvellous views of the *duomo*'. Its ambience is 'decidedly Italian, though all the staff speak English', according to a fan. A returning visitor wrote: 'The staff remain very friendly, accommodation is pleasant.' Breakfasts and cocktails on the flowery roof terrace are 'delightful, especially when the bells of nearby churches are ringing'. There are six floors: a small lift takes you to the fifth-floor reception and the 'beautifully furnished bar/lounge', which provides drinks until late, and has a fire in winter. Bedrooms are smallish, quite plain; beds are comfortable, bathrooms well equipped (many have a spa bath). The higher you go, the better (and more expensive) the room. (*SB, and others*)

Open All year. **Rooms** 28 double. 16 with spa bath. Air conditioning. **Facilities** Lift. Lounge/bar, breakfast room; roof garden/terrace. Unsuitable for ♿. **Location** Central, near Ponte Vecchio. Public garage nearby. **Restriction** No smoking: public areas, 9 bedrooms. **Credit cards** MasterCard, Visa. **Terms** B&B: single €176–€221, double €196–€245.

Loggiato dei Serviti
Piazza SS. Annunziata 3
50122 Florence

Tel (055) 289592
Fax (055) 289595
Email info@loggiatodeiservitihotel.it
Website www.loggiatodeiservitihotel.it

Much loved by *Guide* readers, Rodolfo Gattai's B&B is in 'one of Florence's loveliest squares', 'easily reached from all directions'. Built in 1527 for the order of the Serviti fathers, it is 'rich in atmosphere, tranquillity and comfort'. 'Gracefully restored, in understated style', the stone-vaulted building has polished oak floors, iron or wooden bedsteads, efficient air conditioning, 'beautiful furniture, good, helpful service'. Bedrooms vary in size and quality. 'Ours had views of the floodlit *duomo*, and a handsome canopied bed.' 'Wooden floors, antique furniture. All very tasteful.' Front rooms face the lovely piazza but hear summer jazz concerts, rubbish removal, etc. The rooms at the rear are 'utterly quiet', though some may 'lack character'. 'Excellent buffet breakfast' (stewed and fresh fruit, cheese, ham, hot croissants, yogurt, etc). (*Pat Harman, Donald Reid, and others*)

Open All year. **Rooms** 4 suites, 28 double, 6 single. 5 in annexe. 2 suitable for ♿. Air conditioning. **Facilities** Lift. Lounge, reading room, bar, breakfast room; background music. **Location** Pedestrian zone, 200 m from *duomo*. Garage service. **Restriction** No smoking: public areas, some bedrooms. **Credit cards** All major cards accepted. **Terms** [2004] B&B: single €90–€140, double €130–€205, suite €240–€390. *V* (July/Aug, 15 Nov–28 Feb, except holidays)

Hotel Monna Lisa NEW
Borgo Pinti 27
50121 Florence

Tel (055) 2479751
Fax (055) 2479755
Email monnalisa@florenceby.com
Website www.monnalisa.it

In the city centre, this Renaissance palace is now a 'beautiful and gracious' hotel with 'stunning' lounges filled with antiques and art treasures, and neo-classical drawings and sculpture by Giovanni Duprè, an ancestor of the present owners. Visitors in 2004 thought it even better than during their previous visit 17 years earlier. 'We loved the Mona Lisa spoof paintings in the library. The bar is charming – Gianni, the barman, is a treasure.' Breakfast in a pretty room has good bread, cheese, rolls and fruit, and 'lovely service'. Rooms vary in size: all have antiques, some have a wooden ceiling, some have a balcony facing the 'beautiful garden'. (*Sue Ann and Martin Marcus*)

Open All year. **Rooms** 45. Some in 2 annexes. Air conditioning. **Facilities** Lifts. Lounges, library, bar, breakfast room; gym; conference room. Garden: solarium. **Location** Central, between *duomo* and Ponte Vecchio. Parking (by reservation, with charge). **Restriction** No smoking: public areas, some bedrooms. **Credit cards** All major cards accepted. **Terms** [2004] B&B: single €110–€230, double €270–€350, suite €410–€700.

Hotel Tornabuoni Beacci
Via de' Tornabuoni 3
50123 Florence

Tel (055) 268377
Fax (055) 283594
Email beaccitornabuoni@florenceby.com
Website www.tornabuonihotels.com

'Excellently located', this 'beautifully kept' B&B hotel has been run for many years by its owners, the Bechi family. 'A lovely mixture of antique furnishings and mod cons' (there are tapestries, frescoes and Murano glass lamps), it occupies the top two floors of the historic Palazzo Miniberti Strozzi in this famous street. The bedrooms (some have a balcony) have fine views of rooftops and monuments. 'There are attractive lounges and sitting areas, and a wonderful roof terrace where meals are taken in fine weather,' says a recent visitor. The restaurant serves traditional and international dishes. The buffet breakfast includes meats, hard-boiled eggs and fruit. 'The staff are very friendly.' Children are welcomed. (*KT*)

Open All year. Restaurant closed midday. **Rooms** 2 suites, 29 double, 9 single. Air conditioning. **Facilities** Lift. Lounges, bar, breakfast room, restaurant; conference room. Terrace. Unsuitable for ♿. **Location** Central, near Palazzo Strozzi. Garage nearby; valet parking. **Restriction** No smoking: public areas, some bedrooms. **Credit cards** Most major cards accepted. **Terms** [2004] B&B: single €125–€170, double €185–€230, suite €280–€350. Set dinner €35.

Relais Uffizi NEW
Chiasso del Buco 16
50122 Florence

Tel (055) 2676239
Fax (055) 2657909
Email info@relaisuffizi.it
Website www.relaisuffizi.it

By the Uffizi Gallery, Elisabetta Matucci's B&B is a 15th-century building in a little pedestrianised street (reached under an ancient arch) off the Piazza della Signoria. This is overlooked by the lounge/ breakfast room and some bedrooms: they are spacious, and have antiques and air conditioning. 'Ours was big enough to hold a party,' says the nominator. 'It had a large foyer with desk, ample bathroom with dressing table. Lighting was good. It faced a quiet alley. The ambience is more homey than sophisticated. Reception staff were pleasant, and helpful with restaurant reservations.' (*Claire Lavery*)

Open All year. **Rooms** 13 double. 2 suitable for ♿. Air conditioning. **Facilities** Lounge/breakfast room. **Location** Central: alley off Piazza della Signoria. Parking. **Restrictions** No smoking in public areas. Small dogs only. **Credit cards** Amex, MasterCard, Visa. **Terms** B&B double €140–€200.

FOIANA 39011 Bolzano — Map 11:A4

Hotel Völlanerhof
Via Prevosto 30
Lana, presso Merano

Tel (0473) 568033
Fax (0473) 568143
Email info@voellanerhof.com
Website www.voellanerhof.com

Foiana (Völlan in German) is in superb South Tyrol countryside near Merano: its apple orchards are famous. Monika and Johann Margesin's 'perfectly run' hotel has a magnificent background of wooded hills. 'It is a bit modern for our taste,' says a regular *Guide* correspondent in 2004. 'But service is extremely friendly. In the nice, glass-enclosed restaurant, dinners were excellent, a five-course extravaganza. The waiter recommended some superb local wines.' Another visitor advises: 'Book half board (meals are for residents only), as the town has few other eating places. Once a week there is an amazingly varied dessert buffet. Friday has a fish buffet.' 'Excellent breakfasts: loads of fresh fruit, sausage, cheeses, etc, eggs on request.' There is an attractive covered terrace for meals in good weather, a 'perfectly landscaped' outdoor swimming pool, with plenty of loungers and parasols, a 'beautiful indoor pool', good 'wellness' facilities, etc. Bedrooms are 'spacious, well appointed'; many have a terrace with views. Large public rooms include a 'nicely decorated lounge, and a well-stocked bar'. Families are welcomed. Good walking in the region, and many castles and churches to visit. (*Wolfgang Stroebe, AB*)

Open 26 Mar–20 Nov. **Rooms** 43. **Facilities** Lift. Lounge, piano bar, restaurant; wellness centre, sauna. Indoor and outdoor swimming pools. Garden: children's play area. **Location** 5 km SW of Lana, which is 7 km SW of Merano. Parking. Garage. **Restrictions** No smoking in public areas. No dogs. **Credit cards** MasterCard, Visa. **Terms** [2004] D,B&B €96–€141.

FOLLINA 31051 Treviso — Map 11:A4

Villa Abbazia NEW
Piazza IV Novembre 3

Tel (0438) 971277
Fax (0438) 970001
Email info@hotelabbazia.it
Website www.hotelabbazia.it

Follina, a 'very pretty' village on the Prosecco route in the Venetian pre-Alps, is famous for its 12th-century Cistercian abbey. This can be seen from some bedrooms of the Zanon De Marchi family's luxury hotel (Relais & Châteaux), which, say its nominators, is 'a delight'. The 17th-century summer home of Venetian aristocrats, it has a flowery garden, a dining terrace and a frescoed restaurant, *La Corte*, 'excellent, if a trifle cosmopolitan'. There is a wine bar for light meals, and a café serving 'English afternoon tea as in London'. 'Everything about our room was excellent. Its little terrace overlooked a magical courtyard filled with greenery. The lovely bathroom had pretty tiles. The staff were exceedingly helpful. The owner's wife was at Reception most of the time; her smile was infectious. Her husband, in his blue blazer, was so nice.' Breakfast is a buffet. (*Pat and Jeremy Temple*)

Open 5 Feb–7 Jan. Restaurant closed Sun/Mon midday. **Rooms** 5 suites, 12 double. **Facilities** Salons, café, wine bar, restaurant. Terrace (outside dining); courtyard; garden. **Location** 30 km SW of Belluno. From A27 exit Conegliano, follow signs Pieve di Soligo, then Follina. Small car park. **Restriction** No smoking: public areas, some bedrooms. **Credit cards** All major cards accepted. **Terms** [2004] B&B: single €155–€165, double €207–€220, suite €285–€300. Set meals €45–€65; alc €35–€65.

FONTIGNANO 06070 Perugia Map 11:D4

Romantik Hotel Villa di Monte Solare NEW
Via Montali 7
Colle San Paolo

Tel (075) 832376
Fax (075) 8355462
Email info@villamontesolare.it
Website www.villamontesolare.it

Up a narrow road, this 1780s patrician villa stands amid 'spectacular scenery' in an estate in the hills near Perugia. It was found 'superb' this year. Run in house-party style by its owners, Rosemarie and Filippo Iannarone, it has dignified public rooms (antiques, beams, stone or tiled floors, frescoes). In the grounds are a 17th-century chapel, a 'secret garden', olive groves, vines, walks up to a 'stunning' view of Lake Trasimeno, and much else (see below). Residents meet for drinks before dinner (no choice) at 7.30 pm (*à la carte* meals are served later). Some visitors have found the management 'over-efficient', but this year's reporter wrote: 'Everything is well ordered. The food was inventive, beautifully presented.' Vegetables and fruit are home grown; there is a large cellar of Umbrian wines. Lunch is served under old cedars in an enclosed garden. Breakfast is simple (you decide its time the night before). Bedrooms are 'large and comfortable'; some have views of unspoilt countryside; some are in an old olive press. Other comments: 'Lovely; very good value.' 'Delightful staff.' Children and pets are welcomed. Concerts are held in season; walking and riding holidays are arranged. (*Sue and David Medcalf, and others*)

Open All year. **Rooms** 7 suites, 13 double. Some on ground floor. 10 in 2 farmhouses 150 m. **Facilities** 2 lounges, bar, 2 breakfast rooms, 2 dining rooms; seminar facilities; live music weekly; wine tastings, slide shows. No background music. 60-hectare estate: garden, tennis, 2 unheated swimming pools, riding; chapel. **Location** 25 km W of Perugia, near SE corner of Lake Trasimeno. Parking. **Restriction** No smoking: public areas, some bedrooms. **Credit cards** All major cards accepted. **Terms** [2004] B&B: single €84–€96, double €148–€190, suite €182–€216; D,B&B €31 added per person.

GAIOLE IN CHIANTI 53013 Siena Map 11:D4

Borgo Argenina NEW
Località Argenina
San Marcellino Mont

Tel (0577) 747117
Fax (0577) 747228
Email borgoargenina@libero.it
Website www.borgoargenina.it

Restored over five years by Elena Nappa, run with her daughter, Fiorenza, and 'receptionist dog', Bianca: medieval stone hamlet, now quiet, 'romantic' B&B. Off SS408 15 mins' drive from Gaiole, 28 km NE of Siena. Lounge, breakfast room (buffet with home-made specialities), garden with flowers, lavender and herbs; views of hills and vineyards. Mountain bike rentals; cookery courses. No smoking in public areas. No pets. 7 bedrooms (including suites, some good for families, in Little House, with terrace), some no-smoking. B&B double €130–€180 [2004].

GANGI 90024 Palermo, Sicily — Map 12:B3

Tenuta Gangivecchio BUDGET
C. da Gangivecchio

Tel/Fax (0921) 689191
Email paolotornabene@interfree.it
Website www.tenutagangivecchio.com

'What a fantastic place!' say visitors in 2004. In a former Benedictine abbey (1363), near this hilltop town between Catania and Palermo, an *albergo* and restaurant are owned by the Tornabene family who have lived here since 1856. There are 'beautiful, atmospheric grounds, ruined columns, semi-circular stone seats, welcoming, charming service', also fountains and a swimming pool. The farm produces organic vegetables, olive oil, milk, eggs and cheeses. Paolo Tornabene and his partner, Alda, run a small inn in converted stables: it has a modest dining room where 'very good' no-choice evening meals, based on regional dishes, are served at 8 pm. Its simple bedrooms open on to a long shared terrace above. There is a suite in a cottage. Breakfasts have good coffee, pastry and fruit. Paolo's sister, Giovanna, runs a separate restaurant in a loggia: 'The cooking is excellent, and worth a visit just to walk through the spectacular vaulted entrance to the enclosed courtyard.' There is 'spectacular walking in the surrounding hills, with views for miles'. (*Philip and Maeve Vickery*)

Open All year, except July. **Rooms** 1 suite (in cottage), 8 double, 1 single. **Facilities** Bar, dining room, 2 restaurants; conference room. Park: garden, swimming pool, farm. **Location** 125 km SE of Palermo, 130 km NW of Catania. **Restriction** No smoking in public areas. **Credit cards** MasterCard, Visa. **Terms** [2004] B&B €45; D,B&B €57.

GARDONE RIVIERA 25083 Brescia — Map 11:B3

Villa Fiordaliso NEW
Corso Zanardelli 150

Tel (0365) 20158
Fax (0365) 290011
Email info@villafiordaliso.it
Website www.villafiordaliso.it

In this fashionable resort on the western shore of Lake Garda, this hotel/restaurant is 'a great place', says its 2004 nominator. Owned by the Tosetti family, the 'elegant villa with loads of marble' stands amid pine and olive trees. It is on a busy road (you should ask for a lake-facing room), but it has a 'very beautiful garden', and its restaurant (*Michelin* star) faces the water, where it has a small pier. 'You can lie under trees and swim in the lake, reached through a small, stony beach area. Towards evening, two junior chefs roam the garden for fresh herbs. Dinner is very good, cooking innovative, if a bit showy. Outstanding breakfast. Service was excellent. The whole experience was lovely but very expensive.' Chef Riccardo Camanini's menu includes risotto with scampi; red mullet soup; calf's sweetbreads with coffee and celeriac. The bedrooms are named after flowers (Mimosa, Gardenia, etc), and the suite is called after Mussolini's mistress, Claretta Petacci, who lived in the villa from 1943 for two years. The poet Gabriele D'Annunzio, who stayed here in the 1920s, used to gaze through the villa's stained-glass windows, we are told. (*Wolfgang Stroebe*)

Open 1 Mar–1 Nov. Restaurant closed Mon/Tues midday. **Rooms** 1 suite, 6 double. **Facilities** Hall, piano bar, restaurant (background music). Garden: dining terrace. Private beach. Unsuitable for ♿. **Location** 500 metres from centre of Gardone. 34 km NE of Brescia. Parking. **Restrictions** No smoking: public areas, some bedrooms. Dogs in outdoor restaurant only. **Credit cards** All major cards accepted. **Terms** [2004] B&B: double €230–€400, suite €540. Set lunch €45, dinner €98.

Villa del Sogno — *Tel* (0365) 290181
Via Zanardelli 107 — *Fax* (0365) 290230
Email info@villadelsogno.it
Website www.villadelsogno.it

In 'a splendid position sloping down to Lake Garda', this *fin de siècle* mansion was built by a Viennese silk merchant. 'A lovely place to stay', it is run by the Calderan family. Visitors over the past six years write: 'It is beautiful. The grounds and fabric are meticulously maintained, the staff will bend over backwards to be helpful (the receptionists can do anything in at least four languages), and the view from the terrace where we breakfast and dine is one of the loveliest on the lake.' An earlier correspondent wrote: 'Everything first class; high standards of housekeeping.' Reached up a steep, winding road, the hotel has 'magnificent interiors and paintings; bags of atmosphere'. The large public rooms have flowery padded chairs, oriental rugs, wood panelling, majolica and statuary. In the gardens are lemon and olive trees, cypresses, sculptures and an abundance of flowers. Almost all the bedrooms share the 'wonderful view': some have a balcony. 'Our room, though small, was beautifully decorated.' Another bedroom was 'large, with every comfort'. 'At dinner they use local ingredients and enjoy recommending local goodies.' 'Excellent breakfast: plenty of fresh fruit, good bread.' The 'delightful swimming pool' (with bar) is surrounded by loungers; above it is a 'fine, slightly neglected temple with sensational views'. (*Andrew and Kirsty Muirhead, JD, and others*)

Open 26 Mar–16 Oct. **Rooms** 3 suites, 28 double. 5 on ground floor. Air conditioning. **Facilities** Lift. 2 lounges, TV room, bar, piano bar, restaurant (background music); fitness room. Large garden: dining terrace (background music sometimes); tennis; sauna, unheated swimming pool, bar, solarium, whirlpool; rocky beach. Unsuitable for ♿. **Location** At Fasano, 1 km NE of Gardone Riviera. Parking. **Restrictions** No smoking. No dogs. **Credit cards** All major cards accepted. **Terms** B&B: double €275–€485, suite €450–€500. 30% reduction for single occupancy. Set dinner €50; full alc €75.

GARGNANO 25084 Brescia — Map 11:B3

Villa Giulia — *Tel* (0365) 71022
Viale Rimembranza 20 — *Fax* (0365) 72774
Email info@villagiulia.it
Website www.villagiulia.it

'You would be hard pressed not to fall in love with it.' 'Italian hotel service at its best. A lyrical spot. Scrupulous service.' Always admired, the Bombardelli family's 'civilised hotel', 'elegant, yet relaxed', stands on the western shore of Lake Garda, a short walk from this 'delightful little town with a theatre-set harbour'. 'A beautiful oasis', it has 'stupendous views' over the water to the mountains beyond. 'Our "Romantic" room, with lake and garden views, was beautifully appointed.' 'Ours was spacious, stylish, with lots of wood.' Some bedrooms have a balcony; attic ones have an arched window and sloping ceiling. Some rooms are in chalets among magnolia and palm trees in the large grounds, 'filled with scents and birdsong'. Rooms in the rear annexe are more functional, and lack view and air conditioning. 'Excellent meals', including the 'lavish' breakfast, are served on a 'glorious lakeside terrace' in fine weather. 'At lunch, the salads were something special.' There is a lakeside promenade; also lawns with loungers, a rose garden, a 'delightful' swimming pool surrounded by orange trees and with exercise bicycles. (*Alan Brownlow, Martin and Karen Oldridge, and others*)

Open Approx. Easter–Oct. Restaurant closed Wed evening. **Rooms** 22 double, 1 single. Some in 3 chalets. Some on ground floor. 17 air conditioned. **Facilities** Lounge, bar, piano bar, restaurant; classical background music; Turkish bath, gym; veranda, terrace. Large garden: unheated swimming pool, sauna; private beach. **Location** Lake shore, NW of Gardone. Car park. **Restrictions** No smoking in public areas. Children by arrangement. Small dogs only (max. 10 kg, €16 per day). **Credit cards** Amex, MasterCard, Visa. **Terms** B&B: single €120, double €200–€290. Full alc €50.

GARGONZA 52048 Arezzo **Map 11:D4**

Residence Castello di Gargonza
Monte San Savino

Tel (0575) 847021
Fax (0575) 847054
Email gargonza@gargonza.it
Website www.gargonza.it

Surrounded by woods in the Chianti hills between Arezzo and Siena, this medieval walled village, dominated by a turreted square tower, has for centuries been in the Guicciardini family. It is now run by the 'charming' Conte Roberto Guicciardini more as a centre for conferences and rural activities than a hotel. It 'is super, with such atmosphere', said a reader who spent 'a wonderful week'. Red-roofed cottages, on cobbled alleys, are named after characters in the village's history, eg, Niccolina, a seamstress (one-bedroom flat), Contessa Francesca (two-floor farmhouse). Some are self-catering only; others can be let as modest hotel accommodation. The simple rooms have stone walls, beamed ceiling, tiled floor, plain fabrics. The restaurant, *La Torre di Gargonza*, serves Tuscan specialities, 'delicious, especially the game'. Breakfast, a buffet, is in the old olive press (*frantoio*), also used for meetings, concerts, and as a reading room. Staff are 'excellent'. The lovely garden ('a riot of flowers, Japanese sunshades, lizards, bats, fireflies and glow-worms') is for residents only (a key is provided). The swimming pool, amid olive trees, has panoramic views. No public transport: cars are allowed in only for loading/unloading. Reception sells olive oil and wine; the nearest shops are at Monte San Savino, seven kilometres away. 'Most houses have no private sitting-out area, and there are no washing machines for guests' use, but such is the beauty of Gargonza that none of this matters.' (*Ann Lawson Lucas*)

Open All year, except 5 Nov–2 Dec, 10 Jan–10 Feb. Restaurant closed Tues. **Rooms** 14 suites, 10 double. 8 self-catering cottages (for 2–7). Some on ground floor. **Facilities** Lounge/TV room, bar, restaurant; conference/function facilities. Large estate: garden, unheated swimming pool, woods, farm. Unsuitable for ♿. **Location** 7 km W of Monte San Savino on SS73 to Siena. *Autostrada* A1 exit 27. Follow blue signs. Unguarded parking at entrance. **Restrictions** No smoking in public areas. No dogs. **Credit cards** All major cards accepted. **Terms** [2004] B&B: single €85–€94, double €101–€110, suite €147–€171; D,B&B (min. 3 days) double €158–€167. Full alc €32–€37. *V*

GARLENDA 17033 Savona — Map 11:C2

La Meridiana
Via ai Castelli 11

Tel (0182) 580271
Fax (0182) 580150
Email meridiana@relaischateaux.com
Website www.relaischateaux.com/meridiana

In the Garlenda valley, just inland from the Ligurian Riviera, the Segre family's hotel (Relais & Châteaux) was 'particularly enjoyed' by a regular *Guide* correspondent this year. Visitors returning in 2004 'were warmly welcomed' by the owners, who 'are always about' at this 'lovely place for a relaxing stay'. Earlier guests wrote: 'We love the area as well as the hotel. Our room was uniquely and expensively furnished.' 'Delightful, with a true personal touch. Charming gardens.' The food is almost always enjoyed: the *Rosmarino* restaurant, with its terrace for summer dining under trees, serves modern versions of old Ligurian recipes and has 'a long list of local wines'. Bedroom decor is a mix of antique and local country style. Some rooms have a fireplace; all have a balcony facing gardens or vineyards. 'The comfortable, huge lounge has wonderful large windows.' Drinks can be taken alfresco in a canopied, candlelit area. The pool area (with lifeguard) has 'sumptuous sunbeds' and a 'great drinks and snacks service'. Golf packages are offered (an 18-hole par 72 course is adjacent). Alassio, with its magnificent beach, is near. (*Michael Burns, Pat and Jeremy Temple, and others*)

Open Early Mar–Nov. **Rooms** 14 suites, 14 double. 4 on ground floor. Air conditioning. **Facilities** Lifts. Lounge, TV room, 2 bars, restaurant (background music); sauna, massage. Garden: terrace (meal service), unheated swimming pool, spa pool. Bicycles/mountain bikes available. Golf course adjacent. Beach 15 km. **Location** 6 km SW of Albenga, off *autostrada* A10; 90 km from Genoa airport. Car park. **Restrictions** No smoking: public areas, some bedrooms. No children under 10. **Credit cards** All major cards accepted.

Terms [2004] Room €220–€330, suite €330–€800. Breakfast €20–€24. Set dinner €50–€80; alc €50–€70.

GHIFFA 28823 Verbania — Map 11:A2

Park Hotel Paradiso BUDGET
Via Guglielmo Marconi 20
Tel (0323) 59548
Fax (0323) 59878

In a 'rambling, exotic garden', with banana trees, palms and hydrangeas, this former bishop's palace, on a steep road above Lake Maggiore, is 'a wonderful place to be on a hot summer's evening, looking to hills on the other side, and ferries criss-crossing the water'. 'The decor is astonishing': many Art Nouveau features survive. 'The Anchisi family are the warmest, most simpatico owners of any hotel I have stayed in,' one fan wrote. Other comments: 'Everything about the *Paradiso* is bizarre, but it's offset by the charm, kindness and generosity of the staff.' 'Sweetcorn and basil plants on the dining terrace parapets, tortoises laying eggs on the lawn, lizards darting everywhere – we loved it!' Prices are modest, and the building 'exudes peace and beauty'. The 'sparkly clean' semi-covered swimming pool has panoramic views. Dario Anchisi is 'charming'; Elena, his wife, is a 'talented cook'. 'Our meal comprised deep-fried courgette flowers, fresh from the garden and delicious, stuffed with Parma ham and mozzarella; then gnocchi, then lake fish, gently fried.' Many bedrooms, some with balcony, face the water; some have a small private garden. 'Ours was clean and cool, everything worked.' Some bathrooms are done in Carrara marble. 'Only an hour and a half from Malpensa airport but a world away.' (*S and KM, and others*)

Open 23 Mar–12 Oct. Meals for residents only. **Rooms** 3 suites, 15 double, 5 single (5 in an annexe). **Facilities** Lift. Lounge, TV room, dining room. No background music. Garden: terrace, swimming pool, whirlpool, *bocce*, table tennis. Unsuitable for ♿. **Location** In village. 22 km N of Stresa. Secure parking. **Restriction** No smoking in public areas. **Credit cards** None accepted. **Terms** Room: single €65, double €99. Breakfast €10. Set meals €25; full alc €30.

GROSSETO 58100 — Map 11:D4

Bastiani Grand Hotel NEW
Piazza Gioberti 64
Tel (0564) 20047
Fax (0564) 29321
Email info@hotelbastiani.com
Website www.hotelbastiani.com

This most Italian of Tuscan cities has a surprisingly attractive and unspoiled historic centre, pleasant street cafés, excellent fish restaurants and 'this very well-appointed, comfortable and ideally situated' hotel. Just inside the city walls, and conveniently near the Grosseto South exit from the *autostrada*, the *Bastiani* is moments away from the *duomo*. Elegant shops and restaurants are nearby. 'What the hotel lacks in character,' says its 2004 nominator, 'it makes up for in comfort, efficiency, a very pleasant staff and a wholesome and varied breakfast.' Rooms are 'straightforward and clean with everything you would expect of a modern city hotel'. (*Bing Taylor*)

Open All year. **Rooms** 2 suites, 48 double. Air conditioning. **Facilities** Lift. Hall, bar, Internet point, terrace, breakfast room; meeting room. **Location** Centre of old town, by *duomo*; near Grosseto S. exit. Garage. **Restriction** No smoking: public areas, some bedrooms. **Credit cards** All major cards accepted. **Terms** [2004] B&B: single €84–€124, double €134–€146, suite €169.

ISEO 25049 Brescia — Map 11:B3

Relais I Due Roccoli
Via S Bonomelli

Tel (030) 9822977
Fax (030) 9822980
Email relais@idueroccoli.com
Website www.idueroccoli.com

High above Lake Iseo (one of Italy's smallest lakes), Guido Anessi's 17th-century former hunting lodge (Relais du Silence) is admired for its 'lovely location, pleasing furnishings and superb staff'. Surrounded by woods and steep slopes, it has 'truly magnificent' views over the lake, which can be seen from some bedrooms. Each room has a terrace or balcony. 'From ours,' one couple wrote, 'we watched a prolonged thunderstorm, clouds racing towards us at our level.' Visitors in 2004 enjoyed both the view and the feather pillows. An earlier report told of a room that 'combined rusticity and elegance: beautiful wood-beamed ceiling, painted shutters, iron bed'. Some walls may be thin. The restaurant (with open fire) faces the garden: in summer, guests eat on its stone terrace, adorned with pots of roses and geraniums. 'The food was excellent,' says this year's reporter. 'Breakfast was very good. My husband liked the DIY egg-boiler': there is also a juicer that squeezes whole oranges. The 'courteous service' is praised. The traditional cuisine uses lake fish, home-made ham and salami, organic home-grown fruit and vegetables. Vincenzo Agoni, the manager, 'does not encourage package tours'. Around are the Franciacorta vineyards, which produce Italy's best sparkling wines: 'We had a complimentary glass of it before dinner, a lovely touch. Iseo is a charming town, but the local bus service is such that a car is necessary.' (*Mary Trump*)

Open 15 Mar–31 Oct. **Rooms** 3 suites, 15 double (6 with air conditioning; 1 in cottage), 1 single. 2 suitable for ♿. **Facilities** Lift. Lounge, bar, restaurant (classical background music); dining terrace; function/conference facilities. Park: garden, chapel; unheated swimming pool, tennis, bowling. **Location** 4 km E of Iseo, on road to Polaveno. **Restrictions** No smoking in public areas. No dogs in restaurant. **Credit cards** All major cards accepted. **Terms** Room: single €100, double €133–€150, suite €178. Breakfast €10. D,B&B €102–€135 per person. Full alc €50.

****

Traveller's tale Hotel in Germany. The first room I was shown had a phone but no heat (it was mid-winter). The second room had heat but no phone. I ended up staying in the second and making my call (wearing a coat) in the first.

****

KUENS 39010 Bolzano **Map 11:A4**

Hotel Sonnenhof BUDGET *Tel* (0473) 241160
Dorfstr 48 *Fax* (0473) 241372
Kuens bei Meran *Email* info@hotel-sonnenhof.com
Website www.hotel-sonnenhof.com

The original nominators of the Schrott family's chalet-style hotel, in the 'very beautiful' Passiria valley near Merano, returned for the ninth time in 2004 and wrote: 'It remains a gem, loved by all who visit it. The family constantly seeks to improve it, though improvement on excellence is difficult. The food is delicious and well presented. Meals on the terrace, with magnificent view, are a wonderful experience. The pool and garden are well maintained.' Others said: 'We have never experienced a warmer welcome. Superb value.' The half-board dinner (at about 6.30 pm) is at least five courses (no choice apart from main course). 'Dessert buffet a feast for eyes and palate.' Bedrooms are well appointed. 'Ours, large and comfortable, had stunning views; duvet amusingly arranged like a sculpture.' 'Large corner shower with lovely tiles.' Balconies have loungers. The indoor swimming pool and restaurant have panoramic views. 'The buffet breakfast is wide ranging.' In summer there are *Grillabende* in the garden. Herr Schrott leads a weekly walk including lunch at a mountain *Gasthof*. Wine tastings are held. (*Anne and Philip Eastwood, and others*)

Open Late Mar–early Nov. **Rooms** 17 double, 3 single. Some no-smoking. **Facilities** Lift. Lounge, TV room, bar, restaurant; indoor swimming pool, sauna, gym, solarium; billiard room. No background music. Garden: dining terrace, children's playground. Unsuitable for ♿. **Location** 5 km N of Merano. At *Restaurant Kuenserhof*, turn left. Hotel after 1.5 km. Parking. **Restriction** No smoking in public areas. **Credit cards** MasterCard, Visa. **Terms** [2004] D,B&B €53–€64.

LUCCA **Map 11:C3**

Hotel Ilaria NEW *Tel* (0583) 47615
Via del Fosso 25 *Fax* (0583) 991961
55100 Lucca *Email* info@hotelilaria.com
Website www.hotelilaria.com

Within the walls, in quiet area in SE part of city by garden of Villa Bottini: modern hotel (the villa's converted stables), named after Ilaria del Carretto, whose tomb is in Lucca cathedral. 'Good bedroom and bathroom. Good breakfast. Free hot and cold drinks, pastries, etc, available all day. Free bicycles.' Air conditioning. Lift. Bar/breakfast room; conference room. Terrace. Garden. Parking, garage. No smoking in public areas. All major credit cards accepted. 30 bedrooms. B&B: single €120–€130, double €180–€210 [2004].

Italicised entries indicate a hotel on which we have little information or mixed reports.

Locanda L'Elisa NEW

Via Nuova per Pisa
Massa Pisana
55050 Lucca

Tel (0583) 379737
Fax (0583) 379019
Email elisa@relaischateaux.com
Website www.relaischateaux.com/elisa

Close to the main road to Pisa, but sheltered by mature trees, this striking 19th-century villa is managed by its owner, Alessandro Del Grande. Painted mauve, its windows framed in white, it stands amid lush gardens with a large swimming pool surrounded by lawns, loungers and parasols. Visitors in 2004 were impressed by the 'very personal' welcome. 'A cheerful porter dealt with our car and luggage. The multilingual receptionists are helpful. The small sitting room and bar have good antiques. Our suite, strangely comfortable, quite unlike most luxury hotels, had a fine example of a bourgeois Victorian living room (fabric-covered walls with a large pink/red trellis pattern centred by bouquets of flowers). The carpet was heavily patterned, and there were solid antique chairs. The bedroom had a large antique bed, superb sheets and mattress. The long, narrow bathroom had a ceiling tented in diaphanous fabric, bath and walk-in shower. Everything was well maintained. The view from three windows over the garden was beautiful.' Dinner is in a Victorian-style veranda that opens on to the garden. The buffet breakfast 'needed improvement (packet juices)', but 'staff were cheerful and efficient (one burst into song in the kitchen as he worked)'. Wedding parties, etc, are held. (*David and Kate Wooff*)

Open 11 Feb–7 Jan. **Rooms** 7 suites, 3 double. **Facilities** Lift. Salon, bar, restaurant, conservatory. Garden. **Location** S of Lucca, off SS12 to Pisa. **Restriction** No smoking in public areas. **Credit cards** All major cards accepted. **Terms** [2003] Room €180–€380, suite €285–€450. Breakfast €16. Set meals €40–€80; alc €50–€60.

Hotel La Luna

Via Fillungo, Corte Compagni 12
55100 Lucca

Tel (0583) 493634
Fax (0583) 490021
Email info@hotellaluna.com
Website www.hotellaluna.com

Near the remarkable Piazza Anfiteatro, in one of the most enticing shopping streets of this lovely walled Renaissance city, stands Nino Barbieri's B&B hotel ('modest, if not modestly priced,' says a visitor in 2004). Management, say others, is 'most helpful'. Public rooms are plain; one has a frescoed ceiling, so do some bedrooms. Most rooms are small, 'but nicely done: exposed beams, a good shower' (two have a spa bath). 'Quiet, apart from a local bar's music; we heard birds in the morning.' Earlier visitors described the buffet breakfast as 'modest but generous', but this year it was found 'disappointing' (you can also take a coffee and croissant in the bar). Recommended restaurants include the expensive *Puccini*, the simple *Da Leo* (both in town), and, in the hills looking over the city, *Vipore* (eight kilometres). Lucca is largely pedestrianised, but you can drive to the hotel's garage. (*M and GL, and others*)

Open 7 Feb–7 Jan. **Rooms** 2 suites, 20 double, 7 single. 15 in annexe, 10 m. Air conditioning. **Facilities** Lift. TV/meeting room, bar, breakfast room. No background music. Unsuitable for ♿. **Location** Approach from Piazza S.

Maria inside city walls. Garage 200 m (€10.50). Public car park nearby. **Restrictions** No smoking in public areas. No dogs. **Credit cards** All major cards accepted. **Terms** Room €95–€175. Breakfast €10.50.

Villa La Principessa NEW

Via Nuova per Pisa 1616/G
Massa Pisana
55050 Lucca

Tel (0583) 370037
Fax (0583) 379136
Email info@hotelprincipessa.com
Website www.hotelprincipessa.com

3.5 km S of Lucca, in large grounds on main road to Pisa: 13th-century building, former home of dukes of Lucca, with manager/chefs Susanna and Letitia Mugnani. Spacious public rooms, lavishly decorated (chandeliers, ornate wallpaper, paintings). Salons, bar, vaulted restaurant (closed midday and Tues); meeting/function facilities in separate building. Beautiful garden: terrace (meal service), unheated swimming pool, ancient trees. 'Unfailingly helpful staff,' says visitor in 2004. 'Food well prepared; small dinner menu changes every 2 days.' Open 25 Mar–2 Nov. No smoking in public areas. All major credit cards accepted. 8 suites, 35 bedrooms, some no-smoking. B&B: single €150–€200, double €200–€290, suite €395–€450. Set dinner €39; full alc €60. *V*

MALCESINE 37018 Verona — Map 11:B4

Hotel Maximilian BUDGET

Località Val di Sogno 6

Tel (045) 7400317
Fax (045) 6570117
Email info@hotelmaximilian.com
Website www.hotelmaximilian.com

Surrounded by cypresses and olive trees, on the shores of Lake Garda, with woods and mountains behind, this modern, much-balconied holiday hotel has a strong emphasis on beauty and fitness (see below). 'Staff were fine,' says a visitor this year. 'The grounds are pleasant. Our room had a good-sized balcony facing the lake, its lounge and bathroom were on the floor below; sound insulation was not perfect.' Other visitors had an annexe room with French windows giving on to garden and lake. 'At the excellent breakfast, we were given the dinner menu, so we could order in advance.' The food is thought 'unexciting', but the dining room, bar and reception areas have been renovated this year. Loungers are dotted around the large garden, and there is a private beach. The outdoor swimming pool, 'pleasantly warm', has beautiful views, and 'the indoor pool is inviting'. Some tour groups. (*AG, PG*)

Open Easter–mid-Oct. **Rooms** 38 double, 2 single. Some in annexes. Air conditioning. **Facilities** Lift. Lounges, bars, restaurant; background music; meeting room; fitness/beauty centre: swimming pool, Turkish bath, sauna. Large garden: dining terrace; swimming pool, tennis (€8–€10 an hour); private beach: landing stage, sailing, waterskiing, windsurfing. **Location** 2 km S of Malcesine. Garage. **Restrictions** No smoking in public areas. No pets. **Credit cards** MasterCard, Visa. **Terms** [2004] Room €71–€202. Breakfast €13. D,B&B (min. 3 nights) €81–€111 per person.

Park Hotel Querceto
Località Campiano 17–19

Tel (045) 7400344
Fax (045) 7400848
Email info@parkhotelquerceto.com
Website www.parkhotelquerceto.com

With outstanding views of Lake Garda, Andrea and Giorgia Biasi's Tyrolean-style hotel stands peacefully at the top of a panoramic road on the slopes of Monte Baldo. Much admired by *Guide* readers for 'high quality of rooms, food and facilities', it was built in 1991 using reclaimed timber. It stands in a quiet garden shaded by oak trees (*querceto* means 'tiny wilderness of little oaks'): in one corner is a swimming pool cut into the mountain. 'The dining room and bar open on to a stunning terrace where we dined, watching the sun go down and lights coming on in the town and villages below. Food [including fish from the lake] and wine are excellent.' The bar offers 40 different kinds of *grappa*. Bedrooms, in rustic Tuscan style, have a tiled floor and a balcony; front ones have the views. 'Our room was large, stylish and comfortable.' Malcesine is a 45-minute saunter down paths; you can return in a cable car, or make the 'delightful and scenic' trek on foot. All rooms now have air conditioning.

Open 1 May–8 Oct. **Rooms** 22 double. Air conditioning. **Facilities** TV room, bar, wine cellar, restaurant (background radio); sauna, spa bath. Garden: unheated swimming pool, table tennis. Unsuitable for ♿. **Location** 5 km E of Malcesine. Follow sign to Funivia Monte Baldo. Hotel 3 km along *Strada Panoramica*. Parking. **Restrictions** No smoking. No dogs. **Credit cards** MasterCard, Visa. **Terms** B&B €60–€80; D,B&B €70–€90. Set dinner €20.

MANCIANO 58014 Grosseto — Map 11:D4

Le Pisanelle
Strada Provinciale 32

Tel (0564) 628286
Fax (0564) 625840
Email info@lepisanelle.it
Website www.lepisanelle.it

In the relatively untouristy Maremma in south-west Tuscany, this 18th-century farmhouse has been turned into a guest house by Roberto and Milly Maurelli. 'She loves to entertain her visitors; he is a great cook,' says a recent visitor. 'The location is lovely': the 'beautiful house, very peaceful' stands in a large garden with olive trees, vines and fruit trees (also swimming pool and spa bath). There are some antiques in the spacious public rooms. Dinner is communal, at one long table, and dishes are local, eg, tortelloni with ricotta and truffles; wild boar; ricotta with cognac and hot chocolate. The 'simple but charming' bedrooms, with beamed ceiling, fridge, etc, are on the first floor. Guests have access to the sulphur-water spas at nearby Saturnia. Etruscan and pre-Etruscan remains can be seen in surrounding villages.

Open All year, except 8 Jan–28 Feb, 1 Nov–26 Dec. Restaurant closed midday, Sun, and to non-residents. **Rooms** 6 double. Possibly 2 more in 2005. 1 in annexe. Air conditioning. **Facilities** Lounge, TV room, bar, restaurant; background music. Garden: unheated swimming pool, spa bath, sauna; gazebo. Free mountain bikes. Unsuitable for ♿. **Location** 3 km SE of Manciano, 65 km SW of Orvieto. Parking. **Restrictions** No smoking. No children under 3. No large dogs. **Credit cards** Amex, MasterCard, Visa. **Terms** B&B: single €86–€102, double €92–€112; D,B&B €32 added per person. Set meals €32. *V*

MANTUA 46100 — Map 11:B3

Hotel San Lorenzo NEW
Piazza Concordia 14
46100 Mantua

Tel (0376) 220500
Fax (0376) 327194
Email hotel@hotelsanlorenzo.it
Website www.hotelsanlorenzo.it

Founded by Ottorino Tosi in 1967 and still run by his family, this 'excellent' *albergo* is in Mantua's historic centre where traffic is limited. The staff (all mentioned by name on the hotel's website) are found friendly; service is helpful, but some visitors thought the breakfast 'uninspired'. The bedrooms are well furnished, often with antiques. There are pink marble columns, glass chandeliers and gilded boudoir chairs. From the terrace, there is a panoramic view of ancient Mantua. No restaurant but many are nearby in the Piazza delle Erbe. Visitors this year 'were very happy with *Ristorante Pavesi*', or you could try the *Michelin*-starred *Aquila Nigra*. (*Christopher Maycock, and others*)

Open All year. **Rooms** 7 junior suites, 25 double. 2 suitable for ♿. Air conditioning. **Facilities** 2 lifts. Hall (background music), TV room, bar, breakfast room; meeting room. **Location** Central. Private garage. **Restrictions** No smoking in public areas. No dogs. **Credit cards** All major cards accepted. **Terms** B&B: single €130–€160, double €160–€220, junior suite €190–€240.

MARINA DI CAMPO, Elba 57034 Livorno — Map 11:D3

Hotel Montecristo
Viale Nomellini 11
Isola d'Elba

Tel (0565) 976861
Fax (0565) 976597
Email info@hotelmontecristo.it
Website www.hotelmontecristo.it

The Guide*'s only entry for Elba (reached by ferry from Piombino): modern B&B hotel on edge of large resort on S coast, across promenade from wide, sandy beach, with shallow water, safe bathing. 'Helpful, courteous staff.' Open Easter–mid-Oct. Lift. Hall, piano bar with TV, restaurant (light lunches only, 15 May–15 Sept); sauna, massage. Air conditioning. Terrace. 'Excellent' large outdoor swimming pool. Unsuitable for ♿. Parking. No smoking in public areas. All major credit cards accepted. 43 'comfortable, adequate, clean' bedrooms (some overlook beach, some face car park). B&B €54–€108 [2004].*

> We asked hotels to estimate their 2005 tariffs, but many preferred not to think so far ahead, and gave their 2004 tariffs. Prices should *always* be checked when booking.

MARINA DI VASTO 66054 Chieti — Map 11:E6

Villa Vignola
Località Vignola Nord
SS 16

Tel (0873) 310050
Fax (0873) 310060
Email villavignola@interfree.it
Website www.abruzzocitta.it/villavignola

'A gem': in resort 6 km N of Vasto: Guido Mazzetti's white villa, now fish restaurant-with-rooms. Garden, with fig and lemon trees, direct access to the sea ('shoes needed: no sand, only stones'), lovely views. 'In the evening, Marianne, who speaks good English, tells you what is available, and you choose as many courses as you can eat. Breakfast is dull.' Air conditioning. Lounge, bar, 2 dining rooms. Unsuitable for ♿. Parking. Closed 21–28 Dec. No smoking in public areas. All major credit cards accepted. 5 double bedrooms (some with terrace). B&B: €75–€130. Alc €35.

MATERA 75100 — Map 12:A4

Sassi Hotel
Via San Giovanni Vecchio 89
Sasso Barisano

Tel (0835) 331009
Fax (0835) 333733
Email hotelsassi@virgilio.it
Website www.hotelsassi.it

Famous for its *sassi* (dwellings carved from tufa rock), which were inhabited until the 1960s, and for its rock-hewn churches, some dating back to 8BC, Matera is now a UNESCO world heritage site. This 'enchanting' B&B hotel, also cut into the rock, is in the picturesque, traffic-free old town ('splendidly free of signs and advertisements'). The owner, Raffaele Cristallo, 'is passionate about the restoration', say recent visitors. 'The bedrooms have been beautifully modernised without spoiling the old building.' Each room is unique; each has a terrace or balcony. 'They are not at all damp or cold as you might expect. All are well equipped; ours was smallish, with modern furniture, and a view of the Romanesque cathedral.' 'It was really quiet. The buffet breakfast was fine. The obliging staff spoke excellent English.' No on-site parking, and you have to carry your bags, but a parking permit is provided. The *Sassi*'s brochure promises 'peace away from smog', and sightings of the lesser kestrel. Plenty of restaurants nearby: for local fare in informal surroundings, try *Trattoria Lucana*.

Open All year. **Rooms** 2 suites, 16 double, 4 single. 11 rooms air conditioned. **Facilities** TV room/bar, breakfast room; conference hall. Terrace. No background music. Unsuitable for ♿. **Location** Centre of old town. 65 km SW of Bari. Public parking/garage nearby. **Restrictions** No smoking. Dogs at €5.50 per day. **Credit cards** All major cards accepted. **Terms** [2004] B&B: single €55, double €84–€90, suite €110.

Every entry in the *Guide* is based on a stay of at least one night.

MERANO 39012 Bolzano — Map 11:A4

Castel Fragsburg
Fragsburgerstrasse 3

Tel (0473) 244071
Fax (0473) 244493
Email info@fragsburg.com
Website www.fragsburg.com

High above this pleasant, rather old-fashioned spa resort in the Alto Adige is this 'stunning hotel in a stunning setting', a handsome white former hunting castle (Relais du Silence). Reached by a 'narrow, steep road with few passing places', it stands amid mountains, woods and vineyards. 'Expensive but decent value for money,' says a visitor this year. It is 'impeccably run' by the Ortner family owners, with an 'unfailingly helpful' staff. 'Very comfortable, high standards throughout,' was another comment. Attractive public rooms are in Liberty and Biedermeier style. 'Our vast bedroom faced the mountains at the rear of the hotel (earlier we were offered one with an even better view, but it overlooked the valley and heard the *autostrada*). A complimentary jar of the hotel's own honey awaited us.' The 'marvellous' breakfast buffet has home-made jams, 'wonderful breads'. The restaurant has electrically operated windows to deal with the changing weather. 'Our three dinners were excellent. Wine reasonably priced; a decent, if not extensive selection.' On fine days, meals are served on a terrace above the valley. The sizeable, solar-heated swimming pool in the garden faces the view. 'The extensive beauty and wellness spa has an excellent masseuse.' (*Antony Griew, J and MH, and others*)

Open End Mar–early Nov. Restaurant closed Mon. **Rooms** 12 suites, 6 double, 2 single. **Facilities** Salon, reading room, 3 smoking rooms, 5 dining rooms; sauna, gym, beauty/wellness spa. No background music. Garden: dining terraces; heated swimming pool, children's play area, table tennis, chess. Unsuitable for ♿. **Location** 8 km SE of Merano. Exit Merano Sud from Bolzano–Merano road; follow signs to Hafling; right towards Labers after 3 km. Hotel 5 km along this road. Parking. **Restrictions** Smoking in some bedrooms only. Dogs by arrangement. **Credit cards** MasterCard, Visa. **Terms** D,B&B €100–€150. Set lunch €30–€50, dinner €40–€70; full alc €35.

MERGOZZO 28802 Verbania — Map 11:A2

Hotel La Quartina BUDGET
Via Pallanza 20

Tel (0323) 80118
Fax (0323) 80743
Email laquartina@libero.it
Website www.laquartina.com

On wooded slopes at the northern end of tiny Lake Mergozzo (an extension of Lake Maggiore, and reputedly one of the cleanest lakes in Europe), Laura Profumo's *albergo* stands right by the water. It is 'strongly recommended' this year: 'The atmosphere is friendly and the hotel is spotless.' Some of the 'tastefully decorated' bedrooms have a balcony looking across the lake to mountains. Only drawback: 'The rooms (some are small) are on the second and third floors; no lift, a lot of stairs.' The restaurant shares the view, as does the shady terrace where summer meals are served 'amid a profusion of climbing white roses'. 'Laura prepares exquisite meals' (eg, perch fillets with balsamic vinegar; green ravioli with asparagus and clams). 'The menu is adventurous without being overly long. Breakfast has lovely coffee, hot apricot croissants, fresh rolls. The service is perfect, too. Swimming is tempting, from the small public beach in front of the hotel.' (*Ann Burrows, and others*)

Open 1 Mar–30 Nov. **Rooms** 8 double, 2 single. **Facilities** Lounge, TV room, bar, restaurant. No background music. Terrace (meal service). Garden: solarium, children's playground; beach. Unsuitable for ♿. **Location** 100 m from centre. From A26, exit Verbania (3 km). Parking. **Restriction** No smoking in public areas. **Credit cards** All major cards accepted. **Terms** B&B: single €58–€75, double €90–€110. Set meals €30–€45.

MILAN — Map 11:B3

Antica Locanda dei Mercanti
Via San Tomaso 6
20121 Milan

Tel (02) 8054080
Fax (02) 8054090
Email locanda@locanda.it
Website www.locanda.it

Off the pedestrianised Via Dante, five minutes' walk from the *duomo*, this discreet B&B is on the second and third floors of a 'rather austere' office block in the winding streets of Milan's old commercial centre. No hotel sign: the name and buzzer are on a brass panel by the large green door. A 'tiny, antique' lift takes guests up from a courtyard. The welcome is 'helpful and calm', says a visitor this year. No public rooms, but reception was being enlarged in 2004. Bookings can be guaranteed by credit card, but payment must be made in cash. The 'self-contained but attractive' bedrooms have fresh flowers, pure wool carpet, inter-lined curtains, a small but 'spotless' bathroom (no minibar or TV). Breakfast, in the room, has freshly squeezed orange juice and fresh-baked croissants; ham, cheeses, etc, cost extra. Help is given with parking. The stop for the express train from Malpensa airport (40 minutes) is near, so are excellent restaurants, eg, *Stendhal Antica Osteria*, via Ancona, with 'whirlwind waiter Flavio'. (*Bing Taylor, KC, and others*)

Open All year. **Rooms** 11 double, 3 single. 4 with terrace and air conditioning. 2 in annexe. No TV. **Facilities** No public rooms. No background music. Unsuitable for ♿. **Location** Small street near the Castello Sforzesco, between via Broletto and via Dante. Garages nearby. **Restrictions** No smoking: public areas, 12 bedrooms. No facilities for young children. No dogs. **Credit cards** MasterCard, Visa to guarantee booking; payment in cash. **Terms** Room: single €119–€135, double €155–€200, suite €255–€285. Breakfast €9.

Hotel Manzoni
Via Santo Spirito 20
20121 Milan

Tel (02) 76005700
Fax (02) 784212
Email hotel.manzoni@tin.it
Website www.hotelmanzoni.com

Well located, near chic shopping streets and ten minutes' walk from the *duomo* and La Scala, this unpretentious hotel is a 1950s building in 'an old alley lined with *palazzi*'. It promises 'family environment and the latest technologies'. Recent praise: 'Our spacious, comfortable room had a good bathroom. Staff were welcoming. The buffet breakfast was lovely: hot items, including scrambled eggs, were cooked to order.' Furnishings are 'simple and tasteful'; rates 'very reasonable'. Some rooms might hear noise from nearby houses; most are 'very quiet'. There is a small breakfast area and a bar, and a simple evening meal is available. (*KT*)

Open All year, except 24 Dec–4 Jan, Aug. **Rooms** 3 suites, 22 double, 27 single. Air conditioning. **Facilities** Lift. TV room, bar, breakfast room. Courtyard. Unsuitable for ♿. **Location** Central. Garage. **Restrictions** No smoking in public areas. No dogs. **Credit cards** All major cards accepted. **Terms** [2004] Room €132–€170. Breakfast €15.

Hotel Spadari al Duomo
Via Spadari 11
20123 Milan

Tel (02) 72002371
Fax (02) 861184
Email reservation@spadarihotel.com.it
Website www.spadarihotel.com

'Just round the corner from the magnificent cathedral', this designer B&B hotel was found 'delightful' again this year. 'Very attractive reception floor, comfortable lounge, bright breakfast room/bar. Our large, stylish, quiet bedroom looked over a courtyard. Only failing: inadequate storage for clothes.' 'Room 40, on the seventh floor, has the best view of the *duomo*, but the lift only goes to the sixth floor.' 'Helpful staff, great breakfast' (it includes fruit, freshly squeezed juices, eggs, sausages, etc, and can be served, with a newspaper, in the bedroom for no extra charge). The 'modern-romantic' decor is thought 'charming': a large sculpture and fireplace by Gio Pomodoro in the hall; 'lots of blue, beechwood furniture, pleasing fabrics, extravagant flower arrangements, contemporary paintings'. Snacks are available; 'many good restaurants are nearby, and the staff's recommendations, for eating and shopping, were spot on'. (*Rosemary Viner, CB, and others*)

Open All year, except Christmas. **Rooms** 37 double, 3 single. Air conditioning. **Facilities** Hall, winter garden, American bar/breakfast room; background music. Unsuitable for ♿. **Location** Central, just W of *duomo*. Yellow line underground. Private garage (€20 a night). **Restrictions** No smoking: public areas, some bedrooms. No dogs. **Credit cards** All major cards accepted. **Terms** B&B: single €125–€228, double €165–€288.

MONDELLO 90151 Sicily — Map 12:B2

Villa Esperia NEW/BUDGET
Viale Margherita di Savoia 53
Valdesi Mondello

Tel (091) 6840717
Fax (091) 6841508
Email info@hotelvillaesperia.it
Website www.hotelvillaesperia.it

'Truly Sicilian in feel', this 'very well-run' two-star hotel is a converted 'Liberty-style' villa in a seaside suburb of Palermo, half an hour's bus ride to the centre. 'It stands on a main road: ask for a room at the side or back. Ours was spacious, with excellent bathroom. The dinner was excellent [traditional Sicilian recipes], and very good value. Local families come for celebrations.' The owner, Petrus Salvatore, 'hovers in the background, making sure that all is well'. Meals are served alfresco in summer. Only drawback: 'no garage, but nearby streets suffice'. (*AD Canning-Jones*)

Open All year. **Rooms** 22 double. **Facilities** Bar, restaurant; background music; meeting room. Terrace. Beach 150 m. **Location** 6 km N of Palermo. Street parking. **Restrictions** No smoking in public areas. Small dogs only. **Credit cards** All major cards accepted. **Terms** [2004] B&B: single €68–€85, double €99–€145. Set meals €18; full alc €35.

MONFORTE D'ALBA 12065 Cuneo — Map 11:C2

Albergo Ristorante Giardino da Felicin
Via Vallada 18

Tel (0173) 78225
Fax (0173) 787377
Email albrist@felicin.it
Website www.felicin.it

Each bedroom in this restaurant-with-rooms has a balcony or terrace with 'magnificent views' of the hills, castles and vineyards of the surrounding Barolo wine region. Run by two generations of the 'friendly, multilingual' Rocca family, it has some 'large, comfortable bedrooms', although an annexe room was found 'a bit austere, with two smallish single beds'. A garden area, with tables under a canopy of vines, 'serves as an outdoor lounge': meals are served here in fine weather, and there are two 'classically elegant' dining rooms. 'Nino Rocca, the chef, larger than life, dominates the show.' 'Dinner was a revelation,' say visitors this year, 'a succession of local specialties, the right amount of variety and choice, all delicious.' Others found that 'as residents, we had the most expensive, longest menu: an excellent eight-course meal'. The 'amazing' wine list 'offers good value' and includes some moderately priced Piemonte varieties as well as the expensive Barolos. 'Considering the quality of meals and rooms, the half-board rate is a bargain.' For children there are toys, games, etc. (*Brian and Lesley Knox, Esler and Barbara Crawford, Paul Harman, ER*)

Open 9 Feb–9 Dec. Closed 1–15 July, Sun night/Mon. Restaurant closed midday, except Sat, Sun. **Rooms** 3 suites, 10 double. 1 on ground floor. 2 in annexe 100 m. **Facilities** Lounge, breakfast room, restaurant; veranda. Garden. Unsuitable for ♿. **Location** 17 km S of Alba, 6 km SE of Barolo. **Restriction** No smoking in public areas. **Credit cards** Amex, MasterCard, Visa. **Terms** [2004] B&B: single €85–€90, double €120–€125; D,B&B €100–€110 per person. Set meals €28–€45; full alc €35. *V*

> The *V* sign at the end of an entry indicates that the hotel has agreed to take part in our Voucher scheme and to give *Guide* readers a 25% discount on its room or B&B rates, subject to the conditions explained in *How to read the entries*, and on the back of the vouchers.

MONTECARLO 55015 Lucca **Map 11:C3**

Antica Casa dei Rassicurati NEW/BUDGET *Tel* (0583) 228901
Via della Collegiata 2 *Fax* (0583) 22498
Email info@anticacasadeirassicurati.com
Website www.anticacasadeirassicurati.com

In a 'lovely little medieval walled town', surrounded by vineyards and olive groves, on a hill west of Pescia, this B&B is 'charming and very good value', says the reader who discovered it in 2004. The 18th-century building has been restored in Tuscan style: beamed ceilings, brick floors, etc. 'Run by three friends, Antonella and Marta (both Italian) and Miriam (German), it is very simple, but everything is done with flair and a personal touch.' The bedrooms, each named after a flower, are on two floors. 'Our second-floor room was the only one with a balcony, a tiny triangular space overlooking the street and square.' 'Delicious home-made breakfasts'; in the evening wine and antipasti are served: alfresco in summer, by a fire in winter. For dinner two 'excellent' restaurants just outside the walls are recommended: *Osteria del Vecchio Olivo* and the more pricey *Antico Ristorante Forassiepi*. Children and small dogs are welcomed. (*John Beddoe*)

Open All year. **Rooms** 5 double, 1 single. **Facilities** Bar, breakfast room. No background music. Patio. Unsuitable for ♿. **Location** Centre of town. 15 km E of Lucca. Free parking 50 m. **Restriction** No smoking: public areas, some bedrooms. **Credit cards** MasterCard, Visa. **Terms** [2004] B&B: single €45–€50, double €68–€75. *V*

MONTECASTELLO DI VIBIO 06057 Perugia **Map 11:D5**

Fattoria di Vibio *Tel* (075) 8749607
Località Buchella 9 *Fax* (075) 8780014
Doglio *Email* info@fattoriadivibio.com
Website www.fattoriadivibio.com

With 'glorious views over the valley towards Monte Peglia', in a beautiful part of Umbria, this *Agriturismo* member is run by the Saladini family, Gabriella, Giuseppe and Filippo. Old country houses have been rebuilt keeping the character of the original architecture. Terracotta tiles, wooden beams, open fireplaces and stone walls have been preserved. Bedrooms are 'charmingly decorated' in traditional style: Deruta pottery, wrought iron bedheads, country furniture. There is an emphasis on well-being: 'back to nature massages' and anti-ageing treatments are offered as well as outdoor pursuits (see below). Recent reports vary: some readers have written: 'Very good value.' Others found the food 'inconsistent' and the owners 'not very approachable', but they nevertheless 'had a lovely time'. Evening meals are taken in a beamed room or on a panoramic terrace. Home-produced ingredients, some organic, are used. There is an indoor swimming pool, also a 'superb' one outdoors. Cookery and Italian language courses are held.

Open 3 Mar–10 Jan. **Rooms** 2 cottages, 12 double. **Facilities** Lounge, TV room, bar, *enoteca*, restaurant; background music; indoor swimming pool, sauna. 20-hectare estate: bar, restaurant, swimming pool, tennis, lake, fishing, horse riding, mountain bikes. Unsuitable for ♿. **Location** 43 km SW of Perugia, N of Todi–Orvieto road, between Montecastello and Prodo; follow signs to Prodo–Quadro, then *fattoria*. **Restriction** No smoking in public areas. **Credit cards** All major cards accepted. **Terms** B&B €70–€80; D,B&B €95–€105. Set dinner €30; full alc €40.

MONTEMERANO 58050 Grosseto — Map 11:D4

Caino
Via della Chiesa 4

Tel (0564) 602817
Fax (0564) 602807
Email info@dacaino.it
Website www.dacaino.it

Composed of two adjoining houses, this 'enticing' restaurant (two *Michelin* stars) has three bedrooms on an upper floor. It stands in a narrow street in this medieval hill village ('lovely church') between Orvieto and the coast. Its greatest fans returned in 2004 and still loved 'the food, the people, the supremely tasteful rooms'. Other guests had a 'well-designed small bedroom with a happy mix of antique furniture and modern lighting, great views, an impressive shower room'. 'Goodies to rival a five-star hotel.' Maurizio Menichetti, front-of-house, is helped by his son and daughter; his wife, Valeria Piccini, is the chef: 'A superb meal: seasonal produce used to great effect, portions fairly substantial, combinations sometimes a bit weird.' There is an impressive cheese trolley and a large wine list. Service and welcome are 'impeccable and warm'. Breakfast, in a 'beautiful room' on the first floor, has fresh orange juice, home-made jams, cheeses, 'superb coffee' and 'a wonderfully moist saffron cake'. 'The roads around the village are steep, with many bends.' (*David and Kate Wooff, Pat and Jeremy Temple*)

Open All year, except 24–26 Dec, 8 Jan–26 Feb, 3 weeks July. Restaurant closed Wed/Thurs midday. **Rooms** 3 double. **Facilities** Lounge, restaurant. **Location** 50 km SE of Grosseto, S of Saturnia. **Restrictions** No smoking in public areas. No dogs. **Credit cards** Diners, MasterCard, Visa. **Terms** Room with breakfast €150–€165. Set meals €90; alc €73–€98.

MONTEPULCIANO 53045 Siena — Map 11:D4

Il Riccio NEW/BUDGET
Via Talosa 21

Tel/Fax (0578) 757713
Email info@ilriccio.net
Website www.ilriccio.net

'Convenient and good value', in the old part of this 'lively and friendly' town, near the *duomo*, this *palazzo* has been owned by the local Caroti family since 1949. Part of it is the centre of the Italian School of Mosaics. Since the 1980s, it has also housed this '*meublé*', run by Giorgio and Ivana Caroti with their son, Iacopo, and Giorgio's mother, Antonietta. 'They are very nice,' writes this year's nominator. 'The rooms are simple, quiet and clean' (they have safe, minibar and TV). There is an impressive courtyard, and a 14th-century staircase leads to a solarium which 'is on the highest point of Montepulciano's hill', says the website (wonderful views over the Val Chiana and the lakes). The family's Dalmatian, Indy, is in attendance and small dogs are allowed. No restaurant: good ones nearby include *Borgo Buio*, via Borgo Buio. (*Jann Pasler*)

Open All year. **Rooms** 5 double, 1 single. 2 no-smoking. Air conditioning. **Facilities** Reading room, bar/breakfast room (background music). Sun terrace. Unsuitable for ♿. **Location** Central, near main square. Reserved parking included in room price. **Restriction** No smoking in public areas. **Credit cards** All major cards accepted. **Terms** Room: single €75, double €85. Breakfast €8.

NERVI 16167 Genova **Map 11:C2**

Romantik Hotel Villa Pagoda
Via Capolungo 15

Tel (010) 323200
Fax (010) 321218
Email info@villapagoda.it
Website www.villapagoda.it

Now owned by the Cavaliere family, this 'remarkable building' claims to have been 'witness to eccentric lifestyles'. It stands in a small park, with wide views over the Mediterranean, on the coast south of Genoa. An underground passage connects its cellar to the beach. Built in the early 19th century by a rich merchant, it owes its oriental style to his extensive trade with China and, it is said, his love for a Chinese girl. Later it was the summer residence of the Czar of Russia: much of the furnishing, and the magnificent chandeliers in the public rooms, date from this time. Period furniture abounds; floors are of antique Carrara marble. 'Our room,' say recent visitors, 'had sea-facing balcony and many original features, and was furnished in excellent taste. Its modern bathroom had all one could want.' In the restaurant, *Il Roseto*, 'dinner, excellently prepared, included pasta alla Genovese' (pesto is a local speciality). In the 'luscious' gardens, summer meals are served under white parasols. A gate leads to the 'mostly uninteresting' beach. Indian and traditional massages are available; also bicycle hire. (*A and EA*)

Open Early Feb–end Nov. **Rooms** 4 suites, 13 double. Air conditioning. **Facilities** Lift. Lounge, piano bar, restaurant; background music; conference facilities. Garden; access to beach. Unsuitable for ♿. **Location** 1 km from centre. 10 km SE of Genoa. Parking. **Restrictions** No smoking in public areas. Small dogs only. **Credit cards** All major cards accepted. **Terms** [2004] Room: single €114–€215, double €145–€255, suite €280–€650. Breakfast €13. Set lunch €30, dinner €35; full alc €38. 1-night bookings sometimes refused.

The maps can be found in the colour section of the *Guide*.

ORTA SAN GIULIO 28016 Novara — Map 11:B2

Villa Crespi
Via Fava 18

Tel (0322) 911902
Fax (0322) 911919
Email villacrespi@lagodortahotels.com
Website www.lagodortahotels.com

In 1879 Benigno Crespi, a cotton trader, constructed this astonishing Moorish-style building, complete with minaret, starry vaulted hall, tiles, mosaics, frescoes, chandeliers and arches. It is now 'a great hotel', say fans. Antonio Cannavacciuolo is chef (*Michelin* star in 2004); his wife, Cinzia, manages. 'The setting is magic,' say visitors this year. Others wrote: 'The decorations are breathtaking, beautifully restored. It is worth staying here just to admire the detail.' 'The dinners were superb.' 'Our bedroom, with views over Lake Orta from two sides, was superb, as was the bathroom (with spa bath).' But another couple had a room that 'left a lot to be desired', and thought the garden 'neglected'. Staff are 'very polished, but friendly'. 'The dining terrace is lovely, so is the restaurant. On half board, the food was very good, with local beef specialities, lots of "pre-courses". The wine list includes the best of Italy. We thought it all good value.' In the Shirò health centre you can 'recover your psychophysical harmony', says the brochure. But 'the hotel stands at the corner of two roads which can be noisy with bikers at the weekend' and 'in July and August there was a large marquee, for concerts'. (*Bill Bennett, GB, IGCF, and others*)

Open 14 Feb–1 Jan. Restaurant closed Tues/Wed midday. **Rooms** 8 suites, 6 double. Air conditioning. **Facilities** Lounge, bar, restaurant; background music/pianist; Shirò fitness centre, sauna, solarium, massage. Park: garden, beach. Swimming pool at sister hotel, *L'Approdo*, 1.5 km. Unsuitable for ♿. **Location** Lake shore. From A26 exit Arona/Borgomanero, follow signs Lago d'Orta/Gozzano. **Restrictions** No smoking. Small dogs only. **Credit cards** All major cards accepted. **Terms** B&B: single €120–€175, double €170–€240, suite €240–€480; D,B&B €55 added per person. Set lunch €31, dinner €58–€78; full alc €65. Musical evenings; weddings; gastronomic weeks.

ORVIETO Terni — Map 11:D4

Hotel Maitani
Via L Maitani 5
05018 Orvieto

Tel (0763) 342011
Fax (0763) 342012
Email info@hotelmaitani.com
Website www.hotelmaitani.com

Facing the mosaic-clad facade of 'Italy's most beautiful cathedral', the Morino family's B&B hotel is a converted 13th-century *palazzo* 'superbly located', a few steps from the main square of this magical city. It has Art Deco-style lounges and a collection of modern art: canvases by Vespignani, a Roman follower of Lucien Freud, Valenti, an Umbrian colourist, and others. 'The enthusiastic proprietors are delighted to show and discuss them.' Bedrooms are 'comfortable and efficient', though 'you may have to walk along corridors and up and down a step or two' to reach yours. Breakfast, with local cheeses, sausages, etc, is served in the bar or on a terrace facing the cathedral. Many eating places are nearby – help is given with reservations, 'and across from the cathedral is 'what many regard as the finest ice-cream bar in Italy'.

Open 8 Feb–6 Jan. **Rooms** 8 suites, 23 double, 8 single. Air conditioning. **Facilities** Lift. Lounge, lounge/bar, reading room, breakfast room. **Location** By cathedral. Garage (€12 a night). **Restrictions** No smoking in public areas. No dogs. **Credit cards** All major cards accepted. **Terms** [2004] Room: single €75, double €124–€147, suite €168. Breakfast €10.

Villa Ciconia NEW
Via dei Tigli 69
05019 Orvieto Scalo

Tel (0763) 305582
Fax (0763) 302077
Email villaciconia@libero.it
Website www.hotelvillaciconia.com

In a large park where two rivers meet, just outside Orvieto, this 16th-century villa 'was the quietest of our trip', says the nominator who had a 'delightful' stay. 'Great to wake up to birdsong. Our quite spacious room had wrought iron twin beds, very small shower room with lighting better than in the bedroom. Housekeeping was excellent. Buffet breakfast satisfactory, nothing special.' The restaurant specialises in Umbrian dishes. 'We dined in all three nights of our stay. Roberto, the waiter, was fun. No lift, but our luggage was carried on arrival and departure.' Original features (thick walls, beams, terracotta paving) have survived. One ceiling is painted with allegorical motifs. The Rome–Florence *autostrada* is two kilometres away. (*Claire Lavery*)

Open All year. **Rooms** 12 double. Air conditioning. **Facilities** Bar, restaurant; 2 conference halls. Park: Garden: swimming pool. **Location** 2 km W of Orvieto by SS71. Parking. **Restrictions** No smoking in public areas. No dogs. **Credit cards** All major cards accepted. **Terms** [2004] B&B €65–€145; D,B&B €18 added per person.

OSTUNI 72017 Brindisi — Map 12:A5

Il Frantoio NEW
Strada statale 16, km 874

Tel/Fax (0831) 330276
Email armando@trecolline.it
Website www.trecolline.it

In a large olive farm a few miles from the sea between Bari and Brindisi, this *agriturismo* is 'comfortable, relaxed and enormously friendly, once you get past the worryingly defensive gates', says its nominator in 2004. 'The three generations of owners are great.' Activities range from table tennis to horse riding and mountain biking; there is a well-stocked library, a chapel and, in the grounds, 'orange and lemon gardens and 40,000 olive trees'. Two private beaches (one stony, one sand) are a few miles away. 'Wonderful breakfasts' include home-made jams, fresh fruit and yogurts. 'Everything seems possible: if you want a tomatoey lunch you get choices of different kinds of mozzarella. If you want supper you can have what they are having or go out to one of many nice eateries. Once a week the bell rings at 8 pm and you feast for three hours – endless small courses of wonderfully delicious things, in the courtyard in summer. It cost us €140 per night all in, food, laundry, phone/Internet, farm trips, advice, bicycles, laughs and great fun.' (*Charlie Nairn*)

Open All year. **Rooms** 8 double. **Facilities** Sitting rooms, music room, TV room, library, bar, dining room; courtyard. No background music. 100-hectare farm: 2 gardens, woods. Unsuitable for ♿. **Location** 5 km NE of Ostuni, 42 km NW of Brindisi. Main road towards Bari, exit Ostuni-Villanova to Ostuni then direction Fasano, SS16 to km 874. **Restrictions** No smoking in public areas. Dogs in kennels only. **Credit cards** MasterCard, Visa. **Terms** [2004] B&B: €88–€98. Set meal €49. 1-night bookings sometimes refused July/Aug.

PADUA 35100 — Map 11:B4

Hotel Majestic Toscanelli
Via dell'Arco 2

Tel (049) 663244
Fax (049) 8760025
Email majestic@toscanelli.com

Surrounded by parts of the ancient university, this 'excellent' B&B hotel is in the centre of this 'wonderful city'. Run as a hotel since 1969 by the Morosi family, it is in a car-free piazza, 'almost impossible to reach except on foot', in the old ghetto, with its cafés and boutiques. Decor ranges from '19th-century English to *Barocco Veneziano*'. 'Our charming room, with brocade on bed, windows and walls, was on a quiet courtyard,' said a visitor this year. The 'comfy' large lobby has an Internet terminal. The mezzanine breakfast room, with murals, 'affords an excellent view of the comings and goings on the side street', and 'the buffet is substantial and imaginative', including eggs and bacon. The bar will provide a snack. 'Service was always helpful.' Many restaurants nearby: *Osteria dal Capo*, via Soncin, is recommended this year. (*Christopher Maycock, AW*)

Open All year. **Rooms** 3 suites, 29 double. Some no-smoking. Air conditioning. **Facilities** Lift. Lobby, American bar, breakfast room, conference room. Unsuitable for ♿. **Location** Central (car-free area, valet parking). **Restrictions** No smoking in public areas. Small dogs only. **Credit cards** All major cards accepted. **Terms** [2004] B&B: single €115, double €169.

PALAZZUOLO SUL SENIO 50035 Firenze — Map 11:C4

Locanda Senio NEW
Via Borgo dell'Ore 1

Tel (055) 8046019
Fax (055) 8043949
Email info@locandasenio.it
Website www.locandasenio.it

In an attractive little mountain town amid thickly wooded mountains in north-east Tuscany, this 'small, personal, unsophisticated' inn consists of two old stone buildings that face each other near the church. It is recommended for its 'family atmosphere and very special cooking'. The owners, Ercole and Roberta Lega, are 'most helpful', advising about walks, etc. 'Once, we were driven to the top of a pass, so we could spend the day walking back. Our comfortable bedroom had a modern bathroom. The breakfast room decor could be improved, but the self-service breakfasts were delicious.' The five-course dinners, based on local ingredients (funghi, tartufi, pork, herbs, etc) and medieval recipes, are served on the terrace or in the restaurant with its large fireplace. The *Dispensa della Locanda* sells local delicacies: chestnut honey, wild berry liqueur and 'delicious home-cured meats'. Florence, to the south, is reached via a 'spectacular pass'. (*Clare and Malcolm Dean*)

Open 13 Feb–6 Jan. Restaurant closed Mon/Tues/Wed Nov–Apr; midday, except Sat/Sun. **Rooms** 2 suites (2 m from main building), 5 double, 1 single. **Facilities** Lounge, piano bar, breakfast room, restaurant; children's play room; spa: sauna, Turkish bath, whirlpool. Terrace: meal service, heated swimming pool. Bicycles available. **Location** Central, by church. 56 km NE of Florence. Parking in square. **Restriction** No smoking. **Credit cards** All major cards accepted. **Terms** B&B: single €75–€115, double €135–€160, suite €155–€195; D,B&B (min. 3 days) €95–€115 per person. *V*

PALERMO 90133 Sicily **Map 12:B2**

Palazzo Conte Federico NEW *Tel/Fax* (091) 6511881
Via dei Biacottari 4 *Email* contefederico@contefederico.com
Website www.contefederico.com

A most unusual B&B: it is a baroque suite in a wing of the ancestral home ('one of the most important buildings in Palermo') of Count Federico (a descendant of the Staufen Emperor Friedrich II) and his Austrian wife, a multilingual opera singer. They live here with their two sons. 'It is really suitable only for families or close friends,' the *conte* explains, 'because you must go through the yellow bedroom to reach the other two rooms.' The palazzo, with its high painted ceilings, frescoes, grand stairway, antiques, paintings and sculptures, can be visited by residents, and the count and his wife take an aperitif with them in the evening. 'It was a delight to be with such charming people, so generous with their hospitality, so interested and informed about history, politics, art, etc,' says a visitor this year. 'They are both passionate about music. Beethoven, Schubert and Schumann are in the background all the time. He is a passionate motor-racer: his study is heavily adorned with large silver trophies. We were looked after, turn and turn about, by two young Austrian girls in knee-britches and dashing old-gold jackets, so charming, like Cherubino.' Another visitor wrote: 'Staying here is a unique experience. You are made to feel perfectly at home. The hospitality is faultless. But outside, the building is unremarkable, facing a car park, and the suite gives on to a long, narrow walled well, so in summer noise from neighbours could be a problem (there is no air conditioning).' Breakfast includes sweet Sicilian pastries, fresh fruit, etc: 'You are encouraged to order what you'd like and they buy it from the market, five minutes' walk away.' For dinner, the *Sant'Andrea*, nearby, is warmly recommended: 'Stunning, inventively traditional Sicilian food.' Sometimes the Federicos offer a gala evening with music. (*AL, and others*)

Open All year, except July/Aug. **Rooms** 3. **Facilities** Salon, breakfast room. Unsuitable for ♿. **Location** Central, near cathedral. **Restriction** No smoking in public areas. **Credit cards** None accepted. **Terms** [2004] (min. 2 nights) B&B: single €100, double €330.

PANZANO IN CHIANTI 50020 Firenze — Map 11:C4

Villa Le Barone
Via San Leolino 19

Tel (055) 852621
Fax (055) 852277
Email info@villalebarone.it
Website www.villalebarone.it

Much loved by *Guide* readers, this small hilltop hotel is now owned by Conte Corso Aloisi de Larderel and his 'elegant French wife', Jacqueline, following the death of the 'remarkable' 97-year-old *duchessa*. 'They clearly love their inheritance,' one visitor wrote. The long-serving, 'excellent' manager, Caterina Buonamici, still presides. Praise continued this year: 'No wonder so many people return again and again'; 'In many years of travel, and countless hotel visits, I haven't seen staff as good as this'; 'More like a country house than a hotel'; 'Even better than before'. In the lovely gardens, roses abound and the views over surrounding hills, valleys, vineyards and olive groves are 'to die for'. 'The quiet setting and unsophisticated style make it good for a family holiday.' For others it is 'a perfect place to read, eat, drink and sleep'. 'The food is simple and all the better for that; fresh ingredients, always an interesting pasta dish. Wines are good value.' The 'excellent' breakfast is served on a shady terrace. Light lunches are available. The public rooms are 'tastefully furnished with antiques and floral prints'. Bedrooms vary: 'The better ones are in the main house and the immediate surrounding buildings, but cheaper rooms in the garden have splendid views.' (*Bill Bennett, William Rodgers, Robert Barratt, Jennifer and Michael Hodge, and many others*)

Open 1 Apr–31 Oct. **Rooms** 27 double, 1 single. 20 in 3 garden annexes. 15 air conditioned. **Facilities** Lounges, TV room, 2 bars, restaurant (background music). Garden: unheated swimming pool, bar, tennis, table tennis. Unsuitable for ♿. **Location** 1.5 km SE of Panzano, off SS222 Florence–Siena (both 35 km). Parking. **Restrictions** Smoking banned in public areas, discouraged in bedrooms. No dogs. **Credit cards** Amex, MasterCard, Visa. **Terms** B&B €85–€270; D,B&B €95–€290. Set dinner €34.

Villa Sangiovese NEW
Piazza Bucciarelli 5

Tel (055) 852461
Fax (055) 852463
Email villa.sangiovese@libero.it
Website www.wel.it/villasangiovese

On the corner of the tiny square of this small, unspoilt Tuscan town stands Anne-Marie and Ueli Bleuler-Staerkle's hotel; from the back it commands a 'tremendous view of distant hills and mountains'. 'The dedicated owners give enormous personal attention to detail,' says a report this year. 'I can think of few more pleasant holiday experiences than dining on the terrace overlooking olive groves and vineyards. As the light fades, the hills change colour from green to blue and lights around Florence begin to twinkle. Tagliatelle with porcini mushrooms; super bistecca alla Fiorentina, washed down by Chianti Classico, precede the best sleep of the year.' Another visitor also admired the 'ever-present' owners and their 'helpful and jolly' staff, but thought the food less special. 'Our large room was simple, well ordered and comfortable. No air conditioning, but walls were thick.' The 'beautiful' swimming pool is some way away, down a hill: one couple complained that there was not much shade, and disliked having to carry their sun loungers to and from the pool house. Mountain bikes and maps are provided free of charge. (*David Porter, Tom Mann, and others*)

Open 16 Mar–20 Dec. Restaurant closed Wed. **Rooms** 2 suites, 16 double, 1 single. 11 air conditioned. Some in annexe. **Facilities** 2 lounges, bar, restaurant, library. Terraces: unheated swimming pool down hill. No background music. Unsuitable for ♿. **Location** 30 km Florence, 30 km Siena. Public parking (50 m). **Restrictions** No smoking in public areas. No dogs. **Credit cards** MasterCard, Visa. **Terms** [2004] B&B (min. 3 nights): single €86–€103, double €103–€153, suite €153–€179. Set meals €25–€30. *V* (Mar, Nov/Dec)

PECOL DI ZOLDO ALTO 32010 Belluno **Map 11:A4**

Hotel Valgranda BUDGET
Via Pecol 11

Tel (0437) 789142
Fax (0437) 788767
Email valgranda@dolomiti.it
Website www.dolomiti.it/valgranda

In 'wonderfully located' Dolomite village between Civetta and Pelmo mountains, 30 km NW of Belluno: friendly family-run hotel (on main road; some morning traffic noise). 'Comfortable residents' lounge; well-stocked bar; nice Alpine-style restaurant with good local food, reasonably priced wines; adequate breakfast.' Good sports facilities: indoor pool, gym, Turkish bath, whirlpool; ski room; 'evening baby-club'. 4 suites, 25 double rooms. D,B&B €49–€105; single supplement €21 [2004].

PEDEMONTE 37020 Verona **Map 11:B4**

Villa del Quar
Via Quar 12

Tel (045) 6800681
Fax (045) 6800604
Email info@hotelvilladelquar.it
Website www.hotelvilladelquar.it

'A very nice hotel,' say visitors in 2004. 'Room good. Owners and staff nice and friendly. Restaurant very good.' Quietly set among vineyards on the outskirts of Verona, the Montresor family's luxurious hotel/restaurant (Relais & Châteaux) is a designated national monument, a 16th-century patrician dwelling built over 14th-century foundations. An earlier guest described it as 'the modern Maserati of small Italian hotels, with distinctive style and elegance and properly engineered underpinnings'. Many original features remain; furniture is 'antique neo-classical'. The bedrooms are 'neat but darkish' (some have oak beams and antiques). The public rooms with their 'asymmetrically positioned artefacts' are liked. In the hotel's *Ristorante Arquade*, the chef, Bruno Barbieri, has a *Michelin* star. A wide lawn surrounds the large swimming pool, where there is a bar/gazebo. There is a terrace for outdoor dining, and a jogging track in the large grounds. The village has a museum devoted to the Walsers, an ancient religious order who speak a form of old German. (*Pat and Jeremy Temple*)

Open 14 Mar–5 Jan. Restaurant closed midday on Mon and Tues Mar/April, Nov/Dec. **Rooms** 4 suites, 18 double. Some on ground floor. Some no-smoking. Air conditioning. **Facilities** Salon, bar, tea room, restaurant with veranda (background music, pianist weekends); conference room; sauna, gym; terrace. 3.5-hectare grounds: garden, unheated swimming pool, jogging track; vineyards. Unsuitable for ♿. **Location** 7 km NW of Verona, 4 km W of San Pietro in Cariano. **Restriction** No smoking in public areas. **Credit cards** All major cards accepted. **Terms** [2004] B&B: double €245–€300, suite €345–€550. Set meals €65–€100; alc €60–€80.

PERGINE VALSUGANA 38057 Trento — Map 11:A4

Castel Pergine BUDGET
Via al Castello 10

Tel (0461) 531158
Fax (0461) 531329
Email verena@castelpergine.it
Website www.castelpergine.it

Above a small town (once a Roman settlement) east of Trento, this medieval castle stands in large wooded grounds: 'a marvellous setting'. For 13 years it has been a small hotel, much admired by *Guide* readers. 'It was hard to leave,' one couple wrote in 2004. Its owners are Verena Neff, Swiss, formerly a translator, and Theo Schneider, Austrian, an architect. 'Stunning; totally out of the ordinary', it is approached by a dramatic climb from the valley. Recent comments: 'No bells or mosquitoes disturb the peace.' 'We opened the creaky oak door and found ourselves in a large hall with strange sculptures.' 'Our small room had minimalist furnishing, a view over the Alps, an efficient shower.' 'Ours was splendidly Gothic.' Some bedrooms have solid wood furniture, carved or painted. The lounge/bar is the former throne room. The restaurant, in two 'regally decorated', candlelit medieval rooms, is popular with locals. Our reporters found it 'very good'. The large wine list includes many Trentino varieties at reasonable prices. The buffet breakfast, in the former throne room, includes ham, cheese, fruit juice. Guided tours of the castle, and exhibitions and concerts are held. A lake nearby offers water sports. (*Jannie and Ove Dam, and others*)

Open 24 Mar–7 Nov. Restaurant closed Mon midday. **Rooms** 17 double, 4 single. 14 with facilities *en suite*. 1 on ground floor. No TV. **Facilities** Lounge, TV room/library, bar, restaurant. No background music. Courtyard. Large garden. Unsuitable for ♿. **Restriction** No smoking in public areas. **Location** 2.5 km E of Pergine, 11 km E of Trento towards Padua. **Credit cards** Amex, MasterCard, Visa. **Terms** B&B €32–€51; D,B&B €48–€67. €5 supplement for 1-night stay. Set meals €30; alc from €37.

PERGO DI CORTONA 52040 Arezzo — Map 11:D4

Relais La Corte dei Papi
Via La Dogana 12

Tel (0575) 614109
Fax (0575) 614963
Email info@lacortedeipapi.com
Website www.lacortedeipapi.com

David Papi and his mother have turned their old stone farmhouse near Cortona into this 'small modern hotel with all amenities'. Their 'vision and warmth of welcome' were admired by a recent visitor. The style is 'rustic with discreet glamour': wooden beams, bare stone walls, terracotta tiled floors, big traditional pieces of furniture, spacious bathrooms. 'Most of the handsome bedrooms are in the main building, but our splendid doubles, with ample bed, were in fairy-tale cottages (former dwellings of pigs, cows or dogs) under trees in the grounds. Centrally heated in winter, they must be airily restful hiding places in summer.' Meals are served in a beamed dining room or on a terrace. 'The set menus are organised with originality around the vegetarian, the carnivorous or the fish-eating principle'. Local porcini mushrooms and truffles are used. 'Refined and delicious food served with unobtrusive attentiveness. Good and varied wine list. Elegant, modern table settings.' You need a car to explore this 'delightful borderland between Tuscany and Umbria'. The Papis offer guided tours, cooking classes and sporting activities. Weddings are often held by the swimming pool. (*ALL*)

Open All year. Restaurant open in summer to non-residents. **Rooms** 4 suites, 4 double. 3 on ground floor. Air conditioning. **Facilities** Lounge area, restaurant; 'live music on request'; function/wedding facilities. Garden: bar, outside dining; unheated swimming pool. **Location** 6 km SE of Cortona. **Restrictions** No smoking: public areas, some bedrooms. **Credit cards** All major cards accepted. **Terms** B&B: single €135, double €135–€180, suite €180–€230. Full alc €35. *V*

PIETRASANTA 55045 Lucca — Map 11:C3

Albergo Pietrasanta NEW
Via Garibaldi 35

Tel (0584) 793726
Fax (0584) 793728
Email a.pietrasanta@versilia.toscana.it
Website albergopietrasanta.com

This small town (famous for its marble sculptures), with wooded hills behind and sea stretching out in front, is a 30-minute train ride north of Lucca. In a pedestrianised street, the 16th-century Barsanti-Bonetti palace has been turned into this elegant hotel. 'It has high, ornate ceilings, much *trompe l'œil*, antiques, contemporary art works and huge flower displays,' says the 2004 nominator. 'What it lacks in views it makes up for in all-round quality. Excellent management; highly efficient, bilingual receptionists; every member of staff was caring and courteous. Very good breakfast in large conservatory. Smallish, gravelled courtyard garden with two huge palm trees and much birdsong. Wide Versilia beach ten minutes by taxi.' The bedrooms have antiques and a complimentary decanter of Vino Santo;

some have frescoes. 'Our room, one of the cheapest, though near a lift, was quiet.' No restaurant: light meals are served, and advice is given about local eating places. (*Bev Adams*)

Open All year, except 21 Nov–26 Dec. **Rooms** 7 suites, 11 double, 1 single. Air conditioning. **Facilities** Lifts. Lounges, bar, breakfast room, conservatory; background music; conference room; gym, Turkish bath. Courtyard. Sea 2 km. **Location** Historic centre, near cathedral. 25 km N of Pisa. Garage. **Restriction** No smoking. **Credit cards** All major cards accepted. **Terms** [2004] B&B: single €170–€270, double €300–€420, suite €420–€740.

PISTOIA 51030 — Map 11:C4

Villa Vannini BUDGET
Via Villa 6

Tel (0573) 42031
Fax (0573) 42551
Email info@volpe-uva.it
Website www.volpe-uva.it

On a hill, in large grounds with ancient trees, this 'delightful' yellow-walled villa stands high above this medieval city between Florence and Lucca. It is now run by the Bordonaro family, Marta, Francesca and Luigi (the 87-year-old owner, Maria Vannini, lives in one of the cottages). 'They are friendly, considerate and delightful,' say visitors this year. Others add: 'They achieve that difficult balance between professionalism and an unobtrusive interest in their guests.' The 'wonderful family atmosphere' is liked. 'Our huge room had an anteroom, and a nice view down the valley.' 'A lovely bedroom, elegantly furnished.' 'Superb dinner (a no-choice set menu); delicious Tuscan wine.' 'Good breakfast', in a pretty pink room. There are nooks and crannies to sit in, a 'homely sitting room', a pleasant terrace for drinks and meals. The approach road is narrow and winding: 'Try to arrive by day.' 'The best overall value of the eight hotels we visited,' was one recent plaudit. (*Sam and Philippa Price, NR*)

Open All year. **Rooms** 7 double, 1 single. Some no-smoking. **Facilities** Salon with TV, reading room, smoking room, restaurant; background music. Garden: terrace. Unsuitable for ♿. **Location** 6 km N of Pistoia. From A11 follow signs to Abetone/Modena, then San Felice/Villa di Piteccio. **Restriction** No smoking in public areas. **Credit cards** Amex, MasterCard, Visa. **Terms** B&B: single €45–€60, double €70–€90. Set dinner €40.

POGGIO CATINO 04049 Rieti — Map 11:E5

Borgo Paraelios
Località Valle Collicchia

Tel (0765) 26267
Fax (0765) 26268
Email info@borgoparaelios.it
Website www.borgoparaelios.it

'A really good hotel,' say recent visitors. Regulars add: 'It offers tranquillity and a real feeling of being cosseted by long-serving staff.' Though in the remote hills of Sabina, it is easily reached by minibus from Rome (40 minutes). A Relais & Châteaux member, owned by Adolfo and Andrea Salabé, it is laid out in country club style amid gardens, orchards and terraces. It has many sporting facilities (see below). The rooms, all different, have floral fabrics, antiques and a small terrace; some are in chalets. 'Superbly comfortable beds.' Bathrooms are smart: 'Huge hand basin; corner bath.' 'Services and facilities are excellent.' The public areas are 'sumptuously furnished'; Old Master paintings hang on walls. The billiard room is 'great fun'. Meals are served in a 'lovely vaulted room with tapestries and frescoes' or on terraces. 'The daily-changing menus have been replaced by a seasonal *carte* plus a three-course meal that changes daily. The food is comforting, no aspiration to greatness, but good ingredients', but in 2004, 'unfortunately it was accompanied by the sounds of Richard Clayderman'. As an alternative, you could eat at *Il Poggetto*, 'good, friendly and cheap', in Poggio Mirteto. 'Breakfast is good, but at these prices they should not charge extra for a boiled egg.' There is 'a good selection of light lunches'. (*MB and RC, David and Kate Wooff*)

Open All year. Restaurant closed Tues. **Rooms** 18 double. Air conditioning. **Facilities** Lounge, TV room, breakfast room, restaurant; games room; indoor swimming pool, Turkish bath, sauna; conference facilities; beauty centre; gym. Large grounds: garden, chapel, swimming pool, tennis (all-weather), bowls, 9-hole golf course. Unsuitable for ♿. **Location** 4 km N of Poggio Mirteto. From A1, exit Ponzano/Soratte, go 3 km towards Poggio Mirteto, right on to SS657 for 6 km, left on to SS313 towards Cantalupo, left at T-junction. Parking. **Restrictions** No smoking in public areas. No dogs. **Credit cards** All major cards accepted. **Terms** B&B: single €190–€220, double €280–€300. Alc €75.

PONTEDERA 56025 Pisa — Map 11:C3

Hotel Armonia NEW
Piazza Caduti Divisione Acqui
Cefalonia e Corfù 11

Tel (0587) 278511
Fax (0587 278540
Email reception@hotelarmonia.it
Website www.hotelarmonia.it

In this 'pleasant little town with upmarket shops in a pedestrian zone', this B&B hotel, managed by Claudio Andolfi, stands on the main piazza, near the *duomo*. 'The 19th-century cream-painted *palazzo* has been refurbished to a high standard,' says our inspector. 'Lots of marble, antique furniture and paintings. Bedrooms, though fairly small, are well designed, decorated in excellent taste. Breakfast is the usual Italian buffet (sweet rolls, bread, hard-boiled eggs, cheese, etc); cooked items may be ordered for a supplement. Reception is welcoming, all staff are warm and helpful.' Functions are often held. For meals, *Il Forlì*, a fish restaurant, is recommended, and plenty of other eating places are within walking distance.

Open All year. **Rooms** 4 suites, 23 double. Some on ground floor. Air conditioning. **Facilities** Drawing rooms, reading room, TV room, bar; background music; banqueting/function facilities. **Location** Main square. 25 km from Florence, off SuperStrada to Pisa. Public parking (free on Sun). **Restriction** No smoking in public areas. **Credit cards** All major cards accepted. **Terms** [2004] B&B: single €120, double €150.

PORTONOVO 60020 Ancona — Map 11:C5

Hotel Emilia
Collina di Portonovo 149

Tel (071) 801145
Fax (071) 801330
Email info@hotelemilia.com
Website www.hotelemilia.com

In the Conero Park, in a protected area of great natural beauty near Ancona in the Marche, this large white building was constructed in 1964 by Elia Dubbini and Lamberto Fiorini to house their collection of contemporary art. Now it is a smart hotel run by Raffaella Fiorini (third generation), which visitors in 2004 found 'delightful'. It stands alone on a natural terrace above the sea, amid broom, oaks and lavender fields. In front, a sheer gorse-topped cliff towers above a bay: 'stunning views of sea and coast'. There is an Olympic-sized swimming pool in the 'spacious and attractive' garden, and the poolside bar serves fish dishes that are 'simpler than, but almost as delicious as, those in the main restaurant'. Wine comes from the family's vineyard. 'Our room was plain and of adequate size, but the lighting was poor,' says this year's report. A 'friendly, readily available' *navette* takes guests down to the 'not very appealing' rocky beach. Six electric bicycles are available for guests' use. Alfresco jazz concerts are held in summer. (*Jane and Patrick Gibbs*)

Open 7 Feb–22 Dec. Restaurant closed Oct–Apr, Sun night/Mon midday. **Rooms** 4 suites, 24 double, 2 single. Some suitable for ♿. Air conditioning. **Facilities** Lift. Lounge, TV room, bar, restaurant; background music. Garden: swimming pool, gazebo bar, tennis, golf practice; shuttle to beach (1.5 km). **Location** 12 km SE of Ancona. Parking. **Restrictions** No smoking. No dogs. **Credit cards** All major cards accepted. **Terms** [2004] B&B €75–€200; D,B&B (min. 3 days; obligatory 1 week Aug) €110–€225. Full alc €60.

POSITANO 84017 Salerno — Map 12:B3

Hotel Marincanto NEW
Via Colombo 50

Tel (089) 875130
Fax (089) 875595
Email hotelmarincanto@italyby.com
Website www.italyby.com/marincanto

'Wholeheartedly recommended' in 2004: elegant four-star B&B hotel on six floors, with lovely terraces, splendid views ('even from bathrooms'), high above sea (300 steps down to lovely Incanto beach). 'Charming staff.' Bar, meeting room. Air conditioning. Pets welcome. Paid parking. Open Apr–early Nov. All major credit cards accepted. No smoking in public areas. 25 bedrooms, 'light and airy', all sea-facing, some with balcony, some with spa bath, some no-smoking, some with Internet connection. B&B double €195–€275 [2004].

> Inevitably, some hotels change hands or close after we have gone to press. Please check the ownership when booking, particularly in the case of small places.

Hotel Villa Franca
Via Pasitea 318

Tel (089) 875655
Fax (089) 875735
Email info@villafrancahotel.it
Website www.villafrancahotel.it

The Russo family's 'elegant modern hotel', on Positano's steep hill, is a converted villa, well restored, with stone from Vesuvius and lacquered terracotta vases, in a mainly white decor. Public rooms and most bedrooms look down over the picturesque village and coast. On the panoramic roof terrace is 'the best pool in Positano', said the nominators. 'Our deluxe room was wholly mirrored and tiled, very attractive, not in the least naff. It had a small balcony with table and chairs and a dazzling view over the sea. Its perfectly equipped bathroom had a spa bath.' The restaurant, *Li Galli*, serves 'traditional dishes of the family'. There is a 'wellness centre', with sauna, gym, etc. A free bus 'goes vertically up and down from the town centre' several times a day. There is valet parking ('expensive, but necessary'). (*CH and CE*)

Open 1 Apr–31 Oct. **Rooms** 35 double. 9 in annexe. **Facilities** Restaurant, roof terrace: small unheated swimming pool; wellness centre. No background music. Unsuitable for ♿. **Location** 900 m from centre/beach. Valet parking (€18). **Restriction** No smoking in public areas. **Credit cards** All major cards accepted. **Terms** [2004] B&B double €190–€340; D,B&B €40 added per person.

RADDA IN CHIANTI 53017 Siena — Map 11:D4

Relais Vignale
Via Pianigiani 8

Tel (0577) 738300
Fax (0577) 738592
Email vignale@vignale.it
Website www.vignale.it

'Efficiently run', by its long-serving manager, Silvia Kummer, and 'with a warm welcome, excellent staff, good value', this cluster of old buildings, formerly known as *Fattoria Vignale*, stands in the Chianti hills between Siena and Florence. 'We thoroughly enjoyed our stay for its comfort and the life across the road in Radda,' wrote visitors this year. Behind the sober facade is a 'wonderful interior'. Earlier guests wrote: 'Very good public rooms. Pool and terrace ideal with great views.' Many bedrooms share the views. One couple had 'a terrific room', with small sitting area, large bathroom and view of the well in the courtyard. Others wrote: 'Though near the road, our annexe suite, reached via a zebra crossing, was quiet at night.' Some rooms are small. Some have a small balcony. The *taverna* serves traditional Tuscan food in a cellar or under a pergola on a 'delightful' panoramic terrace, or you can eat at the associated *Ristorante Vignale*, 200 metres away (it has a new chef this year). Breakfast has 'lovely breads'; 'extras requested were brought without charge (including fresh-pressed orange juice)'. In the 18th century, this was a wine-producing estate, and you can buy home-produced wine, olive oil and vinegar. (*Simon and Sally Small, and others*)

Open 19 Mar–11 Dec, 26 Dec–6 Jan. Restaurant closed Thurs, *taverna* closed Wed. **Rooms** 5 suites (2 by pool), 34 double, 3 single. 10 in annexe across street. Air conditioning. **Facilities** 3 lounges, bar, TV room/library, 2 breakfast rooms, *taverna*, terrace (outdoor meals), restaurant; conference room; chapel. No background music. Garden: heated swimming pool. Unsuitable for ♿. **Location** Edge of village. 45 km S of Florence, 33 km N of Siena. Street-facing windows double glazed. Parking. **Restrictions** No smoking: public areas, some bedrooms. No dogs. **Credit cards** All major cards accepted. **Terms** B&B: single €130–€150, double €165–€320, suite €350–€380. Full alc €40 (*taverna*), €60 (restaurant).

RANCO 21020 Varese — Map 11:B2

Il Sole di Ranco
Piazza Venezia 5

Tel (0331) 976507
Fax (0331) 976620
Email ivanett@tin.it
Website www.ilsolediranco.it

Run by the Brovelli family owners since 1850 when it was a simple inn, this smart restaurant-with-rooms (Relais & Châteaux) has a 'beautiful, tranquil' setting on the eastern shore of Lake Maggiore. Named for its sunny position, it is popular with wealthy Milanese. Pretty gardens slope to a lakeside promenade, and in May and June the air is scented by flowering lime trees. Visitors praise the 'warm welcome' and 'first-class staff'. One couple had a 'very fine suite with lake view'; another enjoyed a 'cool and spacious' room with balcony, spa bath and complimentary almond liqueur. In an elegant dining room, or on a vine-covered terrace, Carlo Brovelli, with son Davide, serves 'delicious meals' (*Michelin* star), eg, lobster salad perfumed with orange; breaded lamb with hazelnuts and pistachios. His wife, Itala, runs a *bottega*, selling home-made conserves, etc. A heated outdoor swimming pool is due to open this year. Help is given with tickets for La Scala.

Open 1 Feb–1 Nov. Restaurant closed Mon/Tues, except Mon night off-season. **Rooms** 10 suites, 4 double. In 2 buildings. 1 suitable for ♿. Air conditioning. **Facilities** Lift. Lounge, bar, restaurant; classical background music; function room. Park: terrace (meal service), garden: heated swimming pool; access to lake, fishing. **Location** 45 km NW of Milan. A8 exit Sesto Calende, direction Angera. Secure parking. **Restrictions** No smoking in public areas. No dogs. **Credit cards** All major cards accepted. **Terms** B&B: single €166, double €180, suite from €232; D,B&B €154–€206 per person. Set meals €85–€100; full alc €70–€90.

RAVELLO 84010 Salerno — Map 12:A3

Palazzo Sasso
Via San Giovanni del Toro 28

Tel (089) 818181
Fax (089) 858900
Email info@palazzosasso.com
Website www.palazzosasso.com

High on a cliff, the pink 12th-century palace of the Sasso family, now a 'very fine hotel', has 'spellbinding views' from its terrace over the Amalfi coast. A combination of medieval, baroque and Arabian architecture, it stands in 'delightful', large, sloping, subtropical gardens with 'plenty of shady/sunny spots to relax in'. The manager, Stefano Gegnacorsi, holds a weekly cocktail party for guests: 'Very nice,' said a visitor who returned in 2004. The 'relaxing atmosphere' and 'helpful staff' are praised. The bedrooms, with sea or mountain view, are 'beautifully furnished'. 'Our big room had a lovely balcony.' 'Huge bed, top-quality linens, supremely comfortable.' Many bathrooms have a spa bath. Breakfast has a huge buffet, and you can order cooked dishes and champagne. Light meals and drinks are served in the *Caffè dell'Arte*. The restaurant, *Rossellinis* (*Michelin* star for chef Pino Lavarra, who has worked with Raymond Blanc), is mostly admired. The 'stunning' swimming pool has a window, allowing underwater swimmers to enjoy the view. If you arrive by car, 'park in the square by the church of San Giovanni del Toro, and call Reception – the road beyond is narrow'. (*Wendy Ashworth, and others*)

Open 1 Mar–31 Oct. *Rossellinis* closed midday. **Rooms** 8 suites, 35 double. 1 suitable for ♿. Air conditioning. Internet access (€4 a day). **Facilities** Lift. Library, café, bar (pianist nightly), 2 restaurants (1 for light lunches); mixed background music; conference/banqueting facilities. Garden: terraces, heated swimming pool; sun deck: 2 hydromassage plunge pools. **Location** 300 m beyond square: entry on left *before* 2nd arch. Garage: pre-book (€25). **Restriction** No smoking in public areas. **Credit cards** All major cards accepted. **Terms** [2004] B&B: single/double €200–€600, suite €575–€1,350. Alc €75–€115.

RAVENNA 48100 **Map 11:C4**

Hotel Bisanzio
Via Salara 30

Tel (0544) 217111
Fax (0544) 32539
Email info@bisanziohotel.com
Website www.bisanziohotel.com

In historic centre, near Basilica of San Vitale (famous Byzantine mosaics): Donatella Fabbri's pleasant Art Deco-style B&B hotel (Best Western), with marble, columns, chandeliers. Lounge/bar, breakfast room; background music; meeting room. Air conditioning. Small garden. Unsuitable for ♿, 'but obliging staff help those with lesser disabilities'. 'Excellent breakfasts.' Public parking 40 m (special rates). No smoking: public areas, some bedrooms. All major credit cards accepted. 38 bedrooms (some large, with sitting area; 8 no-smoking). B&B: single €92–€106, double €114–€170.

RIVA DI SOLTO 24060 Bergamo **Map 11:B3**

Hotel Miranda NEW/BUDGET
Via Cornello 8

Tel (035) 986021
Fax (035) 980055
Email info@albergomiranda.it
Website www.albergomiranda.it

On a hillside above *Lago d'Iseo*, one of the smallest of the Italian lakes, stands the Polini family's small modern hotel. Easily reached from Bergamo and Milan airports, it 'offers a warm welcome', says a 2004 visitor. The bedrooms, 'though not lavish, offer a good standard

Europe maps

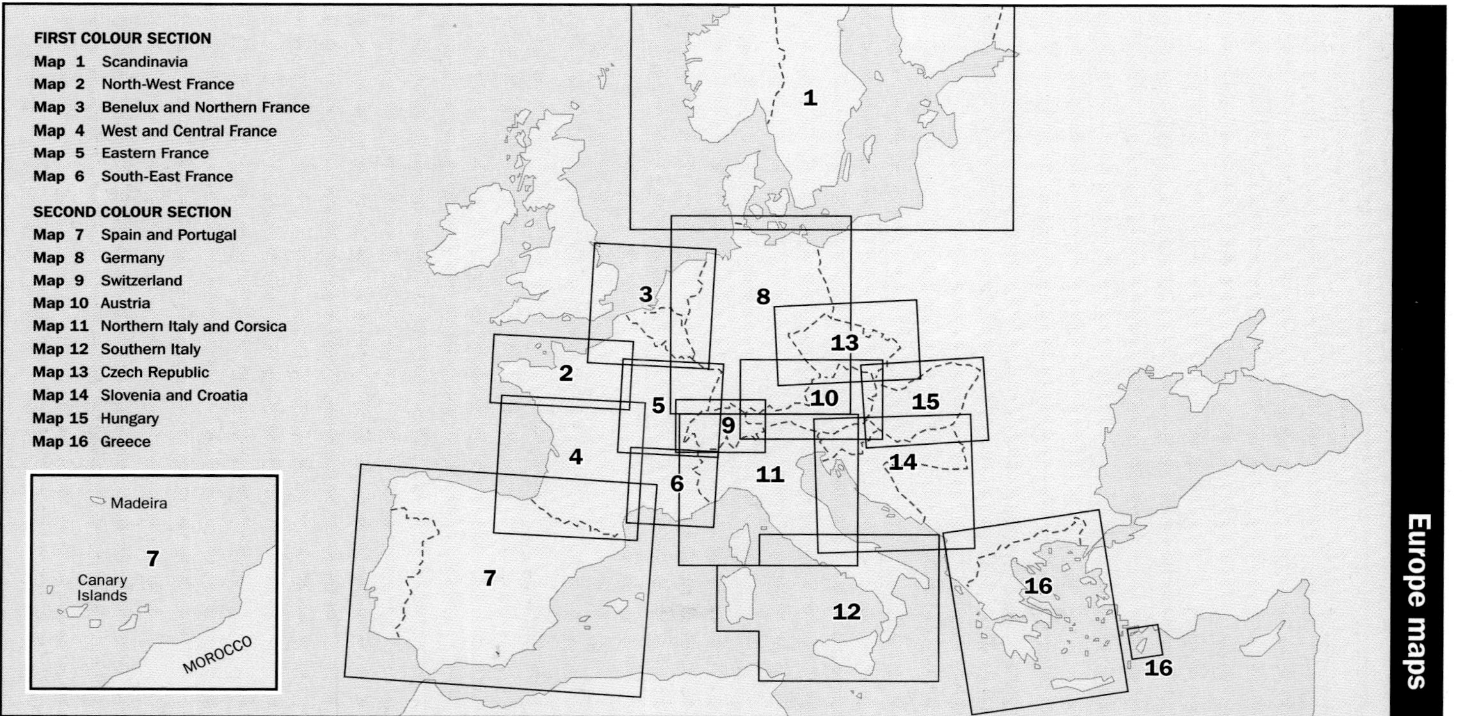
FIRST COLOUR SECTION
Map 1 Scandinavia
Map 2 North-West France
Map 3 Benelux and Northern France
Map 4 West and Central France
Map 5 Eastern France
Map 6 South-East France
SECOND COLOUR SECTION
Map 7 Spain and Portugal
Map 8 Germany
Map 9 Switzerland
Map 10 Austria
Map 11 Northern Italy and Corsica
Map 12 Southern Italy
Map 13 Czech Republic
Map 14 Slovenia and Croatia
Map 15 Hungary
Map 16 Greece
Madeira
7
Canary Islands
MOROCCO
1
2
3
4
5
6
7
8
9
10
11
12
13
14
15
16
16

7 Spain and Portugal

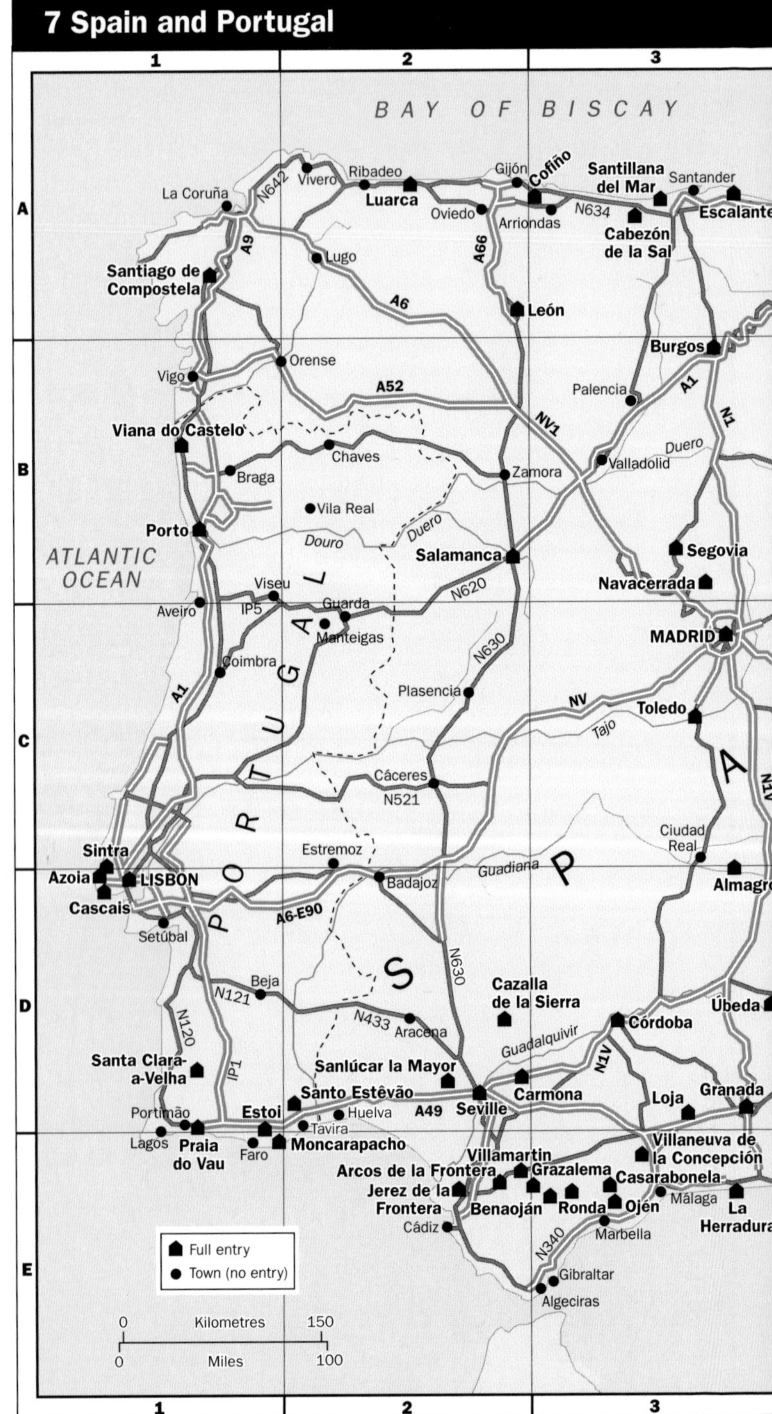

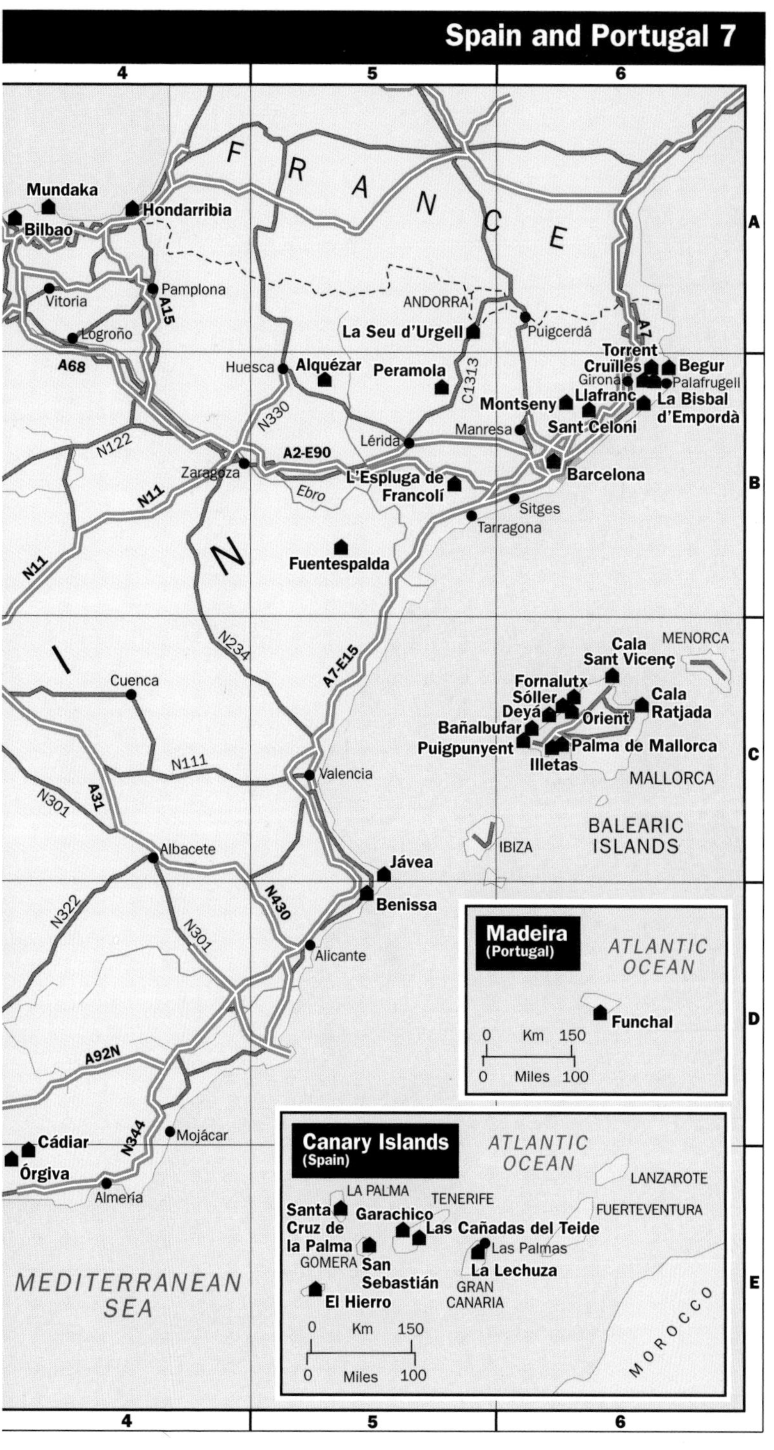

4
5
6
A
B
C
D
E
F R A N C E
S P A I N
Mundaka
Bilbao
Hondarribia
Pamplona
Vitoria
Logroño
A15
A68
ANDORRA
La Seu d'Urgell
Puigcerdá
A7
Torrent
Cruïlles
Begur
Girona
Palafrugell
Llafranc
La Bisbal d'Empordà
Montseny
Sant Celoni
Huesca
Alquézar
Peramola
C1313
N330
Manresa
Lérida
N122
A2-E90
Zaragoza
Barcelona
L'Espluga de Francolí
Ebro
N11
Sitges
Tarragona
Fuentespalda
N234
A7-E15
MENORCA
Cala Sant Vicenç
Fornalutx
Sóller
Cala Ratjada
Deyá
Orient
Bañalbufar
Puigpunyent
Palma de Mallorca
Illetas
MALLORCA
Cuenca
N111
Valencia
N301
A31
IBIZA
BALEARIC ISLANDS
Albacete
Jávea
Benissa
N430
N322
Alicante
Madeira
(Portugal)
ATLANTIC OCEAN
Funchal
0 Km 150
0 Miles 100
A92N
N344
Mojácar
Cádiar
Órgiva
Almería
Canary Islands
(Spain)
ATLANTIC OCEAN
LANZAROTE
LA PALMA
TENERIFE
FUERTEVENTURA
Santa Cruz de la Palma
Garachico
Las Cañadas del Teide
Las Palmas
GOMERA
San Sebastián
La Lechuza
GRAN CANARIA
El Hierro
MEDITERRANEAN SEA
MOROCCO
0 Km 150
0 Miles 100

8 Germany

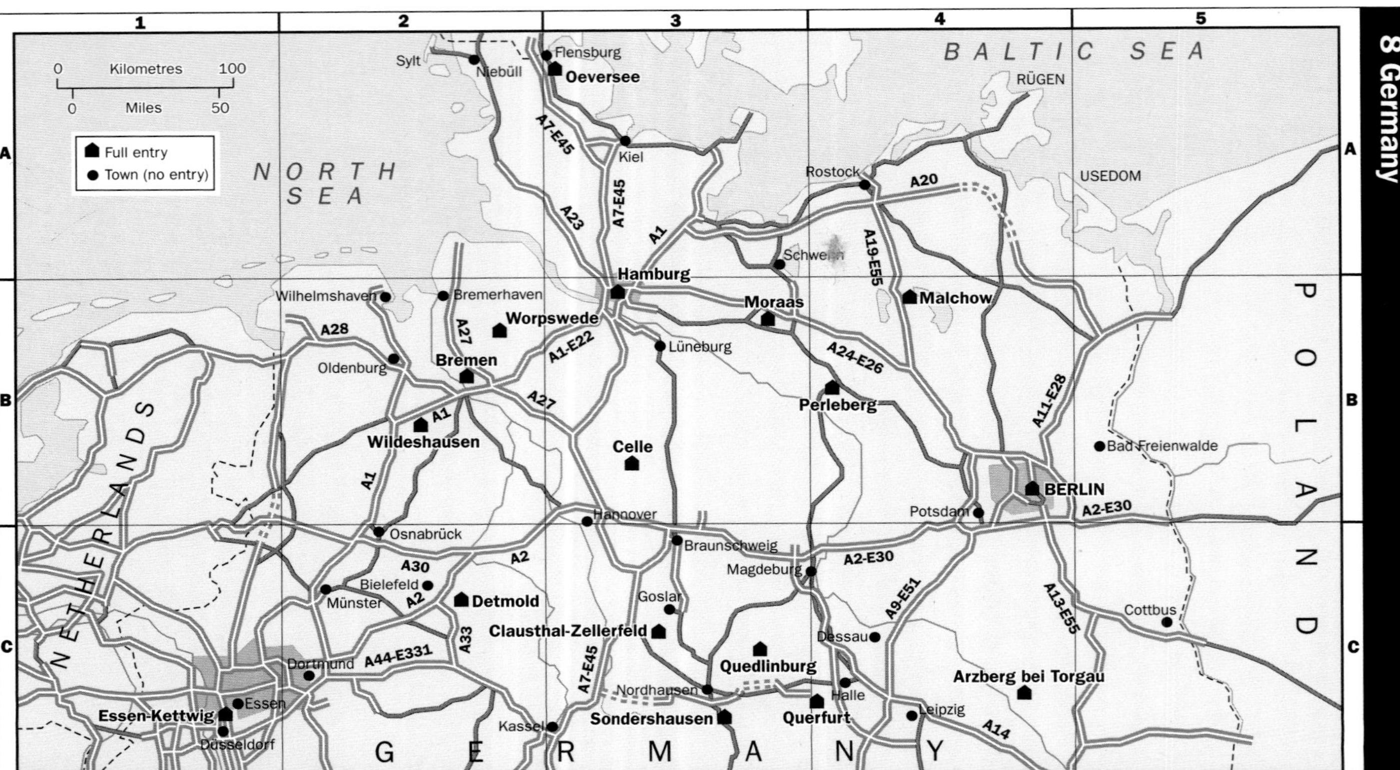
1
2
3
4
5
A
B
C
0
Kilometres
100
0
Miles
50
Full entry
Town (no entry)
NORTH SEA
BALTIC SEA
RÜGEN
USEDOM
POLAND
NETHERLANDS
GERMANY
Sylt
Niebüll
Flensburg
Oeversee
Kiel
Rostock
Schwerin
Hamburg
Moraas
Malchow
Wilhelmshaven
Bremerhaven
Worpswede
Oldenburg
Bremen
Lüneburg
Perleberg
Wildeshausen
Celle
Bad Freienwalde
BERLIN
Potsdam
Hannover
Osnabrück
Braunschweig
Magdeburg
Bielefeld
Münster
Detmold
Goslar
Clausthal-Zellerfeld
Dessau
Cottbus
Quedlinburg
Dortmund
Nordhausen
Halle
Arzberg bei Torgau
Essen
Essen-Kettwig
Düsseldorf
Kassel
Sondershausen
Querfurt
Leipzig
A7-E45
A23
A1
A20
A19-E55
A28
A27
A1-E22
A24-E26
A11-E28
A2-E30
A30
A2
A9-E51
A13-E55
A33
A44-E331
A14

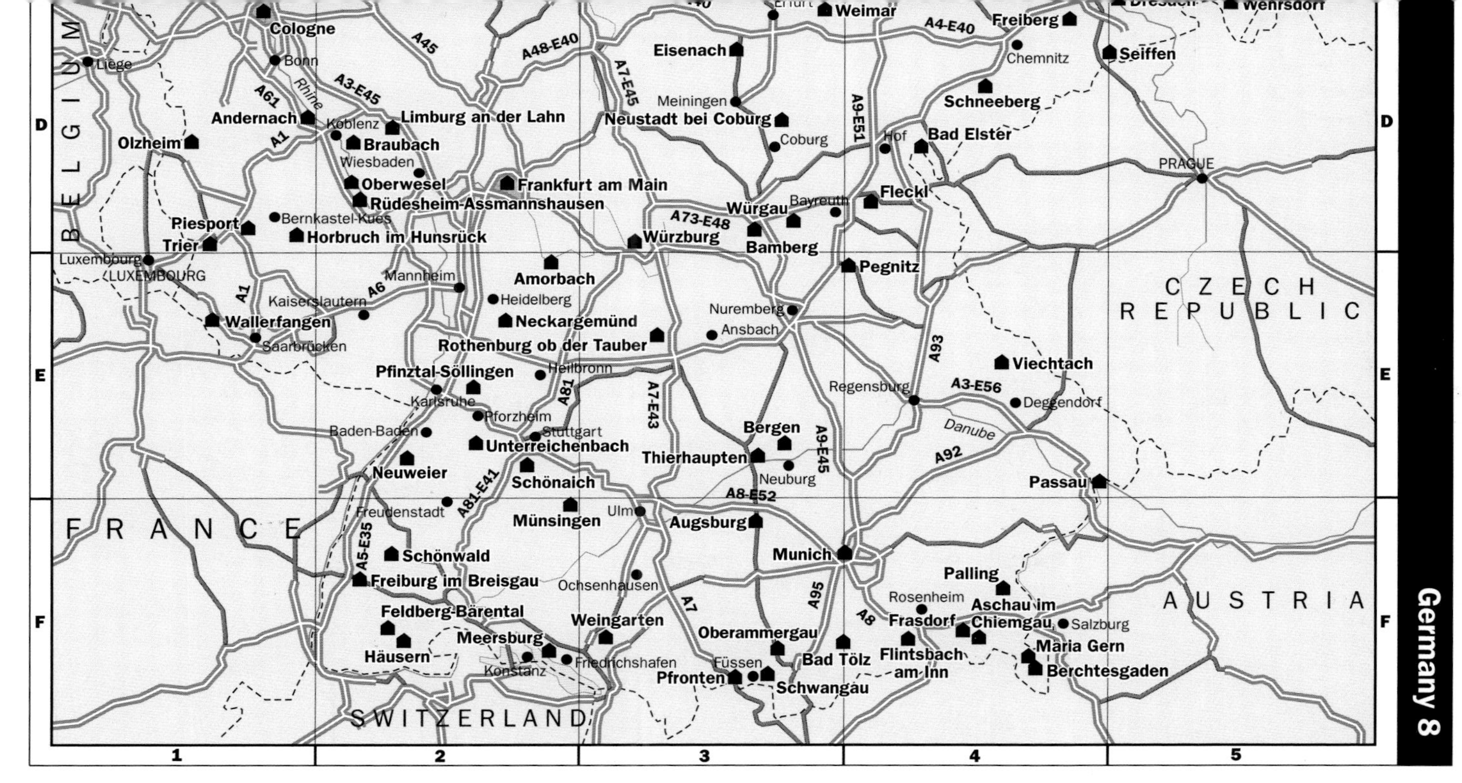
BELGIUM
FRANCE
LUXEMBOURG
SWITZERLAND
AUSTRIA
CZECH REPUBLIC
Cologne
Bonn
Liège
Olzheim
Andernach
Koblenz
Braubach
Limburg an der Lahn
Wiesbaden
Oberwesel
Rüdesheim-Assmannshausen
Bernkastel-Kues
Horbruch im Hunsrück
Piesport
Trier
Luxembourg
Kaiserslautern
Saarbrücken
Wallerfangen
Mannheim
Heidelberg
Neckargemünd
Amorbach
Frankfurt am Main
Eisenach
Meiningen
Neustadt bei Coburg
Coburg
Würzburg
Würgau
Bamberg
Bayreuth
Pegnitz
Nuremberg
Ansbach
Rothenburg ob der Tauber
Heilbronn
Stuttgart
Pforzheim
Karlsruhe
Pfinztal-Söllingen
Baden-Baden
Neuweier
Unterreichenbach
Schönaich
Freudenstadt
Schönwald
Freiburg im Breisgau
Feldberg-Bärental
Häusern
Meersburg
Konstanz
Friedrichshafen
Weingarten
Ochsenhausen
Münsingen
Ulm
Augsburg
Thierhaupten
Bergen
Neuburg
Regensburg
Deggendorf
Viechtach
Passau
Munich
Oberammergau
Füssen
Pfronten
Schwangau
Bad Tölz
Flintsbach am Inn
Rosenheim
Frasdorf
Palling
Aschau im Chiemgau
Maria Gern
Berchtesgaden
Salzburg
Hof
Fleckl
Bad Elster
Schneeberg
Chemnitz
Freiberg
Seiffen
Weimar
PRAGUE
Danube
Rhine
A1
A3-E45
A3-E56
A4-E40
A5-E35
A6
A7
A7-E43
A7-E45
A8
A8-E52
A9-E45
A9-E51
A45
A48-E40
A61
A73-E48
A81
A81-E41
A92
A93
A95
D
E
F
1
2
3
4
5

9 Switzerland

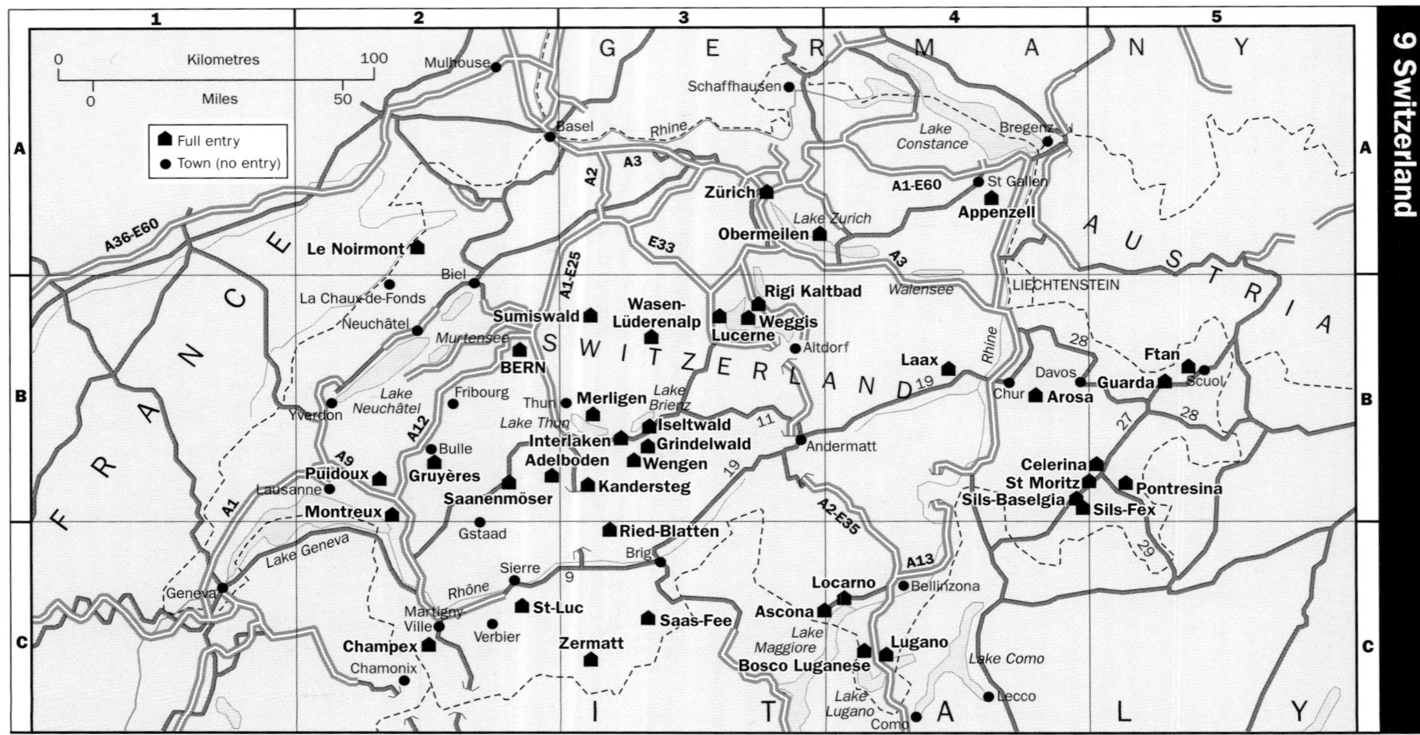

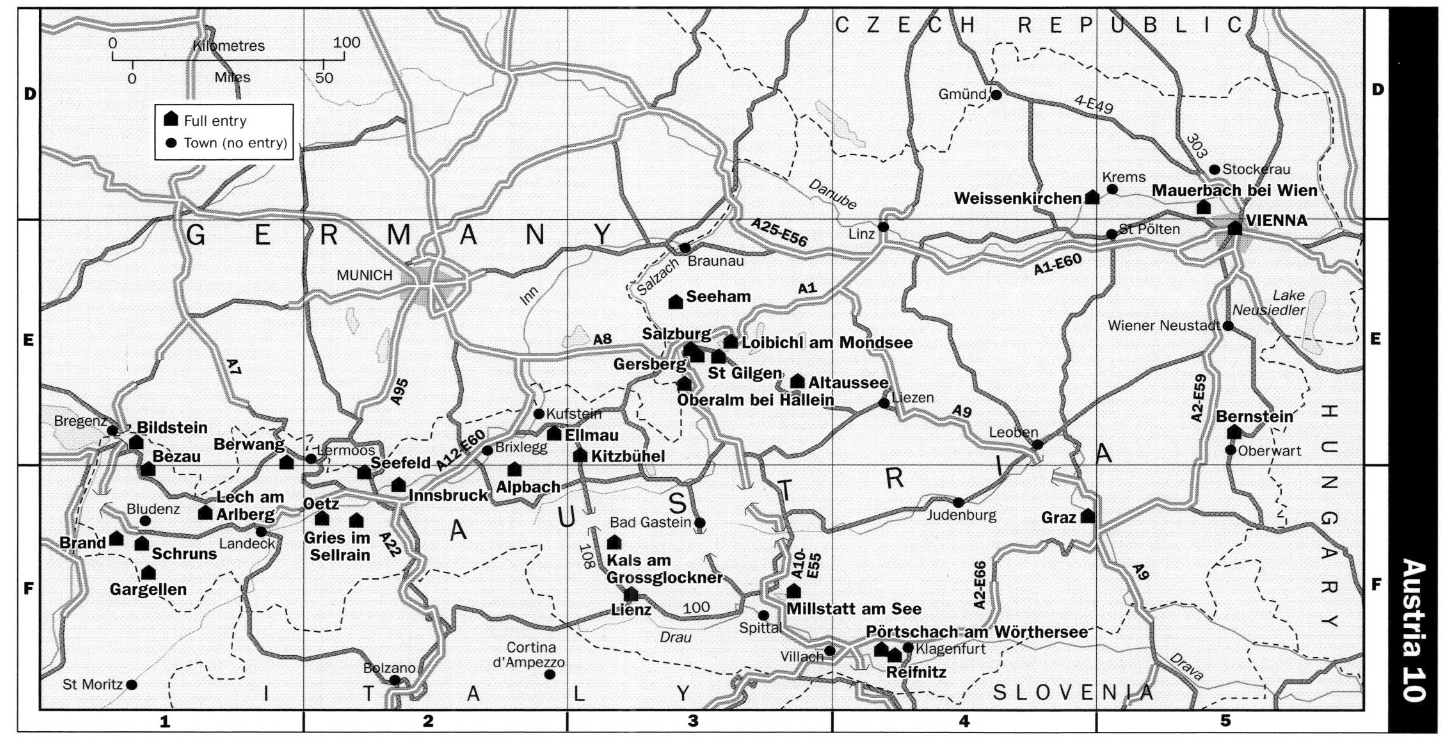
Kilometres 0 100
Miles 0 50
Full entry
Town (no entry)
CZECH REPUBLIC
GERMANY
AUSTRIA
HUNGARY
SLOVENIA
ITALY
Gmünd
4-E49
303
Krems
Stockerau
Weissenkirchen
Mauerbach bei Wien
VIENNA
St Pölten
Danube
Linz
A25-E56
Braunau
Salzach
MUNICH
Inn
A1-E60
A1
Seeham
Lake Neusiedler
Wiener Neustadt
A8
Salzburg
Loibichl am Mondsee
Gersberg
St Gilgen
Altaussee
Oberalm bei Hallein
Liezen
A9
A7
A95
A2-E59
Bernstein
Oberwart
Leoben
Bregenz
Bildstein
Berwang
Kufstein
Ellmau
Bezau
Lermoos
Seefeld
A12-E60
Brixlegg
Kitzbühel
Alpbach
Innsbruck
Lech am Arlberg
Oetz
Bludenz
Gries im Sellrain
Landeck
A22
Brand
Schruns
Gargellen
Bad Gastein
108
Kals am Grossglockner
Lienz
100
A10-E55
Millstatt am See
Spittal
Judenburg
Graz
A2-E66
Pörtschach am Wörthersee
Klagenfurt
Villach
Reifnitz
Drau
Drava
Cortina d'Ampezzo
Bolzano
St Moritz

11 Northern Italy and Corsica

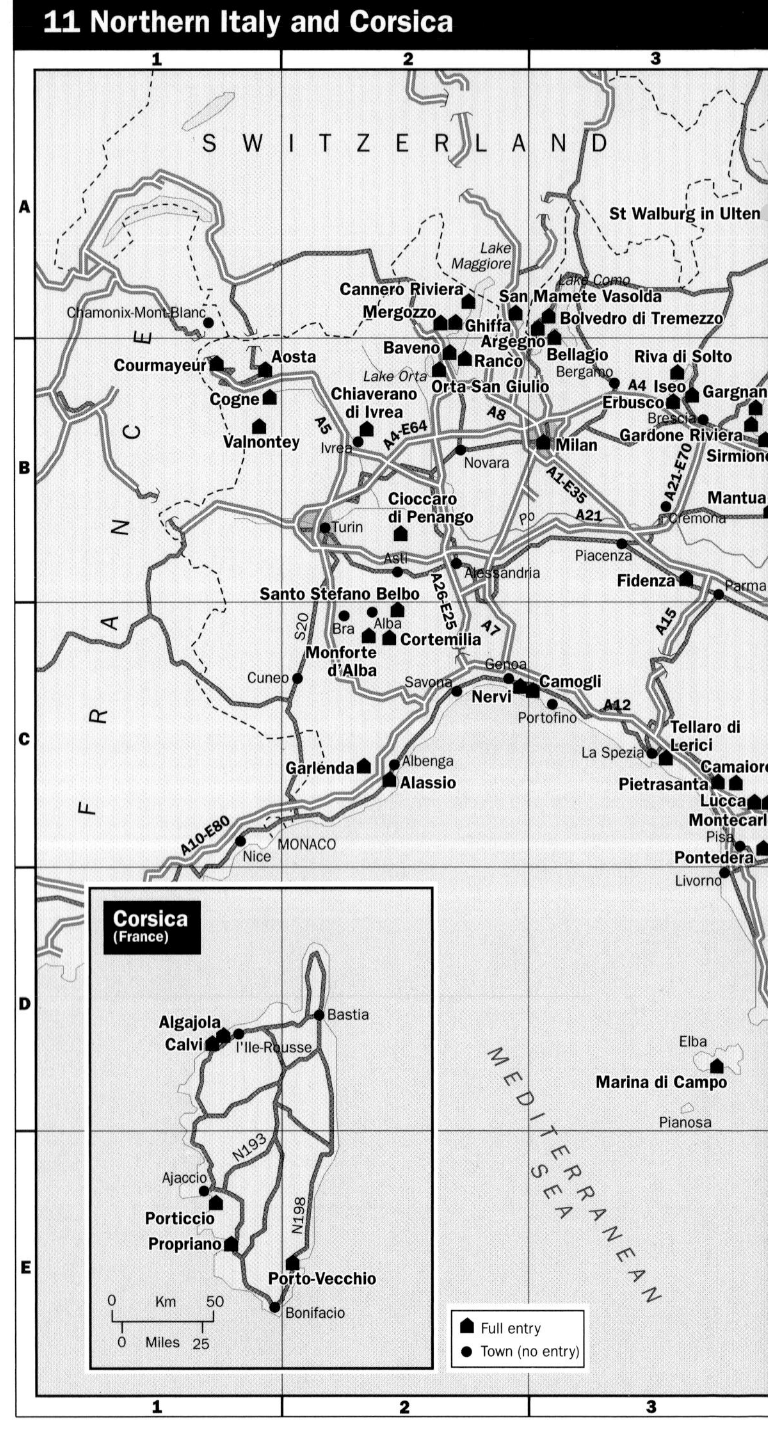

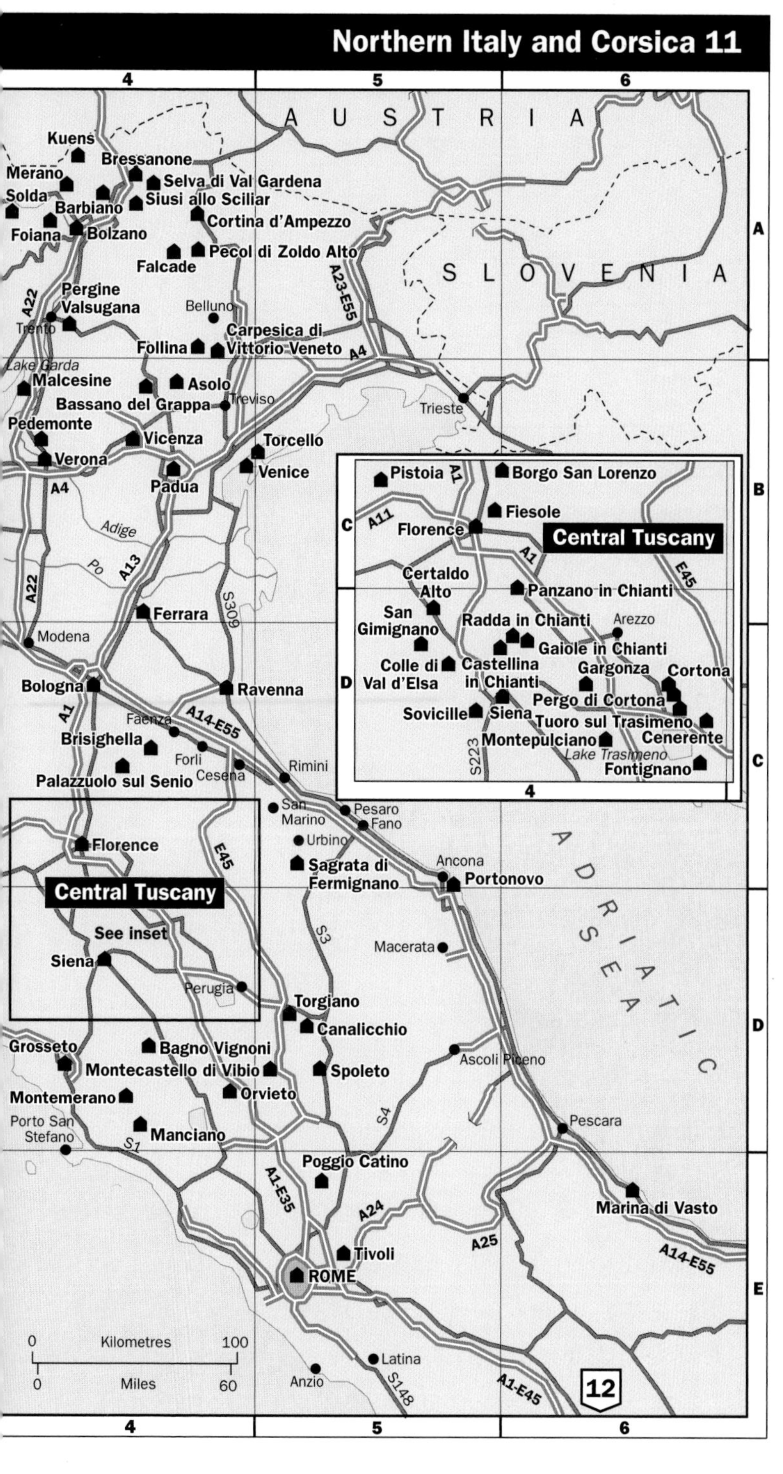
AUSTRIA
SLOVENIA
ADRIATIC SEA
Kuens
Bressanone
Merano
Selva di Val Gardena
Solda
Siusi allo Sciliar
Barbiano
Cortina d'Ampezzo
Foiana
Bolzano
Pecol di Zoldo Alto
Falcade
Pergine Valsugana
Belluno
Trento
Carpesica di Vittorio Veneto
Follina
Lake Garda
Malcesine
Asolo
Bassano del Grappa
Treviso
Trieste
Pedemonte
Vicenza
Torcello
Verona
Venice
Padua
Adige
Po
Ferrara
Modena
Bologna
Ravenna
Faenza
Brisighella
Forlì
Cesena
Rimini
Palazzuolo sul Senio
San Marino
Pesaro
Fano
Urbino
Florence
Sagrata di Fermignano
Ancona
Portonovo
Central Tuscany
See inset
Siena
Macerata
Perugia
Torgiano
Canalicchio
Grosseto
Bagno Vignoni
Montecastello di Vibio
Spoleto
Ascoli Piceno
Orvieto
Montemerano
Porto San Stefano
Manciano
Pescara
Poggio Catino
Marina di Vasto
Tivoli
ROME
Latina
Anzio
Kilometres 0 100
Miles 0 60
12
Central Tuscany
Pistoia
Borgo San Lorenzo
Fiesole
Florence
Certaldo Alto
Panzano in Chianti
San Gimignano
Radda in Chianti
Arezzo
Gaiole in Chianti
Colle di Val d'Elsa
Castellina in Chianti
Gargonza
Cortona
Pergo di Cortona
Sovicille
Siena
Tuoro sul Trasimeno
Montepulciano
Cenerente
Lake Trasimeno
Fontignano
A22
A23-E55
A4
A13
S309
A1
A14-E55
E45
S3
S4
S1
A1-E35
A24
A25
A1-E45
S148
A11
S223

12 Southern Italy

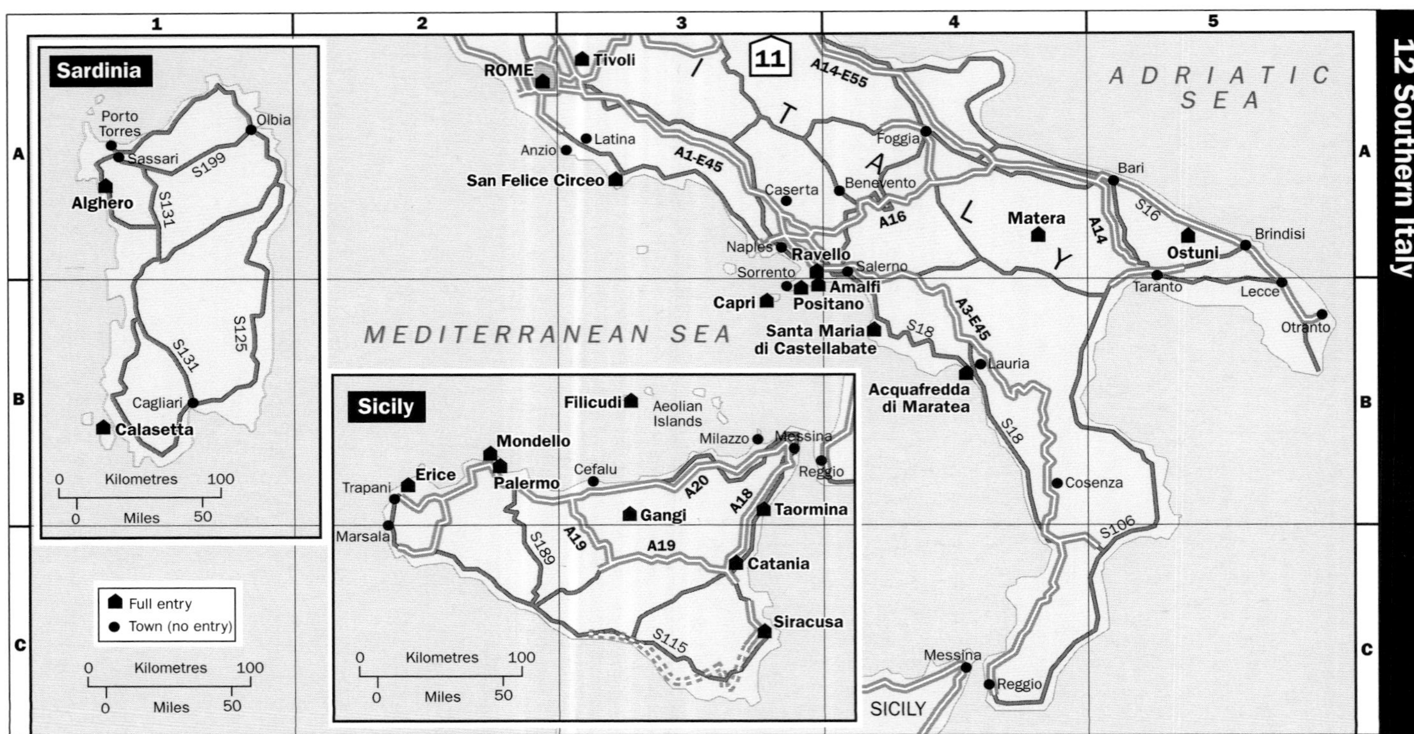

Czech Republic 13
4
5
6
A
B
GERMANY
POLAND
CZECH REPUBLIC
SLOVAKIA
AUSTRIA
Staré Splavy
Karlovy Vary
PRAGUE
Hradec Králové
Ostrava
Plzeň
Olomouc
Zlín
Brno
Jihlava
Luhačovice
Kašperské Hory
České Budějovice
Jindřichův Hradec
Mikulov
Lednice
Český Krumlov
E55
E65
E48
E67
E442
E50
E461
E462
E53
E50-E65
E59
Full entry
Town (no entry)
Kilometres
0
100
Miles
50
Slovenia and Croatia 14
AUSTRIA
HUNGARY
SLOVENIA
CROATIA
BOSNIA-HERZEGOVINA
ADRIATIC SEA
Solčava
Kobarid
Maribor
Selo
Bled
Spodnja Idrija
LJUBLJANA
ZAGREB
Trieste
Piran
Opatija
Rijeka
Rovinj
Marcana
Pula
Plitvice
Zadar
SARAJEVO
Split
Mostar
Palmižana
Mali Ston
Dubrovnik
Lopud
E57
E59
E65
E61
E65-E71
E70
E751
E71
M5
C
D
E
Full entry
Town (no entry)
Kilometres
0
100
Miles
50

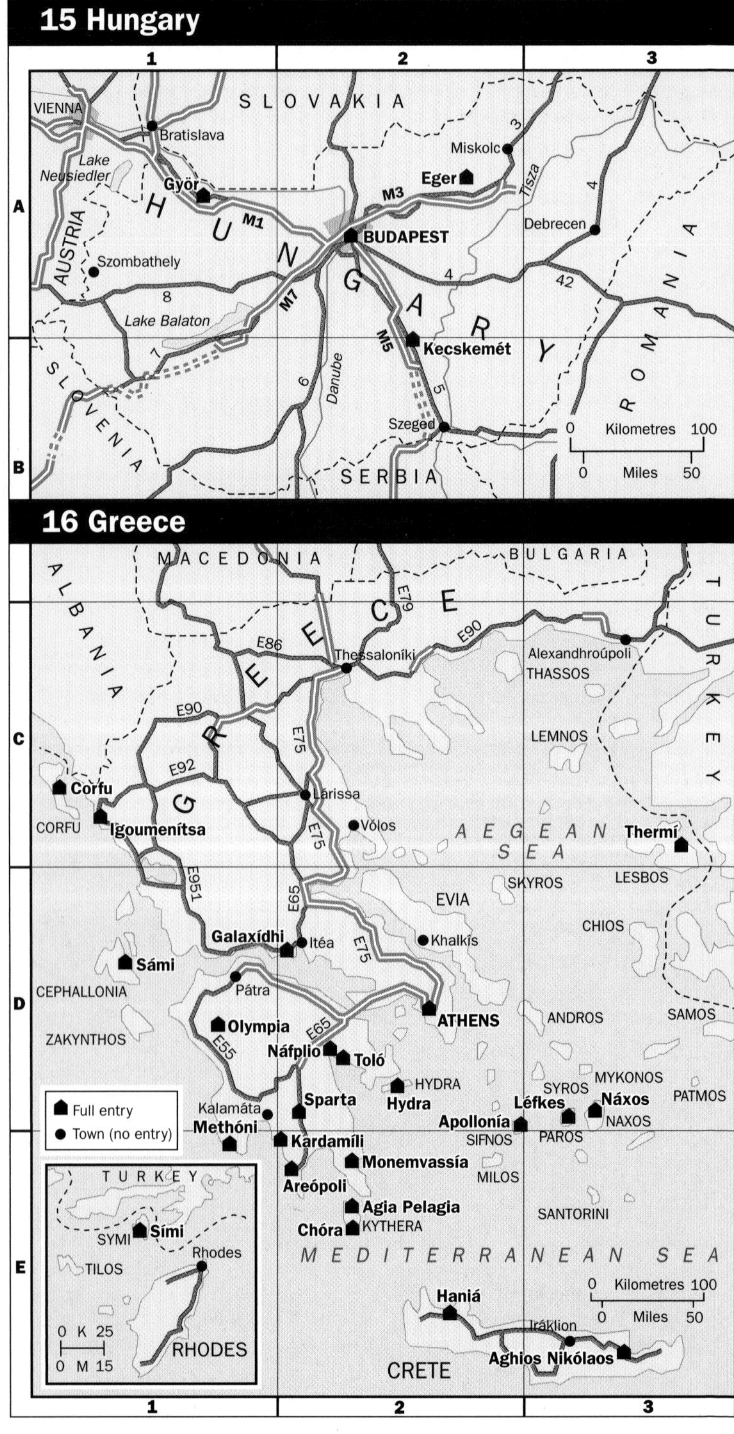
15 Hungary
1
2
3
A
B
SLOVAKIA
VIENNA
Bratislava
Lake Neusiedler
Györ
AUSTRIA
HUNGARY
M1
M3
Eger
Miskolc
3
Tisza
4
Debrecen
BUDAPEST
Szombathely
8
4
42
Lake Balaton
M7
7
M5
Kecskemét
ROMANIA
SLOVENIA
6
Danube
5
Szeged
SERBIA
0 Kilometres 100
0 Miles 50
16 Greece
MACEDONIA
BULGARIA
ALBANIA
GREECE
TURKEY
E79
E86
E90
Thessaloníki
Alexandhroúpoli
THASSOS
E90
E75
LEMNOS
E92
Corfu
CORFU
Igoumenítsa
Lárissa
Vólos
E75
AEGEAN SEA
Thermí
E951
E65
SKYROS
LESBOS
EVIA
CHIOS
Galaxídhi
Itéa
Khalkís
E75
Sámi
CEPHALLONIA
Pátra
ATHENS
ANDROS
SAMOS
Olympia
E65
ZAKYNTHOS
E55
Náfplio
Toló
HYDRA
Hydra
MYKONOS
SYROS
PATMOS
Sparta
Léfkes
Náxos
NAXOS
Kalamáta
Apollonía
SIFNOS
PAROS
Methóni
Kardamíli
Monemvassía
MILOS
Areópoli
Agia Pelagia
SANTORINI
Chóra
KYTHERA
MEDITERRANEAN SEA
Haniá
Iráklion
Aghios Nikólaos
CRETE
0 Kilometres 100
0 Miles 50
Full entry
Town (no entry)
TURKEY
SYMI
Sími
Rhodes
TILOS
0 K 25
0 M 15
RHODES

of comfort' and 'wonderful views of the lake' (all have a balcony). A strong point is the restaurant: 'Food of consistently high standard, attractively presented; charming service. The menu, based on local traditions, has a modern twist, eg, smoked lamb with poached apple, ginger, mustard and honey; steak with truffle sauce.' The 'extensive wine list' includes many excellent local wines, Franciacorte, etc. The terrace looks over ancient olive groves, and there is a swimming pool. (*Andrew Traub*)

Open All year. **Rooms** 23 double, 2 single. 2 suitable for ♿. **Facilities** Lift. Lounge, bar, restaurant with terrace; function rooms. No background music. Garden: unheated swimming pool. **Location** 1.5 km W of Riva di Solto. 40 km NE of Bergamo. Parking. **Restriction** No smoking in public areas. **Credit cards** All major cards accepted. **Terms** B&B: single €47–€53, double €74–€86; D,B&B €46–€65 per person. Set meals €15.50–€35; full alc €35. *V*

ROME — Map 11:E5

Hotel Barocco
Via della Purificazione 4
Piazza Barberini 9
00187 Rome

Tel (06) 4872001
Fax (06) 485994
Email info@hotelbarocco.com
Website www.hotelbarocco.com

'Well located', at the foot of Via Veneto, this historic building is within easy walking distance of the sights of ancient Rome, '*and* the classy shopping streets'. 'Very comfortable' (says a visitor this year), it has cherry wood in the breakfast room, 'antique' stucco and 19th-century prints and oil paintings on the walls, luxurious fabrics, and marble from Trani in the large bathrooms. Front rooms have 'a nice, if noisy' view over the Piazza Barberini; some rooms have a balcony or terrace. Recent comments: 'We could not fault our spacious suite.' 'Our room, not large, had sturdy custom-built furniture and two large windows overlooking a small side street. Efficient air conditioning and comfortable beds ensured a good night's sleep.' 'Everything is spotless.' 'First-rate buffet breakfast.' The manager, Franco Caruso, leads a 'pleasant staff'. 'English afternoon tea' and drinks are served in the small bar. No restaurant; plenty nearby. (*JR*)

Open All year. **Rooms** 5 suites, 26 double, 6 single. Some no-smoking. Air conditioning. **Facilities** Lift. Lobby, TV room, bar, breakfast room; private dining room; classical background music. Unsuitable for ♿. **Location** Central: Piazza Barberini (windows double glazed). Private garage nearby. (Metro: Barberini) **Restriction** No smoking in public areas. **Credit cards** All major cards accepted. **Terms** [2004] B&B: single €165–€216, double €225–€325, suite €300–€516.

Hotel Due Torri NEW
Vicolo del Leonetto 23
00186 Rome

Tel (06) 6876983
Fax (06) 6865442
Email hotelduetorri@interfree.it
Website www.hotelduetorriroma.com

'Near Piazza Navona and within walking distance of all the sights (we didn't use a taxi the whole time we were in Rome), this centrally located hotel is on a quiet little street and I could sleep at night with my window open,' writes the nominator this year. 'Our room was not fancy, but had good water pressure in the shower, comfortable bed, and the continental breakfast had the best selection we have seen.' Once the residence of cardinals and bishops, it is 'not a place of glamour or for luxury-loving guests' but a 'good-value friendly B&B with an old-time, local feeling'. (*Lesley Powell*)

Open All year. **Rooms** 4 suites, 15 double, 7 single. Air conditioning. **Facilities** Lounge, bar, breakfast room. No background music. **Location** Central, near Piazza Navona. Public garage nearby. **Restrictions** No smoking in public areas. Small dogs only. **Credit cards** All major cards accepted. **Terms** B&B: single €114–€165, double €172–€235, suite €235–€315.

Hotel Locarno
Via della Penna 22
00186 Rome

Tel (06) 3610841
Fax (06) 3215249
Email info@hotellocarno.com
Website www.hotellocarno.com

In a quietish street near the Piazza del Popolo, this Art Deco hotel opened in 1925; it recently increased its size by extending into an adjacent building. It has a 'charming internal courtyard', said its nominators: the ample breakfast buffet is served here or on the rooftop terrace. 'The lovely old interiors have a slightly faded air of gentility': many original features survive: antiques and 1950s items create a 'relaxing, undesigned' ambience. 'Our high-ceilinged room had huge windows, a large chandelier, efficient air conditioning so no traffic noise. The large bathroom had an old freestanding cast iron bath. Housekeeping was good.' In the 'comfortable lounge area', light meals and snacks are served. 'Staff are helpful. Bicycles are available.' The business centre has Internet facilities, free to guests. (*P and JT*)

Open All year. **Rooms** 65 double, 18 single. 23 no-smoking. Air conditioning. **Facilities** Lift. Lounge area, bar; background music; business centre. Courtyard. Roof garden. **Location** Central, near Piazza del Popolo. Paid parking nearby. (Metro: Flaminio) **Restrictions** No smoking: public areas, some bedrooms. No dogs. **Credit cards** All major cards accepted. **Terms** [2004] B&B: single €120–€160, double €190–€310, suite €510.

Hotel Lord Byron NEW
Via Giuseppe De Notaris 5
00197 Rome

Tel (06) 3220404
Fax (06) 3220405
Email info@lordbyronhotel.com
Website www.lordbyronhotel.com

On the north side of the Borghese Gardens, this luxury hotel recently underwent a make-over in Art Deco style. It might be a bit out of the way for some travellers (a ten-minute taxi ride to the Spanish Steps), but, write devotees: 'We love its peaceful location, its size, and the fact that it is enticingly stylish compared to the traditional big hotels in central Rome. Reception staff are unfailingly helpful; housekeeping staff perhaps the best we've encountered.' There is an 'expert' barman, and the restaurant, *Sapori del Lord Byron*, serves regional Italian specialities and vegetarian dishes. 'At breakfast, packet juice is standard: ask for freshly squeezed and you'll get it; avoid the "American" coffee: go for espresso.' Portraits of women abound. The bedrooms are 'plushly furnished'. The garden suite, in a separate building, has a terrace where meals can be served. (*David and Kate Wooff*)

Open All year. **Rooms** 9 suites, 20 double, 3 single. Air conditioning. **Facilities** Lift. Lounge/wine bar, restaurant. No background music. Unsuitable for ♿. **Location** N of city, by Borghese Gardens; S of Viale Bruno Buozzi. Public parking nearby. **Restrictions** No smoking. Small dogs only. **Credit cards** All major cards accepted. **Terms** B&B: single €250–€330, double €250–€450, suite €550–€950. Full alc €50.

Hotel Portoghesi
Via dei Portoghesi 1
00186 Rome

Tel (06) 6864231
Fax (06) 6876976
Email info@hotelportoghesiroma.com
Website www.hotelportoghesiroma.com

'One of the best hotels (for the price) that we have stayed in,' says a visitor this year. The Sagnotti family's *palazzo*, a hotel for over 150 years, is within walking distance of most of the main attractions. Named after the exquisite national Portuguese church nearby, it is 'clean and comfortable', with 'helpful staff' and 'excellent soundproofing'. Bedrooms are 'compact, but well decorated'. 'We have not slept in a better bed, except at home,' one couple wrote. Airy corridors and landings are paved with marble. There is a roof terrace, where the 'adequate' breakfast is served under lemon trees in good weather (on cooler days it is in a glassed-in area). Recommended restaurants: *La Campana* ('booking recommended; it is popular with locals'), *Il Bacaro* ('caters more to foreigners'). (*Diana Nairn, and others*)

Open All year. **Rooms** 3 suites (1 with kitchenette), 21 double, 5 single. Air conditioning. **Facilities** Lift. Lounge, breakfast room, roof terrace. Unsuitable for ♿. **Location** Central, between Piazza Navona and Pantheon. Public parking nearby. **Restrictions** No smoking. No dogs. **Credit cards** MasterCard, Visa. **Terms** B&B: single €145–€150, double €180–€190, suite €210–€310.

La Residenza
Via Emilia 22–24
00187 Rome

Tel (06) 4880789
Fax (06) 485721
Email la.residenza@thegiannettihotelsgroup.com
Website www.thegiannettihotelsgroup.com

'A real bargain for Rome', 'superbly located', this old-established B&B hotel is just off Via Veneto, not far from the Borghese Gardens. Yellow-walled, with green shutters and orange awnings, it belongs to the Giannetti group. 'Reception is run by courteous men.' 'Their recommendations for restaurants were perfect,' one reader said. Public rooms are 'inviting' (19th/20th-century decor). There is a weekly drinks party for residents. Free international newspapers, and video films in English and Italian, are available. Everyone admires the lavish breakfast buffet (cheeses, tomatoes, fruit tarts, prosciutto, 'delicious bread', eggs, bacon and sausages). The large front bedrooms are 'comfortable, with a big bath and decent air conditioning', but they hear street noise and the nightclub opposite;

quieter ones at the rear are smaller and darker, but some have a balcony. (*Claire Lavery, Sally R Burt*)

Open All year. **Rooms** 7 suites, 17 double, 5 single. Some no-smoking. Air conditioning. **Facilities** Lift. 2 lounges, library/bar, breakfast room; rooftop terrace. Patio. Unsuitable for ♿. **Location** Central, off Via Veneto (rear rooms quietest). Some parking. (Metro: Barberini) **Restriction** No smoking in public areas. **Credit cards** MasterCard, Visa. **Terms** [2004] B&B: single €83–€93, double €180–€191, junior suite €207–€223.

Teatro di Pompeo
Largo del Pallaro 8
00186 Rome

Tel (06) 68300170
Fax (06) 68805531
Email hotel.teatrodipompeo@tiscali.it
Website www.hotelteatrodipompeo.it

You can see the remains of Pompey's theatre (55BC) in the breakfast room/bar of this small hotel run by the Cavarocchi-Mignoni family. In the historic centre, close to Piazza Navona and the Campo de' Fiori, the four-storey terraced building is on an almost traffic-free, cobbled side street, 'ideally situated for reasonably fit walkers'. The spacious bedrooms are well kept; quietest ones (with shower) overlook the little inner courtyard. 'The staff are pleasant, service is efficient, and the breakfast coffee is good,' one visitor wrote. Another liked the 'unfussy decor, high dark wood ceilings, safe behind a picture (very Poirot) and functional bathroom with a powerful shower'. Many reasonably priced restaurants are within walking distance.

Open All year. **Rooms** 12 double (3 in annexe, 50 m), 1 single. 1 on ground floor. Air conditioning. **Facilities** Lift. Lounge, bar with TV, breakfast room; meeting rooms. No background music. **Location** Central, near Piazza Navona and Campo de' Fiori. Car access from Piazza Vidoni/Vicolo dei Chiodaroli. Public garage nearby. **Restrictions** No smoking in public areas. No dogs. **Credit cards** All major cards accepted. **Terms** B&B: single €130–€150, double €170–€190.

Villa del Parco NEW
Via Nomentana 110
00161 Rome

Tel (06) 44237773
Fax (06) 44237572
Email info@hotelvilladelparco.it
Website www.hotelvilladelparco.it

'Highly recommended; good value', this 'very pleasant' B&B, which the Bernardini family has run for over 40 years, returns to the *Guide* after a time with no reports. A late 19th-century villa, 'beautifully kept, decorated with taste', it is in the embassy district. Fine antiques on landings, public spaces with smart sofas, lamps, books and flower pictures give it a country house air. It stands behind ivy-clad walls, shrubs and plants, on a busy road (front bedrooms have double-glazed windows; other rooms have garden views). 'The welcome is warm,' says a visitor in 2004. 'All the staff are friendly. My room was pleasing, though it faced an office block. Its fine modern bathroom had an interesting shower contraption.' An earlier guest had a 'smallish well-furnished single with fitted carpet (unusual for Italy) and nice extras, like slippers'. The buffet breakfast (fruit, cereals, etc) is in a 'very agreeable' room, or under parasols in the garden. 'They also served a delightful salad lunch to us there.' Children and pets are welcomed; so are disabled guests. The city centre is easily reached by bus. (*Nick Maddock, and others*)

Open All year. **Rooms** 20 double, 9 single. Also 6 'country-style' loft rooms. Some on ground floor. Air conditioning. **Facilities** Lift. Salon, bar, TV room, breakfast room. Garden: terrace. **Location** 1.5 km from centre. Parking: public garage opposite. (Metro: Bologna) **Restriction** No smoking in public areas. **Credit cards** All major cards accepted. **Terms** [2004] B&B: single €75–€120, double €100–€160.

SAGRATA DI FERMIGNANO — Map 11:C5
61033 Pesaro e Urbino

Locanda della Valle Nuova BUDGET *Tel/Fax* (0722) 330303
La Cappella 14
Email info@vallenuova.it
Website www.vallenuova.it

This beguiling eco-friendly small country hotel, on a large organic farm near Urbino, is surrounded by a landscape of gently rolling hills that 'radiate beauty and tranquillity'. The architect owner, Augusto Savini, who believes that 'one should tread lightly on the earth', runs it with his wife, Adriana. 'She loves cooking, every day we looked forward to dinner,' says a visitor this year. 'Service is highly personal.' The simple, attractive bedrooms (now with ceiling fan) are well insulated, the house is solar heated, and in the open-style sitting room/library there is a log fire and a collection of books on ecology and landscaping. The set five-course dinner is based on seasonal ingredients, many grown on the family's surrounding organic farm: 'Adriana and her daughter, Giulia, take pride in telling you what is in each dish' (in autumn there are truffles from the woods). 'Liqueurs after dinner were home made by Giulia from local fruits, nuts and herbs.' 'The *pièce de résistance* is rose jam.' The large swimming pool in the garden is 'lovingly cared for' by Mr Savini. His horses are available for guests to go riding. 'We enjoyed our stay so much that we extended it by a couple of nights.' (*Christopher Beadle, M and GL*)

Open 25 June–7 Nov. Dining room closed midday. **Rooms** 6 double. **Facilities** Lounge/library, dining room. No background music. Garden: unheated swimming pool. 75-hectare organic farm. Unsuitable for ♿. **Location** 3.5 km from Fermignano, 12 km S of Urbino. Awkward to find: consult website. Parking. **Restrictions** No smoking. No children under 12. No dogs. **Credit cards** None accepted. **Terms** (Min. 3 nights) B&B €48; D,B&B €70. Set dinner €27. €20 supplement for single occupancy.

> The 2006 edition of the *Guide*, covering Great Britain and Ireland, will appear in the autumn of 2005. Reports are particularly useful in the spring, and they need to reach us by 15 May 2005 at the very latest if they are to help the 2006 edition.

SAN FELICE CIRCEO 04017 Latina — Map 12:A3

Punta Rossa
Via delle Batterie 37
Località Quarto Caldo

Tel (0773) 548085
Fax (0773) 548075
Email puntarossa@puntarossa.it
Website www.puntarossa.it

In a remote setting on an 'amazing cliffside', this resort complex includes a hotel and a 'fishermen's village' (apartments), in a large botanical park on the coast between Naples and Rome. Its lush grounds slope down to a swimming pool carved into rock (here meals can be served), and then the sea (rocks, no sandy beach), facing the Pontine islands. 'Charming, informal, with obliging staff', it is 'good for children and their grandparents', according to one recent guest. The Battaglia family owners aim to 'create the atmosphere of a private villa'. Every room has a sea view. Some suites have a spa bath. 'Facilities throughout are immaculate.' The restaurant has spectacular views from almost every table. Most visitors find the food 'delicious: the seafood was fresh and well prepared', but one guest thought the dinners, in a 'not-too-appealing' dining room, were 'disappointing', but lunch, alfresco, was 'brilliant'. Breakfast is served on a flowery patio. There is a good wine list. Popular for weddings, meetings, gala dinners, etc. (*JR, and others*)

Open Mar–Nov. **Rooms** 7 suites, 27 double. Air conditioning. **Facilities** Lounge, TV lounge, cafeteria, bar, piano bar July/Aug, restaurant; conference/function facilities; patio (background music); sauna, heated sea-water swimming pool; beauty farm: thalassotherapy. 3-hectare grounds: swimming pool, snack bar; beach. Unsuitable for ♿. **Location** At Quarto Caldo. 4 km W of San Felice Circeo, 36 km SE of Latina. Parking. **Restrictions** No smoking in public areas. No dogs. **Credit cards** All major cards accepted. **Terms** [2004] B&B: single €105–€120, double €180–€250, suite €255–€285; D,B&B (obligatory 1 June–1 Sept) €155–€210 per person. Alc €31–€60. 1-night bookings refused high season weekends.

SAN GIMIGNANO 53037 Siena — Map 11:D4

Hotel Bel Soggiorno
Via San Giovanni 91

Tel (0577) 940375
Fax (0577) 907521
Email hbelsog@libero.it
Website www.hotelbelsoggiorno.it

'This remains one of my favourite hotels in Europe: excellent location, attentive service,' writes a regular *Guide* correspondent in 2004. Just inside the ramparts of this famous medieval town, this 13th-century building has been owned and run as a hotel by the Gigli family since 1886. 'The views are wonderful,' says another returning visitor, 'especially in the morning, as the sun rises and the mist in the valleys evaporates.' Bedrooms (some are small) are clean, air conditioned and 'sensible', with whitewashed walls and terracotta-tiled floor. Some have a balcony; some share a terrace. The panoramic restaurant serves 'specialities from Etruscan kitchens', eg, wild boar with polenta, accompanied by home-made bread and Vernaccia (a local white wine) or Chianti. 'The dinners have returned to their former glory, after a blip last year', and post-dinner, 'there is nothing better than a stroll to the main square for a coffee and a grappa'. 'Breakfast OK: buffet style, with modest fare.' The sister hotel, *Pescille*, outside the walls, has a swimming pool and tennis. (*Garry Wiseman, MG*)

Open All year, except 6 Jan–28 Feb. Restaurant closed 25 Dec. **Rooms** 22 double. Air conditioning. **Facilities** Lift. TV lounge, restaurant; terrace. No background music. Access to unheated swimming pool at sister hotel, *Pescille*. Unsuitable for ♿. **Location** Central. Cars allowed in for unloading. Public car park (P1) at Porta San Giovanni (€12.50 a day). **Restrictions** No smoking in public areas. No dogs. **Credit cards** All major cards accepted. **Terms** B&B: single €70–€90, double €100–€120. Full alc €50.

SAN MAMETE VALSOLDA 22010 Como — Map 11:A2

Hotel Stella d'Italia
Piazza Roma 1

Tel (0344) 68139
Fax (0344) 68729
Email info@stelladitalia.com
Website www.stelladitalia.com

A correspondent who stayed in 1947, as a teenager, at the Ortelli family's hotel on Lake Lugano, returned in 2004 and reported: 'Little seemed to have changed. The welcome was warm, our room was most comfortable, the terms were extremely reasonable.' 'Signor Ortelli [the fourth-generation owner] is ever present, supervising every detail,' said an earlier visitor. 'His pride in the place is warranted.' Unusually for an Italian lakeside hotel, there is no road between it and the water (which most bedrooms face): the view from the balconies 'is outstanding'. Rear rooms hear traffic, and soundproofing in the newer wing might be imperfect. 'Simple, good-value' meals are served in the lakeside terrace restaurant. Breakfast is an 'excellent buffet'. The lounge has easy chairs; there is a library of English books; the colourful terraced gardens have loungers, tables and chairs. Package tours are accommodated. 'A charming, tiny churchyard is a short climb up steep steps.' There are 'delightful walks in the hills behind the village'. The shopping and cultural attractions of Lugano are a ten-minute drive away. (*Bertel Hutchinson, G and VB*)

Open Apr–Oct. **Rooms** 34 double. 28 air conditioned. **Facilities** Lift. Lounge, bar, terrace restaurant. No background music. Garden: dining terrace, direct access to lake; private lido, rowing boats, fishing. Unsuitable for ♿. **Location** 5 km E of Lugano: on lake, between Gandria and Menaggio. Garage (14 cars). **Restriction** No smoking in public areas. **Credit cards** Amex, MasterCard, Visa. **Terms** B&B: single €90–€135, double €115–€150. Set dinner €18; full alc €37.

> We quote either price per room, or else the range of prices per person – the lowest is likely to be for one person sharing a double room out of season, the highest for a single room in high season.

ST WALBURG IN ULTEN 39016 Bolzano Map 11:A3

Gasthof Eggwirt BUDGET

Tel (0473) 795319
Fax (0473) 795471
Email eggwirt@rolmail.net
Website www.eggwirt.it

In a Dolomite village in the Ultental, the Schwienbacher family's *Gasthof* is much loved by *Guide* readers. 'Still excellent value,' wrote a devotee on her 13th visit. Other comments: 'Like stepping into the past.' 'We have never before come across such genuine hospitality.' 'The nearby road can be noisy, and our shower was eccentric, but this was unimportant in view of the beauty of the valley, seen from our balcony, and the warmth of the welcome.' 'Roland and Cristel are wonderfully caring; their daughters, Ulla and Greta, help with language problems.' Some parts of the building are very old; there is much wooden panelling. Bedrooms are 'cosily decorated in Alpine fashion'. The daily-changing half-board dinner has lots of choice. 'Food quite heavy, but tasty.' 'Good house wine.' 'A mighty buffet breakfast.' There is a 'wonderful terrace' for drinks and after-dinner coffee, and concerts in summer. 'The approach is up steep stone steps, and your luggage is not usually carried.' '€42.50 a day half board. We still can't believe it.' 'Funny games' are organised once a week in winter. (*Janice Carrera, and others*)

Open 25 Dec–18 Apr, 9 May–6 Nov. Restaurant closed Tues to non-residents. **Rooms** 18 double, 3 single. **Facilities** TV room, bar, restaurant. Garden: terrace restaurant. Walking, skiing, etc, nearby. Unsuitable for ♿. **Location** Centre of village. 30 km SW of Merano. Parking. **Restriction** No smoking in public areas. **Credit cards** None accepted. **Terms** B&B €28–€34; D,B&B €42.50–€47. Set dinner €15.50.

SANTA MARIA DI CASTELLABATE 84072 Salerno Map 12:B4

Palazzo Belmonte NEW

Tel (0974) 960211
Fax (0974) 961150
Email reservations@palazzobelmonte.it
Website www.palazzobelmonte.com

In a 'luxuriously secluded' setting alongside this lively fishing village, this 17th-century palazzo was built by the family of the Principe di Belmonte as a hunting lodge: the current Principe still lives in one wing. Now an elegant hotel, it stands in a peaceful garden with hibiscus, oleander, roses, jasmine and bougainvillaea and a freshwater swimming pool where lunches are served. A door leads to the private beach. Some suites have a vaulted ceiling, some a private terrace, some face the gardens. 'Ours in a more modern building,' says this year's nominator, 'had a superb sea view.' Mediterranean cuisine is served by torchlight on a terrace. Or you can eat agreeably, and more cheaply, in the village. Dress is 'informal at all times', says the website.

Open Apr–end Oct. **Rooms** 20 suites, 31 double. Some in villa. Air conditioning. **Facilities** Salon, restaurant; conference facilities. 2-hectare grounds: outside dining room, swimming pool, pool restaurant. Private beach. **Location**

Edge of village. 65 km SE of Salerno. **Restriction** No smoking in public areas. **Credit cards** All major cards accepted. **Terms** [2004] B&B: single €140–€200, double €175–€370, suite €220–€650. Set dinner €40.

SANTO STEFANO BELBO 12058 Cuneo — Map 11:C2

Relais San Maurizio
Località San Maurizio 39

Tel (0141) 841900
Fax (0141) 843833
Email info@relaissanmaurizio.it
Website www.relaissanmaurizio.it

'Beautiful, peaceful, a delight,' said its nominators. This converted convent stands amid vineyards, on a hilltop in a picturesque area between Asti and Alba. 'Run with pride and efficiency', it has 'charming young staff' and 'relaxing' lounge areas with huge sofas, easy chairs, piano, paintings (some modern, some old). Old floors and frescoed ceilings have been kept. In the grounds are ancient trees. 'Our welcome was friendly; help with baggage was swift. Our first-floor room, large and light, had heavy beams, antique wardrobe, huge bed, excellent lighting.' The *Ristorante di Guido da Costigliole* (*Michelin* star), in the former refectory in the cellars, serves Piedmontese dishes: 'A superb meal with a different local wine for each course. Amazingly inexpensive.' Breakfast, in a huge room with a painted ceiling, is a large buffet: cooked dishes available if wanted. (*P and JT*)

Open 29 Feb–7 Jan. Restaurant closed Sun night/Mon midday. **Rooms** 30. **Facilities** Lift. Salons, cocktail bar, restaurant; conference facilities; spa with vinotherapy; indoor swimming pool, sauna. Garden. **Location** 3 km from Santo Stefano, 29 km from Asti. **Restriction** No smoking in public areas. **Credit cards** All major cards accepted. **Terms** [2004] (Min. 2 nights at weekends) B&B: single €160–€190, double €205–€295, suite €260–€380. Alc €56–€73.

SELVA DI VAL GARDENA 39048 Bolzano — Map 11:A4

Chalet Portillo NEW
Via Meisules 65

Tel (0471) 795205
Fax (0471) 794360
Email info@chaletportillo.com
Website www.chaletportillo.com

On the edge of this Dolomite resort (Wolkenstein in Gröden in German) at the foot of the impressive Sella massif, this 'superb hotel', 35 years old, is run by its owner, Carlo Senoner (a skiing world champion at Portillo, Chile, 1966), with his wife, son and daughter. 'They are all much in evidence,' say this year's nominators. It is well placed for winter sports (the ski bus stops outside) and has extensive fitness facilities (see below), including a 'most beautiful' indoor swimming pool. 'Superbly appointed, and furnished in Alpine-chalet style, it has a homely, well-organised feel. The bar and lounge are much used in the evening for playing cards and socialising: great atmosphere. The breakfast buffet was excellent. The *en pension* dinners are very good, too: you make your selection at breakfast from a menu with two choices of main course, six of dessert. Good parking arrangements.' Five minutes' walk from the centre, above the main road ('which makes it a little noisy at times'). (*Florence and Russell Birch*)

Open 5 Dec–16 Apr, June–Sept. Dining room closed to non-residents. **Rooms** 31. **Facilities** Lounge, bar, dining room; wellness centre: swimming pool, sauna, Turkish bath, whirlpool, fitness room, solarium. Terrace. **Location** Centre of resort. 42 km NE of Bolzano. Garage. **Restrictions** No smoking. No dogs. **Credit cards** MasterCard, Visa. **Terms** [2004] D,B&B €62–€155.

SIENA 53100 — Map 11:D4

Palazzo Ravizza NEW
Pian dei Mantellini 34

Tel (0577) 280462
Fax (0577) 221597
Email bureau@palazzoravizza.it
Website www.palazzoravizza.com

Well-managed converted 17th-century palazzo *within city walls. 'Elegant public rooms, nine-foot Steinway piano, lovely garden' (which quietest rooms face). Restaurant (closed Sun). Air conditioning. Free Internet service. No smoking in public areas. All major credit cards accepted. 30 bedrooms. B&B double €120–€180. Alc €28–€34.*

Hotel Santa Caterina NEW
Via Enea Silvio Piccolomini 7

Tel (0577) 221105
Fax (0577) 271087
Email info@hscsiena.it
Website www.hscsiena.it

An 18th-century patrician villa has been turned into this small B&B hotel near the Porta Romana, one of the medieval entrances into the *centro storico*: the *Campo* is about 15 minutes' walk away. 'We could not commend it more highly,' says a 2004 visitor. 'It is on a very busy corner, but quadruple glazing and efficient air conditioning mean that noise is minimal. All the bedrooms are elegantly and comfortably furnished, though there is little drawer space. The manageress and her staff were very hospitable and helpful, directing us to excellent local restaurants, summoning taxis, etc. Best of all was the garden, with wonderful views over countryside to Monte Amiata: a perfect spot for drinks after a hot day's sightseeing, and an excellent buffet under trees.' (*Mary Milne-Day*)

Open All year. **Rooms** 18 double, 2 single. Air conditioning. **Facilities** Lift. Lounge/bar. Garden. **Location** 15 mins' walk from centre, outside Porta Romana. Limited parking (€15 daily). **Restriction** No smoking: public areas, some bedrooms. **Credit cards** All major cards accepted. **Terms** B&B: single €75–€105, double €98–€155.

> Don't trust out-of-date editions of the *Guide*. Hotels change hands, deteriorate or go out of business. Each year many hotels are dropped and many new ones are added.

SIRACUSA 96100 Sicily — Map 12:C3

Erbavoglio NEW/BUDGET
Contrada Renaura via Langanelli 8
Tel (0931) 616411
Email sindona.erbavoglio@simail.it
Website www.erbavoglio-siracusa.it

A small country B&B, 'far from hectic traffic', yet a short distance from the historic centre. 'Very relaxing.' It has four 'cosy' bedrooms, says the nominator, recommending it to 'those who are tired of big, impersonal hotels'. A conversion of an old storehouse for farm tools, set amid olive groves, it is ecologically run. It has a nursery of Mediterranean and aromatic plants and a biological vegetable garden. Breakfast, served in a galleried room, consists of 'natural foods', and here, says the website, 'lovers of nature can widen their cultural and scholarly knowledge': there is a library of books about agriculture and botany; botanical walks and other outings are organised. The sea is a short distance away. (*Thérèse Bergman*)

Open All year. **Rooms** 4 double. **Facilities** Hall, library, breakfast room. Garden: barbecue area. **Location** 4 km NE of Siracusa, off SS115. **Restrictions** No smoking: public areas, some bedrooms. 'Tame animals' accepted. **Credit cards** None accepted. **Terms** [2004] B&B €28–€38.

SIRMIONE 25010 Brescia — Map 11:B3

Villa Cortine Palace
Via Grotte 6
Tel (030) 9905890
Fax (030) 916390
Email info@hotelvillacortine.com
Website www.hotelvillacortine.com

'Everything about this hotel is elegant,' says a visitor this year. Other comments: 'Expensive but worth it', 'a haven of peace'. This luxury hotel is a converted 19th-century neo-classical mansion. It stands in a large park above Lake Garda, reached by a 'moderately hair-raising' drive through the town's narrow alleys, crowded in summer. It has a Palladian-style facade, and huge public rooms with chandeliers, frescoes and mosaics. In its beautiful garden are tall trees, a Neptune fountain, a swimming pool and a clay tennis court. Being near the end of the peninsula, it has lake views on both sides. Recent praise: 'An outstanding kitchen.' 'A most enjoyable stay, an excellent room.' A steep walk down, past Roman ruins, leads to the lake, where, in summer, a buffet lunch is served in a pleasant restaurant, and there are sometimes barbecues on the beach. Meals are taken on a large terrace looking over the water. Most bedrooms are in a 'tasteful' 1950s extension: almost all have a balcony and lake view. 'Ours was beautiful.' Occasional concerts are held. (*Richard Lamb, A and GW, and others*)

Open 10 Apr–19 Oct. **Rooms** 2 suites, 4 junior suites, 48 double. Air conditioning. **Facilities** Lift. Salons, bar, restaurant; background music, pianist twice weekly; conference/function facilities. Park: garden, terrace, swimming pool, tennis; beach with bar, restaurant. Unsuitable for ♿. **Location** Near Grotto of Catullus. 35 km W of Verona. Parking. **Restriction** No smoking in public areas. **Credit cards** All major cards accepted. **Terms** [2004] B&B:

double €300–€420, suite €450–€470; D,B&B (compulsory in high season, min. 3 nights): double €430–€680, suite €580–€780. Alc from €55.

SIUSI ALLO SCILIAR 39040 Bolzano — Map 11:A4

Hotel Bad Ratzes BUDGET
Via Ratzes 29

Tel (0471) 706131
Fax (0471) 707199
Email info@badratzes.it
Website www.badratzes.it

Liked for its welcome, 'quietly efficient staff' and 'excellent value for money', this chalet-style hotel is in a 'very beautiful' skiing and summer resort in the South Tyrol nature reserve, at the foot of the Dolomites. Owned by sisters Eva and Waltraud Scherlin, it stands by a stream, on a sunny meadow surrounded by an ancient forest. Recent visitors liked 'the meals, the pool and the scenery'; others wrote: 'Utterly professional; painstaking attention to detail.' 'It is clearly much loved by generations of guests. The happy atmosphere makes everyone friendly.' Children of all ages are well looked after: there is a crèche, equipment for babies, special menus, a supper room, games, a playground 'for the young at heart'. Entertainments for older children include cookery classes, and an 'Indian wigwam' day. 'But there is a strict no-noise policy after 10 pm.' The large swimming pool is separated by a floor-to-ceiling glass wall from the 'huge and lovely' garden. There are log fires, a sauna, sun loungers on the grass. 'Food is copious.' The huge salad and vegetable buffet (often augmented by fondues) is admired, though 'it didn't change much in three days'. Meal service is brisk. Rates include a light lunch and afternoon tea ('the cakes were a disaster for the waistline'). The breakfast buffet has a huge choice. Bedrooms are large, with balcony, and in the big underground garage, a car space is allotted to each room. In summer there is 'wonderful walking in the plateau above the hotel. They provided two buses in the morning to take guests to the cable car.' (*Christina Cheah, Sarah Baxter, Janice Carrera*)

Open 17 Dec–1 Mar, 20 May–2 Oct. **Rooms** 38 double, 10 single. **Facilities** Lift. Lounge, 2 TV rooms, bar (background music), 3 dining rooms, *Stube*; traditional live music weekly; children's playrooms, crèche; heated indoor swimming pool, sauna. 22-hectare grounds: terrace, garden, children's playground. Unsuitable for ♿. **Location** 3 km SE of Siusi, which is 23 km NE of Bolzano. Garage. **Restriction** No smoking. **Credit cards** MasterCard, Visa. **Terms** Full board €65–€100. 3% discount for 14-day stay.

SOLDA 39029 Bolzano — Map 11:A4

Hotel Marlet NEW/BUDGET

Tel (0473) 613075
Fax (0473) 613190
Email hotel.marlet.sulden@rolmail.net
Website www.marlet.com

High above the road, on the far side of the village (Sulden in German), this chalet-style hotel has fine views to the glacier and the Ortler range of mountains. Newly refurbished in modern Alpine style, it has lots of wood panelling and pale wood floors, 'but no kitsch', says the 2004 nominator. The dining room has a large glassed extension facing the valley, there are lots of sitting areas and a sunny terrace. 'Our comfortable room had a fantastic mountain view from the bed. The Signora was charming and efficient. Breakfast is a good buffet. Dinner, served by attractive, well-trained waitresses, had five courses except one evening when it had seven and a zither player. Only criticism: we disliked the muzak in the bar and on the terrace, but the volume was fairly low.' (*Sarah Baxter*)

Open 18 Dec–10 May, July–Sept. Dining room closed to non-residents. **Rooms** 29. **Facilities** Lift. Lounges, conservatory, dining room; billiard room; indoor swimming pool, sauna; children's games area. Terrace. **Location** 96 km W of Bolzano. **Restriction** No smoking in public areas. **Credit cards** MasterCard, Visa. **Terms** [2004] B&B €63–€90 per person. Alc €25–€32.

SOVICILLE 53018 Siena — Map 11:D4

Albergo Borgo Pretale
Località Pretale

Tel (0577) 345401
Fax (0577) 345625
Email info@borgopretale.it
Website www.borgopretale.it

Standing peacefully amid the Tuscan hills near Siena, this medieval stone-built hamlet is now a 'distinctly luxurious' hotel. Around are ancient woods of oak, juniper and myrtle, where wild boar, porcupine, squirrels and deer can sometimes be seen. The bedrooms are in cottages in the large grounds and, beamed and thick-walled, in the central tower: 'Ours was charming, with an interesting shape,' one couple wrote. 'It is so beautiful,' said another, who had 'a peaceful and happy' stay. Others wrote of 'unostentatious comfort' and 'courteous staff'. 'Details were impeccable.' In summer, a buffet lunch is served at tables under trees by the 'lovely, large' swimming pool. Breakfasts are 'delicious and varied'. Tuscan dishes are served in the candlelit restaurant. 'The meals are yummy,' was one comment. But portions are small, and a family with teenagers thought there was 'not enough food'. Tour groups come, but are discreetly handled. (*EW, and others*)

Open Easter–31 Oct. **Rooms** 6 suites, 28 double. 8 in tower. 26 in cottages. Air conditioning. **Facilities** Lounge with TV, piano bar, restaurant; classical background music; meeting room; gym, sauna. Large grounds: terrace, garden, unheated swimming pool (buffet lunch June–Sept), tennis, bowls, mountain bikes, archery. Unsuitable for ♿. **Location** 15 km SW of Sovicille, 20 km SW of Siena (best reached off Fallonica–Colle Val d'Elsa road). Hotel provides detailed directions. Parking. **Restrictions** No smoking: public areas, some bedrooms. No large dogs. **Credit cards** All major cards accepted. **Terms** B&B: single €135, double €205, suite €235; D,B&B: single €175, double €280, suite €320. Set dinner €45.

> Hotels are dropped if we lack positive feedback.

SPOLETO 06049 Perugia — Map 11:D5

Hotel San Luca
Via Interna delle Mura 21

Tel (0743) 223399
Fax (0743) 223800
Email sanluca@hotelsanluca.com
Website www.hotelsanluca.com

Famous for its music festival, this lovely hill town makes a good base for touring eastern Umbria. In its historic centre, the Zuccari family's 'delightful' hotel, once a leather factory, is liked for the 'friendly management and staff'. 'Only drawback, it is difficult to find, reached through a gap in the walls.' Comfortable, very quiet', it has Umbrian floor tiles, antiques, oriental rugs, leather, potted plants and flowers. Large, soundproofed bedrooms (some with terrace or balcony) have 'superb linens'; mattresses are custom-made; there are anti-fog mirrors in the 'excellent' marble bathrooms. 'Everyone is anxious to please,' said recent visitors. 'We were pampered in style.' Breakfast is in a room with murals, or in the courtyard, amid camellias, jasmine and geraniums. Tea and drinks are served in the rose garden. Lunch and dinner are provided by arrangement, and there are some excellent restaurants in town, eg, *Il Panciolle* with wood-burning oven and panoramic terrace. Cookery courses, based on local recipes, are held. (*KB, and others*)

Open All year. **Rooms** 32 double, 3 single. Some no-smoking. 2 suitable for ♿. Air conditioning. **Facilities** Lift. Hall, salon, TV room, breakfast room, restaurant; background music; meeting room. Courtyard, garden. **Location** Approach from Viale Martiri della Resistenza (which runs SW–NE), look for gap in walls halfway along; turn right into Via Interna delle Mura. Free parking in front of hotel; private garage (€13 a day). **Restriction** No smoking in public areas. **Credit cards** All major cards accepted. **Terms** B&B: single €85–€95, double €110–€240.

TAORMINA 98039 Messina, Sicily — Map 12:B3

Villa Belvedere
Via Bagnoli Croce 79

Tel (0942) 23791
Fax (0942) 625830
Email info@villabelvedere.it
Website www.villabelvedere.it

Long enjoyed by *Guide* readers, this tall, pale ochre building has been owned and run by the Franco-Sicilian Pécaut family since 1902. It stands high above the sea (reached by steps or a cable car), amid bougainvillaea, hibiscus, and citrus trees. Inside is a 'tasteful decor in classic style'. The 'delightful front bedrooms, with balcony and views', are admired: 'Our bedroom's beautiful terrace had a view over the garden to the sea.' Sunsets over the sea with Mount Etna behind are 'outrageously romantic'. Rooms are simple (no mini-bar, etc) and those facing the street can be 'poky', but their windows are double glazed, and large tubs with plants and shrubs provide a screen. 'The receptionist could not have been more charming,' was one recent comment. A palm tree grows on an island in the swimming pool in the terraced grounds. In summer, a poolside restaurant serves drinks and light lunches. Breakfast, with fresh orange juice, yogurt, etc, is served in a room with 'great views'. Many restaurants are within walking distance. 'Parking in Taormina is a nightmare; but the hotel, for a small charge, will shoehorn your car in and out of its steep, curving drive.' (*Michael Gwinnell, D and HW, and others*)

Open 9 Mar–20 Nov. Restaurant open 1 Apr–31 Oct (11 am–4 pm). **Rooms** 2 suites (in garden), 42 double, 5 single. Some on ground floor. Some no-smoking. Air conditioning. **Facilities** Lift. TV room, reading room, library, bar, breakfast room. Internet access. No background music. Garden: terraces, unheated swimming pool, summer restaurant. Sea, safe bathing 5 km. Unsuitable for ♿. **Location** 10 mins' walk from centre, near public gardens. Parking. **Restriction** No smoking in public areas. **Credit cards** MasterCard, Visa. **Terms** B&B: single €85–€129, double €110–€205, suite €150–€260. *V* (mid-Mar/Apr, 22 Oct–25 Nov)

Villa Fabbiano — *Tel* (0942) 626058
Via Pirandello 81 — *Fax* (0942) 23732
Email info@villafabbiano.com
Website www.villafabbiano.com

Splendidly situated, on the edge of the town, this 'tasteful-ish and fun' conversion of an old Moorish building has original stonework, carefully preserved. The Fabbiano family owners are 'charming', says a recent visitor, 'their staff are delightful'. There is a 'wonderfully eccentric' tented lounge area. The top-floor dining area, 'a lovely spot', covered but open at the sides in good weather, 'has spectacular, unimpeded views down to the bay and up to the smoking cone of Mount Etna'. Here, guests take a 'good and copious' breakfast, a buffet, but with eggs to order. Bedrooms are 'spacious, with high ceiling'; some have a balcony with sea view. The hotel has reserved space on the beach below, reached by cable car, but some guests feel: 'Why go down, when its pool is so attractive?' Reached by a descending path, past a garden area, it is on a terrace 'with views down and round to bougainvillaea, prickly pear, tall cypresses, and the sea beyond'. Light lunches are served; dinners, too, if ordered well in advance. 'Reliable dinner recommendations' are given. (*LW*)

Open 12 Mar–29 Oct. **Rooms** 14 suites, 12 double. Air conditioning. **Facilities** Lift. Lounge, breakfast room. No background music. Garden: swimming pool. Shuttle service to beach (fee payable). **Location** 500 m from centre. Parking. Transfer from Catania airport €80 for 2. **Restrictions** No smoking. No dogs. **Credit cards** MasterCard, Visa. **Terms** B&B: single €150, double €170–€205, suite €240–€325. Full alc lunch €52.

Grand Hotel Timeo — *Tel* (0942) 23801
Via Teatro Greco 59 — *Fax* (0942) 628501
Email reservation.tim@framon-hotels.it
Website www.framonhotels.it

'When you are sitting under a parasol on the terrace, sucking up a Campari, taking in Etna, the geraniums and the bougainvillaea, and the blue bay far below, it's easy to believe that it's 1953 and Cary Grant is at the next table.' A recent comment on this luxury hotel owned by the

Framon Group, 'grand indeed', which opened in 1873 next to the lovely Greek Theatre, a few minutes' walk uphill from the centre. It has beautiful public rooms, designed to make the best of the views, with arched ceilings, lots of glass and fine wood floors. Its lovely garden, with lily ponds, lemon trees and scented flowers, slopes down the hillside. All bedrooms have a balcony or terrace. 'Ours, not huge, was well thought out, with a smart bathroom,' one couple wrote. Another reporter had 'an elegant suite with a stuccoed bedroom area, two bedrooms with *that view*, and a perfectly equipped, if dimly lit, bathroom, also with the view'. In the restaurant, *Il Dito e la Luna*, Sicilian/Mediterranean cuisine is served. 'The breakfast buffet, served on the terrace, was Lucullan; service was amusing, attentive.' A health centre and an outdoor swimming pool are new this year, and guests can swim at the beach of the sister hotel, *Villa Sant'Andrea*, in Mazzaro at the foot of the hill (reached by cable car or free shuttle service).

Open All year. **Rooms** 22 suites (some in garden, some on ground floor), 34 double. Air conditioning. **Facilities** Lift. 2 salons, piano bar, restaurant; background music; conference/function facilities; health centre; dining terrace. Large grounds: swimming pool. **Location** Pedestrian zone by Greek Theatre. Valet parking. **Restriction** No smoking: public areas, some bedrooms. **Credit cards** All major cards accepted. **Terms** B&B: single €198–€340, double €290–€490; D,B&B €205–€400. Set meals €65–€85; full alc €70.

Villa Ducale NEW
Via Leonardo da Vinci 60

Tel (0942) 28153
Fax (0942) 28710
Email info@villaducale.com
Website www.villaducale.com

'Our favourite small hotel in the world,' says the nominator, who returned for a fourth visit in 2004. 'Its position, above the town, gives it the feel of a private hideaway. The owners, Andrea and Rosaria Quartucci, and their delightful staff offer the perfect *misto* of warmth, hospitality and professionalism.' They serve 'sumptuous breakfasts' of local cheeses, olives, cured meats, marinated vegetables, fruits and Sicilian sweets, on the terrace or in the restaurant (both have 'breathtaking views' of Mount Etna and the Bay of Naxos). All rooms have a flowery balcony or terrace overlooking this 'incredible panorama'. The suites, in a house among lemon trees, face the Straits of Messina. The decor is 'utterly tasteful: hand-painted furnishings and Sicilian damask along with every modern creature comfort'. Romantic flourishes, eg, 'fresh flowers on the pillows', abound. 'In the late afternoon, sitting in the hot tub under the trees while sipping a beverage is heaven.' The owners 'recommend wonderful eateries', and the villa has parking, 'a real plus in Taormina'. (*Gail Pearce*)

Open 15 Feb–30 Nov, 20 Dec–10 Jan. **Rooms** 5 suites, 11 double, 2 single. 1 on ground floor. Air conditioning. **Facilities** Lounge/library, bar, breakfast room; terrace; background music. Garden: whirlpool, swimming pool from May 2005. Courtesy van service to town and beach. **Location** 15 mins' walk from centre. Parking (€10 per day). **Restrictions** No smoking. Small dogs only. **Credit cards** All major cards accepted. **Terms** B&B: single €90–€100, double €130–€250, suite €300–€400.

TELLARO DI LERICI 19030 La Spezia — Map 11:C3

Locanda Miranda
Via Fiascherino 92

Tel (0187) 964012
Fax (0187) 964032
Email locandamiranda@libero.it
Website www.locandamiranda.com

On a cliff-top road outside an old fishing village just south of the Cinque Terre, this restaurant-with-rooms is run by its 'very helpful owners', chef Angelo Cabani and his wife, Giovanna. 'He executes his art with style and flourish,' said a recent visitor, 'she is the versatile *maître d'*; their enormously nice son, Alessandro, runs the front desk.' Others wrote: '*Soigné* but not at all grand.' 'Our lovely room had two balconies overlooking the Golfo dei Poeti.' 'The cooking was an education: fine ingredients, subtle sauces': only fish and pasta are served. 'Signor Cabani took care not to repeat any fish dish over a week – quite an achievement!' There is a huge, well-priced wine list. Breakfast is 'delicious too: freshly squeezed juices and home-made bread'. The hotel is on the road to Tellaro, where it ends: 'No drive-through traffic,' we are assured.

Open 30 Jan–10 Dec. Restaurant closed Mon to non-residents. **Rooms** 7 double. **Facilities** Lounge with TV, restaurant. 2 terraces. Small garden: rock/sand beaches nearby. Unsuitable for ♿. **Location** 4 km SE of Lerici, on main road to Tellaro. Parking. **Restrictions** No smoking. No children under 8. No dogs. **Credit cards** All major cards accepted. **Terms** B&B double €100; D,B&B double €174. Set meals €37–€55; full alc €70. Bookings of more than 1 night preferred.

TIVOLI 00019 Roma — Map 11:E5

Hotel Sirene
Piazza Massimo 4

Tel (0774) 330605
Fax (0774) 330608
Email hotel.sirene@travel.it

'Unpretentious but historic', this is the only hotel in the centre of Tivoli: it has a 'splendid position' on the side of the Aniene gorge, by a waterfall, in the grounds of the Villa di Vospico, and wonderful views of the surrounding countryside and some Roman ruins. It is thought 'good value'. 'An example of Art Deco, it has an elegant curved entrance hall.' Some rooms have a terrace; some are 'quite a walk from Reception'. 'Ours, well planned and comfortable, had a good little balcony from which one could sketch the gorge.' Meals are no longer served, but nearby is a 'very nice restaurant with a big panoramic terrace', the hotel tells us. 'Tivoli has long been a beauty spot where Romans escape to from the heat and dust of the city.' (*MG, J and AL*)

Open All year. **Rooms** 40. Some with terrace. Some no-smoking. Air conditioning. **Facilities** Lift. Lounge, bar, conference room. Panoramic terrace. Unsuitable for ♿. **Location** In grounds of Villa di Vospico, 10 mins' walk from Villa d'Este. Limited private parking; public parking nearby. **Restrictions** No smoking in public areas. No dogs. **Credit cards** All major cards accepted. **Terms** B&B: single €110, double €145, triple €165; D,B&B €18 added per person.

TORCELLO 30012 Venezia — Map 11:B5

Locanda Cipriani
Piazza Santa Fosca 29

Tel (041) 730150
Fax (041) 735433
Email info@locandacipriani.com
Website www.locandacipriani.com

The little island of Torcello, famous for its Romanesque church of Santa Fosca, is 45 minutes by *vaporetto* across the Lagoon from Venice. Here, this 'sophisticated and romantic' restaurant is owned and run by Bonifacio and Daniela Brass: he is the grandson of the founder, Giuseppe Cipriani of the famous hotel-keeping family. Set in 'lovely, well-tended gardens', it is popular with visitors from the city for lunch, served in summer under a pergola. It has two dining rooms, a bar (with wood fire in winter), pictures of Hemingway (who once stayed here), Venetian bas-reliefs, and old copper pots. At night, residents have Torcello for themselves when they stay in the rustic-style rooms (with wooden ceiling and terracotta bricks) above the restaurant. Some rooms face the garden, others the small square and canal in front. 'Ours had cream walls and furniture, loads of books in various languages, flowers, bathrobes in the lilac mosaic-tiled bathroom.' The chef, Renato Ceccato, serves 'classic *Cipriani* dishes', eg, John Dory alla Carlina, and many varieties of pasta, etc. Breakfast includes 'excellent blood orange juice', home-baked pastries and cakes. The Lido is 30 minutes away by *vaporetto*.

Open 10 Feb–5 Jan. Restaurant closed Tues to non-residents. **Rooms** 1 suite, 2 junior suites, 3 single. No TV. Air conditioning. **Facilities** Bar, restaurant; banqueting facilities. No background music. Garden (meal service). Unsuitable for ♿. **Location** Island in Lagoon of Venice. *Vaporetto* Number 14 from San Zaccaria.10 mins' walk from *vaporetto* stop. **Restrictions** No smoking in public areas. No dogs in bedrooms. **Credit cards** All major cards accepted. **Terms** B&B €120–€170; D,B&B €170–€220. Set meals €55–€85.

TORGIANO 06089 Perugia — Map 11:D5

Le Tre Vaselle
Via Giuseppe Garibaldi 48

Tel (075) 9880447
Fax (075) 9880214
Email 3vaselle@3vaselle.it
Website www.3vaselle.it

'Elegant, well equipped and maintained', the Lungarotti family's hotel is in an Umbrian village just off the dual carriageway from Perugia. It takes its name from the three 17th-century Deruta wine jugs in the lobby. It was liked, with some reservations, this year: 'Our split-level room was attractive, but not entirely practical,' one couple wrote. 'The bathroom had a useless shower over a small bath.' Earlier visitors wrote of 'excellent service', 'well-designed rooms' and 'good value'. Luxurious suites, reached by passages and ramps, have frescoed walls, antiques, and rugs on polished tiled floors. Some rooms are in new blocks 'that seem to have been bolted on to the original villa'. All rooms have Internet access. Huge public rooms have beamed ceilings, thick white walls, archways. In the restaurant, *Le Melagrane,* Umbrian dishes are served. The food and wine are generally thought 'excellent' with 'impeccable service', but this can be disrupted when there is a large tour party. Breakfast is 'lavish'. There is a good fitness centre. (*PH, and others*)

Open All year. **Rooms** 18 suites, 40 double, 2 single. 5 in annexe *La Bondanzina* 100 m. Some on ground floor. Some no-smoking. Air conditioning. **Facilities** Lift. Hall (piano bar thrice weekly), reading room, TV room, 2 bars, breakfast room, restaurant; classical background music; games room; sauna, gym, indoor swimming pool; wine museum and shop (wine courses). Garden: terrace (meal service); unheated swimming pool. **Location** Centre; 13 km SE of Perugia, just E of *autostrada*. Parking. Garage (€13). **Restrictions** No smoking in public areas. No dogs. **Credit cards** All major cards accepted. **Terms** B&B: single €150, double €195, suite €245; D,B&B €43 added per person. Full alc €60. *V*

TUORO SUL TRASIMENO 52044 Arezzo — Map 11:D4

Villa di Piazzano
Località Piazzano
Cortona

Tel (075) 826226
Fax (075) 826336
Email info@villadipiazzano.com
Website www.villadipiazzano.com

'Reborn as a delightful hotel', this is one of three hunting lodges of a Renaissance cardinal whose *palazzo* can be seen from here, rising from the flank of Cortona's hill. 'It is a haven of peace and gentle pleasure,' said the nominator, 'restored with a fine sense of understated style, cool, luminous and airy, by the Wimpole family (part Roman, part Australian), whose charm, culture and indefatigable helpfulness create an atmosphere of welcome, balm to the soul. On the first floor, lofty bedrooms (with splendid new bath/shower room), open on to a magnificent central salon with books, sofas, vases of lilies. Great windows look on to spacious views of wooded hills, fields of maize and sunflowers, trees everywhere. There are semi-formal gardens with grass, roses, ancient oaks and a handsome swimming pool. Taking drinks on the gravelled terrace is a delight. Breakfast is a buffet, everything, from blood orange juice to brioches, carefully chosen. Dinner is another pleasure not to be missed, a set meal accompanied by local Merlot (a real treat). Again, ingredients and style demonstrate refined taste.' (*ALL*)

Open 20 Mar–Nov. Restaurant closed Sun. **Rooms** 17. **Facilities** Lift. Sitting room, reading room, bar, 2 dining rooms, meeting room. Garden. Live music sometimes. **Location** 5 km SE of Cortona, NE of Tuoro sul Trasimeno. **Restriction** No smoking. **Credit cards** All major cards accepted. **Terms** B&B: single €120–€155, double €160–€200. Set lunch €25–€30, dinner €40. *V*

> The *V* sign at the end of an entry indicates that the hotel has agreed to take part in our Voucher scheme and to give *Guide* readers a 25% discount on its room or B&B rates, subject to the conditions explained in *How to read the entries*, and on the back of the vouchers.

VALNONTEY 11012 Aosta — Map 11:B1

Hotel La Barme BUDGET

Tel (0165) 749177
Fax (0165) 749213
Email labarme@tiscali.it
Website www.hotellabarme.com

Owned and run by the friendly Herren family, this inexpensive rustic hotel is a converted old wood and stone dairy in a 'tiny, atmospheric' mountain hamlet in the Gran Paradiso national park. It has an 'appealing, simple ambience', one visitor wrote. 'Very clean, tidy; amazingly good value,' says a report this year. It caters for climbers, hikers and skiers: there is a drying room for boots, ice axes, etc (slippers are provided). 'Food was ample, simple and tasty.' A trolley comes briskly round the dining room serving each course in turn (meals are 'not something to linger over'). In summer, guests eat on a wide terrace. Most bedrooms overlook inner alleyways or other buildings ('no views to speak of; no balconies'). 'Our compact room, in a newly built section, had wooden ceiling, pine furniture, a white-tiled shower room.' There is a spacious lounge/bar with ceramic stove; the dining room is on a lower floor (lots of steps). A large car park with play area is adjacent, and can be noisy. (*EC, MG*)

Open 1 Dec–30 Sept. **Rooms** 4 suites, 9 double, 2 single. 2 suitable for ♿. **Facilities** Lounge/bar, restaurant; sauna, massage, solarium. No background music. Garden: children's games, barbecue. **Location** 2 km SW of Cogne, 21 km SE of Aosta. Garage. **Restrictions** No smoking. No dogs. **Credit cards** American Express, MasterCard, Visa. **Terms** B&B €35–€68; D,B&B €10 added. Set meals €15–€23. 1-night bookings sometimes refused.

VENICE — Map 11:B4

Pensione Accademia – Villa Maravege NEW

Fondamenta Bollani
Dorsoduro 1058
30123 Venice

Tel (041) 5210188
Fax (041) 5239152
Email info@pensioneaccademia.it
Website www.pensioneaccademia.it

A 17th-century villa which was the Russian consulate when Venice was an independent republic, this well-known *pensione* has a 'super position' by a side canal, near the Grand Canal at the Accademia bridge. The public rooms are attractive (panelling, chandeliers and Victorian furniture), and there is an upstairs lounge with two large windows. Bedrooms vary in size and quality: the best ones are bright; those not facing the canal are quietest. 'It is slightly more comfortable than 30 years ago,' says a visitor who returned in 2004, 'and it retains a perennial nostalgic charm.' Another reporter called it 'beautiful, elegant and authentic'. Breakfast includes hot dishes and fresh fruit. Book well ahead. (*Dawn Mitchell, Daniel Wentz*)

Open All year, except 9–20 Jan. **Rooms** 27. Some air conditioned. 2 on ground floor. **Facilities** Lounge, TV room, bar. Garden. Unsuitable for ♿. **Location** Vaporetto line 1 or 82 to Accademia stop. **Credit cards** All major cards accepted. **Restrictions** No smoking in public areas. No dogs. **Terms** [2004] B&B: single €80–€125, double €130–€275.

La Calcina NEW
Dorsoduro 780
30123 Venice

Tel (041) 5206466
Fax (041) 5227045
Email la.calcina@libero.it
Website www.lacalcina.com

John Ruskin stayed in this *pensione* on the Dorsoduro in 1877. Now owned by Debora and Alessandro Szemere, who promise 'discreet service and peace', it faces the Giudecca canal and is a short walk from the Accademia, yet away from the throng. 'A far pleasanter spot than the hubbub of St Mark's Square,' says a visitor this year. 'The setting cannot be matched and the standard of accommodation is high. Our corner room, traditionally furnished, had parquet flooring; the side and front windows had breathtaking views.' Breakfast is a generous buffet. 'Very good meals with excellent wines' are served in the informal bar/café/restaurant, *La Piscina*, and its canalside terrace. And the highly rated *Riviera* restaurant is near. (*John Collier*)

Open All year. *La Piscina* closed Mon. **Rooms** 5 suites, 20 double, 7 single. Air conditioning. **Facilities** Hall, lounge; classical background music; bar/café/restaurant with terrace (closed Monday). Background music. Unsuitable for ♿. **Location** On canal facing Giudecca. Lines 51 and 61 Zattere stop; Line 82 Accademia. **Restrictions** No smoking. No children under 16. No dogs. **Credit cards** All major cards accepted. **Terms** B&B: single €75–€106, double €99–€186; suite €136–€239. Full alc €30.

Ca' Pisani Hotel
Rio terà Foscarini
Dorsoduro 979/a
30123 Venice

Tel (041) 2401411
Fax (041) 2771061
Email info@capisanihotel.it
Website www.capisanihotel.it

In a relatively quiet part of the city, by the Accademia, this 16th-century *palazzo* is part of the Design Hotels group. Named after Vettor Pisani, the great admiral of the ancient republic, it is owned and run by Gianni and Marianna Serandrei. The decor is Italian futurist. Visitors in 2004 thought the hi-tech bathrooms 'sensational': they have 'sparkling granite; terrific power shower with water from six different outlets'. Other comments: 'In many ways a design masterpiece.' 'A fab bed. We loved the room: high ceilings with original beams incorporated into Art Deco. Done by Italians it works.' 'A stunning split-level studio.' 'Air conditioning noisy (they will turn it off if you ask).' Some guests find the banks of light switches 'seriously confusing'. The rooftop terrace has 'atmospheric views'. Sitting areas on most floors provide a 'peaceful refuge'. 'How nice to sip an excellent cappuccino with a magazine in the basement bar.' There is a free Internet area. Some cheaper rooms face the blank wall of the Accademia. 'Charming reception staff, so helpful.' 'Good value, particularly for Venice.' But the breakfasts were thought poor. (*Allan Kelly, and others*)

Open All year. Restaurant closed Mon. **Rooms** 29 double. 2 suitable for ♿. Some no-smoking. Air conditioning. **Facilities** Lift, chairlift. Lobby, salon, Internet area, restaurant/bar; background music; roof terrace; Turkish bath. **Location** Central, near Accademia bridge/Zattere water-bus stop. Voucher for parking in Piazzale Roma. **Restriction** No smoking in public areas. **Credit cards** All major cards accepted. **Terms** [2004] B&B: single €194–€275, double €216–€306. Lunch €26–€28; full alc €60. Min. stay 3 nights at weekends.

Hotel Colombina NEW
Calle del Remedio
Castello 4416
30122 Venice

Tel (041) 2770525
Fax (041) 2776044
Email info@hotelcolombina.com
Website www.hotelcolombina.com

'One of the attractions of this gem,' write its 2004 nominators, 'is its location on a junction of canals just behind the Doge's Palace.' In the warren of little streets 100 metres from St Mark's Square, it is a restored 17th century *palazzo*, decorated in 15th-century Venetian style. 'Our large air-conditioned front room, elegantly furnished, overlooked the canals and the Bridge of Sighs. Despite this, we found the area comparatively quiet, apart from the occasional late-night gondola. The breakfast rooms, though in a large cellar, are light and attractive. The buffet has excellent selections of cold and hot dishes. Bar snacks are served. Staff were particularly helpful in providing local directions.' (*David and Pat Hawkins*)

Open All year. **Rooms** 30 double, 2 single. Air conditioning. **Facilities** 2 lounges, bar, 2 breakfast rooms; background music. Unsuitable for ♿. **Location** By St Mark's Square; San Marco water-bus stop. **Credit cards** All major cards accepted. **Restrictions** No smoking: public areas, some bedrooms. 'Small pets only.' **Terms** B&B: single €95–€250, double €180–€410. *V*

Hotel Flora
San Marco 2283/A
30124 Venice

Tel (041) 5205844
Fax (041) 5228217
Email info@hotelflora.it
Website www.hotelflora.it

'Quiet, even by local standards', the Romanelli family's B&B hotel has long been loved by *Guide* readers. It stands at the end of a small street near St Mark's Square by the Contarini Palace (Shakespeare's setting for *Othello*). 'A place of great character', it has an 'old-fashioned' feel that is mostly enjoyed. 'Magical as ever; stuck in a time warp of genuine hospitality, undisturbed by modern management-speak,' said a returning visitor. Bedrooms vary hugely. Some are small (one was found cold in winter), and some bathrooms are 'cramped'. The best rooms overlook the courtyard, 'full of greenery, busts, statuettes of angelic faces and monkeys playing instruments'. In this 'oasis', you can 'take a quiet drink after sightseeing'. 'Good breakfast: scrambled eggs and bacon at extra cost.' 'Our family room was large and comfortable' (children are warmly welcomed). 'Honest good service.' 'Outstandingly helpful desk staff.' The Romanellis also own the *Locanda Novecento* nearby (www.locandanovecento.it). (*FH Potts, JJ, and others*)

Open All year. **Rooms** 38 double, 6 single. 2 on ground floor. Air conditioning. **Facilities** Lift. Lounge, breakfast room. No background music. Courtyard garden: bar. **Location** 300 m W of St Mark's Square. **Restriction** No smoking in public areas. **Credit cards** All major cards accepted. **Terms** [2004] B&B: single €100–€180, double €130–€230.

Londra Palace NEW
Riva degli Schiavoni 4171
30122 Venice

Tel (041) 5200533
Fax (041) 5225032
Email info@hotelondra.it
Website www.hotelondra.it

The proud boast of this opulent hotel is that it has a hundred windows facing the lagoon. A short walk from St Mark's Square, it was built in 1860 and later merged with another hotel next door. It was refurbished in the 1990s at huge cost. It is said to be 'eye-wateringly expensive', but visitors continue to love it: 'Perfectly placed on the waterfront,' says one in 2004. 'Staff were helpful; breakfast was stylish.' Earlier comments: 'A most enjoyable stay. Service was warm, welcoming and efficient. Our room was exceptionally comfortable. Looking out of its window was a constant source of interest.' 'Our balcony, where we enjoyed our evening drink, faced the water.' 'White, fluffy towels and linen sheets replaced daily.' Lavishly decorated bedrooms have silks, brocades, original Biedermeier furniture, a marble bathroom. Some look over red-tiled roofs. Room 106, where Tchaikovsky stayed in 1877, is 'truly lovely'. Public rooms, 'surprisingly small', are in neo-classical style: much glass, Aubusson carpets on marble floors. The *Do Leoni* restaurant, formal, and 'pricey', is 'excellent for Venetian fish'; desserts are 'unusual and delicious'. The bar serves good snacks. The outside terrace, 'most elegant', has a violinist at lunchtime and jazz in the early evening. (*Gillian Bradshaw, Ian and Gill Evett, and others*)

Open All year. **Rooms** 17 junior suites, 36 double. Air conditioning. **Facilities** 3 lounges, bar, restaurant (live music); terrace: bar/restaurant. Unsuitable for ♿. **Location** Facing lagoon, 400 m E of St Mark's Square. **Restrictions** No smoking in public areas. No pets. **Credit cards** All major cards accepted. **Terms** [2004] B&B: double €275–€585, suite €485–€790; D,B&B €60 added per person. Alc €54–€84. 1-night bookings sometimes refused weekends.

VERONA 37100 — Map 11:B4

Hotel Gabbia d'Oro
Corso Porta Borsari 4a

Tel (045) 8003060
Fax (045) 590293
Email gabbiadoro@easyasp.it
Website www.hotelgabbiadoro.it

18th-century palazzo *in* centro storico *(pedestrian street: car access for unloading). Now luxurious B&B hotel, with friendly staff. Stunning decor: beamed ceilings, frescoes, marble, hand-carved doors, chandeliers, opulent fabrics, antiques, elegant knick-knacks, in magnificent public rooms. Lift. Lounge, breakfast room, small panelled bar, orangery for drinks and snacks. Air conditioning. Lavish breakfast. No smoking. Unsuitable for ♿. Parking. No smoking in public areas.*

All major credit cards accepted. 19 suites, 8 double rooms, some with terrace. Room: single €160–€230, double €220–€370, suite €285–€830. Breakfast €23 [2004]. Endorsed this year.

VICENZA 36100 — Map 11:B4

Albergo Due Mori BUDGET
Contrà do Rode 24

Tel (0444) 321886
Fax (0444) 326127
Email info@hotelduemori.com
Website www.albergoduemori.it

'We loved it,' says a visitor this year to this unassuming family-owned B&B, a hotel on a quiet, narrow, pedestrianised street in the *centro storico*. Nearby are Piazza dei Signori and some of Palladio's finest buildings. 'One of the best two-star hotels we have stayed at in Italy. The old building has been refurbished but has nice traditional furniture. The entrance is spacious, giving an impression of luxury unusual in this class of hotel. Our room was enormous. The reception staff were extremely helpful.' 'The large public rooms are beautifully but sparsely furnished in Art Nouveau style,' says another guest. 'The bedrooms are simple, spacious and comfortable.' (*Jane Bloomfield, Elizabeth Ring*)

Open All year. **Rooms** 30. Air conditioning. **Facilities** Lift. Bar, breakfast room. Unsuitable for ♿. **Location** Central. Car park nearby. **Restriction** No smoking in public areas. **Credit cards** All major cards accepted. **Terms** [2004] Room: single €42, double €75. Breakfast ('a bit basic') €5.

Luxembourg

Hôtel du Parc, Clervaux

BOURSCHEID-PLAGE 9164 **Map 3:E5**

Hôtel Theis BUDGET
Rue Buurschter-Plage

Tel 99 00 20
Fax 99 07 34
Email info@hotel-theis.com
Website www.hotel-theis.com

At the bottom of a steep wooded valley in northern Luxembourg, by the grassy banks of the River Sûre (safe, if cool, bathing), stands this solid white-fronted Logis. It is 'efficiently run' by Romain Theis-Milbert ('a rather austere host'). He offers 'exceptional value in beautiful surroundings', say admirers, and the hotel is good for families: 'Our suite gave privacy for parents and a level of independence for children.' Some of the 'excellently furnished' bedrooms have a small balcony. Local dishes are served on Barberye Olivier's traditional menu (no choice), eg, pressé de caille au Porto; gigotin d'agneau, haricots mijotés. Breakfast is a buffet with a wide choice.

The salon and terrace look towards Bourscheid castle. A 'beautiful' wellness centre, built into the rocky bank and free to guests, 'belies the budget nature of the hotel's prices'. 'Difficult to find, but worth the effort.' (*G and VB; also BWR*)

Open 15 Mar–15 Nov. Restaurant closed Wed/Thurs to non-residents. **Rooms** 2 suites, 17 double. Also 12 holiday bungalows. **Facilities** Salon (no-smoking), bistro/bar, restaurant (classical background music); conference facilities; fitness centre: sauna, solarium. 1-hectare grounds: tennis, children's playground; river frontage: bathing, fishing. Unsuitable for ♿. **Location** W of N7, 14 km NW of Diekirch. **Restriction** No dogs. **Credit cards** Diners, MasterCard, Visa (half-board payment by cash or cheque). **Terms** B&B: single €58–€74, double €81–€97, suite €105; D,B&B €60–€96 per person. Set meals €30–€38, full alc €55. 1-night bookings sometimes refused.

CLERVAUX 9701 — Map 3:E5

Hôtel du Parc BUDGET
2 rue du Parc

Tel 92 06 50
Fax 92 10 68
Email hduparc@pt.lu
Website www.hotelduparc.lu

Liked for its family feel and 'slightly faded elegance', this old manor house, owned by Christiane Kämpke and Gert Cox, stands in lovely wooded grounds above the River Clerve. It has magnificent views of this historic little Ardennes town (with castle and Benedictine abbey). The welcome is warm from the 'friendly owners', and 'cheerful staff' ('they lent us a map and we had a fine walk'). Dogs, cats and birds are around; there are 'clocks galore'. Some of the carpeting is 250 years old, and very valuable. 'Our spacious bedroom had a well-designed bathroom.' Dinner is 'varied and excellent'. A 'very special place'; it offers 'good value', say recent guests.

Open Feb–Dec. Restaurant closed Tues. **Rooms** 1 suite, 5 double. 3 no-smoking. **Facilities** Lounge, restaurant (classical background music); sauna, solarium. 2-hectare grounds: terraces. Unsuitable for ♿. **Location** Edge of town. Station 5 mins' walk. **Credit cards** MasterCard, Visa. **Terms** B&B: single €44, double €70, suite €95; D,B&B €58–€70.50 per person. Full alc €40. 1-night bookings refused Sat.

GAICHEL 8469 — Map 3:E5

Hôtel de la Gaichel
5 route de Mersch

Tel 39 01 29
Fax 39 00 37
Email gaichel@relaischateaux.com
Website www.lagaichel.lu

'As nice as ever; it changes very little. We are greeted by Madame or Monsieur, the staff are friendly, professional, the food is very good.' A devotee returns in 2004 to Claudine and Michel Gaul-Jacquemin's smart restaurant-with-rooms (Relais & Châteaux). The old pink building stands in a 'splendid' shady park with stream and nine-hole golf course. 'All rooms have a balcony and a good view. Beds are comfortable. Not a sound at night.' The best bedrooms, and the restaurant, are in a modern extension. *Michelin* awards a star for the 'high-quality' cooking of Claude Lampson, served, in fine weather, on a terrace. 'Lovely lobster salad to start, then lamb, a nice bottle of wine. Not cheap, but one-star quality. The breakfast is traditional continental (no buffet, no muesli or fruit) but great; crisp French bread, croissants, lovely home-made jams, cheese, succulent ham, fresh orange juice.' (*Wolfgang Stroebe*)

Open All year, except 24 Dec, 1 Jan, 9 Jan–10 Feb, 22 Aug–2 Sept, Sun evening/Mon/Tues midday. No accommodation 25 Dec. **Rooms** 9 double, 4 single. **Facilities** Salons, breakfast room, restaurant; classical background music throughout; terrace; sauna; conference facilities. 3-hectare grounds: stream, golf, tennis. Unsuitable for ♿. **Location** 4 km SE of Arlon, 26 km N of Luxembourg city. **Restriction** No dogs. **Credit cards** Amex, MasterCard, Visa. **Terms** [2004] B&B: single €115–€145, double €125–€145; D,B&B €137–€147 per person. Set lunch €40, dinner €55–€90; full alc €100. 1-night bookings sometimes refused.

LUXEMBOURG 1453 — Map 3:E5

Hostellerie du Grünewald
10–16 route d'Echternach
Luxembourg-Dommeldange

Tel 43 18 82
Fax 42 06 46
Email hostgrun@pt.lu
Website www.hotel-romantik.lu

Owned by Brand and Gerhards families: hotel of 'old-fashioned charm' in quiet setting in N suburbs, not far from forest. Good transport to centre. 'Excellent value.' 'Sedate, friendly.' Children welcomed. Business facilities. Pleasant garden. Parking. Access to health facilities at Hilton Hotel *nearby. Good breakfast in pretty setting. 'Superb' if pricey French restaurant (closed 1–20 Jan, 1–17 July, Sat midday, Sun/Mon midday) specialises in lobster, shellfish, game. All major credit cards accepted. 2 suites, 26 bedrooms, 'attractive, comfortable', 5 no-smoking. B&B: single €90–€120, double €120–€145, suite €155–€160; D,B&B €100–€120 per person. Set meals €49–€85 [2004]. Endorsed this year.*

****

Traveller's tale Hotel in Austria. Our overall impression was that this hotel thought itself much classier than it really was. It offered poor value for money. The entrance hall and staircases were drab. And we were asked to let them know when we wanted to use the indoor swimming pool, 'so they could switch the heating on'. The thought of having to pre-plan a swim annoyed us so much that we didn't use the pool.

****

Traveller's tale Hotel in France. When we booked our holiday by email, all hotels but one replied within 24 hours and we booked within 48 hours. This hotel took over a week to respond to the initial query, and nearly three weeks to confirm. To arrive and find the receptionist with her feet on a table and smoking a cigarette was an image which was hard to forget.

****

Netherlands

Canal House Hotel, Amsterdam

ADUARD Groningen **Map 3:A5**

Herberg Onder de Linden NEW

Burg. Van Barneveldweg 3
9831 RD Aduard

Tel (050) 403 14 06
Fax (050) 403 18 14
Email herberg-linden@slenema.nl
Website www.slenema.nl

'Standards are still high' at Geerhard (the chef) and Petra Slenema's *Michelin*-starred restaurant-with-rooms, which returns to the *Guide* after a period without reports. The 'beautiful' red brick, gabled 18th-century building is in a pretty village with a ruined 12th-century Cistercian abbey, near Groningen in northern Holland. The modern French cooking is 'very good', says a report in 2004. Another visior wrote of a 'delicious dinner'. The spacious bedrooms, simply and stylishly furnished, are all different. 'Ours had beams, good bathroom, separate loo. Breakfast included boiled eggs, six kinds of bread, strawberries': it is served, on a terrace overlooking the lovely garden, or by a log fire. 'Not cheap, but you get what you pay for. Our Yorkshire terrier was made very welcome.' Residents are expected to dine in. (*Brenda Hoyle, Elizabeth Ring*)

Open All year, except New Year, 4–11 Feb, 11–24 July, 24–31 Oct, Sun (after breakfast)/Mon. Restaurant closed midday. **Rooms** 5 double. Some no-smoking. **Facilities** Bar, restaurant (background music; no-smoking). Terrace. Garden. Unsuitable for ♿. **Location**. 6 km NW of Groningen. Parking. **Credit cards** All major cards accepted. **Terms** [2004] B&B: single €99.50, double €115. Set dinner €59.50–€69.50; full alc €80.

ALMEN Gelderland — Map 3:B5

De Hoofdige Boer
Dorpsstraat 38
7218 AH Almen

Tel (0575) 43 17 44
Fax (0575) 43 15 67
Email hoofdigeboer@tref.nl
Website www.dehoofdigeboer.nl

Owned by Mr Holtslag and Mrs Leveld, this hotel/café/restaurant has long had a *Guide* entry. It is in an 'immaculate' village in the rural eastern part of the country. The emphasis is on the food: visitors in 2004 had a bedroom that was 'modern, comfortable, with little style'. Fans admire the 'very friendly' staff, the 'informal atmosphere' and the 'high standard of meals'. Regional dishes are 'beautifully served' in an attractive dining room or on a terrace. Breakfast is 'wholesome and plentiful'. There is a small beamed lounge and a pretty garden. Children are well looked after. Residents have free access to Almen's 'enormous and wonderful' open-air public swimming pool, and to an indoor one at Lochem, ten minutes' drive away. Bicycles can be hired in this good area for cycling, 'where most people seem to travel by bicycle or boat'. The fine old town of Zutphen, and the Kröller-Müller museum, with its sculpture park and Van Goghs, are not far. 'The tallest tree of the Netherlands is nearby.' (*Sam and Philippa Price, Elizabeth Ring, and others*)

Open All year, except 1–8 Jan. **Rooms** 1 suite (in annexe), 20 double, 2 single. 4 on ground floor. 1 suitable for ♿. **Facilities** Ramps. Lounge/bar, restaurant (classical background music 'when necessary'); conference room, function room. Garden: tea garden, terrace; bicycle hire. Guests have free access to 2 public swimming pools. **Location** Almen is *c.* halfway between Lochem and Zutphen, just N of N346. Hotel central, near church. Parking. **Restrictions** No smoking: restaurant, many bedrooms. No dogs. **Credit cards** All major cards accepted. **Terms** B&B €50.50–€74.50. Set lunch €9.50, dinner €31.50; full alc €39.50. 1-night bookings refused Christmas.

AMSTERDAM Noord-Holland — Map 3:B4

Ambassade Hotel
Herengracht 341
1016 AZ Amsterdam

Tel (020) 555 02 22
Fax (020) 555 02 77
Email info@ambassade-hotel.nl
Website www.ambassade-hotel.nl

A long-time *Guide* favourite, this 'very decent' B&B hotel is spread among ten 17th-century gabled houses on two of the city's finest canals (Herengracht and Singel). Owned by Mr W Schopman, it is managed by Ireen Wyers and Dick Westerneng; their 'super-efficient, friendly' staff offer a 'seamless service' (regular guests' preferences recorded; umbrellas, bicycle hire and city maps provided). Reception has been redecorated again this year, better to match the paintings on view from the 1950s Dutch Cobra movement; works by Dutch sculptor Ans Hey are also displayed. Public rooms have tall windows, crystal chandeliers, clocks and paintings. 'The sitting room is charming.' The library includes books signed by authors who have stayed (Martin Amis, Salman Rushdie, Umberto Eco, etc). There is a free Internet facility, and a 'float and massage' centre nearby. Bedrooms vary in size according to altitude, and in style, from modern Dutch to period. 'The steep stairs are a challenge, but they added to the charm.' 'Our spacious, clean room had slightly soulless repro furniture.' 'Ours on the fourth floor had a magnificent view.' Front rooms hear street noise, and from the windows of their lower ground-floor room, one couple 'could see only feet of passers-by and wheels of cars and bikes'. Breakfast (7 until 11 am; 11.30 at weekends) is lavish. Many good restaurants nearby; *Zuid Zeebrugge* and *Casa di David* are recommended this year. (*Keith Conlon, Susan B Hanley, Elizabeth Ring, BH, and many others*)

Open All year. **Rooms** 8 suites, 50 double, 1 single. 5 in annexe. Some no-smoking. **Facilities** Lifts. Lobby, 2 lounges, breakfast room (no-smoking); meeting room; library, Internet facility. No background music. Float & Massage centre nearby. Bicycle hire (€12 daily). Unsuitable for ♿. **Location** Central. Meter parking; public garage 5 mins' walk. **Credit cards** All major cards accepted. **Terms** Room: single €155–€165, double €175–€195, suite €250–€340. Breakfast €16.

Canal House Hotel
Keizersgracht 148
1015 CX Amsterdam

Tel (020) 622 51 82
Fax (020) 624 13 17
Email info@canalhouse.nl
Website www.canalhouse.nl

With 'wonderfully faded imperial charm', this unassuming B&B is a 17th-century house on the canal in the Bohemian Jordaan district. Brian and Mary Bennett, the 'amiable' Irish owners, run it with a 'most helpful', mainly Irish staff. The rambling house is 'a treasure trove of wax pictures, carved objects, little tapestries, wrought iron, plants and ecclesiastic bric-a-brac'. 'A very nice room facing the quay and canal' was liked this year; earlier visitors had a quiet garden-facing room, 'tastefully decorated, with a pretty canopied bed'. Some rooms are 'difficult to reach with luggage'. An 'adequate' breakfast is served in a large garden-facing room, with tables permanently laid, a heavy crystal chandelier, and big windows ('pity about the background music'). The bar serves tea and drinks. *Hostaria*, 'excellent Italian', is recommended for meals nearby. (*Keith Conlon, JH, and others*)

Open All year. **Rooms** 22 double, 4 single. 3 on ground floor. No TV. **Facilities** Lift. Lounge/bar, breakfast room; classical background music. Garden: summer house. Unsuitable for ♿. **Location** Central, near Westerkirk.

Street parking; garage nearby. **Restrictions** No smoking: breakfast room, some bedrooms. No children under 12. No dogs. **Credit cards** All major cards accepted. **Terms** B&B: single/double €140–€190.

Hotel de l'Europe
Nieuwe Doelenstraat 2–8
1012 CP Amsterdam

Tel (020) 531 17 77
Fax (020) 531 17 78
Email hotel@leurope.nl
Website www.leurope.nl

The 19th-century building, at the junction of the River Amstel and two canals, may be imposing with grand public rooms, but readers like the 'happy mix of large hotel of character and ambience that goes with family ownership'. Another comment: 'Very expensive, but good service and great food.' Adriaan Grandia is the manager. A collection of Dutch landscapes hangs in the *fin de siècle* lounge; there is a canalside café, a bar, *Freddy's*, a gourmet restaurant, *Excelsior* (with a French chef, Jean-Jacques Menanteau), and a brasserie, *Le Relais*. Meals are also served on a terrace. Some bedrooms have a balcony and windows opening on to the canal; quietest rooms overlook the courtyard. All bathrooms have been redecorated this year. The American breakfast is thought 'splendid'. The fitness centre has a gym and a small Grecian-style swimming pool with a wave machine. Nearby are Rembrandt's house, the Rijksmuseum, and the flower market. (*DJS, and others*)

Open All year. *Excelsior* restaurant closed 1–7 Jan, Sat midday, Sun midday. **Rooms** 6 suites, 17 junior suites, 56 double, 21 single. 2 floors no-smoking. Air conditioning. **Facilities** Lift, ramp. Lounge, café, bar, restaurant (pianist at night); brasserie; banqueting/conference facilities; gym; indoor heated swimming pool, sauna, solarium. Riverside terrace (summer meals). Unsuitable for ♿. **Location** Central, opposite flower market (rooms double glazed; quietest at back). Parking. **Credit cards** All major cards accepted. **Terms** [2004] Room: single €290, double €360, suite €460–€970. Breakfast €25. Set lunch €45, dinner €70; full alc €90.

DELFT Zuid-Holland — Map 3:B4

Hotel de Ark
Koornmarkt 65
2611 EC Delft

Tel (015) 215 79 99
Fax (015) 214 49 97
Email hotel@deark.nl
Website www.deark.nl

Spread over four 17th-century houses facing a canal in the old city, this four-star hotel provides 'reasonable value, good location, spacious rooms', says a visitor this year. 'But there are many changes of level, and the lift serves only one building. Our first-floor room had three floor-to-ceiling windows overlooking the canal. Sparsely furnished (no pictures), it felt a bit stark. The spacious bathroom had twin washbasins, but no separate shower.' Two suites have sauna and whirlpool bath. 'Breakfast, served in a big room looking over the canal, or in the large garden, was unexciting, but the mini-fridge enabled us to picnic in the bedroom. We had some excellent meals in Delft, notably at *L'Escalier* and *Le Vieux Jean*.' (*Michael Gwinnell, and others*)

Open 5 Jan–21 Dec. **Rooms** 2 suites, 23 double, 3 single. 2 on ground floor. Some no-smoking. **Facilities** Lift. Lounge, bar, breakfast room (no-smoking); background music. Terrace, garden. **Location** Centre of Old Delft. 5 mins' walk from station. Garage. **Credit cards** All major cards accepted. **Terms** [2004] B&B: single €98.50, double €124.

Hotel Leeuwenbrug BUDGET
Koornmarkt 16
2611 EE Delft

Tel (015) 214 77 41
Fax (015) 215 97 59
Email sales@leeuwenbrug.nl
Website www.leeuwenbrug.nl

'All the Dutch virtues' are found, by its most devoted fan, at Mr Wubben's patrician house on one of Delft's loveliest canals. It is 'warm, friendly, well organised, clean and unfussy', with 'excellent service'. 'A shirt I had left to be washed between visits was hanging in my room when I returned.' All bedrooms are different: some look over the canal; others face the Nieuwe Kerk; large rear ground-floor rooms in the annexe have picture windows facing a small garden; all have an 'unusually detailed' information folder. The only criticism: 'Smoking is allowed in the breakfast room.' Here, the buffet breakfast, laid out in a narrow entrance hall, was 'even more extensive, pancakes now offered'. Some package tours. (*Andrew Palmer*)

Open 3 Jan–23 Dec. **Rooms** 22 double, 14 single. 5 in annexe. Some on ground floor. **Facilities** Lift. Lounge (background music all day), TV room, bar; conference facilities. Unsuitable for ♿. **Location** S of centre, 5 mins' walk from station. Public parking adjacent (free overnight and Sun). **Restrictions** No smoking in bedrooms. No dogs. **Credit cards** All major cards accepted. **Terms** B&B: single €55–€109, double €80–€125. 1-night bookings occasionally refused. *V* (weekends only)

EDAM Noord-Holland — Map 3:B4

Hotel-Restaurant De Fortuna BUDGET
Spuistraat 3
1135 AV Edam

Tel (0299) 37 16 71
Fax (0299) 37 14 69
Email fortuna@fortuna-edam.nl
Website www.fortuna-edam.nl

'Just the sort of place the *Guide* exists to recommend,' say visitors in 2004 to the Dekker family's restaurant-with-rooms formed from five small 17th-century houses, some in gabled ziggurat style. It has a 'delightful position', by a canal. The friendly owners and their staff 'combine charm and efficiency', said an earlier report. 'Good value,' was another comment. 'Our lovely room, not large but comfortable, overlooked the courtyard garden and canal.' But rooms in the annexe in the garden may have poor soundproofing. The 'excellent' dinner is served in the busy dining room 'full of art, with imaginative lighting, chandeliers, windows and mirrors, like a 17th-century painting'. Breakfasts, are 'particularly good'; 'everything absolutely fresh'. Children are welcomed; only 'small, well-educated dogs' are allowed. A lake with boating and fishing is nearby. (*Nick and Carolyn Carter, and others*)

Open All year. Restaurant closed midday. **Rooms** 22 double, 2 single. In 5 buildings. Some on ground floor. Some suitable for ♿. **Facilities** Lounge, bar, restaurant; background music. Garden: terrace, river. **Location** Central. Ample free parking 100 m, across small bridge. **Credit cards** All major cards accepted. **Terms** [2004] B&B: single €65–€75, double €87.50–€99.50. Set dinner €32.50; full alc €45.

GRONINGEN **Map 3:A5**

Schimmelpenninck Huys
Oosterstraat 53
9711 NR Groningen

Tel (050) 318 95 02
Fax (050) 318 31 64
Email info@schimmelpenninckhuys.nl
Website www.schimmelpenninckhuys.nl

Near the market square of mainly traffic-free old Groningen, this patrician's house (a historic monument) has been restored by the Greek-Dutch Karistinos-Smit family owners, 'much in evidence'. 'A great hotel; difficult to find, but worth it once you do,' said one recent visitor. The lounge, with piano and lots of sofas, is decorated in Jugendstil; 'steep Dutch stairs' lead to the first floor in the main building. Bedrooms, which vary in size, are spread among five buildings around the leafy courtyard where meals are served in fine weather. There are two restaurants: *Parelvisser*, in a building across the garden, specialises in seafood; *Classique*, in an 18th-century room in the front of the house, is traditional French. The family also owns *Akropolis*, said to be the oldest Greek restaurant in the Netherlands. (*DJS*)

Open All year. **Rooms** 6 suites, 43 double, 3 single. In 5 buildings around courtyard. Some on ground floor. **Facilities** Lounge (classical background music), café, 2 restaurants; small conference room. Courtyard garden. Unsuitable for ♿. **Location** Central, off Grote Markt (some rooms hear traffic). Public car park 2 blocks away. **Credit cards** Amex, MasterCard, Visa. **Terms** [2004] Room: single €75.80–€110, double €120, suite €157.50. Breakfast €12.50.

THE HAGUE Zuid-Holland **Map 3:B4**

Parkhotel Den Haag
Molenstraat 53
2513 BJ The Hague

Tel (070) 362 43 71
Fax (070) 361 45 25
Email info@parkhoteldenhaag.nl
Website www.parkhoteldenhaag.nl

Though large by *Guide* standards (with four extra bedrooms this year), this venerable city hotel, down a narrow street in the Hofkwartier (court quarter) of the Dutch capital, is liked for the 'surprisingly personal' service. 'Reception staff learned my name within minutes of my arrival, and remembered it,' reports a recent visitor. The main public room is 'splendid', the staircase 'decidedly elegant'. Bedrooms may be 'anonymous', but they are well equipped for the business traveller. There is a 'charming' courtyard garden, and the breakfast room overlooks the garden of the Noordeinde Palace. No restaurant 'but the city is better endowed with eating places than good hotels': *Garoeda* nearby is recommended ('excellent *rijsttafel*'). (*SH*)

Open All year. **Rooms** 2 suites, 81 double, 37 single. 20 air conditioned. **Facilities** Lounge (background music), bar, breakfast room; 6 conference rooms, business centre. Unsuitable for ♿. **Location** Central, off Prinsestraat, near station. **Restriction** No dogs. **Credit cards** All major cards accepted. **Terms** [2004] B&B: single €140, double €200, suite €375. Weekend packages. 1-night bookings sometimes refused. *V*

MARGRATEN Limburg — Map 3:D5

Hotel Groot Welsden BUDGET

Groot Welsden 27
6269 ET Margraten

Tel (043) 458 13 94
Fax (043) 458 23 55
Email info@hotelgrootwelsden.nl
Website www.hotelgrootwelsden.nl

Liked again this year ('a very friendly welcome'), this small hotel stands in farmland near a village east of Maastricht. Full of character, it is furnished with antiques, old toys, ornaments and *objets d'art*; the bar has an aviary with tiny birds; the lounge has a floodlit fish tank and little night-lights under glass domes. There are 'lots of places to sit, indoors and out'. Residents are offered a four-course dinner at 6.30: no choice until main course, which is selected in advance. 'Food was tasty if unexceptional. Small but adequate wine list. Afterwards they kindly brought us some English magazines, some of them 17 years old, which made for interesting reading.' Some bedrooms are small, three have a whirlpool bath, one has a small roof terrace with plastic grass. 'Our room was filled with religious objects, and had a crucifix on the wall. The excellent breakfast buffet included hot bacon and scrambled eggs.' Light lunches are served. In the large garden, loungers, tables and parasols surround a pond with 'special diving ducks'. Many guests are American: Margraten village has the largest US war cemetery in the Netherlands. (*E and P Thompson*)

Open All year, except carnival time. **Rooms** 14 double. **Facilities** Lounge, bar, garden room (no-smoking), restaurant; classical background music. Garden, tea garden; patio. Bicycle hire. Unsuitable for ♿. **Location** 1 km N of Margraten, off N278, 10 km E of Maastricht. Parking. **Restrictions** No smoking: restaurant, garden room, bedrooms. No pets. **Credit cards** Amex, MasterCard, Visa. **Terms** [2004] B&B: single €58–€74, double €80–€100. Set lunch €11.50, dinner €25; full alc €42. *V*

OUDERKERK AAN DE AMSTEL Noord-Holland — Map 3:B4

't Jagershuis NEW

Amstelzijde 2–4
1184 VA Ouderkerk aan de Amstel

Tel (020) 496 20 20
Fax (020) 496 45 41
Email info@jagershuis.com
Website www.jagershuis.com

In an 'idyllic waterfront location' on the River Amstel, in a village 20 minutes' drive from Schiphol airport, this hotel/restaurant is 'a real find', says the 2004 nominator. 'If you like feeding coots and mallards while relaxing on a canopied terrace perusing the wine list before a modern Dutch dinner in a series of beamed dining rooms, this is for you. Not chi-chi, it is a homely, modern conversion of a fine old building. Throughout are fine paintings, antique furniture and alcoves. The terraces have comfy chairs, and dinner can be eaten outside.' In the restaurant, almost every table has a river view, and Dimitry Mulder's *à la carte* menu has 'surprising specialities'. The bar serves salads, soups, sandwiches. All bedrooms ('good sized, with spotless functional bathroom') face the river. 'Breakfast is guaranteed to put you in a good mood for the day: ham and eggs, muesli that is a nut-lover's dream, a basket of breads. Attentive service.' (*Jon Hughes*)

Open all year, except New Year. Restaurant closed Sat midday. **Rooms** 12 double. Air conditioning. **Facilities** Bar, restaurant; function rooms. Terrace. **Location.** In village 10 km SE of Amsterdam. Parking. **Restriction** No dogs. **Credit cards** All major cards accepted. **Terms** [2004] B&B double €180–€265. Set lunch €38, alc €45–€59.

ROTTERDAM Zuid-Holland — Map 3:C4

Hotel Bazar BUDGET
Witte de Withstraat 16
3012 BP Rotterdam

Tel (010) 206 51 51
Fax (010) 206 51 59
Email all@hotelbazar.nl
Website www.hotelbazar.nl

'For the young at heart': Akbar Tamiz's 'lively, inexpensive' hotel with offbeat decor, on lively street near Museumpark. 'Delicious breakfasts.' Bar, 'fantastic' large North African-themed café/restaurant (background music). 27 bedrooms (best ones spacious): 'amazingly furnished' (eg, shrine to Virgin Mary; photos of Fidel Castro; 'African'). Unsuitable for ♿. All major credit cards accepted. B&B: single €60, double €75–€120. Full alc €23 [2004].

Hotel New York
Koninginnenhoofd 1
3072 AD Rotterdam

Tel (010) 439 05 00
Fax (010) 484 27 01
Email info@hotelnewyork.nl
Website www.hotelnewyork.nl

The 19th-century head office of the Holland America Line has been turned into this lively waterfront hotel. With its symmetrical facade, balconies, dormer windows, towers, wrought iron staircase and carpets with an Art Nouveau motif, it retains the feel of a boat station for transatlantic passengers. Many bedrooms are spacious and high-ceilinged; most have a view of the River Maas; larger ones have the original walnut panelling; all now have high-speed Internet access. Recent praise: 'Friendly staff. Extremely good all-night reception and room service.' 'A wonderfully old-fashioned experience.' There is an oyster bar, and the large café/restaurant, open early until late, attracts non-residents. The new terrace restaurant, *Maaskant*, opens on fine days from 10 am until the early hours. Breakfast is a buffet. The hotel can be reached by subway, or tram, but a water taxi provides the 'most authentic' access.

Open All year. **Rooms** 72 double. 1 suitable for ♿. 1st-floor rooms no-smoking. **Facilities** Lift. Lounge, oyster bar, tea room, café/restaurant, winter garden, terrace restaurant (in fine weather); observation tower; 5 function/

conference rooms. **Location** S of Erasmus Bridge, 1.5 km from centre (tram 20; water taxi). Parking adjacent. **Restriction** No pets. **Credit cards** All major cards accepted. **Terms** [2004] Room €93–€220. Breakfast €10.50–€12.50. Set meal €21.

TILBURG Noord-Brabant — Map 3:C4

Auberg du Bonheur NEW
Bredaseweg 441
5036 NA Tilburg

Tel (013) 468 69 42
Fax (013) 590 09 59
Email info@bonheurhorecagroep.nl
Website www.bonheurhorecagroep.nl

Near campus, on outskirts of 'dull' university town: 'imposing' modern hotel surrounded by trees. 'Friendly; excellent service; comfortable restaurant serves food as good as you can get in Tilburg. Breakfast an excellent buffet.' À la carte *restaurant (closed midday on Sat and Sun); business facilities. All major credit cards accepted. 26 'nicely appointed' bedrooms. B&B: single €95, double €130. Lunch €25, dinner €37–€62 [2004].*

ZUTPHEN Gelderland — Map 3:B5

Eden Hotel NEW
's Gravenhof 6
7201 DN Zutphen

Tel (057) 554 61 11
Fax (057) 554 59 99
Email res.edenzutphen@edenhotelgroup.com
Website www.edenhotelgroup.com

In the centre of this charming town ('like Rye with knobs on,' say visitors in 2004), this 17th-century listed building has been enlarged 'with panache to provide nicely judged light and space'. Now a four-star hotel (Best Western) with a big modern wing, it impressed the nominators: 'Eden is a suitable name.' The interior is a mix of modern and antique: 17th-century prints, and 18th-century wall landscape, and modern sculptures by Kathinka Roovers. Exhibitions are held. There is a conservatory restaurant and a vaulted bar/dining room, *De Gravin*, which serves a monthly-changing menu. The town has good eating places, too; the *Clock* is recommended. The Kröller-Müller museum is near. (*Nigel and Olga Wikeley*)

Open All year. **Rooms** 3 suites, 71 double. Some no-smoking. Some suitable for ♿. **Facilities** Lift. Bar, 2 restaurants; conference/banquet facilities. Terrace. Cycling, walking, canoeing nearby. **Location** Central, opposite St Walburgskerk. Public parking in front. **Credit cards** All major cards accepted. **Terms** [2004] B&B: single €45–€97, double €60–€132, suite €75–€150. Alc €39–€46.

> Italicised entries indicate hotels that are worth considering but which, for various reasons – inadequate information, lack of feedback, ambivalent reports – do not at the moment warrant a full entry.

Norway

Hotel Union Øye, Øye

BERGEN **Map 1:A2**

Hotel Park Pension
Harald Hårfagresgate 35
5007 Bergen

Tel 55 54 44 00
Fax 55 54 44 44
Email booking@parkhotel.no
Website www.parkhotel.no

In a leafy residential quarter near the university and park, Julie Helene and Fredrik Klohs's B&B hotel (*Historiske Hotel*) comprises two late 19th-century white gabled houses, filled with antiques and paintings. Recent visitors had a warm welcome. 'Our room, in the building across the street, was the largest and most comfortable we found anywhere in Norway.' A 'fine' breakfast has fresh rolls, cereal, meats, cheese and fish. Tea and coffee are available (free) all day; snacks and drinks are also served. 'They were happy for us to use the facilities until we caught an afternoon ferry. A good find.' The centre is an easy walk away. (*SAP*)

Open All year, except Christmas, New Year, Easter. **Rooms** 1 suite, 26 double, 6 single. In 2 buildings. Most no-smoking. **Facilities** Reception, breakfast room (no-smoking; background music sometimes). Unsuitable for ♿. **Location** Central, off Strømgaten. Parking 50 Nkr. **Credit cards** All major cards accepted. **Terms** [2004] B&B: single 650–890 Nkr, double 940–1,090 Nkr, suite 1,390–1,490 Nkr.

DALEN 3880 — Map 1:B2

Dalen Hotel
Postboks 54

Tel 35 07 70 00
Fax 35 07 70 11
Email dalenhaa@online.no
Website www.dalenhotel.no

At the head of Bandak lake, in a quiet village by the Telemark Canal, this remarkable hotel, built in 1894, was long popular with European royalty and aristocracy. It remains a 'must-stay', says a *Guide* reader. Built in 'dragon style' with references to local Stave churches, it has swooping pointed ends over layers of balconies, creating a Chinese look. The building fell into disrepair after being confiscated by the Germans during the Second World War. Painstakingly restored in 1994, it is managed by co-owner Olav Underdal. The interiors are 'stunning'; a two-storey entrance hall has a stained-glass ceiling and a gallery. There are carved wooden dragon heads, ornaments, sculptures, polished floors. Bedrooms, 'splendidly old-fashioned', have authentic, sombre colours, stencilling, handmade lace curtains, good lighting. In the dining room, with tall windows and long tables, the no-choice dinner is thought 'simple and excellent'. Summer meals are served under a willow tree in the garden, where a terrace faces a lake with swans.

Open 20 Apr–1 Nov. **Rooms** 1 suite, 36 double, 1 single. Some on ground floor. **Facilities** Ramp. Hall (background music at night), smoking lounge, ladies' lounge, garden lounge, breakfast room, dining room; conference rooms. Garden: outside dining. Lake 300 m (fishing, etc). Unsuitable for ♿. **Location** D45, 20 km W of E134 Drammen–Haugesund, 230 km SW of Oslo. **Restrictions** No smoking: hall, 2 lounges, bedrooms. No dogs. **Credit cards** All major cards accepted. **Terms** [2004] B&B: single 900 Nkr, double 1,150–1,500 Nkr, suite 1,800 Nkr; D,B&B (min. 2 nights) 250 Nkr added per person.

FJÆRLAND 6848 — Map 1:A2

Hotel Mundal

Tel 57 69 31 01
Fax 57 69 31 79
Email hotelmundal@fjordinfo.no
Website www.fjordinfo.no/mundal

One of Norway's oldest hotels, this traditional white clapboard building, on the waterfront of the country's longest and deepest fjord, is still owned and run by the family who built it in 1891. Handed down through the female line, it is managed by Marit Orheim Mauritzen, supported by sister-in-law Billie Orheim (the chef). Other family members help in season: 'Just the kind of warm hosts one hopes to find in a *Guide* hotel,' said a regular visitor. In the public rooms are hand-woven wall hangings and floor coverings, antiques and objects of family interest. The simple bedrooms are in cottage style; some have a sitting area with tea/coffee-making facilities. Modernisation has been done 'with respect for the original style'. The traditional dinners and breakfasts are much liked. A talk on the hotel's history is given over pre-dinner drinks every evening. There's a 'book-café' (the town is noted for its second-hand and antiquarian bookshops), a lounge with a fire, and a music room where you can listen to Grieg CDs. The owners say their hotel is not very suitable for disabled people, but a guest with mobility problems was well looked after. Fjærland is served by a daily boat from Bergen and by buses; some guests arrive by seaplane. (*ES, and others*)

Open 1 May–30 Sept. **Rooms** 26 double, 8 single. **Facilities** Lounge, music room, library/billiard room, book-café, dining room (no-smoking). No background music. Fjordside garden: boats, bicycle hire. Not really suitable for ♿. **Location** Centre of village. 180 km NE of Bergen. Car park. **Restrictions** No smoking. No dogs in public rooms. **Credit cards** Diners, MasterCard, Visa. **Terms** B&B: single 900 Nkr, double 1,300–1,900 Nkr. Set dinner 420 Nkr. *V*

NORDDAL 6214 — Map 1:A2

Petrines Gjestgiveri

Tel 70 25 92 85
Fax 70 25 92 88
Email petrines@petrines.com
Website www.petrines.com

Quietly set near a river in a remote mountain hamlet, this small hotel was 'unreservedly recommended' by *Guide* readers. 'Extremely good value', it promises 'modern comfort in nostalgic surroundings'. Built in 1916 as an old people's home by Helene Petrine Hvidt, a local farmer and apple grower (her photograph can be seen in the restaurant), it became an inn in 1992. Carl Larsson was the inspiration for textile designer Torunn Halseid Marø when she decorated the rooms; they have rugs on pale pine floors, and bright cotton textiles. Eight have facilities *en suite*; four on the ground floor have a wash basin and share a bath and loos. In the 'small, homely' restaurant, specialities include local deer, kid and trout and home-made apple juice (all found 'delicious'). Norddal has the first octagonal church built in the area. Within easy reach is good walking country, and a short drive away is the 'popular but unmissable Geiranger'. (*S and SL*)

Open All year. **Rooms** 12 double. 8 *en suite*. 4 on ground floor. **Facilities** TV room, bar, restaurant; conference/function facilities. **Location** 30 km N of Geiranger, off route 63 to Andalsnes. **Restriction** Smoking in bar only. **Credit cards** All major cards accepted. **Terms** [2004] B&B 350–670 Nkr. Set dinner 250 Nkr.

Exchange rates for countries that do not belong to the European Monetary Union can be found at the back of this volume.

OSLO **Map 1:A3**

Hotel Bondeheimen
Rosenkrantz gate 8
0159 Oslo

Tel 23 21 41 00
Fax 23 21 41 01
Email booking@bondeheimen.com
Website www.bondeheimen.com

City hotel (Best Western) in 'excellent' location near parliament, national theatre, royal palace, nightlife. Endorsed again this year. 'Pleasant, with eager staff.' Good value, especially Fri–Sun. Home-made breads at 'exceptional' buffet breakfast; traditional Norwegian dishes, eg reindeer stew with loganberries, in Kaffistova *(café/restaurant). Lobby/lounge; conference facilities; shop. Some street noise at night. Closed Christmas/New Year, Easter. All major credit cards accepted. 127 bedrooms, in modern Scandinavian style with sophisticated lighting, Internet connection. B&B: single 750–1,095 Nkr, double 990–1,295 Nkr [2004].*

ØYE 6196 **Map 1:A2**

Hotel Union Øye
Norangsfjorden

Tel 70 06 21 00
Fax 70 06 21 16
Email post@unionoye.no
Website www.unionoye.no

Restored to the style of its heyday, this *Historiske Hotel* member was built in the 19th century as a hideaway in a remote setting among mountains of the Norang valley. It was popular with European royalty. The hall, staircase and corridors, dark, old-Norse baronial, 'might be oppressive in bad weather', but it has a magnificent *belle époque* salon, and the porch has fine mountain views. 'A marvellous three days,' say recent visitors. 'Our bedroom, small but comfortable, had a small bathroom and balcony. In wonderful weather, we spent much time in the garden.' Dinner is in two sittings (7 or 8.30 pm). 'At the later one we were able to linger over the delicious food: fish soup and salmon mousse starters; an alcoholic sorbet; pork, beef and lamb cooked to perfection, with good vegetables. The wine list, as everywhere in Norway, was pricey. Breakfast had meat, cheese and fish, cereals, yogurt, wonderful home-baked rolls and preserves.' Tea and coffee are available free of charge in the afternoons. Many mountains to climb in the area, but few flat walks. (*SAP*)

Open Apr–Nov. **Rooms** 21 double. **Facilities** Salon, sitting room, TV room, bar, restaurant. Garden. **Location** Turn right off Hellesylt–Stryn road (route 60), just S of Hellesylt, take Norang valley road (route 655). Hotel 19 km up valley (signposted). **Credit cards** All major cards accepted. **Terms** [2004] B&B: single 940 Nkr, double 1,480 Nkr. Set dinner 395 Nkr.

Italicised entries indicate a hotel on which we have little information or mixed reports.

Portugal

Casa da Calma, Moncarapacho

The Portuguese are proud of their history. Visitors to this country will enjoy a distinctive experience, both in the culture and the cooking: no blandness here. Even in Lisbon, the food is generally traditional, and all the better for that. Fresh fish and salt cod will be found on many menus. Pork features in many regional dishes, often served with clams, a delicious combination.

The Portuguese people have a dignified formality but are not reserved. They have many excellent examples of the kind of hotel the *Guide* likes so much, with character and hands-on owner/managers. Two new entries this year demonstrate this kind of hospitality. Fernando Reino, a retired diplomat, and his wife, Maria Gabriela, offer rural B&B at their *Quinta do Rio Touro*, a restored fruit farm within the Sintra-Cascais natural park. In the peaceful eastern Algarve, Nicole Effenberg has charmingly converted her *quinta*, aptly named *Casa da Calma*. The *Casa Três Palmeiras*, also in the Algarve, continues to be much admired.

In earlier editions of the *Guide* we included a number of members of the state-owned pousada chain, similar to the Spanish paradors. But personally owned and managed places to stay have proliferated, and this year we have only one pousada: the purpose-built one at Viana do Castello.

AZOIA 2705-001 Sintra — Map 7:D1

Convento de São Saturnino

Tel (0219) 28 31 92
Fax (0219) 28 96 85
Email contact@saosat.com
Website www.saosat.com

The restoration of this 12th-century convent, in the 'remote and dramatic valley' of the Sintra-Cascais natural park, has produced an 'eclectic, welcoming, well-run and very personal' small hotel, according to a recent visitor. It was the fruit of three years' work by architect João Kaditch, a medieval enthusiast, and his Scottish business partner, John Nelson Perrie, a designer. 'The furnishings are a remarkably diverse antiquarian mixture.' Bedrooms, 'comfortable and well appointed', have beams; there are attic ceilings, canopy beds and old paintings. The suites are in a modern annexe 50 metres ('and 80 steps') from the main building. The gardens, full of geese, ducks and dogs, are 'decorative and practical'. An 'excellent, if slightly shallow' swimming pool has been created from an old cistern: beside it, in summer, snacks are served. The communal breakfast is sometimes taken in the old kitchens, sometimes at a long table in the dining room which has a period feel. Dinner can be provided, given advance notice. Many restaurants are in the surrounding hills and villages. Beautiful beaches are nearby. (*RWB*)

Open All year. **Rooms** 3 suites (in annexe), 6 double. **Facilities** 2 lounges (background music), TV room, dining room. Garden: swimming pool. Unsuitable for ♿. **Location** 30 km W of Lisbon, off N247 Malveira–Colares. 1st left at village, 2nd left past bar, left at Tourism Rural sign. **Restrictions** No smoking. Small children discouraged. No dogs. **Credit cards** Amex, MasterCard, Visa. **Terms** [2004] B&B: single €120, double €145, suite €160. Set meals €25. 1-night bookings sometimes refused.

Quinta do Rio Touro NEW
Caminho do Rio Touro

Tel (0219) 29 28 62
Fax (0219) 29 23 60
Email info@quinta-riotouro.com
Website www.quinta-riotouro.com

For an experience in eco- and agro-tourism: in 1994, a retired diplomat, Fernando Reino, and his wife, Maria Gabriela, bought this abandoned fruit farm, encircled by hills in a lush valley in the Sintra-Cascais natural park. They now run it as a rural B&B, with bedrooms in its manor house and a guest house, renovated in traditional style. 'A fantastic place: tranquil, beautifully kept,' says the nominator after a 15-day visit in 2004. The multilingual Reinos are seeking an organic certificate for the farm: 'Guests may pick oranges straight from the tree, or try the produce from the ground or off the vine,' they write on their website. The houses are filled with 'antiques and treasures' from their diplomatic travels. Guests have access to the living room, the extensive library, a terrace leading to the garden, a swimming pool and a sauna and exercise room. There are three bedrooms in the main house, and three in the guest house, 100 metres away, which can be taken as a unit. There are seafood restaurants in Azóia, within walking distance, and many sandy beaches are nearby. (*Kevin Kinch*)

Open All year. **Rooms** 4 suites, 2 double. 3 in guest house, 100 m. **Facilities** Lounge, library, bar, breakfast room. No background music. Terrace. Garden: unheated swimming pool. Unsuitable for ♿. **Location** Just outside village. 35 km W of Lisbon. A5 exit 12; turn right for 8 km, left to Azóia; left at *rural turismo* sign. 2nd house along lane. **Restrictions** No smoking. No dogs. **Credit cards** MasterCard, Visa. **Terms** B&B: double €120–€140, suite €140–€200. *V*

CASCAIS **Map 7:D1**

Hotel Albatroz NEW
Rua Frederico Arouca 100
2750-353 Lisbon

Tel (021) 484 73 80
Fax (021) 484 48 27
Email albatroz@albatrozhotels.com
Website www.albatrozhotels.com

On a rocky headland in the old fishing village favoured by the Portuguese royal family in the 19th century, this former summer residence of the dukes of Loulé is now a luxury hotel. 'Liked without qualification', it returns to the *Guide* after a time without reports. 'Ambience, service, situation are all just right,' says this year's report. The *Albatroz* is luxuriously furnished: tiles, frescoes, antiques, rugs and flowers abound. The most opulent rooms are in the old mansion; others, in a modern extension, have a sea-facing balcony. A room in the *Abatroz Palace*, across the road, was 'sumptuous, if not huge, with balcony overlooking the beach (double glazing cut out the noise)'. In the refurbished restaurant, also with sea views, Portuguese and international dishes are served, eg, stuffed crab with prawns; beef Wellington; and meals are sometimes accompanied by a singer or a pianist. On the terrace, a small saltwater swimming pool is surrounded by loungers. (*David Crowe*)

Open All year. **Rooms** 10 suites, 42 double, 1 single. 6 in annexe. Some on ground floor. Air conditioned. **Facilities** 2 lounges, bar, restaurant (background/live music); conference rooms. Terrace: 2 swimming pools. Beach 100 m. **Location** Central, on seafront. Private parking. **Restriction** Only small dogs allowed. **Credit cards** All major cards accepted. **Terms** Room: single €150–€322, double €180–€355, suite €275–€510. Breakfast €15. D,B&B €140–€372 per person. Set meals €35, full alc €55.

'Set meals' refers to fixed-price meals, which may have ample, limited or no choice on the menu. 'Full alc' is the hotel's estimated price per person of a three-course *à la carte* meal with a half bottle of house wine. 'Alc' is the price without wine.

Estalagem Senhora da Guia NEW
Estrada do Guincho
2750-642 Lisbon

Tel (021) 486 92 39
Fax (021) 486 92 27
Email senhora.da.guia@mail.telepac.pt
Website www.senhoradaguia.com

Just outside this fashionable holiday resort, this white-walled hotel stands in 'gorgeously' landscaped grounds on a promontory amid pine trees. It returns to the *Guide* after a time with no reports. A 2004 visitor reports: 'Service throughout was excellent. Relaxing ambience. Our side room, clean, well equipped and air conditioned, had a good balcony which faced a copse of pine trees and part of a golf course. Very secluded. Lots of birds. Reasonable view of the sea.' Some bedrooms hear traffic noise from the main road. Some are in the main house, some in a garden annexe, some in a new sea-facing building, said to be peaceful. Breakfasts are 'gargantuan'. The main dining room was thought 'somewhat drab' this year, but a new, sea-facing restaurant is planned for 2005. In fine weather, meals are served on a terrace that looks across the swimming pool to the sea. 'The food is excellent', and good local restaurants include *Furnas do Guincho*, opposite the hotel. 'To get around, we used local buses and taxis (quickly summoned and not expensive).' 'Good value for money,' was an earlier comment. (*John and June Jennings, and others*)

Open All year. **Rooms** 1 suite, 2 junior suites, 39 double. Some in 2 annexes. Some on ground floor. **Facilities** Lounge/bar, restaurant; classical background music; 2 conference rooms; gym planned for 2005. Garden: unheated swimming pool, solarium, bar. Sandy beach 3 km. Tennis, horse riding nearby. Unsuitable for ♿. **Location** 3 km W of Cascais on coast road to Guincho. Parking. **Restriction** No dogs. **Credit cards** All major cards accepted. **Terms** [2004] B&B: single €105–€230, double €125–€260, suite €225–€340; D,B&B €35 added per person.

ESTOI 8000-661 Algarve — Map 7:D1

Monte do Casal
Cerro do Lobo

Tel (0289) 99 15 03
Fax (0289) 99 13 41
Email reservationsmdc@mail.telepac.pt
Website www.montedocasal.pt

Near an old market town, this 18th-century farmhouse has been turned by owner/manager Bill Hawkins into an 'excellent' small luxury hotel/restaurant. 'It is well run and has a very good restaurant and most helpful staff,' says a visitor this year. The emphasis is on tranquillity: no children under 16. All rooms have a sound system and a sea-facing terrace, where 'breakfast appears, laid on a table, at 9 am'. Seven of the rooms are in a new villa with panoramic views, in the large grounds where there are two swimming pools, bougainvillaea, almond, olive and fruit trees, two waterfalls, rock pools and a stream. This year, bathrooms have been upgraded, the restaurant has been given a new 'antique' decor, and, Mr Hawkins tells us, there is a new suite. 'Its bedroom has its own waterfall, creatively lit at night, and it has a private garden and a rock pool stocked with koi carp.' The eclectic menus are mainly French-based, but 'once it was Thai, and there are occasional British touches, eg, quail's eggs on bubble and squeak'; also some enterprising vegetarian options. A good base for exploring the quieter eastern Algarve. (*Michael Burns, and others*)

Open All year, except 6–20 Jan, 2–16 Dec. **Rooms** 6 suites, 14 double. 7 in villa. Air conditioning. No TV. **Facilities** Lounge, bar, restaurant; background music/live music 5 nights a week; dinner/dance Sat. 3-hectare garden: 3 terraces, 2 heated swimming pools, 2 spa baths. Croquet, putting. Unsuitable for ♿. **Location** 3 km NE of Estoi, *c.* 10 km NE of Faro. Follow signs to SB Alportel and S Bras. From Estoi follow yellow signs. **Restrictions** No smoking: restaurant, bedrooms. No children under 16. No dogs. **Credit cards** Amex, MasterCard, Visa. **Terms** [2004] B&B €62–€144; D,B&B €65–€121. Set dinner €49. *V*

FUNCHAL Madeira — Map 7:D6

Quinta da Bela Vista
Caminho do Avista Navios 4
9000-129 Funchal

Tel (0291) 70 64 00
Fax (0291) 70 64 01
Email info@belavistamadeira.com
Website www.belavistamadeira.com

Splendid views over Funchal Bay are enjoyed from the Ornellas Monteiro family's 'delightful' five-star *estalagem*, a much-extended white 19th-century mansion, which stands in 'stunning' mature gardens on the outskirts of the town. 'The courteous staff are friendly, and will go beyond the norm to help,' said a visitor who enjoyed a week-long stay despite bad weather. The old house is furnished with antiques, paintings and tapestries; a bedroom here was found 'light, well furnished and spotlessly clean'. Good bedside lights, two reading chairs and 'a well-appointed bathroom, but a feeble shower'. Other bedrooms are in two modern wings. A regular visitor advised: 'Pay extra for a big room with a balcony in the *Bay View* annexe.' Two restaurants: the formal *à la carte*, *Casa Mäe*, and the 'very pleasant' *table d'hôte*, *Avista Navios*: 'Excellent service, menu strong on fish, a short but moderately priced wine list.' The bar by the swimming pool 'is a delight, with wonderful views'. 'Breakfast is also good.' A courtesy bus takes guests to the centre. A yacht can be chartered for sea trips. (*NF, and others*)

Open All year. **Rooms** 7 suites, 82 double. Most in 2 annexes. 4 suitable for ♿. Air conditioning. **Facilities** 4 lounges, library, 3 bars, 2 restaurants; classical/jazz background, live piano music; card room, billiard room; fitness room, sauna, spa bath. Garden: terraces, heated swimming pool, snack bar, tennis. Sea 2.5 km (yacht for excursions). **Location** 2.5 km from centre (courtesy minibus). Parking. **Restriction** No dogs. **Credit cards** All major cards accepted. **Terms** B&B: single €148–€254, double €187–€360, suite €360–€432. Set meals €37.50; full alc €53. *V*

> The 2006 edition of the *Guide*, covering Great Britain and Ireland, will appear in the autumn of 2005. Reports are particularly useful in the spring, and they need to reach us by 15 May 2005 at the very latest if they are to help the 2006 edition.

Casa Velha do Palheiro
Palheiro Golf, São Gonçalo
9050-296 Funchal

Tel (0291) 79 03 50
Fax (0291) 79 49 25
Email info@casa-velha.com
Website www.casa-velha.com

In a 'beautiful, peaceful' hillside setting, yet close to overdeveloped, crowded Funchal, this handsome old yellow-fronted hunting lodge stands within the magnificent Palheiro gardens, which have exotic plants from around the world. It has been turned into a luxurious hotel (Relais & Châteaux) by the Blandy family, who live on the estate; James Scott is the manager. It is 'attractively furnished in period style'. 'The staff, especially in the dining room, are very helpful,' said one recent guest. Others wrote: 'Our main memories are of birdsong, frogs croaking, camellias, marvellous food.' In the 'splendid dining room', Benoît Sinthon cooks with 'modern French technique', using Madeiran produce: 'Even the *table d'hôte* dinners are works of art.' Breakfast has 'delicious breads'. 'The swimming pool is excellent; tennis and badminton alongside.' The poolside bar serves snacks; and residents can lunch in the clubhouse of the adjacent Palheiro championship golf course ('magnificent views'). There is a minibus service twice a day to Funchal. (*AS, and others*)

Open All year. **Rooms** 6 suites, 31 double. In 3 buildings. 8 on ground floor. **Facilities** 2 lounges, bar, restaurant (background music at night); TV/games room, billiard room; meeting room; sauna, steam room. 100-acre estate: garden, heated swimming pool, bar; tennis, badminton, table tennis, croquet; golf adjacent; private yacht. Unsuitable for ♿. **Location** 7 km NE of Funchal; follow signs to Palheiro Golf. **Credit cards** Amex, MasterCard, Visa. **Terms** [*to 30 Apr 2005*] B&B: single €124–€171, double €149–€238, suite €279–€371; D,B&B €96–€206 per person. Set lunch €35, dinner €42; full alc €75. *V*

Reid's Palace
Estrada Monumental 139
9000-098 Funchal

Tel (0291) 71 71 71
Fax (0291) 71 71 77
Email reservations@reidspalace.com
Website www.reidspalace.orient-express.com

'Let's sink the myth that *Reid's* is stuffy,' declares a visitor after a 'wonderful week' in 2004 at this famous old hotel. Owned by Orient Express, managed since February 2004 by Bruno Brunner, it nowadays makes an effort to attract families (special rates, a traditional Madeiran Santana house equipped as a games room, and a children's swimming pool). It stands on a south-facing promontory above Funchal Bay (now disfigured by a plethora of high-rise hotels). This year's praise: 'Staff were charming, helpful, informal.' 'A lovely room, the food was fine.' The rambling building has spacious, elegant public rooms. 'Beautifully furnished lounges, flowers everywhere'; 'a superb, prewar-style billiard room'. Sea-facing bedrooms have balcony or terrace. Rooms in the garden wing are quieter and larger than those in the main building. 'We had one of the cheaper rooms; well equipped, with wide views.' In the 'wonderful' gardens, are loungers and parasols. There are three swimming pools on the cliff top, and a tidal pool on the rocks below. 'Fabulous breakfast' (wide-ranging buffet; hot dishes to order). Afternoon tea (with Madeira cake) is served on a terrace. In the 'magnificent' main dining room, food is traditional and men are expected to wear jacket and tie. There is an Italian restaurant, *Villa Cipriani*, and an expensive French one, *Les Faunes* (closed in summer when the alfresco *Brisa do Mar* is open). There are water sports, planned activities and excursions. Funchal is an easy walk down; you can return by the hotel bus or a taxi.' (*Tony Hall, A and BW, and others*)

Open All year. **Rooms** 34 suites, 114 double, 16 single. Some on ground floor. Air conditioning. **Facilities** Lifts. 4 lounges, TV room, cocktail bar (background music all day); breakfast room, 5 restaurants (some have pianist); bridge room, billiard room; Santana house for children; beauty parlour, shops. 5-hectare garden: terraces, 4 swimming pools (2 heated), tennis, children's play area; lift/stairs to sea, windsurfing, fishing. Golf nearby. Unsuitable for ♿. **Location** 1 km from centre. Parking. **Credit cards** All major cards accepted. **Terms** [2004] (Min. stay 10 nights during festive seasons) B&B: single €245–€385, double €295–€630, suite €720–€3,060; D,B&B €54 added per person. Set lunch €32.50, dinner €54; full alc €67.

Vila Vicência BUDGET
Rua da Casa Branca 45
9000-113 Funchal

Tel (0291) 77 15 27
Fax (0291) 77 15 38
Email vicencia@mail.telepac.pt

In a residential area near the Lido complex, Diogo and Gina de Freitas's small B&B hotel is endorsed again in 2004 ('very nice'). Three villas are linked by a 'pretty, well-kept' garden, which has palm trees and a 'small but charming' swimming pool. There are comfortable sitting areas in the main house, and a spacious conservatory where the buffet breakfast is served. 'My room was small but well planned; plenty of storage space.' A superior bedroom had a large terrace with chairs and loungers. Many rooms have a balcony; some might hear traffic (an 'ugly development' surrounds the property). Snacks are served, and the little bar/restaurant in the next-door shopping arcade is recommended for meals, 'or take the bus to the old town and eat there'. The 'friendly staff' will arrange trips into the mountains. (*Margaret Crick, and others*)

Open All year. **Rooms** 7 suites, 21 double, 1 single. **Facilities** Lounge/TV room, bar; conservatory. Garden: terraces, swimming pool. Unsuitable for ♿. **Location** 2.5 km from old town, near *Lido Hotel*, 200 m from sea. **Restrictions** No smoking: lounge, 10 bedrooms. No dogs. **Credit cards** All major cards accepted. **Terms** [2004] B&B: single €30–€35, double €50–€60, suite €65–€70. 1-night bookings sometimes refused. *V*

For details of the Voucher scheme, see page xxvi.

LISBON **Map 7:D1**

As Janelas Verdes
Rua das Janelas Verdes 47
1200-690 Lisbon
Tel (021) 396 81 43
Fax (021) 396 81 44
Email jverdes@heritage.pt
Website www.heritage.pt

Liked for its informal atmosphere, this 18th-century palace, managed by Diogo Laranjo, stands in the cobbled street of the same name ('green windows'). Owned by the Cardoso and Fernandes families, it is filled with paintings, books and memorabilia of the novelist Eça de Queiroz, who once lived here. Portraits line a winding staircase. One reader advises: 'Ask for a room overlooking the port.' Another wrote: 'My spacious bedroom had armchairs and good lighting.' There is a reception lounge, 'soothingly romantic', and a top-floor library (with balcony) where guests can help themselves to a drink (honesty system) or a cup of tea from a small kitchen (biscuits are supplied). An 'excellent' buffet breakfast is served in the lovely walled garden (with water feature, wrought iron tables, huge parasols). Buses stop at the front door (the street can be noisy, but windows are doubled glazed). No restaurant: plenty nearby. The Museu Nacional de Arte Antigua (superb Portuguese primitives) is adjacent; *York House* (*qv*) is across the road. (*CI*)

Open All year. **Rooms** 29 double. Some no-smoking. Air conditioning. **Facilities** Lounge, library/bar. No background music. Garden. Unsuitable for ♿. **Location** 2 km W of centre. **Restrictions** No smoking in some bedrooms. No dogs. **Credit cards** All major cards accepted. **Terms** Room: single €170–€260, double €182–€290. Breakfast €14.

Albergaria Senhora do Monte
Calçada do Monte 39
1170-250 Lisbon
Tel (021) 886 60 02
Fax (021) 887 77 83
Email senhoradomonte@hotmail.com
Website www.maisturismo.pt/sramonte

'We wouldn't stay anywhere else in Lisbon,' say aficionados of this small B&B hotel on one of the city's seven hills. 'It is on the highest point for miles around, the views are stunning. Our room (No. 31), with mini-balcony, had no superfluous space: for those who want more, there are suites. Powerful hot shower. Good value for a capital city.' Earlier praise: 'Modest, impeccably clean, well equipped. Wonderful sunsets.' Some first-floor rooms have a large *azulejo*-tiled terrace. The panoramic rooftop bar/breakfast room, facing city and river, serves cocktails and sandwiches in the evening. Breakfast is 'the usual buffet, particularly well stocked with fruit'; eggs and bacon cost extra. 'It is fun setting out in the slightly scruffy Graca district to catch the handy 28 tram.' The historic Alfama district is a short walk away. *Piteu*, a restaurant near the tram stop, is recommended for 'fresh local produce'. (*Simon and Pearl Willbourn, Richard Parish, PG*)

Open All year. **Rooms** 4 suites, 18 double, 6 single. Some on ground floor with terrace. Some no-smoking. Air conditioning. **Facilities** Lift. TV lounge, rooftop bar/breakfast room (background music). Unsuitable for ♿. **Location** NE of centre. Tram 28; buses 12, 17, 35 nearby. **Restriction** No dogs. **Credit cards** All major cards accepted. **Terms** [2004] B&B double €99–€126.

York House
Rua das Janelas Verdes 32
1200-691 Lisbon

Tel (021) 396 24 35
Fax (021) 397 27 93
Email reservations@yorkhouselisboa.com
Website www.yorkhouselisboa.com

This 17th-century Carmelite convent was turned in the 19th century into a hotel by two Yorkshire women, hence the name. It is on a busy street (some bedrooms face this), but steep steps ('helpful porters' carry luggage) lead to a lovely, peaceful courtyard, shaded by a huge palm tree. Inside are vaulted ceilings, antique furniture, old chests, ceramic tiles, and artefacts. 'The cosy wood-panelled bar has comfortable armchairs. My bedroom, spacious and clean, had an old-fashioned but well-appointed bathroom.' Some rooms have been redesigned in modern style, some have an oblique view of the Tagus; others of Lisbon's big Jesus statue. Breakfast is in the restaurant, a 'bright room with blue *azulejo* tiles' or in the courtyard: a buffet, it includes cake, cheeses, ham, eggs, sparkling wine; but 'poor coffee – ask for an espresso from the kitchen'. The restaurant is thought 'overpriced, fussy'; but there are 'lots of good authentic Portuguese restaurants around'. (*CG, and others*)

Open All year. **Rooms** 7 deluxe, 25 double. 5 no-smoking. Air conditioning. **Facilities** Bar, restaurant; 2 conference rooms. No background music. Courtyard. Unsuitable for ♿. **Location** 2 km W of centre. Public parking (not easy). Buses to centre. **Restriction** No dogs. **Credit cards** All major cards accepted. **Terms** [2004] Room: single €180, double €200–€260. Breakfast €14.

MONCARAPACHO 8700-123 Faro — Map 7:E1

Casa da Calma NEW
Sitio do Pereiro

Tel (0289) 79 10 98
Fax (0289) 79 15 99
Email nicole.effenberg@clix.pt
Website www.casadacalma.com

In the peaceful eastern Algarve, near Tavira, this 'charming' small hotel 'lives up to its name, house of calm', says the nominator (a former *Guide* hotelier). The multilingual owner/manager, Nicole Effenberg, a devotee of eco-tourism, has converted a single-storey 1940s *quinta* in 'well-maintained' gardens, in traditional Portuguese style. 'Our pleasant room had interesting furniture, good lighting, heating for colder nights, books, mineral water, fresh fruit. The tiled bathroom had a bath and separate shower, good towels.' Each room has a veranda with tables and chairs. A 'superb' buffet breakfast, taken on the terrace on sunny days, has 'fresh orange juice from the hotel's own grove, exotic fruit salad, cereals, a cooked egg dish of the day, home-made jams, honey and fresh bread'. An honesty bar, with drinks, snacks and ice cream, is available in the lounge/dining room; complimentary tea, coffee and cake is served in the afternoons. A three-course lunch or dinner is served by arrangement: the 'surprise menu' might include fish or shellfish. In the garden are a swimming pool and sauna. (*Graham Taylor*)

Open All year. **Rooms** 1 suite, 6 double, 1 single. All on ground floor. 5 air conditioned. **Facilities** Lounge/dining room (background music all day). Garden: heated swimming pool, sauna. Beach 7 km. Unsuitable for ♿. **Location** 3 km N of Moncarapacho. A22, exit 15. Car park. **Restriction** Smoking indoors discouraged. **Credit cards** MasterCard, Visa. **Terms** B&B: single €58–€78, double €80–€138, suite €160–€240. Set meals €25–€30. *V*

PORTO 4050-513 — Map 7:B1

Pestana Porto Hotel
Praça da Ribeira 1

Tel (022) 340 23 00
Fax (022) 340 24 00
Email pestana.porto@pestana.com
Website www.pestana.com

A sensitive conversion of old warehouses, built on a section of the medieval city wall, this member of the small Pestana group stands on the historic waterfront, now a World Heritage site. The 'sleek, modern' atmosphere is liked, and 'staff are friendly'. Ask for a bedroom overlooking the River Douro. 'Ours, with a balcony, was large, well appointed. During a festival, we had a magnificent view of the midnight firework display.' The restaurant serves a 'limited but excellent' menu with Portuguese dishes. Breakfast is 'generous and well presented'. Porto has retained its character despite development: trams still run through the streets, and many buildings are clad in colourful *azulejo* tiles.

Open All year. **Rooms** 3 suites, 45 double. 10 no-smoking. Air conditioning. 1 suitable for ♿. **Facilities** Lift, ramps. TV room, bar/café, restaurant; no background music. 4 conference rooms. **Location** Old town, right bank of River Douro. **Restrictions** No smoking in some bedrooms. No dogs. **Credit cards** All major cards accepted. **Terms** [2004] B&B: single €122–€145, double €137–€160, suite €248. Full alc from €28.

PRAIA DO VAU 8501-909 Algarve — Map 7:D1

Casa Três Palmeiras
Apartado 84

Tel (0282) 40 12 75
Fax (0282) 40 10 29
Email dolly@casatrespalmeiras.com
Website www.casatrespalmeiras.com

'In a wonderful setting', on a cliff, this upmarket B&B, 'a peaceful oasis', has glorious views of sea, sky, beach and the rugged coast of the western Algarve. The multilingual Brazilian owner, Dolly Schlingensiepen, and her staff 'could not be more kind and attentive', says the *Guide*'s illustrator, who visited in 2004. 'From the moment you enter the wrought iron gates, you know you are somewhere special. There is an air of tranquillity; life here is stress-free.' Bedrooms, 'of the highest quality', have 'everything you could want': 'superb beds, fridge, fruit, satellite TV'. One room has a large terrace and garden view, the others face the small fish-shaped sea-water swimming pool on a terrace where each room is allotted a space. A path leads to a quiet, sandy beach. Breakfast, ordered the night before, is served after 8.30 am at tables overlooking the sea. It includes fresh juice, eggs, bacon, etc, and 'special touches like a greeting in the guests' language'. Light lunches are available, and advice is given on where to dine. No credit cards: a 40% deposit is required on booking, a further 40% two months before arrival. (*David Brindley, RGW Bing*)

Open Feb–Nov. **Rooms** 5 double. Air conditioning. **Facilities** Lounge with honesty bar; background music if wanted. Terrace. Garden: solar-heated swimming pool. Beach 2 mins' walk. Golf, tennis nearby. **Location** 4 km from Portimão, 62 km W of Faro airport. Directions provided. **Restrictions** No children under 12 (unless all rooms booked by one group). No dogs. **Credit cards** None accepted. **Terms** [2004] B&B: single €153–€179, double €170–€199.

SANTA CLARA-A-VELHA 7665-880 Beja — Map 7:D1

Quinta do Barranco da Estrada BUDGET *Tel* (0283) 93 30 65
Fax (0283) 93 30 66
Email paradiseinportugal@mail.telepac.pt
Website www.paradise-in-portugal.com

Standing above a huge freshwater lake in a remote part of the Alentejo, Frank and Lulu McClintock's home is run in house-party style. It is popular with British families in summer, when children breakfast and take tea together and adults dine round one large table. Organic ingredients are used for the no-choice dinners ('good home cooking'), served under a pergola facing the lake, or indoors by a fire. 'It was fun for our nine- and ten-year-olds, and peaceful for parents,' one visitor wrote. 'Adults read or lazed while the children played in the pretty terraced gardens. From the ladder and diving board on a lakeside wooden jetty, they swam safely in the current-free water out to a pontoon, or borrowed a canoe or sailing dinghy.' The 'cabin-like bedrooms', furnished in simple but tasteful style, have 'lovely lake views'. Frank McClintock, a 'genuine eccentric', keeps bees, takes guests birdwatching; white doves fly from an aviary; there are dogs, cats, lovebirds, chickens and ducks. There are three new bedrooms this year. (*JT*)

Open Feb–Dec, except Christmas. **Rooms** 1 suite, 7 double. All on ground floor. No smoking. No TV/telephone. **Facilities** Ramps. Lounge/bar/dining room; background music at night if wanted; sauna. 2-hectare garden: terrace, children's play area, lake frontage: water sports. 'Not really suitable for ♿.' **Location** 92 km NW of Faro. 14 km N of Santa Clara: turn right to Cortes Pereiras; after 9 km take unmade road at cairn with *Quinta*'s name. Follow cairns for 4 km. Guests met at Santa Clara railway station. **Credit cards** MasterCard, Visa. **Terms** B&B: single €60–€140, double €70–€150, suite €175–€300. Set lunch €15, dinner €25. Birdwatching, painting, well-being holidays. 1-night bookings sometimes refused.

****

Traveller's tale Hotel in Italy. This hotel prides itself on its security. It has a manned gate for guests, and it is locked at night. But the security code was posted on the door, and the gate to the employees' parking lot was open 24 hours a day.

****

SANTO ESTÊVÃO 8800-513 Faro — Map 7:D1

Quinta da Lua BUDGET
Bernardinheiro 1622-X

Tel/Fax (0281) 96 10 70
Email quintadalua@iol.pt
Website www.quintadalua.com.pt

'Simple but stylish. Great value.' A warm endorsement came in 2004 for this small guest house near Tavira, in a rural area of the eastern Algarve ('away from the golfing belt'). Owned and managed by Miguel Martins and Vimal Willems, it stands amid orange trees and vineyards. Earlier visitors thought it 'quiet and well run', with 'comfortable if not over-large rooms in rustic style'. 'The best breakfast we've had in Portugal': with fresh fruit, local cheeses, cakes, etc, it is served on the terrace. The garden has shady sitting areas, and an 'ecological' saltwater pool. 'The orange blossom and herb scents were lovely.' There is an honesty bar and a barbecue. A simple meal is sometimes served by arrangement. 'There are several good restaurants in Santa Lucia on the coast; avoid eating in Tavira.' The sea, with long, sandy beaches, is ten minutes' drive away. (*Michael Green, B and KF*)

Open 15 Dec–15 Nov. **Rooms** 2 suites (with TV), 6 double. **Facilities** Dining room (background music); meeting room. 2-hectare garden: terrace, unheated swimming pool. Beach nearby. Unsuitable for ♿. **Location** 25 km NE of Faro, 4 km NW of Tavira. Santo Estêvão turning off EN125 from Faro. 1st left, 1st right. Look for gateway arch. **Restrictions** No smoking in bedrooms. No children under 15. No dogs. **Credit cards** None accepted. **Terms** B&B: single €50–€100, double €65–€120, suite €90–€140. Set lunch €17, dinner €25. 1-night bookings refused in high season. *V*

SINTRA Lisboa — Map 7:C1

Quinta das Sequóias
Casa da Tapada, Ap. 1004
2710-801 Sintra

Tel (021) 923 03 42
Fax (021) 910 60 65
Email quintadasequoias@hotmail.com
Website www.quintadasequoias.com

Peacefully set on a hill in woodlands outside Sintra, this old manor house, filled with antiques, is run by its owner, Candida Gonzalez, as an upmarket B&B. It has superb views of the coast and the 'fantastic, multi-coloured' royal palace of Pena. Drinks are served in the billiard room, which has videos and a library of CDs. The buffet breakfast is taken at a long table in a high-ceilinged room with a large fireplace and a minstrels' gallery. Bedrooms, furnished with antiques, vary: 'Ours had soft chairs, a tiny balcony. A rustic chandelier hung from the high peaked ceiling. The bathroom was huge, extraordinary: great projecting porous rocks set in its walls; a giant sunken shower had heavy antique brass fittings.' Beyond a wisteria arbour are flowery terraces, fountains and an 'inviting' swimming pool.

Open All year, except Christmas. **Rooms** 6 double. No TV/telephone. **Facilities** Lounge (background music), TV room, billiard room, breakfast room. Garden: unheated swimming pool; spa bath, sauna. Sandy beach 10 km. Unsuitable for ♿. **Location** 4 km W of Sintra, off Monserrate road (signposted). **Restrictions** No smoking. No children. No dogs. **Credit cards** Amex, MasterCard, Visa. **Terms** [2004] (Min. 2 nights) B&B: single €120–€140, double €145–€160.

VIANA DO CASTELO 4901-909 Map 7:B1

Pousada do Monte de Santa Luzia NEW
Apartado 30
Santa Luzia

Tel (0258) 80 03 70
Fax (0258) 82 88 92
Email guest@pousadas.pt
Website www.pousadas.com

High on a hill above the Lima estuary, reached by a twisting road, this purpose-built hotel (1918) has been modernised and turned into a regional pousada. It stands in large, peaceful gardens with a big swimming pool. 'It has spacious public rooms, excellent service,' reports the nominator. 'Our huge bedroom had glorious south-facing views of estuary and coast.' 'Good Portuguese cuisine' (eg, hake gratin with mayonnaise, *torta de Viana*) is served in the formal dining room. (*David Crowe*)

Open All year. **Rooms** 48. Air conditioning. **Facilities** Lift. Lounge, restaurant; conference room. Garden: swimming pool, tennis; fishing. **Location** On hill above town. Parking. **Credit cards** All major cards accepted. **Terms** [2004] B&B: single €87–€147, double €97–€157; D,B&B €23 added per person.

****

Traveller's tale Hotel in Spain. Reception was bored, but not as bored as the waiters in the hideous rooftop restaurant which had boring food and a great view of the city's smog. When we complained to Reception that our bedroom was beside a loudly squeaking lift shaft, boredom was replaced by superciliousness.

****

Traveller's tale Hotel in Germany. Service was slow, though there were only ten diners in the restaurant. The food was OK, but not the *haute cuisine* it was made out to be. When we came to pay, they had no idea what we had eaten or drunk – they were lucky we were honest. The visitors' book had page after page of complaints about appalling service.

****

Traveller's tale Hotel in the Czech Republic. When you opened the door to the hotel bedroom, you entered the bathroom. Walking through that provided access to the beds. The bathroom had the only available seating, other than the two sagging beds. At night a series of express passenger and freight trains seemed to be passing about three feet from the foot of my bed. Other guests opened and closed their doors with such gusto that my door shook.

****

Slovenia

Kendov Dvorec, Spodnja Idrija

'Slovenia was a major surprise,' says a *Guide* correspondent who visited it this year. 'It is so tidy and very beautiful, with marvellous walking country.' Economically, Slovenia has long been the most advanced of all the former 'Socialist' countries, and it is now a part of the EU. For a holiday it has everything, from Alps to Adriatic beaches, old baroque towns, and spas. Piran is an enchanting little Venetian city. Slovenes are a multilingual and romantic people, bursting with poetry and music, and environmentally conscious. Prices are still below Austrian and Italian levels. There are plenty of hotels up to western standards, modestly priced farm guest houses, and some converted castles and manor houses. Hotels tend to be upgraded, rather than new, buildings.

The *Vila Bled* in Bled has long had a *Guide* entry, and we are pleased to welcome back this year the *Lukanc Pension* nearby, at the other end of the price scale. *Kendov Dvorec*, at Spodnja Idrija, is another particularly attractive hotel.

There is no service charge in Slovenia, so clients are expected, if satisfied, to leave a tip of approximately 10%.

BLED 4260 Gorenjska **Map 14:C4**

Vila Bled
Cesta svobode 26
PO Box 53

Tel (04) 57 91 500
Fax (04) 57 41 320
Email hotel@vila-bled.com
Website www.vila-bled.com

'Luxurious yet unpretentious', Slovenia's most sumptuous hotel (Relais & Châteaux) has a 'wonderful setting' by Lake Bled, in a park on a hill, away from the busy resort. Once the summer residence of the Yugoslav royal family, it was remodelled by Tito (you can visit his top-floor concert hall). This year, the bedrooms have been refurnished in 1950s style, and a wellness centre is new. One couple was upgraded to the Presidential Suite: 'The most magnificent hotel accommodation we have ever enjoyed. Enormous bedroom with vast bed, second bedroom for our son, huge sitting room, magnificent views of the lake. Meals a delight, with first-rate service.' Other praise: 'Staff could not have been more friendly.' 'A comfortable visit.' The 'excellent', long-serving manager, Janez Fajfar, is 'jovial'. A red carpet welcomes guests, flowers are abundant; glass, silver and marble shine. Dinners, if not particularly Slovenian, are 'served in grand hotel style', with live music. In summer, 'eating on the terrace while watching fireflies was magical'. 'Good choice at breakfast' (self-help). Guests can use the 'delightful' indoor swimming pool and sauna of the sister *Grand Hotel Toplice*, a kilometre away, and they have special rates at two local golf courses. (*Conrad and Marilyn Dehn, FH Potts, Walter Cottingham*)

Open All year. **Rooms** 20 suites, 10 double. **Facilities** Lifts, ramps. Lounge, bar (pianist in season), breakfast room, restaurant; background music at night; conference room; concert hall; wellness centre. 6-hectare park: terrace, garden, tennis; lake: private lido, bathing, boating. Riding, fishing, golf (25% discount) nearby. Unsuitable for ♿. **Location** 2 km W of Bled (bus-stop Bled-Mlino). **Credit cards** All major cards accepted. **Terms** B&B €80–€200; D,B&B €110–€230. Set dinner €30; full alc €35. *V* (1st night)

****

Traveller's tale Hotel in France. This was utterly disgraceful. A hymn to French poshness and pretension. We thought it would do for a night. 'Can we have a quiet room, please?' 'Certainly, sir.' They failed to tell us about the kitchen ventilator shaft up through the 'quiet' courtyard. It was like Concorde, except that Concorde doesn't have cooking smells. The fan started at about 6 pm. As suppertime approached, it became increasingly smelly. When we reported this, they looked a bit shifty, and said it would finish by 9.30 pm and not start again until 8 am. But by 11.15 pm it was still howling, and our bedroom smelled like a greasy spoon. It started again at 5.50 am. The owner finally admitted that they were in the middle of a two-year court case with the ventilator installers. So why didn't they say so in the first place?

****

KOBARID 5222 Primorska — Map 14:C4

Hotel Hvala BUDGET
and Restauracija Topli Val
Trg svobode 1

Tel (05) 38 99 300
Fax (05) 38 85 322
Email topli.val@siol.net
Website www.topli-val-sp.si

'I cannot speak too highly of it,' says a visitor this year to the Hvala family's spruce modern hotel/restaurant on the main square of this small market town near the Triglav national park. 'The owners are friendly. The rooms are simple but fine. The main reasons for a visit are the lovely scenery and the delicious food.' Others wrote of 'amazingly good value', 'universally helpful staff'. The restaurant, with its white tablecloths and bentwood chairs, is famous for its fish dishes ('delicious seafood platter') and traditional cooking, eg, Kobarid dumplings. 'Good local wines.' Summer meals are served in the garden. Bedrooms are spacious (they can get hot in summer). Breakfast is 'good, with wide choice'. Fishing can be arranged on the Soča River nearby; they will cook your catch for you. In 1917 the Austro-Germans crossed the Alps to defeat the Italians at the battle of Kobarid (Caporetto): the town's museum details this, with a big picture of Hemingway, who later drove an ambulance on this front (see *A Farewell to Arms*). (*Jennifer Potter, and others*)

Open All year, except Feb. **Rooms** 4 suites (1 equipped for ♿), 24 double, 3 single. **Facilities** TV room/lobby, bar, restaurant. Garden: children's playground; summer music. River: swimming, fishing, nearby. **Location** 120 km NW of Ljubljana, near Italian border. Parking. **Credit cards** All major cards accepted. **Terms** [2004] B&B €32–€57.50; D,B&B €42.50–€70.50. Suite €45 added. Alc €26–€30. *V* (low season)

PIRAN 6330 Primorska — Map 14:C4

Hotel Tartini BUDGET
Tartinijev trg 15

Tel (05) 67 11 666
Fax (05) 67 11 665
Email info@hotel-tartini-piran.com
Website www.hotel-tartini-piran.com

On a peninsula pointing into the Adriatic, this tiny medieval seaport, backed by green hills, is a summer haunt of the Ljubljana intelligentsia. Considered by many to be the loveliest of Slovene towns, it was founded by the Venetians, whose influence can still be seen in its small piazzas with statues, its food markets and outdoor seafront restaurants. This unpretentious hotel, painted pink, named after the 18th-century composer Giuseppe Tartini, born in Piran, is in the main square. 'Good value, a fun and trendy decor. Staff were helpful,' was one recent report. But it may be best to eat elsewhere: breakfast has been thought only 'acceptable', evening meals 'disappointing', and the outdoor dining terrace has no view. The bedrooms, all air conditioned, are agreeable if smallish. 'The view from our balcony was like an operetta set.' Rooms overlooking the square can get noise but have double glazing. Quieter ones, at the back, look towards the marina and the sea. On top of the hotel, on different levels, are 'a delightful lawn area', and a small swimming pool. The cheaper sister, the *Hotel Piran*, has a superb seafront setting. (*Robert Barratt, and others*)

Open Early Feb–early Jan. **Rooms** 1 suite, 39 double, 3 single. Air conditioning. **Facilities** Lift. Bar (background music), restaurant (no-smoking); conference room. Terraces: unheated swimming pool. Rocky beach 60 m. **Location** Main square. 25 km SW of Trieste. Parking severely restricted in Piran: produce evidence of hotel booking on arriving. **Credit cards** All major cards accepted. **Terms** [2004] B&B €30–€64; D,B&B €10 added per person.

SELO 4260 Gorenjska **Map 14:C4**

Lukanc Pension NEW/BUDGET *Tel* (04) 57 65 210
Selo pri Bledu 8 *Email* pension.lukanc@siol.net
Website www.slovenia.cc/pen_lukanc

Amid splendid scenery in a village on the edge of a forest near Lake Bled, this 'amazingly cheap' guest house on a working farm was long adored by readers, but it fell from the *Guide* last year for lack of feedback. It returns with two enthusiastic reports in 2004: 'The red carpet at the door was a reliable indication of the excellent hospitality we would receive. Danila Lukanc and her son, Sebastien [Boštjan], gave a wonderfully warm welcome and did everything possible to make our stay enjoyable.' 'Lovely location. Staff very friendly. Satisfying food. Marvellous walking country.' Accommodation is in the old building (where meals are served) and a new house ('spotless, comfortable rooms in local style') up the hill. Earlier comments: 'A wonderful five nights.' 'We were welcomed with vast glasses of home-distilled slivovka.' 'Our spacious room with balcony had stunning Alpine views. The stylish bar has a lovely terrace (more great views).' Breakfast has ham, eggs, pancakes, good coffee. 'Plentiful home-cooked dinners' include 'lashings of soup, big plates of, eg, wiener schnitzel; "kmecka pojedina" ("farmer's feast": smoked meats and sauerkraut); farm vegetables and salads; heavenly pancakes'. Mrs Lukanc ('a star') often comes into the dining room to chat. Also liked: the flowery balconies, pretty garden, waking to the sound of cowbells. A party is held once a week in the bar. (*John Collier, Robert Barratt, and others*)

Open All year. **Rooms** 17 double. 11 in annexe. **Facilities** Sitting room with TV, bar, restaurant (no-smoking); traditional background music when wanted. Garden: terrace. Riding, swimming, skiing nearby. Unsuitable for ♿. **Location** 2 km SW of Bled. Parking. **Credit cards** None accepted. **Terms** [2004] B&B €25; D,B&B €35.

> The 'Budget' label by a hotel's name indicates an establishment where dinner, bed and breakfast are offered at around the foreign currency equivalent of £50 per person, or B&B for about £30 and an evening meal for about £20. These are only a rough guide and do not always apply to single accommodation, nor do they necessarily apply in high season.

SOLČAVA 3335 Štajerska — Map 14:C4

Hotel Plesnik
Logarska dolina 10

Tel (03) 83 92 300
Fax (03) 83 92 312
Email plesnik.doo@siol.net
Website www.plesnik.si

'Once again, we enjoyed the fantastic setting, the peace and quiet, especially at night, the clean air,' say visitors returning in 2004 to the Plesnik family's 'friendly hotel'. 'We still love it,' said others. It is in a national park in the 'pristine' Logar valley 'criss-crossed with walking, cycling and riding trails and dotted with farms where you can eat robust home-made food'. Trim, modern and balconied, informally run 'with great efficiency and charm', this is 'a wonderful place for children'. It has ducks outside the door, and 'fantastic views' of snow-capped mountains from the bedroom balconies. An earlier comment: 'Our room was prettily decorated like the rest of the hotel, which has many pieces of hand-painted furniture.' There are red leather club chairs in the 'cosy' bar. The restaurant serves Slovene specialities. The food can be a bit variable, but the buffet was enjoyed this year, also 'blueberry liqueur on the house, remarkable chocolate cake with blueberry filling', good local cheeses and wines. Breakfast has a 'large and varied buffet', and freshly cooked ham and eggs. Summer drinks and meals are served on a terrace with views. There is a 'good if not enormous' indoor swimming pool facing the mountains, with patio and loungers. Weddings are often held on Saturday. The annexe, *Vila Palenk*, has good family accommodation; or you can stay in the 'cosy' *Na Razpotju Guest House* (ten bedrooms) or the 'unpretentiously simple' *Pleznik Tourist Farm* (five bedrooms). Outdoor activities include hunting, hiking, hang-gliding, caving and skiing. (*Matthew Hamlyn, JB, and others*)

Open All year. **Rooms** 30 double. 11 in *Vila Palenk.* **Facilities** Lift. Lounge, bar, tavern, inn, restaurant (no-smoking); background music; seminar rooms; indoor swimming pool, sauna, whirlpool; massage. Terrace. **Location** Logar valley, 4 km W of Solčava, 70 km NE of Ljubljana. **Credit cards** All major cards accepted. **Terms** [2004] *Hotel Plesnik* B&B €60–€81; D,B&B €69–€91. *Vila Palenk* B&B €51–€64; D,B&B €61–€74.

SPODNJA IDRIJA 5281 Primorska — Map 14:C4

Kendov Dvorec
Na Griču 2

Tel (05) 37 25 100
Fax (05) 37 56 475
Email kendov-dvorec@s5.net
Website www.kendov-dvorec.com

'For those seeking tranquillity and the warmest hospitality.' 'A beautiful house, lovingly restored, exquisite bedlinen, unpretentious food; but what makes it is the quality of the service.' Praise in 2004 for the Svetlik family's hotel (Relais & Châteaux) in the hills west of Ljubljana, near the Italian border. The stylishly converted 14th-century manor house, 'luxuriously furnished with antiques', has 'much ecclesiastical art in small alcoves and windows' and 'a really

Slovene feeling'. 'We were greeted by the charming Ivi Svetlik who treated us like friends visiting her home, rather than paying guests. Staff wore traditional local costume. As evening fell, candles were lit, providing a soft glow throughout the house. Dinner was a relaxed introduction to the finest Slovene cooking', eg, cabbage soup, dumplings, fillet of beef with rosemary. 'In the rather formal dining room, there is no written menu, just a description from Gregor, the *maître d'*. He suggested seriously good bottles for us from the formidable wine list.' There's a panoramic garden terrace for summer eating. 'A splendid breakfast: fruit, cheeses, meats, pots of jam.' 'Our room was delightful: lots of wood, free minibar, decanter of cherry brandy.' 'Beds were "period", but bathroom fittings were modern.' Weddings and banquets are often held. Nearby is 'glorious countryside, an interesting local museum', the medieval town of Skofja Luka, the huge caves at Postojna. (*John Collier, Matthew Hamlyn, JS*)

Open All year. **Rooms** 11 double. **Facilities** Lounges, 3 dining rooms (no-smoking); background music 7 am–11 pm; conference room. 2 gardens (outdoor dining), tennis. River: fishing, swimming nearby. Unsuitable for ♿. **Location** Village centre. 55 km W of Ljubljana. Parking. **Restrictions** Smoking in 1 lounge only. Dogs in 1 bedroom only. **Credit cards** All major cards accepted. **Terms** B&B: single €100–€145, double €125–€170. Set meals €50–€90.

Spain

Hotel San Gabriel, Ronda

We include 23 new entries in our Spanish chapter this year and 19 hotels have been dropped: quite a turnover. Interesting new discoveries include *Hacienda Benazuza*, a 10th-century Moorish farmhouse near Seville, cleverly converted into a luxury hotel. Its restaurant has a *Michelin* star for extraordinarily inventive cooking.

We are pleased to include new hotels in some of Spain's historic cities. *Hotel Neri*, a beautiful conversion of an 18th-century palace in Barcelona's Gothic quarter, adds to our varied selection in this city. We have a fourth entry for Bilbao: the *Petit Palace Arana* is a new minimalist hotel within walking distance of the Guggenheim museum. We have two new entries for Ronda: *La Fuente de la Higuera* is a luxurious small hotel in a valley nearby; *San Gabriel* is a charming B&B in the old town: it returns after a time with no reports.

We include fewer of the members of the national parador chain than we did in the early days of the *Guide* (just four this year). This institution, whose expansion dates back to the Franco era, was established to regenerate rural economies and rescue historic buildings. David Sulkin, who knows the chain well, writes: 'Most paradors are in locations of outstanding natural and historical significance. There are castles, palaces and grand houses with fortifications, on cliffs, on hillsides and in the centre of interesting cities. The parador at the Alhambra in Granada is the flagship: booking must be made months, if not years, ahead. The parador at Santiago de Compostela, just by the cathedral, is also breathtaking. A few paradors are 20th-century built, for example, those at Nerja and Córdoba.

'The restaurant and room staff at paradors are usually exceptionally kind and helpful. The accommodation is always well appointed and spotless. There are large, luxurious bathrooms. The blot on this Spanish landscape is that the reception staff – especially the men – can be haughty and disengaged. Paradors have a huge turnover of guests and the "them in–those out" mentality is sometimes tangible. The Amigo de Paradores, which is the point-collecting, loyalty card system, does not guarantee a warm welcome or a cheery "Goodbye". It is easy to relax and enjoy yourself at a parador, and they represent value for money, but that little bit of extra care and attention, so welcome at the best hotels, may be missing.'

Spain is at its most rewarding when you drive the extra mile to escape the homogenised if efficient hotels where international menus are served. There are many pockets where English is not widely spoken, the cuisine is regional, and the way of life still proudly traditional. Breakfast may sometimes disappoint: in a city or a town, you might be better taking a coffee and croissant (or deep-fried *churros*) in a bar or café. And in mainland Spain you will almost certainly have to change your dining patterns in the evening: dinner, especially in rural areas, is simply not available until 9 pm, and restaurants do not come alive until, at the earliest, 10 pm. You might wish to follow the Spanish custom, taking lunch as the main meal of the day, followed by a siesta. In Mallorca, so popular with British and German visitors, dinner hours are more conventional.

Note There is a 7 per cent tax to pay at all hotels (5 per cent in the Canaries) above the prices quoted here.

ALMAGRO 13270 Ciudad Real **Map 7:D3**

Parador de Almagro
Ronda de San Francisco 31

Tel (926) 86 01 00
Fax (926) 86 01 50
Email almagro@parador.es
Website www.parador.es

In an interesting little town on the plain of La Mancha, this rambling former 16th-century convent, with 14 small galleried courtyards (each with a fountain), is said to be 'one of the most attractive of all the paradors'. 'It was all we expected,' write recent visitors, 'good service, lovely surroundings.' Bedrooms, sparsely furnished 'as befits a former monastery', but spacious, face gardens or swimming pool. The lounges have handsome dark chests and tables, pictures and tapestries. Drinks 'are fairly priced' in the bar, which has huge amphorae. Meals are 'typical parador'; the buffet breakfast is vast. A summer drama festival is held in a Renaissance theatre (Spain's oldest) in the town's splendid main square. (*P and JL*)

Open All year. **Rooms** 3 suites, 49 double, 2 single. 5 on ground floor. 1 suitable for ♿. Air conditioning. **Facilities** 3 lounges, breakfast room, bar, restaurant (background music); conference rooms. Garden: unheated swimming pool. **Location** Central. Parking. **Restriction** No dogs. **Credit cards** All major cards accepted. **Terms** [2004] Room: single €78–€91, double €97–€113, suite €194. Breakfast €10. Set meals €25. D,B&B sometimes obligatory.

ALQUÉZAR 22145 Huesca — Map 7:B5

Villa de Alquézar BUDGET — *Tel/Fax* (974) 31 84 16
Calle Pedro Arnal Cavero 12 — *Website* www.villadealquezar.com

This 'lovely old Pyrenean village, whose houses tumble downhill on both sides of the Vero gorge' is 'off the beaten track but well worth the journey', say recent visitors. In the Parque de la Sierra y los Cañones de Guara, it is a centre for caving, walking and birdwatching. At its top, this 15th-century house, now a B&B hotel, is warmly recommended. 'The Altemir family owners are delightful. Our cool, comfortable room had a good bathroom and a small balcony with view.' Breakfast is 'very good': lots of home-baked rolls, cakes, etc. 'We dined ridiculously cheaply at *La Cocineta* in the square, where we had a splendid view of the floodlit collegiate church (former Moorish *alcazar*) across the ravine.' (*DJH*)

Open All year, except Christmas, 15–30 Jan. **Rooms** 4 suites, 24 double, 3 single. 1 suitable for ♿. Air conditioning. **Facilities** Lift, ramps. Lounge, games room, breakfast room. Garden. **Location** 48 km SE of Huesca. Turn N to Abiego off N240, right fork to Alquézar. Parking. **Restrictions** No smoking: breakfast room, some bedrooms. No dogs. **Credit cards** MasterCard, Visa. **Terms** B&B: single €42, double €50, suite €82.

ARCOS DE LA FRONTERA 11630 Cádiz — Map 7:E2

Hotel El Convento BUDGET — *Tel* (956) 70 23 33
Calle Maldonado 2 — *Fax* (956) 70 41 28
Email hotelelconvento@terra.es
Website www.webdearcos.com/elconvento

In a traffic-free street at the top of the hill of this historic town of whitewashed houses, the Moreno family's 'delightful' converted convent offers a budget alternative to the nearby parador with which it shares the spectacular view over the plain of the Guadalete. This can be enjoyed from some bedrooms, and from the rooftop sun terrace. Some rooms are small; the family tells us that, following a *Guide* comment last year, new mattresses are being fitted, and uncomfortable foot-boards on the beds are being replaced. Staff are 'most helpful', say visitors, and the restaurant, in the arcaded covered patio of a nearby 17th-century palace, is thought 'excellent': it has a *Michelin Bib Gourmand* for its regional cooking, eg, garlic soup; chickpea, haricot bean and pork stew. The family also own the 19-room *Los Olivos del Convento*, a conversion of old houses around a courtyard, down the hill. Arcos's *barrio antiguo* is a national monument. (*R and KF, Y and KF*)

Open All year, except 2 weeks Jan, 1 week July. **Rooms** 10 double, 1 single. Most with balcony or terrace. 1 on ground floor. Air conditioning. **Facilities** Breakfast room/bar (no smoking at breakfast), restaurant (in separate building). No background music. Roof terrace. Unsuitable for ♿. **Location** Top of town; follow directions to parador. Park in Plaza del Cabildo, take Calle Escribanos: hotel signposted. **Restriction** No dogs. **Credit cards** All major cards accepted. **Terms** Room: single €35–€55, double €50–€80. Breakfast €6. Set meals €24; full alc €30.

BAÑALBUFAR 07191 Mallorca — Map 7:C6

Hotel Mar i Vent BUDGET
Carrer Major 49

Tel (971) 61 80 00
Fax (971) 61 82 01
Email marivent@fehm.es
Website www.hotelmarivent.com

Endorsements came again this year (and also a caveat) for the Vives family's unassuming hotel which offers 'good value on a coastline that remains unspoilt by development'. Set above steeply terraced, cultivated slopes that lead down to coves on Mallorca's rugged west coast, it is popular with families in summer, and retired British couples off-season. A visitor over 30 years called both the village and the hotel 'enchanting'. Another guest wrote: 'As good as ever, spotlessly kept, very friendly, and with constant small improvements, eg, air conditioning in some bedrooms.' The 'stunning views' are seen from the bedroom balconies, the pool area (with parasols), the spacious dining room and the terrace where breakfasts (fresh orange juice and 'delicious breads') and drinks are taken. Some find the simple set dinners 'dull', but there are good eating places in the village, eg, *Son Thomás* and *Trattoria Mediterranea* ('very good pasta; excellent vegetarian meals'). *Son Llarg*, at Estellencs, down the coast is also recommended. The rooms, in local style, are simple; some are small, and soundproofing can be poor. 'Our family room in the annexe was spacious, quiet, well furnished.' There is a sheltered tennis court and an unchlorinated swimming pool. 'Snr Vives is everywhere, giving advice on how to find beaches: not easy on this glorious coast.' (*Ann and Sidney Carpenter, Michael Dods, DB, and others*)

Open 30 Jan–30 Nov. Restaurant closed Sun evening. **Rooms** 26 double, 3 single. In 3 buildings. Air conditioning. **Facilities** Lift. 3 salons (1 no-smoking, 2 with TV), bar, restaurant. No background music. Garden: terraces, unheated swimming pool, tennis. Sea coves nearby. Unsuitable for ♿. **Location** Entrance to village. 24 km NW of Palma. Garage, parking. **Restriction** No dogs. **Credit cards** MasterCard, Visa. **Terms** B&B: single €79, double €98; D,B&B €25 added per person. Set meals €25; alc €35. *V*

For details of the Voucher scheme, see page xxvi.

BARCELONA Map 7:B6

Hotel Alexandra
Carrer Mallorca 251
Barcelona 08008

Tel (93) 467 71 66
Fax (93) 488 02 58
Email informacion@hotel-alexandra.com
Website www.hotel-alexandra.com

Well located, between Passeig de Gràcia (where you can see La Pedrera, Gaudí's unusual apartment building without a straight line) and La Rambla, this large, modern hotel 'of elegant appearance' makes 'a comfortable base at a reasonable price'. The decor is contemporary, with much 'brown-beige marble' and strong-coloured fabrics. 'The bedrooms vary in size, but are generally big with good bathroom,' says a regular visitor. Some rooms have a terrace; many are quiet. 'Some fittings (wobbly tabletops, loose cupboard doors) occasionally let down the design. Reception staff are helpful, and there is a pleasant mezzanine bar.' (*CG*)

Open All year. **Rooms** 8 suites, 91 double. Some no-smoking. Some adapted for ♿. Air conditioning. **Facilities** Lobby, bar, restaurant; 5 meeting rooms; shops. **Location** Central, between Passeig de Gràcia and Rambla de Catalunya. Parking. **Restriction** No dogs. **Credit cards** All major cards accepted. **Terms** [2004] Room: single €165–€290, double €195–€330, suite €350–€460. Breakfast €16.

Hotel Claris
Pau Claris 150
Barcelona 08009

Tel (93) 487 62 62
Fax (93) 215 79 70
Email claris@derbyhotels.es
Website www.derbyhotels.es

'More stylish retreat than owner-managed home from home', this designer hotel *gran luxe* in the Eixample district 'delivers a comforting base for forays around the city', say trusted *Guide* correspondents. The neo-classical facade of the 19th-century Palacio Vedruna 'hides a stunning modern interior: acres of marble, honey-coloured woodwork, glass lifts, works of art'; there is a small museum of Egyptian antiquities collected by the owner, Jordi Clos. Everyone praises the staff: 'Courteous, helpful, without a trace of coldness.' One couple had a 'luxurious duplex suite', but another complained of a 'dark, noisy' room. Three restaurants: *Terraza del Claris*, on the rooftop terrace by the 'opulent' swimming pool, has a glass ceiling and a bar ('perfect for a 2 am nightcap on a hot summer night'); *East 47*, with Warhol lithographs, serves 'creative cuisine' ('excellent; rather nouvelle'); *Claris* is for local specialities. Breakfast is a 'beautifully presented' buffet in a pleasant basement room. 'Unabashedly pricey, but we found a good rate on the Internet.' (*David and Kate Wooff, D and AD, and others*)

Open All year. *Terraza* restaurant open June–Oct. **Rooms** 39 suites, 81 double, 4 single. Air conditioning. **Facilities** Bar, 3 restaurants; background music; rooftop swimming pool; fitness centre; museum; conference/function facilities. **Location** Central. (Metro: Passeig de Gràcia) **Credit cards** Amex, MasterCard, Visa. **Terms** Room: single €335, double €372, suite €439. Breakfast €19. Full alc from €50.

Hotel Neri NEW
C/San Sever 5
Barcelona 08002

Tel (93) 304 06 55
Fax (93) 304 03 37
Email info@hotelneri.com
Website www.hotelneri.com

In the historic Gothic quarter by the cathedral, this 18th-century palace has been restored, 'imaginatively and stylishly', as a new small hotel. 'The contemporary artistic decor combines sensitively with the building's character,' say the nominators. 'Judicious lighting, like an operatic stage set, makes it a warm haven within minutes' walk of La Rambla. The staff are unfailingly warm, unobtrusively helpful.' Bedrooms have discreet colours, 'state-of-the-art' furnishings, plasma-screen TV, CD-player; quality fittings and 'excellent showers' in the bathroom. Breakfast, in the 'elegantly modish' restaurant, is a buffet; fresh fruits, fresh-squeezed juice, breads, croissants, 'appetizing cooked dishes'. 'We didn't dine, but the meals are said to be excellent.' (*Paul and Rosalind Bench*)

Open All year. **Rooms** 4 suites, 18 double. Some no-smoking. **Facilities** Bar, lounge/library, restaurant. Roof terrace. **Location** *Barri Gòtic*, near cathedral. (Metro: Jaume I) **Restriction** No dogs. **Credit cards** All major cards accepted. **Terms** [2004] Room: single/double €170–€240, suite €214–€302. Breakfast €15. Alc €50.

Hotel Sant Agustí
Plaça Sant Agustí 3
Barcelona 08001

Tel (93) 318 16 58
Fax (93) 317 29 28
Email hotelsa@hotelsa.com
Website www.hotelsa.com

On an attractive square just off La Rambla, next to the Liceu opera house (and Metro station), this former convent of St Augustin has 'simple, comfortable accommodation – good value'. It claims to be the oldest hotel in the city, and it has been run by one family for four generations. The spacious lounges are 'pleasantly old-fashioned', one reporter wrote. Others said: 'Staff are friendly. The owner was helpful. Our back room, recently decorated, was pleasantly cool, thanks to air conditioning. It had wooden floors, lots of storage space, a safe, excellent marble bathroom, really hot water. Some slight corridor noise.' The quietest, most expensive rooms are in the attic. Front rooms might hear late-night revellers. In the restaurant, facing the square, 'breakfast had fresh baguettes and rolls, a toasting machine, good coffee, but packaged orange juice, alas. It serves Catalan food, but we enjoyed eating at *Les Quinze Nitz* in the nearby Plaça Real: must be the best value in town.' (*DB, and others*)

Open All year. **Rooms** 75. Air conditioning. **Facilities** Lift. Lounge, lobby, bar, restaurant, background music; free Internet connection. **Location** 100 m off Las Ramblas at Calle Hospital. (Metro: Liceu) Parking 80 m. **Credit cards** All major cards accepted. **Terms** [2004] B&B: single €90–€122, double €100–€166.

Hotels are dropped if we lack positive feedback.

Hotel Urquinaona NEW
Ronda de San Pere 24
Barcelona 08010
Tel (93) 268 13 36
Fax (93) 295 41 37
Email info@hotelurquinaona.com
Website www. hotelurquinaona.com

At the top of La Rambla: former hostal *recently turned into small, inexpensive hotel. 'Strongly recommended: unprepossessing entrance, friendly English-speaking staff; absolute quiet.' 18 spacious air-conditioned bedrooms: 'spotless linen', bathroom with power shower. Free Internet access. Coffee shop, restaurant (*Cullera de boix, *specialises in rice dishes, eg, paella). (Metro: Plaça Urquinaona) MasterCard, Visa accepted. Room: single €71, double €90. Breakfast €5 [2004].*

BEGUR

Map 7:B6

Hotel Aigua Blava
Platja de Fornells
Tel (972) 62 20 58
Fax (972) 62 21 12
Email hotelaiguablava@aiguablava.com
Website www.aiguablava.com

Built in the style of a Catalan village around the Fornells cove on a lovely stretch of the Costa Brava, this much-loved hotel ('well run, in a beautiful spot') was thought 'truly wonderful' by a regular *Guide* correspondent this year. Set amid trees and rocks on various levels, it has lush gardens with tables and chairs under parasols, and a large saltwater swimming pool with a bar and plenty of loungers. Many of the staff are long-serving. 'The beautifully converted buildings are very comfortable; some have fabulous views. There is a warm welcome, and service in bar and restaurant is excellent. Sunday lunch was a feast and super value.' Visitors on their 23rd visit in 2004 add: 'The food has improved over its previous good standard.' Another guest advises: 'Choose your accommodation carefully. Sea-view rooms in the main building are best, the higher the better; the gatehouse annexe can be noisy late at night, and end rooms hear the hum from the powerful kitchen ventilation.' You can swim in the sea from tiny beaches or off rocks. (*SP, Harold Metcalfe, Bev Adams*)

Open 26 Feb–1 Nov. **Rooms** 5 junior suites, 75 double, 5 single. In 5 different buildings. Air conditioning. **Facilities** 4 lounges (background music), TV lounge, 3 bars, restaurant/grill; conference/banqueting rooms; boutique, hairdresser. Terrace (meal service). Gardens: tennis, table tennis, volleyball, saltwater swimming pool, paddling pool, children's play area, sand/rock beaches, safe bathing, water sports. Golf nearby. Unsuitable for ♿. **Location** 4 km SE of Begur, 8 km NE of Palafrugell. Garage, car park. **Restriction** No dogs. **Credit cards** All major cards accepted. **Terms** B&B: single €99–€130, double €152–€214, suite €174–€236; D,B&B: single €116, double €208, suite €232. Set meals €36.

The prices quoted for Spain do not include the government tax: 7% in Spain; 5% in the Canary Islands.

BENAOJÁN 29370 Málaga — Map 7:E3

Molino del Santo BUDGET
Bda Estación s/n

Tel (95) 216 71 51
Fax (95) 216 73 27
Email molino@logiccontrol.es
Website www.molinodelsanto.com

'Heartily recommended' again this year, Andy Chapell and Pauline Elkin's converted watermill has a 'superb' setting in the vast mountain landscapes of the Grazalema national park near Ronda. 'Good value for money,' says one visitor in 2004. 'Our delightful room, stylishly furnished, had a small sitting area, balcony, excellent bathroom.' 'A wonderful ten days; a warm and friendly atmosphere,' say others. Particularly liked are the garden rooms, each with terrace, set amid exotic vegetation and cascades of water. Rooms in the main house may hear 'comings and goings'. 'Good heating helps when spring nights are cool.' There is a solar-heated swimming pool, surrounded by loungers and urns. Many residents are British, 'but Dutch, French and local Spanish may fill the restaurant'. 'Appetizing meals' include local specialities, eg, roast kid. Only caveat: 'Loud pop music was played during dinner: they turned it down when asked.' Half board includes afternoon tea with 'delicious home-made cakes'. The 'particularly good' breakfast has fresh orange juice, 'a tempting range of cooked and cold items'. 'Staff are helpful.' Children are welcomed; families are offered alternative mealtimes and menus. 'A sleepy railway station is near, but it is not a problem.' There is good walking, and the Pileta caves, with ancient paintings, are near. (*R Barratt, MH Kershaw, Gail, Ian and Ally Oliver, Carolyn and Robin Orme, B and PL*)

Open 11 Feb–6 Nov. **Rooms** 3 suites, 14 double, 1 single. Some on ground floor. All air conditioned. No TV. **Facilities** Ramp. Lounge, library, bar, restaurant; background music. Terraces. Garden: heated swimming pool, children's pool. Horse riding nearby. Unsuitable for ♿. **Location** Below village, by station. From A376, 2 km N of Ronda, follow signs to Benaoján. Hotel signposted. Parking. **Restriction** No dogs. **Credit cards** Diners, MasterCard, Visa. **Terms** B&B €40–€107; D,B&B (obligatory in season) €64–€130. Full alc €25.

BENISSA 03720 Alicante — Map 7:D5

Casa del Maco BUDGET
Pou Roig

Tel (965) 73 28 42
Fax (965) 73 01 03
Email macomarcus@hotmail.com
Website www.casadelmaco.com

On a ridge in the Lleus valley near the beaches of the Costa Blanca, this 18th-century farmhouse, white-walled and tile-roofed, has been turned into a small rustic hotel/restaurant (Relais du Silence) by a Flemish photographer, Bert de Vooght. It stands in terraced gardens, amid vineyards, olive groves and almond orchards. 'The delightful staff create an atmosphere that must be revisited,' said a visitor who found the place 'outstanding; homely, with excellent facilities'. The comfortable bedrooms have antique furniture; some are beamed. The restaurant, redecorated this year, has a new chef, Luc van Hoof, who serves French *haute cuisine*. Breakfast, 'a true delight', has fresh orange juice, home-baked breads, cheese and ham. Meals are served on a patio on fine days; herbs for the kitchen grow by the swimming pool. (*HC*)

Open All year, except Jan. Restaurant closed Tues. **Rooms** 6 double. Air conditioning. **Facilities** Lounge, restaurant; classical background music. Terrace. Garden: unheated swimming pool. Beaches 2 km. Unsuitable for ♿. **Location** From N332 Calpe–Benissa, take small road on left 1 km after petrol station. Follow signs. **Credit cards** All major cards accepted. **Terms** Room: single €54–€87, double €66–€99. Breakfast €9. D,B&B €69–€123 per person. Set lunch €19, dinner €33–€54.

BILBAO Vizcaya **Map 7:A4**

Iturrienea Ostatua BUDGET
Santa María Kalea 14
Bilbao 48005

Tel (94) 416 15 00
Fax (94) 415 89 29

'An eccentric and enjoyable place,' says a visitor in 2004. Liked by *Guide* readers for its 'amazing value', this simple *pension* is near the cathedral and the lively *Mercado de la Ribera* in the *casco viejo*. Typical praise: 'Extremely welcoming reception.' 'Everything you need, nothing you don't.' The public rooms, 'with an eccentric collection of curios', are found 'cluttered' by some; Basque paintings hang on the walls. The bedrooms, 'with old beams and interesting antique furniture', are 'small but cleverly put together'. 'Ours, at the back, was very quiet, though it had a gloomy outlook.' Some, facing the street, may hear revellers at weekends. There is a little patio with potted plants. Breakfast, served until noon, has 'vast pastries, luscious bread, figs, etc', but 'poor orange juice'. 'No car access, but the amiable staff helped with bags.' The Guggenheim museum is a short journey away by the 'incredibly cheap' Metro. (*MM Davis, CR, and others*)

Open All year. **Rooms** 17 double, 4 single. **Facilities** Breakfast room. No background music. Small patio. Unsuitable for ♿. **Location** Old town, near river. Public parking 200 m (Plaza Berria/Plaza Nueva). **Restrictions** No smoking in breakfast room. No dogs. **Credit cards** Diners, MasterCard, Visa. **Terms** [2004] Room: single €45, double €54. Breakfast €4.

> Most hotels nowadays provide telephone, TV, etc, in the bedrooms. To save space, we do not give such details. If any of these is vital to you, check about availability in advance.

López de Haro
Obispo Orueta 2–4
Bilbao 48009

Tel (94) 423 55 00
Fax (94) 423 45 00
Email lh@hotellopezdeharo.com
Website www.hotellopezdeharo.com

Within walking distance of the Guggenheim museum, this 'very nice city hotel' is part of the Ercilla group. Though perhaps not a typical *Guide* entry, it offers 'excellent value' for a luxury hotel, and the staff win praise ('they gave us directions, suggested restaurants, even returned our hire car'), as do the 'well-appointed bedrooms'. 'Our room was small, but perfectly comfortable; an excellent bathroom.' 'Our quiet suite was large, with an even larger bathroom.' Some bedrooms are for women only. Guests can choose the type of pillow they want, and they have access to nearby gyms. In the public rooms are marble floors, oriental rugs, trailing plants. The small *Club Náutico* restaurant specialises in Basque dishes, 'tapas-style, light and good', and *Zortziko,* one of Bilbao's three *Michelin*-starred restaurants, is round the corner. 'Good buffet breakfast, with fresh orange juice.' (*M and HZ, MB*)

Open All year. Restaurant closed 1–15 Aug. **Rooms** 4 suites, 44 double, 5 single. Air conditioning. **Facilities** Lift. 3 salons, snack bar, tea room, 2 restaurants; background music; conference facilities. Garage. **Location** Central, near Gran Via and river. **Restrictions** No smoking in some bedrooms. No dogs. **Credit cards** All major cards accepted. **Terms** [2004] Room: single €106–€170, double €147–€204, suite €179–€319. Breakfast €12. Set meals €30; full alc €50. Special rates, including admission to Guggenheim museum.

Petit Palace Arana NEW
Bidebarrieta 2
Bilbao 48005

Tel (94) 415 64 11
Fax (94) 416 12 05
Email ara@hthoteles.com
Website www.hthoteles.com

A 19th-century building, 'smack in the city centre', has been converted with a minimalist interior by the small High Tech group. 'The staff are friendly, enthusiastic and informative,' says the nominator. 'My ultra-modern bedroom had a comfortable bed; its unusual shower room, with frosted glass separation, had disconcertingly limited soundproofing.' All rooms have free high-speed Internet access; some have a personal computer and an exercise bicycle. The cost of breakfast, in a 'nicely appointed' beamed room on the top floor, is thought 'out of keeping with the otherwise reasonable prices'. Snacks are served; there are 'lots of eating places nearby', and the hotel is within walking distance of the Guggenheim. (*Andrew Warren*)

Open All year. **Rooms** 45 double, 19 single. Some no-smoking. Air conditioning. **Facilities** Lobby with cyber corner, snack bar/breakfast room; meeting room; business centre. **Location** Opposite Teatro Municipal Arriaga. Parking nearby. **Restriction** No dogs. **Credit cards** All major cards accepted. **Terms** Room: single €75–€150, double €80–€150. Breakfast €11.

Every entry in the *Guide* is updated every year.

Hotel Sirimiri BUDGET
Plaza de la Encarnación 3
Bilbao 48006

Tel (944) 33 07 59
Fax (944) 33 08 75
Email h.sirimiri@hotelsirimiri.com
Website www.hotelsirimiri.com

Endorsed this year: 'clean, comfortable, adequate little hotel' in quiet position on edge of casco viejo *near cathedral, 10 mins by bus/Metro/tram from Guggenheim museum. 'Welcoming, helpful' English-speaking owner, Jon Campo. TV room. Free secure parking, easy access to ferry port. No dogs. All major credit cards accepted. 28 bedrooms (some spacious): single €50, double €70. Breakfast €6.*

LA BISBAL D'EMPORDÀ 17115 Girona — Map 7:B6

Castell d'Empordà NEW
Carretera del Castell

Tel (972) 64 62 54
Fax (972) 64 55 50
Email info@castelldemporda.com
Website www.castelldemporda.com

High on a wooded hillside, with 'wonderful views' of the attractive Empordà countryside, this 14th-century Gothic castle was in ruins when discovered by its Dutch owners, Margo Vereijken and Albert Diks. Restoration over three years has retained the feel of a castle in a conversion to a four-star hotel. 'He respects the traditions of the estate, and has maintained a distinctive Spanish feel,' say the nominators. 'The bedrooms have beautiful antique furniture, from Morocco, India and China.' The eight rooms in the castle vary in size; their bathrooms are impressive; three rooms in the tower are small, and have a shower only. Other rooms are in a new block built into the hillside: 'They might seem box-like, but they have exotic colours, fabulous Indian silks, and massive picture windows with balcony.' Modern dishes ('the lightest risotto, fresh fish') are served in the restaurant, which is decorated in traditional Spanish style. Breakfast has a 'better than average' buffet. The owner's recreation of the battle of Waterloo, with model soldiers, is displayed in a room below the tower. Well placed for touring the Dalí 'triangle'; the museum at Figueres, the artist's home at Port Lligat, and his castle at Púbol. The Costa Brava beaches are 20 minutes' drive away. (*D and JB*)

Open Mar–Nov. **Rooms** 1 suite, 26 double. **Facilities** Bar, restaurant; meeting room; background music. Garden: terrace, swimming pool. **Location** 2 km N of La Bisbal. 28 km from Girona. Parking. **Credit cards** Amex, MasterCard, Visa. **Terms** [2004] B&B: single €110–€140, double €160–€210, suite €270–€350. Set lunch €15; full alc €45. 1-night bookings sometimes refused in season.

> Italicised entries indicate hotels that are worth considering but which, for various reasons – inadequate information, lack of feedback, ambivalent reports – do not at the moment warrant a full entry.

BURGOS Map 7:B3

Landa Palace NEW
Carretera N1 (E5) de Madrid a Irún
Burgos 09001

Tel (947) 25 77 77
Fax (947) 26 46 76
Email landapal@teleline.es
Website www.landapalace.es

South of the city, this 'magnificent and spacious' hotel, built around a 14th-century tower, has baronial public rooms, lots of antiques, and modern extensions. It returns to the *Guide* after a time without reports. 'Our room was excellent and very large,' says a visitor this year. 'The situation next to the motorway is slightly off-putting, but no noise can be heard inside the building, and the large grounds and swimming pool to the rear have beautiful views of the surrounding countryside.' Earlier comments: 'Quirky and pretentious, but worth a visit.' 'Our modern bedroom, beautifully decorated, faced the garden and fields.' Some rooms overlook the hotel car park. Some suites with a terrace are by the swimming pool, which is half indoors, half out. This year's reporters weren't keen on the breakfast or the *tapas* bar. 'We didn't dine in the magnificent dining room, but a fellow traveller reported an excellent meal.' (*Christopher E Ackroyd, and others*)

Open All year. **Rooms** 3 suites, 39 double. Air conditioning. **Facilities** Lift. Lounge, restaurant; conference room; fitness centre, whirlpool; indoor/ outdoor swimming pool. Garden. **Location** 3.5 km S of Burgos on Madrid road. Parking. **Restriction** No dogs. **Credit cards** MasterCard, Visa. **Terms** [2004] Room: single €136–€230, double €170–€200. Breakfast €16. Alc €38.

Mesón del Cid
Plaza de Santa María 8
Burgos 09003

Tel (947) 20 87 15
Fax (947) 26 94 60
Email mesondelcid@mesondelcid.es
Website www.mesondelcid.es

'Splendidly located', in Castile's ancient capital, the López family's hotel is opposite the great Gothic cathedral where the medieval hero lies buried. It is generally thought 'pleasant', though one couple found staff 'rather sullen' during a heatwave. Front bedrooms have 'superb views of the cathedral, floodlit at night'; some rooms face a narrow side street which can be noisy; the annexe rooms are air conditioned. All have a blend of antique and modern furnishings. One couple wrote of a 'very good bathroom'. Breakfast, in a 'canteen-like' room, is thought only 'adequate', but the Castilian cooking in the restaurant is liked, and *Casa Ojeda*, with tables on a quiet square nearby, is also recommended for dinner. A one-way system makes access difficult, but 'there is help with luggage and parking'. (*J and SC, and others*)

Open All year. Restaurant closed 25 Dec, Sun night. **Rooms** 6 suites, 46 double, 3 single. 27, in annexe, air conditioned. **Facilities** Lift. Lounge, bar, restaurant; background music. Unsuitable for ♿. **Location** Opposite cathedral. Private garage nearby; valet parking (€12). **Credit cards** All major cards accepted. **Terms** Room: single €100, double €125, suite €147. Breakfast €10. Set meals €30.

CABEZÓN DE LA SAL 39505 Cantabria — Map 7:A3

El Jardín de Carrejo NEW
Carrejo

Tel (942) 70 15 16
Fax (942) 70 18 71
Email info@eljardindecarrejo.com
Website www.eljardindecarrejo.com

In village, 1.5 km SW of town between Santillana del Mar and San Vicente de la Barquera: stable and straw loft now small guest house: light modern design combined with old beams. Hall, dining room. Big, lovely garden with ancient trees. Closed 3–30 Jan. No dogs. All major credit cards accepted. 10 bedrooms: single €68–€87, double €75–€157. Breakfast €8.

CÁDIAR 18440 Granada — Map 7:E4

Alquería de Morayma BUDGET
Alpujarra

Tel/Fax (958) 34 32 21
Email alqueria@alqueriamorayma.com
Website www.alqueriamorayma.com

A 'beautiful place with enjoyable food' (a comment this year), this *centro agri-turístico* stands on a hillside in the Alpujarras, with wide views across a valley to the snow-capped peaks of the Sierra Nevada. It is informally run by Mariano Cruz Fajardo. His staff are friendly, 'especially Benito, a lovely character who juggles oranges'. Other praise: 'Delightful, good value.' The collection of buildings is on an organic farm with vineyards, an olive grove, orchards, kitchen gardens, hens, doves and farm animals. Guests are encouraged to take part, 'picking fruit, making sausages'. The decor is in local style: white walls, beamed ceilings, 'lovely fabrics, fascinating artefacts'. Bedrooms may be rustic, but bathrooms are modern. There is a library, a museum of the region, a wine cellar and an olive oil press, and an unheated outdoor swimming pool. 'Good, simple local food' is served in the popular restaurant (in two rooms, one large and informal, with fireplace, one smaller, with antiques). Breakfast, on a grassy terrace above the valley, has fresh orange juice, toast, honey, good coffee. Workshops, courses, skiing and climbing trips are organised. You can visit the home of the writer Gerald Brenan, at nearby Yegen. (*R Barratt, C and RO*)

Open All year. **Rooms** 4 suites, 14 double. In 18 units (5 self-catering). All on ground floor. **Facilities** Library, bar (background music), 2 dining rooms; workshops. 38-hectare farm: garden, unheated swimming pool; children's playground. **Location** 3 km SW of Cádiar, on road to Torvizcón; 85 km SE of Granada. **Credit cards** MasterCard, Visa. **Terms** Room: single €48, double €59, suite €63. Breakfast €3. Set meals €11; full alc €17.

> We give details about the credit cards which the hotels tell us that they accept. But please check with them, when booking, that this is still the case.

CALA RATJADA 07590 Mallorca — Map 7:C6

Hotel Ses Rotges
Calle Rafael Blanes 21

Tel (971) 56 31 08
Fax (971) 56 43 45
Email hotel@sesrotges.com
Website www.sesrotges.com

In a village on the north-east tip of Mallorca, this much-admired restaurant-with-rooms (*Michelin* star) is run by the 'delightful' French owner/chef, Gérard Tétard, with his wife, Laurence. Visitors in 2004 had a 'very personal welcome: Cava and fresh strawberries brought to our room in seconds'. The creeper-clad mansion, with 'slightly old-fashioned air, and solid rustic charm', is on a quiet side street. 'Superb' meals are served in the shady courtyard with potted plants and guitar player, or in the beamed dining room. Madame discusses the (no-choice) set menu at breakfast 'and makes amendments as necessary'. Or you could choose from the 'particularly good' *carte*. Local fresh fish is used; there is a wide range of Spanish wines. 'An excellent breakfast, brought to the table.' 'Comfortable, well-maintained' bedrooms have rustic furnishings, flowers, good bathroom. Suites have a small lounge. There is a rooftop terrace with loungers. Cala Ratjada, built around a series of coves, is 'a great contrast to the bucket-and-spade lifestyle of the busier resorts'; 'lovely harbour, nice beaches, good shops'. (*Jon Hughes, Chris Marchant, MK*)

Open Mid-Mar–end-Oct. **Rooms** 5 suites, 17 double, 3 single. Air conditioning. **Facilities** Salon, TV room, bar, restaurant; terrace (summer meals). No background music. Garden. Beach, golf, tennis, horse riding nearby. Unsuitable for ♿. **Location** Near centre: on entering, take 3rd right, 1st left. 80 km NE of Palma. Parking. **Restriction** No dogs. **Credit cards** All major cards accepted. **Terms** [2004] Room: single €72, double €93.50, suite €162. Breakfast €12. D,B&B €46.25 added per person. Set meals €40.50; full alc €60–€70. *V*

CALA SANT VICENÇ 07469 Mallorca — Map 7:C6

Cala Sant Vicenç Hotel
Calle Maressers 2

Tel (971) 53 02 50
Fax (971) 53 20 84
Email info@hotelcala.com
Website www.hotelcala.com

Near the sandy beaches of Mallorca's northern cape, the Suau family's small luxury hotel (Relais & Châteaux) stands quietly in landscaped gardens amid pine trees, in a busy resort. 'A comfortable, pleasant stay,' say returning visitors in 2004. 'Breakfast was superb; the restaurant had significantly improved.' The public rooms and the pool area are 'immaculate'; bedrooms are 'smallish'; many have a balcony; soundproofing can be poor. Two restaurants: one modern and formal, the other a *trattoria*. At lunchtime there is a poolside grill. 'The resort attracts older visitors; this is reflected in the hotel's guest profile: children are there, but there is a quota.' The old port of Pollensa is near. (*Chris Marchant, AR*)

Open 1 Feb–30 Nov. Restaurant closed Sun Feb–Apr. **Rooms** 23 junior suites, 11 double, 4 single. Some suitable for ♿. Air conditioning. **Facilities** Lift. Lounge, TV room, bar, 2 restaurants; live music 2 nights a week, background music; swimming pool, gym, sauna, beauty farm; conference room. Garden: swimming pool (heated in winter), putting. Sandy beach 200 m. Golf nearby. **Location** Centre of village. 10 km NE of Pollensa. Follow road towards sea, turn right. Hotel 100 m on right. Street parking. **Restrictions** Only 4 children under 12 at any time. No dogs. **Credit cards** All major cards accepted. **Terms** (Min. 5 nights Apr–Oct) B&B: single €64–€100, double €163–€246, suite €202–€289. Set dinner €50; full alc €70.

Hotel La Moraleja *Tel* (971) 53 40 10
Fax (971) 53 34 18
Email hotel@lamoraleja.net
Website www.la.moraleja.net

A 'most relaxing' small, hotel composed of two white villas in a residential area of this popular, 'if not particularly appealing', resort. 'Service is excellent,' says a returning visitor this year. Others write: 'Huge bedroom, wonderful bathroom, very private little terraces. Careful landscaping, ingenious water features and a cage of cheery canaries make it a peaceful oasis, though it stands on a main road.' But another visitor advises: 'Avoid the two bedrooms that face the road.' The atmosphere is 'intimate but laid-back', and the hotel is 'beautifully furnished and maintained': 'lots of Spanish paintings and antiques; a particularly nice lounge'. There is a new indoor restaurant this year for evening meals, and a new chef, Santiago Socias: he offers an extensive *à la carte* menu. In the grounds are two swimming pools; the poolside bar serves 'good lunchtime snacks'. Breakfast, taken outdoors on fine days, has a comprehensive cold buffet; hot dishes cooked to order; 'best fresh juice ever'. 'Many guests are English, and middle-aged': unusually for Spain, children under 14 are not allowed. The owner, Gabriel Ramis Esteva, is 'much in evidence'; his collection of vintage cars is on display. Two minutes' walk away is a rock/sand beach. (*John Lunn, R and EU*)

Open 1 May–31 Oct. **Rooms** 1 suite, 16 double. Air conditioning. **Facilities** Lift, ramps. 2 salons, 2 writing rooms, bar, breakfast room, restaurant. No background music. Garden: terraces, 2 swimming pools (1 heated), bar. Unsuitable for ♿. **Location** 1 km inland from centre. 10 km NE of Pollensa. **Restrictions** No children under 14. No dogs. **Credit cards** All major cards accepted. **Terms** [2004] (Min. 3 nights) B&B double €303, suite €338. Full alc €65.

LAS CAÑADAS DEL TEIDE — Map 7:E5
38300 Tenerife, Canary Islands

Parador de Cañadas del Teide *Tel* (922) 38 64 15
Apartado 15, La Orotava *Fax* (922) 38 23 52
Email canadas@parador.es
Website www.parador.es

In a 'spectacular, albeit isolated' setting, this purpose-built parador is 'excellent and inexpensive', says a visitor in 2004, endorsing 'with enthusiasm' its entry in the *Guide*. It is the only building within Tenerife's moonscape Cañadas del Teide national park, 2,000 metres above sea level. Other guests wrote of 'courteous, friendly staff'. The low mountain lodge has dark wood interiors; the lounge/bar has a log fire and big sofas. Bedrooms, 'simple yet elegant', have polished wooden floors. 'Our bed was enormous; the brightly lit bathroom had marble floor and eccentric shower.' Dinner has a Canarian/ cosmopolitan menu: 'Try the rabbit, cod fish cakes, asparagus and lamb, and the local red and white wines.' The buffet breakfast, 'well above Spanish average', includes tortilla and fresh fruits. Tour coaches come to the attached cafeteria, but the parador and its swimming area are off limits to day visitors. The night sky, free from light spill, is 'stunning'. The hotel has a Telescopico Dobsonian, 'but you can wander a few hundred metres and be awe-struck'. 'Unless you are an avid walker, there is not much to do.' (*Simon Bailey, Antony R Fletcher, and others*)

Open All year. **Rooms** 2 suites, 34 double, 1 single. 5 on ground floor. Air conditioning. **Facilities** Lounges, bar, café, restaurant; conference rooms. Garden: small swimming pool. **Location** Centre of island, in Cañadas del Teide national park. 70 km SW of Santa Cruz. **Credit cards** All major cards accepted. **Terms** [2004] Room: single €81, double €101. Breakfast €10. Set meals €24.

CARMONA 41410 Sevilla — Map 7:D2

Parador de Carmona
Calle Los Alcázares

Tel (95) 414 10 10
Fax (95) 414 17 12
Email carmona@parador.es
Website www.parador.es

Liked again in 2004, this converted 14th-century Moorish fortress was once part of Don Pedro the Cruel's summer palace. It has 'style and grandeur'; also wide views over the vast plain and orchards of the River Corbones from its terraces. 'The bedrooms are beautifully cool,' say this year's visitors. 'The views are great and the hotel is smartly run, professional and astonishingly beautiful. The furnishings are perfect. Bathrooms are grand, marble-lined and more than adequate. Breakfast is extensive.' In the 'impressive dining room', the former refectory, specialities include partridge with vegetables; spicy spinach. There is 'a good choice of desserts from the buffet'. 'Dinner was of high quality, with some astonishing bargains on the wine list (service in parador dining rooms can be a touch theatrical, but that can be fun).' Only problem: 'the male reception staff seemed aloof'. Other visitors wrote: 'Our bedroom was well appointed, spacious; no noise, wonderful view.' 'A beautiful swimming pool.' 'Easy to find, plenty of parking.' (*David Sulkin, EB, and others*)

Open All year. **Rooms** 60 double, 3 single. Air conditioning. **Facilities** Lounges, bar, restaurant; background music; conference/function facilities. Gardens, terrace, swimming pool. **Location** Central, signposted. Parking. **Restriction** No dogs. **Credit cards** All major cards accepted. **Terms** [2004] Room: single €96, double €120. Breakfast €10. Set meals €25.

CASARABONELA 29566 Málaga — Map 7:E3

Hotel la Era NEW
Partido Martina
Los Cerrillos

Tel (952) 11 25 25
Fax (952) 11 25 38
Email info@hotellaera.com
Website www.hotellaera.com

On hilltop, 2 km outside small village in Sierra de las Nieves, 46 km NW of Málaga via A357: Francisco and Isabel Diaz's small no-smoking rural hotel, named after threshing stone preserved in large garden (which has unheated swimming pool). 'Pleasing, tasteful; delightful bedrooms and public rooms'; lovely views; home-cooked evening meal. Open 1 Mar–22 Dec. Ramp. Lounge, dining room, Terrace. No children under 12. No dogs. No background music. MasterCard, Visa accepted. 9 bedrooms (1 on ground floor). B&B (min. 2 days): single €87, double €105–€115, suite €135. Set dinner €25. *V*

CAZALLA DE LA SIERRA 41370 Sevilla — Map 7:D2

Hospedería la Cartuja de Cazalla BUDGET

Tel (954) 88 45 16
Fax (954) 88 47 07
Email cartujsv@teleline.es
Website www.skill.es/cartuja

The 'indomitable' Carmen Ladrón de Guevara y Bracho ('ever-present, husky-voiced, eccentric') has devoted 25 years to the restoration of this ruined Carthusian monastery (a national monument). 'A place of utter magic', it stands on a plateau with a natural spring, in the Sierra Norte, north-east of Seville; it is run as a centre of contemporary art and culture. An entranced visitor wrote: 'Carmen appears formidable but has a heart of gold, though she has been known to turn away guests if she finds them uninteresting, or uninterested in the extraordinary project she continues to undertake alone (with two craftsmen).' Bedrooms in the gatehouse of the monastery are 'modestly furnished'; in the cloisters are four suites; a small house with garden is good for a family. Organic ingredients, including local chicken and lamb, and vegetables from the monastery gardens supply the kitchens for the simple meals. There are exhibition and concert rooms, an art gallery and a studio, a swimming pool in the garden, and wide views of the Sierra Morena from a huge panoramic terrace. The surrounding area is full of interest: the acorn-eating pigs for the famous *jamón serrano* are raised here. (*PM*)

Open All year, except 24/25 Dec. **Rooms** 4 suites (in cloisters), 6 double, 2 single. 4 air conditioned. **Facilities** 4 lounges, 4 dining rooms. Concerts. Function rooms. No background music. Terrace, gardens; 2 unheated swimming pools. **Location** 3 km N of Cazalla de la Sierra. From A432 take A455 for 2.5 km towards Constantina. Parking. **Restriction** No smoking: restaurant, bedrooms. **Credit cards** All major cards accepted. **Terms** Room: single €50–€55, double €81–€90, suite €108–€120. Set meals €25. *V*

COFIÑO 33548 Asturias — Map 7:A3

Halcón Palace
c/Cofiño

Tel (98) 584 13 12
Fax (98) 584 13 13
Email info@halconpalace.com
Website www.halconpalace.com

'A wonderful place, deserving all the praise it gets,' says a visitor in 2004. This 17th-century manor house, in a hamlet in the foothills of the Picos de Europa, is run by its Swiss proprietor, Leo Benz, and his Spanish wife, Isabel (both 'charming'). Though surrounded by crenellated walls, and with a medieval-style tower, 'it is not at all grand', says this year's reporter. 'Leo himself said it was a bit shabby.' His brother, Carlos, serves 'hearty Asturian cooking', accompanied by a 'good wine list', and with 'excellent service'. 'When Leo was ill, another brother came from Switzerland to help out.' Bedrooms are 'small, but well equipped'. 'Our bathroom was spotless.' Other comments: 'One of the most marvellous views from a hotel bedroom that we have ever enjoyed.' The only downside is 'background music in the restaurant, but we were always first down to breakfast and were able to switch it off'. Swallows swoop over the small swimming pool, 'nicely sited', with views, in the 'limited but attractive' grounds. (*Meriel Packman, and others*)

Open All year, except Feb, 4 days at Christmas. **Rooms** 1 suite, 17 double, 1 single. 2 on ground floor. **Facilities** 2 lounges, TV lounge, bar, restaurant; function facilities. Garden: terraces, unheated swimming pool. Fishing, riding, canoeing nearby; beaches 15 mins' drive. Unsuitable for ♿. **Location** From Arriondas: AS260 NW to Colunga; after 5 km turn W to Cofiño. **Restriction** No dogs. **Credit cards** All major cards accepted. **Terms** [2004] B&B: single €45–€75, double €58–€93, suite €83–€118; D,B&B €42.50–€88.50 per person. Set meals €13.50.

CÓRDOBA 14003 — Map 7:D3

Hotel Marisa BUDGET
Cardenal Herrero 6

Tel (957) 47 31 42
Fax (957) 47 41 44
Email hotelmarisacor@terra.es
Website www.sol.com/hotel/marisa

Just across a cobbled street from the *Mezquita*, in the *casco antiguo*, stands Antonia Velasco's unassuming and 'pleasant' B&B. The location is 'excellent', say recent visitors, 'but you should ask for a rear room' (some face the inner courtyard). Front rooms are 'subject to an unholy din from the street: cars parking, bad musicians, street cleaners, etc'. Earlier visitors, who commented: 'For a touch of real Spain, look no further', found the staff both 'helpful' and 'charming'. (*Y and KF*)

Open All year. **Rooms** 23 double, 5 single. 4 on ground floor. Air conditioning. **Facilities** TV room/bar. **Location** Old town, opposite *Mezquita* (windows double glazed). Drive along river and watch for signs. Garage. **Credit cards** All major cards accepted. **Terms** Room: single €38–€42, double €60–€65. Breakfast €5.

CRUÏLLES 17116 Girona — Map 7:B6

El Somni NEW
Raval 20

Tel (972) 64 55 90
Fax (972) 64 17 16
Email info@cruilles.com
Website www.cruilles.com

Small B&B hotel in quiet medieval walled village in Gavarres hills, 45 minutes' drive SE from Girona airport. Minimalist conversion (deep colours) by owners, Anna García Cantó (Catalan teacher) and partner, Sandro (Italian artist). Breakfast (continental, Catalan or alc, from €5) in vaulted bar/restaurant or patio garden; background music. All-day snacks. No dogs. All major credit cards accepted. 6 bedrooms (1 on ground floor). B&B: double €65–€195. *V*

DEYÁ 07179 Mallorca — Map 7:C6

Hotel Es Molí
Carretera de Valldemossa

Tel (971) 63 90 00
Fax (971) 63 93 33
Email reservas@esmoli.com
Website www.esmoli.com

On the outskirts of this famous hill village, on a hillside with 'breathtaking views' across olive terraces to the sea, this holiday hotel has long been popular with *Guide* readers. 'Difficult to fault,' was one recent comment. It stands in a 'gorgeous garden' with orange, lemon and ancient olive trees, a bamboo grove, and a pond. Service 'is excellent throughout'; 'drinks, etc, reasonably priced'. Visitors returning after 11 years wrote: 'Even better than we remembered. Staff genuinely friendly; we recognised many from our previous visits.' Bedrooms vary: 'Our lovely room with balcony could have done with more storage space.' 'Our annexe room was large.' 'Our room was small but adequate, spotlessly clean.' Bathrooms are 'excellent'. Rooms near the road get traffic noise. 'Breakfast, dinner and lunch by the large swimming pool were all delicious.' The *Ca'n Quet* restaurant, in a separate building, is also enjoyed. A minibus takes guests to a private beach for sea bathing. 'Pepe's guided walk each Monday is brilliant.' (*JRO, and others*)

Open 29 Apr–29 Oct. **Rooms** 3 suites, 76 double, 8 single. 16 in annexe. Air conditioning. **Facilities** Lift. Lounges, 2 bars, dining room, restaurant (classical background music). Gardens: terrace (dancing twice weekly in summer), heated swimming pool, bar, tennis (extra charge). Free minibus to rocky beach with bar. Unsuitable for ♿. **Location** 500 m from village centre. 29 km NW of Palma. Parking. **Restriction** No dogs. **Credit cards** All major cards accepted. **Terms** B&B: single €125–€139, double €202–€228, suite €360–€400; D,B&B €19 added per person. Set dinner €38; full alc €45.

> Inevitably, some hotels change hands or close after we have gone to press. Please check the ownership when booking, particularly in the case of small places.

S'Hotel d'Es Puig
Es Puig 4

Tel (971) 63 94 09
Fax (971) 63 92 10
Email reservas@hoteldespuig.com
Website www.hoteldespuig.com

'A bargain in a delightful location', this pretty village house on the edge of Deyá is not far from the upmarket *Residencia* (see next entry). It offers similar views at half the price. The managers, Lucian and Ana Maria Rogojina, 'work hard to make guests feel at home', says a *Guide* reader on her fifth visit. 'Peace and quiet is the hallmark: no lively night life.' The 'hotel on the hill' is 'fairly plain: no frills, spotlessly clean; bedrooms have all you need'. The rooms, with ochre walls, terracotta tiles, green shutters, are small, with a tiny *en suite* shower room ('a new shower cubicle with huge showerhead was a great improvement in 2004'). Two rooms have a terrace looking over the pool; so does the penthouse; front rooms look towards the distant sea. Breakfast, a buffet (*churros*, ham, eggs, fruit, etc), is in the garden with lemon trees and views to mountains. There's a small honesty bar. Most guests are English or German. Lots of good restaurants are nearby. Robert Graves, who lived in Deyá, mentioned the building in a short story; he is buried at the church nearby. (*Niki Dixon*)

Open 1 Feb–15 Nov. **Rooms** 1 penthouse, 7 double. Air conditioning. **Facilities** Reception lounge, bar, breakfast room. Patio: unheated swimming pool. Unsuitable for ♿. **Location** Edge of village. Car access up narrow, steep street. Parking nearby. **Restrictions** No smoking in public rooms. No dogs. **Credit cards** All major cards accepted. **Terms** B&B: single €70–€78, double €102–€120, penthouse €170–€190. 1-night bookings sometimes refused.

La Residencia
Finca Son Canals

Tel (971) 63 90 11
Fax (971) 63 93 70
Email reservas@hotel-laresidencia.com
Website www.hotel-laresidencia.com

Exclusive hotel (Orient Express) on edge of village: beautifully converted 17th/18th-century houses (antiques, traditional Spanish furnishings, contemporary art, air conditioning). Lovely grounds: citrus trees, terraces, 2 swimming pools, tennis. Lounges, 2 bars; beauty centre; spa (indoor pool); conference facilities. 2 restaurants: El Olivo, *formal;* Son Fony, *cheaper. Live music sometimes. Private cove 3 km (summer shuttle service). Unsuitable for ♿ (lots of steps). All major credit cards accepted. 62 bedrooms (22 are suites). B&B: single €185–€270, double €225–€565, suite €395–€2,300. Set lunch €45, dinner €69.50 [2004]. Min. stay 5 nights in season. Children under 10 allowed only 1 July–15 Aug, autumn half-term, Christmas. 'Even better than before: first-rate staff, very good food,' say visitors this year.*

****

Traveller's tale Hotel in Austria. We were the only guests at dinner. The solitary waitress stood to attention nearby for the entire meal – it killed conversation.

****

ESCALANTE 39795 Cantabria — Map 7:A3

Hotel San Román de Escalante
Carretera de Escalante a Castillo

Tel (942) 67 77 28
Fax (942) 67 76 43
Email sanromanescalante@mundivia.es
Website www.sanromandeescalante.com

Named after the 12th-century Romanesque chapel in its grounds, this 'lovely, luxurious' hotel (Relais & Châteaux) 'feels like a small village'. The setting, in a forest on the route to Compostela, is peaceful. Fine old buildings, restored 'with love', have been filled with modern art and antiques. 'Some of the art is peculiar,' says one of this year's reports, 'but aesthetic care has gone into the furnishing; the garden, with its quirky sculptures and exotic plants, is well designed.' Some bedrooms have old beams and a chandelier; one is built into a rock face. Jorge Martínez's cooking is liked with caveats: 'Fish was fresh and well cooked, but the menu was limited and did not change; no vegetables or salads. Breakfast was unimaginative.' There are tables, chairs and potted plants in a courtyard, and a swimming pool on a terrace with views ('a great asset, since you have to drive to find a beach'); armchairs and lights are arranged in a glade for after-dinner seating. The co-owner/manager, Juan Melis, is 'a man of culture and humour'. (*M and HZ, CG*)

Open 20 Jan–20 Dec. **Rooms** 3 suites, 13 double. In several buildings. Some on ground floor. Air conditioning. **Facilities** Ramps. Lounge, bar, restaurant (background music); private dining room. Garden: heated swimming pool. Beach 5 km. **Location** 2 km NW of village (go towards Castillo). 39 km E of Santander. **Credit cards** All major cards accepted. **Terms** [2004] Room: single €105–€126, double €126–€152, suite €159–€172. Breakfast €10. Full alc €50. 1-night bookings sometimes refused.

L'ESPLUGA DE FRANCOLÍ 43449 Tarragona — Map 7:B5

Masia del Cadet BUDGET
Les Masies de Poblet

Tel (977) 87 08 69
Fax (977) 87 04 96
Email masiadelcadet@yahoo.es

Run by Corominas-Vidal family owners: old country inn (Relais du Silence) in beautiful setting, 2 km SW of village, near historic monastery at Poblet, NW of Tarragona. 'Excellent meals.' Good walking (nature trails) nearby. Closed Nov. Lift. Salon with TV, bar, restaurant (closed Sun evening/Mon except holidays; background music); function room; terrace (meal service), garden: swimming pool. No dogs. All major credit cards accepted. 12 modern bedrooms, 'attractive, spacious'. B&B: single €72, double €91. Set meals €22; full alc €40.

> We asked hotels to estimate their 2005 tariffs, but many preferred not to think so far ahead, and gave their 2004 tariffs. Prices should *always* be checked when booking.

FORNALUTX 07109 Mallorca Map 7:C6

Ca'n Reus NEW
Carrer de l'Auba 26

Tel (971) 63 11 74
Fax (971) 63 80 41
Email info@canreushotel.com
Website www.canreushotel.com

This attractive village, with cobbled streets and tiled rooftops, in a valley of orange and lemon groves ten minutes' drive from Sóller, stands amid the dramatic mountain scenery of the Sierra de Tramuntana, a paradise for walkers. Here, this 300-year-old house has been run as a small rural hotel since 2003 by Sue and Nick Guthrie (she is the TV journalist, Sue Lloyd-Roberts). They aim for a peaceful, informal atmosphere, and pride themselves on their breakfast, a generous buffet including locally produced tarts, pastries, fruit and jams. At night, the public areas are charmingly lit by candles, on walls, in shallow pools on the floor, and on the stairs. The bedrooms, each named after a mountain, are simple (no CD-player, minibar or TV) and pretty. The most appealing rooms face the view; others overlook a village street. There are old wooden or iron bedheads, capacious armoires, wooden beams, flagged floors and potted plants. Puig Mayor, with its sitting area with rocking chairs, was particularly liked this year. In the small garden, the small swimming pool is surrounded by bougainvillaea, oleanders and loungers. 'Sue is a kind hostess,' say visitors in 2004, 'full of local knowledge.' An enthusiastic walker, she will provide directions for walkers, and sometimes acts as a guide. She provides a comprehensive directory of local restaurants (there are three good ones in the village). Once a week, the Guthries serve a communal no-choice dinner, alfresco in summer. 'Delicious gazpacho; excellent barbecued chicken; a huge roll of goat's cheese; wonderful local pastries' were enjoyed this year, washed down by Mallorcan wines. In winter, a fire warms the small lounge/library. 'Parking seems to depend on the whims of the local mayor', but advice is given. (*A and CR*)

Open All year. **Rooms** 1 suite, 8 double. Some no-smoking. Air conditioning. **Facilities** Entrance hall, lounge, dining room; background music in the morning sometimes. Garden: terraces, unheated swimming pool. Golf, riding, beaches nearby. **Location** NE of Sóller. Directions given on booking. Public parking. **Restrictions** Children under 4 in garden room only. No dogs. **Credit cards** MasterCard, Visa. **Terms** B&B: single €60–€80, double €90–€125, suite €130–€150. Set dinner €30. 1-night bookings sometimes refused May–Sept. *V*

FUENTESPALDA 44587 Teruel Map 7:B5

La Torre del Visco
Apartado de Correos 27

Tel (978) 76 90 15
Fax (978) 76 90 16
Email torredelvisco@torredelvisco.com
Website www.torredelvisco.com

In the remote valley of the Rio de Tastavins, rich in flora and fauna, this fortified 15th-century farmhouse ('Mistletoe Tower') has been sensitively modernised by its 'hands-on' British owners, Jemma Markham and Piers Dutton. A 'quality rural retreat' (Relais & Châteaux), it stands in formal gardens with roses, terraces and fountains, in a huge estate (organically farmed) at the end of a five-kilometre track. Each of the 'elegantly simple' bedrooms (no telephone or TV, but 'four vases of fresh flowers') has its own colour scheme; some have stonework, others antique brickwork. There are good rugs on floors and a collection of lithographs and contemporary paintings on walls. Furnishing varies from 18th-century to Art Deco. One lounge has a Bechstein piano. No background music, but guests may play classical CDs in the library. There is a medieval wine cellar. The daily-changing dinner menu, served in a spacious, modern room or alfresco, uses home-grown and local produce, including organic olive oil. Breakfast (ham, cheese, home-made preserves, eggs and bacon, etc) is served communally in the large kitchen, or on a terrace, until mid-afternoon. For children over four there are 'kites, puzzles, books, games, cats and mountain bikes'. Guided walks, trekking, birdwatching and fishing can be arranged, and courses are held (see below).

Open All year. **Rooms** 4 suites, 11 double. Some no-smoking. No telephone/ TV. **Facilities** 3 lounges, library, bar, dining room. No background music. 220-hectare estate: gardens; river, bathing; farm. Unsuitable for ♿. **Location** 12 km NW of Fuentespalda. A1413 to Valderrobres, A4141 to Fuentespalda. After 6.2 km take track for 5 km. **Restrictions** 'Preferably no children under 4.' No dogs. **Credit cards** MasterCard, Visa. **Terms** D,B&B: single €175, double €220–€270, suite €330–€360. Set meals €38. Courses: cookery, wine, photography, local culture, Spanish, etc. Christmas/New Year packages. 1-night bookings refused weekends. *V* (2-night midweek bookings)

GARACHICO 38450 Tenerife, Canary Islands — Map 7:E5

Hotel El Patio BUDGET
Finca Malpaís, El Guincho

Tel (922) 13 32 80
Fax (922) 83 00 89
Email reservas@hotelpatio.com
Website www.hotelpatio.com

The 'charming' de Ponte family have converted the *quinta* and other buildings on their banana plantation (they have owned it since 1507) into this small rural hotel just outside Garachico. Four brothers look after the plantation, two run the hotel. A visitor returning in 2004 found it 'as good as ever'. Other guests thought it 'wonderful, very good value'. 'A delightful setting' (above a bay on the peaceful north-west corner of the island). Guests can walk through the plantation to a small black sand beach. 'Four gardeners tend the beautiful, large gardens, which have quiet corners with seats, a good-sized swimming pool surrounded by flowers and shrubs.' The bedrooms are in two buildings: each has a lounge with honesty bar. 'We stayed in a converted cattle byre overlooking plantation and hills; traditional furnishings, tiled floors, spotlessly clean. Nice touches, like needle-point no-smoking signs made by one of the daughters.' 'We were upgraded to a room with private terrace.' 'Excellent buffet breakfast: a flow of cooked eggs, bacon and tomatoes, good bread, fruit, wonderful bananas from the estate.' A fixed-price dinner can be ordered at breakfast: 'good plain cooking'. 'Garachico has many restaurants (dinner is around 7.30 here, earlier than in mainland Spain).' 'Do not miss the national park in the volcanic centre of the island.' (*Peter and Celia Gregory, Christopher Beadle, and others*)

Open All year, except 1–12 May, 26 July, 31 Dec. **Rooms** 26 double. All on ground floor. Some in annexe, 800 m. 6 suitable for ♿. **Facilities** Lounges, 2 honesty bars, *bodega*, dining room; games room; meeting room; gym; cellar. 60-hectare estate: patio, gardens, heated swimming pool, tennis, croquet. **Location** On coast, 3 km NE of Garachico. **Restrictions** No smoking: restaurant, bedrooms. No dogs. **Credit cards** Amex, Diners, MasterCard. **Terms** [2004] B&B: single €53–€62, double €75–€94, suite €91–€114. Set dinner €16. *V*

Hotel San Roque
Esteban de Ponte 32

Tel (922) 13 34 35
Fax (922) 13 34 06
Email info@hotelsanroque.com
Website www.hotelsanroque.com

On a cobbled street near the seafront of this interesting little port in the lush north-west of Tenerife, this small designer hotel provides 'a charming blend of style, comfort, cosy ambience, and friendliness', according to a visitor returning in 2004. It is 'very well managed' by the owners, Dominique Carayon ('a courteous man'), his wife Laly (the cook), and son, also Dominique ('very chatty in perfect English'). 'They and their staff could not be nicer; all requests are promptly dealt with.' Painted red, the 17th-century mansion has a Bauhaus/Rennie Mackintosh interior: galleries, arcades, modern art, old woodwork. One patio has a huge futuristic steel sculpture, the other a small swimming pool, and wooden tables for meals. Bedrooms vary greatly: Room 17 has a sleeping area up a steep spiral staircase and a 'beautiful but claustrophobic sitting area (no windows)'. Room 20 has a 'charming sitting area with a good view of the bath'. Some visitors found the lighting difficult to control. The no-choice three-course dinner (booked by 7 pm) is 'elegantly prepared and served: delicious, inventive starters and desserts, but main courses were sometimes less good'. 'Excellent breakfast.' 'Perfect tranquillity.' 'Garachico has no beaches, but lava flows have been creatively sculpted into rock pools and perches.' (*Esler Crawford, Anthony R Fletcher, SW, and others*)

Open All year. Restaurant closed to non-residents. **Rooms** 4 suites, 14 double, 2 single. Air conditioning. **Facilities** Bar, restaurant, 2 patios (1 with swimming pool and bar); weekly live music; sauna, solarium. Mountain bikes. Tennis; free use of public swimming pool nearby; beach, safe bathing 100 m. Unsuitable for ♿. **Location** Centre of village. W end of N coast. Parking. **Restriction** No smoking. **Credit cards** All major cards accepted. **Terms** B&B: single €140–€185, double €165–€235, suite €250–€330. Set dinner €25. 1-night bookings refused 20 Dec–5 Jan.

> The prices quoted for Spain do not include the government tax: 7% in Spain; 5% in the Canary Islands.

GRANADA **Map 7:D3**

Casa Morisca NEW
Cuesta de la Victoria 9
Granada 18010

Tel (958) 22 11 00
Fax (958) 21 57 96
Email info@hotelcasamorisca.com
Website www.hotelcasamorisca.com

In the old Moorish quarter of Granada, below the Alhambra, this 15th-century mansion is now a B&B hotel, 'packed with atmosphere', owned by Carlos Sanchez, and managed by Jesus Candenas. 'Rooms are simple but stylish,' writes its 2004 nominator, 'so is breakfast [in a barrel-vaulted room]. Staff are helpful.' There is a 'small, attractive' galleried patio, with pond, at the back, where drinks are served; it has fine views of the Comares Tower of the Alhambra. Many bedrooms face the Alhambra or the Generalife. 'Buying a cake at the nearby closed nunnery, where you receive it from an invisible vendor, via a revolving door, is an experience. Hard to imagine a better location or hotel at this price.' (*Keith Conlon*)

Open All year. **Rooms** 1 suite, 13 double. Some suitable for ♿. Air conditioning. **Facilities** Breakfast room (no-smoking). No background music. Patio garden. **Location** Moorish quarter, below Alhambra. Public parking. **Restriction** No dogs. **Credit cards** All major cards accepted. **Terms** B&B: single €112–€126, double €191–€216.

Parador de Granada NEW
Calle Real de la Alhambra
Granada 18009

Tel (958) 22 14 40
Fax (958) 22 22 64
Email granada@parador.es
Website www.parador.es

Right in the grounds of the Alhambra, facing the Generalife, this flagship parador is a conversion of a 15th-century Franciscan convent. It has a Moorish decor, fountains, little courtyards, and a view to the Sierra Nevada. Outstanding features are the little chapel and first burial site of Ferdinand and Isabella. Reception can supply tickets for the Alhambra. 'It may be expensive but it deserves a *Guide* entry for its fabulous location, an island of peace and calm amid the scrum that is the Alhambra in the daytime,' says a regular *Guide* correspondent. 'Most of the staff were helpful, and we greatly enjoyed our stay. Our room in the old building was beautifully appointed; we had a lovely view over the fishpond and garden.' Bedrooms in the modern wings are also spacious, if lacking in character. 'The building is a delight; the terrace has comfortable sofas, and we enjoyed beers and *tapas* in the lovely gardens. The breakfast buffet is excellent, with a wide variety of goodies. Dinner is overpriced, but *Les Mimbres*, ten minutes' walk away, by the entrance to the Alhambra, was very good and reasonably priced.' Another visitor called the parador 'as close to heaven in hotels as one can get', and warned that you must book months ahead. (*Niki Dixon, David Sulkin*)

Open All year. **Rooms** 2 suites, 34 double. Air conditioning. **Facilities** Salon, bar, tea room, restaurant; background music; conference room; patios. Garden, terrace. Unsuitable for ♿. **Location** By Alhambra. Parking. **Restriction** No dogs. **Credit cards** All major cards accepted. **Terms** [2004] B&B: single €171, double €214. Breakfast €12. Set dinner €25.

GRAZALEMA 11610 Cádiz — Map 7:E2

Puerta de la Villa NEW
Plaza Pequeña 8

Tel (956) 13 23 76
Fax (956) 13 20 87
Email info@grazhotel.com
Website www.grazhotel.com

Small modern hotel in typical white Andalusian village ('said to be wettest in Spain') within botanically rich Grazalema natural park. Salon, café, restaurant ('good-value dinner'); terrace; conference facilities. 'Smart spa' in basement: swimming pool, whirlpool, gym. 28 air-conditioned bedrooms ('Ours was nice and big; the one next door was twice the size,' says nominator. 2 are suitable for ♿): €98–€120. Breakfast €10. Set meals €27–€36 [2004].

LA HERRADURA 18697 Granada — Map 7:E3

Hotel La Tartana BUDGET
Urb. San Nicolás

Tel/Fax (958) 64 05 35
Email reservations@hotellatartana.com
Website www.hotellatartana.com

'Welcoming' boutique hotel, managed by owners Barry Branham and Penny Jarrett, built in Andalusian style (central courtyard with fountain; beamed ceilings, old monastery doors). In seaside village of whitewashed houses, 50 mins' drive E of Málaga. 'Basic, but adequate bedrooms, stylish public areas.' Salon, bar used by locals, 'enjoyable' restaurant (dinner only, Tues–Sat); background music; meeting facilities. Terrace looking over lovely Mediterranean bay. Beach 5 mins' walk; Cantarrijan naturist beach 10 mins' drive. No dogs. MasterCard, Visa accepted. 1 suite with terrace, 5 double rooms. B&B double €55–€79. Full alc €25.

EL HIERRO 38900 Canary Islands — Map 7:E5

Parador de El Hierro
Las Playas

Tel (922) 55 80 36
Fax (922) 55 80 86
Email hierro@parador.es
Website www.parador.es

One of the remotest of all the paradors, a modern white-painted building by a black lava beach on the smallest, least visited of the Canary Islands. It stands in large gardens with coconut palms and dragon trees, at the end of a 12-kilometre track. All bedrooms face the sea. A visitor this year was 'delighted' to find it in the *Guide*. 'Our pleasant room had a small, comfortable balcony. Snacks and light dishes are served in the bar and veranda all day; welcome if you have treated yourself to lunch at one of the fishing villages.' 'One feels as though one has come to the end of the world,' said last year's nominator. 'At dinner, a brave attempt is made to provide local dishes [poultry and cheese soup; fish; sea urchins, etc]. Excellent breakfasts: sausage, bacon and fried eggs every day. Friendly service. How they do it all in such an isolated place is a mystery. We found the local wines unreliable, but the wine list has some good Tenerife and mainland wines.' A car is essential; 'some of the driving is quite mountainous, and a little daunting'. El Hierro's 'stunning views' are best seen from its seven purpose-built *miradores*. Expect frequent mists, and pounding waves during Atlantic storms. (*Nigel Fletcher, JBH*)

Open All year. **Rooms** 47 double. Air conditioning. **Facilities** Lobby, bar, restaurant. Garden: swimming pool. **Location** From main road from La Estaca: left at 1st crossroads, follow road to parador. **Restriction** No dogs. **Credit cards** All major cards accepted. **Terms** [2004] Room: single €91, double €113. Breakfast €10. Set meals €24.

HONDARRIBIA 20280 Gipuzkoa — Map 7:A4

Hotel Obispo
Plaza del Obispo 1

Tel (943) 64 54 00
Fax (943) 64 23 86
Email recepcion@hotelobispo.com
Website www.hotelobispo.com

On a hill within the ramparts of this interesting old Basque fishing port/seaside resort (also known by its Castilian name, Fuenterrabía), this small B&B hotel is a converted 14th-century palace ('stone and wood predominate'). The owner, Victor Lekuona, is said to be 'very helpful'; his staff are 'very friendly'; there is 'an excellent receptionist with fluent English'. 'Our good-sized top-floor room had a triangular shape, arched doors and windows, and triangular bathroom,' say visitors this year. 'Its ceiling was low, but it was well thought out and neat. It looked out to France and over San Sebastián's little airport; we saw only one small plane all weekend.' Another visitor 'loved her room with its curvy bath'. Earlier comments: 'Our delicious room, shocking pink, had fine old beams, beautiful wooden doors, view of garden and neighbouring pear orchard (lots of sparrows).' 'Delicious orange juice, squeezed to order, came with my tea tray.' The 'excellent' breakfast, in the cafeteria or outdoors, can include bacon and eggs. Plenty of restaurants nearby: the one next door was liked this year, or you could try *Alameda* (*Michelin* star). 'Difficult to find by car: get them to send a map.' The town is 'quiet and tidy; definitely not the Costa del Sol'. (*Andrew and Christine McManus, Jane Northcote, PC*)

Open All year, except 22 Dec–10 Jan. **Rooms** 4 suites, 11 double, 2 single. Most with balcony or terrace. 1 suitable for ♿. **Facilities** Lounge, bar/cafeteria; terrace. No background music. Small walled garden. **Location** 5 mins' walk from centre, in old town. Free parking, garage. **Restriction** No dogs. **Credit cards** All major cards accepted. **Terms** [2004] B&B: single €72–€107, double €79–€132, suite €121–€162.

ILLETAS 07181 Mallorca — Map 7:C6

Hotel Bon Sol
Passeo de Illetas 30

Tel (971) 40 21 11
Fax (971) 40 25 59
Email bonsol@fehm.es
Website www.hotelbonsol.es

On a pine-covered hillside overlooking Palma bay, this large holiday hotel, with mock-Moorish tower, is managed by its owners, Lorraine and Martin Xamena. Praise in 2004: 'An enjoyable visit.' 'Excellent value.' 'Full of colour, warmth and homely luxury. Beautiful paintings, antiques, flowers, stunning views, and those little comforts we Brits love (slippers, the most comfortable I have had, kettle, BBC1). Delicious, plentiful food. Nannies for our children while we ate our four-course dinner in peace.' Low, white, green-shuttered buildings spill down terraces and subtropical gardens to a tiny private cove and beach (a lift and tunnel bypass the road). There are three swimming pools on different levels ('one very warm, one medium warm, one cool'), and a wellness centre. 'Our children adored the playground.' Bedrooms are airy and spacious. In the candlelit restaurant, or on a terrace by the cove, Spanish and international dishes are served: 'Slightly conveyor belt,' thought one visitor, but another wrote of a 'happy atmosphere'. 'Lovely public rooms' include a bar/lounge with pianist each evening. 'Lots of nooks and crannies, indoors and out.' 'Generous buffet breakfast.' (*Walter Cottingham, Helen Garritt, Louise French*)

Open 20 Dec–7 Nov. **Rooms** 8 suites, 91 double, 5 single. Some on ground floor. 28 in gardens. Air conditioning. **Facilities** Lift. 2 lounges, 2 bars (live music nightly), 3 dining rooms; wellness centre; conference room. Gardens: 3 swimming pools, children's play area, sauna, tennis; beach (access by lift/stairs), safe bathing; golf nearby. Unsuitable for ♿. **Location** 8 km W of Palma, on C719. Frequent buses. Parking, garage. **Credit cards** All major cards accepted. **Terms** [2004] B&B €98–€131. Set lunch €15, dinner €25; full alc €34.

JÁVEA 03730 Alicante — Map 7:C5

Hotel El Rodat NEW
Carretera Cabo de la Nao

Tel (966) 47 07 10
Fax (966) 47 15 50
Email info@elrodat.com
Website www.elrodat.com

*Luxury 'hotel village and spa' (*Relais & Châteaux*) on seafront in residential area of Jávea (Xábia) on coast between Alicante (86 km) and Valencia (96 km). Views of Jávea Bay and Montgó national park. 'Lovely rooms and facilities.' 2 restaurants:* H'Anoa *(*haute cuisine, *closed Sun/Mon in winter; live jazz weekly);* L'Arroceri, *with terrace (Mediterranean food); bar; conference facilities; nursery for children in high season; air conditioning. Indoor and outdoor heated swimming pools, tennis. Beaches nearby. All major credit cards accepted. 4 suites, 38 double rooms (in villas among pine and palm trees and flowers): single €123–€175, double €154–€220, suite €196–€280. Breakfast €11. Full alc €35–€45.*

JEREZ DE LA FRONTERA 11407 Cádiz Map 7:E2

Villa Jerez
Avenida de la Cruz Roja 7

Tel (956) 15 31 00
Fax (956) 30 43 00
Email reservas@villajerez.com
Website www.villajerez.com

'Very quiet for a city hotel', this yellow mansion, in the old part, has been converted to a luxury hotel by a small chain; the manager is Sophie De Clerck. 'We slept with the windows open, and heard owls at night, birdsong in the morning,' said recent visitors. The rooms are all different; many face the 'well-maintained' gardens. 'Ours, beautifully furnished, had a luxurious bathroom with lots of goodies. The charming staff were attentive, the meals were excellent.' There is a courtyard with palm trees, an elegant restaurant, *Las Yucas*, and a dining terrace by the 'delightful' swimming pool. 'Expensive but worth it.' Much to see in Jerez: visit one of the sherry *bodegas*, and the Royal Andalusian School of Equestrian Art. (*NG*)

Open All year. **Rooms** 4 suites, 10 double, 2 single. In 3 buildings. Air-conditioning. **Facilities** Lift. Reading room, bar, restaurant; background music; function facilities; gym, sauna, spa bath. Terrace. Large garden: unheated saltwater swimming pool, tennis. **Location** Central, off Plaza del Caballo. Parking, garage. **Restriction** Guide dogs only. **Credit cards** All major cards accepted. **Terms** B&B: single €207–€236, double €272–€309, suite €566–€676; D,B&B €31 added per person. Full alc €42. 1-night bookings sometimes refused.

LA LECHUZA 35320 Gran Canaria, Canary Islands Map 7:E5

Hotel Rural Las Calas NEW/BUDGET
El Arenal 36

Tel (928) 66 14 36
Fax (928) 66 07 53
Email reserva@hotelrurallascalas.com
Website www. hotelrurallascalas.com

The Vega de San Mateo is a protected area in the centre of Gran Canaria island, full of flora and birds, and with farms producing fruit and vegetables. This restored 17th-century manor house is in a hamlet in a fertile valley, 850 metres above sea level. It is now a small rural hotel, warmly nominated this year: 'Fantastic, very good food. Original architecture combined with a touch of design.' The bedrooms surround a central courtyard; there is a garden with fruit trees. The owner, Magüi Carratalá, prides himself on the 'relaxed atmosphere' and Canarian cooking, and can arrange many outdoor activities (see below). (*Mark Raymond*)

Open All year. **Rooms** 2 suites (1 with hydromassage), 5 double. **Facilities** Lounge, library, breakfast room, restaurant; private dining rooms; solarium; small meeting facilities. No background music. Courtyard. Garden, sun terraces. Guided walks, horse riding, mountain biking, golf nearby. Unsuitable for ♿. **Location** 50 m from La Lechuza. 20 mins' drive SW of Las Palmas de Gran Canaria. Parking. **Restriction** No dogs. **Credit cards** MasterCard, Visa. **Terms** B&B: single €50–€60, double €63–€96, suite €72–€120. Set meals €15. 1-night bookings refused. *V*

LEÓN 24001 Map 7:A2

Parador Hostal San Marcos
Plaza de San Marcos 7

Tel (987) 23 73 00
Fax (987) 23 34 58
Email leon@parador.es
Website www.parador.es

With a 'marvellous sense of history, this 'unique' parador is a conversion of a former medieval monastery with an ornate Renaissance facade. The palatial public rooms have antiques and period furniture; tapestries soften cool stone walls; there is a beautiful cloister around a green courtyard, a chapter house and a museum. Most bedrooms are in a modern extension; many have a balcony. Though large and well equipped, some may lack storage space. Some look over the river or garden, and are peaceful. One reader recommends taking one of the suites in the main building; these have a 'magnificent' lounge, so two bedrooms and two bathrooms can easily accommodate two couples or a family; they can cost little more than two doubles. Reserving a table is advised for the 'great dinner, well served' in the large, brightly lit, modern dining room. 'The usual good buffet breakfast.' Reception staff, as in many paradors, may be 'cool and businesslike'. Many package tours. (*M and HZ, and others*)

Open All year. **Rooms** 15 suites, 185 double. Air conditioning. **Facilities** Lift, ramps. 13 salons, bar, restaurant, TV room; background music; conference facilities; beauty parlour. Garden. **Location** On river (signposted). Parking. **Restriction** No dogs. **Credit cards** All major cards accepted. **Terms** Room: single €103–€118, double €128–€147. Breakfast €10. Set meals €27.

LLAFRANC 17211 Girona Map 7:B6

Hotel Restaurant Llevant
Francesc de Blanes 5

Tel (972) 30 03 66
Fax (972) 30 03 45
Email info@hotel-llevant.com
Website www.hotel-llevant.com

On the beach in an unspoilt small Costa Brava resort, the Farrarons family have run their hotel since 1935. 'It is pleasant for a few days at the seaside,' say recent visitors. Bedrooms vary in size from medium to small (the best, sea-facing ones 'can be hard to get'). The rooms are generally 'light, well furnished, with lovely wood floors, good beds and linen' (one reader was reminded by her 'beautifully appointed room' of a luxury yacht). Less liked was a 'somewhat cramped room on the first floor, with a window opening on to a tiny internal courtyard with daylight from a skylight'. Street noise can be a problem in some rooms, but 'the owners and their dedicated staff make up for this'. Meals are served in the 'immaculate' dining room (white tablecloths on ranks of tables) facing the sea, or under huge parasols on the attractive dining terrace. There is always fresh fish on the daily-changing *table d'hôte* dinner menu. The food is liked, but one visitor felt that outside diners were given preference over residents: 'long waits between courses'. 'The beach can be crowded in high season, but the village was quiet in June; a lovely, unspoilt spot on a beautiful coastline.' (*NF, D and GB, and others*)

Open All year, except Nov. Restaurant closed 25 Dec night. **Rooms** 24 double, 2 single. Air conditioning. **Facilities** Lift. 2 lounges, bar, restaurant. Terrace. Unsuitable for ♿. **Location** Seafront of village. 3 km SE of Palafrugell. **Credit cards** Amex, MasterCard, Visa. **Terms** B&B (off-season only): single €52, double €68–€115; D,B&B: single €84–€136, double €129–€267. Set meals €22.50; full alc €40.

LOJA 18300 Granada — Map 7:D3

Hotel La Bobadilla
Finca La Bobadilla
Apartado 144

Tel (958) 32 18 61
Fax (958) 32 18 10
Email info@la-bobadilla.com
Website www.la-bobadilla.com

In a 'beautiful, remote setting', amid olive groves and almond orchards on an Andalusian hilltop, this 'classy' hotel is built in the style of a Moorish village. White-walled villas are reached by winding paths and flowery courtyards; there are colonnades, marble floors, terracotta tiles, a large outdoor swimming pool with fountain, and a chapel. Visitors this year 'had great fun exploring'. The bedrooms are decorated in local style (mahogany furniture, beamed ceilings). 'Our large room had French windows leading on to a grassy terrace.' 'Our enormous King Suite, almost ridiculously well equipped, had walk-in wardrobe, large sitting room, two sun terraces, bath the size of a paddling pool. Genuine comfort; just the right side of stylish.' The restaurants, *La Finca* (*haute cuisine*) and *El Cortijo*, are both thought 'excellent'. 'Outstanding breakfast: buffet filling the room, everything you could think of, fresh-cooked dishes.' In summer, there is an outdoor grill/bar, and flamenco performances. Weddings and concerts are held. 'Fabulous main swimming pool, surrounded by immaculate gardens; a decent gym.' No special rooms for the disabled, but the staff 'couldn't have been more helpful' to a wheelchair-user. (*Jennie Hall, Annie Lade, and others*)

Open All year, except 9–27 Jan. **Rooms** 37 suites, 23 double, 2 single. Air conditioning. **Facilities** Lobby (concerts), reading lounge, TV lounge, bar, breakfast room, 2 restaurants (background music; flamenco in *La Finca* in summer); indoor swimming pool, fitness centre, sauna; meeting/function facilities. 350-hectare grounds: terraces, summer bar/grill, unheated swimming pool, chapel, archery, tennis, children's playground; bicycles, horse riding, *pétanque*, quad bikes. Not really suitable for ♿. **Location** 20 km W of Loja, 65 km SW of Granada. A92/N342 exit 175 direction Villanueva de Tapia and Salinas, turn right off C334. Parking. **Credit cards** All major cards accepted. **Terms** B&B: single €181–€235, double €264–€320, suite €342–€978; D,B&B €47–€49 added per person. Full alc €98. 1-night bookings refused Christmas, Easter.

> We quote either price per room, or else the range of prices per person – the lowest is likely to be for one person sharing a double room out of season, the highest for a single room in high season.

LUARCA 33700 Asturias — Map 7:A2

Hotel Villa la Argentina
Villar de Luarca

Tel (98) 564 01 02
Fax (98) 564 09 73
Email reservas@villalaargentina.com
Website www villalaargentina.com

Owned and run ('with attention to detail') by the Fernández family, this listed *belle époque* villa was built in 1899 by a shipping magnate. It is in a residential area above this charming fishing village in northern Spain. The nominators reported: 'A delightful young man allowed us to choose between two rooms. We had a good bathroom with shower, nice towels. Good lighting.' The suites' bathrooms have hydromassage. A big breakfast (croissants, sandwiches, ham, cheese, tuna empanadas, almond muffins, coffee, etc) is served in a pretty room. In the attractive garden, with exotic plants, is a swimming pool. For dinner, *Restaurant Sport* (fresh fish), was found 'superb'. (*M and HZ*)

Open Mar–Dec. **Rooms** 3 suites, 9 double. **Facilities** Library, bar/coffee shop, breakfast room, restaurant; games room; meeting rooms; chapel. Terrace. Garden: swimming pool, tennis. **Location** Opposite Barrera park in Villar de Luarca; follow hotel signs from village. Parking. **Restriction** No dogs. **Credit cards** All major cards accepted. **Terms** [2004] Room: single €49–€75, double €54–€84, suite €84–€105. Breakfast €6. Set meals €15; full alc €30.

MADRID — Map 7:C3

La Residencia de El Viso NEW
Nervíon 8
Madrid 28002

Tel (91) 564 03 70
Fax (91) 564 19 65
Email reservas@residenciadelviso.com
Website www.residenciadelviso.com

In tree-lined street in chic residential El Viso area (buses to centre a block away): small hotel in house restored in 1930s style. 'Rooms small but comfortable; reasonable rates,' says nominator. Lift, salon/bar, restaurant (closed Sun night); inner courtyard (summer meals), peaceful garden. Air conditioning. No dogs. All major credit cards accepted. 12 air-conditioned rooms: single €77–€103, double €129. Breakfast €10. Set meals (restaurant closed Sun) €31–€57 [2004].

MONTSENY 08640 Barcelona — Map 7:B6

Hotel Restaurant Can Barrina BUDGET
Carretera Palautordera

Tel (93) 847 30 65
Fax (93) 847 31 84
Email info@canbarrina.com
Website www.canbarrina.com

An hour's drive from Barcelona, Frederic Munné's attractive restaurant-with-rooms is a converted farmhouse in the Montseny national park (spectacular views). The chef, Ferran Jaenada, has a *Michelin Bib Gourmand* for his hearty Catalan dishes, which use local fish, mountain raspberries, etc. These are served in a rustic dining room, or on a series of terraces, which enjoy the views. 'Good food, friendly staff,' says a visitor this year, but not everyone enjoyed the piped music. Bedrooms range from 'large and high-ceilinged with garden view' to 'small and dark'. An 'especially good' breakfast is taken on warm days under vines by the swimming pool. Guided walks and horse riding in the mountains can be arranged. A popular wedding venue. (*JAH, and others*)

Open All year, except 15 days over Christmas. **Rooms** 14 double. 6 in annexe. Some on ground floor. **Facilities** Reading room, bar, restaurant (background music); 7 private dining rooms; 2 function/meeting rooms. Garden: 3 terraces: swimming pool. **Location** A7 exit 11; left after toll on to C251 towards Granollers, right on to BV5301 towards Santa María Palautordera/Montseny. **Restriction** No dogs. **Credit cards** Diners, MasterCard, Visa. **Terms** Room: single €58, double €86. Breakfast €9. D,B&B €80 per person. Full alc €40.

MUNDAKA 48360 Vizcaya — Map 7:A4

Atalaya Hotel BUDGET
Itxaropen kalea 1

Tel (94) 617 70 00
Fax (94) 687 68 99
Email reservas@hotel-atalaya-mundaka.com
Website www.hotel-atalaya-mundaka.com

In a Basque resort at the mouth of the Mundaka River (a UNESCO biosphere reserve), linked by a small railway line to the Bilbao metro, this small, modern hotel faces the main square. 'The family owners are very friendly,' says a visitor this year. 'And the terrace café at the back, where snacks are served, is pleasant.' Some bedrooms are small ('as are some beds'), and the ones by the square are noisy (no air conditioning). But a room overlooking the garden was liked: 'Simple but delightful, with a traditional glassed-in gallery.' Breakfast is thought 'excellent'. The 'good value' and the secure parking are appreciated. The restaurants at the harbour serve 'wonderful fish'. The estuary is an important surfing centre.

Open All year, except 24/25 Dec. **Rooms** 10 double, 1 single. **Facilities** 2 salons, bar, cafeteria; background music; meeting room. Garden. Beach 100 m. Unsuitable for ♿. **Location** 37 km NE of Bilbao (rail link). Parking. **Credit cards** All major cards accepted. **Terms** [2004] Room: single €66–€73, double €83–€91. Breakfast €8. 1-night bookings sometimes refused Aug.

NAVACERRADA 28491 Madrid — Map 7:B3

Hotel-Restaurant Las Postas BUDGET
Carretera N501

Tel (918) 56 02 50
Fax (918) 53 11 51
Email postas@hotelaspostas.com
Website www.hotelaspostas.com

Restaurant-with-rooms: converted 19th-century posting house, in mountain town between Madrid (50 km) and Segovia (35 km), popular with Madrileños. *'Stunning views', excellent Spanish cooking: large panoramic gourmet restaurant 'a treat'; less formal restaurant on lower ground floor. Function room. Breakfast in bar/café ('you pay for what you have'). Air conditioning. 'Good walking', some skiing nearby. On road, but quiet at night. Amex, MasterCard, Visa accepted. 22 'rather ordinary' bedrooms: single €50, double €60, suite €96. Breakfast €4. Residents' menu €18; alc €22–€26 [2004].*

OJÉN 29610 Málaga — Map 7:E3

Refugio de Juanar BUDGET
Sierra Blanca

Tel (95) 288 10 00
Fax (95) 288 10 01
Email juanar@juanar.com
Website www.juanar.com

Up a narrow, winding road behind Marbella, in a nature reserve in the foothills of the Sierra Blanca, this former aristocratic hunting lodge has rustic decor and 'modest' bedrooms. 'It is a refuge from the frenzied construction which is destroying the beauty of the area,' one 2004 visitor wrote. 'You can walk directly into the mountains. With vast uncluttered views, it is a delightful place; excellent value for money.' A winter visitor, who stayed in the large room with fireplace where de Gaulle wrote his memoirs in 1970, had 'a warm welcome from a charming young man' but found the building 'chilly'. The restaurant, 'jolly with red gingham and local ceramics', is a favourite lunchtime spot for local families. Game is a speciality (partridge, mountain goat, etc), though the cooking is 'nothing to shout about'. In the grounds are tennis and a swimming pool; from a viewpoint you can watch the sun set over Marbella. (*Hugh SK Peppiatt, Ellin Osmond*)

Open All year. **Rooms** 2 suites, 23 double, 1 single. Some on ground floor. Air conditioning. **Facilities** Lift. 2 salons, TV room, bar, *bodega*, restaurant; background music; function rooms. Garden: swimming pool, tennis. **Location** 9 km W of Ojén, off A355 by narrow road to left (signposted). **Restriction** No dogs. **Credit cards** All major cards accepted. **Terms** Room: single €62–€73, double €82–€95, suite €175–€195. Breakfast €7.50. D,B&B €22 added per person. Set meals €24, full alc €35. *V*

ÓRGIVA 18400 Granada — Map 7:E4

Hotel Taray BUDGET
Carretera A348

Tel (958) 78 45 25
Fax (958) 78 45 31
Email tarayalp@teleline.es
Website www.hoteltaray.com

In a garden beside the Guadalfeo River, with 'spectacular views of the Alpujarras to the south and the snow-capped peaks of the Sierra Nevada to the north', Eladio Cuadros's simple, modern hotel, built in traditional style, was much praised by *Guide* readers this year: 'A bargain; well maintained.' 'Lots of quiet, verdant space, enjoyable food.' 'We had a wonderful time; lovely proprietors, cheerful staff.' The readers who first discovered it returned after two years: 'All is much as before. The garden is a paradise, with colourful flowers, heady scents of orange blossom and jasmine.' The swimming pool, surrounded by grass and olive trees, is 'huge, and properly deep at one end'. The simple bungalow-type bedrooms – 'basic', even 'austere' –

have heating for the cooler months; some have a sitting room, some a private terrace. 'Straightforward satisfying food' is served on a set menu in the restaurant; 'the local dishes are the best'. Breakfast is a 'substantial buffet', with orange juice from fruit in the garden, eggs, ham, cheese, fruit, cereal, home-made quince jelly. 'Only dogs weighing under five kilos' are allowed in the buildings; there are kennels for bigger ones. 'Órgiva has little to detain you, but the mountains and higher villages are a delight.' Granada is an hour's drive away. (*Niki Dixon, R Barratt, Antonia Brandes, Carolyn and Robin Orme*)

Open All year. **Rooms** 3 suites, 3 mini-suites, 9 double. In 2 annexes. Some on ground floor. Air-conditioning. **Facilities** Ramps. Reading/music/TV room, bar, restaurant; background music. Large grounds: unheated swimming pool. **Location** 1.5 km from Órgiva, 60 km SE of Granada. Parking. **Credit cards** All major cards accepted. **Terms** Room: single/double €62, suite €92–€97. Breakfast €5. Set meals €12.

ORIENT 07349 Mallorca — Map 7:C6

L'Hermitage
Carretera de Alaró a Bunyola

Tel (971) 18 03 03
Fax (971) 18 04 11
Email info@hermitage-hotel.com
Website www.hermitage-hotel.com

19th-century monastery, now elegant German-owned hotel. 'Stunning' setting, 2 km W of Orient, in beautiful, remote valley. 'Attentive staff, wonderful food, good selection of Mallorcan and Spanish wines. Ample buffet breakfast.' Open early Feb–early Nov. 2 salons, library, bar, restaurant; background music; chapel. Garden: terrace (outside dining; live music), heated swimming pool, tennis. Unsuitable for ♿. No dogs. All major cards accepted. 'We were given details of fascinating local walks, and keys to allow us into private estates, quite a privilege.' 24 bedrooms (20 in modern annexe; those in the main building may be darker). B&B: single €108–€120, double €169–€219; D,B&B €38 added per person. Set lunch €16; full alc €50 [2004]. *V*

PALMA DE MALLORCA 07012 Mallorca — Map 7:C6

Hotel San Lorenzo
Calle San Lorenzo 14

Tel (971) 72 82 00
Fax (971) 71 19 01
Email info@hotelsanlorenzo.com
Website www.hotelsanlorenzo.com

'A wonderful little hotel,' say visitors this year. 'An excellent welcome; we much enjoyed our junior suite.' Another comment: 'The ambience is beautifully done. The small number of rooms, the lack of a formal reception desk, the security-coded entrance number enable one to come and go as if at home. Not cheap, but it avoids pretension.' Sensitively restored, this tall, narrow, 17th-century house in Palma's old quarter has wrought iron, tiled floors, antique furniture, Mallorcan tiles in the air-conditioned bedrooms on the two top floors (the best rooms have an open fireplace and a terrace). There is a ground-floor patio, an Art Deco bar (brought from Paris) in the bar/breakfast room, and a 'beautiful small swimming pool', surrounded by palms and bougainvillaea, on the second level. The 'delicious' breakfast has fresh orange juice, yogurt, fruit, eggs, and *ensaimada* (flaky pastry). Two bedrooms above an alley can be noisy; rear ones have a balcony or terrace facing the cathedral. The manager, Susanne Kress, is said to be 'capable and charming'; 'her two delightful Spanish assistants handle the operation with a deft touch'. No restaurant; plenty nearby; so is Palma's new modern art museum, Es Baluard. (*Ann and Sidney Carpenter, Bill Hawkins*)

Open All year. **Rooms** 2 junior suites, 4 double. Air conditioning. **Facilities** Bar/cafeteria. No background music. Patios: unheated swimming pool. Unsuitable for ♿. **Location** Old town. Public parking nearby. **Restriction** No dogs. **Credit cards** All major cards accepted. **Terms** [2004] Room: double €130–€180, suite €230. Breakfast €8–€10. 1-night bookings sometimes refused.

PERAMOLA 25790 Lleida — Map 7:B5

Hotel Can Boix
Afueras

Tel (973) 47 02 66
Fax (973) 47 02 81
Email hotel@canboix.com
Website www.canboix.com

Beautifully set among trees at the foot of the craggy Roca del Corb, the Pallarès family's smart, modern hotel is not far from the main Andorra to Lleida road. It is 'very well run, very Spanish', say visitors this year. Most rooms share the 'superb views' of the valley of the Segre; those in the main building have a small balcony. The largest rooms ('grand comfort') are in the annexe. In summer, meals are served under a canopy on a big terrace: 'Huge amounts of good food; meat and game better than fish.' The buffet breakfast is liked. The large swimming pool is surrounded by white loungers, and children are welcomed. Plenty of outdoor activities (see below). (*R and CM*)

Open All year, except 1 month Jan/Feb, 15 days Nov. **Rooms** 41 double. 20 in annexe. Air conditioning. **Facilities** Lift, ramps. Lounge, TV lounge, bar, 2 dining rooms; terrace (meal service); background music; function/conference facilities. Garden: unheated swimming pool, tennis, children's playground. River, fishing, rafting, horse riding, hiking, mountain biking nearby. **Location** 2.5 km NE of village; turn off C14 to Peramola. Parking. **Credit cards** All major cards accepted. **Terms** B&B: single €76–€102, double €101–€134. Set meals €18; alc €49.

PUIGPUNYENT 07194 Mallorca — Map 7:C6

Gran Hotel Son Net
Castillo Son Net

Tel (971) 14 70 00
Fax (971) 14 70 01
Email recepcion@sonnet.es
Website www.sonnet.es

With 'brilliant service' and 'fantastic rooms', David Stein's small luxury hotel, a converted 17th-century palace, is 'strongly recommended' by visitors in 2004. Maria del Mar Soler is its new manager. Painted bright pink, it stands on a small hill amid pine and fruit trees in the Tramuntana mountains in south-west Mallorca. Palm trees, rose bushes and hedges provide privacy for sunbathers beside the 100-foot swimming pool: it has views to olive groves below. There are sculptures in the grounds, and the building is filled with original paintings by Warhol, Chagall and Hockney, and works by Spanish classical masters. The food 'has improved by leaps and bounds': Mediterranean cuisine is served in *L'Orangerie*, the restaurant in an old olive press (meals can also be taken on a terrace or in the courtyard); the *Gazebo* grill and bar by the pool is open in summer. A lavish tea is served in the lounge in winter. 'Good buffet breakfast.' 'Our sumptuous suite had an enormous sitting room and a 14 foot-high ceiling.' (*Helen Moore, Claire and Donald Trelford, and others*)

Open All year. **Rooms** 7 suites (1 in house with private pool), 17 double. 1 suitable for ♿. Air conditioning. **Facilities** Lift. Lounges, restaurant (live music weekend nights); background music in public areas; conference room; gym, sauna, whirlpool. Garden: unheated swimming pool, summer bar/restaurant, tennis; chapel. Beaches 15 km. **Location** 400 m NW of village. 12 km NW of Palma. **Restriction** No dogs. **Credit cards** All major cards accepted. **Terms** [2004] Room €180–€490, suite €590–€1,490. Breakfast €19. Full alc €50–€60. 1-night bookings sometimes refused.

RONDA 29400 Málaga — Map 7:E3

Hotel La Fuente de la Higuera NEW
Partido de los Frontones

Tel (952) 11 43 55
Fax (952) 11 43 56
Email info@hotellafuente.com
Website www.hotellafuente.com

On the site of an old olive mill, in a valley outside Ronda, this 'relaxed, luxurious' small hotel has been created 'in good taste' by the 'laid-back' Dutch owners, Pom and Christina Piek. 'It is cool and pleasant, relying on breezes through the house rather than air conditioning,' says the nominator (fans are also provided). 'Our suite was a delight, with cool, pale colours, large lounge, king-size bed, with mosquito net canopy; private terrace with deckchairs.' Front rooms have views over the valley; rear ones face hillside. A 'well-stocked' honesty bar has drinks and ice cream; home-baked cakes are served every afternoon. 'The three-course dinner, three choices of main course, was good, and Ronda, ten minutes' drive away, has excellent restaurants. Breakfast can be anarchic, as the young waiters concentrate on taking orders for dinner.' There is a 'pleasant small swimming pool'; the valley has 'the usual Spanish soundtrack of dogs, frogs, vans that need a new exhaust, and trains'. (*Niki Dixon*)

Open All year. **Rooms** 8 suites, 3 double. 3 in annexe. **Facilities** Lounge/library (honesty bar), restaurant. No background music. Garden: terrace, swimming pool. **Location** 6 km NW of Ronda. A376 towards Seville; after 2 km turn right on to signposted track; left turn after 1 km; left track after fork. **Restriction** No dogs. **Credit cards** MasterCard, Visa. **Terms** B&B: single €120, double €135, suite €180. Set dinner €35.

Hotel San Gabriel NEW/BUDGET
Calle Marqués de Moctezuma 19

Tel (952) 19 03 92
Fax (952) 19 01 17
Email info@hotelsangabriel.com
Website www.hotelsangabriel.com

In Ronda's charming old town, this 'beautiful 18th-century house with a relaxed atmosphere' has been run as a small B&B hotel since 1998 by the Arnal-Pérez Girón family. It returns to the *Guide*, after a time with no feedback. 'A jewel; elegant and comfortable. The staff couldn't be more friendly,' says this year's report. 'Our lovely superior double was spacious, with good lighting, nice furniture; big shower room. We liked it so much we stayed an extra night, in a standard room, smaller but also lovely.' Many bedrooms overlook tiled roofs. The 'gorgeous' public rooms have heavy Spanish furniture; wooden staircases are lined with gilt-framed pictures. There is a library and a tiny cinema. Breakfast, in the cafeteria/bar converted from the old kitchen, is 'excellent: fresh juice, local breads, good jams'. (*Ellin Osmond*)

Open All year, except 1–7 Jan, 21–31 July, 21–31 Dec. **Rooms** 3 suites, 13 double. Air conditioning. **Facilities** Small lift. Salon, library, billiard room, small cinema, cafeteria/bar, wine cellar. No background music. Patio. Unsuitable for ♿. **Location** Old town. From centre, cross Puente Nuevo, 2nd street on right. **Restrictions** No smoking in cafeteria. No children under 12. No dogs. **Credit cards** Amex, MasterCard, Visa. **Terms** B&B: single €66–€68, double €73–€85, suite €83–€95.

SALAMANCA 37008 Map 7:B2

Hotel Residencia Rector
Paseo Rector Esperabé 10

Tel (923) 21 84 82
Fax (923) 21 40 08
Email hotelrector@telefonica.net
Website www.hotelrector.com

A 'delightful' B&B hotel, well placed for all the principal sights of this lovely university city. 'All members of staff were courteous and most helpful,' says a visitor this year. The 'elegant' building, with pink stone facade, looks like one of Salamanca's old palaces, but it dates from 1945. Despite the location on the busy ring road, bedrooms are quiet: most are grouped around patios. 'Superb breakfast: freshly squeezed orange juice, serrano ham.' 'They recommended an excellent family-run restaurant', or you could try *Chez Victor* (*Michelin* star). (*Anne Folkes; also Peter Crichton*)

Open All year. **Rooms** 1 suite, 11 double, 1 single. Some on ground floor. Some no-smoking. Air conditioning. **Facilities** 2 salons, residents' bar, breakfast room. No background music. Unsuitable for ♿. **Location** Ring road, near Roman bridge/Casa Lis museum. Garage (€10 per day). **Restrictions** No smoking: some bedrooms. No dogs. **Credit cards** All major cards accepted. **Terms** Room: single €89, double €112, suite €146. Breakfast €10.

SAN SEBASTIÁN 38800 La Gomera, Canary Islands Map 7:E5

Parador de la Gomera
Calle Orilla del Llano 1

Tel (922) 87 11 00
Fax (922) 87 11 16
Email gomera@parador.es
Website www.parador.es

Recently entirely refurbished, this stone-built parador stands on a cliff-top overlooking the harbour and marina of the lushest and least spoilt island in the Canaries. Recent visitors wrote: 'Our comfortable room had garden view, air conditioning *and* a roof fan (very *Raffles*), lots of hanging space, spacious, well-lit bathroom equipped with useful items (comb, toothpaste, etc).' Dinner is served by women in traditional costume, in the 'fine, large restaurant with well-spaced tables'. 'It gets off to a good start: complimentary glass of sparkling wine and an *amuse-bouche*'; thereafter it was found a bit variable: 'good rabbit, pork fillet not so good; good puddings; long wine list'. Breakfast was thought 'excellent'. Lots of sitting areas: alcoves and patios. In the well-kept gardens, 'the swimming pool is large, and wonderfully located to catch as much sun as possible'. (*EC*)

Open All year. **Rooms** 2 suites, 56 double. Some on ground floor. Air conditioning. **Facilities** 2 lounges, TV room, 2 bars, restaurant; function room. Large grounds: garden, unheated swimming pool, bar. Beach 15 mins' walk, safe bathing. **Location** 600 m from centre, overlooking port. Parking. **Restriction** No dogs. **Credit cards** All major cards accepted. **Terms** [2004] B&B: single €96, double €120. Breakfast €10. Set meals €24.

SANLÚCAR LA MAYOR 41800 Sevilla Map 7:D2

Hacienda Benazuza NEW
Virgen de las Nieves

Tel (955) 70 33 44
Fax (955) 70 34 10
Email hbenazuza@elbullihotel.com
Website www.elbullihotel.com

Once owned by the dukes of Benazuza, this 'magnificent building' is now a hotel *granlujo* in a village 20 minutes' drive from Seville. It dazzled a visitor in 2004: 'A perfect place; everything you could possibly want under these unequalled roofs. The buildings are on different levels; one vista leads to another, through different-coloured courtyards; everywhere the sound of water. On the lawns are pasha-style bungalows under canopies. Our suite had a tiny enclosed garden; canopied bed, small sitting room where fresh fruit appeared daily; old-fashioned bathroom.' Standard rooms have a small sitting area enclosed by tall hedges. Air conditioning is 'effective and silent'. In the reception rooms, the old olive press machinery and oil vats have been preserved. In *La Alquería*, the main restaurant, Rafael Morales has a *Michelin* star. 'Every meal was an adventure; truly delicious food, inventive in taste, colour and presentation.' Service is by waiters wearing white jackets and gloves. 'The procession of *amuse-bouche* (about 14 of them) was an amazing experience of textures,' add inspectors. Simpler lunches are served in the summer restaurant, cooled by falling water, by the large swimming pool, and the bar provides *tapas*. The 'perfect' *Benazuza* breakfast starts with a small plate with four fresh juices, eg, hibiscus, then come 'exquisite pastries, four kinds of flavoured butter, fresh fig jam, etc; then the menu with lots of egg dishes'. If you don't feel up to this you can ask for orange juice and 'ordinary butter'. Children are flexibly looked after. 'Muzak in the bars only; blissful silence elsewhere.' 'The village is not very exciting, but it has an excellent, simple fish restaurant, *La Coquina*.' (*Katrin Stroh, and others*)

Open All year, except 6–20 Jan. *La Alquería* restaurant closed 6–30 Jan. **Rooms** 17 suites, 26 double, 1 single. Some on ground floor. Air conditioning. **Facilities** Lifts. Reception lounges, 2 bars (background music), TV room; restaurant; billiard room; meeting rooms; business centre. Garden, terraces, herb garden; unheated swimming pool, poolside restaurant. Tennis. **Location** In village. 25 km W of Seville. **Restrictions** No smoking in some bedrooms. No pets. **Credit cards** All major cards accepted. **Terms** Room: single/double €320–€400, suite €430–€510. Breakfast €32. Full alc €100.

SANT CELONI 08470 Barcelona — Map 7:B6

Hotel Suis BUDGET

Calle Major 152

Tel (93) 867 00 02
Fax (93) 867 43 43
Email info@hotelsuis.com
Website www.hotelsuis.com

Sant Celoni may be an 'unprepossessing' town with an 'incomprehensible one-way system', but in *Can Fabes*, it has one of the four *Michelin* three-star restaurants in Spain; and there are regular trains to Barcelona. This 'very pleasant' three-star B&B hotel, in the centre, provides budget accommodation, and has 'a genial proprietor and helpful staff'. Reception is on the first floor. 'Our luggage was cheerfully taken, a delightful maid guided me to a parking garage,' said a recent visitor. 'Our spacious room, on two levels, had an excellent desk, a huge and splendid coatstand, a neat bathroom.' Breakfast, 'a small but well-chosen buffet', is served in the bar.

Open All year. **Rooms** 31 double, 3 single. Air conditioning. 1 suitable for ♿. **Facilities** Lift. Bar; meeting room. No background music. **Location** Main square. 51 km NE of Barcelona. Parking. **Restriction** No dogs. **Credit cards** MasterCard, Visa. **Terms** Room: single €50, double €90. Breakfast €5.

The 2006 edition of the *Guide*, covering Great Britain and Ireland, will appear in the autumn of 2005. Reports are particularly useful in the spring, and they need to reach us by 15 May 2005 at the very latest if they are to help the 2006 edition.

SANTA CRUZ DE LA PALMA 38720 La Palma, Canary Islands — Map 7:E5

Parador de la Palma NEW
El Zumacal
Breña Baja

Tel (922) 43 58 28
Fax (922) 43 59 99
Email lapalma@parador.es
Website www.parador.es

La Palma, the most north-westerly of the Canary Islands, is small and volcanic, less busy than its larger neighbour Tenerife. This parador was built in local style in 1999, on the coast outside the island's capital, near the airport, to replace an existing establishment. 'It has a quiet setting, with views towards Santa Cruz and the wide horizon of the sea,' says the nominator. 'The staff are efficient, and most of them are also friendly.' The large, white building has 'a beautiful open courtyard with plants and small trees, an attractive drawing room and other well-furnished seating areas'. Canarian dishes are served in a 'delightful restaurant' with a panelled ceiling. The buffet breakfast is in a separate room. The swimming pool, surrounded by lawns with parasols and loungers, faces the sea. (*Simon Bailey*)

Open All year. **Rooms** 78 double. Air conditioning. **Facilities** Lift. Lounge/reading room, bar, restaurant; gym, sauna. Garden: swimming pool. **Location** 7 km S of Santa Cruz de la Palma. Parking. **Restriction** No dogs. **Credit cards** All major cards accepted. **Terms** [2004] Room: single €91, double €113. Breakfast €10. Set meals €24.

SANTIAGO DE COMPOSTELA 15703 La Coruña — Map 7:A1

Hotel Virxe da Cerca
Rúa Virxe da Cerca 27

Tel (981) 56 93 50
Fax (981) 58 69 25
Email pousadas@jet.es
Website www.pousadasdecompostela.com

On the old royal road in the famous pilgrimage city, this B&B hotel is a 1999 conversion of a listed building, once a bank, then a Jesuit residence. It belongs to a small group of hotels within the city. Decor is a mix of contemporary and traditional. Visitors have written of the 'helpful and charming staff' and the 'warm welcome'. Many rooms are in rustic style. A superior room, in the old part, was liked: 'It had deep-coloured plaster and honey-stone walls and a view of the market.' Standard rooms, simple and comfortable, with access to a 'small Zen-like rear garden', are in a modern wing at the rear. An 'excellent breakfast buffet' is served in the cafeteria, and there is a limited menu for meals: there is a cabaña-style restaurant in the garden. At the rear is the Belvís public park. 'The location, near all the principal sights, is excellent.' (*CB, and others*)

Open All year. **Rooms** 39. Air conditioning. **Facilities** Lounge, cafeteria, restaurant; background music; function facilities. Garden. Unsuitable for ♿. **Location** Inner ring road, by market. Car park nearby. **Restriction** Guide dogs only. **Credit cards** All major cards accepted. **Terms** [2004] Room: double €85–€95, suite €95–€105. Breakfast €8. Set meals €15–€20.

SANTILLANA DEL MAR 39330 Cantabria — Map 7:A3

Siglo XVIII BUDGET
Revolgo 38

Tel (942) 84 02 10
Fax (942) 84 02 11
Email sigloXVIII@arrakis.es

A small, family-run B&B hotel, loved by regular visitors for its friendliness and 'amazing value'. It is on the outskirts of this medieval town ('very touristy in August'), which is four miles inland despite its name. 'A gem,' say its fans. 'Beautifully maintained. Many small details to impress: chocolates to welcome you; a well-fitted bathroom, good shower, fluffy towels, lots of toiletries, central heating.' The old stone house has tiled floors, old beams, large leather chairs in the bar, where nuts and olives come with drinks. Breakfast has orange juice, plenty of coffee, and cakes: in summer, it is served on a pleasant terrace. There is a swimming pool in the well-tended garden. 'Around are fields with cows and horses.' No restaurant, but 'quite good, substantial' snacks are served and many restaurants are an easy walk away. (*P and JL*)

Open March–12 Dec. **Rooms** 14 double, 2 single. **Facilities** Lounge, bar, breakfast room; games room. Garden: terrace, swimming pool. **Location** Outskirts of town. 25 km W of Santander. S6316 from Barreda. Parking. **Restriction** No dogs. **Credit cards** All major cards accepted. **Terms** [2004] Room €60–€69. Breakfast €4.

SEGOVIA — Map 7:B3

Hotel Infanta Isabel BUDGET
Plaza Mayor 12
Segovia 40001

Tel (921) 46 13 00
Fax (921) 46 22 17
Email admin@hotelinfantaisabel.com
Website www.hotelinfantaisabel.com

'Just what a town hotel should be,' said visitors to this 19th-century house, 'central, pleasantly run', which faces the 'busy, happy' square and beautiful cathedral. It has tasteful *fin de siècle* decor in the public rooms: greens and yellows, damask wall coverings, restrained gilt wall lighting, ornate Spanish stoves. Most bedrooms have a balcony above the square; you might see storks coming to roost on the spires of the cathedral. Double glazing stops most noise, though 'not the chiming of the town clock, but it is quiet at night'. 'Our good-sized room had a well-equipped bathroom with a charming bronze plaque of the Three Graces above the loo.' 'Breakfast was good and varied.' The surrounding streets are full of good eating places.

Open All year. **Rooms** 36 double, 1 single. Air conditioning. **Facilities** Lift. Bar, cafeteria/restaurant; 2 conference rooms; background CDs/radio. Unsuitable for ♿. **Location** Central. Garage (€9). **Restriction** No dogs. **Credit cards** All major cards accepted. **Terms** [2004] Room: single €50–€62, double €78–€97. Breakfast €9. Set meals €20–€30.

All our inspections are anonymous.

Parador de Segovia
Carretera de Valladolid
Segovia 40003

Tel (921) 44 37 37
Fax (921) 43 73 62
Email segovia@parador.es
Website www.parador.es

'Without doubt the main attraction of this parador is its setting, with outstanding views of Segovia from its lounges and the restaurant,' said visitors in 2004 to this modern building on a hilltop facing the old city. They found the ambience of the large, slate-floored open areas on the ground floor 'rather barren and unappealing', but other reporters have found the building 'beautifully designed, constructed and finished'. Bedrooms are large, well furnished, with large bathroom; 'excellent housekeeping' and 'a plentiful selection of freebies'. All rooms have picture windows, and many have a balcony overlooking the city. This year's visitors had 'a lovely room but with only a view of surrounding countryside'. Modern paintings hang in the lobby. The 'ample breakfast buffet' includes fresh orange juice, 'excellent tortilla', and a large selection of pastries. 'Very enjoyable, good-value dinner: pork fillet with apricot sauce; sea bass; an impressive selection of desserts. Service was pleasant and efficient.' In the garden, a swimming pool is surrounded by lawns with parasols and loungers. (*Alex and Beryl Williams, and others*)

Open All year. **Rooms** 7 suites, 93 double, 13 single. Air conditioning. **Facilities** Lift, lounges, bar, TV room, café, restaurant; conference centre; indoor swimming pool, sauna, fitness room. Garden: swimming pool, tennis. **Location** 3 km N of Segovia, on N601. Garage, parking. **Credit cards** All major cards accepted. **Terms** [2004] Double room €120. Breakfast €10. Set meals €25.

LA SEU D'URGELL 25700 Lleida — Map 7:A5

El Castell de Ciutat NEW
Carretera N260

Tel (973) 35 00 00
Fax (973) 35 15 74
Email elcastell@hotelelcastell.com
Website www.hotelelcastell.com

*Converted fortress in valley just S of Pyrenees, 1 km from ancient city (Seo de Urgell, now heavily developed). Tápies family's luxury hotel (Relais & Châteaux). 'Friendly staff, one of the best health spas we've been to,' says visitor this year. Lounges, library, bar, panoramic restaurant (*Michelin *star for Vincente Tonico's monthly-changing menus); background music; 2 conference/banqueting rooms. Garden (dining terrace). Indoor and outdoor swimming pools. Concerts. 'Delightful book of local walks.' Golf packages. Children welcomed. Unsuitable for ♿. All major credit cards accepted. 32 bedrooms (some on ground floor, some rustic, others more modern). B&B: single €130, double €165, suite €255. Full alc €50–€70.*

Italicised entries indicate a hotel on which we have little information or mixed reports.

SEVILLE **Map 7:D2**

Las Casas de la Judería
Callejón de Dos Hermanas 7
Seville 41004

Tel (95) 441 51 50
Fax (95) 442 21 70
Email juderia@casasypalacios.com
Website www.casasypalacios.com

'Ever reliable', this hotel, 'quiet yet central', is composed of a series of buildings round courtyards (some with fountain) in the winding streets of the old Jewish quarter. It is best approached on foot (the 'helpful staff' will park your car). Recent praise: 'Charming: near-luxury comfort, a splendid location.' 'Immaculate bedroom and bathroom.' 'In September, the scent of jasmine in the courtyards added to the ambience.' Original tiles line the corridors. Suites have a sitting room; some rooms have a patio, some are dark. Those in an annexe a few minutes' walk away 'were pleasant, but not as appealing as the hotel proper'. 'In the nice sitting room, drinks and tea were served; a pianist played in the evening.' There is an *à la carte* restaurant, and many other eating places are near. A dissenting view this year on the buffet breakfast, normally found 'excellent': 'The fruit salad wasn't fresh; solid scrambled eggs.' Work was continuing on two swimming pools in 2004. (*Y and KF, R Barratt, and others*)

Open All year. **Rooms** 27 suites, 79 double, 14 single. Some on ground floor. Some no-smoking. 1 suitable for ♿. Air conditioning. **Facilities** Lift. Lounge/piano bar, restaurant. No background music. Courtyards. **Location** Historic centre, off Plaza Santa María la Blanca. Underground car park (€15 a day). **Restriction** No dogs. **Credit cards** All major cards accepted. **Terms** Room: single €89–€183, double €131–€253, suite €225–€380. Breakfast €15. Full alc €45. *V*

Las Casas del Rey de Baeza NEW
Calle Santiago
Plaza Jesús de la Redención 2
Seville 41003

Tel (95) 456 14 96
Fax (95) 456 14 41
Email lascasasdelreydebaeza@hospes.es
Website www.epoquehotels.com

Quietly situated in the Barrio Santa Cruz, within walking distance of the main attractions, this is a 'beautiful old house with internal courtyards and spacious, cool bedrooms furnished in contemporary style with great attention to detail', says the nominator in 2004. Once a palace, it has a white and ochre facade, a white, blue and yellow interior, and lots of potted plants. All bedrooms open on to inner patios where you can order a drink or sit and read. They have wrought iron furniture, white cushions and dark wooden floors. The library and sitting area are decorated in browns and creams with coir rugs on slate floors. A 'deluxe *tapas* menu' is served in a room with a fireplace. 'The plunge pool on the roof terrace is a great treat, and you can order drinks and snacks there.' The 'delicious' breakfast served in a 'beautifully furnished' room has freshly squeezed juices, local hams, egg dishes to order. 'Very friendly young service. A real gem, worth every penny.' Free bicycles are provided. (*Anna Ralph*)

Open All year. Restaurant closed Sun. **Rooms** 5 suites, 36 double. Air conditioning. **Facilities** Lift. Lounge, library, restaurant. Courtyards. Roof terrace:

plunge pool, solarium. **Location** Historic centre, near cathedral. Private parking. **Restriction** No dogs. **Credit cards** All major cards accepted. **Terms** [2004] B&B: single €118–€147, double €142–€182. Set meals €25.70.

SÓLLER 07100 Mallorca — Map 7:C6

Ca's Xorc
Carretera de Deyá

Tel (971) 63 82 80
Fax (971) 63 29 49
Email stay@casxorc.com
Website www.casxorc.com

'The food and setting were superb,' says a visitor in 2004 to this small *Agriturismo*. It stands in 'lovely grounds with great views' in the hills above Sóller. 'The atmosphere is informal, with fairly friendly staff,' said the nominator, who found it 'a delightful spot to get away from it all'. Public rooms are stylish: a Moorish theme adds 'panache'. A deluxe bedroom, with rustic furnishings and poor lighting, was thought to 'lack atmosphere'; but it had 'a good balcony with mountain and sea views' and was quiet. 'Good bathroom: huge tub and walk-in shower.' The more modest rooms are 'excellent value'. The lunch and dinner menus are 'short but well balanced' (the chef is new this year). 'Breakfast, on one of many beautiful terraces, had fresh fruit, pastries, cheeses, meats.' The waiting staff are 'very helpful'. (*Michael Dods, WA*)

Open 3 Mar–15 Nov, Christmas/New Year. **Rooms** 12 double. Air conditioning. **Facilities** Restaurant (background music); meeting room. Garden: terraces, heated swimming pool. Unsuitable for ♿. **Location** 3 km NE of Sóller towards Deyá. **Restriction** No dogs. **Credit cards** All major cards accepted. **Terms** B&B: single €136–€180, double €215–€290. Set meal €61.

TOLEDO — Map 7:C3

Hostal del Cardenal NEW
Paseo de Recaredo 24
Toledo 45004

Tel (925) 22 49 00
Fax (925) 22 29 92
Email cardenal@hostaldelcardenal.com
Website www.hostaldelcardenal.com

The 18th-century residence of the archbishops of Toledo, 'nicely located', just inside the city walls near the Bisagra gate, is now this smart hotel. After a time without reports, it is restored to the *Guide*, 'where it deserves to be', according to a regular correspondent. 'We hauled our cases up stone steps, past terraces with fountains, to the front entrance. We enjoyed dinner in the walled courtyard garden [modelled on the Generalife gardens of the Alhambra] on a balmy September evening: a delightful spot. Not a five-star meal (stewed quail), but service was good, the house wine was excellent. We liked our small bedroom overlooking a quiet internal courtyard; it had attractive wood panelling painted with deep reds, and bird motifs.' Breakfast is a 'typical Spanish buffet'. Close by is a 'useful and unusual moving staircase', leading to the top of the city walls. (*Anthony Stern*)

Open All year, except 24 Dec evening. **Rooms** 2 suites, 22 double, 3 single. Air conditioning. **Facilities** TV room, bar, breakfast room, restaurant; patios, courtyards. No background music. Garden. Unsuitable for ♿. **Location** N side of city, just outside old walls at Puerta de Bisagra (not signposted). Public parking. **Credit cards** All major cards accepted. **Terms** Room: single €52–€66, double €84–€106, suite €114–€145. Breakfast €7.50. Set meals €19; full alc €35.

Parador de Toledo
Cerro del Emperador
Toledo 45002

Tel (925) 22 18 50
Fax (925) 22 51 66
Email toledo@parador.es
Website www.parador.es

'El Greco must have sat near here when he painted his classic picture of the city,' wrote a visitor who enjoyed the 'sensational' view from this parador, which faces the old city across the great gorge of the River Tagus. The building, though modern, 'looks firmly back to antiquity: baronial entrance, repro antique furniture abounds'; the large lounge sometimes has an open fire. A guest who disliked these public areas added: 'Our wonderful room, with balcony and view, had good beds, bathroom with deep bath, two basins, lots of toiletries. Dinners were of high quality for the price: first course almost a meal in itself (eg, mushroom risotto; fish soup); outstanding desserts.' Breakfast, a huge buffet, includes fresh orange juice and fruit, tortilla, fried eggs. 'The front desk was fairly formal, but they couldn't have been more helpful when we were planning a day trip to Madrid (just 50 minutes away by train).' (*MB, AB*)

Open All year. **Rooms** 3 suites, 73 double. **Facilities** Lift. Bar, restaurant; conference facilities. Terrace, garden, swimming pool. **Location** Across Tagus, 3 km by road from city centre. Parking. **Restriction** No dogs. **Credit cards** All major cards accepted. **Terms** [2004] Room: single €96, double €120. Breakfast €10. Set meals €25.

TORRENT 17123 Girona — Map 7:B6

Hotel Mas de Torrent
Afores s/n

Tel (972) 30 32 92
Fax (972) 30 32 93
Email reservas@mastorrent.com
Website www.mastorrent.com

'A hideaway surrounded by fields of wheat, sunflowers and old stone houses', the Figueras family's five-star hotel (Relais & Châteaux) is 'expensive, but worth it', according to a visitor in 2004. The 18th-century honey-coloured stone farmhouse lies between Girona and the Costa Brava coastline. 'It is a haven of relaxation,' says this year's report, 'but more an upmarket restaurant-with-rooms than a hotel: as residents we felt subordinate to a sequence of weddings, conferences, and the smart, vocal local in-crowd in the dining room on a Saturday night.' But earlier guests wrote of a 'warm, personal touch'. The original building has 'handsome public rooms', including 'fabulous upstairs lounges'. 'The views are a treat.' Bedrooms here have antique beds; other rooms are in bungalows in landscaped gardens of orange groves, oleander and olive trees. These, with contemporary decor, 'if slightly less special, are no less indulging'. Each has a private garden with a 'slightly claustrophobic cypress hedge'. Catalan cuisine is served in the restaurant, hung with contemporary paintings, or on a terrace facing the medieval hill town of Pals. Lunch is taken in an informal buffet area by the 'large and glamorous' swimming pool. 'Whoever cooked the gourmet dinner didn't cook the scrambled eggs at breakfast.' (*Bev Adams, and others*)

Open All year. Restaurant closed Sun night/Mon except July/Aug, bank holidays. **Rooms** 17 suites (7 with swimming pool), 22 double. Most in bungalows. Many on ground floor. Air conditioning. **Facilities** Ramps. Reading room, bar, restaurant (background music); games room; conference room. Garden: terrace, swimming pool, tennis, bicycles. **Location** NW of Torrent, which is 4 km NW of Palafrugell. **Credit cards** All major cards accepted. **Terms** [2004] B&B: double €255–€285, suite €295–€550; D,B&B €35 added per person.

ÚBEDA 23400 Jaén — Map 7:D3

Parador de Úbeda NEW
Plaza de Vásquez Molina

Tel (953) 75 03 45
Fax (953) 75 12 59
Email ubeda@parador.es
Website www.parador.es

In the 'exquisite' main square of this Renaissance city, this 'beautiful' parador, a 16th-century stone palace, returns to the *Guide*, 'highly recommended', after a time without reports. 'It is very well run,' says a regular correspondent. 'Polite, competent staff; good value.' Beamed ceilings and fireplaces have been preserved; tiled courtyards off the partly glassed-in courtyard lead to cool bedrooms (many are spacious and high-ceilinged). 'Ours was nicely appointed, though with no view to speak of.' Six rooms and the suite face the square. 'Breakfast and dinner were excellent, with refined service.' The restaurant serves Andalusian specialities, eg, bull's tail in red wine; stewed kid. Úbeda is splendidly preserved and has many fine buildings and churches, including the Sacra Capilla de El Salvador, beside the parador. (*R Barratt*)

Open All year. **Rooms** 1 suite, 35 double. Some on ground floor. Air conditioning. **Facilities** 3 salons, TV room, bar, restaurant; conference facilities. Patio. **Location** Central, near town hall. **Credit cards** All major cards accepted. **Terms** [2004] Room: single €86–€96, double €107–€120. Breakfast €10. Set meals €25.

****

Traveller's tale Hotel in Italy. It is a beautiful place but we will never go back. Everywhere else we met with friendliness and helpfulness. Here, you find incomprehensible restrictions: you must arrive at a certain time, have breakfast at a certain time. It is prohibited to wash your socks in the bathroom, etc. The breakfast was lousy. It was called continental, but you had to pay extra for cheese and ham.

****

VILLAMARTIN 11650 Cádiz Map 7:E2

La Antigua Estación NEW/BUDGET
Apartado 91

Tel (617) 56 03 51
Fax (956) 73 07 02
Email thuster@antiguaestacion.com
Website www.antiguaestacion.com

Built as a station for a railway line that was never completed, this white-painted building in traditional style was converted to a small country hotel in 2002 by husband and wife Thomas Huster and Bettina Zapke Rodriguez. 'It is friendly, quiet, ideal for the independent traveller,' says the nominator. 'I love the relaxing surroundings.' Set amid farmland, it has views towards the distant Grazalema mountains (a national park). The runway of a small private airport runs alongside. The route of the railway, with completed bridges, tunnels and other stations, has been restored as the 'green line' for walking, cycling and horse riding. 'Night-time sounds of water birds. A resident horse and dogs.' An evening meal can be arranged. (*Penelope Dickson-Coleman*)

Open All year. **Rooms** 1 suite, 9 double, 2 single. Some in annexe. Air conditioning. **Facilities** Ramps. Lounge, dining room; flamenco nights sometimes. No background music. 14-hectare grounds: patio, swimming pool. Horse riding, bicycle hire, flying arranged. **Location** Just outside town. E of Jerez de la Frontera, NW of Ronda. **Credit cards** MasterCard, Visa. **Terms** B&B: single €45–€60, double €60–€80, suite €90–€110. Set meals €18.

VILLANUEVA DE LA CONCEPCIÓN 29230 Málaga Map 7:E3

La Posada del Torcal
Partido de Jeva

Tel (952) 03 11 77
Fax (952) 03 10 06
Email hotel@eltorcal.com
Website www.eltorcal.com

In a 'lovely spot', below the limestone outcrops of El Torcal national park, this 'excellent small hotel, less than an hour's drive from Málaga airport', received a warm endorsement from a returning visitor in 2004. The white, modern building, in local style, with ancient beams, antiques and ceramics, looks across almond and olive groves to the rolling Andalusian countryside. Traffic noise can be heard from the road 50 yards away, but the swimming pool, which has the best views, is 'relaxing and quiet'. In summer, *tapas* lunches are served on a poolside terrace. Bedrooms, each named after a Spanish artist, have large bed, sunken bath, balcony and wood-burning stove. 'The food in the restaurant has improved, though it is a little "over-engineered",' says this year's reporter. 'The simpler offerings, such as paella and warm goat's cheese salad, were excellent.' Earlier visitors found the staff 'delightful' and the breakfast (with fried eggs and local bacon) 'excellent' (it is taken on a terrace). The owners, Karen Ducker and Michael Soffe, have many English clients. A 25 per cent non-refundable deposit is requested at the time of booking. (*Niki Dixon, and others*)

Open Feb–Nov, Christmas/New Year. **Rooms** 1 suite, 9 double. 2 on ground floor. All no-smoking. Suite and 1 room air conditioned. **Facilities** Salon, bar, 2 restaurants; classical background music, guitarist twice weekly. 4-hectare grounds: terrace; heated swimming pool, bar, whirlpool, sauna, aromatherapy; *petanca*, tennis, mountain bikes, horse riding, walking. Unsuitable for ♿. **Location** 40 km N of Málaga. 3 km from village (signposted). **Restrictions** No children under 14. No dogs. **Credit cards** All major cards accepted. **Terms** [*until 11 Mar 2005*] (Min. 3 nights Mar–Oct) B&B: single €125, double €155–€180, suite €260. Set meals €35; full alc €49.

Sweden

Värdshuset Clas pä Hörnet, Stockholm

ARILD 260 43 Skåne **Map 1:C3**

Hotel Rusthållargården

Tel (042) 34 65 30
Fax (042) 34 67 93
Email receptionen@rusthallargarden.se
Website www.rusthallargarden.se

On the southern Swedish coast, this 'lovely traditional inn', a handsome 17th-century stone building, has been owned by the Malmgren family for four generations. Liked for its 'great charm and excellent cooking', it has 'beautiful views over the picturesque village of thatched cottages festooned with hollyhocks, roses and geraniums, above a small harbour of blue-and-white boats'. Many bedrooms (each has a name: Poet's, Major's, etc) are in villas in the garden. Local delicacies on the dinner menu include nettle soup with fried salmon and sour cream; baked wolfish and Norwegian lobster with zucchini flowers. Breakfast is an extensive buffet. The hotel has 'an excellent sauna complex'; there is good swimming on nearby beaches, and good walking in the Kullaberg nature reserve. (*A and GT, GKP*)

Open 2 Jan–23 Dec. **Rooms** 49 double, 13 single. 37 in villas, 50–100 m. **Facilities** Lift, ramps. Lounges, bar, restaurant; classical background music; indoor swimming pool. Garden. Sea 200 m. Unsuitable for ♿. **Location** On coast, 30 km NW of Helsingborg. Turn off E6 towards Höganäs. After 10 km follow signs to Mölle. Turn to Arild after 10 km. Hotel off road to harbour. **Restriction** Smoking in 1 lounge only. **Credit cards** All major cards accepted. **Terms** B&B: single 975–1,420 Skr, double 1,350–1,980 Skr; D,B&B: single 1,175–1,575 Skr, double 2,750 Skr. Set lunch 180 Skr, dinner 435 Skr; full alc 570 Skr.

BÅLSTA 74693 Uppsala län — Map 1:B4

Krägga Herrgård

Tel (0171) 532 80
Fax (0171) 532 65
Email info@kragga.se
Website www.kragga.se

On the shores of Lake Mälaren, 45 minutes' drive from Stockholm, this 19th-century manor house is now an 'excellent' luxury hotel, managed by its owner, Leif Bonér. A recent report: 'A warm welcome. The public rooms in the manor house, filled with beautiful cut flowers, include a charming library.' Two modern wings enclose a lakeside garden. Bedrooms are attractive, with their pine furniture and matching flowery wallpaper and fabrics. The dining room and a lounge were given a facelift in 2004. The four-course gourmet dinner is found 'excellent', with a 'comprehensive wine list'. 'Good breakfast' (it includes fruit, eggs and 'a special Swedish treat, "fil"'). In February, you can walk or skate on the frozen lake, 'beautiful in the winter sun'. There is a waterside pavilion where special meals are sometimes served, and a Lapland-style tepee for wine tastings, etc. Conferences are held during the week; there are good weekend rates. Under the same ownership: *Thoresta Herrgård*, an 18th-century manor house hotel at Bro, ten kilometres to the south. (*S and LG*)

Open All year, except perhaps Christmas/New Year. Restaurant closed Sun. **Rooms** 4 suites, 24 double, 15 single. 1 on ground floor. **Facilities** Lounge, library, TV room, bar, 2 restaurants; background music. Garden: tennis. **Location** Take Bålsta exit from E18 NW of Stockholm. Follow signs to Krågga. Parking. **Restriction** No smoking: bedrooms, restaurant. **Credit cards** All major cards accepted. **Terms** [2004] B&B: single 1,200 Skr, double 1,600 Skr, suite 2,900 Skr. Set lunch 165 Skr, dinner 610 Skr. *V*

GÄVLE 803 11 Dalarna — Map 1:A4

Hotell Gävle
Staketgatan 44

Tel (026) 66 51 00
Fax (026) 66 51 50
Email info.gavle@swedenhotels.se
Website www.hotellgavle.se

In small city (with 'uncommonly good' National Railway Museum), 200 km N of Stockholm: family-owned B&B hotel. 'Efficient, but with family atmosphere; charming in its own way. Nondescript building, but bedrooms nicely furnished 'and soundproofed'. Extensive breakfast buffet in pleasant lounge; snacks available all day; many restaurants nearby. Lift. Sauna. Ample free parking. Garage. Bicycle hire. All major credit cards accepted. 50 bedrooms. B&B double 840–1,140 Skr [2004].

KNIVSTA 741 95 Uppland **Map 1:A4**

Åby Gård BUDGET

Tel (0183) 88 218
Fax (0183) 88 123
Email aby@abygard.se
Website www.abygard.se

On their large working farm 50 km north-west of Stockholm, Fredrik Johansson and his 'very helpful' wife, Ulla Larsson, offer rustic B&B. 'A real Swedish experience; perfect for those on a limited budget,' said one visitor. Four bedrooms are in a wing (formerly the kitchen and laundry block); two interconnecting rooms are in the 17th-century farmhouse. 'We shared the main building with the hosts and their children, and were treated like family, with all that entails (no locks on doors, even on the shower/loo).' Breakfast includes a wide selection of home-smoked cold meats, eggs, muesli, etc. Advice is given on local attractions and restaurants. The farm's smokery produces smoked meat and sausages, which can be bought in the farm shop.

Open All year, except 20 Dec–10 Jan. **Rooms** 1 family, 4 double, 1 with facilities *en suite*. 4 in separate wing. **Facilities** TV lounge, breakfast room. 1-hectare garden on 250-hectare farm. 7 golf courses nearby. Unsuitable for ♿. **Location** 20 km N of Arlanda airport, NW of Stockholm towards Uppsala: junction of routes 77/273. **Restriction** No smoking. **Credit cards** Diners, MasterCard, Visa. **Terms** [2004] B&B 250–300 Skr.

STOCKHOLM **Map 1:B4**

Berns Hotel
Näckströmsgatan 8
111 47 Stockholm

Tel (08) 566 32200
Fax (08) 566 32201
Email frontoffice@berns.se
Website www.berns.se

A large building by Berzelii Park has, since 1863, contained restaurants, bars and a theatre. Part of it is now this 'discreet and exclusive' boutique hotel. The bedrooms have been designed by Olle Rex, they are done in cherry wood and oak; one reporter found their decor 'a bit stern'; another called it 'cosy yet stylish'. Trouble has been taken with the single rooms: many have a sofa under a bay window. The doubles are in two sizes (described in the brochure as 'large and somewhat smaller'). Some rooms have a big balcony facing the harbour. Breakfasts are 'spectacularly lavish'. Terence Conran designed the restaurant, in an ornate former music hall: it has huge mirrors and chandeliers, oak panelling, contemporary paintings and fabrics. It serves brunch, lunch and dinner (often to live jazz). Or you can eat in the *Crustacea Bar*. In summer when the restaurant is closed (Stockholm empties in July), meals are served on a terrace.

Open All year, except Christmas week. Main restaurant closed July. **Rooms** 3 suites, 43 double, 23 single. **Facilities** Salon, 5 bars, *Crustacea Bar*, restaurant (live music Wed–Sat), terrace (summer restaurant); nightclub; conference facilities. **Location** Central, by Berzelii Park. **Credit cards** All major cards accepted. **Terms** [2004] B&B: single 2,150 Skr, double 2,500–3,700 Skr, suite 4,700–6,400 Skr.

Central Hotel
Vasagatan 38
111 20 Stockholm

Tel (08) 566 208 00
Fax (08) 24 75 73
Email centralhotel@profilhotels.se
Website www.profilhotels.se

By main bus and railway stations, large, 'environmentally conscious' chain-owned hotel, managed by Per Bengtsson. 'Great value; personal service; attentive staff.' Good buffet breakfast, served in garden on fine days ('excellent breads'). Reception/lounge/bar (occasional background music at night; tea/coffee buffet except in summer; snacks available); conference room. All major credit cards accepted. 93 'quiet, comfortable', recently refurbished bedrooms. B&B: single 850–1,650 Skr, double 1,150–2,490 Skr [2004].

Värdshuset Clas pä Hörnet
Surbrunnsgatan 20
113 48 Stockholm

Tel (08) 165 130
Fax (08) 612 5315
Email hotel@claspahornet.com
Website www.claspahornet.com

Named after its first landlord (in 1731), 'Clas on the Corner' is a low, wooden building surrounded by high-rises at what was one of Stockholm's northern toll gates (an 'interesting and varied' neighbourhood). There is easy access to the old city by public transport. The owners, Kjell Appelgren and Cecilia Lewenhagen, who pride themselves on the inn's 'feeling of tradition', have renovated and furnished it under the eye of the City Museum of Stockholm. 'Rarely have I felt a hotel more welcoming,' was one recent comment. In the restaurant, the traditional Swedish cooking is praised ('my best meal in Stockholm'). The bar and the patio, where summer meals are served, are 'inviting'. The bedrooms, all different, have antiques and 18th-century decor; they are 'simple, quiet, satisfactory in every way'. A suite is new this year.

Open All year, except perhaps Christmas. **Rooms** 1 suite, 8 double, 2 single. **Facilities** Bar, restaurant; conference/banqueting/function facilities. Patio. **Location** 1 mile N of centre. Street parking. **Credit cards** All major cards accepted. **Terms** [2004] Room: single 795–1,295 Skr, double 1,090–1,745 Skr, suite 1,995–2,395 Skr. Set meals 395 Skr.

Exchange rates for countries that do not belong to the European Monetary Union can be found at the back of this volume.

Lady Hamilton Hotel
Storkyrkobrinken 5
111 28 Stockholm

Tel (08) 506 40100
Fax (08) 506 40110
Email info@lady-hamilton.se
Website www.lady-hamilton.se

The philosophy of the Bengtsson family, owners of a trio of hotels in the pedestrianised old town (Gamla Stan), is that 'hotel corridors should not be boring'. Nelson enthusiasts, they also own the *Victory* (see next entry) and *Lord Nelson* ('Sweden's narrowest hotel'). This conversion of three old houses, near the cathedral and royal palace, is dedicated to Lady Hamilton: George Romney's portrait of her as Bacchante hangs in the lobby. Small wooden rocking horses and old wooden chests stand on landings, and throughout the building are collections of model ships, antique boxes, china and much more. Recent visitors liked their attic room, with its huge old beams, wide seat under attic windows. 'Not much storage space, good shower room, smallish towels.' Some rooms face the street, 'charming but noisy'; top ones can be hot in summer. A self-service breakfast is served in a room hung with embroidered pictures of ships. Salads and sandwiches are available. Plenty of eating places are near.

Open All year. **Rooms** 16 double, 18 single. **Facilities** Lift. Lobby, bistro/breakfast room (background music); conference rooms; sauna, plunge pool. Unsuitable for ♿. **Location** Old Town, by cathedral. Valet parking. **Restrictions** No smoking: bistro during breakfast, some bedrooms. No dogs. **Credit cards** All major cards accepted. **Terms** [2004] B&B: single 1,050–1,990 Skr, double 1,950–2,690 Skr.

Victory Hotel
Lilla Nygatan 5
111 28 Stockholm

Tel (08) 506 40000
Fax (08) 506 40010
Email info@victory-hotel.se
Website www.victory-hotel.se

'Still sailing well', this 17th-century house (Relais & Châteaux) in the Old Town is the flagship of the Bengtsson family's group of three Stockholm hotels (see also *Lady Hamilton*, above). Dedicated to the memory of Lord Nelson, it is crammed with memorabilia, figure-heads, etc. A letter from Nelson to Lady Hamilton is displayed in the lobby. Visitors in 2004 found the staff 'efficient and friendly', and enjoyed 'the usual admirable breakfast'. 'Our daughter loved the furniture and the nautical theme': each bedroom is named after a sea captain from the great age of sailing ships. 'Our roof-top junior suite presented the usual challenges (like controlling the roof-light blinds), and an ideal space for an extra bed.' The bistro/bar serves drinks and snacks. The smart *Leijontornet* restaurant (built around the ruins of a 14th-century fortified tower) has a good-value *table d'hôte* menu each night; fish is a speciality. 'Ideally situated for sightseeing', the hotel is in a traffic-free area (but a busy road system is nearby). (*Brian, Lesley and Fenella Knox*).

Open All year, except Christmas. **Rooms** 4 apartments, 4 suites, 23 double, 18 single. Air conditioning. **Facilities** Lift. Library, restaurant with bar; background music; terrace; 15 conference rooms; sauna, unheated plunge pool. Courtyard (summer meal service). Unsuitable for ♿. **Location** Old

Town island. Valet parking. **Restrictions** No smoking: restaurant, most bedrooms. No dogs. **Credit cards** All major cards accepted. **Terms** B&B: single 1,250–2,390 Skr, double 1,950–3,590 Skr, suite 2,750–5,990 Skr. Set dinner 450 Skr; full alc 750 Skr.

STRÄNGNÄS 645 30 Södermanland — Map 1:B4

Hotell Laurentius — *Tel* (152) 104 44
Östra Strandvägen 12 — *Fax* (152) 104 43
Email info@hotellaurentius.com
Website www.hotellaurentius.com

'Staying with us is like living in the centre of Swedish history,' says Jürgen Lüdtke, a 'transplanted Austrian who loves electronic gadgets'. He and his Swedish wife, Lena, are the 'congenial hosts' of this small B&B 'of character'. A. converted dormitory of a girls' school, it stands opposite the steam boat landing on Lake Mälaren in this historic town which has a 13th-century cathedral, Sweden's second school (founded 1626), and its first printing works. Bedrooms, 'simple, clean, comfortable', are up flights of stairs off a hall. Breakfast is served alfresco in summer; on cold days it is in the Green Room (lounge), with fireplace and views of Ulfhäll bay. Other meals are for groups only, but the hotel has a drinks licence. A restaurant is opposite; chairs stand on the lawn in summer. A small beach is nearby. Bicycles can be hired and golf packages are offered.

Open All year. **Rooms** 9 double, 3 single. **Facilities** Breakfast room/lounge; sauna; conference room. Garden. Bicycle hire; golf nearby. Unsuitable for ♿. **Location** Opposite pier, on Lake Mälaren. **Restrictions** No smoking. No dogs. **Credit cards** All major cards accepted. **Terms** [2004] B&B: single 595–850 Skr, double 895–1,095 Skr.

****

Traveller's tale Hotel in Germany. We were offered a room in the annexe. It was between a road and a railway line, in a 'garden' that was overrun with weeds. Window boxes had been unattended. The room was dirty. Cobwebs in windows. A number of electric lights did not work. The large bedroom was dominated by an enormous partners' desk with two uncomfortable swivel office chairs. The covering of the door handle to the bathroom had become detached, making the handle potentially dangerous.

****

Traveller's tale Hotel in France. After our long journey a bath was called for. The water ran dangerously hot for two minutes and then turned cold. If turned off and back on, it ran hot for a minute and then cold. We dragged Madame up to look at the problem and she said her husband would sort it out. When he looked at it, he said I was running the water too fast. The following morning we had had enough. We told the proprietor we were leaving. He asked me if I thought his hotel was 'horrible'. I was tempted to say yes, but resisted.

****

Switzerland

Romantik Hotel Florhof, Zürich

Swiss hotel standards are among the world's highest, in terms of smooth professional service, cleanliness, comfort, well-equipped bedrooms and bathrooms, and food that is well prepared and presented. But prices can be correspondingly high. And, surprisingly few – even at the top end – provide air conditioning, though summer temperatures can be high. Many of the classic resort hotels cater for a staid clientele and are sedate by today's standards, but, increasingly, 'fitness facilities' are being introduced, to attract the younger generation, and families.

In the last decade, there has been a renewed interest in simple *Berghotels* (mountain inns), aimed at walkers and nature-lovers. Many of these have dormitory accommodation only, but some have a few simple private bedrooms too.

Food is usually served copiously, and breakfast is generally a buffet, especially in German-speaking areas. Some hotels have a bland 'international' menu, but quite a number serve local Swiss specialities, fondue, raclette, etc, or modern cuisine. We mention *Michelin*'s stars and *Bib Gourmand*, as in other countries covered by this guide.

Service is included in all bills; only in expensive places are you expected to leave a few extra francs for special service.

ADELBODEN 3715 Bern — Map 9:B2

Parkhotel Bellevue
Bellevuestrasse 15

Tel (033) 673 80 00
Fax (033) 673 80 01
Email info@parkhotel-bellevue.ch
Website www.parkhotel-bellevue.ch

Adelboden, one of the older Swiss ski resorts in the western part of the Bernese Oberland, has changed little over the years, nor has this holiday hotel, now run by the third generation of the Richard family. 'Ideal in all seasons', according to fans, it has splendid mountain views. In the large grounds are old trees, a spa, a heated saltwater outdoor swimming pool in which you can swim while snow falls, and there is an 'outstanding' indoor pool. Buses, gondolas and a two-horse charabanc can be taken for trips to local villages, and 'splendid walks' are all around. The buffet breakfast, taken on the garden terrace in fine weather, is 'ample and varied'. Drinks are served in the *Scotch Club* and the *Intermezzo* bar; meals are in the gourmet *Fidelio* restaurant and the rustic *Stübli*. The seasonal menu always has a vegetarian option and a salad course, and there is an extensive wine list. Staff are found 'charming'; most are tri-lingual. Spacious bedrooms have sofa and easy chairs; many have a terrace. Bathrooms have 'an abundance of white, fluffy towels'. (*Mr Aldwinkle, D and GR*)

Open All year, except May. **Rooms** 50 (including suites and family apartments). All no-smoking. **Facilities** Lounge, 2 bars, 2 restaurants; pianist in winter, background music; children's playroom. Large grounds: fitness centre: indoor and outdoor heated swimming pools, sauna, massage, therapies, etc; 'relaxation pavilions'; mountain bikes. Climbing, tennis, curling, paragliding nearby. Unsuitable for ♿. **Location** 5 mins' walk from centre; hotel pick-up from bus station. Car park. **Credit cards** Amex, MasterCard, Visa. **Terms** [2004] (Min. 7 nights, supplement for shorter stays) D,B&B 130–260 Sfrs.

APPENZELL 9050 Eastern Switzerland — Map 9:A4

Haus Lydia BUDGET
Eggerstandenstrasse 53

Tel (071) 787 42 33
Fax (071) 367 21 70
Email contact@hauslydia.ch
Website www.hauslydia.ch

'Unusually good value', Emil and Lydia Mock-Inauen's good-value, modern Appenzeller chalet, says a regular correspondent, is 'an interesting cross between B&B and *hotel garni*'. It is part of a family home in a residential area. The guest rooms and apartments have separate entrances. 'All are comfortable, nicely decorated in regional style, with a ceiling partly inlaid with wood. Shower rooms are fine.' The town centre, with cafés, restaurants and shops, is a short walk away. Indoor and outdoor swimming pools are a 15-minute walk. 'Slight traffic noise from a highway behind the house; in front is a lovely view of mountains. Breakfast, in an attractive area, includes two kinds of bread, meat, cheese, etc; seconds of everything offered. Several languages are spoken by the family members [there are five sons, Reto, Benno, Raphael, Emil and Kuno], and they try hard to meet individual needs.' Drinks are on sale in the foyer. 'This combination of price and facilities is hard to beat.' (*CB*)

Open All year. **Rooms** Two 2-room apartments (1 suitable for ♿), 4 double. 1 on ground floor. Some no-smoking. **Facilities** Library, breakfast room. No background music. Garden: table tennis, barbecue. **Location** 15 mins' walk from centre. Parking. **Credit cards** MasterCard, Visa. **Terms** [2004] B&B 39–60 Sfrs.

AROSA 7050 Graubünden — Map 9:B4

Hotel Prätschli

Tel (0813) 771 861
Fax (0813) 771 148
Email info@praetschli.ch
Website www.praetschli.ch

'Ideal for winter sports': modern hotel, 1,900 m above Arosa, at edge of snowfields: 'You can almost ski into the Ski Halle.*' Open Dec–Apr. Free bus to village (20 mins). Pleasantly furnished rooms, excellent bathrooms, friendly service. 'Food all one could wish for.' Lift. Lounge, bar, 2 restaurants (1 for fondue, raclette),* locanda *with music; sauna, gym, hairdresser. Panoramic views. Parking. All major credit cards accepted. B&B: single 180–390 Sfrs, double 260–420 Sfrs, suite 550–750 Sfrs; D,B&B (min. 3 nights) 30 Sfrs added per person [2004].*

ASCONA 6612 Ticino — Map 9:C3

Hotel Casa Berno
Via Gottardo Madonna 15

Tel (091) 791 32 32
Fax (091) 792 11 14
Email hotel@casaberno.ch
Website www.casaberno.ch

The views over Lake Maggiore are 'wonderful' from this modern four-star hotel (Relais du Silence) on a wooded hillside. They can be enjoyed from the bedroom balconies (now with sun blind), the restaurant, and the terraced garden, 'where you can lounge in privacy on comfortable chairs'. Returning visitors in 2004 found 'nearly all the staff still the same: they enjoy working here'. The 'very high standards in all departments' are admired. 'Cleanliness is absolute.' The food is thought 'impressive, with extremely fresh produce and imaginative menus'. 'Menus never the same in a week.' Dinner is often accompanied by a piano or violins; on Fridays it is a six-course candlelit affair. All the bedrooms face south. 'Breakfast on the terrace in summer is heaven.' The swimming pool is 'a delight, warm and a good size'. The 'charming' directors, Pierre Goetschi and Ingeborg Schmitt, 'keep a keen eye on things', arranging motorboat and bicycling trips, barbecues, walks, and a golf competition in June; mountain bikes are provided free of charge. (*Alex and Beryl Williams, SC*)

Open Late Mar–late Oct. **Rooms** 11 suites, 43 double, 7 single. **Facilities** Lift. Lounges, grill room, restaurant with terrace; live music sometimes; sauna, massage, solarium, fitness room, ladies' hairdresser; roof garden with bar. Garden: swimming pool, putting. Golf, tennis, water sports nearby. **Location** Between Monte Verità and Ronco, 3 km above Ascona (shuttle service). **Credit cards** All major cards accepted. **Terms** [2004] D,B&B 212–288 Sfrs; B&B 20 Sfrs reduction. *V*

Romantik Hotel Castello Seeschloss *Tel* (091) 791 01 61
Piazza Motta *Fax* (091) 791 18 04
Email castello-seeschloss@bluewin.ch
Website www.castello-seeschloss.ch

By Lake Maggiore, at the end of a traffic-free promenade, this 13th-century castle, with its pointed arch windows and flowery courtyard, is now an elegant hotel, owned by the Ris brothers. 'Not cheap but worth every penny,' say recent visitors. The 'helpful staff' are praised. 'Our well-appointed room had a balcony overlooking the swimming pool, immediately behind the main building.' Some bedrooms are in one of the original medieval towers, facing the lake. Many rooms have frescoes, some are beamed; some are suitable for a family. In the 'well-laid-out' gardens are 'plenty of places in which to relax'. The gourmet restaurant, *De Ghiriglioni*, serves 'very good food', on a lakeside terrace in fine weather. Light lunches can be taken in the garden in summer. There is a cellar bar, and a pavilion in the garden for cocktail parties, etc. 'Remarkably good breakfasts, with a wide range of fruit.' (*PH, and others*)

Open 1 Mar–9 Nov. **Rooms** 5 suites, 37 double, 4 single. Some in 2 annexes (20 m). 50 air-conditioned. **Facilities** Lift. Lounge, bar, dining room, 2 restaurants; conference/function facilities; courtyard. Garden: swimming pool (heated Apr–Oct), lakeside terrace, summer restaurant; pavilion (for functions; occasional piano music). Beach 1 km. Unsuitable for ♿. **Location** Central, by lake and port. Parking, garage (19 Sfrs daily). **Credit cards** All major cards accepted. **Terms** B&B: single 164–304 Sfrs, double 248–428 Sfrs, suite 468–548 Sfrs; D,B&B 38 Sfrs added per person. Set menus 23–48 Sfrs; full alc 110 Sfrs. *V*

BERN 3011 **Map 9:B2**

Hotel Belle Époque *Tel* (031) 311 43 36
Gerechtigkeitsgasse 18 *Fax* (031) 311 39 36
Email info@belle-epoque.ch
Website www.belle-epoque.ch

On a handsome street in the lower old part of Bern, Jürg and Bice Musfeld-Brugnoli's small hotel is filled with turn-of-the-19th-century furniture and paintings. Each bedroom, a celebration of Art Nouveau, is individually decorated. The suites, on the top floor, have a modern music system. 'Rooms at the back are the quietest; ours was eminently comfortable, especially the bed,' said one visitor. 'The foyer is cramped, but the welcome, often from the owner himself, is typically Swiss.' Meals are served inside or on the terrace. 'The menu is not large, but every dish is delicious. The buffet breakfast is more than adequate' (it can include champagne or sparkling wine). Light lunches are served. (*AB*)

Open All year. **Rooms** 3 junior suites, 14 double. 4 no-smoking. **Facilities** Lift. Foyer, bar, restaurant; live jazz/background music. Terrace. **Location** 500 m from centre, NW of cathedral. **Credit cards** All major cards accepted. **Terms** [2004] Room: single 195–245 Sfrs, double 280–340 Sfrs, suite 245–590 Sfrs. Breakfast 19 Sfrs. Set dinner 62 Sfrs; alc 46–96 Sfrs.

BOSCO LUGANESE 6935 Ticino — Map 9:C4

Villa Margherita NEW

Tel (091) 611 51 11
Fax (091) 611 51 10
Email margherita@relaischateaux.com
Website www.relaischateaux.com/margherita

'Expensive but worthwhile', according to its nominator in 2004, this 'beautiful' hotel (Relais & Châteaux) stands in large grounds up a winding road above Lugano. It has magnificent views of the lake. Owned by the Herzog and Poretti families, it started life as a small *pension*. 'It is now quite big, but doesn't feel like this, being housed in various buildings. The touch is personal. We felt welcome from the moment we were met at Lugano station. Our junior suite had balcony, big sitting area, big bathroom.' There is an indoor saltwater swimming pool, and an outdoor one in the landscaped grounds where there are green alleyways, Mediterranean plants, plenty of loungers, and a terrace for summer meals. 'We found the dinner, usually five courses, delicious' (in cool weather it is served in a 'classic' dining room). 'Buffet breakfast equally good.' (*Maureen Sharkey*)

Open 7 Apr–17 Oct. **Rooms** 6 suites, 26 double. **Facilities** Salon, restaurant; spa: swimming pool, sauna, hammam; conference facilities. Garden: dining terrace, swimming pool. **Location** 7 km NW of Lugano. From N2 exit Lugano go towards Ponte Tresa; 2 km after roundabout take 1st traffic lights. Parking, garage. **Credit cards** All major cards accepted. **Terms** [2004] B&B: double 368–484 Sfrs, suite 512–616 Sfrs; D,B&B 58 Sfrs added per person. Set meals 50–84 Sfrs; alc 40–98 Sfrs.

CELERINA 7505 Graubünden — Map 9:B5

Chesa Rosatsch NEW
Via San Gian 7

Tel (0818) 37 01 01
Fax (0818) 37 01 00
Email hotel@rosatsch.ch
Website www.rosatsch.ch

'A superb family hotel with universally friendly staff', discovered in 2004 by a regular *Guide* correspondent. It stands on the River Inn, in the centre of a 'lovely, cosy' village. 'The real plus is the eating arrangements, amazing for a small hotel. The main restaurant, 300 years old, with tremendous ambience, serves truly gourmet food on four-course menus ranging from 78 to 95 Swiss francs. You can eat just two courses at lower prices but not lower quality. There is a second area, the *Stuva Bacharia*, wood-clad in local style, and the really casual restaurant, *La Cuort*, with domed glass roof, serves breakfast, and local specialities (basic and not-so-basic) in the evening. The bedrooms are cosy with lots of wood, and lots of wardrobe/shelf space, great for all the skiing clobber.' Hiking paths and gondolas are nearby. Celerina's ski facilities connect with those of 'rather built-up' St Moritz. 'The truly adventurous can take an accompanied ride on the Olympic bob track which finishes near the village. A heart-stopping 80-second thrill of a lifetime (210 francs).' (*Oliver Schick*)

Open 11 June–12 Apr. Main restaurant closed midday. **Rooms** 1 suite, 33 double (some family). Some no-smoking. **Facilities** Lounge, bar, 3 restaurants; small spa; function facilities. **Location** Central, near San Gian church. 3 km NE of St Moritz. **Credit cards** All major cards accepted. **Terms** B&B: single 99–144 Sfrs, double 153–234 Sfrs; D,B&B 68 Sfrs added per person. Set meals 78–95 Sfrs; alc 37–116 Sfrs.

Hotel-Restaurant Saluver
Via Maistra 128

Tel (081) 833 13 14
Fax (081) 833 06 81
Email mail@saluver.ch
Website www.saluver.ch

At entrance of attractive village (with winter and summer sports) 3 km NE of St Moritz: owner/chef Christian Jurczyk's modern, Engadine-style building in traditional beige, brown and grey. 'My comfortable room had well-designed bathroom, excellent towels,' says nominator. Rustic Swiss decor, lots of pine. Restaurant, popular with locals, has 'wide-ranging' menu. Outdoor terrace café in summer. Small lift, lounge; sauna. 'Standard' buffet breakfast. Parking. Garage (12 Sfrs). All major credit cards accepted. 23 bedrooms, most with balcony. B&B 110–120 Sfrs; D,B&B 45 Sfrs added per person [2004].

CHAMPEX 1938 Valais — Map 9:C2

Relais Le Belvédère BUDGET
Champex-Lac

Tel (027) 783 11 14
Fax (027) 783 25 76
Email belvedere@dransnet.ch
Website www.le-belvedere.ch

In a 'charming family resort', surrounded by pine-covered, snow-capped mountains, this simple country inn is run by the Favre-Holzhacker family, Gabriel, Sarah and Irène. 'Quiet and friendly', the chalet-style building makes a good base for walking. Nearby is a lake with boating, fishing in summer, skating in winter. 'Fantastic setting. Memorable views,' says a visitor in 2004. The view from the dining room over the St-Bernard valley is spectacular. Much of the action takes place in the café/bistro where everyone sits, eats and drinks, including passing locals. The owner/chefs 'have a sense of humour'. 'Mme Favre is delightful, helpful, fluent in English'; her daughter is 'highly efficient'. The food is thought 'of a high standard' by some, 'ordinary' by others (robust portions, regional fare, fondues and raclettes, etc). 'Breakfast was fine.' Spotless bedrooms have panelled walls, stripped pine furniture and one or two balconies; some may be small with a 'tiny shower room'. (*Brian Beach, AW*)

Open All year, except 1 week before Easter, 15 Nov–20 Dec. Closed Wed off-season. **Rooms** 1 for 4, 8 double, 1 single. No telephone. **Facilities** Salon with TV, library, restaurant, café/bistro; folk music/background radio. Garden: terrace. Lake 5 mins' walk: boating, fishing, etc. **Location** In village (turn right by Mitsubishi garage). 15 km S of Martigny-Ville. Car park. **Restriction** Smoking discouraged. **Credit cards** MasterCard, Visa. **Terms** B&B: single 85–90 Sfrs, double 140–160 Sfrs; D,B&B 90–105 Sfrs per person. Set lunch 18 Sfrs, dinner 50 Sfrs; full alc 65 Sfrs. 1-night bookings sometimes refused high season.

FTAN 7551 Graubünden — Map 9:B5

Hotel Haus Paradies

Tel (081) 861 08 08
Fax (081) 861 08 09
Email info@hotelhausparadies.ch
Website www.relaischateaux.com/paradies

Just outside this charming cliffside village, in 'one of the least touristy areas of Switzerland', this smart hotel (Relais & Châteaux) is built on a hill on several levels, in a style more Le Corbusier than Swiss (plenty of stone, wood, leather and glass). The setting, on a minor, winding road, is 'magnificent', amid flower meadows. 'You can do a different walk every day without using a car,' one fan wrote. Manager/chef Eduard Hitzberger has two *Michelin* stars for his ambitious modern cooking in the gourmet restaurant, *La Bellezza* (book well ahead); his wife, Waltraud, is 'full of charm'. The cheaper *Stüva* serves fondue chinois and local specialities; half-board guests dine in the *Bellavista* (a four-course daily-changing set menu). Breakfast, 'a delight', has home-made breads. The young staff are helpful. Every bedroom has a mountain view, sitting area and balcony or terrace. The library has a grand piano (concerts are held once a week). Major changes (new spa, a lift, more bedrooms) are planned for 2005. (*KRW*)

Open 19 Dec–29 Mar, 20 May–25 Oct. *Bellezza* closed Mon/Tues; *Bellavista* closed midday. **Rooms** 14 suites, 6 double, 5 single. **Facilities** Lift. Lounge (classical background music), library, TV room, reading room, bar, 3 restaurants (no-smoking); classical background music; live piano sometimes; small spa: sauna, solarium, massage; weekly music evening. Large grounds: terrace; putting. Unsuitable for ♿. **Location** 8 km W of Scuol. Parking, garage (15–20 Sfrs). **Credit cards** All major cards accepted. **Terms** [2004] B&B: single 240–270 Sfrs, double 425–460 Sfrs, suite 545–1,250 Sfrs; D,B&B 88 Sfrs added per person. Set meals 65–198 Sfrs; full alc 62–108 Sfrs.

GRINDELWALD 3818 Bern — Map 9:B3

Hotel Belvedere

Tel (033) 854 57 57
Fax (033) 853 53 23
Email belvedere@grindelwald.ch
Website www.belvedere-grindelwald.ch

In the beautiful Jungfrau region of the Bernese Oberland, this classic hotel was built by the Hauser family in 1904. Silvia and Urs Hauser are now the 'hands-on' proprietors; they and their multinational staff are 'warmly welcoming', and 'everything works efficiently', say admirers. The tall pink concrete building is 'easily spotted as one drives into Grindelwald'. Its 'institutional' appearance belies a 'charming' interior, and it has spectacular views of the Eiger and the Wetterhorn. 'Our suite had two patio doors on to its large balcony.' 'Our spacious room had a narrow veranda, a bit vertigo-inducing.' The food 'was excellent, served in large quantities', says one reporter; another thought it 'sometimes over-elaborate'. The dining room is 'comfortable' and the hors d'œuvre buffet is admired. In summer, 'breakfasting and dining on the terrace is magic', and Urs Hauser leads hiking and cycling expeditions. There are family rooms, special menus for children, and a games room. (*Esler Crawford, A and BW, and others*)

Open 10 Dec–20 Oct. Restaurant closed 15 Apr–15 May. **Rooms** 6 suites, 45 double, 4 single. Some no-smoking. Some suitable for ♿. **Facilities** Lift. 2 lounges, piano/smokers' bar, children's games room, restaurant; indoor swimming pool, whirlpool. Large garden. Paragliding, river rafting, canyon jumping available. Unsuitable for ♿. **Location** 200 m from centre. Parking. **Restriction** No smoking: restaurant, 1 lounge, some bedrooms. **Credit cards** Diners, MasterCard, Visa. **Terms** B&B: single 215–270 Sfrs, double 250–470 Sfrs, suite 420–500 Sfrs; D,B&B 120–290 Sfrs per person. Full alc 65 Sfrs. 1-night bookings refused Christmas/New Year. *V* (off-season only)

Hotel-Restaurant Kirchbühl

Tel (033) 853 35 53
Fax (033) 853 35 18
Email hotel@kirchbuehl.ch
Website www.kirchbuehl.ch

'A great hotel. What makes it special is the warmth of the owners, and the quality of the food,' says a visitor to this chalet hotel (Relais du Silence) on a hillside. 'Mr and Mrs Brawand are warm, hearty hosts, who truly want their guests to enjoy themselves; the younger generation are also involved, so there is always a Brawand around. From the best ['Eiger deluxe'] rooms, I don't think I have had better views. The food is the kind you can eat every day. On the daily-changing half-board menu, we enjoyed fried pike-perch; rib lamb cutlets. The breakfast buffet is lavish.' There are three restaurants: *La Marmite* serving international dishes, and the *Hilty-Stübli* and *Eiger-Stube* for Swiss specialities (fondue, etc). In fine weather, meals are taken on the 'wonderful' terrace with 'fantastic' Alpine views. There is a 'luxurious sauna'. 'The hotel is child-friendly, but not at the expense of adults.' Some tour groups, 'which sometimes leave a little noisily early in the morning'. (*Susan Hanley*)

Open Early Dec–Easter Mon, early May–23 Oct. Restaurant may close in early spring. **Rooms** 4 junior suites, 39 double, 5 single. 1 suitable for ♿. Also some apartments. **Facilities** Lift. Lounge, bar, 3 restaurants; classical background music. Garden, terrace. Free access to Grindelwald's sports centre (swimming pool, etc). **Location** On hill above church. 1 km from station (transport provided). Parking. Garage (10 Sfrs). **Credit cards** All major cards accepted. **Terms** B&B: single 145–215 Sfrs, double 110–175 Sfrs, suite 165–195 Sfrs; D,B&B 45 Sfrs added per person. Set meals 22–45 Sfrs; full alc 70 Sfrs.

Romantik Hotel Schweizerhof

Tel (033) 853 22 02
Fax (033) 853 20 04
Email info@hotel-schweizerhof.com
Website www.hotel-schweizerhof.com

'One of our favourites': on their third visit in ten years, regular *Guide* correspondents again loved this double-gabled chalet hotel with rustic decor. The owners, Anneliese and Otto Hauser, 'are always around', they say, and 'their high standards ensure a most comfortable stay'. The building is central, but it stands back from the road in a 'pretty, but noisy' garden. The attractive lounge and restaurant (with zither player) have spectacular Alpine views. 'Breakfast and dinner are eagerly anticipated.' Meals are thought 'good, though not *haute cuisine*'; vegetarians are catered for. Summer meals are served alfresco. The bedrooms, with much panelling, are good-sized and immaculate. 'Our junior suite faced the Jungfrau, Mönch and Eiger.' In summer, Grindelwald is full of tourists, 'but by taking a ski lift you can quickly be in the mountains, surrounded by breathtaking scenery, wild flowers, peace and quiet'. There are many interesting walks, well signposted, and cogwheel trains from the village go to the Jungfraujoch (at 3,454 metres, the highest railway station in Europe). Excellent rail and postbus services make many other attractive villages easily accessible. (*Roger and Jean Cook, and others*)

Open 18 Dec–23 Mar, 26 May–2 Oct. **Rooms** 16 suites, 27 double, 6 single. **Facilities** Lift. Bar, library, Internet corner, TV room, restaurant (zither player Tues–Sun); swimming pool, sauna, steam room; games room; bowling alley. Terrace (meal service). Large garden. Parking. Unsuitable for ♿. **Location** 200 m from centre. 2 mins' walk from station. **Credit cards** All major cards accepted. **Terms** [2004] D,B&B (min. 3 nights): single 200–265 Sfrs, double 370–490 Sfrs, suite 460–590 Sfrs. Set lunch 18–30 Sfrs, dinner 48 Sfrs; full alc 80 Sfrs.

GRUYÈRES 1663 Fribourg — Map 9:B2

Hostellerie des Chevaliers
Ruelle des Chevaliers

Tel (026) 921 19 33
Fax (026) 921 25 52
Email chevaliers@gruyeres-hotels.ch
Website www.gruyeres-hotels.ch/chevaliers

This 'most attractive' small town, famous for its castle, medieval houses and cheese, is a popular base for holidays. On its edge, this large white building (Relais du Silence) stands amid green lawns, backed by a snow-capped mountain. Recent praise: 'It is comfortable, well run, with excellent breakfasts' (the buffet includes home-made jams, cheese, thick local cream, etc). 'The atmosphere was relaxed. Reception staff were friendly but unobtrusive. No unnecessary extra facilities, hence the reasonable rates. From our balcony the view was spectacular, up to ramparts and castle on one side, over a valley to the sub-Alps in the other.' Sometimes you might see deer or red kites. The bedrooms, with rustic decor, are in an extension reached through an art gallery. The restaurant is in three rooms (one a winter garden). One couple thought it 'overpriced'; another found it 'airy, well decorated, with wonderful views and unelaborate, excellent food'. Only reservation: 'The menu in the evening didn't change.' But 'good food – raclette, fondue, quiche, etc – can be found almost anywhere in Gruyères'. Good walking nearby. (*K and SM, J and CC*)

Open All year, except Jan. Restaurant closed Sun night/Mon. **Rooms** 34. **Facilities** Lounge, breakfast room, restaurant; art gallery; conference room. Garden: terrace. **Location** In village. SE of Bulle, just off A12. Parking. **Credit cards** All major cards accepted. **Terms** B&B: single 100–160 Sfrs, double 160–260 Sfrs; D,B&B (min. 3 nights) 45 Sfrs added per person. Set lunch 25 Sfrs; alc 42–83 Sfrs.

GUARDA 7545 Graubünden — Map 9:B5

Hotel Meisser
Dorfstrasse 42

Tel (081) 862 21 32
Fax (081) 862 24 80
Email info@hotel-meisser.ch
Website www.hotel-meisser.ch

'Wonderfully situated' in a quiet village high above the Inn valley, the Meisser family's spruce yellow-painted hotel dates from 1658. The atmosphere is 'homely' (books, magazines, family photos in the lounge). Most visitors were enthusiastic this year: 'Benno Meisser was most helpful,' one wrote. Bedrooms range from handsome, large ones to tiny garrets. 'Our rooms were comfortable and quiet.' 'Ours had a balcony and superb views.' 'Our suite in the beautifully restored annexe *Chasa Pepina*, across the street, had panelled walls and ceiling, some lovely antiques, a smart bathroom.' One couple thought their room in the main building 'cheaply furnished'. The Jugendstil dining room, once a hay barn, has tall windows and bare floorboards; there is a panoramic *à la carte* restaurant. One visitor found the *en pension* menu 'excellent, with good choice', but another wrote of 'bizarre combinations of products'. The bar has a pool table and 'cigar lounge'. Two terraces have parasols and awnings – grills and snacks are served in summer; two wide lawns have loungers. (*Alex, Beryl and Jonathan Williams, RK, and others*)

Open Christmas–Easter, mid-May–mid-Nov. **Rooms** 5 suites (in annexe, across road), 17 double, 2 single. Some on ground floor. **Facilities** Salon, bar, dining room, restaurant. Garden: 2 terraces (summer meals), table tennis. Unsuitable for ♿. **Location** Centre of village (shuttle to station). 42 km E of Davos. Parking. **Restriction** No smoking: dining room, some bedrooms. **Credit cards** All major cards accepted. **Terms** [2004] B&B 75–210 Sfrs; D,B&B (min. 3 nights) 40 Sfrs added. Full alc 70 Sfrs.

INTERLAKEN 3800 Bern — Map 9:B3

Hotel Beau-Site
Seestrasse 16

Tel (033) 826 75 75
Fax (033) 826 75 85
Email info@beausite.ch
Website www.beausite.ch

'We couldn't fault it,' says a visitor in 2004 to this traditional hotel owned by the 'charming' Max and Ria Ritter. It has magnificent views of the Jungfrau massif. An inspector wrote of 'very friendly staff'. The quietest bedrooms face the garden where there is an aviary with chickens, geese and turkeys. 'Our room was bright, well lit, clean, and extremely well appointed without being fussy.' Breakfast is 'superb, plenty of choice and good rolls and lovely jams', but one visitor found the dinners 'quite expensive' and less good. The lake has good bathing and sailing, and a grass beach is nearby. (*Jane Smith and others*)

Open All year. **Rooms** 47 double, 3 single. **Facilities** Lift. Lounge, *Stübli*, veranda restaurant. Large garden: children's playground. Beach 2 km. **Location** 6 mins' walk from centre. Garage (20 Sfrs a night). **Credit cards** All major cards accepted. **Terms** [2004] Room: single 100–200 Sfrs, double 150–340 Sfrs. Full alc 50 Sfrs.

ISELTWALD 3807 Bern — Map 9:B3

Hotel Kinners Bellevue

Tel (033) 845 11 10
Fax (033) 845 12 77
Email geniessen@kinners.ch
Website www.kinners.ch

On the shore of Lake Brienz, Hanspeter and Rosmarie Kinner's modern, chalet-style restaurant-with-rooms (Relais du Silence) is 'heartily recommended' for its food and 'beautiful setting'. Backed by steep woods, it has a 'superb' lakeside terrace, shaded by trees, for drinks and meals, and a small lounge. 'A place to unwind.' The views are stunning. 'Wonderfully quiet.' One visitor, who enjoyed 'a very good meal and a great swim in the lake', found the bedrooms 'very small': they are 'plain and clean'. 'Our first-floor front room had a large balcony looking over the lake.' The decor is 'very Swiss': much use of wood and folk-weave fabrics. The dining room and panelled grill room are popular locally. 'Excellent' dinners include 'wonderful' local fish, and steaks cooked on an open fire. Frau Kinner presides over the 'fabulous' breakfast buffet. Iseltwald is a tiny, picturesque fishing village. (*SBH, and others*)

Open Mar–Dec. Restaurant closed Tues except July–Sept, Wed Oct–Mar. **Rooms** 9 double, 1 single. **Facilities** Salon, 2 dining rooms. Garden. On lake: beach, sailing. Unsuitable for ♿. **Location** S shore of lake. Iseltwald is 10 km E of Interlaken. **Credit cards** All major cards accepted. **Terms** Room with breakfast 86–172 Sfrs. Set meals 19.50–68.50 Sfrs; alc 55–119 Sfrs.

Every entry in the *Guide* is based on a stay of at least one night.

KANDERSTEG 3718 Bern Map 9:B3

Waldhotel Doldenhorn

Tel (033) 675 81 81
Fax (033) 675 81 85
Email doldenhorn@compuserve.com
Website www.doldenhorn-ruedihus.ch

'Delightful' and smart, the Maeder family's chalet-style hotel is on the outskirts of the village. 'Cosy in winter', it has 'a lovely large lounge' with open fire, gallery, and large, tartan-covered chairs. 'We were warmly welcomed,' said Christmas visitors. 'The food was excellent throughout our stay.' Meals are in the wood-panelled *Burestube* (Swiss cuisine), the *Grüne Saal* or, 'for the connoisseur', *Au Gourmet* (15 *Gault Millau* points for, eg, beef with wild mushrooms and stuffed pepper; lobster with truffle sauce). Meals are also served in the winter garden and, in summer, on a terrace. The bedrooms, all different, are light and modern: the largest have a balcony and a spa bath. Children are welcomed. The hotel bus sometimes takes guests on outings. The *Landgasthof Ruedihus*, serving Swiss specialities, five minutes' walk away, is under the same ownership. 'It has lovely rooms and a 19th-century atmosphere.' (*JBB, and others*)

Open 15 Dec–17 Apr, 7 May–31 Oct. Main restaurant closed Tues. **Rooms** 6 suites, 25 double, 4 single. **Facilities** Lift. Lounge, bar (live music), 3 restaurants (background music); conference room; fitness centre: saunas, whirlpool, solarium. Terrace (meals). Large grounds. **Location** 15 mins' walk from centre. Parking. **Credit cards** All major cards accepted. **Terms** [2004] B&B: single 110–220 Sfrs, double 200–310 Sfrs, suite 300–600 Sfrs; D,B&B 45 Sfrs added per person. Set lunch 30 Sfrs, dinner 45 Sfrs; full alc 90 Sfrs.

Hotel Restaurant Ermitage BUDGET

Tel (033) 675 80 20
Fax (033) 675 80 21
Email info@ermitage-kandersteg.ch
Website www.ermitage-kandersteg.ch

This village, at the western end of the Bernese Oberland, is good all year round for a holiday: skiing and glaciers in winter, 'a hiker's paradise' in summer. Just above it is the Oeschinensee, a delightful oval lake overlooked by mountain peaks. It can be reached by the chairlift that starts near this friendly little chalet hotel, which was thought 'fabulous' by a visitor in 2004. 'Wonderful location. Our room had a mountain view. We could see three waterfalls from our balcony and hear the nearby rushing river.' A party of four adults and four children spent a week in 2004 and 'were sad to leave'. The owners, Rosemarie and Karl Bieri (she is the cook, he the 'attentive but unobtrusive host'), live here with their two children, Tamara and Joel, and they welcome families. They serve refreshments all day, and the garden restaurant is popular with locals. The rooms are well equipped: some have a spa bath. Earlier praise: 'From the moment you enter, you feel welcome. Staff are excellent.' 'Blissfully quiet.' 'Food is the strong point' (there is an emphasis on organic ingredients). 'The meals for residents were simple and no-choice, but always well cooked.' 'Terrific breakfast buffet.' 'Our children played pool enthusiastically every evening. Excellent value. We were impressed.' (*Justin Rogan, Susan Lawlor, and others*)

Open Mid-Dec–end Mar, mid-May–end Oct. Restaurant closed Mon, except July/Aug. **Rooms** 1 family, 12 double, 2 single. Some no-smoking. 1 suitable for ♿. **Facilities** Bar, winter garden, 2 dining rooms, sauna; conference room. Garden: terrace, children's playground. Skiing, lake (boating, etc) nearby. **Location** 10 mins' walk from centre, by path along Oeschinen brook. Parking. Free transfer from station. **Credit cards** All major cards accepted. **Terms** [2004] B&B 75–110 Sfrs; D,B&B (min. 3 nights) 25 Sfrs added.

LAAX 7031 Graubünden **Map 9:B4**

Hotel Posta Veglia
Via Principala 54

Tel (081) 921 44 66
Fax (081) 921 34 00
Email info@poestlilaax.ch
Website www.poestlilaax.ch

Maja and René Meyer's rustic hotel/restaurant in old part of small village ('The Lakes') in Surselva valley (Romansch-speaking area), 25 km W of Chur. 'Warm reception; first-class cooking.' Restaurant (closed Mon in summer) popular with locals; alfresco meals on terrace with view of mountains. Lounge. Buffet breakfast. Free parking. 7 attractive bedrooms (some beamed; some with panoramic views). Closed mid-Apr–June. B&B 75–170 Sfrs; D,B&B 115–210 Sfrs. Full alc 100 Sfrs. *V*

LOCARNO 6648 Ticino **Map 9:C4**

Hotel-Restaurant Navegna au Lac
Via alla Riva 2, Minusio

Tel (091) 743 22 22
Fax (091) 743 31 50
Email hotel@navegna.ch
Website www.navegna.ch

'The location is perfect, the views are spectacular': separated only by a footpath from the water, the Ravelli family's hotel stands by Lake Maggiore. It makes a peaceful retreat from Locarno, 20 minutes' stroll away along the esplanade. The bedrooms, though not large, are 'clean, and simply furnished', say recent visitors. Best ones have a balcony. Front rooms are 'beautifully quiet'; the few rear ones face a railway line. Meals, including the wide-ranging buffet breakfast, are served on a raised terrace looking over the lake, or in a pretty dining room. 'Food was of high quality; prices were reasonable. Staff are friendly.' 'Superb cooking, particularly the home-made ravioli and the Châteaubriand.' There is a small, shady garden with sun loungers, a swimming area in front of the hotel. (*AR, MPW*)

Open Mar–30 Nov. Restaurant open Mar–26 Dec, closed Tues except 15 June–15 Sept. **Rooms** 20. Some no-smoking. Air conditioning. **Facilities** Restaurant; function facilities. Garden on lake: dining terrace, bathing, water sports. **Location** 2 km E of centre: follow signs for Bellinzona. Parking. **Credit cards** MasterCard, Visa. **Terms** [2004] Room: single 90–100 Sfrs, double 85–125 Sfrs; D,B&B 28 Sfrs added per person.

LUCERNE Map 9:B3

Hotel zum Rebstock
St-Leodegarstrasse 3
6006 Lucerne

Tel (041) 410 35 81
Fax (041) 410 39 17
Email rebstock@hereweare.ch
Website www.hereweare.ch

A couple inter-railing round Europe in 2004 arrived unannounced, 'exhausted and grubby', at this yellow-painted hotel in a quiet street near the centre of this popular resort. 'The owner, Claudia Moser, spirited us up to a beautiful, well-furnished, bright front room with lake and mountain views, comfortable sitting area and modern, spacious bathroom with great shower. The cathedral bells ring every 15 minutes, but the double glazing was 100 per cent effective. Breakfast was a huge buffet with cooked dishes on offer.' In the 'beautiful little restaurant', 'dinner was good, honest cooking. Great atmosphere.' The house speciality, the Rebstock Plate, consists of beef fillet with red wine and herb butter, veal fillet rolled in Parma ham, and pork fillet with a whisky cream sauce, all served with leek and potato gratin and fresh vegetables. Other visitors wrote: 'Our room, charming though small, had everything we needed. Service was excellent.' The historic character of the 12th-century building has been kept – wooden floors, beams everywhere. Tables stand under parasols in front of the building in summer, and meals are also served in the garden at the back. 'When we left, they insisted on driving us to the station, though it is only a short walk away.' (*Jane Smith, and others*)

Open All year. **Rooms** 1 suite, 14 double, 15 single. **Facilities** TV/computer room, bar, 3 dining rooms; meeting room. No background music. Garden, terrace. Unsuitable for ♿. **Location** Near station and Kunstmuseum. Parking (18 Sfrs a night). **Credit cards** All major credit cards accepted. **Terms** B&B: single 160–190 Sfrs, double 260–295 Sfrs, suite 350–500 Sfrs; D,B&B 30 Sfrs added per person. Set meals 20–50 Sfrs; full alc 60 Sfrs.

Romantik Hotel Wilden Mann
Bahnhofstrasse 30
6000 Lucerne

Tel (041) 210 16 66
Fax (041) 210 16 29
Email mail@wilden-mann.ch
Website www.wilden-mann.ch

'Splendidly located' on the edge of the Old Town, Charles and Ursula Zimmermann's former 16th-century tavern is named after a mythical giant. It stands by the River Reuss which runs into the lake: a steamer service operates from a nearby landing stage. 'Everything impressed,' said a visitor this year, 'quick, courteous reception, a fine suite with super sitting room, decor of a high standard.' Other comments: 'Expensive but good value: everything you would expect from a high-class hotel.' 'Good amenities, lovely linen, beautiful furniture.' 'Atmosphere of a historic hotel combined with modern efficiency.' Returning visitors were impressed to find their details from a previous visit on the registration form. But a single room by the service lift was noisy early ('clattering trolleys and cleaning staff'). 'Generous breakfasts' include 'freshly baked rolls'. For meals there are the gourmet *Wilden Mann Stube* (international menu), the cheaper *Burgerstube* (regional specialities), and the geranium-bedecked terrace. (*SP, and others*)

Open All year. **Rooms** 8 junior suites, 31 double, 11 single. Some no-smoking. **Facilities** Lift. Lounge, 2 restaurants; background music all day; function/conference facilities; terrace. Unsuitable for ♿. **Location** 500 m W of main railway station. Public parking 50 m. **Credit cards** Diners, MasterCard, Visa. **Terms** B&B: single 165–200 Sfrs, double 265–380 Sfrs, suite 340–430 Sfrs. Set lunch 19.50–26 Sfrs, dinner 59 Sfrs; full alc 60 Sfrs.

LUGANO Ticino — Map 9:C4

Hotel du Lac
Riva Paradiso 3
6902 Lugano-Paradiso

Tel (091) 986 47 47
Fax (091) 986 47 48
Email dulac@dulac.ch
Website www.dulac.ch

On lake, 2 km from centre: Kneschaurek family's modern B&B hotel, architecturally undistinguished, but with 'typical Swiss efficiency; exceptionally helpful staff; good restaurant: good-value Monday buffet'. Lift. Large lounge, veranda bar (live music), restaurant, L'Arazzo *(tapestry); fitness room, sauna, whirlpool, solarium. Garden: big heated swimming pool (also used by locals); landing stage, lake bathing. Unsuitable for ♿. Closed 16 Dec–19 Mar. All major credit cards accepted. Garage (18 Sfrs), parking (10 Sfrs). 53 bedrooms (most are spacious, some no-smoking). B&B: single 140–210 Sfrs, double 266–350 Sfrs, suite 310–500 Sfrs; D,B&B (min. 3 nights) 50 Sfrs added per person [2004].*

Parkhotel Villa Nizza
Via Guidino 14
6902 Lugano-Paradiso

Tel (091) 994 17 71
Fax (091) 994 17 73
Email hotelnizza@swissonline.ch
Website www.villanizza.com

Built on the foundations of a Renaissance villa, this large, white hotel is on a private road at the start of a path up to the summit of Monte San Salvatore. Much admired, it has beautiful views of the lake, and a large garden (which the quietest bedrooms overlook) with Alpine and Mediterranean flora, palm trees, birdsong, and a 'decent-sized' solar-heated swimming pool. The building is 'nicely decorated' ('we liked the small display of historic household items'). Best bedrooms have a balcony facing Lake Lugano and surrounding snow-peaked mountains, but they might hear trains and city noise from below. 'The staff could not have been more helpful,' one fan wrote. Summer meals are served on a terrace. 'From the *carte* we enjoyed delicious house specialities.' Organic produce and wines come from the home farm. 'The excellent breakfast included torta di pane, and interesting jams.' There is a solarium, and a 'relaxed winter garden with sweet-water spa'. 'Every week we offer our guests a sympathetic cocktail party and a very special farmer breakfast,' write the owners, Ari and Ruth Quadri-Müller. Barbecues with music are sometimes held.

Open 11 Mar–16 Oct. **Rooms** 4 suites, 18 double. **Facilities** Lift. 2 lounges (1 no-smoking), bar, 2 dining rooms (no-smoking); background music; conference room; spa, solarium. Garden: dining terrace, grotto; heated swimming pool; children's playground. **Location** 20 mins' walk from centre. From autoroute, exit Lugano Sud, turn right after McDonald's, go to stop sign, turn left. **Credit cards** Amex, MasterCard, Visa. **Terms** [2004] B&B: single 120–135 Sfrs, double 170–260 Sfrs, suite 270–300 Sfrs. Set dinner 39.50–46 Sfrs. *V*

MERLIGEN 3658 Bern — Map 9:B3

Seehotel Restaurant du Lac NEW
Seestrasse

Tel (033) 251 37 31
Fax (033) 251 12 08
Email info@merligen-hoteldulac.ch
Website www. merligen-hoteldulac.ch

The Kropf-Michael family's 'small, friendly, good-value' hotel on Lake Thun was discovered by a *Guide* reader in 2004. 'Management and guests very friendly, relaxed feel, good atmosphere round the swimming pool, everything well maintained and clean. Excellent buffet breakfast: we liked the DIY system of boiling eggs. Our medium-size room had balcony, good bathroom, lake view. The young staff spoke good English. We really enjoyed our stay.' The suites (Niesen, Jungfrau, Mönch) have panoramic views (no lift). Five minutes' walk away is the boat service to Thun and Interlaken. There is a panoramic restaurant and, in summer, a pizzeria in the garden. 'The B&B price includes a moonlight drink on the terrace.' (*Maureen Sharkey*)

Open All year. **Rooms** 22. **Facilities** Restaurant; function facilities. Garden: terrace, pizzeria, swimming pool. **Location** 13 km SE of Thun. Parking. **Credit cards** MasterCard, Visa. **Terms** [2004] D,B&B 60–120 Sfrs; B&B 75 Sfrs discount. Set meals from 18 Sfrs.

MONTREUX 1815 Vaud — Map 9:B2

L'Ermitage
Rue du Lac 75
Montreux-Clarens

Tel (021) 964 44 11
Fax (021) 964 70 02
Email ermitage.krebs@bluewin.ch
Website www.ermitage-montreux.com

'It is near perfect,' says a visitor returning in 2004 to this smart restaurant-with-rooms in a villa on the shores of Lake Geneva. Earlier he wrote: 'Marvellous service, marvellous food, a lovely room.' Owned and run by Étienne and Isabelle Krebs (he is the chef), it looks across the water towards snow-capped mountains. In summer, tables and chairs stand under white parasols on the terrace by the pretty garden. All bedrooms (each is different) face the lake; some have a balcony where breakfast can be served. In the 'Hollywood-style' bathroom of the 'exotic suite', a palm tree towers over the bath. The 'outstanding' *cuisine de saison et du marché* (*Michelin* star, 17 *Gault Millau* points) might include red mullet with spring vegetables; chocolate *semifreddo* with passion fruit. Dogs are welcomed. Jean-Jacques Rousseau set *La Nouvelle Héloise* in Clarens. (*Christopher McCall*)

Open 26 Jan–22 Dec. Restaurant closed Sun/Mon off-season. **Rooms** 3 junior suites, 3 double, 1 single. **Facilities** Restaurant. Terrace (meal service). No background music. Garden on lake. Unsuitable for ♿. **Location** 1 km from centre, towards Vevey. Car park. Landing stage on lake. **Credit cards** All major cards accepted. **Terms** B&B: single 180–200 Sfrs, double 300 Sfrs, suite 340–480 Sfrs. Set lunch 65 Sfrs, dinner 98–175 Sfrs; full alc 195 Sfrs.

LE NOIRMONT 2340 Jura — Map 9:A2

Restaurant et Hôtel Georges Wenger
Rue de la Gare 2

Tel (032) 957 66 33
Fax (032) 957 66 34
Email georges-wenger@swissonline.ch
Website www.georges-wenger.ch

A correspondent this year loved her second visit to this famous restaurant-with-rooms (Relais & Châteaux) by the station of a village high in the Jura near the French border. 'Fruit and home-made fruit juice were brought to our beautifully furnished room minutes after our arrival. Dinner was inventive. Breakfast was outstanding. Georges and Andrea Wenger are an unassuming couple for all their deserved success.' Earlier visitors wrote: 'Service is faultless.' 'Smart but welcoming, so popular you must book well in advance.' Herr Wenger's cooking (*Michelin* star) is based on local produce, eg, truite du lac à la compote d'herbes sauvages. On the 'formidable' wine list, 'every Swiss wine-growing region is represented'. 'Our favourite room has French windows leading on to a terrace where we breakfast (heavenly home-baked breads) in the sunshine, overlooking local activities.' 'Furnishings a mix of classical and modern.' Two suites have oriental touches and a grand bathroom. Some noise from trains and local traffic. Loungers stand in the small garden. Local museums include one for vintage cars, another for watches.

Open 22 Jan–22 Dec. Restaurant closed Mon/Tues. **Rooms** 4 suites, 1 double. **Facilities** Smoking salon, restaurant (no-smoking; background music); terrace. Garden. Unsuitable for ♿. **Location** By station. 19 km NE of La Chaux-de-Fonds. Windows triple glazed. Large car park. **Credit cards** All major cards accepted. **Terms** [2004] B&B: double 290–320 Sfrs, suite 340–390 Sfrs. Set meals 75–185 Sfrs; full alc 150 Sfrs.

OBERMEILEN 8706 Zürich — Map 9:A3

Gasthof Hirschen am See
Seestrasse 856

Tel (01) 925 05 00
Fax (01) 925 05 01
Email reservations@hirschen-meilen.ch
Website www.hirschen-meilen.ch

'What a find,' says a 2004 visitor to this lakeside hotel. Easily reached from Zürich (20 minutes by train, followed by a short walk or bus journey), it is well clear of the city's bustle. 'It looks like nothing from outside, but one's impression changes the moment one walks through the door.' It is worth paying a little extra for one of the eight quiet bedrooms that face the lake. 'Ours had a small sitting area. On the covered terrace facing the water, dinner was very good.' No lounge area, but there is a 'very pleasant' bar, a French restaurant (very popular, booking advised), and a *taverna* with a little garden. An earlier guest wrote: 'Everything is most comfortable; staff are helpful. Splendid meals with professional service. The bedrooms are delightfully furnished, well lit.' The 'excellent' buffet breakfast has 'loads of cereals, yogurts, fresh fruit salad, breads, cheeses; eggs on request'. (*Wolfgang Stroebe, and others*)

Open All year. Restaurant closed Mon Jan–Apr. **Rooms** 14 double, 2 single. **Facilities** Bar, *taverna*, restaurant; conference room. Terrace (meal service). **Location** On Lake Zürich, 15 km SE of Zürich towards Rapperswill. **Credit cards** All major cards accepted. **Terms** [2004] B&B: single 110–135 Sfrs, double 185–260 Sfrs, junior suite 300 Sfrs; D,B&B 58 Sfrs added per person. Set meals 39–85 Sfrs; alc 43–109 Sfrs.

PONTRESINA 7504 Graubünden — Map 9:B5

Hotel garni Chesa Mulin

Tel (081) 838 82 00
Fax (081) 838 82 30
Email info@chesa-mulin.ch
Website www.chesa-mulin.ch

In this upmarket resort, good for a winter or a summer holiday, the Schmid/Isepponi family have been 21 years at their 'cosy' B&B hotel. Formed of two chalets, it is admired for its 'high standards of personal service' and rustic style. Public areas (renovated this year) have much panelling and wooden ceilings. In the 'pleasantly decorated' bedrooms are lots of stripped pine, good reading lights. The views are 'terrific', and the village centre and sports facilities are nearby. No restaurant, 'but the breakfast spread is enough to see you through the day', and snacks are served. Parasols, tables and chairs stand in the big garden in summer.

Open Dec–Apr, June–Oct. **Rooms** 24 double, 6 single. 1 designed for ♿. **Facilities** Lift. Lounge, snack bar, breakfast room (background music); sauna. Garden, terrace. **Location** Central. 7 km E of St Moritz. Garage, parking. **Restrictions** No smoking: breakfast room, some bedrooms. No dogs. **Credit cards** Diners, MasterCard, Visa. **Terms** B&B 85–140 Sfrs. 1-week bookings preferred in winter. Off-season rates for senior citizens.

PUIDOUX 1070 Vaud — Map 9:B2

Hôtel du Signal de Chexbres NEW

Chemin du Signal
Puidoux-Gare

Tel (021) 946 05 05
Fax (021) 946 05 15
Email info@hotelsignal.ch
Website www.hotelsignal.ch

'It focuses on the essentials and gets them right,' says the nominator of this large four-star hotel (Relais du Silence), in a 'superb position' above Lake Leman which most bedrooms face. Set in big grounds, it belongs to the Swiss Golf Hotels group. 'Even in foggy November weather, it was a delight. The "porter" who carried our bags turned out to be the owner, Herr Gunten: very personable, he seems to be around night and day, eager to see to his guests' comfort. His staff set a pleasant tone. The beds are comfortable, the rooms almost too warm in cold weather. Good lighting.' The older bedrooms are spacious, though some floors may be creaky; newer rooms are smaller but have a balcony. 'Bathrooms are good, and we liked the towels in two different colours.' There is an 'amazing indoor pool for serious swimming', and a terrace for summer meals. 'In the very pleasant dining room, breakfasts were good, and the *demi-pension* dinners were excellent. Portions not too large, and they were very amenable about making changes.' Returning in 2004, the nominator added: 'The hotel is lovely in summer with its huge lawn and views over Lake Leman. There were many elderly guests who clearly have been coming for decades. The staff were very kind to them.' (*Susan B Hanley*)

Open Early Mar–end Nov. **Rooms** 70. **Facilities** Lift. Lounges, library, bar, restaurants; 25-metre indoor swimming pool, sauna; conference facilities. Large grounds: terrace (outside dining), garden, tennis, solarium. Golf nearby. **Location** 1 km SW of Puidoux by industrial zone. 14 km E of Lausanne. **Credit cards** All major cards accepted. **Terms** [2004] B&B 99–158 Sfrs; D,B&B 30–40 Sfrs added.

RIED-BLATTEN 3919 Valais — Map 9:C3

Hotel Nest- und Bietschhorn
Lötschental

Tel (027) 939 11 06
Fax (027) 939 18 22
Email nest-bietsch@loetschental.ch
Website www.nest-bietsch.ch

Popular with walkers, climbers and skiers, this small chalet-style hotel is in the upper part of the Lötschental, a beautiful and unspoilt area and UNESCO heritage site. 'Well appointed, clean, comfortable, and attractively decorated with mountaineering appurtenances', it is run by its owners, Erwin and Helene Bellwald-Grob. He is the chef, proud of his local specialities, eg, jambon cru, raclette, viande séchée. 'The food is excellent': there is a five-course *table d'hôte* dinner, an *à la carte* menu with 'adequate choice, a good selection of wines from the Valais. Light dishes are available all day. 'Splendid breakfast buffet: perfect fruit, home-made muesli, cold meats, etc.' The postbus from Goppenstein railway station stops at the door.

Open 20 Dec–2 weeks after Easter, 20 May–5 Nov. **Rooms** 12 double, 5 single. **Facilities** Lounge, TV room, dining room, restaurant; background music everywhere; sauna. Terrace. Garden. Unsuitable for ♿. **Location** 38 km NW of Brig. **Credit cards** All major cards accepted. **Terms** B&B: single 70–90 Sfrs, double 135–170 Sfrs; D,B&B 33 Sfrs added per person. *V*

> The *V* sign at the end of an entry indicates that the hotel has agreed to take part in our Voucher scheme and to give *Guide* readers a 25% discount on its room or B&B rates, subject to the conditions explained in *How to read the entries*, and on the back of the vouchers.

RIGI KALTBAD 6356 Rigi Kaltbad — Map 9:B3

Hotel Bergsonne

Tel (041) 399 80 10
Fax (041) 399 80 20
Email info@bergsonne.ch
Website www.bergsonne.ch

'What a splendid place,' says a visitor in 2004. An earlier reporter called it 'an extraordinary hotel in an unrivalled position'. Willy and Dorly Camps-Stalder's modern chalet hotel stands high on the southern face of the Rigi mountain, in this traffic-free resort. 'Uninspiring from the outside, unusual inside, it has that "*je ne sais quoi*" which demands that you go back,' says one of its many admirers. It has magnificent views of the Alps and Lake Lucerne, 'sunrise above the clouds with the lake below'. Arriving 'is an adventure': the *Bergsonne* is reachable only by rack railway or cable car (guests are given a tourist pass, which cuts the cost). 'The lower station of the cable car is some distance from the landing stage uphill' and 'the golf buggy ride round steep bends from the cable car adds to the experience'. Visitors write of 'good value for money', 'a spacious room', 'an excellent family suite'. Dorly Camps-Stalder's cooking is 'of an unusually high standard'. 'Some of the best food we have eaten: wonderful fresh fish from the lake.' 'The excellent wine list (mostly French) adds to the experience.' 'Breakfast's a banquet.' No lounge or bar, but there is a sun terrace, and two nearby hotels have a bar. 'The hotel would make an ideal setting for a Poirot mystery, but do not attempt the walk down unless you want to use muscles you never knew you had.' (*Garry Wiseman, RC, and others*)

Open Dec–Mar, May–Nov. Restaurant closed Tues in summer. **Rooms** 4 suites, 13 double. **Facilities** Restaurant (closed Tues in summer), 2 *Stübli*; sun terrace. Garden. Unsuitable for ♿. **Location** 3 km NE of Weggis. No access by car: take rack railway from Vitznau or cable car from Weggis. **Credit cards** MasterCard, Visa. **Terms** B&B: single 90–120 Sfrs, double 180–230 Sfrs, suite 230 Sfrs; D,B&B (min. 3 nights) 48–55 Sfrs added per person.

SAANENMÖSER 3777 Bern — Map 9:B2

Hotel Hornberg

Tel (033) 748 66 88
Fax (033) 748 66 89
Email hornberg@gstaad.ch
Website www.hotel-hornberg.ch

Liked again in 2004 ('comfort, excellent food, an exceptional standard of courtesy and friendliness'; 'I cannot think of a Swiss hotel in which the family are more in evidence'), this chalet hotel (Relais du Silence) is in a beautiful walking area of the Saanenland, below the high Hornberg. It looks over a valley towards Gstaad, ten minutes away on foot. The owner/managers Peter and Elisabeth von Siebenthal run it with Brigitte, their 'delightful daughter', Christian Hoefliger, and Darek, their dog. Good for a family holiday, it has lots of wood panelling, large windows, airy public rooms, family suites, a lawn with deckchairs and much else (see next page). Most bedrooms look on to the garden and along the valley, and are quiet. Some have a south-facing balcony. 'Our room was well equipped and well lit.' One visitor was given on arrival a smallish north-facing room, 'but an hour later they moved me, with apologies, to a much bigger room next door on the same terms'. 'The restaurant is smart.' 'There are always at least two members of the family on duty at breakfast and dinner.' In the dining room are pine tables, simple decor, superb views and flowers. The food is 'a blend of traditional and light modern'. A vegetarian menu is available. The breakfast buffet has 'great choice'. In summer, the family arranges twice-weekly outings with picnic, tables and chairs (sometimes in an old military vehicle), to local beauty spots. 'Almost all the other guests had been coming for many years.' (*Ralph Kenber, and others*)

Open 6 Dec–11 Apr, 21 May–22 Oct. **Rooms** 5 suites (in chalet connected by tunnel, 100 m), 24 double, 8 single. **Facilities** Lounge/bar (background CDs), TV room, dining room, restaurant; 2 meeting rooms; children's playroom; indoor swimming pool, sauna. Large garden: terrace, swimming pool, children's play area, garden chess. Golf, river rafting, mountain biking nearby. Unsuitable for ♿. **Location** 9 km N of Gstaad, on Zweisimmen road. Parking. **Credit cards** All major cards accepted. **Terms** [2004] B&B 150–270 Sfrs; D,B&B 30 Sfrs added per person. Set dinner 45–89 Sfrs; full alc 80 Sfrs.

SAAS-FEE 3906 Valais — Map 9:C3

Romantik Hotel Beau-Site

Tel (027) 958 15 60
Fax (027) 958 15 65
Email hotel.beau-site@saas-fee.ch
Website www.romantikhotels.com/saas-fee

With a backdrop of mountain peaks and glaciers, this traffic-free resort is popular with holidaymakers in both winter and summer. Here, Urs and Marie-Jeanne Zurbriggen's chalet hotel, with decor in local Valais style, was enjoyed again in 2004: 'Family run; high level of service.' Others wrote: 'Our fifth visit in six years. Food was first rate. The owners are closely involved. Breakfasts were excellent: 12 different varieties of bread.' Earlier visitors had 'a charming room with two balconies giving breathtaking views of snow-covered mountains'. Two restaurants, one gourmet, and one that specialises in local dishes. Staff wear traditional dress. The residents' dining room serves a short set menu. 'The menu is displayed in the morning and they were very helpful if there was anything we didn't want.' There is a 'pleasant lounge', with open fire, a games room and playground for children, and a 'relax centre' (small swimming pool with waterfall; sauna; massage, etc). Family apartments are at one end of the building; these have a small separate bedroom for children; some have a little cooking area; some of the bathrooms may be 'dated'. In summer, Urs Zurbriggen sometimes leads organised walks; packed lunches are available. (*Annie Lade, and others*)

Open 13 Dec–17 Apr, 12 June–25 Sept. *La Ferme* restaurant closed May. **Rooms** 16 family apartments, 3 suites, 10 double, 3 single. **Facilities** Lounge/bar, children's games room, residents' dining room (no-smoking; pianist weekly), 2 restaurants, wine cellar; relax centre; heated swimming pool, sauna, solarium, whirlpool. Garden: children's playground. Unsuitable for ♿. **Location** Central. No cars in resort (large car park at entrance). **Restriction** No dogs. **Credit cards** Diners, MasterCard, Visa. **Terms** [2004] Room with breakfast 193–376 Sfrs; D,B&B 50 Sfrs added per person. Alc 41–91 Sfrs. 1-night bookings refused high season.

ST-LUC 3961 Valais — Map 9:C2

Hotel Bella Tola & St-Luc
Rue principale

Tel (027) 475 14 44
Fax (027) 475 29 98
Email info@bellatola.ch
Website www.bellatola.ch

At the entrance of this village in the beautiful Val d'Annivers, Anne-Françoise and Claude Buchs-Favre's large white, blue-shuttered hotel dates from 1859. It has fine views of mountains including the Matterhorn, and is well placed for skiing in the St-Luc and Chandolin areas. A family with two teenage daughters loved it in 2004: 'Atmosphere warm and welcoming. Our spacious room was comfortable. We enjoyed all our meals and still remember the fragrance of the bowls of pot-pourri throughout the building.' The decor is attractive, in restrained style: carved beds, parquet floors, polished furniture; neutral curtains in the bedrooms. 'Spectacular floral arrangements.' The old salon is used for musical weekends and lectures. There are two dining rooms, each with frescoed ceiling: one serves fondues, raclette, salads, etc, the other sophisticated French cuisine. In summer, guests take tea under ancient trees in the garden. A spa with swimming pool, sauna, etc, is new this year. Hiking trips, with picnic, can be arranged. (*Helena Knight*)

Open Mid-Dec–mid-Apr, mid-June–end Oct. **Rooms** 1 junior suite, 28 double, 3 single. **Facilities** Lift. 2 lounges, library, piano bar, breakfast room, restaurant; background music; games room; spa: swimming pool, sauna, solarium. Garden: terrace, children's playground. **Location** From Sierre: at entrance to resort, on left. Free parking 100 m downhill. **Restriction** No smoking: breakfast room, bedrooms. **Credit cards** MasterCard, Visa. **Terms** [2004] D,B&B 128–250 Sfrs. Set lunch 21 Sfrs, dinner 46 Sfrs; full alc 75 Sfrs.

ST MORITZ 7500 Graubünden — Map 9:B5

Hotel Languard
Via Veglia 14

Tel (081) 833 31 37
Fax (081) 833 45 46
Email languard@bluewin.ch
Website www.languard-stmoritz.ch

'I was happy to have found this superlative little hotel,' says a reader who visited the *Languard* out of season and plans to come back for a longer stay. Owned by Giovanni Trivella and his family, it is in a quiet side street, off the beaten track but near the pedestrianised town centre. 'The owners were gracious; the breakfast arrangements were friendly.' Other comments: 'You feel like a guest in someone's home.' 'Very reasonably priced in a town where rates can be high.' 'We had a breathtaking view of lake and mountains from the large picture windows in our room. With white duvet covers and pine panelling, it was rather austere (we liked this). It had a sitting area with sofa and chairs, an immaculate bathroom.' No restaurant: plenty in town, particularly in Via dal Bagn in the direction of St Moritz-Bad. The cable car is three minutes' walk away, the lake about twenty. (*Don Maxwell, and others*)

Open 3 Dec–24 Apr, 3 June–23 Oct. **Rooms** 8 suites, 10 double, 4 single. Some on ground floor. **Facilities** Lift. Breakfast room. No background music. **Location** St Moritz-Dorf, near pedestrian zone. Parking. **Credit cards** All major cards accepted. **Terms** [2004] B&B: single €59–€150, double €117–€270, suite €165–€324.

SILS-BASELGIA 7515 Graubünden — Map 9:B4

Hotel Margna

Tel (081) 838 47 47
Fax (081) 838 47 48
Email info@margna.ch
Website www.margna.ch

Converted from a hunting lodge in 1871, this large, pink-washed building is just off the main street of a mountain hamlet between two lakes, near St Moritz. 'A model of an unpretentious four-star hotel', it is 'well modernised, warm and comfortable'. 'My favourite hotel, excellent as ever,' said a returning visitor this year. The managers, Regula and Andreas Ludwig, 'keep a discreet watch', and many of their staff have been here for years. The typical Engadine decor includes much wood panelling. The 'high standard of personal service' is admired: 'A shining example of Swiss hospitality of the old style.' Bedrooms are 'immaculate' (some have a sitting area), and there is an evening turn-down service. Food is 'excellent, with subtle flavours': home-made pasta, local cèpes and locally produced sausages are on the long menus. Plenty to do in the large grounds (see below), and in winter you can sit in a whirlpool bath looking out at the snow. (*Michael Burns, and others*)

Open 13 Dec–12 Apr, 12 June–9 Oct. **Rooms** 13 suites, 30 double, 26 single. **Facilities** Lift. Lounges, kindergarten, piano bar, 3 restaurants; games room; sauna, whirlpool, massage, etc. Garden: terrace, tennis, 6-hole golf course. Unsuitable for ♿. **Location** 10 km SW of St Moritz, off main road to Maloja. Do not approach from Sils-Maria (road is barred). Parking. **Credit cards** MasterCard, Visa. **Terms** [2004] D,B&B 185–350 Sfrs; B&B 35 Sfrs reduction.

SILS-FEX 7514 Graubünden — Map 9:B4

Hotel Fex
Valfex

Tel (081) 826 53 55
Fax (081) 826 57 54
Email info@hotelfex.ch
Website www.hotelfex.ch

At end of remote valley, 11 km SW of St Moritz, at c. *2,000 m: Reto Gilly's old-fashioned 100-year-old 'perfect place' of a hotel, all wood, overlooking glaciers, waterfalls, Alpine meadows. 'Comfy rooms, delicious food in astonishing setting. Huge breakfast. Good value. Lovely terrace. Public transport by horse-drawn omnibus.' Lounge, TV room, breakfast room, dining room, restaurant. Parking. Open 10 June–20 Oct, 20 Dec–15 Apr. Amex, MasterCard, Visa accepted. 15 bedrooms. D,B&B 95–140 Sfrs [2004].*

SUMISWALD 3454 Bern — Map 9:B3

Landgasthof Bären NEW/BUDGET
Marktgasse 1

Tel (034) 431 10 22
Fax (034) 431 23 24
Email hotel@baeren-sumiswald.ch
Website www.baeren-sumiswald.ch

Four-storey, 14th-century building, much modernised behind historic facade, by church of village 3 km W of Wasen between Bern and Lucerne. 'Quality furnishings; bedrooms comfortable if lacking character; bathrooms with heated floor. Good buffet breakfast in old-fashioned restaurant' (traditional Swiss cooking by owner/chef, Stefan Hiltbrunner). Lift. Car park. Closed Mon, 2 weeks Feb, 2 weeks Mar, last week July/1st week Aug. All major credit cards accepted. 17 bedrooms (1 suitable for ♿; some may hear traffic). B&B: single 90 Sfrs, double 150–160 Sfrs. Set meal 18.50 Sfrs; alc 32–83 Sfrs [2004].

WASEN-LÜDERENALP 3457 Bern — Map 9:B3

Hotel Restaurant Lüderenalp

Tel (034) 437 16 76
Fax (034) 437 19 80
Email hotel@luederenalp.ch
Website www.luederenalp.ch

Owned by the Held-Kugler family for four generations, this modern chalet-style hotel 'combines Swiss efficiency with charm'. The setting is 'entrancing', and it is 'neither imposing nor sophisticated', say visitors who were 'captivated by the comfort and friendliness'. Set up a small, twisting road, it has fine views of the Emmental valley. 'On a clear day we could see the Eiger, Mönch and Jungfrau from our good-sized balcony' (the best rooms face south). The rooms are 'modern [lots of blond wood], and comfortable'. Some have a shower down the corridor. No lounge: the large restaurant, with big terrace, is popular with groups for 'lunch with a view', especially on Sunday: 'At night, it was more relaxed. Excellent dinners, with much use of local ingredients. The good breakfast had wonderful aged Emmental cheese. In summer, we were lulled to sleep by the bells on cows enjoying the luscious flower-strewn grass of the summer pasture.' A car is virtually essential, although there is a regular postbus service in summer ('useful for returning to the hotel after following one of the many downhill trails').

Open All year, except 14 days Dec, Christmas, 14 days Jan. Restaurant sometimes closed Mon/Tues in winter. **Rooms** 20. 14 in 2 annexes. **Facilities** Lift. 3 restaurants (1 with terrace); background music; meeting room; sauna. Garden: children's play area. Unsuitable for ♿. **Location** SW of Lucerne,

10 km SE of Wasen, at high point of road to Langnau. **Credit cards** All major cards accepted. **Terms** [2003] B&B: single 85–145 Sfrs, double 158–210 Sfrs. Set meals 25–35 Sfrs; full alc 55–70 Sfrs.

WEGGIS 6353 Bern — Map 9:B3

Hotel Albana NEW
Luzernerstrasse 26

Tel (041) 390 21 41
Fax (041) 390 29 59
Email albanaweggis@access.ch
Website www.albana-weggis.ch

Owned by the Wolf family for four generations, this quite large four-star hotel stands quietly in big grounds, up a steep hill from the centre of town. It is nominated in 2004 by someone who has been visiting since 1962: 'The views, the cuisine, and the great attention by the multilingual staff, are the reasons for our many visits. Guests of many nationalities arrive. Room service is free.' Most bedrooms have balcony with deckchairs and outstanding Alpine views. 'They are large and comfortable, with excellent bathroom, good storage space and adaptable lights for reading in bed. On the roof is an area with deckchairs where you can enjoy the sun and the view.' There are stately lounges with painted ceiling. The *Panorama* restaurant looks over the Vierwaldstättersee. There is a good library ('not guests' left-overs'); occasional music evenings (classical, chamber or light) are held; bicycles can be hired. (*Maria Goldberg*)

Open 26 Jan–8 Dec. **Rooms** 57. **Facilities** Lounges, bar, restaurant; meeting rooms. Roof terrace. Garden. **Location** Up hill from centre. 21 km E of Lucerne. Parking. **Credit cards** All major cards accepted. **Terms** [2004] Room with breakfast 190–360 Sfrs. Set meals 48–120 Sfrs; alc 65–122 Sfrs.

Hôtel Beau Rivage
Gotthardstrasse 6

Tel (041) 392 79 00
Fax (041) 390 19 81
Email info@beaurivage-weggis.ch
Website www.beaurivage-weggis.ch

'Wow! What service, what a room, what a view, what a very good dinner.' One of many tributes this year to this much-loved hotel on Lake Lucerne. Other praise: 'Excellent as ever.' 'A magical place. Sitting on the terrace having breakfast, or in the garden facing the lake, is wonderful.' Run with 'great warmth' by its 'charming owners' Dorly and Urs-Peter Geering and their 'attentive staff', it has fine views over the lake, and is protected from northerly winds by Mount Rigi. There is a broad lakeside terrace for summer meals, a lovely garden with a swimming pool kept warm until late September, and a solarium. Some bedrooms are small. Back ones face a small street. One couple had a 'beautiful first-floor room with a patio overlooking the lake'. 'Busy steamboats, and ice-capped mountains across the water.' 'We liked being able to choose each day whether we wanted to be on *demi-pension*.' 'Substantial five-course dinner, very reliable [13 *Gault Millau* points]. Wide and varied wine list.' On Tuesday evenings there is a 'wonderful' buffet with local specialities. Desserts are 'irresistible'. 'Each night Mrs Geering visited the tables to chat.' 'Not cheap, but worth it.' 'In off-season excellent value.' The cable car up to Rigi Kaltbad is 15 minutes' walk away. (*Jane Smith, E and P Thompson, Alex and Beryl Williams, Florence and Russell Birch, Julia Hummel*)

Open 5 Apr–31 Oct. **Rooms** 4 suites, 28 double, 9 single. Some no-smoking. Some suitable for ♿. **Facilities** Lift. Lounge, bar, restaurant (band/pianist three times weekly). Garden: heated swimming pool, whirlpool, steam bath, solarium; lakeside terrace; beach. **Location** Near quay. Regular boat service to Lucerne. Garages, parking. **Credit cards** All major cards accepted. **Terms** B&B: single 127–172 Sfrs, double 214–334 Sfrs, suite 352–414 Sfrs; D,B&B 50 Sfrs added per person. Set meals 40–60 Sfrs; full alc 70 Sfrs.

WENGEN 3823 Wengen — Map 9:B3

Hotel Alpenrose

Tel (033) 855 32 16
Fax (033) 855 15 18
Email info@alpenrose.ch
Website www.alpenrose.ch

'A model of a friendly small hotel,' say visitors returning in 2004. Owned by the von Allmen family, it has a 'wonderful position' in the lower part of the village. Others wrote: 'Everything runs smoothly. Warm welcome. Well-trained staff. Excellent meals. It's like a club: one guest had been coming for 30 years.' There are large, light public rooms, a lounge with open fire, a rustic bar, a flowery garden in summer. The best bedrooms ('comfortable rather than luxurious') face south; many have a balcony with 'chocolate box views of the Alps'. 'Our charming room had pine panelling and furniture.' The 'delightful' Frau Allmen (she is Scottish) produces a five-course, no-choice set dinner, 'always excellent', 'well thought-out', and served by 'particularly pleasant waiting staff'. Vegetarians are catered for. 'The Friday option of fondue bourguignonne has a breathtaking penumbra of sauces.' 'Wide choice' at breakfast, including 'crispy bacon and eggs'. Children are welcomed. Guests are collected by electric bus from the cogwheel railway which climbs up from Lauterbrunnen. Car-free Wengen is one of the prettiest year-round resorts in the Swiss Alps: 'cowbells tinkle everywhere'. (*David and Anna Sefton, Sheila and John Cotton, RC*)

Open Mid-May–end Sept, mid-Dec–mid-Apr. **Rooms** 39 double, 9 single. 5 in chalet. Some no-smoking. **Facilities** Lounges, bar, restaurant (no-smoking). No background music. Large garden: terrace. Unsuitable for ♿. **Location** 6 mins' walk from centre. **Restriction** No dogs. **Credit cards** Amex, MasterCard, Visa. **Terms** D,B&B 105–192 Sfrs. Set dinner 39.50 Sfrs.

> 'Set meals' refers to fixed-price meals, which may have ample, limited or no choice on the menu. 'Full alc' is the hotel's estimated price per person of a three-course *à la carte* meal with a half bottle of house wine. 'Alc' is the price without wine.

ZERMATT 3920 Valais — Map 9:C3

Hotel Alex

Bodmenstrasse 12

Tel (027) 966 70 70
Fax (027) 966 70 90
Email info@hotelalexzermatt.com
Website www.hotelalexzermatt.com

'Efficient, enjoyable, individual', the *Alex* has views of the towering Matterhorn. Its 'kind owners', Alex and Gisela Perren, offer 'old-fashioned hospitality', say their fans. The decor, found 'kitsch' by one visitor, is loved for its quirkiness by others: 'Lots of stained glass, bar seats like chamois (with horns, and bells around their necks), old prams with dolls, plaster frogs supporting lily pads, dried and artificial flower arrangements everywhere.' 'Our quiet rooms had carved pine-panelled walls, proper down duvets, plenty of cupboard space, spa bath with underwater illumination.' In the beamed, candlelit dining rooms: 'dinner was excellent, with prompt service; Frau Perren, in an exotic outfit each night, went round the tables, chatting to guests'. Her husband, a former mountain guide, 'gives advice on ski routes and mountain restaurants' (access to ski slopes is close by). The newly renovated cocktail bar has music and dancing, wines by the glass, 'healthy cocktails' and cigars. 'Substantial buffet breakfast.' A terrace for summer meals. The indoor swimming pool resembles a grotto.

Open 26 Nov–1 May, 11 June–17 Oct. **Rooms** 31 suites, 44 double, 10 single. **Facilities** Lift. 2 lounges, TV room, 2 Internet corners, lounge bar (music, dancing), bar, grill, restaurant (no-smoking); card room, games rooms; conference facilities; indoor heated swimming pool, spa bath, sauna, steam bath, gym, tennis, squash; terrace. Garden. Unsuitable for ♿. **Location** 2 mins' walk from station. No cars in Zermatt. **Credit cards** Amex, MasterCard, Visa. **Terms** [2004] D,B&B: single 160–277 Sfrs, double 320–608 Sfrs; B&B 20 Sfrs reduction per person.

Hotel Metropol

Matterstrasse 9

Tel (027) 966 35 66
Fax (027) 966 35 65
Email metropol.zermatt@reconline.ch
Website www.reconline.ch/metropol

'Ten wonderful days. My favourite hotel anywhere,' wrote a devotee who celebrated his 80th birthday at Franziska and Gabriel Taugwalder's chalet hotel. 'A very friendly, well-maintained establishment,' was another comment. Near the centre but in a 'tranquil part of town', it has 'amazing' views: from the south-facing balconies you can see the Matterhorn, six kilometres away. The bedrooms (most are decent-sized, but singles are small) have 'simple but tasteful' furniture, large wardrobe; 'everything important is good'; 'no fake antiques'. On the ground floor is a large sitting area with open fire, and a panoramic *à la carte* restaurant with adjoining terrace and garden. Cooking is traditional. Breakfasts are copious. The fitness centre has a 'nice-sized' swimming pool (its huge windows look over the town); also sauna, whirlpool, etc. The sister hotel next door, *Alfa*, slightly cheaper, is also recommended. A little electric taxi meets guests at the station. (*RP, Peter and Angela Mynors*)

Open 27 Nov–24 Apr, 3 June–23 Oct. Restaurant closed Mon. **Rooms** 4 suites, 16 double, 2 single. Some no-smoking. **Facilities** Lift. Lounge, TV room, bar, restaurant; fitness centre: swimming pool. No background music. Garden: terrace. Unsuitable for ♿. **Location** 2 mins' walk from centre; 10 mins' walk from station (hotel will meet). No cars in Zermatt. **Restrictions** No smoking: restaurant during breakfast, 11 bedrooms. No dogs. **Credit cards** All major cards accepted. **Terms** [2004] B&B: single 140–250 Sfrs, double 230–398 Sfrs. Set lunch 38 Sfrs, dinner 50 Sfrs; full alc 55 Sfrs. *V*

ZÜRICH 8001 — Map 9:A3

Romantik Hotel Florhof
Florhofgasse 4

Tel (01) 250 26 26
Fax (01) 250 26 27
Email info@florhof.ch
Website www.florhof.ch

Visitors in 2004 to Brigitte and Beat Schiesser's hotel loved this 'wonderfully old-fashioned' place, from the complimentary glass of Prosecco on arrival and fresh fruit in the bedroom, to the chocolate bar on departure. In the old part of the city, near the university, theatre and art museum, the *Florhof* is a listed 16th-century building, 'well furnished, quiet and comfortable'. Previous admirers wrote of 'a civilised place with helpful staff'; 'delightful room and bathroom'. The restaurant ('French Mediterranean' cooking) has 15 *Gault Millau* points: one visitor thought it 'excellent if unduly expensive'; vegetarians are catered for, and there is a children's menu. The 'charming' dining terrace, with fountain, overlooks the flowery garden. Breakfast is a buffet ('but juices were packaged'). (*Ian Young, AB, and others*)

Open All year. Restaurant closed Christmas/New Year, Sat/Sun, bank holidays. **Rooms** 2 suites (air conditioned), 23 double, 10 single. 10 shower only. Some on ground floor. Some no-smoking. **Facilities** Reading room, restaurant (classical background music); terrace. Garden. Unsuitable for ♿. **Location** Old town, near university. Parking. **Credit cards** All major cards accepted. **Terms** [2004] B&B: single 240–290 Sfrs, double 340–380 Sfrs, suite 480–580 Sfrs. Full alc 120 Sfrs.

****

Traveller's tale Hotel in Spain. The public areas are imposing and spacious, but the bedrooms do not exude the same air of opulence. Ours had one small window, tiny bathroom with no ventilation, and a loo of the electric 'mince it all up and don't watch too closely' kind. The furniture was indeed old. Whether it was antique should be left to the imagination.

****

Traveller's tale Hotel in Paris. I was amazed to be charged for the phone call made by a member of staff to reserve a restaurant table for me. The basic breakfast is awful, and they charge for anything extra, a euro for a pat of butter. One morning, I ordered scrambled eggs: when it came, it was an old boiled egg which had been mashed.

****

Alphabetical list of hotels

In this index, prepositions, articles and the following words are omitted from the beginning of hotel names: albergaria, albergo, auberge; gasthof; Grand Hotel; hostal, hostellerie, hostería; hotel, hôtel, hôtellerie, hotel-restaurant; locanda; pension, pensione; relais; Romantikhotel; villa.

Austria

Belgium

Germany

Hotels in Central and Eastern Europe

Last year, we asked readers' help in recommending hotels in countries for Central and Eastern European countries for which we do not have a chapter. We are very grateful to the readers who responded to this plea, notably Charles Belair, Gillian Bradshaw, John and Theresa Stewart, AD Lloyd, David Crowe, Judith Harrison, and Roger and Hannelore Diamond.

Here is a random selection of hotels, in alphabetical order by country.

BOSNIA AND HERZEGOVINA

SARAJEVO

Omega Ambassador Hotel. Five minutes from the centre of this interesting city: a modern business hotel. 28 bedrooms, some no-smoking. 'Outstanding buffet breakfast in lounge or on covered terrace. Rooms small but spotless. Very efficient management; helpful reception staff.'

ESTONIA

TALINN

Park Consul Schlössle Hotel, www.tallink.fi. On a quiet residential street in the Old Town: 'medieval ambience and antique decor; deluxe accommodation' (23 bedrooms). 'Sumptuous meals' in *Stenhus* restaurant.

Rotermanni Viiking Hotell, www.vikinghotel.ee. Hotel with about 20 rooms: opened in the 1990s in a former goods warehouse behind street-front buildings between the Old Town and the ferry/harbour area (both a few minutes' walk away). About €55 for single use of a double room meeting all needs, including buffet breakfast. 'Inexpensive, well run, but short on style (IKEA abounds)'.

TARTU

Tampere Maja. Inexpensive, well run and well located: four guest rooms in a cultural centre/guest house in an 18th-century wooden building of heritage value. Run by city of Tampere, Finland, in a sophisticated and attractive university city in south-east Estonia (Tampere and Tartu are twinned; 'Maja' means 'house' or 'inn' in Estonian). About €40 for single use of a pleasant IKEA-styled double room, including buffet breakfast, use of a residents' lounge, free Internet access.

LATVIA

RIGA

Elizabetes Maja, www.allhotels.lv. In a wooden 18th-century building a couple of blocks north of the Old Town, in an area full of 18th/19th-century buildings of architectural interest. 14 individually decorated rooms on two floors. The breakfast room (unusually) is in the basement, but it offers gourmet fare for a non-buffet breakfast. At-door parking if you reserve in advance. Two storeys. No lift. Small rear garden.

Gutenbergs Hotel, www.gutenbergs.lv. Opposite the cathedral, built 1880 for a German printer, now a hotel. 'Its public spaces are wonderfully decorated in Venetian style (tapestries, antiques, etc).' 38 comfortable bedrooms with Internet connection, flowers in summer, etc.

Konventa Sēta, www.konventa.lv. 'Most attractive, with rambling charm'; a conversion of nine medieval buildings, originally part of a 15th-century convent, in the city centre. 141 bedrooms, decorated in Scandinavian style, round internal courtyards, most are quiet. Plentiful buffet breakfast, attractive bar, restaurant. Under the same management as the *Hotel de Rome* (below).

Hotel Metropole, www.metropole.lv. 'The oldest continually running hotel in Riga. Now Swedish-owned, recently renovated in Scandinavian style. On the south edge of the Old Town. 80 rooms in a former (1920s and 1930s) locale for foreign intrigue. 'Excellent breakfast buffet and nice rooms, but breakfast is served on low tables in the hotel bar.'

Multilux B&B, www.multilux.lv/BB. Seven rooms, one floor up in office building three tram stops from Old Town. Amazing value off-season, a bit higher in summer: about €45 for single use of double room, including breakfast, dinner, free transport to and from airport. Very professionally run; inexpensive.

Hotel de Rome, www.derome.lv. On liveliest street of Old Town: large (88 rooms), comfortable, efficient business hotel. Atrium, lobbies, gallery. Ample buffet breakfast. Bar/café; top-floor restaurant with good international cuisine.

LITHUANIA

KAUNAS

Metropolis Hotel (formerly Lietuva Hotel), www.takiojineris.com. In an interesting city, capital of independent Lithuania between the wars: 'an experience', an attractive 1920s period hotel under a preservation order, retaining all its important original design features. In the city centre just inside the pedestrian zone, but with access to a guarded car park at the rear and from there into the hotel. 'Some nice rooms; some others need renovation.' Two storeys; no lift. 'Amazingly cheap in 2003 with newly lowered prices (about €18 for a single room with buffet breakfast), but breakfast is taken two blocks away at another (very forgettable) 1980s hotel under same ownership.'

Santakos Hotel. 19th-century building, now 40-bedroom hotel (Best Western), on the edge of the Old City. 'Our room was large and well equipped, staff were helpful, but the breakfast room was overwhelmed by a coach party.' Swimming pool; sauna.

VILNIUS

Narutis Hotel, www.narutis.com. 'On a pedestrian road near the university, this 16th-century building, beautifully restored, is in very good condition, with all the facilities one would expect. The staff were very helpful, and free bicycles are provided.' The Art Deco-style *Kristupo Café* faces lively Pilieu Street, the main street of the Old Town. The hotel's restaurant, in a Gothic cellar, gives a 30% reduction to residents, and there are many other restaurants around. 50 bedrooms.

Hotel Victoria, www.victoria.lv. A former Soviet training centre and trainee guest house in the Lithuanian capital. Now Swedish-owned, it has 25 good-value rooms in an 'unprepossessing but quite adequate style' in a largish building on the north side of the river across from the Old Town, about a five-minute (€2) taxi ride away. 'Friendly, competent staff. Nice buffet breakfast. Easy street parking. Two storeys; no lift. They will call a reliable taxi for you, but you have to bargain for a different taxi back to the hotel. All taxis are very cheap here, though, so it does not really matter a lot to a foreigner (and the drivers know that).'

POLAND

BEBLO

Zajazd Krystyna, www.zajazd-krystyna.com.pl. A well-appointed modern hotel, 'very cheap; adequate in everything, except no plug for basin and bath'. Set back from the main road to Kraków.

KRAKÓW

Hotel Saski, www.hotelsaski.com.pl. In a side street, close to the city's medieval central square, this two-storey hotel was recently refurbished. 'Reception staff extremely helpful. Elegant old lift. Good restaurant and breakfast. Caters to all levels of affordability; not all rooms *en suite*; very communal wash areas, all very clean. Our room was quiet with period decor.'

Senacki Hotel, www.senacki.krakow.pl. A good-quality small hotel (20 bedrooms), very central in the pedestrianised area of the Old Town (but noisy), overlooking Grodzka Street. 'Top-floor rooms are cramped. Very helpful staff. Good buffet breakfast.' Restaurant serving lunch and dinner. 'Good value, but no air conditioning.'

KRASICZYN
Hotel Zamkowy, www.krasiczyn.com.pl. A former hunting lodge in the grounds of a castle (now being restored), at Krasiczyn, near Przemysl. A 'comfortable, rather old-fashioned' three-star hotel. Spacious bedrooms. 'Good breakfast buffet in lodge. Excellent dinner in castle.'

NIEDZICA
Niedzica Zamek, www.hotelspoland.com. Near the Polish/Slovak border: this well-preserved medieval castle overlooks a lake. 'Our comfortable room was furnished with Polish antiques. Good value.' The restaurant by the castle serves lunch and dinner by arrangement. 14 bedrooms.

SANOK
Hotel Restauracja Jagielloński, www.jagiellonski.webpark.pl. 'A hotel such as we have never stayed in. Very cheap, clean, welcoming, amazing. The furnishings and contents of our bedroom were more than idiosyncratic. Our bedclothes were striped satin. Dinner not up to scratch. Breakfast OK.'

WETLINA
Pensjonat Leśny Dwór, www.bieszczady.pl. A peaceful hunting lodge, now a hotel, in the Bieszczady national park, in the foothills of the Carpathians. 'The long-bearded proprietor and wife take huge pride in providing good service. Food goodish. Excellent value.'

ROMANIA

SIBIU
Imparătul Romanilor, www.hotelsromania.com. 2 km from centre, in pedestrianised street: large, traditional hotel of faded grandeur. 'Amazing dining room with roof that opens: good food and exceptional wine. Excellent value.'

RUSSIA

MOSCOW
Hotel Budapest, www.allrussiahotels.com. In the historic centre, near the Kremlin, Duma, etc. 121-room hotel, built 1876. 'Good service. Comfortable rooms.'

Hotel Metropole, www.russia.travelmall.com. A central five-star hotel, in restored Art Nouveau building. Bars, restaurant with fine glass ceiling; health club.

President Hotel, www.moscow-hotels.net/president-hotel. Four-star hotel, built 1983, owned by administrative department of Russian president. 210 bedrooms, modern, spacious, air conditioned.

ST PETERSBURG
Angleterre Hotel, www.angleterrehotel.com. Opposite St Isaac's cathedral, within walking distance of the Hermitage, a four-star hotel with 193 bedrooms, owned by Rocco Forte. Brasserie, business centre, nightclub, casino. 'Helpful staff. Breakfast had fantastic choice.'

Hotel Astoria, www.astoria.spb.ru. Next to the *Angleterre*: classic grand (five-star) hotel, a restored Art Nouveau building, owned by Rocco Forte. 'Decor a blend of Russian nobility and European elegance.' 198 bedrooms, modernised with good bathroom. Historic lobby lounge, winter garden. 'Excellent food in *Davidov* restaurant.' Gym.

UKRAINE

L'VIV
Hotel Grand, www.about.lviv.ua. 100-year-old building, now a 60-room hotel. 'Excellent, spacious bedrooms with *en suite* bathroom. Excellent dining room for breakfast and dinner.' Lunch, drinks, etc, in pavement café. 'Helpful staff.'

ODESSA
Hotel Londonskaya, www.allrussiahotels.com. In the historic centre, built 1867 in early Renaissance style, restored in 1988. 'Grand, calm and elegant.' 56 bedrooms.

Hotel Mozart, www.allrussiahotels.com. New 25-room hotel in the centre, opposite the opera house. Classic design. Liked for comfort and food.

Useful websites
Baltic states: www.balticsww.com/tourist
Poland: www.travelpoland.com
Romania: www.rotravel.com

How to contact the *Guide*:
By mail: From anywhere in the UK write to: *Good Hotel Guide*, Freepost, PAM 2931, London W11 4BR (no stamp needed)
From outside the UK: *Good Hotel Guide*, 50 Addison Avenue, London W11 4QP, England
By telephone or fax: (020) 7602 4182
By email: goodhotel@aol.com
Via our website: www.goodhotelguide.com

Reviews of the *Good Hotel Guide*

What the media says

'It's about as honest and disinterested as a hotel guide can be.' *The Sunday Times*, 2004

'Perfect whether you want to fling yourself across crevasses or slump in a spa.' *Your Wedding*, 2004

'A truly independent view of more than 800 places to stay.' *Oxford Times*, 2004

'This is a must for frequent travelers or those who just want to let someone make the beds and cook the food occasionally… Every glove compartment should have one.' *Ink Magazine*, 2003

'The reviews are as honest and thorough as it gets. Everything from idyllic B&Bs to our finest country houses.' *Wedding Day*, 2003

'The leading guide to British and Irish hotels of quality and character… The *GHG* is unique, written with wit and evocative style… The perfect guide for people who care about where they stay.' *The American*, 2003

'Must Buy… *Good Hotel Guide: Great Britain & Ireland*… finding somewhere perfect to spend your first night is so much simpler.' *Brides* magazine, 2004

'A bible for the discerning traveller.' *Sunday Independent*, Dublin, 2003

'The most rigorous is the *Good Hotel Guide*, which relies on a small, unpaid army of inspectors who always stay overnight.' *Independent on Sunday*, 2003

'The *Good Hotel Guide: Great Britain & Ireland* is unbiased and dishes the details on 800 fabulous hotels and B&Bs.' *Brides* magazine, May 2003

'The *Good Hotel Guide*… gives colourful, witty and unbiased information about interesting and attractive hotels.' *Pipedown*, 2003

'The travel writers' bible.' *Executive Woman*, May 2003

'The *Good Hotel Guide: Continental Europe* is a useful companion for finding great value-for-money accommodation. Every option is covered, be it a city hotel, a grand château or a rural farmhouse retreat… Written by truly independent contributors who accept no payment for staying at the establishments listed, you need never stay anywhere less than perfect again.' *Daily Express*, 2003

What hotels say

'The *GHG* not only brings in numbers of guests, but we also judge "media" by the quality of the guests, and the *GHG* just has to be one of the top scorers.' Philip Ross, owner of *Bromley Court*, Ludlow

'Word of mouth and independent guides are the source of our business. We appreciate your reviews.' Murray Inglis, owner of *The Masons Arms* at Branscombe

'The *Good Hotel Guide* is consistently our third highest source of business (after word-of-mouth and company bookings) exceeding Johansens, AA, RAC, *Which* and the Internet.' Francis Young, proprietor of *The Pear Tree at Purton*

'We have long regarded the *Guide* as the bible of the industry.' Christopher and Alison Davy, owners of *The Rose and Crown* at Romaldkirk

'We renew our thanks to be associated with the success of your *Guide*. It is the key which opens the gate of British tourism.' *Hôtel Beatus*, Cambrai, France

'The best thing about the *Good Hotel Guide* is just this – that the *Guide* brings us very nice guests.' *Hotel Mundal*, Fjærland, Norway

'We get a lot of very good business from being in the *Good Hotel Guide*.' Les Scott of *Strattons*, Swaffham

What readers say

'No one in their right mind would go near a hotel without your advice.' David Taylor, August 2004

'We do realise the value of a book like the *Good Hotel Guide* after experiences like this…' Kate and Jim Craddock, April 2004

'We can't imagine booking anywhere without your guide.' Roger and Jean Cook, August 2004

'As ever the *GHG* is priceless. Or, in words often heard here in the Deep South, now taken generically as referring to the book, its editors and its contributors: "You da MAN!"' John Stege, Macon, Georgia, USA, April 2004

'My husband can't understand why I spend so much time writing reports [for you], but your guide is still by far the best way to find a hotel, so I feel an obligation. And it's fun too!' Susan Hanley, Seattle, Washington, USA, September 2003

'Thank you for helping to make our travels happy ones.' Sue Ann and Martin Marcus, Wilmette, Illinois, USA, September 2004

Exchange rates

The exchange rates given below were correct at the time of printing, but in some cases may be wrong by the time of publication. Please check for up-to-date information.

	£1 sterling	US$1
Euro	1.46	1.22
Denmark (Danish Krone: Dkr)	10.88	6.07
Norway (Norwegian Krone: Nkr)	12.24	6.82
Sweden (Swedish Krona: Skr)	13.25	7.39
Switzerland (Swiss Franc: Sfr)	2.26	1.26

International telephone codes

Austria	43
Belgium	32
Croatia	385
Czech Republic*	420
Denmark	45
France	33
Germany	49
Greece*	30
Hungary*	36
Italy*	39
Luxembourg	352
Netherlands	31
Norway	47
Portugal	351
Slovenia	386
Spain*	34
Sweden	46
Switzerland	41

* The first digit of the national area code that follows the international code should be omitted when the number is dialled from abroad, except in the case of the Czech Republic, Greece, Hungary, Italy and Spain.

Belgium, Denmark, Greece, Luxembourg and Norway have no area codes.

Champagne winners: Report of the Year competition

Each year we award two dozen bottles of champagne for the best reports of the year. A dozen bottles have already been distributed to contributors to the volume for Great Britain and Ireland, which was published in September 2004. A bottle apiece will go to the following generous and eloquent readers for their contributions to this volume.

John Collier, of Bristol
David Crowe, of Beckenham
Gareth and Ros Gunning, of Chelmsford
John Hillman, of London
Sally Holloway, of Harrogate
Bertel Hutchinson, of Derby
Brian and Rosalind Keen, of Amersham
Dawn Mitchell, of Kew
William and Ann Reid, of Edinburgh
Jane Smith, of Crieff
Katrin Stroh, of London
Rosemary Winder, of Teddington

Join the *Good Hotel Guide* Readers' Club

Send us a brief review of your favourite British or Irish hotel.

As a member of the club, you will be entitled to:

1. Special pre-publication discount offers
2. Personal advice on hotels
3. Advice if you are in dispute with a hotel

The best review will win a bottle of vintage champagne.

Send your review via:

Our website: www.goodhotelguide.com
or email: goodhotel@aol.com
or fax: 020-7602 4182
or write to: *Good Hotel Guide*
Freepost PAM 2931
London W11 4BR
or
from outside the UK:
Good Hotel Guide
50 Addison Avenue
London W11 4QP
England

Hotel reports

Readers' reports are the lifeblood of the *Good Hotel Guide.* As we explain in the Introduction, it is sadly likely that this is the last continental volume of the *Guide*, but its sister volume, covering hotels in Great Britain and Ireland, is still going strong, and we welcome reports on hotels in the 2005 volume, and nominations for hotels to be included in its 2006 edition. You may use the following report forms but this is not essential. We get many reports by letter and email. But please write each report on a separate piece of paper, and nominate only hotels you have visited in the past 12 months.

Please give as much detail as possible about the building, the public rooms, bedrooms, food and service, and the grounds. We also welcome information about the location, places to visit and, in the case of B&B hotels, recommendable restaurants. If you can enclose a brochure with your report, or tell us about a website, that will be very helpful.

In the case of an existing entry, even a short endorsement helps, though longer reports are much more useful. For a new nomination we need plenty of detail; often we cannot consider a potentially attractive hotel because of an inadequate report. We get routine information about number of rooms, facilities and prices from the hotels. We want readers to give information that is not accessible elsewhere.

Please do *not* tell a hotel that you intend to file a report. Anonymity is essential to objectivity.

Nominations for the 2006 edition of the *Good Hotel Guide: Great Britain & Ireland*, which will appear in September 2005, should reach us not later than 15 May 2005. The latest date for comments on existing entries is 1 June 2005.

If you need more report forms, please ask.

Our address for **UK correspondents** (no stamp needed) is:

Good Hotel Guide, Freepost, PAM 2931, London W11 4BR.

Reports posted **outside the UK** should be stamped normally and addressed to:

Good Hotel Guide, 50 Addison Avenue, London W11 4QP, England.

Reports can be faxed to us on (020) 7602 4182, or emailed to goodhotel@aol.com.

[2005]

To: *The Good Hotel Guide*, Freepost PAM 2931, London W11 4BR

NOTE: No stamps needed in UK, but letters posted outside the UK should be addressed to 50 Addison Avenue, London W11 4QP, England, and stamped normally. Unless asked not to, we shall assume that we may publish your name. If you would like more report forms please tick ☐

Name of Hotel______________________________________

Address ____

____

Date of most recent visit   Duration of visit

☐ New recommendation   ☐ Comment on existing entry

Report:

Please continue overleaf

I am not connected directly or indirectly with the management or proprietors

Signed ____

Name (CAPITALS PLEASE) ____________________________

Address _______________________________________

____

Email ____

[2005]

To: *The Good Hotel Guide*, Freepost PAM 2931, London W11 4BR

NOTE: No stamps needed in UK, but letters posted outside the UK should be addressed to 50 Addison Avenue, London W11 4QP, England, and stamped normally. Unless asked not to, we shall assume that we may publish your name. If you would like more report forms please tick ☐

Name of Hotel ____

Address ____

____

Date of most recent visit

Duration of visit

☐ New recommendation

☐ Comment on existing entry

Report:

Please continue overleaf

I am not connected directly or indirectly with the management or proprietors

Signed ____

Name (CAPITALS PLEASE) ______________________________

Address ____

____

Email ____

[2005]

To: *The Good Hotel Guide*, Freepost PAM 2931, London W11 4BR

NOTE: No stamps needed in UK, but letters posted outside the UK should be addressed to 50 Addison Avenue, London W11 4QP, England, and stamped normally. Unless asked not to, we shall assume that we may publish your name. If you would like more report forms please tick ☐

Name of Hotel________________________________

Address ________________________________

____

Date of most recent visit Duration of visit

☐ New recommendation ☐ Comment on existing entry

Report:

Please continue overleaf

I am not connected directly or indirectly with the management or proprietors

Signed ____

Name (CAPITALS PLEASE) ____________________________

Address _______________________________________

____

Email ____

[2005]

To: *The Good Hotel Guide*, Freepost PAM 2931, London W11 4BR

NOTE: No stamps needed in UK, but letters posted outside the UK should be addressed to 50 Addison Avenue, London W11 4QP, England, and stamped normally. Unless asked not to, we shall assume that we may publish your name. If you would like more report forms please tick ☐

Name of Hotel____

Address ____

____

Date of most recent visit Duration of visit

☐ New recommendation ☐ Comment on existing entry

Report:

Please continue overleaf

I am not connected directly or indirectly with the management or proprietors

Signed ____

Name (CAPITALS PLEASE) ____________________________

Address ____

____

Email ____

[2005]

To: *The Good Hotel Guide*, Freepost PAM 2931, London W11 4BR

NOTE: No stamps needed in UK, but letters posted outside the UK should be addressed to 50 Addison Avenue, London W11 4QP, England, and stamped normally. Unless asked not to, we shall assume that we may publish your name. If you would like more report forms please tick ☐

Name of Hotel ______________________________

Address ______________________________

____

Date of most recent visit

Duration of visit

☐ New recommendation

☐ Comment on existing entry

Report:

Please continue overleaf

I am not connected directly or indirectly with the management or proprietors

Signed ____

Name (CAPITALS PLEASE) ________________________________

Address ____

____

Email ____

[2005]

To: *The Good Hotel Guide*, Freepost PAM 2931, London W11 4BR

NOTE: No stamps needed in UK, but letters posted outside the UK should be addressed to 50 Addison Avenue, London W11 4QP, England, and stamped normally. Unless asked not to, we shall assume that we may publish your name. If you would like more report forms please tick ☐

Name of Hotel ____

Address ____

____

Date of most recent visit Duration of visit

☐ New recommendation ☐ Comment on existing entry

Report:

Please continue overleaf

I am not connected directly or indirectly with the management or proprietors

Signed ______________________________

Name (CAPITALS PLEASE) ______________________________

Address ______________________________

____

Email ______________________________

[2005]

To: *The Good Hotel Guide*, Freepost PAM 2931, London W11 4BR

NOTE: No stamps needed in UK, but letters posted outside the UK should be addressed to 50 Addison Avenue, London W11 4QP, England, and stamped normally. Unless asked not to, we shall assume that we may publish your name. If you would like more report forms please tick ☐

Name of Hotel____

Address ____

____

Date of most recent visit

Duration of visit

☐ New recommendation

☐ Comment on existing entry

Report:

Please continue overleaf

I am not connected directly or indirectly with the management or proprietors

Signed ____

Name (CAPITALS PLEASE) ______________________________

Address ____

____

Email ____